Dictionary of 2oth Century History

D0809102

Dictionary of 20th Century History

Collins

HarperCollins*Publishers*
Westerhill Road, Glasgow G64 2QT

www.collins.co.uk

First published 2004

© 2004 Research Machines Plc
Helicon Publishing is a division of Research Machines

Reprint 10 9 8 7 6 5 4 3 2 1 0

ISBN 0 00 716556 0

A catalogue record for this book is available from the British Library.

Typeset by Davidson Pre-Press Graphics Ltd, Glasgow

Printed and bound in Great Britain by Clays Ltd, St Ives plc.

INTRODUCTION

The *Collins Dictionary of 20th Century History* is a new and comprehensive guide to our recent past, covering the people, the events and the social and political upheavals which have changed the nature of our world.

A special feature of this dictionary is the inclusion of long explanatory entries on countries, entries that are designed to be especially helpful for students.

Also included is a list of essential websites to provide guidelines for further research, from the Russian-Japanese war to genocide studies.

The book is organized alphabetically, with each headword appearing in bold. The order is decided as if there are no spaces between words, for example:

> **Africa, the scramble for**
> **African National Congress**
> **African nationalism**
> **African union**
> **Afrika Korps**
> **Agadir incident**
> **Aga Khan**

Cross references are indicated by an asterisk * in front of the entry being cross-referenced. Cross referencing is selective; a cross reference is shown when another entry contains material directly relevant to the subject matter of an entry, and to where the reader may not otherwise think of looking.

The text for this book has been prepared by Helicon Publishing, a division of Research Machines Plc. The entries have been taken from their major educational encyclopedic database. Collins would like to thank Jane Horwood for her assistance in selecting and editing the entries, and Alice Goldie for compiling the website selection.

A

Abacha, Sani (1943–1998) Nigerian soldier, politician, and president (1993–98). In 1983 he took part in the coup that ended the Second Republic. In 1993 he seized power following presidential elections in which Chief Moshood *Abiola appeared to be the winner. He arrested Abiola and suppressed a strike by oil workers. The Abacha regime received international condemnation for the hanging of the environmentalist and human-rights campaigner Ken Saro-Wiwa in 1995.

Abbas, Ferhat (1899–1985) Algerian nationalist leader and politician. He was the first president of the exile-based Gouvernement Provisoire de la République Algérienne (GPRA) 1958–61, and was elected president of the national assembly after independence.

Abd al-Karim (1880–1963) also known as **Abd al-Karim el-Khettabi**, Moroccan chief known as the 'Wolf of the Riff'. With his brother Muhammad, he led the **Riff revolt** against the French and Spanish invaders, defeating the Spanish at Anual in 1921. For five years he ruled his own Republic of the Riff, centred on Melilla. Then the Spanish sought military assistance from the French (who governed northern Morocco); a joint army of 160,000 under Marshal Pétain subdued the rebellion in 1925 and Abd al-Karim surrendered in 1926.

abdication crisis in British history, the constitutional upheaval of the period 16 November 1936 to 10 December 1936, brought about by the British king *Edward VIII's decision to marry Wallis *Simpson, a US divorcee. The marriage of the 'Supreme Governor' of the Church of England to a divorced person was considered unsuitable and the king abdicated on 10 December and left for voluntary exile in France. He was created Duke of Windsor and married Mrs Simpson on 3 June 1937.

Abdullah, ibn Abdul Aziz al-Saud (1924–) Saudi Arabian prince, first deputy prime minister from 1982. On the assassination, in 1975, of King *Faisal, he became second deputy prime minister and he was designated Crown Prince and first deputy prime minister on the death of his half-brother King Khalid in 1982. After his half-brother King *Fahd suffered a stroke, power was temporarily ceded to Abdullah, his legal successor, in January 1996.

Abdullah, Sheikh Muhammad (1905–1982) Indian politician, known as the 'Lion of Kashmir'. He headed the struggle for constitutional government against the Maharajah of Kashmir, and in 1948, following a coup, became prime minister. He agreed to the accession of the state to India, but was dismissed and imprisoned from 1953 (with brief intervals of freedom) until 1966, when he called for Kashmiri self-determination. He became chief minister of Jammu and Kashmir in 1975, accepting the sovereignty of India.

Abdullah ibn Hussein (1882–1951) King of Jordan 1946–51. In 1921, after the collapse of the Ottoman empire, he became emir of the British mandate of Transjordan, covering present-day Jordan, and became king when the mandate ended in May 1946. In May 1948 King Abdullah attacked the newly established state of Israel, capturing large areas. He retained the area called the West Bank (Arab

Palestine) after a ceasefire in 1949 and renamed the country the Hashemite Kingdom of Jordan. He was assassinated in July 1951 by a Palestinian Arab fanatic.

Abdullah ibn Hussein (1962–) King of Jordan from 1999. Abdullah was crowned king of Jordan after his father, *Hussein ibn Talal, who had ruled the Hashemite Kingdom since 1952, died. Abdullah, who was an army major general, and untested in the affairs of state, became the fourth leader of this small but strategically vital state. He promised to maintain Hussein's legacy, continuing the course of moderation and commitment to Middle East peace.

Abernathy, Ralph D (1926–1990) US Baptist clergyman and civil rights activist. Martin Luther *King Jr's chosen successor as head of the Southern Christian Leadership Conference (SCLC), Abernathy went on to devote his attention to religious ministry and the issues of worldwide peace.

Abiola, Moshood Kastumawo (1937–1998) Nigerian politician, president in 1993. First elected to parliament as a National Party member in 1979, he won the 1993 presidential elections as the Social Democratic Party candidate, but was arrested and charged with treason following a military coup. After spending a year in prison his detention was declared illegal but the election result remained invalid. He died as his release was being negotiated.

Abkhazia (or Abkhaziya) autonomous republic in northwestern *Georgia; area 8,600 sq km/3,320 sq mi; population (1993 est) 516,600. The region is located between the main range of the Caucasus Mountains and the Black Sea, with a subtropical climate on the latter's shores, and with densely wooded foothills. Most of the population, including that of the capital, Sokhumi, and the cities of Ochamchire and Gagra, is located in the lowland of the coastal area.

Industries include the mining of tin and coal, and lumbering and sawmilling, but agriculture, including fruit, tobacco, and tea cultivation, is still the leading occupation. Tourism and health resorts on the coast and on Lake Ritsa are also important.

Abu Nidal (1934–2002) also known as **Sabri Khalil al-Banna,** Palestinian-Arab terrorist. During the late 1950s he joined Yassir *Arafat's Fatah guerrilla group, which was linked to the Palestinian Liberation Organization (PLO). However, he was critical of what he saw as its moderate stance and, when expelled in 1973, set up his own, more extreme Palestinian Arab terrorist organization, known as the 'Al-Fatah Revolutionary Command', also known as 'Black June'. This clandestine body was responsible for a series of ruthless assassinations, hijackings, and kidnappings of Israeli, Western, and 'moderate Palestinian' targets. The Abu Nidal Group's activities have been condemned by the PLO, which sentenced Abu Nidal to death, in 1974.

The Abu Nidal Group's attempted assassination, in June 1982, of the Israeli ambassador in London, Shlomo Argov, gave Israel the pretext to launch an invasion of Lebanon, while its December 1985 attacks on passengers at Rome and Vienna airports led to US bombing reprisals against Libya. Abu Nidal received backing initially from Iraq and then, in the early 1980s, from Syria and Libya. Iraqi assistance was resumed in 1990.

Acheampong, Ignatius Kutu (1931–1979) Ghanaian army officer and politician, military ruler of Ghana 1972–78. He led the coup of January 1972 that overthrew the president, Dr Busia, and was himself replaced by his deputy, Frederick Akuffo, in a bloodless coup in 1978.

Acheson, Dean (Gooderham) (1893–1971) US politician. As undersecretary of state 1945–47 in Harry Truman's Democratic administration, he was associated with George C Marshall in preparing the *Marshall Plan, and succeeded him as secretary of state 1949–53.

Acheson's foreign policy was widely criticized by Republican members of Congress, especially Senator Joe *McCarthy, for an alleged weak response to communist advances in Southeast Asia, especially after the outbreak of the Korean War. Acheson advocated containment of the USSR. He survived a vote calling for his resignation, but left the State Department in 1952 following the election to the presidency of the Republican Dwight D Eisenhower. Acheson was highly critical of the UK's foreign-policy aims, notably of the claim to a 'special relationship' with the USA.

Adams, Gerry (1948–) born **Gerard Adams**, Northern Irish politician, leader (president) of *Sinn Fein from 1983, member of Parliament for Belfast West 1983–92 and since 1997. He has been a key figure in Irish peace negotiations. In 1994 he was the main architect of the IRA ceasefire and in 1997 Adams entered into multiparty talks with the British government which, on Good Friday, 10 April 1998, resulted in an agreement accepted by all parties. He has since been a member of the Northern Ireland Assembly created by the peace process.

Adams was interned 1972 and 1973–77 on suspicion of involvement in terrorist activity. In 1993 it was revealed that he had held talks about a possible political solution with the leader of the Social Democratic and Labour Party, John *Hume, and with representatives of the British government. In August 1994, when Adams announced an IRA ceasefire, the British government removed all restrictions on his public appearances and freedom to travel to mainland Britain (in force since 1988).
The unwillingness of the IRA to decommission its arms prior to full

British troop withdrawal from Northern Ireland led to a delay in the start of all-party peace talks in 1995, and the resumption of IRA violence in February 1996 was a setback. Nevertheless, in September 1998, he met the Ulster Unionist leader, David Trimble, at Stormont, Belfast, in an historic meeting, the first of its kind for several generations.

Addams, Jane (1860–1935) US social reformer, feminist, and pacifist. In 1889 she founded and led the social settlement of Hull House in the slums of Chicago, Illinois, one of the earliest community welfare centres. She was vice-president of the National American Woman Suffrage Alliance 1911–14, and in 1915 led the Women's Peace Party and the first Women's Peace Congress. She shared the Nobel Prize for Peace in 1931 with Nicholas Murray Butler for her support of women's suffrage.

Aden Arabic **'Adan**, main port and commercial centre of Yemen, on a rocky peninsula at the southwest corner of Arabia, commanding the entrance to the Red Sea; population (1995) 562,000. The city's economy is based on oil refining, fishing, shipping, and light industries, including boatbuilding. A British territory from 1839, Aden became part of independent South Yemen in 1967; it was the capital of South Yemen until 1990.

Adenauer, Konrad (1876–1967) German Christian Democrat politician, chancellor of West Germany 1949–63. With the French president Charles de Gaulle he achieved the post-war reconciliation of France and Germany and strongly supported all measures designed to strengthen the Western bloc in Europe.

Adenauer was mayor of his native city of Cologne from 1917 until his imprisonment by Hitler in 1933 for opposition to the Nazi regime. After the war he headed the Christian Democratic Union (CDU) and became chancellor, combining the office with that of foreign minister. He was re-elected chancellor in 1953 and retained the post of foreign minister until 1955.

Admin Box, Battle of the in World War II, the first major victory over the Japanese for British and Indian troops at Sinzewa, Burma (now Myanmar), in February 1944.

Admiralty, Board of the in the UK, the controlling department of state for the Royal Navy from the reign of Henry VIII until 1964, when most of its functions – apart from that of management – passed to the Ministry of Defence. The 600-year-old office of Lord High Admiral reverted to the sovereign.

Advisory, Conciliation, and Arbitration Service ACAS, in the UK, government-funded independent body for the improvement of industrial relations through its advisory, conciliation, and arbitration services. Set up in 1974 as the Conciliation and Arbitration Service, it adopted its current name in 1975, and became a statutory body in January 1976 under the Employment Protection Act (1975). Specifically, ACAS aims to encourage the extension of collective bargaining and, wherever possible, the reform of collective-bargaining machinery. In 2001 it had some 800 staff.

Adwa, Battle of defeat of the Italians by the Ethiopians at Adwa in 1896 under Emperor Menelik II. It marked the end of Italian ambitions in this part of Africa until Mussolini's reconquest in 1935.

affirmative action, USA policy of positive discrimination pursued in the USA for the advancement of disadvantaged US citizens. First promoted by US president Lyndon Johnson's Executive Order 11246 (1965), it was furthered by a 1970 Department of Labor order to federal contractors to develop 'an acceptable affirmative action program', and the Equal Opportunities Act (1972). Aimed in particular at black American and Hispanic American ethnic groups, it also covered gender discrimination. Stemming from the *civil-rights movement of the 1960s, it was argued that education and employment should be biased towards non-white ethnic groups to overcome the effects of centuries of prejudice. Affirmative action was enforced in organizations receiving public funds, and many private employers adopted similar programmes. The policy began to falter in the 1980s, when the Civil Rights Commission called it 'unjustified discrimination'. In the 1990s a series of court cases declared it illegal, as it promoted 'reverse discrimination', preferential treatment of one ethnic group over another. Nevertheless, affirmative action had challenged white-American domination in education, employment, and government.

Afghanistan mountainous, landlocked country in south-central Asia, bounded north by Tajikistan, Turkmenistan, and Uzbekistan, west by Iran, and south and east by Pakistan, India, and China.

Afghan Wars three wars waged between Britain and Afghanistan to counter the threat to British India from expanding Russian influence in Afghanistan.

First Afghan War (1838–42): the British invaded Afghanistan to protect their own interests after Persia, encouraged by Russia, became involved in the region. Although successful at first, a later Afghan rising drove them out of Afghanistan, and of the 4,000 British who formed the garrison of Kabul only one arrived safely at Jalalabad. Another British expedition was dispatched, which captured Kabul, released British prisoners there, and then evacuated the country.

Second Afghan War (1878–80): General Roberts captured Kabul in 1879 and relieved Kandahar.

Third Afghan War (1919): peace followed the dispatch by the UK of the first aeroplane ever seen in Kabul.

'Aflaq, Michel (1910–1989) Syrian political philosopher, founder of the Ba'ath (Arab Resistance) Party in the early 1940s. During 1949 'Aflaq was briefly education minister, under President Hashem al-Atassi. He failed twice in bids to be elected to the Syrian parliament, in 1947 and 1949, but remained influential as secretary general of the Ba'ath Party. After Ba'ath came to power, in a March 1963 coup, he became marginalized as the party's military wing gained the ascendancy. After the military wing's coup in 1966, 'Aflaq left Syria and became based mainly in Baghdad, Iraq, where the Iraqi Ba'ath Party seized power in 1968.

Africa, the scramble for drive by European nations to establish colonies in Africa. It began in the 1880s, and by 1914 only two African countries remained completely independent. They were Ethiopia, which had been a kingdom for about 2,000 years, and Liberia, established in 1822 as a homeland for freed black slaves. The rest were under the control of seven European powers: Belgium, Britain, France, Germany, Italy, Portugal, and Spain. Britain and France had the most colonies. All these colonies were short-lived, and the majority attained their independence in the 1960s and 1970s.

African National Congress ANC, South African political party, founded in 1912 as a multiracial nationalist organization with the aim of extending the franchise to the whole population and ending all racial discrimination. Its president from 1997 is Thabo *Mbeki.

The ANC was banned by the government from 1960 to January 1990. Talks between the ANC and the South African government began in December 1991 and culminated in the adoption of a non-racial constitution in 1993 and the ANC's agreement to participate in a power-sharing administration, as a prelude to full majority rule. In the country's first universal suffrage elections in April 1994, the ANC won a sweeping victory, capturing 62% of the vote, and Nelson Mandela was elected president. The ANC also won a majority in South Africa's first democratic local government elections in November 1995, when it won 66.3% of the vote.

The ANC won 66% of the vote in the country's second non-racial election in June 1999, but fell just short of a two-thirds majority in parliament. The ANC government secured the coveted two-thirds majority needed to change aspects of the South African constitution by making a deal with a small Indian-led party. Through a coalition agreement with the Minority Front, the ANC secured the single extra seat it needed after the national election, taking it to 267 seats out of 400.

Although originally non-violent, in exile in Mozambique from 1960 the ANC developed a military wing, **Umkhonto we Sizwe**, which engaged in sabotage and guerrilla training.

The armed struggle was suspended in August 1990 after Mandela's release from prison and the organization's headquarters were moved from Zambia to Johannesburg.

Its vice-president from 1991 is Walter *Sisulu. Former ANC leaders include Solomon Plaatje, Albert Luthuli, and Oliver Tambo. Several imprisoned leaders were released in October 1989, Mandela in February 1990. Chris Hani was leader of the military wing from 1987 until his assassination in 1993. In October 1992, accusations of inhumane treatment of prisoners held in ANC camps outside South Africa led Mandela to institute an inquiry and promise an end to such abuses.

The ANC's successes in constitutional negotiations from 1991 were seen as a threat by *Inkatha and by white, right-wing politicians, and during the early 1990s fighting between supporters of the ANC and Inkatha left hundreds dead.

African nationalism political movement for the unification of Africa (*pan-Africanism) and for national self-determination. Early African political organizations included the Aborigines Rights Protection Society in the Gold Coast in 1897, the African National Congress in South Africa in 1912, and the National Congress of West Africa in 1920.

African Union AU; formerly **Organization of African Unity (1963–2001),** association established in 1963 as the Organization of African Unity (OAU) to eradicate colonialism and improve economic, cultural, and political cooperation in Africa. The secretary general is Amara Essy of Côte d'Ivoire (from 2001). Its headquarters are in Addis Ababa, Ethiopia. There are 53 members representing virtually the whole of central, southern, and northern Africa.

Afrika Korps German army in the western desert of North Africa 1941–43 during World War II, commanded by Field Marshal Erwin Rommel. They were driven out of North Africa by May 1943.

Agadir Incident or **the Second Moroccan Crisis,** international crisis provoked by Kaiser Wilhelm II of Germany, July–November 1911. By sending the gunboat *Panther* to demand territorial concessions from the French, he hoped to drive a wedge into the Anglo-French entente. In fact, German aggression during the Second Moroccan Crisis merely served to reinforce Anglo-French fears of Germany's intentions. The crisis gave rise to the term 'gunboat diplomacy'.

Aga Khan III (1877–1957) also known as **Sir Sultan Muhammad Aga Khan,** Spiritual head (*imam*) of the Ismaili Muslim sect, born in Karachi, India (now Pakistan). He succeeded to the title in 1885.

agitprop (Russian **'agitation propaganda')** Soviet government bureau established in September 1920 in charge of communist agitation and propaganda. The idea was later developed by left-wing groups in the West for the use of theatre and other arts to convey political messages.

Agnew, Spiro (Theodore) (1918–1996) US vice-president 1969–73, a Republican. He was governor of Maryland 1966–69, and vice-president under Richard *Nixon. Agnew took the lead in a campaign against the press and opponents of the *Vietnam War. Although he was one of the few administration officials not to be implicated in the *Watergate affair, he resigned in 1973, shortly before pleading 'no contest' to a charge of income-tax evasion.

agrarian revolution until the 1960s historians believed that there had been an 18th-century revolution in agriculture, similar to the revolution that occurred in industry. They claimed that there had been sweeping changes, possibly in response to the increased demand for food from a rapidly expanding population. Major events included the enclosure of open fields; the development of improved breeds of livestock; the introduction of four-course crop rotation; and the use of new crops such as turnips as animal fodder.

Recent research, however, has shown that these changes were only part of a much larger, slower, ongoing process of development: many were in fact underway before 1750, and other breakthroughs, such as farm mechanization, did not become common until after 1945.

agriculture, 19th-century British after a period of depression following the Napoleonic Wars, agriculture developed rapidly during the 19th century. The landed interests countered the post-war slump in agriculture with protective legislation, although the implementation of the Corn Laws led to rural poverty and discontent in the first half of the 19th century and contributed to the distress in Ireland caused by the potato famine. Following the repeal of the Corn Laws in 1846, the expanding urban population and improvements in transport opened up a greater market and led to what has been called the 'golden age' in British farming (1850–70). This, however, was followed by a great depression in agriculture that lasted until 1914, as rising imports of cheap foodstuffs undercut the British farmer.

Aguinaldo, Emilio (1869–1964)
Filipino revolutionary leader.
He became a militant nationalist on Luzon island during the 1890s and led a year-long insurrection against the Philippines' Spanish colonial rulers in 1896, which ended with his exile to Hong Kong in 1897. After the outbreak of the Spanish-American War in April 1898, Aguinaldo, with assistance from the USA, returned to Luzon to lead an anti-Spanish insurrection, at the same time as US attacks. He established a 'Visayan Republic', with its capital at Malolos and himself as president.
He opposed the peace treaty that concluded the Spanish-American War in 1899 and led a two-year-long rebellion against US occupying forces, which claimed 4,000 American and 10,000 Filipino lives. In July 1901 Aguinaldo made an oath of allegiance to the USA, in return for an amnesty. In 1935 he ran unsuccessfully for president, being defeated by Manuel Quezon.

Aguiyi-Ironsi, Johnson (1925–1966)
Nigerian politician and soldier, head of state in 1966. He commanded the Nigerian contingent during the UN involvement in the Congo from 1960, and was appointed commander-in-chief in 1965. He assumed power following the officers' coup of January 1966, but was killed in the counter-coup led by Yakuba *Gowon in July 1966.

Ahern, Bertie (1951–)   Irish politician, Taoiseach (prime minister) from 1997, leader of Fianna Fáil from 1994. After the May 1997 election he formed a minority government as Ireland's youngest Taoiseach. His promotion of peace negotiations culminated in the 1998 Good Friday Agreement between Northern Ireland's contending parties, which received 94% backing in a referendum in the Irish Republic in May 1998.

Ahidjo, Ahmadou (1924–1989)
Cameroonian politician, president 1960–82. He became president following the amalgamation of most of the British Cameroons with the French Cameroons in 1960, and was re-elected to that post in 1972, 1975, and 1980. After his resignation in 1982, he went into voluntary exile in France. His one-party state, although severe on the rival, but outlawed, Union des Populations Camerounaises (UPC), was relatively successful economically and less repressive than many West African states.

Aidid, Muhammad Farah (1936–1996)
Somali soldier and politician. A one-time colleague of the Somali president Siad Barre, in 1990 he established an anti-Barre paramilitary organization, the United Somali Congress (USC), which eventually drove the president from office in 1991. Rivalry subsequently developed within the ruling coalition and Somalia was again plunged into civil war. During 1993 United Nations peacekeeping forces (principally US Marines) targeted Aidid as the principal villain in the conflict and conducted an abortive mission to capture him. He was killed in faction fighting in August 1996.

Aisne, Battles of   three battles between Allied and German forces in northern France during World War I. The first battle in September 1914 was inconclusive and left both sides entrenched along lines they held for most of the rest of the war. The second battle April–May 1917 cost both the French and Germans heavy casualties and was one of the prime causes of the mutinies in the French army the following month. In the final battle June 1918, the Germans nearly succeeded in breaking through to Paris.

Akihito (1933–) Emperor of Japan from 1989, succeeding his father Hirohito (Showa). His reign is called the Heisei ('achievement of universal peace') era.

Akko formerly **Acre; New Testament Ptolemais**, seaport in northwest Israel, situated on the Mediterranean Sea; population (1995 est) 48,300. The city was built on a small promontory which, with Mount Carmel to the south, forms a semicircular bay. From being part of British-mandated Palestine, it became part of Israel in 1948. Industries include tourism, fishing, and light manufactures.

Alamein, El, battles of two decisive battles of World War II in the western desert of northern Egypt. In the first (1–22 July 1942), the British 8th Army under *Auchinleck held off the German and Italian forces under *Rommel; in the second (23 October–4 November 1942), *Montgomery defeated Rommel.

Alanbrooke, Alan Francis Brooke (1883–1963) 1st Viscount Alanbrooke, British army officer. He was Chief of Staff in World War II and largely responsible for the strategy that led to the German defeat.

Albania country in southeastern Europe, bounded north by Serbia and Montenegro, east by the Former Yugoslav Republic of Macedonia, south by Greece, and west and southwest by the Adriatic Sea.

Albert I (1875–1934) King of the Belgians from 1909, the younger son of Philip, Count of Flanders, and the nephew of Leopold II. In 1900 he married Duchess Elisabeth of Bavaria. In World War I he commanded the Allied army that retook the Belgian coast in 1918 and re-entered Brussels in triumph on 22 November.

Albright, Madeleine (1937–) US diplomat and Democrat politician, Secretary of State 1997–2001. An adviser to leading Democrat politicians from the early 1970s, she was US ambassador to the United Nations 1993–97.

Alcalá Zamora y Torres, Niceto (1877–1949) Spanish politician, first president of Spain 1931–36. In April 1936 a Socialist motion in the Cortes (national assembly) censuring the president was carried and he resigned.

Alcock, John William (1892–1919) English aviator. On 14 June 1919, he and Arthur Whitten-Brown made the first non-stop transatlantic flight, from Newfoundland to Ireland. He was awarded the KBE in 1919.

Alekseev, Mikhail Vasilievich (1857–1918) Russian general. He was twice appointed Chief of Staff, under the supreme commanders in chief Nicholas II (1915) and Kerenski (1917), with a brief period inbetween as commander-in-chief of all Russian armies. In 1918 he organized in the Kuban region the first anti-Bolshevik volunteer army.

Alessandri Palma, Arturo (1868–1950) Chilean president 1920–25 and 1932–37. Social and political reforms proposed in his first presidential term were blocked by an opposition-controlled congress. Forced into exile, he returned to achieve a measure of economic recovery at the expense of the repression of opponents, a policy that made him a controversial figure in Chilean history. During his second term, he established a central bank and introduced monetary reform to stabilize the national currency.

Alexander (1893–1920) King of the Hellenes (Greece), second son of King Constantine I, on whose dethronement 1917 he ascended the throne. His government, with Eleutherios Venizelos as premier, enjoyed the confidence of the Western powers. During his reign the boundaries of Greece were much extended.

Alexander I, Karageorgevich (1888–1934) Regent of Serbia 1912–21 and king of Yugoslavia 1921–34, as dictator from 1929. The second son of Peter I, King of Serbia, he was declared regent for his father in 1912 and on his father's death became king of the state of South Slavs – Yugoslavia – that had come into being in 1918.

Alexander, Harold Rupert Leofric George (1891–1969) 1st Earl Alexander of Tunis, British field marshal, a commander in World War II in France, Burma (now Myanmar), North Africa, and the Mediterranean. He was governor general of Canada 1946–52 and UK minister of defence 1952–54. He was appointed KCB in 1942, Viscount in 1946, and Earl Alexander of Tunis in 1952, and was awarded the OM in 1959.

Alexandra (1936–) Princess of the UK. Daughter of the Duke of Kent and Princess Marina, she married Angus Ogilvy (1928–), younger son of the Earl of Airlie. They have two children, James (1964–) and Marina (1966–).

Alexandra Feodorovna (1872–1918) Last tsarina of Russia 1894–1917. She was the former Princess Alix of Hessen and granddaughter of Britain's Queen Victoria. She married *Nicholas II and, from 1907, fell under the spell of *Rasputin, a 'holy man' brought to the palace to try to cure her son of haemophilia. She was shot with the rest of her family by the Bolsheviks in the Russian Revolution.

Alexeyev, Mikhail (1855–1918) Russian military commander during World War I, chief of staff 1915–17. In 1914 he was chief of staff to General Ivanoff on the Southeast Front, becoming chief of staff to the Russian Army 1915. After the March 1917 revolution he was replaced by General *Brusilov, and following the October Revolution he helped found the Volunteer Army, fighting with the counter-revolutionary 'Whites' against the Bolsheviks.

Alfonsín Foulkes, Raúl Ricardo (1927–) Argentine politician and president 1983–89. Becoming president at the time of the country's return to civilian government, he set up an investigation of the army's human-rights violations, with the subsequent trial and detention of many former military and political leaders. Economic problems caused him to seek help from the International Monetary Fund and introduce austerity measures, leading to debt restructuring and fiscal reform.

Alfonso XIII (1886–1941) King of Spain 1886–1931. He assumed power in 1906 and married Princess Ena, granddaughter of Queen Victoria of Great Britain, in the same year. He abdicated in 1931 soon after the fall of the Primo de Rivera dictatorship 1923–30 (which he supported), and Spain became a republic. His assassination was attempted several times.

Algeciras Conference international conference held Jan–April 1906 when France, Germany, Britain, Russia, and Austria-Hungary, together with the USA, Spain, the Low Countries, Portugal, and Sweden, met to settle the question of Morocco. The conference was prompted by increased German demands in what had traditionally been seen as a French area of influence, but it resulted in a reassertion of Anglo-French friendship and the increased isolation of Germany. France and Spain gained control of Morocco.

Algeria country in North Africa, bounded east by Tunisia and Libya, southeast by Niger, southwest by Mali and Mauritania, northwest by Morocco, and north by the Mediterranean Sea.

Algiers, Battle of bitter conflict in Algiers 1954–62 between the Algerian nationalist population and the French colonial army and French settlers. The conflict ended with Algerian independence in 1962.

Ali, (Chaudri) Muhammad (1905–1980) Pakistani politician, prime minister 1955–56. In 1932 he was made accountant general of Bahawalpur state and re-established its finances. In 1936 he became private secretary to the Indian finance minister and in 1945 was the first Indian to be appointed financial adviser of war and supply. In 1947, on the partition of India, he became the first secretary general of the Pakistan government, in 1951 finance minister, and in 1955 prime minister. He resigned in 1956 because of lack of support from members of his own party, the Muslim League.

Ali, Maulana Muhammad (1878–1931) Muslim Indian political activist. Following a period of imprisonment 1915–19, with his brother, Maulana Shaukat *Ali, he joined the *Khilafat movement to protest against British policy towards the sultan of Turkey, who was also caliph of Islam. Muhammad became its leader and allied with the Indian National Congress, adopting Mahatma Gandhi's *satyagraha , a strategy of nonviolent resistance to British rule. He was elected president of the Congress in 1923.

Ali, Maulana Shaukat (1873–1938) Muslim Indian political activist. The brother of Maulana Muhammad *Ali, he organized *Anjuman-i-Khuddam-i-Kaaha* in 1913 to provide support for Muslim causes in the Middle East. He later joined the *Khilafat movement and allied with the Indian National Congress.

Ali, Tariq (1943–) British political activist and writer. He was born in Lahore (then part of British India, now in Pakistan) and came to the UK in 1963 to study at Oxford University. A prominent revolutionary in the 1960s, Ali was particularly associated with the Vietnam Solidarity Campaign and student radicalism. He was a member of the (Trotskyist) International Marxist Group, editor of the radical publications *Black Dwarf* and *Red Mole*, and later joined the editorial board of *New Left Review*. His application for membership of the Labour Party was rejected in 1983.

Alia, Ramiz (1925–) Albanian communist politician, head of state 1982–92. He gradually relaxed the isolationist policies of his predecessor, Enver Hoxha, and following public unrest introduced political and economic reforms, including free elections in 1991, when he was elected executive president. In September 1994 Alia was convicted of abuse of power while in office and sentenced to eight years' imprisonment, but was released in July 1995 following an appeal court ruling. In October 1997 the Albanian prosecutor general dropped genocide charges against Alia.

Aliyev, Geidar Alirza (1923–2003) Azerbaijani politician, president 1993–2003. An Azeri Muslim veteran of the Communist Party of the Soviet Union (CPSU), of which he was a full Politburo member 1982–87, he returned to politics in his newly independent homeland in 1991. He became president in June 1993, after Albufaz Elchibey was overthrown in a military coup, and was elected in October 1993 in a contest boycotted by the opposition. His authoritarian regime has developed closer ties with Russia, while gradually promoting market-centred economic reforms. He was re-elected in 1995 and 1998.

Allenby, Edmund Henry Hynman (1861–1936) 1st Viscount Allenby, British field marshal. In World War I he served in France before taking command 1917–19 of the British forces in the Middle East. After preparations in Egypt, he captured Gaza, Beersheba and, in 1917, Jerusalem. His defeat of the Turkish forces at Megiddo in Palestine in September 1918 was followed almost at once by the capitulation of Turkey. He was high commissioner in Egypt 1919–35. KCB 1915, Viscount 1919.

Allende (Gossens), Salvador (1908–1973) Chilean left-wing politician, president 1970–73. Elected president as the candidate of the Popular Front alliance, Allende never succeeded in keeping the electoral alliance together in government. His failure to solve the country's economic problems or to deal with political subversion allowed the army, backed by the Central Intelligence

Agency (CIA), to stage the 1973 coup that brought about the death of Allende and many of his supporters.

Allende, born in Valparaíso and educated as a physician at the University of Chile, became a Marxist activist in the 1930s and was elected to congress in 1937 and the senate in 1945. He rose to prominence as a presidential candidate in 1952, 1958, and 1964. In each election he had the support of the socialist and communist movements but was defeated by the Christian Democrats and nationalists. As president, his socialism, land reforms, and nationalization of banking and US-owned copper mines led the CIA to regard him as a communist and to their involvement in the coup that replaced him by General Augusto Pinochet.

Alliance for Progress programme of US assistance to Latin American countries, initiated by President Kennedy in 1961 under the auspices of the *Organization of American States.

Allies, the in World War I, the 27 Allied and Associated powers aligned against the Central Powers (Germany, Austro-Hungary, Turkey, and Bulgaria) and represented at the Treaty of Versailles (1919); they included France, Italy, Russia, the UK, Australia and other Commonwealth nations, and, in the latter part of the war, the USA. In World War II they were some 49 countries allied against the *Axis Powers (Germany, Italy, and Japan), including France, the UK, Australia and other Commonwealth nations, the USA, and the former Soviet Union.

Alpini elite Italian mountain military force founded 1872. Expanded during World War I into 8 special regiments and 38 companies of militia, they used mule transport and were all adept mountaineers and skiers. Among their exploits was the capture April 1916 of the Adamello Glacier during a snowstorm from an Austrian force at an altitude of over 3,000 m/10,000 ft.

***Altmark* incident** naval skirmish in World War II. The *Altmark*, a German auxiliary cruiser, was intercepted on 15 February 1940 by the British destroyer *Intrepid* off the coast of Norway. It was carrying the captured crews of Allied merchant ships sunk by the German battleship *Admiral Graf Spee* in the South Atlantic, and took refuge in Jösing fjord, where it was cornered by HMS *Cossack*, under Captain Vian, and ran aground. Vian's men released 299 British merchant sailors.

Amado, Jorge (1912–2001) Brazilian novelist. His first novel, *O país do carnaval/The Country of the Carnival* (1932), follows a youthful member of the intelligentsia seeking political answers in the wake of the revolution of 1930. Amado's next few novels outlined his personal manifesto and highlighted the cause of various exploited groups in society. *Gabriela, cravo e canela/Gabriela, Clove and Cinnamon* (1952) marked a change in style and emphasis and focused on sociopolitical change.

He was imprisoned for his leftist political beliefs in 1935 and spent several years in exile, though he briefly represented the Communist Party of Brazil as federal deputy of the Brazilian parliament 1946–47.

Amal radical Lebanese Shiite military force, established by Musa Sadr in the 1970s; its headquarters are in Borj al-Barajneh. The movement split into extremist and moderate groups in 1982, but both sides agreed on the aim of increasing Shiite political representation in Lebanon.

Amanullah Khan (1892–1960) Emir (ruler) of Afghanistan 1919–29, who assumed the title of king in 1926. Third son of Habibullah Khan, he seized the throne on his father's assassination and concluded a treaty with the British, but his policy of westernization led to rebellion in 1928. Amanullah had to flee, abdicated in 1929, and settled in Rome, Italy.

Amato, Giuliano (1938–) Italian law professor and socialist politician, prime minister 1992–93 and 2000–01. Heading a centre-left government, Amato was sworn in as Italy's prime minister in April 2000, having served as prime minister 1992–93 and as treasury minister 1999–2000. He was one of the country's few leading socialists to emerge unscathed from the corruption scandals of the early 1990s. As prime minister, Amato showed that he was not afraid to tackle notoriously difficult issues.

Ambrose, Stephen (1936–2002) US historian. A prolific writer, he published more than 30 books, many of them on World War II. Several of his books, including *Band of Brothers* (1993), *D-day* (1994), and *Undaunted Courage* (1996) became bestsellers. He was also known for his biographies of US presidents Dwight D Eisenhower and Richard Nixon, and American Civil War leaders Crazy Horse and Gen George Custer.

American Expeditionary Force AEF, US forces sent to fight in Europe after the USA entered World War I in April 1917. Although initially only a token force of one division went to France under General Pershing, by November 1918 the AEF comprised three armies each of three corps, a total of 1,338,000 combat troops.

American Legion community organization in the USA, originally for ex-servicemen of World War I, founded 1919. It has approximately 2.9 million members, and has admitted veterans of World War II, the Korean War, and the Vietnam War. Veterans of more recent wars are also eligible to join.

***Amethyst* Incident** UK–China episode arising 20 April 1949 when a British frigate, HMS *Amethyst*, sailing on the Chang Jiang (Yangtze) River, was fired at by communist Chinese forces. The ship was trapped for 14 weeks before breaking free and completing the journey to the sea. The temporary detention of this British vessel has been interpreted as an attempt by the Chinese to assert their sovereignty over what had been considered an international waterway.

Amin (Dada), Idi (1925–2003) Ugandan politician, president 1971–79. He led the coup that deposed Milton Obote in 1971, expelled the Asian community in 1972, and exercised a reign of terror over his people during which an estimated 300,000 people were killed. After he invaded Tanzania in 1978, the Tanzanian army combined with dissident Ugandans to counter-attack. Despite assistance from Libya, Amin's forces collapsed and he fled in 1979, settling in Saudi Arabia.

Amin was commissioned into the new Ugandan army in 1962 and an alliance with President Obote led to rapid promotion; by 1966 he was commander of the armed forces. Mounting evidence of Amin's corruption and brutality had convinced Obote to replace him at the end of 1970, but Amin seized power before he could do so. He suspended the constitution and all political activity and took legislative and executive powers into his own hands. During his brutal regime a large proportion of the educated elite were killed or fled into exile, as well as significant numbers of the Acholi and Langi peoples and Christians. His so-called 'economic war' against foreign domination resulted in the mass expulsion of the Asian population in 1972, appropriation of their assets promoting further collapse in the economy.

Amnesty International human-rights organization established in the UK in 1961 to campaign for the release of prisoners of conscience worldwide; fair trials for all political prisoners; an end to the death penalty, torture, and other inhuman treatment of all prisoners; and the end of extrajudicial (outside of the law) executions and 'disappearances'. It has no political or economic ties. By 2001 Amnesty International had more than a million members and supporters in some 160 countries and territories, and section offices in over 50 countries. The organization was awarded the Nobel Prize for Peace in 1977 for its work to secure the release of political prisoners. It is based in London.

Amritsar Massacre or **Jallianwalah Bagh massacre**, the killing of 379 Indians (and wounding of 1,200) in Amritsar, at the site of a Sikh religious shrine in the Punjab in 1919. British troops under Gen Edward Dyer opened fire without warning on a crowd of some 10,000, assembled to protest against the arrest of two Indian National Congress leaders (see *Congress Party).

Anastasia (1901–1918) Russian Grand Duchess, youngest daughter of *Nicholas II. During the Russian Revolution she was presumed shot with her parents by the Bolsheviks after the Revolution of 1917, but it has been alleged that Anastasia escaped.

Ancre, Battle of the in World War I, one of the last of the series of battles in the Somme area 1916–17. In three days of fighting November 1916, British forces attempted to capture a heavily fortified German salient based on the village of Beaumont-Hamel. They captured the village and advanced about a mile until difficult weather conditions made fighting impossible.

Andean Group Spanish **Grupo Andino**, South American organization aimed at economic and social cooperation between member states. It was established under the Treaty of Cartagena (1969), by Bolivia, Chile, Colombia, Ecuador, and Peru. Venezuela joined in 1973, but Chile withdrew in 1976 and Peru suspended membership and became an observer in 1992. The Andean Pact was established in 1992 to create a free trade area. The organization is based in Lima, Peru.

Anders, Wladyslaw (1892–1970) Polish general and leader of Polish forces in exile during World War II.

Andorra landlocked country in the east Pyrenees, bounded north by France and south by Spain.

Andreotti, Giulio (1919–) Italian Christian Democrat politician, a fervent European. He headed seven post-war governments: 1972–73, 1976–79 (four successive terms), and 1989–92 (two terms). In addition he was defence minister eight times, and foreign minister five times. In 1993 Andreotti was among several high-ranking politicians accused of possible involvement in Italy's corruption network; he went on trial in September 1995 charged with using his influence to protect Mafia leaders in exchange for political support. He was acquitted in October 1999.

Andrew, Andrew Albert Christian Edward (1960–) Prince of the UK, Duke of York, second son of Queen Elizabeth II. He married Sarah Ferguson in 1986; their first daughter, Princess Beatrice, was born in 1988, and their second daughter, Princess Eugenie, was born in 1990. The couple separated in 1992 and were officially divorced in May 1996. Prince Andrew was a naval helicopter pilot and served during the Falklands War, and in 1999 accepted a naval post in international relations.

Andropov, Yuri (1914–1984) Soviet communist politician, president of the USSR 1983–84. As chief of the KGB 1967–82, he established a reputation for efficiently suppressing dissent.

Andropov was politically active from the 1930s. His part in quelling the Hungarian national uprising of 1956, when he was Soviet ambassador, brought him into the Communist Party secretariat 1962 as a specialist on East European affairs. He became a member of the Politburo in 1973 and succeeded Brezhnev as party general secretary in 1982. Elected president in 1983, he instituted economic reforms.

Angels of Mons visions of St George accompanied by angels, mounted horsemen, medieval cavalry, and similar apparitions reportedly seen in the sky by British troops retreating after their defeat at the Battle of Mons in August 1914. The testimony of soldiers who took part in the retreat is generally ascribed to fatigue-induced hallucinations.

Anglo-Irish Agreement or **Hillsborough Agreement**, concord reached in 1985 between the UK prime minister Margaret Thatcher and Irish prime minister Garret FitzGerald. One sign of the improved relations between the two countries was increased cooperation between police and security forces across the border between Northern Ireland and the Republic of Ireland.

The pact also gave the Irish Republic a greater voice in the conduct of Northern Ireland's affairs. However, the agreement was rejected by Northern Ireland Unionists as a step towards renunciation of British sovereignty. Following further talks in March 1988, the UK and Irish prime ministers issued a joint statement in Northern Ireland. The statement did not envisage any particular outcome, but specified that the consent of the majority of the people of Northern Ireland was required before there could be any constitutional change.

All-party peace talks were planned during the Irish Republican Army (IRA) ceasefire from 1994 to 1996, but were delayed by the IRA's unwillingness to decommission its arms prior to full British troop withdrawal from Northern Ireland. After the ceasefire was restored in July 1997, multiparty peace talks on the future of Northern Ireland started in September 1997.

Anglo-Irish Treaty in Irish history, articles of agreement between Britain and southern Ireland signed in London in December 1921, which confirmed the end of the *Anglo-Irish War (1919–21) but then precipitated the Irish Civil War (1922–23). The settlement created the *Irish Free State within the British Commonwealth and endorsed the creation of Northern Ireland. (Previously, the 1920 Government of Ireland Act had provided for partition of Ireland and two home rule parliaments.) Republicans split into pro-Treaty and anti-Treaty factions, opposition mainly centring on the subjugation of the Irish to the British monarchy, by the appointment of a British governor general, and an oath of allegiance to Britain required by members of the Parliament of the Irish Free State. Civil war was initiated by the provisional government of the Free State in 1922 to crush the anti-Treaty movement.

Anglo-Irish War or **the War of Independence**, conflict in Ireland 1919–21, between the *Irish Republican Army (IRA), the paramilitary wing of Sinn Fein, and British government forces, reinforced by the ex-service Auxiliaries and *Black and Tans. Its outbreak is usually dated to the IRA's killing of two policemen in Soloheadbeg, County Tipperary, on 21 January 1919. Following a war of guerrilla tactics, ambushes, assassinations, and reprisals, a truce negotiated in July 1921 led to the *Anglo-Irish Treaty, which established the *Irish Free State. Over 550 soldiers and police and more than 750 volunteers and civilians died during the conflict.

Angola country in southwest Africa, bounded west by the Atlantic Ocean, north and northeast by the Democratic Republic of Congo (formerly Zaire), east by Zambia, and south by Namibia. The Cabinda enclave, a district of Angola, is bounded west by the Atlantic Ocean, north by the Congo River, and east and south by the Democratic Republic of Congo.

Annales school or **total history**, group of historians formed in France in 1929, centred on the journal *Annales d'histoire économique et sociale* that pioneered new methods of historical enquiry. Its leading members included Fernand

*Braudel, who coined the term 'total history', and Marc Bloch. Their view was that to arrive at worthwhile conclusions on broad historical debates, all aspects of a society had to be considered. Thus they widened the scope of research away from political history to include social and economic factors as well.

Annam former country of Southeast Asia, incorporated in Vietnam in 1946 as Central Vietnam. Its capital was Hué. A Bronze Age civilization was flourishing in the area when China conquered it in about 111 BC. The Chinese named their conquest An-Nam, 'peaceful south'. Independent from 1428, Annam signed a treaty with France in 1787 and became a French protectorate, part of Indochina in 1884. During World War II, Annam was occupied by Japan.

Annan, Kofi (1938–) Ghanaian diplomat, secretary general of the United Nations (UN) from 1997. Heading the peacekeeping department of the UN from 1993, he oversaw its peacekeeping operations in Somalia from 1993 and in Bosnia-Herzegovina from 1995. He was re-elected in 2001. In the same year, he shared the 2001 Nobel Prize for Peace with the UN itself.

Anne, Anne Elizabeth Alice Louise (1950–) Princess of the UK, second child of Queen Elizabeth II, declared Princess Royal in 1987. She is actively involved in global charity work, especially for children. An excellent horse rider, she won silver medals in both individual and team events in the 1975 European Championships, and competed in the 1976 Olympics.

Anschluss (German **'union'**) the annexation of Austria with Germany, accomplished by the German chancellor Adolf Hitler on 12 March 1938.

Antarctic Treaty international agreement between 13 nations aiming to promote scientific research and keep Antarctica free from conflict, dating from 1961. In 1991 a 50-year ban on

mining activity was secured. An environmental protection protocol, addressing the issues of wildlife conservation, mineral exploitation, and marine pollution, came into effect in January 1998 after it was ratified by Japan. Antarctica is now a designated 'natural reserve devoted to peace and science'.

Anti-Comintern Pact or Anti-Communist Pact, agreement signed between Germany and Japan 25 November 1936, opposing communism as a menace to peace and order. The pact was signed by Italy in 1937 and by Hungary, Spain, and the Japanese puppet state of Manchukuo in 1939. While directed against the USSR, the agreement also had the effect of giving international recognition to Japanese rule in Manchuria.

Antigua and Barbuda country comprising three islands in the eastern Caribbean (Antigua, Barbuda, and uninhabited Redonda).

Antonescu, Ion (1886–1946) Romanian general and politician. He headed a pro-German government during World War II, which enforced the Nazis' anti-Semitic policies, and was executed for war crimes in 1946.

Anzac acronym for **Australian and New Zealand Army Corps**, general term for all troops of both countries serving in World War I, particularly one who fought at *Gallipoli, and to some extent in World War II. It began as a code name based on the initials of the Corps in January 1915. The term may also be used generally of any Australian or New Zealand soldier, though 'digger' is more usual.

Anzac Cove cove on the west coast of the *Gallipoli peninsula in Turkey where Australian and New Zealand troops landed on 25 April 1915 during World War I. The name was adopted a few days after the landing. In 1990 it was the site of an international gathering to mark the 75th anniversary of the event.

Anzio, Battle of in World War II, the beachhead invasion of Italy 22 Jan–23 May 1944 by Allied troops; failure to use information gained by deciphering German codes led to Allied troops being stranded temporarily after German attacks.

ANZUS acronym for **Australia, New Zealand, and the United States** (Pacific Security Treaty), a military alliance established in 1951. It was replaced in 1954 by the Southeast Asia Treaty Organization (SEATO).

Aosta, Duke Amadeo (1898–1942) Italian general, cousin of King Emmanuel of Italy. During World War II, he was a general of the Italian Air Force and Viceroy of Abyssinia (now Ethiopia).

apartheid (Afrikaans 'apartness') racial-segregation policy of the government of South Africa from 1948 to 1994. Under the apartheid system, non-whites – classified as Bantu (black), coloured (mixed), or Indian – did not share full rights of citizenship with the white minority. For example, black people could not vote in parliamentary elections, and until 1990 many public facilities and institutions were restricted to the use of one race only. The establishment of Black National States was another manifestation of apartheid. In 1991, after years of internal dissent and violence and the boycott of South Africa, including the imposition of international trade sanctions by the United Nations (UN) and other organizations, President F W *de Klerk repealed the key elements of apartheid legislation and by 1994 apartheid had ceased to exist.

The term apartheid has also been loosely applied to similar movements and other forms of racial separation, for example social or educational, in other parts of the world.

apartheid policies The term 'apartheid' was coined in the late 1930s by the South African Bureau for Racial Affairs (SABRA), which called for a policy of 'separate development' of the races. It was first legislated in 1948, when the Afrikaner National Party gained power under Prime Minister *Malan. The principal measures adopted included the prohibition of mixed marriages (1949) and sexual relations between individuals of different race (1950); the introduction of the 'pass laws' of 1950, which required all black people over the age of 16 to carry identity documents; and the provision of separate transport and other public facilities for non-whites, which was introduced under the Separate Amenities Act of 1953. These measures were further reinforced in 1950 by a forced resettlement policy, by which the government segregated the population into different areas on the basis of ethnic background; and by legislation in education, which first set out a restricted curriculum for black school children (under the Bantu Education Act of 1953), and later led to the establishment, in 1959, of five 'ethnic' universities and the banning of non-white students from all other universities. In the 1970s the Bantu Homelands Citizenship Act provided for all blacks to eventually become citizens of segregated 'homelands', and for their South African citizenship to be revoked.

Internally, organizations opposed to apartheid were banned, including the *African National Congress (ANC) and the *United Democratic Front (UDF). Some leading campaigners for its abolition, like Steve *Biko, were killed; others, such as Archbishop Desmond *Tutu, were harassed.

opposition to apartheid As well as the ANC and UDF (which were founded in 1912 and 1983 respectively), a number of other anti-apartheid organizations were active in South African politics during the years of apartheid. Even as the government first began to legislate apartheid policies, the ANC's leaders joined with coloured and Indian groups in the 'defiance campaign' of 1952, holding peaceful demonstrations to draw attention to their grievances. The campaign collapsed within a few months, however, and its leaders, including Albert *Luthuli, were banned or imprisoned, while new legislation was introduced to block further demonstrations. Other opposition to the Afrikaner National Party included the multiracial Liberal Party, which was set up in 1953 and eventually included universal suffrage among its aims, as well as the Pan Africanist Congress (PAC) and the Progressive Party, which were both formed in 1959.

uprisings Anti-apartheid feeling resulted in many uprisings, including the *Sharpeville uprising of 1960, which took place during a campaign launched by the pan-Africanist Congress against the pass laws; the Soweto riots of 1976, which were prompted by the government's ruling that Afrikaans was to be the language used in African schools; and unrest at the Crossroads squatter camps in 1986. During this period, thousands of the regime's opponents were imprisoned without trial and many anti-apartheid leaders were exiled, while others joined guerrilla forces outside South Africa.

appeasement   historically, the conciliatory policy adopted by the British government, in particular under *Neville Chamberlain, towards the Nazi and fascist dictators in Europe in the 1930s in an effort to maintain peace (see *United Kingdom: history 1914–45, **policy of appeasement**). It was strongly opposed by *Winston Churchill, but the *Munich Agreement of 1938 was almost universally hailed as its justification. Appeasement ended when Germany occupied Bohemia–Moravia in March 1939.

Aquino, (Maria) Corazon (1933–) called '**Cory**'; born **Maria Corazon Conjuangco**, Filipino centrist

politician, president 1986–92. She was instrumental in the nonviolent overthrow of President Ferdinand *Marcos in 1986. As president, she sought to rule in a conciliatory manner, but encountered opposition from the left (communist guerrillas) and the right (army coup attempts), and her land reforms were seen as inadequate.

Arab–Israeli Wars   series of wars and territorial conflicts between Israel and various Arab states in the Middle East since the founding of the state of Israel in May 1948. These include the war of 1948–49; the 1956 Suez War between Israel and Egypt; the Six-Day War of 1967, in which Israel captured territory from Syria and Jordan; the October War of 1973; and the 1982–85 war between Israel and Lebanon. In the times between the wars tension has remained high in the area, and has resulted in skirmishes and terrorist activity taking place on both sides.

first Arab–Israeli War (1948–1949) As soon as the independent state of Israel was proclaimed on 14 May 1948, it was invaded by combined Arab forces and full-scale war broke out, which ended finally with Israeli victory and a series of armistices. Israel retained the western part of Jerusalem, Galilee, and the Negev, and went on to annex territory until it controlled 75% of what had been Palestine under British mandate. The Arab states subsequently imposed an economic boycott on Israel and continued to make raids across the border, which eventually prompted an Israeli attack on the Egyptian garrison in the Gaza Strip in February 1955. The war also produced a flood of Arab refugees from Israel and the war areas.

second Arab–Israeli War (29 October–5 November 1956) After Egypt had taken control of the Suez Canal and blockaded the Straits of Tiran, causing the *Suez Crisis, Israel, with British and French support, invaded and captured Sinai and the Gaza Strip. Under heavy US pressure, and after the entry of a United Nations (UN) force in 1957, Israel finally withdrew its forces.

third Arab–Israeli War, the Six-Day War (5–10 June 1967) In the events leading up to the war of 1967, Egypt (then the United Arab Republic) blockaded the Straits of Tiran, and introduced troops into Sinai. Israel launched a pre-emptive attack on three fronts (against Egypt, Jordan, and Syria) on 5 June 1967 and within six days its armed forces achieved a victory that resulted in the capture of the Golan Heights from Syria; the eastern half of Jerusalem and the West Bank from Jordan; and, in the south, the Gaza Strip and Sinai peninsula as far as the Suez Canal from Egypt. This victory earned only a limited degree of peace, although the occupied territories – which doubled the area under Israel's control – greatly enhanced the Israelis' feelings of security.

fourth Arab–Israeli War, the October War or **Yom Kippur War** (6–24 October 1973) This war was so called because the Israeli forces were taken by surprise on Yom Kippur (the Day of Atonement), a Jewish holy day. In recognition of their failures since 1948 Egypt and Syria chose to start the war on the day when the Israelis would be at their most vulnerable, as the whole country effectively shuts down for the 24 hours of Yom Kippur. It started with the crossing of the Suez Canal by Egyptian forces, who made initial gains, though, in the face of Israeli counter-attacks, there was some later loss of ground by the Syrians in the north. The war had 19,000 casualties, and also led to a shift of certain sectors of international opinion against Israel.

fifth Arab–Israeli War (6 June 1982–1984) From 1978 the presence of Palestinian guerrillas in Lebanon led to Arab raids on Israel and Israeli retaliation, and on 6 June 1982 Israel launched a full-scale invasion of Lebanon. By 14 June Beirut was encircled, and the *Palestine Liberation Organization (PLO) and Syrian forces were evacuated (mainly to Syria) 21–31 August. In December 1982 multinational peace-keeping forces were sent in to keep the warring factions in Beirut apart. In February 1984 there was a unilateral withdrawal of the multinational forces. However, Israel maintained a 'security zone' in southern Lebanon, and supported the South Lebanese Army militia as a buffer against Palestinian and *Hezbollah guerrilla incursions.

events in the 1990s In July 1993, following the killing of seven Israeli soldiers in south Lebanon, Israel launched a week-long attack on the area. In July 1994, Israel and Jordan sign a declaration ending the 46-year-old 'state of war' between them. In April 1996, after Hezbollah guerrillas fired rockets into northern Israel from south Lebanon, Israel launched a seventeen-day attack on the country, known as the 'Grapes of Wrath'. In May 2000, Israeli troops were withdrawn from south Lebanon, and were replaced by Lebanese and UN forces. However, negotiations with Syria regarding the Golan Heights failed to reach agreement. Intensive negotiations to push forward the *Israel–Palestine peace process, hosted by US president Bill Clinton at Camp David, collapsed at the beginning of 2001.

Arab League or **League of Arab States**, organization of Arab states established in Cairo in 1945 to promote Arab unity, primarily in opposition to Israel. The original members were Egypt, Syria, Iraq, Lebanon, Transjordan (Jordan 1949), Saudi Arabia, and Yemen. They were later joined by Algeria, Bahrain, Comoros, Djibouti, Kuwait, Libya, Mauritania, Morocco, Oman, Palestine, the PLO, Qatar, Somalia, Sudan, Tunisia, and the United Arab Emirates. In 1979 Egypt was suspended and the league's headquarters transferred to Tunis in protest against the Egypt–Israeli peace, but Egypt was readmitted as a full member in May 1989, and in March 1990 its headquarters returned to Cairo. Despite the strains imposed on it by the 1990–91 Gulf War, the alliance survived. The secretary general is Amr Mohammed Musa, a former Egyptian foreign minister, from 2001.

Arafat, Yassir (1929–) born **Muhammad Yassir Abdul-Ra'ouf Arafat As Qudwa al-Husseini,** Palestinian nationalist politician, cofounder of the al-*Fatah (Movement for the National Liberation of Palestine) resistance group in 1958, leader of the *Palestine Liberation Organization (PLO) from 1969, and president of the Palestinian National Authority (PNA) from 1994. He was a key player in peace talks with Israel regarding the status of the Palestinian territories of the Gaza Strip and the West Bank within Israel (see *Israel–Palestine peace process). His power as president of the PNA was diminished by his failure to control Palestinian extremists during the intifada (uprising) against Israel that began in September 2000, and the appointment in 2003 of a prime minister to run day-to-day government in the PNA. In 1994, he shared the Nobel Prize for Peace with Israeli prime minister Yitzhak *Rabin and foreign minister Shimon *Peres for their agreement of an accord on Palestinian self-rule.

Arakan or **Rakhine,** state of *Myanmar (formerly Burma) on the Bay of Bengal coast, some 645 km/ 400 mi long and strewn with islands; population (1994 est) 2,482,000. Most of Arakan is mountainous or hilly land, originally covered with tropical forest, though this has now mainly been destroyed by shifting cultivation and has been replaced by a dense growth of bamboo. Only 10% of the area, mainly in river deltas, is cultivated, with rice and tobacco being leading

crops. The chief town is Sittwe. It is bounded along its eastern side by the Arakan Yoma, a mountain range rising to 3,000 m/10,000 ft. It shares a short border with Bangladesh to the north. The ancient kingdom of Arakan was conquered by Burma in 1785.

Arapaho (**Arapaho 'trader'**) member of an American Indian people who moved from Minnesota and North Dakota to the upper Missouri River area in the 17th century, where they became close allies of the Cheyenne. Their language belongs to the Algonquian family. Originally a farming people in the eastern woodlands, they acquired horses and adopted the nomadic existence of the Plains Indians, hunting buffalo, and raiding other peoples and Anglo-American settlers. They also became known as great traders. The Arapaho now live on reservations in Wyoming and Oklahoma, and number about 5,000 (1990).

Arbenz Guzmán, Jácobo (1913–1971) Guatemalan social democratic politician and president from 1951 until his overthrow in 1954 by army rebels led by Carlos Castillo Armas, operating with the help of the US Central Intelligence Agency (CIA).

Archangel, Expedition to joint Allied (British, French, and US) operation 1918–19 to stabilize the Eastern Front following the Russian Revolution and safeguard the large concentration of military stores which had been sent to Archangel and other Western military interests in the area. The Allied force succeeded in capturing Murmansk in July 1918 and then bombarded Archangel by air and sea, taking the city in August 1918. The Bolsheviks were driven from the area and a new local government established. However by early 1919, Archangel was little more than an enclave in an otherwise almost entirely Bolshevik country and it was evacuated August–September 1919.

Arctic convoys in World War II, series of supply convoys sailing from the UK to the USSR around the North Cape to Murmansk, commencing October 1941.

Arendt, Hannah (1906–1975) German-born US political philosopher. Her concerns included totalitarianism, the nature of evil, and the erosion of public participation in the political process. Her works include *Eichmann in Jerusalem* (1963) and *On Violence* (1972).

Arens, Moshe (1925–) Israeli politician and engineer, deputy leader of the Likud Party from 1992. He was elected to the Knesset (Israeli parliament) in 1974. In 1982 he was appointed ambassador to the USA and in 1986 he was given responsibility for Israeli–Arab affairs. Although instinctively right-wing in his views, he was also a pragmatist and, although initially opposed to dealings with the Palestine Liberation Organization (PLO), accepted the need for compromise.

Arevalo Bermejo, Juan José (1904–1990) Guatemalan president 1945–51, elected to head a civilian government after a popular revolt in 1944 ended a 14-year period of military rule. During his years in power, there were more than 20 attempts to oust him. He sought to promote social justice, with labour law and educational reforms, and health projects. He also renewed the dispute with the UK over Belize. However, many of his reforms were later undone by subsequent military rulers.

Argentina country in South America, bounded west and south by Chile, north by Bolivia, and east by Paraguay, Brazil, Uruguay, and the Atlantic Ocean.

Arias Navarro, Carlos (1908–1989) Spanish politician. As a state prosecutor in the Spanish Civil War, he gained notoriety as the 'Butcher of Málaga' during the nationalists' savage repression of the province. He became prime minister after the assassination of Luis Carrero Blanco in December 1973, and was confirmed as the first prime minister of the monarchy following Franco's death in 1975.

He resigned in 1976 under Juan Carlos I, having proved too hardline to effect the transition to democracy.

Arias Sánchez, Oscar (1940–) Costa Rican politician, president 1986–90, and secretary general of the left-wing National Liberation Party (PLN) from 1979. He advocated a neutralist policy and in 1987 was the leading promoter of the Central American Peace Plan, which brought peace to neighbouring Nicaragua. He lost the presidency to Rafael Angel Caldéron Fournier in 1990. He was awarded the Nobel Prize for Peace in 1987 for promoting peace in Central America.

Aristide, Jean-Bertrand (1953–) President of Haiti 1990–91, 1994–95, and from 2001. A left-wing Catholic priest opposed to the right-wing regime of the Duvalier family, he relinquished his priesthood in 1994 to concentrate on the presidency. He initially campaigned for the National Front for Change and Democracy, representing a loose coalition of peasants, trade unionists, and clerics. His return to power in 2001 on a similar platform was accompanied by parliamentary success for his new party of supporters, the Fanmi Lavalas (FL).

aristocracy (Greek *aristos* 'best', *kratos* 'power')** social elite or system of political power associated with landed wealth, as in Western Europe; with monetary wealth, as in Carthage and Venice; or with religious superiority, as were the Brahmans in India. Aristocracies are also usually associated with monarchy but have frequently been in conflict with the sovereign over their respective rights and privileges. In Europe, their economic base was undermined during the 19th century by inflation and falling agricultural prices, leading to their demise as a political force after 1914.

Armenia country in western Asia, bounded east by Azerbaijan, north by Georgia, west by Turkey, and south by Iran.

Armenian massacres series of massacres of Armenians by Turkish soldiers between 1895 and 1915. In 1894–96 demands for better treatment led to massacres of Armenians in eastern Asia Minor. Over 50,000 Armenians were killed by Kurdish irregulars and Ottoman troops. The killing was stopped by the major European powers, but in 1915 Ottoman suspicions of Armenian loyalty led to further massacres and deportations. The Turks deported 1.75 million Armenians to Syria and Palestine; 600,000 to 1 million were either killed or died of starvation during the journey.

armistice cessation of hostilities while awaiting a peace settlement.
The Armistice refers specifically to the end of World War I between Germany and the Allies on 11 November 1918. On 22 June 1940, following the German invasion of France, French representatives signed an armistice with Germany in the same railway carriage at Compiègne as in 1918. No armistice was signed with either Germany or Japan in 1945; both nations surrendered and there was no provision for the suspension of fighting. The Korean armistice, signed at Panmunjom on 27 July 1953, terminated the Korean War 1950–53.

Armistice Day anniversary of the armistice signed 11 November 1918, ending World War I.

arms trade sale of conventional weapons, such as tanks, combat aircraft, and related technology, from a manufacturing country to another nation. Arms exports are known in the trade as 'arms transfers'. Most transfers take place between governments and can be accompanied by training and maintenance agreements. International agreements, such as the *Nuclear Non-Proliferation Treaty, outlaw the transfer of nuclear weapons and weapons of biological or chemical warfare. There are also agreements not to supply certain countries with conventional weapons, such as Iraq and Libya which may use weapons for internal repression or neighbour disputes. However, an active black market means that these arms embargoes are typically overcome. Around a half of the world's arms exports end up in countries of the developing world. Iraq, for instance, was armed in the years leading up to the 1991 Gulf War mainly by the USSR but also by France, Brazil, and South Africa.

Arnhem, Battle of in World War II, airborne operation by the Allies, 17–26 September 1944, to secure a bridgehead over the Rhine, thereby opening the way for a thrust towards the Ruhr and a possible early end to the war. It was only partially successful, with 7,600 casualties.

Arras, Battle of battle of World War I, April–May 1917; an effective but costly British attack on German forces in support of a French offensive, which was only partially successful, on the *Siegfried Line. British casualties totalled 170,000 as compared to 75,000 German casualties.

Asanuma, Inejiro (1898–1960) Japanese politician, leader of the Japan Socialist Party. In 1946 he was elected to the lower house of the Diet (parliament) in the first post-war election and repeatedly thereafter. He was stabbed to death by a 17-year-old right-wing assassin as he made a public speech in 1960.

Ashdown, Paddy (Jeremy John Durham) (1941–) British politician, leader of the Liberal Democrat party 1988–99. His party significantly increased its seat holding in the 1997 general election, winning more seats than it had had since the 1920s, and cooperated in areas such as constitutional reform with the new Labour government of Tony Blair. From 1997 Ashdown sat with Blair on a joint cabinet committee, whose scope was extended from constitutional issues in November 1998 to cover areas such as health, education, and Europe. Ashdown stood down as Liberal Democrat leader in 1999 and was replaced by Charles Kennedy, elected in August. Ashdown retired as a member of Parliament in June 2001.

Asquith, Herbert Henry (1852–1928) 1st Earl of Oxford and Asquith, British Liberal politician, prime minister 1908–16. As chancellor of the Exchequer, he introduced old-age pensions in 1908. He limited the powers of the House of Lords and attempted to give Ireland *home rule.

Assad, Hafez al (1930–2000) Syrian Ba'athist politician, president 1971–2000. He became prime minister after a bloodless military coup in 1970. The following year he became the first president to be elected by popular vote. Having suppressed dissent, he was re-elected in 1978, 1985, 1991, and 1999. He was a Shia (Alawite) Muslim.

He ruthlessly suppressed domestic opposition, and was Iran's only major Arab ally in its war against Iraq. He steadfastly pursued military parity with Israel, and made himself a key player in any settlement of the Lebanese civil war or Middle East conflict generally. His support for United Nations action against Iraq following its invasion of Kuwait in 1990 raised his international standing. In 1995, following intense US diplomatic pressure, he was close to reaching a mutual peace agreement with Israel. However, the assassination of Yitzhak *Rabin in November 1995 and the return of a Likud-led government in Israel seriously threatened the peace process. Upon his death in June 2000 he was succeeded by his son, Bashar.

Association of South East Asian Nations ASEAN, regional alliance formed in Bangkok in 1967; it took over the non-military role of the Southeast Asia Treaty Organization in 1975. Its members are Indonesia, Malaysia, the Philippines, Singapore, Thailand, (from 1984) Brunei, (from 1995) Vietnam, (from 1997) Laos and Myanmar, and (from 1999) Cambodia; its headquarters are in Jakarta, Indonesia. North Korea took part in the organization for the first time at the 2000 annual meeting of foreign ministers.

Astor, Nancy (1879–1964) born **Nancy Witcher Langhorne**, US-born British Conservative politician, the first woman member to sit in the House of Commons. After marrying into the wealthy Anglo-American Astor family, Nancy Astor entered Parliament in 1919. She was a keen advocate of women's rights, social reform, and temperance movements. She wrote an early biography *My Two Countries* (1923).

Astor, Waldorf, 2nd Viscount Astor of Cliveden (1879–1952) British politician and newspaper proprietor. Astor was Conservative and Unionist MP for Plymouth 1910–19, when he was raised to the peerage. During his political career, he held several junior ministerial posts.

Atatürk, Kemal (1881–1938) born **Mustafa Kemal Pasha, (**Turkish **'Father of the Turks')** Turkish politician and general, first president of Turkey from 1923. After World War I he established a provisional rebel government and in 1921–22 the Turkish armies under his leadership expelled the Greeks who were occupying Turkey. He was the founder of the modern republic, which he ruled as a virtual dictator, with a policy of consistent and radical Westernization.

Kemal, born in Thessaloniki, was banished in 1904 for joining a revolutionary society. Later he was pardoned and promoted in the army and was largely responsible for the successful defence of the Dardanelles against the British in 1915. In 1918, after Turkey had been defeated, he was sent into Anatolia to implement the demobilization of the Turkish forces in accordance with the armistice terms, but instead he established a provisional government opposed to that of Constantinople (modern Isanbul, then under Allied control) and in 1921 led the Turkish armies against the Greeks, who had occupied a large part of Anatolia. He checked them at the Battle of the Sakaria, 23 August–13 September 1921, for which he was granted the title of Ghazi ('the Victorious'), and within a year had expelled the Greeks from Turkish soil. War with the British was averted by his diplomacy, and Turkey in Europe passed under Kemal's control. On 29 October 1923 Turkey was proclaimed a republic with Kemal as first president.

Atlantic, Battle of the German campaign during World War I to prevent merchant shipping from delivering food supplies from the USA to the Allies, chiefly the UK. By 1917, some 875,000 tons of shipping had been lost. The odds were only turned by the belated use of naval convoys and depth charges to deter submarine attack.

Atlantic Charter declaration issued during World War II by the British prime minister Winston Churchill and the US president Franklin D Roosevelt after meetings in August 1941. It stressed their countries' broad strategy and war aims and was largely a propaganda exercise to demonstrate public solidarity among the Allies.

Attlee, Clement (Richard) (1883–1967) 1st Earl Attlee, British Labour politician. In the coalition government during World War II he was Lord Privy Seal 1940–42, dominions secretary 1942–43, and Lord President of the Council 1943–45, as well as deputy prime minister from 1942. As prime minister 1945–51 he introduced a sweeping programme of nationalization and a whole new system of social services.

Auchinleck, Claude John Eyre (1884–1981) called 'the Auk', British commander in World War II. He commanded the First Battle of El *Alamein in 1942 in northern Egypt, in which he held Rommel's allied German and Italian forces at bay. In 1943 he became commander-in-chief in India and founded the modern Indian and Pakistani armies. In 1946 he was promoted to field marshal; he retired in 1947.

Aung San (1916–1947) Burmese (Myanmar) politician. He was a founder and leader of the Anti-Fascist People's Freedom League, which led Burma's fight for independence from the UK. During World War II he collaborated first with Japan and then with the UK. In 1947 he became head of Burma's provisional government but was assassinated the same year by political opponents. His daughter *Suu Kyi spearheaded a nonviolent pro-democracy movement in Myanmar from 1988.

Auriol, Vincent (1884–1966) French Socialist politician. He was president of the two Constituent Assemblies of 1946 and first president of the Fourth Republic 1947–54.

Auschwitz Polish Oswiecim, town near Kraków in Poland; the site of the notorious Auschwitz-Birkenau *concentration camp used by the Nazis in World War II to exterminate Jews and other political and social minorities, as part of the 'final solution'; population (1992 est) 45,100. The camp's four gas chambers, disguised as bathhouses and with crematoria attached, had a combined capacity to kill over 12,000 people a day.

Ausgleich compromise between Austria and Hungary on 8 February 1867 that established the Austro-Hungarian Dual Monarchy under Habsburg rule. It endured until the collapse of Austria-Hungary in 1918.

Australia country occupying all of the Earth's smallest continent, situated south of Indonesia, between the Pacific and Indian oceans.

    government Australia is an independent sovereign nation within the Commonwealth, retaining the

British monarch as head of state, represented by a governor general. The constitution came into effect on 1 January 1901. As in the British system, the executive, comprising the prime minister and cabinet, is drawn from the federal parliament and is answerable to it. The parliament consists of two chambers: an elected Senate of 76 (12 for each of the six states, two for the Australian Capital Territory, and two for the Northern Territory); and a House of Representatives of 147, elected by universal adult suffrage. Senators serve for six years, and members of the House for three years.

Voting is compulsory; the Senate is elected by proportional representation, but the House of Representatives is elected as single-member constituencies with preferential voting. Each state has its own constitution, governor (the monarch's representative), executive (drawn from the parliament), and legislative and judicial system. Each territory has its own legislative assembly. The last relics of UK legislative control over Australia were removed in 1986.

federal versus state powers On the foundation of the Commonwealth of Australia, the division of powers between the state and federal governments was made, broadly, on the principle that those powers that were concerned solely with internal affairs should be vested in the states (as the colonies now became). The restrictions thus imposed on federal action have at times proved irritating, and on occasions have prevented the government from pursuing policies it has considered necessary both for the economic development of the country and for the improvement of social conditions within the community.

Frequent attempts have been made to amend the constitution, but with little success. Nearly all proposed amendments have been designed to increase federal powers, but with the exception of 1946, when the Commonwealth was given control of social services, these proposals have been rejected by the electorate. The Commonwealth has desired full powers over trade, commerce, industrial matters, trusts, and monopolies, but though these have been denied it, judicial review and its financial supremacy have enabled it to exert an increasing influence over state policy.

government before World War I The factors that had induced the formation of a federation, and had helped shape the constitution, largely dictated the issues to which the Commonwealth parliament first turned its attention. Within a decade legislation had been passed to establish an Australian navy and military force, to impose a protective tariff, and to implement the 'White Australia' policy (aimed at barring Asian immigration), and the first steps towards a welfare state had been taken with the granting of old-age pensions.

The Labor government that came into power in 1910 was already beginning to chafe under the limits imposed by the constitution when the outbreak of World War I overshadowed domestic affairs.

Australia in World War I At the outbreak of war, all parties pledged themselves to support the Allied cause. A division of troops was immediately placed at the disposal of the imperial government in Britain, and a small force was promptly sent to German New Guinea. At no time did Australia adopt conscription, though two attempts were made to introduce it. Both times a majority of the people voted against it, and the issue split the Labor Party. Despite this opposition to compulsory overseas service, out of the population of 5 million, 400,000 men enlisted. Total casualties were approximately 220,000, including 55,585 dead. The Victoria Cross was awarded to 63 Australians.

Australian troops formed part of Anzac (the Australian and New Zealand Army Corps), and took part in many of the crucial battles of the war, most notably in the *Gallipoli campaign. They also fought in defence of the Suez Canal and on the Salonika front in the early years of the war, and later in Palestine, Flanders, and France. Other forces took German New Guinea, Nauru, and the Bismarck Archipelago. These former German possessions were subsequently subject to Australian administration under a League of Nations mandate. The Australian navy also served in the war, its most famous feat being the sinking of the German cruiser *Emden* off the Cocos Islands in 1914.

governments and parties in the 1920s At the termination of hostilities, Australia was represented at the Paris Peace Conference and became a member of the League of Nations, but external affairs quickly faded into the background. Australians were more concerned to get their forces home as quickly as possible and to get back to the problem of developing the continent and improving social conditions.

There was a change in emphasis, in outlook, and in actual policy in the period after World War I. Material questions were to dominate the 1920s. The Labor Party had been in the ascendancy before the war but after the split over conscription it lost control, not only in the Commonwealth but in all states except Queensland. By 1924 it had recaptured most of the state governments, but not until 1929 did it regain control in the Commonwealth parliament. William *Hughes led a Nationalist government until 1923, and Stanley *Bruce a Nationalist–Country Party coalition until 1929.

industrial unrest Throughout the period there was a series of industrial disputes, and government-sponsored arbitration seemed powerless to avert them. The situation was aggravated by the division of arbitration powers between the Commonwealth and the states – by 1919 all states had established some form of arbitration or wage regulation.

The Commonwealth government had tried to make arbitration work, but it failed to persuade the electorate to enlarge its industrial powers and only embittered industrial relations with the introduction of increased penalties for breach of arbitration rulings. The increasingly hard line against the trade unions taken by Bruce's Nationalist–Country Party coalition during the 1920s helped to bring about its defeat at the hands of the electorate in 1929.

development and immigration in the 1920s By 1929 the collapse of the economic plans of Bruce's defeated government was also evident. It had concentrated throughout the 1920s on an attempt to force the pace of economic development, and to this end had generously encouraged immigration and imported capital. Except for a few years before the war, there had been no large-scale immigration to Australia for a considerable time, and the growth of population depended largely on natural increase.

In cooperation with the British government (which provided the capital) and the states (which helped settle the immigrants), the Commonwealth sponsored ambitious immigration schemes, under which £34 million was to be made available for land settlement and associated public works. In fact the target came nowhere near being realized, for only £9 million of the loan money was spent and only 200,000 immigrants had arrived when signs of the coming depression brought the schemes to an end.

the great depression Australia was one of the first countries to feel the effects of the great depression that followed the *Wall Street crash of 1929.

Bad seasons and a disastrous fall in the price of wheat had already brought to an end the period of optimistic expansion by the time of the 1929 election.

The new Labor government showed some hesitation in dealing with the situation. Tariffs were raised still higher, but the pursuit of the traditional objectives of economic retrenchment and deflation caused dissension in Labor ranks, for it was seen by some to involve greater hardships for workers than for other sections of the community. A compromise policy calling for conversion of loans and a limited amount of inflation was finally evolved. However, the Labor Party had been seriously weakened. It was defeated in the 1931 elections and remained in opposition for ten years.

Though economic recovery was comparatively rapid, economic problems continued to preoccupy the government throughout the 1930s. The government was acquiescent when Britain pursued a policy of appeasement in Europe, and though 1934 saw the beginning of rearmament, it was not until war became imminent that real efforts were made to provide any adequate defence measures.

Australia in World War II On the outbreak of World War II the Australian prime minister Robert *Menzies followed Britain's lead, and on 3 September 1939 Australia declared war on Germany. The country was in many ways unprepared, and it took some time to organize an effective war effort. From the beginning Australia cooperated in the Empire Air Training scheme, compulsory military training was introduced, and before the end of 1939 the Australian Imperial Force had sailed for the Middle East. In the first two years of the war Australian troops fought in Greece, Syria, and North Africa.

The domestic political situation in the early years of the war was

unstable. The 1940 elections had resulted in the House of Representatives being evenly divided between Labor and non-Labor, with two independents holding the balance. Menzies remained prime minister and the Labor Party rejected his repeated proposals for an all-party government, though consenting to be members of an all-party advisory war council. In August 1941 Menzies resigned and after a brief period Labor assumed control. Labor had not questioned the participation in the war but merely the disposition of troops, and with the attack on Pearl Harbor in December 1941 the cause of the dispute disappeared.

In the same month the new Labor prime minister John *Curtin made his famous appeal to the USA for help – an appeal that was interpreted by some as the severing of the link with Britain. Britain was too occupied in the European theatre of war to provide effective assistance in the defence of Australia, which, as the Japanese pushed south, had only one armoured division and seven skeleton divisions of semi-equipped untrained militia to defend it. February 1942 saw the surrender of 15,000 Australian troops to the Japanese at the fall of Singapore, the bombing of Darwin on the Australian mainland, and the recall by Curtin of two of the three Australian divisions in the Middle East. The British prime minister Winston Churchill had wanted these diverted to defend Burma, but Curtin insisted that they return to Australia.

The rest of the war saw close cooperation between US and Australian forces. Australia became the base for the Allied campaign in the Pacific, and under the supreme command of Gen Douglas MacArthur the Allied forces halted the Japanese drive in 1942–43, and in mid-1943 began the recapture of the islands and the slow reconquest of the New Guinea coastline. In 1943 the 9th Division, which had remained in the Middle East and had assisted in checking the German advance into Egypt, had been recalled to join the fighting in New Guinea and the nearby islands. The last campaign in which Australian troops fought was the invasion of Borneo in July 1945.

At home, the impact of the war on the life of the community had been considerable even before the Japanese attack prompted much more extensive government controls. At first the government showed some reluctance to interfere with traditional economic freedoms, but by 1942 it had rationed a wide range of articles, pegged wages, controlled prices, and undertaken the direction of labour. Manpower had become a serious problem as the Australian manufacturing industry expanded under the pressure of the increased demands made upon it, once Australia became the base for US and Australian forces and a source of supplies. The result was a significant change in the structure of the economy, with the establishment of new industries and the expansion of existing ones.

post-war policy The maintenance of full employment was for many years a basic consideration in post-war policy. Even before hostilities ended the government drew up plans for projects that would be undertaken if unemployment threatened. In fact this did not happen, and the immediate post-war years were a period of rapid expansion, rising wages, and over-full employment.

The two objectives that have so often shaped Australian policies, the improvement of social conditions and the economic development of the continent, again dominated policy in the post-war period. The welfare state had actually been extended during the war, with family allowances being paid from 1941, and in 1945 a comprehensive scheme of unemployment and sickness benefits was introduced.

further immigration The war had emphasized Australia's relative

emptiness, and the labour shortage continued after the war. This encouraged the development of a government-sponsored immigration scheme, starting in 1948. It was initially decided that an intake of 70,000 a year, together with natural increase, would result in a 2% population increase annually, this being considered the maximum increase possible without economic strain (although later this maximum was revised).

Old immigration policies were abandoned: no longer were immigrants settled on the land, and no longer was immigration only encouraged from Britain, as it was realized that the large number of displaced persons in Europe offered a ready source of immigrant labour. Numerically, the programme was very successful. In the first three decades following the war over 2 million new immigrants settled in Australia, including about one-third from Britain, which included children who were shipped from UK orphanages from the end of World War II until the late 1960s.

the Menzies era It had been expected that large-scale immigration would relieve the labour shortage, but by creating new demands, notably in housing, schools, and hospitals, it aggravated the situation and was one of the contributing factors to post-war inflation, which reached a crisis point in 1951. High wool prices, heavy private investment, home building, and huge public-works programmes were contributory causes.

In 1952 the Menzies government (elected in 1949 as a Liberal–Country Party coalition, and re-elected in 1954, 1955, 1958, 1961, and 1963) decided that it had become necessary to reimpose certain controls, notably import restrictions, in order to halt inflation. These measures temporarily slowed the pace of expansion and intake of immigrants, but were reasonably successful in restoring economic stability. A prolonged period of economic prosperity followed, and active federal encouragement of immigration was revived. Australia's post-war economic expansion survived inflationary pressures and periodic waves of acute industrial unrest, in which control of the largest unions by the extreme left played a leading part.

Politically, the period was notable as one of great crisis for the Labor Party, continuously out of office from 1949 to 1972, and from 1954 deeply divided against itself. Australian political life as a whole suffered from its consequences.

foreign affairs Australia became much more conscious of its relationship with non-Commonwealth countries after World War II. The danger of Japanese invasion during the war had emphasized the need to make adequate defence arrangements, and the search for powerful allies resulted in attempts to achieve closer association with the USA. In the Cold War period Australia joined two regional defence alliances, becoming a member of Anzus (with New Zealand and the USA) in 1951, and of the Southeast Asia Treaty Organization (SEATO) in 1954.

The need to establish friendly relations with Asian countries became increasingly important, particularly following the emergence of an expansionist Indonesia, which claimed some of Australia's trusteeship territories. To this end Australian diplomatic representation in many Asian countries was increased, and Australia made aid contributions under the Colombo Plan. In 1964, during the Indonesian threat to Malaysia, the Australian government introduced selective conscription.

In the early 1960s there was uncertainty in Australia regarding its future political and economic relations with Britain should the latter gain entry to the European Economic Community (EEC). A new trade agreement between the two countries in 1957 had safeguarded the preferences laid down by the Ottawa agreements of 1932, and many Australians considered that British membership of the EEC would imperil Australia's economy and entail the dissolution of the British Commonwealth. By this time Australia was, however, far less dependent upon British imports than it had been before 1939. Nevertheless when Britain did join the European Community (EC) in 1973, it was felt by many Australians that Britain had turned its back, and a new strain of nationalism began to emerge.

a succession of Liberal prime ministers In 1966 Sir Robert Menzies retired and was succeeded by Harold *Holt, who, a year later, was presumed drowned in a swimming accident. John *Gorton became prime minister in 1968 but lost a vote of confidence in the House of Representatives. Holt had increased the number of Australian troops committed to the *Vietnam War, and under Gorton the country became increasingly split over the issue. Gorton was succeeded by a Liberal–Country Party coalition under William McMahon in 1971. In December 1972 McMahon was defeated in the general election by the Labor Party under Gough *Whitlam – the first Labor victory since 1949.

Whitlam's Labor government In April 1974 Whitlam dissolved both houses of parliament because of persistent deadlock, but a month later he was re-elected, despite having a reduced majority in the House of Representatives. During 1974 the Australian economy became progressively more unstable (partly owing to the international economic situation), with an unfavourable balance of trade, growing unemployment, and trade-union unrest.

On 1 January 1975, Australia introduced new laws on immigration.

These restricted the number of unskilled and semiskilled workers allowed into the country, in order to ease the unemployment situation. They also abolished preferential treatment of immigrants from Britain, except in cases of family reunion.

In mid-1975 the Whitlam government narrowly survived accusations of unorthodox international loan-raising activities. The affair led to the dismissal or resignation of several senior government ministers and damaged Labor's standing. Opposition to the government's monetary policy became stronger in October when the opposition-dominated Senate exercised its constitutional right in blocking budget bills concerning money supply.

Whitlam replaced by Fraser
An impasse developed and the government rejected the Senate's proposal for a general election in mid-1976. On 11 November 1975 the governor general, Sir John Kerr, took the unprecedented step of dismissing the government and installing a caretaker ministry under Malcolm *Fraser, the Liberal leader, to govern until elections could be held. The wisdom of this action was questioned by many, and there were widespread demonstrations supporting Whitlam. Kerr himself resigned in 1977.

The Liberals won a majority in the December 1975 elections with Fraser forming a coalition (Liberal–National Country Party). Whitlam was succeeded as leader of the Labor Party by Bill *Hayden. In the 1977 general election Fraser's coalition government was returned with a reduced majority, which was further reduced in the 1980 elections.

the Hawke era In the 1983 general election the coalition was eventually defeated and the Australian Labor Party under Bob *Hawke again took office. Hawke called together employers and unions to a National Economic Summit to agree to a wage

and price policy and to deal with unemployment. In 1984 he called a general election 15 months early and was returned with a reduced majority. Hawke placed even greater emphasis than his predecessors on links with Southeast Asia, and imposed trading sanctions against South Africa as a means of influencing the dismantling of apartheid.

In the 1987 general election Labor marginally increased its majority in the House but did not have an overall majority in the Senate, where the balance was held by the Australian Democrats. The 1990 election was won by Labor, led by Hawke, with a reduced majority in the House of Representatives, for a record fourth term in office. The Australian Democrats maintained the balance of power in the Senate. In August 1991 Hawke announced that agreement had been reached on greater cohesion of the states' economies.

Keating as prime minister
In December 1991 Hawke's leadership of the Labor Party was successfully challenged by Paul *Keating, who became the new party leader and prime minister. Hawke retired from politics in January 1992. Despite Keating's 'kickstart' plan – announced in February 1992 – to boost a stagnant economy, Australia's unemployment rate reached a record 11.1% in July. Keating's inability to tackle the effects of the recession was seen as the main reason for his waning popularity. An expansionary budget outlined in August was criticized by the opposition as an attempt to gain support for the Labor Party in preparation for the 1993 elections. In December 1992 the Citizenship Act was amended so as to remove the oath of allegiance to the British crown.

In March 1993 Keating's premiership was confirmed when the Labor Party won a surprising general election victory, entering an unprecedented fifth term of office. John Hewson resigned as Liberal Party leader in May 1994 and was succeeded by Alexander Downer, who in turn was replaced by John Howard in January 1995.

In general elections held in March 1996, Keating's Labor Party was defeated by John Howard's Liberal–National coalition, giving the country its first conservative government for 13 years. Their overwhelming victory was seen as likely to make a republican future for Australia more distant. Despite his opposition to Keating's aim of holding a referendum before the year 2000 on whether Australia should become a republic, Howard pledged to set up a convention in 1997 to examine reforms to Australia's 19th-century written constitution. The Australian Constitutional Convention sat in Canberra. Delegates voted 13 February 1998 to replace the Queen as head of state with a president chosen by a bipartisan parliamentary majority. The vote was 89 to 52 (with 11 abstentions).

The ruling Liberal-National government, led by John Howard, narrowly retained power after the October 1998 general election, with majority of only six seats. Labor improved its performance, while the extremist One Nation party, led by Pauline Hanson and which called for less immigration, secured 8% of the vote, but won no seats. The introduction of a new 10% goods-and-services tax (GST) from July 2000 was confirmed in June 1999 by government legislation.

Australians voted in a referendum in November 1999 to retain their constitutional links with Britain and keep the queen as head of state. 55% voted 'no' in a referendum that offered them a historic opportunity to shed their colonial past, and chose not to become a republic with their own head of state. They also rejected a separate proposal to insert a preamble to the constitution, recognizing Aborigines as the first Australians. Following the referendum results, Howard said that, as far as he was concerned, constitutional reform was no longer on the political agenda. But republican yearnings would not disappear overnight, and the constitutional debate would undoubtedly be revived at the next general election in 2001, if not before.

Prime Minister Howard, regarded by many Australians as the architect of the referendum defeat, faced a cabinet as divided as the rest of the country. Critics pointed out that Howard had tinkered with the referendum question itself. Voters were asked whether they wanted Australia to become a republic, with the Queen and Governor-General replaced by a president appointed by two-thirds of parliament. Thus, Australians were asked two questions, not one: whether they wanted a republic and whether they favoured a particular method of electing the president. But the second question did not mention that candidates would be nominated by the public before they were approved by parliament. The referendum failed largely because many republicans thought they would have no say in choosing the president.

population in the 1990s Australia's population reached 19 million in August 1999. Natural increase accounted for 53% of the rise from 18 million, and net overseas migration contributed 47%.

In 2000, the Olympic Games was held in Sydney. It was estimated that the event brought over A$3 billion in new business to the Australian economy.

At the end of August 2000, Australia's government decided not to cooperate further with United Nations (UN) committees, complaining that the UN was interfering in domestic politics. Australia was angered by UN criticism of its treatment of Aboriginal Australians and asylum-seekers.

torrential floods Torrential rains in much of eastern Australia during late

November 2000 caused widespread flooding in rural areas. In western Queensland and New South Wales, rivers flooded farmland, destroyed crops, including more than a million tonnes of wheat, and isolated towns and homesteads.

welfare changes for New Zealanders In December 2000, the Australian government decided to stop the automatic right of New Zealand migrants to Australian government benefits such as the dole. Only New Zealanders who meet the requirements for permanent residency will receive benefits. The change is expected to save about A\$1 billion over 10 years. About 30,000 New Zealanders migrate to Australia annually, and 400,000 New Zealanders already live in the country.

Between July and December 2000, over 1,000 illegal immigrants had arrived from Indonesia by boat, and in December, at least 160 drowned when storms sank the boats.

In February 2001, the ruling Liberal party lost in state elections in Queensland and Western Australia. The following month, it lost a by-election in Queensland, as Australia's economy suffered a sharp slowdown. In late June, Peter Hollingworth, the former Anglican archbishop of Brisbane, took over from William Deane as governor-general.

oil and gas deal with East Timor East Timor and Australia signed an agreement in July 2001 to divide royalties from future oil and gas fields in the Timor Sea, which divides the two countries. Because most of the fields are in East Timorese waters, East Timor will receive 90% of the royalties, Australia 10%. The Australian foreign minister, Alexander Downer, said that Australia wanted to provide East Timor with a long-term revenue flow to support its development. The agreement superceded the 1989 Timor Gap Treaty, which split revenues 50–50 between Australia and Indonesia, which at that time controlled East Timor.

asylum crisis In August, a Norwegian freighter carrying 433 asylum seekers rescued from a sinking Indonesian ferry was refused permission to land them in Australia. In an unprecedented move, Australian troops prevented the mainly Afghan refugees from landing and 40 soldiers boarded the freighter, the MV *Tampa*, threatening to sail it out of territorial waters. After an eight-day stand-off, the unwanted asylum-seekers transferred to the HMAS *Manoora*, which took them to Papua New Guinea from where they were flown to New Zealand and Nauru, where applications for refugee status would be processed. However, the Australian government received a humiliating setback on 11 September when the Federal Court ruled that it had acted illegally in refusing the refugees permission to apply for asylum in the country and that they must be allowed to land. The government responded by launching an appeal against the ruling. In October, nine Sri Lankans were jailed for up to five years in the state of Western Australia for smuggling refugees as part of continuing the crackdown on unauthorized arrivals to Australia ordered by Prime Minister Howard. The asylum issue was expected to be a dominant concern in the general election scheduled for November.

2001 elections John Howard was returned to office with an increased majority for a third term as prime minister in elections held on 10 November. Howard's harsh asylum policies proved popular, and gained the Liberal party 70% of the vote. Taking responsibility for the electoral defeat of the Australian Labor Party, Kim Beazley resigned as leader and was replaced by Simon Crean. However, the new Liberal government came under attack in February 2002 for allegedly misleading voters about an incident involving asylum seekers during the 2001 election campaign.

Prime Minister Howard refused to comment on the use of edited photographs to claim that a number of asylum seekers on a boat had thrown their children into the sea to force the Australian navy to intervene. The photographs and the story were used to garner support for the party's hard-line stance on political asylum during the campaign. Parliament began an enquiry into the allegations.

bush fires In December 2001 and January 2002, Australia's biggest bush fires for eight years destroyed more than 150 homes in New South Wales. Some fires reached the outskirts of Sydney. The fires did not cause any deaths or serious injuries to humans, but killed thousands of sheep and native animals, and forced the evacuation of more than 5,000 people. By 1 January, the fires had consumed 300,000 ha/741,000 acres of bush. Police detained 21 people on suspicion of arson.

asylum controversy continues Hundreds of asylum-seekers in the Woomera detention camp ended a 16-day hunger strike on 29 January 2002 after the government said it would speed up consideration of their applications. Many of the 370 hunger strikers had sewn their lips together, while other inmates had attempted or threatened suicide. However, he Australian government faced mounting international pressure over its asylum policy, and the United Nations commissioner for human rights, Mary Robinson, asked to send an envoy to inspect the Woomera camp to ensure that Australia was meeting its international obligations. Public protest at the conditions at Woomera continued, with protesters helping over 50 asylum seekers to escape in March by knocking down fences and giving bolt-cutters to the detainees.

The government came under further attack in February for allegedly misleading voters about an incident involving asylum seekers during the 2001 election campaign. Prime Minister Howard refused to comment on the use of edited photographs to claim that a number of asylum seekers on a boat had thrown their children into the sea to force the Australian navy to intervene. The photographs and the story were used to garner support for the party's hard-line stance on political asylum during the campaign. The Australian parliament began an enquiry into the allegations.

Austria landlocked country in central Europe, bounded east by Hungary, south by Slovenia and Italy, west by Switzerland and Liechtenstein, northwest by Germany, north by the Czech Republic, and northeast by the Slovak Republic.

government Austria is a federal republic consisting of nine provinces (*Länder*), each with its own provincial assembly (Landtag), provincial governor, and councillors. The 1920 constitution was amended in 1929, suspended during *Hitler's regime, and reinstated in 1945. The two-chamber federal assembly consists of a national council (Nationalrat) and a federal council (Bundesrat). The Nationalrat has 183 members, elected by universal suffrage through proportional representation, for a four-year term. The Bundesrat has 64 members elected by the provincial assemblies for varying terms. Each province provides a chair for the Bundesrat for a six-month term. The federal president, elected by popular vote for a six-year term, is formal head of state and chooses the federal chancellor on the basis of support in the Nationalrat. The federal chancellor is head of government and chooses the cabinet.

Austria in the 1920s Following the defeat of the *Austro-Hungarian Empire in 1918, the last Habsburg emperor was overthrown, and Austria became a republic, comprising only Vienna and its immediately surrounding provinces. The Treaty of St Germain, signed in 1919 by Austria and the Allies, established Austria's present boundaries.

The political history of the new republic was characterized from the outset by a bitter struggle between the Social Democrats and the Christian Socialists (who had substantial middle-class support). The workers of Vienna, which now dominated the new state, had played a decisive part in establishing the republic, and as a result socialism had great influence in the National Assembly immediately after the overthrow of the Dual Monarchy. The first chancellor was the Socialist leader, Karl *Renner, who made it an aim of his domestic policy to establish a working agreement between the Social Democrats and the Christian Socialists. For a considerable time the chief issues were the Tirol question and the Anschluss, or union, with Germany. The two issues were linked, in that both were of concern to those with pro-German sympathies.

The Tirol question concerned the protection of the German-speaking minorities in the South Tirol (that part of the old Austrian crownland that passed to Italy after 1918), and was of considerable importance even outside the two countries immediately affected. The practical acquiescence of successive Austrian governments in the Tirol situation as it had been decided in the peace treaty drove many moderate but patriotic Austrians into the extreme pan-German camp. Austria's unstable economic position, producing as it did chronic poverty and unemployment, led to the growth of extreme leftist groups in Vienna itself, and this led to equal extremism among the non-socialists. It also led many Austrians to decide that Austria would never have a stable government until it achieved greater economic stability, and this was increasingly considered to mean union, at least economic union, with Germany.

internal tensions increase In 1927 there was serious Social Democrat rioting in Vienna. One result of this was the formation of the Heimwehr, or bourgeois private army, which was designed as a challenge to the activities of the socialists' illegal armed bands, which, in times of stress, patrolled Vienna. In the elections of 1930 the Social Democrats replaced the Christian Socialists as the largest single party, but they too had to rely on the support of the pan-German group. In 1931, in the face of Austria's worsening economic position, caused by the world depression, a customs union with Germany was concluded in the face of much international opposition. Two months later the biggest bank in Austria failed; the government fell, and the Christian Socialists returned to power. The customs union was immediately renounced.

Internal tension was growing. In 1932 Engelbert *Dollfuss, a Christian Socialist, became chancellor. He allied with the Heimwehr group to maintain his position, and adopted a line independent of both the pan-Germans (by now Nazi in character) and the socialists. To do this he had to resort to dictatorial methods. In February 1934 the socialists rose in revolt against the Heimwehr, and for several days there was civil war in Vienna and in some of the larger provincial towns. The rising was crushed with heavy loss of life to the socialists, and their leaders were executed. Dollfuss, who had suppressed the rising, forfeited much of the support he had previously gained abroad for his resistance to the German Nazis, besides driving some socialists into a conspiracy with the Austrian Nazis to overthrow his government.

Stringent laws against political violence were now introduced, and a new constitution introduced suspending democracy and making Austria a corporative state. Some of the Nazi conspirators were imprisoned, with the result that in July there was a sudden (unsuccessful) Nazi revolt, in which Dollfuss was assassinated. He was succeeded as chancellor by Kurt von *Schuschnigg.

annexation by Germany and World War II After 1934 Austrian independence was gravely threatened by the annexationist ambitions of Adolf Hitler (himself Austrian-born), and the pressure on Austria further increased following Italy's alliance with Germany in 1936. In February 1938 Schuschnigg was forced to accept a Nazi minister of the interior, and finally, in March 1938, the Germans occupied the country. The Austrian president was forced to resign, and Schuschnigg was imprisoned. The army was incorporated with that of Germany, which also took over diplomatic representation abroad. The Austrian Diet was dissolved, the German mark substituted for the Austrian schilling, and the country subordinated to the Reich as the German province of 'Ostmark'(East Mark), under Hitler's dictatorship. The German annexation met with no armed resistance, and the Anschluss (union) became an accomplished fact.

In World War II Austria's armed forces, subsumed under German control, were used on the Eastern Front throughout the campaign against the USSR (for more details of the Eastern Front see *World War II). Though many Austrians had originally welcomed the Anschluss, serious opposition to it, though largely unorganized, had existed from the start. Certainly by 1943, once the war had begun to turn against Germany, the attitude of the Austrian people generally was anti-Nazi; this was manifested in acts of sabotage in agriculture, and by opposition from industrial workers, who suffered heavy losses at the hands of Nazi execution squads. But Austria was useful to Germany as an air-raid shelter, and affluent Germans evacuated their families to Austria, even before the mass evacuation to the Alpine districts. Hence Austria suffered from a shortage of houses and food, and in 1943 the population was 10 million compared with 7 million before the war.

At the Moscow Conference in October 1943 Britain, the USA, and the USSR pledged to restore Austrian independence. By April 1945 Russian armies had crossed the Austrian frontier, and on 13 April Vienna was captured.

the restoration of Austrian independence On 27 April 1945 a provisional Austrian government was set up in Vienna, and in October this was recognized by the Allies as the rightful Austrian government. Its constitutional structure was based on the constitution of 1920. Elections held in November 1945 resulted in a coalition of the Socialist Party of Austria (SPÖ) and the Austrian People's Party (ÖVP, the Catholic party). Subsequently Leopold Figl of the People's Party became chancellor, while Karl Renner, the veteran Socialist, became president.

After the cessation of hostilities Austria was divided into British, US, French, and Soviet zones of occupation. Vienna, within the 1937 boundaries of the city, was jointly occupied by armed forces of the four Allied powers, and its administration directed by an inter-Allied governing authority of commandants appointed by the respective commanders in chief. At a meeting in September 1945 the Allied council of foreign ministers decided that the frontier of Austria would not be changed save for minor rectifications, and this decision therefore barred the restoration to Austria of the South Tirol, of which it had been deprived in 1919. At various times since 1945, incidents in the German-speaking areas of the Italian Tirol have led to renewed popular support in Austria for a revision of the Tirol frontiers in Austria's favour.

The post-war Austrian government concentrated on reconstruction. Vienna had suffered severe damage, and major rehousing programmes were begun. But the division of Austria and Vienna into separate zones hindered economic recovery. In 1955 a peace treaty was signed by Britain, France, the USA, and the USSR recognizing Austria's sovereignty. The occupation forces were withdrawn, and Austria's future neutrality was stipulated, which continued throughout the Cold War. Reparations were to be paid by Austria to the USSR over a ten-year period.

Austria suffered few crises in the post-war years. Prosperity returned, helped by good labour relations and tourism, and in 1960 Austria became a founding member of the *European Free Trade Association (EFTA). From 1953 Austria was governed by a coalition of the ÖVP and the SPÖ. Until 1961 the chancellor was Julius Raab. In 1966 the ÖVP formed the government alone (the first non-coalition government since the war) with Josef Klaus as chancellor.

the Kreisky years The SPÖ formed a minority government under Bruno *Kreisky in 1970 and increased its majority in the 1971 and 1975 general elections. The government was nearly defeated in 1978 over proposals to install the first nuclear power plant. The plan was abandoned, but nuclear energy remained a controversial issue. The SPÖ lost its majority in 1983, and Kreisky resigned, refusing to join a coalition. The SPÖ decline was partly attributed to the emergence of two environmentalist groups, the United Green Party (VGÖ) and the Austrian Alternative List (ALÖ). Fred Sinowatz, the new SPÖ chair, formed a coalition government with the Freiheitliche Partei (FP; Freedom Party).

the Waldheim controversy When Kurt *Waldheim, former UN secretary general, became president in 1986, he was diplomatically isolated by many countries because of controversy over his service in the German army during World War II. Later that year Sinowatz resigned as chancellor and was succeeded by Franz *Vranitzky. The SPÖ–FP coalition broke up when an extreme right-winger, Jörg Haider, became FP leader. Vranitzky remained as chancellor with the ÖVP leader, Alois Mock, as vice-chancellor. Sinowatz denounced the new coalition as a betrayal of socialist principles and resigned as chair of the SPÖ.

entering the European Union In the 1990 general election the Socialists won a clear lead over other parties and Vranitzky began another term as chancellor. Thomas Klestil, the candidate of the ÖVP, replaced Waldheim as president in 1992. A referendum held in June 1994 gave a clear endorsement of Austria's application for European Union (EU) membership. Despite gains for far-right parties, including the FP, in the October 1994 general election, the SPÖ–ÖVP coalition continued under Vranitzky's leadership, and in January 1995 Austria left EFTA to become a full EU member.

The governing coalition collapsed in October 1995 following disagreements over the budget and popular disillusion with EU membership, and the strict convergence criteria for monetary union. In the ensuing general election in December 1995 the SPÖ emerged as the winner, but in February 1996, after seven weeks of negotiations, the SPÖ and the ÖVP agreed on renewing the coalition led by Vranitzky. In January 1997 he was replaced by Viktor Klima.

In March 1998, the government ruled out membership of NATO for at least five years. In April, President Klestil was re-elected for a second six-year term.

coalition government includes the far right In February 2000, a new coalition government was elected, headed by People's Party's Wolfgang

Schüssel and including the far-right FP, led by Jörg Haider, then governor of the region of Carinthia. The coalition marked the inclusion of the far right in a Western European government for the first time since World War II, and was met with protests from the Austrian electorate and across Europe, especially since it was revealed that Haider had Nazi links and sympathies. The EU's 14 other member states pledged to impose political sanctions on Austria, Israel removed its ambassador immediately, and the USA recalled its ambassador for a decision to be made. The visit of the Prince of Wales, heir to the British throne, was cancelled.

Haider soon announced he would resign as leader of the FP in May, though he denied that his decision was a result of international pressure. The FP retained its position in the coalition government, and when Haider officially stepped down, he was replaced by Susanne Riess-Passer, a successor he picked himself and who pledged to stay loyal to his policies. In May the Austrian finance minister threatened to delay payment of its EU contributions and disrupt business in response to the sanctions that had been imposed. These were lifted in September 2000, after an EU report found Austria's human rights record to be satisfactory, and it was decided that continued sanctions would only promote nationalism in the country. In October the FP did poorly in provincial elections in Styria, though the People's Party did well, and the following month, its participation in the coalition government was called into question by the resignation of a third minister from the party since February. In March 2001, it received only 20% of the vote in Vienna city elections, and the Social Democrats secured a clear victory.

On 1 January 2002, euro notes and coins were introduced as the national currency.

A row over a Czech nuclear power plant at Temelin, near the Austrian border, resumed in January 2002 after Jörg Haider again called for it to be closed. The government had recently agreed to a compromise with the Czech government that would leave it open. However, a petition launched by the FP demanding a veto on the Czech Republic's EU membership was signed by more than 915,000 people, nearly a sixth of Austria's voters. On 22 January, the EU commissioner responsible for enlargement warned Austria that it must keep to its agreement with the Czech government.

Austro-Hungarian Empire the Dual Monarchy established by the Habsburg Franz Joseph in 1867 between his empire of Austria and his kingdom of Hungary (including territory that became Czechoslovakia as well as parts of Poland, the Ukraine, Romania, Yugoslavia, and Italy).

It collapsed in the autumn of 1918 with the end of World War I. Only two king-emperors ruled: Franz Joseph and Karl.

Axis alliance of Nazi Germany and fascist Italy before and during World War II. The **Rome–Berlin Axis** was formed in 1936, when Italy was being threatened with sanctions because of its invasion of Ethiopia (Abyssinia). It became a full military and political alliance in May 1939. A ten-year alliance between Germany, Italy, and Japan (**Rome–Berlin–Tokyo Axis**) was signed in September 1940 and was subsequently joined by Hungary, Bulgaria, Romania, and the puppet states of Slovakia and Croatia. The Axis collapsed with the fall of Mussolini and the surrender of Italy in 1943 and Germany and Japan in 1945.

Ayub Khan, Muhammad (1907–1974) Pakistani soldier and president 1958–69. He served in the Burma Campaign 1942–45, and was commander-in-chief of the Pakistan army in 1951. In 1958 Ayub Khan assumed power after a bloodless army coup. He won the presidential elections in 1960 and 1965, and established a stable economy and achieved limited land reforms. His militaristic form of government was unpopular, particularly with the Bengalis. He resigned in 1969 after widespread opposition and civil disorder, notably in Kashmir.

Azad, Maulana Abul Kalam (1888–1958) Indian Muslim scholar, author, journalist, and politician. During World War I he advocated a programme of non-cooperation with the British, which influenced Mahatma *Gandhi and for which he was imprisoned. He was elected president of the Indian National Congress in 1940 and was also president of the Congress Party during negotiations for India's independence. After independence, he was in charge of the ministry of education.

Azaña, Manuel (1880–1940) Spanish politician, prime minister 1931–33 and 1936. He was the first prime minister of the second Spanish republic, and the last president of the republic during the Civil War 1936–39, before the establishment of a dictatorship under General Francisco Franco.

Azcona del Hoyo, José Simon (1927–) Honduran politician, president 1986–90. A moderate conservative, he signed the American Peace Accord of 1987 despite his government's quiet acceptance of the presence in Honduras of Nicaraguan contras backed by the USA. He was barred by law from seeking a second term.

Azerbaijan country in western Asia, bounded south by Iran, east by the Caspian Sea, west by Armenia and Georgia, and north by Russia.

Azhari, Ismail (1902–1969) Sudanese politician, first prime minister of Sudan 1954–56 and president 1964–69. Imprisoned by the British for nationalist agitation, he was elected head of the National Unionist Party in 1952, and led the country in the two years preceding full independence.

Azikiwe, Nnamdi (1904–1996) Nigerian politician and president 1963–66. A leading nationalist in the 1940s, he advocated self-government for Nigeria. He was prime minister of Eastern Nigeria 1954–59 and on independence became governor general of the Federation of Nigeria 1960–63. During the civil war triggered by the secession of Biafra 1967–70 he initially backed his own ethnic group, the Ibo, but switched his support to the federal government in 1969.

Aziz, Tariq (1936–) born **Mikhail Yuhanna**, Iraqi politician, deputy prime minister 1979–2003, and foreign minister 1983–91. Saddam Hussein's right-hand man, Aziz was a loyalist who remained staunchly faithful to the Iraqi leader. After 1983, and especially during the Gulf War, Aziz was the chief international spokesperson for Iraqi policy. He visited Egypt in 1983 in the first formal contact between the two nations since 1978. In the summer of 1990 he led Iraq's intimidation of its erstwhile Arab allies, culminating in the invasion of Kuwait in August of that year. Throughout his tenure, Aziz was credited with bringing Iraqi diplomacy more into the mainstream.

Aznar, José María (1953–) Spanish politician, prime minister 1996–2004. He became premier of the Castile-León region in 1987. Elected leader of the right-of-centre Popular Party (PP) in 1989, Aznar and the PP lost to the ruling Social Workers' Party (PSOE) in the elections of 1989 and 1993. A minority PP government headed by Aznar was installed in 1996. He was outspoken in his support of the US-led Iraq War in 2003, despite overwhelming public disapproval. His party's defeat in the 2004 elections was widely attributed to public anger at the government's reaction to the terrorist bombings in Madrid, in March 2004, that killed around 200 people.

B

Baader–Meinhof gang popular name for the West German left-wing guerrilla group the *Rote Armee Fraktion/Red Army Faction*, active from 1968 against what it perceived as US imperialism. The three main founding members were Andreas Baader, Gudrun Ensslin, and Ulrike Meinhof.

Ba'ath Party Party of Arab Renaissance, ruling political party in Iraq and Syria. Despite public support of pan-Arab unity and its foundation in 1943 as a party of Arab nationalism, its ideology has been so vague that it has fostered widely differing (and often opposing) parties in Syria and Iraq.

Babangida, Ibrahim (1941–) Nigerian politician and soldier, president 1985–93. He became head of the Nigerian army in 1983, and in 1985 led a coup against President Muhammadu Buhari, assuming the presidency himself. From 1992 he promised a return to civilian rule but resigned in 1993, his commitment to democracy increasingly in doubt.

Baden-Powell, Robert Stephenson Smyth (1857–1941) 1st Baron Baden-Powell, British general, founder of the Scout Association. He was commander of the garrison during the 217-day siege of Mafeking (now Mafikeng) in the Second South African War (1899–1900). After 1907 he devoted his time to developing the Scout movement, which rapidly spread throughout the world.

Bader, Douglas Robert Steuart (1910–1982) British fighter pilot. He lost both legs in a flying accident in 1931, but had a distinguished flying career in World War II. He was credited with 221/2 planes shot down (20 on his own and some jointly)

before himself being shot down and captured in August 1941. The film *Reach for the Sky* (1956) was based on his experiences; he was played by Kenneth More.

Badoglio, Pietro (1871–1956) Italian soldier and fascist politician. He served as a general in World War I and subsequently in the campaigns against the peoples of Tripoli and Cyrenaica. In 1935 he became commander-in-chief in Ethiopia, adopting ruthless measures to break patriot resistance. He was created viceroy of Ethiopia and duke of Addis Ababa in 1936. He resigned during the disastrous campaign into Greece in 1940 and succeeded Mussolini as prime minister of Italy from July 1943 to June 1944, negotiating the armistice with the Allies.

Baedeker raids series of German air raids directed at British provincial towns and cities April–Oct 1942.

Baghdad Pact military treaty of 1955 concluded by the UK, Iran, Iraq, Pakistan, and Turkey, with the USA cooperating; it was replaced by the *Central Treaty Organization (CENTO) when Iraq withdrew in 1958.

Bahamas country comprising a group of about 700 islands and about 2,400 uninhabited islets in the Caribbean, 80 km/50 mi from the southeast coast of Florida. They extend for about 1,223 km/760 mi from northwest to southeast, but only 22 of the islands are inhabited.

Bahrain country comprising a group of islands in the Gulf, between Saudi Arabia and Iran.

Bakhtiar, Shahpur (1914–1991) Iranian politician, the last prime minister under Shah *Pahlavi, in 1979. He was a supporter of the political leader Muhammad Mossadeq in the 1950s, and was active in the National Front opposition to the shah from 1960. He lived in exile after the 1979 Islamic revolution, until his assassination by Islamic zealots at his home in Paris.

Balaguer Ricardo, Joaquín Videla (1906–2002) Dominican Republic centre-right politician, president 1960–62, 1966–78, and 1986–96. The country's figurehead president in 1960 under the dictator Rafael *Trujillo Molina, he formed the Christian Social Reform Party (PRSC) in 1965, and was elected president in 1966. He established a more democratic regime and closer links with the USA, but faced coup attempts, right-wing terrorism, and left-wing guerrilla incursions. He retired in 1978, but failure of the economic policies of the left-of-centre Dominican Revolutionary Party (PRD) brought him back to power in 1986.

Balbo, Count Italo (1896–1940) Italian aviator and politician. He was one of the main figures in Mussolini's 'March on Rome' but later quarrelled with him over the alliance with Germany.

Baldwin, Stanley (1867–1947) 1st Earl Baldwin of Bewdley, British Conservative politician, prime minister 1923–24, 1924–29, and 1935–37. He weathered the general strike of 1926, secured complete adult suffrage in 1928, and handled the *abdication crisis of Edward VIII in 1936, but failed to prepare Britain for World War II.

Balfour Declaration letter, dated 2 November 1917, from British foreign secretary A J Balfour to Lord Rothschild (chair, British Zionist Federation) stating: 'HM government view with favour the establishment in Palestine of a national home for the Jewish people.' It helped form the basis for the foundation of *Israel in 1948.

Balkan Wars two wars 1912–13 and 1913 (preceding World War I) which resulted in the expulsion by the Balkan states of Ottoman Turkey from Europe, except for a small area around Istanbul.

Ball, Albert (1896–1917) British fighter pilot and air ace. He was awarded the MC, DSO and Bar, and, posthumously, the Victoria Cross. At the time of his death May 1917 he had attained the rank of captain and was credited with over 40 enemy aircraft shot down.

Banda, Hastings Kamuzu (1905–1997) Malawi politician, physician, and president (1966–94). He led his country's independence movement and was prime minister of Nyasaland (the former name of Malawi) from 1964. He became Malawi's first president in 1966 and was named president for life in 1971; his rule was authoritarian. Having bowed to opposition pressure and opened the way for a pluralist system, Banda stood in the first free presidential elections for 30 years in 1994, but was defeated by Bakili Muluzi. In January 1996 he and his former aide, John Tembo, were acquitted of the murders of three senior politicians and a lawyer in 1983.

Bandaranaike, Sirimavo (1916–2000) born **Sirimavo Ratwatte Dias Bandaranaike**, Sri Lankan politician, prime minister 1994–2000. She succeeded her husband Solomon *Bandaranaike to become the world's first female prime minister, 1960–65 and 1970–77, but was expelled from parliament in 1980 for abuse of her powers while in office. Her daughter Chandrika Bandaranaike Kumaratunga was elected president in 1994. She resigned her position on 10 August 2000 because of poor health, and was replaced by Ratnasiri Wickremanayake.

Bandaranaike, Solomon West Ridgeway Dias (1899–1959) Sri Lankan nationalist politician. In 1952 he founded the Sri Lanka Freedom Party and in 1956 became prime minister, pledged to a socialist programme and a neutral foreign policy. He failed to satisfy extremists and was assassinated by a Buddhist monk.

Bandung Conference first conference, in 1955, of the Afro-Asian nations, proclaiming anticolonialism and neutrality between East and West. It was organized by Indonesia, Myanmar, Sri Lanka, India, and Pakistan.

Bangladesh country in southern Asia, bounded north, west, and east by India, southeast by Myanmar, and south by the Bay of Bengal.

Bani-Sadr, Abu'l-Hassan (1933–) Iranian politician, first president of Iran, 1980–81, after the Islamic Revolution of 1979. He was an important figure in the Iranian Revolution of 1978–79, serving as a bridge between the political intelligentsia and the Islamic clergy opposition to the shah's regime. After the revolution, Bani-Sadr became foreign and economics minister in November 1979 and was elected the first president of the Islamic Republic in January 1980, and chair of the defence council. After his dismissal by Ayatollah *Khomeini, he fled to France.

Bantustan or **homeland**, name until 1978 for a Black National State in the Republic of South Africa.

Bapaume, Battle of battle between German and British forces during World War I in Nord *département*, France; the second phase of the successful British offensive of 21 August–2 September 1918. The British pushed the Germans back 8 km/5 mi, capturing 34,250 prisoners and 270 guns as well as vital strategic positions, including the German strongpoint at Mont St Quentin. The battle was very similar to the Battle of the Somme 1916, starting from more or less the same positions and following the same general plan.

Barak, Ehud (1942–) born **Ehud Brog,** Israeli Labour politician, prime minister 1999–2001, former chief of staff of the Israeli army, and the most decorated soldier in the nation's history. As prime minister, Barak formed a government consisting of seven parties of differing political views, the 'One Israel' alliance. He often faced difficulties in keeping the coalition alive, as he depended on the support of three ultra-Orthodox Jewish parties. His campaign emphasized progress in the Middle East peace process, and he withdrew Israeli forces from Lebanon, the Golan Heights (Syria), and much of the West Bank. Talks stalled in May 2000 over the future of Jerusalem and violence from October led to Barak's resignation in December and subsequent defeat in prime ministerial elections in February 2001 and resignation as Labour leader.

Barbados island country in the Caribbean, one of the Lesser Antilles. It is about 483 km/300 mi north of Venezuela.

Barbarossa, Operation in World War II, German code name for the plan to invade the USSR, launched on 22 June 1941. The plan was initially successful but by the end of 1941, the German advance had stalled. Large sections of the USSR, particularly the Ukraine, remained in German hands until 1944 and fighting continued elsewhere until then, notably the sieges of Leningrad and Stalingrad.

Barbie, Klaus (1913–1991) German Nazi, a member of the *SS paramilitary organization from 1936. During World War II he was involved in the deportation of Jews from the occupied Netherlands from 1940 to 1942 and in tracking down Jews and Resistance workers in France from 1942 to 1945. He was arrested in 1983 and convicted of crimes against humanity in France in 1987.

Barnard, Christiaan Neethling (1922–2001) South African surgeon who performed the first human heart transplant in 1967 at Groote Schuur Hospital in Cape Town. The 54-year-old patient lived for 18 days.

**Barre, Raymond Octave Joseph
(1924–)** French centre-right
politician, prime minister 1976–81
under President Valéry *Giscard
d'Estaing, when he gained a reputation
as a tough and determined budget-
cutter.

**Barrès, (Auguste-) Maurice
(1862–1923)** French writer and
nationalist activist. In a trilogy of
novels collectively entitled *Le Culte du
moi/The Cult of the Ego* 1888–91 he
expounded an individualistic
philosophy, the need to cultivate all
aspects of a personality. He emerged
as a champion of regionalism and
nationalism in his second trilogy of
novels, *Le Roman de l'énergie nationale/
The Novel of National Energy* 1897–1902.

Barrow, Errol Walton (1920–1987)
Barbadian left-of-centre politician,
prime minister 1961–76 and 1986–87.
He co-founded the Democratic Labour
Party (DLP) in 1955, becoming its chair
in 1958, and leading the DLP to victory
following independence in 1961.
Defeated in 1976 by the BLP, led by
Tom Adams, he returned to power
with a decisive majority in 1986. A
critic of the US intervention in Grenada
in 1983, Barrow oversaw a review
of Barbadian participation in the
US-backed regional security system.

Baruch, Bernard Mannes (1870–1965)
US financier. He was a friend of the
British prime minister Winston
Churchill and a self-appointed,
unpaid adviser to US presidents
Woodrow Wilson, Franklin D Roosevelt,
and Harry Truman. He strongly
advocated international control of
nuclear energy.

Basque the people inhabiting the
Basque Country of central northern
Spain and the extreme southwest of
France. The Basques are a pre-Indo-
European people whose language
(**Euskara**) is unrelated to any other
language. Although both the Romans
and, later, the Visigoths conquered
them, they largely maintained their
independence until the 19th century.

During the Spanish Civil War
(1936–39), they were on the republican
side defeated by Franco. The Basque
separatist movement *Euskadi ta
Askatasuna (ETA; 'Basque Nation and
Liberty') and the French organization
Iparretarrak ('ETA fighters from the
North Side') have engaged in guerrilla
activity from 1968 in an attempt to
secure a united Basque state.

At the beginning of the 10th century
the Basques to the south of the
Pyrenees were brought into the
kingdom of Navarre and were granted
fueros (charters) allowing them
autonomy. The fueros were lost by
the French Basques in the French
Revolution and by the Spanish Basques
in the 19th century. Their long tradition
of self-government helps to explain
their continued fight for separatism.
The declaration of the republic in
Spain divided their allegiances, and
its defeat sent many Basques into exile
in North and South America.

Bataan peninsula in Luzon, the
Philippines, which was defended
against the Japanese in World War II
by US and Filipino troops under
Gen MacArthur from 1 January to
9 April 1942. MacArthur was
evacuated, but some 67,000 Allied
prisoners died on the **Bataan Death
March** to camps in the interior.

**Batista (y Zaldívar), Fulgencio
(1901–1973)** Cuban right-wing
dictator, dictator-president 1934–44
and 1952–59. Having led the
September 1933 coup to install Ramón
Grau San Martín in power, he forced
Grau's resignation in 1934 to become
Cuba's effective ruler, as formal
president from 1940. Exiled in the
USA 1944–49, he ousted President
Carlos Prío Socarrás in a military coup
in 1952. His authoritarian methods
enabled him to jail his opponents
and amass a large personal fortune.
He was overthrown by rebel forces led
by Fidel *Castro in 1959. Batista fled
to the Dominican Republic and later
to Portugal. He died in Spain.

Batlle y Ordóñez, José (1856–1929)
Uruguayan statesman, political reformer, and president 1903–07 and 1911–15. Many industries were nationalized by the state during his administration and significant improvements were made in the areas of working hours, pensions, and unemployment benefits. He also gave women the vote. Proposals made during his presidency subsequently influenced changes to the nation's constitution in 1917, with the creation of national socialist governance.

Battenberg, (Mountbatten) Prince Louis Alexander (1854–1921)
British admiral. A member of a British family of German extraction, Battenberg joined the Royal Navy and became an admiral. In 1914 he was First Sea Lord but was forced to retire due to anti-German public feeling as a result of World War I.

battleship class of large warships with the biggest guns and heaviest armour. The *Dreadnought class of battleship, built by the British Navy after 1906, revolutionized battleship design, as it was an 'all-big-gun' ship. Until World War II battleships were the dominant unit in modern navies, when naval aircraft became more useful in naval battles.

Baudouin (1930–1993) King of the Belgians 1951–93. In 1950 his father, *Leopold III, abdicated and Baudouin was known until his succession in 1951 as *Le Prince Royal*. During his reign he succeeded in holding together a country divided by religion and language, while presiding over the dismemberment of Belgium's imperial past. In 1960 he married Fabiola de Mora y Aragón (1928–), member of a Spanish noble family. They were unable to have any children, and he was succeeded by his brother, Albert, in 1993.

Beatrix, (Wilhelmina Armgard) (1938–) Queen of the Netherlands. The eldest daughter of Queen *Juliana, she succeeded to the throne on her mother's abdication in 1980. In 1966 she married West German diplomat Claus von Amsberg, who was created Prince of the Netherlands. Her heir is Prince Willem Alexander.

Beatty, David (1871–1936) 1st Earl Beatty, British admiral in World War I. He commanded the cruiser squadron 1912–16 and bore the brunt of the Battle of *Jutland in 1916.

Beaverbrook, (William) Max(well) Aitken (1879–1964) 1st Baron Beaverbrook, Canadian-born British financier, proprietor and publisher of the *Daily Express* group of newspapers, and a UK government minister in cabinets during both world wars. He bought a majority interest in the *Daily Express* in 1916, founded the *Sunday Express* in 1918, and bought the London *Evening Standard* in 1923. He served in David Lloyd George's World War I cabinet and Winston Churchill's World War II cabinet.

Bechuanaland former name (to 1966) of *Botswana.

Beck, Józef (1894–1944) Polish soldier and politician, foreign minister of Poland 1932–39. He served in Józef *Piłsudski's Polish Legion against the Russians in 1914, and took part in the Polish attack that drove the Soviet Union from Polish territory in 1919–20. As foreign minister in Piłsudski's military government, he tried to preserve Polish independence by signing non-aggression pacts with both Germany and the USSR. After the fall of Poland to Nazi forces, Beck fled to Romania, where he died.

Bedell Smith, Walter (1895–1961) US general; Eisenhower's staff officer for much of World War II. Among his many achievements was the negotiation of the Italian surrender 1943 and the surrender of German forces in northwestern Europe 1945.

beer-hall putsch or **Munich beer-hall putsch**, unsuccessful uprising at Munich led by Adolf Hitler, attempting to overthrow the government of Bavaria in November 1923. More than

2,000 Nazi demonstrators were met by armed police, who opened fire, killing 16 of Hitler's supporters. At the subsequent trial for treason, General Ludendorff, who had supported Hitler, was acquitted. Hitler was sentenced to prison, where he wrote *Mein Kampf.*

Begin, Menachem (1913–1992) Israeli politician. He was leader of the extremist Irgun Zvai Leumi organization in Palestine from 1942 and prime minister of Israel 1977–83, as head of the right-wing Likud party. Following strong encouragement from US president Jimmy *Carter, he entered into negotiations with President Anwar *Sadat of Egypt, which resulted in the Camp David Agreements. He shared the Nobel Prize for Peace in 1978 with Anwar Sadat for their efforts towards the Israel-Egypt peace treaty of 1979. In 1981 Begin won a new term of office but his health was failing. The death of his wife in 1982 was a grave blow, resulting in his retirement in September 1983. For the rest of his life he was a virtual recluse.

Belarus or **Byelorussia** or **Belorussia**, country in east-central Europe, bounded south by Ukraine, east by Russia, west by Poland, and north by Latvia and Lithuania.

Belaúnde Terry, Fernando (1913–2002) Peruvian politician and president 1963–68 and 1980–85. He championed land reform and the construction of roads to open up the Amazon valley. He fled to the USA in 1968 after being deposed by a military junta. After his return, his second term in office was marked by rampant inflation, a devaluation of the currency in 1967, enormous foreign debts, terrorism, mass killings, and human-rights violations by the armed forces.

Belgium country in Western Europe, bounded to the north by the Netherlands, to the northwest by the North Sea, to the south and west by France, and to the east by Luxembourg and Germany.

Belize country in Central America, bounded north by Mexico, west and south by Guatemala, and east by the Caribbean Sea.

Belleau Wood in World War I, US victory over the Germans, June 1918, during the Allied drive to expel the Germans from northern France. After their success at Château-Thierry, US Marines attacked German positions in Belleau Wood 6 June. The Marines spent almost three weeks clearing the wood in the face of strong German defences.

Ben Ali, Zine el Abidine (1936–) Tunisian politician, president from 1987. After training in France and the USA, he returned to Tunisia and became director general of national security. He was made minister of the interior and then prime minister under the ageing president for life Habib *Bourguiba, whom he deposed in 1987 in a bloodless coup with the aid of ministerial colleagues. He ended the personality cult established by Bourguiba and moved towards a pluralist political system. He was re-elected in 1994, with 99% of the popular vote.

Ben Barka, Mehdi (1920–1965) Moroccan politician. He became president of the National Consultative Assembly in 1956 on the country's independence from France. He was assassinated by Moroccan agents with the aid of the French secret service.

Ben Bella, Muhammad Ahmed (1916–) Algerian politician. He was among the leaders of the Front de Libération Nationale (FLN), the first prime minister of independent Algeria 1962–63, and its first president 1963–65. His centralization of power and systematic purges were among the reasons behind his overthrow in 1965 by Houari *Boumédienne. He was detained until 1979. In 1985 he founded a new party, Mouvement pour la Démocratie en Algérie (MDA), and returned to Algeria in 1990 after nine years in exile. The cancellation of the 1991 legislative elections led to his exile for the second time, and his party was banned in 1997.

Benelux acronym for **BElgium, the NEtherlands, and LUXembourg,** customs union of Belgium, the Netherlands, and Luxembourg, an agreement for which was signed in London by the three governments in exile in 1944, and ratified in 1947. It came into force in 1948 and was further extended and strengthened by the Benelux Economic Union Treaty in 1958. The full economic union between the three countries came into operation in 1960. The three Benelux countries were founder-members of the European Economic Community (now the *European Union), for which the Benelux union was an important stimulus.

Beneš, Edvard (1884–1948) Czechoslovak politician. He worked with Tomás Masaryk towards Czechoslovak nationalism from 1918 and was foreign minister and representative at the League of Nations. He was president of the republic from 1935 until forced to resign by the Germans and headed a government in exile in London during World War II. He personally gave the order for the assassination of Reinhard *Heydrich in Prague in 1942. Having signed an agreement with Joseph Stalin, he returned home as president in 1945 but resigned again after the communist coup in 1948.

Bengal former province of British India, in the northeast of the subcontinent. It was the first major part of India to come under the control of the British East India Company (the 'Bengal Presidency'). When India gained independence in 1947, Bengal was divided into West Bengal, a state of India, and East Bengal, which from 1972 onwards became part of the newly independent state of *Bangladesh.

Ben-Gurion, David (1886–1973) adopted name of **David Gruen,** Israeli statesman and socialist politician. He was one of the founders of the state of Israel, the country's first prime minister 1948–53, and again 1955–63. He retired from politics in 1970, but remained a lasting symbol of the Israeli state.

Benin country in west Africa, bounded east by Nigeria, north by Niger and Burkina Faso, west by Togo, and south by the Gulf of Guinea.

Benn, Tony (Anthony Neil Wedgwood) (1925–) British Labour politician, formerly the leading figure on the party's left wing. He was minister of technology 1966–70 and secretary of state for industry 1974–75, but his campaign against entry to the European Community (EC; now the European Union) led to his transfer to the Department of Energy 1975–79. A skilled parliamentary orator, he twice unsuccessfully contested the Labour Party leadership. Benn stood down in May 2001 as an MP after 50 years in Parliament, but remained politically active.

Bennett, Richard Bedford (1870–1947) 1st Viscount Bennett, Canadian Conservative politician, prime minister 1930–35. He was minister of finance in 1926. In the election of 1935 he was heavily defeated because of his failure to cope with the effects of the economic depression. He was succeeded as premier by Mackenzie *King.

Ben Zvi, Izhak (1884–1963) Israeli politician, president 1952–63. He was born in Poltava, Russia, and became active in the Zionist movement in Ukraine. In 1907 he went to Palestine but was deported in 1915 with David *Ben-Gurion. They served in the Jewish Legion under Field Marshal Allenby, who commanded the British forces in the Middle East. In 1952 he succeeded Chaim *Weizmann as the second president of the newly formed state.

Berchtesgaden   village in southeastern Bavaria, Germany, site of Hitler's country residence, the Berghof, which was captured by US troops 4 May 1945 and destroyed.

Beriya, Lavrenti Pavlovich (1899–1953) Georgian communist. He was USSR commissar (minister) for internal affairs 1938–45 and deputy prime minister under Stalin, in charge of security matters, 1941–53. In 1945 he was made a marshal of the Soviet Union. Beriya ended the Great Purge by liquidating his predecessor Yezhov and many NKVD (Soviet secret police) officials, and organized the deportation of hundreds of thousands from eastern Poland, the Baltic States, and areas formerly occupied by the Germans. He was also in charge of the security police in the satellite states of Eastern Europe.

Berlin, Battle of   in World War II, series of 16 heavy bombing attacks on Berlin by the RAF November 1943–March 1944. Some 9,111 bomber sorties were flown during the course of the campaign and immense damage was done to the city. Almost 600 bombers were lost during the battle, into which the Germans threw their entire air defence capability.

Berlin, Battle of   final battle of the European phase of World War II, 16 April–2 May 1945; Soviet forces captured Berlin, the capital of Germany and seat of government and site of most German military and administrative headquarters. Hitler committed suicide on 30 April as the Soviets closed in and General Karl Weidling surrendered the city on 2 May. Soviet casualties came to about 100,000 dead; German casualties were unknown but some 136,000 were taken prisoner and it is believed over 100,000 civilians died in the course of the fighting. After the war, Berlin was divided into four sectors – British, US, French, and Soviet – and until 1948 was under quadripartite government by the Allies.

Berlin blockade   the closing of entry to Berlin from the west by Soviet Forces from June 1948 to May 1949. It was an attempt to prevent the other Allies (the USA, France, and the UK) unifying the western part of Germany. The British and US forces responded by sending supplies to the city by air for over a year (the **Berlin airlift**). In May 1949 the blockade was lifted; the airlift continued until September. The blockade marked the formal division of the city into Eastern and Western sectors. In 1961 East Berlin was sealed off with the construction of the *Berlin Wall.

Berlinguer, Enrico (1922–1984) Italian communist who freed the party from Soviet influence. Secretary general of the Italian Communist Party from 1972, by 1976 he was near to the premiership, but the murder in 1978 of former prime minister Aldo Moro by Red Brigade guerrillas prompted a shift in popular support towards the socialists.

Berlin Olympics   Olympic Games held in Berlin in 1936. Adolf Hitler and the Nazi party attempted to use the occasion for propaganda purposes and to demonstrate German physical prowess.

Berlin Wall   dividing barrier between East and West Berlin from 1961 to 1989, erected by East Germany to prevent East Germans from leaving for West Germany. Escapers were shot on sight.

Bermuda   British overseas territory in the Northwest Atlantic Ocean; area 54 sq km/21 sq mi; population (1994 est) 60,500. The colony consists of 138 small islands, of which 20 are inhabited; the 6 principal islands are linked by bridges and causeways. The capital and chief port is Hamilton. Bermuda is Britain's oldest colony, officially taken by the crown in 1684. Under the constitution of 1968, it is fully self-governing, with a governor (John Vereker from 2002), senate, and elected House of Assembly (premier from 1998 Jennifer Smith, Progressive

Labour Party). The principal economic activities are tourism and finance, especially insurance. Industries include pharmaceuticals and growing Easter lilies. The currency used in the colony is the Bermuda dollar, the main language spoken is English, and the main religion is Christianity.

Bernadotte, Count Folke (1895–1948) Swedish diplomat and president of the Swedish Red Cross. In 1945 he conveyed Nazi commander Heinrich Himmler's offer of capitulation to the British and US governments, and in 1948 was United Nations mediator in Palestine, where he was assassinated by Israeli Stern Gang guerrillas. He was a nephew of Gustaf VI of Sweden.

Bernhard Leopold, Prince of the Netherlands (1911–) Formerly Prince Bernhard of Lippe-Biesterfeld, he married Princess *Juliana in 1937. When Germany invaded the Netherlands in 1940, he escaped to England and became liaison officer for the Dutch and British forces, playing a part in the organization of the Dutch Resistance.

Berri, Nabih (1939–) Lebanese politician and soldier, leader of Amal ('Hope'), the Syrian-backed Shiite nationalist movement. He became minister of justice in the government of President Amin *Gemayel in 1984. In 1988 Amal was disbanded after defeat by the Iranian-backed Hezbollah ('Party of God') during the Lebanese civil wars, and Berri joined the cabinet of Selim Hoss in 1989. In December 1990 Berri was made minister of state in the newly formed Karami cabinet, and in 1992 retained the same post in the cabinet of Rashid al-Sohl. He subsequently became president of the national assembly.

Betancourt, Rómulo (1908–1981) Venezuelan president 1959–64 whose rule was plagued by guerrilla violence and economic and political division. He expanded welfare programmes, increased expenditure on education, encouraged foreign investment, and tried to diversify the Venezuelan economy to decrease its dependence on oil exports.

Bethlen, István (1874–1947) Count Bethlen, Hungarian prime minister 1921–31. After World War I, when Béla Kun headed the communist revolution, Bethlen was a leader of the successful counter-revolution. As prime minister, he settled the western frontier amicably with Austria, and in 1923 obtained suspension of the reparations order against Hungary and a loan from the League of Nations. In 1927 he signed a treaty with fascist Italy. From 1931 to 1935 he was leader of a conservative group in opposition. He resisted the Nazis during World War II.

Bethmann Hollweg, Theobald Theodor Friedrich Alfred von (1856–1921) German politician, imperial chancellor 1909–17. He was largely responsible for engineering popular support for World War I in Germany, but his power was overthrown by a military dictatorship under Erich von *Ludendorff and Paul von Hindenburg.

Bevan, Aneurin (Nye) (1897–1960) British Labour politician. Son of a Welsh miner, and himself a miner at 13, he was member of Parliament for Ebbw Vale 1929–60. As minister of health 1945–51, he inaugurated the National Health Service (NHS); he was minister of labour from January to April 1951, when he resigned (with Harold Wilson) on the introduction of NHS charges and led a Bevanite faction against the government. In 1956 he became chief Labour spokesperson on foreign affairs, and deputy leader of the Labour party in 1959. He was an outstanding speaker.

Beveridge, William Henry (1879–1963) 1st Baron Beveridge, British economist. A civil servant, he acted as Lloyd George's lieutenant in the social legislation of the Liberal government before World War I. His *Report on Social Insurance and Allied Services* (1942), known as the *Beveridge Report, formed the basis of the welfare state in Britain.

Beveridge Report, the in Britain, popular name of *Social Insurance and Allied Services*, a report written by William Beveridge in 1942 that formed the basis for the social-reform legislation of the Labour government of 1945–50.

Bevin, Ernest (1881–1951) British Labour politician. Chief creator of the Transport and General Workers' Union, he was its general secretary 1921–40. He served as minister of labour and national service 1940–45 in Winston Churchill's wartime coalition government, and organized the 'Bevin boys', chosen by ballot to work in the coalmines as war service. As foreign secretary in the Labour government 1945–51, he played a leading part in the creation of the *North Atlantic Treaty Organization (NATO).

Bhattari, Krishna Prasad (1925–) Nepalese politician, prime minister 1990–91. As an opponent of absolute monarchy, he was in hiding for 12 years until 1990, when, as leader of the centrist Nepali Congress Party, he became prime minister in the wake of the revolution that year, which ended the uncontested rule of King *Birendra. However, in 1991, in Nepal's first multiparty elections in three decades, he offered his resignation to the king after losing his own seat in the 205-member House of Representatives to the Marxist leader of the United Communist Party, Madan Bhandari.

Bhindranwale, Sant Jarnail Singh (1947–1984) Indian Sikh fundamentalist leader who campaigned for the creation of a separate state of Khalistan during the early 1980s, precipitating a bloody Hindu–Sikh conflict in the Punjab. Having taken refuge in the Golden Temple complex in Amritsar and built up an arms cache for guerrilla activities, Bhindranwale, along with around 500 followers, died at the hands of Indian security forces who stormed the temple in 'Operation Blue Star' in June 1984.

Bhumibol Adulyadej (1927–) King of Thailand from 1946. Born in the USA and educated in Bangkok and Switzerland, he succeeded to the throne on the assassination of his brother. In 1973 he was active, with popular support, in overthrowing the military government of Marshal Thanom Kittikachorn and thus ended a sequence of army-dominated regimes in power from 1932.

Bhutan mountainous, landlocked country in the eastern Himalayas (southeast Asia), bounded north and west by Tibet (China) and to the south and east by India.

Bhutto, Benazir (1953–) Pakistani politician. She was leader of the Pakistan People's Party (PPP) from 1984, a position she held in exile until 1986. Bhutto became prime minister of Pakistan from 1988 until 1990, when the opposition manoeuvred her from office and charged her with corruption. She returned as prime minister (1993–96), but was removed again under suspicion of corruption. In 1999, while living in self-imposed exile in London, Bhutto (and her husband, Asif Ali Zardari) was found guilty of corruption and given a five-year prison sentence, but in April 2001 Pakistan's Supreme Court quashed the convictions and ordered a retrial.

Bhutto, Zulfikar Ali (1928–1979) Pakistani politician, president 1971–73, and prime minister from 1973 until the 1977 military coup led by General *Zia ul-Haq. In 1978 Bhutto was sentenced to death for conspiring to murder a political opponent and was hanged the following year. He was the father of Benazir Bhutto.

Biafra, Republic of African state proclaimed 1967 when fears that Nigerian central government was increasingly in the hands of the rival Hausa tribe led the predominantly Ibo Eastern Region of Nigeria to secede under Lt-Col Odumegwu Ojukwu. On the proclamation of Biafra, civil war ensued with the rest of the federation. In a bitterly fought campaign federal forces confined the Biafrans to a shrinking area of the interior by 1968, and by 1970 Biafra ceased to exist. Around 1 million Biafrans died in the famine caused by the civil war.

Bidault, Georges Augustin (1899–1983) French Christian Democrat politician, cofounder of the Mouvement Républicain Populaire (MRP) and prime minister 1946 and 1949–50.

Biggs, Ronald (1929–) English criminal, member of the gang responsible for the robbery of the London–Glasgow mail train in the UK on 8 August 1963. He was sentenced to 30 years imprisonment but escaped from Wandsworth prison, London, in July 1965 and fled, first to Australia, and later to Rio de Janeiro, Brazil. Unable to be extradited under Brazilian law, he lived there until May 2001, when he returned voluntarily to the UK, and was arrested on his arrival.

Bikini Atoll atoll in the *Marshall Islands, western Pacific, where the USA carried out 23 atomic- and hydrogen-bomb tests (some underwater) from 1946 to 1958.

Biko, Steve (1946–1977) born **Bantu Stephen Biko**, South African civil-rights leader. An active opponent of *apartheid, he was arrested in August 1977, and died in detention on 12 September. Following his death in the custody of South African police, he became a symbol of the anti-apartheid movement. An inquest in the late 1980s found no one was to blame for Biko's death.

Five former security policemen confessed to being involved in Biko's murder in January 1997. They applied for an amnesty to the Truth and Reconciliation Commission (TRC), the body charged with healing South Africa by exposing its past and laying foundations for a more peaceful future. The amnesty application angered Biko's family, and his widow

challenged the legitimacy of the TRC in the Constitutional Court.

bin Laden, Osama (1957–) Saudi-born, Afghanistan-based, Islamic fundamentalist terrorist leader who is believed to have masterminded a number of terrorist attacks directed at US targets since the early 1990s. The 11 September 2001 destruction of the World Trade Center in New York, by suicide hijackers of two commercial airliners, and two other aircraft hijackings, claimed around 3,000 lives. It was the worst act of terrorism on record. US president George W Bush responded by launching a War on Terrorism, with a US-led international coalition mounting military strikes on Afghanistan in an attempt to force its *Taliban government to give bin Laden up. Earlier bin Laden was thought to have engineered attacks including the February 1993 bombing of the World Trade Center in which 6 people died, the June 1996 bombing of the US military complex in Saudi Arabia, killing 19, the August 1998 bombings of US embassies in Kenya and Tanzania, killing 224, and an October 2000 suicide bomb attack on the USS *Cole* in Yemen, which killed 17 US sailors. Bin Laden promotes jihad (holy war) against the USA with the aim of liberating Islam's three holiest places – Mecca, Medina, and Jerusalem.

Bird, Vere Cornwall (1910–1999) Antiguan politician, chief minister 1960–67, and prime minister 1967–71 and 1976–94. He formed the centre-left Antigua Labour Party (ALP) in 1968, but lost power to George Walter, leader of the Progressive Labour Movement (PLM), in 1971. Having regained control in 1976, he earned the title 'father of the nation' by negotiating Antigua's independence from British colonial rule in 1981. A political conservative, Bird pursued a policy of political non-alignment, although in 1983 Antigua assisted the USA in its invasion of Grenada.

Birendra, Bir Bikram Shah Dev (1945–2001) King of Nepal from 1972, when he succeeded his father Mahendra; he was formally crowned in 1975. King Birendra oversaw Nepal's return to multiparty politics and introduced a new constitution in 1990. He was murdered by Crown Prince Dipendra, along with eight other members of the royal family, in June 2001. His brother Gyanendra replaced him as king.

Birkenhead, F(rederick) E(dwin) Smith (1872–1930) 1st Earl of Birkenhead, British lawyer and Conservative politician. He was a flamboyant and ambitious character, and played a major role in securing the Anglo-Irish Treaty in 1921, which created the Irish Free State (now the Republic of Ireland). As a lawyer, his greatest achievement was the Law of Property Act of 1922, which forms the basis of current English land law.

Bishop, Maurice (1944–1983) Grenadian socialist politician, president 1979–83. Founder of the New Jewel Movement (NJM) in 1973, a mass anti-colonial Marxist–Leninist organization, he became prime minister of a provisional revolutionary government in 1979, after Eric *Gairy was ousted in a coup. Radical elements within the NJM embarked on a socialist economic programme, aligning the country with communist Cuba and the USSR, and in October 1983 Bishop, who had tried to improve relations with a concerned USA, was deposed. He was killed by the military under General Hudson Austin, who had seized power as a Revolutionary Military Council. These events precipitated armed intervention on 25 October 1983 by a US–Caribbean 'liberation force'.

Bismarck German battleship of World War II. Launched in February 1939, it was a constant threat to Allied convoys in the Atlantic until sunk by the British in May 1941. The largest battleship afloat at the time, it weighed 47,000 tonnes.

Bitar, Salah Eddin (1912–1980) Syrian politician, prime minister several times between 1963 and 1964 and in 1966. He was, with Michel 'Aflaq, a cofounder of the pan-Arab socialist doctrine of Ba'athism, which was particularly influential in Syria and Iraq. When the Ba'ath Party split into several factions in 1966 he left Syria for exile in Beirut, Lebanon.

Biya, Paul (1933–) Cameroonian politician, prime minister 1975–82 and president from 1982. He entered politics under the aegis of President Ahmadou *Ahidjo, becoming prime minister in 1975. When Ahidjo retired unexpectedly in 1982, he became president and reconstituted the government with his own supporters. He survived a coup attempt in 1984, reputedly instigated by Ahidjo, and was re-elected president in 1988 with more than 98% of the vote.

Bjelke-Petersen, Joh(annes) (1911–) Australian right-wing politician, leader of the Queensland National Party (QNP) and premier of Queensland 1968–87.

Black and Tans nickname of a special auxiliary force of the Royal Irish Constabulary formed from British ex-soldiers on 2 January 1920 and in action in Ireland March 1920–December 1921. They were employed by the British government to combat the killing of policemen by the Irish Republican Army (IRA), the military wing of the Irish nationalist *Sinn Fein government, during the *Anglo-Irish War, or War of Independence (1919–21). The name derives from the colours of their improvised khaki and black uniforms, and was also the name of a famous pack of hounds.

Black Muslims religious group founded in 1930 in the USA. Members adhere to Muslim values and believe in economic independence for black Americans. Under the leadership of Louis *Farrakhan and the group's original name of the *Nation of Islam, the movement has undergone a resurgence of popularity in recent years. In October 1995 more than 400,000 black males attended a 'Million Man March' to Washington DC. Organized by the Nation of Islam, it was the largest ever civil-rights demonstration in US history.

Black Power movement towards black separatism in the USA during the 1960s, embodied in the **Black Panther Party** founded in 1966 by Huey *Newton and Bobby Seale. Its declared aim was the creation of a separate black state in the USA to be established by a black plebiscite under the aegis of the United Nations. Following a National Black Political Convention in 1972, a National Black Assembly was established to exercise pressure on the Democratic and Republican parties.

Black September guerrilla splinter group of the *Palestine Liberation Organization formed 1970. Operating from bases in Syria and Lebanon, it was responsible for the kidnappings at the Munich Olympics 1972 that led to the deaths of 11 Israelis, and subsequent hijack and bomb attempts. The group was named after the month in which Palestinian guerrillas were expelled from Jordan by King Hussein.

Black Thursday day of the Wall Street stock market crash on 24 October 1929, which precipitated the depression in the USA and throughout the world.

Blair, Tony (1953–) born **Anthony Charles Lynton Blair**, British Labour politician, leader of the Labour Party from 1994, prime minister from 1997. A centrist in the manner of his predecessor John *Smith, he became Labour's youngest leader by a large majority in the first fully democratic elections to the post in July 1994. He moved the party away from its traditional socialist base towards the 'social democratic' political centre, under the slogan 'New Labour', securing approval in 1995 of a new

Labour Party charter, which removed the commitment to public ownership. During the 2003 US-led Iraq War, he was a firm ally of US president George W *Bush, despite strong opposition from within sections of the Labour Party and the public. This damaged his public standing, amid accusations that his government had overstated the military threat posed by Iraqi president Saddam Hussein.

Blair and his party secured landslide victories in the 1997 and 2001 general elections, with 179-seat and 167-seat majorities respectively. During his first term as prime minister, Blair retained high public approval ratings and achieved a number of significant reforms, including Scottish and Welsh devolution, reform of the House of Lords, ceding control over interest rates to the Bank of England, a national minimum wage, the creation of an elected mayor for London, and a peace agreement in Northern Ireland. His government pursued a cautious economic programme, similar to that of the preceding Conservative administrations, involving tight control over public expenditure and the promotion, in the Private Finance Initiative, of 'public–private partnerships'. This achieved steady economic growth and higher levels of employment, providing funds for greater investment in public services during Blair's second term, from 2001. In 2003, public support for Blair fell, both because of concerns that investment in public services had not delivered clear improvements, and because of criticism of his stance on the Iraq War.

Blair's presidential style of governing involves delegating much to individual ministers, but intervening in key areas in an effort to build up public support. He was supported by a large team of political advisers and media 'spin doctors', who emphasized the importance of image and presentation. In his second term,

Blair spent more time on international diplomacy, trying to act as a bridge between the USA and European Union countries in the run-up to the Iraq War.

Blaize, Herbert Augustus (1918–1989) Grenadian centrist politician, prime minister in 1967 and 1984–89. Cofounder of the centrist Grenada National Party (GNP), he led the official opposition after full independence in 1974. In hiding from 1979, following the left-wing coup by Maurice *Bishop, he returned after the US invasion of 1983, and led a reconstituted New National party (NNP) to power in 1984. Suffering from terminal cancer, he relinquished the NNP leadership to Keith Mitchell early in 1989, and was succeeded as prime minister by Ben Jones.

Blake, George (1922–1994) British double agent who worked for MI6 and also for the USSR. Blake was unmasked by a Polish defector in 1961 and imprisoned, but escaped to the Eastern bloc in 1966. He is said to have betrayed at least 42 British agents to the Soviet side.

Blamey, Thomas Albert (1884–1951) Australian field marshal. Born in New South Wales, he served at Gallipoli, Turkey, and on the Western Front in World War I. After his recall to Australia in 1942 and appointment as commander-in-chief, Allied Land Forces, he commanded operations on the Kokoda Trail and the recapture of Papua.

Blitz, the (German **Blitzkrieg** 'lightning war') German air raids against Britain September 1940–May 1941, following Germany's failure to establish air superiority in the Battle of *Britain. It has been estimated that about 42,000 civilians were killed, 50,000 were injured, and more than two million homes were destroyed and damaged in the Blitz, together with an immense amount of damage caused to industrial installations.

Blitzkrieg (German 'lightning war') swift military campaign, as used by Germany at the beginning of World War II (1939–41). It was characterized by rapid movement by mechanized forces, supported by tactical air forces acting as 'flying artillery' and is best exemplified by the campaigns in Poland in 1939 and France in 1940.

The abbreviated **Blitz** was applied to the attempted saturation bombing of London by the German air force between September 1940 and May 1941.

Blomberg, Werner Eduard Fritz von (1878–1943) German field marshal. After a sound but unremarkable career in World War I, Blomberg became minister of war January 1933 and commander-in-chief of German armed forces May 1935. Hitler forced him to resign shortly after he was appointed field marshal 1936.

Bloody Sunday shooting dead of 13 unarmed demonstrators in Londonderry, Northern Ireland, on 30 January 1972, by soldiers from the British Army's 1st Parachute Regiment. One wounded man later died from an illness attributed to the shooting. The demonstrators were taking part in a march to protest against the British government's introduction of internment without trial in Northern Ireland on 9 August 1971. The British government-appointed Widgery Tribunal found that the paratroopers were not guilty of shooting dead the 13 civilians in cold blood. In January 1998, however, British prime minister Tony Blair announced a new inquiry into the events of Bloody Sunday.

Blum, Léon (1872–1950) French socialist politician, parliamentary leader of the Section Française de l'Internationale Ouvrière (SFIO) in the inter-war period and the first socialist prime minister of France 1936–37, when his Popular Front government introduced paid holidays and the 40-hour working week in France. He was prime minister again in 1938 and 1946.

Blumentritt, Gunther (1892–1967)
German general. A general staff officer,
he was chief of operations for Field
Marshal von *Rundstedt throughout
the Polish and French campaigns
1939–40, and planned French
counterinvasion defences 1942.
He commanded several units in his
own right 1944–45 then surrendered
to the British May 1945.

Blunt, Anthony Frederick (1907–1983)
English art historian and double agent.
As a Cambridge lecturer, he recruited
for the Soviet secret service and, as a
member of the British Secret Service
1940–45, passed information to the
USSR. In 1951 he assisted the defection
to the USSR of the British agents
Guy *Burgess and Donald Maclean
(1913–1983). He was the author of
many respected works on Italian and
French art, including a study of
Poussin 1966–67. Unmasked in 1964,
he was given immunity after his
confession.

boat people illegal emigrants
travelling by sea, especially those
Vietnamese who left their country after
the takeover of South Vietnam in 1975
by North Vietnam. In 1979, almost
69,000 boat people landed in Hong
Kong in a single year. By 1988, it was
decided to treat all boat people as
illegal immigrants unless they could
prove they qualified for refugee status.
In all, some 160,000 Vietnamese fled to
Hong Kong, many being attacked at
sea by Thai pirates, and in 1989 50,000
remained there in cramped, squalid
refugee camps. The UK government
began forced repatriation in 1989,
leaving only 18,000 in Hong Kong by
1996. Before taking over Hong Kong in
1997, the Chinese authorities made it
clear that they wanted all the
Vietnamese cleared out of the territory.
At the end of 1997, 3,364 refugees were
still living in Hong Kong. In January
1998, the Hong Kong Executive
Council ended the policy of granting
asylum to the boat people. A UN-backed
plan to accelerate the repatriation of
around 38,000 boat people living in
Southeast Asia was announced in
January 1996. Hong Kong closed its
last camp for boat people in May 2000,
after a decision made in February of
that year to give the Vietnamese
refugees residency in Hong Kong.

Boelke, Captain Oskar (1889–1916)
German fighter pilot in World War I.
By 1916 he had more enemy aircraft to
his credit than any other German flier
and received the *Order pour le Merite*.
At the time of his death in October
1916, he was credited with 40 victories.

Bofors gun light 40-mm anti-aircraft
gun designed by the Bofors company
of Sweden 1929 and used by almost all
combatants in World War II. They were
highly effective against low-flying
ground attack aircraft.

Bokassa, Jean-Bédel (1921–1996)
Central African Republic president
1966–79 and self-proclaimed emperor
1977–79. Commander-in-chief from
1963, in December 1965 he led the
military coup that gave him the
presidency. On 4 December 1976 he
proclaimed the Central African Empire
and one year later crowned himself
emperor for life.
His regime was characterized by
arbitrary state violence and cruelty.
Overthrown in 1979, Bokassa was
in exile in Côte d'Ivoire until 1986.
Upon his return he was sentenced
to death, but this was commuted to
life imprisonment in 1988.

Bolger, Jim (1935–) born **James
Brendan Bolger**, New Zealand
National Party centre-right politician,
prime minister 1990–97. His
government improved relations with
the USA, which had deteriorated
sharply when the preceding Labour
governments had banned nuclear-
powered and nuclear-armed ships
from entering New Zealand's
harbours. It also oversaw an upturn
in the economy. However the October
1996 general election, held for the first
time under a mixed-member system
of proportional representation, was

inconclusive and Bolger was forced to form a coalition government, with the New Zealand First Party leader, Winston Peters, as his deputy. In November 1997 he resigned and was replaced as prime minister by his transport minister, Jenny Shipley, who had led a right-wing revolt against his leadership. He remained in Shipley's government until April 1998, when he became ambassador to Washington (until 2001).

Bolivia landlocked country in central Andes mountains in South America, bounded north and east by Brazil, southeast by Paraguay, south by Argentina, and west by Chile and Peru.

Bolshevik (from Russian *bolshinstvo* 'a majority') member of the majority of the Russian Social Democratic Party who split from the *Mensheviks in 1903. The Bolsheviks, under *Lenin, advocated the destruction of capitalist political and economic institutions, and the setting up of a socialist state with power in the hands of the workers. The Bolsheviks set the *Russian Revolution of 1917 in motion. They changed their name to the Russian Communist Party in 1918.

Bombay former province of British India; the capital was the city of Bombay (now Mumbai). In 1960 the major part became the two new states of Gujarat and Maharashtra.

bombing campaigns, World War II air raids conducted against civilian and industrial targets by both the Allied and Axis powers from 1940 to 1945. Their aim was to destroy the morale of civilian populations and undermine the military capability of the enemy, although their long-term effect on the war is disputed. Small-scale bombing raids had occurred during World War I using German airships, but *World War II saw the advent of city or area bombing on an unprecedented scale. The bombing of civilians was considered as important as the bombing of military and

industrial production facilities. Thousands were injured, killed, or made homeless during the *Blitz on Britain 1940–41, and the area bombing of German cities, such as the *thousand-bomber raid over Cologne in 1942.

Bongo, Omar (1935–) adopted name of **Albert-Bernard Bongo**, Gabonese politician, president from 1967. Minister of national defence 1964–65 and vice-president in 1967 under President Léon M'ba, he succeeded as president, prime minister, and secretary general after M'ba's death in 1967, and established the Gabonese Democratic Party (PDG) as the only legal party in 1968. He converted to Islam in 1973, and presided over the exploitation of Gabon's rich mineral resources without notably diminishing inequalities. In 1993 he was re-elected for the fourth time and from 1995 remained in power as president only. He won more than two-thirds of the vote in a presidential election in December 1998 and was expected to remain in power for another seven years.

Bonham-Carter, (Helen) Violet (1887–1969) Baroness Asquith of Yarnbury, British president of the Liberal party 1945–47. A close supporter of Winston Churchill, she published *Winston Churchill as I Knew Him* in 1965. She was the daughter of H H Asquith. She was created a DBE in 1953 and Baroness in 1964.

Bonner, Yelena (1923–) Russian human-rights campaigner. Disillusioned by the Soviet invasion of Czechoslovakia in 1968, she resigned from the Communist Party (CPSU) after marrying her second husband, Andrei *Sakharov in 1971, and became active in the dissident movement.

Bono, Sonny (1935–1998) adopted name of **Salvatore Phillip Bono**, US pop singer and Republican politician. He was the male half of the popular 1960s musical duo, Sonny and Cher, who rose to fame with the 1965 hit record 'I Got You Babe'. Bono's latter-day involvement in politics led to his 1988 election as mayor of Palm Springs, California. In 1994 he became the city's elected representative in the US Congress.

Bonomi, Ivanoe (1873–1952) Italian socialist politician, prime minister 1921–22 and 1944–45. An opponent of Mussolini's seizure of power, he left politics in 1924, but after 1942 was a leading figure in the anti-fascist struggle. He replaced Pietro *Badoglio as prime minister in 1944 and established a broad, antifascist coalition government. In 1945 he was forced to resign in favour of the more radical Ferruccio Parri. He became president of the senate in 1948.

Boothby, Robert John Graham (1900–1986) Baron Boothby, British politician, born in Scotland. He became Unionist member of Parliament for East Aberdeenshire in 1924 and was parliamentary private secretary to Winston Churchill 1926–29. He advocated the UK's entry into the European Community (now the European Union).

Boothroyd, Betty (1929–) British Labour politician, Speaker of the House of Commons 1992–2000. A Yorkshire-born daughter of a textile worker and a weaver, and a former West End dancer, she was elected member of Parliament for West Bromwich in the West Midlands in 1973 and was a member of the European Parliament 1975–77. The first woman to hold the office of Speaker, she controlled parliamentary proceedings with a mixture of firmness and good humour. She announced in July 2000 that she would retire from her official duties as Speaker at the end of summer 2000.

Borden, Lizzie (Andrew) (1860–1927) US alleged murderess from Fall River, Massachusetts. Borden was arrested and tried for the axe-murders of her father and stepmother in 1892. She was acquitted in 1893. Her alleged deed was immortalized, and exaggerated, in the quatrain 'Lizzie Borden took an axe / And gave her mother forty whacks; / And when she saw what she had done / She gave her father forty-one'.

Borden, Robert Laird (1854–1937) Canadian Conservative politician, prime minister 1911–20. Throughout World War I he represented Canada at meetings of the Imperial War Cabinet, and he was the chief Canadian delegate at the Paris Peace Conference in 1919. He played an important role in transforming Canada from a colony to a nation, notably by insisting on separate membership of the League of Nations in 1919.

Boris III (1894–1943) Tsar of Bulgaria from 1918, when he succeeded his father, Ferdinand I. From 1934 he was a virtual dictator until his sudden and mysterious death following a visit to Hitler. His son Simeon II was tsar until deposed in 1946.

Bormann, Martin (1900–1945) German Nazi leader. He took part in the abortive Munich *beer-hall putsch (uprising) in 1923 and rose to high positions in the Nazi Party, becoming deputy party leader in May 1941 following the flight of Rudolf Hess to Britain.

Bornu kingdom of the 9th–19th centuries to the west and south of Lake Chad, western central Africa. Converted to Islam in the 11th century, Bornu reached its greatest strength in the 15th–18th centuries. From 1901 it was absorbed in the British, French, and German colonies in this area, which became the states of Niger, Cameroon, and Nigeria. The largest section of ancient Bornu is now the **state of Bornu** in Nigeria.

borstal in the UK, formerly a place of detention for offenders aged 15–21, first introduced in 1908. From 1983 borstal institutions were officially known as youth custody centres, and have been replaced by **young offender institutions**.

Bosch, (Gavino) Juan Domingo (1909–2001) Dominican Republic writer and socialist politician, president in 1963. His left-wing Partido Revolucionario Dominicano (PRD; Dominican Revolutionary Party) won a landslide victory in the 1962 elections. In office, he attempted agrarian reform and labour legislation, but was opposed by the USA as a 'communist sympathizer', overthrown by the army, and forced into exile. Attempts to restore Bosch to power in 1965 led to civil war and intervention by US Marines. After his return in 1970, he formed the Dominican Liberation Party (PLD) in 1973, but his bids for the presidency in 1982, 1986, and 1990 were unsuccessful. His achievement was to establish a democratic political party after three decades of dictatorship.

Bose, Subhas Chandra (1897–1945) Indian nationalist politician, president of the Indian Congress Party 1938–39. During World War II, he recruited Indian prisoners of war to fight the British in his Indian National Army (INA).

Bosnia-Herzegovina Serbo-Croat **Bosna-Hercegovina**, country in central Europe, bounded north and west by Croatia, and east by Serbia and Montenegro.

Botha, Louis (1862–1919) South African soldier and politician. He was a commander in the Second South African War (Boer War). In 1907 he became premier of the Transvaal and in 1910 of the first Union South African government. On the outbreak of World War I in 1914 he rallied South Africa to the Commonwealth, suppressed a Boer revolt, and conquered German South West Africa.

Botha, P(ieter) W(illem) (1916–) South African politician, prime minister 1978–89. He initiated a modification of *apartheid, which later slowed down in the face of Afrikaner (Boer) opposition, and made use of force both inside and outside South Africa to stifle *African National Congress (ANC) party activity. In 1984

he became the first executive state president. After suffering a stroke in 1989, he unwillingly resigned both party leadership and presidency and was succeeded by F W *de Klerk.

Botswana landlocked country in central southern Africa, bounded south and southeast by South Africa, west and north by Namibia, and northeast by Zimbabwe.

Bottai, Giuseppe (1895–1959) Italian politician. One of the founders of the Fascist Party, Bottai took an active part in the *March on Rome in October 1922. He was among the Fascist Grand Council members who demanded Mussolini's resignation in July 1943. Sentenced to death by the Republic of Salò and to life imprisonment by the Italian authorities after World War II, he escaped and joined the French Foreign Legion. He returned to Italy on being offered amnesty.

Bougainville, Battle of in World War II, Allied campaign November 1943–April 1944 to recover the most northerly of the Solomon Islands from the Japanese. Bougainville was taken by the Japanese March 1942 and became an important refuelling and supply base for their operations against Guadalcanal and the other Solomon Islands. An estimated 8,500 Japanese were killed in fighting on the island and a further 9,000 died of illness and malnutrition.

Boumédienne, Houari (1925–1978) adopted name of **Muhammad Boukharouba**, Algerian politician who brought the nationalist leader Mohammed *Ben Bella to power by a revolt in 1962 and superseded him as president in 1965 by a further coup. During his 13 years in office, he presided over an ambitious programme of economic development and promoted Algeria as an active champion of the developing world. In late 1978 he died of a rare blood disease.

Bourassa, Henri (1868–1952) Canadian politician and journalist.

Elected in 1896 to the Dominion House of Commons as a Liberal, he resigned in 1899 as a protest against Canadian participation in the Boer War and was triumphantly re-elected as a Nationalist. He left the Dominion Parliament in 1907 and was a member of the Québec legislature 1908–12. In 1910 he established the Montréal nationalist newspaper *Le Devoir*.

Bourgeois, Léon Victor Auguste (1851–1925) French politician. Entering politics as a Radical, he was prime minister in 1895, and later served in many cabinets. He was awarded the Nobel Prize for Peace in 1920 for his pioneering advocacy of the League of Nations and international cooperation.

Bourguiba, Habib ben Ali (1903–2000) Tunisian politician, first president of Tunisia 1957–87. He became prime minister in 1956 and president (for life from 1975) and prime minister of the Tunisian republic in 1957; he was overthrown in a bloodless coup in 1987.

Boutros-Ghali, Boutros (1922–) Egyptian diplomat and politician, deputy prime minister 1991–92, secretary general of the United Nations (UN) 1992–96. He worked towards peace in the Middle East in the foreign ministry posts he held from 1977 to 1991. The first Arab and African to become UN secretary-general, his term saw lengthy and difficult peacekeeping operations in Bosnia, Somalia, and Rwanda, and other challenges in Haiti and the post-Cold War world. The USA, a permanent member of the UN security council, was dissatisfied with his independent leadership and ensured he did not get a second term. In December 1996 he was replaced by Kofi *Annan. In 1997–2002, Boutros-Ghali was secretary general of La Francophonie, a 49-member grouping of French-speaking nations.

Boxer member of the *I ho ch'üan* ('Righteous Harmonious Fists'), a society of Chinese nationalists dedicated to fighting Western influence in China. They were known as Boxers by Westerners as they practised boxing training which they believed made them impervious to bullets. In 1898 the Chinese government persuaded the Boxers to join forces to oppose foreigners. In 1900 the *Boxer Rebellion was instigated by the empress Zi Xi and thousands of Chinese Christian converts and missionaries were murdered.

Boxer Rebellion or **Boxer Uprising**, rebellion of 1900 by the Chinese nationalist *Boxer society against Western influence. European and US legations in Beijing (Peking) were besieged and many missionaries and Europeans were killed. An international punitive force was dispatched and Beijing was captured on 14 August 1900. In September 1901 China agreed to pay reperations.

Braddock, Elizabeth Margaret (Bessie) (1899–1970) British union activist and Labour politician. Born in Liverpool, she was a city councillor in Liverpool from 1930 until 1961. She was Liverpool's first Labour and first female member of Parliament, winning the Exchange division in 1945 and holding this until 1970. A right-winger, she was a powerful and caustic platform speaker and a stout defender of working people's rights to better health and education services. She turned down the offer of a post in the 1964 Labour government.

Bradley, Omar Nelson (1893–1981) US general in World War II. In 1943 he commanded the 2nd US Corps in their victories in Tunisia and Sicily, leading to the surrender of 250,000 Axis troops, and in 1944 led the US troops in the invasion of France. His command, as the 12th Army Group, grew to 1.3 million troops, the largest US force ever assembled.

Bradshaw, Robert Llewellyn (1916–1978) St Kitts and Nevis politician, prime minister 1967–78. After universal adult suffrage had been granted by the British colonial rulers in

1952, Bradshaw led the St Kitts Labour Party (SKLP) to electoral victory and became trade minister in 1956. He became chief minister of the three-island colony of St Kitts–Nevis–Anguilla in 1966, and in 1967, after associate statehood was secured, his position was designated 'prime minister'.

Brandt, Willy (1913–1992) adopted name of **Karl Herbert Frahm**, German socialist politician, federal chancellor (premier) of West Germany 1969–74. He played a key role in the remoulding of the Social Democratic Party (SPD) as a moderate socialist force (leader 1964–87). As mayor of West Berlin 1957–66, Brandt became internationally known during the Berlin Wall crisis of 1961. He was awarded the Nobel Prize for Peace in 1971 for his contribution towards reconciliation between West and East Germany.

Branting, Karl H(jalmar) (1860–1925) Swedish astronomer, editor, political activist, and prime minister. Branting shared the Nobel Prize for Peace in 1921 with Norwegian pacifist and historian Christian Louis Lange for his lifelong commitment to constitutional pacifism and his role in international diplomacy.

Bratianu, Ion (1864–1927) Romanian premier and virtual dictator during World War I and almost until his death. He concluded with the Entente powers (Britain, France, and Russia) a treaty on the basis of which Romania declared war on Germany and Austria in August 1916. He was in opposition from 1919 to 1921. He was the son of Ioan Constantin Bratianu.

Brauchitsch, (Heinrich Alfred) Walther von (1881–1948) German field marshal. A staff officer in World War I, he became commander-in-chief of the army and a member of Hitler's secret cabinet council 1938. He resigned after a heart attack and his failure to repel Marshal *Zhukov's counterattack outside Moscow 1941. He was captured 1945, but died before he could be tried in the *Nuremberg trials.

Braudel, (Paul Achille) Fernand (1902–1985) French historian. While in a German prisoner-of-war camp during World War II he wrote *La Mediterranée et le monde mediterranéen à l'époque de Philippe II/The Mediterranean and the Mediterranean World in the Age of Philip II* 1949, a work which revolutionized the writing of history by taking a global view of long-term trends.

Braun, Eva (1912–1945) German mistress of Adolf Hitler. Secretary to Hitler's photographer and personal friend, Heinrich Hoffmann, she became Hitler's mistress in the 1930s and married him in the air-raid shelter of the Chancellery in Berlin on 29 April 1945. The next day they committed suicide together.

Brazil largest country in South America (almost half the continent), bounded southwest by Uruguay, Argentina, Paraguay and Bolivia; west by Peru and Colombia; north by Venezuela, Guyana, Suriname, and French Guiana; and northeast and southeast by the Atlantic Ocean.

Brest-Litovsk, Treaty of bilateral treaty signed on 3 March 1918 between Russia and Germany, Austria-Hungary, and their allies. Under its terms, Russia agreed to recognize the independence of Georgia, Ukraine, Poland, and the Baltic States, and to pay heavy compensation. Under the November 1918 armistice that ended World War I, it was annulled, since Russia was one of the winning allies.

Bretton Woods township in New Hampshire, USA, where the United Nations Monetary and Financial Conference was held in 1944 to discuss post-war international payments problems. The agreements reached on financial assistance and measures to stabilize exchange rates led to the creation of the International Bank for Reconstruction and Development in 1945 and the International Monetary Fund (IMF).

Breyer, Stephen G(erald) (1938–)
US Supreme Court associate justice.
He served on the Watergate Special
Prosecution Force in 1973. He
contributed to the deregulation of the
airlines in the 1970s. Able to grasp and
clearly explain legal complexities, he
was nominated to the US Supreme
Court by President Bill Clinton in 1994.

Brezhnev, Leonid Ilyich (1906–1982)
Soviet leader. A protégé of Joseph
Stalin and Nikita Khrushchev, he came
to power (after he and Aleksei
*Kosygin forced Khrushchev to resign)
as general secretary of the Communist
Party of the Soviet Union (CPSU)
1964–82 and was president 1977–82.
Domestically he was conservative;
abroad the USSR was established as
a military and political superpower
during the Brezhnev era, extending
its influence in Africa and Asia.

Brezhnev, born in the Ukraine,
joined the CPSU in the 1920s. In 1938
he was made head of propaganda by
the new Ukrainian party chief,
Khrushchev, and ascended in the local
party hierarchy. After World War II he
caught the attention of the CPSU
leader Stalin, who inducted Brezhnev
into the secretariat and Politburo in
1952. Brezhnev was removed from
these posts after Stalin's death in 1953,
but returned in 1956 with Khrushchev's
patronage. In 1960, as criticism of
Khrushchev mounted, Brezhnev was
moved to the ceremonial post of state
president and began to criticize
Khrushchev's policies openly.

Brezhnev stepped down as president
in 1963 and returned to the Politburo
and secretariat. He was elected CPSU
general secretary in 1964, when
Khrushchev was ousted, and gradually
came to dominate the conservative and
consensual coalition. In 1977 he
regained the additional title of state
president under the new constitution.

He suffered an illness (thought to
have been a stroke or heart attack)
March–April 1976 that was believed to
have affected his thought and speech

so severely that he was not able to
make decisions. These were made by
his entourage, for example, committing
troops to Afghanistan to prop up the
government. Within the USSR,
economic difficulties mounted; the
Brezhnev era was a period of caution
and stagnation, although outwardly
imperialist.

Brezhnev Doctrine   Soviet doctrine
of 1968 designed to justify the invasion
of Czechoslovakia. It laid down for the
USSR as a duty the direct maintenance
of 'correct' socialism in countries
within the Soviet sphere of influence.
In 1979 it was extended, by the
invasion of Afghanistan, to the direct
establishment of 'correct' socialism in
countries not already within its sphere.
The doctrine was renounced
by Mikhail *Gorbachev in 1989.
Soviet troops were withdrawn from
Afghanistan, and the satellite states of
Eastern Europe were allowed to decide
their own forms of government, under
what was dubbed the 'Sinatra
doctrine'.

Briand, Aristide (1862–1932)   French
republican politician, 11 times prime
minister 1909–29. A skilful
parliamentary tactician and orator,
he was seldom out of ministerial office
between 1906 and 1932. As foreign
minister 1925–32, he was the architect,
with the German chancellor Gustav
*Stresemann, of the 1925 Locarno Pact
(settling Germany's western frontier)
and the 1928 Kellogg–Briand Pact
(renouncing war). In 1930 he outlined
an early scheme for the political and
economic unification of Europe.
He shared the Nobel Prize for Peace
in 1926 with Stresemann for their work
for European reconciliation.

Britain, Battle of   World War II air
battle between German and British air
forces over Britain from 10 July to
31 October 1940. The height of the
battle occurred 30–31 August.

British Broadcasting Corporation
BBC, the UK state-owned
broadcasting network. It operates

television and national and local radio stations, and is financed by the sale of television (originally radio) licences. It is not permitted to carry advertisements but it has an additional source of income through its publishing interests and the sales of its programmes. The BBC is controlled by a board of governors, each appointed by the government for five years. The BBC was converted from a private company (established in 1922) to a public corporation under royal charter in 1927. Under the charter, news programmes were required to be politically impartial. The first director-general was John *Reith from 1922 to 1938.

British Empire, Order of the   British order of knighthood instituted in 1917 by George V. There are military and civil divisions, and the ranks are GBE, Knight Grand Cross or Dame Grand Cross; KBE, Knight Commander; DBE, Dame Commander; CBE, Commander; OBE, Officer; MBE, Member.

British Expeditionary Force   BEF, during World War I (1914–18) the term commonly referred to the British army serving in France and Flanders, although strictly speaking it referred only to the forces sent to France in 1914; during World War II it was also the army in Europe, which was evacuated from Dunkirk, France in 1940.

British Honduras   former name (to 1973) of *Belize.

British Legion   organization to promote the welfare of British veterans of war service and their dependants. Established under the leadership of Douglas Haig in 1921 (royal charter 1925) it became the **Royal British Legion** in 1971; it is nonpolitical.

British Somaliland   British protectorate 1884–1960 comprising over 176,000 sq km/67,980 sq mi of territory on the north Somali coast of East Africa, opposite its base at Aden. In 1960 British Somaliland united with Italian Somaliland to form the independent state of Somalia. British authorities were harassed from 1899 by Somali nationalists, led by the Muslim leader Muhammad bin Abdullah Hassan (Sayyid Maxamed Cabdulle Xasan), who held the interior until his death in 1920.

Brookeborough, Basil Stanlake Brooke (1888–1973)   Viscount Brookeborough, Northern Irish Unionist politician and prime minister 1943–63. He was born in Colebrook, County Fermanagh, and educated at Winchester and Sandhurst. A conservative unionist and staunch advocate of strong links with Britain, he entered the Northern Ireland House of Commons in 1929 and held ministerial posts 1933–45. His regime, particularly in the 1950s and 1960s, saw moderate improvements in economic prosperity and community relations but maintained an illiberal stance towards Northern Ireland's Catholic minority, and made no real attempt at significant political or economic reform.

Brown, George Alfred (1914–1985)   Baron George-Brown of Jevington, British Labour politician. He entered Parliament in 1945, was briefly minister of works in 1951, and contested the leadership of the party on the death of Hugh Gaitskell, but was defeated by Harold Wilson.

Brown, George (Scratchley) (1918–1978)   US pilot who flew heavy bombers during World War II. As commander of the 7th Air Force in Saigon 1968–70, he was accused of falsifying reports about air strikes in Cambodia 1969–70. President Richard Nixon appointed him chairman of the Joint Chiefs of Staff in 1974.

Browning automatic rifle   US light machine gun used for infantry support, adopted by the US Army 1917 and standard issue until the early 1950s. It used a 20-shot magazine and fired at 500 rounds per minute.

Browning machine gun   US medium machine gun. A water-cooled, tripod-mounted, belt-fed gun of 30-in calibre, it was adopted by the US Army 1917 and is still in use in most countries. Resembling the Vickers and Maxim guns, the original design was operated by recoil force and fired at about 500 rounds per minute.

Brown v. Board of Education in full *Brown v. Board of Education of Topeka, Kansas,* landmark US Supreme Court decision of 1954 which ruled that racially segregated educational facilities were intrinsically unequal and therefore in violation of the Fourteenth Amendment. This ruling negated the long-standing 'separate but equal' doctrine of the *Plessy* v. *Ferguson* case of 1896, and helped fuel the *civil-rights movement in the USA.

Bruce, Stanley Melbourne (1883–1967) 1st Viscount Bruce of Melbourne, Australian National Party politician, prime minister 1923–29. He introduced a number of social welfare measures and sought closer economic ties with the UK, campaigning for 'Imperial Preference'. With the economy worsening, he lost the 1929 general election and also his seat, but emerged as an energetic diplomat, serving as Australia's high commissioner to London from 1933 to 1945.

Brundtland, Gro Harlem (1939–) Norwegian Labour politician, prime minister 1981, 1986–89 and 1990–96 and director-general (head) of the World Health Organization (WHO) 1998–2003. She entered politics in 1974, when invited to become environment minister (to 1976), and became the country's first female major party leader and prime minister in 1981. She held office as prime minister for 7 months in 1981 and returned to office in 1986. Her government was forced to push through austerity measures, after the collapse of world petroleum prices. She resigned as leader of the Norwegian Labour Party in 1992 but continued as prime minister. From 1993, she led a minority Labour

government committed to European Union membership, but failed to secure backing for the membership application in a 1994 national referendum and resigned as prime minister in 1996.

Brunei country comprising two enclaves on the northwest coast of the island of Borneo, bounded to the landward side by Sarawak and to the northwest by the South China Sea.

Brüning, Heinrich (1885–1970) German politician. Elected to the Reichstag (parliament) in 1924, he led the Catholic Centre Party from 1929 and was federal chancellor 1930–32 when political and economic crisis forced his resignation.

Brusilov, Aleksei Alekseevich (1853–1926) Russian general, military leader in World War I who achieved major successes against the Austro-Hungarian forces in 1916. Later he was commander of the Red Army 1920, which drove the Poles to within a few miles of Warsaw before being repulsed by them.

Brusilov Offensive in World War I, major Russian assault led by General Alexei Brusilov against the southern sector of the Eastern Front June 1916 in order to relieve pressure on the Western and Italian Fronts by drawing German forces east. The offensive met this immediate objective but also had far broader effects: it cost the Russians almost one million casualties, which demoralized the army and aided the revolutionary cause; it brought Romania into the war on the Allied side, resulting in the eventual conquest of Romania by German forces; and the decimation of Austro-Hungarian forces made the German Army the dominant partner among the Central Powers thereafter.

Brussels, Treaty of pact of an economic, political, cultural, and military alliance established in 17 March 1948, for 50 years, by the UK, France, and the Benelux countries, joined by West Germany and Italy in

1955. It was the forerunner of the North Atlantic Treaty Organization and the European Community (now the European Union).

Bryan, William Jennings (1860–1925) US politician who campaigned unsuccessfully for the presidency three times: as the Populist and Democratic nominee in 1896, as an anti-imperialist Democrat in 1900, and as a Democratic tariff reformer in 1908. He served as President Woodrow Wilson's secretary of state 1913–15. In the early 1920s he was a leading fundamentalist and opponent of Clarence Darrow in the *Scopes monkey trial.

Bryant, Arthur Wynne Morgan (1899–1985) British historian who produced studies of Restoration figures such as Pepys and Charles II, and a series covering the Napoleonic Wars including *The Age of Elegance* 1950. Knighted 1954.

B-Specials armed, part-time section of the *Royal Ulster Constabulary. The B-Specials helped to police Northern Ireland between their formation in 1920 to their abolition in 1969. They were replaced by the Ulster Defence Regiment (UDR) in 1970.

Buchanan, Pat(rick Joseph) (1938–) US right-wing Republican activist and journalist. Although a TV and radio commentator, he often attacked the mass media. He was a candidate for the Republican nomination for president in 1992 and 1996.

Buchenwald site of a Nazi *concentration camp from 1937 to 1945 at a village northeast of Weimar, eastern Germany.

Budenny, Semyon Mikhailovich (1883–1973) Soviet general. A sergeant-major in the Tsar's army, Budenny joined the Bolsheviks 1917 and rose rapidly, commanding a cavalry army by 1920 and being made Marshal of the Soviet Union 1935. One of Stalin's 'Old Guard', he survived the Great Purge of Red Army Officers 1936–38 and after the German

invasion of the USSR 1941 became commander-in-chief in the Ukraine and Bessarabia.

Buhari, Muhammadu (1942–) Nigerian politician and soldier, president 1983–85. He led the military coup that ousted Shehu *Shagari in 1983. Having assumed the presidency himself, he imposed an authoritarian regime of austerity measures, and was deposed in a coup led by Ibrahim *Babangida in 1985. He was detained until 1988.

Bukharin, Nikolai Ivanovich (1888–1938) Soviet politician and theorist. A moderate, he was the chief Bolshevik thinker after Lenin. Executed on Stalin's orders for treason in 1938, he was posthumously rehabilitated in 1988.

Bulganin, Nikolai Aleksandrovich (1895–1975) Soviet politician and military leader. His career began in 1918 when he joined the Cheka, the Soviet secret police. He helped to organize Moscow's defences in World War II, became a marshal of the USSR in 1947, and was minister of defence 1947–49 and 1953–55. On the fall of Georgi Malenkov he became prime minister (chair of the council of ministers) 1955–58 until ousted by Nikita Khrushchev.

Bulgaria country in southeast Europe, bounded north by Romania, west by Serbia and Montenegro and Macedonia, south by Greece, southeast by Turkey, and east by the Black Sea.

Bulge, Battle of the or **Ardennes offensive**, in World War II, Hitler's plan (code-named 'Watch on the Rhine') for a breakthrough by his field marshal Gerd von *Rundstedt, aimed at the US line in the Ardennes from 16 December 1944 to 28 January 1945. Hitler aimed to isolate the Allied forces north of the corridor which would be created by a drive through the Ardennes, creating a German salient (prominent part of a line of attack, also known as a 'bulge'). There were 77,000 Allied casualties and 130,000 German, including Hitler's last powerful reserve of elite Panzer units. Although US troops were encircled for some weeks at Bastogne, the German counteroffensive failed.

The Germans deployed three panzer armies in the operation and initially made good progress along a 113 km/70 mi sector of the front. However, once the Allies had recovered from the initial surprise of an attack along a previously quiet section of the front, they launched a serious counterattack to the north and south of the 'bulge'. Improvements in the weather also allowed Allied air support to take effect and by January most of the German attack had been contained and repulsed.

Bunche, Ralph Johnson (1904–1971) US diplomat. He was principal director of the United Nations Department of Trusteeship 1948–54 and UN undersecretary 1955–67, acting as mediator in Palestine 1948–49 and as special representative in the Congo in 1960. He became UN undersecretary general in 1968. He was awarded the Nobel Prize for Peace in 1950 for negotiating the Arab-Israel truce of 1949.

Bundy, McGeorge (1919–1996) US public official and educator. He was special national security adviser to presidents John F Kennedy and Lyndon Johnson 1961–66 and played a prominent role in pursuing the Vietnam War.

Burger, Warren Earl (1907–1995) US jurist, chief justice of the US Supreme Court 1969–86. Appointed to the court by President Richard Nixon because of his conservative views, Burger showed himself to be pragmatic and liberal on some social issues, including abortion and desegregation. It was Burger's ruling against presidential executive privilege in 1974, at the height of the Watergate scandal, that forced the release of damning tapes and documents that were to prompt the resignation of Nixon.

Burgess, Guy Francis de Moncy (1911–1963) British spy, a diplomat recruited in the 1930s by the USSR as an agent. He was linked with Kim *Philby, Donald Maclean (1913–1983), and Anthony *Blunt.

Burkina Faso formerly **Upper Volta**, landlocked country in west Africa, bounded east by Niger, northwest and west by Mali, and south by Côte d'Ivoire, Ghana, Togo, and Benin.

Burma War war 1942–45 during which Burma (now *Myanmar) was occupied by Japan. Initially supported by *Aung San's Burma National Army, the Japanese captured Rangoon and Mandalay 1942, forcing the withdrawal of General Alexander's British forces to India. During 1943, Chindit guerrilla resistance was organized and after a year's heavy fighting at Imphal and Kohima, British, Commonwealth, American, and Chinese nationalist troops reopened the 'Burma Road' between India and China January 1945. Rangoon was recaptured May 1945.

Burnham, (Linden) Forbes (Sampson) (1923–1985) Guyanese Marxist-Leninist politician. He was prime minister from 1964 to 1980 in a coalition government, leading the country to independence in 1966 and declaring it the world's first cooperative republic in 1970. He was executive president 1980–85. Resistance to the US landing in Grenada 1983 was said to be due to his forewarning the Grenadans of the attack.

Burns, John Elliot (1858–1943) British labour leader, born in London of Scottish parentage. He was sentenced to six weeks' imprisonment for his part in the Trafalgar Square demonstration on 'Bloody Sunday', 13 November 1887, and was leader of the strike in 1889 securing the 'dockers' tanner' (wage of 6d per hour). An Independent Labour member of Parliament 1892–1918, he was the first working-class person to be a member of the cabinet, as president of the Local Government Board 1906–14.

Burundi country in east central Africa, bounded north by Rwanda, west by the Democratic Republic of Congo, southwest by Lake Tanganyika, and southeast and east by Tanzania.

Bush, George Herbert Walker (1924–) 41st president of the USA 1989–93, a Republican. He was vice-president 1981–89 and director of the Central Intelligence Agency (CIA) 1976–81. The Bush presidency marked a turning point in world affairs, as the collapse of the USSR ended the Cold War and heralded a 'new world Order' dominated by the USA as the only global superpower. Active in foreign affairs, Bush sent US troops to depose his former ally, Gen Manuel *Noriega of Panama, and, in the 1991 Gulf War, to remove Iraq from Kuwait. These raised his public standing, but domestic economic problems led to defeat in the 1992 presidential elections by the Democrat Bill *Clinton. His eldest son, George W *Bush, became president in 2001, and another son, Jeb (John Ellis) Bush (1953–), governor of Florida in 1999.

Bush, George W(alker), Jr (1946–) 43rd president of the USA from 2001. Republican governor of Texas 1994–2000 and son of former US president George *Bush, he was elected president after defeating Democrat Al *Gore in a hotly disputed contest and with a smaller share (48.1%) of the popular vote than his Democrat rival (48.3%). The presidency was conceded to Bush 36 days after the election, following a narrow decision by the divided US Supreme Court. Inexperienced in foreign affairs, Bush is supported in his administration by his father's former defense secretary, Dick *Cheney, who is vice-president, and the former head of the armed forces, Colin *Powell, who is secretary of state. In 2003 Bush instigated a US-led war against Iraq, as part of his broader 'war against terrorism' and to overthrow Iraqi president Saddam Hussein. However, this action, along with decisions to withdraw from the antiballistic missile agreement and not to adopt the Kyoto Protocol on the environment, led to concerns of increasing US unilateralism in international affairs.

Busia, Kofi (1913–1978) Ghanaian politician and academic, prime minister 1969–72. He became a leader of the National Liberation Movement 1954–59, in opposition to Kwame *Nkrumah, and went into exile in 1959. Following the 1966 coup, he returned as adviser to the National Liberation Council and then founded the Progress Party, leading it to electoral victory in 1969. He was ousted as prime minister in a military coup in 1972, and returned to exile in the same year.

Bustamante, (William) Alexander (1884–1977) born William Alexander Clarke, Jamaican centre-right politician, prime minister 1962–67. Founder of the Bustamante Industrial Trade Union for sugar plantation workers in 1938, he was imprisoned by the British colonial authorities 1941–42 for his union and political activities. In 1943 he established the Jamaica Labour Party (JLP) as the political wing of his union and served as chief minister 1953–55. As leader of the Labour Party, he became Jamaica's first prime minister on independence in 1962. He pursued a conservative policy programme and developed close ties with the USA. He was knighted in 1955.

Buthelezi, Chief Mangosuthu Gatsha (1928–) South African Zulu leader and politician, president of the Zulu-based *Inkatha Freedom Party (IFP), which he founded as a paramilitary organization for attaining a nonracial democratic society in 1974 and converted into a political party in 1994. He was appointed home affairs minister in the country's first post-apartheid government, led by *African National Congress (ANC) leader Nelson *Mandela, in 1994. In June 1999 Buthelezi was offered the post of deputy president of South Africa by the new president Thabo *Mbeki but Buthelezi refused the post.

Butler, Richard Austen (1902–1982) Baron Butler of Saffron Walden; called **'Rab'**, British Conservative politician. As minister of education 1941–45, he was responsible for the 1944 Education Act that introduced the 11-plus examination for selection of grammar school pupils; he was chancellor of the Exchequer 1951–55, Lord Privy Seal 1955–59, and foreign minister 1963–64. As a candidate for the prime ministership, he was defeated by Harold Macmillan in 1957 (under whom he was home secretary 1957–62), and by Alec Douglas Home in 1963.

Butskellism UK term for political policies tending towards the middle ground in an effort to gain popular support; the term was coined 1954 after R A *Butler (moderate Conservative) and Hugh *Gaitskell (moderate Labour politician).

Buzek, Jerzy Karol (1940–) Polish politician, prime minister of Poland from 1997. A chemical-engineering professor and a veteran trade-union activist, he was named prime minister of a new centre–right coalition in October 1997, after the Solidarity Electoral Action (AWS) emerged victorious in general elections. Outlining his new government's programme, he promised to push for rapid integration with the North Atlantic Treaty Organization (NATO) and the European Union (EU), to cut bureaucracy, decentralize finances, and expedite privatization plans.

Byng, Julian Hedworth George (1862–1935) 1st Viscount Byng of Vimy, British general in World War I, commanding troops in Turkey and France, where, after a victory at Vimy Ridge, he took command of the Third Army.

Cabral, Amilcar (1924–1973) Guinean nationalist leader. He founded the African Party for the Independence of Portuguese Guinea and Cape Verde (PAIGC) in 1956 and, after abortive constitutional discussions with the Portuguese government, initiated a revolutionary war in 1963. He was murdered in 1973 just as his aim was being achieved. His brother, Luiz Cabral, became the first president of an independent Guinea-Bissau in 1974.

Cabral, Luiz de Almeida (1931–) Guinean nationalist leader and politician, first president of the republic of Guinea-Bissau 1974–80. As a member of the African Party for the Independence of Portuguese Guinea and Cape Verde (PAICG), he went into exile in 1960 and took part in the guerrilla struggle to win independence. Success made him the president of the new republic in 1974, but he was later overthrown in a coup. He was the brother of the nationalist leader Amilcar *Cabral.

Caetano, Marcello José des Neves Alves (1906–1980) Portuguese right-wing politician. Professor of administrative law at Lisbon from 1940, he succeeded the dictator António Salazar as prime minister from 1968 until his exile after the military coup of 1974. He was granted political asylum in Brazil.

Cai Yuanpei (or Ts'ai Yüan-p'ei) (1863–1940) Chinese educator, scholar, and politician. In 1911 he became the first minister of education of the new Chinese Republic, presiding over the creation of a new school system. He resigned in 1912 but continued to be active in educational affairs, helping to promote a work-study programme for Chinese students in France. Appointed chancellor of Beijing (Peking) University in 1916, he encouraged free debate and scholarship at the university, transforming it into one of the country's foremost intellectual centres.

Calamity Jane (c. 1852–1903) US frontier woman, an expert markswoman and rider who dressed as a man. Allegedly a pony express rider and then a scout for General George Custer in Wyoming in the 1870s, she was companion to 'Wild Bill' Hickok and nursed the sick during a 1878 smallpox epidemic. Many fictional accounts of the Wild West featured her exploits.

calendar division of the year into months, weeks, and days and the method of ordering the years. From year one, an assumed date of the birth of Jesus, dates are calculated backwards (BC 'before Christ' or BCE 'before common era') and forwards (AD, Latin *anno Domini* 'in the year of the Lord', or CE 'common era'). The **lunar month** (period between one new moon and the next) naturally averages 29.5 days, but the Western calendar uses for convenience a **calendar month** with a complete number of days, 30 or 31 (February has 28). For adjustments, since there are slightly fewer than six extra hours a year left over, they are added to February as a 29th day every fourth year (**leap year**), century years being excepted unless they are divisible by 400. For example, 1896 was a leap year; 1900 was not.

Callaghan, (Leonard) James (1912–) Baron Callaghan of Cardiff, British Labour politician, prime minister and party leader 1976–79. He became prime minister in April 1976 after the unexpected retirement of Harold *Wilson and he headed a minority government, which stayed in power from 1977 through a pact with the Liberal Party. A Labour moderate, he held power at a time when trade unions and the party's left wing had increasing influence, and he was forced to implement austerity measures agreed with the International Monetary Fund (IMF). Callaghan was previously chancellor of the Exchequer 1964–67, home secretary 1967–70, and foreign secretary 1974–76.

Calles, Plutarco Elías (1877–1945) Mexican political leader, president 1924–28. His administration saw the construction of new roads and irrigation works, as well as land reforms. In 1928 he retired to become a landowner and financier, but founded the National Revolutionary Party in 1929 through which he controlled succeeding presidents.

Calley, William L(aws), Jr (1943–) US soldier. In 1968, he led a platoon into the hamlet of My Lai, South Vietnam, and supervised his men as they massacred some 500 elderly men, women, and children. In 1971 he was convicted of the murder of 22 Vietnamese and was sentenced to life imprisonment. He was released by President Richard Nixon in 1974.

Cambodia formerly **Khmer Republic (1970–76), Democratic Kampuchea (1976–79), and People's Republic of Kampuchea (1979–89),** country in southeast Asia, bounded north and northwest by Thailand, north by Laos, east and southeast by Vietnam, and southwest by the Gulf of Thailand.

Cambrai, Battles of two battles in World War I at Cambrai in northeastern France as British forces attempted to retake the town from the occupying Germans, eventually succeeding on 5 October 1918.

Cameroon country in west Africa, bounded northwest by Nigeria, northeast by Chad, east by the Central African Republic, south by the Republic of the Congo, Gabon, and Equatorial Guinea, and west by the Atlantic.

Camorra Italian secret society formed about 1820 by criminals in the dungeons of Naples and continued once they were freed. It dominated politics from 1848, was suppressed in 1911, but many members eventually surfaced in the US Mafia. The Camorra still operates in the Naples area.

Campaign for Nuclear Disarmament CND, nonparty-political British organization advocating the abolition of nuclear weapons worldwide. Since its foundation in 1958, CND has sought unilateral British initiatives to help start, and subsequently to accelerate, the multilateral process and end the arms race.

The movement was launched by the philosopher Bertrand Russell and Canon John Collins and grew out of the demonstration held outside the government's Atomic Weapons Research Establishment at Aldermaston, Berkshire, at Easter 1956. CND held annual marches from Aldermaston to London from 1959 to 1963, after the initial march in 1958 which was routed from London to Aldermaston. From 1970 CND has also opposed nuclear power.

Its membership peaked in the early 1980s, during the campaign against the presence of US Pershing and cruise nuclear missiles on British soil, which left in 1991. It is part of Abolition 2000, a global network, founded in 1995 and with organized support in 76 countries, to press for the elimination of nuclear weapons.

Camp David Agreements two framework accords agreed in 1978 and officially signed in March 1979 by Israeli prime minister *Begin and Egyptian president *Sadat at Camp David, Maryland, USA, under the guidance of US president *Carter. They cover an Egypt–Israel peace treaty and phased withdrawal of Israel from Sinai, which was completed in 1982, and an overall Middle East settlement including the election by the *West Bank and *Gaza Strip

Palestinians of a 'self-governing authority'. The latter issue has stalled repeatedly over questions of who should represent the Palestinians and what form the self-governing body should take.

Canada country occupying the northern part of the North American continent, bounded to the south by the USA, north by the Arctic Ocean, northwest by Alaska, east by the Atlantic Ocean, and west by the Pacific Ocean.

government The Canada Act of 1982 gave Canada power to amend its constitution and added a charter of rights and freedoms. This represented Canada's complete independence, though it remains a member of the British *Commonwealth.

Canada is a federation of ten provinces: Alberta, British Columbia, Manitoba, New Brunswick, Newfoundland, Nova Scotia, Ontario, Prince Edward Island, Québec, and Saskatchewan; and two territories: Northwest Territories and Yukon. Each province has a single-chamber assembly, popularly elected; the premier (the leader of the party with the most seats in the legislature) chooses the cabinet. The two-chamber federal parliament consists of the Senate, whose maximum of 112 members are appointed by the government for life or until the age of 75 and must be resident in the provinces they represent; and the House of Commons, which has 282 members, elected by universal suffrage in single-member constituencies.

The federal prime minister is the leader of the best-supported party in the House of Commons and is accountable, with the cabinet, to it. Parliament has a maximum life of five years. Legislation must be passed by both chambers and then signed by the governor general.

modern history In 1867 the British North America Act united Ontario, Québec, Nova Scotia, and New Brunswick in the Dominion of Canada. After confederation the dominion went on incorporating new provinces and stretching its boundaries to the north and the west – not without cost to the American Indian peoples, many of whom lost their land and were forced onto reservations. Lack of consultation also led to two rebellions of the Métis (French-Indian people) led by Louis Riel, one in 1869 and the other in 1885.

In 1870 the province of Manitoba was added to the confederation; British Columbia joined in 1871 and Prince Edward Island followed in 1873. The new provinces of Alberta and Saskatchewan were created from the Northwest Territories in 1905. The issue of whether some of these new western provinces should be officially bilingual led to divisions between French- and English-speaking Canadians.

Between the years 1881 and 1885 the Canadian Pacific Railway was built, helping to open up the west to settlement. An improving economy led to vast areas of fertile prairie land being developed for agriculture, especially wheat. The discovery of gold and other metals, the exploitation of forests for lumber and paper, the development of fisheries and tourism, and investment from other countries gradually transformed Canada's economy into one of the most important manufacturing and trading nations in the world.

politics and foreign affairs, 1867–1918 The decades following 1867 were dominated by the Conservative prime minister John Macdonald. His death in 1891 broke up the Conservative Party, and in 1896 Wilfrid Laurier and the Liberals were returned to power. They remained in office until 1911, when their policy of establishing a reciprocal trade agreement with the USA was defeated and the Conservatives under Robert *Borden were returned.

Canada sent a contingent to the second South African War (the Boer

War, 1899–1902), and in World War I landed its first contingent in Britain on 6 October 1914. However, the issue of supporting Britain in both these wars caused further divisions between French- and English-speaking Canadians. The former favoured isolationism and the latter an active pro-British policy, and this division was exacerbated by the introduction of conscription in 1917. In World War I, Canadian troops fought in the Second Battle of Ypres, at St Julien, Festubert, Vimy Ridge, Hill 70, Passchendaele, the Somme, and Cambrai, among other engagements. During the period of the war the Houses of Parliament in Ottawa were destroyed by fire (February 1916), and there was a disastrous munitions explosion at Halifax, Nova Scotia (December 1917).

Canada in the 1920s In 1919 the Prince of Wales made an official tour of Canada, laying the foundation stone of the tower of the new Parliament buildings in Ottawa. In the same year the Canadian National Railways were organized. Robert Borden was succeeded by Arthur *Meighen as premier in 1920, but his Conservative ministry soon fell, and W L Mackenzie *King, a Liberal, became premier (December 1921) and held office till 1926. In 1926 Meighen once again became premier, but was defeated in the House immediately and resigned, and Mackenzie King again became premier, but was severely defeated in the 1930 general elections. Taxation and protective tariffs were the dominant issues in Canadian politics during the 1920s.

the depression period Canada suffered with other countries in the world depression following the Wall Street crash of 1929. Factories closed, the wheat market collapsed, and the demand for manufactured and agricultural products fell to disastrous levels. The Conservative R B *Bennett became prime minister in 1930 at a time of increasing unemployment, and was pledged to an upward revision of tariffs to exclude imports of manufactured goods, especially from the USA. The overwhelming Liberal victory in the provincial elections of 1934 was followed by Bennett's heavy defeat in the general election of 1935, when Mackenzie King once more became premier. In 1935 Lord Tweedsmuir (John Buchan) became governor general, one of the most popular in the country's history.

The year 1930 marked the end of the era of the rise of the wheat empire, which had begun with the construction of the railways. By 1933 thousands of farmers were on welfare relief, their savings wiped out, and innumerable farms were abandoned. Though grain continued to be important, the west had great natural resources awaiting development, and in 1930 control of the exploitation of these resources was transferred from the dominion government to the Prairie Provinces. The depression also encouraged new political movements. In Alberta the Social Credit Party advocated drastic changes in the control of banking and money, and gained control of the provincial legislature.

Despite the economic depression, the 1930s were not devoid of substantial achievements. Following the 1931 Statute of Westminster, which had granted the British dominions complete autonomy in external affairs, this was a period of constitutional development in Canada, which played a leading part in the transformation from British Empire to Commonwealth.

In domestic affairs, the Prairie Farm Rehabilitation Act of 1935, passed by the Conservative government, provided for a programme of research involving the cooperation of dominion and provincial governments. Through the efforts of farmers and scientists, the latitude at which arable agriculture was possible was pushed gradually further north in Saskatchewan and Alberta. Radio and flying, too, helped in the expansion northwards, freight being carried through the Northwest Territories and even to the Arctic islands.

Canada in World War II Despite Mackenzie King's previous vacillation over giving aid to Britain in time of crisis and his insistence on parliamentary approval, there was little doubt of Canada's resolve in 1939 to join the Allies. However, the Canadian Parliament, in order to underline Canada's independence, allowed a week to pass after Britain's declaration of war on Germany before declaring war itself (10 September 1939).

In World War II, Canada provided troops at corps strength in both Sicily and Italy (1943–45) and in northwest Europe (1944–45), and Canadian naval units played a prominent part in the Battle of the Atlantic. Canada also operated the British Commonwealth air-training plan, and provided 48 operational air squadrons.

the US-Canadian alliance
A landmark in Canadian history was the creation on 18 August 1940 of the US-Canadian Permanent Joint Board of Defence, following an agreement signed at Ogdensburg by Mackenzie King and President F D Roosevelt. By this agreement the signatories in effect declared their determination to cooperate fully 'in the defence of the northern half of the Western hemisphere'.

The Ogdensburg agreement marked a new stage not only in the relations of Canada and the USA, but in the relations of the USA with the British Commonwealth. For the first time in its history the USA had signed a permanent military agreement with a member of the Commonwealth, and had recognized Canada as its closest friend and associate. For the first time, too, Canada had shown that it was bound to join with its neighbour in defence of the common continent, while remaining free to offer military support to other Commonwealth nations.

With the end of World War II and the beginning of the Cold War, the alliance began to take on a new significance. Early in 1946 the confidence of the Canadian public in the integrity of the USSR, its former wartime ally, was shaken by the 'Gouzenko spy case', which revealed an organized Soviet espionage ring in Canada. The Gouzenko case no doubt helped to make Canada one of the leading proponents of the North Atlantic Treaty Organization (NATO), which came into being when Canada joined the other 11 signatories of the North Atlantic Treaty in Washington DC on 4 April 1949. In the Korean War (1950–53) Canada supported the US-led United Nations effort by sending an army brigade, three destroyers, and an air-transport squadron, all of which it maintained in the field throughout the war.

post-war constitutional changes
After World War II many further constitutional changes were carried through. In 1947 residents of Canada became 'Canadian citizens' as well as British subjects, and Canada was declared to be of equal status to Great Britain within the Commonwealth. In 1949 it was decided that there would be no further appeals from the Supreme Court of Canada to the Privy Council in London. The governor general was authorized to sign treaties on the advice of the government of Canada alone, and the power to amend the Canadian constitution in matters lying solely within federal jurisdiction was transferred from the British Parliament to the Canadian Parliament. In 1952 Vincent Massey was named governor general of Canada, the first Canadian to hold the post.

A domestic event of great importance occurred at the same time, when Newfoundland joined the Canadian confederation on 31 March 1949. This led to a considerable improvement in the economic welfare of the former colony.

politics and the economy in the post-war period Mackenzie King retired in November 1948 after holding office for a total of 23 years since 1921. His successor, Louis St Laurent, a Québec lawyer who had entered politics only in 1941, proceeded in 1949 to win a landslide electoral victory.

Both World War II and then the Korean War gave impetus to Canada's industrial and mineral development, which began at this time to gather real momentum. Despite a fresh round of inflation the country was so prosperous that in 1953 the St Laurent government achieved another great electoral sweep. In 1957, following a general election, the St Laurent government was defeated and the Progressive Conservatives under J G *Diefenbaker were returned to power after 22 years of consecutive Liberal government. Canada was experiencing an economic boom: industry was expanding rapidly, aided by a rising immigration rate, and the whole face of the country was changing. Canada's self-confidence was exemplified in the opening of the St Lawrence Seaway in 1959.

Subsequently depression set in: unemployment rose and confidence waned. Uncertainty was exacerbated by Britain's efforts, during 1960–61, to enter the European Economic Community (EEC), which Canadians feared would have a deleterious affect on their own economy. In the elections in June 1962 Diefenbaker lost his overall majority but remained premier, and immediately announced an austerity programme to remedy the economic situation. He resigned in February 1963 after the Social Credit members, who had held the balance of power since the previous election, voted against the government on defence.

the Pearson governments In the subsequent elections the Liberals emerged as the strongest single party and their leader, Lester *Pearson, became prime minister. Canada's economic position had now improved, but the country faced a serious political problem in French-speaking Québec (see below). Various government scandals in 1964 added to Pearson's difficulties, and there was growing concern in some quarters that US influence in Canada, notably in the economic and business spheres, was being allowed to become too great. Divisions among his political opponents, however, enabled his minority government to survive into 1965 despite its apparent lack of positive leadership. The general election in November 1965 produced an inconclusive result, the Liberals still failing to gain an overall majority, but continuing in office. The Pearson government, despite its failure to win the overwhelming support of the Canadian people, did establish a modern welfare system that improved the lot of many Canadians.

Québec and national identity In Québec, partly under pressure of a delayed industrial revolution in that province, a strong nationalist movement had emerged, whose extremist wing advocated Québec 's secession from the rest of Canada and was prepared to achieve this by force if necessary. There were even fears for the life of Queen Elizabeth II on her tour of Canada in October 1964, but in the event the tour passed off safely – although the Queen met with a frigid reception in Québec City.

In an effort to consolidate national unity in the face of the growing Québécois separatist movement, the Pearson government had in 1963 established the Royal Commission on Bilingualism and Biculturalism. In 1965 this body published a preliminary report that highlighted the sense of national crisis and called for positive steps to be taken to remove the growing sense of grievance among French Canadians.

In December 1964, after months of bitter argument, final approval was given to a new national flag, intended to replace the Canadian red ensign (with its British Union Jack in one corner) and to act as a unifying symbol between Canada's different ethnic and linguistic groups. The new 'maple leaf' flag was flown for the first time in February 1965. Canadian feelings of national identity received a great impetus from the holding of the international exhibition Expo 67 in Montréal on the occasion of Canada's centenary. Other centennial projects across the country such as the building of theatres or community centres helped to engender pride in Canadian individuality. The mood was shattered somewhat by the visit of the French president Charles de Gaulle, who caused a diplomatic furore when in a speech he proclaimed '*Vive le Québec libre!*' ('Long live free Québec!').

the Trudeau era In 1967–68 both Diefenbaker and Pearson were replaced by new party leaders. Robert Stanfield, a lean and phlegmatic Nova Scotian, won the Progressive Conservative leadership contest, and Pierre *Trudeau, an attractive and dynamic young lawyer from Montréal who had joined the party in 1965, won the Liberal leadership.

In the election of 1968, in an outbreak of what was called 'Trudeaumania', Trudeau swept to power with the first majority government since 1958. He retained this parliamentary position, except for the two years after the 1972 election when his hold on power was nearly ended by the Conservatives, but the 1974 election again provided him with a majority government. During these years much of the glamorous aura surrounding Trudeau dissipated, and he was seen by many as intellectually arrogant and contemptuous of parliamentary rights.

Problems of inflation increased the difficulties of the government, forcing it eventually to attempt to curb wages and prices contrary to its pledges in the 1974 election campaign. Criticism also centred on foreign policy, where Canadian nationalists were impatient with Canada's unwillingness to dissociate itself more completely from the shadow of US foreign policy, especially in regard to the Vietnam War.

Nevertheless Trudeau's belief in federalism and his series of conferences to sort out the problems of federal–provincial power-sharing did help for a time to stem the tide of separatism in Québec. He placed great emphasis on developing bilingualism, and a carefully planned programme to promote this was begun in 1970. Trudeau was also helped by the excesses of some separatists who in 1970 kidnapped a British trade commissioner and murdered a Québec minister.

The issue of separatism came to the fore again in the mid-1970s, and the Québec prime minister René *Lévesque stated, after the success of his Parti Québécois in the November 1976 election, that a referendum would be held to ascertain whether the people of Québec wished their province to become an independent nation. The referendum, held in 1980, rejected independence.

In 1979, with no party having an overall majority in the Commons, the Progressive Conservatives formed a government under Joe *Clark. Later that year Trudeau announced his retirement from politics, but when in December 1979 Clark was defeated on his budget proposals, Trudeau reconsidered his decision and won the 1980 general election with a large majority.

Trudeau's third administration was concerned with 'patriation' – that is, the extent to which the British Parliament should determine Canada's constitution. The position was resolved with the passing of the Constitution Act 1982, the last piece of UK legislation to have force in Canada.

the return of the Progressive Conservatives In 1983 Clark was replaced as leader of the Progressive Conservatives by Brian *Mulroney, a corporate lawyer who had never run for public office, and in 1984 Trudeau retired to be replaced as Liberal Party leader and prime minister by John Turner, a former minister of finance. Within nine days of taking office Turner called a general election, and the Progressive Conservatives, under Mulroney, won 211 seats, the largest majority in Canadian history.

Soon after taking office, Mulroney began an international realignment, placing less emphasis on links established by Trudeau with Asia, Africa, and Latin America, and more on cooperation with Europe and a closer relationship with the USA. The election of 1988 was fought on the issue of free trade with the USA, and the Conservatives won with a reduced majority. Despite the majority of voters opting for the Liberals or New Democratic Party (NDP), who both opposed free trade, an agreement was signed with the USA in 1989. Turner and Ed Broadbent, leader of the NDP, both resigned in 1989.

Other notable events in foreign relations during the Mulroney administration include Canada's participation in the coalition opposing Iraq's invasion of Kuwait in 1990–91, and the announcement in February 1992 that Canada, a key partner in NATO, would embark on a phased withdrawal of its forces in Europe.

constitutional reform In 1987 a compromise had been reached between the Canadian provinces aimed at getting Québec's acceptance of the 1982 constitutional reforms. This agreement, known as the Meech Lake Accord, collapsed in 1990.

In September 1991, Mulroney presented a new constitutional reform package to Parliament, designed primarily to persuade Québec to remain as part of the Canadian federation. The plan, known as the Charlottetown Accord, was passed in August 1992, giving greater autonomy to Québec, increased powers to all provinces, and a reformed Senate. A subsequent national referendum in November 1992 rejected the plan, although its reforms were supported by all major Canadian parties except the Reform Party and the Bloc Québécois (for opposed reasons).

Another important constitutional development occurred in May 1992, when an Inuit self-governing homeland was approved by voters in Canada's Northwest Territories.

Conservatives routed by Liberals In February 1993 Mulroney resigned the leadership of the Progressive Conservative Party but remained prime minister until June 1993 when Kim Campbell succeeded him as Canada's first woman premier. In the same month the Canadian Parliament ratified the North American Free Trade Agreement (NAFTA) with the USA and Mexico.The October 1993 general election brought a humiliating defeat for the Progressive Conservatives, their seat tally in the House of Commons falling from 169 to 2, with Kim Campbell losing her own seat. The Liberals won 178 seats and their leader, Jean *Chrétien, became prime minister. The Bloc Québécois, led by Lucien Bouchard, won 54 seats and became the official opposition. Kim Campbell resigned as leader of the Progressive Conservatives in December 1993. Under Chrétien, the Liberal Party went on to win the next two general elections, in June 1997 and November 2000.

referendum in Québec In a 1995 referendum in Québec, voters narrowly rejected a proposal that their province should become an independent sovereign state. The separatist Parti Québécois, which held power in Québec under Jacques Parizeau, drew strong support from the province's French-speaking majority, attracting 49% of the vote. In August 1998 the supreme court ruled that if Québec votes to secede, it can only do so with the federal government's consent, and in December 1999 the federal government published a bill which would make secession even more difficult.

Prime Minister Chrétien appointed Adrienne Clarkson to succeed Romeo LeBlanc as governor general in October 1999. She was the first immigrant to be governor general, having come to Canada from Hong Kong in 1952 as a refugee of Chinese origin.

In September 2000, Stockwell Day and Joe Clark, the leaders of Canada's two rival right-of-centre parties, the Canadian Alliance and the Progressive Conservatives, each won by-elections for seats in the federal parliament. However, the Liberal Party won the general election two months later by a large margin. The win was seen as a blow to Québec separatist tendencies, and in January 2001, the premier of Québec, Lucien Bouchard, resigned after clashing with hardline separatists in the Parti Québécois. He was replaced by Bernard Landry. In May, the Alliance party split, with 8 of its 66 members of parliament seceding from the party, and calling for the resignation of Alliance's leader, Stockwell Day.

In July, Canada legalized the widespread medicinal use of cannabis. New regulations allowed thousands of people suffering from chronic illnesses to grow and smoke the drug.

In by-elections in Québec in October, the Parti Québécois lost much of its support, reducing the likelihood of a new referendum on Québecois secession.

In a sweeping government reshuffle in January 2002, Chrétien named John Manley, formerly the foreign minister, as his deputy and eventual replacement. Chrétien said he himself would remain in office at least until December.

canal artificial waterway constructed for drainage, irrigation, or navigation. **Irrigation canals** carry water for irrigation from rivers, reservoirs, or wells, and are designed to maintain an even flow of water over the whole length. **Navigation and ship canals** are constructed at one level between locks, and frequently link with rivers or sea inlets to form a waterway system. The Suez Canal in 1869 and the Panama Canal in 1914 eliminated long trips around continents and dramatically shortened shipping routes.

Canaris, Wilhelm Franz (1887–1945) German admiral and intelligence expert. A U-boat commander during World War I, he remained in the navy after the war and became an intelligence specialist. He ran the Abwehr, the German armed forces Intelligence Service, from 1935 until his arrest after the *July Plot against Hitler 1944.

Cape Verde country formed by a group of islands in the Atlantic, west of Senegal (West Africa).

government The 1992 constitution provides for a multiparty political system – although religious and geographically based parties are prohibited – with a 79-member national people's assembly and a president, both directly elected and serving five-year terms. The president must secure an absolute majority, while the assembly needs only a simple majority. The prime minister is nominated by the assembly and appointed by the president.

history The Cape Verde islands were first settled in the 15th century by Portugal, the first black inhabitants being slaves imported from West Africa. Over the next five centuries of Portuguese rule the islands were gradually peopled with Portuguese, African slaves, and people of mixed African-European descent who became the majority. The Cape Verdians kept some African culture but came to speak Portuguese or the Portuguese-derived Creole language, and became Catholics.

A liberation movement developed in the 1950s. The mainland territory to which Cape Verde is linked, Guinea-Bissau, achieved independence 1974, and a process began for their eventual union. A transitional government was set up, composed of Portuguese and members of the African Party for the Independence of Portuguese Guinea and Cape Verde (PAIGC).

after independence In 1975 a national people's assembly was elected, and Aristides Pereira, PAIGC secretary general, became president and head of government of Cape Verde. The 1980 constitution provided for the union of the two states but in 1981 this aspect was deleted because of insufficient support, and the PAIGC became the African Party for the Independence of Cape Verde (PAICV). From 1981 to 1990 the PAICV was the only permitted political party. Pereira was re-elected, and relations with Guinea-Bissau improved. Under President Pereira, Cape Verde adopted a non-aligned policy and achieved considerable respect within the region. An opposition party, the Independent Democratic Union of Cape Verde (UCID), operated from Portugal.

end of the one-party system In the first multiparty elections, held in January 1991, a new centre party, Movimento para a Democracia (MPD; Portuguese for Movement for Democracy), won a majority in the assembly. After a very low turnout the following month, Mascarenhas Monteiro was elected president in succession to Pereira. He appointed Carlos Viega as his prime minister. A new constitution was adopted in 1992. Monteiro was re-elected president in February 1996 and in 2000 Gualberto do Rosário, leader of the MPD, became prime minister. In January 2001, the opposition socialist Partido Africano da Independência de Cabo Verde (PAICV; African Party of Independence of Cape Verde) defeated the MPD in parliamentary elections. In February, José Maria Neves became prime minister, and socialist and former prime minister Pedro Pires was peacefully elected president.

Capone, Al(phonse) (1899–1947) called **'Scarface'**, US gangster. During the Prohibition period, he built a formidable criminal organization in Chicago. He was brutal in his pursuit of dominance, killing seven members of a rival gang in the St Valentine's Day Massacre of 1929. He was imprisoned from 1931 to 1939 for income-tax evasion, the only charge that could be sustained against him.

Caporetto, Battle of in World War I, joint German-Austrian victory over the Italian Army October 1917. The battle took place at Caporetto, a village on the River Isonzo in northwest Slovenia. The German commander, General Karl von Bülow, broke through Italian lines on the Isonzo and forced an Italian retreat to fall back onto the Piave line.

Cárdenas, Lázaro (1895–1970) Mexican centre-left politician and general, president 1934–40. A civil servant in early life, Cárdenas took part in the revolutionary campaigns 1913–28 that followed the fall of President Porfirio Díaz. As president of the republic, he attempted to achieve the goals of the revolution by building schools, distributing land to the peasants, developing workers' cooperatives, nationalizing foreign oil properties, and developing transport and industry. Although he was popular, the constitution restricted him to one term in office. He was minister of defence 1943–45.

Caribbean Community and Common Market CARICOM, organization for economic and foreign policy coordination in the Caribbean region, established by the Treaty of Chaguaramas in 1973 to replace the former Caribbean Free Trade Association. Its members are Antigua and Barbuda, Bahamas, Barbados, Belize, Dominica, Grenada, Guyana, Haiti, Jamaica, Montserrat, St Kitts and Nevis, St Lucia, St Vincent and the Grenadines, and Trinidad and Tobago. The Bahamas is a member of the Community but not of the Caribbean Single Market and Economy (CSME).

The British Virgin Islands and the Turks and Caicos Islands are associate members, and Anguilla, the Dominican Republic, Mexico, Haiti, Puerto Rico, and Venezuela are observers. CARICOM headquarters are in Georgetown, Guyana.

Carl XVI Gustavus (1946–) or **Carl XVI Gustaf**, King of Sweden from 1973. He succeeded his grandfather Gustavus VI, his father having been killed in an air crash in 1947. Under the new Swedish constitution, which became effective on his grandfather's death, the monarchy was stripped of all power at his accession.

Carlist supporter of the claims of the Spanish pretender Don Carlos de Bourbon (1788–1855), and his descendants, to the Spanish crown. The Carlist revolt continued, primarily in the Basque provinces, until 1839. In 1977 the Carlist political party was legalized and Carlos Hugo de Bourbon Parma (1930–) renounced his claim as pretender and became reconciled with King Juan Carlos.

Carlsson, Ingvar (Gösta) (1934–) Swedish socialist politician. Leader of the Social Democratic Labour Party (SDAP) from 1986, he was deputy prime minister 1982–86 and prime minister 1986–91 and 1994–96.

Carmichael, Stokely (1941–1998) also known as **Kwame Touré**, Trinidad-born US civil-rights activist. He coined the term *Black Power. As leader of the Black Panthers (1967–69), he demanded black liberation rather than integration, and called for armed revolution. He then moved to Guinea, changed his name, and worked for the pan-African movement.

Carmona, Antonio (1869–1951) Portuguese politician and general. After a military coup in 1926 he was made prime minister and minister of war, with dictatorial powers. In 1928 he was elected president for life by plebiscite, and in 1932 he appointed António *Salazar as prime minister and virtual dictator.

Carniola former crownland and duchy of Austria, most of which was included in Slovenia, part of the kingdom of the Serbs, Croats, and Slovenes (later Yugoslavia) between 1919 and 1991. The western districts of Idrija and Postojna, then allocated to Italy, were transferred to Yugoslavia in 1947. Carniola is now part of independent Slovenia.

Carol II (1893–1953) King of Romania (1930–40). Son of King Ferdinand, he married Princess Helen of Greece and they had a son, Michael. In 1925 he renounced the succession because of his affair with Elena Lupescu and went into exile in Paris. Michael succeeded to the throne in 1927, but in 1930 Carol returned to Romania and was proclaimed king.

In 1938 he introduced a new constitution under which he practically became an absolute ruler. He was forced to abdicate by the pro-Nazi *Iron Guard in September 1940, went to Mexico, and married his mistress in 1947.

Carranza, Venustiano (1859–1920) Mexican revolutionary leader, president 1914–20. His presidency was marked by civil unrest and his reluctance to implement reforms set out in the 1917 constitution.

carrier warfare naval warfare involving aircraft carriers. Carrier warfare was conducted during World War II in the battle of the Coral Sea May 1942, which stopped the Japanese advance in the South Pacific, and in the battle of Midway Islands June 1942, which weakened the Japanese navy through the loss of four aircraft carriers. The US Navy deployed six aircraft carriers during the Gulf War 1991.

Carrington, Peter Alexander Rupert (1919–) 6th Baron Carrington, British Conservative politician. He was defence secretary 1970–74, and led the opposition in the House of Lords 1964–70 and 1974–79. While foreign secretary 1979–82, he negotiated independence for Zimbabwe, but resigned after failing to anticipate the Falklands crisis. He was secretary general of NATO 1984–88 and chaired the European Community-sponsored peace talks on Yugoslavia in 1991. He was knighted in 1958.

Carson, Edward Henry (1854–1935) Baron Carson, Anglo-Irish politician and lawyer who played a decisive part in the trial of the writer Oscar Wilde. In the years before World War I he led the movement in Ulster to resist Irish *home rule by force of arms if need be. He was knighted in 1896, and made a baron in 1921.

Carter, Howard (1873–1939) English Egyptologist. He discovered the virtually intact tomb of Tutankhamen, an Egyptian king of the 18th dynasty. This important archaeological find was made in 1922 in the Valley of the Kings at Luxor with the British archaeologist Lord Carnarvon, although the sealed door was not opened until February 1923.

Carter, Jimmy (1924–) born **James Earl Carter**, 39th president of the USA 1977–81, a Democrat. Features of his presidency were the return of the Panama Canal Zone to Panama, the introduction of an amnesty programme for deserters and draft dodgers of the Vietnam War, and the Camp David Agreements for peace in the Middle East. During the 1990s he emerged as a mediator and peace negotiator, securing President Jean-Bertrand Aristide's safe return to Haiti in October 1994. He was awarded the Presidential Medal of Freedom in 1999 and the Nobel Prize for Peace in 2002.

Carter Doctrine assertion 1980 by President Carter of a vital US interest in the Gulf region (prompted by the Soviet invasion of Afghanistan and instability in Iran): any outside attempt at control would be met by military force if necessary.

Casablanca Conference World War II meeting of the US and UK leaders Roosevelt and Churchill, 14–24 January 1943, at which the Allied demand for the unconditional surrender of Germany, Italy, and Japan was issued.

Casement, Roger David (1864–1916) British diplomat and Irish revolutionary. While in the British consular service, he exposed the ruthless exploitation of the people of the Belgian Congo and Peru, for which he was knighted in 1911 (degraded 1916). He was hanged for treason by the British for his involvement in the Irish nationalist cause.

Casey, Richard Gardiner (1890–1976) Baron Casey, Australian diplomat, Liberal politician, and governor general 1965–69. In 1924 he was involved in the formulation of the *Statute of Westminster and from 1931 served in the House of Representatives as a United Australian (now Liberal) Party deputy and, from 1935, minister. In 1940 he was appointed minister plenipotentiary in Washington, DC, beginning Australia's formal diplomatic representation overseas. He was a member of the British war cabinet in World War II and governor of Bengal, India, 1944–46. Re-elected to the Australian federal parliament in 1949, he was minister for external affairs 1951–60, working to build up Australia's relations with Asia and to foster the alliance with the USA. Unable to work harmoniously with Prime Minister Robert *Menzies, he retired in 1960 and was granted a life peerage.

Cassin, René-Samuel (1887–1976) French jurist, professor, humanitarian, and internationalist. Cassin was a distinguished proponent of the legal and moral recognition of human rights. His life's work was based on the belief that if states recognize the dignity of man in their laws then human responses will be constructive. He was awarded the Nobel Prize for Peace in 1968 at the age of 81 for his contribution to the protection of human worth and the rights of man.

Cassino, Battles of in World War II, series of costly but ultimately successful Allied assaults January–May 1944 on heavily fortified German positions blocking the Allied advance to Rome. Both sides sustained heavy losses in the operation. Cassino is in southern Italy, 80 km/50 mi northwest of Naples, at the foot of Monte Cassino.

Castelo Branco, Humberto de Alencar (1900–1967) Brazilian politician and president 1964–67. His government succeeded in stabilizing the economy, reorganizing the financial system, and renegotiating foreign debt, but failed to alter traditional patterns of authority and prevent the emergence of hardline factions amongst the military, which established the 'tutelary regime' that survived until 1985. He was succeeded in office by his war minister Artur da Costa e Silva in 1967.

Castle, Barbara Anne (1911–2002) Baroness Castle; born Barbara Betts, British Labour politician; a cabinet minister in the Labour governments of the 1960s and 1970s. She led the Labour group in the European Parliament 1979–89 and became a life peer in 1990.

Castro, Cipriano (1858–1924) Venezuelan military leader and dictator 1899–1908, known as 'the Lion of the Andes'. When he refused to pay off foreign debts in 1902, British, German, and Italian ships blockaded the country, leaving the nation almost bankrupt. He presided over a corrupt government and is renowned for being one of the most corrupt leaders in South American history. There were frequent rebellions during his rule,

and opponents of his regime were exiled or murdered.

Castro (Ruz), Fidel (Alejandro) (1927–) Cuban communist politician, prime minister 1959–76, and president from 1976. He led the revolution that overthrew the right-wing regime of the dictator Fulgencio *Batista in 1959. He improved education and health and raised the standard of living for most Cubans, but dealt harshly with dissenters. From 1991, deprived of the support of the USSR and experiencing the long-term effects of a US trade embargo, Castro began to make reforms limiting state control over the economy; foreign ownership was permitted in major areas of commerce and industry from 1995 (the USA continued its economic embargo)

Cat and Mouse Act popular name for the **Prisoners, Temporary Discharge for Health, Act 1913**; an attempt by the UK Liberal government under Herbert Asquith to reduce embarrassment caused by the incarceration of *suffragettes accused of violent offences against property.

Catt, Carrie Chapman (1859–1947) US women's suffrage leader; president of the National American Woman Suffrage Association 1900–04 and 1915–47. Working at both state and federal levels, she played a major role in pushing through the Nineteenth Amendment to the US Constitution (adopted in 1919 and ratified in 1920), which guaranteed women aged 21 and over the right to vote in the USA.

Cavaco Silva, Anibal (1939–) Portuguese politician, finance minister 1980–81, and prime minister and Social Democratic Party (PSD) leader 1985–95. Under his leadership Portugal joined the European Community in 1985 and the Western European Union in 1988.

Cavell, Edith (Louisa) (1865–1915) English nurse. As matron of a Red Cross hospital in Brussels, Belgium, in World War I, she helped Allied soldiers escape to the Dutch frontier. She was court-martialled by the Germans and condemned to death. The British government made much propaganda from her heroism and execution, which was cited as an example of German atrocities.

Ceausescu, Nicolae (1918–1989) Romanian politician, leader of the Romanian Communist Party (RCP), in power from 1965 to 1989. He pursued a policy line independent of and critical of the USSR. He appointed family members, including his wife Elena Ceausescu (1919–1989), to senior state and party posts, and governed in an increasingly repressive manner, zealously implementing schemes that impoverished the nation. The Ceausescus were overthrown in a bloody revolutionary coup in December 1989 and executed on Christmas Day that year.

CEDA acronym for **Confederación Español de Derechas Autónomas**, federation of right-wing parties under the leadership of José Maria Gil Robles, founded during the Second Spanish Republic 1933 to provide a right-wing coalition in the Spanish Cortes. Supporting the Catholic and monarchist causes, the federation was uncommitted as to the form of government.

Central African Federation CAF, grouping imposed by the British government in 1953, incorporating the territories of Nyasaland and Northern and Southern Rhodesia. Although it established representative government along federal and multiracial lines, an underlying function was to prevent the spread of Afrikaner nationalism into central Africa. It was dismembered 1963 in the face of African demands for independence in Nyasaland and Northern Rhodesia, and the intransigence of the minority white community in Southern Rhodesia.

Central African Republic landlocked country in Central Africa, bordered northeast and east by Sudan, south by the Democratic Republic of Congo and the Republic of the Congo, west by Cameroon, and northwest by Chad.

Central American Common Market CACM; Spanish Mercado Común Centroamericana (MCCA), economic alliance established in 1961 by El Salvador, Guatemala, Honduras (seceded in 1970), and Nicaragua; Costa Rica joined in 1962. Formed to encourage economic development and cooperation between the smaller Central American nations and to attract industrial capital, CACM failed to live up to early expectations: nationalist interests remained strong and by the mid-1980s political instability in the region and border conflicts between members were hindering its activities. Its offices are in Guatemala City, Guatemala.

Central Command military strike force consisting of units from the US army, navy, and air force, which operates in the Middle East and North Africa. Its headquarters are in Fort McDill, Florida. It was established in 1979, following the Iranian hostage crisis and the Soviet invasion of Afghanistan, and was known as the Rapid Deployment Force until 1983. It commanded coalition forces in the Gulf War in 1991.

Central Intelligence Agency CIA, US intelligence organization established in 1947. It has actively intervened overseas, generally to undermine left-wing regimes or to protect US financial interests; for example, in the Democratic Republic of Congo (formerly Zaire) and Nicaragua. From 1980 all covert activity by the CIA had by law to be reported to Congress, preferably beforehand, and to be authorized by the president. In 1994 the CIA's estimated budget was around US$3.1 billion. John M Deutsch became CIA director in 1995 after the Agency's standing was diminished by a scandal involving Aldrich Arnes, a CIA agent who had been a longtime mole for the KGB. George Tenet became director in 1997.

Central Treaty Organization CENTO, military alliance that replaced the

*Baghdad Pact in 1959; it collapsed when the withdrawal of Iran, Pakistan, and Turkey in 1979 left the UK as the only member.

Centre Party   German *Zentrumspartei*, German political party established in 1871 to protect Catholic interests. Although alienated by Chancellor Bismarck's *Kulturkampf* 1873–78, in the following years the *Zentrum* became an essential component in the government of imperial Germany. The party continued to play a part in the politics of Weimar Germany before being barred by Hitler in the summer of 1933.

Cerezo Arévalo, Mario Vinicio (1942–) Guatemalan politician, president 1986–91. He led the centre-left Guatemalan Christian Democratic Party (PDCG) to victory in congressional and presidential elections in 1985, to become the country's first civilian president in two decades. He was criticized for failing to tackle economic problems and for being too accommodating to the military, but his period in office helped to consolidate military rule. He was debarred by the constitution from standing for a second term, and his PDCG successor, Alfonso Cabrera, was defeated by the right-wing Jorge Serrano Elias in the 1990 presidential election.

Céspedes, Carlos Manuel de (1871–1939) Cuban revolutionary and politician, president in 1933. He participated in the revolution of 1895 and the Spanish–American War of 1898. Céspedes became provisional president in August 1933, following the overthrow of Gerardo Machado after a coup directed by Fulgencio *Batista. However, he was forced to resign after a further coup in September 1933 by Batista and a student junta, which installed Ramón Grau San Martín in his stead.

Chaco War   war between Bolivia and Paraguay (1932–35) over boundaries in the north of Gran Chaco, settled by arbitration in 1938.

Chad   landlocked country in central North Africa, bounded north by Libya, east by Sudan, south by the Central African Republic, and west by Cameroon, Nigeria, and Niger.

Chadli, Benjedid (1929–) Algerian politician, president 1979–92. An army colonel, he supported Houari *Boumédienne in the overthrow of Mohammed *Ben Bella in 1965, and succeeded Boumédienne in 1979, pursuing more moderate policies. Following the victory of the Front Islamique du Salut (FIS) in the first round of legislative elections in 1991, Benjedid, under pressures from the army, resigned in January 1992.

Chain, Ernst Boris (1906–1979) German-born British biochemist who was awarded a Nobel Prize for Physiology or Medicine in 1945, together with Alexander *Fleming and Howard Florey (Fleming for his discovery of the bactericidal effect of penicillin, and Chain and Florey for their isolation of penicillin and its development as an antibiotic drug). Chain also discovered penicillinase, an enzyme that destroys penicillin. Chain was knighted in 1969.

Chamberlain, (Arthur) Neville (1869–1940) British Conservative politician, son of Joseph Chamberlain. He was prime minister 1937–40; his policy of appeasement toward the Italian fascist dictator Benito Mussolini and German Nazi Adolf Hitler (with whom he concluded the *Munich Agreement in 1938) failed to prevent the outbreak of World War II. He resigned in 1940 following the defeat of the British forces in Norway.

Chamberlain, (Joseph) Austen (1863–1937) British Conservative politician, elder son of Joseph Chamberlain; foreign secretary 1924–29. He shared the Nobel Prize for Peace in 1925 with Charles G *Dawes for his work in negotiating and signing the Pact of *Locarno, which fixed the boundaries of Germany. In 1928 he also signed the *Kellogg–Briand pact to outlaw war and provide for peaceful settlement of disputes.

Chamorro, Violeta (1929–)   Barrios de, Nicaraguan newspaper publisher and politician, president 1990–96. With strong US support, she was elected to be the candidate for the National Opposition Union (UNO) in 1989, winning the presidency from Daniel *Ortega Saavedra in February 1990 and thus ending the period of *Sandinista rule and the decade-long *Contra war. She brought greater stability and democracy to the country, but chose not to contest the 1996 presidential election, and was succeeded by Arnoldo Alemán of the right-of-centre Liberal Alliance.

Chamoun, Camille (Nimer) (1900–1987)   Arabic Kamil Sham'un, Lebanese Maronite Christian politician, president 1952–58. As president, he pursued pro-Western policies, antagonizing leftist-Nasserists, and, after being accused of rigging the 1957 elections, became increasingly authoritarian. His refusal as president to support Lebanon's possible accession into Syria and Egypt's new United Arab Republic and rumours that he was seeking a second term led to civil war in June–July 1958, which was ended by the landing of US troops and by the election of army commander General Fuad Shihab (Chehab) as president. Chamoun responded by founding the National Liberal Party, but was to return only briefly to government, in 1975–76 and 1984.

Charles, Charles Philip Arthur George (1948–)   Prince of the UK, heir to the British throne, and Prince of Wales since 1958 (invested 1969). He is the first-born child of Queen Elizabeth II and the Duke of Edinburgh. He studied at Trinity College, Cambridge, (1967–70), before serving in the Royal Air Force and Royal Navy. The first royal heir since 1660 to have an English wife, he married *Diana, Princess of Wales (then Lady Diana Spencer), daughter of the 8th Earl

Spencer, in 1981. There are two sons and heirs, William (1982–) and Henry (1984–). Amid much publicity, Charles and Diana separated in 1992 and were divorced in 1996. Following the death of Diana, Princess of Wales in 1997 Charles' popularity with the British public seemed in some doubt; however opinion polls in 1998 indicated that public feeling had warmed towards him and to his long-standing relationship with Camilla Parker Bowles (1946–).

Charles, (Karl Franz Josef) (1887–1922)   Emperor of Austria and king of Hungary from 1916, the last of the Habsburg emperors. He succeeded his great-uncle Franz Josef in 1916 but was forced to withdraw to Switzerland in 1918, although he refused to abdicate. In 1921 he attempted unsuccessfully to regain the crown of Hungary and was deported to Madeira, where he died.

Charles, (Mary) Eugenia (1919–) Dominican centre-right politician, prime minister 1980–95; cofounder and first leader of the cente-right Dominica Freedom Party (DFP). Two years after Dominica's independence the DFP won the 1980 general election and Charles became the Caribbean's first female prime minister. In 1993 she resigned the leadership of the DFP, but remained as prime minister until the 1995 elections, which were won by the opposition United Workers' Party (UNP). She then announced her retirement from politics.

Charles (XVI) Gustavus (1946–) born **Carl Gustaf Folke Hubertus**, King of Sweden (1973–). He was the only son of Prince Gustavus Adolphus (1906–47) and Princess Sibylla of Saxe-Coburg And Gotha (1908–72). Although Crown Prince from 1950, he did not succeed to the throne of Sweden until 1973, on the death of his grandfather, Gustavus (VI) Adolphus. In June 1976 he married Silvia Sommerlath. Soon after his succession Charles oversaw major constitutional changes in Sweden that have rendered the monarchy little more than a symbolic position.

Charter 77   Czechoslovak human rights movement founded 1977 to lobby for Czech conformity to the UN Declaration of Human Rights.

Château-Thierry, Battle of   in World War I, US victory over German troops May–June 1918 in northern France during the German offensive on the Marne.

Chavez, Cesar Estrada (1927–1993) US labour organizer who in 1962 founded the National Farm Workers Association (NFWA), now known as the United Farm Workers (UFW), and, with the support of the AFL-CIO (Federation of North American Trade Unions) and other major unions, embarked on a successful campaign to unionize California grape workers. Chavez strove to call the public's attention to the struggles of farm workers for better pay and safer working conditions, leading to strikes and boycotts of citrus fruits, lettuce, and grapes in the early 1970s, but disagreement and exploitation of migrant farm labourers continued despite his successes.

Checkpoint Charlie   Western-controlled crossing point for non-Germans between West Berlin and East Berlin, opened in 1961 as the only crossing point between the Allied and Soviet sectors. Its dismantling in June 1990 was seen as a symbol of the ending of the *Cold War.

Chehab, Fuad (1901–1973)   Lebanese soldier and president. He was educated at the French military academies of Damascus and St Cyr. He served in the army under the French mandate, becoming commander-in-chief on independence in 1946. During a break in his military career he was prime minister for six days during an emergency in September 1952. As president 1958–64 he restored stability to Lebanon, which had been shaken by the 1958 civil war.

Cheka   secret police operating in the USSR between 1917 and 1923. It originated from the tsarist Okhrana (the security police under the tsar from 1881 to 1917), and became successively the OGPU (GPU) (1923–34), NKVD (1934–46), MVD (1946–53), and the *KGB from 1954.

Chelmsford, Frederick John Napier Thesiger, 1st Viscount Chelmsford (1868–1933)   English colonial administrator. In Australia, he was governor of Queensland 1905–09 and of New South Wales 1909–13. He was viceroy of India 1916–21, and was briefly First Lord of the Admiralty in 1924.

chemical warfare   use in war of gaseous, liquid, or solid substances intended to have a toxic effect on humans, animals, or plants. Together with biological warfare, it was banned by the Geneva Protocol in 1925, and the United Nations, in 1989, also voted for a ban. In June 1990 the USA and USSR agreed bilaterally to reduce their stockpile to 5,000 tonnes each by 2002. The USA began replacing its stocks with new nerve-gas binary weapons. In 1993 over 120 nations, including the USA and Russian Federation, signed a treaty outlawing the manufacture, stockpiling, and use of chemical weapons. The Russian parliament ratified the treaty in 1997.

Ch'en I (1901–1972)   Vice-Premier and Foreign Minister of the People's Republic of China. In 1941 Ch'en was given command of the New Fourth Army in the war against Japan. In the civil war which followed he was commander of the Third Field army in eastern China and as such took Shanghai in 1949. He was mayor of Shanghai from 1949–58. Concurrently he held several important posts in the national government. In 1958 he became foreign minister and frequently represented his country abroad. During the Cultural Revolution he was attacked by the Red Guards, but, thanks to Chou En-lai's protection, was spared humiliation.

Chen Boda (or **Ch'en Po-ta**) **(1905–1989)**
Chinese political propagandist.
He became chief editor of the party
organ, *Hongqi* (*Red Flag*), in 1958,
and during the Cultural Revolution
1966–69 he became associated with
the radicals and was appointed to the
Politburo in 1969. In the campaign
against leftist excesses the following
year, however, he was arrested and
expelled from the Chinese Communist
Party (CCP). In 1980–81 he was tried
along with the *Gang of Four and
sentenced to 18 years in prison but
was reportedly released later the
same year.

Chen Duxiu (1879–1942) Chinese
communist politician, party leader
1921–27. A founder member of the
Chinese Communist Party (CCP)
and its leader from July 1921, Chen
followed conventional Leninist
thinking and sought to foment a
socialist revolution in China through
CCP-led workers' uprisings in the
country's coastal cities. Discredited
both by the failure of his efforts and by
his association with Trotskyist groups,
Chen was replaced as CCP leader by
Li Lisan. He was expelled from the
CCP in 1929 and died in Sichuan.

Cheney, Dick (1941–) born **Richard
Bruce Cheney**, US Republican
politician, vice-president from 2001.
He was the youngest-ever chief of staff
1975–77 under President Gerald Ford,
a member of Congress 1979–89, and
defense secretary 1989–93 under
President George H W Bush. He was
selected in 2000 as the running-mate of
Bush's son, George W *Bush, to bring
experience in federal matters and
foreign policy to the electoral ticket.

Chen Yi (or **Ch'en I**) **(1901–1972)**
Chinese communist military and
political leader, foreign minister
1958–69. A member of the Chinese
Communist Party from 1923, he
emerged as a supporter of *Mao Zedong
in the struggle with the Kuomintang
(*Guomindang nationalist party), and
took a leading role in the military
campaign against the Japanese

occupying forces. He was created
marshal of the People's Republic in
1955 and served as mayor of Shanghai
1949–58.

**Chen Yun (1905–1995) adopted name
of Liao Chenyun**, Chinese communist
politician and economic planner.
An economics expert, he was the
second-ranking 'party elder' at the
time of his death. A veteran of the
Long March of 1934–35, he was a
member of the Chinese Communist
Party (CCP) Politburo for a record
53 years (1934–87). He favoured
a planned economy in which market
forces would be allowed to operate in
a controlled manner, 'like a bird in a
cage'. Formerly an ally of China's
paramount leader Deng Xiaoping,
Chen became a conservative opponent
in his later years, voicing concern at
the destabilizing effects of Deng's
'uncaged' market socialism.

**Chernenko, Konstantin Ustinovich
(1911–1985)** Soviet politician, leader
of the Communist Party of the Soviet
Union (CPSU) and president 1984–85.
He was a protégé of Leonid Brezhnev
and from 1978 a member of the
Politburo.

**Chernov, Viktor Mikhailovich
(1873–1952)** Russian politician.
He was leader of the Socialist
Revolutionaries, occupying a central
position in the party. In 1917 he was
minister of agriculture in Aleksandr
Kerensky's provisional government.
In 1918 he was elected chair of the
Constituent Assembly. He emigrated
in 1920 and died in the USA.

**Cheshire, (Geoffrey) Leonard
(1917–1992)** English pilot and
philanthropist. Commissioned into
the Royal Air Force on the outbreak of
World War II, he was decorated several
times. A devout Roman Catholic, he
founded the first **Cheshire Foundation
Home** for the Incurably Sick in 1948.
In 1959 he married Susan Ryder
(1923–), who established a foundation
for the sick and disabled of all ages
and became a life peeress in 1978.

Chicherin, Georgi Vasilievich (1872–1936) Russian diplomat. After graduating from St Petersburg University he worked in the archives department of the Russian Foreign Office. In 1904 he emigrated to Berlin, Germany, and there joined the Russian Social Democratic Workers' party, becoming a prominent member of the *Menshevik faction. For many years he was active in the labour movements of Britain, France, and Germany. After the Bolsheviks seized power in Russia in 1917, Chicherin became a Bolshevik, and was imprisoned in Brixton Prison for having enemy associations. In January 1918 he was released and expelled from Britain in exchange for George Buchanan. He then returned to Russia. Chicherin was appointed commissar (minister) for Foreign Affairs; he negotiated and signed the Treaty of Rapallo with Germany in 1922 and subsequently played a role in the formation of the USSR.

Chifley, Ben (Joseph Benedict) (1885–1951) Australian Labor prime minister 1945–49. He united the party in fulfilling a welfare and nationalization programme 1945–49 (although he failed in an attempt to nationalize the banks in 1947) and initiated an immigration programme and the Snowy Mountains hydroelectric project.

Childers, (Robert) Erskine (1870–1922) English civil servant and writer, Irish republican, author of the spy novel *The Riddle of the Sands* (1903).

Chile South American country, bounded north by Peru and Bolivia, east by Argentina, and south and west by the Pacific Ocean.

China the largest country in East Asia, bounded to the north by Mongolia; to the northwest by Tajikistan, Kyrgyzstan, Kazakhstan, and Afghanistan; to the southwest by India, Nepal, and Bhutan; to the south by Myanmar, Laos, and Vietnam; to the southeast by the South China Sea; to the east by the East China Sea, North Korea, and Yellow Sea; and to the northeast by Russia.

government China is divided into 22 provinces, five autonomous regions, and three municipalities (Beijing, Shanghai, and Tianjin), each with an elected local people's government with policy-making power in defined areas. Ultimate authority resides in the single-chamber National People's Congress (NPC), composed of about 2,970 deputies indirectly elected every five years through local people's congresses. Deputies to local people's congresses are directly elected through universal suffrage in constituency contests. The NPC, the 'highest organ of state power', meets annually and elects a permanent, 155-member standing committee to assume its functions between sittings. The committee has an inner body comprising a chair and 16 vice-chairs. The NPC also elects for a five-year term a State Central Military Commission (SCMC), leading members of the judiciary, the vice-president, and the state president, who must be at least 45 years old. The president is restricted to two terms in office and performs primarily ceremonial functions. Executive administration is effected by a prime minister and a cabinet (state council) that includes three vice premiers, departmental ministers, state commission chiefs, the auditor general, the secretary general, and the governor of the Bank of China. The state council is appointed by and accountable to the NPC.

China's controlling force is the Chinese Communist Party (CCP). It has a parallel hierarchy comprising elected congresses and committees functioning from village level upwards and taking orders from above. A national party congress every five years elects a central committee of about 319 members (189 of whom have full voting powers) that meets twice a year and elects a Politburo of about

20 members and a five-member secretariat to exercise day-to-day control over the party and to frame state and party policy goals. The Politburo meets weekly and is China's most significant political body.

There have been, in recent years, moves towards increased democratization and decentralization, with allegedly competitive elections to the NPC's standing committee 1988 and secret voting introduced within the NPC from 1993. Efforts have also been made to more clearly demarcate state and party responsibilities and to reduce CPP interference in state decision-taking. China does not allow human-rights monitors into the country.

history For details of Chinese history prior to the establishment of the People's Republic, see *China: prehistoric and ancient history to 221 BC ; *China: late imperial history 1279–1900; *China: history 1900–49.

In 1949, after years of civil war, the Communists finally eliminated Nationalist (*Guomindang) resistance on the mainland. The Communists proceeded to inaugurate the People's Republic of China (PRC), with *Mao Zedong as chairman, the Nationalists having withdrawn to *Taiwan.

early reforms and reconstruction The first major reform of the Communist regime was a general redistribution of land and reduction of rents while the civil war was still in progress, followed 1949–52 by an extension (albeit more muted) of agrarian reform to former Guomindang territories. Landlord property was divided among poor peasants, but rich and 'middle' peasants were spared confiscation. Another major social reform was the 1950 Marriage Law, which gave women equal rights in marriage, divorce, and property ownership.

When peace had been restored, economic reconstruction and industrialization were priorities.

Mechanisms were put in place to ensure central direction of the economy, but at first the capitalist sector of the economy was left alone. A centralized Soviet-style constitution was adopted in 1954, and by February 1956 some 99% of privately-owned businesses had 'entered into partnerships with the state' (in other words, they were nationalized). Compensation to former owners – the 'national capitalists' – was paid in the form of interest right up to (and perhaps beyond) the Cultural Revolution.

the 'Anti' campaigns During the period 1949–53 the Party grew from 4.5 to 6.6 million members. Other sections of the population such as workers, youth, women, and children were also recruited into mass organizations. Two major political campaigns took place, the '3 Anti' campaign of 1951, which was directed against corruption, waste, and bureaucracy, and the '5 Anti' campaign of 1952, directed principally against bribery, tax evasion, fraud, illegal use of public property, and stealing of economic secrets. The '3 Anti' campaign was designed to whip the growing bureaucracy into line. The '5 Anti' campaign was a major blow against bourgeois remnants in the new China.

collectivization After the 1949–53 land reforms mutual-aid teams were formed to share tasks in farming smallholdings. Soon 'lower-level cooperatives' came into being, in which payment to individual peasants was based partly on the amount of work done and partly on the amount of land contributed. Compared with the USSR under Stalin, collectivization in the PRC was carried out with caution and a degree of sensitivity. The next stage in 1956 was the formation of 'advanced cooperatives', which rewarded labour only.

the Hundred Flowers and anti-rightist campaigns In 1956 Mao initiated the *Hundred Flowers campaign to encourage criticism of bureaucracy in the party and administration. This was partly in response to the problems highlighted by the Hungarian uprising of 1956. By April 1957 the campaign had generated unwelcome heat, and was called off in June. An 'anti-rightist' campaign followed in which those who had spoken out most forthrightly were themselves criticized.

foreign affairs in the 1950s Early PRC foreign policy leant towards the USSR, which was the first country to recognize the new government (Britain did so in January 1950). In February 1950 *Zhou Enlai (Chou En-lai), then premier and foreign minister, signed a treaty of friendship, alliance, and mutual assistance with the USSR, which over the next decade extended considerable aid to China. In 1950 Chinese troops overran *Tibet, which later became an autonomous region of China. Opposition to Chinese rule there has been rigorously repressed.

The Chinese involvement in the *Korean War (1950–53) ruled out any question of reconciliation with the USA, and intensified the 'left turn' of the regime domestically. China entered the war in November 1950 when US-led UN troops crossed the 38th parallel and reached the Chinese border, ignoring Chinese warnings. Victories against the better-equipped UN forces strengthened national pride. After the 1953 armistice the USA continued to withhold diplomatic recognition from the People's Republic. The USA also forbade trade with the PRC, blocked its entry into the UN, and continued to protect the Nationalist regime in Taiwan. The Communists made no attempt to invade Taiwan, but began bombardment of the offshore islands of Quemoy and Matsu in 1958. Ritual bombardments continued for many years.

the Sino-Soviet split At the end of the 1950s the Sino-Soviet alliance

began to break down. There were many reasons for this development. The USSR had often ignored or trampled on the interests of the Chinese Communist Party (CCP). Chinese sources later revealed that after 1949 China was forced to trade with the USSR on disadvantageous terms. The PRC leadership saw the establishment of a policy of 'peaceful coexistence' between the USSR and the USA after the 1962 *Cuban missile crisis as a betrayal. Ideological differences, culminating in the late 1960s in Chinese charges of Soviet 'revisionism' and 'social imperialism', also played a role. Finally, China's promotion of its own developmental strategy at the expense of the Soviet model provoked withdrawal of Soviet aid and consequently much economic hardship in China.

China's attacks on the USSR began obliquely in 1960 with condemnations of Yugoslav revisionism. The split became irrevocable in 1962 when the USSR sided with India during a brief Sino-Indian border war. In 1963 the dispute became public and increasingly bad-tempered. During the 1960s the PRC entered into competition with the USSR for influence not only in the world Communist movement but also among the developing nations. In December 1963–February 1964 Zhou Enlai toured Africa and visited Burma (now Myanmar), Pakistan, and Ceylon (now Sri Lanka). This was part of China's *non-aligned strategy, projecting itself as the voice of the developing world, although it achieved nuclear capability by 1964.

the Great Leap Forward The first step in the evolution of an indigenous development strategy was the 'Great Leap Forward' of 1958. This called for the promotion of small-scale labour-intensive industry alongside the large-scale modern sector, a combination known as 'walking on two legs'. At the same time 700,000 agricultural collectives were merged into 26,000 'People's Communes' in an attempt to boost food output. The ideological aim was to achieve classless 'true communism'.

The Great Leap failed, largely because it was wasteful of human and material resources and misdirected investment. The communes, at least in their immediate tasks, failed because their over-centralized structure alienated the peasants. These agricultural and industrial crises were compounded by terrible natural disasters in 1959 and 1960 and the Soviet withdrawal of blueprints and technicians in 1960. More than 20 million Chinese died as a result of floods and famine in this period.

economic recovery The failure of the Great Leap reduced Mao's influence 1962–65, and a successful 'recovery programme' was begun under President *Liu Shaoqi. In March 1962 Zhou Enlai announced a new strategy, which gave agriculture first priority. Private farming plots and markets were reintroduced, communes reduced in size, and income differentials and material incentives restored. The period 1961–66 saw economic recovery, but at the expense of Mao's 'revolutionary' goals, and pragmatism and professionalism prevailed in the 'Red versus expert' debate. Mao himself came under veiled attack from liberal intellectuals, and retired for a time to the 'second line' – from where he began to set in motion a campaign to destroy the new balance of forces at the top.

the Cultural Revolution Mao's plotting was to culminate in the eruption in 1966 of the 'Great Proletarian *Cultural Revolution', a 'rectification campaign' directed against 'rightists' and 'capitalist-roaders' in the CCP and seeking to re-establish the supremacy of (Maoist) ideology over economics. Mao's aim was to repudiate bourgeois ideology and revisionism, inject fresh blood into

a simplified administration, and revolutionize Chinese youth. Mao was supported by *Lin Biao, chief of the People's Liberation Army (PLA), and the Shanghai-based *Gang of Four (led by Mao's wife *Jiang Qing). Millions of student Red Guards – owing allegiance only to Mao – were encouraged to organize themselves against the party and government elite throughout China. The chief targets were Liu Shaoqi, *Deng Xiaoping (head of the CCP secretariat), and Peng Zhen (mayor of Beijing), all of whom were forced out of office. Some 500,000 people are thought to have been killed during the Cultural Revolution, and millions of intellectuals and professionals were sent to work on communes. The education system was reduced to chaos.

Government institutions fell into abeyance and in the resulting disorder the PLA acquired unprecedented power. New 'Three-Part Revolutionary Committees', comprising Maoist party officials, trade unionists, and PLA commanders, took over the administration of the country. With the emergence of independent 'ultra-left' currents among Chinese youth and increasing resistance by many army units and cadres to Beijing, the Maoist centre reversed the radical tide after 1967. By 1968 schools were reopened, and millions of Red Guards 'sent down' to remote rural areas. The reconstruction of the party and administration began. By 1970 Mao had sided with pragmatic prime minister Zhou Enlai and started restoring order and creating a more balanced system.

normalization and détente In 1972 the Chinese government announced that Mao's named successor, Lin Biao, had been killed in an aeroplane crash the previous year while fleeing to the USSR after an unsuccessful coup attempt. Military influence waned, but remained above pre-1966 levels. In 1972–73 Deng Xiaoping, finance minister Li Xiannian, and others were rehabilitated. This reconstruction movement climaxed in the summoning of the National People's Congress (NPC) in 1975 for the first time in 11 years to ratify a new constitution and approve an economic plan termed the 'Four Modernizations' – agriculture, industry, armed forces, and science and technology – that aimed at placing China on a par with the West by the year 2000.

The early 1970s also witnessed the emergence of a policy of détente towards the USA. After the 1968 invasion of Czechoslovakia by Soviet-led Warsaw Pact forces, the CCP leaders perceived a growing danger of Soviet invasion of China, especially after small border clashes began to occur in 1969 in the disputed Ussuri River region. Combined with prospects of US disengagement from the *Vietnam War, the increased Sino-Soviet tensions prompted the PRC to seek normalization of relations with the USA, thus creating a more complex international alignment of forces. The visit of US President Nixon to China was followed by the visit of Japanese premier Kakuei Tanaka in 1972. In October 1971 the PRC was admitted to the UN, from which Taiwan was now excluded. Full diplomatic relations were established with the USA in 1979.

after Mao The deaths of Zhou Enlai and Mao Zedong in 1976 unleashed a violent succession struggle between the leftist Gang of Four, led by Jiang Qing, and moderate 'rightists', grouped around the vice premier, Deng Xiaoping. Deng was forced into hiding by the Gang; and Mao's moderate protégé *Hua Guofeng became CCP chair and head of government in 1976. Hua arrested the Gang on charges of treason and held power 1976–78 as a stopgap leader, continuing Zhou Enlai's modernization programme. His authority was progressively challenged, however, by Deng Xiaoping, who returned to office in 1977 after campaigns in Beijing.

Deng in power By 1979, after further popular campaigns, Deng had gained effective charge of the government, controlling a majority in the Politburo. State and judicial bodies began to meet again, the late Liu Shaoqi was rehabilitated as a party hero, and economic reforms were introduced. These involved the dismantling of the commune system, the introduction of direct farm incentives under a new 'responsibility system', and the encouragement of foreign investment in 'Special Economic Zones' in coastal enclaves.

By June 1981 Deng's supremacy was assured when his protégés *Hu Yaobang and *Zhao Ziyang had become party chair and prime minister respectively, and the Gang of Four were sentenced to life imprisonment. In 1982, Hua Guofeng and a number of senior colleagues were ousted from the Politburo, and the NPC adopted a definitive constitution, restoring the post of state president (abolished in 1975) and establishing a new code of civil rights.

modernization The new administration was a collective leadership, with Hu Yaobang in control of party affairs, Zhao Ziyang overseeing state administration, and Deng Xiaoping (a party vice-chair and chair of the State Central Military Commission) formulating long-term strategy and supervising the PLA. The triumvirate streamlined the party and state bureaucracies and promoted to power new, younger, and better-educated technocrats. They sought to curb PLA influence by retiring senior commanders and reducing personnel numbers from 4.2 million to 3 million. The economy was modernized by extending market incentives and local autonomy, and by encouraging foreign trade and investment.

the emergence of the pro-democracy movement These economic reforms met with substantial success in the agricultural sector (output more than doubled 1978–85) but had adverse side effects, widening regional and social income differentials and fuelling a mass consumerism that created balance-of-payments problems. Contact with the West brought demands for full-scale democratization in China. These calls led in 1986 to widespread student demonstrations, and party chief Hu Yaobang was dismissed in 1987 for failing to check the disturbances. Hu's departure imperilled the post-Dengist reform programme, as conservative forces, grouped around the veteran Politburo members Chen Yun and Peng Zhen, sought to halt the changes and reestablish central party control. Chen Yun, Peng Zhen, and Deng Xiaoping all retired from the Politburo in October 1987, and soon after *Li Peng took over as prime minister, Zhao Ziyang having become CCP chair.

the Tiananmen Square massacre With inflation spiralling, an austerity budget was introduced in 1989. This provoked urban unrest and a student-led pro-democracy movement, launched in Beijing, rapidly spread to provincial cities. There were mass demonstrations during Soviet leader Mikhail Gorbachev's visit to China in May 1989. Soon after Gorbachev's departure, a brutal crackdown was launched against the demonstrators by Li Peng and President *Yang Shangkun, with Deng Xiaoping's support. Martial law was proclaimed and in June 1989 more than 2,000 unarmed protesters were massacred army troops in the capital's *Tiananmen Square. Arrests, executions, martial law, and expulsion of foreign correspondents brought international condemnation and economic sanctions.

return to conservatism After the massacre, Communist Party general secretary Zhao Ziyang was ousted and replaced by Jiang Zemin (the Shanghai party chief and new protégé of Deng Xiaoping), a move that consolidated

the power of the hardline faction of President Yang Shangkun and Li Peng. Deng officially retired from the last of his party and army posts but remained a dominant figure. A crackdown on dissidents was launched as the pendulum swung sharply away from reform towards conservatism. Jiang Zemin replaced Yang Shangkun as state president in 1993. By the summer of 1995 there was increasing concern over the failing health of Deng Xiaoping, whose reign as 'paramount leader' appeared to be nearing an end. In December 1995 Wei Jingsheng, a leading pro-democracy campaigner, was sentenced to 14 years' imprisonment for criticizing the government and calling for independence for Tibet.

By 1992 China's economy, after stalling in 1989–90, began to expand again, with a significant increase in industrial output, as the country entered a new phase of economic reform. In 1993 it grew by 13% and in 1994 by a further 9%. In March 1996 Li Peng announced to parliament that China's GDP had quadrupled between 1980 and 1995. The USA renewed the country's most-favoured-nation (MFN) trade status in May 1996.

death of Deng Xiaoping Deng Xiaoping died in February 1997 at the age of 92. He had been the country's leader since 1978 and was a promoter of market economic reforms and the 'opening to the West', which led to a trebling in per-capita incomes as the economy grew at 9% per annum. Afflicted with Parkinson's disease and barely able to walk or talk, Deng had not been seen in public for two years.

Effective power had already passed to a collective leadership headed by Deng's chosen successor, Jiang Zemin, state president and Communist Party leader. It also included Li Peng, the prime minister, who was more conservative, Qiao Shi, head of the National People's Congress and former security chief, and Zhu Rongji, the deputy prime minister who was committed to economic modernization. Little change in the existing direction, which involved combining economic reforms with strict political control by the Communist Party, was expected in the short term.

foreign affairs in the 1980s and 1990s In the 1980s there was a partial rapprochement with the USSR, culminating in Mikhail Gorbachev's visit in May 1989. However, a new rift became evident in 1990, when the Chinese government denounced the Soviet leader's 'revisionism'. However, Jiang Zemin visited the USSR in May 1991 for talks with Gorbachev, the first visit to the USSR of a CCP leader since 1957, and an agreement on the demarcation of the Sino-Soviet border was signed.

In April 1997 closer relations with Russia were established when a joint declaration was signed in Moscow opposing the world domination of one superpower (the United States) following the end of the Cold War. In November Russian President Boris Yeltsin and Jiang Zemin signed an agreement to implement the 1991 Sino-Soviet border agreement.

Relations with Vietnam, a close ally of the Soviet Union, had been poor, especially following China's military incursion into Vietnam in February–March 1979 to punish Vietnam for its treatment of its ethnic Chinese population. But in November 1991 Vietnam's Communist Party leader and prime minister visited Beijing, after which relations were normalized and a trade agreement was signed.

Relations with the much of the West were warm, with economic contacts widening. China used its UN Security Council vote to back much of the policy of the US-led anti-Iraq alliance during the Gulf crisis of 1990–91, although it abstained in the vote authorizing the war. In 1991 Japan and the European Community dropped most of the sanctions imposed in the wake of the Tiananmen massacre. In September 1991 British prime minister John Major became the first Western leader to pay an official visit to China since 1989. In 1992 China established full diplomatic relations with Israel, and Beijing received the first-ever state visit by a Japanese emperor.

In November 1998 Jiang Zemin became the first Chinese head of government to make a state visit to Japan; the host country conveyed its 'deep remorse' for atrocities committed in China in the 1930s and 1940s.

In contrast, relations with the USA remained strained, officially because of China's poor human-rights record and its indiscriminate sale of weapons technologies around the world. In May 1996 Liu Gang, one of the leaders of the 1989 pro-democracy uprising in Tiananmen Square and the government's third most-wanted political dissident, escaped to the USA.

In January 1996, Li Peng declared that reunification with Taiwan would become a priority once *Hong Kong and Macau were returned to China in 1997 and 1999 respectively. A Hong Kong takeover panel was appointed in February 1996, and the former British colony was handed back to China in July 1997.

separatist violence Three bombs placed on buses in Urumqi in February 1997 killed nine people and injured 74. The bombs, timed to go off following Deng Xiaoping's memorial ceremony in Beijing, were assumed to be the work of separatist Muslim forces. Policing in Xinjiang province had been stepped up in early February after anti-Chinese riots in Yining City in which ten people were killed and more than 100 injured when Chinese soldiers opened fire on demonstrators. Another bomb exploded in March on a bus in one of Beijing's main shopping streets during the rush hour, reportedly killing two people and injuring 30. Exiled Uighur separatists claimed responsibility for the bomb, and vowed to stage more attacks until they had gained complete freedom for Xinjiang. Xinjiang is home to China's biggest concentration of Muslims – mostly Uighurs, but also Kazakhs, Kirzhis, and Hui – and for decades China had been unable to quell outbursts of violent separatist activity.

leadership shake-up The 15th Congress of the Chinese Communist Party closed in September 1997 with the retirement of several Deng-era leaders, underlining the commanding position secured by party leader and state president Jiang Zemin. Qiao Shi, the head of the NPC and widely viewed as an important rival to Jiang, and a perceived liberal who had helped rebuild the rule of law, stepped down from the party's Central Committee and Politburo. In March 1998 he was replaced by the more hardline Li Peng, who was due to retire as prime minister. The 69-year-old deputy prime minister, Zhu Rongji, an economic reformer who had defused pro-democracy demonstrations in Shanghai in 1989 without resorting to force, moved to third place in the CP hierarchy and was elected to succeed Li Peng as prime minister. Jiang Zemin was re-elected as president; the 55-year-old Hu Jintao was elected vice-president.

improved relations with USA and Russia In September 1997 urban unemployment was officially reported to have reached 4%. In October President Jiang visited the USA for the first Chinese-American summit since 1985. It marked an improvement in relations, which had been strained since the 1989 Tiananmen Square crackdown. President Clinton lifted a ban on the export of non-military nuclear reactors to China. In November 1997, during a visit to China by Russian president Boris Yeltsin, a joint declaration was signed on the basis of a May 1991 agreement, ending years of tension over the demarcation of the eastern sector of the Chinese border.

downsizing of military and bureaucracy It was announced at the September 1997 Congress that the 3-million-strong Chinese army, air force, and navy (the People's Liberation Army) would be modernized and also reduced by 0.5 million over the coming three years. In March 1998 the NPC approved an overhaul of the state bureaucracy, entailing scrapping or merging 15 of the government's 40 ministries and departments, creating four new 'super ministries', and sacking half of the 8 million staff.

dissidents released In November 1997 the prominent pro-democracy dissident, Wei Jingsheng, was released from prison on medical parole after 18 years of intermittent internment; he immediately went to the USA for treatment for hypertension. In April 1998, Wang Dan, a leader of the dissident student protest movement in 1989, was released from prison on medical grounds and allowed to leave for the USA.

Zhu Rongji as prime minister Zhu Rongji was voted China's new prime minister in March 1998, winning 98% of the delegates' votes in the National People's Congress. Zhu's election came as no surprise, but marked what many believed could be a new era in Chinese politics. He announced that he would serve only one term, and should therefore be able to drive through his ambitious reform plans without needing to be overly wary of making enemies. Zhu stated that he planned savage cuts in China's bloated bureaucracy and intended to overhaul loss-making state enterprises. Millions of state jobs would go during his five-year term.

human rights For the first time since the 1989 Tiananmen Square crackdown, China did not face a motion condemning the country's record at the 1998 meeting of the UN Human Rights Commission. Following in the footsteps of the EU, the USA decided not to sponsor an anti-China resolution, citing improvements in human rights on the mainland. Washington's decision had been bolstered by Beijing's announcement that China intended to sign the UN International Covenant on Civil and Political Rights.

In December 1998, the dissident Xu Wenli was sentenced to 13-years' imprisonment for 'attempting to overthrow the state,' after trying to set up China's first opposition party, the Chinese Democratic Party. Xu had already spent ten years in jail for participating in the 1978–79 Democracy Wall movement.

Dissidents in China in early January 1999 formed an independent labour party, the Chinese Labour Party. Previously, the Communist Party rulers had imprisoned leaders of another would-be opposition group, the China Democracy Party, in its most severe suppression of dissent in three years.

Chinese authorities prepared for the tenth anniversary of the Tiananmen Square killings by blocking access to some Internet sites and closing some foreign television channels. In an unprecedented legal action, an underground network of families who lost relatives in the 1989 massacre submitted evidence to a Chinese court demanding a criminal investigation into the role played by troops and officials. While the action's chances of success in Beijing were slim, the organization would pledge simultaneously to champion it in the international courts. While security forces on the Chinese mainland ensured there would be no mass gathering to commemorate the Tiananmen anniversary on 4 June, officials in Hong Kong did nothing to stop the traditional rally marking the event.

status of Macau In May 1998 a Preparatory Committee for the Establishment of the Macau Special Administrative Region (SAR) was formed. It comprised representatives from China and Macau and would oversee the transfer of sovereignty. By this date, nearly four-fifths of 'leading and directing' posts in the Macau civil service were held by local, as opposed to Portuguese-expatriate, officials. In December 1998 the Preparatory Committee agreed procedures for the establishment of a 200-member Nomination Committee, to elect members of the territory's first government after its handover to China in December 1999.

economic crisis Amidst a global economic crisis in the region, it was revealed in December 1998 that Guangdong Enterprises, the Chinese government's holding company for businesses in the province, had debts of almost $3 billion. This raised fears that China might default on some of its debts or make Western investments worth far less by devaluing the currency. In December 1998 the government announced that the economy had grown by 7.8% during 1998.

In February 1999, in an endorsement of the market economy, it was announced that the constitution would be amended to add the ideas of the late Deng Xiaoping to its state ideology of 'Marxist-Leninist Mao Zedong thought'. In July 1999 it was announced that the country had developed a neutron bomb, and in September 1999 Hu Jintao, the current vice-president, was appointed vice-chair of the Central Military Commission (CMC), which oversees China's armed forces. In November 1999 after 13 years of discussion, a deal was reached to allow foreign firms access to China's markets, in exchange for China's entry to the *World Trade Organization (WTO). In May 2000 a US bill gave China permanent trade status with the USA, and represented another step on the path to China's inclusion in the WTO.

Falun Gong In July 1999, China banned the Falun Gong ('Wheel of Law'), a spiritual movement founded in 1992 that preached salvation from an immoral world and practised a form of martial arts and meditation known as qigong. The ban followed a silent vigil in Beijing in April, by 10,000 members of the movement in protest against what they claimed was official harassment. The government claimed the Falun Gong cheated people and threatened social chaos, and later characterized it as an 'evil cult'. It had become increasingly alarmed at the group's tight organization and the large number of Chinese officials, intellectuals, and party members – up to 700,000 – who had become involved.

The ensuing crackdown, condemned by human rights groups, involved burning the books of the Falun Gong's founder, Li Hongzhi, who was accused of plotting to overthrow the Communist Party, and exposing members. In October 1999, Falun Gong members were arrested after protesting in Beijing's Tiananmen Square, but continued their campaign of civil disobedience.

In April 2000, China succeeded in preventing a UN vote on a US-backed motion condemning Beijing for suppressing religion and crushing dissent. The same month saw further protests and arrests. In early October 2000, members of the Falun Gong demonstrated on the anniversary of China's Communist revolution, and more than 300 were beaten and arrested. In December a further 700 members were arrested. In January 2001, five members doused themselves with petrol and set themselves ablaze in Tiananmen Square; one woman died. The government broadcast graphic footage of the protest as part of its media campaign to legitimate its crackdown on the group.

crackdown on corruption
A government crackdown against internal corruption began in July 2000,

with the execution of Cheng Kehie, a former deputy chairman of the National People's Congress who was convicted of taking bribes worth US$5 million, and was the most senior official to be executed since the Communists came into power in 1949. Human rights group Amnesty International reported in February 2000 that in 1998 China had executed 1,769 people, more than the rest of the world combined, for crimes that included drunk driving and tax fraud. In July, the presidents of China, Kazakhstan, Kyrgyzstan, Russia, and Tajikistan met in Dushanbe, Tajikistan to pledge cooperation in fighting terrorism, religious extremism, and drug trafficking.

The boldest strike against corruption came in September 2000, when the government executed for bribery Cheng Kejie, a former deputy chairman of the National People's Congress, and arrested the country's former second-ranked policeman for dishonesty. The cases coincided with the trials of at least 200 officials accused of evading tariffs on the importing of US$6.6 billion worth of cars, other luxury goods, and raw materials. The first verdicts in November resulted in 14 people being sentenced to death.

In a crackdown on religion in December, the authorities closed 450 unauthorized churches, destroying 210 of them.

military spending In March 2001, the Chinese government announced military spending plans of US$17 billion over the next year, an annual increase of 18%. The announcement followed a warning from China to the USA not to sell advanced weapons to Taiwan. The USA said it would continue to sell Taiwan enough weapons to defend itself.

explosions An explosion in a school in Fanglin, eastern China, killed 41 people, many of them children, in March 2001. The cause was not confirmed, and the government denied local reports that it was an accident with fireworks being made by the children to raise money for the school. Later in the month, four explosions occurred in the northern city of Shijiazhuang, destroying residential blocks and killing at least 108 people. A man was arrested the following week, and reportedly confessed to the explosions, citing personal revenge against some of the residents of the blocks. However, there was concern that he was being made a scapegoat, and the explosions may have been the work of disgruntled factory workers who had caused explosions in the past. More than one million textile workers had lost their jobs since the late 1990s.

US spy plane crisis A US spy plane and a Chinese fighter jet collided in mid-air on 1 April 2001. The fighter crashed and the pilot was killed, while the US EP-3 surveillance plane was forced to make an emergency landing on China's Hainan Island. It was not resolved who was at fault: the Chinese demanded an apology and an explanation, while the USA demanded the return of the plane and its 24 crew members. The apology and subsequent release of the crew occurred on 11 April, but China did not return the US$80 million plane. The crisis was finally resolved on 24 May, when China accepted US proposals to dismantle the plane and fly it out of the country in crates. China had insisted that allowing the plane to be flown out of the country would be regarded as a national humiliation.

tense relations with USA
Diplomatic tensions with the US government, already strained by the spy plane crisis, were further damaged by visits by the Dalai Lama and Chen Shui-bian, the president of Taiwan, to the White House in late May 2001. China protested that the USA was interfering in its domestic affairs.

2000 census Results from the national census, carried out in November 2000, were published in June. The population of mainland China and Taiwan had grown by 132 million since 1990, to a total of 1.26 billion.

China carried out 2,468 documented judicial executions in 2001, about three-quarters of the world's total, according to a report by Amnesty International released in April 2002. The crackdown on crime had led to more than 1,700 people being put to death between April and June 2001 alone.

membership of the WTO
In September 2001, China secured a groundbreaking deal on its membership of the World Trade Organization (WTO), opening the country to unprecedented economic cooperation with capitalism. China had agreed to cut tariffs from 21% to an overall average of 8% and eliminate subsidies for farmers and state-owned enterprises. The agreement ended 15 years of negotiations between the Chinese and the 142-nation WTO. It provided for Chinese entry by the end of 2001, and set a strict timetable to open the country's economy. March 2002, the National People's Congress was informed that welfare spending would have to increase by 28% to combat the effects of unemployment caused by WTO membership.

China: prehistoric and ancient history to 221 BC the fossil remains of the first known inhabitant of China, the famous Peking man, a form of *Homo erectus* who lived about 750,000–500,000 years ago, were discovered at Choukoutien, near Beijing (Peking), in 1927. In November 1998, however, Chinese archaeologists announced the discovery in Fanchang County in east China's Anhui Province of 180 stone tools dating back 2.4 million years. In Manchuria all stages of Stone Age culture from Palaeolithic to Mesolithic and Neolithic have been found; and Neolithic sites have been discovered in the whole range of the Huang He (Yellow River) valley from Gansu to Shandong provinces. There were farming settlements on these sites from around 4000 BC.

The painted-pottery culture of Yangshao (in Henan), from around the 4th–3rd millenia BC, was founded on agriculture and animal husbandry, and used stone and bone implements. It may have overlapped with the black-pottery culture of Longshan (in Shandong), which seems to have flourished around 1800 BC. This period marks the beginnings of petty states in China.

China: late imperial history 1279–1900 for the earlier history of China, see *China: prehistoric and ancient history to 221 BC .

The period 1279 to 1900 opened with the establishment of the vast Mongol Empire and the subsequent Yuan dynasty under Kublai Khan, but his successors after 1294 were less able. The Chinese regained control with the Ming dynasty (1368–1644), although it was more famous for its art and culture than its military might. The Manchu invaded from the north in 1619, establishing the Qing, or Manchu dynasty, (the last imperial dynasty of China) in 1644.

China: history 1900–49 for Chinese history prior to 1900, see *China: prehistoric and ancient history to 221 BC and *China: late imperial history 1279–1900.

the foundation of the Chinese republic After the *Boxer Uprising of 1900 (which had been supported by the empress dowager Zi Xi) the Manchu dynasty was again forced to make concessions in the direction of reform. Between 1901 and 1905 the old civil-service examination system was abolished and military reform promised. After Japan's impressive victory over Russia in 1905 clamour for a constitutional monarchy revived and the court promised steps towards constitutional government. But reforms were made too little and too late. Republicanism grew ever stronger, fostered by the United League of *Sun Zhong Shan (Sun Yat-sen). Risings took place in 1910, but the decisive rising took place in Wuhan on 10 October 1911 under United League leadership.

The movement, which was more antidynastic than republican, rapidly spread, and soon embraced most of the southern provinces of China. In December 1911 Sun Zhong Shan, the inspiration behind the revolution, returned to China from the USA and was elected president of the republic at a convention in Nanjing where the provisional government was set up. Meanwhile the Manchu court had called on Yuan Shihkai, the commander of the modern northern army, who came to their aid on being granted unqualified powers. Yuan's temporizing tactics paid off when in February 1912 the emperor abdicated and Yuan was elected president of the new republic by agreement with Sun.

struggles in the early republic Almost immediately the struggle between the president and parliamentarians began. The parliamentarians organized themselves into the *Guomindang in 1912. Yuan was censured by the National Assembly in 1913 for negotiating a large foreign loan, and in July southern provincial governors belonging to the Guomindang rose against him in a second revolution, which was crushed. Sun Zhong Shan fled to Japan, the Guomindang was dissolved, and parliament rigged.

In 1914 Japan attacked the German-leased territory of Kiaochow and on 7 November captured Qingdao (Tsingtao). Japan also occupied Chinese districts in Shandong, thus violating Chinese neutrality. Protests were met by the notorious *Twenty-one demands, by which Japan effectively demanded the control of China. An ultimatum forcing acceptance of these was delivered to

China on 7 May 1915. Yuan partly accepted Japan's demands and thereby lost support for his scheme to become emperor, which was already halfway to realization. Widespread protests forced him to renounce any such ambition in March 1916 and he died shortly afterwards.

In different parts of country military leaders declared their provinces independent, and set themselves up as warlords. The Beijing government continued, but was ineffective, while a rival revolutionary government was set up in Guangzhou.

the 4th May Movement After World War I the Treaty of Versailles, which the Chinese government accepted and which would have awarded Shandong to Japan, sparked off a movement of protest that was the first to involve ordinary citizens. Known as the 4th May Movement (1919) it was started by Beijing University students and spread to the workers and shopkeepers of Shanghai. The government was forced to dismiss the minister of foreign affairs and two other junior ministers previously responsible for the negotiations with Japan.

The students and their tutors realized that China's backwardness was deep-rooted and that the whole pattern of Chinese feudal thought was an anachronism in the modern world. The student movement then turned to questioning the value of the whole traditional pattern of Chinese thought and custom.

The most remarkable achievement of this movement was the reform of the education system. Hitherto the classical language had been the medium of instruction; now school textbooks were written in the vernacular and a modern curriculum adopted. Within a year over 400 newspapers and magazines changed their style from the classical language to the vernacular, and since then a huge amount of literature, including short stories, novels, plays, and poetry,

has been produced in the vernacular. At the same time proposals were made for the future replacement of the complicated Chinese writing system with a phonetic alphabet. The movement was hailed with some justification as the 'Chinese Renaissance'.

On the political side, it was in this movement that some young intellectuals, among whom was *Mao Zedong, started the pioneer work of organizing first a Marxism study group, and then the Chinese Communist Party (1921), which was soon destined to lead the entire nation on to a totally different road.

the establishment of Guomindang rule The Soviet Union created a favourable impression in China by formally relinquishing all extraterritorial rights in 1923. In contrast the Western powers earned only more ill will by refusing to recognize the Guangzhou government. The Soviets also lent practical aid to the Chinese revolution. In 1922 and 1923 their envoy, Adolf Joffe, met Sun Zhong Shan in Shanghai and Sun accepted Soviet help in streamlining and centralizing the Guomindang organization, agreeing at the same time to cooperate with the new-born Chinese Communist Party (CCP).

Sun now envisaged an initial period of 'party tutelage' of the country, prior to the introduction of democracy. The First National Congress of the Guomindang was held in Guangzhou in 1924, where Sun's 'Three People's Principles' (nationalism, democracy, and people's livelihood) were proclaimed.

The following year Sun died in Beijing while on a fruitless mission to negotiate the reunion of north and south. A second popular movement developed after demonstrating students were shot down in Shanghai by British-led International Settlement police on 30 May 1925, thus giving a boost to anti-imperialism and incidentally helping to prepare the way for the northward drive of the forces of the Guangzhou government, which began in July 1926 under the command of *Jiang Jie Shi (Chiang Kai-shek). Jiang had been head of the Huangpu (Whampoa) Military Academy set up by Sun in 1924 and staffed by Soviet advisers. By autumn the Northern Expedition had taken Changsha and Wuhan, where the Guangzhou government transferred to set in motion a social revolution. In March 1927 both Nanjing and Shanghai fell to the southern armies.

A clash with the foreign powers on account of the murder of foreign nationals in Nanjing seemed imminent when Jiang Jie Shi, who had no sympathy with the leftist government in Wuhan, swooped on his erstwhile communist allies, executed thousands of them, and set up his own right-wing government in Nanjing. After much manoeuvring the communists were expelled from Wuhan and the Guomindang government united in Nanjing. The northern expedition was resumed under Jiang in 1928. In alliance with the warlords, Feng Yuxiang (Feng Yu-hsiang) and Yen Hsi-shan (Yan Xishan), Jiang defeated the local despot presiding over Beijing. The seat of government, however, remained Nanjing. Meanwhile the Communist Red Army had been formed from a nucleus of the old Fourth Army, and communist bases set up in southern provinces relying on peasant support.

the Guomindang–communist conflict The Guomindang seemed now in a position to rebuild China's fortunes, but in fact little progress was made. The warlords who had allied themselves with Jiang reasserted their independence and in 1929 civil wars recommenced. The Guomindang had little popular appeal and Jiang's recourse to a modified Confucianism hardly inspired the youth of the

nation; the more politically inclined among them were more receptive to the call of the beleaguered communists, not only because of their progressive social policies, but also because they alone seemed determined to resist Japanese imperialism, now clearly the biggest threat to China's security.

The Second Sino-Japanese War began when Japan overran Manchuria in 1931, and the next year set up the puppet state of Manchukuo there, with the ex-emperor of China, Henry *P'u-i as titular head of state. They then attacked Shanghai in 1932, and took control of Chengde (Jehol) in 1933, after which they thoroughly infiltrated northeast China.

Jiang Jie Shi's policy was to avoid conflict with the Japanese until internal rebellion had been suppressed. Hence from 1930 to 1934 his main efforts were directed to destroying the communist bases, the main one being the Jiangxi Soviet. Growing pressure on the base forced the communists to break out of the Guomindang encirclement in 1934 and begin the famous *Long March, which took them first to the frontiers of Tibet and then back into Shanxi (northwest China) where they settled at Yan'an (Yenan) in October 1935. From the march Mao Zedong emerged as practically undisputed leader of the CCP.

a united front against the Japanese The troops entrusted with the suppression of the communists in their new base were under Zhang Xueliang (Chang Hsüeh-liang). Zhang had been expelled from Manchuria by the Japanese and was more interested in joining with the communists to fight the Japanese. Hence when Jiang Jie Shi flew to Xi'an in December 1936 to press for an offensive Zhang imprisoned him. He was released only after he had agreed with Zhou Enlai (Chou En-lai), one of Mao's chief supporters in the Communist Party, to form a united front against Japan.

war with Japan The Japanese wasted little time after this pact in manufacturing an excuse to launch a full-scale invasion of China. The *Marco Polo bridge incident on 7 July 1937 provided the necessary pretext. Chinese forces fought effectively, resisting at Shanghai for three months and winning a notable victory at Dai Er Zhuang (Tai Erh Chuang), but Japanese superiority in armament, especially aircraft, enabled them to take all the eastern provinces within the year. The Japanese set up puppet governments in Beijing and Nanjing. The headquarters of the Chinese government were withdrawn westward to Wuhan, and then, when that city fell in October 1938, to Chongqing (Chungking) where it remained for the rest of the war.

At this stage of the war the initiative passed into the hands of the communist armies, organized into the Eighth Route Army and the New Fourth Army, which carried on guerrilla warfare in occupied areas, and at the same time made political gains among the peasants. Hostility between Guomindang and communists soon revived, reaching its high point in January 1941, when Guomindang troops surrounded and destroyed the New Fourth Army headquarters south of the Chang Jiang. In the last years of the war, once Britain and the USA were also at war with Japan (see *World War II), the communists had increasing success in limited campaigns against the Japanese despite being deprived of Allied logistical help, while the Guomindang front was static.

the civil war resumes When Japan capitulated at the end of World War II its troops still garrisoned northern and eastern China, and the communists hoped to take over those northern provinces in which their armies were operating. However, the USA recognized the nationalists (the Guomindang) as the legally constituted government of China, and helped them to take the surrender of all Japanese garrisons by providing an airlift for Guomindang troops. The Soviets, who had occupied Manchuria, likewise refused to yield the cities to the communists. When the Soviets departed, stripping the region of its industrial plant, the Guomindang controlled the key points.

Neither communists nor nationalists could long tolerate the existence of the other. While negotiations went on between them, with the US envoy Gen George C. Marshall mediating, sporadic outbreaks of fighting occurred and both sides jockeyed for position. Marshall gave up his attempt at mediation in January 1947, and open war was resumed. The communists fought the same sort of campaign as against the Japanese, cutting communications, isolating enemy units, and bringing superior force to bear when they chose to fight. Nationalist strongholds in Manchuria and northern China fell one after another.

In government-controlled southern China galloping inflation and the depredations of the secret police did nothing to rally the people to the nationalist cause. Nationalist generals defected to the enemy, and Beijing was handed over intact on 31 January 1949. The newly named People's Liberation Army crossed the Chang Jiang in April and met little resistance in its march south. Jiang Jie Shi fled with his government to *Taiwan, and the People's Republic of China was established in Beijing on 1 October 1949.

For subsequent developments in Chinese history see *China and *Taiwan.

Chinese Exclusion Act 1882 legislation prohibiting the entry of Chinese labourers into the USA. The initial act, passed in 1882 for a period of ten years, was renewed in 1892 and then made permanent in 1902. US immigration laws against the Chinese were finally repealed during World War II.

Chinese Revolution series of great political upheavals in China between 1911 and 1949 which eventually led to Communist Party rule and the establishment of the People's Republic of China. In 1912 a nationalist revolt overthrew the imperial Manchu dynasty. Under the leaders *Sun Zhong Shan (Sun Yat-sen) (1923–25) and *Jiang Jie Shi (Chiang Kai-shek) (1925–49), the Nationalists, or *Guomindang, were increasingly challenged by the growing communist movement. The 10,000-km/6,000-mi *Long March to the northwest, undertaken by the communists from 1934 to 1935 to escape Guomindang harassment, resulted in the emergence of *Mao Zedong as a communist leader. During World War II the various Chinese political groups pooled military resources against the Japanese invaders, but in 1946 the conflict reignited into open civil war; see *China: history 1900–49, **the civil war resumes**. In 1949 the Guomindang were defeated at Nanjing and forced to flee to *Taiwan. Communist rule was established in the People's Republic of China under the leadership of Mao Zedong.

Chirac, Jacques René (1932–) French right-of-centre Gaullist politician and head of state, president from 1995 and prime minister 1974–76 and 1986–88, 'co-habiting' on the second occasion with the socialist president François *Mitterrand. Chirac led the Gaullist party 1974–95, refounding it in 1976 as the Rally for the Republic (RPR), now part of the Union for a Popular Movement (UMP). He also served as the first elected mayor of Paris 1977–95. In 2003 Chirac fell out with US president George W Bush over the US-led war against Iraq, which France refused to support, preferring a UN solution.

Chisholm, Shirley (1924–) born **Anita St Hill**, US Democrat representative and social activist. The first black American woman elected to Congress, in 1969, she served until 1983. In 1982 she ran for the Democratic nomination for president. She was a champion of minority education and employment opportunities.

Chissano, Joaquim Alberto (1939–) Mozambique nationalist politician, president from 1986; foreign minister 1975–86. In October 1992 he signed a peace accord with the leader of the rebel Mozambique National Resistance (MNR) party, bringing to an end 16 years of civil war. In 1994 he won the country's first free presidential elections, and was re-elected in 1999. A pragmatic Marxist, his governments have implemented economic reforms, and he took Mozambique into the Commonwealth in 1995.

Chrétien, (Joseph Jacques) Jean (1934–) French-Canadian politician, prime minister of Canada 1993–2003. He won the leadership of the Liberal Party in 1990 and defeated Kim Campbell of the governing Progressive Conservative Party by a landslide margin in the October 1993 election. Although himself a Québécois, he has been consistently opposed Québéc's separatist ambitions, advocating instead national unity within a federal structure. His Liberal Party was re-elected in the 1997 and 2000 general elections. He retired as prime minister in December 2003, being replaced by Paul Martin.

Christian X (1870–1947) King of Denmark and Iceland from 1912, when he succeeded his father Frederick VIII. He married Alexandrine, Duchess of Mecklenburg-Schwerin, and was popular for his democratic attitude. During World War II he was held prisoner by the Germans in Copenhagen. He was succeeded by Frederick IX.

Christian Democracy ideology of a number of parties active in Western Europe since World War II, especially in Italy, the Federal Republic of Germany, and France, and (since 1989) in central and Eastern Europe. Christian Democrats are essentially moderate conservatives who believe in a mixed economy and in the provision of social welfare. They are opposed to both communism and fascism but are largely in favour of European integration.

Chulalongkorn (1853–1910) also known as **Rama V**, King of Siam (modern Thailand) from 1868. He studied Western administrative practices and launched an ambitious modernization programme after reaching his majority in 1873. He protected Siam from colonization by astutely playing off French and British interests.

Churchill, Winston (Leonard Spencer) (1874–1965) British Conservative politician, prime minister 1940–45 and 1951–55. In Parliament from 1900, as a Liberal until 1924, he held a number of ministerial offices, including First Lord of the Admiralty 1911–15 and chancellor of the Exchequer 1924–29. Absent from the cabinet in the 1930s, he returned in September 1939 to lead a coalition government from 1940 to 1945, negotiating with Allied leaders in World War II to achieve the unconditional surrender of Germany in 1945. He led a Conservative government between 1951 and 1955. His books include a six-volume history of World War II (1948–54) and a four-volume *History of the English-Speaking Peoples* (1956–58). *War Speeches 1940–45* (1946) contains his most memorable orations. He was awarded the Nobel Prize for Literature in 1953.

Ciano, Galeazzo, Count (1903–1944) Italian fascist politician. Son-in-law of the dictator Mussolini, he was foreign minister and member of the Fascist Supreme Council 1936–43. He voted against Mussolini at the meeting of the Grand Council in July 1943 that overthrew the dictator, but was later tried for treason and shot by the fascists.

Ciller, Tansu (1946–) Turkish politician, prime minister 1993–96 and a forthright exponent of free-market economic policies. She won the leadership of the centre-right True Path Party and the premiership on the election of Suleyman *Demirel as president. Her support for a military, as opposed to a diplomatic, approach to Kurdish insurgency provoked international criticism; in 1995 relations with her coalition partners deteriorated, and a general election was called for December. The result was inconclusive and, after prolonged attempts to form a new coalition, she agreed in 1996 to have a rotating premiership with the Motherland Party leader, Mesut Yilmaz. However, this arrangement foundered in June 1996 following allegations of corruption against Ciller. In October 1997 her husband was charged with changing figures on the balance sheet of a US firm owned by the family.

CIS abbreviation for *Commonwealth of Independent States, established in 1992 by 11 former Soviet republics.

Cisneros, Henry (Gabriel) (1947–) US mayor and secretary of Housing and Urban Affairs 1993–97. As mayor of his home city of San Antonio, Texas, 1982–90, he gained a national reputation for being a Latin American progressive in charge of a large American city.

Civic Forum Czech Obcanske Forum, Czech democratic movement, formed in November 1989, led by Václav *Havel. In December 1989 it participated in forming a coalition government after the collapse of communist rule in Czechoslovakia. The party began to splinter during 1991: from it emerged the right-of-centre Civic Democratic Party, led by Václav Klaus, the social-democratic Civic Movement, led by Jiri Dienstbier, and the centre-right Civic Democratic Alliance (CDA).

civil-rights movement US movement especially active during the 1950s and 60s that aimed to end segregation and discrimination against blacks, as well as affirm their constitutional rights and improve their status in society. Organizations such as the *National Association for the Advancement of Colored People (NAACP) helped bring about important legislation, including the 1954 * *Brown* v. *Board of Education* decision, desegregating schools. Further legislation followed, such as the Civil Rights Acts 1964 and the Voting Rights Act 1965, under President Lyndon Johnson. Prominent civil-rights activists such as Martin Luther *King inspired nonviolent protest and helped effect these changes.

Civil War, Irish in Irish history, a conflict, 1922–23, that followed the signing of the *Anglo-Irish Treaty (1921), which established the *partition of Ireland into the *Irish Free State and Northern Ireland. In June 1922 the Irish government, led by Michael *Collins, attacked the headquarters of the anti-Treaty faction (mostly from the *Irish Republican Army (IRA)) at the Four Courts in Dublin. Fighting continued until April 1923, when the IRA gave up the fight. There were over 900 casualties.

Civil War, Spanish war (1936–39) precipitated by a military revolt led by General Franco against the Republican government. Inferior military capability led to the gradual defeat of the Republicans by 1939, and the establishment of Franco's dictatorship.

Franco's insurgents (Nationalists, who were supported by fascist Italy and Nazi Germany) seized power in the south and northwest, but were suppressed in areas such as Madrid and Barcelona by the workers' militia. The loyalists (Republicans) were aided by the USSR and the volunteers of the International Brigade, which included several writers, among them George Orwell.

   chronology 18 July 1936 Military rebellion led by General Franco.
   November 1936 Republicans successfully defend Madrid. German

and Italian governments recognize Franco's government.
   February 1937 Málaga falls to the Nationalists.
   1937 Bilbao, Guernica, and the Basque country are bombed into submission by the Nationalists. By the third week of October, Republican resistance in the north is decimated.
   1938 Air raids are launched against Barcelona, and Cataluña is cut off from the main Republican territory. In September, there is heavy fighting in Andalusia and Estremuda as well.
   January 1939 Barcelona falls to the Nationalists.
   29 March 1939 Madrid is occupied by Nationalist troops. Franco goes on to establish a dictatorship.

Clark, Alan Kenneth McKenzie (1928–1999) British Conservative politician and military historian. He served as a minister of state for defence 1989–92 but failed to achieve Cabinet rank. In 1997 he returned to politics as MP for Kensington and Chelsea. His *Diaries* (1993), a record of his political career, have been labelled as frequently indiscreet.

Clark, Joe (Charles Joseph) (1939–) Canadian Progressive Conservative politician who became party leader in 1976, and in May 1979 defeated Pierre *Trudeau at the polls to become the youngest prime minister in Canada's history. Following the rejection of his government's budget, he was defeated in a second election in February 1980. He became secretary of state for external affairs (foreign minister) in 1984 in the government of Brian *Mulroney.

Clark, Mark Wayne (1896–1984) US general in World War II. In 1942 he became Chief of Staff for ground forces, and deputy to General Eisenhower. He led a successful secret mission by submarine to get information in north Africa to prepare for the Allied invasion, and commanded the 5th Army in the invasion of Italy. He remained in this command until the end of the war when he took charge of the US occupation forces in Austria.

Clarke, Kenneth Harry (1940–)
British Conservative politician. A cabinet minister 1985–97, he held the posts of education secretary 1990–92 and home secretary 1992–93. He succeeded Norman Lamont as chancellor of the Exchequer in May 1993, bringing to the office a more open and combative approach. Along with his colleagues Malcolm Rifkind, Tony Newton, and Patrick Mayhew, in 1996 he became the longest continuously serving minister since Lord Palmerston in the early 19th century.

Clay, Lucius DuBignon (1897–1978)
US commander-in-chief of the US occupation forces in Germany 1947–49. He broke the Soviet blockade of Berlin 1948 after 327 days, with an airlift – a term he brought into general use – which involved bringing all supplies into West Berlin by air.

Cleaver, (Leroy) Eldridge (1935–1998)
US political activist. He joined the Black Panthers in 1967 (see *Black Power), becoming minister of information, and stood for US president in 1968. After a fight with the police, he fled to Cuba in 1968 and Algeria in 1969. His political autobiography, *Soul on Ice*, was published in 1968.

Clerides, Glafkos John (1919–)
Greek Cypriot lawyer and politician, president of Cyprus from 1993. Leader of the right-of-centre Democratic Rally, he unsuccessfully contested the presidency in 1978, 1983, and 1988, and then won it by a narrow majority in 1993 at the age of 73. His personal ties with the Turkish leader Rauf Denktas raised expectations that he might be more successful than his predecessors in resolving his country's divisions, and peace talks resumed in June 1996. He was narrowly re-elected in February 1998, and in March 1998 began talks with the European Union on the country's possible accession.

Clinton, Bill (1946–) born **William Jefferson Blythe IV Clinton**, 42nd president of the USA 1993–2001. A Democrat, he served as governor of Arkansas 1979–81 and 1983–93, establishing a liberal and progressive reputation. As president, he sought to implement a New Democrat programme, combining social reform with economic conservatism as a means of bringing the country out of recession. He introduced legislation to reduce the federal deficit and cut crime. Clinton presided over a period of unchecked expansion for the US economy, which regained global pre-eminence, and he sought, with mixed success, to promote peace and stability in the Balkans, Middle East, and Northern Ireland. He was the first Democrat since Franklin Roosevelt to be elected for a second term. Following accusations of perjury and obstruction of justice Clinton underwent an impeachment trial (the second such trial in US history) in early 1999 but was acquitted.

Clinton, Hillary Diane Rodham (1947–)
US lawyer, Democrat senator, and former first lady. In 1993 her husband President Bill *Clinton appointed her to head his task force on the reform of the national health-care system, but her proposal of health insurance for all US citizens was blocked by Congress in 1994. She was elected senator for New York in November 2000, becoming the first first lady to hold public office.

Coates, Joseph Gordon (1878–1943)
New Zealand Reform Party centre-right politician, prime minister 1925–28.

Cohn-Bendit, Daniel (1945–) German student activist and politician. His 22nd March Movement was prominent amongst the leftist movements that took part in the students' and workers' demonstrations in France in May 1968. Expelled from France on the orders of the interior minister, Cohn-Bendit re-emerged in the 1980s as a prominent activist in the German Green Party, running an alternative bookshop in Frankfurt. In 1998 he was invited to head the French Green Party list for the European elections in June 1999.

Colditz castle in eastern Germany, near Leipzig, used as a high-security prisoner-of-war camp (Oflag IVC) in World War II. Among daring escapes was that of British Captain Patrick Reid (1910–1990) and others in October 1942, whose story contributed much to its fame. It became a museum in 1989. A highly successful British TV drama series called *Colditz* (1972) was based on prisoners' experiences.

Cold War ideological, political, and economic tensions from 1945 to 1989 between the USSR and Eastern Europe on the one hand and the USA and Western Europe on the other. The Cold War was fuelled by propaganda, undercover activity by intelligence agencies, and economic sanctions; and was intensified by signs of conflict anywhere in the world. Arms-reduction agreements between the USA and USSR in the late 1980s, and a reduction of Soviet influence in Eastern Europe, led to a reassessment of positions, and the 'war' was officially ended in December 1989.

The term 'Cold War' was first used by Bernard *Baruch, advisor to US President Truman, in a speech made in April 1947. He spoke about Truman's intent for the USA to 'support free peoples who are resisting attempted subjugation by armed minorities or by outside pressures' (see *Truman Doctrine).

origins Mistrust between the USSR and the West dated from the Russian Revolution of 1917 and contributed to the disagreements which arose during and immediately after World War II over the future structure of Eastern Europe. The *Atlantic Charter, signed in 1941 by the USA and the UK, favoured self-determination; whereas the USSR insisted on keeping the territory obtained as a result of the Hitler–Stalin pact of August 1939. After the war the USA was eager to have all of Europe open to Western economic interests, while the USSR,

afraid of being encircled and attacked by its former allies, saw Eastern Europe as its own sphere of influence and, in the case of Germany, was looking to extract reparations. As the USSR increased its hold on the countries of Eastern Europe, the USA pursued a policy of 'containment' that involved offering material aid to Western Europe (the *Marshall Plan) and to Nazi-victimized countries such as Greece and Turkey. The USSR retaliated by setting up *Comecon to offer economic aid to countries within its sphere of influence. Berlin became the focal point of East–West tension (since it was zoned for military occupational governments of the USA, UK, France, and USSR, yet was situated within what was then Soviet-controlled East Germany). This culminated in the Soviet blockade of the US, British, and French zones of the city in 1948, which was relieved by a sustained airlift of supplies (see *Berlin blockade). In 1961 the East Berlin government began construction on the *Berlin Wall to prevent the flow of East German people to the West.

increasing tensions The growing divisions between the capitalist and *communist worlds were reinforced by the creation of military alliances: the *North Atlantic Treaty Organization (NATO) was set up in the West in 1949, and was followed in the East by the *Warsaw Pact in 1955. Tensions between the two blocs increased significantly at a number of points during the following two decades, and were prompted on the one hand by the USSR's military suppression of anticommunist revolutions – the *East German revolt in 1953, the Hungarian uprising in 1956 and the revolt known as the *Prague Spring in Czechoslovakia in 1968; and on the other hand by US participation in the *Vietnam War (1961–75) and the *Cuban missile crisis of 1962, during which the two superpowers came closer than ever before to nuclear war.

The crisis was initiated by the siting of Soviet rockets in *Cuba in October 1962, after which US President *Kennedy, by means of military threats and negotiation, forced the Soviet leader Nikita *Khrushchev to back down and dismantle the missiles. During the 1960s the *non-aligned movement appeared – a group of nations which adopted a position of strategic and political neutrality towards the USA which was accused of pursuing a policy of US imperialism; and towards the USSR, who was seen to be promoting communist ideology through Soviet imperialism.

During the late 1970s and 1980s, tensions between the two blocs were exacerbated still further: first by the USSR's invasion of *Afghanistan in 1979 and the resultant war which continued until 1987; and then by the aggressive foreign policy pursued between 1981 and 1989 by US President Ronald *Reagan. In 1980 and 1981, for example, the USA supported the newly formed *Solidarity trade-union movement in Poland, and in 1983, Reagan publicly referred to the USSR as an 'evil empire'. The major point of tension, however, arose with the increasing intensification of the arms race (see *nuclear warfare), which placed heavy demands upon the economies of both countries, and was given a quite new direction by Reagan's insistence on militarizing space through the *Strategic Defense Initiative, popularly known as Star Wars. President *Gorbachev's reforms finally fuelled the end of the Cold War: the Berlin Wall was opened in 1989, and subsequently dismantled, and the USSR was dissolved in 1991.

collectivization policy pursued by the Soviet leader Joseph Stalin in the USSR after 1929 to reorganize agriculture by taking land into state ownership or creating collective farms. Much of this was achieved during the first two five-year plans but only by forcible means and with much loss of life among the peasantry. Stalin's ruthless pursuit of collectivization in *Ukraine created a totally artificial famine that led to the deaths of several million peasants. Stalin denied that the famine was occurring, and continued to present the collectivization policy as necessary and popular.

Collins, Michael (1890–1922) Irish nationalist. He was a *Sinn Fein leader, a founder and director of intelligence of the *Irish Republican Army (IRA) in 1919, a minister in the provisional government of the Irish Free State in 1922 (see *Ireland, Republic of), commander of the Free State forces in the civil war, and for ten days head of state before being killed by Irish republicans.

Born in County Cork, Collins joined the Irish Republican Brotherhood while working in London, and in 1916 returned to Ireland to fight in the *Easter Rising. Following his release from prison in December 1916, he became a leading republican organizer and in 1918 was elected Sinn Fein member to the Dáil (Irish parliament). Appointed minister of home affairs and then minister for finance, he continued to maintain a dominant position in the Irish Volunteers (later the IRA) as a director of organization and intelligence. During the *Anglo-Irish War (1919–21) he was noted for his skilful infiltration of the British intelligence system in Ireland and ruthless assassination of its operatives. In 1921 Collins helped vice-president Arthur *Griffith to negotiate the Anglo-Irish Treaty, and encouraged the support of key IRA figures. He became chairman of the pro-treaty provisional government and, during the ensuing civil war, commander-in-chief of the national army which crushed the opposition in Dublin and the large towns within a few months. When Griffith died on 12 August 1922, Collins became head of state but was ambushed and killed near Cork on 22 August.

Collor de Mello, Fernando Affonso (1949–) Brazilian politician, president 1990–92. He founded the right-wing Partido de Reconstrução Nacional (PRN; National Reconstruction Party) in 1989. As its candidate, he won the first public presidential election in 29 years to become the youngest ever Brazilian president, promising to root out government corruption and entrenched privileges. His administration was based on renewed economic stability and sustained development, although his attempts to reduce inflation were unsuccessful.

However, rumours of his own past wrongdoing led to his constitutional removal from office by a vote of impeachment in congress in October 1992.

Colombia country in South America, bounded north by the Caribbean Sea, west by the Pacific Ocean, northwestern corner by Panama, east and northeast by Venezuela, southeast by Brazil, and southwest by Peru and Ecuador.

Comecon acronym for **COuncil for Mutual ECONomic Assistance; or CMEA**, economic organization from 1949 to 1991, linking the USSR with Bulgaria, Czechoslovakia, Hungary, Poland, Romania, East Germany (1950–90), Mongolia (from 1962), Cuba (from 1972), and Vietnam (from 1978), with Yugoslavia as an associated member. Albania also belonged between 1949 and 1961. Its establishment was prompted by the *Marshall Plan. Comecon was formally disbanded in June 1991.

Cominform contraction of **Communist Information Bureau**, organization 1947–56 established by Soviet politician Andrei Zhdanov (1896–1948) to exchange information between European communist parties. The Cominform was a revival of the Communist International (see *International, the) or Comintern, which had been formally disbanded in 1943. Yugoslavia was expelled in 1948.

Commons, House of lower chamber of the UK Parliament. It consists of 659 elected members of Parliament, each of whom represents a constituency. Its functions are to debate, legislate (pass laws), and to oversee the activities of government. Constituencies are kept under continuous review by the Parliamentary Boundary Commissions (1944). The House of Commons is presided over by the Speaker. Proceedings in the House of Commons began to be televised from November 1989. After the 1997 election, the Commons included a record 120 women members, including 101 female Labour MPs; this fell to 118 after the 2001 election.

Commonwealth, the (British) voluntary association of 54 sovereign (self-ruling) countries and their dependencies, the majority of which once formed part of the British Empire and are now independent sovereign states. They are all regarded as 'full members of the Commonwealth'; the newest member being Mozambique, which was admitted in November 1995. Additionally, there are 13 territories that are not completely sovereign and remain dependencies of the UK or one of the other fully sovereign members, and are regarded as 'Commonwealth countries'. Heads of government meet every two years, apart from those of Nauru and Tuvalu; however, Nauru and Tuvalu have the right to take part in all functional activities. The Commonwealth, which was founded in 1931, has no charter or constitution, and is founded more on tradition and sentiment than on political or economic factors. However, it can make political statements by withdrawing membership; a recent example was Nigeria's suspension between November 1995 and May 1999 because of human-rights abuses. Fiji was readmitted in October 1997, ten years after its membership had been suspended as a result of discrimination against its ethnic Indian community.

On 15 May 1917 Jan Smuts, representing South Africa in the Imperial War Cabinet of World War I, suggested that 'British Commonwealth of Nations' was the right title for the British Empire. The name was recognized in the Statute of Westminster in 1931, but after World War II a growing sense of independent nationhood led to the simplification of the title to the Commonwealth.

In 2000 Queen Elizabeth II was the formal head but not the ruler of 17 member states; 5 member states had their own monarchs; and 33 were republics (having no monarch). The Commonwealth secretariat, headed from April 2000 by London-born Canadian Don McKinnon as secretary general, is based in London. The secretariat's staff come from a number of member countries, which also pay its operating costs.

Commonwealth of Independent States CIS, successor body to the *Union of Soviet Socialist Republics, initially formed as a new commonwealth of Slav republics on 8 December 1991 by the presidents of the Russian Federation, Belarus, and Ukraine. On 21 December, eight of the nine remaining non-Slav republics – Moldova, Tajikistan, Armenia, Azerbaijan, Turkmenistan, Kazakhstan, Kyrgyzstan, and Uzbekistan – joined the CIS at a meeting held in Kazakhstan's former capital, Alma-Ata (now Almaty). Georgia joined in 1994. The CIS formally came into existence in January 1992 when President Gorbachev resigned and the Soviet government voted itself out of existence. It has no formal political institutions and its role is uncertain. There is a 2,000-strong CIS bureaucracy in Moscow, Russian Federation.

communism (French *commun* 'common, general') revolutionary socialism based on the theories of the political philosophers Karl Marx and Friedrich Engels, emphasizing common ownership of the means of production and a planned, or command economy. The principle held is that each should work according to his or her capacity and receive according to his or her needs. Politically, it seeks the overthrow of capitalism through a proletarian (working-class) revolution. The first communist state was the *Union of Soviet Socialist Republics (USSR) after the revolution of 1917. Revolutionary socialist parties and groups united to form communist parties in other countries during the inter-war years. After World War II, communism was enforced in those countries that came under Soviet occupation. Communism as the ideology of a nation state survives in only a few countries in the 21st century, notably *China, *Cuba, *North Korea, *Laos, and *Vietnam, where market forces are being encouraged in the economic sphere. China emerged after 1961 as a rival to the USSR in world communist leadership, and other countries attempted to adapt communism to their own needs. The late 1980s saw a movement for more individual freedom in many communist countries, ending in the abolition or overthrow of communist rule in Eastern European countries and Mongolia, and further state repression in China. The failed hard-line coup in the USSR against President Gorbachev in 1991 resulted in the abandonment of communism there. However, in December 1995 the reform-socialist Communist Party of the Russian Federation (CPRF) did well in Russian parliamentary elections, with the party's leader, Gennady Zyuganov, running high in the opinion polls. Reform communist parties have also recovered some strength in other states in central and Eastern Europe, forming governments. In Hungary the ex-communist Hungarian Socialist Party achieved power in a coalition government in 1994; in Lithuania, the ex-communist Democratic Labour Party (LDLP) won a parliamentary majority and the presidency in 1993; and in Poland the ex-communist Democratic Left Alliance (SLD) and Polish Peasant Party (PSL) polled strongly in the December 1993 elections. Communist parties also remain the largest parliamentary forces in Moldova (in March 1998 elections the Moldovan Communist Party (PCM) won the biggest share (30% of the popular vote) and the Ukraine (since 1994 an alliance of communist and socialist parties have formed the largest bloc).

Comoros country in the Indian Ocean between Madagascar and the east coast of Africa, comprising three islands – Njazidja (Grande Comore), Nzwani (Anjouan), and Mwali (Moheli). A fourth island in the group, Mayotte, is a French dependency. Together the islands are known as the Comoros Islands.

Compaoré, Blaise (1952–) Burkinabè politician; president of Burkina Faso from 1987, and chair of the Popular Front of Burkina Faso. An army officer, Compaoré was second-in-command to President Thomas Sankara, under whom he served as minister of state and as a member of the National Council for the Revolution (CDR). In 1987 Sankara was killed in the coup that brought Compaoré to power. Compaoré tolerated the development of multparty politics and his government was not considered severely repressive. He was re-elected by popular vote in 1991.

Compton, John George Melvin (1926–) St Lucian centrist politician, prime minister 1964–79 and 1982–96. He left the St Lucia Labour Party (SLP) to form the breakaway United Workers' Party (UWP) in 1961, becoming chief minister in 1964. After St Lucia left the Windward Islands federation in 1967, he was redesignated prime minister, with the finance and planning portfolios, and guided the country to independence within the British Commonwealth in 1979. In opposition to SLP governments from 1979, he led the UWP to a decisive victory in 1982. He retired in 1996 and was knighted in 1997.

concentration camp prison camp for civilians in wartime or under totalitarian rule. Concentration camps called *reconcentrados* were used by the Spanish in Cuba in 1896, to 'reconcentrate' Cubans in urban areas (and in which 200,000 were believed to have died), and by the British during the Second Boer War in South Africa in 1899 for the detention of Afrikaner women and children (with the subsequent deaths of more than 20,000 people). A system of hundreds of concentration camps was developed by the Nazis in Germany and occupied Europe (1933–45) to imprison Jews and political and ideological opponents after Adolf *Hitler became chancellor in January 1933. The most infamous camps in World War II were the extermination camps of *Auschwitz, Belsen, *Dachau, Maidanek, *Sobibor, and *Treblinka. The total number of people who died at the camps exceeded 6 million, and some inmates were subjected to medical experimentation before being killed.

concordat agreement regulating relations between the papacy and a secular government, for example, that for France between Pius VII and the emperor Napoleon, which lasted from 1801 to 1905; Mussolini's concordat, which lasted from 1929 to 1978 and safeguarded the position of the church in Italy; and one of 1984 in Italy in which Roman Catholicism ceased to be the Italian state religion.

Congo, Democratic Republic of country in central Africa, formerly Zaire (1971–97), bounded west by the Republic of the Congo, north by the Central African Republic and Sudan, east by Uganda, Rwanda, Burundi, and Tanzania, southeast by Zambia, and southwest by Angola. There is a short coastline on the Atlantic Ocean.

Congo, Republic of country in west-central Africa, bounded north by

Cameroon and the Central African Republic, east and south by the Democratic Republic of Congo, west by the Atlantic Ocean, and northwest by Gabon.

Congress of Racial Equality CORE, US nonviolent civil-rights organization, founded in Chicago in 1942 by James Farmer. CORE first concentrated on housing, then sponsored Freedom Rides into the South in 1961 and a lengthy campaign of voter registration. Its work helped achieve such results as the 1965 Voting Rights Act. In recent years, CORE's politically conservative approach has drawn criticism from more militant African-Americans, and its role has been diminished.

Congress Party Indian political party, founded in 1885 as the Indian National Congress. It led the movement to end British rule and was the governing party from independence in 1947 until 1977, when Indira Gandhi lost the leadership she had held since 1966. Congress also held power from 1980 to 1989 and from 1991 to 1996. Heading a splinter group, known as **Congress (I)** ('I' for Indira), she achieved an overwhelming victory in the elections of 1980, and reduced the main Congress Party to a minority. The 'I' was dropped from the name in 1993 following the assassination of Rajiv *Gandhi in 1991, and a small split occurred in the party in 1995.

The **Indian National Congress**, founded by the British colonialist Allan Hume (1829–1912), was a moderate body until World War I. Then, under the leadership of Mahatma Gandhi, it began a campaign of nonviolent noncooperation with the British colonizers. It was declared illegal 1932–34, but was recognized as the paramount power in India at the granting of independence in 1947. Dominated in the early years of Indian independence by Prime Minister Nehru, the party won the elections of 1952, 1957, and 1962. Under the leadership of Indira Gandhi from 1966, it went on

to win the elections of 1967 and 1971, but was defeated for the first time in 1977. It has since held power 1980–89 and 1991–96. Despite Rajiv Gandhi's widow, Sonia, taking on the party's leadership, it finished well behind the Hindu Bharatiya Janata Party (BJP) in the February 1998 general election. In May 1999 Sonia Gandhi resigned as the party's leader after three senior politicians said it should not be ruled by a foreigner; they were nevertheless expelled from the party and later in May Gandhi resumed her leadership.

Connolly, James (1870–1916) Irish socialist and revolutionary. Born in Edinburgh of immigrant Irish parents, Connolly combined a Marx-inspired socialism with a Fenian-inspired republicanism. He helped found the Irish Socialist Republican Party in Dublin in 1896, and organized a strike of transport workers in 1913 with the Irish Labour leader James *Larkin. His Irish Citizen Army took part in the *Easter Rising against British rule in 1916, for which he was executed by the British.

After establishing the Irish Socialist Republican Party and founding *The Workers' Republic*, the first Irish socialist paper, Connolly grew disillusioned with his political progress and moved to the USA in 1903, where he was active in the International Workers of the World. Returning to Ireland in 1910, he became involved in trade-union, industrial, and political affairs in Belfast and Dublin and played a key role in the establishment the Irish Labour Party.

Connolly the international socialist opposed World War I, but Connolly the Irish republican hoped to take advantage of it to begin an anti-British rebellion. Consequently he committed his small Irish Citizen Army to a joint operation with the Irish Republican Brotherhood that resulted in the Easter Rising. Connolly was a signatory of the declaration of the Irish Republic, and was responsible for its more socially radical sentiments.

He was commandant general of the Dublin Division in the rising and was wounded in the fighting. News of his execution while sitting propped-up in a chair was said to have fuelled the indignation of Irish nationalists at the government's treatment of the rebels.

His books *Irish History* (1910) and *The Reconquest of Ireland* (1915), exercised profound influence on Irish socialist thought long after his death.

Conservative Party UK political party, one of the two historic British parties; the name replaced **Tory** in general use from 1830 onwards. Traditionally the party of landed interests (those owning substantial land or property), it broadened its political base under Benjamin Disraeli's leadership in the 19th century. In recent history, the Conservative Party was in power under Margaret *Thatcher (1979–90) and John *Major (1990–97). After the party's defeat in the 1997 general election, John Major resigned as party leader and was succeeded by William Hague, who in turn resigned following defeat in the 2001 general election. He was replaced by Iain Duncan Smith, who was in turn replaced in 2003 by Michael Howard. The party's Central Office is located in Smith Square, London, and the current party chairman is Michael Ancram. In 2001, the party had 325,000 members.

Constantine I (1868–1923) King of the Hellenes (Greece) 1913–17 and 1920–22. He insisted on Greek neutrality in World War I and was forced by the rebel government of Eleuthérios Venizelos and the Allies to give up the throne. He was recalled in 1920 but after a military revolt he abdicated in favour of his son, George II. He married Sophia Dorothea, sister of Emperor William II of Germany, in 1889.

Constantine II (1940–) King of the Hellenes (Greece). In 1964 he succeeded his father Paul I, went into exile in 1967, and was formally deposed in 1973.

Contadora Group alliance formed between Colombia, Mexico, Panama, and Venezuela in January 1983 to establish a general peace treaty for Central America and a Central American parliament (similar to the European Parliament).

containment US policy (adopted from the late 1940s) designed to prevent the spread of communism from the USSR. It was first stated by George Kennan, then director of the State Department's policy planning staff, in July 1947. The policy evolved from the *Truman Doctrine (March 1947), under which the US government justified sending military support to the Greek and Turkish governments against communist rebels.

Contra member of a Central American right-wing guerrilla force attempting to overthrow the democratically elected Nicaraguan Sandinista government between 1979 and 1990. The Contras, many of them mercenaries or former members of the deposed dictator Somoza's guard (see *Nicaraguan Revolution), operated mainly from bases outside Nicaragua, mostly in Honduras, with covert US funding, as revealed by the *Irangate hearings of 1986–87.

convoy system grouping of ships to sail together under naval escort in wartime. In World War I (1914–18) navy escort vessels were at first used only to accompany troopships, but the convoy system was adopted for merchant shipping when the unrestricted German submarine campaign began in 1917. In World War II (1939–45) the convoy system was widely used by the Allies to keep the Atlantic sea lanes open.

Coolidge, (John) Calvin (1872–1933) 30th president of the USA 1923–29, a Republican. As governor of Massachusetts in 1919, he was responsible for crushing a Boston police strike. As Warren *Harding's vice-president 1921–23, he succeeded to the presidency on Harding's death.

He won the 1924 presidential election, and his period of office was marked by economic growth.

Cooper, (Alfred) Duff, 1st Viscount Norwich (1890–1954) English Conservative politician. He was elected Conservative member of Parliament in 1924 and was secretary of war 1935–37, but resigned from the Admiralty in 1938 over Neville Chamberlain's appeasement policy. He served as minister for information 1940–42 under Winston Churchill and as ambassador to France 1944–47.

Cooperative Party former political party founded in Britain in 1917 by the cooperative movement to maintain its principles in parliamentary and local government. A written constitution was adopted in 1938. The party had strong links with the Labour Party; from 1946 Cooperative Party candidates stood in elections as Cooperative and Labour Candidates and, after the 1959 general election, agreement was reached to limit the party's candidates to 30.

Corfu incident international crisis 27 August–27 September 1923 that marked the first assertion of power in foreign affairs by the Italian fascist government. In 1923 an international commission was determining the frontier between Greece and Albania. On 27 August 1923, its chief, Italian general Tellini, was found (with four of his staff) murdered near the Albanian border, but on Greek territory. The Italian government under Benito Mussolini, backed by Italians, fascist and antifascist, sent an ultimatum to the Greek government demanding compensation, which was rejected. On 31 August Mussolini ordered the Italian bombardment and occupation of the Greek island of Corfu. The Greeks appealed to the League of Nations and, under pressure from Britain and France, Mussolini withdrew from Corfu on 27 September 1923. Greece had to accept most of the Italian demands, including the payment of a large indemnity.

Cosgrave, Liam (1920–) Irish politician, Taoiseach (prime minister) 1973–77, leader of Fine Gael 1965–77. Cosgrave signed the ill-fated Sunningdale agreement of December 1973 with the British government and representatives of the moderate unionist and nationalist parties in Northern Ireland. The agreement, which proposed a power-sharing executive in Northern Ireland, coupled with cross-border institutions to deal with security and common socioeconomic matters, collapsed under extremist unionist pressure in 1974. At home, Cosgrave was prepared to make few concessions to reformist opinion on the Republic's social legislation, and even fewer towards traditional republicanism. He presided over severely repressive legislation to curb the Irish Republican Army (IRA) in the Republic, including the declaration of a state of emergency in September 1976.

Cossack people of southern and southwestern Russia, Ukraine, and Poland, predominantly of Russian or Ukrainian origin, who took in escaped serfs and lived in independent communal settlements (military brotherhoods) from the 15th to the 19th century. Later they held land in return for military service in the cavalry under Russian and Polish rulers. After 1917, the various Cossack communities were incorporated into the Soviet administrative and collective system.

There are many Cossack settlements in the northern Caucasus. Cossack movements demand the restoration of their traditional military role (granted in part by a 1993 decree) and collective ownership of land.

Costa Rica country in Central America, bounded north by Nicaragua, southeast by Panama, east by the Caribbean Sea, and west by the Pacific Ocean.

Côte d'Ivoire country in West Africa, bounded north by Mali and Burkina Faso, east by Ghana, south by the Gulf of Guinea, and west by Liberia and Guinea.

Coty, René (1882–1962) French centrist politician and head of state. As second president of the Fourth Republic 1954–59, Coty called on the National Assembly to invest General Charles *de Gaulle as prime minister following the coup in Algiers in May 1958, and backed this with the threat of his own resignation.

Council of Europe body constituted in 1949 to achieve greater unity between European countries, to help with their economic and social progress, and to uphold the principles of parliamentary democracy and respect for human rights. It has a **Committee** of foreign ministers, a **Parliamentary Assembly** (with members from national parliaments), and a **European Commission on Human Rights**, established by the 1950 European Convention on Human Rights.

Coupon Election British general election of 1918, named after the letter issued November 1918 by the ruling Liberal–Conservative coalition under Lloyd George and Bonar Law jointly endorsing their candidates. Asquith, who had been ousted as prime minister by Lloyd George in 1916, referred to this letter as a 'coupon', evoking the language of wartime rationing. The coalition won a massive victory 14 December 1918, securing a majority of 262, and Lloyd George remained in office.

Cousins, Frank (1904–1986) British trade unionist and politician. He was general secretary of the Transport and General Workers' Union (TGWU) 1956–69, and was minister of technology 1964–66 and Labour member of Parliament for Nuneaton 1965–66.

Couve de Murville, Jacques Maurice (1907–1999) French politician and diplomat, prime minister 1968–69. He was minister of foreign affairs 1958–68 and succeeded Georges Pompidou as prime minister. He was president of the foreign affairs committee of the National Assembly 1973–81.

Craig, James (1871–1940) 1st **Viscount Craigavon**, Ulster Unionist politician; first prime minister of Northern Ireland 1921–40. Elected to Westminster as MP for East Down 1906–18 (Mid-Down 1918–21), he was a highly effective organizer of the Ulster Volunteers and unionist resistance to home rule before World War I. In 1921 he succeeded Edward *Carson as leader of the Ulster Unionist Party, and was appointed prime minister later that year. As leader of the Northern Ireland government he carried out systematic discrimination against the Catholic minority, abolishing proportional representation in 1929 and redrawing constituency boundaries to ensure Protestant majorities.

Craxi, Bettino (Benedetto) (1934–2000) Italian socialist politician, leader of the Italian Socialist Party (PSI) 1976–93, prime minister 1983–87. In 1993 he was one of many politicians suspected of involvement in Italy's corruption network; in 1994 he was sentenced in absentia to eight and a half years in prison for accepting bribes, and in 1995 he received a further four-year sentence for corruption. In April 1996, with other former ministers, he was found guilty of further corruption charges, and received a prison sentence of eight years and three months, but avoided imprisonment by living in self-imposed exile in Tunisia.

Crerar, Henry Duncan Graham (1888–1965) Canadian general. Appointed Chief of the Canadian General Staff 1940, he was sent to Britain to organize the training of Canadian troops as they arrived. He resigned 1941 and took a drop in rank to command the 1st Canadian Corps which he led in the invasion of Sicily 1944. He commanded 1st Canadian Army in the *D-Day invasion of France. His force was later involved in clearing the Schelde Estuary and 1945 broke the *Siegfried Line and entered Germany.

Cresson, Edith (1934–) born **Edith Campion**, French socialist politican, the first woman prime minister of France 1991–92. A longstanding supporter of François *Mitterrand, she served under his presidency as minister for agriculture 1981–83, tourism 1983–84, trade 1984–86, and European affairs 1988–90. Outspoken in promoting and protecting French trade, her government lacked clear direction and proved unpopular. Replaced as prime minister by former finance minister Pierre Bérégovoy, Cresson was appointed to the European Commission in 1994. In February 2000 she faced allegations of fraud dating back to her term as education minister, during which time it was claimed that she received large payments from Elf, a French oil company. After Belgium submitted a request to the European Commission, Cresson lost her parliamentary immunity from prosecution.

Crete, Battle of in World War II, costly but successful German operation to capture the island of Crete from the Allies May 1941. Both sides suffered massive casualties, in particular the German airborne forces which sustained a casualty rate of over 50%. *Hitler was so appalled at this that he forbade any further major airborne operations.

Cripps, (Richard) Stafford (1889–1952) British Labour politician, representing Bristol East 1931–52, and expelled from the Labour Party 1939–45 for supporting a 'Popular Front' against Chamberlain's appeasement policy. Prominent in the Socialist League during the 1930s, he was solicitor general 1930–31, ambassador to the USSR 1940–42, minister of aircraft production 1942–45, and chancellor of the Exchequer 1947–50. Knighted 1930.

Croatia Serbo-Croat **Hrvatska**, country in central Europe, bounded north by Slovenia and Hungary, west by the Adriatic Sea, and east by Bosnia-Herzegovina and Serbia and Montenegro.

Cronkite, Walter Leland, Jr (1916–) US broadcast journalist. He was one of the first US journalists to cover World War II, writing about the European front for United Press, a news agency, and was anchor of the national evening news programme for CBS, a US television network, from 1962 to 1981. He covered nearly every presidential election and convention 1952–1980. An influential journalist and public figure, he was identified as 'most trusted man' by the American public in opinion polls during the Watergate scandal.

Crosland, (Charles) Anthony (Raven) (1918–1977) British Labour politician, president of the Board of Trade 1967–69, secretary of state for local government and regional planning 1969–70, secretary of state for the environment 1974–76, and foreign secretary 1976–77. He entered Harold Wilson's first government in 1964, and after holding junior office, he entered the cabinet as secretary of state for education.

Crossman, Richard Howard Stafford (1907–1974) British Labour politician. He was minister of housing and local government 1964–66 and of health and social security 1968–70. His posthumous 'Crossman Papers' (1975) revealed confidential cabinet discussions.

Cuba island country in the Caribbean Sea, the largest of the West Indies, off the south coast of Florida and to the east of Mexico.

Cuban missile crisis confrontation in international relations in October 1962 when Soviet rockets were installed in Cuba and US president John F *Kennedy compelled Soviet leader Nikita *Khrushchev, by military threats and negotiation, to remove them. This event prompted an unsuccessful drive by the USSR to match the USA in nuclear weaponry.

The USSR began sending nuclear weapons to Cuba, a *Cold War ally, in 1962 to prepare for a possible US invasion of the island. Reports of the arms were received in July in the USA, and in October a US spy plane sighted a missile on a launch site. The close presence of nuclear weapons that could destroy the Eastern seaboard within minutes of launching greatly alarmed the USA. After contemplating air strikes or full invasion of Cuba, the USA imposed a naval 'quarantine' (blockade) around the island on 22 October 1962, with the intent to seize any Soviet weapons or military equipment being shipped. The two superpowers came closer to possible nuclear war than at any other time. On 28 October Khrushchev gave way to Kennedy's demands to withdraw the missiles, after Kennedy promised not to invade Cuba. Kennedy also secretly undertook to dismantle US missile bases in Turkey (a US ally that bordered the USSR). However, this was not made public, so most Americans believed that the USSR was forced to back down solely because of US military pressure. On 2 November Kennedy announced that Soviet missile bases in Cuba were being dismantled.

Cultural Revolution   Chinese mass movement from 1966 to 1969 begun by Communist Party leader *Mao Zedong, directed against the upper middle class – bureaucrats, artists, and academics – who were killed, imprisoned, humiliated, or 'resettled'. Intended to 'purify' Chinese communism, it was also an attempt by Mao to renew his political and ideological pre-eminence inside China. Half a million people are estimated to have been killed.

The 'revolution' was characterized by the violent activities of the semi-military Red Guards, most of them students. Many established and learned people were humbled and eventually sent to work on the land, and from 1966 to 1970 universities were closed. Although the revolution was brought to an end in 1969, the resulting bureaucratic and economic chaos had many long-term effects. The ultra-leftist *Gang of Four, led by Mao's wife *Jiang Qing and defence minister Lin Biao, played prominent roles in the Cultural Revolution. The chief political victims were *Liu Shaoqi and *Deng Xiaoping, who were depicted as 'bourgeois reactionaries'. After Mao's death, the Cultural Revolution was criticized officially and the verdicts on hundreds of thousands of people who were wrongly arrested and persecuted were reversed. See also *China, Cultural Revolution.

Cunningham, Andrew Browne (1883–1963)   1st Viscount Cunningham of Hyndhope,   British admiral in World War II, commander-in-chief in the Mediterranean 1939–42, maintaining British control; as commander-in-chief of the Allied Naval Forces in the Mediterranean Feb–Oct 1943 he received the surrender of the Italian fleet. He then became First Sea Lord and Chief of Naval Staff until 1946. KCB 1939, Baron 1945, Viscount 1946.

Cunningham, John (1917–)   British air ace of World War II. He was among the first pilots to be given airborne radar for night fighting. His successes with this led to his nickname 'Cats-Eyes Cunningham', a public relations stunt to conceal the fact that radar was in use.

Cunninghame-Graham, Robert Bontine (1852–1936)   Scottish writer, politician, and adventurer. He wrote many travel books based on his experiences in Texas and Argentina 1869–83 and in Spain and Morocco 1893–98. He became the first president of the Scottish Labour Party in 1888 and the first president of the Scottish National Party in 1928.

Cuno, Wilhelm Carl Josef (1876–1933) German industrialist and politician who was briefly chancellor of the Weimar Republic in 1923.

Cuomo, Mario Matthew (1932–)   US Democrat politician. He was governor of New York State 1983–95. One of his party's foremost thinkers, he was for many years seen as a future president. His key concern was that rich and poor America should unite.

Curragh 'Mutiny' demand in March 1914 by the British general Hubert Gough and his officers, stationed at Curragh, Ireland, that they should not be asked to take part in forcing Protestant Ulster to participate in home rule. They were subsequently allowed to return to duty, and after World War I the solution of partition was adopted.

Curtin, John Joseph Ambrose (1885–1945) Australian Labor politician, prime minister and minister of defence 1941–45. He was elected leader of the Labor Party in 1935. As prime minister, he organized the mobilization of Australia's resources to meet the danger of Japanese invasion during World War II. He died in office before the end of the war.

Curzon, George Nathaniel (1859–1925) 1st Marquess Curzon of Kedleston, British Conservative politician, viceroy of India 1899–1905. During World War I, he was a member of the cabinet 1916–19. As foreign secretary 1919–24, he negotiated the Treaty of Lausanne with Turkey.

Cyprus island in the Mediterranean Sea, off the south coast of Turkey and west coast of Syria.

Czechoslovakia former country in eastern central Europe, which came into existence as an independent republic in 1918 after the break-up of the *Austro–Hungarian empire at the end of World War I. It consisted originally of the Bohemian crown lands (Bohemia, Moravia, and part of *Silesia) and *Slovakia, the area of Hungary inhabited by Slavonic peoples; to this was added as a trust, part of Ruthenia when the Allies and associated powers recognized the new republic under the treaty of St Germain-en-Laye. Besides the Czech and Slovak peoples, the country included substantial minorities of German origin, long settled in the north, and of Hungarian (or Magyar) origin in the south. Despite the problems of welding into a nation such a mixed group of people, Czechoslovakia made considerable political and economic progress until the troubled 1930s. It was the only East European state to retain a parliamentary democracy throughout the interwar period, with five coalition governments (dominated by the Agrarian and National Socialist parties), with Tomas Masaryk serving as president.

Czech Republic landlocked country in east-central Europe, bounded north by Poland, northwest and west by Germany, south by Austria, and east by the Slovak Republic.

D

Dachau site of a Nazi *concentration camp during World War II, in Bavaria, Germany. The first such camp to be set up, it opened early in 1933 and functioned as a detention and forced labour camp until liberated in 1945.

Dahomey former name (until 1975) of the People's Republic of *Benin.

Daladier, Edouard (1884–1970) French Radical politician, prime minister in 1933, 1934, and 1938–40, when he signed the Munich Agreement in 1938 (ceding the Sudeten districts of Czechoslovakia to Germany). After declaring war on Germany in September 1939, his government failed to aid Poland and, at home, imprisoned pacificists and communists. After his government resigned in March 1940, Daladier was arrested by the Vichy authorities, tried with Léon Blum at Riom in 1942, then deported to Germany, 1943–45. He was re-elected as a deputy 1946–58.

Daley, Richard Joseph (1902–1976) US politician and controversial mayor of Chicago 1955–76. He built a formidable political machine and ensured a Democratic presidential victory 1960 when J F Kennedy was elected. He hosted the turbulent national Democratic convention 1968.

Dalton, (Edward) Hugh (John Neale) (1887–1962) Baron Dalton, British Labour politician and economist, born in Wales. Chancellor of the Exchequer from 1945, he oversaw nationalization of the Bank of England, but resigned in 1947 after making a disclosure to a lobby correspondent before a budget speech. Baron 1960.

Dardanelles campaign in World War I, unsuccessful Allied naval operations 1915 against the Turkish-held Dardanelles, a narrow channel between Asiatic and European Turkey, forming a passage between the Mediterranean and the Sea of Marmora and thence to the Black Sea. After a series of unsuccessful naval attacks January–March 1915, the idea of a purely naval attack was abandoned, and instead planning began for a military action against the *Gallipoli peninsula. The only real impact of the naval attack was to alert the Turkish army so that they had time to reinforce and fortify the area before the Gallipoli landings.

Darlan, Jean Louis Xavier François (1881–1942) French admiral and politician. He entered the navy 1899, and was appointed admiral and commander-in-chief 1939. He commanded the French navy 1939–40, took part in the evacuation of Dunkirk, and entered the Pétain cabinet as naval minister. In 1941 he was appointed vice premier, and adopted a strongly pro-German stance in the hope of obtaining better conditions for the French people, with little success. When Pétain was replaced by *Laval 1942, he was dropped from the cabinet and sent to North Africa, where he was assassinated by a French monarchist 24 December.

Darnand, André Joseph Auguste (1897–1945) French admiral and extreme-rightwing activist, founder of the Service d'Ordre Légionnaire (SOL) in 1941 and its successor, the Milice Française in 1943, whose security police collaborated with the German army and Gestapo. Decorated for bravery in World War I, Darnand moved in the inter-war period between the Action Française's leagues, Jacques Doriot's fascistic Parti Populaire Français, and the Cagoule. After the

1940 Armistice he supported *Pétain and joined the Waffen SS as an officer in 1943, taking the oath of allegiance to Hitler before becoming the Vichy minister of interior in 1944. At the Liberation he fled to Germany, was captured in Italy and returned to France, where he was tried and executed by firing squad in October 1945.

Das, Chitta Ranjan (1870–1925) Bengali patriot and politician. He participated in the campaign against the partition of Bengal, chaired the Bengal Provincial Congress in 1917 and the Indian National Congress in 1918. He joined Mahatma Gandhi's noncooperation movement in 1920 and helped form the *Swarajiya Party in 1922. Opposed to Hindu communalism, he was popular with both Muslim and Hindu communities in Bengal. He was elected mayor of Calcutta City Corporation in 1924.

Davis, Angela Yvonne (1944–) US left-wing activist for African-American rights, prominent in the student movement of the 1960s. In 1970 she went into hiding after being accused of supplying guns used in the murder of a judge, who had been seized as a hostage in an attempt to secure the release of three black convicts. She was captured, tried, and acquitted. At the University of California she studied under Herbert Marcuse, and was assistant professor of philosophy at the Los Angeles campus 1969–70. In 1980 she was the Communist vice-presidential candidate.

Dawes, Charles Gates (1865–1951) US Republican politician. In 1923 the Allied Reparations Commission appointed him president of the committee that produced the Dawes Plan, a loan of $200 million that enabled Germany to pay enormous war debts after World War I. It reduced tensions temporarily in Europe but was superseded by the Young Plan (which reduced the total reparations bill) in 1929. Dawes was made US vice-

president (under Calvin Coolidge) in 1924, and he shared the Nobel Prize for Peace in 1925 with Austen *Chamberlain for his reorganization of German reparation payments. He was ambassador to the UK 1929–32.

Dayan, Moshe (1915–1981) Israeli general and politician. As minister of defence 1967 and 1969–74, he was largely responsible for the victory over neighbouring Arab states in the 1967 Six-Day War, but he was criticized for Israel's alleged unpreparedness in the 1973 October War and resigned along with Prime Minister Golda *Meir.

D-day 6 June 1944, the day of the Allied invasion of Normandy under the command of General Eisenhower to commence Operation Overlord, the liberation of Western Europe from German occupation. The Anglo-US invasion fleet landed on the Normandy beaches on the stretch of coast between the Orne River and St Marcouf. Artificial harbours known as 'Mulberries' were constructed and towed across the Channel so that equipment and armaments could be unloaded on to the beaches. After overcoming fierce resistance the allies broke through the German defences; Paris was liberated on 25 August, and Brussels on 3 September. D-day is also military jargon for any day on which a crucial operation is planned. D+1 indicates the day after the start of the operation.

Deakin, Alfred (1856–1919) Australian politician, prime minister 1903–04, 1905–08, and 1909–10. In his second administration, he enacted legislation on defence and pensions.

Déat, Marcel (1894–1955) French politician, a leading collaborator with Nazi Germany. He was minister of labour under the *Vichy government in 1940, and founded the so-called 'unity' party, the Rassemblement National Populaire in the same year. He was condemned to death for treason 1945, but spent the last decade of his life in hiding in an Italian monastery.

De Bono, Emilio (1866–1944) Italian general and Fascist politician. He took part in Mussolini's *March on Rome in 1922 and was later governor of Tripolitania 1925–28. As colonial minister 1929–35, he spent much of his time preparing for the conquest of Abyssinia (Ethiopia), and commanded the Italian forces in Abyssinia in 1935. He voted against Mussolini in 1943 and was shot as a traitor.

Debray, Régis (1941–) French Marxist theorist. He was associated with Che *Guevara in the revolutionary movement in Latin America in the 1960s. In 1967 he was sentenced to 30 years' imprisonment in Bolivia but was released after three years. His writings on Latin American politics include *Strategy for Revolution* (1970). He became a specialist adviser to President Mitterrand of France on Latin American affairs.

Debré, Michel Jean-Pierre (1912–) French Gaullist politician and prime minister. He was minister of justice 1958, the chief author of the Fifth Republic's constitution and its first prime minister 1959–62. He accepted *de Gaulle's negotiations for Algerian independence despite his own attachment to keeping Algeria French. He was later minister of finance and deputy premier 1966–68, minister for foreign affairs 1968–69, and minister of defence 1969–73 before standing for the presidency in 1981, when he was eliminated on the first ballot.

Debs, Eugene V(ictor) (1855–1926) US labour leader and socialist who organized the Social Democratic Party in 1897 (known as the Socialist Party from 1901). He was the founder and first president of the American Railway Union in 1893, and was imprisoned for six months in 1894 for defying a federal injunction to end the 1894 Pullman strike in Chicago. An ardent socialist and union man, he ran for the US presidency five times as the Socialist Party's candidate.

decolonization gradual achievement of independence by former colonies of the European imperial powers, which began after World War I. The process of decolonization accelerated after World War II with 43 states achieving independence between 1956 and 1960, 51 between 1961 and 1980, and 23 from 1981. The movement affected every continent: India and Pakistan gained independence from Britain in 1947; Algeria gained independence from France in 1962, the 'Soviet empire' broke up 1989–91.

Defence of the Realm Act act granting emergency powers to the British government August 1914. The Act, popularly known as DORA, was revised several times in World War I and allowed the government to requisition raw materials, control labour, and censor cables and foreign correspondence. It was superseded by the Emergency Powers Act 1920.

De Gasperi, Alcide (1881–1954) Italian politician. A founder of the Christian Democrat Party, he was prime minister 1945–53 and worked for European unification.

de Gaulle, Charles André Joseph Marie (1890–1970) French general and first president of the Fifth Republic 1958–69. He organized the *Free French troops fighting the Nazis 1940–44, was head of the provisional French government 1944–46, and leader of his own Gaullist party. In 1958 the national assembly asked him to form a government during France's economic recovery and to solve the crisis in Algeria. He became president at the end of 1958, having changed the constitution to provide for a presidential system, and served until 1969.

Born in Lille, he graduated from Saint-Cyr in 1911 and was severely wounded and captured by the Germans in 1916. In June 1940 he refused to accept the new prime minister Pétain's truce with the Germans and on 18 June made his historic broadcast calling on the French to continue the war against

Germany. He based himself in England as leader of the Free French troops fighting the Germans 1940–44. In 1944 he entered Paris in triumph and was briefly head of the provisional government before resigning over the new constitution of the Fourth Republic in 1946. In 1947 he founded the Rassemblement du Peuple Français, a non-party constitutional reform movement, then withdrew from politics in 1953. When national bankruptcy and civil war in Algeria loomed in 1958, de Gaulle was called to form a government. As prime minister he promulgated a constitution subordinating the legislature to the presidency and took office as president in December 1958. Economic recovery followed, as well as Algerian independence after a bloody war. A nationalist, he opposed 'Anglo-Saxon' influence in Europe.

de Klerk, F(rederik) W(illem) (1936–) South African National Party politician, president 1989–94. A pragmatic conservative who sought gradual reform of the *apartheid system, he ended the ban on the *African National Congress (ANC) opposition movement in 1990 and released its effective leader Nelson *Mandela. By June 1991 he had repealed all racially discriminating laws. After a landslide victory for Mandela and the ANC in the first elections open to all regardless of race, in April 1994, de Klerk became second executive deputy president in a government of national unity formed by Mandela. He shared the 1993 Nobel Peace Prize with Mandela for their work in dismantling apartheid and negotiating the transition to a non-racial democracy.

Delcassé, Théophile (1852–1923) French politician. He became foreign minister 1898, but had to resign 1905 because of German hostility; he held that post again 1914–15. To a large extent he was responsible for the *Entente Cordiale 1904 with Britain.

Delors, Jacques Lucien Jean (1925–) French socialist politician, economy and finance minister 1981–84 under François *Mitterrand's presidency, and president of the European Commission, 1985–94. In the latter role, he oversaw significant budgetary reform, the introduction of the single European market, and the negotiation and ratification of the 1992 *Maastricht Treaty on European Union.

Demirel, Süleyman (1924–) Turkish politician, president 1993–2000. Leader from 1964 of the Justice Party, he was prime minister 1965–71, 1975–77, 1979–80, and 1991–93. He favoured links with the West, full membership of the European Union, and foreign investment in Turkish industry.

Democratic Party older of the two main political parties of the USA, founded in 1792. It tends to be the party of the working person, as opposed to the Republicans, the party of big business, but the divisions between the two are not clear cut. Its stronghold since the Civil War has traditionally been industrial urban centres and the southern states, but conservative southern Democrats were largely supportive of Republican positions in the 1980s and helped elect President Reagan. Bill Clinton became the first Democrat president for 13 years in 1993. The party lost control of both chambers of Congress to the Republicans in November 1994, and increasing numbers of southern Democrat politicians later defected. However, in November 1996 Clinton became the first Democrat president since Franklin D Roosevelt to be elected for a second term, winning 31 states, chiefly in the northeast and west. Al Gore, who was vice-president under Clinton, lost the 2000 presidential election to Republican George Bush, Jr.

Originally called Democratic Republicans, the party was founded by Thomas Jefferson to defend the rights of the individual states against the centralizing policy of the Federalists. Democrat government during 1828–60 straddled the demands of various conflicting factions, including states' rights, the issue of Westward expansion, and abolitionism. Slavery eventually emerged as the key issue, dividing the party. The Democrats controlled all the southern states that seceded from the Union in 1860–61. In the 20th century, under the presidencies of Grover Cleveland, Woodrow Wilson, Franklin D Roosevelt, Harry Truman, John F Kennedy, Lyndon B Johnson, Jimmy Carter, and Bill Clinton, the party has adopted more liberal social-reform policies than the Republicans.

From the 1930s, the Democratic Party pursued a number of policies that captured the hearts and minds of the US public, as well as making a significant contribution to their lives. They included Roosevelt's *New Deal and Kennedy's New Frontier which was implemented by Lyndon Johnson. The New Deal aimed at pulling the country out of the 1930s depression and putting it back to work, whereas the *Great Society programme – encompassing the Economic Opportunity Act, the Civil Rights Act (1964), the *Medicare and Voting Rights Act (1965), and the Housing, Higher Education, and Equal Opportunities acts – sought to make the USA a better place for the ordinary, often disadvantaged, citizen.

The Democratic Party has never been a homogenous unit and in the early 1990s it comprised at least five significant factions: the southern conservative rump, the Conservative Democratic Forum (CDF); the northern liberals, moderate on military matters but interventionist on economic and social issues; the radical liberals of the Midwest agricultural states; the Trumanite 'Defense Democrats', liberal on economic and social matters but military hawks; and the non-Congressional fringe, led by Jesse *Jackson and seeking a 'rainbow' coalition of African Americans, Hispanics, feminists, students, peace campaigners, and southern liberals.

Bill Clinton led a reformist 'New Democrat' wing of the party, centred around the Democratic Leadership Council (DLC), which is fiscally conservative, but liberal on social issues.

Democratic Unionist Party DUP, Northern Ireland political party orientated towards the Protestant Unionist community. It opposes union with the Republic of Ireland. The DUP originated in 1971 as a breakaway from the Official Ulster Unionist Party. It was co-founded by the Reverend Ian *Paisley, a Presbyterian minister and militant Unionist MP for North Antrim, who continues to lead it. The party gained 18.1% of votes in the June 1998 elections to the new 108-seat Belfast assembly, holding 21 seats; and took 5 seats in Westminster in the 2001 general election.

Deng Xiaoping (or **Teng Hsiao-ping) (1904–1997)** Chinese political leader. A member of the Chinese Communist Party (CCP) from the 1920s, he took part in the *Long March (1934–36). He was in the Politburo from 1955 until ousted in the *Cultural Revolution (1966–69). Reinstated in the 1970s, he gradually took power and introduced a radical economic modernization programme. He retired from the Politburo in 1987 and from his last official position (as chair of the State Military Commission) in March 1990. He was last seen in public in February 1994. He appointed President Jiang Zemin to succeed him on his death in 1997.

Deng, born in Sichuan province into a middle-class landlord family, joined the CCP as a student in Paris, where he adopted the name Xiaoping ('Little Peace') in 1925, and studied in Moscow in 1926. After the Long March, he served as a political commissar to the People's Liberation Army during the civil war of 1937–49. He entered the CCP Politburo in 1955 and headed the secretariat during the early 1960s, working closely with President Liu Shaoqi. During the Cultural Revolution Deng was dismissed as a 'capitalist roader' and sent to work in a tractor factory in Nanchang for 're-education'.

Deng was rehabilitated by his patron *Zhou Enlai in 1973 and served as acting prime minister after Zhou's heart attack in 1974. On Zhou's death in January 1976 he was forced into hiding but returned to office as vice premier in July 1977. By December 1978, although nominally a CCP vice-chair, state vice premier, and Chief of Staff to the PLA, Deng was the controlling force in China. His policy of 'socialism with Chinese characteristics', misinterpreted in the West as a drift to capitalism, had success in rural areas. He helped to oust *Hua Guofeng in favour of his protégés *Hu Yaobang (later in turn ousted) and *Zhao Ziyang.

His reputation, both at home and in the West, was tarnished by his sanctioning of the army's massacre of more than 2,000 pro-democracy demonstrators in *Tiananmen Square, Beijing, in June 1989. When Deng officially retired from his party and army posts, he claimed to have renounced political involvement, but in 1992 publicly announced his support for market-oriented economic reforms. A subsequent purge of military leaders was later claimed to have been carried out at Deng's instigation.

Denikin, Anton Ivanovich (1872–1947) Russian general. He distinguished himself in the *Russo-Japanese War 1904–05 and World War I. After the outbreak of the Bolshevik Revolution 1917 he organized a volunteer army of 60,000 Whites (loyalists) but was routed 1919 and escaped to France. He wrote a history of the Revolution and the Civil War.

Denktas, Rauf Raif (1924–) Turkish-Cypriot nationalist politician. In 1975 the Turkish Federated State of Cyprus (TFSC) was formed in the northern third of the island, with Denktas as its head, and in 1983 he became president of the breakaway Turkish Republic of Northern Cyprus (TRNC), which was recognized internationally only by Turkey. He was re-elected in 1995 and 2000. Successive talks between Denktas and Greek Cypriot leaders failed to reach agreement on the reunification of the island.

Denmark peninsula and islands in northern Europe, bounded to the north by the Skagerrak arm of the North Sea, east by the Kattegat strait, south by Germany, and west by the North Sea.

Derby, Earl of title borne by the English Stanley family since 1485. Notable members include Edward (George Geoffrey Smith) Stanley, 14th Earl of Derby, and Edward George Villiers Stanley, 17th Earl of Derby. The 18th Earl is Edward John Stanley (1918–), who succeeded to the title in 1948.

Desai, Morarji Ranchhodji (1896–1995) Indian politician. An early follower of Mahatma Gandhi, he was independent India's first non-Congress Party prime minister 1977–79, as leader of the Janata party, after toppling Indira Gandhi. Party infighting led to his resignation of both the premiership and the party leadership.

Desert Rats nickname of the British 7th Armoured Division in North Africa during World War II. Their uniforms had a shoulder insignia bearing a jerboa (a North African rodent, capable of great leaps). The Desert Rats' most famous victories include the expulsion of the Italian army from Egypt in December 1940 when they captured 130,000 prisoners, and the Battle of El *Alamein. Their successors, the 7th Armoured Brigade, fought as part of the British 1st Armoured Division in the 1991 Gulf War.

Desert Storm, Operation code-name of the military action to eject the Iraqi army from Kuwait during 1991. The build-up phase was code-named **Operation Desert Shield** and lasted from August 1990, when Kuwait was first invaded by Iraq, to January 1991 when Operation Desert Storm was unleashed, starting the *Gulf War. Desert Storm ended with the defeat of the Iraqi army in the Kuwaiti theatre of operations in late February 1991. The cost of the operation was $53 billion.

de Valera, Éamon (1882–1975) Irish nationalist politician, president/Taoiseach (prime minister) of the Irish Free State/Eire/Republic of Ireland 1932–48, 1951–54, and 1957–59, and president 1959–73. Repeatedly imprisoned, de Valera participated in the *Easter Rising of 1916 and was leader of the nationalist *Sinn Fein party 1917–26, when he formed the republican *Fianna Fáil party. He opposed the Anglo-Irish Treaty (1921) but formulated a constitutional relationship with Britain in the 1930s that achieved greater Irish sovereignty.

De Valera was born in New York, the son of a Spanish father and an Irish mother, and sent to Ireland as a child. After studying at Blackrock College and the Royal University at Dublin, he became a teacher of mathematics, French, and Latin in various colleges. He was sentenced to death for his part in the Easter Rising, but the sentence was commuted to penal servitude for life, and he was released under an amnesty in 1917 because he was born in New York. In the same year he was elected to Westminster as MP for East Clare, and president of Sinn Fein. He was rearrested in May 1918, but escaped to the USA in 1919. He returned to Dublin in 1920 from where he directed the struggle against the British government. He authorized the negotiations of 1921, but refused to accept the ensuing treaty arguing that external association with Britain rather than the lesser status of dominion was attainable.

His opposition to the Anglo-Irish Treaty contributed to the civil war that followed. De Valera was arrested by the Free State government in 1923, and spent a year in prison. In 1926 he formed a new party, Fianna Fáil, which secured a majority in 1932. De Valera became Taoiseach and foreign minister of the Free State, and at once instituted a programme of social and economic protectionism. He played the leading role in framing the 1937 constitution by which southern Ireland became a republic in all but name. In relations with Britain, his government immediately abolished the oath of allegiance and suspended payment of the annuities due under the Land Purchase Acts. Under an agreement concluded in 1938 between the two countries, Britain accepted £10 million in final settlement, and surrendered the right to enter or fortify southern Irish ports. Throughout World War II de Valera maintained a strict neutrality, rejecting an offer by Winston Churchill in 1940 to recognize the principle of a united Ireland in return for Eire's entry into the war. He lost power at the 1948 elections but was again prime minister 1951–54 and 1957–59, and thereafter president of the Republic 1959–66 and 1966–73.

Dewar, Donald Campbell (1937–2000) British Labour politician, born in Scotland, secretary of state for Scotland from 1997 and first minister of the newly elected Scottish parliament from May 1999. He joined the Labour Party while at university and contested the Aberdeen South parliamentary seat at the age of 27, later winning it 1966–70. Following a period out of Parliament, he represented Glasgow Garscadden from 1978. He was opposition spokesperson on Scottish affairs 1981–92 and on social security 1992–95, and then opposition chief whip 1995–97. He successfully oversaw the passage of legislation in 1997 to create a devolved parliament for Scotland, and in 1998 was elected Labour leader for the Scottish parliament.

de Wet, Christiaan Rudolf (1854–1922)
Boer general and politician. He served
in the South African Wars 1880 and
1899. When World War I began, he
headed a pro-German rising of 12,000
Afrikaners but was defeated, convicted
of treason, and imprisoned. He was
sentenced to six years' imprisonment
for his part in the uprising, but was
released 1915.

Dewey, Thomas Edmund (1902–1971)
US public official and governor of New
York 1942–54. Dewey was twice the
Republican presidential candidate,
losing to Franklin D Roosevelt in 1944
and to Harry Truman in 1948, the latter
race being one of the greatest electoral
upsets in US history.

Diana, Princess of Wales (1961–1997)
born **Diana Frances Spencer**,
Daughter of the 8th Earl Spencer,
Diana married Prince Charles in
St Paul's Cathedral, London, in 1981.
She had two sons, William and Harry,
before her separation from Charles in
1992. In February 1996, she agreed to
a divorce, after which she became
known as Diana, Princess of Wales.
Her worldwide prominence for charity
work contributed to a massive
outpouring of public grief after her
death in a car crash in Paris on
31 August 1997. Her funeral proved
to be the biggest British televised event
in history.

Diaz, Armando (1861–1928)   Italian
general in World War I. After the Battle
of Caporetto November 1917 he
replaced Cadorna as Italian
commander-in-chief and held the
Austro-Hungarian advance on the line
of the Piave. He comprehensively
defeated the Austrians along their
whole line October–November 1918.

dictatorship of the proletariat
Marxist term for a revolutionary
dictatorship established during the
transition from capitalism to
*communism after a socialist
revolution. In the USSR the communist
rule from 1917 till the adoption of the
Stalin Constitution in 1936, was

officially termed the dictatorship of the
proletariat.

Diefenbaker, John George (1895–1979)
Canadian Progressive Conservative
politician, prime minister 1957–63.
In 1958, seeking to increase his
majority in the House of Commons,
Diefenbaker called for new elections;
his party won the largest majority in
Canadian history. In 1963, however,
Diefenbaker refused to accept atomic
warheads for missiles supplied by the
USA, and the Progressive Conservative
Party was ousted after losing a no-
confidence vote in parliament.

Dien Bien Phu, Battle of   decisive
battle in the Indochina War at a French
fortress in North Vietnam, near the
Laotian border. French troops were
besieged 13 March–7 May 1954 by the
communist Vietminh, and the eventual
fall of Dien Bien Phu resulted in the
end of French control of Indochina.

Dieppe Raid   in World War II,
a disastrous Allied attack August 1942
on the German-held seaport on the
English Channel about 305 km/190 mi
northwest of Paris. The limited-
objective raid was partly designed
to obtain practical experience of
amphibious landing techniques and
German defences, but mostly to
placate the Soviet leader Stalin, who
was agitating for a second front in
Europe. The raid was a dismal failure
which cost the Allies heavily in
casualties and strained relations
between Canada and Britain for some
time, although a number of valuable
lessons about landing on hostile
beaches were learned and applied in
the *D-Day landings 1944.

**Dimitrov, Georgi Mikhailovich
(1882–1949)**   Bulgarian communist,
prime minister from 1946. He was
elected a deputy in 1913 and from 1919
was a member of the executive of
the Comintern, an international
communist organization (see the
*International). In 1933 he was arrested
in Berlin and tried with others in
Leipzig for allegedly setting fire to the

parliament building (see *Reichstag Fire). Acquitted, he went to the USSR, where he became general secretary of the Comintern until its dissolution in 1943.

Diouf, Abdou (1935–) Senegalese left-wing politician, president 1981–2000. He became prime minister in 1970 under President Léopold Senghor and, on his retirement, succeeded him, being re-elected in 1983, 1988, and, in multiparty elections, in 1993. Despite a controversial law passed in 1998 making him president for life, presidential elections were held in March 2000 in which he was defeated by Abdoulaye Wade. He stepped down as president and six months later he announced his withdrawal from politics. His presidency was characterized by authoritarianism, aimed at maintaining the dominance of the Senegalese Socialist Party, which Diouf led.

Diplock court in Northern Ireland, a type of court established in 1972 by the British government under Lord Diplock (1907–1985) to try offences linked with guerrilla violence. The right to jury trial was suspended and the court consisted of a single judge, because potential jurors were allegedly being intimidated and were unwilling to serve. Despite widespread criticism, the Diplock courts continued to operate into the 1990s.

disarmament reduction of a country's weapons of war. Most disarmament talks since World War II have been concerned with nuclear-arms verification and reduction, but biological, chemical, and conventional weapons have also come under discussion at the United Nations and in other forums. Attempts to limit the arms race (initially between the USA and the USSR and since 1992 between the USA and Russia) have included the Strategic Arms Limitation Talks (SALT) of the 1970s and the *Strategic Arms Reduction Talks (START) of the 1980s–90s.

disestablishment the formal separation of a church from the State by ceasing to recognize it as the official church of a country or province. The special status of the Church of Ireland, created by Henry VIII in 1541, was a major source of grievance to Irish Catholics in the 19th century and it was disestablished by Gladstone in 1869, with its endowments converted to charitable ends. In 1920, after a bitter struggle lasting over 50 years, the Welsh Anglican Church was disestablished as the Church in Wales; it gained its own archbishop and was detached from the province of Canterbury. There have been several attempts to disestablish the Church of England which would involve the abolition of the Royal Supremacy over the Church and the concomitant right of the Prime Minister to advise the Crown on episcopal appointments.

dissident in one-party states, a person intellectually dissenting from the official line. Dissidents have been sent into exile, prison, labour camps, and mental institutions, or deprived of their jobs. In the former USSR the number of imprisoned dissidents declined from more than 600 in 1986 to fewer than 100 in 1990, of whom the majority were ethnic nationalists. In China the number of prisoners of conscience increased after the 1989 Tiananmen Square massacre. The most prominent pro-democracy activist, Wang Dan, was sentenced to 11 years' imprisonment in 1996 for allegedly plotting to overthrow the government (he was released on medical grounds in April 1998 and allowed to visit the USA).

Distributism campaign for land reform publicized by English writer G K Chesterton in his group the Distributist League, the journal of which he published from 1925. The movement called for a revival of smallholdings and a turn away from industrialization. Supporters included many Conservatives and traditional clergy.

Djibouti country on the east coast of Africa, at the south end of the Red Sea, bounded east by the Gulf of Aden, southeast by Somalia, south and west by Ethiopia, and northwest by Eritrea.

Djilas, Milovan (1911–1995) Yugoslav dissident and political writer. A close wartime colleague of Marshal *Tito, he was dismissed from high office in 1954 and twice imprisoned 1956–61 and 1962–66 because of his advocacy of greater political pluralism and condemnation of the communist bureaucracy. He was formally rehabilitated in 1989.

D-notice in the UK, a censorship notice issued by the Department of Defence to the media to prohibit the publication of information on matters alleged to be of national security. The system dates from 1922.

Dobrynin, Anatoly Fedorovich (1919–) Soviet diplomat, ambassador to the USA 1962–86, emerging during the 1970s as a warm supporter of détente.

Doe, Samuel Kanyon (1950–1990) Liberian politician and soldier, head of state 1980–90. After seizing power in a coup, Doe made himself general and army commander-in-chief. As chair of the People's Redemption Council (PRC) he was the first Liberian ruler to come from an indigenous Liberian group, ending the political dominance of the US-Liberian elite. He lifted the ban on political parties in 1984 and was elected president in 1985, as leader of the newly formed National Democratic Party of Liberia. Despite alleged electoral fraud, he was sworn in during January 1986. Having successfully put down an uprising in April 1990, Doe was deposed and killed by rebel forces in September 1990. His regime was notable for incompetence and a poor human-rights record.

Doi, Takako (1929–) Japanese socialist politician. She was elected Speaker of the House of Representatives in 1993, and led the Social Democratic Party of Japan (SDJP), formerly the Japan Socialist Party (JSP), 1986–1991.

The country's first female major party leader, she was largely responsible for the SDJP's revival in the late 1980s. Her resignation followed the party's crushing defeat in local elections in April 1991. In 1996 she was persuaded to lead the Social Democratic Party (SDP) again in the general election campaign, but could not prevent its support falling further.

Dole, Bob (Robert Joseph) (1923–) US Republican politician, leader of his party in the Senate 1985–87 and 1995–96. He unsuccessfully stood as a candidate for the Republican presidential nomination in 1980 and 1988; in 1996 he captured the nomination, but lost the presidential election to Democrat Bill Clinton. Regarded initially as a hardline right-of-centre 'mainstreet' Republican, his views later moderated, particularly in the social sphere. He retired from politics in 1996 and became a special counsel to a Washington law firm.

dollar diplomacy disparaging description of US foreign policy in the early 20th century. The USA sought political influence over foreign governments (China 1909 and 1912; Haiti 1910; Nicaragua and Honduras 1911; Dominican Republic 1916) by encouraging American financiers to make loans to countries whose indebtedness could then be used to promote US interests.

Dollfuss, Engelbert (1892–1934) Austrian Christian Socialist politician. He was appointed chancellor in 1932, and in 1933 suppressed parliament and ruled by decree. In February 1934 he crushed a protest by the socialist workers by force, and in May Austria was declared a 'corporative' state. The Nazis attempted a coup on 25 July; the Chancellery was seized and Dollfuss murdered.

Dominica island in the eastern Caribbean, between Guadeloupe and Martinique, the largest of the Windward Islands, with the Atlantic Ocean to the east and the Caribbean Sea to the west.

Dominican Republic country in the West Indies (eastern Caribbean), occupying the eastern two-thirds of the island of Hispaniola, with Haiti covering the western third; the Atlantic Ocean is to the east and the Caribbean Sea to the west.

domino theory idea popularized by US president Eisenhower in 1954 that if one country came under communist rule, adjacent countries were likely to fall to communism as well.

Dönitz, Karl (1891–1980) German admiral, originator of the wolf-pack submarine technique, which sank Allied shipping in World War II. He succeeded Hitler in 1945, capitulated, and was imprisoned 1946–56.

DORA in the UK, acronym for the **Defence of the Realm Act**, passed in November 1914, which conferred extraordinary powers on the government for the duration of World War I. Their general tenor was to prevent communication with the enemy, prevent spreading of false reports, and secure the safety of the armed forces, but beneath that lay a multitude of regulations and orders affecting the entire population.

Dos Santos, José Eduardo (1942–) Angolan left-wing politician, president from 1979, a member of the People's Movement for the Liberation of Angola (MPLA). By 1989, he had negotiated the withdrawal of South African and Cuban forces, and in 1991 a peace agreement to end the civil war. In 1992 his victory in multiparty elections was disputed by Jonas Savimbi, leader of the rebel group National Union for the Total Independence of Angola (*UNITA), and fighting resumed, escalating into full-scale civil war in 1993. Representatives of the two leaders signed a peace agreement in 1994. Dos Santos' proposal to make Savimbi vice-president was declined by the latter in 1996.

Douaumont in World War I, French fort near the village of the same name in the *département* of the Meuse. The fort was the scene of heavy fighting during the attack on Verdun and was eventually captured by the Germans February 1916. The village itself was taken by the Germans March 1916 and subsequently changed hands several times before both were finally retaken by the French October 1916.

Douglas-Home, Alec (1903–1995) **Baron Home of the Hirsel;** born **Alexander Frederick Douglas-Home**, British Conservative politician. He was foreign secretary 1960–63, and succeeded Harold Macmillan as prime minister in 1963. He renounced his peerage (as 14th Earl of Home) and re-entered the Commons after successfully contesting a by-election, but failed to win the 1964 general election, and resigned as party leader in 1965. He was again foreign secretary 1970–74, when he received a life peerage. The playwright William Douglas-Home was his brother. He was knighted in 1962.

Doumer, Paul (1857–1932) French politician. He was elected president of the Chamber in 1905, president of the Senate in 1927, and president of the republic in 1931. He was assassinated by Gorgulov, a White Russian emigré.

Doumergue, Gaston (1863–1937) French prime minister December 1913–June 1914 (during the time leading up to World War I); president 1924–31; and premier again February–November 1934 at head of a 'national union' government.

Dowding, Hugh Caswall Tremenheere, 1st Baron Dowding (1882–1970) British air chief marshal. He was chief of Fighter Command at the outbreak of World War II in 1939, a post he held through the Battle of Britain 10 July– 12 October 1940.

Downing Street street in Westminster, London, leading from Whitehall to St James's Park, named after Sir George Downing (died 1684), a diplomat under Cromwell and Charles II. **Number 10** is the official residence of the prime minister and **number 11** is the residence of the chancellor of the Exchequer. **Number 12** is the office of the government whips. After his appointment as prime minister in May 1997, Tony Blair chose to use Number 11 to accommodate his family, using Number 10 as his office and for Cabinet meetings. The chancellor of the Exchequer, Gordon Brown, retained his office in Number 11 but used the flat above Number 10 as his residence.

Downing Street Declaration statement, issued jointly by UK prime minister John *Major and Irish premier Albert *Reynolds on 15 December 1993, setting out general principles for holding all-party talks on securing peace in Northern Ireland. The Declaration was warmly welcomed by mainstream politicians in both the UK and the Republic of Ireland, but the reception by Northern Ireland parties was more guarded. However, after initial hesitation, republican and Loyalist cease-fires were declared in 1994 and an Ulster framework document, intended to guide the peace negotiations, was issued by the UK and Irish governments in February 1995.

Dreadnought class of battleships built for the British navy after 1905 and far superior in speed and armaments to anything then afloat. The first modern battleship to be built, it was the basis of battleship design for more than 50 years. The first Dreadnought was launched in 1906, with armaments consisting entirely of big guns.

Drees, Willem (1886–1988) Dutch socialist politician, prime minister 1948–58. Chair of the Socialist Democratic Workers' Party from 1911 until the German invasion of 1940, he returned to politics in 1947, after being active in the resistance movement. In 1947, as the responsible minister, he introduced a state pension scheme.

Dreyfus, Alfred (1859–1935) French army officer, victim of miscarriage of justice, anti-Semitism, and cover-up. Employed in the War Ministry, in 1894 he was accused of betraying military

secrets to Germany, court-martialled, and sent to the penal colony on Devil's Island, French Guiana. When his innocence was discovered in 1896 the military establishment tried to conceal it, and the implications of the Dreyfus affair were passionately discussed in the press until he was exonerated in 1906.

Dreyfus was born in Mulhouse, eastern France, of a Jewish family. He had been a prisoner in the French Guiana penal colony for two years when it emerged that the real criminal was a Major Esterhazy; the high command nevertheless attempted to suppress the facts and used forged documents to strengthen their case. After a violent controversy, in which the future prime minister Georges Clemenceau and the novelist Emile Zola championed Dreyfus, he was brought back for a retrial in 1899, found guilty with extenuating circumstances, and received a pardon. In 1906 the court of appeal declared him innocent, and he was reinstated in his military rank.

Duarte, José Napoleón (1925–1990) El Salvadorean politician, president 1980–82 and 1984–88. He was mayor of San Salvador 1964–70, and was elected president in 1972, but was soon exiled by the army for seven years in Venezuela. He returned in 1980, after the assassination of Archbishop Romero had increased support for the Christian Democratic Party (PDC), and became president, with US backing. He lost the 1982 presidential election, but was successful in May 1984. On becoming president again, he sought a negotiated settlement with the left-wing guerrillas in 1986, but resigned in mid-1988, as he had terminal liver cancer.

Dubček, Alexander (1921–1992) Czechoslovak politician, chair of the federal assembly 1989–92. He was a member of the Slovak resistance movement during World War II, and became first secretary of the Communist Party 1967–69.

He launched a liberalization campaign (called the *Prague Spring) that was opposed by the USSR and led to the Soviet invasion of Czechoslovakia in 1968. He was arrested by Soviet troops and expelled from the party in 1970. In 1989 he gave speeches at pro-democracy rallies, and after the fall of the hardline regime, he was elected speaker of the National Assembly in Prague, a position to which he was re-elected in 1990. He was fatally injured in a car crash in September 1992.

Du Bois, W(illiam) E(dward) B(urghardt) (1868–1963) US educator and social critic. Du Bois was one of the early leaders of the National Association for the Advancement of Colored People (NAACP) and the editor of its journal *Crisis* 1909–32. As a staunch advocate of African-American rights, he came into conflict with Booker T *Washington, opposing the latter's policy of compromise on the issue of race relations.

Dukakis, Michael Stanley (1933–) US Democrat politician, governor of Massachusetts 1974–78 and 1982–90, presiding over a high-tech economic boom, the 'Massachusetts miracle'. He was a presidential candidate in 1988.

Dulles, John Foster (1888–1959) US lawyer and politician. Senior US adviser at the founding of the United Nations, he was largely responsible for drafting the Japanese peace treaty of 1951. As secretary of state 1952–59, he was an architect of US *Cold War foreign policy and secured US intervention in South Vietnam after the expulsion of the French in 1954. He was highly critical of the UK during the *Suez Crisis in 1956.

Duma in Russia, before 1917, an elected assembly that met four times following the short-lived 1905 revolution. With progressive demands the government could not accept, the Duma was largely powerless. After the abdication of Tsar Nicholas II, the Duma directed the formation of a provisional government.

Dumbarton Oaks 18th-century mansion in Washington, DC, USA, used for conferences and seminars. It was the scene of a conference held in 1944 that led to the foundation of the United Nations.

Duvalier, François (1907–1971) Right-wing president of Haiti 1957–71. Known as **Papa Doc**, he ruled as a dictator, organizing the Tontons Macoutes ('bogeymen') as a private security force to intimidate and assassinate opponents of his regime. He rigged the 1961 elections in order to have his term of office extended until 1967, and in 1964 declared himself president for life. He was excommunicated by the Vatican for harassing the church, and was succeeded on his death by his son Jean-Claude Duvalier.

Duvalier, Jean-Claude (1951–) Right-wing president of Haiti 1971–86. Known as **Baby Doc**, he succeeded his father François Duvalier, becoming, at the age of 19, the youngest president in the world. He continued to receive support from the USA but was pressured into moderating some elements of his father's regime, yet still tolerated no opposition. In 1986, with Haiti's economy stagnating and with increasing civil disorder, Duvalier fled to France, taking much of the Haitian treasury with him.

Dzerzhinsky, Feliks Edmundovich (1877–1926) Polish **Feliks Dzierzynski**, Polish-born Russian revolutionary and founder of the *Cheka secret police, forerunner of the *KGB.

E

EAM-ELAS acronym for *Ethnikon Apelevtherotikon Metopon*, 'National Liberation Front', the largest Greek resistance movement in World War II. It was under communist control. Formed in September 1941; its military wing, Ethnikos Laikos Apeleftherotikos Stratos (ELAS), was founded in December 1942. EAM-ELAS fought rival non-communist resistance as well as Italians and Germans. By German withdrawal in 1944 EAM controlled two-thirds of the country. Attempts to form a united front with the Greek government-in-exile failed, and the British suppressed an ELAS coup in Athens in December 1944. ELAS officially surrendered in February 1945 to the Greek government, but EAM-ELAS leaders continued fighting for the communist cause during the Greek Civil War 1946–49.

Earhart, Amelia (1898–1937) US aviation pioneer and author, who in 1928 became the first woman to fly across the Atlantic. With copilot Frederick Noonan, she attempted a round-the-world flight in 1937. Somewhere over the Pacific their plane disappeared.

Eastern Front battlefront between Russia and Germany/Austria-Hungary during World War I. In 1914 it was effectively the borders of eastern Prussia/Russia, Germany/Poland, Galicia/Poland, and Galicia/Russia. In present-day terms the front ran roughly from Kaliningrad in Russia via Białystok, southwesterly to Torun in Poland, south to Katowice, east to Lviv, and southeast to the mouth of the River Danube.

Eastern Front battlefront between the USSR and Germany during World War II. Initially running along the line of the Polish eastern border agreed between Germany and the Soviet Union in the Ribbentrop–Molotov pact 1939 (more or less where the border lies today), the front fluctuated wildly during the course of the campaign. At the time of the front's most eastern extent it ran from Petsamo in northern Finland, parallel with the Finnish border, skirted Leningrad, then ran southeast in front of Moscow, through Voronezh to Stalingrad, then down toward the Caucasus and looped back to the west to end on the Black Sea close to Novorossiysk.

Easter Rising or **Easter Rebellion**, in Irish history, a republican insurrection against the British government that began on Easter Monday, April 1916, in Dublin. The rising was organized by the Irish Republican Brotherhood (IRB), led by Patrick *Pearse, along with sections of the Irish Volunteers and James *Connolly's socialist Irish Citizen Army. Although a military failure, it played a central role in shifting nationalist opinion from allegiance to the constitutional Irish Parliamentary Party (IPP) to separatist republicanism.

Arms from Germany intended for the IRB were intercepted, but the rising proceeded regardless with the seizure of the Post Office and other buildings in Dublin by 1,500 volunteers. The rebellion was crushed by the British Army within five days, both sides suffering major losses: 250 civilians, 64 rebels, and 132 members of the crown forces were killed and around 2,600 injured. Pearse, Connolly, and about a dozen rebel leaders were subsequently executed in Kilmainham Jail. Others, including the future

Taoiseach (prime minister) Éamon de Valera, were spared due to US public opinion, and were given amnesty in June 1917.

East German revolt 1953, rebellion by the workers against the communist policies of the German Democratic Republic (East Germany) 16–19 June 1953. It was sparked by food shortages in spring 1953 and a subsequent 10% increase in the work norms, the amount of production required from each worker. A strike that broke out on 16 June spread to most of East Germany's industries, and quickly spiralled into demands for democracy. The USSR, which had previously ordered the East German government to compromise with the workers, sent in the *Red Army to restore order. The revolt led to repressive measures and the continued presence of Red Army forces in East Germany until the collapse of the communist regime in 1989.

East Timor in full **Democratic Republic of East Timor**, country in southeast Asia, on the island of Timor in the Malay Archipelago.

Eban, Abba (1915–2002) born **Aubrey Solomon**, South African-born Israeli diplomat and politician. He was Israeli ambassador to the United Nations (UN) 1948–59 and, simultaneously, Israel's ambassador in Washington 1950–59. Returning to Israel, he was elected to the Knesset and subsequently held several government posts, culminating in that of foreign minister 1966–74.

Ebert, Friedrich (1871–1925) German socialist politician. He was the first president of the German Republic, from February 1919 until his death. He became socialist leader of the Reichstag in 1916 and succeeded Prince Max of Baden as chancellor in 1918.

Ebro, Battle of principal battle of the *Spanish Civil War 24 July–18 November 1938, in the vicinity of Gandesa, about 40 km/25 mi south of Lleida. By the time the battle ended 18 November, the Republicans had lost about 30,000 dead, 20,000 wounded, and 20,000 prisoners, while the Nationalists lost 33,000 killed and wounded. This defeat effectively destroyed the International Brigades and put an end to any hope of Republican victory.

EC abbreviation for **European Community**, former name (to 1993) of the *European Union.

Ecevit, Bulent (1925–) Turkish social democrat politician and prime minister (1974, 1977, 1978–79, and from 1999). During his first term of office, he was responsible for ordering the military invasion of Cyprus. He was later imprisoned by the military dictatorship in Turkey in the 1980s. In 1987 he became chairman of the Party of the Democratic Left.

Economic Community of West African States ECOWAS; or **Communauté Economique des Etats de l'Afrique de l'Ouest**, organization promoting economic cooperation and development, established in 1975 by the Treaty of Lagos. Its members include Benin, Burkina Faso, Cape Verde, Gambia, Ghana, Guinea, Guinea-Bissau, Côte d'Ivoire, Liberia, Mali, Mauritania, Niger, Nigeria, Senegal, Sierra Leone, and Togo. Its headquarters are in Abuja, Nigeria.

Ecuador country in South America, bounded north by Colombia, east and south by Peru, and west by the Pacific Ocean.

Eden, (Robert) Anthony (1897–1977) 1st Earl of Avon, British Conservative politician, foreign secretary 1935–38, 1940–45, and 1951–55; prime minister 1955–57, when he resigned after the failure of the Anglo-French military intervention in the *Suez Crisis.

Edward VIII (1894–1972) King of Great Britain and Northern Ireland January–December 1936, when he renounced the throne to marry Wallis Warfield *Simpson (see *abdication crisis). He was created Duke of Windsor and was governor of the Bahamas 1940–45.

Edward, Edward Antony Richard Louis (1964–), Prince of the UK, third son of Queen Elizabeth II. He is seventh in line to the throne after Charles, Charles's two sons, Andrew, and Andrew's two daughters. In 1999 he married Miss Sophie Rhys-Jones at Windsor Castle and the couple became the Earl and Countess of Wessex.

Egypt country in northeast Africa, bounded to the north by the Mediterranean Sea, east by the Palestinian-controlled Gaza Strip, Israel, and the Red Sea, south by Sudan, and west by Libya.

government The 1971 constitution provides for a single-chamber people's assembly of 454, ten nominated by the president and 444 elected (400 from party lists and 44 as independents) by 222 constituencies. The assembly serves a five-year term. The president is nominated by the assembly and then elected by popular referendum for a six-year renewable term. The president appoints at least one vice-president and a council of ministers, headed by a prime minister. There is also a 258-member consultative council (Majlis ash-Shura), partly elected and partly appointed, with advisory powers.

the Arab conquest In 639, during the caliphate of Umar, the second caliph of Islam, an Arab army of 4,000 men was sent to take Egypt, then a part of the Byzantine Empire. They defeated the Byzantines at Heliopolis in 640, and the conquest of Egypt proceeded with very little difficulty, being complete by 642. That part of the population that had adhered to the old gods embraced the faith of Islam, but the Copts remained Christians. The Arabic language gradually superseded Egyptian; it eventually replaced Greek as the official administrative language in 706. In 661 Egypt came under the Umayyad dynasty, that took over the caliphate in that year. They were succeeded by the Abbasid dynasty in 750.

The Christian Copts of Egypt were generally tolerated, although there was the occasional persecution. In 829–30 the Copts raised a serious revolt, and Motasin, the local feudal lord, failed to suppress them. The caliph Ma'mun came to Egypt to assist and the Copts were defeated, and subjugated with great cruelty. Conversion to Islam accelerated after this, although Copts have continued to hold important government posts in Egypt right up to the present day. In 868 Egypt was given as a fief to a Turkish general called Bayikbeg, the son of a slave, who had risen in the caliph's service. In the same year a virtually autonomous local dynasty, that of the Tulunids (868–905), was established by Ahmad ibn Tulun, who even managed to take advantage of Abbasid distractions over a slave revolt in Iraq to annex Syria in 879–80. Following a period of strong government, Egypt declined into a period of instability and power struggles until the appointment of Muhammad Ibn Tughj as governor (896–935). He was followed by the briefly successful rule of the Ikshidid dynasty (until 968), and then in 969 the Shiite Fatimids conquered Egypt. They founded Al-Azhar university in 972 and the present-day city of Cairo (Al-Qahirah, 'the Victorious') in 973, and under the Fatimids Egypt thrived as a centre of literature, philosophy, and science. International trade also flourished, encouraged by the political stability of the country and the laissez-faire policy of the Fatimid rulers.

Saladin and his dynasty In the 1160s the Fatimids were eclipsed by the power struggles between various government officials, who summoned the aid of foreign armies. Thus in 1164 a Christian army from the Crusader states of Syria and Palestine joined a usurper called Shawar, but they were defeated in 1169 by a Syrian army led by Shirguh and his nephew Saladin. Saladin overthrew the Fatimid caliphate in 1171, took the title of sultan, and restored Sunni Islam and allegiance to the Abbasid caliphate in Baghdad. He took for himself the title of sultan, and established his own Ayyubid dynasty in Egypt as well as in Syria, being succeeded by his son Othman.

the Mamelukes The later years of the Ayyubid dynasty are marked by various power struggles. During this period freed Turkish slaves known as Mamelukes formed the sultan's bodyguard and, after the death of the Ayyubid sultan Nagm-al-din, they seized power in 1250, forming a dynasty that was to rule Egypt and Syria for nearly 300 years. Under the Mamelukes Egypt became the centre of power and of Arabic culture, distinguished by major achievements in architecture and literature, in the eastern Mediterranean world. A Mameluke army decisively defeated the Mongols in 1260, at Ayn Jalut in Palestine, stopping the Mongol advance in southwest Asia, and in 1291 the Mamelukes completed their rule over Syria with their capture of Acre, the last possession of the crusaders in the region. However, a variety of factors, including the Black Death, the devastating campaigns of Tamerlane, and the emergence of the Portuguese as rivals in the trade with India, helped to weaken the Mameluke state.

the Ottoman conquest There had long been a rivalry between the Ottoman Turks and the Mamelukes over the control of the region to the north of Syria, and in 1516 the Ottoman sultan Selim I invaded Syria. Selim defeated the Mamelukes and incorporated Egypt into the *Ottoman Empire in 1517.

As a Turkish province, Egypt became something of a backwater, and entered a period of economic and cultural decline. It was governed by Turkish viceroys (pashas), although many Mamelukes still held important posts in both the government and the army. In the 17th and 18th centuries the Mamelukes of this informal elite,

known as beys, entered a period of factional strife among themselves. Although the Mamelukes continued to acknowledge the suzerainty of the Turkish sultan in Constantinople, by the later 18th century they had achieved autonomous rule over Egypt. An Ottoman army attempted to end Mameluke rule in Egypt in 1786, but was unsuccessful.

Napoleon's expedition to Egypt Napoleon's military expedition to Egypt in 1798 was ostensibly to suppress the Mamelukes and restore the authority of the Turkish sultan in Constantinople. However, Napoleon's real ambition was to conquer Egypt and establish a strong French presence between Britain and India. After taking Alexandria, Napoleon defeated the Mameluke army of Murad Bey and Ibrahim Bey at the Battle of the Pyramids. He then established a municipal council in Cairo, and the French exercised dictatorial power. The French fleet was destroyed by Nelson and the British in the Battle of Aboukir Bay in 1798.

Napoleon set off on an expedition to Syria, from where any Turkish attack on Egypt was likely to come. He left French governors in Cairo, Alexandria, and Upper Egypt (the Nile valley south of the delta). The Syrian expedition was unsuccessful, and Napoleon returned to France. The Turks sent a double expedition to recover Egypt by force. The French general Jean-Baptiste Kléber defeated the Turks, and a certain amount of order was restored. Kléber was assassinated, and Gen (Baron) Abd Allah Jacques de Menou, a former French aristocrat who had become a convert to Islam, succeeded in command. His declaration of a French protectorate over Egypt convulsed the country again.

In 1801 the British landed at Aboukir and occupied Alexandria. The combined British and Turkish armies under Hely Hutchinson and

Yusuf Pasha marched to Cairo, and Gen Belliard, the French commander, finding himself overwhelmed, agreed to evacuate Cairo and leave Egypt with his troops. De Menou in Alexandria was compelled to accept the same conditions, and both left for France, thus terminating the French occupation of Egypt.

Mehmet Ali comes to power
Troubles arose almost at once. The Turks tried to exterminate the Mamelukes, and the Albanian soldiers in the Ottoman army rebelled against the Turks successfully, forcing Muhammad Khosrev, the Turkish viceroy of Egypt, to flee. Mehmet Ali (or Muhammad Ali), an Albanian commander, allied himself to the Mamelukes. This was the beginning of further struggles. One faction of the Albanians put Ahmed Pasha Khorshidin (Khorshid Pasha, or Khurshid Pasha) in the seat of government, and Kurdish troops were sent from Syria to Cairo to strengthen Khorshid. However, the Kurds behaved with such ferocity that Mehmet Ali was hailed by the people as their leader and saviour. A furious and bloody struggle took place between the forces of the two rivals. Khorshid was recalled to Turkey, and Mehmet Ali made himself pasha of Egypt.

When the beys (Mamelukes) disputed his authority, Mehmet Ali had them massacred. In 1807 a British force arrived in Egypt. The troops entered Rosetta without opposition, but were trapped in the narrow streets and suffered heavy casualties. Mehmet Ali allied himself to his enemies, the beys, for the purpose of driving out the British, and marched to Cairo, and the British were forced to retire. Mehmet Ali then massacred the remaining beys and made himself sole undisputed possessor of Egypt. He recognized the suzerainty of the Ottoman sultan, and complied with the command of the Ottoman government in

Constantinople to send an army against the Wahabis in Arabia in a war that lasted from 1811 until 1818. In 1820 Mehmet Ali extended his rule into Sudan, intending to control and profit from slave trading and to use Sudan as a source of new army recruits.

Egypt under Mehmet Ali Mehmet Ali now turned his attention to Egyptian domestic affairs. He created for himself a monopoly of the industries of the country, and by nationalizing the land became the owner of all the cultivated soil of Egypt. He started and encouraged the cotton-growing industry in the delta, and ordered the digging of the new canal between Cairo and Alexandria, at a cost of 20,000 labourers' lives. He has been credited with setting up the basis of a modern agricultural and educational system and with making the first important cultural contacts with Europe. Mehmet Ali also reorganized his army, with Arabs and black Africans replacing Turks and Albanians.

The Ottoman sultan also appointed Mehmet Ali as governor of Crete, where he crushed the revolt by the Greeks in 1822. In 1824 a fleet of 60 Egyptian vessels sailed to mainland Greece to assist the Turks against the Greek insurgents. Such was their success that the European powers intervened and defeated a combined Turkish-Egyptian fleet at the Battle of Navarino. In 1833, two years after an invasion led by his son Ibrahim, the sultan appointed Mehmet pasha of Syria and the district of Adana, so that Mehmet now became the sole ruler of a large empire, while he was only responsible for a small tribute to the sultan. In the view of the European powers Mehmet was becoming too strong and too aggressive, and in 1841 they compelled him to submit to certain restrictions. He died in 1849 at the age of 80.

Mehmet's successors Mehmet's son Ibrahim was already dead, so Mehmet was succeeded by his grandson Abbas I. During his reign the railway from Alexandria to Cairo was commenced at the suggestion of the British government. Abbas was murdered by his own slaves after only six years' rule. He was succeeded by Said, the fourth son of Mehmet. During his rule the French engineer Ferdinand de Lesseps obtained the concession for the construction of the *Suez Canal (completed in 1869). The British secured the right to start the Telegraph Company and established the Bank of Egypt. The national debt was commenced under Said, who died in 1863.

Ismail, who succeeded Said, did a great deal to reorganize the government. In 1867 he was awarded the title of khedive by the Turkish sultan, a title also borne by his successors up to 1914. However, his extravagance landed him in bankruptcy, and he sold his shares in the Suez Canal to the British government in 1875, thereby paving the way for Anglo-French control of the khedive's affairs. He was compelled to submit to a constitutional government, but he soon found means of getting rid of it. Ismail was immediately deposed by the sultan in 1879 at the request of the French and British, and his son Tewfik (or Tawfiq) succeeded him as khedive.

Anglo-French control In the same year the British and French established direct financial and political control, the two countries being represented in Egypt by Evelyn Baring (afterwards Lord Cromer) and de Blignières respectively. A movement now began among Arab troops in the Egyptian army to remove the foreigners. The nationalist movement was led by an Arab officer, Ahmed Arabi (better known as Arabi Pasha or Urabi Pasha), who was made undersecretary for war, and then a member of the cabinet. At the instigation of an Arab faction a massacre took place in Alexandria in 1882, and, fearing a serious revolt, both Britain and France sent fleets.

The British government decided to employ military force. The French declined to share the responsibility and Britain acted alone. Troops were landed under the command of Sir Garnet Wolseley, and the revolt was crushed at the Battle of Tall al-Kabir. The khedive returned to Cairo, and a fresh ministry was formed. Arabi was sentenced to death, but his life was spared and he was banished. The task of restoring the country to order fell to Lord Dufferin, the high commissioner, and the practical carrying out of this general scheme was undertaken by Evelyn Baring, who was appointed consul general in 1883.

development under the British The most difficult problem that Baring faced was that of finance. The Convention of London (1885) enabled Egypt to raise a loan of £9 million. In 1892 the khedive Tewfik died, and his son Abbas Hilmi succeeded. Egypt began to increase in prosperity. In 1907 Baring (now Lord Cromer) resigned, having restored solvency, improved irrigation, and arranged the construction of the first Aswan dam, thereby building up a country that was steadily progressing and prospering. The British also helped the Egyptians to suppress a number of rebellions in Sudan, the last being crushed at the Battle of Omdurman in 1898 by Gen Horatio Kitchener, and from 1899 Sudan was administered as an Anglo-Egyptian condominium.

The *Entente Cordiale of 1904 between Britain and France recognized the British occupation of Egypt. Baring was succeeded by Eldon Gorst in 1907, and the resignation of Gorst in 1911 was followed by the appointment of Kitchener as British agent and consul general. Under Kitchener the policy of his predecessor was to a certain extent reversed, and any measure of independence that Egyptian ministers had previously enjoyed was withdrawn.

Egypt in World War I World War I brought Kitchener back to Britain, and in August 1914 he became secretary of state for war. Great Britain declared war on Turkey in November. This was followed in December by Britain declaring Egypt to be a British protectorate. The khedive Abbas Hilmi was deposed and his uncle, Hussein Kamil (or Kamel), was proclaimed sultan of Egypt, so ending Turkey's nominal sovereignty over Egypt. In October 1917 Hussein Kamil died and was succeeded by his brother, Ahmed Fuad. Throughout the war Egypt was used as a base for British military operations against the Turks in the Middle East, and the Suez Canal was successfully defended against a Turkish attack in 1915.

nominal independence Following World War I there was a resurgence of Egyptian nationalism led by Saad Zaghlul Pasha, a former minister of education and minister of justice, who in 1918 demanded complete independence for Egypt. The British government recalled the high commissioner and exiled Zaghlul and other leading nationalists. Rioting and strikes followed, but Field Marshal *Allenby, who had been appointed special high commissioner, succeeded in restoring order, and Zaghlul and his fellow exiles were allowed to return to Egypt. Acting on Allenby's recommendation, the British government proclaimed the end of the British protectorate, and Egypt was recognized as an independent sovereign state in February 1922.

This proclamation was subsequently ratified by the British Parliament, but Egypt's independence was qualified by the reservation of certain points for later settlement. Thus Britain retained control over Sudan and the defence of Egypt against foreign attack, and also retained the right to protect European

interests and to protect the security of communications between various parts of the British Empire (most importantly the Suez Canal). The sultan Ahmed Fuad became King Fuad I. In April 1923 the constitution of the kingdom of Egypt as a hereditary constitutional monarchy was proclaimed.

nationalist agitation and further autonomy In the following period there was a struggle for power between the king, the nationalist *Wafd party (led by Zaghlul Pasha and then by Nahas Pasha), and the British. It led to violence, and in November 1924 Gen Sir Lee Stack, governor general of the Sudan, was assassinated by Egyptian nationalists in Cairo. The British government insisted on the withdrawal of detachments of Egyptian troops from Sudan.

Four years later, in 1928, the Muslim Brotherhood was founded by Hasan al-Banna as an Islamic revivalist movement. It was to become an increasingly politicized and activist Arab nationalist movement after 1938, calling for the establishment of a Muslim state governed by Islamic law. It was eventually banned after an assassination attempt on Prime Minister Gamal Nasser in 1954. It continued to be very powerful through the social programmes it operated among the poor.

Egyptian nationalism continued to increase during the interwar years among the people, but as yet the movement was largely unorganized and unstable and could only express itself in isolated acts of violence. The accession of an inept monarch, Farouk, in 1936 was to give this nationalism a left-wing direction that would transform it completely.

In August 1936 an Anglo-Egyptian treaty of alliance was signed, by which Britain agreed to recognize Egypt's full independence, announcing a phased withdrawal of British forces over 20 years, except from the Suez Canal

Zone, Alexandria, and Port Said, where Britain had naval bases. By the Convention of Montreux of May 1937, Britain recognized that the responsibility for the lives and property of foreigners in Egypt belonged to the Egyptian government.

Egypt in World War II During World War II Germany and Italy made every effort to persuade Egypt to betray Britain, but Egypt as a whole stood by its treaty obligations. Until the middle of 1942 there was no definite military threat to Egypt proper, although in 1940 the Italian forces of Gen Graziani had reached Sidi Barrani. But at the beginning of July 1942 German and Italian forces under Erwin Rommel were actually marching on the Nile delta, and for some days the military position was precarious. However, the Axis advance was held by the British 8th Army at the First Battle of El *Alamein, and the tide turned after the Second Battle. For more details of the North Africa Campaign, see *World War II.

Although Egypt did not take an active military part in the war, it severed diplomatic relations with the Axis powers. Under the Anglo-Egyptian Treaty of 1936 it was not obliged to make active war upon Britain's enemies, and the Egyptian army was not in a condition to take on the Italians or the Germans. Moreover it was an open secret that some of the Egyptian army leaders with good connections in the palace favoured the Axis, whose political principles appealed to them more than those of the Western democracies. Indeed, it was from the palace that the chief opposition came to cooperation with the Allies throughout the war.

The crisis came in February 1942 when the British 8th Army had just been driven back from Libya into Egypt for the second time. It was then that the British ambassador demanded an audience with King Farouk and supported his demands by surrounding the Abdin Palace with British troops. It was on the ambassador's insistence that the king appointed Nahas Pasha as premier. Although Nahas was the leader of the nationalist Wafd, the British calculated that as Nahas had signed the Anglo-Egyptian Treaty he might be most relied upon to uphold its terms. Nahas continued in power for the ensuing two years, in face of increasing political and economic difficulties, until a corruption scandal gave the king an opportunity to dismiss him and his party.

agitation for British withdrawal In December 1945 the Egyptian government demanded a revision of the 1936 treaty, stating that it had been made in the midst of an international crisis and that the war had exhausted the treaty's principal objectives. The Egyptian government also declared that the presence of foreign troops was wounding to national dignity and could only be interpreted by public opinion as a tangible sign of mutual mistrust. Britain expressed its willingness to discuss the matter, but things did not move swiftly enough for the nationalists, who were now far stronger and more organized and articulate than in prewar days. There were serious anti-British riots, with loss of life and property, in Cairo and Alexandria.

In January 1947 the Egyptian government broke off negotiations with Britain, and later appealed to the Security Council of the United Nations (UN) to instruct Britain to withdraw troops from Egypt and Sudan, and also to withdraw the existing administrative regime in Anglo-Egyptian Sudan. The Security Council, however, did not make any recommendation. Nevertheless the British government evacuated its troops from Alexandria and Cairo early in 1947.

the First Arab–Israeli War Egypt was involved in the Arab–Jewish struggle over the partitioning of Palestine, which had been administered by Britain under a League of Nations mandate since the end of World War I. Partition of the territory between Arabs and Jewish settlers was recommended in November 1947 by a committee appointed by the General Assembly of the UN, but the Arab League refused to recognize partition. Following the termination of the British mandate and the declaration by Jewish settlers of the state of Israel, Egyptian troops invaded the territory in the south, while the Transjordan Arab Legion and Syrian and Lebanese troops invaded from the north and east in May 1948. A truce was agreed in June, by which date the Egyptian army had reached Isdud, 32 km/20 mi south of Tel Aviv, and occupied positions running southeast from Magdala through Faluja to Beersheba and linked up with the Arab Legion at Bethlehem.

When hostilities were resumed the Arabs sustained several defeats and accepted a renewal of the ceasefire in July. Israeli troops then decided to take the offensive against Egypt and a large Egyptian force was surrounded at Faluja, 32 km/20 mi northeast of Gaza. Egypt then became the sole target of Israeli pressure. Israeli troops entered Egyptian territory in December but were driven back and a truce was finally arranged for January 1949, and a general armistice was signed in Rhodes in February.

Nasser comes to power In effect the Egyptian army had been decisively defeated in the war, in part because of an arms scandal. King Farouk was blamed for his failure to prevent the creation of Israel, and his position was undermined. Anti-British demonstrations reached a climax in January 1952 with violent riots in Cairo, and in July 1952 a group of radical army officers, calling themselves the Free Officers, carried out a bloodless coup. The coup had

popular backing, and resulted in the abdication of King Farouk. The 1923 constitution was suspended and all political parties were banned.

For a short time Farouk's infant son Ahmed Fuad II reigned, but in June 1953 Gen Muhammad Neguib proclaimed Egypt a republic with himself as president and prime minister. In less than a year (April 1954) he was compelled to resign his official offices by the Revolutionary Council after a power struggle with Lt Col Gamal Abdel *Nasser, the real leader of the coup, and ceased to be president. A council of ministers carried on the affairs of state until March 1956, when a government was formed with Nasser as prime minister. The same year the presidency was strengthened by a new constitution, and Nasser was elected president, unopposed.

towards the Suez Crisis
In February 1953 an Anglo-Egyptian agreement was signed, ending the condominium of Sudan. In October 1954 another agreement was signed for the withdrawal of British troops from the Suez Canal Zone (which took place in 1956). At home Nasser embarked on a programme of social reform, which included setting close limits on land-holding to benefit the cultivator class and expanding educational opportunities, saddling the country with a vast student population and an inflated bureaucracy to provide them with employment. Abroad he began to assert his position both in the Arab and the developing world, becoming a major force for Arab unity and a leader of the *non-aligned movement.

Meanwhile, in December 1955 it was announced that the USA and the UK would give Egypt financial support for the construction of the proposed Aswan High Dam. There were formal qualifications regarding ratifications by the governments concerned. Further sums of money in support of the project were expected, and indeed assured, by the World Bank. The initial sum of money involved was estimated at $1,300,000.

In July 1956 the offer of assistance was suddenly withdrawn by both the USA and the UK as 'not being feasible in the present circumstances'. These 'circumstances' were presumably associated with Egypt's acceptance of military equipment and military advice from the Communist bloc and Nasser's changing role from that of a conventional president to that of a dictator. Nasser's reaction was decisive. In July, in Alexandria, he announced that the Egyptian government had nationalized the Suez Canal Company.

Suez and the Second Arab–Israeli War The seizure of the canal was regarded as illegal in Western Europe and the USA, but it was soon obvious that no effective joint action by the protesting states against Egypt was possible. Only in Britain and France was there any serious demand for stern action against Egypt.

Israel, provoked by frequent Egyptian raids into its territory, reached a secret understanding with Britain and France, and invaded Egypt in October 1956, advancing into Sinai with the avowed purpose of destroying Egyptian strong points and other places from which the raids were taking place. The Egyptian forces in Sinai were defeated, although the political gains for Egypt were considerable, as Israel was seen as the aggressor.

France and Britain called on both belligerents to cease fighting, and when this did not occur a joint Anglo-French force invaded Egypt from the air and occupied Port Said (5–6 November). The British and French governments claimed their main objective was the protection of the Suez Canal, free navigation of which was threatened by the invading Israeli forces. The Egyptian air force suffered crippling destruction on the ground, and, although there was some organized resistance to the Anglo-French force, the latter could probably have occupied the whole length of the canal. The Anglo-French action resulted in Egypt's blocking the Suez Canal and making it impassable, the very thing that Britain and France had tried to avoid.

World opinion, with which both the USA and USSR concurred, was ranged against this use of force by the UK and France, and Western influence in the Middle East was destroyed for several years as the result of their action. Britain, France, and Israel were branded as aggressors at the UN and called upon to cease their military activities. US pressure brought about an Anglo-French withdrawal in December, and Israeli forces withdrew in March 1957. A UN force was organized to safeguard the canal from further attacks and to prevent further outbreaks of violence between Israel and Egypt in Sinai. The blockships sunk by Egypt in the canal were later removed by engineers acting under orders from the UN, and the canal was reopened in March 1957.

The apparent success of Nasser's policy in the UN, and the fait accompli of his seizure of the canal, more than outweighed the effect of Egypt's military defeats. Nasser's, and thus Egypt's, prestige soared within the Arab world. The Anglo-French action pushed Egypt into closer dependence on the Soviet bloc, obliging the USA to realign its policy in the Middle East. Another consequence was the confiscation of property owned by British and French nationals in Egypt.

attempts at union In February 1958 Egypt and Syria proclaimed the union of their two countries, under the name of the United Arab Republic (UAR), and with Nasser as president. Yemen subsequently joined the union. Egypt retained the name 'United Arab Republic' until 1971, when it became the 'Arab Republic of Egypt'. The UAR collapsed with Syria's withdrawal in 1961, due to Syrian resentment of Egyptian domination in the centralized state that they had created. After its failure Nasser attempted to create a second merger, but this time on federal lines. In April 1963 an agreement signed in Cairo between the UAR, Iraq, and Syria appeared to do this, but the new federation never had any reality.

relations with the Arab world and in Africa Nevertheless, despite these setbacks, Nasser's position as leader of Arab nationalism remained virtually unchallenged. Gradually, however, his left-wing and interventionist attitudes alienated several other Arab states. Jordan had never been on good terms with him, and Saudi Arabia became increasingly hostile. When Nasser supported the republican side in the civil war in North Yemen, Saudi Arabia countered by aiding the Yemeni royalists. This produced a stalemate that was most damaging to UAR interests and prestige. It seriously bogged down a whole army and contributed to the defeat in the 1967 war with Israel. In addition, Morocco and Tunisia were not prepared to accept the implications of Nasser's anti-Israel policies, and Iraq embarked on policies that were independent of the UAR, whose influence appeared increasingly confined to the 'left fringe' of Arab politics.

The UAR used both the UN General Assembly and the Organization of African Unity (OAU; later African Union) to propagate its views, and for some years held a unique position in African affairs. Nasser established close personal links with President Nkrumah of Ghana, and this alliance long seemed formidable. But Nkrumah's overthrow in 1966 and Ghana's subsequent immediate withdrawal from the UAR orbit illustrated the weakness of this connection; few other African political leaders were prepared to subscribe fully to the UAR's particular interpretation of pan-Africanism. The majority of African states did not follow the UAR in breaking off diplomatic relations with Britain over the Rhodesia issue in December 1965 (see *Zimbabwe).

domestic affairs under Nasser Nasser carried through many social reforms in Egypt, redistributing land, nationalizing the economy, and establishing in 1962 the sole political organization, the Arab Socialist Union (ASU). The Aswan High Dam, on which work began in January 1961, was intended to revolutionize Egypt's economy and to solve some of the country's serious energy and agricultural problems (it also created unforeseen ecological problems for the future). But by the end of 1966 the state of the country had deteriorated badly, not least because of Egypt's rapidly growing population (nearing 60 million). Another factor was Egypt's involvement in the North Yemen civil war, which was a major economic and military drain on Egypt's energies until troops were finally withdrawn in 1967.

the Third Arab–Israeli War and its aftermath This period came to a climax with the major miscalculation of the 1967 war with Israel. Mounting tensions between Israel and its Arab neighbours led Egypt into a military alliance with Syria and Jordan. Egypt blocked the Strait of Tiran (Israel's only means of access to the Red Sea) and ordered the withdrawal of the UN Emergency Force in Sinai. Israel's response was a devastating surprise attack, which effectively destroyed the armed forces of Egypt, Jordan, and Syria in six days. Sinai was occupied by Israeli forces up to the Suez Canal.

Nasser offered to resign but was prevented by popular acclaim. He retained his authority in Egypt and the Arab world, although, inevitably, it was somewhat diminished. He was faced with a formidable array of problems: keeping the military pressure on Israel (which involved increasing the Soviet military presence in Egypt); searching for some diplomatic means of obtaining Israel's withdrawal; and domestic political and economic problems. There were serious demonstrations in November 1968 in Alexandria and El Mansûra. Nasser's death in 1970 was an occasion of national grief.

Sadat assumes the presidency

Nasser was succeeded as president by his vice-president, Col Anwar *Sadat. In 1971 the title Arab Republic of Egypt was adopted. Sadat continued Nasser's policy of promoting Arab unity, but proposals to create a federation of Egypt, Libya, and Syria again failed.

In May 1971 Sadat successfully resisted a challenge to his authority from the vice-president Ali Sabri, supported by the war minister Gen Fauzi. Thereafter Sadat, while publicly maintaining adherence to Nasserism, set about modifying the Egyptian economic and social structure. In 1971 the country's first permanent constitution was introduced, containing measures of liberalization, in particular in the field of civil rights. However Sadat frequently protested that the same year would see decisive action taken against Israel. Considerable unrest followed when nothing happened.

In 1972 Sadat reversed Egypt's dependence on the Soviet Union by dismissing the 20,000 Russian military advisers present in the country. In a deadlocked position of neither war nor peace (which obviously benefited Israel) Sadat faced much criticism and numerous disturbances. In March 1973 Sadat assumed the office of prime minister together with the presidency he already held. Meanwhile he carefully cultivated good relations with Saudi Arabia, and transformed his position within Egypt and the Arab world by launching an unexpected war against Israel in October 1973.

the Fourth Arab–Israeli War

On 6 October 1973 Egyptian forces swept across the Suez Canal to attack the Israelis occupying Sinai. Syria immediately joined Egypt and within a few days Jordan, Iraq, Kuwait, Saudi Arabia, Sudan, Tunisia, Algeria, and Morocco announced varying degrees of military support for Egypt and Syria. Two weeks of fierce fighting followed. Egypt established its army on the east bank of the Suez Canal, holding a front about 12 km/7.5 mi east of the canal, but elsewhere the Israelis crossed the canal to establish a bridgehead on the west bank between Ismailia and the Great Bitter Lakes. Yet more important than the military struggle was the political. Israel relied heavily for military supplies on the USA, and Egypt and its allies relied on Soviet equipment. Through the UN the two superpowers were instrumental in effecting an agreement to a ceasefire between Egypt and Israel on 22 October 1973.

The political prestige gained enabled Egypt, through the mediation of the US secretary of state Henry *Kissinger, to negotiate two interim withdrawal agreements with Israel in January 1974 and September 1975, accompanied by the establishment of a UN buffer zone separating the rival armies. The shift from Soviet influence was symbolized in the visits made by the US president Richard Nixon to Egypt in 1974 and by Sadat to the USA in 1975. At home, too, Sadat changed direction, releasing political prisoners, and reversing Nasser's economic policies by encouraging foreign investment and activity in the country. This economic liberalism was known as *infitah* ('opening').

the Camp David agreements

In 1977 Sadat went to Israel to address the Israeli parliament and plead for peace. Other Arab states were dismayed by this move, and diplomatic relations with Syria, Libya, Algeria, and South Yemen, as well as the Palestine Liberation Organization (PLO), were severed and Egypt was expelled from the Arab League in 1979. Despite this opposition, Sadat pursued his peace initiative, and at the *Camp David talks in the USA he and the Israeli prime minister Menachem Begin signed two agreements.

The first laid a framework for peace in the Middle East, and the second a framework for a treaty between the two countries. In 1979 a treaty was signed and Israel began a phased withdrawal from Sinai. As a consequence, Egypt's isolation in the Arab world grew, and the economy suffered from the withdrawal of Saudi subsidies. US aid became vital to Egypt's survival, and links between the two governments grew steadily closer.

position in the Arab world In 1981 Sadat was assassinated by a group of Muslim fundamentalists who opposed him. He was succeeded by Lt Gen Hosni *Mubarak, who had been vice-president since 1975. Mubarak continued the policies of his predecessor. In the 1984 elections the National Democratic Party (NDP), formed by Sadat in 1978, won an overwhelming victory in the assembly, strengthening Mubarak's position. Although Egypt's treaty with Israel remained intact, relations between the two countries became strained, mainly because of Israel's pre-emptive activities in Lebanon and the disputed territories. Egypt's relations with other Arab nations improved, and only Libya maintained its trade boycott; the restoration of diplomatic relations with Syria in 1989 paved the way for Egypt's resumption of its leadership of the Arab world. In 2000, Egypt and Sudan formally resumed diplomatic ties, which were broken in 1995 when Egypt accused Sudan of an abortive assassination attempt against President Mubarak.

Mubarak as peace broker Mubarak played a growing role in the search for Middle East peace, acting as an intermediary between the Israelis and Palestinians, and the choice of the country's deputy prime minister, Dr Boutros Boutros-Ghali, as UN secretary general was regarded as evidence of international respect for Egypt's diplomatic successes. At home, problems with Islamic fundamentalists increased but Mubarak was re-elected by referendum for a second term in October 1987. The 1990 general election was boycotted by the main opposition parties, leaving the NDP with 348 of the 444 elected seats. Egypt was a member of the UN coalition forces that sought an economic embargo against Iraq in 1990 for annexing Kuwait, and its armed forces joined in the military action against Iraq in 1991.

fundamentalist violence From May 1992 outbreaks of violence between Muslim and Christian militants became more common, and in 1993 an Islamic militant campaign by the Gama'a el-Islamiya and the Egyptian branch of Islamic Jihad to unseat the government began in deadly earnest, with politicians and other people prominent in public life being targeted. Acts of terrorism have also been directed against foreign tourists, in an effort to destroy Egypt's valuable tourism industry – the massacre of over 60 tourists at Luxor in 1997 had a deeply damaging effect on tourism revenues. A government crackdown began in 1993 and in July, amid continuing violence, Mubarak was re-elected for a third term of office. He survived an assassination attempt in June 1995, and the ruling NDP won a clear victory in the November–December assembly elections of that year. In January 1996 Kamal Ahmed Ganzouri replaced Atef Sidki as prime minister. In September 1999 President Mubarak was awarded a fourth six-year term in a popular referendum. He went on to appoint Atef Obeid, an economist and former minister in charge of the country's privatisation programme, as his prime minister.

Obeid replaced Kamal Ganzouri in what was the most wide-ranging government reshuffle in Muburak's 18 years in power. It was anticipated that the pace of economic reform would speed up.

Violence continued into 2000 when at least 20 people were killed in clashes in southern Egypt in January. It was the worst violence to occur between Christians and Muslims in Egypt in living memory.

In elections held in November 2000, opposition parties did much better than usual and the banned Muslim Brotherhood won 17 seats, re-establishing their presence in parliament for the first time in a decade. A week later, 15 members of the Brotherhood arrested the previous year were given prison sentences.

rights for women Egypt's parliament passed a controversial family status law at the end of January 2000 which makes divorce easier for women by allowing them to sue for divorce on the grounds of incompatibility. The previous legislation stated that a woman had to prove ill-treatment before she could apply for divorce. However, the parliament also rejected an article that would have allowed wives to travel without their husband's permission.

train disaster At least 363 people died in Egypt's worst train disaster on 20 February 2002, when a train travelling between Cairo and Luxor caught fire. The transport minister and the head of the railway authority resigned two days later.

Egyptology the study of ancient Egypt. Interest in the subject was aroused by the Napoleonic expedition's discovery of the Rosetta Stone in 1799. Various excavations continued throughout the 19th century and gradually assumed a more scientific character, largely as a result of the work of the British archaeologist Flinders *Petrie from 1880 onwards and the formation of the Egyptian Exploration Fund in 1882.

In 1922 another British archaeologist, Howard Carter, discovered the tomb of Tutankhamen, the only royal tomb with all its treasures intact.

Eichmann, (Karl) Adolf (1906–1962) Austrian Nazi. As an *SS official during Hitler's regime 1933–45, he was responsible for atrocities against Jews and others, including the implementation of genocide. He managed to escape at the fall of Germany in 1945, but was discovered in Argentina in 1960, abducted by Israeli agents, tried in Israel in 1961 for *war crimes, and executed.

Einaudi, Luigi (1874–1961) Italian politician and economist; president of Italy 1948–55. As budget minister from 1947 he devised a rigorous deflationary policy of tight monetary control and high interest rates that continued until 1950. While this contributed to high unemployment and may have delayed Italy's post-war industrial recovery, it also helped to revive confidence in the lira and laid the foundation for growth in the post-1950 era.

Eire name of southern Ireland as prescribed in the 1937 Constitution.

Eisenhower, Dwight David ('Ike') (1890–1969) 34th president of the USA 1953–60, a Republican. A general in World War II, he commanded the Allied forces in Italy in 1943, then the Allied invasion of Europe, and from October 1944 all the Allied armies in the West. As president he promoted business interests at home and conducted the *Cold War abroad. His vice-president was Richard Nixon.

Eisenhower was born at Denison, Texas. A graduate of West Point military academy in 1915, he served in a variety of staff and command posts before World War II. He became commander-in-chief of the US and British forces for the invasion of North Africa in November 1942, commanded the Allied invasion of Sicily in July 1943, and announced the surrender of Italy on 8 September 1943.

In December he became commander of the Allied Expeditionary Force for the invasion of Europe and was promoted to General of the Army in December 1944. After the war he served as commander of the US Occupation Forces in Germany, then returned to the USA to become Chief of Staff. He served as president of Columbia University and chair of the joint Chiefs of Staff 1949–50. Eisenhower became supreme commander of the Allied Powers in Europe in 1950, and organized the defence forces in the North Atlantic Treaty Organization (NATO). He resigned from the army in 1952 to campaign for the presidency; he was elected, and re-elected by a wide margin in 1956.

A popular politician, Eisenhower held office during a period of domestic and international tension, although the USA was experiencing an era of post-war prosperity and growth. Major problems during his administration included the ending of the *Korean War, the growing civil-rights movement at home, and the *Cold War. His proposals on disarmament and the control of nuclear weapons led to the first International Conference on the Peaceful Uses of Atomic Energy, held under the auspices of the United Nations at Geneva in 1955.

Elizabeth II (1926–) born **Elizabeth Alexandra Mary Windsor**, Queen of Great Britain and Northern Ireland from 1952, the elder daughter of George VI. She married her third cousin, Philip, the Duke of Edinburgh, in 1947. They have four children: Charles, Anne, Andrew, and Edward.

Elizabeth, the Queen Mother (1900–2002) Wife of King George VI of Great Britain. She was born Lady Elizabeth Angela Marguerite Bowes-Lyon, and on 26 April 1923 she married Albert, Duke of York, who became King George VI in 1936. Their children are Queen Elizabeth II and Princess Margaret.

Ellis Island island in New York harbour, USA, 1.5 km/1 mi from Manhattan Island; area 0.1 sq km/ 0.04 sq mi. A former reception centre for immigrants during the immigration waves between 1892 and 1943 (12 million people passed through it from 1892 to 1924), it was later used (until 1954) as a detention centre for nonresidents without documentation, or for those who were being deported. Ellis Island is now a national historic site (1964) and contains the Museum of Immigration (1989).

El Salvador country in Central America, bounded north and east by Honduras, south and southwest by the Pacific Ocean, and northwest by Guatemala.

Enigma German enciphering machine of World War II and, by extension, the codes generated by it. The code was cracked by the British in spring 1940 and the Allies gained much useful intelligence as the Germans believed the code unbreakable.

enosis (Greek 'union') movement, developed from 1930, for the union of *Cyprus with Greece. The campaign (led by *EOKA and supported by Archbishop Makarios) intensified from the 1950s. In 1960 independence from Britain, without union, was granted, and increased demands for union led to its proclamation in 1974. As a result, Turkey invaded Cyprus, ostensibly to protect the Turkish community, and the island was effectively partitioned.

Entente Cordiale (French 'friendly understanding') agreement reached by Britain and France in 1904 recognizing British interests in Egypt and French interests in Morocco. It was expressly designed to check the colonial ambitions of the German Second Empire under *William II. Though not a formal alliance, the Entente generated tripartite cooperation between Britain, France, and Russia from 1907 (the Triple Entente), and formed the basis for

Anglo French military collaboration before the outbreak of World War I in 1914.

Enver Pasha (1881–1922) Turkish politician and soldier. He led the military revolt of 1908 that resulted in the Young Turks' revolution (see *Turkey). He was killed fighting the Bolsheviks in Turkestan.

EOKA acronym for **Ethnikí Organósis Kipriakóu Agónos** (National Organization of Cypriot Struggle), an underground organization formed by General George *Grivas in 1955 to fight for the independence of Cyprus from Britain and ultimately its union (*enosis*) with Greece. In 1971, 11 years after the independence of Cyprus, Grivas returned to the island to form EOKA B and to resume the fight for *enosis*, which had not been achieved by the Cypriot government.

Equatorial Guinea country in west-central Africa, bounded north by Cameroon, east and south by Gabon, and west by the Atlantic Ocean; also five offshore islands including Bioko, off the coast of Cameroon.

Erhard, Ludwig (1897–1977) German economist and Christian Democrat politician, chancellor of the Federal Republic 1963–66. He became known as the 'father of the German economic miracle'. As economics minister 1949–63 he instituted policies driven by his vision of a 'social market economy', in which a capitalist free market would be tempered by an active role for the state in providing a market-friendly social welfare system. His period as chancellor was less distinguished.

Eritrea country in East Africa, bounded north by Sudan, south by Ethiopia, southeast by Djibouti, and east by the Red Sea.

Erlander, Tage Fritiof (1901–1985) Swedish politician. Elected to parliament as a Social Democrat in 1933, he was minister without portfolio in the wartime coalition government from 1944, and was minister for ecclesiastical affairs when chosen to succeed Per Albin Hansson as party leader and prime minister in 1946. He made way for the younger Olof *Palme in 1969.

Ershad, Hussain Muhammad (1930–) Military ruler of Bangladesh 1982–90. He became chief of staff of the Bangladeshi army in 1979 and assumed power in a military coup in 1982. As president from 1983, Ershad introduced a successful rural-oriented economic programme. He was re-elected in 1986 and lifted martial law, but faced continuing political opposition, which forced him to resign in December 1990.

Erzberger, Matthias (1875–1921) German politician. Long a hate figure for the German right, he first attracted controversy as an advocate of peace without annexations in 1917. Subsequently, as a member of the armistice delegation, he supported acceptance of the terms of the Treaty of Versailles despite fierce German opposition. He resigned in 1921 after an unsuccessful libel action against a political opponent, and was assassinated in August 1921.

Estonia country in northern Europe, bounded east by Russia, south by Latvia, and north and west by the Baltic Sea.

Ethiopia country in East Africa, bounded north by Eritrea, northeast by Djibouti, east and southeast by Somalia, south by Kenya, and west and northwest by Sudan. It was known as Abyssinia until the 1920s.

ethnic cleansing the forced expulsion of one ethnic group by another to create a homogenous population, for example, of more than 2 million Muslims by Serbs in Bosnia-Herzegovina 1992–95. The term has also been used to describe the killing of Hutus and Tutsis in Rwanda and Burundi in 1994, and for earlier mass exiles, as far back as the book of Exodus.

Eurocommunism policy followed by communist parties in Western Europe during the 1970s and 1980s to seek power within the framework of national political structures rather than by revolutionary means. By 1990 it had lost significance with the collapse of communism across Central and Eastern Europe.

European Community EC, collective term for the European Economic Community (EEC), the European Coal and Steel Community (ECSC), and the European Atomic Energy Community (Euratom). The EC is now a separate legal entity with the *European Union (EU), which was established under the *Maastricht Treaty (1992) and includes intergovernmental cooperation on security and judicial affairs.

European Free Trade Association EFTA, organization established in 1960 and consisting of Iceland, Norway, Switzerland, and (from 1991) Liechtenstein, previously a non-voting associate member. There are no import duties between members. Of the original EFTA members, Britain and Denmark left in 1972 to join the *European Community (EC), as did Portugal in 1985; Austria, Finland, and Sweden joined the *European Union (EU) in 1995.

European Union EU, political and economic grouping, comprising 25 countries (in 2004). The six original members – Belgium, France, (West) Germany, Italy, Luxembourg, and the Netherlands – were joined by the United Kingdom, Denmark, and the Republic of Ireland in 1973, Greece in 1981, Spain and Portugal in 1986, Austria, Finland, and Sweden in 1995, and Cyprus, the Czech Republic, Estonia, Hungary, Latvia, Lithuania, Malta, Poland, the Slovak Republic, and Slovenia in 2004. East Germany was incorporated on German reunification in 1990. The *European Community (EC) preceded the EU, and comprised the European Coal and Steel Community (set up by the

1951 Treaty of Paris), the European Economic Community, and the European Atomic Energy Community (both set up by the 1957 Treaties of *Rome). The EU superseded the EC in 1993, following intergovernmental arrangements for a common foreign and security policy and for increased cooperation on justice and home affairs policy issues set up by the *Maastricht Treaty (1992). Other important agreements have been the Single European Act (1986), the Amsterdam Treaty (1997), and the Treaty of Nice (2000). The basic aims of these treaties have been the expansion of trade, the abolition of restrictive economic practices, the encouragement of free movement of capital and labour, and establishment of a closer union among European peoples.

The main consultative and decision-making institutions of the EU are the European Commission, the Council of the European Union (and the European Council), the European Parliament, the European Court of Justice and the Court of Auditors. Other important bodies include the **Economic and Social Committee** (including workers' and employers' representatives) and the **Committee of the Regions**. The **European Investment Bank** is the EU's financing institution, providing long-term loans for capital investment.

The most important policy areas of the EU include the common agricultural policy, economic and monetary union (and the creation of the single European currency or euro), the single European market, enlargement, security, and judicial and home affairs. The EU also agrees measures on environmental protection, regional development (through several structural funds), research, employment and social affairs, transport, and energy.

Budget revenue comes from levies on agricultural imports from non-member countries, customs duties, the proceeds of value-added tax receipts, and contributions from member states based on gross national product (the 'own resources' financing system). The United Kingdom gets an annual budget rebate (which has been in place since 1984).

Euskadi ta Askatasuna ETA; or **Basque Nation and Liberty**, illegal organization of militant Basque separatists, founded in 1959, and committed to the independence of the Basque Country from Spain. Its main strategy has been based on violence, with more than 800 deaths attributed to the group over the period 1968–2000. It had links with the former political party Herri Batasuna (HB), and its French counterpart is Iparretarrak ('ETA fighters from the North Side').

Evans, Arthur John (1851–1941) English archaeologist. His excavations at Knossos on Crete uncovered a vast palace complex, and resulted in the discovery of various Minoan scripts. He proved the existence of a Bronze Age civilization that predated the Mycenean, and named it Minoan after Minos, the legendary king of Knossos.

Eyadema, (Etienne) Gnassingbé (1935–) Togolese army officer and politician. In 1967, after serving in the French army, he overthrew President Grunitzky to become Togo's unelected president. A 1972 national referendum confirmed his presidency. He won a hollow victory in the 1993 elections because all the main opposition parties refused to take part and their supporters boycotted the polls.

F

Fabian Society UK socialist organization for research, discussion, and publication, founded in London in 1884. Its name is derived from the Roman commander Fabius Maximus, and refers to the evolutionary methods by which it hopes to attain socialism by a succession of gradual reforms. Early members included the playwright George Bernard Shaw and Beatrice and Sidney Webb. The society helped to found the Labour Representation Committee in 1900, which became the Labour Party in 1906.

Fabius, Laurent (1946–) French politician, leader of the Socialist Party (PS) 1992–93. As prime minister 1984–86, he introduced a liberal, free-market economic programme, but his career was damaged by the 1985 *Greenpeace sabotage scandal.

Fahd (1923–) in full **Fahd ibn Abdul Aziz al-Saud**, King of Saudi Arabia from 1982. He encouraged the investment of the country's enormous oil wealth in infrastructure and new activities – such as petrochemical industries – in order to diversify the economy, and also built up the country's military forces. When Iraq invaded neighbouring Kuwait in August 1990, King Fahd joined with the USA and other international forces in 'Operation Desert Storm' in the course of the 1990–91 Gulf War, in which Saudi Arabia was used as the base from which Kuwait was liberated in February 1991.

Falling oil prices, since the 1980s, led to a gradual reduction in the country's financial reserves, and to some retrenchment and, in the 1990s, gradual privatization. From the early 1990s King Fahd's absolutist regime faced twin pressures from liberals, campaigning for democratic elections, and from fundamentalist Islamic groups, which opposed the monarchy and sought the full imposition of Islamic *sharia* law. In May 1993 a group of Islamic activists, led by Muhammad al-Masari, formed a Committee for the Defence of Legitimate Rights to monitor the regime's adherence to Islamic principles. In response to pro-democracy pressures, in August 1993 the king established an advisory Shura Council, comprising 60 members of the national elite, drawn from outside the royal family, and also established a system of regional government. In November 1995 King Fahd suffered a stroke, and in January 1996 he temporarily ceded power for one month to Crown Prince Abdullah, his legal successor.

Fair Deal the policy of social improvement advocated 1945–48 by Harry S Truman, as president of the USA 1945–53. The Fair Deal proposals, first mooted in 1945 after the end of World War II, aimed to extend the *New Deal on health insurance, housing development, and the laws to maintain farming prices. Although some bills became law – for example a Housing Act, a higher minimum wage, and wider social security benefits – the main proposals were blocked by a hostile Congress.

Faisal I (1885–1933) King of Iraq from 1921. During his reign, which included the achievement of full independence in 1932, he sought to foster pan-Arabism and astutely maintained a balance between Iraqi nationalists and British interests. He was succeded by his only son, **Ghazi I**, who was killed in a car accident in 1939.

Faisal Ibn Abd al-Aziz (1905–1975)
King of Saudi Arabia from 1964.
Ruling without a prime minister, he
instituted a successful programme of
economic modernization, using Saudi
Arabia's vast annual oil revenues,
which grew from $334 million in 1960
to $22.5 billion in 1974, after the
quadrupling of world oil prices in
1973–74. A generous welfare system
was established, including free medical
care and education to postgraduate
level, and subsidized food, water, fuel,
electricity, and rents; slavery was
outlawed; and financial support was
given to other Arab states in their
struggle with Israel. In March 1975
Faisal was assassinated by a mentally
unstable nephew, Prince Museid, and
his half-brother Khalid became king.

Falange (Spanish **'phalanx'**) also
known as Falange Española. Former
Spanish Fascist Party, founded in 1933
by José Antonio Primo de Rivera
(1903–1936), son of military ruler
Miguel *Primo de Rivera. It was
closely modelled in programme and
organization on the Italian fascists and
on the Nazis. In 1937, when *Franco
assumed leadership, it was declared
the only legal party, and altered its
name to Traditionalist Spanish Phalanx.

**Falkenhayn, Erich Georg Anton
Sebastian von (1861–1922)** German
soldier. Falkenhayn served on the
expedition to China 1900 and became
minister of war 1913. On the outbreak
of World War I he became chief of the
general staff and remained in this post
until he was removed by the Kaiser
August 1916 after the failure of the
German attacks on Verdun. He was
sent to the Eastern Front where he
succeeded in subduing Romania before
handing over his command to General
von Mackensen 1917. He then took up
an unsuccessful command in support
of the Turks against the British in the
Middle East and was recalled
March 1918.

Falklands War war between Argentina
and Britain over disputed sovereignty

of the Falkland Islands initiated when
Argentina invaded and occupied the
islands on 2 April 1982. On the
following day, the United Nations
Security Council passed a resolution
calling for Argentina to withdraw.
A British task force was immediately
dispatched and, after a fierce conflict in
which more than 1,000 Argentine and
British lives were lost, 12,000 Argentine
troops surrendered and the islands
were returned to British rule on
14–15 June 1982.

Fanfani, Amintore (1908–1999)
Italian right-wing politician. He was
a Christian Democrat premier of Italy
in 1954, 1958–59, and 1960–63.
Subsequently he became foreign
minister and was noted for his
'European' policy. He was again
premier 1982–83 and 1987.

Fang Lizhi (1936–) Chinese political
dissident and astrophysicist. He
advocated human rights and political
pluralism and encouraged his students
to campaign for democracy. After the
Red Army massacred the student
demonstrators in Tiananmen Square,
Beijing, in June 1989, Fang and his wife
took refuge in the US embassy in Beijing
until June 1990, when they received
official permission to leave China.

Farinacci, Roberto (1892–1945)
Italian politician. Fascist Party
Secretary from 1924 to 1926, he became
a member of the Fascist Grand Council
in 1935 and was appointed minister of
state in 1938. An ardent racist and anti-
Semite, notorious for his extremism
and pro-Nazi tendencies, he edited
the *Regime Fascista*, the party organ.
He was shot while attempting to flee
to Switzerland.

Farouk (1920–1965) King of Egypt.
He succeeded the throne on the death
of his father *Fuad I. His early
popularity was later overshadowed by
his somewhat unsuccessful private life,
and more importantly by the
humiliating defeat of the Egyptian
army in 1948. In 1952 a group called
the 'Free Officers', led by Muhammad

Neguib and Gamal Abdel Nasser, forced him to abdicate, and he was temporarily replaced by his son Ahmad Fuad II. Exiled for the remainder of his life, he died in Rome in 1965.

Farrakhan, Louis (1933–) born **Louis Eugene Walcott**, African-American religious and political figure. Leader of the *Nation of Islam, Farrakhan preached strict adherence to Muslim values and black separatism.

His outspoken views against Jews, homosexuals, and whites caused outrage. In 1995 he organized the 'Million Man March' in Washington, DC; an estimated 400,000 people attended.

fascism political ideology that denies all rights to individuals in their relations with the state; specifically, the *totalitarian nationalist movement founded in Italy in 1919 by *Mussolini and followed by Hitler's Germany in 1933.

Fascism came about essentially as a result of the economic and political crisis of the years after World War I. Units called *fasci di combattimento* (combat groups), from the Latin *fasces*, were originally established to oppose communism. The fascist party, the *Partito Nazionale Fascista*, controlled Italy 1922–43. Fascism protected the existing social order by suppressing the working-class movement by force and by providing scapegoats for popular anger such as minority groups: Jews, foreigners, or blacks; it also prepared the citizenry for the economic and psychological mobilization of war.

The term 'fascism' is also applied to similar organizations in other countries, such as the Spanish *Falange and the British Union of Fascists under Oswald *Mosley.

Neo-fascist groups still exist in many Western European countries, in the USA (the Ku Klux Klan and several small armed vigilante groups), France (National Front), Germany (German

People's Union), Russia (Pamyat), and elsewhere. Germany experienced an upsurge in neo-fascist activity in 1992 and again in 1998, with rioting in several major cities. The winning of a London local-government seat by the British National Party in 1993 raised fears of the growth of right-wing racism in Britain. In Italy the discrediting of the Christian right-of-centre parties resulted in a triumph for right-wing groups, including the neo-fascist National Alliance, in the 1994 elections. However, by 1998 the National Alliance had adopted a less extremist programme and claimed to be a mainstream conservative party.

Fatah, al- Palestinian nationalist organization, founded in 1957 to bring about an independent state of Palestine. Also called Tahir al-Hatani al Falastani (Movement for the National Liberation of Palestine), it is the main component of the *Palestine Liberation Organization (PLO).

Fateh Singh, Sant (1911–1972) Sikh religious leader. Born in the Punjab, India, he was a campaigner for Sikh rights and was involved in religious and educational activity in Rajastan, founding many schools and colleges there. In 1942 he joined the *Quit India Movement, and was imprisoned for his political activities. During the 1950s he agitated for a Punjabi-speaking state, which was achieved once Haryana was created as a separate state in 1966.

Faulkner, (Arthur) Brian (Deane) (1921–1977) Baron **Faulkner of Downpatrick**, Northern Irish Unionist politician and the last prime minister of Northern Ireland 1971–72 before the Stormont parliament was suspended. Elected to the Northern Ireland House of Commons in 1949, he held various ministerial posts 1959–71, and became leader of the Unionist Party in 1971. As prime minister he adopted a tough stance against republicans, reintroducing internment in 1971, but also tried to win middle-class Catholic support by offering nationalists a role in the parliamentary committee system. In 1973 he committed his party to the ill-fated Sunningdale power-sharing agreement.

Faure, Edgar (1908–1988) French Radical politician, prime minister 1952 and 1955–56, when he was the first prime minister since 1876 to dissolve the national assembly rather than resign after a no-confidence vote. As education minister after the student revolt of 1968, he reformed the curriculum and university management, giving institutions autonomy and introducing staff–student representation. He was president of the national assembly 1973–78.

February Revolution first of the two political uprisings of the *Russian Revolution in 1917 that led to the overthrow of the tsar and the end of the Romanov dynasty.

Federal Bureau of Investigation FBI, agency of the US Department of Justice that investigates violations of federal law not specifically assigned to other agencies, and is particularly concerned with internal security.

The FBI was established in 1908 and built up a position of powerful autonomy during the autocratic directorship of J Edgar Hoover 1924–72. The director is Robert Mueller, a former federal prosecutor, from 2001.

federalist in Australian history, one who supported the federation of the six self-governing colonies into the Commonwealth of Australia which occurred on 1 January 1901.

Feng Guozhang (or Feng Kuo-chang) (1859–1919) Chinese militarist. He served as a provincial military governor before becoming acting president of the Chinese Republic 1917–18. During his one year in office China declared war on Germany.

Feng Yuxiang (or Feng Yü-hsiang or Fung Yü-hsiang) (1882–1948) called **'the Christian General'**, Chinese warlord. Born in Hsing-chi-chen, Hopeh Province, he rose through the ranks to command an independent force and contested for control of northern China with Zhang Zuolin and other warlords between 1920 and 1926. In 1924 Feng Yuxiang took Beijing (then Peking), and set up a government that included members of the Nationalist Party. He supported the Nationalist government in 1927, but became apprehensive of the growing personal power of Chiang Kai-shek and joined in two successive revolts, both of which failed. In 1930 he was ousted by Zhang Zueliang and Chiang Kai-shek's Nationalist army.

Ferdinand (1861–1948) King of Bulgaria 1908–18. Son of Prince Augustus of Saxe-Coburg-Gotha, he was elected prince of Bulgaria in 1887 and, in 1908, proclaimed Bulgaria's independence from Turkey and assumed the title of tsar. In 1915 he entered World War I as Germany's ally, and in 1918 abdicated.

Ferdinand (1865–1927) King of Romania from 1914, when he succeeded his uncle Charles I. In 1916 he declared war on Austria. After the Allied victory in World War I, Ferdinand acquired Transylvania and Bukovina from Austria-Hungary, and Bessarabia from Russia. In 1922 he became king of this Greater Romania. His reign saw agrarian reform and the introduction of universal suffrage.

Ferdinand, Franz (or Francis) (1863–1914) Archduke of Austria. He became heir to Emperor Franz Joseph, his uncle, in 1884 but while visiting Sarajevo on 28 June 1914, he and his wife were assassinated by a Serbian nationalist. Austria used the episode to make unreasonable demands on Serbia that ultimately precipitated World War I.

Ferraro, Geraldine Anne (1935–) US Democratic politician, vice-presidential candidate in the 1984 election.

Festival of Britain artistic and cultural festival held in London May–September 1951 both to commemorate the 100th anniversary of the Great Exhibition and to boost morale after years of post-war austerity. The South Bank of the Thames formed the focal point of the event and the Royal Festival Hall built specially for the festival is a reminder of the modernist style of architecture promoted at the time.

Fianna Fáil (Irish 'Soldiers of Destiny') Republic of Ireland political party, founded by the Irish nationalist Éamon *de Valera in 1926, and led since 1994 by Bertie *Ahern. A broad-based party, it is conservative socially and economically, and generally right of centre. It was the governing party in the Republic of Ireland 1932–48, 1951–54, 1957–73, 1977–81, 1982, 1987–94 (from 1993 in coalition with Labour), and from 1997. Its official aims include the establishment of a united and completely independent all-Ireland republic.

fifth column group within a country secretly aiding an enemy attacking from without. The term originated in 1936 during the Spanish Civil War, when General Mola boasted that Franco supporters were attacking Madrid with four columns and that they had a 'fifth column' inside the city.

Fiji Islands country comprising 844 islands and islets in the southwest Pacific Ocean, about 100 of which are inhabited.

Fine Gael (Irish 'family of the gael') Republic of Ireland political party founded in 1933 by William Cosgrave and led by John Bruton from 1990. It has been socially liberal in recent years but fiscally conservative. Though it formed a coalition government with the Labour and Democratic Left parties 1994–97, it has typically been the main opposition party.

Finland country in Scandinavia, bounded to the north by Norway, east by Russia, south and west by the Baltic Sea, and northwest by Sweden.

Fisher, Andrew (1862–1928) Australian Labor politician. Born in Scotland, he went to Australia in 1885.

He entered the Australian parliament in 1901 and became Labor Party leader in 1907. He was prime minister 1908–09, 1910–13, and 1914–15, and Australian high commissioner to the UK 1916–21.

Fitt, Gerry (Gerard) (1926–) Baron Fitt, Northern Ireland politician. From 1962 to 1972 he represented the Dock Division of Belfast as a Republican Labour member of the Northern Ireland parliament, then founded and led the Social Democratic Labour Party (SDLP). He was an SDLP MP for nine years, resigning the leadership in 1979 to sit as an Independent socialist. He lost his Belfast seat in the 1983 general election.

FitzGerald, Garret Michael (1926–) Irish politician, leader of the Fine Gael party 1977–87. As Taoiseach (prime minister) 1981–82 and 1982–87, he attempted to solve the Northern Ireland dispute, ultimately by participating in the *Anglo-Irish Agreement in 1985. He tried to remove some of the overtly Catholic features of the constitution to make the Republic more attractive to Northern Protestants.

Fitzgerald, 'Honey Fitz' (1863–1950) born **John Francis Fitzgerald**, US businessman and mayor. He ran a newspaper and was a state senator and Republican US Representative for Massachusetts, before he became mayor of Boston (1906–08, 1910–14). His administrations were plagued by charges of corruption and political patronage.

Fleming, Alexander (1881–1955) Scottish bacteriologist who was awarded a Nobel Prize for Physiology or Medicine in 1945 for his discovery of the bactericidal effect of penicillin in 1928. In 1922 he had discovered lysozyme, an antibacterial enzyme present in saliva, nasal secretions, and tears. While studying this, he found an unusual mould growing on a culture dish, which he isolated and grew into a pure culture. This led to his discovery of penicillin, which came into use in 1941. He shared the award with Howard W Florey and Ernst B *Chain, whose research had brought widespread realization of the value of penicillin with its isolation and its development as an antibiotic drug.

Flying Tigers nickname given to the American Volunteer Group in World War II, a group of US pilots recruited to fight in China by Maj-Gen Chennault 1940–41. The group proved an effective force against the Japanese over southern China and Burma 1941–42, destroying some 300 enemy aircraft. It was absorbed into the regular US air forces as the 14th Air Force with Chennault as its commander 1942.

Foch, Ferdinand (1851–1929) Marshal of France during World War I. He was largely responsible for the Allied victory at the first battle of the *Marne in September 1914, and commanded on the northwestern front October 1914–September 1916. He was appointed commander-in-chief of the Allied armies in the spring of 1918, and launched the Allied counter-offensive in July that brought about the negotiation of an armistice to end the war.

Foot, Michael Mackintosh (1913–) British Labour politician and writer. A leader of the left-wing Tribune Group, he was secretary of state for employment 1974–76, Lord President of the Council and leader of the House 1976–79, and succeeded James Callaghan as Labour Party leader 1980–83.

Football War popular name for a five-day war between El Salvador and Honduras which began on 14 July 1969, when Salvadorean planes bombed Tegucigelpa. Its army entered Honduras, but the *Organization of American States arranged a ceasefire, by which time about 2,000 lives had been lost.

Forbes, George William (1869–1947) New Zealand centre-right politician, prime minister 1930–35. He was Liberal Party whip from 1912 and leader between 1925–28. He became leader again, when it had become the United Party, in 1930, and also prime minister. A genial, uncomplicated politician, described as a 'plain man without frills', Forbes led the country through the difficulties of the Great Depression, heading a United Party–Reform Party coalition. However, his inflexibility as unemployment increased led to a crushing electoral defeat in 1935 and a first-ever victory for the Labour Party, led by Michael *Savage.

Ford, Gerald R(udolph) (1913–) 38th president of the USA 1974–77, a Republican. He was elected to the House of Representatives in 1948, was nominated to the vice-presidency by Richard Nixon in 1973 on the resignation of Spiro *Agnew, and became president in 1974, when Nixon was forced to resign following the *Watergate scandal. He granted Nixon a full pardon in September 1974.

Foreign Legion volunteer corps of foreigners within a country's army. The French **Légion Etrangère**, founded in 1831, is one of a number of such forces. Enlisted volunteers are of any nationality (about half are now French), but the officers are usually French. Headquarters until 1962 was in Sidi Bel Abbés, Algeria; the main base is now Corsica, with reception headquarters at Aubagne, near Marseille, France.

The French foreign legion was founded by Louis-Philippe 'to clear France of foreigners' and since then has always taken cast-offs and undesirables, including those from the French army itself.

Levels of desertion are relatively high, around 6%.

Fort Knox US army post and gold depository in northern Kentucky, established in 1917 as a training camp and named after the US soldier and politician Henry Knox. The maximum security US Treasury gold-bullion vaults were built at the fort in 1936, opening in 1937.

Foster, William Zebulon (1881–1961)
US Communist leader. Secretary of the
American Communist Party, he was
the party's presidential candidate three
times. He was indicted with 11 others
on charges of advocating the
overthrow of the US government, but
was excused trial because of illness.

Fourteen Points the terms proposed
by President Wilson of the USA in his
address to Congress of 8 January 1918,
as a basis for the settlement of *World
War I. The creation of the *League of
Nations was one of the points.

France country in western Europe,
bounded to the northeast by Belgium,
Luxembourg, and Germany, east by
Germany, Switzerland, and Italy, south
by the Mediterranean Sea, southwest
by Spain and Andorra, and west by the
Atlantic Ocean.

government Under the 1958 Fifth
Republic constitution, amended in
1962 and 1995, France has a two-
chamber legislature and a 'shared
executive' government. The legislature
comprises a national assembly, with
577 deputies elected for five-year terms
from single-member constituencies
following a two-ballot run-off majority
system, and a senate, whose 321
members are indirectly elected, a third
at a time, triennially for nine-year
terms from groups of local councillors.

Twenty-two national-assembly and
13 senate seats are elected by overseas
départements (administrative regions)
and territories, and 12 senate seats by
French nationals abroad. The national
assembly is the dominant chamber.
The senate can temporarily veto
legislation, but its vetoes can be
overridden by the national assembly.

France's executive is functionally
divided between the president and
prime minister. The president, elected
by direct universal suffrage after
gaining a majority in either a first or
second run-off ballot, functions as head
of state, commander in chief of the
armed forces, and guardian of the
constitution. A referendum in 2000

reduced the term of the president from
seven years to five years, starting in
2002. The president selects the prime
minister, presides over cabinet
meetings, countersigns government
bills, negotiates foreign treaties, and
can call referenda and dissolve the
national assembly (although only one
dissolution a year is permitted).

The prime minister is selected from
the ranks of the national assembly.
According to the constitution,
ultimate control over policymaking
rests with the prime minister and
council of ministers.

The president and prime minister
work with ministers from political
and technocratic backgrounds, assisted
by a skilled and powerful civil service.
A nine-member constitutional council
(selected every three years in a
staggered manner by the state
president and the presidents of the
senate and national assembly, and
serving nine-year, non-renewable
terms) and a *Conseil d'Etat* ('council of
state'), staffed by senior civil servants,
rule on the legality of legislation
passed. At the local level there are
21 regional councils concerned with
economic planning. Below these are
96 *département* councils and almost
36,000 town and village councils.
Corsica has its own directly elected
61-seat parliament with powers to
propose amendments to national-
assembly legislation.

There are four overseas *départements*
(French Guiana, Guadeloupe,
Martinique, and Réunion) with their
own elected general and regional
councils, two overseas 'collective
territories' (Mayotte and St Pierre and
Miquelon) administered by appointed
commissioners, and four overseas
territories (French Polynesia, the
French Southern and Antarctic
Territories, New Caledonia, and the
Wallis and Futuna Islands) governed
by appointed high commissioners,
which form constituent parts of the
French Republic, returning deputies
to the national legislature.

the aftermath of World War II

Although Paris was physically undamaged in World War II, many cities, such as Brest, Rouen, Lorient, Le Havre, and Caen, were in ruins. The French had suffered considerable economic privations during the years 1940–44; and France in 1944 was in the midst of an inflation that was threatening the very existence of the middle class.

France's internal problems were not its only ones. The pre-1939 French colonial empire was on the verge of disintegration. Syria and Lebanon had already achieved independence; the French West Africa possessions were demanding at least a measure of self-government, and some nationalists were calling for outright independence. In Indochina (now Vietnam, Cambodia, and Laos) the communists and other nationalists soon launched a full-scale war of independence against France (the Indochina War). These colonial problems drained France's economy severely in the post-war years and had considerable repercussions on internal French politics.

towards a new constitution

A constituent assembly charged with drawing up a constitution for a Fourth Republic was elected in 1945, an election in which women voted in France for the first time. The Communists were returned as the strongest party because of their important role in the wartime resistance, closely followed by the Socialists and a new political organization known as the Mouvement Républicain Populaire (MRP), a group of the progressive centre drawing considerable strength from former Catholic resistance fighters.

When the constituent assembly met, Charles *de Gaulle returned to the people the powers he had exercised as head of the provisional government formed at the liberation in 1944. Having been given a new mandate, he formed a government drawn from the three main parties, and pledged to implement a far-reaching social programme. However, de Gaulle resigned in January 1946 because he did not want to be a figurehead president in the manner of the Third Republic, yet already found himself dependent on the political parties, especially the Communists and Socialists.

Throughout 1946 France was searching for a new constitution. The reconciliation of a sovereign legislature with a stable executive was the stumbling block, though the seriousness of the country's economic position clearly pointed to the need for a strong government. A new constitution was eventually approved in a referendum in October. Under the new constitution a second chamber, the Council of the Republic, with members chosen by indirect election, was given a voice, though not a decisive one, in the legislature; the president was to be elected by the two chambers in joint session. There were also provisions for the organization of the French Union – the new term for France's depleted colonial empire.

the Fourth Republic (1946–58): general characteristics and developments Despite attempts to correct some of the flaws of the Third Republic, the new constitution once again provided for a weak executive and a powerful national assembly. With 26 impermanent governments being formed during the period of the Fourth Republic, real power passed to the civil service, which, by introducing a new system of 'indicative economic planning', engineered rapid economic reconstruction.

The peaceful decolonization of Morocco and Tunisia in 1956 and the creation of the European Economic Community (EEC) in 1958 were also important achievements. In contrast, the forcible expulsion of the French from Indochina in 1954 was for many a national humiliation, and the bitter colonial conflict in Algeria was to bring about the demise of the Fourth Republic itself.

the Blum government of 1946–47 In the November 1946 elections, which created the first national assembly of the Fourth Republic, the Socialists fell to third place among the leading parties. The Communists were still the strongest single party, but the majority in the assembly was anticommunist. In the new conditions of equipoise between Communists and the MRP, the Socialists, despite their depleted numbers, secured the vital position in the middle of the political seesaw, and it was in these circumstances that in December Léon *Blum formed a purely Socialist government.

Blum's stopgap government launched an attack on the price rises and on financial instability. Attempts were also made to settle the Indochinese question, where the French were attempting to regain control of their colonies from the nationalists, who had themselves ousted the Japanese-sponsored regime at the end of World War II. The government also laid the foundations of a new Anglo-French entente. In January 1947 the assembly installed as first president of the new republic the Socialist Vincent Auriol, a close friend and colleague of Blum.

governments and events from 1947 to 1957 Blum resigned for reasons of health and was succeeded by Paul Ramadier (also Socialist), who headed a coalition. The change of government did not interfere with the negotiations for a treaty of alliance with the UK, and the treaty was eventually signed at Dunkirk on 4 March 1947. However, the economic situation was deteriorating, and there soon appeared a deepening division in the government between the Communists and the rest of the ministers.

This period was also marked by the formation of the Rassemblement du Peuple Français (RPF, 'rally of the

French people'). The RPF was an organization fostered by de Gaulle as a nationwide movement of national union, and though he was accused by the left, especially the Communists, of favouring reactionary elements, the movement constituted a new and popular force that for a time materially affected the political balance in France.

But meanwhile the economic situation was growing steadily worse. The political situation was further weakened by the refusal of the Communists to vote for the funding of military operations against the nationalists in Indochina and to suppress a revolt in Madagascar. The Communists then left the government in 1947.

In September 1948 a coalition under the Radical Socialist Henri Queuille took office, and a period of relative political stability followed. The following year France joined the *North Atlantic Treaty Organization (NATO) as a founder member. In July 1949 Queuille's government fell. There was a series of rapid changes of government before political stability returned with Georges *Bidault as premier.

By early 1950 the situation in Indochina was becoming extremely serious. Jean de *Lattre de Tassigny was appointed commander in chief of the army and French high commissioner there in an attempt to retrieve the situation; his subsequent premature death probably put the seal on certain French defeat in the area. In May 1950 Robert Schuman, the French foreign minister, put forward his 'Schuman Plan', which eventually developed into the European Coal and Steel Community, the basis of what is now the European Union.

By mid-1951 many observers believed that de Gaulle's return to power was imminent. After a temporary improvement, the economic situation was weakening again, a bitter domestic battle was raging on the question of state aid to church schools, and abroad the Indochina crisis continued. In relation to the planned European Defence Community there was considerable controversy in France about whether a European army should include West German forces, both because would involve the recreation of a German army, regarded by many French people as synonymous with the recreation of German 'militarism', and because it would subsume French forces within a supranational army.

After a series of short-lived governments, René Pleven became premier in August 1951, and was succeeded at the beginning of 1952 by Edgar *Faure, a Radical Socialist. Faure reopened the question of Tunisian independence, but his government lasted only a few weeks, and in March 1952 Antoine Pinay, an Independent Republican, succeeded him.

In July the Gaullists split on a question of party discipline, and after this time de Gaulle's prospects of a return to power receded rapidly, despite the country's blatant political instability, illustrated by constant changes of government. In May 1953, conscious of a loss of popular support, de Gaulle resigned from the leadership of the RPF, and withdrew from politics.

After a prolonged period without a government, France got a new premier, Laniel, in June 1953. In October 1953 the National Assembly voted in favour of continuing the Indochina War, although the French position there was rapidly becoming untenable. The fall of *Dien Bien Phu in May 1954 shocked French public opinion deeply, and the following month the government was defeated on an Indochina issue.

The new premier was the Radical Socialist Pierre Mendès-France. In July the fighting in Indochina was ended by an agreement reached at Geneva. This was generally regarded in France as a crushing surrender; the 80-year French occupation of Indochina came

formally to an end on 29 April 1955. Mendès-France's North Africa policy eventually led to his defeat in the assembly in February 1955, and he was succeeded by Faure.

The Franco-Tunisian home-rule agreements were signed in Paris in June 1955, and in October the former Moroccan sultan, deposed by the French two years earlier, was restored to his throne. But by this time the bitter armed conflict between nationalists and the French army and settlers in Algeria was becoming serious. At home political stability and possibly the Fourth Republic itself were temporarily threatened by the rise of the violently right-wing *poujadist movement, although its popularity was only transient. The Saarland referendum in October, with its overwhelming victory for the pro-German parties, was another blow to France. In November Faure's government was defeated on a question of electoral reform.

The general elections of January 1956 produced an indecisive result, but in February the Socialist Guy Mollet became premier. Although governing with a precariously balanced coalition, he was premier longer that any other holder of the office under the Fourth Republic. Moroccan independence was announced in March 1956; but it was the increasingly critical Algerian situation that was basically responsible for the defeat of Mollet's government in June 1957, and of its successors.

At the beginning of 1958 the European Economic Community (EEC) came into being. In March 1957 France had been one of the signatories of the Treaty of Rome, which had established the EEC, but in 1958 it seemed that France would not be able to provide it with the expected leadership. There was inflation and economic stagnation at home, and the insoluble Algerian problem across the Mediterranean. France appeared to be moving rapidly towards chaos.

the coming of the Fifth Republic

In May 1958 a revolt of French settlers and army officers in Algeria against what they regarded as the effeteness of the government in Paris and its handling of the Algerian war led to the overthrow of the Fourth Republic. De Gaulle was swept back to power on a wave of popular enthusiasm. He indicated that this time he must be given the means to take whatever measures he deemed necessary to save France, and his policies were approved by a referendum in September. A new constitution establishing the Fifth Republic came into force in October.

the de Gaulle era, 1958–69

In December 1958 de Gaulle was elected as the Fifth Republic's first president, with wide executive powers. The franc was devalued, and a series of drastic measures enacted, aimed at stabilizing the economy. In the longer term, the de Gaulle era was one of economic growth and large-scale rural-to-urban migration. The relationship between France and its overseas possessions was re-examined: those territories wishing to retain ties with France entered the *French Community, which had superseded the French Union. Guinea, however, voted for separation from France and became an independent state without French connections in October 1958. By 1961 so many overseas possessions had gained independence within the French Community that the Community itself was dissolved.

France's economy grew stronger through the succeeding years, though some underlying weaknesses remained, and its foreign policy developed distinctive traits. France took steps to become an independent military nuclear power just when Britain was abandoning the role. Although retaining friendly relations with Britain and the USA at the start of his regime (he paid a successful state visit to Britain in 1960 and had cordial talks in Paris with President Kennedy

in 1961), de Gaulle took the decisive step of actively promoting closer Franco-German relations, and so officially ended a period of hatred and mistrust between the two countries that had been virtually continuous since 1870. Close economic and cultural links were established between France and the German Federal Republic, and in January 1963 de Gaulle and the German chancellor Konrad Adenauer signed the Franco-German 'reconciliation treaty' in Paris.

Meanwhile de Gaulle's decision that the Algerian problem could be solved only by granting full independence to the nationalists caused bitterness among the settlers and officers who had brought him to power in the expectation that he would win the war there for France. There were abortive revolts against de Gaulle in Algeria in 1960 and 1961, and several attempts were made on his life, then and later, by supporters of the Organization de l'Armée Secrète (OAS), which during 1960–61 carried out a systematic terrorist campaign in both Algeria and France. As time passed it attracted some of de Gaulle's foremost original supporters, such as Gen Raoul Salan, Georges Bidault, and Jacques Soustelle, but by 1963 the OAS was a spent force. Algeria became independent in 1962, after a referendum had approved de Gaulle's policy there.

Although there was at times considerable criticism of de Gaulle's government, not merely among extremists but among moderates who felt that he was riding roughshod over democratic principles, his supporters won an overall majority over all other parties in the elections in November 1962. Under de Gaulle, France dominated the European Economic Community, and in January 1963 vetoed Britain's application to join it. De Gaulle distrusted Britain's motives, and was suspicious of Britain's ties with the USA at a time when France was attempting to become the leader of a third 'European' force, which would be independent of both the Soviet and the 'Anglo-Saxon' (Anglo-American) blocs. This pronouncedly independent line was to show itself in France's withdrawal of its fleets from NATO commands, in its first atomic-bomb test in 1960 and hydrogen-bomb test in 1968, and in de Gaulle's outspoken criticism in 1965 of US policy in Vietnam.

In 1965 de Gaulle was re-elected president under the new constitutional arrangement whereby the president was chosen by universal suffrage. However, the election was close: the first ballot failed to give him an outright majority, and in the second ballot his left-wing opponent François *Mitterrand polled nearly 45% of the vote. De Gaulle continued with his independent approach to foreign policy. He took tough action with the EEC in the course of 1966, and in the same year announced the French withdrawal from the integrated military command of NATO, with complete withdrawal to occur in 1969. Nevertheless, de Gaulle's position seemed uncertain. His paternalistic approach to domestic affairs, reflected in censorship and centralization, brought about a public reaction, and in the general elections of 1967 the Gaullists and the 'right coalition' won only a bare majority.

In May 1968 a student revolt, largely in the Latin Quarter of Paris, was followed by the most extensive wave of strikes that France had known since 1936. The government was severely shaken, but de Gaulle recovered; the elections of 1968 returned an enormous Gaullist majority, and a new phase of Gaullism seemed to be inaugurated by the appointment of Maurice *Couve de Murville as prime minister. By November de Gaulle was in a sufficiently strong position to refuse to devalue the franc. But the referendum of 1969, which sought to reform the Senate and local

government, went against de Gaulle. He resigned in April 1969 and took no further part in French public life.

Pompidou's presidency, 1969–74
De Gaulle's former prime minister Georges *Pompidou was elected president on de Gaulle's resignation. Pompidou maintained some Gaullist principles in foreign policy, such as retaining independent possession of nuclear weapons, the desire for understanding with communist countries, and a critical attitude towards Israel. But he was more subtle and more conciliatory in many spheres, particularly towards Great Britain's membership of the EEC, which his meeting with the British prime minister Edward Heath in 1971 made possible. At home Pompidou was cautious. He was alarmed both by the increase of left-wing support (as shown in the elections of 1973 that reduced the Gaullist majority) and by the number of scandals affecting Gaullist politicians. But France remained prosperous, and Pompidou saw no threat to his position, until he was stricken with illness and died in April 1974.

Giscard's presidency, 1974–81
At first it seemed that Pompidou's successor would be the former Gaullist prime minister Jacques Chaban-Delmas. But a revolt among certain Gaullists, led by Jacques *Chirac, and the prestige of Valéry *Giscard d'Estaing, leader of the centre-right Independent Republicans, proved too much. In the second ballot Giscard d'Estaing rallied most of the Gaullists and moderates, as well as the right wing, to beat the Communist–Socialist coalition, led by Mitterrand, which must also have received some Gaullist and moderate support.

Giscard attempted to present an informal image, and encouraged the impression of a France governed by young and dynamic men and women. In domestic policies he was too conservative to be an innovator, but in social matters he emphasized the quality of life and sought to improve conditions for women by laws that made it easier to obtain divorce and abortion. He also lowered the minimum age of voting from 21 to 18, relaxed censorship, and reformed the education system. He followed Gaullist principles by insisting on the primacy of French interests and of French nuclear weapons, but followed Pompidou in being conciliatory and cautious. In the European Community he played a more active and cooperative role than his predecessors.

Giscard faced opposition, however, from his 'right coalition' partner Jacques Chirac, who was prime minister 1974–76; he also had to contend with deteriorating international economic conditions. France performed better than many of its European competitors in the period 1974–81, with the president launching a major nuclear-power programme to save on energy imports and, while Raymond *Barre was prime minister (1976–81), a new, liberal 'freer market' economic strategy. During this period the Union pour la Démocratie Française (UDF; Union for French Democracy) was formed to unite several centre-right parties. However, with 1.7 million unemployed, Giscard was defeated by Socialist Party leader François Mitterrand in the 1981 presidential election.

Mitterrand and the 'left coalition' Mitterrand's victory was the first presidential success for the 'left coalition' during the Fifth Republic, and was immediately succeeded by a landslide victory for the Parti Socialiste (PS; Socialist Party) and Parti Communiste Français (PCF; French Communist Party) in the 1981 elections to the national assembly. The new administration introduced a radical programme of social reform, decentralization, and nationalization, and passed a series of reflationary budgets aimed at reducing unemployment.

Financial constraints forced a switch towards a more conservative policy of *rigueur* ('austerity') in 1983. A U-turn in economic policy was completed in 1984 when the prime minister, Pierre *Mauroy, was replaced by Laurent *Fabius, prompting the resignation of PCF members of the cabinet. An international scandal was created in July 1985 when the ship *Rainbow Warrior*, belonging to the environmental organization Greenpeace, whose opposition to nuclear testing annoyed France, was sunk in New Zealand by French secret-service agents. Unemployment rose to over 2.5 million in 1985–86, increasing racial tension in urban areas. The extreme-rightwing Front National (FN; National Front), led by Jean-Marie *Le Pen, benefited from this and gained seats in the March 1986 national assembly elections. The 'left coalition' lost its majority, the PCF having been in decline for some years. The PS, however, had emerged as France's single most popular party.

Mitterrand and Chirac From 1958 to 1986 the president and prime minister had been drawn from the same party coalition, and the president had been allowed to dominate in both home and foreign affairs. In 1986 Mitterrand was obliged to appoint as prime minister the leader of the opposition, Jacques Chirac, who emerged as the dominant force in the 'shared executive'. Chirac introduced a radical 'new conservative' programme of denationalization, deregulation, and 'desocialization', using the executive's decree powers and the parliamentary guillotine to steamroller measures through. His educational and economic changes encountered serious opposition from militant students and striking workers, necessitating embarrassing policy concessions. Chirac was defeated by Mitterrand in the May 1988 presidential election.

Rocard's progressive programme In the national assembly elections of

June 1988, the Socialists emerged as the largest single political party. Mitterrand duly appointed Michel *Rocard, a moderate social democrat, as prime minister heading a minority PS government that included several centre-party representatives. Rocard implemented a progressive programme, aimed at protecting the underprivileged and improving the quality of life. In June 1988 he negotiated the Matignon Accord, designed to solve the New Caledonia problem, which was later approved by referendum. Between 1988 and 1990 France enjoyed a strong economic upturn and attention focused increasingly on quality of life, with Les Verts (the Green Party) gaining 11% of the national vote in the European Parliament elections of June 1989.

racial tensions Although the extreme right FN had been virtually eliminated from the national assembly in 1988 by the reintroduction of single-member constituencies, it continued to do well in municipal elections, pressurizing the government into adopting a hard line against illegal immigration. New programmes were announced for the integration of Muslim immigrants – from Algeria, Tunisia, and other areas with French colonial ties – into mainstream French society. Religious and cultural tensions increased. A commission set up to look at the problems of immigrant integration reported in 1991 that France's foreign population was 3.7 million (6.8% of the population), the same as in 1982. However, 10 million citizens were of 'recent foreign origin'.

the Gulf War In September 1990, after Iraqi violation of the French ambassador's residence in Kuwait, the French government dispatched 5,000 troops to Saudi Arabia. Despite France's previously close ties with Iraq (including arms sales), French military forces played a prominent role within the US-led coalition in the 1991 Gulf War. Defence minister Jean-Pierre Chevènement resigned in February 1991 in opposition to this strategy, but the majority of people in the country – which has the largest Muslim population in western Europe – supported the government's stance.

Mitterrand's popularity in decline In April 1991 the neo-Gaullist Rassemblement pour la République (RPR; Rally for the Republic) and the Union pour la Démocratie Française (UDP; Union for French Democracy), France's main, usually factious, right-of-centre opposition parties, signed a formal election pact. In May, after disagreements over economic policy, Mitterrand replaced Rocard with Edith *Cresson, saying that her experience as a former member of the European Parliament and minister for European affairs would be important for France's future in Europe. Mitterrand became the Fifth Republic's longest-serving president in September 1991.

However, with the economy in recession, racial tensions increasing, discontent among farmers, militancy among public-sector workers, and the reputation of the PS tarnished by a number of financial scandals, Mitterrand's popularity fell from over 50% in September 1991 to barely 35% in January 1992.

By the close of 1991, the popularity rating of Cresson was the lowest ever for a premier in the Fifth Republic, and in the March 1992 regional council elections the PS captured only 18% of the national vote. Mitterrand appointed Pierre Bérégovoy to replace Cresson in April 1992. As finance minister, he had been blamed by Cresson for the nation's economic troubles, but he was respected by the country's financial community. In a referendum in September 1992 the Maastricht Treaty on European union was narrowly endorsed.

Balladur's premiership The PS suffered a heavy defeat in the March 1993 national-assembly elections, which were held during the midst of economic recession, with the unemployment rate exceeding 10%. The PS's national poll share was its lowest since the parliamentary election of 1968. Mitterrand appointed Edouard Balladur of the conservative RPR as prime minister, to head the second 'cohabitation' government of his presidency. In the aftermath of the PS defeat, Bérégovoy committed suicide. Michel Rocard was chosen to replace him as PS leader, but resigned in June 1994 after the PS polled poorly in the European elections. He was replaced by Henri Emmanuelli.

Balladur proved a popular prime minister but encountered opposition to his tight immigration and privatization policies and his proposals for local-government funding of private schools, which put him at odds with President Mitterrand. His employment legislation, reducing the minimum wage paid to young workers, was criticized by unions and the PS, and he abandoned these proposals after protest demonstrations were followed by a revival of the left in local elections. With Mitterrand in failing health, Balladur emerged as the dominant force in the 'cohabitation' administration, compounding his popularity by engineering a recovery in the French economy. However, in the autumn of 1994 his popularity rating slumped after several of his ministers were implicated in corruption scandals and resigned. Financial scandals also damaged the PS, made worse by the revelation of the use of HIV-infected blood in transfusions under earlier Socialist governments.

French influence in central Africa was severely weakened by the fall of president Mobutu in Zaire, following the collapse in 1994 of the regime France had supported in Rwanda.

Chirac becomes president
Evidence of a split within the conservative RPR emerged in the run-up to the 1995 presidential elections when it became clear that both Jacques Chirac, former premier and party leader, and Prime Minister Balladur intended to contest the presidency. Balladur, whose reputation had suffered from his alleged involvement in a telephone-tapping affair and his admission that he had profited from share dealings, rapidly lost ground to Chirac, who presented himself as a 'man of the people', promising action against 'social exclusion', more jobs, higher public-sector wages, and a more relaxed economic policy to stimulate recovery. After the PS took a surprising lead in the first ballot, Balladur dropped out of the contest. Chirac, at the head of a 'right coalition', was elected president in May, securing a comfortable majority over the PS candidate Lionel Jospin. He appointed the former foreign minister and pro-European Alain Juppé as prime minister, and began his presidency with the controversial announcement that France planned to resume nuclear-weapons testing in the Pacific region. The decision to resume nuclear testing was widely condemned and the first test on Mururoa atoll provoked anticolonial riots in Tahiti. At home, national security measures were announced in the wake of a terrorist bombing campaign mounted by Algerian guerrillas, and the position of Juppé appeared under threat owing to his implication in a housing scandal. Significant amendments to the constitution were approved in July 1995, but by the end of the year popular support for President Chirac had slumped dramatically, with nationwide public-sector strikes – the worst since 1968 – in November and December bringing the nation's transport system to a virtual standstill.

events in 1996–97 In January 1996 the government announced an end to its nuclear-weapons testing programme in the south Pacific and called for a worldwide test ban.

In March a treaty with the USA and Britain was signed that made the south Pacific a nuclear-free zone. In the same month former defence minister François Léotard replaced Giscard as head of the centre-right UDF, the junior partner in the ruling coalition.

Pledging a reduction in the country's fiscal deficit and a commitment to a single European currency, in August the government agreed to cut government spending by 2% in real terms in 1997 in an effort to qualify for European Monetary Union in 1999, in spite of high unemployment and lack of growth in the economy.

In May 1996 a fresh outbreak of terrorist violence by the outlawed National Corsican Liberation Front ended the truce called in January and jeopardized future talks with the French government. In December François Santoni, leader of the hardline Corsican separatist A Cuncolta Naziunalista wing of the front, was captured by French police, but the organization continued to mount a wave of bombings in Corsica and Nice in January 1997. In May 1998 Corsican separatists ended a three-month ceasefire with a bombing in southern France.

1997 elections – Socialists come to power In March 1997 unemployment reached a post-war record of 12.8% of the workforce. However, the rise was slowing and the economy was beginning to pick up. This persuaded President Chirac to announce in late April that a general election would be held a year early. His intention was that the government should receive a mandate to carry out further austerity measures that would enable France to meet the financial targets required for membership of a single European currency in 1999, and would assure Chirac a majority in the national assembly until the end of his presidential term. His tactic backfired, however, when the elections were won by the PS, who opposed the previous

government's austerity measures. The PS leader Lionel Jospin became prime minister in June 1997. His left-wing coalition government claimed victory in French regional elections in mid-March 1998, but fell short of the sweeping successes it had expected. Although the far-right FN fell short of the record nationwide score predicted by opinion polls, it seemed to have matched, or slightly exceeded, the 15% it achieved in the 1997 parliamentary election.

Jospin's plans In September 1997 unemployment was 3.2 million, or 12.6%, and still rising. The new PS government unveiled plans to create 35,000 new jobs in the public sector over the coming two and a half years, implementing a manifesto comment. The jobs would go to 18–25-year-olds, over a quarter of whom were currently unemployed, and they would be given five-year contracts of a level of at least the minimum wage, with 80% of the cost underwritten by the government. However, in policy U-turns, it allowed privatization to continue with the sale of holdings in Air France and France Telecom, and broke a promise to abolish tough immigration laws introduced by the preceding government.

In January 1998 the government faced nationwide protests by unemployed people, who marched and occupied welfare offices, demanding additional financial assistance. Prime Minister Jospin offered to create a FFr 1 billion fund to help the unemployed through retraining and other measures. In February the National Assembly passed a law to reduce the working week from 39 hours to 35 hours, starting in 2000. When this did come into effect, in February 2000 there were protests, notably by French lorry drivers who blocked roads and border checkpoints in anger at the attempt by employers to use the new legislation to break down traditional working patterns and to impose a wage freeze.

regional elections and party splits

In regional elections in March 1998, the ruling PS, Verts, and PCF coalition performed well, winning 37% of the vote, while the FN, with 15% of the vote, held the balance of power in 19 of the 22 regions. The 'mainstream right', comprising the RPR and the UDF, won 36% of the vote, but was thrown into disarray by divisions over whether to accept FN support to take control of regions. Four UDF members, including the former defence minister, Charles Millon, defied the party's leadership and retained their regional presidencies with FN support. They were consequently banned from the UDF. Millon, president of Rhône-Alpes region, responded in April 1998, by forming a new party. In May 1998 the Démocratie Libérale (DL; Liberal Democracy), led by Alain Madelin, broke away from the UDF. Also in May, the FN narrowly lost its one National Assembly seat in a by-election. In April 1998 the National Assembly voted in favour of France's involvement in the European single currency.

In September 1998, François Bayrou, a former education minister and the leader of Democratic Force, was elected leader of the opposition centre-right UDF. The vacancy had been created by the resignation of François Léotard, who was under investigation in connection with allegations of illicit funding of the defunct Republican Party. In November 1999 Michèle Alliot-Marie, a lawyer, was elected head of the RPR, making her the first woman to lead one of France's main political parties.

In December 1998, the FN, the most successful far-right party in Western Europe, broke into two factions, led respectively by Le Pen and his rebel deputy, Bruno Mégret, each claiming to be the true standard-bearer of the French ultra-right. Mégret was elected president in late January 1999 of what his supporters claimed was the authentic version of the FN.

The Mégret wing of the party – called the Mouvement National Républicain (MNR; National Republican Movement) claimed to be patriotic rather than xenophobic and concerned principally with the threats of the present (immigration, globalism, US cultural imperialism, and European federalism). A court ruled in May 1999, however, that the right to use the name, symbols, and campaign subsidiaries of the FN belonged to Le Pen and not to Mégret. The ruling was a severe rebuff for the breakaway party.

In December 1998, it was announced that GDP grew by 3.1% during 1998, the strongest performance during the 1990s, leading to high levels of public support (above 60%) for Prime Minister Jospin. The unemployment rate fell to 11%.

Corsica The government of Prime Minister Jospin survived a vote of censure in May 1999 in the National Assembly. It had been brought by the conservative opposition in protest at the government's handling of a scandal in Corsica, which led to the sacking and detention of the prefect there. The issue of rule in Corsica was addressed by Jospin in July 2000 when he unveiled a plan for limited autonomy for the government there. In an attempt to end 20 years of violence on the island, he proposed a single political and administrative body with limited independent law-making powers. The proposals marked a great departure from the tradition of heavy-handed government from Paris, and were overwhelmingly approved by the Corsican Assembly (the regional parliament). The plan was conditional on an end to violence.

BSE In October 1999, France refused to join other European countries in lifting a ban on British beef which had been enforced in response to cases of BSE, a disease in cows, being transferred to humans through beef,

causing Creutzfeldt–Jakob disease, a brain disease. The British government reacted angrily to France's refusal to resume imports of British beef. In October 2000, fears over BSE in French cattle rose as three supermarket chains were discovered to have sold meat from infected herds.
The following month, President Chirac called for an immediate ban on cattle remains in all French animal feed and schools took beef off the menu.

On 25 July 2000, an Air France Concorde aircraft crashed soon after take-off in Paris, killing all 113 people on board and leading to all Concordes being grounded.

fuel protests A wave of disruptive protests over fuel prices supplemented by high taxes upon petrol and other oil products hit Europe in August and September 2000. Popular protests began in France at the end of August, when protests involving the blockading of oil refineries, halting deliveries of fuel, by lorry drivers, farmers, ambulance workers and taxi drivers were successful as the government made tax concessions on fuel. The actions of the French government inspired similar protests in Germany, Spain, the UK, Ireland, and Belgium.

Elf-Aquitaine corruption scandal In January 2001, the trial began of the former foreign minister, Roland Dumas, his ex-mistress, and others, on charges of corruption in relation to Elf-Aquitaine, a state-owned oil company. In February, Alfred Sirven, a former leading executive at Elf, was extradited from the Philippines to face corruption charges, and act as a key witness in the case involving Dumas. In May, the trial resulted in prison sentences for most of the accused, including Dumas who was convicted of embezzlement and sentenced to six months in jail. It was one of the biggest corruption trials in French history.

Paris mayoral elections In March 2001, Paris elected its first Socialist

mayor, Bertrand Delanoe, since 1871. Delanoe was also one of the country's few openly gay politicians.

Chirac under investigation In March 2001, President Chirac refused on constitutional grounds to testify before a tribunal investigating corrupt financing of his party in Paris when he was mayor. He had been implicated in October 2000, when an investigation uncovered a videotape of a bribe allegedly being given his presence in 1986. Further allegation were made in June, and magistrates announced that they wanted to question Chirac, as well as his wife and daughter, over cash payments for trips made when he was mayor of Paris. In July, Chirac rejected suggestions that he had received £240,000 in bribes, allegedly spent on holidays for himself and his family and friends.

On 1 January 2002, euro notes and coins were introduced as the national currency.

presidential elections In the second round of the presidential election on 5 May, Chirac, won by a landslide with 82.2% of the vote (the highest ever margin of victory in the Fifth Republic) over Jean-Marie Le Pen, the leader of the FN. Socialist voters switched their allegiance to Chirac following the elimination of Lionel Jospin in the first round, reflecting their hostility to Le Pen's perceived fascism. However, Le Pen attracted 5.5 million votes (720,000 more than in the first round) in an 80% turnout, provoking widespread European concern about the increasing popularity of far-right parties.

In June 2002, in the concluding round of parliamentary elections in France, the centre-right won a landslide victory, taking 399 of the National Assembly's 577 seats. The Union pour la Majorité Présidentielle (UMP; Union for the Presidential Majority), an alliance of the RPR and the DL supporting President Chirac, secured 355 seats, the UDF 29 seats, and other right-wing candidates 15 seats. The left lost its former parliamentary majority as the PS dropped by 101 seats to 140 and its allies won only a further 38.

Franchet d'Esperey, Louis Félix Marie François (1856–1942) French soldier. In World War I, he fought in the first Battle of the Marne September 1914, then held the Aisne bridgeheads. He was placed in command of the Armies of Eastern France April 1916, and of the Armies of the North January 1917. He was appointed supreme commander of the Allied armies in the East June 1918, accepting the surrender of Bulgaria September 1918. He commanded the Allied forces in Turkey until 1920 and was created Marshal of France 1921.

Franco, Francisco (Paulino Hermenegildo Teódulo Bahamonde) (1892–1975) Spanish dictator from 1939. As a general, he led the insurgent Nationalists to victory in the Spanish *Civil War 1936–39, supported by fascist Italy and Nazi Germany, and established a dictatorship. In 1942 Franco reinstated a Cortes (Spanish parliament), which in 1947 passed an act by which he became head of state for life.

Franco was born in Galicia, northwestern Spain. He entered the army in 1910, served in Morocco 1920–26, and was appointed chief of staff in 1935, but demoted to governor of the Canary Islands in 1936. Dismissed from this post by the Popular Front (Republican) government, he plotted an uprising with German and Italian assistance, and on the outbreak of the Civil War organized the invasion of Spain by North African troops and foreign legionaries. He took command of the Nationalists and proclaimed himself caudillo (leader) of Spain. The defeat of the Republic with the surrender of Madrid in 1939 brought all Spain under his government. The war and first years

of power were marked by the execution of tens of thousands of his opponents.

On the outbreak of World War II, in spite of Spain's official attitude of 'strictest neutrality', his pro-Axis sympathies led him to send aid, later withdrawn, to the German side. His government was at first ostracized as fascist by the United Nations, but with the development of the Cold War, Franco came to be viewed more as an anti-communist, which improved relations with other Western countries.

At home, he curbed the growing power of the *Falange Española (the fascist party), and in later years slightly liberalized his regime, though he was never a popular ruler. In 1969 he nominated *Juan Carlos as his successor and future king of Spain. He relinquished the premiership in 1973, but remained head of state until his death.

Franjiyeh, Suleiman (1910–) also known as **Sulayman Franjiyya**, Lebanese Maronite Christian politician, president 1970–76. He emerged as a fierce rival of the conservative Maronite political clans of Chamoun and Gemayel and from 1960 sat in the Lebanese parliament, serving as a minister in 1960–61 and 1968–70. He was elected president, by the parliament, in August 1970, when he defeated Elias Sarkis by a single vote.

Frankfurter, Felix (1882–1965) Austrian-born US jurist and Supreme Court justice. As a supporter of liberal causes, Frankfurter was one of the founders of the American Civil Liberties Union in 1920. Appointed to the US Supreme Court in 1939 by F D Roosevelt, he opposed the use of the judicial veto to advance political ends.

Fraser, (John) Malcolm (1930–) Australian Liberal politician, prime minister 1975–83; nicknamed 'the Prefect' because of a supposed disregard of subordinates.

Fraser, Peter (1884–1950) New Zealand Labour politician, prime minister 1940–49. A member of the

New Zealand parliament from 1918, Fraser was minister of health and education 1935–40 and when Michael *Savage died in office, he became prime minister. During his period as prime minister he coordinated the New Zealand war effort. After 1945 he concentrated on problems of social legislation, encouraged state control over key industries, and, in 1949, promoted controversial legislation to bring in military conscription.

Frederick IX (1899–1972) King of Denmark from 1947. He was succeeded by his daughter who became Queen *Margrethe II.

Free French in World War II, movement formed by Gen Charles *de Gaulle in the UK in June 1940, consisting of French soldiers who continued to fight against the Axis after the Franco-German armistice. They took the name **Fighting France** in 1942 and served in many campaigns, among them Gen Leclerc's advance from Chad to Tripolitania in 1942, the Syrian campaigns of 1941, the campaigns in the Western Desert, the Italian campaign, the liberation of France, and the invasion of Germany. Their emblem was the Cross of Lorraine, a cross with two bars.

Frei (Montalva), Eduardo (1911–1982) Chilean president 1964–70. Elected as the only effective anti-Marxist candidate, he pursued a moderate programme of 'Chileanization' of US-owned copper interests.
His regime, characterized by social reform, was plagued by inflation and labour unrest, but saw considerable economic development.

Frelimo acronym for *FREnte de Libertação de Moçambique*, 'Front for the Liberation of Mozambique', nationalist group aimed at gaining independence for Mozambique from the occupying Portuguese. It began operating from southern Tanzania in 1962 and continued until victory in 1975.

French, John Denton Pinkstone (1852–1925) 1st Earl of Ypres, British field marshal. In the second South African War 1899–1902, he relieved Kimberley and took Bloemfontein; in World War I he was commander-in-chief of the British Expeditionary Force in France 1914–15; he resigned after being criticized as indecisive and became commander-in-chief home forces. KCB 1900, Viscount 1916, Earl 1922.

French Community former association consisting of France and those overseas territories joined with it by the constitution of the Fifth Republic, following the 1958 referendum. Many of the constituent states withdrew during the 1960s, and it no longer formally exists, but in practice all former French colonies have close economic and cultural as well as linguistic links with France.

French Equatorial Africa federation of French territories in West Africa. Founded in 1910, it consisted of Gabon, Middle Congo, Chad, and Ubangi-Shari (now the Central African Republic), and was ruled from Brazzaville. The federation supported the Free French in World War II and was given representation in the French Fourth Republic 1944–58. In 1958, the states voted for autonomy and the federation was dissolved.

French India former French possessions in India: Pondicherry, Chandernagore, Karaikal, Mahé, and Yanam (Yanaon). They were all transferred to India by 1954.

French Revolution the period 1789–1799 that saw the end of the monarchy in France. The revolution began as an attempt to create a constitutional monarchy, where the powers of the king would be limited by a parliament. By late 1792, however, demands for long-overdue reforms resulted in the proclamation of the First Republic and the execution of King Louis XVI in January 1793.
The violence of the revolution, attacks by other nations, and bitter factional struggles, riots, and counter-

revolutionary uprisings across France severely weakened the republic. This helped bring the extremists to power, and the bloody Reign of Terror followed. French armies then succeeded in holding off their foreign enemies and one of the generals, Napoleon Bonaparte, seized power in 1799.

the States General In the decades before the French Revolution, France was involved in the Seven Years' War (1756–1763) and the American Revolution (1775–1783), also known as the War of American Independence. The cost of these wars brought about a financial crisis. The French government did not have the money to pay for the wars, so borrowed large amounts of money at high rates of interest to finance them. By 1787 it was clear that the French monarchy and government was bankrupt, and King Louis XVI and his government were forced to seek new solutions to their problems.

In 1788 King Louis XVI decided to summon the States General (three 'estates' of clergy (first), nobles (second), and commons (third)) in order to raise taxes. It was the first time that the States General had been called since 1614, indicating major weakness in the monarchy. By calling the States General, King Louis XVI was admitting that the monarchy was in a desperate position, leaving him at the mercy of his enemies in France.

The States General met in May 1789. During the meeting, the representatives of the third estate (all the people of France who were neither nobles nor Catholic priests) insisted that the three estates should be merged into a single national assembly. The demand was designed to force the king to recognize the rights of the French nation and people. Priests from the first estate soon joined the deputies of the third estate, along with many liberal-minded nobles from the second estate. When Louis XVI tried to lock the doors of the National Assembly hall, the deputies

met in a nearby tennis court, and issued the 'Tennis Court Oath'. In this statement they swore that they would never stop meeting until Louis XVI recognized their rights.

Louis was forced to back down and accept the existence of the National Assembly. At the same time, however, large numbers of soldiers were gathering on the hills surrounding Paris. Their intentions were unclear, but the people of Paris were unlikely to believe that their king was entirely peaceful towards them. The combination of the attempt to stop the creation of a national assembly and the presence of troops around Paris created a highly tense atmosphere in Paris by the second week of July 1789.

the National Assembly Louis's actions led to the storming of the Bastille prison by the Paris mob on 14 July 1789. On the same day the price of bread in Paris had reached its highest ever level. The Bastille was the symbol of the repressive power of the monarchy. It was also believed to hold ammunition that would allow the Parisians to defend themselves against the king's soldiers. The storming of the Bastille was followed by the formation of a revolutionary city government in Paris, known as the Paris Commune, and a number of peasant uprisings outside Paris.

In August the National Assembly introduced the 'Declaration of the Rights of Man and of the Citizen', which contained the ideas of liberty and equality; the right to own property; and the right of all citizens to resist oppressive treatment. The king refused to agree to the Declaration, however, and in October there were more uprisings in Paris. In 1791 the royal family attempted to flee the country in the 'flight of Varennes', but Louis XVI was captured and was later forced to accept a new constitution.

the constitution of 1791 The new constitution established a constitutional monarchy. It reduced

Louis's powers and gave authority over lawmaking and financial matters to the National Assembly. Power had passed from the hands of the monarchy to the representatives of the French people. Under the constitution, France was reorganized into 83 *départements*. This was for the purposes of efficiency and to mark a break with the past. The constitution also reformed the court system by abolishing the old *parlements* which had been dominated by the nobility. It also gave government control over the *Roman Catholic Church by requiring both judges and priests to be elected to office, as well as extending religious tolerance to Protestants and Jews. The National Assembly also took ownership of much of the Catholic Church's vast lands and property, which were sold off in order to pay off the nation's debts.

war with Austria and Prussia
During this period some of the aristocracy moved abroad, and tried to encourage other nations to fight against the revolutionary government. These aristocrats were known as émigrés, and many settled in Prussian (German) towns in the *Rhineland. They used their fortunes to raise armies and produce propaganda pamphlets against the revolution. They wanted to get the Prussians and Austrians to launch a war to restore Louis XVI and the monarchy to its pre-1789 position in France. The émigrés were particularly confident of getting the Austrians to attack the revolution, as the Austrian emperor, Joseph II, was the brother of Marie Antoinette, the French queen.

The revolution's supporters outside France were also suffering increased attack, and France eventually went to war with Austria and Prussia (who supported Louis XVI) on 20 April 1792. The Austrian and Prussian armies invaded France, and for a time the war threatened to destroy the revolution. The armies of the revolution lost every

battle they fought with the Austrians and Prussians, and it seemed inevitable that Paris and the revolution would soon fall. By 2 September 1792 the Austrians had captured the fortress at *Verdun and the road to Paris was open to them.

However, on 10 August the Paris mob had stormed the Tuileries Palace, where Louis XVI had been living, and had imprisoned the king and his family. The constitutional monarchy established by the 1791 constitution was brought to an end.

On 20 September 1792 the French won a crucial victory at the Battle of Valmy and effectively saved the revolution. A National Convention had been formed by election and, on 21 September, the Convention abolished the monarchy and declared France a republic. Louis XVI was put on trial, found guilty of treason, and executed at the guillotine on 21 January 1793.

the Reign of Terror In the period after Louis XVI's death, tensions within the National Convention resulted in a power struggle between the moderate Girondins and the more radical Jacobins, led by Maximilien Robespierre, Georges Jaques Danton, and Jean Paul Marat. The Jacobins arrested the Girondin leaders in June 1793, and control of the country was passed to the infamous Committee of Public Safety, which was headed by Robespierre, Lazare Carnot, and Bertrand Barère. The committee announced a policy of terror against all those seen as rebels or opponents of the revolution, supporters of the king, and Girondin sympathizers. During the Reign of Terror, an estimated 18,000 citizens were sent to the guillotine (though figures vary), and many more died in prison without being formally brought to trial. One of the more famous victims of the Terror was Marie Antoinette, the widow of Louis XVI.

Freyberg, Bernard Cyril (1889–1963)
1st Baron Freyberg, English-born New

Zealand soldier and administrator, governor general 1946–52. During World War II he commanded the 2nd New Zealand Expeditionary Force in the Middle East; the Commonwealth forces in Greece, Crete, and North Africa, during 1941; and the New Zealand Corps in Italy 1944–45.

Frunze, Mikhail Vasilievich (1885–1925) Russian revolutionary general. He defeated the Russian admiral Aleksander Kolchak in 1919 and the general Peter Nicolaievich Wrangel in 1920. In 1924 he became president of the Revolutionary Military Council, and in January 1925 became people's commissar (minister), for military and naval affairs, replacing Trotsky, who was ousted by Stalin.

Fuad I (1868–1936) King of Egypt from 1923. Son of the Khedive Ismail, he succeeded his elder brother Husse in Kamel as sultan of Egypt in 1917. Egypt was declared independent in 1922 and the promulgation of the 1923 constitution enabled him to assume the title of king. His pretension to be king of Sudan as well was not realized. Opposed to the constitution, he favoured the restoration of the autocracy of the ruling family and was almost constantly in conflict with the nationalists, represented by the Wafd.

Fuchs, (Emil Julius) Klaus (1911–1988) German spy who worked on atom-bomb research in the USA in World War II, and subsequently in the UK. He was imprisoned 1950–59 for passing information to the USSR and resettled in eastern Germany.

Fujimori, Alberto (Kenya) (1938–) Peruvian politician, president 1990–2000. He pursued free-market economic policies that led to economic growth and a widening gap between rich and poor. In 1992 he sided with the military in a coup to increase his powers and fight domestic terrorism. He was forced from office in 2000 by popular protests against government corruption and tampered elections, and he fled to Japan. He was succeeded by Alejandro Toledo.

Fukuda, Takeo (1905–1995) Japanese politician, prime minister 1976–78. First elected to the Diet (parliament) in 1952, he became a powerful faction leader in the conservative Liberal Democratic Party and continued to wield great influence until he relinquished the leadership of his faction in 1986.

Fulbright, (James) William (1905–1995) US Democratic politician. A US senator 1945–75, he was responsible for the **Fulbright Act** 1946, which provided grants for thousands of Americans to study abroad and for overseas students to study in the USA. Fulbright chaired the Senate Foreign Relations Committee 1959–74, and was a strong internationalist and supporter of the United Nations.

G

Gabon country in central Africa, bounded north by Cameroon, east and south by the Congo, west by the Atlantic Ocean, and northwest by Equatorial Guinea.

Gairy, Eric Matthew (1922–1997) Grenadian centre-left politician, chief minister 1957–62 and prime minister 1967–79. Initially a champion of the rural poor, he founded the Grenada United Labour Party (GULP) in 1950. He became chief minister of the Federation of the West Indies in 1957. As prime minister he led Grenada to independence within the British Commonwealth in 1974, but his regime became increasingly autocratic and corrupt, imposing restrictions on the media and unions, and order through his 'Mongoose Gang' of thugs. In 1979 he was ousted in a left-wing coup and, unsuccessful in further elections, he retired as GULP leader in 1996.

Gaitskell, Hugh (Todd Naylor) (1906–1963) British Labour Party leader from 1955. In 1950 he became minister of economic affairs, and then chancellor of the Exchequer until October 1951. As party leader, he tried to reconcile internal differences on nationalization and disarmament.

Galland, Adolf (1912–1996) German air ace of World War II. He served in the Spanish Civil War 1936–39 and then the Polish and French campaigns 1939 and the Battle of Britain 1940. By June 1941 he had claimed 70 enemy aircraft and was the first German pilot to be awarded the Swords to the Knight's Cross.

Gallegos Freire, Rómulo (1884–1969) Venezuelan politician and writer. He was Venezuela's first democratically elected president in 1948 before being overthrown and exiled by a military coup the same year. He was also a professor of philosophy and literature. His novels, focusing on Venezuelan life, include *La trepadora/The Climber* (1925) and *Doña Bárbara* (1929). He returned to Venezuela in 1958.

Gallipoli port in European Turkey, giving its name to the peninsula (ancient name **Chersonesus**) on which it stands. In World War I, at the instigation of Winston Churchill, an unsuccessful attempt was made between February 1915 and January 1916 by Allied troops to force their way through the Dardanelles and link up with Russia. The campaign was fought mainly by Australian and New Zealand (*Anzac) forces, who suffered heavy losses. An estimated 36,000 Commonwealth troops died during the nine-month campaign.

Galtieri, Leopoldo Fortunato (1926–2003) Argentine general and president 1981–82. A leading member from 1979 of the ruling right-wing military junta and commander of the army, Galtieri became president in December 1981. Under his leadership the junta ordered the seizure in 1982 of the Falkland Islands (Malvinas), a British colony in the southwestern Atlantic claimed by Argentina. After the surrender of his forces he resigned as army commander and was replaced as president. He and his fellow junta members were tried for abuse of human rights and court-martialled for their conduct of the war; he was sentenced to 12 years in prison in 1986, but only served a small portion of his sentence. In January 2000, warrants were issued in Spain for the arrest of Galtieri and other high-ranking members of his junta, accusing them of crimes against humanity and genocide during their period of power in Argentina.

Gambia, The country in west Africa, bounded north, east, and south by Senegal and west by the Atlantic Ocean.

Gamelin, Maurice Gustave (1872–1958) French commander-in-chief of the Allied armies in France at the outset of World War II 1939. Replaced by Maxime Weygand after the German breakthrough at Sedan 1940, he was tried by the *Vichy government as a scapegoat before the Riom 'war guilt' court 1942. He refused to defend himself and was detained in Germany until released by the Allies 1945.

Gandhi, Indira Priyadarshani (1917–1984) born **Indira Priyadarshani Nehru**, Indian politician, prime minister of India 1966–77 and 1980–84, and leader of the *Congress Party 1966–77 and subsequently of the Congress (I) party. She was assassinated in 1984 by members of her Sikh bodyguard, resentful of her use of troops to clear malcontents from the Sikh temple at Amritsar.

Her father, Jawaharlal Nehru, was India's first prime minister. She married Feroze Gandhi in 1942 (died 1960, not related to Mahatma Gandhi) and had two sons, Sanjay Gandhi (1946–1980), who died in an aeroplane crash, and Rajiv *Gandhi, who was assassinated in 1991. In 1975 the validity of her re-election to parliament was questioned, and she declared a state of emergency. During this time Sanjay Gandhi implemented a social and economic programme (including an unpopular family-planning policy) that led to his mother's defeat in 1977.

Gandhi, Mahatma (1869–1948) honorific name of **Mohandas Karamchand Gandhi,** (Sanskrit *Mahatma* '**Great Soul'**) Indian nationalist leader. A pacifist, he led the struggle for Indian independence from the UK by advocating non-violent non-cooperation (*satyagraha* 'truth and firmness') from 1915. He was imprisoned several times by the British authorities. He was influential in the nationalist Congress Party and in the independence negotiations in 1947. He was assassinated by a Hindu nationalist in the violence that followed the partition of British India into India and Pakistan in 1948. Religious violence in India and Pakistan soon waned, and his teachings came to inspire non-violent movements in other parts of the world, notably in the USA under civil-rights leader Martin Luther King Jr, and in South Africa under Nelson Mandela.

Gandhi began to develop the principles of *satyagraha*, the practice of non-violent resistance, while practising as a lawyer in South Africa, where he lived from 1893. He led the Indian community there in opposition to racial discrimination until 1914, when the South African government made important concessions to his demands. He returned to India in January 1915 and became the leader in the country's complex struggle for independence from British rule. He organized hunger strikes, boycotts of British goods, and events of civil disobedience, and campaigned for social reform. In 1920, when the British failed to make amends, Gandhi proclaimed an organized campaign of non-cooperation. Indians in public office resigned, government agencies were boycotted, and Indian children were withdrawn from government schools. Gandhi was arrested by the British, but they were soon forced to release him.

India's economic independence was an important issue for Gandhi's *Swaraj* (self-ruling) movement. As a remedy for the extreme poverty affecting Indian villagers as a result of exploitation by British industrialists, Gandhi advocated the revival of cottage industries. He began to use a spinning wheel as a token of the renewal of native Indian industries and the return to the simple village life he expounded.

In 1921 the Indian National Congress, the group that spearheaded the movement for independence, gave Gandhi complete executive authority. However, a series of armed revolts against Britain broke out and Gandhi withdrew from active politics 1924–30. In 1930, he led a 265 km/165 mi march from Ahmadabad, Gujarat, to the Arabian Sea, and produced salt by evaporating sea water as a gesture of defiance against the British monopoly in salt production. In 1932, he began to fast as a method of protest. The fasts were effective measures against the British, because revolution could well have broken out had he died. He formally resigned from politics in 1934, but continued to travel through India teaching ahimsa (non-violence) and demanding the eradication of 'untouchability', the policy of shunning members of India's lowest caste. In real terms, his political power remained immense and, in 1939, he returned to active political life because of the pending federation of Indian principalities with the rest of India. Gandhi stood steadfastly against the partition of India, but ultimately had to concede to it, hoping that internal peace would be achieved after the Muslim demand for separation had been met.

Gandhi, Rajiv (1944–1991) Indian politician, prime minister from 1984 (following his mother Indira Gandhi's assassination) to November 1989. As prime minister, he faced growing discontent with his party's elitism and lack of concern for social issues. He was assassinated at an election rally.

Gang of Four in Chinese history, the chief members of the radical faction that played a key role in directing the *Cultural Revolution and tried to seize power after the death of the communist leader *Mao Zedong in 1976. It included his widow *Jiang Qing; the other members were three young Shanghai politicians: Zhang Chunqiao, Wang Hongwen, and Yao Wenyuan. The coup failed and the Gang of Four were arrested. Publicly tried in 1980, they were found guilty of treason.

Gang of Four in the UK, term referring to four members of the Labour Party who in 1981 resigned to form the *Social Democratic Party: Roy Jenkins, David Owen, Shirley Williams, and William Rodgers.

Garand rifle US rifle M1, standard US military rifle from 1936 until the late 1950s. The first automatic rifle to be adopted as standard by any major power, its undoubted success in combat led to a reappraisal of this type of weapon by all combatants.

Garang, John (1945–) Sudanese guerrilla leader of the southern rebels in the country's civil war. He defected from the army in 1970 and joined the Anya Nya rebels. In 1983 he set up the Sudanese People's Liberation Army (SPLA), which raided government installations in southern Sudan. In 1984 he formed the Sudanese People's Liberation Movement (SPLM). In 1991 the SPLM formed a government in exile with Garang as leader. His position was weakened by opposition to his authoritarian style of leadership and the overthrow of his ally in Ethiopia *Mengistu Haile Mariam. In August 1997 South African president Nelson *Mandela invited Garang and Sudanese president al-Bashir to take part in peace talks.

García Perez, Alan (1949–) Peruvian politician and president 1985–90; leader of the moderate, reformist left-wing American Popular Revolutionary Alliance party (APRA; Aprista Party). He inherited an ailing economy and was forced to trim his socialist programme. His government was marked by scandals, economic crisis, and the failure to confront growing political violence caused by guerrillas and drugs traffickers. He lost to political novice Alberto Fujimori in the 1990 presidential elections.

Garner, John Nance (1868–1967) US political leader and vice-president of the USA 1933–41. He served in the US House of Representatives 1903–33. A Democratic leader in the House, he was chosen as Speaker 1931. He later served as vice-president during Franklin Roosevelt's first two terms. Opposing Roosevelt's re-election in 1940, Garner retired from public life.

Garvey, Marcus (Moziah) (1887–1940) Jamaican political thinker and activist, an early advocate of black nationalism. He led a Back to Africa movement for black Americans to establish a black-governed country in Africa.

The Jamaican politico-religious movement of Rastafarianism is based largely on his ideas.

gaullism political philosophy deriving from the views of Charles *de Gaulle but not necessarily confined to Gaullist parties, or even to France. Its basic tenets are the creation and preservation of a strongly centralized state and an unwillingness to enter into international obligations at the expense of national interests. President Chirac's Rally for the Republic is an influential neo-Gaullist party in contemporary France, and was the first main political party in France to appoint a woman as head, when Michèle Alliot-Marie was elected its leader in November 1999.

Gaza Strip strip of land on the Mediterranean Sea, 10 km/6 mi wide and 40 km/25 mi long, extending northeast from the Egyptian border; area 363 sq km/140 sq mi; population (2001 est) 1,022,200, mainly Palestinians, plus about 6,000 Israeli settlers, most of whom arrived during the 1990s and who occupy a fifth of the territory. The Gaza Strip was captured by Israel from Egypt in 1967 during the Six-Day War and occupied by Israel until 1994, when responsibility for its administration was transferred to the Palestine National Authority (PNA). The capital is Gaza; other main centres of population are Khan Yunis and Rafah. Prior to the great influx of Palestinian refugees in 1948 the area was rural, and is geographically part of the Negev. The area is dependent on Israel for the supply of electricity. Agriculture is the main activity and occupies three-quarters of the area; citrus fruit (much of which is exported to Europe), wheat, and olives are farmed. Industry is on a small scale, including handmade goods, such as olive wood carvings, for Israel's tourist industry. Living standards in the area are low, with limited water supplies, inadequate sewage systems, and a very high level of unemployment; about a tenth of the population commutes daily to work in Israel. International relief agencies provide important support for the economy.

An international airport was opened at Daniyeh, in the south of the Gaza Strip, in November 1998.

Gemayel, Amin (1942–) Lebanese politician, a Maronite Christian; president 1982–88. He succeeded his brother, president-elect **Bechir Gemayel** (1947–1982), on his assassination on 14 September 1982. The Lebanese parliament was unable to agree on a successor when his term expired, so separate governments were formed under rival Christian and Muslim leaders. Following the end of his term of office as president, Gemayel was largely instrumental in ending Lebanon's civil war in 1989.

Gemayel, Bechir (1947–1982) also known as **Bashir Jumayyil**, Lebanese Maronite Christian soldier and politician, assassinated in 1982 while president elect. By the systematic elimination of rival Maronite Christian militia, by 1980 he had uncontested control of a Maronite enclave in East Beirut. The evident distancing of his Phalangist party from Israeli support, and its wish to expel all foreign influence from Lebanese affairs, effected his election as president on 22 August 1982. Having twice escaped assassination, he was killed 22 days later in a car bomb explosion.

General Agreement on Tariffs and Trade GATT, agreement designed to provide an international forum to encourage regulation of international trade. The original agreement was signed in 1947, shortly after World War II. It was followed in 1948 by the creation of an international organization, within the United Nations, to support the agreement and to encourage free trade between nations by reducing tariffs, subsidies, quotas, and regulations that discriminate against imported products. The agency GATT was effectively replaced by the *World Trade Organization (WTO) in January 1995, following the Uruguay Round. The legal agreement still exists although it was updated in 1994 to reflect a shift from trade in goods to trade in goods, services, and intellectual property. The new GATT agreements are administered by the WTO.

General Belgrano Argentine battle cruiser torpedoed and sunk on 2 May 1982 by the British nuclear-powered submarine *Conqueror* during the *Falklands War. At the time of the attack it was sailing away from the Falklands.

general strike refusal to work by employees in several key industries, with the intention of paralysing the economic life of a country. In British history, the General Strike was a nationwide strike called by the Trade Union Congress (TUC) on 3 May 1926 in support of striking miners. Elsewhere, the general strike was used as a political weapon by anarchists and others (see *syndicalism), especially in Spain and Italy.

The immediate cause of the 1926 general strike was the report of a royal commission on the coal-mining industry (*Samuel Report* (1926)) which, among other things, recommended a cut in wages. The mine-owners wanted longer hours as well as lower wages. The miners' union, under the leadership of A J Cook, resisted with the slogan 'Not a penny off the pay, not a minute on the day'. A coal strike started in early May 1926 and the miners asked the TUC to bring all major industries out on strike in support of the action; eventually it included more than 2 million workers. The Conservative government under Stanley Baldwin used troops, volunteers, and special constables to maintain food supplies and essential services, and had a monopoly on the information services, including BBC radio. After nine days the TUC ended the general strike, leaving the miners – who felt betrayed by the TUC – to remain on strike, unsuccessfully, until November 1926. The Trades Disputes Act of 1927 made general strikes illegal.

Geneva Convention international agreement of 1864 regulating the treatment of those wounded in war, and later extended to cover the types of weapons allowed, the treatment of prisoners and the sick, and the protection of civilians in wartime. The rules were revised at conventions held in 1906, 1929, and 1949, and by the 1977 Additional Protocols.

Genscher, Hans-Dietrich (1927–) German politician, chair of the West German Free Democratic Party (FDP) 1974–85, and foreign minister 1974–92. A skilled and pragmatic tactician, Genscher became the reunified Germany's most popular politician.

Gentile, Giovanni (1875–1944) Italian philosopher and politician, whose writings formed the basis of the Italian Fascist state under Mussolini. As minister of education from 1924, he reformed both the school and university systems. He edited the *Encyclopedia Italiana* and wrote the entry in it for 'fascism'. He was assassinated by partisans.

George II (1890–1947) King of Greece 1922–23 and 1935–47. He became king on the expulsion of his father Constantine I in 1922 but was himself overthrown in 1923. Restored by the military in 1935, he set up a dictatorship under Joannis *Metaxas, and went into exile during the German occupation 1941–45.

George V (1865–1936) King of Great Britain and Northern Ireland from 1910, when he succeeded his father Edward VII. He was the second son, and became heir in 1892 on the death of his elder brother Albert, Duke of Clarence. In 1893, he married Princess Victoria Mary of Teck (Queen Mary), formerly engaged to his brother. During World War I he made several visits to the front. In 1917, he abandoned all German titles for himself and his family. The name of the royal house was changed from Saxe-Coburg-Gotha to Windsor.

George VI (1895–1952) King of Great Britain and Northern Ireland from 1936, when he succeeded after the abdication of his brother Edward VIII, who had succeeded their father George V. Created Duke of York in 1920, he married in 1923 Lady Elizabeth Bowes-Lyon (1900–2002), and their children are Elizabeth II and Princess Margaret. During World War II, he visited the Normandy and Italian battlefields.

Georgia country in the Caucasus of southeastern Europe, bounded north by Russia, east by Azerbaijan, south by Armenia and Turkey, and west by the Black Sea.

Germany in full **Federal Republic of Germany**, country in central Europe, bounded north by the North and Baltic Seas and Denmark, east by Poland and the Czech Republic, south by Austria and Switzerland, and west by France, Luxembourg, Belgium, and the Netherlands.

government With reunification in 1990 the German government remained almost identical to that of former West Germany. It is based on the West German constitution (the Basic Law), drafted in 1948–49 by the Allied military governors and German provincial leaders in an effort to create a stable, parliamentary form of government, to diffuse authority, and to safeguard liberties. It borrowed from British, US, and neighbouring European constitutional models. It established, firstly, a federal system of government built around ten (11 including West Berlin, which did not have full status; the number rose to 16 since reunification) *Länder* (federal states), each with its own constitution, elected parliament, and government headed by a minister-president. The *Länder* have original powers in education, police, and local government, and are responsible for the administration of federal legislation through their own civil services. They have local taxation powers and are assigned shares of federal income tax and VAT revenues, being responsible for 50% of government spending.

The constitution, secondly, created a new federal parliamentary democracy, built around a two-chamber legislature comprising a directly elected 672-member lower house, the Bundestag (federal assembly), and an indirectly elected 69-member upper house, the Bundesrat (federal council). Bundestag representatives are elected for four-year terms by universal suffrage under a system of 'personalized proportional representation' in which electors have one vote for an ordinary constituency seat and one for a *Land* party list, enabling adjustments in seats gained by each party to be made on a proportional basis.

Political parties must win at least 5% of the national vote to qualify for shares of 'list seats'. Bundesrat members are nominated and sent in blocs by *Länder* governments, each state being assigned between three and five seats depending on population size. The Bundestag is the dominant parliamentary chamber, electing from the ranks of its majority party or coalition a chancellor (prime minister) and cabinet to form the executive government. Once appointed, the chancellor can only be removed by a 'constructive vote of no confidence' in which a majority votes positively in favour of an alternative leader.

Legislation is effected through all-party committees. The Bundesrat has few powers to initiate legislation, but has considerable veto authority. All legislation relating to *Länder* responsibilities requires its approval, constitutional amendments need a two-thirds Bundesrat (and Bundestag) majority, while the Bundesrat can temporarily block bills or force amendments in joint Bundestag–Bundesrat 'conciliation committees'. Bundestag members also join an equal number of representatives elected by *Länder* parliaments in a special Bundesversammlung (federal convention) every five years to elect a federal president as head of state. The president, however, has few powers and is primarily a titular figure.

The 1949 constitution is a written document. Adherence to it is policed by an independent federal constitutional court based at Karlsruhe which is staffed by 16 judges, who serve terms of up to 12 years. All-party committees from the Bundestag and Bundesrat select eight each.

The court functions as a guarantor of civil liberties and adjudicator in Federal–*Land* disputes. (Similar courts function at the *Land* level.)

Germany divided In 1949 Germany was divided by the Allied powers and the USSR, forming the German Democratic Republic (East Germany) in the eastern part of the country (formerly the Soviet zone of occupation), and the Federal Republic of Germany (West Germany) in the west (comprising the British, US, and French occupation zones under Allied military control following Germany's surrender at the end of World War II in 1945).

For the next four and a half decades West and East Germany were divided by the policies of the *Cold War, with West Germany becoming the strongest European NATO power, and East Germany a vital member of *Comecon and the *Warsaw Pact. During the era of Soviet leader Leonid Brezhnev, Soviet medium-range nuclear missiles were stationed on East German soil.

the formation of the Federal Republic In post-war West Germany, a policy of demilitarization, decentralization, and democratization was instituted by the Allied control powers and a new, intentionally provisional, constitution framed, which included eventual German reunification. The Federal Republic (West Germany) came into existence on 23 May 1949, when the Basic Law, or constitution, was signed by members of the Parliamentary Council in the presence of the Allied military governors (thereafter called commissioners).

West Berlin was blockaded by the Soviet Union 1948–49 (see *Berlin blockade), but survived to form a constituent *Land* in the Federal Republic, after an airlift operation by the Allied powers.

Adenauer comes to power in West Germany Politics during the Federal Republic's first decade were dominated by the Christian Democratic Union (CDU), led by the popular Konrad *Adenauer.

The first elections to the Bundestag, or lower house of the German Federal parliament, were held on 15 August 1949, the Christian Democrats emerging as the strongest party. Theodor Heuss was elected first president of the Republic, and Adenauer was elected first German Federal chancellor (16 September). The first government of the Republic was a right-wing coalition. In the declaration of policy of his government on 20 September Adenauer voiced the determination of his ministers to cooperate closely with the Western powers. In retaliation for the institution of the German Federal Republic, an East German state, the German Democratic Republic, was established under Soviet auspices in the eastern zone of Germany in October 1949.

economic recovery under Adenauer Chancellor Adenauer and his economics minister, Ludwig *Erhard, established a successful approach to economic management, termed the 'social market economy', which combined the encouragement of free-market forces with strategic state intervention on the grounds of social justice.

This new approach, combined with aid under the *Marshall Plan and the enterprise of the labour force (many of whom were refugees from the partitioned East), brought rapid growth and reconstruction during the 1950s and 1960s, an era termed the 'miracle years'. In additional factor in Germany's economic performance was that it did not have the rearmament burden of the other leading Western countries.

Western defence alliances During this period, West Germany was also reintegrated into the international community. Adenauer's government supported the Federal Republic's proposed participation in West European collective defence. This subject, raising the question of a recreated German army and possible conscription, caused considerable controversy in West Germany over the next few years, and in many other countries, especially France, where the prospect of a new German army was viewed with much popular misgiving, in the light of recent history.

The German Social Democrats (SPD) were opposed to the Federal Republic tying itself militarily to the West, primarily because they claimed that this would prejudice any chance of German reunification with East Germany; and this fear was played upon by Soviet propaganda. However,

Adenauer had the necessary majority to carry through his policy, with only minor modifications. In the elections of 1953 his party increased its majority.

In 1952 it was agreed that on West Germany's formal joining of the proposed European Defence Community (EDC) the Allied occupation should end, although Allied troops would continue to be stationed in the Federal Republic or German and European defence purposes. The London and Paris agreements, which followed French rejection of the EDC in 1954, resulted in West Germany being invited to join NATO and officially restored to the Federal Republic full sovereignty. French distrust of the German rearmament that this involved was allayed by various safeguards. As a result, the Western European Union, of which the Republic was a member, came into being on 7 May 1955; and seven days later the Federal Republic formally joined NATO, becoming a loyal supporter of the USA. A small regular army was soon built up; but conscription was not started until 1956–57.

In 1955 Adenauer visited Moscow. As a result, diplomatic relations were established between the USSR and West Germany and the USSR returned to Germany several thousand German prisoners still detained in the USSR.

European integration West Germany was admitted to the Organization for European Economic Cooperation (OEEC; the predecessor of the OECD) in 1949; and became a full member of the Council of Europe in 1951. It was one of the founder members of the European Coal and Steel Community.

When in 1955, against Adenauer's advice, the inhabitants of Saarland voted against 'Europeanization', and by implication, in favour of union with West Germany, relations between France and the Federal Republic were temporarily strained. Agreement was eventually reached, however, as a result of which Saarland was united to West Germany at midnight on 31 December 1956.

West Germany was one of the signatories of the Treaty of Rome in 1957, under which the European Economic Community (EEC) came into being on 1 January 1958. Germany has continued to play a dominant role in the EEC and its successors, the European Community (EC) and European Union (EU), and has been a constant advocate of closer European integration.

After Charles de Gaulle's return to power in France in May 1958 relations between France and West Germany grew closer, due partly to a personal friendship between Adenauer and de Gaulle. In January 1963 a 'treaty of reconciliation' between the two countries was signed in Paris. When Adenauer retired from the chancellorship later in the year, however, the warmth of Franco-German relations began to diminish and differences between the two countries concerning the future course of such organizations as the EEC and NATO became more open.

government in East Germany
The People's Council, elected in 1948, and consisting mainly of a communist-dominated Socialist Unity Party (SED), was converted into a People's Chamber (Volkskammer) on the establishment of the Democratic Republic of Germany (7 October 1949). After that all elections were on the pattern of a one-party list of candidates.

East Germany dissolved its five *Länder* (Brandenburg, Mecklenburg–West Pomerania, Saxony, Saxony–Anhalt, and Thuringia) in 1952, and its Chamber of States, or upper house, in 1958, vesting local authority in 15 *Bezirke*, or administrative districts. Under the 1968 constitution the supreme legislative and executive body in the German Democratic Republic was the Volkskammer (people's chamber), whose 500 members (including 66 from East Berlin) were elected every five years by universal suffrage.

the sovietization of East Germany
On the inauguration of East Germany, Wilhelm *Pieck became the president, Otto Grotewohl (former leader of the SPD in the East) became premier, and Walter *Ulbricht deputy premier. From the beginning the real power resided with Ulbricht, who was first secretary of the SED Politburo. After Pieck's death in 1960 the presidency was abolished, and a council of state was elected by the Volkskammer. Its chairman, who was given dictatorial powers, was Ulbricht. His position was further strengthened after Grotewohl's death in 1964.

The years immediately after 1949 saw the rapid establishment of a communist regime on the Soviet model, involving the nationalization of industry, the formation of agricultural collectives, and the creation of a one-party political system. East Germany made periodic suggestions for talks on German reunification, but its drafts invariably included clauses designed to perpetuate forcibly its own communist regime, and were rejected by the Western powers and by West Germany.

Shortly after its inauguration, East Germany recognized the Oder–Neisse line as its permanent boundary with Poland, and acknowledged the expulsion of over 2 million Germans from the *Sudeten area of Czechoslovakia as 'permanent and just'.

the 1953 revolt From its inception the poverty of East Germany contrasted markedly with the prosperity of West Germany, and the curbs on personal liberties added to a discontent that found expression in the thousands of refugees who poured into West Berlin, and thence to the Federal Republic, from the eastern sector. In June 1953 opposition to sovietization led, during food shortages, to severe rioting in East Berlin and in several other East German towns (see *East German revolt). In Berlin only the intervention of Soviet tanks restored order.

The revolt was followed by repressive measures, and though the Democratic Republic was proclaimed a sovereign state in 1954 (recognized at first only by the communist powers), large Soviet forces continued to be stationed there until the collapse of the communist regime in 1989.

the Berlin crisis of 1960–61 Friction between East and West Germany came to a head in 1960–61, because of the continuing flow of refugees entering West Berlin from the east. This had caused the population of East Germany to decline sharply between 1949 and 1961 and was undoubtedly affecting its economy adversely.

On 13 August 1961 East Germany closed the Berlin border, and subsequently built a heavily policed wall along it (see *Berlin Wall). The flow of refugees was thus virtually stopped, though a limited number of sensational successful escapes continued to be made, together with many equally sensational and often fatal failures, which severely shocked public opinion in the West.

From December 1963 an agreement was reached between the East and West Berlin authorities under which West Berliners could visit relatives in East Berlin and the Democratic Republic for limited periods at festive seasons, and some elderly citizens of East Germany were permitted to go and settle with their relatives in the West.

Adenauer gives way to Erhard In 1959 Heuss was succeeded as West German president by Heinrich Lubke. After the elections of 1961 the Christian Democrats lost ground, and governed in a coalition with the Free Democrats (FDP). Though the economic boom continued, the CDU and its allies lost prestige on account of various government scandals, and an increasingly public rift between the ageing Chancellor Adenauer and his economics minister, Erhard, centring on the question of Adenauer's retirement.

The emergence of a new and youthful SPD leader, Willy *Brandt – who had vaulted to international prominence as mayor of West Berlin during the construction of the Berlin Wall – suggested a strong threat to future CDU dominance of West German politics. Erhard eventually succeeded Adenauer as chancellor in 1963 and resigned in 1966.

Erhard had to face differences within his own party, and public controversy on such matters as to whether the law should be amended to allow for trials of war criminals to take place after May 1965 (when they would normally have qualified for the 20-year indemnity exemption). Additionally, relations with several Arab states were strained by West Germany's agreement to establish ambassadorial relations with Israel, to whom, by 1965, it had completed payment of large reparations for the *Holocaust.

A closer understanding with Britain was reflected in a highly successful state visit of Queen Elizabeth II to West Germany in 1965, and by a subsequent agreement between the two countries on a West German contribution towards the support costs of the British Army of the Rhine. In September 1965 Erhard led his party to victory in the federal general election.

Brandt and Ostpolitik During the 1960s Willy Brandt played a major role in shifting the SPD away from its traditional Marxist affiliation towards a more moderate position. Support for the SPD steadily increased after this policy switch and the party joined the CDU in an uneasy 'grand coalition' (1966–69), with Brandt as the junior partner and foreign minister to CDU chancellor Kurt Georg *Kiesinger.

But by the later 1960s most younger people felt that the time had come to face realities and regularize West Germany's relations with its eastern neighbours. This mood found expression in Brandt's foreign policy of *Ostpolitik ('eastern policy'), which sought reconciliation with Eastern Europe as a means of improving contacts between East and West Germany.

The SPD, with Brandt as chancellor, gained power in 1969, with the support of the FDP under Walter Scheel (1919–). Under Brandt's moderate socialist government, West Germany concluded treaties with Poland and the USSR (1970), treaties that normalized relations, recognized the de facto boundaries, and provided for limited cooperation in various fields. In 1972 a treaty was effected with East Germany, acknowledging East Germany's borders and separate existence and enabling both countries to enter the United Nations in 1973.

In 1974 Brandt was forced to resign after the revelation that his personal assistant (Günther Guillaume) had been an East German spy, and was succeeded by Helmut *Schmidt. Also in 1974, Gustav Heinemann (1899–1976), president since 1969, was succeeded by Walter Scheel.

developments in East Germany in the 1960s and 1970s Apart from the unsuccessful uprisings of 1953, East Germany proved a notably quiescent member of the Eastern bloc. By the 1970s there was a considerable improvement in living standards and the availability of consumer goods. East Germany's policy of economic austerity had yielded good results, and by 1969 it had a higher per-capita GNP (gross national product) than Austria, Japan, and Italy, almost two-thirds that of West Germany, and it was the world's 10th industrial power.

During the 1970s there was some relaxation in government rigidity, a more moderate political stance

was adopted, and the Stalinist Walter Ulbricht was replaced as leader of the Socialist Unity Party (SED) by the pragmatic Erich *Honecker. Economic and diplomatic relations with the West were extended. In 1972–73 the number of countries officially recognizing East Germany soared, and East Germany achieved international status as an independent state, although the West German constitution continued to declare that there was only one German nationality.

Schmidt's centrist course As SPD chancellor of West Germany, Helmut Schmidt adhered to Ostpolitik and emerged as a leading advocate of European cooperation. In the 1976 general election Schmidt's SDP–FDP coalition won a narrow majority over the CDU–CSU alliance headed by Dr Helmut *Kohl. The CSU (Christian Social Union) is the more right-wing sister party of the CDU in Bavaria, and in the 1980 election the CDU–CSU alliance was headed by the CSU leader, the controversial Franz-Josef *Strauss, but was once more comfortably defeated by the SPD–FDP coalition.

Between 1980 and 1982, the left wing of the SPD and the liberal FDP were divided over military policy (in particular the proposed stationing of US nuclear missiles in West Germany) and economic policy.

Chancellor Schmidt fought to maintain a moderate, centrist course but the FDP eventually withdrew from the federal coalition in 1982 and joined forces with the CDU, led by Helmut Kohl, to unseat the chancellor in a 'positive vote of no confidence'. Helmut Schmidt immediately retired from politics and the SPD, led by Hans-Jochen Vögel, was heavily defeated in the Bundestag elections in 1983, losing votes on the left to the new environmentalist Green Party.

Kohl's chancellorship in the 1980s The new Kohl administration, with the FDP's Hans-Dietrich *Genscher remaining as foreign minister, adhered closely to the external policy of the previous chancellorship, while at home a freer market approach was introduced.

Unemployment rose to 2.5 million in 1984, problems of social unrest emerged, and violent demonstrations greeted the installation of US nuclear missiles on German soil in 1983–84. Internally, the Kohl administration was rocked by scandals over illegal party funding, which briefly touched the chancellor himself. However, a strong recovery in the German economy from 1985 enabled the CDU–CSU–FDP coalition to gain re-election in the federal election in 1987.

During 1988–89, after the death of the CSU's Franz-Josef Strauss, support for the far-right Republican Party began to climb, and it secured 7% of the vote in the European Parliament elections of June 1989. In 1989–90 events in East Germany and elsewhere in Eastern Europe caused half a million economic and political refugees to enter the Federal Republic (see below); they also prompted the reopening of the debate on reunification (*Wiedervereinigung*). This resulted in West German politics becoming more highly charged and polarized. The CDU gave strong support to swift, graduated moves towards 'confederative' reunification, if desired, following free elections in East Germany.

exodus to West Germany In East Germany Honecker had been urged by the liberalizing Soviet leader Mikhail Gorbachev since 1987 to accelerate the pace of domestic economic and political reform; his refusal to do so increased grassroots pressure for liberalization. In September 1989, after the violent suppression of a church and civil-rights activists' demonstration in Leipzig, an umbrella dissident organization, Neue Forum (New Forum), was illegally formed.

The communist regime was further destabilized between August and October 1989 both by the exodus of more than 30,000 of its citizens to West Germany through Hungary (which had opened its borders with Austria in May) and by Honecker's illness during the same period.

reform in East Germany On 6 and 7 October 1989 the Soviet leader Mikhail Gorbachev visited East Berlin, and made plain his desire to see greater reform. This catalyzed the growing reform movement, and a wave of demonstrations (the first since 1953) swept East Berlin, Dresden, Leipzig, and smaller towns. At first, under Honecker's orders, they were violently broken up by riot police. However, the security chief, Egon Krenz, ordered a softer line and in Dresden the reformist Communist Party leader, Hans Modrow, actually marched with the protesters.

Faced with the rising tide of protest and the increasing exodus to West Germany (between 5,000 and 10,000 people a day), which caused grave disruption to the economy, Honecker was replaced as party leader and head of state by Krenz (18–24 October). In an attempt to keep up with the reform movement, Krenz sanctioned far-reaching reforms in November that effectively ended the SED monopoly of power and laid the foundations for a pluralist system. The Politburo was purged of conservative members; Modrow became prime minister and a new cabinet was formed; New Forum was legalized, and opposition parties allowed to form; and borders with the West were opened and free travel allowed, with the Berlin Wall being effectively dismantled.

moves towards reunification In December 1989 West German Chancellor Kohl announced a ten-point programme for reunification of the two Germanys. While the USA and USSR both called for a slower assessment of this idea, reunification was rapidly achieved on many administrative and economic levels.

By mid-December the Communist Party had largely ceased to exist as an effective power in East Germany.

political crisis in East Germany Following revelations of high-level corruption during the Honecker regime, Krenz was forced to resign as SED leader and head of state, being replaced by Gregor Gysi (1948–) and Manfred Gerlach (1928–) respectively. Honecker was placed under house arrest awaiting trial on charges of treason, corruption, and abuse of power, and the Politburo was again purged. (Honecker was finally allowed to leave Germany for exile in Chile in January 1993.) An interim SED–opposition 'government of national responsibility' was formed in February 1990. The political crisis continued to deepen, with the opposition divided over reunification with West Germany, while the popular reform movement showed signs of running out of control after the storming in January of the former security-police (Stasi) headquarters in East Berlin. The economy continued to deteriorate – a total of 344,000 people had fled to West Germany in 1989 and 1,500 continued to leave daily – and countrywide work stoppages increased.

East German elections in March 1990 were won by the centre-right Alliance for Germany, a three-party coalition led by the CDU. Talks were opened with the West German government on monetary union and a treaty unifying the economic and monetary systems signed in July 1990.

reunification Official reunification came about on 3 October 1990, with Berlin as the capital (although the seat of government initially remained in Bonn). In mid-October new *Länder* elections were held in former East Germany, in which the conservative parties did well. The first all-German elections since 1932 took place on 2 December 1990, resulting in victory for Chancellor Kohl and a coalition government composed of the CDU,

CSU, and FDP, with only three former East German politicians. In Berlin, which became a *Land*, the ruling SPD lost control of the city council to a new coalition government. The former states of East Germany resumed their status as *Länder*.

social conflict During 1991 divisions grew within the newly united nation as the economy continued to boom in the west, while in the east unemployment rose rapidly. More than 90% of Ossis (easterners) said they felt like second-class citizens, and those in work received less than half the average pay of the Wessis (westerners). Hundreds of racist attacks on foreigners took place, mainly in the east. Public support for Kohl slumped, notably after taxes were raised in order to finance both the rebuilding of the east and the German contribution to the US-led coalition against Iraq.

economic crisis in the east Eastern Germany's GDP fell by 15% during 1990 and was projected to decline by 20% during 1991, with a third of the workforce either unemployed or on short time. There were large anti-Kohl demonstrations and outbreaks of right-wing racist violence in eastern cities March–April 1991 as the economic crisis deepened. In western Germany, the ruling CDU suffered reverses in state elections during the spring of 1991 as Wessi voters reacted against Kohl's backtracking on his promise not to raise taxes to finance the east's economic development.

Defeat in Kohl's home *Land* of Rhineland–Palatinate in 1991 meant that the CDU lost, to the SPD, the majority it had held in the Bundesrat (upper chamber) since October 1990. In May 1991 Björn Engholm, the minister-president of Schleswig-Holstein since 1988, was elected chair of the SPD. He replaced Hans-Jochen Vögel, who continued as the SPD's leader within the Bundestag.

In June 1991 the Bundestag (lower chamber) voted to move to Berlin.

The Bundesrat (upper chamber) the following month voted to remain in Bonn, agreeing to reconsider its decision in later years.

racist violence Throughout 1991 and 1992, neo-Nazi and other far-right groups continued their campaign of violence against foreigners. A shift to the right emerged in elections in Bremen in September 1991, with support for the CDU and the right-wing, anti-foreigner German People's Union rising significantly.

recession By January 1993 unemployment exceeded 7% and, as recession gripped the country, a 1% decline in national output was predicted for the year ahead. Rudolf Scharping took over as SPD leader in April 1993. In July, parliament introduced restrictions on asylum seekers (more refugees from the Balkan civil wars had been received by Germany than by all other countries combined). In a state election in Hesse in March 1993 support for the CDU slumped while the extreme-right Republicans captured 8% of the vote.

Kohl elected to fourth successive term In May 1994 Chancellor Kohl's nominee, Roman Herzog, was elected president. A resurgence of the German economy helped the ruling CDU–CSU–FDP coalition to secure a narrow 10-seat majority in the October 1994 Bundestag elections. Support for the opposition SPD and the Greens increased, while the reform-communist Party of Democratic Socialism – strong in the east – achieved the election of 30 deputies. The following month Kohl was re-elected to an unprecedented fourth successive term as chancellor.

At the start of 1995 the government banned leading neo-Nazi groups in a determined effort to curb right-wing racial violence, and in June the Bundestag broke with a 50-year taboo and approved the deployment of 1,500 soldiers and medical staff in the Balkans region. This followed a 1994 constitutional court ruling that allowed for armed missions outside of the NATO region provided they were for humanitarian reasons. Support for the SPD slumped to a post-war low of 23% in state elections in Berlin in October 1995, and the following month Oskar Lafontaine replaced Rudolf Scharping as SPD leader.

worsening economic conditions By the end of 1995 unemployment had reached a post-war high of 3.8 million and in January 1996 the Kohl government announced a 50-point reflation plan to tackle the problem. In a bid to reduce the public sector deficit to 3% of GDP by 1997, enabling entry into the European Union's economic and monetary union (EMU) in 1999, a DM 70 billion ($46 billion) savings package was announced. Plans to reform the welfare system by cutting sick pay and job protection, raising the retirement age, and freezing public-sector pay for two years were rejected by trade unions and employers and a spate of warning strikes by public sector workers accompanied the country's entry into recession. Federal tax reforms were rejected by the country's 16 states (*Länder*) in May 1996. In a referendum in the same month voters in Brandenburg rejected a merger with Berlin.

In November 1996 the government announced plans for emergency spending cuts to hold the budget deficit below 3%, the ceiling set for participation in European economic and monetary union. Measures to cut social welfare benefits, including unemployment benefit and sick pay, caused widespread industrial unrest.

In January 1997 unemployment rose to a post-war record of 4.7 million, representing 12.2% of the labour force (10.6% in western Germany and 18.7% in eastern Germany).

The Social Democrats (SPD), led by the reformist Gerhard Schroeder, won the September 1998 general election, to end the 16-year chancellorship of Helmut Kohl. Schroeder formed a coalition government with the Greens, with Joschka Fischer of the Greens becoming foreign minister. Oskar Lafontaine became the new finance minister, and its former leader, Rudolf Scharping, became defence minister. Kohl resigned as leader of the Christian Democrats (CDU), and was replaced by Wolfgang Schäuble. Theo Waigel, the former finance minister and leader of the Bavarian-based Christian Social Union (CSU), one of the CDU's coalition allies, also stepped down, and was replaced as CSU leader by Edmund Stoiber, Bavaria's state premier.

In November 1998 the new chancellor, Gerhard Schroeder, in his inaugural speech to parliament, stated that job creation was his government's top priority, although it would be constrained by inherited 'financial burdens.' He also pledged to create a federal republic of the new centre (*Neues Mittel*), and stated that he would take personal charge of eastern German reconstruction. Dual citizenship was awarded to many of the seven million foreigners living in the country. Schroeder confirmed plans for the closure of nuclear power plants, but through cooperation with those within the energy sector. In January 1999, following French and British criticisms, the German government agreed to postpone a ban on the reprocessing of nuclear waste, and to delay legislation phasing out German nuclear power.

In November 1998 President Herzog moved his office from Bonn to Berlin, becoming the first federal agency to do so. The chancellor and most ministries were scheduled to move there in September 1999.

In November 1998 the ex-communist Party of Democratic Socialism (PDS) entered a governing coalition for the first time when they formed a coalition government with the Social Democratic Party (SPD) in the east German state of Mecklenberg-Western Pomerania.

Reichstag reopened The refurbished Reichstag, which was burned down in February 1933, was officially reopened in April 1999.

racial legislation The parliament, in May 1999, put an end to the 'Blood Law' of the Second Reich, under which 'Germanness' was deemed to reside only in the genes. An estimated four million immigrants would be able to claim German passports under an amended nationality law which was adopted by the Bundestag with a massive majority.

After a bomb in Dusseldorf in July 2000, and a series of attacks on asylum seekers in Germany, hundreds of Germans protested at neo-Nazi violence in their country in August 2000. The government responded to fears about neo-Nazis by setting up an investigation into one of Germany's far-right parties, and on 16 August announced a heavily funded government programme aimed at German youth to educate against Nazi values.

presidential election 1999 Johannes Rau, a Social Democrat, was elected German president in May 1999. Rau, the former prime minister of North Rhine-Westphalia, was chosen by an electoral college of MPs and delegates. It was only the second time in its 50-year history that Federal Germany had a Social Democrat president.

corruption scandal In 1999 Kohl admitted to having received secret (and therefore illegal) donations on behalf of the Christian Democrats while he was chancellor, and the ensuing inquiry sought to establish whether the payments were connected to arms deals. In January 2000, he resigned from the honorary leadership of the party, seemingly a direct result of the revelations of the criminal investigation which also incriminated other members of the party; Schäuble resigned as leader of the Christian Democrats after admitting that in 1994 he had accepted payment from an arms dealer on behalf of his party. Manfred Kanther, party chairman, admitted financial irregularities in previous positions as aide to Kohl and former regional chief of the Christian Democrats. Friedrich Merz, the deputy leader, was elected to lead the party in parliament. The general secretary, Angela Merkel, took over the national leadership.

Kohl, meanwhile, was left to raise millions to help his party to pay the fine incurred by illegal financing under his leadership. In June 2000, he testified before a parliamentary committee investigating the scandal, but refused to name donors who contributed 2 million marks/ US$950,000 to his party, as well as denying that the contributions had bought any government favours. In February 2001, he was fined 300,000 marks/US$143,000, but spared a criminal trial.

BSE crisis The first two cases of BSE (bovine spongiform encephalopathy), or mad cow disease, detected in German-born cattle were announced on 24 November 2000. Chancellor Gerhard Schroeder banned the sale of meat-and-bone meal in all animal feed. Sales of beef in Germany slumped and farmers' organizations said the industry was on the verge of collapse. On 21 December, Austria banned all imports of German cattle and beef. The German government unveiled plans to promote organic farming and tighten controls on meat production in January 2001, but the ministers for health and for agriculture resigned a week later. At the end of January 2001, 20 cases of BSE had been confirmed in Germany, and the government, under pressure from the EU, ordered the destruction of 400,000 cattle. It also set the target that by 2006 10% of German farmland should be under organic production (the current figure was less than 3%).

foreign minister investigated In February 2001, prosecutors announced that Germany's foreign minister, Joschka Fischer, would be formally investigated regarding allegations that he had lied in court in January regarding his revolutionary past. The court case in question was the trial of a friend of Fischer's, Hans-Joachim Klein, who was accused of taking part in a terrorist attack on ministers from the Organization of Petroleum-Exporting Countries (OPEC) in Vienna, Austria, in 1975.

new FDP leader Guido Westerwelle became leader of the opposition FDP in May 2001.

On 1 January 2002, euro notes and coins were introduced as the national currency. In the same month, Edmund Stoiber was selected by the CDU and the CSU as their candidate for chancellor in the general elections schedules for later in the year.

industrial action Thousands of industrial workers staged strikes in April 2002 in support of demands by IG Metall, the metalworkers' union, for a 6.5% wage rise in the country's biggest industries. The union promised further industrial action if employers did not increase their 2% offer.

Germany, East formerly **German Democratic Republic (GDR)**, country 1949–90, formed from the Soviet zone of occupation in the partition of Germany following World War II. East Germany became a sovereign state in 1954, and was reunified with West Germany in October 1990. For history, see *Germany.

Gestapo (contraction of **Geheime Staatspolizei**) Nazi Germany's secret police, formed in 1933, and under the direction of Heinrich *Himmler from 1934.

Geyl, Pieter (1887–1966) Dutch historian awarded international recognition for his services to history. He was made CBE in 1959.

Ghana country in West Africa, bounded north by Burkina Faso, east by Togo, south by the Gulf of Guinea, and west by Côte d'Ivoire.

Gheorgiu-Dej, Gheorghe (1901–1965)
Romanian communist politician. A
member of the Romanian Communist
Party from 1930, he played a leading
part in establishing a communist
regime in 1945. He was prime minister
1952–55 and state president 1961–65.
Although retaining the support of
Moscow, he adopted an increasingly
independent line during his final years.

Giap, Vo Nguyen (1910–) Vietnamese
military leader and communist
politician. When *Ho Chi Minh formed
the Vietminh in 1941 in China, Giap
organized the army that returned to
Indochina in 1944 to fight the Japanese
and liberated Hanoi on 19 August
1945. As commander-in-chief of a
guerrilla force of 60,000, he led the
struggle against the French colonial
forces, conclusively defeating them
at Dien Bien Phu on 7 May 1954. With
the growth of US influence in South
Vietnam, Giap sent North Vietnamese
troops to help the Vietcong (the
National Liberation Front), and he took
direct control of communist military
operations in South Vietnam in 1967,
launching the *Tet Offensive in
February 1968. He was responsible for
the defeat of the US army in 1973.

Born in Quangbiln Province, then
part of the French protectorate of
Indochina, Giap joined the Communist
Party in 1930. With a doctorate in law
from the University of Hanoi 1938,
he fled to China when the party was
banned in 1939, and became military
aide to Ho Chi Minh. When Vietnam
was partitioned in 1954, he became
commander-in-chief of the North
Vietnam army. His training manual
on guerrilla warfare 1960 was
published in English as *People's War,
People's Army* (1962). He was minister
of national defence and deputy prime
minister of Vietnam 1976–80.

Gierek, Edward (1913–2001) Polish
communist politician. He entered the
Politburo of the ruling Polish United
Workers' Party (PUWP) in 1956 and
was party leader 1970–80.

Giraud, Henri Honoré (1879–1949)
French general. He put up stiff
resistance to the German invasion
of France but was captured and
imprisoned by the Germans 1940–42,
when he escaped to Algiers. He
succeeded Admiral *Darlan as local
commander of the Free French in
Algiers December 1942. He became
co-president, with de Gaulle, of the
National Committee for Liberation
May 1943 and was made commander-
in-chief of the French Army, liberating
Corsica September 1943. However,
de Gaulle's political manoeuvring
led to him resigning his co-presidency
October 1943 and his command in
North Africa April 1944.

Giscard d'Estaing, Valéry (1926–)
French centre-right politician,
president of France 1974–81.
Committed to developing closer
European unity, during his presidency
he helped initiate the new Exchange
Rate Mechanism in 1978 and direct
elections to the European Parliament
from 1979. He also introduced
liberalizing social reforms, including
divorce and abortion law reforms and
reducing the voting age to 18. Faced
with a worsening economy, in 1976 he
brought in Raymond *Barre as prime
minister to manage a deflationary
programme, but was defeated by the
Socialist leader François *Mitterrand
in 1981. In 1984 he was re-elected to
the National Assembly but resigned
in 1989 in order to sit in the European
Parliament.

Giuliani, Rudolph W (1944–) US
Republican politician, mayor of New
York City 1993–2001. A former federal
prosecutor, he was elected mayor of
the traditionally Democrat-dominated
New York City, at the second attempt,
in 1993. As a result of demographic
shifts and his own, non-partisan
'quality of life' programme, the crime
rate fell dramatically and the economy
expanded. In November 1997, he
became the first Republican since
Florio La Guardia in 1937 to be

re-elected. He was widely admired for his calm leadership in the aftermath of the terrorist attacks on New York on 11 September 2001.

glasnost (Russian **'openness'**) Soviet leader Mikhail *Gorbachev's policy of liberalizing various aspects of Soviet life, such as introducing greater freedom of expression and information and opening up relations with Western countries. *Glasnost* was introduced and adopted by the Soviet government in 1986.

Glenn, John Herschel, Jr (1921–) US astronaut and politician. On 20 February 1962, he became the first US astronaut to orbit the Earth, doing so three times in the spacecraft *Friendship 7*. The flight lasted 4 hours 55 minutes. On 29 October 1998, Glenn became the oldest person in space when, at the age of 77, he embarked on a nine-day mission aboard the shuttle *Discovery*.

Glubb, John Bagot (1897–1986) called 'Glubb Pasha', British military commander, founder of the Arab Legion (the Jordanian army), which he commanded 1939–56. Under his leadership the Legion grew in number from 1,000 to 9,000, becoming the most powerful Arab military force. Knighted 1956.

Goebbels, (Paul) Joseph (1897–1945) German Nazi leader. As minister of propaganda from 1933, he brought all cultural and educational activities under Nazi control and built up sympathetic movements abroad to carry on the 'war of nerves' against Hitler's intended victims. On the capture of Berlin by the Allies, he committed suicide.

Goering, Hermann Wilhelm (1893–1946) Nazi leader, German field marshal from 1938. He was part of Hitler's inner circle, and with Hitler's rise to power was appointed commissioner for aviation from 1933 and built up the Luftwaffe (air force). He built a vast economic empire in occupied Europe, but later lost favour and was expelled from the party in

1945. Tried at Nuremberg for war crimes, he poisoned himself before he could be executed.

Gokhale, Gopal Krishna (1866–1915) Indian political adviser and friend of Mahatma Gandhi, leader of the Moderate group in the Indian National Congress before World War I.

Goldman, Emma (1869–1940) US political organizer, feminist and co-editor of the anarchist monthly magazine *Mother Earth* 1906–17. In 1908 her citizenship was revoked and in 1919 she was deported to Russia. Breaking with the Bolsheviks in 1921, she spent the rest of her life in exile. Her writings include *My Disillusionment in Russia* (1923) and *Living My Life* (1931).

Goldwater, Barry (Morris) (1909–1998) US Republican politician; presidential candidate in the 1964 election, when he was overwhelmingly defeated by Lyndon Johnson. As senator for Arizona 1953–65 and 1969–87, he voiced the views of his party's right-wing faction. Many of Goldwater's conservative ideas were later adopted by the Republican right, especially the Reagan administration.

Gombos, Gyula (1886–1936) Hungarian Premier between October 1932 and October 1936. He brought Hungary closer to an alliance with Hitler's Germany and his internal policies were inspired by Italian fascism.

Gómez, Juan Vicente (1857–1935) Venezuelan dictator 1908–35 and president. The discovery of oil during his rule attracted US, British, and Dutch oil interests and made Venezuela one of the wealthiest countries in Latin America. Gómez amassed a considerable personal fortune and used his well-equipped army to dominate the civilian population.

Gomułka, Władysław (1905–1982) Polish communist politician, party leader 1943–48 and 1956–70. He introduced moderate reforms, including private farming and tolerance for Roman Catholicism.

Gonne, Maud (1865–1953) married name **Maud MacBride**, Irish nationalist and actor, a founder-member of *Sinn Fein. A celebrated society beauty, she became acquainted with the poet W B Yeats in the 1890s through her support for Irish nationalism. Gonne refused Yeats's offer of marriage, and in 1903 married Major John MacBride, who had fought against the British in the Boer War and was ultimately executed for his part in the *Easter Rising in 1916. Their son Seán MacBride was foreign minister of the Irish Republic from 1948–51 and winner of the Nobel Peace Prize.

González Márquez, Felipe (1942–) Spanish socialist politician, leader of the Socialist Workers' Party (PSOE), and prime minister 1982–96. His party was re-elected in 1989 and 1993, but his popularity suffered as a result of economic upheaval and revelations of corruption within his administration. During 1995 he was himself briefly under investigation for alleged involvement with anti-terrorist death squads in the 1980s, and in March 1996, he and his party were narrowly defeated in the general elections.

Good Friday Agreement multiparty settlement proposed on 10 April 1998 in the *Northern Ireland peace process.

Good Neighbor policy the efforts of US administrations between the two world wars to improve relations with Latin American and Caribbean states. The phrase was first used by President F D Roosevelt in his inaugural speech March 1933 to describe the foreign policy of his *New Deal.

Goose Green in the Falklands War, British victory over Argentina at Goose Green, south of San Carlos, on 28 May 1982 during the advance on Port Stanley.

Gorbachev, Mikhail Sergeyevich (1931–) Russian politician, leader and president of the USSR 1985–91. He attempted to revive the faltering Soviet economy through economic reforms (*perestroika) and liberalize society and politics through *glasnost (openness) and competition in elections, and to halt the arms race abroad through arms reduction agreements with the USA. He pulled Soviet troops out of Afghanistan and allowed the Soviet-bloc states in central Europe greater autonomy, a move which soon led to the break-up of the USSR and end of the *Cold War. He was awarded the Nobel Prize for Peace in 1990 for promoting greater openness in the USSR and helping to end the Cold War.

Gorbachev radically changed the style of Soviet leadership, but encountered opposition to the pace of change from both conservatives and radicals. His reforms failed to improve the economy and resulted in ethnic and nationalist tensions within the USSR, culminating in demands for independence in the Baltic and Caucasus regions. Communist hardliners briefly overthrew Gorbachev in August 1991 and within months the USSR had dissolved and Gorbachev resigned as president. He contested the Russian presidential elections in June 1996, but polled only 0.5% of the vote.

Gore, Al(bert Arnold, Jr) (1948–) US Democratic politician, vice-president 1993–2001. A member of the House of Representatives 1977–79 and senator for Tennessee 1985–92, he was on the conservative wing of the party, but held liberal views on such matters as women's rights, environmental issues, and abortion. As vice-president he was unusually active in foreign affairs, and also advocated reforms in government through cutting red tape and improving efficiency. He narrowly failed to win the 2000 presidential election, winning 500,000 more votes but four fewer electoral-college seats than his Republican opponent, George W *Bush.

Gorshkov, Sergei Georgievich (1910–1988) Soviet admiral,

Gort, John Standish Surtees Prendergast Vereker, 1st Viscount Gort (1886–1946) British general who in World War II commanded the British Expeditionary Force 1939–40, conducting a fighting retreat from Dunkirk, France. Although he had no experience of major command, he handled the BEF with great skill in the face of the German onslaught and French collapse, taking the vital decision 23 May 1940 to withdraw the British Army via Dunkirk before it was entirely destroyed. 6th Viscount (Irish peerage) 1902, Viscount (UK) 1945.

Gorton, John Grey (1911–2002) Australian Liberal politician, prime minister 1968–71. A member of the Senate, he was elected party leader and prime minister following the death of Harold *Holt in 1968. He then transferred to the lower house, winning Holt's vacant seat. His prime ministership was marred by conflicts with his colleagues over his style of leadership and lack of consultation, while divisions over the continuing involvement of Australia in the Vietnam War led to a drop in electoral support. In 1971, following the resignation of his defence minister, Malcolm *Fraser, a party vote of confidence resulted in a tied ballot and Gorton resigned rather than use his casting vote to stay in power.

Gottwald, Klement (1896–1953) Czechoslovakian communist president. He criticized the Munich capitulation in 1938, and went into exile in Moscow, where he remained until 1945, meeting Edvard Beneš, the head of the Czechoslovakian government in exile, in 1943. Vice premier in the Czechoslovakian coalition government of 1945, he became premier after the elections in the following year. He used this position to complete the communist seizure of power in 1948, and in 1948 he succeeded Beneš as president.

Goulart, João (1918–1976) **Marquis of Belquior,** Brazilian politician and president 1961–64. A weak and vacillating leader, he alienated moderate opinion by flirting with nationalist and left-wing groups. His administration was plagued with economic problems and with the growing influence of communist party members. He was ejected by a coup in 1964, engineered by the army and supported by powerful conservative politicians in the Brazilian Democratic Union (UDN).

governor-general representative of the British government in a Commonwealth country that regards the British sovereign as head of state. The first Commonwealth country to receive such a representative was Canada in 1929. In almost all Commonwealth countries the governor-general is now a citizen of that country.

Gowon, Yakubu (1934–) Nigerian politician, head of state 1966–75. He became army chief of staff following a coup in January 1966, and five months later seized power in a further coup. Unsuccessful in his efforts to prevent the secession of the eastern region of *Biafra, Nigeria was plunged into civil war 1967–70. After leading the federal army to victory, he reunited the country with his policy of 'no victor, no vanquished'. His later administration was plagued by allegations of corruption and Gowon's failure to timetable a return to civilian rule. Deposed by a bloodless coup in 1975, he went into exile in the UK, returning to Nigeria in 1983.

Graf Spee, Admiral German pocket battleship of World War II. It sailed from Germany just before the outbreak of war and sank nine British merchant ships in the Atlantic. It was damaged in the Battle of the *River Plate December 1939 and sailed into Montevideo, Uruguay, for repairs. Its captain, Langsdorff, fearful that the ship would be sunk as soon as it left the safety of the harbour, scuttled it 17 December 1939.

Gramsci, Antonio (1891–1937) Italian Marxist who attempted to unify social theory and political practice. He helped to found the Italian Communist Party in 1921 and was elected to parliament in 1924, but was imprisoned by the Fascist leader Mussolini from 1926; his *Quaderni di carcere/Prison Notebooks* were published posthumously in 1947.

Grandi, Dino, Count (1895–1988) Italian politician who challenged Mussolini for leadership of the Italian Fascist Party in 1921 and was subsequently largely responsible for Mussolini's downfall in July 1943.

Graziani, Rodolfo, Marquess (1882–1955) Italian general. He was commander-in-chief of Italian forces in North Africa during World War II and had some initial success in an advance into Egypt but was comprehensively defeated by British forces 1940, and subsequently replaced. Later, as defence minister in the new Mussolini government, he failed to reorganize a republican fascist army, was captured by the Allies 1945, tried by an Italian military court, and finally released 1950. He remained active in neo-fascist politics until his death.

Great Depression world economic crisis 1929–late 1930s, sparked by the *Wall Street crash of 29 October 1929. It was the longest and most devastating depression in the Western world in modern history.

The Great Depression was precipitated by the Wall Street crash when millions of dollars were wiped off US share values in a matter of hours. This forced the closure of many US banks involved in stock speculation and led to the recall of US overseas investments. This loss of US credit had serious repercussions on the European economy, especially that of Germany, and led to a steep fall in the levels of international trade as countries attempted to protect their domestic economies. Although most European countries experienced a slow recovery during the mid 1930s, the main impetus for renewed economic growth was provided by rearmament programmes later in the decade.

Great Leap Forward change in the economic policy of the People's Republic of China introduced by *Mao Zedong under the second five-year plan of 1958 to 1962. The aim was to achieve rapid and simultaneous agricultural and industrial growth through the creation of large new agro-industrial communes. The inefficient and poorly planned allocation of state resources led to the collapse of the strategy by 1960 and the launch of a 'reactionary programme', involving the use of rural markets and private subsidiary plots. More than 20 million people died in the Great Leap famines of 1959 to 1961. See also *China, **the Great Leap Forward**.

Great Society political slogan coined 1965 by US President Lyndon B Johnson to describe the ideal society to be created by his administration (1963–68), and to which all other nations would aspire. The programme included extensive social welfare legislation, most of which was subsequently passed by Congress.

Grechko, Andrei Antonovich (1903–1976) Soviet soldier, marshal of the Soviet Union and minister of defence from 1967. He had a successful career in the cavalry army and as a coordinator of multinational armies.

Greece country in southeast Europe, comprising the southern part of the Balkan peninsula, bounded to the north by the Former Yugoslav Republic of Macedonia and Bulgaria, to the northwest by Albania, to the northeast by Turkey, to the east by the Aegean Sea, to the south by the Mediterranean Sea, and to the west by the Ionian Sea.

government The 1975 constitution provides for a parliamentary system of government, with a president who is head of state, a prime minister who is head of government, and a single-chamber parliament. The president, elected by parliament for a five-year term, appoints the prime minister on the basis of assembly support and the cabinet. Parliament has 300 members, all elected by universal suffrage for a four-year term, and the prime minister and cabinet are collectively responsible to it. Bills passed by parliament must be ratified by the president, whose veto can be overridden by an absolute majority of the total number of members. In 1986 the constitution was amended, limiting the powers of the president in relation to those of the prime minister.

war with Turkey Following the defeat of Turkey in World War I, the Treaty of *Sèvres (1920) awarded to Greece practically all of Thrace outside Constantinople (Istanbul) and, in the western part of Asian Turkey, a mandate over Smyrna (Izmir) and the territory around it. In October 1920 King *Alexander died, and in the subsequent elections Eleuthérios *Venizelos, who had forced Alexander's father, *Constantine I to abdicate, was defeated and left Greece. A referendum held shortly afterwards favoured the return of Constantine.

In 1921 Greece invaded Anatolia (Asian Turkey), and in the war that followed, Greece was deserted by the other European powers, France favouring the Turks. Greece was forbidden to attack Constantinople, and in September 1922 the Turks captured Smyrna. This was followed by the second abdication of Constantine, who retired to Palermo in Sicily and died in the following year. He was succeeded by his son *George II. By the Treaty of Lausanne (1923) Greece lost eastern Thrace, the boundary between Greece and Turkey being fixed at the River Maritsa.

Shortly afterwards, in August 1923, Greece was embroiled with Italy over the murder of Gen Tellini, the Italian delegate, with the other members of the commission investigating the Albanian boundary, while on Greek soil. Following an Italian ultimatum Corfu was bombarded, and although the Italians were forced by the League of Nations to evacuate Corfu in September, Greece paid a large indemnity.

the dictatorship of Metaxas
An unsuccessful counter-revolution against the 'revolutionary government' brought the monarchy into discredit, and in 1924 Greece was proclaimed a republic. The republic endured with varying fortunes until 1935, when, following a rigged referendum organized by Gen Kondylis, the monarchy was restored by an overwhelming majority and George II was recalled. Venizélos, Kondylis, and Tsaldaris all died in 1936, and Gen Joannis *Metaxas became premier.

Metaxas established a dictatorship; parliament was dissolved and political parties suppressed, and in 1938 he was made premier for life. A treaty was signed with Turkey to last for ten years, under which each country undertook to remain neutral if one of them were attacked, while each would prevent the transport of troops or munitions through its territory to any state attacking either of them. At the same time Greek and Turkish troops entered the Thracian frontier territory, which for 15 years had been demilitarized under the Treaty of Lausanne.

the Italian invasion in World War II
When World War II broke out in 1939, Greece remained neutral. But in October 1940 the Italian Fascist dictator Mussolini suddenly and without declaring war launched an attack on Greece from Italian-held Albania. Mussolini had expected either surrender or a merely nominal resistance, but he found the country united and the small Greek army full of patriotic fervour. A small contingent of the British air force had been sent to cooperate with the Greek defence and, in November, while the Italians were still being pressed steadily back through the Albanian mountains,

British planes delivered a crippling blow at the main Italian fleet lying in Taranto harbour, thereby reversing the balance of naval power in the eastern Mediterranean.

Under commander in chief Alexandros Papagos the Greek army displayed brilliant tactical skill in mountain warfare, turning one position after another by seizing points of vantage that dominated it. By the end of the year they had pushed the Italians back out of Greece, conquered nearly one-third of Albania, and were approaching Tepelenë. Heavy reinforcements, however, were now reaching the Italian armies and for two months the position remained essentially unchanged.

the German intervention In April 1941 the German armies crossed the Bulgarian frontier into Macedonia, and – despite spirited resistance by the Greek forces, aided by a British expeditionary force of some 60,000 men – the odds were so overwhelming that in a few weeks the whole of Greece was in German hands and the British forces had been evacuated. The practical value of sending a British army to Greece was later disputed by *Papagos.

After Metaxas's death in 1941 political uncertainty in Greece increased. King George and his ministers withdrew to Egypt and finally reached Britain in September. German forces entered Athens in April and set up a puppet government. There followed a period of appalling privation for the capital and for the whole country. Italian troops entered Athens in June and formally took over the occupation of the country from the German garrison; but the Germans continued to control all communications, the coastline, and the airfields, besides being in control of Crete. At the end of the first 15 months of the Axis occupation of Greece some 100,000 of a population of 1 million in Athens and Peiraias had died of starvation.

Greek resistance Guerrilla warfare by Greek resistance fighters got under way in 1942. Attacks against Axis troops, and sabotage of railways and supply stores, were frequent, despite reprisals. An agreement between Britain and the exiled Greek government was signed in March respecting the organization and employment of Greek armed forces, and the two governments agreed that among the objects of the war were the 'complete liberation of Greece and the re-establishment of her freedom and independence'. *Lend-lease agreements were also made between Britain and Greece, and between the USA and Greece.

As time went by, differences of political opinion began to undermine the unity of purpose of the various guerrilla bands. Now that the king had once more left Greece – though under force of circumstances – the old republican animosities were revived against him for having kept Metaxas in office. The king tried to smooth over differences by issuing declarations promising, when he should return, to consult the will of the people on the political and constitutional status of the country.

The British, concerned that political disagreements could have a negative effect on the resistance effort of the 'Antartes' (irregular guerrilla bands), sent liaison officers into Greece, and in July 1943 it was announced that the Greek guerrilla bands had come under the Supreme Allied Command in the Middle East. There nevertheless remained five separate resistance organizations, the chief being ELAS (National Popular Liberation Army), an offshoot of EAM (National Liberation Front) – both with a strong communist element – and EDES (National Democratic Greek Army). With the collapse of Italy the Germans revoked the division of Greece into German and Italian zones of occupation and resumed control of all communications. Early in 1944 British liaison officers succeeded in getting the representatives of the various rival guerrilla forces to agree to end hostilities among themselves and to cooperate in the fight against the Germans. Yet unrest in the Greek forces remained, and there were mutinies in both the army and navy based in Egypt.

George Papandreou, then leader of the Democratic Socialist Party, escaped at this time from Greece and went to Cairo to urge the cause of national unity. In June 1944 the king entrusted Papandreou with the formation of a government, but the various parties drifted farther apart. By October the southern areas of Greece were nearly free of Germans, although in the north fighting was still going on. On 14 October Athens and Peiraias were occupied by British troops.

liberation and political uncertainty
Now that Greece was liberated from the Germans, EAM emerged as the largest political party. The fact that EAM wanted to create a socialist state and was openly against the king's return was responsible for a wave of monarchist feeling among the nationalists or right-wing elements, and EAM, favouring a republican form of government, was reluctant to demobilize the forces of ELAS while in control of much of the country.

The Papandreou government, with the support of Lt Gen Sir Robert Scobie, the British commander in chief of the Greek army, then announced its determination to disband these forces by 10 December 1944 and to re-form the Greek army to supersede the resistance groups as the regular armed force of the nation. At the end of December, following a visit to Athens by British prime minister Winston Churchill and his foreign secretary Anthony Eden on Christmas Day, the king appointed Archbishop Damaskinos regent of Greece. Additional British troops were now

sent to Athens, and street by street the capital was cleared of irregular troops. A peace agreement was signed in February 1945. One of its clauses was that a referendum should be held to decide finally on the constitutional question, under the supervision of the Allies.

But this agreement did not bring political harmony. No fewer than six cabinets held office during 1945. In 1946 in some areas, especially in the north, armed bands resumed their activities despite the truce. Meanwhile, the royalist Greeks won the elections of March 1946, the first for ten years, and eventually a referendum again resulted in a majority in favour of the return of the king, who soon afterwards left Britain for Athens. He died in April 1947 and was succeeded by his brother, *Paul.

the civil war resumes In 1947 the civil war flared up again. That Greece did not fall under communist influence was undoubtedly partially due to the massive aid the government received from the USA, under the provisions of the *Truman Doctrine. US aid in the end more than outweighed the help that the communist insurgents were receiving from the USSR and its satellites. Untold hardship was caused to the people in northern Greece by the continual warfare, and large numbers of Greeks were deported to communist countries.

By 1949 the internal situation was again critical for the government in Athens. The rebels appeared to be gaining ground, were in control of northern Greece, and were slowly paralysing the country's economy. Papagos was recalled from retirement and appointed commander in chief of the armed forces, with very wide powers. Eight months later, in August 1949, the Greek communists admitted total defeat, Papagos's successes against them having been fortuitously helped by the quarrel between Marshal Tito of Yugoslavia and the USSR.

Greece in the 1950s From 1951 until his death in 1955 Papagos dominated Greek politics, his Greek Rally Party gaining an overwhelming majority in the elections of 1952. Though his rule was authoritarian, the mass of Greeks welcomed it as providing stability after all the years of enemy occupation, civil war, and vacillating coalitions. In addition, Papagos had the personal appeal of a national hero. The economy of the country revived, and in 1953 a treaty of friendship was signed between Greece, Turkey, and Yugoslavia, by which the Greeks who had been taken into Yugoslavia during the civil war were repatriated. In 1951 Greece became a member of NATO.

From 1953 onwards Greek politics became increasingly dominated by the *Cyprus question, the court and government soon identifying themselves with the popular desire for *enosis*, the union of Cyprus with Greece. Greece's open sympathy and tacit support for EOKA (the Cypriot movement pressing for this union) soon strained its relations with Turkey and Britain, and consequently NATO strength in the eastern Mediterranean was threatened. However, in 1959 the Zürich and London agreements, in which Greece participated, established an independent Cyprus, with Archbishop *Makarios as first president. This ended the crisis for the time being, even though the settlement rejected *enosis*, on which Greece and the Greek Cypriots had always insisted in the past.

political crises of the 1960s Under Constantinos *Karamanlis, premier from 1955 until 1963, Greece made steady economic progress. New roads and industries were established and tourism greatly expanded, but there was no comparable advance in agriculture. The drift to the towns and a high emigration rate, both to the USA and to Western Europe, continued, and the gap between rich and poor remained wide.

In April 1963 an incident in London, involving Queen Frederika of Greece – whose pronounced anticommunist views and alleged authoritarianism had made her a controversial figure both in and outside Greece – temporarily jeopardized the proposed state visit to London of the Greek king and queen later that year. Karamanlis resigned when King Paul insisted on making the visit, which then took place as planned, though there were hostile demonstrations by various left-wing elements in Britain.

In December 1963 the Cyprus crisis broke out again, when Makarios advocated the unilateral repeal of the Zürich and London agreements. Greece once more was closely involved, and its relations with Turkey and Britain again suffered.

In November 1963 the veteran politician George Papandreou had become premier as head of the Centre Union Party. In March 1964 King Paul died and was succeeded by his son, Constantine II, who later in the year married Princess Anne-Marie of Denmark. The popularity of the young king and the political stability of the whole country were threatened in July 1965 by a bitter conflict between Constantine and Papandreou. This was touched off by the alleged discovery within the army of a conspiracy involving Papandreou's son, the socialist Andreas *Papandreou. Following a dispute over tenure of the ministry of defence, Constantine dismissed Papandreou.

In the agitation that followed there were signs that democratic government in Greece might soon be gravely endangered. The political crisis was temporarily settled by the formation in September 1965 of a coalition government, which included some of Papandreou's former supporters. Prospects for settlement of the crisis appeared good when, in late 1966, the leaders of the two main parties, George Papandreou (Centre

Union) and Panayiotis Kanellopoulos
(National Radical Union), agreed to
proceed to elections.

the Colonels seize power These
elections were scheduled for May 1967,
but before they could take place there
was a military coup, and a junta
headed by Col George Papadopoulos,
Col Nicholas Makarezos, and Brig
Stylianos Pattakos seized power in
April 1967. The official pretext for the
coup was the need to forestall an
armed communist uprising. Mass
arrests, mainly of left-wingers,
followed. All political parties were
abolished, while large-scale purges
were instituted in the armed forces.

Although power in the new regime
clearly lay with the military, the
nominal prime minister was a civilian,
Konstantine Kollias. King
Constantine's attitude towards the new
regime was reserved, and in December
1967 he launched a counter-coup
against 'the Colonels', as the regime
had come to be known. The counter-
coup was unsuccessful, and
Constantine fled into exile in Italy. This
was the signal for direct military rule.
Gen Zoitakis became regent, while
Col Papadopoulos, who had emerged
as the strong man of the regime,
assumed the premiership. Further
purges of royalist officers who had
supported the king's coup ensued.

In September 1968 a new and
authoritarian constitution was approved
by a large majority in a referendum;
but, as martial law was still in force,
this could not be regarded as a true test
of opinion. Even after the enactment of
the new constitution many of its
provisions remained in abeyance.

Although there was an initial degree
of acquiescence in some sectors of
society the Colonels' regime never
enjoyed any degree of popularity.
Opposition was ruthlessly suppressed
and, following the findings of the
European Commission of Human Rights,
Greece was obliged to withdraw from
the Council of Europe. Power was

increasingly concentrated in the hands
of Papadopoulos, who became regent
as well as prime minister.

growing opposition to the Colonels
Despite the regime's growing
unpopularity there were few signs of
large-scale resistance. In early 1973,
however, there were increasing signs
of restlessness among Greek students.
This was followed in late May by a
naval mutiny, which led to the
precipitate abolition of the monarchy.
Papadopoulos proclaimed the creation
of a 'presidential republic'. This was
ratified by a 78% vote in a referendum
held in July, although martial law still
remained in force in Athens and
Peiraias. Papadopoulos, the only
candidate, was elected president.
He declared an amnesty and promised
the holding of elections within
18 months. To oversee these elections
he appointed a former politician,
Spyros Markezinis, as prime minister.

The strategy of a move towards a
'guided' democracy met with
opposition from university students.
An occupation of the Athens
Polytechnic in November 1973 was
suppressed with severe brutality.
At least 34 students were killed and
many hundreds more were wounded.
The Polytechnic massacre was
followed by Papadopoulos's
overthrow in a bloodless coup by
Brig Gen Demetrios Ioannidis,
the commander of the military police
(ESA), which had assumed the leading
role in the hounding of opponents of
the regime. Although Ioannidis ruled
through a civilian cabinet there was
no doubt it was he who held effective
power. He soon showed that he had
no solution to his country's pressing
political and economic problems
(inflation was running at 30% per
annum in 1973).

The regime's foreign policy was
characterized by increasing belligerence
towards Turkey and towards President
Makarios in Cyprus. This culminated
in the pro-enosis coup, inspired from

Athens, mounted against Makarios in July 1974. This was quickly followed by a Turkish invasion of the island. Both Greece and Turkey mobilized, and in the ensuing turmoil the Ioannidis regime collapsed after threats from the commander of the Third Army Corps stationed in Salonika.

return to democracy The exiled Karamanlis was summoned back from Paris to defuse the tension that existed with Turkey and to liquidate the legacy of seven years of military dictatorship. Under Karamanlis's Government of National Salvation the Greek armed forces were demobilized and Karamanlis embarked on the precarious task of returning Greece to democratic rule. Karamanlis legalized the Greek Communist Party, which had been banned since 1947, and other political parties, and ended martial law and press censorship. In elections in November 1974 Karamanlis's New Democracy Party (ND) won 54% of the vote and 220 out of 300 seats in parliament. Following a referendum in December 1974 that decisively rejected a restoration of the monarchy, a new constitution for a democratic 'Hellenic Republic' was adopted, with Constantine Tsatsos as president.

During the course of 1975 a number of trials were held of ringleaders of the dictatorship and their accomplices. In August the three prime movers of the April 1967 coup were sentenced to death, later commuted to life imprisonment. Disappointment with US policy towards the dictatorship (which it had helped to keep in power) and over Cyprus led Greece to apply for accelerated membership of the European Community (EC; the precursor of the European Union), an application welcomed by the existing member countries.

The ND won the 1977 general election with a reduced majority, and in 1980 Karamanlis resigned as prime minister and was elected president. In 1981 Greece became a full member of the European Community, having been an associate since 1962.

Greek socialism The Panhellenic Socialist Movement (PASOK) won an absolute majority in parliament in the 1981 general election. Its leader, Andreas Papandreou, became Greece's first socialist prime minister. PASOK had been elected on a radical socialist platform, which included withdrawal from the EC, the removal of US military bases, and a programme of domestic reform. Important social changes, such as lowering the voting age to 18, the legalization of civil marriage and divorce, and an overhaul of the universities and the army, were carried out; but instead of withdrawing from Europe, Papandreou was content to obtain a modification of the terms of entry, and, rather than close US bases, he signed a five-year agreement on military and economic cooperation. In 1983 he also signed a ten-year economic-cooperation agreement with the USSR.

Despite introducing austerity measures to deal with rising inflation, PASOK won a comfortable majority in the 1985 elections. Criticism of Papandreou grew during 1989 when close aides were implicated in a banking scandal. He lost the general elections in 1989 and Tzanis Tzannetakis, an ND backbencher, formed Greece's first all-party government for 15 years. However, this soon broke up, and after months of negotiation Xenophon Zolotas (PASOK) put together a government of unity, comprising communists, socialists, conservatives, and nonpolitical figures.

Constantine Mitsotakis of the ND was sworn in as premier in April 1990 and formed a new all-party government after his party failed to win an outright majority in the elections. In June Karamanlis was again elected president. Papandreou was cleared of all corruption charges in January 1992. In September 1993 Mitsotakis dissolved parliament after the ND lost its overall majority (three of its members had defected to the newly formed left-of-centre Political Spring party). PASOK won an outright majority in the October 1993 elections and Papandreou was returned as prime minister. In March 1995 Costis Stephanopoulos, PASOK's candidate, was elected president. Papandreou, his health rapidly deteriorating, resigned in January 1996, and Costas Simitis became prime minister. Simitis appointed the pro-Europe Theodoros Pangalos as foreign minister. Papandreou was declared well and released from hospital in March, but died in June. In September 1996 PASOK was returned to power with 41.4% of the vote, signifying a slightly reduced majority.

foreign relations in the 1990s
An agreement on the siting of US bases in Greece was signed in 1990. In 1992 Greece refused to recognize the independence of the breakaway Yugoslav republic of Macedonia, saying it implied territorial claims on the Greek province of the same name. The republic was granted United Nations membership under the provisional name of the Former Yugoslav Republic of Macedonia in 1993. The Greek decision to impose a trade embargo against Macedonia in February 1994 brought widespread condemnation, and in April 1994 the European Commission took the unprecedented step of prosecuting Greece in the European Court of Justice. A compromise agreement was reached, and in September 1995 Greece recognized Macedonia and lifted its embargo. In July 1997 Greece and Turkey agreed to resolve all future disputes by peaceful means. In August 1999 Greece dropped its objections of principle to Turkey becoming, one day, a full member of the EU. It also sent aid to victims of earthquakes in Turkey in August and November 1999.

September 1999 earthquake
An earthquake, measuring 5.9 on the Richter scale, struck in September 1999, with its epicentre in a suburb 16 km/ 12 mi north of Athens. At least 127 people were killed and 70,000 were left homeless in the earthquake which was the strongest to hit the country since 1981. The government put the cost of reconstruction at $200 million. Turkey returned the aid that Greece had offered it after its own August earthquake; this reciprocation helped to improve relations between the two countries, and in January 2000 Greece and Turkey signed a series of agreements aimed at improving relations between them.

Simitis returns to power In general elections in April 2000 Costas Simitis was re-elected as prime minister, winning by only 1% in the tightest political contest ever in Greece. He pledged to continue with his preparations for entering the European single currency, and with his efforts to work on relations with Turkey. He formally submitted Greece's application to join the European single currency.

internal problems 2000 Greek workers brought Athens to a stop on 10 October 2000, with a general strike in protest against the government's planned labour reforms. The protest came in the wake of general condemnation of the Greek ferry system, which links the mainland with the many Greek islands, following the shipwreck of a passenger ferry which caused many deaths. The ensuing enquiry found that a large proportion of ferries in use did not come up to Greek or European seaworthiness standards.

Greece joined the euro in January 2001, with euro notes and coins becoming national currency on 1 January 2002.

In October 2001, Prime Minister Simitis was re-elected leader of PASOK.

Greenham Common   site of a continuous peace demonstration on public land near Newbury, Berkshire, UK, outside a US airbase. The women-only camp was established in September 1981 in protest against the siting of US cruise missiles in the UK. The demonstrations ended with the closure of the base. Greenham Common reverted to standby status, and the last US cruise missiles were withdrawn in March 1991.

Green Party political party aiming to 'preserve the planet and its people', based on the premise that continual economic growth is unsustainable. The leaderless party structure reflects a general commitment to decentralization. Green parties sprang up in Western Europe in the 1970s and in Eastern Europe from 1988. Parties in different countries are linked to one another but unaffiliated with any pressure group.

Greenpeace international environmental pressure group, founded in Vancouver, Canada, in 1971, with a policy of non-violent direct action backed by scientific research. During a protest against French atmospheric nuclear testing in the South Pacific in 1985, its ship *Rainbow Warrior* was sunk by French intelligence agents, killing a crew member. In 1995, it played a prominent role in opposing the disposal of waste from an oil rig in the North Sea, and again attempted to disrupt French nuclear tests in the Pacific. In 2004, Greenpeace (now headquartered in the Netherlands) had a global membership of 2.8 million in 41 countries.

Grenada island country in the Caribbean, the southernmost of the Windward Islands.

Grey, Edward (1862–1933) 1st Viscount Grey of Fallodon, British Liberal politician, MP for Berwick on Tweed 1885–1916, nephew of Charles Grey. As foreign secretary 1905–16 he negotiated an entente with Russia in 1907, and backed France against Germany in the *Agadir Incident of 1911. He published his memoirs, *Twenty-Five Years* in 1925. Baronet 1882, Viscount 1916.

Griffith, Arthur (1872–1922) Irish journalist, propagandist and politician. He was active in nationalist politics from 1898 and united various nationalist parties to form Sinn Fein 1905. When the provisional Irish parliament declared a republic in 1919, he was elected vice-president and signed the treaty that gave Eire its independence in 1921. He was elected the country's first president in 1922, dying in office later that year.

Grimond, Jo(seph), Baron Grimond (1913–1993) British Liberal politician, born in St Andrews, Scotland. As leader of the Liberal Party 1956–67, he aimed at making it 'a new radical party to take the place of the Socialist Party as an alternative to Conservatism'. An old-style Whig and a man of culture and personal charm, he had a considerable influence on post-war British politics, although he never held a major public position. During his term of office, the number of Liberal seats in Parliament doubled.

Grivas, George (Georgios Theodoros) (1898–1974) Greek Cypriot general who from 1955 led the underground group EOKA's attempts to secure the union (Greek *enosis*) of Cyprus with Greece.

Gromyko, Andrei Andreyevich (1909–1989) President of the USSR 1985–88. As ambassador to the USA from 1943, he took part in the Tehran, Yalta, and Potsdam conferences; as United Nations representative 1946–49, he exercised the Soviet veto 26 times. He was foreign minister 1957–85. It was Gromyko who formally nominated Mikhail Gorbachev as Communist Party leader in 1985.

Grosz, Károly (1930–1996) Hungarian communist politician, prime minister 1987–88. As leader of the ruling Hungarian Socialist Workers' Party (HSWP) 1988–89, he sought to establish a flexible system of 'socialist pluralism'.

Gruzenberg, Mikhail (1884–1952) born **Mikhail Markovich Borodin**,

Russian communist. From 1918 he worked as an agent of the Communist International. In 1923 he was invited by Sun Zhong Shan (Sun Yat-sen) to China, and until 1927 acted as high adviser to the Central Executive Committee of the *Guomindang. He returned to Russia, was arrested in a Stalinist purge in 1949, and died in a Siberian labour camp.

Guadalcanal, Battle of   in World War II, important US operation 1942–43 on the largest of the Solomon Islands. The battle for control of the area began when the US discovered the Japanese were building an airfield and landed marines to take the site August 1942. The Japanese sent reinforcements by sea to recapture the airfield and a series of bitter engagements took place on land for control of the airfield and at sea as each side attempted to reinforce their own troops and prevent the other from doing so. The naval operations began to dwarf those on the land they were supposedly supporting and both sides lost large numbers of ships and aircraft. The engagements on land and sea were inconclusive until the Japanese concluded such heavy naval losses could not be justified by one island and evacuated 7 February 1943.

Guatemala   country in Central America, bounded north and northwest by Mexico, east by Belize and the Caribbean Sea, southeast by Honduras and El Salvador, and southwest by the Pacific Ocean.

Guderian, Heinz Wilhelm (1888–1954)   German general in World War II. He created the Panzer (German 'armour') divisions that formed the ground spearhead of Hitler's *Blitzkrieg* attack strategy, achieving a significant breakthrough at Sedan in Ardennes, France 1940, and leading the advance to Moscow 1941.

Guevara, Che (Ernesto) (1928–1967)   Latin American revolutionary. He was born in Rosario, Argentina, and trained there as a doctor, but left his homeland

in 1953 because of his opposition to the right-wing president Juan Perón. In effecting the Cuban revolution of 1959 against the Cuban dictator Fulgencio Batista, he was second only to Castro and Castro's brother Raúl. Between 1961 and 1965, he served as Cuba's minister of industry. In 1965 he went to the Congo to fight against white mercenaries, and then to Bolivia, where he was killed in an unsuccessful attempt to lead a peasant rising near Vallegrande. He was an orthodox Marxist and renowned for his guerrilla techniques.

In November 1995 the location of the mass grave in which Guevara's body was buried was revealed by a witness to the burial to be in the village of Valle Grande in Bolivia. The remains of Guevara were unearthed in 1997 and returned to Cuba for a hero's burial.

Guinea   country in West Africa, bounded north by Senegal, northeast by Mali, southeast by Côte d'Ivoire, south by Liberia and Sierra Leone, west by the Atlantic Ocean, and northwest by Guinea-Bissau.

Guinea-Bissau   country in West Africa, bounded north by Senegal, east and southeast by Guinea, and southwest by the Atlantic Ocean.

Gulf Cooperation Council   GCC, Arab organization for promoting peace in the Gulf area, established 1981. Its declared purpose is 'to bring about integration, coordination, and cooperation in economic, social, defence, and political affairs among Arab Gulf states'. Its members include Bahrain, Kuwait, Oman, Qatar, Saudi Arabia, and the United Arab Emirates; its headquarters are in Riyadh, Saudi Arabia.

Gulf War   war 16 January–28 February 1991 between Iraq and a coalition of 28 nations led by the USA. The invasion and annexation of Kuwait by Iraq on 2 August 1990 provoked a build-up of US troops in Saudi Arabia, eventually totalling over 500,000.

The UK subsequently deployed 42,000 troops, France 15,000, Egypt 20,000, and other nations smaller contingents.

An air offensive lasting six weeks, in which 'smart' weapons came of age, destroyed about one-third of Iraqi equipment and inflicted massive casualties. A 100-hour ground war followed, which effectively destroyed the remnants of the 500,000-strong Iraqi army in or near Kuwait.

Guomindang or **Kuomintang,** Chinese National People's Party formed in 1912 after the overthrow of the Manchu Empire, and led by *Sun Zhong Shan (Sun Yat-sen). The Guomindang was an amalgamation of small political groups, including Sun's *Hsin Chung Hui* ('New China Party'), founded in 1894. During the *Chinese revolution (1927–49) the right wing, led by *Jiang Jie Shi, was in conflict with the left, led by *Mao Zedong (though the sides united during the Japanese invasion of 1937–45). Zedong emerged victorious in 1949. Guomindang survived as the dominant political party of Taiwan (until 2000), where it is still spelled **Kuomintang**. However, in recent years there have been splits between mainland-born hardliners and moderates, led by *Lee Teng-hui, president of Taiwan 1988–2000 and Kuomintang leader 1988–2001.

Gursel, Cemal (1895–1966) Turkish soldier and politician. Became commander-in-chief of the Turkish land forces in 1958. After leading an army coup in 1960 he became president of the Committee of National Unity, head of state, and prime minister (1960–61). He was elected president in October 1961 after the resumption of constitutional government. After illness he was replaced as president in March 1966.

Gush Emunim (Hebrew **'bloc of the faithful'**) Israeli fundamentalist group, founded 1973, which claims divine right to settlement of the West Bank, Gaza Strip, and Golan Heights as part of Israel. The claim is sometimes extended to the Euphrates.

Gustavus V (or **Gustaf V) (1858–1950)** King of Sweden from 1907, when he succeeded his father Oscar II. He married Princess Victoria, daughter of the Grand Duke of Baden 1881, thus uniting the reigning Bernadotte dynasty with the former royal house of Vasa.

Gustavus VI (or **Gustaf VI) (1882–1973)** King of Sweden from 1950, when he succeeded his father Gustavus V. He was an archaeologist and expert on Chinese art. He was succeeded by his grandson *Carl XVI Gustavus.

Guyana country in South America, bounded north by the Atlantic Ocean, east by Suriname, south and southwest by Brazil, and northwest by Venezuela.

H

Haakon VII (1872–1957) King of Norway from 1905. Born Prince Charles, the second son of Frederick VIII of Denmark, he was elected king of Norway on the country's separation from Sweden, and in 1906 he took the name Haakon. On the German invasion in 1940 he refused to accept Vidkun *Quisling's collaborationist government, and instead escaped to London and acted as constitutional head of the government-in-exile. He served as a powerful personification of Norwegian nationhood.

Habré, Hissène (c. 1930–) Chadian nationalist and politician, prime minister in 1978 and president 1982–90. Formerly a leader of the Chadian National Liberation Front (Frolinat), he joined the Armed Forces of the North (FAN) in the early 1970s, but made peace with President Félix Malloum and was appointed prime minister in 1978. After Malloum was overthrown by the Frolinat leader Goukouni Oueddi in 1979, Habré became defence minister, and in 1982 he seized control, aided by the CIA. With French military assistance and support from African heads of state, he forced Libya to withdraw from northern Chad but was ousted in a coup led by his military commander Idriss Deby in 1990. Habré was indicted for torture and barbarity by a court in Senegal in February 2000. He had been living in Senegal since he was overthrown in 1990, He is accused of the responsibility for the torture and killing of tens of thousands of Chadians during his eight-year rule.

Habyarimana, Juvenal (1937–1994) Rwandan politician and soldier, president 1973–94. In 1973, as fighting between the Tutsi and Hutu tribes recommenced, he led a bloodless coup against the government of President Grégoire Kayibanda and established a military regime. He founded the National Revolutionary Development Movement (MRND) as the only legally permitted political organization and promised an eventual return to constitutional government; civilian rule was adopted in 1980. In April 1994 Habyarimana and Burundian president Cyprien Ntaryamira were killed when their plane was shot down over Kigali, sparking an escalation in the civil war and a wave of atrocities against Tutsi civilians.

Hacha, Emil (1872–1945) Czech politician, president, and lawyer. He succeeded Beneš as President after the 1938 Munich Pact. As German forces entered the country on 14 March 1939, he was forced to sign a declaration in Berlin placing his country under German 'protection'. In 1945 he was arrested as a war criminal but died before he could come to trial.

Haganah Zionist military organization in Palestine. It originated under the Turkish rule of the Ottoman Empire before World War I to protect Jewish settlements, and many of its members served in the British forces in both world wars. After World War II it condemned guerrilla activity, opposing the British authorities only passively. It formed the basis of the Israeli army after Israel was established in 1948.

Hague Convention, 1899 agreement relating to the rights and duties of belligerents in wartime. It was reached by delegates of the peace conference that took place in the Hague, Netherlands, between May and July 1899. Its most important result was the establishment of a **Permanent Court of Arbitration** at the Hague, popularly

known as the **Hague Tribunal**.
The court arbitrated on cases of
international dispute, but has lost
much of its importance to the
International Court of Justice, also
at the Hague. A second *Hague
Convention followed in 1907.

Hague Convention, 1907 agreement
relating to the rights and duties of
belligerents in wartime. It was reached
by delegates of the peace conference
that took place in the Hague,
Netherlands, between June and
October 1907. Its provisions included
the humane treatment of prisoners of
war and the outlawing of the use of
poisons as weapons of war. Some of
the principles are also incorporated
in the *Geneva Convention, which,
largely because of its more limited
aims, have been implemented more
successfully. It followed the *Hague
Convention of 1899.

Haider, Jörg (1950–) Austrian
politician and former leader of the
Austrian Freedom Party (*Freiheitliche
Partei Österreichs*) 1986–2000. As leader
of Austria's far-right, anti-immigrant
Freedom Party, Jörg Haider formed a
coalition government in early February
2000 with Wolfgang Schüssel's
mainstream conservative People's
Party. Schüssel was named as the
leader of the government, while
Haider remained governor of the
region of Carinthia, and a senior
partner in the new coalition.
This marked the inclusion of the far
right in a West European government
for the first time since World War II,
and was met with protests from the
Austrian electorate and across Europe,
including the imposition of political
sanctions by the 14 other member
states of the European Union (EU).
Haider resigned his position as leader
of the Freedom Party on May 1, 2000.
He denied that his decision was a
result of international pressure, and
the Freedom Party retained its position
in the new Austrian coalition
government. Diplomatic sanctions

were lifted in September, after an EU
report found Austria's human rights
record to be satisfactory.

Haig, Alexander Meigs (1924–)
US general and Republican politician.
He became President Nixon's White
House chief of staff at the height of
the *Watergate scandal, was NATO
commander 1974–79, and secretary of
state to President Reagan 1981–82.

**Haig, Douglas (1861–1928) 1st Earl
Haig**, Scottish army officer,
commander-in-chief in World War I,
born in Edinburgh, Scotland. His
Somme offensive in France in the
summer of 1916 made considerable
advances only at enormous cost to
human life, and his Passchendaele
offensive in Belgium from July to
November 1917 achieved little at a
similar loss. He was created field
marshal in 1917 and, after retiring,
became first president of the *British
Legion in 1921.

**Haile Selassie, Ras (Prince) Tafari
(1892–1975)** called 'the Lion of
Judah', Emperor of Ethiopia 1930–74.
He pleaded unsuccessfully to the
League of Nations against the Italian
conquest of his country 1935–36, and
was then deposed and fled to the UK.
He went to Egypt in 1940 and raised
an army, which he led into Ethiopia in
January 1941 alongside British forces,
and was restored to the throne on
5 May. He was deposed by a military
coup in 1974 and died in captivity the
following year. Followers of the
Rastafarian religion believe that he
was the Messiah, the incarnation of
God (Jah).

**Hailsham, Quintin McGarel Hogg,
Baron Hailsham of St Marylebone
(1907–2001)** British Conservative
politician and lawyer. Having
succeeded as 2nd Viscount Hailsham
in 1950, he renounced the title in 1963
to re-enter the House of Commons,
and was then able to contest the
Conservative Party leadership
elections. He took a life peerage in
1970 on his appointment as Lord

Chancellor 1970–74 and was Lord Chancellor again 1979–87.

Haiti country in the Caribbean, occupying the western part of the island of Hispaniola; to the east is the Dominican Republic.

Haldane, Richard Burdon (1856–1928) 1st Viscount Haldane, British Liberal politician, born in Scotland. As secretary for war 1905–12, he sponsored the army reforms that established an expeditionary force, backed by a territorial army and under the unified control of an imperial general staff. He was Lord Chancellor 1912–15 and in the Labour government of 1924. His writings on German philosophy led to accusations of his having pro-German sympathies. Viscount 1911.

Halder, Franz (1884–1971) German general. As chief of staff from September 1938, he was responsible for much of the planning for the invasion of the USSR in 1941, though it seems he did not dare draw attention to possible problems. He was arrested in the aftermath of the *July Plot against Hitler in 1944 and imprisoned in Dachau concentration camp. Liberated by US troops in 1945, he gave evidence for the prosecution at the *Nuremberg trials of Nazi war criminals.

Halévy, Elie (1870–1937) French historian. In 1898 he became professor at the Ecole Libre des Science Politiques. *Histoire du Socialisme européen* (1948), based on notes on his lectures, was published posthumously.

Halifax, Edward Frederick Lindley Wood, 1st Earl of Halifax (2nd creation) (1881–1959) British Conservative politician, viceroy of India 1926–31. As foreign secretary 1938–40 he was associated with Chamberlain's 'appeasement' policy. He received an earldom in 1944 for services to the Allied cause while ambassador to the USA 1941–46. Baron in 1925, succeeded as viscount in 1934, created earl in 1944.

Hallowes, Odette Marie Celine (1912–1995) French-born war heroine. From 1942 she worked as a British agent in German-occupied France. She was captured, tortured, and sent to Ravensbruck concentration camp. In 1945 she escaped. Her outstanding courage and endurance won her the MBE (1945), the George Cross (1946), and the Legion of Honour (1950).

Halsey, William Frederick (1882–1959) US admiral. A highly skilled naval air tactician, his handling of carrier fleets in World War II played a significant role in the eventual defeat of Japan. He was appointed commander of US Task Force 16 in the Pacific 1942 and almost immediately launched the Doolittle raid on Tokyo. He took part in operations throughout the Far East, including Santa Cruz, Guadalcanal, Bougainville, and the Battle of *Leyte Gulf. He was promoted to fleet admiral 1945 and retired 1947.

Hamaguchi, Osachi (or Yuko**) (1870–1931)** Japanese politician, prime minister 1929–30. His policies created social unrest and alienated military interests. His acceptance of the terms of the London Naval Agreement 1930 was also unpopular.

Hamas or **Islamic Resistance Movement,** (Arabic **'zeal'**) Islamic fundamentalist organization formally founded by Sheikh Yassin Ahmed in 1988. Its militant wing, the Izzedine Al Qassam Brigades, played a major role in the *Intifada, the Palestinian uprising in the Israeli-occupied territories from 1987, particularly in the economically deprived *Gaza Strip, the Hamas heartland. Responsible for attacks on Israeli soldiers and civilians and for suicide bombings, the group gained a reputation for ruthlessness and unpredictability. A radical 'rejectionist' group, which opposes negotiations with Israel by the *Palestine Liberation Organization (PLO) and does not recognize the right of Israel to exist, it rejects the 1993

Oslo Peace Accords which led to the establishment of the Palestine National Authority and its campaign of violence within Israel has been aimed at disrupting the *Israel–Palestine peace process. The short-term aim of Hamas is a complete Israeli withdrawal from the Palestinian territories and its long-term goal is the establishment of an Islamic state on the land of Palestine. Hamas also has a social role, running hospitals and schools.

Hammarskjöld, Dag (Hjalmar Agne Carl) (1905–1961) Swedish secretary general of the United Nations (UN) 1953–61. His role as a mediator and negotiator, particularly in areas of political conflict, helped to increase the prestige and influence of the UN significantly, and his name is synonymous with the peacekeeping work of the UN today. He was killed in a plane crash while involved in a controversial peacekeeping mission in Congo (now the Democratic Republic of Congo). He was posthumously awarded the Nobel Prize for Peace in 1961 for his peacekeeping work as secretary general of the UN.

Hara, Takashi (Kei) (1856–1921) Japanese politician, president 1918–21. As the head of the majority party in the Diet (parliament), he became prime minister in 1918 and presided over the first party cabinet since the establishment of the Meiji Constitution. He proved to be a conservative premier, moving cautiously on political and social reform. Although he expanded the electorate by lowering tax qualifications, he did not endorse the principle of universal manhood suffrage.

Hardie, (James) Keir (1856–1915) Scottish socialist, the first British Labour politician, member of Parliament 1892–95 and 1900–15. He worked in the mines as a boy and in 1886 became secretary of the Scottish Miners' Federation. In 1888 he was the first Labour candidate to stand for Parliament; he entered Parliament independently as a Labour member in 1892, he became chair of the Labour party 1906–08 and 1909–10, and in 1893 was a chief founder of the *Independent Labour Party.

Harding, Warren G(amaliel) (1865–1923) 29th president of the USA 1921–23, a Republican. As president he concluded the peace treaties of 1921 with Germany, Austria, and Hungary, and in the same year called the Washington Naval Conference to resolve conflicting British, Japanese, and US ambitions in the Pacific. He opposed US membership of the *League of Nations. There were charges of corruption among members of his cabinet (the *Teapot Dome Scandal), with the secretary of the interior later convicted for taking bribes.

Harriman, (William) Averell (1891–1986) US diplomat. He was administrator of *lend-lease in World War II and warned of the Soviet Union's aggressive intentions from his post as ambassador to the USSR 1943–46. He became Democratic secretary of commerce 1946–48 in Harry Truman's administration, governor of New York 1955–58, and negotiator of the Nuclear Test Ban Treaty with the USSR in 1963. He served the Lyndon Johnson administration 1968–69 in the opening rounds of the Vietnam War peace talks at which he was chief negotiator.

Harris, Arthur Travers (1892–1984) British marshal of the Royal Air Force in World War II. Known as 'Bomber Harris', he was commander-in-chief of Bomber Command 1942–45.

Hassan II (1929–1999) King of Morocco 1961–99. He succeeded the throne upon the death of his father Mohamed V. Following riots in Casablanca in 1965, he established a royal dictatorship and survived two coup attempts. The occupation of the former Spanish Western Sahara in 1976 enabled him to rally strong popular support and consolidate his power. He returned to constitutional government in 1984, with a civilian prime minister leading a government of national unity. He was succeeded by his 35-year-old son Muhammad.

Hatoyama, Ichiro (1883–1959) Japanese conservative politician, prime minister 1954–56. In 1945 he organized the conservative Japan Liberal Party (Nihon Jiyuto), which gained a victory in the elections the following year. On the verge of becoming prime minister, he was purged from official life by the US occupation authorities for his role in supporting the military cabinets of the 1930s. Although he was rehabilitated in 1951, he found that leadership of the Liberal Party was now firmly in the hands of *Shigeru Yoshida. He formed a new conservative party, the Japan Democratic Party (Nihon Minshuto), which successfully ousted Yoshida from power in 1954, and became premier. During his premiership relations with the USSR were normalized, thus paving the way for Japan's entry into the United Nations in 1956, and the two conservative parties were merged in 1955 to form the Liberal Democratic Party (Jiyu Minshuto).

Hatton, Derek (1948–) British left-wing politician, former deputy leader of Liverpool city council. A leading member of the Militant Tendency, Hatton was removed from office and expelled from the Labour Party in 1987.

Haughey, Charles James (1925–) Irish politician; Taoiseach (prime minister) 1979–81, 1982, and 1987–92; leader of Fianna Fáil 1979–92. He succeeded Jack Lynch as Fianna Fáil leader and Taoiseach in 1979, to be confronted with serious economic problems and an intensely difficult period in Anglo-Irish relations, as the UK's Thatcher government attempted to face down the IRA hunger strikes of 1980 and 1981. Haughey lost office in 1981 after an early general election and regained it for a short period in 1982. His final period of office, beginning in 1987, was mired in difficulty, and saw Haughey forced to accept coalition with the Progressive Democrats. In 1998 the Irish Director of Public Prosecutions elected to prosecute him for his alleged attempts to obstruct an earlier hearing into payments made to politicians in the 1980s.

Havel, Václav (1936–) Czech dramatist, civil rights activist, and politician, president of Czechoslovakia 1989–92 and of the Czech Republic 1993–2003. A noted playwright, he participated in the 'Prague spring' liberal reforms in 1968, but his plays were banned after the Soviet clampdown later in the year. In 1977 he formed the human rights organization *Charter 77, which pressed for democratic reforms, and was subsequently imprisoned 1979–83 and 1989 for dissident activity. He was popularly elected president after the bloodless 'velvet revolution' of November–December 1989, which saw the overthrow of the Communist Party following popular protests, and he became a much respected international statesman.

Hawke, Bob (Robert James Lee) (1929–) Australian Labor politician, prime minister 1983–91, on the right wing of the party. He was president of the Australian Council of Trade Unions 1970–80. He announced his retirement from politics in 1992.

Haya de la Torre, Víctor Raúl (1895–1979) Peruvian politician, political thinker, and founder of the American Popular Revolutionary Alliance (APRA; Aprista Party) in 1924. The voice of radical nationalistic dissent in Peru, APRA advocates that indigenous peoples should have an equal voice in the political and educational affairs of their countries. In 1963 he made an unsuccessful bid for the Peruvian presidency. He is the author of *Adónde va Indoamérica/ The Future of Indoamerica* (1935).

Hayden, Bill (1933–) born **William George Hayden**, Australian Labor politician. He was leader of the Australian Labor Party and of the opposition 1977–83, minister of foreign affairs 1983–88, and governor general 1989–96.

Haywood, William Dudley (1869–1928) called **'Big Bill'**, US labour leader. Elected treasurer-secretary of the Western Federation of Miners (WFM) in 1900, a member of the Socialist Party from 1901, and one of the founders of the Industrial Workers of the World (IWW, 'Wobblies') in 1905, his goal was to unite all unions in 'one big union'. In 1905 Haywood was charged with involvement in the murder of Frank Stenunenberg, an anti-union politician and former governor of Idaho, and his acquittal in 1907 made him a hero of the labour movement. Arrested again for sedition during World War I, he spent his later years in exile in the USSR.

Healey, Denis Winston (1917–) **Baron Healey**, British Labour politician. While secretary of state for defence 1964–70 he was in charge of the reduction of British forces east of Suez. He was chancellor of the Exchequer 1974–79. In 1976 he contested the party leadership, losing to James Callaghan, and again in 1980, losing to Michael Foot, to whom he was deputy leader 1980–83. In 1987 he resigned from the shadow cabinet.

Heath, Edward (Richard George) (1916–) British Conservative politician, party leader 1965–75. As prime minister 1970–74 he took the UK into the European Community (EC) but was brought down by economic and industrial-relations crises at home. He was replaced as party leader by Margaret Thatcher in 1975, and became increasingly critical of her policies and her opposition to the UK's full participation in the EC. During John Major's administration 1990–97, he undertook missions in Iraq in 1990 and 1993 to negotiate the release of British hostages, but also continued his attacks on 'Eurosceptics' within the party. He stepped down as an MP in 2001.

Heffer, Eric Samuel (1922–1991) British Labour politician, member of Parliament for Walton, Liverpool 1964–91. He held a ministerial post 1974–75, joined Michael Foot's shadow cabinet in 1981, and was regularly elected to Labour's National Executive Committee, but found it difficult to follow the majority view.

Heflin, James (Thomas) (1869–1951) US politician. A lawyer and state representative, he filled vacancies in the US House of Representatives as a Democrat representative of Alabama (1904–20) and the Senate (1920–31), afterwards working for the Federal government in Alabama. Heflin was born in Louina, Alabama.

Hekmatyar, Gulbuddin (1949–) Afghani leader of the Mujahedin (Islamic fundamentalist guerrillas), prime minister 1993–94 and 1996. Strongly anticommunist and leading the Hezb-i-Islami (Islamic Party) faction, he resisted the takeover of Kabul by moderate Mujahedin forces in April 1992 and refused to join the interim administration, continuing to bombard the city until being driven out. In June 1993, under a peace agreement with President Burhanuddin Rabbani, Hekmatyar was re-admitted to the city as prime minister, but his forces renewed their attacks on Kabul during 1994. He was subsequently dismissed from the premiership, but returned to Kabul in June 1996, when he became combined prime minister, defence minister, and finance minister. However, in September he was driven out of Kabul by the Taliban (fundamentalist student army) who had seized control of much of Afghanistan.

Heligoland Bight, Battle of World War I naval battle between British and German forces 28 August 1914 fought in the Heligoland Bight, the stretch of water between Heligoland island and the German mainland used by the

German fleet for exercises. The British launched a surprise raid on the German vessels exercising in the Bight and succeeded in sinking three light cruisers and a destroyer, a severe blow to German naval morale.

Helms, Jesse (1921–) US Republican senator. Born in Monroe, North Carolina, he attended Wingate College and Wake Forest College and served in the US navy 1942–45. He was administrative assistant to US senator Willis Smith 1951–53 and to US senator Alton Lennon in 1953. He was elected to the US Senate in 1972, and re-elected in 1978, 1984, 1990, and 1996.

Helsinki Conference international meeting in 1975 at which 35 countries, including the USSR and the USA, attempted to reach agreement on cooperation in security, economics, science, technology, and human rights. This established the Conference on Security and Cooperation in Europe, which is now known as the Organization for Security and Cooperation in Europe.

Henderson, Arthur (1863–1935) British Labour politician and trade unionist, leader of the Labour Party 1914–1918, born in Scotland. He helped to transform the Labour Party from a pressure group into a party of government, and was home secretary 1924–29 in the first Labour government. As foreign secretary 1929–31 he accorded the Soviet government full recognition. He was awarded the Nobel Prize for Peace in 1934 for his work for international disarmament.

Henderson Field airfield established on Guadalcanal island during World War II; originally begun by the Japanese, it was completed by US forces 1942 and named after a US Marine major killed at the Battle of *Midway. The Guadalcanal campaign was fought over possession of the airfield, since its position was essential for command of the area around the Solomon Islands.

Heng Samrin (1934–) Cambodian politician, national leader 1981–91. A Khmer Rouge commander 1976–78, he became disillusioned with its brutal tactics. He led an unsuccessful coup against *Pol Pot in 1978 and established the Kampuchean People's Revolutionary Party (KPRP) in Vietnam, before returning in 1979 to head the new Vietnamese-backed government, becoming KPRP leader in 1981. He was replaced as prime minister by the reformist Hun Sen in 1985 but retained control over the government until 1991 as KPRP leader.

Henlein, Konrad (1898–1945) Sudeten-German leader of the Sudeten Nazi Party in Czechoslovakia, and closely allied with Hitler's Nazis. He was partly responsible for the destabilization of the Czechoslovak state in 1938, which led to the *Munich Agreement and secession of Sudeten to Germany.

Herriot, Edouard (1872–1957) French radical politician. A leading parliamentarian of the inter-war period, Herriot was president of his party (1919–26, 1931–35, and 1945–56) and prime minister (1924–25, 1926, and 1932). As president of the chamber of deputies 1936–40 and a staunch republican, he challenged the legality of the 1940 parliamentary vote establishing the Vichy regime.

Hertzog, James Barry Munnik (1866–1942) South African politician, prime minister 1924–39, founder of the Nationalist Party in 1913 (the United South African National Party from 1933). He opposed South Africa's entry into both world wars.

Herzl, Theodor (1860–1904) Austrian founder of the Zionist movement. The *Dreyfus case convinced him that the only solution to the problem of anti-Semitism was the resettlement of the Jews in a state of their own. His book *Der Judenstaad/Jewish State* (1896) launched political *Zionism, and he became the first president of the World Zionist Organization in 1897.

Herzog, Chaim (1918–1997) Irish-Israeli soldier, lawyer, writer, politician, and president of Israel (1983–93). He served as Israel's ambassador and permanent representative to the United Nations between 1975–78. Returning to Israel, he joined the Labour Party and was elected to the Knesset in 1981. His public standing made him an obvious choice for the presidency in 1983.

Heseltine, Michael (Ray Dibdin) (1933–) British Conservative politician, deputy prime minister 1995–97. A member of Parliament from 1966 (for Tavistock 1966–74 and for Henley from 1974), he was secretary of state for the environment 1990–92 and for trade and industry 1992–95.

Hess, (Walter Richard) Rudolf (1894–1987) German Nazi leader. Imprisoned with Adolf Hitler 1924–25, he became his private secretary, taking down *Mein Kampf* from his dictation. In 1933 he was appointed deputy *Führer* to Hitler, a post he held until replaced by Goering in September 1939. On 10 May 1941 he landed by air in the UK with his own compromise peace proposals and was held a prisoner of war until 1945, when he was tried at Nuremberg as a war criminal and sentenced to life imprisonment. He died in *Spandau prison, Berlin.

Heuss, Theodor (1884–1963) German politician and writer, first president of the Federal German Republic 1949–59. After World War II he became leader of the Free Democratic party in West Germany and played an important role in the drafting of the Basic Law (constitution) of the Federal Republic.

He Xiangning (or Ho Hsiang-ning) (1880–1972) Chinese revolutionary and feminist. She was one of the first Chinese women publicly to advocate nationalism, revolution, and female emancipation, and one of the first to cut her hair short. An active advocate of links with the communists and

Russia, she went to Hong Kong in 1927 when Chiang Kai-shek broke with the communists, and was an outspoken critic of his leadership. She returned to Beijing (Peking) in 1949 as head of the overseas commission.

Heydrich, Reinhard Tristan Eugen (1904–1942) German Nazi, head of the *Sicherheitsdienst* (SD), the party's security service, and Heinrich *Himmler's deputy. He was instrumental in organizing the final solution, the policy of genocide used against Jews and others. 'Protector' of Bohemia and Moravia from 1941, he was ambushed and killed the following year by three members of the Czechoslovak forces in Britain, who had landed by parachute. Reprisals followed, including several hundred executions and the massacre in *Lidice.

Hezbollah or **Hizbollah, ('Party of God')** extremist Muslim organization founded by the Iranian Revolutionary Guards who were sent to Lebanon after the 1979 Iranian revolution. Its aim is to spread the Islamic revolution of Iran among the Shiite population of Lebanon. Hezbollah is believed to be the umbrella movement of the groups that held many of the Western hostages taken from 1984.

In 1996 Hezbollah guerrillas, opposed to the Middle East peace process, engaged in renewed hostilities with Israeli forces stationed in southern Lebanon.

Higgins, Henry Bournes (1851–1929) Irish-born Australian politician and judge. An expert in constitutional law, Higgins was critical of the terms of federation within the British Empire when Australia became a self-governing Commonwealth in 1901. He was a popular figure within the Australian labour movement, especially for establishing the principles of arbitration in industrial disputes and the minimum wage.

Hill, Joe (c. 1872–1915) born Joel Emmanuel Hagglung, Swedish-born

US labour organizer. A member of the Industrial Workers of the World (IWW, 'Wobblies'), he was convicted of murder on circumstantial evidence in Salt Lake City, Utah, in 1914. Despite calls by President Wilson and the Swedish government for a retrial, Hill was executed in 1915, becoming a martyr for the labour movement.

Hillery, Patrick (John) (1923–) Irish politician, president 1976–90. As minister of foreign affairs, he successfully negotiated Ireland's entry into the European Economic Community (EEC, now the European Union) in 1973. Thereupon he became Ireland's first EEC Commissioner. Hillery served as president for two terms until 1990.

Hillsborough Agreement another name for the *Anglo-Irish Agreement (1985).

Himmler, Heinrich (1900–1945) German Nazi leader, head of the *SS elite corps from 1929, the police and the *Gestapo secret police from 1936, and supervisor of the extermination of the Jews in Eastern Europe. During World War II he replaced Hermann Goering as Hitler's second-in-command. He was captured in May 1945 and committed suicide.

Hindenburg Line German western line of World War I fortifications running from Arras, through Cambrai and St Quentin, to Soissons, built 1916–17. Part of the line was taken by the British in the third battle of *Arras, but it generally resisted attack until the British offensive of summer 1918.

Hirohito (1901–1989) regal name **Showa**, Emperor of Japan from 1926, when he succeeded his father Taish (Yoshihito). After the defeat of Japan in World War II in 1945, he was made a figurehead monarch by the US-backed constitution of 1946. He is believed to have played a reluctant role in General *Tojo's prewar expansion plans. He was succeeded by his son *Akihito.

Hiroshima industrial city and port on the south coast of Honshu Island, Japan; population (1994) 1,077,000. On 6 August 1945 it was destroyed by the first wartime use of an atomic bomb. The city has been largely rebuilt since then. The main industries include food processing and the manufacture of cars and machinery.

Towards the end of *World War II the city, which was the seventh largest in Japan, was utterly devastated by the first US atomic bomb dropped by the *Enola Gay*; the strike on Nagasaki followed three days later. More than 10 sq km/4 sq mi were obliterated, with very heavy damage outside that area. Casualties totalled at least 137,000 out of a population of 343,000: 78,150 were found dead, others died later. By 1995, the estimated death toll, which included individuals who had died from radiation-related diseases in the intervening years, had climbed to about 192,000. An annual commemorative ceremony is held on 6 August.

Hiss, Alger (1904–1996) US Democrat Department of State official and diplomat imprisoned in 1950 for perjury when he denied dealings with former Soviet agent Whittaker Chambers. The Hiss case contributed to the climate of fear and suspicion that led to communist witch hunts of the 1950s (see *McCarthyism). Doubts have since been raised about the justice of his conviction.

Hitler, Adolf (1889–1945) German Nazi dictator, born in Austria. He was *Führer* (leader) of the Nazi Party from 1921 and wrote *Mein Kampf/My Struggle* (1925–27). As chancellor of Germany from 1933 and head of state from 1934, he created a dictatorship by playing party and state institutions against each other and continually creating new offices and appointments. His position was not seriously challenged until the *July Plot of 1944, which failed to assassinate him. In foreign affairs, he reoccupied the Rhineland and formed an alliance with the Italian Fascist Benito *Mussolini in

1936, annexed Austria in 1938, and occupied Sudeten under the *Munich Agreement. The rest of Czechoslovakia was annexed in March 1939. The Ribbentrop–Molotov pact was followed in September by the invasion of Poland and the declaration of war by Britain and France (see *World War II). He committed suicide as Berlin fell.

Hitler was born in Braunau-am-Inn and spent his early years in poverty in Vienna and Munich. After serving as a volunteer in the German army during World War I, he was employed as a spy by the military authorities in Munich and in 1919 joined, in this capacity, the German Workers' Party. By 1921 he had assumed its leadership, renamed it the National Socialist German Workers' Party (Nazi Party for short), and provided it with a programme that mixed nationalism with anti-Semitism. Having led an unsuccessful uprising in Munich in 1923, he served nine months in prison, during which he wrote his political testament, *Mein Kampf*.

The party did not achieve national importance until the elections of 1930; by 1932, although Field Marshal Hindenburg defeated Hitler in the presidential elections, it formed the largest group in the Reichstag (parliament). As the result of an intrigue directed by Chancellor Franz von *Papen, Hitler became chancellor in a Nazi–Nationalist coalition on 30 January 1933. The opposition was rapidly suppressed, the Nationalists removed from the government, and the Nazis declared the only legal party. In 1934 Hitler succeeded Hindenburg as head of state. Meanwhile, the drive to war began; Germany left the *League of Nations, conscription was reintroduced, and in 1936 the Rhineland was reoccupied.

Hitler and Mussolini, who were already both involved in the Spanish Civil War, formed an alliance (the *Axis) in 1936, joined by Japan in 1940. Hitler conducted the war in a ruthless but idiosyncratic way, took and ruled most of the neighbouring countries with repressive occupation forces, and had millions of Slavs, Jews, Romanies, homosexuals, and political enemies killed in *concentration camps and massacres. He narrowly escaped death on 20 July 1944 from a bomb explosion at a staff meeting, prepared by high-ranking officers. On 29 April 1945, when Berlin was largely in Soviet hands, he married his mistress Eva Braun in his bunker under the chancellery building and on the following day committed suicide with her.

Hoare–Laval Pact plan for a peaceful settlement to the Italian invasion of Ethiopia in October 1935. It was devised by Samuel Hoare (1880–1959), British foreign secretary, and Pierre *Laval, French premier, at the request of the *League of Nations. Realizing no European country was willing to go to war over Ethiopia, Hoare and Laval proposed official recognition of Italian claims. Public outcry in Britain against the pact's seeming approval of Italian aggression was so great that the pact had to be disowned and Hoare was forced to resign.

Ho Chi Minh (1890–1969) adopted name of **Nguyen Tat Thanh**, North Vietnamese communist politician, prime minister 1954–55, and president 1954–69. Having trained in Moscow shortly after the Russian Revolution, he headed the communist *Vietminh from 1941 and fought against the French during the Indochina War 1946–54, becoming president and prime minister of the republic at the armistice. Aided by the communist bloc, he did much to develop industrial potential. He relinquished the premiership in 1955, but continued as president. In the years before his death, Ho successfully led his country's fight against US-aided South Vietnam in the *Vietnam War 1954–75.

Hodza, Milan (1878–1944) Czechoslovak politician, prime minister 1936–38. He and President Edvard *Beneš were forced to agree to the secession of the Sudeten areas of Czechoslovakia to Germany before resigning on 22 September 1938 (see *Munich Agreement).

Hoffa, Jimmy (James Riddle) (1913–1975) US labour leader, president of the International Brotherhood of Teamsters (lorry drivers' union) from 1957. He was jailed 1967–71 for attempted bribery of a federal court jury after he was charged with corruption. He was released by President Richard Nixon with the stipulation that he did not engage in union activities, but was evidently attempting to reassert influence when he disappeared in 1975. He is generally believed to have been murdered.

Hoffman, Abbie (Abbot) (1936–1989) US left-wing political activist, founder of the Yippies (Youth International Party), a political offshoot of the hippies. He was a member of the Chicago Seven, a radical group tried for attempting to disrupt the 1968 Democratic Convention.

Hofmeyr, Jan Hendrik (1894–1948) South African statesman and historian. In the coalition government of 1933 he was minister for the interior, education, and public health. But his sympathies for the Bantu people soon made him unpopular with many of the Afrikaners. In 1936 he strongly opposed the bill to destroy the Cape native franchise, and in 1938 he resigned. When the Second World War broke out Hofmeyr rejoined the government as minister of finance and in 1943 was appointed deputy prime minister. In the 1948 elections his liberal attitude towards the non-European races alienated many electors, but his party supported him and he remained in the forefront of the opposition to the Prime Minister Daniel Malan's policy of segregation.

Holland, Sidney George (1893–1961) New Zealand National Party right-of-centre politician, prime minister 1949–57. He removed wartime controls, abolished the Legislative Council (the upper house of parliament), pursued a market-centred economic strategy, and participated in conferences on the Suez Crisis in 1956. He was knighted in 1957, but, with his health deteriorating, retired in September 1957 and was replaced as prime minister and party leader by Keith *Holyoake.

Holocaust, the or **Shoah**; Hebrew 'whirlwind', the annihilation of an estimated 16 million people by the Nazi regime between 1933 and 1945, principally in the numerous extermination and *concentration camps, most notably *Auschwitz (Oswiecim), *Sobibor, *Treblinka, and Maidanek in Poland, and Belsen, *Buchenwald, and *Dachau in Germany. Camps were built on railway lines to facilitate transport. Of the victims, around 6 million were Jews (over 67% of European Jews); around 10 million Ukrainian, Polish, and Russian civilians and prisoners of war, Romanies, socialists, homosexuals, and others (labelled 'defectives') were also imprisoned and/or exterminated. Victims were variously starved, tortured, experimented on, and worked to death. Millions were executed in gas chambers, shot, or hanged. It was euphemistically termed the final solution (of the Jewish question). The precise death toll will never be known. Holocaust museums and memorial sites have been established in Israel and in other countries, and many Jews remember those who died by observing Yom Ha-Shoah, or Holocaust Remembrance Day.

Holt, Harold Edward (1908–1967) Australian Liberal politician, prime minister 1966–67. His brief prime ministership was dominated by the Vietnam War, to which he committed increased Australian troops.

Holyoake, Keith Jacka (1904–1983) New Zealand National Party right-of-centre politician, prime minister in 1957 (for three months) and 1960–72, during which time he was also foreign minister. During his second period as prime minister he secured electoral victories for the National Party on three occasions, developed closer ties with Australia, supported the USA in Vietnam, and negotiated special access for New Zealand dairy produce to the UK market, within the European Community. He was knighted (GCMG) on his retirement in 1972 and, between 1977–80, became the first former prime minister to serve as governor general.

Home Guard unpaid force formed in Britain in May 1940 to repel the expected German invasion, and known until July 1940 as the Local Defence Volunteers. It consisted of men aged 17–65 who had not been called up, formed part of the armed forces of the Crown, and was subject to military law. Over 2 million strong in 1944, it was disbanded on 31 December 1945, but revived in 1951, then placed on a reserve basis in 1955. It ceased activity in 1957.

homeland or **Bantustan**, before 1980, name for the Black National States in the Republic of South Africa.

home rule, Irish movement to repeal the Act of Union of 1801 that joined Ireland to Britain, and to establish an Irish parliament responsible for internal affairs. In 1870 Isaac Butt formed the Home Rule Association and the movement was led in Parliament from 1880 by Charles Stewart Parnell. After 1918 the demand for an independent Irish republic replaced that for home rule.

Homestead Act in US history, an act of Congress in May 1862 that encouraged settlement of land in the west by offering plots of up to 65-ha/160-acres, cheaply or even free, to citizens aged 21 years and over, or heads of family. In return, they had to promise to stay on the plot for five years, and to cultivate and improve the land, as well as build a house. The law

was designed to prevent people from controlling vast amounts of land in order to make a quick fortune. By 1900 about 32 million ha/80 million acres had been distributed. Homestead lands are available to this day.

Honduras country in Central America, bounded north by the Caribbean Sea, southeast by Nicaragua, south by the Pacific Ocean, southwest by El Salvador, and west and northwest by Guatemala.

Honecker, Erich (1912–1994) German communist politician, in power in East Germany 1973–89, elected chair of the council of state (head of state) in 1976. He governed in an outwardly austere and efficient manner and, while favouring East–West détente, was a loyal ally of the USSR. In 1989, following a wave of pro-democracy demonstrations, he was replaced as leader of the Socialist Unity Party (SED) and head of state by Egon Krenz, and expelled from the Communist Party. He died in exile in Chile.

Hong Kong special administrative region directly under the central government in the southeast of China, comprising Hong Kong Island, the mainland Kowloon Peninsula and New Territories, and many small islands, of which the largest is Lantau; area 1,070 sq km/413 sq mi; population (2001 est) 6,708,400 (57% Hong Kong Chinese, most of the remainder are refugees from the mainland). A long-established and continuing policy of free trade has helped the rise of Hong Kong as one of the world's major commercial and financial centres. The capital buildings are located in Victoria (Hong Kong City), and other towns and cities include Kowloon and Tsuen Wan (in the New Territories). A former British crown colony, it reverted to Chinese control in July 1997.

From 1997 an enclave of Guangdong province, China, Hong Kong has one of the world's finest natural harbours.

Hong Kong Island is connected with Kowloon by undersea railway and ferries. A world financial centre, its stock market has four exchanges. Main exports are textiles, clothing, electronic goods, office machinery, clocks, watches, cameras, and plastic products; tourism is also important to the economy. Entrepôt trade is very significant: a large proportion of the exports and imports (mainly consumer goods, raw materials and semi-manufactured goods) of southern China are transshipped here. The currency used is the Hong Kong dollar; the languages spoken are English and Chinese; religions include Confucianism, Buddhism, and Taoism, with Muslim and Christian minorities.

Hooks, Benjamin (Lawson) (1925–) US judge, public official, and civil-rights reformer. He gained national recognition as the first African-American to serve on the Federal Communications Commission (FCC) 1972–77, where he became a driving force to improve both the portrayal of and employment opportunities for African-Americans in the electronic media. He succeeded Roy Wilkins as executive director of the National Association for the Advancement of Colored People (NAACP) 1977–93 and pushed the organization to be more vocal and activist in pro-black concerns. He was producer and host of a number of television programmes airing racial issues.

Hoover, Herbert (Clark) (1874–1964) 31st president of the USA 1929–33, a Republican. He was secretary of commerce 1921–28. Hoover lost public confidence after the stock-market crash of 1929, when he opposed direct government aid for the unemployed in the Depression that followed.

Hoover, J(ohn) Edgar (1895–1972) US lawyer and director of the Federal Bureau of Investigation (FBI) from 1924 until his death. He built up a powerful network for the detection of organized crime, including a national fingerprint

collection. His drive against alleged communist activities after World War II and his opposition to the Kennedy administration brought much criticism for abuse of power.

Hopkins, Harry Lloyd (1890–1946) US government official. Originally a social worker, in 1935 he became head of the WPA (Works Progress Administration), which was concerned with Depression relief work. After a period as secretary of commerce 1938–40, he was appointed supervisor of the *lend-lease programme in 1941, and undertook missions to the UK and the USSR during World War II.

Hore-Belisha, (Isaac) Leslie (1893–1957) 1st Baron Hore-Belisha, British politician. A National Liberal, he was minister of transport 1934–37, introducing a number of traffic reforms including the introduction of a driving test for motorists, traffic lights, and Belisha beacons to mark pedestrian crossings. He was war minister from 1937, until removed by Chamberlain in 1940 on grounds of temperament, and introduced peacetime conscription in 1939.

Horrocks, Brian Gwynne (1895–1985) British general. He served in World War I, and in World War II under Montgomery at Alamein and with the British Liberation Army in Europe. KBE 1945.

Horthy, Miklós Horthy de Nagybánya (1868–1957) Hungarian politician and admiral. Leader of the counter-revolutionary White government, he became regent in 1920 on the overthrow of the communist Béla *Kun regime by Romanian and Czechoslovak intervention. He represented the conservative and military class, and retained power until World War II, trying (although allied to Hitler) to retain independence of action. In 1944 he tried to negotiate a surrender to the USSR but Hungary was taken over by the Nazis and he was deported to Germany. He was released from German

captivity the same year by the Western
Allies. He was not tried at Nuremberg,
however, but instead allowed to go to
Portugal, where he died.

Houphouët-Boigny, Félix (1905–1993)
Côte d'Ivoire right-wing politician,
president 1960–93. He held posts in
French ministries, and became
president of the Republic of Côte
d'Ivoire on independence in 1960,
maintaining close links with France,
which helped to boost an already
thriving economy and encourage
political stability. Pro-Western and
opposed to communist intervention
in Africa, Houphouët-Boigny was
strongly criticized for maintaining
diplomatic relations with South Africa.
He was re-elected for a seventh term
in 1990 in multi-party elections, amid
allegations of ballot rigging and
political pressure.

**House Un-American Activities
Committee** HUAC, Congressional
committee, established in 1938 as
the Special Committee to Investigate
Un-American Activities under the
chairmanship of Martin Dies. Noted
for its public investigation of alleged
subversion, particularly of
communists, it was renamed the
House Internal Security Committee in
1969. It achieved its greatest notoriety
during the 1950s through its hearings
on communism in the movie industry.
It was abolished in 1975.

**Howe, (Richard Edward) Geoffrey
(1926–)** **Baron Howe of Aberavon**,
British Conservative politician,
member of Parliament for Surrey East.
As chancellor of the Exchequer
1979–83 under Margaret Thatcher,
he put into practice the monetarist
policy that reduced inflation at the
cost of a rise in unemployment.
In 1983 he became foreign secretary,
and in 1989 deputy prime minister
and leader of the House of Commons.
On 1 November 1990 he resigned
in protest at Thatcher's continued
opposition to the UK's greater
integration in Europe.

Hoxha, Enver (1908–1985) Albanian
communist politician, the country's
leader from 1954. He founded the
Albanian Communist Party in 1941,
and headed the liberation movement
1939–44. He was prime minister
1944–54, also handling foreign affairs
1946–53, and from 1954 was first
secretary of the Albanian Party of
Labour. In policy he was a Stalinist
and independent of both Chinese
and Soviet communism.

Following World War II, in
November 1945, Hoxha's government
obtained allied recognition on
condition that free elections were held.

On 2 December 1945 a communist-
controlled assembly was elected, and
Albania declared a republic on
11 January 1946.

Hoyte, (Hugh) Desmond (1929–)
Guyanese politician and president
1985–92. He held a number of
ministerial posts before becoming
prime minister under Forbes Burnham.
On Burnham's death in 1985 he
succeeded him as president.

Hrawi, Elias (1930–) Lebanese
Maronite Christian politician,
president 1989–98. He implemented
the 1989 Taif peace agreement,
which he had helped to draw up,
ending Lebanon's 14-year civil war,
and which reduced the president's
executive powers. His position was
strengthened in 1990 when the
Syrians, with whom he enjoyed
good relations, put down a rebellion
by the Christian militia leader
General Michel Aoun. In 1991 a treaty
was signed with Syria. In 1995 the
term of the presidency (six years)
was extended by a further three years
to allow Hrawi to continue and
provide stability while Prime Minister
Rafiq al-Hariri pressed ahead with
economic reconstruction.

**Hrushevsky, Mikhail Sergeevich
(1866–1934)** Ukrainian historian
and politician. After the *February
Revolution of 1917, he joined the party
of Ukrainian Socialist Revolutionaries

and was president of the short-lived Ukrainian Central Council.
He emigrated in 1918, but returned to Kiev, Ukraine, in 1924, and became a member of the Ukrainian Academy of Sciences, and in 1929 of the USSR Academy of Sciences. In 1930 he was arrested and deported from Kiev.

Hua Guofeng (or Hua Kuofeng) (1920–) Chinese politician, leader of the Chinese Communist Party (CCP) 1976–81, premier 1976–80. He dominated Chinese politics 1976–77, seeking economic modernization without major structural reform. From 1978 he was gradually eclipsed by Deng Xiaoping. Hua was ousted from the Politburo in September 1982 but remained a member of the CCP Central Committee.

Huai-Hai, Battle of decisive campaign 1948–49 in the Chinese Civil War (1946–49). The name is derived from the two main defensive positions held by the nationalist *Guomindang force: the Huang (Huai) River in Shandong and Jiangsu provinces, and the Lung Hai railway. Communist forces from the east and west captured Suzhou (Soochow), a key railway junction, on 1 December 1948. On 6 January 1949 they secured a crushing victory at Yungchung to the southwest, facilitating an advance on Shanghai, which fell in the spring of 1949.

Hudson's Bay Company chartered company founded by Prince Rupert in 1670 to trade in furs with North American Indians. In 1783 the rival North West Company was formed, but in 1821 it merged with the Hudson's Bay Company. In 1912 the company planned a chain of department stores in western Canada, and became Canada's leading retail organization, which it remains today. It also has oil and natural gas interests.

Huerta, Victoriano (1854–1916) Mexican soldier and political leader, president 1913–14. As provisional president, he established a military dictatorship in 1913. Military pressure from insurgents, notably Venustiano *Carranza, Pancho *Villa, and Emiliano *Zapata, forced him to resign in July 1914 and flee to Europe.

Hughes, Billy (William Morris) (1862–1952) Australian politician, prime minister 1915–23; originally Labor, he headed a national cabinet. After resigning as prime minister in 1923, he helped Joseph *Lyons form the United Australia Party in 1931 and held many other cabinet posts 1934–41. He joined the Liberal Party in 1944.

Hughes, Howard (Robard) (1905–1976) US industrialist, aviator, and film producer. Inheriting wealth from his father, the industrialist Howard Robert Hughes, who had patented a revolutionary oil-drilling bit, he took control of the family firm, the Hughes Tool Corporation, in 1923, to create a financial empire. A skilled pilot, he manufactured and designed aircraft. He also formed a Hollywood film company in 1926, and produced and directed several films including *Hell's Angels* (1930), *Scarface* (1932), and *The Outlaw* (1944). From his middle years he was a recluse.

Hull, Cordell (1871–1955) US Democratic politician. As F D Roosevelt's secretary of state 1933–44, he was a vigorous champion of free trade, and opposed German and Japanese aggression. He was identified with the Good Neighbor policy of nonintervention in Latin America. An advocate of collective security after World War II, he was called by Roosevelt 'the father of the United Nations'. He was awarded the Nobel Prize for Peace in 1945 for his work in organizing the United Nations (UN).

human rights civil and political rights of the individual in relation to the state. Under the terms of the *United Nations Charter human rights violations by countries have become its proper concern, although the implementation of this obligation is hampered by Article 2 (7) of the charter prohibiting interference in domestic affairs. The Universal Declaration of *Human Rights, passed by the General Assembly on 10 December 1948, is based on a belief in the inherent (natural) rights, equality, and freedom of human beings, and sets out in 28 articles the fundamental freedoms – civil, political, economic – to be promoted. The declaration has considerable moral force but is not legally binding on states.

Human Rights, Universal Declaration of charter of civil and political rights drawn up by the United Nations in 1948. They include the right to life, liberty, education, and equality before the law; to freedom of movement, religion, association, and information; and to a nationality.

Under the **European Convention of Human Rights** of 1950, the Council of Europe established the **European Commission of Human Rights**, which investigates complaints by states or individuals. Its findings are examined by the **European Court of Human Rights** (established in 1959), whose compulsory jurisdiction (legal power) has been recognized by a number of states, including the UK.

Hume, John (1937–) Northern Ireland politician, leader of the Social Democratic and Labour Party (SDLP) from 1979. Hume was a founder member of the Credit Union Party, which later became the SDLP. An MP since 1969, and a member of the European Parliament, he has been one of the chief architects of the peace process in Northern Ireland. He shared the Nobel Prize for Peace in 1998 with David Trimble for their efforts to further the peace process. Hume announced his resignation in September 2001.

Humphrey, George (Magoffin) (1890–1970) US industrialist and cabinet member. A lawyer, he became president of the Hanna iron ore company, and in 1929 he created National Steel which flourished despite the depression. President *Eisenhower's surprising choice for secretary of the treasury 1952–56, he checked inflation and balanced the budget before returning to National Steel.

Hundred Flowers campaign in Chinese history, a movement from 1956 to 1957 of open political and intellectual debate, encouraged by *Mao Zedong.

The campaign was intended to rouse the bureaucracy and to weaken the position of the Chinese Communist Party's then dominant pro-Soviet 'right wing'. It rapidly got out of hand, resulting in excessive censure of party personnel.

Hungarian uprising national uprising against Soviet dominance of Hungary in 1956.

Hungary country in central Europe, bounded north by the Slovak Republic, northeast by Ukraine, east by Romania, south by Serbia and Montenegro and Croatia, and west by Austria and Slovenia.

Hurd, Douglas (Richard) (1930–) Lord of Westwell, British Conservative politician, home secretary 1985–89 and foreign secretary 1989–95. A moderate 'Heathite' Conservative, he was passed over for the cabinet during Margaret Thatcher's first term as prime minister, but was appointed Northern Ireland secretary in 1984. In November 1990 he was an unsuccessful candidate in the Tory leadership contest following Margaret Thatcher's unexpected resignation.

Husák, Gustáv (1913–1991) Czechoslovak politician, leader of the Communist Party of Czechoslovakia (CCP) 1969–87 and president 1975–89. After the 1968 Prague Spring of liberalization, his task was to restore control, purge the CCP, and oversee the implementation of a new, federalist constitution. He was deposed in the popular uprising of November–December 1989 and expelled from the CCP in February 1990.

Hussein, Saddam (1937–) Iraqi leader, in power from 1968, president

1979–2003. He presided over the Iran–Iraq war 1980–88, and harshly repressed Kurdish rebels seeking independence in northern Iraq. He annexed Kuwait in 1990 but was driven out by a US-dominated coalition army in February 1991. Defeat in the *Gulf War led to unrest, and both the Kurds in the north and Shiites in the south rebelled. His savage repression of both revolts led to charges of genocide. In 2003 US-led forces invaded Iraq on the grounds that Saddam had weapons of mass destruction (WMD) and was in contravention of UN resolutions requiring Iraqi disarmament. Saddam went into hiding and was captured by coalition forces in December 2003.

Saddam joined the Arab Ba'ath Socialist Party in 1957 and soon became involved in revolutionary activities. In 1959 he was sentenced to death for the attempted assassination of the head of state, General Kassem, and took refuge in Syria and Egypt. A coup in 1963, which overthrew Kassem, made his return possible, although in the following year Saddam was imprisoned for plotting to overthrow the new regime. After his release he took a leading part in the 1968 revolution, removing the civilian government and establishing a Revolutionary Command Council (RCC). Initially, he wielded influence from behind the scenes, but he progressively eliminated real or imagined opposition to become president in 1979. He governed autocratically, supported by a clique of loyal supporters drawn from his home region and secret police who ruthlessly suppressed dissent. In all, an estimated 300,000 suspected political opponents were killed during his 24 years in power.

Hussein ibn Ali (1856–1931)   born **Sharif Husayan Hussein ibn Ali**, King of the Hejaz 1916–24 and founder of the modern Hashemite dynasty. Emir (grand sherif) of the Muslim holy city of Mecca 1908–16, at the start of World War I he sided with the Turks and Germany. However, T E *Lawrence persuaded him, in 1916, to join an Arab Revolt against Turkish rule, when he was proclaimed the independent King of the Hejaz region of Arabia. In 1919 he proclaimed himself king of all the Arab countries. This led to conflict with *Ibn Saud of the neighbouring emirate of Nejd. Hussein accepted the caliphate in 1924, but was forced to abdicate in 1924 by Ibn Saud. He took refuge in Cyprus and died in Amman, Jordan.

Hussein ibn Talal (1935–1999)   King of Jordan 1952–99. By 1967 he had lost all his kingdom west of the River Jordan in the Arab-Israeli Wars, and in 1970 suppressed the Palestine Liberation Organization acting as a guerrilla force against his rule on the remaining East Bank territories. Subsequently, he became a moderating force in Middle Eastern politics, and in 1994 signed a peace agreement with Israel, ending a 46-year-old state of war between the two countries.

Hutton, Barbara (1912–1979) US heiress, granddaughter of retail magnate F W Woolworth, notorious in her day as the original 'poor little rich girl'. Her seven husbands included the actor Cary Grant.

Hu Yaobang (1915–1989)   Chinese politician, Communist Party (CCP) chair 1981–87. A protégé of the communist leader Deng Xiaoping, Hu presided over a radical overhaul of the party structure and personnel 1982–86. His death ignited the pro-democracy movement, which was eventually crushed in *Tiananmen Square in June 1989.

Huysmans, Camille (1871–1968) Belgian politician. He entered parliament as a Socialist in 1910. From 1905–21 he was secretary of the Second International, and between the World Wars held several posts in the Belgian Cabinet. He served as burgomaster of Antwerp (1933–40), but escaped to

England during World War II; he was reinstated as burgomaster in 1944. He was prime minister in a post-war coalition government (1946–47) and subsequently minister of education (1947–49). Huysmans was born in Bilsen, and was educated in Liège, Belgium.

hydrogen bomb bomb that works on the principle of nuclear fusion. Large-scale explosion results from the thermonuclear release of energy when hydrogen nuclei are fused to form helium nuclei. The first hydrogen bomb was exploded at Enewetak Atoll in the Pacific Ocean by the USA in 1952.

Ibarruri, Dolores (1895–1989) called 'La Pasionaria' (the passion flower), Spanish Basque politician, journalist, and orator; she was first elected to the Cortes (Spanish parliament) in 1936. She helped to establish the Popular Front government and was a Loyalist leader in the Civil War. When Franco came to power in 1939 she left Spain for the USSR, where she was active in the Communist Party. She returned to Spain in 1977 after Franco's death and was re-elected to the Cortes (at the age of 81) in the first parliamentary elections for 40 years.

Ibn Saud (1880–1953) born **Abdul Aziz al-Saud**, First king of Saudi Arabia from 1932. His personal hostility to *Hussein ibn Ali, the British-supported political and religious leader of the Al Hijaz (Hejaz) region of western Arabia, meant that he stood back from the Arab Revolt of World War I, organized by T E *Lawrence and in which *Abdullah ibn Hussein and *Faisal I, of Iraq, participated. However, after the war, supported by the Wahabi-inspired Ikhwan (Brethren), Ibn Saud extended his dominions to the Red Sea coast, capturing Jedda and the Muslim holy cities of Mecca and Medina (with their lucrative pilgrimage revenue). By 1921, all central Arabia had been brought under his rule, and in 1924 he successfully invaded the Hejaz, defeating Hussein ibn Ali, who, in 1919, had proclaimed himself king of all the Arab countries. In January 1926, at Mecca, he was proclaimed King of Hejaz and Nejd and in 1932 the territories were unified, under the title 'Kingdom of Saudi Arabia'. In 1934 Saudi forces attacked Yemen and captured further territories in the south, including the towns of Najran and Jizan.

Oil was discovered in 1938, with oil concessions being leased to US and British companies, and exports began in 1946. During the 'first oil boom' (1947–52), the country was transformed from a poor pastoral kingdom into an affluent modernizing state, as annual oil revenues increased from $10 million to $212 million. During World War II, Ibn Saud remained neutral, but sympathetic towards the UK and the USA. In 1945 he founded the Arab League to encourage Arab unity.

His father was the son of Faisal, the sultan of Nejd (Najd), in central Arabia, at whose capital, Riyadh, Ibn Saud was born. The al-Saud family had dominated central Arabian politics since the mid-18th century, when it had established itself as the standard bearer of the Wahabi fundamentalist Islamic sect. In 1891 a rival north Arabian dynasty, the Rashidis, seized Riyadh, and Ibn Saud went into exile with his father, who resigned his claim to the throne in favour of his son, who was brought up in Kuwait. In 1902, following a Bedouin (nomadic Arab tribe) revolt, Ibn Saud recaptured Riyadh and recovered the kingdom. By 1914 he controlled much of the former Turkish possessions along the Gulf, and in 1915 Britain recognised him as Emir of Hasa (eastern Arabia) and Nejd.

Iceland island country in the North Atlantic Ocean, situated south of the Arctic Circle, between Greenland and Norway.

Ichikawa, Fusaye (1893–1981) Japanese feminist and politician. In 1924 she formed the Women's Suffrage

League in Japan. Following World War II she became head of the New Japan Women's League, which secured the vote for women in 1945, and went on to fight for their wider rights. She campaigned against legalized prostitution and served in the Japanese Diet (parliament) 1953–71, where she continued to press for an end to bureaucratic corruption. After defeat in 1971 she was returned to parliament in 1974 and 1980.

Idris I (1889–1983) also known as **Muhammad Idris al-Mahdi**, Libyan head of the Sanusiya order and king 1951–69. He played a major role in both the struggle for independence from the Italians and the preservation of his country's unity and integrity. His pro-Western attitude, especially towards the presence of US and British military bases, was a source of friction between him and President *Nasser of Egypt.

Ikeda, Hayato (1899–1965) Japanese politician and economist, prime minister 1960–64. He introduced an 'income doubling policy' of economic growth and higher living standards. He was a supporter of the US–Japan Security Treaty of 1960, and developed a low-key style in international relations during the post-war recovery period.

Iliescu, Ion (1930–) Romanian president 1990–96, and from 2000. A former member of the Romanian Communist Party (PCR) and of Nicolae Ceausescu's government, Iliescu swept into power on Ceausescu's fall as head of the National Salvation Front.

Immelmann, Max (1890–1916) German fighter ace in World War I. He developed the 'Immelmann Turn', a manoeuvre in which, pursued, he would climb suddenly in a half-loop, roll, and then dive back at his pursuer. Decorated by the Kaiser January 1915, he was shot down and killed near Lens by Lt George McCubbin 18 June 1916.

Imphal, Battle of in World War II, Allied operation in 1944 to hold Japanese forces back from an important road junction in the Manipur district of northeast India, 600 km/375 mi northwest of Kolkata (formerly Calcutta); the turning point in the Burma campaign.

Inchon, Battle of in the Korean War, successful US Marines amphibious operation on 15 September 1950 at Inchon, 32 km/20 mi west of Seoul, South Korea. The Marines secured the city within two weeks and broke the North Korean forces' hold on the Pusan area.

Independent Labour Party ILP, British socialist party, founded in Bradford in 1893 by the Scottish politician Keir *Hardie. In 1900 it joined with trades unions and Fabians in founding the Labour Representation Committee, the nucleus of the *Labour Party. Many members left the ILP to join the Communist Party in 1921, and in 1932 all connections with the Labour Party were severed. After World War II the ILP dwindled, eventually becoming extinct. James Maxton (1885–1946) was its chair 1926–46.

India country in southern Asia, bounded to the north by China, Nepal, and Bhutan; east by Myanmar and Bangladesh; northwest by Pakistan and Afghanistan; and southeast, south, and southwest by the Indian Ocean.

government India is a federal republic whose 1949 constitution contains elements from the US and British systems of government. It comprises 28 self-governing states, administered by a governor, appointed by the federal president for a five-year term. Each state has its own legislature (legislative assembly), popularly elected for a five-year term, from which a council of ministers (headed by a chief minister) is drawn. A number of the larger states have a second chamber (legislative council). The states have primary control over education, health, police, and local government and work in consultation with the centre in the economic sphere.

In times of crisis, central rule ('president's rule') can be imposed. There are also seven union territories (including Delhi), administered by a lieutenant governor appointed by the federal president. The central (federal) government has sole responsibility in military and foreign affairs and plays a key role in economic affairs.

The titular, executive head of the federal government is the president, who is elected for a five-year term by an electoral college composed of members from both the federal parliament and the state legislatures. However, real executive power is held by a prime minister and cabinet drawn from the majority party or coalition within the federal parliament.

The two-chamber federal parliament has a 542-member lower house, Lok Sabha (house of the people), which has final authority over financial matters and whose members are directly elected for a maximum term of five years from single-member constituencies by universal suffrage, and a 245-member upper house, Rajya Sabha (council of states), 237 of whose members are indirectly elected, one-third at a time for six-year terms, by state legislatures on a regional quota basis. (The remaining two seats in the Lok Sabha are reserved for Anglo-Indians, while eight representatives of the Rajya Sabha are also presidential nominees.) Bills to become law must be approved by both chambers of parliament and receive the president's assent.

independence and partition

In August 1947 the first prime minister of independent India, Jawaharlal *Nehru, declared; 'Long years ago we made a tryst with destiny and now the time comes when we shall redeem our pledge'. India became independent from Britain at midnight on 14–15 August 1947. Lord Mountbatten, who had been sent as the last imperial viceroy to administer the handing over of power, remained as India's first governor general, and until 1949 India temporarily remained under the supervision of a governor general appointed by the British monarch while a new constitution was framed and approved. India remained within the *Commonwealth.

The Muslims of British India had insisted on the creation of a separate Muslim state, and independence had been accompanied by the partition of the subcontinent into two states: the predominantly Muslim *Pakistan, and the predominantly Hindu and Sikh India. Hundreds of thousands died in the communal violence accompanying the resultant mass migrations of Hindus, Muslims, and Sikhs.

The intervention of Mahatma *Gandhi in Bengal largely stemmed the violence, but in January 1948 he was assassinated by a Hindu fanatic. Gandhi had led the Indian National Congress (see *Congress Party) in its campaign for independence, and although he no longer held any official position, few decisions could be taken without his approval. His power over the masses was symbolized by the success his numerous fasts had on stemming communal violence. His ideal of satyagraha, passive nonviolent resistance (see *noncooperation movement), has greatly influenced Indian politics.

the Princely States and the Kashmir question Congress, the party that had won independence, ruled with little opposition. In addition to having to deal with the virtual civil war in the Punjab caused by the mass migrations, the new government had to deal with the problems associated with the Princely States, the territories in the subcontinent that were ruled by native princes, not directly under British rule.

By the terms of independence from Britain, each of the Princely States could choose whether to join either Pakistan or India, or whether to remain independent. None chose the latter course. Hyderabad and Junagadh both had Muslim rulers and Hindu populations, but after the rulers of both decided to join Pakistan, their territories were forcibly annexed by India. In *Kashmir the majority of the population are Muslim, but the Hindu maharaja opted to join India and called for Indian intervention when Muslims marched from the north on Srinagar. Fighting between Indian and Pakistani troops was brought to an end by a UN ceasefire on 30 October 1948, but Kashmir continued to be a source of tension and conflict between India and Pakistan.

Shock and sorrow at the death of Gandhi briefly improved relations between India and Pakistan, but this did not last long. In 1949 India stopped coal supplies to Pakistan, claiming that the latter was holding up supplies of raw jute. East Bengal (then East Pakistan, now Bangladesh), which before partition had produced over 75% of India's jute, was left with unsold stocks, while the mills in West Bengal had no material to process. Further cross-border migrations took place.

the Congress government and the new constitution At independence the most important member of the Indian cabinet was not Nehru, the prime minister, but V J *Patel, the minister with responsibility for home affairs and the states (as the former provinces had become). Gandhi's moral authority conditioned the relations between the two. The new structure of the country was formed largely by Patel and his secretary, V P Menon. But Nehru had free rein in international affairs, where he excelled. Under Patel the new Indian government took over the public services, and most of their personnel, almost intact. Despite opposition from Hindu extremists, India was to be secular and a compromise language formula was found, with English remaining the official language for 15 years.

The constitution adopted in 1949 was almost purely Western in character, drawing not only upon the 1935 Government of India Act, but also upon the US constitution and those of Europe, including that of the Soviet Union.

Communist opposition After the death of Patel, Nehru became the unchallenged leader of India. In the first general elections (1951–52) 173 million people voted and Congress depended for its massive success on Nehru's charisma. Although there were 59 other parties, Congress had a landslide victory. The Communists, having unsuccessfully tried revolution in the Telengana district of Hyderabad between 1948 and 1951, turned instead to the democratic process.

In the 1957 elections the Communist Party polled 12 million votes to become the largest opposition party in the central parliament. The Communist Party enjoyed great popularity in Kerala, a poor but literate state, where it governed, carrying out successful reforms from 1957 until 1959 when the 'president's rule' was imposed from the centre. In 1960 the Communists in Kerala polled 44% of the vote, and in the 1962 elections they formed the major opposition party in Andhra Pradesh and West Bengal.

The power of Congress depended on its heroic past, but its early self-sacrifice turned to corruption, and the social and economic reforms that were endorsed by the party were often not carried out. Nehru himself threatened to resign after Congress's vote was reduced in the 1957 election, and Kerala lost to the Communists, citing what he called his party's 'deep malaise'.

the language issue The demand, backed by violence, for the states to be organized on linguistic grounds, was a major problem. When a Telugu-speaking leader died from his fast, Nehru capitulated and new boundaries were drawn up for the state of Andhra, and a new commission advocated the creation of states on a linguistic basis. The seeds of a Punjabi-speaking state were sown when the Sikhs demonstrated, threatening a return to the partition riots. A compromise was found and the formation of a Punjabi-speaking state delayed until after Nehru's death. The States Reorganization Bill was passed in 1956. Nehru's indecisiveness allowed this bill to give power to reactionary elements intent on frustrating social and economic change.

the first and second five-year plans Nehru's hopes for reform were embodied in centralized direction of the economy, through a series of five-year plans, administered by the Planning Commission set up in 1950. The first five-year plan from 1951 to 1956 was a success, concentrating mainly on agriculture, a base from which the second plan could proceed to concentrate on industry. But no cure had been produced to curtail the endemic poverty of the country, and Nehru recognized the need for a greater ideological framework.

In 1955 the 'socialist pattern of society' was set down as the objective of planning. Neglect of agriculture in the second plan in 1956 led to catastrophe, and drastic action was taken to save it. The weakness of the plan had been agricultural overconfidence and over-concentration on industry. Huge imports of grain were necessary by the beginning of the third plan in 1961. Nehru realized that there was a gap between the ideal and reality in Indian politics, stressing in 1957 'how poisoned we are to the very core'.

leadership of the developing world Nehru's foreign policy was summed up in the Pancha Sila, or five principles of coexistence, first announced in a joint statement with the Chinese premier Zhou Enlai in 1954. This policy influenced emerging Afro-Asian countries in the late 1950s and the 1960s. Equally influential was the

Chinese and Indian stance of non-alignment in the ideological conflict between the Soviet bloc and the West (see *non-aligned movement). Nehru's claim that India was nonviolent and Gandhian became the image that India presented to the world. At the meeting of the members of the Colombo Plan in 1954 India asserted itself as 'leader of the developing nations'. At the Bandung Conference in 1955 Nehru and Zhou Enlai successfully advocated the Pancha Sila, and from then until the Belgrade Conference in 1961 (which was the first official meeting of the non-aligned movement) these ideals were embraced by 24 countries.

conflict with China India's leadership of the developing world led to isolation, and when the Chinese attacked India in 1962 the non-aligned were reluctant in their support for India. In 1950 the Chinese invaded Tibet and India could do nothing but protest. When India placed check posts along the northern frontier with China the Chinese protested, but India was obdurate throughout the diplomatic exchanges of the 1950s.

Anti-Chinese feeling built up in India when the Dalai Lama and many other refugees fled from Tibet in 1959 following a failed uprising against Chinese rule. An accidental border clash was dubbed by India as 'deliberate aggression'. Throughout negotiations, attempts by Nehru at conciliation were greeted in India by uproar. Chinese penetration of the Himalayas border area of Aksai Chin was, however, regarded by India as an invasion of Indian territory.

As a diversion in 1961, to prove the government's bellicosity to China, India invaded the tiny Portuguese colony of Goa, in southwest India. The Indian navy and airforce were used against a territory with a mere 2,500 troops, an antique frigate, and an empty airfield. The unreality of India's attitude to China was summed up in the words of the home minister: 'If the

Chinese will not vacate the areas occupied by her India will have to repeat what she did in Goa.' (France's few small colonies in India, including Pondicherry, had been transferred to India in 1954.)

The clash with China was partly provoked by India's intransigence, contrasting with China's apparent attempts at conciliation. China had nothing to fear from India and yet Nehru announced his belief that China would not retaliate. When in 1962 the Chinese army invaded Assam the Indian army collapsed. The shock for Nehru and India was immense, but having made their point the Chinese withdrew, and what had been thought of as a full-scale invasion turned out to be a punitive expedition. The image of India and Nehru was tarnished, and the result for India was a greater dependence on the USA and Britain, and a questioning of the policy of non-alignment.

Shastri and renewed conflict with Pakistan Nehru died in 1964 and was replaced as president by Lal Bahadur *Shastri. The ministry of external affairs, which had been held by Nehru, went to Swaran Singh. In 1964 president's rule was again imposed in Kerala, where there had been a Communist victory, and the Communist Party in India split into pro-Chinese and pro-Soviet wings.

In 1965 a skirmish known as the 'War of the Rann of Kutch' took place with Pakistan, but a ceasefire followed the mediation of the British prime minister Harold Wilson. A major war between the two powers broke out in Kashmir in August, which ended in a precarious ceasefire. China supported Pakistan and demanded that India dismantle military works on the Tibetan side of the Chinese border. In January 1966, under Soviet mediation, Shastri and the Pakistani president Ayub Khan signed a formal ceasefire agreement in Tashkent. Shastri died soon afterwards. Meanwhile, in

1965–66 there were severe famine conditions in Maharashtra state.

the early years of Indira Gandhi's premiership Under the new prime minister Indira *Gandhi (Nehru's daughter), ideological changes took place. Her encouragement of foreign investment was seen as a deviation from Nehru's non-aligned and socialist policies. In the same year the rupee was devalued by 36.5% and a new Hindu-majority province, Haryana, was created in the Punjab.

By 1967 the power of Congress was being eroded. In the elections it gained only 8 out of 17 states. A serious challenge to the leadership came from Morarji *Desai. Kerala and Bengal were dominated by the Communists, and in the latter state sieges of managers by workers called 'gheraos' had become commonplace. More serious, however, was a peasant rising in the Bengali village of Naxalbari, from where the pro-Chinese *Naxalites emerged to create a reign of anarchy and terror in Bengal.

Sino-Indian relations became tense again when Indian diplomats alleged ill-treatment in Beijing. By the following year, president's rule had extended to the states of West Bengal, Uttar Pradesh, Bihar, and the Punjab, and Congress's relations with Communist-controlled Kerala were strained. In an extraordinary political conflict in 1969 Indira Gandhi, while retaining majority support in Congress, was sacked from the party by a working committee of its bosses. The result was a split into the Opposition Congress and Indira Gandhi's Ruling Congress. The fourth five-year plan concentrated on food production, and stressed its socialist framework by nationalizing 14 banks. In 1970 the Ruling Congress formed a coalition with the Communist Party of India in Kerala, and the Communist Party (Marxist) was weakened.

the 1971 war with Pakistan In 1971 agitation by separatist groups in East

Pakistan led to violent suppression by forces loyal to West Pakistan, and there were mass migrations of people from East to West Bengal. Indian troops intervened to support the separatists, and the ensuing war with Pakistan led to the creation of *Bangladesh from the ruins of East Pakistan. Much of India's newly increased revenue was absorbed by Bangladesh.

Indian relations with the USA were weakened by US partisan support for Pakistan in the war. India moved closer to the Soviet bloc, and on 9 August 1971 a 20-year treaty of friendship with the Soviet Union was signed. This provided for immediate consultations between the USSR and India if either country suffered attack or threat of attack by a third country, and prohibited either from entering into a military alliance that was directed against the other. Mrs Gandhi emphasized that India's policy of non-alignment had not been reversed. India supported the Arabs in the1973 Arab–Israeli War, and the same year a further 15-year economic and military assistance agreement was signed with the USSR. In June 1974 India carried out its first underground nuclear test, leading Pakistan to demand from the West a 'nuclear umbrella' to defend itself.

the state of emergency In 1973 prices soared as a result of the worldwide increase in oil prices, and the fifth five-year plan, which concentrated on increasing the production of food grains, was launched. In 1974 the fifth plan was revised to cope with increases in oil prices, and food riots took place in Maharashtra and Gujarat.

In 1975, having been found guilty of electoral malpractice during the 1971 election, Indira Gandhi imposed a state of emergency and imprisoned almost 1,000 political opponents. She was cleared of malpractice by the Supreme Court in November 1975, but the 'emergency' continued for two years, during which period a harsh compulsory birth-control programme was introduced.

The state of emergency was lifted in March 1977 for elections in which the opposition Janata Party was swept to power, led by Morarji *Desai. The new government was undermined by economic difficulties and internal factional strife. Desai was toppled as prime minister in 1979, and a coalition under Charan Singh was soon overthrown. In January 1980 the Congress (I) Party, led by Indira Gandhi, was returned to power with a landslide victory.

the Amritsar massacre The new Gandhi administration was economically successful, but the problems of intercaste violence and regional unrest were such that the Congress (I) Party lost control of a number of states. The greatest unrest was in Punjab, where Sikh demands for greater religious recognition and for resolution of water and land disputes with neighbouring states escalated into calls for the creation of a separate state of 'Khalistan'.

In 1984, troops were sent into the Sikhs' most holy shrine, the Golden Temple at Amritsar, to dislodge the armed Sikh extremist leader Sant Jarnail Singh Bhindranwale, resulting in the deaths of Bhindranwale and hundreds of his supporters. The ensuing Sikh backlash brought troop mutinies, culminating in the assassination of Indira Gandhi by her Sikh bodyguards in October 1984. In Delhi, retaliating Hindus massacred 3,000 Sikhs before the new prime minister Rajiv *Gandhi (Indira's elder son) restored order.

In December 1984, Bhopal in central India became the site of a major industrial accident caused by the US multinational company Union Carbide failing to adhere to safety standards. More than 2,500 people were killed.

Rajiv Gandhi's premiership In the elections of December 1984, Congress (I), benefiting from a wave of public sympathy, gained a record victory. As prime minister, Rajiv Gandhi pledged to modernize and inject greater market efficiency into the Indian economy and to resolve the Punjab, Assam, and Kashmir disputes.

Early reforms and the spread of technology, with India launching its first space satellite, augured well. Progress was made towards resolving the ethnic disputes in Assam and the hill areas, with 25 years of rebellion ended in Mizoram, which was made a new state of the Indian Union. However, Gandhi was unable to resolve the Punjab problem, with Sikh–Hindu ethnic conflict continuing, while in northern India Hindu–Muslim relations deteriorated.

Gandhi's enthusiasm for economic reform also waned from 1986, and his personal reputation was sullied by the uncovering of the 'Bofors scandal' by finance minister V P *Singh, involving alleged financial kickbacks received by government-connected organizations from a $1,400-million arms contract with the Swedish Bofors Corporation.

In northern Sri Lanka, where an Indian Peacekeeping Force (IPKF) had been sent in July 1987 at the Sri Lankan government's request as part of an ambitious peace settlement, Indian troops became bogged down in a civil war.

Despite bumper harvests in 1988–89, Gandhi's popularity continued to fall. V P Singh, who had been dismissed from Congress (I) in 1987, attacked Gandhi's increasingly dictatorial style and became the recognized leader of the opposition forces, which united under the Janata Dal umbrella in October 1988.

V P Singh's coalition government
In the general election of November 1989 a broad anti-Congress electoral pact was forged, embracing the Janata Dal (People's Party), Bharatiya Janata Party (BJP) – both factions of the Communist Party – and the regional-level Telugu Desam. This ensured that Congress (I) failed to secure a working majority. V P Singh, widely respected for his incorruptibility, took over at the head of a minority National Front coalition.

Singh's main objective was the lowering of racial tensions. However, in January 1990 Muslim separatist violence erupted in Kashmir, forcing the imposition of direct rule and leading to a deterioration of relations with Pakistan. Relations were improved with the neighbouring states of Bhutan, Nepal (which had been subject to a partial border blockade by India during 1989), and Sri Lanka, with whom a date (31 March 1990) was agreed for the withdrawal of the IPKF. President's rule was imposed over Jammu and Kashmir in July 1990 and over Assam in November 1990, as a result of the rising tide of separatist violence. Punjab, where interethnic murders climbed to record heights from November, had been under president's rule since 1983.

During the summer and early autumn of 1990 V P Singh's government was rocked by a series of events, including the prime minister's decision to employ more low-caste workers in government and public-sector jobs, which resulted in protests by high-caste students and a split in the Janata Dal. Chandra Shekhar, a long-time Singh opponent, emerged as the leader of a rebel faction.

Hindu militants (the Vishwa Hindu Parishad) announced that on 30 October 1990 they would begin to build a 'birthplace' temple dedicated to the warrior god Ram on the site of a mosque in the northern city of Ayodhya. (Some Hindus believed that the mosque had been built on the site of a Hindu temple, considered to be the birthplace of Ram, and it remained a disputed site.) This precipitated serious communal tensions, which the government was unable to quell. On 7 November, after troops had fired on Hindu fanatics who were attempting to storm the Ayodhya mosque, the Singh government was voted out of office.

Chandra Shekhar's minority government A new minority government was formed by Chandra Shekhar, who led a tiny Janata Dal socialist faction comprising 56 deputies and was assured of outside support by the Congress Party of Rajiv Gandhi. Violence continued, with a total of 890 people killed and 4,000 injured in Hindu–Muslim riots, and 3,560 people killed in the continuing ethnic strife in Punjab in 1990. The higher oil prices due to the crisis in the Gulf hit India's economy badly. At the end of January 1991 Shekhar dismissed the opposition-led government of the large southern state of Tamil Nadu, citing the presence of Tamil Tiger rebels from northern Sri Lanka. In March, Shekhar fell out with his backers, Congress (I), and tendered his resignation, but continued as caretaker premier until elections in May 1991.

the 1991 elections On 21 May 1991, a day after the first round of voting had taken place in the general election, Rajiv Gandhi was assassinated at Sriperumpudur, near Madras (now Chennai), by a suicide bomber. She was one of the Liberation Tigers of Tamil Eelam (LTTE), who resented the presence of Indian forces in Sri Lanka. P V Narasimha Rao, an experienced southerner, became Congress (I) party president.

Gandhi's assassination occurred in the wake of what had been the most violent election campaign in Indian history, with several hundred dying in election-related violence in northern India where Hindu, Muslim, and Sikh communal tensions were acute. Fortunately, there was subsequent calm, with polling being delayed until mid-June 1991 in seats not already contested.

Benefiting from a sympathy vote, Congress (I) emerged as the largest single party, capturing, along with its allies, around 240 of the 511 seats

contested. The BJP, which had performed particularly strongly before Rajiv Gandhi's assassination, captured 125 seats and 25% of the popular vote, V P Singh's National Front and Left Front (Communist Party) allies captured 125 seats, while the Samajwadi Janata Party of the outgoing premier Chandra Shekhar captured only five seats. Congress (I) polled well in central and southern India, but was defeated by the BJP in its traditional northern Hindu-belt heartland of Uttar Pradesh, where a BJP state government was subsequently formed. The BJP's rise was the most striking development during this election.

A Congress (I) minority government was established, headed by Rao. In a new industrial policy, subsidies were slashed, inward foreign investment encouraged, and industrial licensing scrapped, bringing an end to the 'permit raj'.

sectarian violence continues
The president's rule was extended over Jammu and Kashmir in September 1991 for a further six months and was imposed in Meghalaya in October 1991. In Punjab, where killings averaged 600 a month during 1991, the president's rule was to remain in force until state elections in February 1992. In September 1991 a Places of Worship Bill was passed, prohibiting the conversion of any place of worship that existed at the time of independence in 1947, thus debarring Hindus from converting mosques into temples. Despite the mosque in Ayodhya being exempted from its terms, the bill was opposed by the Hindu-chauvinist BJP.

The position of Rao's minority government was strengthened in January 1992 when a split occurred in the opposition Janata Dal and a number of its deputies left and sought alliance with Congress (I). In elections held in February 1992 in strife-torn Punjab, Congress (I) won control of the state assembly and a majority in parliament. However, despite heavy security, turnout was only 28%, with the main Sikh nationalist party opponents of Congress boycotting the contest.

In December 1992 Hindu extremists demolished the Muslim mosque in Ayodhya, spreading communal violence across the country and resulting in over 1,200 deaths, two-thirds of which were Muslims. In response, Prime Minister Rao dismissed four state governments controlled by the Hindu-chauvinist BJP and ordered the arrest of senior opposition leaders and the banning of extremist religious organizations.

foreign relations Despite the break-up of the USSR in 1991, economic and military links with Russia remained close. A thaw in relations with China resulted in December 1991 after the visit to India of Li Peng, the first Chinese premier to visit India since the border conflict of 1962. In January 1992 full diplomatic relations with Israel were established.

developments and events, 1993–95 In July 1993, Rao narrowly survived a confidence vote but in December 1993, with the addition of ten formerly independent members to Congress (I), the government established a clear parliamentary majority. An earthquake in Maharashtra state had earlier killed tens of thousands, and president's rule remained in force in Manipur, Tripura, and Kashmir, where 114 soldiers, 820 militants, and 577 civilians died in January–September 1993 as a result of the ongoing civil war. An outbreak of pneumonic plague in the western city of Surat in September 1994 claimed more than 50 lives.

Congress (as the party had been redesignated) suffered losses in four state elections in November–December 1994, and in the spring of 1995 lost control of Maharashtra and Gujarat to the Hindu-chauvinist Shiv Sena and BJP. It was also defeated in Bihar.

In October 1995 direct rule was imposed in Uttar Pradesh following caste clashes and the collapse of a coalition government, which included the BJP. A report published in 1995 by the independent Vohra Commission showed large areas of northern India to be under the control of mafia gangs, backed by local politicians, and in January 1996 a number of politicians, including the leader of the BJP, were charged with corruption.

the 1996 elections In national elections held in April 1996 the BJP emerged as the largest parliamentary bloc, but failed to win a majority. The second-largest number of votes was won by the leftist National Front–Left Front (NF–LF) group, followed by Congress, which suffered its worst election defeat since independence.

Rao resigned and dissolved parliament and in May 1996 the BJP formed a minority government under Atal Behari Vajpayee, but this collapsed after only 13 days.

the United Front governments A new coalition of centrist and leftist parties was formed in June, headed by H D Deve Gowda of the NF–LF (now the United Front), which enjoyed the tacit backing of the Congress Party. The new finance minister Palaniappan Chidambaram continued the liberalizing economic reforms instituted by Rao, with cuts in public spending and plans to streamline state-controlled firms and boost foreign and private investment. The United Front coalition government pledged to concentrate on the 'concerns of the poor', including rural development and social welfare.

In August 1996. a bill was passed changing the name of Madras to Chennai. Amid allegations of involvement in political bribery, Rao resigned as president of Congress in September 1996 and was replaced by Sitaram Kesri. In strife-torn Kashmir in October the National Conference Party (which wants the state to remain within India) won a sweeping victory in the first local elections for nearly a decade. In Uttar Pradesh, inconclusive elections and the lack of a stable majority resulted in the imposition of direct central rule.

In December 1996, the former prime minister P V Narasimha Rao, who faced charges in three separate fraud trials, resigned as parliamentary leader of the Congress Party. The party's president Sitaram Kesri took over as parliamentary leader in January 1997; he criticized the programme of economic liberalization that had been introduced six years earlier, believing that the reforms had been implemented too quickly and with too great a burden being placed on the poor.

In February 1997, in state elections in the northern province of Punjab, the Sikh Akali Dal and its ally the Hindu nationalist BJP won a decisive victory over the Congress Party, which had restored peace during its five years in power. In the same month the United Front government cut income tax by 10%, as well as corporate taxes and import duties, in a pro-business budget.

In April 1997, the minority 13-party United Front government of Deve Gowda fell after the Congress Party, led by the ambitious 79-year-old Sitaram Kesri, withdrew its support and it was defeated on a confidence vote. This action by Congress was believed to have been triggered by Gowda's authorization of police investigations of its members accused of corruption. A new United Front government was formed, with Congress backing, later in the month. It was headed by the respected 77-year-old socialist and former foreign minister Inder Kumar Gujral, The new government included virtually all members of the preceding Gowda cabinet.

The Congress Party withdrew support from India's ruling coalition late November 1997, forcing the prime minister to resign in the third government collapse in less than two years. Congress abandoned IK Gujral's seven-month-old, 14-party United Front government after accusing one of its members of supporting rebels linked to the 1991 assassination of party leader and former Prime Minister, Rajiv Gandhi. Gujral was the second prime minister to lead the nation and the United Front, after Congress withdrew support from a previous Front chief deemed ineffective March 1996.

the 1998 general election
The results of the general election held in India late February–early March 1998 showed that no party won the 273-seat majority needed to control the lower house of parliament. However, the country's Hindu nationalist Bharatiya Janata Party (BJP) was the single largest party, and India's president, R K Narayanan, asked BJP's leader, Atal Behari Vajpayee, 71, to head a coalition government. The widow of slain prime minister Rajiv Gandhi, Sonia, became president of Congress.

In response to demands for greater local autonomy, in August 1998 the government proposed the creation of three new states – Uttaranchal, Vananchal (later to be called Jharkhand), and Chhattisgarh – to be carved out of parts of the states of Uttar Pradesh, Bihar, and Madhya Pradesh. Chhattisgarh, Uttaranchal, and Jharkhand were created in November 2000.

nuclear testing India mid-May 1998 fuelled regional tensions and angered the world's opinion by conducting nuclear tests. Three nuclear weapons, which included an H-bomb, were tested in the Rajasthan desert. Reports on the explosions contributed to further increase of tension between India and Pakistan, and in late May Pakistan conducted five nuclear explosion on its territory.

International reaction to the testing in India soon followed: Australia and New Zealand recalled their high commissioners, Japan threatened to cut off aid, and China and UN secretary general Kofi Annan expressed concern. US President Clinton announced that he intended to implement the economic sanctions of America's 1994 Nuclear Proliferation Prevention Act. President Clinton announced the full implementation of the sanctions a few days later when India reported the explosion of two further nuclear weapons. Implementation of the US sanctions would mean blocking aid, barring bank loans and banning exports of equipment, such as computers, that might have a military use. In September 1998, India announced that it was now prepared to sign the Comprehensive Test Ban Treaty and would conduct no further nuclear tests, apart from those that are still legal under the treaty.

In November 1998, US economic sanctions were partially lifted. This was a reward for India's announcement of a voluntary moratorium on further tests, its commitment to the treaty, and the resumption of dialogue with Pakistan over disputed Kashmir.

state elections In November 1998, in the four northern and central states of Delhi, Rajasthan, Madhya Pradesh, and Mizoram, the opposition Congress polled strongly, securing its best election results for a decade and attracting back support from the young, Muslims and dalits (formerly 'untouchables'). It swept the ruling Hindu-nationalist BJP from power in Delhi and Rajasthan and retained control of Madhya Pradesh. The results were viewed as a reflection of public approval for Sonia Gandhi's leadership of Congress and a reflection of public disenchantment with recent sharp food price rises under the eight-month-old BJP national government of Atal Behari Vajpayee.

In April 1999, the BJP-led coalition government was defeated on a confidence vote in parliament. In the following month the parliament was dissolved. A general election was planned for late September or October. Sonia Gandhi, the Italian-born widow of Rajiv Gandhi, resigned as president of India's Congress Party in May 1999 after senior officials said it should not be led by a foreigner. Later in May, however, Sonia Gandhi withdrew her resignation and resumed control of the party.

India's Supreme Court in May 1999 confirmed death sentences on four people involved in the assassination of former prime minister Rajiv Gandhi.

civil unrest and continuing conflict over Kashmir Late 1998 and early 1999 saw a rise of religious unrest and a dramatic escalation of the terror campaign against Christians, mainly in the state of Gujarat.

For the first time in 20 years, India used air power in May 1999 to attack what it called 'infiltrators' in Kashmir. Indian aircraft attacked guerrillas operating in the Indian part of Kashmir. The persisting conflict between the two nuclear powers caused concern in capitals worldwide. The USA, Britain, China, the UN, and the EU called for the two sides to show restraint. Pakistan and India agreed in June to discuss ways to bring peace to Kashmir. The warlike conflict eased a little in July after Pakistani prime minister Sharif had a hastily arranged meeting with President Bill Clinton in Washington, DC.

A full-scale Indo-Pakistani war appeared to have been averted in July 1999 after Pakistan announced a truce with India over Kashmir, and as India's air strikes stopped and Pakistani militants from mountains in Kashmir began to withdraw.

Indian forces in August 1999 faced continued attacks by militants. Nevertheless, after celebrating the 52nd anniversary of India's independence, Prime Minister Vajpayee unveiled a formal nuclear weapons doctrine, based on a 'credible minimum deterrent' that would be used only after a first strike against the country by an enemy. Although the announcement did not mention the Comprehensive Test Ban Treaty which India, as well as Pakistan, was under intense pressure to sign before the end of September deadline, the world community was at least reassured by the doctrine's commitment to no first use.

The ruling Hindu BJP-led alliance in October 1999 narrowly won India's third election in less than four years. Vajpayee and Sonia Gandhi won their own seats. Several small parties did well. The main winners in the most populous state, Uttar Pradesh, were two lower-caste parties, the Samajwadi Party and the Bahujan Samaj Party.

In the Congress party's first electoral test since Sonia Gandhi took over as party president, it performed poorly, finishing with fewer seats than in the previous elections. It appeared that Sonia Gandhi's lack of political experience, her weak grasp of Hindi, and her foreign birth had all taken their toll.

Prime Minister Vajpayee made economic reform his top priority. His programme also included several important constitutional reforms: fixed terms for the Lok Sabha and state assemblies, the need for a third of people in legislatures to be women, and the creation of the three new states first proposed in 1998 – Uttaranchal, Jharkand, and Chhattisgarh.

natural disasters The coastal state of Orissa was hit in October 1999 by the fiercest cyclone for 28 years. The government, which had been criticized for a slow response to the tragedy, said in November that the confirmed death toll from the storm had reached 9,504. Officials said they did not expect the toll to exceed 10,000. Millions of people lost their homes and livelihoods, and the state was strewn with potentially disease-causing human corpses and animal carcasses. The government said almost 300,000 cattle had been reported killed.

rising tensions with Pakistan
India's celebrations to mark 50 years as a republic in January 2000 were overshadowed by rising tensions with Pakistan. India accused Pakistan of involvement in a week-long hijacking of an Indian airliner by Kashmiri militants who demanded the release of terrorists imprisoned by India. Pakistan denied any involvement. The Indian government agreed to release three prisoners, including the Islamic religious leader Maulana Masood Azhar, who subsequently appeared in public on Pakistani soil. Shelling and clashes in Kashmir heightened tension just before the visit to the area scheduled to be made by US President Clinton. Both sides denied responsibility for attacks. The following April, India announced a record 28% increase in defence spending for the next year.

Pakistani-backed fighters in Kashmir, the Hizbol Mojahedin, declared a three-month ceasefire in July 2000, and expressed willingness to talk to the government. In response to this, the Indian army suspended all offensive operations for the first time during the 11 years of violence in which more than 30,000 people had died. However, India refused to allow the involvement of Pakistan in the peace talks, and the mutual ceasefire was cancelled after only 15 days, with rebel activity and retaliation attacks recommencing. However, in November, India announced a unilateral ceasefire to coincide with Ramadan, Islam's holy month. The ceasefire was rejected by militant groups, but despite further killings, India held to its promise, though it was still not prepared to hold talks with Pakistan on the future of Kashmir.

internal problems 300,000 workers in India's state telecommunications industry went on strike in September 2000, claiming that employment was placed at risk by privatization plans. The same month, ex-premier

Narasimha Rao was convicted of bribing MPs in the crucial no-confidence vote he faced in 1993. He appealed against the ruling. In October the Supreme Court rejected an application by an environmental group to halt construction of the controversial Sardar Sarovar dam on the Narmada River in Gujarat.

earthquake in Gujarat
An estimated 50,000 people were killed after the most powerful earthquake in India for 50 years struck the northwest state of Gujarat on 26 January 2001. The quake, measuring 7.9 on the Richter scale, injured a further 150,000 people, and left more than 1 million in need of food, shelter, and clean drinking water. It laid waste to towns and cities throughout Gujarat state; two large towns, Bhuj and Anjar, were virtually destroyed. Aftershocks continued to affect the region during the first half of February.

bribery scandal Increased privatization and tax cuts were unveiled in the annual budget in February, which promised a 'new deal' designed to encourage economic growth. Quantitative restraints on 715 categories of imports were lifted. However, India's coalition government began to fall apart when videotapes of high officials taking bribes in set-up arms deals were released in March 2001. Bangaru Laxman – the president of the BJP, the main party in the coalition – and the defence minister George Fernandes, were among those forced to resign. One of the parties withdrew its nine members of parliament from the coalition.

ceasefire in Kashmir India repeatedly extended its unilateral ceasefire in December 2000, January 2001, and February, though pro-Pakistan militant groups continued to deride it as an attempt to win international sympathy. In mid-January, a separatist suicide squad tried to storm Srinagar's airport. The ensuing gun battle with Indian security forces left 11 dead and a dozen injured, and led to large-scale protests. However, the ceasefire extensions received a guarded welcome from the All-Party Hurriyat Conference, the main mouthpiece of peaceful Kashmiri separatists. India unexpectedly ended the ceasefire in Kashmir on 24 May 2001, and announced that it would invite Pakistan's military ruler, Gen Pervez Musharraf, to Delhi to discuss the future of the disputed territory. The ceasefire had been ignored by militants; the continuing violence had led to the deaths of around 1,200 people since its inception.

1 billion India's population was estimated at 1.027 billion on 1 March 2001, making it the second country in the world after China to cross the 1 billion mark. It grew by 181 million in the preceding ten years. However, its growth rate slowed from 2.1% per year in the 1980s to 1.9% per year in the 1990s.

state elections Elections in five key states in May saw the opposition Congress party gain victories in the states of Kerala, Assam, and Pondicherry. An ally of Congress, the All-India Anna Dravida Munnetra Kazhagam (AIADMK; All-India Anna Dravida Progressive Federation), won in Tamil Nadu. The Communist Party won in West Bengal, becoming the world's longest-serving elected communist administration.

summit with Pakistan In early July, the government announced the release of more than 400 Pakistani prisoners as a goodwill gesture before the summit meeting on 14 July. However, despite the talks, fighting between separatist rebels and soldiers killed 49 people in the two days leading up to the summit. A strike also closed down the Kashmir Valley, and protesters and police battled for hours in Srinagar, leaving five Indian soldiers and seven separatist rebels dead. Musharraf and Vajpayee began their first summit meeting in Agra. Although the talks remained inconclusive, they were described as cordial and constructive, and the dialogue was due to continue with Vajpayee accepting an invitation from Musharraf to a meeting in Pakistan.

protests over Naga truce Police shot dead 13 people in June when a mob set fire to the state assembly building in Imphal, the capital of Manipur. The rioters were protesting against the Delhi government's truce with Naga separatists in the state.

'Bandit Queen' murdered Phoolan Devi, member of Parliament for Mirzapur in Uttar Pradesh state, India, and a former outlaw, was shot dead in Delhi on 25 July 2001. Known as the 'Bandit Queen', in the early 1980s she led a criminal gang that carried out violent robberies in northern and central India, and became a popular media figure. Surrendering in 1983, she served an 11-year prison sentence, and turned to politics on her release. Championing the poor and defying the caste system, she was twice elected MP as a member of the Samajwadi party.

parliament building attacked Five armed assailants broke into the Indian parliament building in December 2001. No members of Parliament were harmed, but the ensuing battle resulted in the deaths of the attackers and nine others, including police officers. India demanded that Pakistan take action against Lashkar-e-Taiba, the Pakistani-based Islamic militant group accused of carrying out the attack. Tension between the two nuclear powers further escalated when India accused Pakistan's intelligence services of actively supporting the attack. India recalled its high commissioner from Islamabad and announced it was halting bus and rail links with Pakistan. The two countries exchanged shellfire on 23 December and New Delhi acknowledged that it had mobilized forces near the border with Pakistan, and that its troops were on high alert. The violence continued in

January 2002, as four Indian policemen died when armed militants attacked a US cultural centre in Kolkata. Two separate Islamic militant groups claimed responsibility for the attack. Clashes and deaths in fighting along the Kashmir border continued late January and early February. However, Prime Minister Vajpayee said in late January that his country would not go to war with Pakistan, and that the disputes could be resolved by diplomacy.

Hindu–Muslim violence increases Tensions rose between Hindus and Muslims in India in February 2002. A train carrying Hindu worshippers from a religious celebration at Ayodhya, where militant Hindus demolished the Babri Masjid (Mosque of Babur) in 1992, was set on fire by a Muslim crowd, killing at least 57 people. Most of the victims were activists with the Vishwa Hindu Parishad (VHP; World Hindu Council), who had planned to start building a temple at Ayodhya on 15 March in defiance of court orders. The death toll in Hindu–Muslim clashes in the western state of Gujarat had risen to more than 700 by the middle of March.

anti-terrorism bill In March, parliament approved a controversial anti-terrorism bill that set strict rules for arrest, interrogation, and investigation, and allowed detention of suspects for up to 30 days without appearing before a court. Opposition parties objected, saying they feared its powers would be misused, and Sonia Gandhi, leader of the Indian National Congress, claimed the bill posed a larger threat to the freedom of ordinary people than to terrorists.

threat of war The government accused Pakistan of backing Islamic militant incursions into Indian-administered Kashmir in May 2002, bringing the two countries close to war. A large troop build-up on the Kashmir line of control was ordered, as Pakistan heightened the tension by test-firing missiles capable of carrying nuclear warheads. There was widespread international concern. In June, under diplomatic pressure from the USA, the government announced a series of measures to reduce tension with Pakistan, including withdrawing its navy from waters near Pakistan and ending a ban on Pakistani civil aircraft entering its airspace.

new president In July 2002, Abdul Kalam was elected by an electoral college for a five-year term as the 12th president and head of state of India. Despite his scientific rather than political background, Kalam has enjoyed nationwide popularity as the creator of India's nuclear weapons development programme.

India Acts legislation passed in 1858, 1919, and 1935 which formed the basis of British rule in India until independence in 1947. The 1858 Act abolished the administrative functions of the British East India Company, replacing them with direct rule from London. The 1919 Act increased Indian participation at local and provincial levels but did not meet nationalist demands for complete internal self-government (*Montagu-Chelmsford reforms). The 1935 Act outlined a federal structure but was never implemented.

Indonesia country in southeast Asia, made up of 13,677 islands situated on or near the Equator, between the Indian and Pacific oceans. It is the world's fourth most populous country, surpassed only by China, India, and the USA.

Industrial Workers of the World IWW, labour movement founded in Chicago, USA in 1905, and in Australia in 1907, the members of which were popularly known as the **Wobblies**. The IWW was dedicated to the overthrow of capitalism and the creation of a single union for workers, but divided on tactics.

Inkatha Freedom Party IFP, (from the grass coil worn by Zulu women for carrying head loads; its many strands give it strength) South African political party, representing the nationalist aspirations of the country's largest ethnic group, the Zulus. It was founded as a paramilitary organization in 1975 by its present leader, Chief Mangosuthu *Buthelezi, with the avowed aim of creating a non-racial democratic political situation. The party entered South Africa's first multiracial elections in April 1994, after an initial violent boycott, and emerged with 10% of the popular vote.

Inönü, Ismet (1884–1973) Turkish politician and soldier, president 1938–50, and prime minister 1923–38 and 1961–65. He continued the modernization and westernization of Turkey begun by the republic's founder Kemal Atatürk, and kept his country out of World War II. After 1945 he attempted to establish democratic institutions.

International, the coordinating body established by labour and socialist organizations, including: **First International** or **International Working Men's Association** (1864–72), formed in London under Karl Marx; **Second International** (1889–1940), founded in Paris; **Third (Socialist) International** or **Comintern** (1919–43), formed in Moscow by the Soviet leader Lenin, advocating from 1933 a popular front (communist, socialist, liberal) against the German dictator Hitler; **Fourth International** or **Trotskyist International** (1938), somewhat indeterminate, anti-Stalinist; **Revived Socialist International** (1951), formed in Frankfurt, Germany, a largely anticommunist association of social democrats.

International Atomic Energy Agency IAEA, agency of the United Nations established in 1957 to advise and assist member countries in the development and peaceful application of nuclear power, and to guard against its misuse.

It has its headquarters in Vienna, and is responsible for research centres in Austria and Monaco, and the International Centre for Theoretical Physics, Trieste, Italy, established in 1964. It conducts inspections of nuclear installations in countries suspected of developing nuclear weapons, for example Iraq and North Korea.

International Labour Organization ILO, specialized agency of the United Nations, originally established in 1919, which formulates standards for labour and social conditions. Its headquarters are in Geneva, Switzerland. It was awarded the Nobel Peace Prize in 1969. By 1997, the agency was responsible for over 70 international labour conventions.

internment detention of suspected criminals without trial. Internment had been practised since the 18th century in times of crisis under the suspension of the writ of habeus corpus. In the 20th century a number of public order and security acts were passed by the UK or Irish governments, making provision for internment after the Easter Rising in 1916, and during the *Anglo-Irish War, the Irish Civil War, and the *Irish Republican Army (IRA) bombing campaigns of World War II and 1957–62. In 1971 internment was reintroduced by the UK government for the detention of people suspected of terrorist acts in Northern Ireland. The practice was suspended in December 1978, and the legislation for internment lapsed in 1980.

internment, Japanese the evacuation of all people of Japanese ancestry living on the West coast of the USA to detention centres in 1942, after Japan's attack on *Pearl Harbor during World War II.

Intifada (Arabic 'resurgence' or 'throwing off') Palestinian uprising, specifically between December 1987 and September 1993, during which time a loosely organized group of Palestinians (the **Liberation Army of Palestine**, also called Intifada) rebelled against armed Israeli troops in the occupied territories of the Gaza Strip and the West Bank. Their campaign for self-determination included strikes, demonstrations, stone-throwing, and petrol bombing. It was organized at grass-roots level by the Unified National Command, dominated by the *al-Fatah faction of the *Palestine Liberation Organization (PLO), but the Islamic fundamentalist group *Hamas also played a key role, particularly in the Gaza Strip. The September 1993 peace accord between Israel and the PLO provided limited autonomy for Gaza and the town of Jericho and initiated the *Israel–Palestine peace process. However, extremist groups that had participated in the Intifada, notably the militant wing of Hamas, opposed the accord and continued a campaign of violence within Israel.

A second Intifada began in September 2000, after a visit by right-wing Israeli politician Ariel *Sharon to the holy site of Haram al-Sharif (Temple Mount) in Jerusalem. This continued into 2001, with Hamas again playing a key role and Palestinian public opinion being hardened by Israel's stern counter-measures. A grass-roots body, the National and Islamic Forces (NIF), emerged, which began to bring together the secular and Islamic nationalists of al-Fatah and Hamas. By August 2001, more than 500 Palestinians and 150 Israelis had been killed in this second Intifada.

Inukai, Tsuyoshi (1855–1932) Japanese politician, prime minister 1931–32. He first achieved a ministerial position in 1898 and after a long political career eventually became prime minister in 1931. His policies angered the military and he was assassinated in an attempted coup in May 1932.

Invergordon Mutiny incident in the British Atlantic Fleet, Cromarty Firth, Scotland, on 15 September 1931. Ratings refused to prepare the ships for sea following the government's cuts in their pay; the cuts were consequently modified.

Iorga, Nicolae (1871–1940) Romanian historian, writer, and politician. He was for many years chief of the Nationalist Party. Tutor and friend of Carol I, he was largely instrumental in securing his return from exile and restoration to the throne. In 1931 he became premier of a non-party Cabinet.

Iran country in southwest Asia, bounded north by Armenia, Azerbaijan, the Caspian Sea, and Turkmenistan; east by Afghanistan and Pakistan; south and southwest by the Gulf of Oman and the Gulf; west by Iraq; and northwest by Turkey.

Irangate US political scandal in 1987 involving senior members of the Reagan administration (the name echoes the Nixon administration's *Watergate). Congressional hearings 1986–87 revealed that the US government had secretly sold weapons to Iran in 1985 and traded them for hostages held in Lebanon by pro-Iranian militias, and used the profits to supply right-wing Contra guerrillas in Nicaragua with arms. The attempt to get around the law (Boland amendment) specifically prohibiting military assistance to the Contras also broke other laws in the process.

Iran–Iraq War war between Iran and Iraq (1980–88), claimed by the former to have begun with the Iraqi offensive on 21 September 1980, and by the latter with the Iranian shelling of border posts on 4 September 1980. Occasioned by a boundary dispute over the Shatt-al-Arab waterway, it fundamentally arose because of Saddam Hussein's fear of a weakening of his absolute power base in Iraq by Iran's encouragement of the Shiite majority in Iraq to rise against the Sunni government. An estimated 1 million people died in the war.

The war's course was marked by offensive and counter-offensive, interspersed with extended periods of stalemate. Chemical weapons were used, cities and the important oil installations of the area were the target

for bombing raids and rocket attacks, and international shipping came under fire in the Gulf (including in 1987 the US frigate *Stark*, which was attacked by the Iraqi airforce). Among Arab states, Iran was supported by Libya and Syria, the remainder supporting Iraq. Iran also benefited from secret US arms shipments, the disclosure of which in 1986 led to considerable scandal in the USA, *Irangate.

The intervention of the USA 1987, ostensibly to keep the sea lanes open, but seen by Iran as support for Iraq, heightened, rather than reduced, tension in the Gulf, and United Nations attempts to obtain a ceasefire failed. The war ended in August 1988 after ceasefire talks in Geneva.

Iraq country in southwest Asia, bounded north by Turkey, east by Iran, southeast by the Gulf and Kuwait, south by Saudi Arabia, and west by Jordan and Syria.

Ireland, Republic of country occupying the main part of the island of Ireland, in northwest Europe. It is bounded to the east by the Irish Sea, south and west by the Atlantic Ocean, and northeast by Northern Ireland.

government The 1937 constitution provides for a president, elected by universal suffrage for a seven-year term, and a two-chamber national parliament, consisting of a senate, Seanad Éireann, and a house of representatives, Dáil Éireann, both serving five-year terms. The senate has 60 members, 11 nominated by the prime minister (Taoiseach) and 49 elected by panels representative of most aspects of Irish life. The Dáil consists of 166 members elected by universal suffrage through the single-transferable vote form of proportional representation. The president appoints a prime minister who is nominated by the Dáil, which is subject to dissolution by the president if the government loses its house majority during its five-year term.

history The Anglo-Irish Treaty of December 1921 had given Southern Ireland dominion status within the *Commonwealth, and it was now referred to as the Irish Free State. Six out of the nine counties of Ulster remained part of the UK, with limited self-government.

the civil war The Anglo-Irish Treaty was narrowly ratified by the Dáil Éireann (parliament) in January 1922 (by 64 votes to 57) and a provisional government of the Irish Free State was set up. The Irish Free State was accepted by *Irish Republican Army (IRA) leader Michael *Collins, as a stepping stone to the goal of greater freedom, but not by many of his colleagues, who refused to accept the partition of Ireland and shifted their allegiance to the more radical Republican leader Éamon *de Valera.

A bitter civil war ensued, but after a period of guerrilla fighting the 'Irregulars' of the splinter anti-Treaty faction of the IRA were suppressed by the Free State army under Gen Richard Mulcahy. During this period the president, Arthur *Griffith, died (in August 1922), and Collins took over as head of state. However, Collins was assassinated ten days later, on 22 August, at Béal-na-mBláth in west Cork in an ambush by anti-Treaty IRA men.

W T *Cosgrave then became prime minister (or more accurately, president of the executive council), and T M Healy was nominated as governor general. The aftermath of Collins's killing saw a hardening of the Free State government's tactics towards the anti-Treaty Irregulars in a war that was to bequeath to Ireland a lasting legacy of bitterness.

T M Healy was succeeded as governor general in 1928 by James McNeill. Cosgrave's pro-Treaty party Cumann na Gaedheal (the predecessor of *Fine Gael) remained in power until 1932.

the oath of allegiance
The Republican *Fianna Fáil party founded by de Valera in 1926 – which represented the anti-Treaty, more militantly republican side of the Irish Civil War (1922–23) split – put forward candidates at parliamentary elections, but these, when successful, could not sit in the Dáil because of their refusal to take the oath of allegiance to the British crown (one of the provisions of the 1921 Anglo-Irish Treaty).

In 1927 the Dáil passed an Electoral Amendment Act making it necessary for parliamentary candidates to subscribe to the oath in order to be eligible for election. The Fianna Fáil candidates thereupon took the oath, declaring beforehand that they regarded it as an 'empty formula'.

After the general election of February 1932, Fianna Fáil, by uniting with Labour and Independent members, secured a majority in the Dáil, and a government under de Valera's leadership took office. A bill was introduced to abolish the oath of allegiance; it was passed by the Dáil but was rejected by the Senate.

the Land Annuities issue A more serious issue was the government's decision not to continue the payment to Great Britain of the 'Land Annuities', which had originated in the various Land Purchase Acts, under which Irish tenants were enabled to purchase their holdings through loans from the British state. The annual sum due was £3 million.

The British government endeavoured to collect the money by imposing tariff duties on Free State exports to the UK, and the Free State retaliated with duties on UK imports. The question was settled in April 1938 by an agreement signed in London, under which the Irish government paid £10 million in commutation of the annuities, the special trading duties were amended, and the British government relinquished the rights in the Irish naval ports (such as Cobh and Lough Swilly) that it had been given by the treaty of 1921.

the constitution of 1937 In 1935 the Dáil passed bills to abolish the Senate and university representation. The office of governor general was abolished. These matters were, however, reconsidered before a new constitution was framed in 1937.

The new constitution declared Ireland (now called 'Eire') to be a sovereign, independent state; no mention was made of the British crown, but the External Relations Act of 1936 remained in force, giving the crown certain functions in the concluding of treaties and the accrediting of diplomatic representatives. The government of the UK and the dominions agreed that the constitution should not effect a fundamental alteration in the position of Ireland in the Commonwealth.

general developments during and after World War II When World War II broke out, the Irish government declared the neutrality of the state, a position that was maintained throughout the war. A large number of Irish men and women from Southern Ireland, however, joined the British forces, and many others found war work in the UK. During and after the war the IRA continued its fight for an independent, unified Ireland through a campaign of violence, mainly in Northern Ireland, but also on the British mainland and, to a lesser extent, in the South.

The post-war years saw considerable economic advance in the Republic, despite the high rate of emigration of Irish citizens to the UK and elsewhere. Agricultural methods improved and new industries were established, attracting foreign capital. Tourism, notably from the UK and the USA, became one of the Republic's most important industries.

In 1973 Ireland joined the European Community at the same time as Britain and has played an active part in that organization since. Similarly it has shouldered global responsibilities as a member of the United Nations, providing observers and troops for peace-keeping operations in a number of areas.

post-war politics In 1948 a coalition government under John Costello of Fine Gael replaced de Valera's Fianna Fáil administration. The last formal links with the British Commonwealth were severed in April 1949 by the coming into force of the Republic of Ireland Act 1948. This event caused no bitterness in either Britain or the Republic of Ireland. The Ireland Act 1949 (of the UK Parliament) subsequently recognized the secession of the Republic of Ireland from dominion status, and confirmed citizens of the Republic in the rights that they had hitherto enjoyed in the UK.

In 1951 Costello was defeated at the polls by de Valera's Fianna Fáil party, but was again returned to power in the general election of 1954. At the general election of March 1957 Costello was defeated and de Valera again became Taoiseach (prime minister). He resigned in 1959 and from that year until 1973 was president of the Republic, although obtaining a reduced majority in the presidential election of 1966. He was succeeded as premier by his deputy, Seán Lemass, who was in office until 1966 when Jack *Lynch, also of Fianna Fáil, took his place.

politics in the 1970s After the 1973 election, the Fianna Fáil government was replaced by a Fine Gael–Labour coalition headed by Liam *Cosgrave. The success of the Labour Party in the 1973 election was evidence of the growth of an urban proletariat and an increased demand for more widespread social benefits. Erskine H Childers became president in 1973, and was succeeded on his death in 1974 by Cearbhall (Carroll) Ó Dálaigh.

Following the murder in July 1976 of the British ambassador in Dublin, a state of emergency was declared in the Irish Republic in August 'arising out of the armed conflict now taking place in

Northern Ireland'. An Emergency Powers Bill and a Criminal Law Bill were approved by the Dáil in September and were subsequently signed into law by President Ó Dálaigh, but following criticism by the minister of defence, Patrick Donegan, he resigned in late October, and Patrick *Hillery was elected unopposed as his successor.

In the general election of June 1977 Fianna Fáil gained a parliamentary majority of 20 over the Fine Gael–Labour coalition, the largest ever achieved in the history of the Irish Republic, and Jack Lynch again became prime minister. Lynch resigned in 1979, and was succeeded by Charles *Haughey, also of Fianna Fáil. Haughey's aim was a united Ireland, with considerable independence for the six northern counties.

the Troubles in the North Until 1969, cooperation between Northern Ireland and the Republic, on both political and economic matters, had been increasing. However the outbreak of violence in the North and the activities of the IRA which, although illegal in the South, was frequently based there, revived old allegiances, bitterness, and party quarrels.

Northern Ireland once again dominated Irish politics, and relations between the Republic and Britain deteriorated sporadically. They were at a particularly low ebb after the introduction of internment in the North, and in 1971 the Republic laid a formal complaint against Britain before the European Commission of Human Rights over the treatment of 'political' prisoners. However the Republic took part in the Sunningdale Conference in 1973 on the future of Ireland and, as the violence became more acute and predictably spread into the South, strenuous efforts were made against the IRA by the government of the South. In 1979 IRA violence intensified: on the same day in August, Earl Mountbatten was murdered in

the Republic and 18 British soldiers were killed in County Down, Northern Ireland.

the Anglo-Irish Agreement In 1983 all the main Irish and Northern Irish political parties initiated the New Ireland Forum as a vehicle for discussion. Its report was rejected by Margaret Thatcher's Conservative government in the UK, but discussions between London and Dublin resulted in the signing of the Anglo-Irish Agreement in 1985, providing for regular consultation and exchange of information on political, legal, security, and cross-border matters. The agreement also said that the status of Northern Ireland would not be changed without the consent of a majority of the people. The agreement was criticized by the Unionist parties of Northern Ireland, who asked that it be rescinded.

politics in the 1980s After the 1981 election Garret *FitzGerald, leader of Fine Gael, formed another coalition with Labour but was defeated the following year on budget proposals and resigned. Haughey returned to office with a minority government, but he too had to resign later that year, resulting in the return of FitzGerald. FitzGerald's coalition ended in 1986, and the February 1987 election again returned Fianna Fáil and Charles Haughey.

In 1988 relations between the Republic of Ireland and the UK were at a low ebb because of disagreements over decisions relating to the extradition of republican prisoners. In 1989 Haughey called an election and, after failing to win a majority, entered into a coalition with the Progressive Democrats (a breakaway party from Fianna Fáil), putting two of their members into the cabinet. In November 1990, after being dismissed as deputy prime minister, Brian Lenihan was defeated in the presidential election by the left-wing-backed Mary *Robinson.

Haughey resigns The Progressive Democrat leader Desmond O'Malley withdrew from the coalition after allegations against Haughey, in January 1992, of illegal telephone-tapping. As a result, Haughey lost his parliamentary majority and resigned as Fianna Fáil leader and prime minister. He was succeeded in February 1992 by Albert *Reynolds, leading a reconstructed cabinet.

In a national referendum in June 1992, Ireland showed its approval of the Maastricht Treaty on European union when 69% voted in favour in a turnout of 57%.

the Fianna Fáil–Labour coalition Having failed to win a confidence vote in the Dáil, Reynolds called a general election in November 1992. The result gave no party a working majority, although Labour made substantial gains under Dick Spring. In January 1993, after prolonged negotiations, Reynolds succeeded in forming a Fianna Fáil–Labour coalition, with Spring as deputy to Reynolds in the post of minister for foreign affairs. In October 1993 a six-year National Development Plan (NDP) was unveiled, aimed at a 'transformation of Ireland'.

The new coalition began working closely with the UK government in seeking an end to the violence in Northern Ireland, culminating in the *Downing Street Declaration in December 1993, in which both Reynolds and UK prime minister John Major offered constitutional talks with all parties if violence was renounced.

After lengthy, behind-the-scenes negotiations on both sides of the Irish border, the IRA formally ended its 'military operations' in August 1994, and in October Protestant paramilitaries announced an end to their campaign of violence as long as the IRA cessation held.

Fine Gael joins forces with Labour In November 1994 Labour leader Dick Spring withdrew his support from the governing coalition in protest over a controversial judicial appointment made by Reynolds. Having lost his parliamentary majority, Reynolds resigned as premier and as leader of Fianna Fáil. For a time it appeared that the new Fianna Fáil leader, Bertie *Ahern, would succeed him as premier, but in December 1994 Spring announced the formation of a new coalition of Fine Gael, Labour, and the Democratic Left Party.

Fine Gael leader John Bruton, as the new premier, stressed his commitment to the Northern Ireland peace process and, with Spring retaining the post of deputy and foreign minister, Anglo-Irish negotiations resumed. A framework peace document, published in February 1995, contained the Republic's agreement to renounce its claim to Northern Ireland and a proposal for joint North–South administrative bodies with limited powers. In November 1995 the Irish public narrowly voted to legalize divorce in a national referendum.

Following June 1997 elections, Ireland's centre-left government conceded defeat to Bertie Ahern's Fianna Fáil party and its Progressive Democrat allies and Independents. In November 1997 Mary McAleese was elected president. Overall, the Dublin governments of the 1990s showed an enthusiasm to work with London for an end to the conflict in Northern Ireland. The twin aims of this policy were to enable nationalists to make significant progress through constitutional politics, and to reassure unionists that their consent would be required prior to constitutional change. As such, it was hoped that neither republicans nor loyalists would seek or find justification for paramilitary violence.

Following the IRA's second ceasefire, proclaimed in July 1997, Anglo-Irish negotiations continued, and multiparty talks, known as Stormont talks, resumed in January 1998 in Belfast.

On 10 April 1998 the Northern Ireland Political Talks Document, also known as the Good Friday agreement, was released. Amongst its fundamental principles were: the establishment of a Northern Ireland Assembly with considerable executive and legislative powers; the founding of a North–South Ministerial Council that would be accountable to a Northern Ireland Assembly as well as to the Irish parliament; the establishment of a British-Irish Council that would liaise between the two governments and devolved administrations of Scotland, Wales, and Northern Ireland; and a new British–Irish agreement that would supersede the Anglo-Irish Agreement of 1985. The date of a referendum designed to take place simultaneously in the Republic of Ireland and in Northern Ireland, in which the proposed settlement would be decided, was set for 22 May 1998.

On that day, the Good Friday agreement was overwhelmingly endorsed by 94.39% (1,442,583 votes) in the Republic of Ireland and 71.12% of voters (676,966 votes) in Northern Ireland. 5.61% (85,748 voters) in the Republic and 28.88% of the electorate (274,879 voters) in Northern Ireland voted 'No' to the agreement. The average turnout in the Republic was 55.59% (as compared with 80.98% in the north), that is, 1,528,331 out of 2,749,208 people eligible to vote. Support reached 92% in Kerry and Cavan Monaghah and 93% in Donegal.

In February 2001, John Bruton resigned as leader of Fine Gael after losing a vote of confidence. He was replaced by Michael Noonan.

rejection of the Treaty of Nice
Voters in the Republic rejected the Treaty of Nice by 54% to 46% in a referendum held in June 2001. The treaty had laid down the minimum changes required to permit eastward expansion of the European Union (EU), and needed to be ratified by all 15 EU countries before it could go

ahead. However, the European Commission controversially declared that enlargement of the EU would go ahead despite the result.

An attempt by the government to further tighten the country's already strict anti-abortion laws was rejected on 7 March 2002 by a narrow margin in a constitutional referendum. Proposals that included removing the threat of suicide as grounds for abortion were defeated by 50.42% to 49.58%.

2002 elections Fianna Fáil, led by Prime Minister Ahern, retained power in a May general election. Increasing its representation to 81 seats in the Dáil Éireann, the party narrowly fell short of an overall majority, but it was the first time in over 30 years that voters had re-elected a government. The opposition Fine Gael lost seats, with only 31 of its previous 54. Sinn Fein won five seats – an increase of four.

Irgun short for **Irgun Zvai Leumi** (National Military Society), a Jewish guerrilla group active against the British administration in Palestine (1946–48). Their bombing of the King David Hotel in Jerusalem in 22 July 1946 resulted in 91 fatalities.

Irish Free State name of the former state of southern Ireland 1922–37, established as a result of the Anglo-Irish Treaty (1921). It was replaced by Eire in 1937 and the Republic of *Ireland in 1949. The treaty established a 26-county dominion, which exercised a significant degree of autonomy but was formally subordinated to the British crown through the appointment of a governor general and an oath of fidelity to be taken by its representatives.

Irish National Liberation Army
INLA, guerrilla organization committed to the end of British rule in Northern Ireland and Irish reunification. The INLA, founded in 1974, is a left-wing offshoot of the *Irish Republican Army (IRA). Among its activities was the killing of British

politician Airey Neave in 1979. The INLA initially rejected the IRA's call for a ceasefire in 1994; its assassination in 1997 of loyalist leader Billy Wright threatened to destabilize the peace process and bomb attacks occurred in London in 1998. However, after the Omagh bomb atrocity in 1998 the INLA became the first republican subversive group to state explicitly that the war was over and voice strong support for the peace process.

Irish Republican Army IRA, militant Irish nationalist organization formed in 1919, the paramilitary wing of *Sinn Fein. Its aim is to create a united Irish socialist republic including Ulster. To this end, the IRA has frequently carried out bombings and shootings. Despite its close association with Sinn Fein, it is not certain that the politicians have direct control of the military, the IRA usually speaking as a separate, independent organization. The chief common factor shared by Sinn Fein and the IRA is the aim of a united Ireland.

Irish Republican Brotherhood secret revolutionary society that grew out of the Fenian movement, in the wake of the failed insurrection of 1867, in an effort to reform its organization and improve its security precautions. Although very successful in the 1870s and 1880s in attracting membership and in encouraging secret agrarian agitation, internal frictions over the question of support for home rule hampered the movement thereafter. By the early 1910s, thanks to increasing frustration with constitutional politicians and the organizational skills of Tom Clarke (1857–1916) and Sean MacDermott the movement had revived and was a considerable force behind both the 1916 Easter Rising and the *Anglo-Irish War. Damaged by splits among its leaders over the *Anglo-Irish Treaty, the brotherhood was said to have been dissolved in 1924, but rumours that it has survived in the USA, until the time of the

Northern Ireland peace process, have persisted.

Iron Curtain in Europe after World War II, the symbolic boundary between capitalist West and communist East during the *Cold War. The term was popularized by the UK prime minister Winston Churchill from 1946.

An English traveller to Bolshevik Russia, Ethel Snowden (1881–1951), used the term with reference to the Soviet border in 1920. The Nazi minister Goebbels used it a few months before Churchill in 1945 to describe the divide between Soviet-dominated and other nations that would follow German capitulation.

Iron Guard profascist group controlling Romania in the 1930s. To counter its influence, King Carol II established a dictatorship in 1938 but the Iron Guard forced him to abdicate in 1940.

Ironside, (William) Edmund, 1st Baron Ironside (1880–1959) Scottish field marshal. He served in the South African War 1899–1902 and World War I. In 1939 during World War II, he replaced Viscount Gort as Chief of the Imperial General Staff because the minister of war, Leslie Hore-Belisha, found him more congenial. In May 1940 he sided with Gort against Churchill in a disagreement over the possibility of the British Expeditionary Force breaking out to the south. Churchill transferred Ironside to the Home Forces, but he handed the post over to *Alanbrooke in July 1940 and retired. KCB 1919, Baron 1941.

Israel country in Southwest Asia, bounded north by Lebanon, east by Syria and Jordan, south by the Gulf of Aqaba, and west by Egypt and the Mediterranean Sea.

government Israel has no written constitution. In 1950 the single-chamber legislature, the Knesset, voted to adopt a state constitution by evolution over an unspecified period of time. As in the UK, certain laws are considered to have particular constitutional significance and could, at some time, be codified into a single written document.

Supreme authority rests with the Knesset, whose 120 members are elected by universal suffrage, through a system of proportional representation, for a four-year term. It is subject to dissolution within that period. The president is constitutional head of state and is elected by the Knesset for a five-year term, renewable only once. The prime minister and cabinet are mostly drawn from, and collectively responsible to, the Knesset, but occasionally a cabinet member may be chosen from outside. Since 1996 the prime minister has been popularly elected for a four-year term.

history Following the Jewish revolts against the Roman occupation of 66–73 and 135, many of the Jewish population of Palestine (broadly the area now covered by Israel, the Gaza Strip, and the West Bank) were either killed or dispersed to other parts of the Mediterranean world (the diaspora). Palestine was further Hellenized, and when Christianity was adopted as the official religion of the Roman Empire in the 4th century, many churches were built around the sites holy to Christians, which became centres of pilgrimage.

Palestine under Muslim rule With the collapse of the Western Roman Empire in the 5th century, Palestine remained under the rule of the Eastern Roman (Byzantine) Empire, until Jerusalem was captured by the Persians in 614. This was followed in 637 by the conquest of the whole area by the Muslim Arabs. From the 11th to the 13th centuries, a number of European Crusades attempted to recover what Christians regarded as the Holy Land from the Muslims. The First Crusade was perhaps the most successful, capturing Jerusalem in 1099 and establishing a Christian kingdom that lasted a century before falling to the sultans of Egypt.

In 1517, Palestine was conquered by the Ottoman Turks, and became part of the *Ottoman Empire for four centuries. At the end of the 19th century, the Zionist movement emerged, advocating the re-establishment of a Jewish homeland in Palestine as a refuge for the persecuted Jews of eastern Europe. In 1897, Theodor *Herzl organized the First Zionist Congress in Basel to publicize Jewish claims to Palestine, where numbers of Jews began to settle.

the British mandate In World War I, Britain and France were at war with Turkey, and made plans regarding the post-war division of the Ottoman Empire, by which Syria would be occupied by the French, while Palestine would fall to the British. In 1917, in order to encourage Jewish support for the war effort, the British foreign secretary A J Balfour wrote to Lord Rothschild, a leading British Zionist, stating that the British government 'view with favour the establishment in Palestine of a national home for the Jewish people' – the so-called Balfour Declaration. In 1918 British forces expelled the Turks from Palestine, and in 1920, under a League of Nations mandate, Palestine came under British administration.

Jewish immigration continued in the 1920s, bringing about conflict with the resident Arabs. In 1929 there was severe communal violence around Jerusalem, and in 1933 there were Jewish riots in protest at British attempts to restrict Jewish immigration. Arab discontent culminated in an uprising in 1936. In an attempt to resolve the problem, the Peel Report of 1937 recommended partition of Palestine between Jews and Arabs, but with a British region that would include Jerusalem and the shrines sacred to the three major religions. This was accepted by most Jews, but rejected by the Arabs, and fighting ensued. With war looming in

Europe the British government also decided not to accept the proposals, and with the outbreak of World War II in 1939, postponed plans for independence.

the formation of Israel and the First Arab–Israeli War In Europe, the Nazi *Holocaust had killed about 6 million Jews, and hundreds of thousands tried to get to Palestine before, during, and after World War II. Jewish–Arab violence increased after the war, and Zionist guerrilla groups such as *Irgun and the *Stern Gang attacked British forces. Britain announced that it would surrender its mandate to the United Nations, which in 1947 voted for the partition of Palestine.

Virtual war broke out in March 1948 between the unofficial Jewish forces (*Haganah and Irgun) and local Arabs, including the Jordan Arab Legion. The main fighting was for control of the road between Tel Aviv-Yafo and Jerusalem, which the Jews managed to keep open, although a group of Jewish settlements south of the city was destroyed by the Legion. The Jewish forces gained complete control in Haifa, Jaffa, Safed, and Tiberias.

On 14 May 1948, the day before the British mandate was due to end, the state of Israel was proclaimed, with David *Ben-Gurion, of Mapai (the Israeli Workers' Party, forerunner of the Israeli Labour Party), as prime minister. The neighbouring Arab states (Egypt, Lebanon, Jordan, and Syria) immediately sent forces to crush Israel but failed, and when a ceasefire agreement was reached in January 1949, Israel controlled more land than had been originally allocated to it (for more details of the fighting, see *Egypt). Israel retained the western part of Jerusalem, Galilee, and the Negev Desert. Most of the remainder of Palestine, known as the *West Bank (an area to the west of the River Jordan), was occupied by Jordan, while in the south Egypt occupied the

*Gaza Strip. The Arab states continued to refuse to recognize Israel, and imposed an economic boycott.

The creation of the state of Israel resulted in the displacement of much of the Arab population of the region. The war produced 700,000 Arab refugees from Israel and the war areas, many settling in refugee camps in the Gaza Strip and the West Bank. Jewish immigration on a large scale was encouraged, and Israel's population doubled within three years of independence. By 1962, about 2 million Jews had arrived from all over the world. In 1964, a number of Palestinian Arabs in exile founded the *Palestine Liberation Organization (PLO), aiming to overthrow Israel.

the Suez Crisis and the Second Arab–Israeli War The Arabs continued to regard Israel's existence as illegitimate, and raids across the border took place. From 1952, Egypt stepped up the blockade of Israeli ports and its support of Arab guerrillas based in the Gaza Strip, and in February 1955 Israel attacked the Egyptian garrison in Gaza.

The nationalization of the Suez Canal by the Egyptian leader Col *Nasser, and the growing local tensions, contributed to the outbreak of the *Suez Crisis and the Second Arab–Israeli War in 1956. Under a secret agreement with England and France, Israel invaded Egypt in October 1956, advancing into the Gaza Strip and Sinai with the avowed purpose of destroying Egyptian strong points and places from which cross-border raids were taking place. In November, French and British forces intervened in Egypt to reoccupy the Canal Zone. US pressure brought about an Anglo-French withdrawal in December, and Israeli forces withdrew in March 1957.

Israeli politics in the 1950s and 1960s In its first two decades, Israel was sustained by a steady flow of funds from abroad, while the development of agriculture became a major and successful concern. Foreign relations were orientated generally towards the West, and the USA has continued to be Israel's closest ally. Relations were gradually improved with West Germany, which until 1966 paid reparations for the damage inflicted on its Jewish population during World War II. In 1960, a leading Nazi war criminal, Adolf *Eichmann, was kidnapped in Argentina by Israeli agents. He was tried in Israel and executed in 1962.

Israel's system of proportional representation generally results in the formation of coalition governments, and in the early decades of Israel's existence these were all dominated by left-of-centre parties. Ben-Gurion, who was prime minister almost continuously from 1948, resigned in 1963, to be succeeded by Levi Eshkol. Eshkol's government lasted until 1967, forming a new coalition in the build-up towards a third Arab–Israeli war. The coalition included Moshe *Dayan, a hero of the 1956 war, as defence minister.

the Six-Day War Tensions between Israel and its Arab neighbours continued through the 1960s. In 1967 Egypt blockaded the Straits of Tiran (Israel's only means of access to the Red Sea), and introduced troops into Sinai. A third Arab-Israeli war broke out on three fronts, with Egypt, Jordan, and Syria, in June 1967, but within six days Israel's armed forces had defeated their Arab opponents. Israeli forces seized the Gaza Strip and Sinai from Egypt, the West Bank (including east Jerusalem, bringing all of Jerusalem under Israeli control) from Jordan, and part of the Golan Heights from Syria, and these occupied territories were placed under Israeli law.

This victory produced only a very limited degree of peace, even though the occupied territories greatly enhanced the Israelis' feelings of security. Palestinian fighters, such as the PLO, increased their activities, particularly from Jordan until King Hussein suppressed them in 1970–71.

developments between 1968 and 1973 In 1968, three of the left-of-centre coalition parties combined to form the Israel Labour Party. The following year, Levi Eshkol died in February and was unexpectedly succeeded by Golda *Meir, a former foreign minister. Her tenure of office was marked by a hardening of attitudes towards the Palestinians and the question of withdrawal from occupied territories. Public and government opinion was particularly divided on the latter subject, but as long as peace moves seemed remote and US pressure slight, Israel felt able to contain bouts of military tension and international criticism.

In the atmosphere of comparative peace, the disparities between Jews of North African and Middle Eastern origins and those of European and American origins showed themselves in social unrest. The 1967 victory attracted immigration, and an unexpected increase came after the USSR relaxed its emigration restrictions in 1971. By 1972, the 3 million Jewish immigrants had arrived. In spite of efforts by the Israeli armed forces, Palestinian guerrillas managed to enter the country, and in one of the worst attacks at the time, 28 people were killed at Lod airport in May 1972. Such attacks became an international phenomenon, and Israeli aircraft and personnel were frequent targets; 11 Israeli athletes were killed at the Olympic Games in Munich in September 1972.

the Fourth Arab–Israeli War However, the euphoria following the 1967 victory bred a sense of over-confidence in Israel, which led to the belief that Arab forces would not mount a major attack, having insufficient airpower. Thus Israeli forces were badly surprised by the

simultaneous attacks on Yom Kippur
(the Jewish Day of Atonement),
6 October 1973, by Egyptian forces
across the Suez Canal and by the
Syrians in the Golan Heights. Within
a few days, Jordan, Iraq, Kuwait, Saudi
Arabia, Sudan, Tunisia, Algeria, and
Morocco announced varying degrees
of military support for Egypt and
Syria. There followed over two weeks
of hard fighting, in which Israeli
casualties were very high – about
3,000 killed or missing. The USA and
USSR, who supplied Israel and its
enemies respectively with military
equipment, were instrumental in
effecting a ceasefire through the UN,
on 22 October 1973.

the effects of the war The war
had a deep effect on Israeli society.
International opinion at the UN, in
part under the influence of the Arab
oil-producers' embargo, shifted against
Israel. Internally the government was
discredited, and the right-wing Likud
group, formed in 1973, made electoral
gains. Meir announced her resignation
in April 1974, and in June was
succeeded by Gen Yitzhak *Rabin,
heading another Labour-led coalition.
Concessions imposed by the USA led
to interim agreements with Egypt
(involving staged Israeli withdrawals
from Sinai) and Syria. In November
1973 the PLO was recognized, at the
Arab Summit in Algiers, as the 'sole
representative of the Palestinian
people.' In November 1974 the UN
granted the PLO observer status and
recognized Palestinian rights to
independence and self-determination.
The PLO was promoted as a
negotiating partner, something that the
Israeli government found abhorrent.

In 1975, immigration fell to 20,000,
the lowest figure for a decade and
about equalling the number that
emigrated. Inflation was high, and
the Israeli pound was repeatedly
devalued. Expenditure on the armed
forces took about 40% of the national
budget, and Israelis were one of the
most highly taxed people in the world.

the Camp David Agreements
The 1977 election resulted in a first
victory for the right-wing Likud,
which formed a coalition government
with the religious parties, with
Menachem *Begin as prime minister.
Although Likud claimed indivisible
sovereignty over the whole of the
biblical Land of Israel (including Gaza
and the West Bank), within five
months relations between Egypt and
Israel changed dramatically, mainly
owing to peace initiatives by President
*Sadat of Egypt, encouraged by US
president Jimmy *Carter. Setting a
historical precedent for an Arab leader,
Sadat visited Israel to address the
Knesset in November 1977, and the
following year the Egyptian and Israeli
leaders met at Camp David, Maryland,
to sign agreements for peace in the
Middle East. A treaty was signed in
1979, and in 1980 Egypt and Israel
exchanged ambassadors, to the dismay
of most of the Arab world. Israel had
totally withdrawn from Sinai by 1982,
but continued to occupy the Golan
Heights.

the Fifth Arab–Israeli War In March
1978, in reprisal for a PLO raid, Israeli
troops entered Lebanon, destroying
Palestinian guerrilla bases, and
engaging with Syrian forces stationed
in Lebanon. UN troops were then sent
to police the area as Israeli soldiers
withdrew. In June 1982, Israeli forces
launched a full-scale invasion of
Lebanon and surrounded West Beirut,
in pursuit of 6,000 PLO fighters who
were trapped there. A split between
Egypt and Israel was avoided by the
efforts of the US special negotiator
Philip Habib, who secured the
evacuation from Beirut to other Arab
countries of about 15,000 PLO and
Syrian fighters in August. However,
massacres in two Palestinian refugee
camps at Sabra-Shatila by Lebanese
Christian militias with Israel's alleged
complicity increased Arab hostility.

Talks between Israel and Lebanon,
between December 1982 and May 1983,

resulted in an agreement, drawn up by US Secretary of State George Shultz, calling for the withdrawal of all foreign forces from Lebanon within three months. Syria refused to acknowledge the agreement, and left some 30,000 troops, with about 7,000 PLO members, in the northeast; Israel retaliated by refusing to withdraw its forces from the south, but did make a phased withdrawal from elsewhere in the country.

Shamir and Peres share power
During this time, Begin faced growing domestic problems, including rapidly rising inflation and opposition to his foreign policies. In 1983 he resigned, and Likud's Yitzhak *Shamir formed a shaky coalition. Elections in July 1984 proved inconclusive, with the Labour Alignment, led by Shimon *Peres, winning 44 seats in the Knesset, and Likud, led by Shamir, 41. Neither leader was able to form a viable coalition, and it was eventually agreed that a 'government of national unity' would be formed, with Peres as prime minister and Shamir as his deputy for the first 25 months, then a reversal of the positions in October 1986. By this time, the government had successfully brought inflation to within manageable levels.

Israeli forces withdraw from Lebanon Meanwhile, the problems in Lebanon continued. In 1984, under pressure from Syria, President Gemayel of Lebanon declared the 1983 treaty with Israel to be void. In February 1985, Israel stepped up its withdrawal of troops in Lebanon, despite the possibility of this leading to civil war in southern Lebanon. The Shiite guerrilla group *Hezbollah took advantage of the situation by attacking the departing Israeli troops. Israel retaliated by attacking Shiite villages. The withdrawal was virtually complete by June 1985, though Israel maintained a 'security zone' in southern Lebanon, supporting the South Lebanese Army militia as

a buffer against PLO and Hezbollah guerrilla incursions into Israel.

the Palestinian question and the Intifada By 1984, the Arab world was split into two camps, with the moderates represented by Egypt, Jordan, and Yassir *Arafat's PLO, with whom King Hussein of Jordan had established a relationship. The more militant radicals included Syria, Libya, and the rebel wing of the PLO. In 1985, Hussein and Arafat put together a framework for a Middle East peace settlement, to involve bringing together all interested parties. Israel objected to the involvement of the PLO, though Peres met Hussein secretly in the south of France, and later, in a speech to the UN, said he would not rule out the possibility of an international conference on the Middle East. Shamir, however, was not as welcoming towards the idea. Arafat also had talks with Hussein and later, in Cairo, Egypt, renounced PLO guerrilla activity outside Israeli-occupied territory.

In December 1987, an organized Palestinian uprising in the occupied territories, the *Intifada, began. It continued sporadically until September 1993, with Palestinians demanding self-government and the establishment of a state of Palestine. In April 1988, the military commander of the PLO, Abu Jihad, was assassinated in Tunis, allegedly by the Israeli secret service. This triggered further violence in the occupied territories. In July, Hussein transferred responsibility for the West Bank to the PLO. Egyptian president Hosni *Mubarak proposed a ten-point programme for elections in the occupied territories leading towards an unspecified form of autonomous self-rule. Labour, but not Likud, quickly agreed to the provisions, and the USA approved the plan.

The November 1988 general election resulted in a hung parliament, and

Shamir formed another coalition with Peres and the Labour Party after lengthy negotiations. In December, Arafat repudiated terrorism and recognized Israel's right to exist. In 1989, Likud accepted some of the provisions of Mubarak's ten-point plan, but Shamir continued to take a hard line with both the Palestinian protests and the PLO, while Peres was more conciliatory. These differences broke the coalition partnership in March 1990. After a three-month political crisis, Shamir succeeded in forming a new coalition government, including members of Likud and far-right nationalist and religious parties. Israel's crackdown on Palestinians in the occupied territories drew widespread international condemnation.

in search of peace In January 1991, the Gulf War erupted with UN-coalition air raids against Iraq. In retaliation, Scud missiles were launched against Israel and Israel's nonretaliation was widely praised. Shamir agreed to an amended Middle East peace plan in August 1991, and in September released a number of Palestinian prisoners as part of a hostage exchange. Negotiations with Jordan and Syria began in October in Madrid, Spain. However, progress was slow due to Shamir's intransigence and the continuing policy of establishing Jewish settlements in the Palestinian territories. But Israel's participation in the peace process was too much for fundamentalists in Shamir's coalition, who withdrew their support in January 1992. Shamir had to call a general election to try to restore his majority in the Knesset.

In June 1992, the Labour Party, now led by former premier Yitzhak Rabin, defeated Likud in the general election, and a month later Rabin was confirmed as prime minister, heading the first Labour-dominated government since 1977. In August 1992, US–Israeli relations improved

when US president George Bush and Rabin agreed a loan pact to aid Israel's absorption of several hundreds of thousands of Jewish émigrés from the former USSR. The move solved an issue considered to be a major obstacle in the Middle East peace talks.

events of 1993 and the Israeli–PLO peace accord In December 1992, 415 Palestinians, alleged to be members of the outlawed *Hamas Islamic Resistance Movement, were expelled from Israel and the occupied territories. They were refused asylum in Lebanon and so forced to set up camp in 'no man's land' on the Lebanese border. Despite UN condemnation of the expulsion, the Israeli government initially refused to reconsider its decision. Although 100 of the deportees were allowed to return in February 1993, the vast majority remained in exile until December.

The *Israel–Palestine peace process, discussions regarding the status of the West Bank and Gaza Strip that continued throughout the 1990s and into the new millennium, began in earnest in January 1993, when the ban on contacts with the PLO was formally lifted. In March 1993, Binyamin *Netanyahu succeeded Yitzhak Shamir as leader of Likud. Face-to-face talks between Palestinians and Israelis began in Washington in April.

Israel renewed attacks against southern Lebanon in July in an attempt to force the Lebanese government to take action against Hezbollah units based there, which had been attacking Israeli targets, and had killed seven Israeli soldiers. The scale and ferocity of the Israeli action brought widespread international criticism. A peace deal, brokered by the USA and Syria, stipulated that neither side would attack unless the other did so first, and both sides also pledged to avoid hitting civilian targets.

In September 1993, Israel officially recognized the right of the PLO to participate in the peace process, and Rabin and Arafat reached a preliminary peace agreement in Washington, providing for limited autonomy in the Gaza Strip and the West Bank town of Jericho, and a phased withdrawal of Israeli troops from the occupied territories.

advancements in peace In July 1994, the 46-year-old 'state of war' with Jordan was formally ended and a future peace with Syria seemed credible. In October 1994, Rabin, Arafat, and foreign minister Shimon Peres were jointly awarded the Nobel Peace Prize. In September 1995, agreement was finally reached on the second phase of the 1993 peace agreement – the transfer of control of Palestinian areas in the West Bank to the PLO and the holding of elections to a Palestinian council. Six weeks later, in November, Rabin was assassinated by a young Jewish extremist on leaving a peace rally. Peres took over as prime minister, and launched into negotiations with Syria. Progress was made, but the talks suspended after Hamas bombings in February and March 1996.

The first free elections to an 88-member Palestine National Council (PNC), held in January 1996, were won by the PLO. Concurrently, Yassir Arafat was elected PNC president.

further unrest in Lebanon By mid-April 1996, the number of Hezbollah attacks on Israel had risen to more than a hundred since the beginning of the year, and Israel began a 17-day campaign in southern Lebanon in which Israeli helicopter gunships rocketed Beirut for the first time since 1982. In less than a week, 26 deaths were recorded in Israel's attacks, 23 of which were civilians. The raid came a day after Hezbollah fired rockets into northern Israel (injuring 36 people), and in the wake of an escalating cycle of violence that had gripped Lebanon in preceding weeks. The Israeli campaign was linked to the Israeli election scheduled for May; by launching the air attack on Beirut, Peres hoped to convince the Israeli electorate that Hezbollah was being punished. A ceasefire was negotiated by the USA, Syria, Israel, and Lebanon.

Netanyahu becomes premier In May 1996, Likud leader Binyamin Netanyahu became the first directly elected prime minister. In the concurrent Knesset elections, Labour won 34 of the 120 seats, and Likud 32, forcing Netanyahu to rely on support from other, mainly religious, parties. The more conservative government stalled on peace negotiations and continued to establish new Jewish settlements in the occupied territories.

Israeli police began inquiries into allegations of corruption in Netanyahu's government that were completed in April 1997. The police later announced that they had insufficient evidence to indict Netanyahu on corruption charges, but doubts about his probity remained and opposition politicians demanded his resignation.

In September 1997, Israeli agents attempted, but failed, to assassinate Hamas leader Khalid Mashaal, living in Jordan, leading to a crisis in relations between Israel and Jordan. Criticism of Netanyahu's government inside and outside the country grew, and in January 1998 he survived a no-confidence vote in the Knesset. In April 1998, Israel celebrated its 50th anniversary.

A new Middle East peace deal was produced after US-brokered talks at Wye Plantation, Maryland, in September 1998. However, Netanyahu failed to win the support of the Knesset, forcing him to call an early 1999 election, scheduled for May. In January 1999, he suspended the Wye accord timetable.

Barak comes to power In the most divisive election campaign in the country's history, Ehud *Barak, leader of the Labour Party from June 1997, defeated Netanyahu in May 1999 to become Israel's prime minister. Since Barak's Labour Party did less well, he was forced to put together a coalition government including all three ultra-Orthodox parties, but excluding Likud. As he was sworn in, he pledged to achieve peace with Syria, Lebanon, and the Palestinians.

In early June, the Israeli-supported South Lebanon Army withdrew from the Jezzine area of southern Lebanon, badly harassed by Hezbollah guerrillas. The Lebanese government declined to send its army to control the area, despite its assurance under the Wye agreement to afford Israel protection from Hezbollah guerrillas. To Barak's anger, before leaving office, Netanyahu ordered Israeli warplanes to make raids on various targets in Lebanon in retaliation to Hezbollah guerrilla rocket-attacks on Israel.

Golan Heights discussions Talks between Syria and Israel resumed in the USA in December 1999 after a four-year break. The main issue for discussion was Israel's withdrawal from the Golan Heights, but Barak wished to negotiate concurrently over Syria's relationship with Lebanon, the disarmament of Hezbollah, and an end to Israel's occupation of the Golan Heights. Syria accused Israel of a lack of good faith. In January 2000, the talks were postponed indefinitely by Israel. No reason was given, although Israel rejected Syria's demand to commit to a full Israeli withdrawal from the Golan Heights, and said that negotiations would not be resumed until Syria was seen to control the Hezbollah.

political corruption allegations in 2000 President Weizman, who had been elected in 1993 and again in 1998, became the first head of state in the nation's history to become the subject of a criminal inquiry when, in January 2000, he admitted that he had accepted large sums of money from a French millionaire while serving in parliament and as a minister. Despite calls for his resignation, he made it clear that he would not be giving up his office, protesting that he had done nothing illegal. Investigations had also begun on Binyamin Netanyahu in September 1999, who was accused of misusing public funds when in office. Charges were dropped in September 2000 for lack of evidence. Other investigations condemned Barak's election team for grave financial irregularities in the campaign of 1999.

renewed fighting in Lebanon
In February 2000, six Israeli soldiers in Lebanon were killed after the breakdown of talks with Syria. In response, Israel withdrew from the 1996 ceasefire agreement, and began a bombing campaign, first targeting three power transformers providing power to Lebanese cities. Syria refused to negotiate until Israel committed to withdrawing from the Golan Heights, while the Israeli government voted for tougher rules in any deal with Syria.

Barak defeated a motion of no confidence and insisted that, before Israel pulled out from Lebanon, he would exhaust all chances of a deal with Syria and Lebanon. Meanwhile, the UN threatened to withdraw some of its frontline outposts in southern Lebanon if the battles between Israeli occupying troops and Hezbollah guerrillas continued. At a meeting of the 22-nation Arab League, there was universal condemnation of Israel's actions. In March, the bombing campaign intensified, but Arab-Israeli peace talks reopened, and Israel's cabinet confirmed Barak's commitment to withdraw Israeli troops from southern Lebanon by July.

Israeli withdrawal from Lebanon
Ordered by the Supreme Court, Israel released 13 Lebanese detainees in April 2000, who had been held without trial for more than ten years. While this was a conciliatory move, the following month Israel bombed two more Lebanese power stations after Lebanese rockets were shot into

northern Israel. Israel's bombing had cost Lebanon dearly in terms of power and finance, and appeared to push a peaceful withdrawal further away. But popular Israeli demands for a withdrawal grew, and morale in the Israeli-backed South Lebanon Army was diminishing. Fears grew that if Israel withdrew from Lebanon without reaching an agreement with Syria, the Middle East would become a war zone. However, the UN Middle East representative confirmed that peacekeepers would be deployed on the border between Lebanon and Israel after Israel's withdrawal.

In late May, the Israeli army staged a hasty withdrawal from the region. It was a risky step towards peace for Barak, as Hezbollah and the Israelis were left without a buffer zone on the border, and the retreat seemed to represent an embarrassment to Israel as a military superpower. However, within two months, Hezbollah forces in the frontier area were replaced with Lebanese government troops, joining almost 400 UN soldiers on the border.

problems with the coalition Barak's coalition government was unsettled in June 2000 when the ultra-Orthodox Shas party said it would pull out of the coalition over a disagreement regarding funding for its religious schools. The left-wing secular Meretz party then resigned from the coalition in a move designed to palliate the Shas party. The row was just one in a series of setbacks that Barak had suffered as a result of the uneasy alliance formed by having several parties represented in his government. In July, the Knesset elected Moshe Katsav, a right-wing Iranian-born member of the Likud party who opposed Barak's peace initiative, to replace Ezer Weizman as president. On the eve of Barak's departure for the Camp David talks in July 2000, the prime minister narrowly survived a no-confidence vote in parliament, and entered the summit with only a minority of supporters in

government. There were further no-confidence votes following Barak's return from Camp David, which he again survived, but his foreign minister, David Levy, resigned in protest at the concessions that Barak had made during the talks. Under severe political pressure, Barak's cabinet voted in September to abolish the Religious Affairs Ministry, representing a first step towards Barak's promised secularization. Barak also planned to give Israel a written constitution that would loosen the grip of the Orthodox establishment on citizens, proposing to introduce civil marriage and to consolidate women's rights.

renewed violence In September 2000, following a controversial visit by the Likud leader, Ariel Sharon, to the holy site of Haram al-Sharif (Temple Mount), clashes between Palestinians and Israeli security forces spread to other disputed areas including the West Bank and Gaza, leading to over 300 deaths by December. An Arab summit in October, the first for four years, condemned Israel's part in the violence, but did not lead to a break in diplomatic relations with Israel. The conflict intensified in late November.

Barak resigns On 9 December, Barak suddenly announced his immediate resignation, calling a special election for prime minister, in which he would stand, for February 2001. Both former prime minister Binyamin Netanyahu and Ariel Sharon announced their intention to stand. However, Netanyahu linked his candidacy to a call for fresh general elections, and had to withdraw from the race in January 2001 when Shas, the Knesset's third-biggest party, decided to oppose this call.

A US-led commission of inquiry into the violence, headed by former US senator George Mitchell, agreed at a summit held in Sharm el-Sheikh,

Egypt, on 17 October, made its first visit to the region on 11 December.

Sharon becomes premier

In February 2001, Sharon won the special elections called by Barak, a result that many felt would damage the peace process. Turnout was at a record low (62%), especially among Arab Israelis (18%). Sharon formed a broad-based coalition government that included the Labour party, with Shimon Peres as foreign secretary. Labour had previously voted to join the government, after Ehud Barak resigned as leader. Violence in the Palestinian territories escalated in the following months. In April 2001, Rabbi Ovadia Yosef, the spiritual leader of Israel's influential Shas party, preached a sermon calling for God's annihilation of Arabs. He was heavily criticized by many Israeli politicians. Days later, Sharon repudiated every concession considered by Barak, and the Israeli army launched an attack on Syrian radar targets in eastern Lebanon, killing at least three soldiers, in retaliation for the killing of an Israeli soldier by Hezbollah guerrillas.

In May 2001 the Mitchell commission called for an end to Palestinian terrorism, a freeze on Israeli settlement building, a lifting of the Israeli blockade of Palestinian self-rule territories, and a ceasefire. In June 2001 the Israelis showed restraint after a Palestinian suicide bomber killed 20 young Israelis at a Tel Aviv-Yafo beach-front discotheque. In response Arafat committed his forces to an unconditional ceasefire, and on 13 June Israel joined in accepting a ceasefire brokered by US Central Intelligence Agency director George Tenet. The Palestinian ceasefire largely held in areas controlled by the Palestine National Authority, but not in occupied parts of the West Bank or Gaza. There were demonstrations against the ceasefire in Gaza city and Ramallah by Palestinians who had been radicalized by the conflict, and

Arafat was unable to control Hamas and Islamic Jihad terrorists.

In August 2001, following further suicide bombing attacks on Israelis, Sharon ordered the closure of the Palestinians' political headquarters in Orient House, Jerusalem. He backed efforts by foreign minister Shimon Peres to hold ceasefire talks with Arafat, but the ceasefire was effectively over, with violence mounting again. Israel launched an assassination policy of 'targeted killings' in an effort to combat the threat of suicide bombers and to stop attacks on soldiers and settlers in Palestinian areas. Several prominent Palestinian political and military leaders were eliminated, but at the cost of further retaliation by suicide bombers. By August 2001 the death toll since the Intifada had begun in September 2000 had reached more than 500 Palestinians and 150 Israelis.

Israel–Palestine peace process ongoing talks between *Israel and the *Palestine Liberation Organization (PLO). The process can be said to have begun in January 1993 when an Israeli ban on contact with the PLO was formally lifted, and in September of that year Israel officially recognized the PLO's right to participate in the peace process, and agreed an initial peace accord. The peace process continued throughout the 1990s and into the 21st century, and suffered many setbacks. Although Israel handed over control of parts of the *Gaza Strip and the *West Bank to a Palestine National Authority (PNA), the final status of these areas remained unresolved.

Italy country in southern Europe, bounded north by Switzerland and Austria, east by Slovenia, Croatia, and the Adriatic Sea, south by the Ionian and Mediterranean seas, and west by the Tyrrhenian and Ligurian seas and France. It includes the Mediterranean islands of Sardinia and Sicily.

government The 1948 constitution provides for a two-chamber parliament consisting of a senate and a 630-member chamber of deputies. Both are elected for a five-year term by universal suffrage and have equal powers. Constitutional reforms adopted in 1993 amended the voting system – one of proportional representation – to allow for 75% of the chamber of deputies to be elected by simple majority voting. The revisions also allowed Italian expatriates to vote in national elections and required elected deputies to retire after 15 years. The senate's 315 elected members are regionally representative, and there are also seven life senators. The president is constitutional head of state and is elected for a seven-year term by an electoral college consisting of both houses of parliament and 58 regional representatives. The president appoints the prime minister and cabinet (council of ministers), and they are collectively responsible to parliament. Although Italy is not a federal state, each of its 20 regions enjoys a high degree of autonomy, with a regional council elected for a five-year term by universal suffrage.

history The consolidation of the politically unified Italy was slow and difficult, owing to the great social and economic differences between the wealthier industrialized north and the poor agrarian south. In 1878 King Victor Emmanuel II died and was succeeded by Umberto I, and in the same year Pope Pius IX was succeeded by Leo XIII.

the later 19th century Umberto I's reign was characterized by electoral reform (1881) and foreign colonization. The formation of a colonial empire began in 1869 with the purchase of land on the Bay of Assab, on the Red Sea, from the local sultan. In the next 20 years the Italians occupied all of *Eritrea, which was made a colony in 1889. Somaliland, along the northeast coast of Africa, was acquired between 1880 and 1890. Italy's claims upon Abyssinia (Ethiopia) led to war, which

ended in an Italian defeat at Adowa (1896) and the restoration of all land to Abyssinia by the Treaty of Addis Ababa (1896).

In 1882 Italy joined Germany and Austria in the Triple Alliance, largely owing to its distrust of France. Alliance with Austria also implied a renunciation of Italy's claims on Austrian possessions in the north (the Trentino and the South Tirol) and along the Adriatic coast of the Balkans.

the years before World War I In 1900 Umberto was assassinated and was succeeded by his only son, Victor Emmanuel III. At the beginning of the new century Italy entered upon more friendly relations with France, and in the disputes over Morocco in 1906–11 supported France against Germany, while France acquiesced in Italian colonial ambitions in Tripolitania (an area of modern Libya), then part of the Turkish Ottoman Empire.

In September 1911 war broke out between Italy and Turkey in connection with the rights and privileges of Italian subjects in Tripolitania. In November of the same year the Italian government formally proclaimed the annexation of Tripolitania and the neighbouring area of Cyrenaica. In 1912 Italy also acquired the Dodecanese Islands from Turkey.

Meanwhile, at home, the industrialization of Italy gave rise to acute problems of social reform, and led to the rise of left-wing political groups, centred in the north.

Italy in World War I After the outbreak of war in 1914 between the Allies (including Britain, France, and Russia) and the Central Powers (Germany, Austria-Hungary, and Turkey), Italy was at first neutral. As the price of continued neutrality, Italy demanded territorial concessions from Austria in the Trentino, Istria, Dalmatia, and Albania. Austria rejected all but a small extension of the Italian frontier.

Giorgio Sonnino, the Italian foreign minister, then opened negotiations with the Allies, and finally, in April 1915, the secret Treaty of London was signed, by which fulfilment of Italy's territorial claims was promised together with an immediate loan of £50 million. In May 1915 Italy declared war on Austria-Hungary.

The Italian army was poorly equipped, and only some 400,000 men were available for the main offensive launched on the River Isonzo and for the operations in the Trentino. Not until 1916 did Italy become actively at war with Germany. As a result of Sonnino's foreign policy the unity and independence of Albania were proclaimed under the protection of Italy, while in April 1917 the Treaty of St Jean-de-Maurienne was concluded with France and Britain, defining Italy's share in the post-war partition of Asia Minor (Asiatic Turkey).

In October 1917 the Italians suffered a massive defeat at the hands of German-Austrian forces at Caporetto (see *Caporetto, Battle of). This defeat stiffened Italian resistance, and in June and October 1918 the reorganized Italian army defeated the Austrians at the Second and Third Battles of the Piave, and in October Austria sued for an armistice.

post-war territorial issues At the end of World War I the resources of Italy were exhausted. Its losses in men amounted to half a million, and the country was bankrupt. The fact, however, that for Italy the war ended with a military victory encouraged a nationalist movement, which demanded the port of Fiume (Rijeka, now in Croatia) as well as the territorial gains promised in the Treaty of London. The Adriatic question was unsolved, and Italian dissatisfaction with the peace treaty caused the resignation of the prime minister, Vittorio *Orlando in 1919.
He was succeeded by the liberal Francesco*Nitti.

Domestic unrest in Italy was heightened by the feeling aroused over the Allied intervention in Fiume, following the coup d'état of Gabriele D'Annunzio, who in September 1919 occupied the city with a band of Italian volunteers. The 'Adriatic question' was settled tentatively by the Treaty of Rapallo (1920), whereby Italy surrendered the Dalmatian coast of the Adriatic to the new state of Yugoslavia, but secured sovereignty over Zara (Zadar, now in Croatia), while Fiume was made an independent state.
It remained for Mussolini to reach a definite settlement, known as the Treaty of Rome, in January 1924, whereby Yugoslavia exercised control over Port Baroc and the Delta, and Italy over Fiume.

the advent of Mussolini and the Fascists Benito *Mussolini became prime minister in 1922, having been the leader of the Fasci di Combattimenti, first organized by him in 1919 (see *fascism). Italian fascism was an eclectic phenomenon, drawing both on the violent rhetoric of extreme nationalism and syndicalism. By 1921 the Fascists increasingly projected themselves as a movement capable of overcoming the bitter conflicts between capital and labour, although the development of agrarian fascism in the Po Valley, which in the same year transformed a minority group into a mass movement, showed that, despite the movement's ambiguities, its crucial support came from the right.

In 1921 the Fascists reorganized into a political party and returned 30 members to parliament, allying themselves with the Nationalists. In 1922, taking advantage of the weak government leadership and the continuing social unrest throughout the country – which rallied much moderate opinion to their support – Mussolini organized the Fascist March on Rome. The black-shirted Fascist columns advanced on Rome in October, and two days later Mussolini arrived from Milan in response to a royal summons. He at once formed a cabinet in which he combined the premiership with the ministries of foreign affairs and the interior. At the elections held in April 1924 the Fascists, after modifying the electoral laws in their favour, gained an absolute majority.

Following the murder of the Socialist Giacomo Matteoti, Mussolini came under pressure from his followers to take a hard line against all opposition. This resulted in the suspension of democratic rights in January 1925, a ruthless campaign against real and suspected opponents, and the gradual establishment of Mussolini's dictatorship. By 1928 Mussolini was absolute dictator, and adopted the title of Duce (leader). Superficially at least, Italy took on the appearance of a corporative state.

The 1929 *Lateran Treaties, establishing the pope's territorial sovereignty over the Vatican City State, and subsequent moderation by Mussolini on religious questions, gave him at least passive support from many devout Catholics who never became active Fascists.

Italian expansionism in the 1930s
In foreign affairs Italy successfully surmounted many difficulties with Yugoslavia over Fiume; with Greece over the murder of Gen Tollini of the Albanian Frontier Commission, followed by the Italian occupation of Corfu; with France over the treatment of Italian minorities in France and Tunisia; and with Turkey over Turkish fears of an Italian annexation of Anatolia. Italy was also a signatory to the Locarno treaties on European security (see *Locarno, Pact of).

A rapid increase in population and a shortage of war materials, coupled with the bankruptcy of the regime's domestic policy and the need to create new support, led Italy along the road of imperialism. Notwithstanding the existence of various treaties and conventions guaranteeing the integrity of Ethiopia, Mussolini announced his intention of annexing the country and by May 1936 Italian forces were occupying the Ethiopian capital. Thus, in addition to the areas of Libya conquered in 1911, vast new regions were added in 1936; yet the number of Italians settled in the Italian possessions in northeast Africa scarcely ever exceeded 30,000.

The League of Nations considered collective action against Italy, but the idea was eventually abandoned. Mussolini, together with Hitler, also committed forces to the right-wing cause of Gen Franco in the Spanish Civil War (1936–39). After the *Munich Agreement (1938), Mussolini's prestige rose considerably as a result of his part in the settlement. This event further strengthened the ties between Italy and Germany (already strong since the formation of the Rome–Berlin *Axis in October 1936), even though the German annexation of Austria earlier in 1938 had appeared to frustrate Mussolini's ambition of achieving a dominant position in southeast Europe.

Mussolini's aggressive intentions became increasingly obvious: Italian claims were launched for Djibouti, Tunisia, Corsica, and Nice. In April 1939 Italian troops invaded Albania. King Zog fled, the country was occupied, and Victor Emmanuel III became king of Albania. In May, Italy and Nazi Germany signed a treaty of alliance.

increasing authoritarianism
At home, the Duce strengthened his autocratic position by the abolition of the Chamber of Deputies. In its place a Chamber of Fasci and Corporations was set up, having 800 members from the National Council of the Fascist Party and the National Council of Corporations, nominated by Mussolini. The government had the right to issue decrees with the force of law, which were then placed before the Chamber. The Chamber dealt with constitutional

laws, budget estimates, and also any other matters that Mussolini authorized it to discuss.

The real ruling authority was the Gran Consiglio del Fascismo (Fascist Grand Council), which was composed of the quadrumviri of the March on Rome, appointed for an indefinite period, a certain number of members (ministers and other high dignitaries) appointed for as long as they held their offices, and an indeterminate number of members appointed for three years by the head of the government.

early campaigns in World War II
On the outbreak of World War II in 1939, Italy was at first neutral, though obviously friendly to Germany. Nevertheless the following year, with the decline of Allied fortunes in Western Europe, Mussolini became convinced of an eventual Germany victory and on 10 June Italy declared war on France and Great Britain, and shortly afterwards launched an attack on Egypt from Libya. But, contrary to Mussolini's probable belief, the collapse of France did not bring the war to an end and Italy gained few territorial benefits. Economic conditions in Italy became increasingly bad. In October 1940 Italy launched an attack on Greece, but the stout resistance maintained by the Greeks caused the campaign to linger on through the winter with catastrophic results for the Italians. Moreover the Italian navy was severely crippled by the British air force attack on the naval base of Taranto (November 1940).

Military disasters continued: an Italian army was routed in Albania by the Greeks in March 1941, the province of Cyrenaica was lost to the Allies (see *North Africa Campaign), and the Ethiopians launched a successful revolt, which, aided by British arms, resulted in the loss of Eritrea in March and the fall of Addis Ababa in April.

Germany, however, succeeded in retrieving Italian fortunes in both North Africa and the Balkans.

The reflected prestige helped to maintain the Fascist regime in Italy, which fell more and more under the control of Germany.

Italy was associated with Germany in the defeat of Yugoslavia and gained some land on the Dalmatian coast. Italy also provided an occupying force for Greece, which had been defeated by the Germans. By June 1941 Italy was at war with the USSR (although Hitler had given no notice to Mussolini of his intention to invade the USSR), and by the end of the year with the USA. Italy's economic situation deteriorated still further and its industry was entirely tied to Germany's war machine. With German help, efforts were made to strengthen the hold of the Fascist Party. At the instigation of Germany, the Fascists also started to deport large number of Italian Jews to the Nazi death camps. At the end of 1941 Italy occupied Nice and Corsica at the same time as the Germans moved into southern France.

the fall of Mussolini The year 1943 saw the fall of Mussolini and the surrender of Italy to the Allies. After the Allied invasion of Sicily, Mussolini made a last bid to prepare the mainland of Italy against invasion and to ensure the loyalty of the Fascist Party by excluding several leading members from the government. Dissension within the Fascist Party, however, broke into open revolt when Mussolini, after two meetings with Hitler in July, was unable to obtain a promise of adequate German support against the coming invasion.

By order of the king, Mussolini was arrested and Pietro *Badoglio, another Fascist, was called upon to form a government. A secret armistice with the Allies was agreed while the Germans, in anticipation of some such move, tightened their grip in northern Italy and also occupied the Rome airfields. On 8 September, following the Allied landing at Salerno, the armistice was declared. Badoglio set up his government in British-occupied territory and on 11 October Italy declared war on Germany.

In the meantime, Mussolini, after a dramatic airborne rescue carried out by German paratroopers, set up a republican Fascist regime in the north, named the Republic of Salò. He avenged himself on those of his former supporters who had betrayed him but were now in his power. Among them were Count Galeazzo *Ciano and Emilio *De Bono who were tried and shot in January 1944.

liberation In June 1944 the Allied armies entered Rome and Victor Emmanuel retired in favour of his son, Prince Umberto. He did not, however, abdicate. Badoglio resigned and Ivanoe Bonomi, a veteran socialist statesman from the days before fascism, formed a new government. With an Italian government in Rome, most of the occupied areas of southern Italy were handed over to Italian control, and the government was recognized diplomatically by the United Nations.

On 28 April 1945 Mussolini, his mistress, and 12 members of his cabinet were shot by members of the largely left-wing partisan resistance movement, which had been fighting the Fascists and Germans in occupied Italy since 1943, and had also organized general strikes. On 2 May 1945 the German army in Italy surrendered, and the liberation of Italy was completed.

the establishment of the republic Bonomi, who considered his interim task now at an end, resigned and a coalition government under Ferrucio Parri succeeded him. Parri resigned in November 1945, after a consultative assembly had been established and a new government comprising six parties was formed by the Christian Democrat Alcide De Gasperi. By this time the Allied military government had handed over to the Italian government the control of all territory except Venezia Giulia and the Udine

province, while the economic situation was eased by supplies that reached Italy from foreign sources through the agency of the UN.

In May 1946 Victor Emmanuel formally abdicated and his son was proclaimed king as Umberto II. However, a referendum on the future of the monarchy held in June resulted in a majority in favour of a republic. Umberto abdicated in June, and subsequently went into exile in Portugal.

Elections were held for the Constituent Assembly under a new system of proportional representation, which resulted in a gain of 207 seats for the Christian Democratic Party, 115 for the Socialists, and 104 for the Communists out of a total of 556. The Constituent Assembly met in June and proclaimed a republic, electing de Nicola as provisional president. De Gasperi continued as premier of a reconstructed coalition government, the first for 25 years to consist of freely elected deputies.

the peace treaty The first event that confronted the new government was the peace treaty with the Allies, signed on 10 February 1947. The terms of the treaty, whereby Istria, Fiume, and land east of the River Isonzo were ceded to Yugoslavia (with the exception of the newly created Free Territory of Trieste) were considered a sad blow to Italy, and neither did they satisfy Yugoslav ambitions. The treaty also stipulated the cession of the Tenda-Briga area in the Maritime Alps to France and the Dodecanese Islands to Greece, while Italy also lost its colonies in Africa and agreed to respect the independence of Ethiopia.

Italy also agreed to pay substantial reparations over seven years, and provisions were made for the demilitarization of frontiers and of islands in the Mediterranean and for the limitation of armed forces.

De Gaspari's governments 1947–53 De Gasperi, at the head of a new coalition government in January 1947, weathered the storm created by the peace treaty. Further unrest was being caused by shortages of raw materials and other economic difficulties. In May the Communists, who had supported the government since 1944, were expelled from the coalition, and De Gasperi formed a further government dependent mainly on the Christian Democrats. The new constitution became law on 1 January 1948. In May 1948 Luigi Einaudi was elected president of Italy for a seven-year term.

The general election of 1948 established the Christian Democrats as the major party of the right. The successive De Gasperi administrations (he headed eight between 1945 and 1953) always had to rely on support from other parties, latterly more and more right-wing Socialists and the Liberals; for, though the Christian Democrats were the largest single party in parliament, they never had an overwhelming majority over all other parties combined.

As time went by the left-wing parties in the coalitions became increasingly dissatisfied with the government's internal policy, which they regarded as insufficiently progressive. Various attempts at social reform were, however, carried out by De Gasperi and his successors, notably in the sphere of land reform, which especially affected southern Italy, but with little real success.

In 1949 De Gasperi's foreign policy brought Italy into NATO, and in the same year Italy became a founder member of the Council of Europe. His moderate influence soon reestablished Italy's status in West European politics, but his alliances with the West were bitterly opposed by the Communists.

The Christian Democrats lost ground in the general election in 1953 after an attempt to alter the electoral laws in their favour. In July De Gasperi formed his eighth and last ministry. Only his own party members joined it and it lasted only a few days. After 1953

various attempts were made to build a new coalition formula around the weakened Christian Democrat Party.

the later 1950s The 12 years, 1950–62, saw the Italian 'economic miracle', during which its gross national product doubled, and it was able to sustain one of the highest growth rates in the world (6%) for an even longer period.

In October 1954 Italy and Yugoslavia finally reached agreement over the Trieste problem, thus settling a nine-year dispute. Under it, Italy obtained an area including Trieste city and Yugoslavia the area around it, where the population was mainly non-Italian. Trieste was to remain a free port. It was on the whole a solution more favourable than Italy could have envisaged at the end of the war. In 1955 Giovanni Gronchi succeeded Luigi Einaudi as president of the Republic.

The late 1950s were a period of considerable uncertainty. The Soviet invasion of Hungary in 1956 led to a regrouping of the left-wing parties, and a less intransigent position was adopted by Pietro Nenni's Socialist Party. At the level of local government a certain amount of cooperation between the Socialist and Centre parties became possible. These developments had as their background the rapid expansion of the country's economy, which was symbolized in 1957 by the signing of the Treaty of Rome, which gave Italy an important position in the new European Economic Community (EEC) and illustrated the degree of recovery achieved since the war.

the shift to the left in the 1960s The 1960s ushered in a decade of political and economic difficulties. The organization of the EEC itself, together with the fiercer climate of international competition, began to reveal weaknesses in Italy's export-led economic boom. Higher rates of employment meant that the low-wage policies that had nurtured the boom had to be abandoned in the face of mounting discontent, and the parties of the left increasingly gained support.

During the brief premiership of Fernando Tambroni in 1960, an attempt was made to find a new right-wing coalition, drawing on monarchists and neo-fascists. The venture seemed to point the way to an experiment in presidential government, and the resulting outcry led not only to Tambroni's fall but also to a series of attempts to find an 'opening to the left', a coalition based on the Christian Democrats that would include the left rather than the traditional centre and right. new liberalism of the Vatican after the election of Pope John XXIII in 1958, which made cooperation between clerical politicians and the Socialists a practical possibility. The spectacular economic growth of the 1950s had also converted many previous disciples of laissez-faire among the Christian Democrats, who were now ready to accept some degree of state planning and intervention.

The Christian Democrat Amintore *Fanfani guided the first move to the left in his coalition government of 1960–62, but in the attempt to find a programme acceptable to the Socialists he lost the support of sections of his own party. After heavy losses in the 1963 elections Fanfani stood down, but after a caretaker government the experiment was successfully resumed by Aldo *Moro (Christian Democrat prime minister December 1963–June 1968), who was able to obtain the support of Nenni's Socialist Party. The alliance was strained by the government's deflationary policies, and also by the revelation of a supposed conspiracy in which the Secret Service (SIFAR) was heavily implicated. This led to a further split within the Socialist Party and the formation of a Party of Proletarian Unity by Nenni's discontented followers.

In 1964 the divided Christian Democrats had been unable to decide on a candidate, and the Social Democrat, Giuseppe Saragat, was elected president. Despite its early promise the Moro coalition achieved little in the way of practical reforms, and the Socialists paid the price in the elections of 1968. A new centre–left coalition, including Republicans and various socialist groups, was formed by Mariano Rumor in December 1968, but it was unable to survive the violent outbursts of discontent amongst both students and industrial workers in the following year.

the South Tirol problem
A continuing problem has been the existence of non-Italian-speaking minorities, who number about 250,000. Some of these are the German-speaking people who live in the South Tirol, the area round Bolzano (Bozen) on the borders of Switzerland and Austria. After World War II many of these German-speakers demanded a severance of the ties with Italy; some hoped for an independent Tirolean state, others called for reunion with Austria. In an agreement to settle the issue in 1946, Austria acknowledged the existing Brenner frontier with Italy, and Italy in turn promised local self-government or autonomy within the framework of the Italian state for the province of Bolzano and the few mixed-language communes in the province of Trento to the south. After several years of tension in the province, including terrorist incidents in the early 1960s, the Italian and Austrian governments found a mutually acceptable policy that restored peace to the area.

the north–south divide The plight of southern Italy (the Mezzogiorno) has presented one of the most permanent and intractable problems since the formation of the Italian state in 1870. Existing poverty and backwardness in the south was further aggravated by the industrialization of the north in the late 19th century, and the reforms introduced by Giovanni Giolitti (prime minister several times in the late 19th and early 20th centuries) had little success. The massive wave of overseas emigration in the decade before 1914 provides an index of the deteriorating conditions in the south.

Despite early promises, however, the area was again neglected by the Fascist regime. After liberation in 1944 the south once again became the scene of bitter peasant risings and attempts to occupy uncultivated estates. De Gasperi's government in 1950 introduced agrarian reforms and established a special bank, the Cassa del Mezzogiorno, to encourage investment in the south. The renewed massive emigration of the 1950s and 1960s indicated that such measures were inadequate.

Other government plans to create incentives for investment in the south, the Vanoni Plan (1954) and the Pieraccini Plan (1965) were never implemented, and the Alfa Romeo factory built near Naples rapidly proved to be a costly blunder. The funds of the Cassa have often been directed to political, rather than economic, ends, and although some improvements have occurred, the gap between the north and south has tended to increase since the end of the war.

the turbulent 1970s Against a continuing background of unrest and violence, notably in the city of Reggio di Calabria, a new reforming ministry was formed by Emilio Colombo (July 1970–June 1971). The election of a new president, the Christian Democrat Giovanni Leone, in December 1971 was followed by a dissolution of parliament a year before the expiry of its term (for the first time in post-war Italy), and under the more conservative leadership of Giulio *Andreotti the Christian Democrats held up well in the ensuing elections.

In addition to industrial disputes and economic problems, Italian politics were dominated by two other issues in the earlier 1970s. In July 1970 the law creating new regional assemblies came into force, and the first elections to the regional councils were held. In general, support was shown for parties of the government coalition, but in the local elections of 1975 Italian politics received one of their sharpest jolts since the war when the Communists made landslide gains.

The second major issue was that of the referendum on the Divorce Bill introduced in 1970. The referendum was delayed until 1974, but the favourable vote was seen as a further blow to the traditional clerical parties and an indication of the Roman Catholic Church's declining influence in Italian politics.

In January 1976 Moro's coalition government resigned after the withdrawal of support by the Socialists. He formed a minority Christian Democrat administration in February, but lacking adequate support was forced to resign in April. In the June elections, the Communists greatly increased their share of the vote (receiving over 34% as against 27% in 1972). The Christian Democrats maintained their 38% share by taking votes from the extreme right and the smaller centre parties.

In the wake of their electoral success the Communists pressed for what they called the 'historic compromise', a broad-based government with representatives from the Christian Democratic, Socialist, and Communist parties, which would, in effect, be an alliance between Communism and Roman Catholicism. The Christian Democrats rejected this. Apart from a brief period in 1977–78, the other parties excluded the Communists from power-sharing, forcing them to join the opposition.

At the end of July 1976 Giulio Andreotti formed a government of

Christian Democrats, assured of the abstention of the Communist deputies, and the new government proceeded to introduce severe measures to cope with the continuing economic crisis. Andreotti continued as prime minister until 1979.

Political violence continued through this period. On the extreme left, the Red Brigade were responsible for a number of terrorist acts, including the kidnapping and shooting of former prime minister Aldo Moro in 1978. The Red Brigade were also initially thought to be responsible for the bombing of Bologna railway station in 1980, in which 82 people died, but this was later found to be the work of far-right elements.

Italy in the 1980s In 1980 the Socialists returned to share power with the Christian Democrats and Republicans and participated in a number of subsequent coalitions. In 1983, the leader of the Italian Socialist Party (PSI), Bettino *Craxi, became the republic's first Socialist prime minister, leading a coalition of Christian Democrats, Socialists, Republicans, Social Democrats, and Liberals. In the same year Italy played an important part in the multinational peacekeeping force in Beirut.

Under Craxi's government, which lasted until 1987, the state of the economy improved, although the north–south divide in productivity and prosperity persisted, despite attempts to increase investment in the south. Various short-lived coalition governments followed; in 1989, the veteran Giulio Andreotti put together a new coalition of Christian Democrats, Socialists, and minor parties.

the early 1990s In 1990 the Communist Party abandoned Marxism–Leninism and adopted the name Democratic Party of the Left (PDS). Its leader, Achille Occhetto, was elected secretary general of the renamed party. A referendum held in 1991 overwhelmingly approved reform

of the voting procedure in an attempt to eliminate electoral corruption and to reduce the political influence of the Mafia. The 1992 general election resulted in the ruling coalition losing its majority and the need for the Christian Democrats to forge a new alliance.

President Cossiga carried out his threat to resign if a new coalition was not formed within a reasonable time. The election of Oscar Luigi Scalfaro as president in May 1992 was followed in June by the swearing in of Giuliano Amato, leader of the PSI, as premier. In September 1992, after unprecedented currency speculation, the government devalued the lira and suspended its membership of the Exchange Rate Mechanism of the European Monetary System.

corruption scandals In February 1993, judges investigating Italy's corruption network accused PSI leader, Bettino Craxi, of involvement. He resigned the leadership and was succeeded by Giorgio Benvenutu. In March 1993 corruption investigations (Mani Puliti), instigated in 1992 by the crusading Milan magistrate Antonio di Pietro, revealed the extensive involvement of many of Italy's notable politicians, including seven-times prime minister, Giulio Andreotti, whose name was linked with Mafia leaders. In May 1993 parliament voted to retain former Socialist leader Bettino Craxi's immunity from prosecution on several charges of corruption, despite widespread criticism.

constitutional reform An April 1993 referendum showed 82.7% of the Italian people to be in favour of a new majority electoral system and a 'cleaner' democracy. Prime Minister Giuliano Amato announced his resignation, marking the start of a transition towards a Second Republic. Carlo Azeglio Ciampi, the Christian Democrat governor of the Bank of Italy, was asked to form a new government. In May, Giorgio Benvenutu was replaced as PSI leader by Ottaviano del Truro. Constitutional reform proposals were approved by parliament in August 1993.

Berlusconi's right-wing alliance, 1994 In January 1994 Ciampi resigned to make way for a general election. A number of new political parties subsequently formed, including the right-of-centre Forza Italia, transformed from a pressure group into a full-fledged political party under media magnate Silvio Berlusconi.

Despite fundamental differences in policy between the federalist Northern League (LN, or Lombardy League) and the neofascist National Alliance, the two parties joined forces with Berlusconi's Forza Italia to fight the March 1994 elections, winning a resounding victory. Berlusconi succeeded in forming a right-wing coalition government but, within months of assuming office, faced a crisis of confidence arising from alleged conflicts of interest between his business concerns and his national responsibilities. In December 1994, after his coalition lost its parliamentary majority, he resigned.

Dini's premiership, 1995–96 Lamberto Dini, a former banker and independent member of Berlusconi's administration, was chosen to form a new government in January 1995. He led a cabinet of nonelected technocrats and sought to reduce the budget deficit by reform of the state pension system, but was fiercely opposed by Berlusconi's Forza Italia and in October 1995 narrowly survived a no-confidence vote by agreeing to step down at the end of the year. Dini formally resigned in January 1996 but, after the failure of Antonio Maccanico to form a broad-based coalition on the instruction of President Scalfaro, continued as caretaker premier until the election in spring.

Prodi as prime minister In the general election of April 1996, the centre-left 'Olive Tree alliance'

emerged victorious with about 45% of the vote. Its leader, Romano Prodi, was appointed prime minister.

In the same month as the general election, former prime ministers Berlusconi, Craxi, and Andreotti, and former foreign minister Gianni de Michelis, former chief prosecutor Antonio di Pietro, together with fashion designers Giorgio Armani, Krizia, and Santo Versace were arraigned on corruption charges. Di Pietro was subsequently cleared of all allegations.

In September 1996, Northern League leader Umberto Bossi, blaming the southern states for Italy's economic decline, proposed an independent Republic of Padania to embrace the whole of northern Italy, including Milan, Florence, and Venice. In November 1996 the lira re-entered the Exchange Rate Mechanism of the European Monetary System. Di Pietro resigned from the Prodi government in November amid renewed allegations of corruption.

In January 1997 Berlusconi's brother, Paolo, was cleared of plotting against Antonio di Pietro. Prime Minister Prodi survived a no-confidence vote in parliament in April 1997, but resigned in October rather than suffer a 'no confidence' vote. There were immediate attempts to form a grand coalition, but later, with the promise of support from the Communists, Prodi agreed to continue. In December 1997 former prime minister Silvio Berlusconi was sentenced to 16 months' imprisonment for false accounting, but the sentence was immediately quashed; in the same month Prodi was cleared of corruption charges. In February 1998 former prime minister Berlusconi went on trial for alleged tax fraud and in July was given a 33-months' prison sentence for bribing tax officials.

In October 1998, the Olive Tree Alliance coalition government of Romano Prodi collapsed after its hard-left allies, the Refounded Communists, withdrew support and it was defeated on a confidence vote. The Refounded Communists' leader Massimo d'Alema put together a new coalition government. The coalition included Communists, Greens and the ex-Christian Democrats of Francesco Cossiga. Carlo Azeglio Ciampi remained as treasury minister.

d'Alema as prime minister In May 1999 Ciampi was elected president by MPs and regional representatives. He has never been affiliated to any party, and made it his mission to introduce the economic rigour and sacrifices required to meet the criteria for the single European currency.

Amid disputes with his coalition, Prime Minister Massimo d'Alema resigned in late December 1999, but two days later was asked to form another government, and presented a centre-left administration, excluding the three rebel parties that caused problems to his first government. When d'Alema's coalition was beaten in regional elections by a right-wing alliance led by former prime minister Silvio Berlusconi, Giuliano Amato was sworn in as prime minister of a centre-left coalition, Italy's 58th government since 1945.

Amato as prime minister Seven referendums held in Italy in late May 2000, including one that proposed abolishing proportional representation in parliamentary elections, were all declared to be invalid as only 32% of the electorate voted, far below the minimum 50% required to give force to the verdict.

In September, Amato surprisingly conceded leadership of the centre-left coalition in the next general election to Franceso Rutelli, the popular mayor of Rome.

Berlusconi returns to power In May 2001, the election was won by former prime minister Silvio Berlusconi, leading a centre-right coalition, who promised tax cuts to regenerate the economy. After a month of bitter wrangling with his allies, Berlusconi finally named his government in June. The National Alliance's Gianfranco Fini was named deputy prime minister, and Umberto Bossi, whose Northern League party until recently wanted an independent northern Italian state, was named Minister of Institutional Reform and Devolution. Giulio Tremonti, a former tax lawyer, took over as treasury minister, and Renato Ruggiero, a former head of the World Trade Organization (WTO), was put in charge of foreign affairs.

In a final report released in September 2001, an Italian parliamentary committee investigating allegations of brutality and disorganization by police during the Group of Eight (G8) summit in Genoa in July effectively absolved the police force.

In December, Berlusconi came under unprecedented pressure from the EU to accept proposals for a wide-ranging EU arrest warrant, which Italy alone was blocking on the grounds that fraud and corruption be removed from the list of crimes to which the warrant could be applied. The foreign minister, Renato Ruggiero, resigned on 5 January 2002 claiming his pro-European stance made him increasingly isolated within the government. Berlusconi took on the post himself two days later.

In March, Berlusconi urged trade unions to call off a planned general strike and to discuss controversial labour-law reforms. The plea followed the murder of Marco Biagi, the economic adviser to the government who had recommended the reforms which aimed to make it easier for employers to dismiss staff. The Brigate Rosse per la Costruzione del Partito Comunista Combattente (BR-PCC; Red Brigades for the Construction of the Fighting Communist Party) left-wing terrorist group claimed responsibility for Biagi's death. Despite the assassination and Berlusconi's plea, the trade-union confederation CGIL held a huge rally in Rome protesting against the proposals, and the country's three largest unions called a general strike just days later.

Iwo Jima, Battle of intense fighting between Japanese and US forces 19 February–17 March 1945 during World War II. In February 1945, US marines landed on the island of Iwo Jima, a Japanese air base, intending to use it to prepare for a planned final assault on mainland Japan. The 22,000 Japanese troops put up a fanatical resistance but the island was finally secured on 16 March. US casualties came to 6,891 killed and 18,700 wounded, while only 212 of the Japanese garrison survived.

Izetbegovic, Alija (1925–2003) Bosnia-Herzegovinan politician, president 1990–96 and member of the rotating three-person collective presidency 1996–2000. A lifelong opponent of communism, he founded the Stranka Demokratski Akcije (SDA; Party of Democratic Action) in 1990, ousting the communists in the multiparty elections that year. He represented the Bosnian Muslims on the rotating presidency agreed under the Dayton peace accord until his retirement in 2000.

J

Jackson, Jesse Louis (1941–) US Democratic politician, cleric, and campaigner for minority rights. He contested his party's 1984 and 1988 presidential nominations in an effort to increase voter registration and to put black issues on the national agenda. He is an eloquent public speaker, and in 1998 emerged as a spiritual adviser to President Bill Clinton. He withdrew from politics indefinitely after it emerged in January 2001 that he had fathered a child during an extramarital affair in 1998.

Jackson, Robert (Houghwout) (1892–1954) US Supreme Court justice. He served as counsel to the Bureau of Internal Revenue 1934–36 and to the Department of Justice 1936–40. He was US attorney general 1940–41 and served on the US Supreme Court 1941–54.

Jagan, Cheddi Berret (1918–1997) Guyanese left-wing politician, president 1992–97. With his wife, Janet Jagan, he co-founded the People's Progressive Party (PPA) in 1950, of which he was the leader, and was the first prime minister of British Guyana 1961–64. As presidential candidate in August 1992, he opposed privatization as leading to 'recolonization'. The PPA won a decisive victory, and Jagan became president (succeeding Desmond Hoyte). Vice-president Samuel Hinds succeeded to the presidency on Jagan's death, but in elections in December 1997, Jagan's wife, Janet, was elected as president.

Jakeš, Miloš (1922–) Czech communist politician, a member of the Politburo from 1981 and party leader 1987–89. A conservative, he supported the Soviet invasion of Czechoslovakia in 1968. He was forced to resign in November 1989 following a series of pro-democracy mass rallies.

Jamaica island in the Caribbean Sea, south of Cuba and west of Haiti.

Jameson, Leander Starr (1853–1917) Scottish colonial administrator, born in Edinburgh, Scotland. In South Africa, early in 1896, he led the **Jameson Raid** from Mafeking into the Transvaal to support the non-Boer colonists there, in an attempt to overthrow the government (for which he served some months in prison). Returning to South Africa, he succeeded Cecil *Rhodes as leader of the Progressive Party of Cape Colony, where he was prime minister 1904–08. He was made 1st baronet in 1911.

Janata Dal or **People's Party**, Indian centre-left coalition, formed in October 1988 under the leadership of V P *Singh and comprising the Janata, Lok Dal (B), Congress (S), and Jan Morcha parties. In a loose alliance with the Hindu fundamentalist Bharatiya Janata Party and the Communist Party of India, the Janata Dal was victorious in the November 1989 general election, taking power out of the hands of the Congress (I) Party. Following internal splits, its minority government fell in November 1990. Since 1992, several breakaway Janata Dal factions have been formed. The party has drawn particularly strong support from Hindu lower castes and, with its secular outlook, recently from Muslims. It formed the core of the new government of H D Deve Gowda in June 1996 and that of Inder Kumar Gujral in April 1997. In the 1998 general election the party formed part of the United Front, an alliance with regional parties, which lost much support and finished third in the hung parliament.

Japan country in northeast Asia, occupying a group of islands of which the four main ones are Hokkaido, Honshu, Kyushu, and Shikoku. Japan is situated between the Sea of Japan (to the west) and the north Pacific (to the east), east of North and South Korea.

government Japan's 1946 constitution, revised in 1994, was framed by the occupying Allied forces with the intention of creating a consensual, parliamentary form of government and avoiding an over-concentration of executive authority. The emperor, whose functions are purely ceremonial, is head of state. The Japanese parliament, the Diet (Kokkai), is a two-chamber body composed of a 252-member house of councillors and a 511-member house of representatives. The former chamber comprises 152 representatives elected from 47 prefectural constituencies by the 'limited-vote' system and 100 elected nationally by proportional representation. Each member serves a six-year term, the chamber being elected half at a time every three years. Representatives to the lower house are elected by universal suffrage for four-year terms, 300 from single-member constituencies and 200 by proportional representation in 11 regions throughout the country (this system, approved by parliament in 1994, replaced one under which representatives had been elected from large multi-member constituencies by the 'limited-vote' system). Many representatives are elected to the Diet from the bureaucracy. The house of representatives is the most powerful chamber, able to override (if a two-thirds majority is gained) vetoes on bills imposed by the house of councillors, and enjoying supremacy on financial questions. Legislative business is effected through a system of standing committees. Executive administration is entrusted to a prime minister, chosen by parliament, who selects a cabinet that is collectively responsible to parliament.

history For earlier Japanese history, see *Japan: history 1869–1912.

Japan in defeat The surrender of Japan at the end of World War II to the Allies – formally concluded on 2 September 1945 – marked the opening of a new epoch in the history of eastern Asia. For the preceding half century Japan had pursued a policy of militaristic expansionism. On the basis of unquestioning loyalty to the imperial throne, the whole nation had been taught to face any hardships that might be entailed in following the national destiny; the throne itself had been exalted from a temporal to a quasi-divine institution, and the servants of the throne down to the humblest private soldier had been encouraged to regard themselves as a race apart from the rest of humanity, participating in the godlike characteristics of emperor and nation.

Some of the hardline Japanese leaders sought suicide. Hajime Sugiyama, chief of the Japanese General Staff and minister of war in several crucial cabinets, committed suicide on 12 September, and Gen Hideki *Tojo tried to kill himself when US officers went to arrest him.

territorial losses After Japan's defeat, Korea was made independent, Manchuria and Formosa (Taiwan) were returned to China, and the Pacific islands mandated to Japan after World War I – the Caroline, Marshall, Mariana, and Palau islands – were placed by the United Nations (UN) under US trusteeship. It also lost some of its outlying islands to the USA and the USSR. It regained the Ryukyu Islands in 1972 and the Bonin and Volcano Islands in 1968 from the USA, but continues to agitate for the return from Russia of the Northern Territories (the islands of the Shikotan and Habomai group) and the southernmost Kuril Islands (Kunashiri and Etorofu).

Allied occupation and control An Allied control commission took charge of Japan itself, and

Gen Douglas *MacArthur, US supreme commander of the Allied forces of occupation (mostly consisting of US troops), had little difficulty in carrying out his instructions for the disarmament of Japan and for the destruction of its war potential both in the moral and material sphere. The land forces were disarmed and disbanded, all aircraft were confiscated, and the Japanese navy was virtually disbanded.

After the dissolution of the Imperial General Headquarters, and the arrest of many prominent individuals preparatory to their indictment as war criminals, came the entire control by Allied authorities of the commercial and industrial life of Japan. This involved the break-up of landlord holdings among peasant proprietors, and the diversion of productive capacity into a programme to provide the people with the necessaries of life. There was also a major 'democratization campaign', involving radical social and educational reform.

The speed of social reform, and especially the abolition of the Tokubetsu Koto Keisatsu, or special higher police (also known as *shiso keisatsu*, 'thought police'), in October 1945, led to the reconstruction of a Japanese government. The new administration gave an assurance that the political power of the military clique and of the bureaucrats of the old type had been broken, and that the aim of the administration was to inaugurate a regime in which policy would be determined by the will of the electorate.

Experience throughout 1946 showed that MacArthur could rely upon Japanese cooperation in the task of attempting to restore normal social and economic conditions in the chaos of the post-1945 period, when Japan experienced near-starvation, soaring inflation, innumerable strikes, and rampant criminality. Perhaps the greatest contrast with the Allied occupation of Germany was that, instead of being split up into administrative zones, Japan was administered as a whole by the single controlling authority, the Supreme Commander's Headquarters, working through the Japanese government, and in the provinces through the Allied Military Government, which, despite its name, was in fact entirely staffed by US personnel. After 1948 the occupation authorities enforced the deflationary Dodge Line, curbed labour excesses, and, following the victory of the Communists in China, made an about-turn in prodding the Japanese towards rearmament. Allied rule continued in Japan until April 1952.

the 1946 constitution A year after the surrender, the Japanese house of representatives in Tokyo adopted by an overwhelming majority a new draft constitution. This 'Peace Constitution' superseded the Meiji constitution of 1889. Based largely upon US ideas, the new constitution based the foundations of the state not upon divine mandate, but upon the will of the electorate. It restricted the functions of the emperor Hirohito (era name Showa), who renounced his claims to divinity and became a powerless figurehead ruler. Article IX of the constitution renounced warfare as an instrument of public policy and banned the maintenance of any armed forces by which war could be waged, although it implicitly reserved the right to maintain self-defence forces as authorized by the UN charter.

In the elections of April 1946, women voted for the first time in Japanese history, and there were 38 women among the candidates elected. The voting age had been reduced from 25 to 20.

reconstruction and Westernization Through all the vicissitudes of total defeat, total demilitarization, and total occupation, the Japanese succeeded in adhering to the three things considered essential to future reconstruction: the emperor system, the national structure of government, and the close-knit official bureaucratic machine (which had survived virtually intact, being essential for the efficient administration of the US occupation).

From the outbreak of the Korean War in 1950, reconstruction proceeded rapidly, and, with vast US financial aid, the re-industrialization of Japan was considerably accelerated. This new industrial revolution, unlike that of 50 years previously, brought a great improvement in living standards to the workers involved. A strong and now legalized trade-union movement helped to consolidate this.

The increased urbanization and Westernization of Japan brought with it some serious social problems, on a scale not hitherto encountered in Japan. Legalized abortion drastically reduced the birth rate, thus diminishing Japan's population problem, but raising the possibility of an acute labour shortage and imbalance of population in the future. The memories of Hiroshima and Nagasaki encouraged the growth of a strong pacifist movement among young Japanese intellectuals; this was fostered by the Japanese Communist Party, because of its anti-American implications.

In 1951 a peace treaty was signed in San Francisco, USA, between Japan and the representatives of 48 countries. In the same year a Security Treaty was signed with the USA that gave the USA the right to maintain troops and bases in Japan. Under the Mutual Defence Pact of 1954 the USA supplied most of the equipment needed by the Japanese armed forces, which had been revived by MacArthur as a 'national police reserve' (subsequently renamed 'self-defence force') in 1950, despite Communist and pacifist protests. With its military defence assured by the USA, Japan tended towards neutrality in foreign affairs.

Japan's growing prosperity led to a decline in Communist influence there after 1952, while a fusion of non-Communist left-wing groups resulted in increased political stability. In 1956 Japan became a member of the United Nations Organization. In 1959 the 'democratization' of the Japanese royal family was exemplified in the crown prince's marriage to a commoner. Anti-Americanism in Japan remained a powerful enough force to organize such violent demonstrations in Tokyo in 1960 that the Japanese government asked the US president Dwight Eisenhower to put off indefinitely his projected visit to Japan, as it could not guarantee his safety there.

Liberal Democratic hegemony

Post-war politics in Japan were dominated by the Liberal Democratic Party (LDP), formed in 1955 from the merger of existing pro-capitalist conservative parties and providing a regular succession of prime ministers. Real decision-making, however, centred around a broader, consensual grouping of politicians, senior civil servants, and directors of the major *keiretsu* (post-war finance and industrial houses, much less closely integrated than the former family-dominated *zaibatsu*). Through a paternalist, guided approach to economic development, epitomized by the operations of the Ministry for International Trade and Industry (MITI), the Japanese economy expanded dramatically during the 1950s and 1960s, with gross national product (GNP) increasing by 10% per year.

The LDP won the general election in November 1960, and was again returned to power in 1963. Despite the challenge from the left, which loomed large in the 1950s, the Liberal Democrats continued to hold a majority in the Diet, although in the 1974 house of councillors elections they were scarcely able to maintain their dominance.

The proposed extension, without revision, of the 1951 Security Treaty with the USA led to demonstrations and, in 1968–69, to attacks by the Red Army guerrilla organization protesting against US domination. In 1970 the crisis had been surmounted, partly because the government of Eisaku *Sato, who was prime minister 1964–72, had secured in 1969 a promise from the US president Richard Nixon that Okinawa would be restored to Japan in 1972. In 1972 Sato's successor, Kakuei *Tanaka, gained a similar success in foreign affairs by normalizing Japanese relations with Communist China in the wake of Nixon's visit to Beijing.

Over the next two years, economic difficulties and allegations of personal misconduct resulted in a loss of support for Tanaka's leadership, and he resigned in December 1974, being succeeded by Takeo Miki. The eruption in February 1976 of a scandal over huge bribes received from the US Lockheed corporation, and the subsequent arrest of Tanaka, had a serious effect on the political situation. A split developed within the LDP, and Miki was forced to resign following elections held on 5 December 1976, when the LDP won 249 seats, thus losing the overall majority that it had held since the merger of the two parties in 1955.

However, shortly after the elections the LDP re-established its majority by gaining the support of a sufficient number of independents, and an LDP government was formed under Takeo Fukuda. Elections to the house of councillors were held on 10 July 1977, the LDP gaining 63 of the 126 seats being contested.

reasons for conservative dominance Apart from the political skill of Liberal Democrat leaders there have been four basic factors that explain the conservative dominance in Japanese politics. One is the fragmentation of the opposition.

Not only did the Socialists split into two separate parties in 1960, but they failed to gain the expected support of the fast-growing urban proletariat. Much of this vote was won in the 1960s by the Komeito, the political arm of the new religious sect Soka Gakkai, and in the early 1970s by the dramatically revived Japan Communist Party.

Another factor was the distorted electoral system, which gave much greater weight to rural areas, where conservative support was strong, partly because the government assured farmers a high price for rice. In addition, to win elections in Japan has always been exceptionally costly, and massive support from business has given the Liberal Democrats a huge advantage over their opponents. Finally, and most important, Liberal Democratic rule witnessed unparalleled economic growth, averaging 10% a year in the two decades preceding 1973.

After the 1973 oil crisis, however, Japan experienced unaccustomed zero growth, but even before then, the need for some reconsideration of the single-minded pursuit of economic growth was being increasingly felt, for Japan was also being afflicted by environmental pollution to an unprecedented extent.

economic impact abroad Japanese economic growth was maintained during the 1970s, though at a reduced average annual rate for the decade of 4.5%, and the country made a major impact in the markets of North America and Europe as an exporter of electronics, machinery, and motor vehicles. This created resentment overseas as economic recession began to grip Europe and the USA, and led to calls for Japan to open up its internal market to foreign exporters and to assume a greater share of the defence burden for the Asia–Pacific region. During the premierships of Miki (1974–76), Fukuda (1976–78), Masayoshi Ohira (1978–80), and Zenko

Suzuki (1980–82), Japan resisted these pressures, and in 1976 the Japanese government placed a rigid limit of 1% of gross national product on military spending.

liberalization A review of policy was instituted by Prime Minister Yasuhiro *Nakasone, who assumed power in 1982. He favoured a strengthening of Japan's military capability, a re-evaluation of attitudes towards the country's past, and the introduction of a more liberal, open-market economic strategy at home. The yen was revalued in 1985.

Nakasone's policy departures were controversial and only partly implemented. However, he gained a landslide victory in the 1986 elections, and became the first prime minister since Sato (1964–72) to be re-elected by the LDP for more than one term. Before the defeat in 1987 of his plans for tax reform, Nakasone was able to select Noboru *Takeshita as his successor.

political scandals Takeshita continued Nakasone's domestic and foreign policies, introducing a 3% sales tax in 1988 and lowering income-tax levels to boost domestic consumption. The new sales tax was electorally unpopular, and the government's standing during 1988–89 was further undermined by revelations of insider share-dealing (the Recruit scandal), in which more than 40 senior LDP and opposition figures, including Takeshita, Nakasone, and the finance minister Kiichi Miyazawa, were implicated. Takeshita was forced to resign in June 1989.

This marked an inauspicious start to the new *Heisei* ('attaining peace') era proclaimed on the death in January 1989 of Hirohito and the accession of his son Akihito as emperor. The new prime minister Sosuke Uno, the former foreign minister, was dogged by a sex scandal and resigned after only 53 days in office. He was replaced by Toshiki Kaifu, a member of the LDP's small scandal-free Komoto faction. Elections in February 1990 were won by the LDP, but with large gains for the Japanese Socialist Party (JSP), led by Ms Takako Doi.

support for the Gulf Allies When another insider trading scandal emerged in the autumn of 1990, it was overshadowed by the crisis in the Gulf, caused by Iraq's annexation of Kuwait. Although Japan is constitutionally debarred from sending troops abroad, the Diet's refusal to pass a bill authorizing the sending of unarmed, non-combatant military personnel damaged Kaifu's standing. However, Japan pledged US$13 billion to support the US-led anti-Iraq coalition in the Gulf War. After the war, in 1991, Japan contributed over US$2.6 million towards the environmental cleanup, sent teams of experts to help repair desalination plants and remove oil spills, and donated US$110 million for the relief of the Kurds and other displaced people.

Miyazawa's troubled government In November 1991 Kaifu was succeeded as LDP leader, and hence prime minister, by Kiichi Miyazawa, whose government included a surprisingly large number of 'rehabilitated' members tainted by the Lockheed and Recruit scandals. During 1992 the Miyazawa government was rocked by a succession of damaging bribery and corruption scandals, the most serious being centred on the Tokyo Sagawa Kyubin company and its enormous political donations and links with organized crime. More than 100 politicians, a seventh of the Diet membership, were implicated, and in October it forced the resignation from the Diet of Shin Kanemaru (1914–), the LDP's deputy chair and most influential figure.

economic decline and recovery A precipitous fall in the stock market in the summer of 1992 was stopped short in September by an economic rescue package of 10.7 trillion yen

(US$87 billion), mainly in extra public spending. In 1993 Japan entered its worst recession of the post-war era. Despite record trade surpluses in 1992 and 1993, Japan remained in recession until the end of 1995. With annual GDP growth exceeding 5% in June 1996, the Bank of Japan officially announced the end of recession.

developments and events in 1993–94 Prime Minister Miyazawa dissolved parliament in June 1993 after losing a vote of confidence over proposed electoral reforms, and called a general election for July. In the meantime new parties were formed by dissidents from the LDP, among them Shinseito (Japan Renewal Party), led by Tsutomu Hata, and the Japan New Party (Nihon Shinto, JNP), led by Morohiro Hosokawa. The LDP failed to win an overall majority in the July elections, ending 38 years in power. Miyazawa resigned as LDP leader and was succeeded by Yohei Kono.

Morohiro Hosokawa of the JNP was chosen as prime minister in August 1993, at the head of a non-LDP coalition. In February 1994 Hosokawa secured parliamentary approval of a compromise political-reform package, aimed at curbing corruption. The reforms included restriction of political donations and restructuring of the system by which members of the chamber of deputies were elected. In April 1994 accusations of corruption forced Hosokawa's resignation. Tsutomu Hata of the Shinseito party was appointed to replace him but, within hours of taking office, the Social Democratic Party of Japan (SDPJ) withdrew their support, leaving him heading a minority coalition government.

An improbable 'grand coalition' was formed in June 1994, with the SDPJ's chairman Tomiichi Murayama serving as prime minister, and the LDP's president Yohei Kono as foreign minister and deputy prime minister. Passage of the final version of a long-debated political-reform package was achieved in November 1994. A new reform-orientated opposition grouping, Shinshinto (New Frontier Party, NFP), was formed in December 1994. Led by the popular former LDP premier Toshiki Kaifu, it comprised 214 Diet members and represented a serious electoral threat to the LDP.

developments and events in 1995 In January 1995 an earthquake hit the city of Kobe, claiming more than 4,000 lives. The government came under fire for its poor handling of the relief programme, and later made a public apology. Two months later a nerve-gas attack on the Tokyo subway, carried out by the Aum Shinriky religious sect, killed 10 people and injured 5,000. Throughout 1995 the political mood remained uncertain as the economy was afflicted by recession, and in July 1995 the SDPJ polled poorly in elections to the house of representatives. Murayama remained in power, and in August 1995 made a formal apology for Japanese atrocities during World War II. The populist-conservative trade and industry minister Ryutaro Hashimoto replaced Yohei Kono as LDP leader in September 1995, and in December Ichiro Ozawa became the new leader of Shinshinto, the main opposition party.

developments and events in 1996 Prime Minister Murayama resigned in January 1996 and was replaced by Ryutaro Hashimoto. In August 1996 the new Democratic Party of Japan (DPJ) was formed by dissidents from the right-of-centre Shinto Sakigate and SDPJ. A general election in October produced an inconclusive result and a minority LDP government was subsequently formed.

In September 1996, following an agreement by the USA in April to close a number of its military bases on Okinawa (leaving around 47,000 troops and a large air base), the islanders voted for a further large reduction of the US presence. The long-standing irritant of the US military presence had been compounded by a recent high-profile rape case involving three US personnel and a local teenage girl, the three men having been given jail terms in Japan in March 1996.

In December 1996, the former prime minister Tsutomu Hata, one of the leading figures in the opposition Shinshinto party, along with 12 lower-house deputies, left to form a new party, the Taiyoto (Sun Party). Hata had been critical of the forceful leadership style of Shinshinto president Ichiro Ozawa.

economy in the late 1990s
In January 1997 the new government of Ryutaro Hashimoto pledged a break from Japan's past policy of seeking to promote economic recovery through increased expenditure, and placed priority on reducing the budget deficit and overhauling the economic and social system. Previously, trade surpluses reached record levels in 1992 and 1993 but Japan remained in recession until the end of 1995. With annual GDP growth exceeding 5% in June 1996, the Bank of Japan officially announced the end of recession. However, in November 1997 the country faced its biggest corporate failure since the World War II, following the collapse of the country's fourth-largest stockbroker, Yamaichi Securities. Yamaichi announced that it was closing down with debts of about £15 billion. The brokerage employed 7,500 people at 117 domestic branches and more than 30 branches overseas.

Japanese authorities confirmed mid-June 1998 that the country's economy had plunged into recession. Markets throughout Asia slumped after Japan announced that output had fallen for the second consecutive quarter. Figures published in June showed that Japan's gross domestic product (GDP) had shrunk by 1.3% in the three months to the end of March 1998. Following a decline in the last quarter of 1997, it left Japan's GDP 0.7% lower than

a year before. It represented the first full-year decline since 1974, following the first shock of the oil crisis. Japan came under intense pressure in late June 1998 to get its economy in order to stop the Asian crisis from deepening and spreading to the West. After a disastrous performance by his Liberal Democratic Party in the upper house elections, Prime Minister Ryutaro Hashimoto announced his resignation on 13 July 1998. On 30 July Keizo Obuchi, who had been decisively elected leader of the Liberal Democratic Party on 24 July, was declared prime minister. The former prime minister, Kiichi Miyazawa, an economics expert, reluctantly agreed to become finance minister, at a time of mounting concern over the country's economic and financial condition. Obuchi led the largest faction within the LDP, the Keiseikai, which was seen as being still controlled from behind the scenes by the former prime minister, Noboru Takeshita.

The 1998 changes were seen as indicative, after a flirtation with reform, of a return to traditional factional politics within the LDP. In the economic sphere, it was expected that there would be renewed emphasis on expansion of public works programmes at a time when seven of the country's ten regions were in a slump.

parliamentary coalition The LDP entered into a coalition in mid-January 1999 with Ichiro Ozawa, who once forced it from office after 38 years in power. Prime Minister Keizo Obuchi announcement of the alliance between LDP and Ozawa's Liberal Party had followed two months of negotiations. The government's increased parliamentary presence would make it easier to avoid the parliamentary bickering that had held up important financial legislation during summer 1998.

In November 1998, the government unveiled a US$200 billion economic stimulus package, including US$70 billion for public works projects and US$50 billion in tax cuts, after the GDP shrank by 2% in 1998. Komei and Shinto Heiwa (New Peace Party) merged to form New Komeito, which, led by Takenori Kanzaki, was the second largest opposition force in the Diet (lower house), with 65 seats. Soka Gakkai, the wealthy lay Buddhist organization, withdrew its backing from the opposition Liberal Party.

In January 1999 Prime Minister Keizo Obuchi, of the LDP, effectively formed a coalition government with the opposition Liberal Party, led by the right-wing Ichiro Ozawa, which had 47 seats in the lower house. The Liberal Party deputy leader, Takeshi Noda, was brought into the cabinet. However, the government lacked a majority in the upper house, and suffered pressure from opposition parties who threatened to boycott parliament in protest against the government's forcing through legislation to reduce the number of seats elected by proportional representation, which would benefit larger political parties.

In early April 2000, Prime Minister Obuchi suffered a sudden stroke, generally blamed on the punishing work schedule he adopted, and lapsed into a coma. Yoshiro Mori, the secretary-general of the ruling Liberal Democratic Party, was appointed as Japan's prime minister; Obuchi died six weeks later in mid-May. In parliamentary elections in June 2000, the LDP lost its majority. However, Prime Minister Mori was able to remain in power because of support for his coalition partners, the Buddhist Komei-to (Clean Government Party), and the Hoshu-to (Conservative Party). Over the next six months, the stock market remained weak, Mori's poll ratings sank to a new low – below 10% at times – and three ministers resigned from the government amid a series of scandals. In January 2001, unemployment reached a post-war

high, and in March shares on Tokyo's stock market reached a 16-year low. The drop was caused partly by the ongoing crisis in the Japanese government, and partly in response to a sharp overnight fall in the US stock market.

Japanese trawler sunk by US submarine In February 2001, a Japanese fishing trawler was sunk by a US submarine, drowning nine people. The accident, which occurred nine miles off Pearl Harbour in the Pacific Ocean, was caused by the submarine's sonar operator not seeing the trawler. He admitted that his work had been hindered by the civilians who had been on board the vessel.

Mori resigns Prime Minister Mori resigned in mid-April 2001 as Japan's financial crisis continued. He was replaced by Junichiro Koizumi. Makiko Tanaka became foreign minister, and Masajuro Shiokawa became finance minister. Koizumi pledged to push through market-centred reforms, including privatization, deregulation, and reform of the banking system, to help revive the economy. In July, the LDP coalition retained its majority in elections to the upper house of parliament. The result was widely ascribed to Prime Minister Koizumi's personal popularity – before his election as party president, the party had looked certain to lose.

diplomatic tensions with USA Relations between Japan and the USA were strained in July 2001 by a delay in handing over to the Japanese authorities a US pilot suspected of raping a Japanese woman in Chatan, Okinawa. The attack had threatened to overshadow a meeting at Camp David, Maryland, between US president George W Bush and the Japanese prime minister, Junichiro Koizumi, and prompted renewed calls for a reduction in the numbers of US troops on the island of Okinawa.

BSE A case of bovine spongiform encephalopathy (BSE), or mad cow disease, was reported in mid-

September 2001 on a farm in Chiba, near Tokyo. It was the first Asian case of the disease, and China, South Korea, and Malaysia immediately banned the import of Japanese beef.

In October 2001, Prime Minister Koizumi apologized for South Korean suffering during his country's occupation of the peninsula in World War II.

Makiko Tanaka, Japan's first female foreign minister, was abruptly sacked in January 2002, days after publicly breaking down in tears over a long-running feud with her own civil servants. On 1 February, Prime Minister Koizumi moved quickly to halt criticism of his decision to fire Tanaka by replacing her with another woman, former environment minister Yoriko Kawaguchi, and vowing to push ahead with economic reforms. In April, Koichi Kato, an ally of Koizumi, resigned from parliament over allegations of misuse of campaign money. The departure of Kato, a powerful former cabinet minister long seen as a future prime minister, was seen as damaging to Koizumi. This was reflected in opinion polls showing that the prime minister's public support had fallen from a peak of 90% when he first took office, to under 50%.

Japan: history 1869–1912 The period 1869 to 1912 is also known as the Meiji era. Following the restoration of imperial power under Emperor Mutshohito *Meiji in 1869, Japan entered a rapid period of Westernization, modernization, and industrialization. By the early years of the 20th century, Japan had become a power capable of defeating Russia.

Jarrow Crusade in Britain, march in 1936 from Jarrow to London, protesting at the high level of unemployment following the closure of Palmer's shipyard in the town.

Jaruzelski, Wojciech Witold (1923–) Polish army general, appointed first secretary of the Polish United Workers Party (PUWP) in 1981. He was responsible for the imposition of martial law in Poland in December 1981. He was prime minister 1981–85 and president 1985–90. During martial law he attempted to suppress the *Solidarity trade union, interning its leaders and political dissidents. In 1989 he approved the 'Round Table' talks with the opposition that led to partially free parliamentary elections and to the appointment of a coalition government under a noncommunist prime minister, Tadeusz Mazowiecki.

Jaurès, (Auguste Marie Joseph) Jean (Léon) (1859–1914) French socialist politician. He was considered a commanding intellectual presence within the socialist movement in France, through his writings (which included a magisterial social history of the French revolution), his oratory, and his journalism. In the decade leading up to the outbreak of World War I, Jaurès' impassioned opposition to the rising tide of militarism in Europe brought him centre stage within the Second International.

Jawara, Dawda Kairaba (1924–) Gambian politician, prime minister 1965–70 and president 1970–94. After entering politics in 1960 he progressed rapidly, becoming minister of education and then premier in 1962. Following full independence within the Commonwealth in 1965 he became prime minister and, with the adoption of republican status in 1970, he assumed the presidency. An abortive coup against him in 1981 was thwarted by Senegalese troops bringing the two countries closer together into the Senegambia confederation of 1982–89. He lost power in 1994 following a military coup.

Jayawardene, Junius Richard (1906–1996) Sri Lankan politician. Leader of the United Nationalist Party from 1973, he became prime minister in 1977 and the country's first president 1978–88. Jayawardene embarked on a free-market economic strategy, but was confronted with increasing Tamil–Sinhalese ethnic unrest, forcing the imposition of a state of emergency in 1983.

Jellicoe, John Rushworth (1859–1935) **1st Earl Jellicoe**, British admiral who commanded the Grand Fleet 1914–16 during World War I; the only action he fought was the inconclusive battle of *Jutland. He was First Sea Lord 1916–17, when he failed to push the introduction of the convoy system to combat U-boat attacks. KCVO 1907, Viscount 1918, 1st Earl 1925.

Jenkins, (David) Clive (1926–1999) Welsh trade union leader. Jenkins was well known as a militant negotiator and a fluent controversialist, and as an advocate of British withdrawal from the European Economic Community. He was a member of the TUC (Trades Union Congress) General Council from 1974. He was a Metropolitan borough councillor (1954–60), editor of *Trade Union Affairs*, and author of several publications, including *The Kind of Laws the Unions Ought to Want* (1968), co-authored with J Mortimer, and *Computers and the Unions* (1978), co-authored with Barrie Sherman.

Jenkins, Roy Harris (1920–2003) **Baron Jenkins of Hillhead**, British politician, born in Monmouthshire, Wales. He became a Labour minister in 1964, was home secretary 1965–67 and 1974–76, and chancellor of the Exchequer 1967–70. He was president of the European Commission 1977–81. In 1981 he became one of the founders of the Social Democratic Party and was elected as an SDP MP in 1982, but lost his seat in 1987. In the same year, he was elected chancellor of Oxford University and made a life peer. In 1997 he was appointed head of a commission, set up by the Labour government, to recommend, in 1998, a new voting system for elections to Parliament.

Jesuit or **the Society of Jesus**, member of the largest and most influential Roman Catholic religious order founded by Ignatius Loyola in 1534, with the aims of protecting Catholicism against the Reformation and carrying out missionary work. During the 16th and 17th centuries Jesuits took a leading role in the Counter-Reformation, the defence of Catholicism against Protestantism – many, for instance, came to England to work to undermine the Elizabethan religious settlement. Others worked as missionaries in Japan, China, Paraguay, and among the North American Indians. The order had (1991) about 29,000 members (15,000 priests plus students and lay members). There are Jesuit schools and universities.

history The Society of Jesus received papal approval in 1540. Its main objects were defined as educational work, the suppression of heresy, and missionary work among nonbelievers (its members were not confined to monasteries). Loyola infused into the order a spirit of military discipline, with long and arduous training. Their political influence resulted in their expulsion during 1759–68 from Portugal, France, and Spain, and suppression by Pope Clement XIV in 1773. The order was revived by Pius VII in 1814, but has since been expelled from many of the countries of Europe and the Americas, and John Paul II criticized the Jesuits in 1981 for supporting revolution in South America. Their head (general) is known as the 'Black Pope' from the colour of his cassock; Pieter-Hans Kolvenbach was elected general in 1983.

Jewish Agency administrative body created by the British mandate power in Palestine in 1929 to oversee the Jewish population and immigration. In 1948 it took over as the government of an independent Israel.

Jiang Jie Shi (or Chiang Kai-shek) (1887–1975) Chinese nationalist Kuomintang (*Guomindang) general and politician, president of China 1928–31 and 1943–49, and of *Taiwan from 1949, where he set up a US-supported right-wing government on his expulsion from the mainland by the communist forces.

Jiang Qing (or Chiang Ching) (1914–1991) Chinese communist politician, third wife of the party leader *Mao Zedong. In 1960 she became minister for culture, and played a key role in the 1966–69 *Cultural Revolution as the leading member of the Shanghai-based *Gang of Four, who attempted to seize power in 1976. She was imprisoned in 1981.

Jiang Zemin (1926–) Chinese communist politician, leader of the Chinese Communist Party (CCP) 1989–2002 and state president 1993–2003. He succeeded *Zhao Ziyang as Communist Party leader after the *Tiananmen Square massacre of 1989, and during the next decade he steered a middle course of market-centred economic reform while maintaining the CCP's monopoly of political power. Chinese exports were heavily promoted and foreign investment was attracted, leading to significant economic growth but also growing corruption. Jiang stepped down as party leader in November 2002 and as state president in March 2003, but retained significant power as chairman of the central military commission, overseeing the armed forces.

Jim Crow laws laws designed to enforce racial segregation and deny black Americans their civil rights. These laws originated in the 1880s and were common in the southern USA until the 1960s. The US Supreme Court decision * *Plessy* v. *Ferguson* (1896) legitimized these laws by affirming segregation under the 'separate but equal' doctrine. Jim Crow laws were eroded by US Supreme Court decisions during the 1950s and 60s such as *Brown* v. *Board of Education* in 1954 – a landmark ruling which declared that segregation in schools was unconstitutional – and civil-rights legislation such as the Civil Rights Act 1964 and Voting Rights Act 1965. (See also *civil-rights movement.)

Jinnah, Muhammad Ali (1876–1948) Indian politician, Pakistan's first governor general from 1947. He was president of the *Muslim League in 1916 and 1934–48, and by 1940 was advocating the need for a separate state of Pakistan. At the 1946 conferences in London he insisted on the partition of British India into Hindu and Muslim states.

Jodl, Alfred (1890–1946) German general. In World War II he was in effect responsible for most German operations outside the USSR and he drew up the Nazi government's plan for the attack on Yugoslavia, Greece, and the USSR. In January 1945 he became Chief of Staff and headed the delegation that signed Germany's surrender in Reims 7 May 1945. He was tried for war crimes in Nuremberg 1945–46 and hanged.

Joffre, Joseph Jacques Césaire (1852–1931) Marshal of France during World War I. He was chief of general staff in 1911. The German invasion of Belgium in 1914 took him by surprise, but his stand at the First Battle of the *Marne resulted in his appointment as supreme commander of all the French armies in 1915. His failure to make adequate preparations at Verdun in 1916 and the military disasters on the *Somme led to his replacement by Nivelle in December 1916.

John, Patrick (1937–) Dominican centre-left politician, chief minister 1974–78 and prime minister 1978–80. Having succeeded Edward Le Blanc as chief minister, John led the Dominica Labour Party (DLP) to victory in 1975, and became the country's first prime minister after independence within the British Commonwealth was secured in 1978. His increasingly authoritarian style of government, which included attempts to restrict trade-union and media freedoms, led to violent demonstrations, and in 1980 he was obliged to resign. In 1985 he was found guilty of complicity in a plot to overthrow Prime Minister Eugenia

*Charles in 1981, and sentenced to 12-years' imprisonment.

Johnson, Amy (1903–1941) English aviator. She made a solo flight from England to Australia in 1930, in $9^1/_2$ days, and in 1932 made the fastest ever solo flight from England to Cape Town, South Africa. Her plane disappeared over the English Channel in World War II while she was serving with the Air Transport Auxiliary.

Johnson, Hiram Warren (1866–1945) US politician. He was the 'Bull Moose' party candidate for vice-president in Theodore Roosevelt's unsuccessful bid to regain the presidency in 1912. Elected to the Senate 1917, Johnson served there until his death. He was an unyielding isolationist, opposing US involvement in World War I as well as membership in the League of Nations and World Court.

Johnson, Lyndon Baines (1908–1973) 36th president of the USA 1963–69, a Democrat. He was a member of Congress 1937–49 and the Senate 1949–60. Born in Texas, he brought critical Southern support as J F Kennedy's vice-presidential running mate in 1960, and became president on Kennedy's assassination.

After Kennedy's assassination, Johnson successfully won congressional support for many of Kennedy's *New Frontier proposals, obtaining enactment of an \$11 billion tax cut, a sweeping Civil Rights Act, and an Economic Opportunity Act, all during 1964. He moved beyond the New Frontier to declare 'war on poverty' and outlined a vast programme of economic and social welfare legislation designed to create what he termed the 'Great Society' in his first State of the Union message of May 1964.

Jordan country in southwest Asia, bounded north by Syria, northeast by Iraq, east, southeast, and south by Saudi Arabia, south by the Gulf of Aqaba, and west by Israel.

government Jordan is a constitutional monarchy, with the king effectively head of state and government. The 1952 constitution, amended in 1974, 1976, and 1984, provides for a two-chamber national assembly comprising a 40-member senate, appointed by the king for an eight-year term (one-half rotating every four years), and an 80-member house of representatives (house of deputies), elected by universal suffrage for a four-year term. The house is subject to dissolution within that period. The king governs with the help of a council of ministers whom he appoints and who are responsible to the assembly. The prime minister is the most senior member of the council. Political parties were banned in 1963, partially restored in 1971, banned again in 1976, then finally legalized in 1992 (although they remain subject to government approval).

history The area forming the kingdom of Jordan was occupied by the independent Nabataeans from the 4th century BC and perhaps earlier, until AD 106 when it became part of the Roman province of Arabia. It was included in the Crusaders' kingdom of Jerusalem 1099–1187. Palestine (partly in the disputed West Bank) and Transjordan (the present-day East Bank) were part of the Turkish Ottoman Empire until its dissolution after World War I. Both were then placed under British administration by the League of Nations.

end of British mandates Transjordan acquired greater control of its own affairs than Palestine and separated from it in 1923, achieving full independence when the British mandate expired in 1946. The mandate for Palestine ran out in 1948, whereupon Jewish leaders claimed it for a new state of Israel. Israel was attacked by Arab nations and fought until a ceasefire was agreed in 1949. By then Transjordan forces had occupied part of Palestine to add to what they called the new state of

Jordan. The following year they annexed the West Bank. In 1952 Hussein ibn Tal Abdulla el Hashim came to the Jordanian throne at the age of 17 upon the mental incapacity of his father; he was officially made king in 1953. In 1958 Jordan and Iraq formed an Arab Federation, which ended five months later when the Iraqi monarchy was overthrown. In 1967, following the Six-Day War (see *Arab-Israeli Wars), Israelis captured the West Bank.

search for peace King Hussein survived many upheavals in his own country and neighbouring states, including attempts on his life, and kept control of Jordan's affairs as well as playing a central role in Middle East affairs. Relations with his neighbours fluctuated, but he was generally a moderating influence. After Israel's invasion of Lebanon in 1982, Hussein played a key role in attempts to bring peace to the area, establishing a relationship with *Palestine Liberation Organization (PLO) leader Yassir *Arafat. By 1984 the Arab world was split into two camps, with the moderates represented by Jordan, Egypt, and Arafat's PLO, and the militant radicals by Syria, Libya, and the rebel wing of the PLO. In 1985 Hussein and Arafat put together a framework for a Middle East peace settlement, to involve bringing together all interested parties, but Israel objected to the PLO being represented. Further progress was hampered by the PLO's alleged complicity in a number of guerrilla operations in that year. Hussein tried to revive the search for peace by secretly meeting the Israeli prime minister in France and persuading Yassir Arafat to renounce publicly PLO violence in territories not occupied by Israel.

greater democratization In response to mounting unrest within Jordan in 1989, Hussein promised greater democratization and elections to a new 80-member house of representatives were held. (From 1986, there had been in each chamber of parliament equal representation for the east and west (occupied) banks of the river Jordan, but in 1988 Hussein decided to relinquish authority of the West Bank and the number of seats were reduced.) Martial law (in force since 1967) was ended, and political parties legalized in 1992. Assembly elections in 1993 were won by deputies loyal to the king (mainly independents), with several leading Islamic fundamentalists failing to win back their seats.

moves towards peace Following the Iraqi invasion and annexation of Kuwait in August 1990, Hussein unsuccessfully attempted to act as a mediator. Meanwhile the United Nations' trade embargo on Iraq and the exodus of thousands of refugees into Jordan strained the country's resources. Jordan attended the historic Middle East peace conference in Spain in 1991. However, the king's image as a peace broker had been damaged by his support for Saddam Hussein and in 1993 he publicly distanced himself from the Iraqi leader. Later that year he concluded a 'common agenda' for peace with Israel. In January 1994 an economic cooperation pact was signed with the PLO, and in July a treaty with Israel to end the 46-year-old 'state of war' – as a precursor to serious boundary negotiations.

In February 1996 Abdul-Karim Kabariti was appointed prime minister. Widespread riots followed a steep rise in bread prices in August 1996. Pro-government candidates were successful in the November 1997 assembly elections. In August 1998 Fayez Tarawneh was appointed prime minister.

King Hussein in late January 1999 dismissed his brother as heir-apparent to the Hashemite throne, installing his eldest son, the 36-year-old half-English Prince Abdullah ibn Hussein, as crown prince. The move drew a mixed reaction from Jordanians, confused by the speed of the decision days after King Hussein returned from six months of cancer treatment in the USA.

The nation was united in mourning the death of King Hussein on 7 February 1999; his funeral was attended by hundreds of foreign dignitaries. Crown prince *Abdullah ibn Hussein succeeded his father and was sworn in by the Jordanian parliament in February. In the following month, King Abdullah II appointed an ally of his father, Abdul-Raouf Rawabdeh, prime minister. The new King Abdullah attained the rank of major-general in the army in 1998, and was also interested in economics and development issues.

In May 1999 King Abdullah held talks with Yassir Arafat to forge a united Arab position, before the renewal of peace negotiations with Israel. To the end of renewing Israeli peace talks, the offices of Hamas, the Palestinian Islamist movement in Jordan which opposes the Israeli-Palestinian peace process, were closed down by the Jordanian government. On his first visit to Israel, in April 2000, King Abdullah called for Jerusalem to be the joint capital of Israel and a future Palestine state. However, the main emphasis of the talks with Israeli Prime Minister Barak was on Israeli-Jordanian economic relations, especially water management.

In June 2000 King Abdullah dismissed the conservative prime minister, Abdul-Raouf Rawabdeh, and replaced him with Ali Abu al-Ragheb, a US-educated economist, and appointed more liberal members of parliament to work alongside him. The new prime minister was given the task of pushing through reforms which had been approved by the International Monetary Fund (IMF).

In April 2001, as a result of continuing economic and political stability, King Abdullah extended the term of the House of Representatives by two years.

Joseph, Keith Sinjohn (1918–1994) Baron Joseph, British Conservative politician. A barrister, he entered Parliament in 1956. He held ministerial posts in 1962–64, 1970–74, 1979–81, and was secretary of state for education and science 1981–86. He was made a life peer in 1987.

Jospin, Lionel Robert (1937–) French socialist politician, first secretary of the Socialist Party (PS) 1981–88 and 1995–97, then prime minister 1997–2002, under President Jacques *Chirac, heading a 'pluralist left' coalition with communist, green, and left-wing radical parties. A moderate within the PS, he was a close ally of François *Mitterrand. He retired from politics in May 2002, after being defeated in the first round of the presidential elections, finishing in third place behind the far-right extremist Jean-Marie *Le Pen.

Jouhaux, Léon Henri (1879–1954) French trade unionist, the most prominent non-communist trade-union leader in France in the 20th century. Jouhaux served as secretary general of the General Confederation of Labour (CGT) 1909–47 and played a key role in the negotiations with Léon *Blum's Popular Front government that gave French workers paid holidays and the 40-hour week. He was awarded the Nobel Prize for Peace in 1951 for his role as cofounder of the International Confederation of Free Labour Unions.

Joyce, William (1906–1946) Born in New York, son of a naturalized Irish-born American, he carried on fascist activity in the UK as a 'British subject'. During World War II he made propaganda broadcasts from Germany to the UK, his upper-class accent earning him the nickname **Lord Haw Haw**. He was hanged for treason.

Juan Carlos (1938–) King of Spain. The son of Don Juan, pretender to the Spanish throne, he married Princess Sofia, eldest daughter of King Paul of Greece, in 1962. In 1969 he was nominated by *Franco to succeed on the restoration of the monarchy intended to follow Franco's death; his father was excluded because of his known liberal views. Juan Carlos became king in 1975, and played a vital role in the smooth transition to democratic stability. He was instrumental in the defeat of an attempted military coup in 1981.

Juin, Alphonse Pierre (1888–1967) French general. A fellow-student of *de Gaulle at the St Cyr military academy, in World War II he was captured by the Germans May 1940. He was released July and offered the post of war minister in the *Vichy government. He refused and instead became commander-in-chief North Africa, succeeding General *Weygand. When the Allies invaded Africa 1942 he promptly joined them and later led French forces against the Germans in Tunisia and Italy. He became Chief of Staff of the Free French and took part in the liberation of France 1944. He was posthumously appointed Marshal of France by de Gaulle.

Juliana (1909–2004) Queen of the Netherlands 1948–80. The daughter of Queen Wilhelmina (1880–1962), she married Prince Bernhard of Lippe-Biesterfeld in 1937. She abdicated in 1980 and was succeeded by her daughter *Beatrix.

July Plot or **July Conspiracy**, in German history, an unsuccessful attempt to assassinate the dictator Adolf Hitler and overthrow the Nazi regime on 20 July 1944. Colonel von *Stauffenberg planted a bomb in a briefcase under the conference table at Hitler's headquarters at Rastenburg, East Prussia. Believing that Hitler had been killed, Stauffenberg flew to Berlin to join Field Marshal von Witzleben and General von Beck to proclaim a government headed by resistance leader and former lord mayor of Leipzig Carl Goerdeler. However, in his absence someone moved the briefcase, so Hitler was only slightly injured, though five senior officers

were killed. Telephone communications remained intact, counter measures were taken in Berlin by Major Otto Ernst Remer (1912–97), and the conspirators fumbled their coup attempt. Reprisals were savage: the conspirators and their sympathizers were given the choice of committing suicide or being hanged. At least 250 officers died this way, including Field Marshal *Rommel, and some 10,000 people were sent to concentration camps.

Jumblatt, Walid (1949–) Lebanese Druze Muslim politician. His charismatic father, Kamal, was founder of the Progressive Socialist Party (PSP) in 1949, and he became PSP leader in March 1977 after Kamal's assassination and subsequently played an important role in Lebanese politics. He made strategic alliances with Syria and with the moderate Shia Amal militia of Nabih Berri in defence of the semi-autonomous Druze enclave against encroaching Maronite Christian forces.

junta (Spanish **'council'**) the military rulers of a country, especially after an army takeover, as in Turkey in 1980. Other examples include Argentina, under Juan Perón and his successors; Chile, under Augusto Pinochet; Paraguay, under Alfredo Stroessner; Peru, under Manuel Odría; Uruguay, under Juan Bordaberry, and Myanmar since 1988. Juntas rarely remain collective bodies, eventually becoming dominated by one member.

Juppé, Alain Marie (1945–) French neo-Gaullist politician, foreign minister 1993–95 and prime minister 1995–97. In 1976, as a close lieutenant of Jacques Chirac, he helped to found the right-of-centre Rally for the Republic (RPR) party, of which he later became secretary general, then president. He was appointed premier by newly-elected president Chirac in May 1995 but, within months, found his position under threat as a result of a housing scandal. Opposition to his government's economic programme, particularly welfare cuts, provoked a general strike in November 1995.

Justo, Agustín Pedro (1876–1943)
Argentine military leader and president 1932–38. During his administration, economic and political problems, left over from the previous administrations, were rife. He was instrumental – along with his foreign minister, Carlos Saavedra Lamas – in ending the Chaco War between Bolivia and Paraguay 1932–35.

Jutland, Battle of   World War I naval battle between British and German forces on 31 May 1916, off the west coast of Jutland. Its outcome was indecisive, but the German fleet remained in port for the rest of the war.

K

Kabila, Laurent (Desiré) (1939–2001) Congolese soldier and politician, president of the Democratic Republic of Congo (formerly Zaire) 1997–2001. Opposed to the oppressive regime of President Mobutu, his Tutsi-led uprising was supported by the presidents of neighbouring Angola, Rwanda, and Uganda, becoming the Alliance of Democratic Forces for the Liberation of Congo (ADFL) from November 1996. The ADFL, led by Kabila, made rapid advances westwards from the Great Lakes region, reaching the outskirts of the capital, Kinshasa, in May 1997. After President Mandela of South Africa failed to broker a political agreement Mobutu fled the country, and Kabila declared himself president. In August 1998 Rwanda and Uganda supported the launch of the Congolese Assembly for Democracy (RCD), a rebel offensive against Kabila, but Angola and Zimbabwe maintained their backing for the president. He was assassinated in January 2001, allegedly by one of his bodyguards. He was succeeded by his son, Joseph.

Kádár, János (1912–1989) Hungarian communist leader, in power 1956–88, after suppressing the national uprising. As leader of the Hungarian Socialist Workers' Party (HSWP) and prime minister 1956–58 and 1961–65, Kádár introduced a series of market-socialist economic reforms, while retaining cordial political relations with the USSR.

Kaganovich, Lazar Moiseevich (1893–1991) Soviet politician who was in charge of the enforced collectivization of agriculture in 1929–34, and played a prominent role in the purges of the Communist Party carried out under Joseph Stalin in the 1930s. He was minister of transport 1935–44, and the Moscow metro underground system was built under his direction.

Kalinin, Mikhail Ivanovich (1875–1946) Soviet politician, founder of the newspaper *Pravda*. He was prominent in the 1917 October Revolution, and in 1919 became head of state (president of the Central Executive Committee of the Soviet government) until 1937, then president of the Presidium of the Supreme Soviet until 1946.

Kamenev, Lev Borisovich (1883–1936) born **Lev Borisovich Rosenfeld**, Russian leader of the Bolshevik movement after 1917 who, with Stalin and Zinovyev, formed a ruling triumvirate in the USSR after Lenin's death in 1924. His alignment with the Trotskyists led to his dismissal from office and from the Communist Party by Stalin in 1926. Arrested in 1934 after Kirov's assassination, Kamenev was secretly tried and sentenced, then retried, condemned, and shot in 1936 for allegedly plotting to murder Stalin.

Kang Sheng (or K'ang Sheng) (1899–1975) Chinese politician. A prominent member of the Communist Party during the 1960s, he exercised considerable influence behind the scenes in his capacity as head of party security. During the Cultural Revolution he was associated with the radical left group led by Mao Zedong's wife, *Jiang Qing. Since Mao's death in 1976, Kang's role in the persecution of party members and intellectuals during the Cultural Revolution has been condemned.

KANU acronym for **Kenya African National Union**, political party founded in 1944 and led by Jomo

*Kenyatta from 1947, when it was the Kenya African Union (KAU); it became KANU on independence in 1964. The party formed Kenyatta's political power base in 1963 when he became prime minister; in 1964 he became the first president of Kenya. KANU was the sole political party 1982–91.

It secured an overwhelming majority in multiparty elections in 1993, but opposition parties disputed the results and their claims of malpractices were partly supported by independent Commonwealth observers.

Karadzic, Radovan (1945–) Montenegrin-born leader of the Bosnian Serbs' unofficial government 1992–96. He co-founded and became president of the Serbian Democratic Party of Bosnia-Herzegovina (SDS-BH) in 1990 and called for a single country that would unite all ethnic Serbs. In 1992 he launched the siege of Sarajevo, plunging the country into a prolonged and bloody civil war. He pursued a ruthless military campaign that involved *ethnic cleansing of tens of thousands of Bosnian Muslims to create 'pure' Serb areas. In 1995 he was charged with genocide and crimes against humanity by the Yugoslav War Crimes Tribunal in The Hague, Netherlands, but he continued to evade arrest.

Karamanlis, Constantinos (1907–1998) Greek politician of the New Democracy Party. A lawyer and an anticommunist, he was prime minister 1955–58, 1958–61, and 1961–63 (when he went into self-imposed exile because of a military coup). He was recalled as prime minister on the fall of the regime of the 'colonels' in July 1974, and was president 1980–85.

Karami, Rashid (1921–1987) Lebanese politician, prime minister of Lebanon 1955–56, 1958–60, 1961–64, and five times subsequently between 1965 and 1976. His final term of office began in 1984. Karami was a member of the predominantly Muslim National Front, but tried to ensure stability for

Lebanon by sharing power with representatives of the Maronite Christian community. To this end, he headed a coalition government formed by the Christian president Amin *Gemayel in 1984, which it was hoped would end the country's bitter civil war, but was assassinated three years later.

Karmal, Babrak (1929–1996) Afghani communist politician, president 1979–86. In 1965 he formed the People's Democratic Party of Afghanistan (PDPA). As president, with Soviet backing, he sought to broaden the appeal of the PDPA but encountered wide resistance from the Mujahedin (Muslim guerrillas).

Kasavubu, Joseph (1910–1969) Congolese politician, first president of the Republic of Congo 1960–65. After winning a power struggle with prime minister Patrice *Lumumba when the Congo gained independence from Belgium, he fought off a challenge from Sese Seko *Mobutu in the ensuing civil war. However, he was later ousted by Mobutu in a coup in November 1965.

Kashmir former part of Jammu state in the north of British India with a largely Muslim population, ruled by a Hindu maharajah, who joined it to the republic of India in 1947. Fighting took place between the pro-India Hindu ruling class and the pro-Pakistan Muslim majority involving Indian and Pakistani troops, until a UN ceasefire was agreed on 30 October 1948. There was open war between the two countries 1965–66 and 1971. It is today divided under the terms of the 1972 Simla Agreement between the Pakistani area of Kashmir and the Indian state of Jammu and Kashmir. Since 1990 it has been riven by Muslim separatist violence, with more than 150,000 Indian troops deployed in Kashmir in 1993. These were criticized by human-rights groups for torture, rape, and killing. Estimates of casualties 1990–93 range from 8,000 to

20,000. Separatist violence escalated during 1995 and several Westerners were taken hostage, with one being killed by the militant separatist group Al-Faran. The main political party in Jammu and Kashmir, the separatist Jammu and Kashmir Liberation Front (JKLF), is divided into Indian- and Pakistan-based factions. In October 1996 the National Congress Party, which aims to retain the area within India, won the first local elections to be held since the separatist violence broke out in 1990. In September 1997 cross-border shelling by Pakistani and Indian forces led to 50 deaths. More than 100 were killed in August 1998 in intensified shelling duels between India and Pakistan.

Katayama, Tetsu (1887–1978) Japanese politician. He headed a coalition government in 1947–48, becoming the country's first socialist prime minister. His government created a new ministry of labour, enacted an anti-monopoly law, and presided over the dissolution of the pre-war financial combines (zaibatsu), but became increasingly unpopular when economic crisis forced it to impose price and wage controls. After his resignation in 1948 he became identified with the party's right wing, and later, in 1950, helped to form the moderate Democratic Socialist Party, which supported the 1951 Security Treaty with the USA.

Kato, Taka-akira (1860–1926) Japanese politician, prime minister 1924–26. After a long political career with several terms as foreign minister, Kato led probably the most democratic and liberal regime of the Japanese Empire.

Katyn Forest forest near Smolensk, southwest of Moscow, Russia, where 4,500 Polish officer prisoners of war (captured in the German-Soviet partition of Poland 1940) were shot; 10,000 others were killed elsewhere. In 1989 the USSR accepted responsibility for the massacre.

Kaunda, Kenneth David (1924–) Zambian politician, president 1964–91. Imprisoned 1958–60 as founder of the Zambia African National Congress, in 1964 he became the first president of independent Zambia. In 1972 he introduced one-party rule. He supported the nationalist movement in Southern Rhodesia (now Zimbabwe) and survived a coup attempt in 1980. In 1990, widespread anti-government demonstrations forced him to accept a multiparty political system and he was defeated in multiparty elections in 1991 by Frederick Chiluba.

Kautsky, Karl Johann (1854–1938) German socialist theoretician who opposed the reformist ideas of Edouard Bernstein from within the Social Democratic Party. In spite of his Marxist ideas he remained in the party when its left wing broke away to form the German Communist Party (KPD).

Kawakami, Hajime (1879–1946) Japanese Marxist academic. As an economics professor at Kyoto University, Kawakami was the author of the best-selling *Tale of Poverty* (1916). He moved towards Marxism after the October Revolution and joined the underground Communist Party in 1932. Arrested in 1933, he was imprisoned until 1937.

Kazakhstan country in central Asia, bounded north by Russia, west by the Caspian Sea, east by China, and south by Turkmenistan, Uzbekistan, and Kyrgyzstan.

Keating, Paul John (1944–) Australian politician, Labor Party (ALP) leader, and prime minister 1991–96. As prime minister he introduced labour market and training reforms and historic indigenous legislation, which recognized the land rights of Australia's Aboriginal people, and focused Australia's foreign policy towards the Asian region. Viewed as the father of modern Australian republicanism, he set up a committee in 1993 to look at the changes needed for Australia to become a federal republic within a decade. He and his party lost the February 1996 general election to John Howard, leader of the Liberal Party.

Kefauver, (Carey) Estes (1903–1963) US Democratic politician. He served in the House of Representatives 1939–49 and in the Senate 1949 until his death. He was an unsuccessful candidate for the Democratic presidential nomination in 1952 and 1956, losing to Adlai Stevenson both times.

Keita, Modibo (1915–1977) Mali politician, president of the Independent Republic of Mali 1960–68. A pan-Africanist (see *pan-Africanism) radical who was influenced by the Ghanaian leader Kwame *Nkrumah, he was deposed in a military coup led by Moussa Traore and imprisoned until his death.

Keitel, Wilhelm (1882–1946) German field marshal in World War II, chief of the supreme command from 1938 and Hitler's chief military adviser. He dictated the terms of the French armistice in 1940 and was a member of the court that sentenced many officers to death for their part in the *July Plot 1944. He signed Germany's unconditional surrender in Berlin on 8 May 1945. Tried at Nuremberg for war crimes, he was hanged.

Kekkonen, Urho Kaleva (1900–1986) Finnish politician, prime minister of Finland four times in the early 1950s and president 1956–81. An advocate of détente, he was the prime mover behind the *Helsinki Conference on European security (1975), an important superpower summit.

Kellogg–Briand Pact agreement negotiated in 1928 between the USA and France to renounce war and seek settlement of disputes by peaceful means. It took its name from the US secretary of state Frank B Kellogg (1856–1937) and the French foreign minister Aristide Briand. Most other nations subsequently signed. Some successes were achieved in settling South American disputes, but the pact

made no provision for measures against aggressors and became ineffective in the 1930s, with Japan in Manchuria, Italy in Ethiopia, and Hitler in central Europe.

Kelly, Petra (1947–1992) German politician and activist. She was a vigorous campaigner against nuclear power and other environmental issues and founded the German Green Party in 1972. She was a member of the Bundestag (parliament) 1983–90, but then fell out with her party.

Kennedy, Edward Moore ('Ted') (1932–) US Democratic politician. He aided his brothers John and Robert Kennedy in their presidential campaigns of 1960 and 1968, respectively, and entered politics as a senator for Massachusetts in 1962. He failed to gain the presidential nomination in 1980, largely because of questions about his delay in reporting a car crash at Chappaquiddick Island, near Cape Cod, Massachusetts, in 1969, in which his passenger, Mary Jo Kopechne, was drowned.

Kennedy, John F(itzgerald) ('Jack') (1917–1963) 35th president of the USA 1961–63, a Democrat; the first Roman Catholic and the youngest person to be elected president. In foreign policy he carried through the unsuccessful Bay of *Pigs invasion of Cuba, and secured the withdrawal of Soviet missiles from the island in 1962. His programme for reforms at home, called the *New Frontier, was posthumously executed by Lyndon Johnson. Kennedy was assassinated while on a visit to Dallas, Texas, on 22 November 1963. Lee Harvey Oswald (1939–1963), who was within a few days shot dead by Jack Ruby (1911–1967), was named as the assassin.

background The son of financier Joseph Kennedy, he was born in Brookline, Massachusetts, educated at Harvard and briefly at the London School of Economics, and served in the navy in the Pacific during World War II, winning the Purple Heart and the Navy and Marine Corps medal.

early political career After a brief career in journalism he was elected to the House of Representatives in 1946. At this point he was mainly concerned with domestic politics and showed few signs of the internationalism for which he later became famous. In 1952 he was elected to the Senate from Massachusetts, defeating Republican Henry Cabot Lodge, Jr, one of Eisenhower's leading supporters. In 1953 he married socialite Jacqueline Lee Bouvier (1929–1995).

presidential candidate Kennedy made his name as a supporter of civil-rights legislation and as a prominent internationalist, but his youth and his Roman Catholicism were considered serious barriers to the White House. His victory in all seven primaries that he entered, however, assured his place as Democratic candidate for the presidency in 1960. His programme was a radical one, covering promises to deal with both civil rights and social reform. On television Kennedy debated well against the Republican candidate Richard *Nixon, yet went on to win the presidency by one of the narrowest margins ever recorded.

presidency Critics suggest style was more important than substance in the Kennedy White House, but he inspired a generation of idealists and created an aura of positive activism. He brought academics and intellectuals to Washington as advisers, and his wit and charisma combined with political shrewdness disarmed many critics. His inaugural address, with its emphasis on the 'new frontier', was reminiscent of Franklin D Roosevelt. In fact Kennedy did not succeed in carrying through any major domestic legislation, though, with the aid of his brother Robert *Kennedy, who was attorney general, desegregation continued and the Civil Rights Bill was introduced. He created the *Peace Corps – volunteers who give various types of health, agricultural, and educational aid overseas – and he proposed the *Alliance for Progress for aid to Latin America.

foreign affairs It was in foreign affairs that Kennedy's presidency was most notable. Early in 1961 came the fiasco of the Bay of Pigs, which, though partially carried over from the previous administration, was undoubtedly Kennedy's responsibility. This was redeemed by his masterly handling of the *Cuban missile crisis in 1962, where his calm and firm approach had a prolonged effect on US–Soviet relations. The Nuclear *Test Ban Treaty of 1963 achieved a further lessening of tension. Kennedy's internationalism won him a popular European reputation not attained by any of his predecessors. He visited Western Europe in 1961 and 1963, and was tumultuously received on each occasion. The US involvement in the Vietnam War began during Kennedy's administration.

assassination On 22 November, while on a tour of Texas, Kennedy was shot while being driven through Dallas and died shortly afterwards. His presumed assassin, Lee Harvey Oswald, was himself shot on 24 November while under arrest. Kennedy's death caused worldwide grief and his funeral was attended by heads of state and their representatives from all over the world. He was buried in Arlington National Cemetery.

Kennedy, Joseph (Patrick) (1888–1969) US industrialist and diplomat. As ambassador to the UK 1937–40, he was a strong advocate of appeasement of Nazi Germany. He groomed each of his sons – Joseph Patrick Kennedy, Jr (1915–1944), John F *Kennedy, Robert *Kennedy, and Edward *Kennedy – for a career in politics.

Kennedy, Robert Francis (1925–1968) US Democratic politician and lawyer. He was presidential campaign manager for his brother John F *Kennedy in 1960, and as attorney general 1961–64 pursued a racket-busting policy and worked to enforce federal law in support of civil rights. He was assassinated during his campaign for the 1968 Democratic presidential nomination.

He was also a key aide to his brother. When John F Kennedy's successor, Lyndon Johnson, preferred Hubert H Humphrey for the 1964 vice-presidential nomination, Kennedy resigned as attorney general and was elected senator for New York. When running for president, he advocated social justice at home and an end to the Vietnam War. During a campaign stop in California, he was shot by Sirhan Bissara Sirhan (1944–).

Kent, Bruce (1929–) English peace campaigner who was general secretary of the Campaign for Nuclear Disarmament 1980–85. He has published numerous articles on disarmament, Christianity, and peace. He was a Catholic priest until 1987.

Kenya country in east Africa, bounded to the north by Sudan and Ethiopia, to the east by Somalia, to the southeast by the Indian Ocean, to the southwest by Tanzania, and to the west by Uganda.

Kenyatta, Jomo (c. 1894–1978) adopted name of Kamau Ngengi, Kenyan nationalist politician, prime minister from 1963, as well as the first president of Kenya from 1964 until his death. He led the Kenya African Union from 1947 (KANU from 1963) and was active in liberating Kenya from British rule.

A member of the Kikuyu ethnic group, Kenyatta was born near Fort Hall, son of a farmer. Brought up at a Church of Scotland mission, he joined the Kikuyu Central Association (KCA), devoted to recovery of Kikuyu lands from white settlers, and became its president. He spent some years in the UK, returning to Kenya in 1946. He became president of the Kenya African Union (successor to the banned KCA in 1947). In 1953 he was sentenced to seven years' imprisonment for his

management of the guerrilla organization *Mau Mau, though some doubt has been cast on his complicity. Released to exile in northern Kenya in 1958, he was allowed to return to Kikuyuland in 1961 and became prime minister in 1963 (also president from 1964) of independent Kenya. His slogans were *'Uhuru na moja'* (Freedom and unity) and *'Harambee'* (Let's get going).

Kerekou, Mathieu Ahmed (1933–) Benin socialist politician and soldier, president 1980–91 and from 1996. In 1972, while deputy head of the army, he led a coup to oust the ruling president and establish his own military government. He embarked on a programme of 'scientific socialism', changing the country's name to Benin to mark the change of direction. In 1987 he resigned from the army and confirmed a civilian administration. He was re-elected president in 1989, but lost to Nicéphore Soglo in the 1991 presidential elections. He won the 1996 presidential elections, despite claims of fraud, and was re-elected in 2001.

Kerensky, Alexandr Feodorovich (1881–1970) Russian revolutionary politician, prime minister of the second provisional government before its collapse in November 1917, during the *Russian Revolution. He was overthrown by the Bolshevik revolution and fled to France in 1918 and to the USA in 1940.

Kerr, John Robert (1914–1990) Australian lawyer who as governor general 1974–77 controversially dismissed the prime minister, Gough *Whitlam, and his government in 1975.

Kesselring, Albert (1885–1960) German field marshal in World War II, commander of the Luftwaffe (air force) 1939–40, during the invasions of Poland and the Low Countries and the early stages of the Battle of Britain. He later served under Field Marshal Rommel in North Africa, took command in Italy in 1943, and was commander-in-chief on the western front March in 1945. His death sentence for war crimes at the Nuremberg trials in 1947 was commuted to life imprisonment, but he was released in 1952.

KGB secret police of the USSR, the **Komitet Gosudarstvennoy Bezopasnosti** (Committee of State Security), which was in control of frontier and general security and the forced-labour system. KGB officers held key appointments in all fields of daily life, reporting to administration offices in every major town. On the demise of the USSR in 1991, the KGB was superseded by the Federal Counterintelligence Service, which was renamed the Federal Security Service (FSB) in April 1995, when its powers were expanded to enable it to combat corruption and organized crime, and to undertake foreign-intelligence gathering. Its main successor is the Russian Federal Security Service (FSB), which focuses on 'economic security' and combating foreign espionage.

Khaddhafi (or Gaddafi or Qaddafi), Moamer al- (1942–) Libyan revolutionary leader, in power since 1969. Charismatic and unpredictable, he set out to establish himself as leader of the Arab world. His sponsorship of anti-Western terrorist organizations and rebels in Chad the 1980s and 1990s, and attempts at territorial expansion, led to Libya's exclusion from the international community and to the imposition of international sanctions. However, from 1999 Khaddhafi sought to improve relations with the West and in 2003 Libya announced that it was giving up efforts to develop weapons of mass destruction.

Khaddhafi's complicity in international terrorism led to his country's diplomatic isolation in the 1980s and 1990s. In 1986 US president Ronald Reagan ordered the bombing of Khaddhafi's compound in Tripoli, after Libya was linked to a terrorist bombing in Berlin which killed a member of the US military. In 1992 UN air, arms, and oil equipment sanctions were imposed against Libya after Khaddhafi's refusal to allow extradition of two suspects in the 1988 Lockerbie and 1989 Union de Transports Aériens bombings. With growing economic problems at home and anxious to modernize Libya's oil industry, from the late 1990s Khaddhafi sought to mend fences with the West. In 1999 the two Lockerbie suspects were handed over and UN sanctions suspended. Their trial ended in January 2001, with one suspect convicted and the other acquitted, and in September 2003 UN sanctions were lifted after Libya admitted responsibility for the Lockerbie bombing and agreed to pay $2 billion in compensation to the families of the Lockerbie victims. In 2000 Libya also mediated a hostage crisis in the Philippines, in which the Abu Sayyaf Muslim guerrillas kidnapped people of various nationalities who were holidaying in the area. Libya paid $24 million in ransom money for the remaining hostages in September 2000.

khaki election snap election in October 1900 called by the Conservative prime minister, the Earl of Salisbury, in the wake of British successes in the 2nd Boer War. Salisbury hoped to build on the public euphoria at the victories in South Africa to restore his government, but although he won a slightly increased majority he did not manage to make good the losses in his majority since 1895. It is called the 'khaki' election after the colour of the army's uniform in South Africa.

Khalid Ibn Abd al-Aziz (1913–1982) King of Saudi Arabia 1975–82. The fourth son of King Abdul Aziz *Ibn Saud, the founder of the Saudi dynasty, he succeeded to the throne in 1975 when his half-brother, King *Faisal, was assassinated. Khalid did not enjoy good health, and ruled for only seven years, during which time he effected moderate influence in

Middle Eastern politics. He was succeeded by his half-brother *Fahd.

Khama, Seretse (1921–1980)
Botswanan politician, prime minister of Bechuanaland in 1965, and first president of Botswana 1966–80. He founded the Bechuanaland Democratic Party in 1962 and led his country to independence in 1966. Botswana prospered under his leadership, both economically and politically, and he won every post-independence election until his death in July 1980. He was knighted in 1966.

Khamenei, Ayatollah Said Ali (1939–)
Iranian Muslim cleric and politician, president of Iran 1981–89 and Supreme Spiritual Leader from 1989. From the early 1960s Khamenei founded the Council of Militant Clerics and was an active supporter of Ayatollah Ruhollah *Khomeini's movement against Shah Reza Pahlavi. He was arrested in 1963 and detained in prison 1967–69 and 1974–75, before being exiled in 1977. After the revolution in 1979, Khamenei founded the Islamic Republican Party (IRP), which became the ruling party, and served as a Majlis (parliament) deputy, commander of the Revolutionary Guard, and deputy defence minister. Wounded in an assassination attempt in June 1981, four months later he was elected state president. He was re-elected in August 1985, defeating two opponents, but on Khomeini's death in June 1989, resigned to become the country's Supreme Spiritual Leader and was given the religious title of Ayatollah. Somewhat less extreme than his predecessor, Ayatollah Khamenei sought to 'unfreeze' relations with the USA and to improve an economy that had been shattered by the 1980–88 Iran–Iraq War.

Khan, Habibullah (1872–1919)
Afghan politician. He was emir of Afghanistan (1901–19). He renewed the arrangement with Britain by which the control of foreign relations was delegated to the British government.

He also supported Britain during World War I. He was assassinated.

Kharkov, Battle of in World War II, series of battles 1941–43 between Soviet and German forces over possession of Kharkov, the fourth most important city in the USSR, about 480 km/300 mi east of Kiev. The city changed hands several times before finally being recaptured by Soviet forces in August 1943.

khedive title granted by the Turkish sultan to his Egyptian viceroy in 1867, retained by succeeding rulers until 1914.

Khe Sanh in the Vietnam War, US Marine outpost near the Laotian border and just south of the demilitarized zone between North and South Vietnam. Garrisoned by 4,000 Marines, it was attacked unsuccessfully by 20,000 North Vietnamese troops 21 January–7 April 1968.

Khilafat movement campaign by Indian Muslims after World War I to protect the office of khalifa from abolition by the British, and to protest against partition of Turkey under the Treaty of Sèvres 1920, which was seen as an organized attempt to eliminate all centres of Muslim power. It was the only time that Muslims and Hindus united in active anti-British alliance. The khalifa was the religious and temporal head of the Sunni branch of Islam, and was situated in Constantinople.

Khmer Rouge communist movement in Cambodia (Kampuchea) formed in the 1960s. Controlling the country 1974–78, it was responsible for mass deportations and executions under the leadership of *Pol Pot. Since then it has conducted guerrilla warfare, and in 1991 gained representation in the governing body.

Khomeini, Ayatollah Ruhollah (1900–1989) Iranian Shiite Muslim leader. Exiled from 1964 for his opposition to Shah Pahlavi, he returned when the shah left the country in 1979, and established a fundamentalist Islamic republic.

His rule was marked by a protracted war with Iraq, and suppression of opposition within Iran, executing thousands of opponents.

Khrushchev, Nikita Sergeyevich (1894–1971) Soviet politician, secretary general of the Communist Party 1953–64, premier 1958–64. He emerged as leader from the power struggle following Stalin's death and was the first official to denounce Stalin, in 1956. His de-Stalinization programme gave rise to revolts in Poland and Hungary in 1956. Because of problems with the economy and foreign affairs (a breach with China in 1960; conflict with the USA in the *Cuban missile crisis of 1962), he was ousted by Leonid Brezhnev and Alexei Kosygin.

Born near Kursk, the son of a miner, Khrushchev fought in the post-Revolutionary civil war 1917–20, and in World War II organized the guerrilla defence of his native Ukraine. He denounced Stalinism in a secret session of the party in February 1956.

Many victims of the purges of the 1930s were either released or posthumously rehabilitated, but when Hungary revolted in October 1956 against Soviet domination, there was immediate Soviet intervention. In 1958 Khrushchev succeeded Bulganin as chair of the council of ministers (prime minister). His policy of competition with capitalism was successful in the space programme, which launched the world's first satellite (Sputnik). Because of the Cuban crisis and the personal feud with Mao Zedong that led to the Sino-Soviet split, he was compelled to resign in 1964, although by 1965 his reputation was to some extent officially restored. In April 1989 his 'secret speech' against Stalin in February 1956 was officially published for the first time.

Kiesinger, Kurt Georg (1904–1988) West German Christian Democrat politician. He succeeded Ludwig *Erhard as chancellor in 1966, heading a 'grand coalition' of the Christian Democrats (CDU) and the Social Democrats (SPD) until 1969, when Willy *Brandt took over as chancellor.

Kiev, Battle of in World War II, German victory August 1941 over Soviet forces. Kiev, the third-largest Soviet city at the time, remained in German hands until liberated by the 1st Ukrainian Front November 1943.

Kim Dae Jung (1924–) South Korean social-democratic politician, president from 1998. As a committed opponent of the regime of General Park Chung Hee, he suffered imprisonment and exile. He was awarded the Nobel Prize for Peace in 2000 for his work for peace and reconciliation with North Korea, and for his support of democracy and human rights in South Korea and East Asia.

Kim Il Sung (1912–1994) North Korean communist politician and marshal. He became prime minister in 1948 and led North Korea in the *Korean War 1950–53. He became president in 1972, retaining the presidency of the Communist Workers' party. He liked to be known as the 'Great Leader' and campaigned constantly for the reunification of Korea. His son **Kim Jong Il**, known as the 'Dear Leader', succeeded him.

Kim Jong Il (1942–) North Korean communist politician, national leader from 1994, when he succeeded his father, *Kim Il Sung in what was the first dynastic succession in the communist world. Despite his official designation 'Dear Leader', he lacked his father's charisma and did not automatically inherit the public adulation accorded to him. In October 1997 he formally became general secretary of the ruling communist party amid famine in North Korea.

King, Martin Luther, Jr (1929–1968) US civil-rights campaigner, black leader, and Baptist minister. He first came to national attention as leader of the Montgomery, Alabama, bus boycott of 1955–56, and was one of the organizers of the march of 200,000 people on Washington, DC in 1963 to demand racial equality, during which he delivered his famous 'I have a dream' speech. He was awarded the Nobel Prize for Peace in 1964 for his work as a civil-rights leader and an advocate of nonviolence. He was assassinated on 4 April 1968 in Memphis, Tennessee.

In 1957 King founded the Southern Christian Leadership Conference, a civil-rights organization. A charismatic and moving speaker, he was the leading figure in the campaign for integration and equal rights for black Americans in the late 1950s and early 1960s. In the mid-1960s his moderate approach was criticized by black militants. He was the target of intensive investigation by the federal authorities, chiefly the FBI under J Edgar Hoover. King's nonviolent campaign to end segregation drew national attention in 1963, when police turned dogs and fire hoses on demonstrators, many of whom were children, in Birmingham, Alabama. King was jailed along with large numbers of his supporters. His 'Letter from the Birmingham Jail' eloquently expressed his philosophy of nonviolent direct action.

By the mid-1960s, King's actions and those of civil-rights activists across the nation had led to significant achievements in equal rights, notably the Civil Rights Act 1964 and the Voting Rights Act 1965. In the late 1960s King turned his attention to promoting economic opportunities for minorities and the disadvantaged, and to protesting against the Vietnam War.

King, W(illiam) L(yon) Mackenzie (1874–1950) Canadian Liberal prime minister 1921–26, 1926–30, and 1935–48. He maintained the unity of the English- and French-speaking populations, and was instrumental in establishing equal status for Canada with the UK.

'King and Country' debate controversial debate in Britain in February 1933 in which the Oxford Union, the university's debating society, passed the motion 'this House will in no circumstances fight for its King and its Country'. The debate sent shockwaves throughout the country as many saw it as signalling that Britain's young elite had lost their sense of patriotism, although it probably more accurately reflected a commitment to disarmament after the horrors of World War I.

Kinnock, Neil Gordon (1942–) British Labour politician, party leader 1983–92 and European Union commissioner 1995–2004. As party leader, succeeding his ally Michael Foot, he moderated his strongly left-wing position and made Labour a centre-left mainstream party once again. He expelled members of the hard-left Militant Tendency and reversed policies on unilateral nuclear disarmament, withdrawal from the European Union, and large-scale nationalization that he had once advocated. He resigned as party leader after the 1992 general election defeat, and in 1995 became a European commissioner, with the transport portfolio. From 1999 to 2004 he was vice-president of the European Commission with responsibility for internal reform.

Kiowa (Kiowa *kai-gwa* **'principal people'**) member of an American Indian people who moved from the Rocky Mountains of Montana to the Great Plains of South Dakota in the 1600s. Their language belongs to the Kiowa-Tanoan family. Originally hunter-gatherers, they acquired horses and adopted the nomadic culture of the Plains Indians, hunting buffalo and raiding Spanish and Apache settlements as far south as Texas and Mexico. The Kiowa were one of the last Plains Indians to capitulate to the US government, after which they settled on reservations in Oklahoma. Today the Kiowa-Comanche-Apache Business Committee, a joint business corporation, manages Kiowan interests. The population is some 8,600 (2000).

Kiribati   republic in the west central
Pacific Ocean, comprising three groups
of coral atolls: the 16 Gilbert Islands,
8 uninhabited Phoenix Islands, 8 of the
11 Line Islands, and the volcanic island
of Banaba.

Kirk, Norman Eric (1923–1974)   New
Zealand Labour centre-left politician,
prime minister 1972–74. He withdrew
New Zealand troops from the Vietnam
War, attempted to block French nuclear
tests in the Pacific, and developed
closer ties with Australia, as a
counterbalance to UK's entry to the
European Economic Community
(EEC; now the European Union).
He died in office and was succeeded as
prime minister by his finance minister,
Wallace Rowling.

**Kirkpatrick, Jeane Duane Jordan
(1926–)**   US politician and professor
of political science. She served as
US ambassador to the United Nations
1981–85. Originally a Democrat, she
often spoke out against communism
and left-wing causes. She joined the
Republican Party 1985.

Kirov, Sergei Mironovich (1886–1934)
Russian Bolshevik leader who joined
the party in 1904 and played a
prominent part in the 1918–20 civil
war. As one of *Stalin's closest
associates, he became first secretary
of the Leningrad Communist Party.
His assassination, possibly engineered
by Stalin, led to the political trials held
during the next four years as part of
the *purge.

Kishi, Nobusuke (1896–1987)
Japanese right-wing politician and
prime minister 1957–60. A government
minister during World War II and
imprisoned in 1945, he was never put
on trial and returned to politics in
1953. During his premiership, Japan
began a substantial rearmament
programme and signed a security
treaty with the USA that gave rise
to massive protests both in the Diet
(parliament) and on the streets.

Kissinger, Henry (Alfred) (1923–)
German-born US diplomat. After
a brilliant academic career at Harvard
University, he was appointed national
security adviser in 1969 by President
Nixon, and was secretary of state
1973–77. His missions to the USSR
and China improved US relations with
both countries, and he took part in
negotiating US withdrawal from
Vietnam in 1973 and in Arab-Israeli
peace negotiations 1973–75. He shared
the Nobel Prize for Peace in 1973 with
North Vietnamese diplomat *Le Duc
Tho for their efforts in securing the
peace settlement of the Vietnam War.

His secret trips to Beijing and
Moscow led to Nixon's visits to both
countries and a general détente. In 1976
he was involved in the negotiations
in Africa arising from the Angola and
Rhodesia crises. In 1983, President
Reagan appointed him to head a
bipartisan commission on Central
America. He was widely regarded
as the most powerful member of
Nixon's administration.

Kita, Ikki (1883–1937)   Japanese
political activist whose convictions
were a mixture of socialism, anti-
Westernism. and nationalism. These
ideas influenced the young officers
who attempted an unsuccessful coup
against the government in February
1936. In the subsequent repression,
Kita was arrested and executed.

**Kleist, (Paul Ludwig) Ewald von
(1881–1954)**   German field marshal.
Commissioned into the cavalry 1902,
he was a lieutenant-general by 1935
and retired 1938. He was recalled 1939
and given command of XXII Army
Corps in Poland, then led Panzer
Group Kleist in France 1940. He then
led 1 Panzer Group in the Balkans and
1 Panzer Army in the invasion of the
USSR. Promoted to field marshal
November 1942, he commanded Army
Group A in the Ukraine. He retired for
the second time 30 March 1944, but
when the Soviets occupied Germany
he was captured and remained
a prisoner until he died.

Kluge, (Hans) Gunther von (1882–1944) German field marshal. He served in the invasions of Poland and France and was promoted to field marshal July 1940. He led 4th Army in the invasion of the USSR, later succeeding von Bock as commander of Army Group Centre. He replaced von *Rundstedt as commander-in-chief in the West July 1944, with orders to throw the Allies back into the sea. After the disaster at the Falaise Gap he was relieved and replaced by *Model. He was caught up in the aftermath of the failed *July Plot against Hitler, although not involved in it himself and was 'invited' to commit suicide.

Knox, Philander Chase (1853–1921) US lawyer, politician, and cabinet member. He practised industrial law in Pittsburgh, Pennsylvania (1877–99). As President William McKinley's attorney general (1901–04), he filed an antitrust suit that prevented J P Morgan's western railroad monopoly. A Republican serving Pennsylvania, he was a mid-term senator (1904–09). He became secretary of state (1909–13), initiating 'dollar diplomacy' to protect US investments overseas. He returned to the Senate (1917–21). Knox was born in Brownsville, Pennsylvania.

Kohima, Battle of one of the most savage battles of World War II, April–May 1944, as the Allied garrison at Kohima, a town in Manipur province, northeast India, repulsed a wave of Japanese attacks with severe casualties.

Kohl, Helmut (1930–) German conservative politician, leader of the Christian Democratic Union (CDU) 1976–98, West German chancellor (prime minister) 1982–90, and German chancellor from 1990–98. He oversaw the reunification of East and West Germany 1989–90 and in 1990 won a resounding victory to become the first chancellor of a reunited Germany. His miscalculation of the true costs of reunification and their subsequent effects on the German economy led to a dramatic fall in his popularity, but as the economy recovered, so did his public esteem, enabling him to achieve a historic fourth electoral victory in 1994. He was defeated by Gerhard Schroeder of the Social Democratic Party (SDP) in the elections of September 1998, a year in which unemployment reached record levels. In December 1999, Kohl admitted to receiving secret and therefore illegal payments on behalf of his party when he was chancellor, and he was fined 300,000 marks/US$143,000 in January 2001.

Kohl studied law and history before entering the chemical industry. Elected to the Rhineland-Palatinate *Land* (state) parliament in 1959, he became state premier in 1969. After the 1976 Bundestag (federal parliament) elections Kohl led the CDU in opposition. He became federal chancellor in 1982, when the Free Democratic Party (FDP) withdrew support from the socialist Schmidt government, and was elected at the head of a new coalition that included the FDP. His close working relationship with President Mitterrand of France was the foundation for accelerating progress towards closer European integration, and Kohl was a strong backer of the idea of a single European currency.

From 1984 Kohl was implicated in the Flick bribes scandal over the illegal business funding of political parties, but he was cleared of all charges in 1986. However, in December 1999 he admitted to keeping secret party bank accounts when he was chancellor. He refused to name the source of the illegal payments, which amounted to two million marks/US$950,000.

Koivisto, Mauno Henrik (1923–) Finnish politician, prime minister 1968–70 and 1979–82, and president 1982–94. He was finance minister 1966–67 and led a Social Democratic Party coalition as prime minister 1968–70. He became interim president in 1981 after the resignation of Urho

Kekkonen, and was elected president the following year. As president he shared power with Centre Party prime minister Esko Aho in Finland's unusual 'dual executive'.

Kolchak, Alexander Vasilievich (1874–1920) Russian admiral, commander of the White forces in Siberia after the Russian Revolution. He proclaimed himself Supreme Ruler of Russia in 1918, but was later handed over to the Bolsheviks by his own men and shot.

Komsomol Russian name for the All-Union Leninist Communist Youth League of the former Soviet Union. Founded in 1918, it acted as the youth section of the Communist Party.

Koniev, Ivan Stepanovich (1898–1973) Soviet marshal who in World War II liberated Ukraine from the invading German forces 1943–44 and then in 1945 advanced from the south on Berlin to link up with the British-US forces. He commanded all Warsaw Pact forces 1955–60.

Konoe, Fumimaro, Prince (1891–1945) Japanese politician and prime minister 1937–39 and 1940–41. He helped to engineer the fall of the *Tojo government in 1944 but committed suicide after being suspected of war crimes.

Koo, Vi Kyuin Wellington (1888–1985) Chinese Nationalist politician, and diplomat. Born in Shanghai, as Ku Wei-chun, he studied in the USA, at Columbia University. At the conclusion of World War I, Koo represented Republican China at the 1919 Paris Peace Conference and during the inter-war years served as foreign minister 1922–24 and 1931–32, and as finance minister 1926–27. Thereafter, as the Kuomintang (Guomindang, nationalist) regime which he supported was forced on the retreat, by the twin challenges of the communists and the Japanese, Koo concentrated on a diplomatic career.

Korean War war from 1950 to 1953 between *North Korea (supported by China) and *South Korea, aided by the United Nations (the troops were mainly US). North Korean forces invaded South Korea on 25 June 1950, and the Security Council of the United Nations, owing to a walk-out by the USSR, voted to oppose them. The North Koreans held most of the South when US reinforcements arrived in September 1950 and forced their way through to the North Korean border with China. The Chinese retaliated, pushing them back to the original boundary by October 1950; truce negotiations began in 1951, although the war did not end until 1953. The Korean War established that the USA was prepared to intervene militarily to stop the spread of *communism. After 1953 the Korean peninsula remained a *Cold War battleground.

By September 1950, the North Koreans had overrun most of the South, with the United Nations (UN) forces holding a small area, the Pusan perimeter, in the southeast. The course of the war changed after the surprise landing of US troops later the same month at Inchon on South Korea's northwest coast. The troops, led by General Douglas *MacArthur, fought their way through North Korea to the Chinese border in little over a month. On 25 October 1950, Chinese troops attacked across the Yalu River, driving the UN forces below the *38th parallel.

Truce talks began in July 1951, and the war ended two years later, with the restoration of the original boundary on the 38th parallel. The armistice was signed 27 July 1953 with North Korea, but South Korea did not participate, and a peace treaty did not follow.

Kornilov, Lavr Georgyevich (1870–1918) Russian general, commander-in-chief of the army, who in August 1917 launched an attempted coup, backed by officers, against the revolutionary prime minister, *Kerensky. The coup failed, but brought down the provisional government, clearing the way for the Bolsheviks to seize power.

Kosygin, Alexei Nikolaievich (1904–1980) Soviet politician, prime minister 1964–80. He was elected to the Supreme Soviet in 1938, became a member of the Politburo in 1946, deputy prime minister in 1960, and succeeded Khrushchev as premier (while Brezhnev succeeded him as party secretary). In the late 1960s Kosygin's influence declined.

Kotoku, Shusui (1871–1911) Japanese journalist and political activist. A prolific writer, Kotoku moved from social democracy to pacifism to anarchist communism. In 1903, just before the Russo–Japanese War of 1904–05, he launched the anti-war *Heimin Shinbun* (*Common People's Newspaper*). First imprisoned in 1905, he was arrested again in 1910 in the infamous High Treason Incident and executed in 1911.

Krasin, Leonid Borisovich (1870–1926) Russian Bolshevik politician and diplomat. An early confederate of *Lenin, he played a leading role in the Russian Revolution of 1905. Following the success of the 1917 October Revolution, he held various official appointments within the new Soviet Union, and helped normalize its relations with other countries.

Kreisky, Bruno (1911–1990) Austrian Social Democrat politician and diplomat, chancellor of Austria 1970–83. He headed Austria's first Socialist government since the war, and consolidated his position when the 1975 general election gave his party an absolute majority. He stepped down after being defeated in elections in 1983.

Krishna Menon, Vengalil Krishnan (1897–1974) Indian politician who was a leading light in the Indian nationalist movement. He represented India at the United Nations 1952–62, and was defence minister 1957–62, when he was dismissed by Nehru following China's invasion of northern India.

Kristallnacht ('night of (broken) glass') night of 9–10 November 1938 when the Nazi Sturmabteilung (SA) militia in Germany and Austria mounted a concerted attack on Jews, their synagogues, homes, and shops. It followed the assassination of a German embassy official in Paris by a Polish-Jewish youth. Subsequent measures included German legislation against Jews owning businesses or property, and restrictions on their going to school or leaving Germany. It was part of the *Holocaust.

Kronstadt uprising revolt in March 1921 by sailors of the Russian Baltic Fleet at their headquarters in Kronstadt, outside Petrograd (now St Petersburg). On the orders of the leading Bolshevik, Leon Trotsky, Red Army troops, dressed in white camouflage, crossed the ice to the naval base and captured it on 18 March. The leaders were subsequently shot.

Krueger, Walter (1881–1967) US general. After building his reputation as a trainer, he took command of 6th US Army in Australia 1943, under *MacArthur. He soon made it into a highly efficient force that served in New Guinea, New Britain, and the Admiralty Islands. He invaded the Philippines in October 1944, finally taking Manila after a month of house-to-house fighting.

Kubitschek, Juscelino (1902–1976) Brazilian president 1956–61. His term as president saw political peace, civil liberty, and rapid economic growth at the cost of high inflation and corruption. He had a strong commitment to public works and the construction of Brasília as the nation's capital.

Kucan, Milan (1941–) Slovene politician, president of Slovenia from 1990. He served as chair of the parliament 1978–86 and became chair of the communist party 1986–89. He became president of Slovenia in April 1990.

kulak Russian term for a peasant who could afford to hire labour and often acted as village usurer. The kulaks resisted the Soviet government's policy of collectivization, and in 1930 they were 'liquidated as a class', with up to 5 million being either killed or deported to Siberia.

Kun, Béla (1886–1937) Hungarian politician. He created a Soviet republic in Hungary in March 1919, which was overthrown in August 1919 by a Western blockade and Romanian military actions. The succeeding regime under Admiral *Horthy effectively liquidated both socialism and liberalism in Hungary.

Kunaev, Dimmukhamed Akhmedovich (1912–1993) Kazakh politician. He worked his way up the Kazakh party ladder in the 1940s and 1950s, coming into close contact with Leonid Brezhnev and being made first secretary in 1960. He was demoted by Nikita Khrushchev in 1962, but was reappointed in 1964 by Brezhnev, who also brought him into full membership of the Politburo. His dismissal by Mikhail Gorbachev in 1986 led to riots in Alma Ata, but these were countered by charges of extensive corruption.

K'ung, H H (or Hsiang-hsi) (1881–1967) Chinese politician and banker. As governor of the Bank of China and minister of finance 1933–44, he attempted to increase the government's financial control of the modern sector. Through control of the four major banks, the government floated more bond issues to finance its military projects. K'ung's abandonment of the silver standard in favour of a managed paper currency in 1935 was to lead ultimately to hyperinflation in the 1940s.

Kursk, Battle of in World War II, an unsuccessful German offensive against a Soviet salient in July 1943. Kursk was the greatest tank battle in history and proved to be a turning point in the Eastern Front campaign. With nearly 6,000 tanks and 2 million troops involved the battle was hard fought, reaching its climax with the pitched battle on 12 July between 700 German and 850 Soviet tanks.

Kuwait country in southwest Asia, bounded north and northwest by Iraq, east by the Gulf, and south and southwest by Saudi Arabia.

Kuznetsov, Vasilly (1894–1964) Soviet general of World War II. A young general when he defended Kiev 1941, he was afterwards made a scapegoat for its loss, though General *Budenny was really at fault. Remarkably, Kuznetsov survived and was given a command at Stalingrad, where he performed well, and then became deputy commander of the Southwest Front, fighting from the Don to Berlin.

Kyoto Protocol international protocol to the United Nations Framework Convention on Climate Change (UNFCCC) that was agreed at Kyoto, Japan, in December 1997. It commits the 186 signatory countries to binding limits on carbon dioxide and other heat-trapping 'greenhouse gases', which many scientists believe contribute to global warming. For industrialized nations, Kyoto requires cuts in greenhouse gas emissions to an average of 5.2% below 1990 levels by 2012. Developing countries are also committed to emissions targets. The text of the UNFCCC was adopted in 1992 and promoted at the climate summit held in Rio de Janeiro, Brazil, in June 1992. The convention entered into force in 1994, with 166 countries as signatories. The protocol was adopted at the December 1997 Kyoto conference on the UNFCCC. It will come into force on the 90th day after it is ratified by at least 55 parties to the convention which accounted in total for at least 55% of global carbon dioxide emissions in 1990.

Kyrgyzstan or **Kirghizia**, country in central Asia, bounded north by Kazakhstan, east by China, west by Uzbekistan, and south by Tajikistan.

Labor Party in Australia, a political party based on socialist principles. It was founded in 1891 and first held office in 1904. It formed governments 1929–31 and 1939–49, but in the intervening periods internal discord provoked splits, and reduced its effectiveness. It returned to power under Gough Whitlam 1972–75, and again under Bob Hawke in 1983, he was succeeded as party leader and prime minister by Paul Keating in 1991, who subsequently lost the 1996 general election.

Labour Party UK political party based on socialist principles, originally formed to represent workers. It was founded in 1900 and first held office in 1924. The first majority Labour government 1945–51 introduced nationalization and the National Health Service, and expanded *social security. Labour was again in power 1964–70, 1974–79, and from 1997 (winning the 2001 general election). The party leader (Tony *Blair from 1994) is elected by an electoral college, with a weighted representation of the Parliamentary Labour Party (30%), constituency parties (30%), and trade unions (40%). In 2000, the membership of the Labour Party was 361,000.

Labour Representation Committee in British politics, a forerunner (1900–06) of the Labour Party. The committee was founded in February 1900 after a resolution drafted by Ramsay *MacDonald, and moved by the Amalgamated Society of Railway Workers (now the Rail, Maritime, and Transport Union), was carried at the 1899 Trades Union Congress (TUC). The resolution called for a special congress of the TUC parliamentary committee to campaign for more Labour members of Parliament. Ramsay MacDonald became its secretary. Following his efforts, 29 Labour members of Parliament were elected in the 1906 general election, and the Labour Representation Committee was renamed the Labour Party.

Ladysmith town in province of KwaZulu-Natal (formerly Natal), South Africa, 185 km/115 mi northwest of Durban, near the Klip River; population (1991) 12,700. It has textile, clothing, and other light industries, and has an important railway depot. Founded in 1851, it was besieged for 118 days during the Boer War. It was named after the wife of the governor of Natal, Sir Harry Smith.

La Follette, Robert Marion (1855–1925) US political leader. A senator 1906–25, he was a leader of the national progressive reform movement and unsuccessfully ran for president on the Progressive ticket in 1924. He was popularly known as 'Fighting Bob'.

Lafontaine, Oskar (1943–) German socialist politician, federal deputy chair of the Social Democrat Party (SPD) from 1987 and chair from 1995. Leader of the Saar regional branch of the SPD from 1977 and former mayor of Saarbrucken, he was nicknamed 'Red Oskar' because of his radical views on military and environmental issues. His attitude became more conservative once he had become minister-president of Saarland in 1985.

La Guardia, Fiorello (Henry) (1882–1947) US Republican politician. He was mayor of New York 1933–45. Elected against the opposition of the powerful Tammany Hall Democratic Party organization, he improved the administration of the

city, suppressed racketeering, and
organized unemployment relief, slum-
clearance schemes, and social services.
Although nominally a Republican, he
supported the Democratic president
Franklin D Roosevelt's *New Deal.

Lajpat Rai, Lala (1865–1928)   Indian
politician and writer. His published
articles advocated technical education
and industrial self-help and criticized
the Congress as being a gathering of
English-educated elites. Arguing that
Congress should openly and boldly
base itself on the Hindus alone, he led
a wave of nationalism in Punjab
1904–07. The Congress split in the
Surat session in 1907 and he formed
the 'extremist' trio of Lal, Pal and Bal,
with Bal Gangadhar Tilak (1856–1920)
and Bipin Chandra *Pal. Deported on
charges of inciting the peasants, he led
the noncooperation movement in
Punjab in 1921.

Lancaster House Agreement   accord
reached at a conference held in
September 1979 at Lancaster House,
London, between Britain and
representative groups of Rhodesia,
including the Rhodesian government
under Ian Smith and black nationalist
groups. The agreement enabled a
smooth transition to the independent
state of Zimbabwe in 1980.

Landsbergis, Vytautas (1932–)
Lithuanian politician, president
1990–93. He became active in
nationalist politics in the 1980s,
founding and eventually chairing
the anticommunist Sajudis
independence movement in 1988.
When Sajudis swept to victory in the
republic's elections in March 1990,
Landsbergis chaired the Supreme
Council of Lithuania, becoming,
in effect, president. He immediately
drafted the republic's declaration of
independence from the USSR, which,
after initial Soviet resistance, was
recognized in September 1991.
In October 1996, after a general
election, he took the chair of the
new parliament.

Lange, David Russell (1942–)   New
Zealand Labour centre-left politician,
prime minister 1983–89. A skilled
parliamentary debater, he became
Labour's deputy leader in 1979, and
in 1983 replaced Wallace Rowling as
party leader. Taking advantage of
economic difficulties and a changing
public mood, Lange led Labour to a
decisive win in the 1984 general
election, replacing Robert *Muldoon
of the National Party as prime
minister. The centrepiece of his policy
programme was non-nuclear military
policy. This was put into effect, despite
criticism from the USA, becoming
law in 1987. It prevented US nuclear-
armed or nuclear-powered ships
visiting New Zealand's ports and
resulted in the USA suspending its
defence obligations to New Zealand
under the ANZUS treaty. Lange's
government also introduced a free-
market economic policy, which was a
significant and controversial departure
for Labour, and improved Maori
rights and the position of women.
His government was re-elected in
1987, but in August 1989 Lange
unexpectedly resigned, as a result
of health problems but also pressure
being exerted by supporters of the
right-wing former finance minister,
Roger Douglas. Lange, who had
become a critic of Douglas' liberalizing
policies, had dismissed Douglas in
1988. Lange was replaced as prime
minister by Geoffrey Palmer and
served under him as attorney general
until 1990.

Lansbury, George (1859–1940)   British
Labour politician, leader in the
Commons 1931–35. He was a member
of Parliament for Bow from 1910–12 –
when he resigned to force a by-election
on the issue of votes for women, which
he lost – and again 1922–40. In 1921,
while mayor of the London borough
of Poplar, he went to prison with most
of the council rather than modify their
policy of more generous unemployment
relief.

Laos landlocked country in southeast Asia, bounded north by China, east by Vietnam, south by Cambodia, west by Thailand, and northwest by Myanmar.

Largo Caballero, Francisco (1869–1946) Spanish politician; leader of the Spanish Socialist Party (PSOE). He became prime minister of the Popular Front government elected in February 1936 and remained in office for the first ten months of the Civil War before being replaced in May 1937 by Juan Negrín (1887–1956).

Larkin, James (1876–1947) Irish labour leader. He founded the Irish Transport and General Workers' Union (ITGWU) in 1909. Depressed by his failure in the 1913 Dublin lockout, he went to the USA in 1914. He returned to Ireland in 1923, only to be embroiled in a bitter dispute with William O'Brien, who had built up the ITGWU in his absence. Larkin eventually joined the Labour Party, and was elected to the Dáil (Irish parliament) in 1943.

Laski, Harold Joseph (1893–1950) English political theorist. Professor of political science at the London School of Economics from 1926, he taught a modified Marxism and was active in the Socialist League during the 1930s. He published *A Grammar of Politics* (1925), a central text of Fabian political science, and *The American Presidency* (1940). He was chair of the Labour Party 1944–45.

Lateran Treaties series of agreements that marked the reconciliation of the Italian state with the papacy in 1929. They were hailed as a propaganda victory for the fascist regime. The treaties involved recognition of the sovereignty of the *Vatican City State, the payment of an indemnity for papal possessions lost during unification in 1870, and agreement on the role of the Catholic Church within the Italian state in the form of a concordat between Pope Pius XI and the dictator Mussolini.

Latin American Integration Association (Spanish **Asociación Latino-Americana de Integración (ALADI)**), organization aiming to create a common market in Latin America; to promote trade it applies tariff reductions preferentially on the basis of the different stages of economic development that individual member countries have reached. Formed in 1980 to replace the Latin American Free Trade Association (formed in 1961), it has 11 members: Argentina, Bolivia, Brazil, Chile, Colombia, Ecuador, Mexico, Paraguay, Peru, Uruguay, and Venezuela. Its headquarters are in Bogotá, Colombia.

Lattre de Tassigny, Jean de (1889–1952) French general. He served in World War I, and in World War II commanded the 14th Division during the German invasion 1940. He was imprisoned by the Germans after the armistice but escaped to the UK 1943 and joined General de Gaulle's *Free French forces. He was the French signatory to the German surrender in Berlin 9 May 1945. Following the war he commanded NATO Land Forces Europe 1948 and was commander-in-chief Indo-China (now Vietnam) 1950–52.

Latvia country in northern Europe, bounded east by Russia, north by Estonia, north and northwest by the Baltic Sea, south by Lithuania, and southeast by Belarus.

Lausanne, Treaty of peace settlement in 1923 between Greece and Turkey after Turkey refused to accept the terms of the Treaty of Sèvres in 1920, which would have made peace with the western Allies. It involved the surrender by Greece of Smyrna (now Izmir) and East Thrace to Turkey and the enforced exchange of the Greek population of Smyrna for the Turkish population of Greece.

Laval, Pierre (1883–1945) French extreme-rightwing politician, he gravitated between the wars from socialism through the centre ground (serving as prime minister and foreign secretary 1931–32 and again 1935–36) to the extreme right. As head of the Vichy government and foreign minister 1942–44, he was responsible for the deportation of Jews and for requisitioning French labour to Germany.

Law, Andrew Bonar (1858–1923) British Conservative politician, born in New Brunswick, Canada, of Scottish descent. He succeeded Balfour as leader of the opposition in 1911, became colonial secretary in Asquith's coalition government 1915–16, chancellor of the Exchequer 1916–19, and Lord Privy Seal 1919–21 in Lloyd George's coalition. He formed a Conservative cabinet in 1922, but resigned on health grounds.

Lawrence, T(homas) E(dward) (1888–1935) called 'Lawrence of Arabia', British soldier, scholar, and translator. Appointed to the military intelligence department in Cairo, Egypt, during World War I, he took part in negotiations for an Arab revolt against the Ottoman Turks, and in 1916 attached himself to the emir Faisal. He became a guerrilla leader of genius, combining raids on Turkish communications with the organization of a joint Arab revolt, described in his book *The Seven Pillars of Wisdom* (1926).

Lawson, Nigel, Baron Lawson of Blaby (1932–) British Conservative politician. A former financial journalist, he was financial secretary to the Treasury 1979–81, secretary of state for energy 1981–83, and chancellor of the Exchequer 1983–89. He resigned as chancellor after criticusm by government adviser Alan Walters, supported by prime minister Margaret Thatcher, over his policy of British membership of the European Monetary System.

League of Nations international organization formed after World War I to solve international disputes by arbitration. Established in Geneva, Switzerland, in 1920, the League included representatives from states throughout the world, but was severely weakened by the US decision not to become a member, and had no power to enforce its decisions. It was dissolved in 1946. Its subsidiaries included the **International Labour Organization** and the **Permanent Court of International Justice** in The Hague, the Netherlands, both now under the *United Nations (UN).

Lease, Mary Elizabeth (1853–1933) US political activist and lawyer. Her most famous work, *The Problem of Civilization Solved* (1895), contained elements of both Marxism and racism. A fiery, uncompromising figure, she frequently feuded with other activists, and after the election of 1896, moved to New York City, where she was a political writer for the *World* and practised law on the Lower East Side. She allied herself briefly with the Theosophists, and, for a time, with Christian Science, and she was a member of the Socialist Party from 1899.

Lebanon country in western Asia, bounded north and east by Syria, south by Israel, and west by the Mediterranean Sea.

government Under the 1926 constitution, amended in 1927, 1929, 1943, 1947, and 1990, legislative power is held by the national assembly, whose 128 members (half of whom are Christians, and half Muslims) are elected by universal adult suffrage, through a party list system of proportional representation. The assembly serves a four-year term. The president is elected by the assembly for a six-year term and appoints a prime minister and cabinet who are collectively responsible to the assembly. Under the 1943 amended constitution the president is Christian, the prime minister is Sunni Muslim, and the speaker of the national assembly is Shiite Muslim. The 1990 amendment reflects the Muslim majority that has emerged since 1947.

The powers of the president have been much diminished, although the post is still reserved for a Maronite Christian.

history The area now known as Lebanon was once occupied by Phoenicia, an empire that flourished from the 5th century BC to the 1st century AD, when it came under Roman rule. Christianity was introduced during the Roman occupation, and Islam arrived with the Arabs in 635. Lebanon was part of the Turkish Ottoman Empire from the 16th century, until administered by France under a League of Nations mandate 1920–41. It was declared independent in 1941, became a republic in 1943, and achieved full autonomy in 1944.

Lebanon has a wide variety of religions, including Christianity and many Islamic sects. For many years these coexisted peacefully, giving Lebanon a stability that enabled it, until the mid-1970s, to be a commercial and financial centre. Beirut's thriving business district was largely destroyed in 1975–76, and Lebanon's role as an international trader has been greatly diminished.

PLO presence in Lebanon After the establishment of Israel in 1948, thousands of Palestinian refugees fled to Lebanon, and the *Palestine Liberation Organization (PLO), founded in Beirut in 1964, had its headquarters in Lebanon 1971–82 (it moved to Tunis in 1982). The PLO presence in Lebanon was the main reason for Israeli invasions and much of the subsequent civil strife.

Fighting was largely between left-wing Muslims, led by Kamul Jumblatt of the Progressive Socialist Party, and conservative Christian groups, mainly members of the Phalangist Party. There was also conflict between pro-Iranian traditional Muslims, such as the Shiites, and Syrian-backed deviationist Muslims, such as the Druze.

civil war In 1975 the fighting developed into full-scale civil war.

A ceasefire was agreed in 1976, but fighting began again in 1978, when Israeli forces invaded Lebanon in search of PLO guerrillas. The United Nations (UN) secured Israel's agreement to a withdrawal and set up an international peacekeeping force, but to little avail. In 1979 Major Saad Haddad, a right-wing Lebanese army officer, with Israeli encouragement, declared an area of about 1,800 sq km/ 700 sq mi in southern Lebanon an 'independent free Lebanon', and the following year Christian Phalangist soldiers took over an area north of Beirut. Throughout this turmoil the Lebanese government was virtually powerless. In 1982 Bachir Gemayel (youngest son of Pierre Gemayel, the founder of the Phalangist Party) became president. He was assassinated before he could assume office and his brother Amin took his place. Israeli forces again invaded in 1982, driving to Beirut and forcing the expulsion of PLO guerrillas and leaders to Syrian-held areas and to Tunisia.

efforts to end hostilities In 1983, after exhaustive talks between Lebanon and Israel, under US auspices, an agreement declared an end to hostilities and called for the withdrawal of all foreign forces from the country within three months. Syria refused to recognize the agreement and left about 40,000 troops, with about 7,000 PLO fighters, in northern Lebanon. Israel responded by refusing to take its forces from the south. Meanwhile, a full-scale war began between Phalangist and Druze soldiers in the Chouf Mountains, ending in a Christian defeat and the creation of a Druze-controlled ministate. The multinational force was drawn gradually but unwillingly into the conflict until it was withdrawn in the spring of 1984. Unsuccessful attempts were made in 1985 and 1986 to end the civil war. Meanwhile, Lebanon, and particularly Beirut, became a battlefield for the Iranian-backed

Shiite *Hezbollah and Syrian-backed Shiite Amal factions.

In 1988 President Assad of Syria, with the agreement of the Lebanese government and Iran, sent his troops into South Beirut in an attempt to restore order and secure the release of hostages believed to be held there. Gemayel's term as president ended and, after failure to agree a suitable Maronite Christian successor, the outgoing president appointed Gen Michel Aoun to head a caretaker military government. The civil war in Beirut continued, with the East Beirut 'administration' of Gen Aoun, backed by Christian army units and Lebanese militia forces (although 30% of them were Muslim), pitted against the West Beirut 'administration' (Muslim) of Premier Selim al-Hoss, supported by the Syrian army and Muslim militia allies, including Walid Jumblatt's Progressive Socialist Party (Druze).

ceasefire agreed In May 1989 the Arab League secured a ceasefire agreement and, despite Aoun's opposition, in November René Muawad, a Maronite Christian, was made president; within days he was killed by a car bomb. Another Maronite, Elias Hrawi, was named as his successor. Aoun continued to defy the elected president for a further year, but eventually surrendered and took refuge in the French embassy; he was later pardoned.

hostages released In 1990 it was estimated that 18 Westerners, including eight Americans, were being held hostage in Lebanon by pro-Iranian Shiite Muslim groups; many had been held incommunicado for years. In August the release of the hostages began. By November 1990 the Hrawi administration had regained control of Beirut and proposals for a new constitution for a Second Republic were being discussed. By 1992, due to improved relations with Syria and Iran and the efforts of the UN secretary general, all Western hostages had been

released. The 15 years of civil war were estimated to have left 144,240 dead, 17,415 missing, and 197,505 injured.

Gradually, a sense of normality returned to Lebanon, and particularly Beirut, with Syrian troops helping to maintain order. The 1992 general election was boycotted by many Christians, but the re-election of the pro-Syrian administration, with the moderate businessman Rafik al-Hariri as prime minister, offered promise of a lasting peace. Hezbollah guerrillas, however, remained active in the south of the country, provoking intermittent raids by Israeli forces which continued to occupy a buffer zone.

In April 1996 Israel began an attack on southern Lebanon in which helicopter gunships rocketed Beirut for the first time since 1982. Within less than a week 26 deaths were recorded in Israel's attacks, 23 of these were civilians. The raid came the day after Hezbollah fired rockets into northern Israel (injuring 36 people), and in the wake of an escalating cycle of violence that had gripped Lebanon in preceding weeks. This series of attacks and counter-attacks marked the end of the 1993 Israeli-Hezbollah agreement. A new ceasefire was proposed by the USA, Israel, Syria, and Lebanon. In 1996, fighting between Muslim guerrillas and Israeli forces and their militia allies in South Lebanon killed 255 people, an increase of 80 on 1995 figures. In what was Israel's greatest military humiliation in Lebanon since 1985, 12 Israeli soldiers were killed in an ambush in southern Lebanon in September 1997.

In 1998 General Emile Lahoud, a Christian Maronite, was elected president. Within months of his election, Rafik al-Hariri resigned his position as prime minister, and was replaced with Salim al-Hoss.

There were strong indications, following the May 1999 Israeli elections won by Ehud Barak, that the South Lebanon Army (SLA), Israel's proxy army in southern Lebanon, would shortly withdraw from a large part of the zone it has occupied. The SLA withdrew in June from the Jezzine area, badly harassed by Hezbollah guerrillas. The Lebanese government declined to send its army to control the area. Nevertheless, Israeli warplanes bombed Beirut and Baalbek in northeast Lebanon in June 1999, destroying power stations and bridges.

Israel's outgoing government refused to attend the international monitoring committee set up under the 1996 pact to hear complaints. After Israel withdrew from the 1996 ceasefire agreement in February 2000, there was renewed fighting between Israel and Lebanon. Following the fighting, Israeli Prime Minister Barak defeated a motion of no confidence and insisted that, before Israel pulled out from Lebanon, he would exhaust all chances of a deal with Syria and Lebanon. He declared that it was the responsibility of Syria to control Hezbollah guerrillas operating against Israel in south Lebanon.

After Arab-Israeli peace talks were reopened in March 2000, Israel's cabinet confirmed Prime Minister Barak's commitment to withdraw Israeli troops from south Lebanon by July 2000. However, the bombing campaign which had gained strength since Israel bombed three Lebanese power stations in February continued despite, and perhaps as a result of, universal condemnation of Israel's actions at a recent meeting of the 22-nation Arab League. In an attempt to prevent Israel's withdrawal from the Golan Heights being under fire, US president Clinton and Syrian president Assad attempted to frame a deal which would lead to a peaceful withdrawal, and would include the UN Security Council.

Ordered by the Supreme Court, Israel released 13 Lebanese detainees in April 2000, who had been held without trial for more than ten years. While this was a conciliatory move, the following month Israel bombed two more Lebanese power stations after Lebanese rockets shot into northern Israel. Israel's bombing cost Lebanon dearly in terms of power and finance, and continued to push a peaceful withdrawal further away. Fears grew that if Israel went ahead with a withdrawal from Lebanon without reaching an agreement with Syria, the Middle East would become a war zone. The UN Middle East representative confirmed that peacekeepers would be deployed on the border between Lebanon and Israel after Israel's withdrawal.

In May 2000, when morale was low in the Israeli-sponsored army controlling southern Lebanon, following Israeli popular demands to quit the region, and threats made by the Hezbollah against the Lebanese soldiers and citizens working with Israel, the Israeli army staged a hasty withdrawal from the region. While it was not the controlled and stately withdrawal that Barak had planned, it remained the case that he had ordered the first step, albeit a risky one, in an attempted peace in the Middle East. The retreat, which represented an embarrassment to Israel, left the Hezbollah and Israelis without a buffer zone on the border. However, the intent was to bring peace between Israel and the Hezbollah, which would have an effect on talks with the Syrians and Palestinians. More than two months after the Israeli withdrawal from southern Lebanon, Hezbollah forces in the frontier area were replaced with Lebanese government troops, together with almost 400 UN soldiers on the border.

In October 2000, Rafik al-Hariri, former prime minister of Lebanon, again became prime minister after a landslide victory in September's parliamentary elections. He went on to criticize Syria for keeping 35,000 troops in south Lebanon. In February 2001, the UN extended the mandate of the UN Interim Force in Lebanon until August 2001. In June, 6,000 Syrian troops were recalled from Lebanon. In August, the Lebanese army arrested 150 members of two right-wing Christian groups, including students and party officials, opposed to the Syrian military presence.

Lebrun, Albert (1871–1950) French politician. He became president of the senate in 1931 and in 1932 was chosen as president of the republic. In 1940 he handed his powers over to Marshal Pétain.

Leclerc, Phillipe (1902–1947) born **Jacques Phillipe de Hautecloque**, General in the Free French forces of World War II. A captain in the 4th French Infantry Division, he refused to surrender to the Germans in 1940. He was captured but escaped to the UK. He was appointed general officer commanding French Equatorial Africa and governor of Chad and Cameroun for the Free French, and changed his name to avoid repercussions against his family in France. Leclerc's troops joined the British in North Africa and the US 3rd Army under *Patton for the *D-Day landings on 6 June 1944. Leclerc received the German surrender of Paris on 25 August 1945, and then took his division to Alsace to liberate Strasbourg.

Le Duc Tho (1911–1990) North Vietnamese diplomat who shared the Nobel Prize for Peace in 1973 with Henry *Kissinger for his part in the negotiations to end the Vietnam War. He indefinitely postponed receiving the award.

Lee, Jennie (Janet) (1904–1988) Baroness Lee of Asheridge, British socialist politician. She became a member of Parliament for the Independent Labour Party representing North Lanark at the age of 24, and in 1934 married Aneurin *Bevan. Representing Cannock 1945–70, she was on the left wing of the Labour

Party. She was on its National Executive Committee 1958–70, became a privy councillor from 1966, and was minister of education 1967–70, during which time she was responsible for founding the Open University in 1969. She was made a baroness in 1970.

Lee Kuan Yew (1923–) Singaporean politician, prime minister 1959–90. Lee founded the anticommunist Socialist People's Action Party in 1954 and entered the Singapore legislative assembly in 1955. He was elected the country's first prime minister in 1959, and took Singapore out of the Malaysian federation in 1965. He remained in power until his resignation in 1990, and was succeeded by Goh Chok Tong. Until 1992 he held on to the party leadership.

Lee Teng-hui (1923–) Taiwanese right-wing politician, vice-president 1984–88, president 1988–2000, and Kuomintang (see *Guomindang) party leader 1988–2001. The country's first island-born leader, he was viewed as a reforming technocrat. He was directly elected president in March 1996, defying Chinese opposition to the democratic contest.

Leguía, Agusto Bernardino (1863–1932) Peruvian politician and president 1908–12 and 1919–30. During his first term, he actively embarked on a programme of fiscal, social and public infrastructural reform. He participated in the negotiations that ultimately resolved the territorial boundary disputes between his own country, Brazil, and Bolivia. His second term in office was marked by his severance of ties with the old Peruvian oligarchy. In 1920, he promulgated a new constitution, and ruled dictatorially, vigorously suppressing all opposition.

Leigh-Mallory, Trafford Leigh (1892–1944) British air chief marshal in World War II. He took part in the Battle of Britain and was commander-in-chief of Allied air forces during the invasion of France.

Le May, Curtis E(merson) (1906–)
US air force general. He commanded
305 Bomber Group, one of the first US
units to arrive in the UK in World War
II, and devised most of the tactics
employed by the 8th Air Force. He
took charge of 20th Bomber Command
in the India-Burma-China theatre 1944
and carried out long-range B-29 raids
against Formosa and western Japan.
He then moved to 21 Bomber
Command in the Marianas January
1945, and began a strong offensive
against Japanese cities. The B-29
bombers which dropped the atom
bombs August 1945 were under Le
May's command. He was a candidate
in the 1968 vice-presidential campaign.

lend-lease   in US history, an act of
Congress passed in March 1941 that
gave the president power to order
'any defense article for the government
of any country whose defense the
president deemed vital to the defense
of the USA'. During World War II, the
USA negotiated many lend-lease
agreements, notably with Britain and
the USSR.

Lenin, Vladimir Ilyich (1870–1924)
adopted name of **Vladimir Ilyich
Ulyanov,** Russian revolutionary, first
leader of the USSR, and communist
theoretician. Active in the 1905
Revolution, Lenin had to leave Russia
when it failed, settling in Switzerland
in 1914. He returned to Russia after
the February revolution of 1917 (see
*Russian Revolution). He led the
Bolshevik revolution of November
1917 and became leader of a Soviet
government, concluded peace with
Germany, and organized a successful
resistance to White Russian (pro-
tsarist) uprisings and foreign
intervention during the *Russian civil
war 1918–21. His modification of
traditional Marxist doctrine to fit
conditions prevailing in Russia became
known as **Marxism-Leninism,**
the basis of *communist ideology.

Lenin was born on 22 April 1870 in
Simbirsk (now renamed Ulyanovsk),
on the River Volga, and became a
lawyer in St Petersburg. His brother
was executed in 1887 for attempting
to assassinate Tsar Alexander III.
A Marxist from 1889, Lenin was sent
to Siberia for spreading revolutionary
propaganda 1895–1900. He then edited
the political paper *Iskra* ('The Spark')
from abroad, and visited London
several times. In *What is to be Done?*
(1902), he advocated that a
professional core of Social Democratic
Party activists should spearhead the
revolution in Russia, a suggestion
accepted by the majority (*bolsheviki*)
at the London party congress 1903.
From Switzerland he attacked socialist
support for World War I as aiding
an 'imperialist' struggle, and wrote
*Imperialism, the Highest Stage of
Capitalism* (1917).

After the renewed outbreak of
revolution February–March 1917,
he was smuggled back into Russia in
April by the Germans so that he could
take up his revolutionary activities and
remove Russia from the war, allowing
Germany to concentrate the war effort
on the Western Front. On arriving in
Russia, Lenin established himself at
the head of the Bolsheviks, against the
provisional government of Kerensky.
A complicated power struggle ensued,
but eventually Lenin triumphed on
8 November 1917; a Bolshevik
government was formed, and peace
negotiations with Germany were
begun, leading to the signing of the
Treaty of *Brest-Litovsk on 3 March 1918.

From the overthrow of the
provisional government in November
1917 until his death, Lenin effectively
controlled the USSR, although an
assassination attempt in 1918 injured
his health. He founded the Third
(Communist) *International in 1919.
With communism proving inadequate
to put the country on its feet, he
introduced the private-enterprise
New Economic Policy in 1921.

Leningrad, Siege of   in World War II,
German siege of the Soviet city of

Leningrad (now St Petersburg, Russia) 1 September 1941–27 January 1944. Some 1 million inhabitants of the city are believed to have died during the 900 days of the siege, either from disease, starvation, or enemy action. Leningrad was awarded the title of 'Hero City' for withstanding the siege.

Leopold III (1901–1983) King of the Belgians 1934–51. Against the prime minister's advice he surrendered to the German army in World War II in 1940. Post-war charges against his conduct led to a regency by his brother Charles and his eventual abdication in 1951 in favour of his son Baudouin.

Le Pen, Jean-Marie (1928–) French extreme-rightwing politician, founder of the National Front (FN) in 1972.

His skill as a public speaker, his demagogic mixing of nationalism with law-and-order populism – calling for immigrant repatriation, stricter nationality laws, and the restoration of capital punishment – and his hostility to the European Union attracted a wide swathe of electoral support in the 1980s and 1990s, and in the 2002 presidential election progressed to the run-off round, but was heavily defeated by Jacques *Chirac.

Lesotho landlocked country in southern Africa, an enclave within South Africa.

Lettow-Vorbeck, Paul Emil von (1870–1964) German general. He served in the Boxer Rebellion in China 1900 and after in German Southwest Africa. In World War I, he was military commander in German Southeast Africa (now Tanzania) where he kept the Allies at bay for most of the war despite being vastly outnumbered.

Lévesque, René (1922–1987) French-Canadian politician, premier of Québec 1976–85. In 1968 he founded the Parti Québecois, with the aim of an independent Québec, but a referendum rejected the proposal in 1980.

Lewis, John L(lewellyn) (1880–1969) US labour leader. President of the United Mine Workers (UMW) 1920–60, he was largely responsible for the adoption of national mining safety standards in the USA. His militancy and the miners' strikes during and after World War II led to President Truman's nationalization of the mines in 1946.

Lewis and Clark expedition US government expedition conducted 1804–06 to map uncharted territory bought from France under the Louisiana Purchase (1803), and to find a land route to the Pacific coast. The survey, ordered by President Thomas Jefferson, was led by Meriwether Lewis and William Clark. The round trip from St Louis, Missouri to the mouth of the Columbia River covered some 13,000 km/8,000 mi. Information gathered by the explorers, and the opening of a new route to the Pacific, helped to fuel the Westward expansion of the USA; one immediate effect was an influx of US mountain men (fur traders) to the Rocky Mountain regions. The **Lewis and Clark National Historic Trail**, opened in 1978, marks the route taken by the explorers.

The expedition followed the Missouri River northwest from St Louis to the Three Forks in western Montana. From there, they took the Jefferson River southwest to its head, crossed the Continental Divide at Lemhi Pass, traversed the Bitterroot Range at Lolo Pass, descended the Clearwater River to the Snake (originally Lewis) River; followed the Snake to the Columbia River; and finally rafted down the Columbia to the Pacific, ending their journey at Oregon's Fort Clatsop. On their return east, the explorers also investigated the routes taken by the Marias and Yellowstone rivers, in Montana.

Lexington town in Middlesex County, east Massachusetts; population (2000 est) 30,400. It is located 17 km/11 mi northwest of Boston, of which it is a mainly residential suburb. Industries include printing and publishing.

Lexington is also an electronic, optical, and scientific research centre. First called Cambridge Farms, after European settlement in 1642, Lexington was incorporated in 1713.

Leyte Gulf, Battle of the   in World War II, US naval victory over Japan 17–25 October 1944, to the east of the Philippines. The biggest naval battle in history, involving 216 US warships, 2 Australian vessels, and 64 Japanese warships, it resulted in the destruction of the Japanese navy.

Liao Zhongkai (or Liao Chung-k'ai) (1878–1925)   Chinese politician. Born in the USA, he studied in Japan before becoming the leading financial expert of the *Guomindang (Kuomintang) after 1912. Associated with the left wing of the party, he supported the United Front with the communists in 1923, advocating a planned economy along socialist lines. In 1924 he played an important role in setting up both the workers' and peasants' departments under Guomindang auspices as part of its new strategy of mass mobilization.

Liaquat Ali Khan, Nawabzada (1895–1951)   Indian politician, deputy leader of the *Muslim League 1940–47, first prime minister of Pakistan from 1947. He was assassinated by objectors to his peace policy with India.

Liberal Democrats   UK political party of the centre, led since 1999 by Charles Kennedy. Britain's third main party, the Liberal Democrats are successors to the *Liberal Party and the *Social Democratic Party, which merged in 1998 to form the Social and Liberal Democrats (SLD). The name Liberal Democrats was adopted in 1989. It is a progressive party, which supports closer integration within the European Union, constitutional reform (including proportional representation and regional government), and greater investment in state education and the National Health Service, financed by higher direct taxes. The party has strong libertarian and environmentalist

wings. It has been in coalition, with Labour, in the Scottish Parliament since 1999, and in the Welsh Assembly since 2000. It won 52 seats at the June 2001 general election – the best result for the Liberals and their successors for more than 70 years.

Liberal Party   British political party, the successor to the Whig Party, with an ideology of liberalism. In the 19th century it represented the interests of commerce and industry. Its outstanding leaders were Palmerston, Gladstone, and Lloyd George. From 1914 it declined, and the rise of the Labour Party pushed the Liberals into the middle ground. The Liberals joined forces with the Social Democratic Party (SDP) as the Alliance for the 1983 and 1987 elections. In 1988 a majority of the SDP voted to merge with the Liberals to form the Social and Liberal Democrats (SLD), which became known as the *Liberal Democrats from 1989. A minority have retained the name Liberal Party.

The Liberal Party was officially formed on 6 June 1859, although the term 'Liberals' had been increasingly in use since the 1832 Reform Act. Its formal establishment marked a shift of support for the party from aristocrats to include also progressive industrialists, backed by supporters of the utilitarian reformer Jeremy Bentham, Nonconformists (especially in Welsh and Scottish constituencies), and the middle classes. During the Liberals' first period of power, from 1830 to 1841, they promoted parliamentary and municipal government reform and the abolition of slavery, but their *laissez-faire* theories led to the harsh Poor Law of 1834. Except for two short periods, the Liberals were in power from 1846 to 1866, but the only major change was the general adoption of free trade. Liberal pressure forced Prime Minister Robert Peel to repeal the Corn Laws of 1846, thereby splitting the ruling Conservative (or Tory) party.

Extended franchise (1867) and Gladstone's emergence as leader began a new phase, dominated by the Manchester school with a programme of 'peace, retrenchment, and reform'. Gladstone's 1868–74 government introduced many important reforms, including elementary education and vote by ballot. The party's left, composed mainly of working-class Radicals and led by Charles Bradlaugh (a lawyer's clerk) and Joseph Chamberlain (a wealthy manufacturer), repudiated *laissez faire* and inclined towards republicanism, but in 1886 the Liberals were split over the policy of home rule for Ireland, and many became Liberal Unionists or joined the Conservatives.

Except for the period 1892 to 1895, the Liberals remained out of power until 1906, when, reinforced by Labour and Irish support, they returned with a huge majority. Old-age pensions, National Insurance, limitation of the powers of the Lords, and the Irish Home Rule Bill followed. Lloyd George's alliance with the Conservatives from 1916 to 1922 divided the Liberal Party between him and his predecessor Asquith, and although reunited in 1923 the Liberals continued to lose votes. They briefly joined the National Government (1931–32). After World War II they were reduced to a handful of members of Parliament. However, Liberal thinkers, notably John Maynard Keynes and William Beveridge, had a profound influence on post-war governments in terms of creation of a welfare state and ideas about government intervention to help manage the economy.

A Liberal revival began under the leadership (1956–67) of Jo Grimond and continued under Jeremy Thorpe, who resigned after a period of controversy within the party in 1976. After a caretaker return by Grimond, David Steel became the first party leader in British politics to be elected by party members who were not MPs.

Between 1977 and 1978 Steel entered into an agreement to support Labour in any vote of confidence in return for consultation on measures undertaken. After the 1987 general election, Steel suggested a merger of the Liberal Party and the SDP, and the SLD was formed on 3 March 1988, with Paddy Ashdown elected leader in July of that year. From 1989 the SLD became known as the Liberal Democrats.

Unlike the Council for Social Democracy, which was wound up in 1990, a rump Liberal Party remained after the 1988 Liberal–SDP merger. In 2001 it had 30 local councillors. It contested 14 parliamentary constituencies at the June 2001 general election but won less than 1% of the vote, except in Liverpool West Derby, where, with 15% of the vote, its candidate finished in second position, ahead of the Liberal Democrats.

Liberal Party, Australian political party established 1944 by Robert Menzies, after a Labor landslide, and derived from the former United Australia Party.

After the voters rejected Labor's extensive nationalization plans, the Liberals were in power 1949–72 and 1975–83 and were led in succession by Harold Holt, John Gorton, William McMahon, Billy Snedden, Malcolm Fraser, John Hewson, Alexander Downer, and John Howard. It returned to power in 1996 in a coalition with the National Party.

Liberia country in West Africa, bounded north by Guinea, east by Côte d'Ivoire, south and southwest by the Atlantic Ocean, and northwest by Sierra Leone.

Libya country in North Africa, bounded north by the Mediterranean Sea, east by Egypt, southeast by Sudan, south by Chad and Niger, and west by Algeria and Tunisia.

government The 1977 constitution created an Islamic socialist state, and the government is designed to allow the greatest possible popular involvement, through a large congress and smaller secretariats and committees. There is a General People's Congress (GPC) of 1,112 members that elects a secretary general who is intended to be head of state. The GPC is serviced by a general secretariat, which is Libya's nearest equivalent to a legislature. The executive organ of the state is the General People's Committee, which replaces the structure of ministries that operated before the 1969 revolution. The Arab Socialist Union (ASU) is the only political party, and, despite Libya's elaborately democratic structure, ultimate power rests with the party and its leader.

history The area now known as Libya was inhabited by North African nomads until it came successively under the domination of Phoenicia, Greece, Rome, the Vandals, Byzantium, and Islam, and from the 16th century was part of the Turkish *Ottoman Empire. In 1911 it was conquered by Italy, becoming known as Libya from 1934.

After being the scene of much fighting during World War II, in 1942 it was divided into three provinces: Fezzan, which was placed under French control; Cyrenaica; and Tripolitania, which was placed under British control. In 1951 it achieved independence as the United Kingdom of Libya, Muhammad Idris-as-Sanusi becoming King Idris.

revolution The development of oil reserves during the 1960s transformed the Libyan economy. The country enjoyed internal and external stability until a bloodless revolution in 1969, led by young nationalist officers, deposed the king and proclaimed a Libyan Arab Republic. Power was vested in a Revolution Command Council (RCC), chaired by Col Moamer al-Khaddhafi, with the Arab Socialist Union (ASU) as the only political party. Khaddhafi soon began proposing schemes for Arab unity, none of which was

permanently adopted. In 1972 he planned a federation of Libya, Syria, and Egypt and later that year a merger between Libya and Egypt. In 1980 he proposed a union with Syria and in 1981 with Chad.

Islamic socialism Khaddhafi attempted to run the country on socialist Islamic lines, with people's committees pledged to socialism and the teachings of the Koran. The 1977 constitution made him secretary general of the general secretariat of the GPC, but in 1979 he resigned the post in order to devote more time to 'preserving the revolution'.

conflict with the West Khaddhafi's attempts to establish himself as a leader of the Arab world brought him into conflict with Western powers, particularly the USA. The Reagan administration objected to Libya's presence in Chad and its attempts to unseat the French-US-sponsored government of President Habré. The USA linked Khaddhafi to worldwide terrorist activities, despite his denials of complicity, and the killing of a US soldier in a bomb attack in Berlin in 1986 by an unidentified guerrilla group prompted a raid by US aircraft, some of them British-based, on Tripoli and Benghazi. Libyan terrorists were also blamed for the bombing of Pan American World Airways Flight 103 over Lockerbie, Scotland, in 1988, which killed 270 people; and for the 1989 bombing of UTA (Union de Transports Aériens) Flight 772 over Niger.

international sanctions In 1988 Khaddhafi embarked on a dramatic programme of liberalization, freeing political prisoners and encouraging private businesses to operate, and in the same year offered to recognize Chad's independence and to give material help in the reconstruction of the country. In January 1989 he did not retaliate when two fighter jets were shot down over the Mediterranean off Libya by the US Navy, and appeared to be moving towards improving external relations, effecting a reconciliation with Egypt in October 1989. However in April 1992 international sanctions were imposed against Libya after Khaddhafi repeatedly refused to extradite six suspects linked to the Lockerbie and UTA bombings. Foreign air links were severed and Libyan diplomatic staff in several countries were expelled. A US request for tougher sanctions was rejected by the United Nations in April 1995.

In April 1999 the Libyan government handed over the two men suspected of planting a bomb on the aircraft which crashed over Lockerbie, Scotland, for trial in the Netherlands.

In July 1999 the UK restored full diplomatic relations with Libya, broken off after British police officer Yvonne Fletcher was shot outside the Libyan embassy in London in 1984. The move followed Libya's acceptance of responsibility for the murder, and after the Libyan authorities paid an undisclosed sum in compensation to the family, British foreign secretary Robin Cook said he expected a British ambassador to take up position in Libya in December, making the last conciliatory step in the lifting of sanctions between Libya and Britain.

In March 2000, a day after Khaddhaffi sacked his prime minister and abolished half of his government, he surprised the outside world by proposing that Libya install a formal head of state. The General People's Congress, the highest-ranking legislative body, endorsed reform in the government, abolishing twelve ministries and devolving powers to local level, and named a new prime minister, Mubarak al-Shamikh.

Lockerbie trial Eight months after the two suspects were handed over by Libya in April 1999, it was ruled that they should be tried (under Scots law) on every count they faced, enabling the broadest possible amount of evidence to be put before the court. The trial

opened in early May 2000 at Camp Zeist, a specially convened Scottish court sitting in the Netherlands. It ended in January 2001, with one of the two suspects, Abdelbaset Ali Mohmed al-Megrahi, being found guilty of murdering 270 people. His co-defendant was found not guilty. Khaddhafi denounced the ruling, claiming to have proof of al-Megrahi's innocence. The UK and USA insisted that sanctions against Libya would not be fully lifted until it accepted responsibility for the bombing and agreed to pay compensation to the victims' families.

international relations Libya became involved in a hostage crisis in the Philippines in September 2000 as hostages held by the Abu Sayyaf Muslim guerrilla group were released in small numbers. Despite some international criticism, Libya agreed to pay $24 million/£16 million for the remaining hostages. The money would come from the Khaddhafi International Association for Charitable Organizations, with Khaddhafi appearing to hope that by ending the crisis his image on the international stage would be further enhanced and his country might win a more respectable role.

Li Dazhao (or Li Ta-chao) (1888–1927) Chinese revolutionary. He was one of the founders of the Chinese Communist Party, and his interpretation of Marxism as applied to China had a profound influence on *Mao Zedong. In 1927, when the Manchurian military leader, Zhang Zuolin (Chang Tsolin), then occupying Beijing (Peking), raided the Soviet Embassy, Li was captured and executed.

Liddell Hart, Basil Henry (1895–1970) British military strategist. He was an exponent of mechanized warfare, and his ideas were adopted in Germany in 1935 in creating the 1st Panzer Division, combining motorized infantry and tanks. From 1937 he advised the UK War Office on army reorganization. Knighted in 1966.

Lidice Czechoslovak mining village, replacing one destroyed by the Nazis on 10 June 1942 as a reprisal for the assassination of Reinhard *Heydrich. The men were shot, the women sent to concentration camps, and the children taken to Germany. The officer responsible was hanged in 1946.

Lie, Trygve Halvdan (1896–1968) Norwegian Labour politician and diplomat. He became secretary of the Labour Party in 1926. During the German occupation of Norway in World War II he was foreign minister in the exiled government 1941–46, when he helped retain the Norwegian fleet for the Allies. He became the first secretary general of the United Nations 1946–53, but resigned over Soviet opposition to his handling of the Korean War.

Liebknecht, Karl (1871–1919) German socialist, son of Wilhelm Liebknecht. A founder of the German Communist Party, originally known as the Spartacus League (see *Spartacist), in 1918, he was one of the few socialists who refused to support World War I. He led an unsuccessful revolt with Rosa *Luxemburg in Berlin in 1919 and both were murdered by army officers.

Liechtenstein landlocked country in west-central Europe, bounded east by Austria and west by Switzerland.

Ligachev, Egor Kuzmich (1920–) Soviet politician. He joined the Communist Party (CPSU) in 1944, and became a member of the Politburo in 1985. He was replaced as the party ideologist in 1988 by Vadim Medvedev.

Likud (Hebrew **'consolidation'** or **'unity'**) alliance of right-wing Israeli political parties, formed in 1973 by Menachem *Begin, uniting Herut ('freedom'), the Liberal Party of Israel, Laam ('for the nation'), and Ahdut. It defeated the Labour Party coalition in the May 1977 election, bringing Begin to power. Under the leadership of Yitzhak *Shamir 1983–93, Likud became part of an uneasy national coalition with Labour 1984–90, but

was defeated by the Labour Party in the 1992 general election. Under the leadership of Binyamin *Netanyahu 1993–99 and Ariel *Sharon since 1999, it adopted a much harder line than Labour in the Middle East peace process. In May 1996, Netanyahu became Israel's first directly-elected prime minister, and formed a Likud-led government. He was defeated in May 1999 by Ehud Barak of the Labour party, who was in turn defeated by Sharon in February 2001.

Lillie, Gordon William (1860–1942) called **'Pawnee Bill'**, US frontiersman and showman. Enchanted by stories of the Old West, he left home at age 15 and lived among the Pawnee Indians and learned their language. He held various jobs in Oklahoma and Texas – buffalo hunter, teacher, cattle rancher – and after 1883 he travelled with Buffalo Bill's show and similar 'wild west' shows as an interpreter and guardian of the Pawnee. In 1888 he set out with his own show, 'Pawnee Bill's Historic Wild West', but it soon failed. Settling in Wichita, Kansas, he led 'boomers' in the opening of the Oklahoma Territory (1889). He regrouped his wild west show in 1890 and it was extremely popular until 1909, when it merged with Buffalo Bill's. He feuded with Buffalo Bill and in 1913 retired to his 809-ha/2,000-acre ranch near Pawnee, Oklahoma, where he bred cattle and participated in civic affairs. Lillie was born in Bloomingdale, Indiana.

Lima Declaration agreement sponsored by US President Franklin D Roosevelt at the pan-American Conference December 1938 which held that a threat to the peace, security, or territory of any of the American republics would be a source of concern to all the republics. It was designed primarily to safeguard the American continent from the spread of fascism from Europe and to provide the USA and other states with a general mandate for intervention if necessary.

Lin Biao (or **Lin Piao) (1908–1971)**
Chinese communist soldier and
politician, deputy leader of the Chinese
Communist Party 1969–71. He joined
the communists in 1927, became a
commander of *Mao Zedong's Red
Army, and led the Northeast People's
Liberation Army after 1945 during the
*Chinese revolution (1927–49).
He became defence minister in 1959,
and as vice-chair of the party from
1969 he was expected to be Mao's
successor. In 1972 the government
announced that Lin had been killed
in an aeroplane crash in Mongolia on
17 September 1971 while fleeing to
the USSR following an abortive coup
attempt.

**Linlithgow, John Adrian Louis Hope,
1st Marquess Linlithgow (1860–1908)**
British administrator, son of the 6th
earl of Hopetoun, first governor
general of Australia 1900–02. Earl 1873,
Marquess 1902.

Li Peng (1928–)   Chinese communist
politician, a member of the Politburo
from 1985, and prime minister 1987–98.
A conservative hardliner, during the
pro-democracy demonstrations of 1989
he supported the massacre of students
by Chinese troops and the subsequent
execution of others. He sought
improved relations with the USSR
and favoured maintaining firm central
and party control over the economy.
In March 1998 Li stepped down as
prime minister, being replaced by the
more reformist Zhu Rongji, and was
elected chairman of the National
People's Congress (China's parliament).
He stepped down as NPC chairman in
March 2003.

Lithuania   country in northern Europe,
bounded north by Latvia, east by
Belarus, south by Poland and the
Kaliningrad area of Russia, and west
by the Baltic Sea.

Little Entente   series of alliances
between Czechoslovakia, Romania,
and Yugoslavia 1920–21 for mutual
security and the maintenance of

existing frontiers. Reinforced by the
Treaty of Belgrade 1929, the entente
collapsed upon Yugoslav cooperation
with Germany 1935–38 and the
Anglo-French abandonment of
Czechoslovakia in 1938.

Little Red Book   book of aphorisms
and quotations from the speeches and
writings of *Mao Zedong, in which he
adapted Marxist theory to Chinese
conditions. Published in 1966, the book
was printed in huge numbers and read
widely at the start of the *Cultural
Revolution.

Litvinov, Maxim (1876–1951)   adopted
name of **Meir Walach**, Soviet
politician, commissioner for foreign
affairs under Stalin from January 1931
until his removal from office in May
1939.

Liu Shaoqi (or **Liu Shao-chi)
(1898–1969)**   Chinese communist
politician, president 1960–65 and the
most prominent victim of the 1966–69
leftist *Cultural Revolution.
A Moscow-trained labour organizer,
he was a firm proponent of the Soviet
style of government based around
disciplined one-party control, the use
of incentive gradings, and priority for
industry over agriculture. This was
opposed by *Mao Zedong, but began
to be implemented by Liu while he
was state president 1960–65. Liu was
brought down during the *Cultural
Revolution.

Livingstone, Ken(neth) (1945–)
British Labour politician, mayor of
London from 2000. The leader of the
Greater London Council (GLC)
1981–86 and member of Parliament for
Brent East 1987–2001, he ran as an
independent in the London mayoral
election in 2000, opposing Frank
Dobson, the Labour Party's official
candidate. This led to his expulsion
from the Labour Party for five years;
he was readmitted by the party in
January 2004. As mayor, he introduced
the pioneering initiative of a
'congestion charge' on vehicles
entering central London.

Livonia German **Livland**, one of the former Baltic States, divided in 1918 between the modern states of Estonia and Latvia. Livonia belonged to the Teutonic Knights from the 13th to 16th centuries, to Poland from 1561, Sweden from 1629, and Russia from 1721.

Li Xiannian (1909–1992) Chinese communist politician, member of the Chinese Communist Party (CCP) Politburo from 1956, and state president 1983–88. He fell from favour during the 1966–69 Cultural Revolution, but was rehabilitated as finance minister in 1973, by *Zhou Enlai, and proceeded to implement cautious economic reform.

Lloyd, (John) Selwyn (Brooke) (1904–1978) Baron Selwyn Lloyd, British Conservative politician. He was foreign secretary 1955–60 and chancellor of the Exchequer 1960–62. He was made a baron in 1976.

Lloyd George, David, 1st Earl Lloyd-George of Dwyfor (1863–1945) British Liberal politician, prime minister 1916–22. A pioneer of social reform and the welfare state, as chancellor of the Exchequer 1908–15 he introduced old-age pensions in 1908 and health and unemployment insurance in 1911. High unemployment, intervention in the Russian Civil War, and use of the military police force, the *Black and Tans, in Ireland eroded his support as prime minister. The creation of the Irish Free State in 1921 and his pro-Greek policy against the Turks following the Greek invasion of Anatolia (Asian Turkey) caused the collapse of his coalition government.

Born in Manchester of Welsh parentage, Lloyd George was brought up in north Wales, became a solicitor, and was member of Parliament for Caernarvon Boroughs from 1890. During the Boer War, he was prominent as a pro-Boer. His 1909 budget (with graduated direct taxes and taxes on land values) provoked the Lords to reject it, and resulted in the Act of 1911 limiting their powers. He held ministerial posts during World War I until 1916 when there was an open breach between him and Prime Minister *Asquith, and he became prime minister of a coalition government. Securing a unified Allied command, he enabled the Allies to withstand the last German offensive and achieve victory. After World War I he had a major role in the Versailles peace treaty. In the 1918 elections, he achieved a huge majority over Labour and Asquith's followers. He had become largely distrusted within his own party by 1922, and never regained power. He was made an earl in 1945.

Locarno, Pact of series of diplomatic documents initialled in Locarno, Switzerland, on 16 October 1925 and formally signed in London on 1 December 1925. The pact settled the question of French security, and the signatories – Britain, France, Belgium, Italy, and Germany – guaranteed Germany's existing frontiers with France and Belgium. Following the signing of the pact, Germany was admitted to the League of Nations.

Lodge, Henry Cabot, II (1902–1985) US diplomat. He served as the US representative at the United Nations 1953–60. He was the Republican Party's unsuccessful candidate for vice-president in 1960. During the Vietnam War he was ambassador to South Vietnam 1963–64 and 1965–67, and President Nixon's negotiator in the peace talks of 1969.

Lomé Convention convention in 1975 that established economic cooperation between the European Economic Community and developing countries of Africa, the Caribbean, and the Pacific (ACP). It was renewed in 1979, 1985, 1989, and 2000.

London, Treaty of secret treaty signed on 26 April 1915 between Britain, France, Russia, and Italy. It promised Italy territorial gains (at the expense of

Austria-Hungary) on condition that it entered World War I on the side of the Triple Entente (Britain, France, and Russia). Italy's intervention did not achieve the rapid victories expected, and the terms of the treaty (revealed by Russia 1918) angered the USA. Britain and France refused to honour the treaty and, in the post-war peace treaties, Italy received far less territory than promised.

Londonderry, Charles Stewart Henry Vane-Tempest-Stewart (1878–1949) British statesman. He was secretary of state for air 1931–35. Churchill considered that the great achievement of Londonderry's period of office was the designing and promotion of the Hurricane and Spitfire fighters, which proved vital in the Battle of Britain.

Long, Huey (Pierce) 'the Kingfish' (1893–1935) US Democratic politician. As governor of Louisiana 1928–32 and senator for Louisiana 1932–35, he became legendary for his political rhetoric. He was popular with poor white voters for his programme of social and economic reform, which he called the 'Share Our Wealth' programme. It represented a significant challenge to F D Roosevelt's *New Deal economic programme.

Longford, Frank (Francis Aungier) Pakenham (1905–2001) 7th Earl of Longford, British Labour politician. He was brought up a Protestant but became a leading Catholic and an advocate of penal reform. He worked in the Conservative Party Economic Research Department 1930–32, yet became a member of the Labour Party and held ministerial posts 1948–51 and 1964–68. Earl 1961.

Long March in Chinese history, the 10,000-km/6,000-mi trek undertaken from 1934 to 1935 by *Mao Zedong and his communist forces from southeast to northwest China, under harassment from the Guomindang (nationalist) army; see *China: history 1900–49, **the Guomindang–communist conflict.**

Long Range Desert Group highly mobile British penetration force formed in July 1940 to carry out reconnaissance and raids deep in the desert of North Africa.

Loos, Battle of in World War I, unsuccessful French-British offensive September 1915 to recover the mining district around the towns of Loos and Lens from the Germans. This was the first action in which the British used gas, but the wind shifted and blew the gas back over British lines.

Lords, House of upper chamber of the UK Parliament. Following the House of Lords Act 1999, the number of hereditary peers (those with an inherited title) sitting in the upper chamber was reduced from 750 to a maximum of 92. In October 2001 there were 711 members of the House of Lords: 91 hereditary peers, 620 life peers (with title granted for the remainder of their lifetime), 2 archbishops, and 24 bishops. Together the hereditary and life peers form the Lords Temporal, of whom 26 are 'law lords'; the archbishops and bishops are the Lords Spiritual. In October 2001 the hereditary peers included 50 Conservative, 4 Labour, and 31 independent 'cross-bench' members. Of the life peers, 172 were Conservative, 193 Labour, and 145 'cross-benchers'. There were 117 women peers.

Lubbers, Rudolph Franz Marie (Ruud) (1939–) Dutch politician, prime minister of the Netherlands 1982–94. Leader of the right-of-centre Christian Democratic Appeal (CDA), he became minister for economic affairs in 1973. In October 2000, he was appointed United Nations High Commissioner for Refugees.

Ludendorff, Erich von (1865–1937) German general, chief of staff to Hindenburg in World War I, and responsible for the eastern-front victory at the Battle of Tannenberg in 1914. After Hindenburg's appointment as chief of general staff and

Ludendorff's as quartermaster-general in 1916, he was also politically influential and the two were largely responsible for the conduct of the war from then on. After the war he propagated the myth of the 'stab in the back', according to which the army had been betrayed by the politicians in 1918. He took part in the Nazi rising in Munich in 1923 and sat in the Reichstag (parliament) as a right-wing Nationalist.

Luftwaffe German air force used both in World War I and (as reorganized by the Nazi leader Hermann Goering in 1933) in World War II. The Luftwaffe also covered anti-aircraft defence and the launching of the flying bombs *V1 and V2.

Germany was not supposed to have an air force under the terms of the Treaty of Versailles 1918, so the Luftwaffe was covertly trained and organized using Lufthansa, the national airline, as a cover; its existence was officially announced 1 April 1935. It was an entirely tactical force under the command of Hermann *Goering but headed by Field Marshal Milch from 1936, subordinated to the General Staff as a direct support arm for the army, and was one of the vital components of the *Blitzkrieg* tactics. Although some officers advocated strategic long-range bombing, they were ignored, and except for maritime reconnaissance, the Luftwaffe never operated any long-range aircraft. The Luftwaffe was also responsible for Germany's anti-aircraft defences, operating both guns and aircraft.

Lugard, Frederick John Dealtry (1858–1945) 1st Baron Lugard, British colonial administrator. He served in the army 1878–89 and then worked for the British East Africa Company, for whom he took possession of Uganda in 1890. He was high commissioner for northern Nigeria 1900–06, governor of Hong Kong 1907–12, and governor general of Nigeria 1914–19.

Lumumba, Patrice Emergy (1925–1961) Congolese politician, prime minister of the Republic of the Congo (now the Democratic Republic of Congo) in 1960. Founder of the National Congolese Movement in 1958, he led his party to victory in the elections following independence in 1960. However, the country collapsed into civil war, and Lumumba was ousted in a coup led by Mobutu in September 1960, and murdered a few months later.

Lunacharski, Anatoli Vasilievich (1873–1933) Russian politician and literary critic. From the October Revolution until 1929, he was people's commissar for education in the Russian Federal Republic. Modernistic experimentation in schools ended with his removal from the ministry. Later, liberal Soviet literary critics referred to Lunacharski's views to support an easing of cultural policy.

Lüneburg Heath German **Lüneburger Heide**, low, sandy area in Lower Saxony, Germany, between the Elbe and Aller rivers and southeast of Hamburg; area 200 sq km/77 sq mi. The chief city on it is Lüneburg. It was here that more than a million German soldiers surrendered to British General Montgomery on 4 May 1945. It has been a nature park since 1920.

Lusitania ocean liner sunk by a German submarine on 7 May 1915 with the loss of 1,200 lives, including some US citizens; its destruction helped to bring the USA into World War I.

Luthuli (or Lutuli), Albert John (c. 1898–1967) South African politician, president of the *African National Congress 1952–67. Luthuli, a Zulu tribal chief, preached nonviolence and multiracialism. He was awarded the Nobel Prize for Peace in 1960 for his advocacy of a nonviolent struggle against *apartheid.

Luxembourg landlocked country in Western Europe, bounded north and west by Belgium, east by Germany, and south by France.

Luxemburg, Rosa (1870–1919)
Polish-born German communist.
She helped found the Polish Social
Democratic Party in the 1890s, the
forerunner of the Polish Communist
Party. She was a leader of the left wing
of the German Social Democratic Party
from 1898 where she collaborated
with Karl *Liebknecht in founding
the Spartacus League in 1918 (see
*Spartacist). Imprisoned during World
War I for opposing the continuation
of the war, she was also critical of
the decision to launch an uprising in
November 1918. She disagreed with
leading Polish left-wing ideologists
on the issue of Polish nationalism.
Luxemburg was also the author of
a Marxist critique of capitalist
imperialism, *The Accumulation of
Capital*. She was murdered, together
with Liebknecht, in January 1919 by
the Frei Corps who put down the
Spartacist uprising.

**Lyautey, Louis Gonzalve Hubert
(1854–1934)** French administrator
and soldier. Lyautey proved a able
colonial administrator in the new
French protectorate of Morocco, where
he was put in charge by Poincaré in
1912. Owing to his enlightened policy,
Morocco remained loyal to France in
World War I. In 1916–17 he was briefly
minister for war.

Lynch, Jack (John Mary) (1917–1999)
Irish politician, Taoiseach (prime
minister) 1966–73 and 1977–79, and
leader of Fianna Fáil 1966–79.

Lyons, Joseph Aloysius (1879–1939)
Australian politician, founder of the
United Australia (now Liberal) Party
in 1931, prime minister 1931–39.
Lyons followed the economic
orthodoxy of the time, drastically
cutting federal spending. He also
cracked down on communism and
introduced tough censorship laws.

Maastricht Treaty treaty establishing the *European Union (EU). Agreed in 1991 and signed in 1992, the treaty took effect on 1 November 1993 following ratification by member states. It advanced the commitment of member states to economic and monetary union (but included an opt-out clause for the United Kingdom); provided for intergovernmental arrangements for a common foreign and security policy; increased cooperation on justice and home affairs policy issues (though the Social Chapter was rejected by the UK until a change of government in 1997); introduced the concept of EU citizenship (as a supplement to national citizenship); established new regional development bodies; increased the powers of the European Parliament; and accepted the principle of subsidiarity (a controversial term defining the limits of European Community involvement in national affairs).

McAliskey, Bernadette Josephine (1947–) born **Bernadette Josephine Devlin**, Northern Irish political activist, prominent in the civil rights movement in Northern Ireland in the late 1960s. In 1969, at the age of 21, she was elected a member of the Westminster Parliament. In the same year she was arrested while leading Catholic rioters in the Bogside, Londonderry, and was sentenced to six months' imprisonment. She stood down as an MP at the 1974 general election. In 1981, along with her husband, Michael McAliskey, whom she married in 1973, she survived an assassination attempt after actively supporting IRA hunger strikers. She went on to chair the Independent Socialist Party of Ireland.

MacArthur, Douglas (1880–1964) US general in World War II, commander of US forces in the Far East and, from March 1942, of the Allied forces in the southwestern Pacific. After the surrender of Japan he commanded the Allied occupation forces there. During 1950 he commanded the UN forces in Korea, but in April 1951, after expressing views contrary to US and UN policy, he was relieved of all his commands by President Truman.

MacBride, Seán (1904–1988) Irish revolutionary, politician, lawyer, and peace campaigner. He became chief of staff of the IRA in 1936 but left the movement after the 1937 constitution, and broke with it completely over its 1939 bombing campaign. He won a reputation as a great barrister for his defence of IRA suspects during the war years and founded Clann na Poblachta (Children of the Republic) in 1946. He took his party into coalition as part of the interparty government, 1948–51, in which he was minister for external affairs, and split the second interparty government in 1957 over its handling of the IRA's border campaign. He shared the Nobel Prize for Peace in 1974 with Japanese politician Eisaku *Sato for his campaign for human rights.

McCarthy, Eugene Joseph (1916–) US politician. He was elected to the House of Representatives in 1948 and to the Senate in 1958. An early opponent of the Vietnam War, he ran for president in 1968. Although his upset victory in the New Hampshire primary forced incumbent Lyndon Johnson out of the race, McCarthy lost the Democratic nomination to Hubert Humphrey.

McCarthy, Joe (Joseph Raymond) (1908–1957) US right-wing Republican politician. His unsubstantiated claim in 1950 that the State Department had been infiltrated by communists started a wave of anticommunist hysteria, wild accusations, and blacklists, which continued until he was discredited in 1954. He was censured by the Senate for misconduct.

McCarthyism period of political persecution during the 1950s, led by US senator Joe *McCarthy, during which many public officials and private citizens were accused of being communists or communist sympathizers. Although McCarthy was officially censured by the Senate for misconduct in 1954 (most of his evidence was fabricated), his claims induced an atmosphere of suspicion and paranoia that destroyed many careers. The term has come to signify any type of reckless political persecution or witch hunt.

MacDonald, (James) Ramsay (1866–1937) British politician, first Labour prime minister January–October 1924 and 1929–31, born in Morayshire, Scotland. He left the party to form a coalition government in 1931, which was increasingly dominated by Conservatives, until he was replaced by Stanley Baldwin in 1935.

Macdonald, Hector Archibald (1852–1903) British soldier, known as 'Fighting Mac'. At 18 he enlisted in the Gordon Highlanders. He was taken prisoner at Majuba in the first Boer war (1881), but Boer commander Gen Joubert returned him his sword on account of his bravery. He routed the Mahdi's troops at the Battle of Omdurman (1898).

Macedonia landlocked country in southeast Europe, bounded north by Serbia, west by Albania, south by Greece, and east by Bulgaria.

McGovern, George (Stanley) (1922–) US Democratic politician. He was elected to the US House of Representatives in 1956, served as an adviser to the Kennedy administration, and was a senator 1963–81. A strong opponent of the Vietnam War, he won the Democratic presidential nomination in 1972, but was soundly defeated by the incumbent, Richard Nixon.

Machel, Samora Moises (1933–1986) Mozambique nationalist leader, president 1975–86. Machel was active in the liberation front *Frelimo from its conception in 1962, fighting for independence from Portugal. He became Frelimo leader in 1966, and Mozambique's first president from independence in 1975 until his death in a plane crash near the South African border.

Maclean, Donald Duart (1913–1983) English spy who worked for the USSR while in the UK civil service. He defected to the USSR in 1951 together with Guy *Burgess.

Macmillan, (Maurice) Harold (1894–1986) 1st Earl of Stockton, British Conservative politician, prime minister 1957–63; foreign secretary 1955 and chancellor of the Exchequer 1955–57. In 1963 he attempted to negotiate British entry into the European Economic Community (EEC), but was blocked by the French president Charles de Gaulle. Much of his career as prime minister was spent defending the UK's retention of a nuclear weapon, and he was responsible for the purchase of US Polaris missiles in 1962.

McNamara, Joseph D (1934–) US police chief, detective writer, and research fellow. Known for his best-selling detective novels, he spent 35 years in active law enforcement, which included serving as police chief of Kansas City, Missouri (1973–76), and police chief of San Jose, California (1976–91). He was a criminal justice fellow at Harvard Law School (from 1969) and was named a research fellow at the Hoover Institution at Stanford University in 1991. In addition to detective thrillers such as *Fatal Command*, he was the author of *Safe and Sane*, a crime prevention textbook, among several other non-fiction works, and numerous articles. McNamara was born in New York City.

MacSwiney, Terence (1879–1920) Irish writer and revolutionary. In March 1920 he was elected Lord Mayor of Cork, following the murder of his predecessor by police. In August he was arrested for possession of a Royal Irish Constabulary cipher and sentenced to two years' imprisonment. He immediately began a hunger strike, demanding his unconditional release. He died in Brixton Prison after a fast of 74 days, which attracted worldwide attention.

McVeigh, Timothy (1968–2001) former US Army soldier who was convicted for the 1995 Oklahoma City bombing in Oklahoma, the worst terrorist attack in US history. He was executed in 2001.

Madagascar island country in the Indian Ocean, off the coast of East Africa, about 400 km/280 mi from Mozambique.

Madariaga, Salvador de (1886–1978) Spanish author and diplomat. His works include *Shelley and Calderón and other Essays* 1920; 'Don Quixote' 1934, an introductory essay; *The World's Design* 1938; *Christopher Columbus* 1939; *Hernán Cortes* 1941; *The Fall of the Spanish-American Empire* and *The Rise of the Spanish-American Empire* both 1947; *Bolívar* 1952; *Democracy versus Liberty* 1958; and *Latin America between the Eagle and the Bear* 1962.

Madero, Francisco Indalecio (1873–1913) Mexican liberal politician, president 1911–13. He took over the presidency from Porfirio Díaz after his resignation following political unrest. However, internal divisions and the continuing civil war paralysed the government. In February 1913, Victoriano *Huerta, the commander of the government

forces, plotted with rebels in Mexico City and assassinated Madero's brother. He then imprisoned Madero on charges of treason, and usurped power. Madero was murdered on 22 February 1923, after he had allegedly sought to escape.

Mafeking, Siege of Boer siege, during the South African War, of the British-held town (now **Mafikeng**) from 12 October 1899 to 17 May 1900. The British commander Col Robert Baden-Powell held the Boers off and kept morale high until a relief column arrived and relieved the town. The raising of the siege was a great boost to morale in Britain.

Maginot Line French fortification system along the German frontier from Switzerland to Luxembourg built 1929–36 under the direction of the war minister, André Maginot. It consisted of semi-underground forts joined by underground passages, and was protected by antitank defences; lighter fortifications continued the line to the sea. In 1940 German forces pierced the Belgian frontier line and outflanked the Maginot Line.

Maguire Seven seven Irish victims of a miscarriage of justice. In 1976 Annie Maguire, five members of her family, and a family friend were imprisoned in London for possessing explosives. All seven of the convictions were overturned in June 1991.

Mahathir bin Muhammad (1925–) Malaysian politician, prime minister 1981–2003. Leader of the New United Malays' National Organization (UMNO Baru), his 'look east' economic policy, which emulated Japanese industrialization, met with considerable success, but faced its first serious challenge in 1997 when the Malaysian currency came under attack from international speculators. This forced austerity measures in 1998, including the repatriation of many foreign workers. He stepped down as prime minister in October 2003.

Major, John (1943–) British Conservative politician, prime minister 1990–97. He was foreign secretary in 1989 and chancellor of the Exchequer 1989–90. His low-key, consensus style of leadership contrasted sharply with his predecessor Margaret *Thatcher. He launched a joint UK–Irish peace initiative on Northern Ireland in 1993, which led to a general ceasefire in 1994. His Back to Basics campaign to restore traditional values was undermined by a series of scandals involving Conservative ministers, and continuing party divisions led to his resigning as party leader in June 1995 to force a leadership vote, which he won narrowly. The Conservatives were heavily defeated in the 1997 general election, after which Major stepped down as party leader. In 2001 he retired from the House of Commons to pursue a career in business.

Makarios III (1913–1977) born **Mikhail Christodoulou Mouskos**, Cypriot politician and Greek Orthodox archbishop 1950–77. A leader of the Greek-Cypriot resistance organization *EOKA, he was exiled by the British to the Seychelles 1956–57 for supporting armed action to achieve union with Greece (*enosis*). He was president of the republic of Cyprus 1960–77 (briefly deposed by a Greek military coup July–Dec 1974).

Makhno, Nestor Ivanovich (1889–1935) Ukrainian Anarchist leader. He commanded a peasant army during the Civil War, then allied himself with the Red Army in 1919–20. A new conflict soon broke out between the Soviets and Makhno's force and he was defeated. He then emigrated.

Malan, Daniel François (1874–1959) South African right-wing politician, prime minister 1948–54. He founded the Purified National Party in 1934. His policy of *apartheid was implemented in a series of acts of parliament including the Group Areas Act, the Mixed Marriages Act, and the Immorality Act.

Malawi country in southeast Africa, bounded north and northeast by Tanzania; east, south, and west by Mozambique; and west by Zambia.

Malayan Emergency civil conflict in British-ruled Malaya, officially lasting from 1948 to 1960. The Communist Party of Malaya (CPM) launched an insurrection, calling for immediate Malayan independence. Britain responded by mounting a large-scale military and political counter-insurgency operation, while agreeing to eventual independence. In 1957 Malaya became independent and the state of emergency was ended in 1960, although some CPM guerrillas continue to operate.

Malaysia country in southeast Asia, comprising the Malay Peninsula, bounded north by Thailand, and surrounded east and south by the South China Sea and west by the Strait of Malacca; and the states of Sabah and Sarawak in the northern part of the island of Borneo (southern Borneo is part of Indonesia).

Malcolm X (1926–1965) adopted name of **Malcolm Little**, US black nationalist leader. After converting to Islam, he joined the *Nation of Islam sect, became a persuasive speaker about white exploitation of black people, and gained a large popular following, especially among black youth. He opposed the *civil-rights movement and, instead of integration and equality, advocated black separatism and self-dependence, using violent means if necessary for self-defence. His *Autobiography of Malcolm X*, written with Alex Haley, was published in 1965.

Maldives group of 1,196 islands in the north Indian Ocean, about 640 km/ 400 mi southwest of Sri Lanka; only 203 of them are inhabited.

Malenkov, Georgi Maximilianovich (1902–1988) Soviet prime minister 1953–55, Stalin's designated successor but abruptly ousted as Communist Party secretary within two weeks of Stalin's death by *Khrushchev, and forced out as prime minister in 1955 by *Bulganin.

Mali landlocked country in northwest Africa, bounded to the northeast by Algeria, east by Niger, southeast by Burkina Faso, south by Côte d'Ivoire, southwest by Senegal and Guinea, and west and north by Mauritania.

Malik, Yakob Alexandrovich (1906–1980) Soviet diplomat. He was permanent representative at the United Nations 1948–53 and 1968–76, and it was his walkout from the Security Council in January 1950 that allowed the authorization of UN intervention in Korea (see *Korean War).

Malinovsky, Rodion Yakovlevich (1898–1967) Russian soldier and politician. In World War II he fought at Stalingrad, commanded in the Ukraine, and led the Soviet advance through the Balkans to capture Budapest in 1945 before going east to lead the invasion of Manchuria. He was minister of defence 1957–67.

Malta island in the Mediterranean Sea, south of Sicily, east of Tunisia, and north of Libya.

Manchuria European name for the northeastern region of China, comprising the provinces of Heilongjiang, Jilin, and Liaoning. It was united with China by the Manchu dynasty in 1644, but as the Chinese Empire declined, Japan and Russia were rivals for its control.

The Russians were expelled after the *Russo-Japanese War 1904–05, and in 1932 Japan consolidated its position by creating a puppet state, **Manchukuo**, nominally led by the Chinese pretender to the throne Henry P'u-i. At the end of World War II the Soviets occupied Manchuria in a two-week operation in August 1945. Japanese settlers were expelled when the region was returned to Chinese control.

mandate in history, a territory whose administration was entrusted to Allied states by the League of Nations under the Treaty of Versailles after World

War I. Mandated territories were former German and Turkish possessions (including Iraq, Syria, Lebanon, and Palestine). When the United Nations replaced the League of Nations in 1945, mandates that had not achieved independence became known as trust territories.

Mandela, Nelson (Rolihlahla) (1918–) South African politician and lawyer, president 1994–99. He was president of the *African National Congress (ANC) 1991–97. Imprisoned from 1964, as organizer of the then banned ANC, he became a symbol of unity for the worldwide anti-*apartheid movement. In February 1990 he was released, the ban on the ANC having been lifted, and entered into negotiations with the government about a multiracial future for South Africa. In May 1994 he was sworn in as South Africa's first post-apartheid president after the ANC won 62.65% of the vote in universal-suffrage elections. He shared the Nobel Prize for Peace in 1993 with South African president F W *de Klerk for their work towards dismantling apartheid and negotiating the transition to a non-racial democracy. In June 1999 he stepped down as president and was succeeded by ANC president, Thabo Mbeki.

Mandela was born near Umtata, south of Lesotho, the son of a local chief. In a trial of several ANC leaders, he was acquitted of treason in 1961, but was once more arrested in 1964 and given a life sentence on charges of sabotage and plotting to overthrow the government. In February 1990 he was released from prison on the orders of state president F W de Klerk and in July 1991 was elected, unopposed, to the presidency of the ANC. In December 1991 the ANC began constitutional negotiations with the government and in February 1993 Mandela and President de Klerk agreed to the formation of a government of national unity after free, non-racial elections (that took place in 1994). Relations between Mandela and de Klerk deteriorated when former members of de Klerk's security forces were prosecuted in March 1996, and de Klerk announced his decision to withdraw his Nationalist party from the coalition in May 1996. Mandela stepped down as ANC president in December 1997 and was replaced by his former deputy Thabo Mbeki. He was appointed as UN mediator for the seven-year civil war in Burundi in January 2000.

Mandela married the South African civil-rights activist Winnie *Mandela in 1958. They separated in 1992 and were divorced in 1996. In 1998 he married Graca Machel, the widow of the Mozambique nationalist leader. His autobiography, *Long Walk to Freedom* (1994) was widely acclaimed, and his state visit to Britain in July 1996 was a resounding success.

Mandela, Winnie Madikizela (Nomzamo) (1934–) South African civil-rights activist, former wife of Nelson Mandela. A leading spokesperson for the African National Congress (ANC) during Nelson Mandela's imprisonment 1964–90, in 1991 she received a six-year prison sentence for her role in the kidnapping and assault of four youths. Her sentence was later waived and in May 1994, following the ANC's victory in the country's first universal-suffrage elections, she was given a deputy ministerial post in the new government. In 1995 she was dismissed from her cabinet post, following allegations of dereliction of duty. In 2003 she was found guilty of fraud and theft, and was sentenced to five years in prison.

Manley, Norman Washington (1893–1969) Jamaican centre-left politician, chief minister 1955–59 and prime minister 1959–62. With his cousin Alexander *Bustamante, he dominated Jamaican politics until his death. Manley formed the democratic-socialist People's National Party (PNP), the country's first political party, in 1938. As chief minister, he helped create the Federation of the West Indies in 1958. After internal self-government was achieved in 1959, Manley embarked on a programme of economic development, promoting the tourist and bauxite industries, and land reform.

Mann Act US Act of Congress of 1910 that was introduced by Republican Representative James Mann, in response to fears of trafficking in women (the 'white slave trade'). The Act made it an offence to transport a woman across state borders 'for the purposes of prostitution or debauchery, or for any other immoral purpose'. Subsequently the Act became notorious for its widespread use by the FBI as a catch-all offence used against those for whom a better charge could not be found, for example heavyweight boxer Jack Johnson, Charlie Chaplin, and Chuck Berry. In the 1960s this misuse of the Act was increasingly eliminated.

Mannerheim, Carl Gustav Emil von (1867–1951) Finnish general and politician, leader of the conservative forces in the civil war 1917–18 and regent 1918–19. He commanded the Finnish army 1939–40 and 1941–44, and was president of Finland 1944–46.

Manstein, (Fritz) Erich von (1887–1973) adopted name of **Erich von Lewinski**, German field marshal. He served as Chief of Staff to von *Rundstedt in the Polish and French campaigns 1939–40 and commanded a Panzer corps in the invasion of the USSR 1941. He was given the task of capturing Leningrad August 1942, but was then moved to Army Group Don and ordered to relieve the German 6th Army trapped in Stalingrad. He was unable to help the trapped army but dealt with the subsequent Soviet offensive and captured Kharkov. He fought at the Battle of Kursk

July 1943, after which he conducted the withdrawal of Army Group South. After a series of arguments with Hitler over this withdrawal he was dismissed and took no further part in the war. He was imprisoned as a war criminal 1945–53.

Manuel II (1889–1932) King of Portugal 1908–10. He ascended the throne on the assassination of his father, Carlos I, but was driven out by a revolution in 1910, and lived in England.

Mao Dun (or Mao Tun) (1896–1981) pseudonym of **Shen Yanbin (or Shen Yen-ping)**, Chinese writer. He wrote a trilogy of novellas, published as *Shi (Eclipse)* (1930); a best-selling novel, *Ziye (Midnight)* (1932), about financial exploiters in the decadent Shanghai of the time; and a collection of short stories. In 1930 he helped to organize the influential League of Left-Wing Writers. After the Communists came to power in 1949 he was China's first minister of culture 1949–65, and founder editor of the literary journal *People's Literature* 1949–53.

Mao Zedong (or Mao Tse-tung) (1893–1976) Chinese communist politician and theoretician, leader of the Chinese Communist Party (CCP) 1935–76. Mao was a founder of the CCP in 1921, and became its leader in 1935. He organized the *Long March 1934–35 and the war of liberation 1937–49, following which he established a People's Republic and communist rule in China. He was state president until 1959, and headed the CCP until his death. His influence diminished with the failure of his 1958–60 *Great Leap Forward, but he emerged dominant again during the 1966–69 *Cultural Revolution, which he launched in order to promote his own antibureaucratic line and to purge the party of 'revisionism'.

Mao adapted communism to Chinese conditions, as set out in the *Little Red Book* (1960), in which he stressed the need for rural rather than urban-based revolutions in Asia; for reducing rural–urban differences; and for perpetual revolution to prevent the emergence of new elites. He advocated a 'mass line' form of leadership, involving the broad mobilization of the people in economic, social, and political movements. He was also an advocate of a non-aligned strategy for the developing world, and helped to precipitate the Sino-Soviet split after 1960, which arose when the USSR withdrew military and technical support from China. His writings and thoughts dominated the functioning of the People's Republic 1949–76, and some 740 million copies of his *Quotations* have been printed to date, while his works as a whole total over 2,000 publications.

Mapai acronym for *Miphlegeth Poale Eretz Israel*, **'Party of the Workers of the Land of Israel'**, Israeli Workers' Party or Labour Party, founded in 1930. Its leading figure until 1965 was David Ben-Gurion. In 1968, the party allied with two other democratic socialist parties to form the Israeli Labour Party.

Marchais, Georges (1920–1997) French communist politician. As general secretary of the French Communist Party (PCF) 1972–94, Marchais presided over his party's decline, its vote dropping in parliamentary elections from 21% in 1973 to 10% in 1986, and in presidential elections to under 8% in 1988.

March on Rome, the means by which fascist leader Benito Mussolini came to power in Italy in 1922. A protracted crisis in government and the threat of civil war enabled him to demand the formation of a fascist government to restore order. On 29 October 1922, King Victor Emmanuel III invited Mussolini to come to Rome to take power. The 'march' was a propaganda myth: Mussolini travelled overnight by train from Milan to Rome, where he formed a government the following day, 30 October. Some 25,000 fascist Blackshirts were also transported to the city, where they marched in a ceremonial parade on 31 October.

Marco Polo bridge incident conflict in 1937 between Chinese and Japanese army troops on the border of Japanese-controlled Manchukuo and China that led to full-scale war between the two states. It lasted until the Japanese surrender in 1945.

Marcos, Ferdinand Edralin (1917–1989) Filipino right-wing politician, dictator-president 1965–86, when he was forced into exile in Hawaii by a popular front led by Corazon *Aquino.

Marcos, Imelda Romualdez (1930–) Filipino politician and socialite, wife of the dictator-president Ferdinand *Marcos, and known as the 'Iron Butterfly'.

Margai, Milton A(ugustus) S(triery) (1895–1964) Sierra Leone nationalist leader and politician, prime minister 1959–64. Appointed a member of the protectorate assembly in 1940, he helped found the Sierra Leone People's Party (SLPP) in 1951, and played a major role in pressing for independence. He was chief minister 1954–58 and, as prime minister of a coalition government from 1959, steered Sierra Leone to full independence in 1961. In international affairs he exercised a moderating influence on his contemporaries in other African States. On his death he was succeeded as party leader and prime minister by his half-brother Albert Margai (1910–1980).

Margaret (1930–2002) Margaret Rose, Princess of the UK, younger daughter of George VI and sister of Elizabeth II. In 1960 she married Anthony Armstrong-Jones, later created Lord Snowdon, but they were divorced in 1978. Their children are David, Viscount Linley (1961–) and Lady Sarah Chatto (1964–).

Margrethe II (1940–) Queen of Denmark from 1972, when she succeeded her father Frederick IX. In 1967, she married the French diplomat Count Henri de Laborde de Monpezat, who took the title Prince Hendrik. Her heir is Crown Prince Frederick (1968–).

Market Garden, Operation in World War II, unsuccessful operation by British and US forces to cross the Meuse, Waal, and Neder-Rijn rivers in Holland in September 1944.

Markievicz, Constance Georgina, Countess Markievicz (1868–1927) born **Constance Georgina Gore Booth**, Irish socialist, revolutionary, and politician. Founder of Na Fianna, the republican youth organization, in 1909, she joined the Irish Citizen Army and took part in the *Easter Rising of 1916; her resulting death sentence was commuted. In 1918 she was elected to Westminster as a Sinn Fein candidate (technically the first British woman MP), but did not take her seat, instead serving as minister for labour in the first Dáil Éireann (then the illegal republican parliament) 1919–22.

Markov, Georgi (1929–1978) Bulgarian playwright and novelist who fled to the UK 1971; he was assassinated by being jabbed with a poisoned umbrella.

Marne, Battles of the in World War I, two unsuccessful German offensives in northern France. In the **First Battle** 6–9 September 1914, German advance was halted by French and British troops under the overall command of the French general Joseph Joffre; in the **Second Battle** 15 July–4 August 1918, the German advance was defeated by British, French, and US troops under the French general Henri Pétain, and German morale crumbled.

Marshall, George C(atlett) (1880–1959) US general and diplomat. He was army chief of staff in World War II, secretary of state 1947–49, and secretary of defence September 1950–September 1951. He was awarded the Nobel Prize for Peace in 1953 for initiating the *Marshall Plan for European economic recovery in 1947.

Marshall, Thurgood (1908–1993) US jurist and civil-rights leader. As a prominent civil-rights lawyer, he frequently presided over landmark cases such as * *Brown* v. *Board of Education* (1954). Marshall was named director of the *National Association for the Advancement of Colored People (NAACP) Legal Defense and Education Fund in 1940. He was named to the US Court of Appeals in 1961 and served as solicitor general 1965–67. In 1967 President Johnson appointed him to the US Supreme Court, a post he held until 1991. The first black Supreme Court justice, Marshall was a strong voice for civil and individual rights throughout his career.

Marshall Islands country in the west Pacific Ocean, part of Micronesia, occupying 31 atolls (the Ratak and Ralik chains).

Marshall Plan programme of US economic aid to Europe, set up at the end of World War II, totalling $13.3 billion throughout the life of the programme from 1948 to 1952 (equivalent to more than $88 billion late 1990s dollars). Post-war Europe was in a state of economic collapse and physical ruin and the USA, as the world's richest nation, intended to resurrect the European economy and combat the perceived danger of a communist takeover in Europe. Officially known as the European Recovery Program, it was announced by Secretary of State George C *Marshall in a speech at Harvard in June 1947, but it was in fact the work of a State Department group led by Dean *Acheson.

Martens, Wilfried (1936–) Belgian politician; prime minister 1979–92. He was president of the Dutch-speaking Social Christian Party (CVP) 1972–79 and, as prime minister, headed several coalition governments in the period 1979–92, when he was replaced by Jean-Luc Dehaene heading a new coalition.

Martov, Yuly Osipovich (1873–1923) adopted name of **Yuly Osipovich Tsederbaum**, Russian revolutionary. He was a member of the Social Democratic Party from 1892 and leader of the Mensheviks. He cooperated with Lenin at first, but broke with him in 1903. After the October Revolution he became official leader of the Menshevik party.

Mary, Queen (1867–1953) Consort of George V of Great Britain and Ireland. She was the only daughter of the Duke and Duchess of Teck, the latter a grand-daughter of George III. In 1891 she was engaged to marry Prince Albert Victor (born 1864), Duke of Clarence and eldest son of the Prince of Wales (later Edward VII), but he died in 1892, and in 1893 she married his brother George, Duke of York, who succeeded to the throne in 1910.

Masaryk, Jan Garrigue (1886–1948) Czechoslovak politician, son of Tomáš Masaryk. He was foreign minister from 1940, when the Czechoslovak government was exiled in London in World War II. He returned in 1945, retaining the post, but as a result of political pressure by the communists committed suicide.

Masire, Quett Ketumile Joni (1925–) Botswanan politician; president 1980–98. In 1962, with Seretse *Khama, he founded the Botswana Democratic Party (BDP) and in 1965 was made deputy prime minister. After independence in 1966, he became vice-president and, on Khama's death in 1980, president, continuing a policy of non-alignment. He retired in March 1998 and was succeeded by Festus Mogae of the BDP.

Massey, (Charles) Vincent (1887–1967) Canadian Liberal Party politician.

He was the first Canadian to become governor general of Canada 1952–59.

Massey, William Ferguson (1856–1925) New Zealand right-of-centre politician, prime minister 1912–25. He concentrated initially on controlling militant unions and the newly formed Federation of Labour. He drew upon fellow farmers, 'Massey Cossacks', to act as special constabulary strike breakers in the goldfields and Wellington docks in 1912–13. He also led the country through World War I, supporting the UK war effort, although he was intellectually an isolationist. He attended the Paris Peace Conference at the war's conclusion and was re-elected with a large majority in December 1919. He died in office, and remains today New Zealand's longest-serving prime minister.

Mata Hari (1876–1917) stage name of **Margaretha Geertruida Zelle**, Dutch courtesan, dancer, and probable spy. In World War I she had affairs with highly placed military and government officials on both sides and told Allied secrets to the Germans. She may have been a double agent, in the pay of both France and Germany. She was shot by the French on espionage charges.

Matapan southernmost cape of mainland Greece, off which, on 28 March 1941, during World War II, a British fleet under Admiral Cunningham sank an Italian squadron.

Matsuoka, Yosuke (1880–1946) Japanese politician, foreign minister 1940–41. A fervent nationalist, Matsuoka led Japan out of the League of Nations in 1933 when it condemned Japan for the seizure of Manchuria. As foreign minister, he allied Japan with Germany and Italy. At the end of World War II, he was arrested as a war criminal but died before his trial was concluded.

Matteotti, Giacomo (1885–1924) Italian socialist politician. After Mussolini gained power in 1922, Matteotti was an outspoken opponent

of the Fascist regime. He was, consequently, murdered in June 1924.

Maudling, Reginald (1917–1979) British Conservative politician, chancellor of the Exchequer 1962–64, contender for the party leadership in 1965, and home secretary 1970–72.

Mau Mau Kenyan secret guerrilla movement 1952–60, an offshoot of the Kikuyu Central Association banned in World War II. Its aim was to end British colonial rule. This was achieved in 1960 with the granting of Kenyan independence and the election of Jomo Kenyatta as Kenya's first prime minister.

A state of emergency was declared in 1952, and by 1956 colonial government forces had killed more than 11,000 Kikuyu. More than 100 Europeans and Asians and 2,000 progovernment Kikuyu were killed by the Mau Mau. The state of emergency was ended in 1960, and three years later Kenya achieved independence.

Mauritania country in northwest Africa, bounded northeast by Algeria, east and south by Mali, southwest by Senegal, west by the Atlantic Ocean, and northwest by Western Sahara.

Mauritius island country in the Indian Ocean, east of Madagascar.

Mauroy, Pierre (1928–) French socialist politician, prime minister 1981–84. He oversaw the introduction of a radical reflationary programme. He was first secretary (leader) of the Socialist Party 1988–1992.

Maurras, Charles Marie Photius (1868–1952) French writer. The leading spirit of the extreme nationalist movement Action Française, he was imprisoned 1945–52 as a collaborator during the German occupation of France. His works include criticism, prose tales, and poetry, and his collected writings about World War I were published as *Les Conditions de la victoire/The Terms of Victory* 1916–18.

Maxton, James (1885–1946) Scottish politician, chair of the Independent

Labour Party 1926–40, and member of Parliament for Bridgeton, Glasgow, from 1922 until his death. One of the most turbulent 'Red Clydesiders', he was expelled from the House of Commons in 1923 for calling a minister a murderer. As chair of the Independent Labour Party, he led its secession for the Labour Party in 1932, and became increasingly isolated from mainstream Labour politics. His extreme views won few supporters, but his sincerity won the respect of many.

May 4th Movement Chinese student-led nationalist movement ignited by demonstrations in Beijing in 1919. It demanded that China's unpopular warlord government reject the decision by the Versailles peace conference to confirm Japan's rights over the Shandong peninsula that had been asserted in the *Twenty-one demands in 1915.

Maya member of a prehistoric American Indian civilization originating in the Yucatán Peninsula in Central America about 2600 BC, with later sites in Mexico, Guatemala, and Belize. Their language belonged to the Totonac-Mayan family. From AD 325 to 925 (Classical Period) the Maya culture dominated the region, after which it declined under pressure from the Toltec and, from the 16th century, the Spanish. The Maya are known for their ceremonial centres, which included stepped pyramids, ball courts, and astronomical observatories. Today Maya live in Yucatán, Guatemala, Belize, and western Honduras, and number 8–9 million (1994 est). Many speak Maya along with Spanish, but they are now Roman Catholic.

Mbeki, Thabo (1942–) South African politician, first executive deputy president from 1994 and president from 1999. As chair of the *African National Congress (ANC) from 1989, he played an important role in the constitutional talks with the de Klerk government that eventually led to the adoption of a nonracial political system. In December 1997 he replaced Nelson Mandela as ANC President, and in June 1999 succeeded him as president.

Mboya, Tom (Thomas Joseph) (1930–1969) Kenyan politician and trade unionist. He helped found the Kenya African National Union (*KANU) in 1960, becoming its secretary general. A prominent pan-Africanist, he was elected chair of the All-African People's Conference in Ghana during 1958. He served as minister of labour prior to independence in 1963, and became minister of economic affairs from 1964 until his assassination.

Means, Russell (1939–) US Oglala Sioux activist. In 1970 he founded the second chapter of the American Indian Movement (AIM) in Cleveland, Ohio. His flair for guerrilla theatre, including the seizure of the Mayflower II on Thanksgiving in 1970 and the Trail of Broken Treaties in 1972, helped bring AIM to national attention. In response to clashes between police and AIM supporters in South Dakota, he and 200 followers seized control of Wounded Knee in 1973 for 71 days.

Medicare US health-care insurance programme, administered and financed by the federal government, providing medical benefits to citizens aged 65 or over. Originally proposed by President John F Kennedy as part of his 'New Frontier' programme to attack poverty, it was introduced by President Lyndon B Johnson in 1965. Unlike the US health-care programme Medicaid, Medicare largely escaped cutbacks in federal spending during the Republican presidency of Ronald Reagan (1981–88), but was subject to budgetary pressures under Republican president George Bush (1989–92). With the federal budget moving towards surplus, in 1998 the Democrat president Bill Clinton proposed increased spending on Medicare.

Médici, Emilio Garrastazú (1905–1986)
Brazilian dictator-president 1969–74.
He was elected to presidental office by
a military junta in 1969, succeeding
president Artur da Costa e Silva.
His reign was marked by strong
oppression and dictatorial powers,
but his administration governed the
nation successfully and brought about
economic vibrancy. He was replaced
in 1974 by his own appointed
successor, Ernesto Giesel.

medicine, 19th-century the 19th
century was a period of enormous
medical change and progress.
Many diseases that had been fatal in
1800 were either treatable by 1900,
or a cure would be found very early
in the 20th century using techniques
developed by 19th-century scientists.
Doctors, chemists, and scientists
investigated medicine using the new
scientific technology made available
by the Industrial Revolution, and made
discoveries that changed the face of
medical practice. Government
involvement in medicine and public
health also changed dramatically
during the 19th century. In 1800
governments refused to act to protect
the health of the public, but by 1900
the principle of government
responsibility had been well
established in many European countries.
The training of doctors and nurses
was fundamentally altered, along
with the organization of hospitals.
Most important was the development
of germ theory by Louis Pasteur,
a discovery that gave doctors and
scientists the key to understanding,
treating, and preventing disease.

Meighen, Arthur (1874–1960)
Canadian Conservative politician.
He was prime minister 1920–21 and
1926–27. Between 1913 and 1920 he
successively held the posts of solicitor
general, secretary of state, and minister
of the interior.

Meiji, Mutsuhito (1852–1912)
Emperor of Japan from 1867, under the
regnal era name Meiji ('enlightened').
During his reign Japan became a world
industrial and naval power. His
ministers abolished the feudal system
and discrimination against the lowest
caste, established state schools,
reformed the civil service, and
introduced conscription, the Western
calendar, and other measures to
modernize Japan, including a
constitution in 1889.

Mein Kampf (German **'my struggle'**)
book dictated by the Nazi leader
Adolf *Hitler to his deputy Rudolf Hess
1923–24, during their imprisonment in
the Bavarian fortress of Landsberg for
attempting the 1923 Munich *beer-hall
putsch. Part autobiography, part
political philosophy, the book presents
Hitler's ideas of German expansion,
anticommunism, and anti-Semitism,
and formed the blueprint for the racist
ideology of National Socialism. It was
published in two volumes, in 1925
and 1927.

Meir, Golda (1898–1978) born
Golda Mabovitch, later **Golda Myerson**,
Israeli Labour politician; foreign
minister 1956–66 and prime minister
1969–74. Criticism of the Israelis' lack
of preparation for the 1973 Arab-Israeli
War led to election losses for Labour
and, unable to form a government,
she resigned.

Born in Russia, she emigrated to the
USA in 1906, and in 1921 went to
Palestine.

Mellon, Andrew William (1855–1937)
US financier who donated his art
collection to found the National
Gallery of Art, Washington, DC, in
1937. He was secretary of the Treasury
1921–32, pursuing tax-cutting policies.

Menchú Tum, Rigoberta (1959–)
Guatemalan campaigner for the rights
of indigenous peoples. She was
awarded the Nobel Prize for Peace
in 1992 for her efforts to promote
intercultural peace and she returned
from exile to live and campaign in
Guatemala.

Menderes, Adnan (1899–1961)
Turkish politician. In 1945 he became
one of the leaders of the new
Democratic Party and was made prime
minister when it came to power in 1950.
Re-elected in 1954 and 1957, he was
deposed in 1960 and superseded by
General Cemal Gursel following an army
coup. He was put on trial and hanged.

**Mendès-France, Pierre Isaac Isadore
(1907–1982)** French centre-left
politician. His premiership, July
1954–February 1955, secured France's
negotiated withdrawal from Indochina
in August 1954, the granting of
political autonomy to France's
Tunisian protectorate, and a major
package of economic reforms,
introducing a regional dimension to
economic planning and also a value-
added tax. Such controversial policies
combined with his Jewish background
to make him the target of anti-Semitic
attacks from the far right (paralleling
Léon *Blum's experience in the 1930s).

Menem, Carlos (Saul) (1930–)
Argentine politician, president
1989–99; leader of the Peronist Partido
Justicialista (PJ; Justicialist Party).
Although gaining electoral support
from the poor, he introduced sweeping
privatization and cuts in public
spending to address Argentina's
economic crisis and stimulate the free
market. He pardoned hundreds of
human rights violators connected with
Argentina's period of military rule
(1976–83) and imprisoned under his
predecessor Raúl Alfonsín. He also
improved relations with Britain.

Mengistu, Haile Mariam (1937–)
Ethiopian soldier and socialist
politician, head of state 1977–91
(president 1987–91). He seized power
in a coup, and instituted a regime of
terror to stamp out any effective
opposition. Confronted with severe
problems of drought and secessionist
uprisings, he survived with help from
the USSR and the West until his violent
overthrow by rebel forces.

**Menshevik (Russian *menshinstvo*
'minority')** member of the minority of
the Russian Social Democratic Party,
who split from the *Bolsheviks in 1903.
The Mensheviks believed in a large,
loosely organized party and that,
before socialist revolution could occur
in Russia, capitalist society had to
develop further. During the Russian
Revolution they had limited power
and set up a government in Georgia,
but were suppressed in 1922.

Menzies, Robert Gordon (1894–1978)
Australian conservative politician,
leader of the United Australia
(now Liberal) Party and prime minister
1939–41 and 1949–66.

A Melbourne lawyer, he entered
politics in 1928 as a Nationalist in the
Victoria parliament, was attorney
general in the federal parliament
1934–39, and in 1939 succeeded Joseph
*Lyons as prime minister and leader of
the United Australia Party, resigning in
1941 when colleagues were dissatisfied
with his leadership of Australia's war
effort. In 1949 he became prime
minister of a Liberal–Country Party
coalition government, and, exploiting
divisions in a divided Labor Party
oposition, was re-elected in 1951, 1954,
1955, 1958, 1961, and 1963; he followed
the USA's lead in committing Australia
to the Vietnam War and retired soon
after, in 1966. A conservative and an
ardent royalist, who unsuccessfully
tried to ban the Communist Party in
1950, he was viewed by critics as a
'frozen Edwardian'. They argued that
he did not show enough interest in
Asia, and supported the USA and
white African regimes too uncritically.
His defenders argued that he provided
stability in domestic policy and
national security. KT 1963.

**Mercosur or South American
Common Market**; Portuguese
**Mercosul, (Spanish *Mercado del Sur*
'Market of the South')** free-trade
organization, founded in March 1991
on signature of the Asunción Treaty

by Argentina, Brazil, Paraguay, and Uruguay, and formally inaugurated on 1 January 1995. With a GNP of $800,000 million and a population of more than 190 million, Mercosur constitutes the world's fourth-largest free-trade bloc after the European Economic Area, the *North American Free Trade Agreement, and the Asia-Pacific Economic Cooperation Conference.

Mesopotamian Campaign in World War I, British campaign to secure the oil installations along the Tigris and the Euphrates and safeguard the route to India. A small force from the Indian Army was sent to the area in November 1914 and quickly took Basra in modern-day Iraq but then made slow progress. In the aftermath of the disastrous Dardanelles Campaign of 1915, a counterattack was authorized on Baghdad but this failed and the army retreated to Kut-al-Imra, where 10,000 prisoners were taken. The War Office in London took charge of the campaign directly, and a further force of 120,000 troops was sent. The British made steady progress, taking Baghdad in March 1917 and then moved swiftly through the rest of the region until the Turks in Mesopotamia surrendered in October 1918. The cost to Britain and India was about 16,000 dead, and almost 100,000 casualties and it was criticized as having little military basis or control.

Metaxas, Ioannis (1870–1941) Greek general and politician, born in Ithaca. He restored *George II (1890–1947) as king of Greece, under whom he established a dictatorship as prime minister from 1936, and introduced several necessary economic and military reforms. He led resistance to the Italian invasion of Greece in 1941, refusing to abandon Greece's neutral position.

Meuse, Battles of the in World War I, battles between French and German forces in August 1914 on the line of the River Meuse in northern France. The French won a remarkable victory in stemming at least part of the German invasion but did not fully exploit their advantage.

Mexico country in the North American continent, bounded north by the USA, east by the Gulf of Mexico, southeast by Belize and Guatemala, and southwest and west by the Pacific Ocean; population (2000 est) 13,083,400 It is the northernmost country in Latin America.

government Mexico is a federal republic of 31 states and a federal district, based in Mexico City. The constitution dates from 1917 and is broadly based on the US model. Legislative power rests with a two-chamber national congress of senate, chamber of deputies, and directly elected president. The senate has a six-year term and the deputies serve for three years. The president serves a six-year term and chooses the cabinet. The senate has 128 members, each state and the federal district being represented by four senators. Three of these are elected by majority election and the fourth by proportional representation. The chamber has 500 members: 300 representing single-member constituencies and 200 elected by proportional representation so as to give due weight to minority parties. Members of congress are elected by universal suffrage. Each state has an elected governor and chamber of deputies, elected for a six-year term.

history The first humans probably reached Mexico from the north some time after 14,000 years ago. Some of the earliest evidence of human occupation in Mexico has been found at Tlapacoya, and comprises a series of hunting camps with clipped tools and animal bones. At the end of the last ice age (around 8000 BC) hunting became more intensive with an advanced stone-tool inventory based on the Clovis and leaf spearpoints also found elsewhere in North America. Large game, such as mammoth, mastodon and horse, were hunted to extinction by about 7000 BC.

After around 7000 BC economies became more generalized and there is evidence of intensive plant collecting and incipient cultivation of avocados, squash, chilli peppers, and amaranth. The greatest agricultural achievements were the domestication of corn (maize) and three kinds of bean between 5000 and 3000 BC, forming a diet so complete in proteins that scarcely any meat was consumed. The only domestic animal was the turkey.

the Preclassic period The Formative or Preclassic period of Mexican civilization (c. 2000 BC–c. AD 250) developed on this sound agricultural basis, and irrigation was widely used. Pottery had appeared in around 2450 BC on the Pacific coast, and small ritualistic figurines featured in certain houses in the villages. By 1500 BC ceremonial architecture was constructed in Oaxaca and on the coast of the Gulf of Mexico.

The Gulf coast was the centre of the first great culture, the Olmec (c. 1200–400 BC). This was based on the temple cities of San Lorenzo and La Venta, which comprised platforms, plazas, and huge sculptured heads of basalt. La Venta was planned along the axis of a ceremonial routeway with a pyramid as its focus. Olmec art was based on the mythology of the jungle, and it is suggested that the later gods of Mesoamerica, including such Aztec gods as Quetzalcoatl (the feathered serpent) and Tlaloc (the rain god), had their origins with the Olmec. The Olmec developed hieroglyphic writing and a calendar based on detailed astronomical observation. Trade with the highlands and Central America provided the Olmec with minerals, stones, and other resources.

the Classic period By the early centuries AD the cultural pivot of

Mexico shifted to the highlands, and particularly to the ceremonial cities of Monte Albán – one of the most important centres of the Zapotecs – and Teotihuacán. However, in the Yucatán Peninsula, the great *Maya civilization also flourished throughout the Classic period (c. AD 250–900). In this period art, architecture, metalwork, and science reached high levels of sophistication.

Teotihuacán was the supreme religious centre, a vast city laid out on a planned grid in the Valley of Mexico. It had a large complex of pyramids and palaces at its centre, decorated with friezes and frescoes, and suburbs of merchants, craftsmen, and foreigners. The city was a great political and economic force, establishing an empire over much of south Mexico and having trade links and embassies in the great Mayan cities of the Yucatán (see *Maya). Trade was in luxury goods – obsidian, jade, feathers, gold – as well as foodstuffs. At its peak in around AD 450–650, Teotihuacán had a population of some 200,000, making it the largest city in the world at that time. Teotihuacán collapsed in AD 750 for reasons that are not entirely understood, although hundreds of years later was revived as a religious centre by the Aztecs. The Classic period ended around AD 900 with the collapse of other great Mesoamerican cities.

the Postclassic period In the Postclassic period (AD 900–1250) the Mixtec kingdom (capital Cholula) spread across south Mexico, and overran the wealthy Zapotec state in Oaxaca, seizing their capital, Monte Albán. Evidence of conquest there has been excavated to reveal the tomb of a Mixtec lord with rich grave goods, including amber, jade, coral and jet beads, and the bones of many servants. Mixtec art and influence was spread beyond their territory by trade.

In the north was the great Toltec

kingdom, based in the city of Tula, northeast of Mexico City. Tula was an impressive urban centre covering 5 sq km/2 sq mi, with carved monoliths depicting gods and soldiers erected on top of the main decorated pyramid. Mythology tells of a struggle between two gods: Quetzalcoatl (the feathered serpent), representing the traditional peaceful priesthood, and Tezcatlipoca (smoking mirror), whose followers were warlike. The followers of Quetzalcoatl were expelled and fled ultimately to the Yucatán, where they built the city of Chichén Itzá. Following the collapse of the Toltecs in the 12th century, their territories were taken over by the Aztecs and the Maya.

the Aztecs and the Spanish conquest The Aztecs moved south into the Valley of Mexico in the 12th century, and in around 1325 started to build their great capital of Tenochtitlán. They came to dominate the surrounding tribes, creating a large empire in central Mexico.

Aztec civilization collapsed within two years of the coming of the Spanish conquistadores under Hernán Cortés in 1519. The last Aztec king, Montezuma II, was killed in 1520, and, with the assistance of the peoples who had been subjugated by the Aztecs, Cortés captured Tenochtitlán in 1521. The indigenous population was reduced from 21 million in 1519 to 1 million by 1607, with many deaths from Old World diseases to which they had no resistance.

Spanish colonial rule and independence In 1535 Mexico became the viceroyalty of New Spain, and was governed by a viceroy and council for nearly 300 years. Colonial rule became increasingly oppressive, and the struggle for independence began in 1810. A confused and prolonged war of independence culminated in 1821, when a conservative faction in Mexico declared the country's independence from an innovating liberal government in Spain. One of the conservative military leaders, Agustín de Iturbide, made himself emperor in 1822, establishing the short-lived Mexican Empire of 1822–23.

civil wars and war with the USA Iturbide's enforced abdication precipitated 50 years of conflict and civil war between liberals demanding the abolition of military, clerical, and guild privileges and conservatives defending them. Dominating this period was the dictator Antonio López de Santa Anna. Political instability and economic backwardness exposed Mexico to the intervention of the USA, which annexed Texas in 1835. This brought about the Mexican War 1846–48, in the course of which Mexico suffered further losses to the USA, including New Mexico and California, in return for a negligible indemnity. Santa Anna was overthrown in 1855 by Benito Juárez, whose liberal reforms included many anticlerical measures.

Habsburg rule In 1861, enticed by the offer of 30% of the proceeds, France planned to intervene in the recovery of 79 million francs owed to a Swiss banker by former Mexican president Miguel Miramón, who had been overthrown and exiled by Juárez in 1860. Seeking to regain power, in 1862 Miramón appealed to Empress Eugénie, consort of Napoleon III, saying that steps must be taken against Juárez and his 'anti-Christian' policies. Eugénie proposed Maximilian, the brother of Emperor Francis Joseph of Austria, as monarch of Mexico. Napoleon III agreed, since the plan suited his colonial ambitions, and in 1864 Maximilian accepted the crown offered him by conservative opponents of Juárez. Juárez and his supporters continued to fight against this new branch of the Habsburg empire, and in 1867 the monarchy collapsed and Maximilian was executed.

Díaz's capitalist dictatorship Juárez returned to the presidency (1867–72), and attempted unsuccessfully to turn the impoverished indigenous peoples into prosperous small farmers, but he was unable to bring stability to Mexico. Only the ruthless opportunism of Porfirio Díaz – who was dictator of Mexico 1877–80 and 1884–1911 – made political stability and economic expansion possible. However, Díaz's handling of the economy made him deeply unpopular, and only a small landowning and industrialist class benefited from his programme.

the Mexican Revolution The gap between rich and poor widened, and the result of festering resentments was the explosion known as the Mexican Revolution. The Revolution, which started in 1910, was precipitated by the liberal movement led by Francisco Madero, which triggered off unrest among the peasants (led by Emiliano *Zapata), artisans, and the expanding urban working class. By 1911 Madero had ousted Díaz and reestablished a liberal regime, but was himself assassinated in 1913. The Revolution brought changes in land ownership, labour legislation, and reduction in the powers of the Roman Catholic Church.

Following Madero's death Victoriano Huerta seized power, but was forced to resign in 1914 by the USA, where it was widely believed that he had pro-German sympathies. The same was also suspected of Francisco 'Pancho' Villa (1877–1923), who established a revolutionary government in the north of Mexico. In 1915 Venustiano Carranza established a regime more acceptable to the USA than that of Huerta, and in 1916 Carranza gave the US army permission to pursue Villa into Mexico after a raid across the US border. US forces withdrew early in 1917, having failed to kill Villa. Relations with the USA remained poor following the interception by British Naval Intelligence of a message in early 1917 from the German foreign minister

Alfred Zimmermann to the German ambassador to Mexico, which suggested that Mexico ally itself with Germany and reconquer the territory lost to the USA in the 19th century. Although Mexico denied any involvement in this proposal, it helped to precipitate the USA's entry into World War I. Carranza stayed in power until his murder in 1920, which was followed by three years of civil war.

the Revolution institutionalized After the civil war Mexico experienced gradual agricultural, political, and social reforms. In 1927 military leaders responded to economic dislocation and political instability by forming a single political party, the Mexican Revolutionary Party, which was renamed the Partido Revolucionario Institucional (PRI; Institutional Revolutionary Party) in 1946. The broadly based PRI has dominated Mexican politics ever since, pursuing moderate, left-of-centre policies, and carefully exploiting the revolutionary myth.

The Revolution had clearly lost its impetus until 1934, when the new president, Lázaro *Cárdenas, confronted by a wave of discontent among the peasants and urban workers, announced a drastic reform programme, including measures for oil nationalization, land redistribution, and industrial expansion. In 1938 all foreign-owned oil wells were nationalized, but compensation was not agreed until 1941. During the Spanish Civil War Mexico exported considerable amounts of arms and ammunition to the Spanish Republican government.

Mexico in World War II The government of Manuel Avila Camacho (president 1940–46) realized the danger to Mexico implicit in the aggressive designs of the Axis powers, and readily responded to the various proposals made by the USA in 1941 for closer cooperation and the settlement of outstanding differences. The murder in Mexico in 1940 of Leon Trotsky, who had been granted asylum some years previously, involved the government in difficulties with the communists, who were assumed to be involved in the assassination. In June 1942 Mexico formally declared war on the Axis powers as a response to Axis sinkings of Mexican ships, and a squadron of the Mexican air force fought in the Pacific theatre in 1945.

Mexico in the post-war decades None of the successors of Cárdenas maintained the speed of social change that he instigated in the 1930s, although economic expansion from 1945 to the 1970s was dramatic. But prosperity was confined to a small upper class and an expanding urban middle class, while conditions amongst the underprivileged groups generally failed to improve. Resentments exploded in a wave of peasant, trade-union, and student unrest in the 1960s, which was ruthlessly repressed, and large sections of the population remained alienated.

President Luis Echeverría, on assuming office in 1970, emphasized the uniqueness of the Mexican Revolution and promised a nationalistic capitalism, a tolerance of limited opposition, and a degree of sympathy towards the reforms instituted by the democratically elected Marxist president of Chile, Salvador Allende. In practice, however, the only opposition party to be permitted to flourish was the extreme right-wing Partido Acción Nacional (PAN; National Action Party). Mexico nevertheless continued to present a democratic face to the world, and in 1974 broke off diplomatic relations with the Spanish government of Gen Franco because of the undemocratic manner in which Basque rebels were treated.

economic problems From the 1970s the popularity of the PRI was damaged by the country's poor economic performance and soaring international debts. However, despite criticisms from vested-interest groups such as the trade unions and the church, the PRI scored a clear win in the 1985 elections. The government's problems increased later that year when an earthquake in Mexico City caused thousands of deaths and made hundreds of thousands homeless, and in 1986 the government was forced to sign an agreement with the International Monetary Fund (IMF).

the PRI under challenge The PRI faced its strongest challenge in the 1988 elections. However, despite claims of fraud, the PRI candidate, Carlos Salinas de Gortari, was declared president by the electoral college. During his term, around 250 political opposition activists were killed.

Salinas led campaigns against corrupt trade unions and drug traffickers, and worked closely with the US administration of President Bush to negotiate debt reductions. In April 1992 public outrage followed a gas sewer-line explosion in Mexico's second-largest city, Guadalajara, in which 194 died and 1,400 were injured. In the July 1992 state-governor elections, the PRI suffered its second defeat in 63 years in Chihuahua state, losing to a PAN candidate. The PRI nominated Donaldo Colosio Murrieta as its presidential candidate, to succeed Salinas in September 1993. In the same month important electoral reforms were introduced, aimed at curbing corruption, and in November 1993 the *North American Free Trade Agreement (NAFTA) with the USA and Canada was ratified by the Mexican senate.

the Zapatista rebellion and political violence An uprising in the southeastern state of Chiapas by a newly formed rebel group, the Zapatista National Liberation Army (Ejército Zapatista Liberación National; EZLN), in January 1994 was harshly put down by government troops. The

EZLN opposed the recent NAFTA agreement, which they claimed would benefit only the better-off members of society, and demanded political reform and redistribution of land. The government offered a unilateral cease-fire and awarded the rebels political recognition as the Zapatista National Liberation Front (Frente Zapatista Liberación National; FZLN), and a peace accord was signed in March.

In the same month Murrieta, the PRI presidential candidate, was assassinated. He was replaced by Ernesto Zedillo Ponce de León, who went on to win the August 1994 presidential elections. The following month the PRI secretary general, José Francisco Ruiz Massieu, was assassinated. Subsequent investigations into his killing suggested a conspiracy involving senior members of the PRI and a Mexican drug cartel, and in March 1995 the former president, Carlos Salinas, went into exile after his brother Raúl was charged in connection with the murder. Meanwhile, allegations of electoral fraud in state-governor elections in Chiapas had led the EZLN to swear in a rival candidate to the official PRI winner.

the currency crisis of 1994–95
Share prices plunged in December 1994, when, contrary to earlier assurances, the government devalued Mexico's currency, the peso, allowing it to float freely on international markets. By January 1995 the peso had lost a third of its value, forcing President Zedillo to announce an austerity programme, to which the USA and the international community responded by authorizing loans worth nearly $50 billion. Zedillo also signed an electoral-reform pact, which included an agreement to rerun elections in Chiapas and one other state. At the end of 1994, Mexico's trade deficit was $28 billion.

accord with the Zapatistas
In February 1995 the PRI suffered a landslide defeat in the key state of Jalisco, the third and most damaging defeat in its history. In the same month Zedillo ordered government forces into areas occupied by the EZLN, but later recalled them and announced his willingness to resume talks. In November 1995, government and EZLN representatives reached an agreement providing for greater autonomy for the indigenous Mayan people of Chiapas. EZLN and government representatives signed the first of six peace accords in February 1996 recognizing the right of American Indians to adopt traditional forms of government within their communities and to have adequate representation in the national parliament. Peace talks stalled soon afterwards but were reopened in August. However, violent attacks against the government by the new leftist Popular Revolutionary Army (EPR; Ejército Popular Revolucionario) increased.

the 1997 elections In July 1997 the PRI suffered dramatic setbacks in city, state, and parliamentary elections at the hands of both the left-wing and conservative opposition. The party lost Mexico City for the first time to the social democrats, and two of the six state governorships at stake to the conservative National Action Party. The PRI retained control of the upper house but won only 36% of the nationwide vote for the 500-seat lower house.

ethnic unrest Paramilitary gunmen killed 45 American Indians and wounded 11 others in an attack on a village in the Chiapas state of Mexico in late December 1997. Many of the victims were women and children. Thousands of Tzotzil American Indians fled their villages for the northern Chiapas highlands or were evacuated to Polho, a village populated mainly by Zapatista sympathizers. International outrage over the massacre put pressure on president Zedillo to investigate the paramilitary groups believed to be behind the massacre. As the result, the governor of Chiapas resigned in January 1998. In March 1998 the government announced that the lapsed peace accord with the Zapatista rebels would be reactivated and that a bill would be introduced to ensure indigenous rights. However, talks between the government and the rebels broke down in December 1998.

student demonstrations A long-running student strike against proposed increases in student fees (plans which the authorities later abandoned) at the Autonomous University of Mexico (UNAM) turned violent in February 2000. Injuries numbered 37 and arrests 745 when the students were evicted from a university building.

crackdown on crime In March 2000 President Zedillo announced a crackdown on organized crime. Days after the announcement, the police chief of the northern border city of Tijuana was murdered by a drug gang.

trade agreement In June, Mexico signed a free-trade agreement with El Salvador, Guatemala, and Honduras, to eliminate duties on 80% of their exports and 65% of Mexico's. Later in the year, the Mexican peso fell to a 16-month low against the US dollar.

2000 elections After 71 years, the Institutional Revolutionary Party (PRI) lost power in Mexico. In early July 2000 Vicente Fox, the candidate of the conservative National Action Party, won the country's presidential election by an unexpectedly wide margin. He promised national unity, job creation, and to attack government corruption. In concurrent legislative elections, the PRI lost control of both houses of congress and the mayoralty of Mexico City.

Fox's cabinet included several business people, former government officials, and left-wing academics, but few politicians. In his first actions as president, in early December, Fox sent a bill on indigenous rights to Congress as a step towards trying to settle the Zapatista rebellion in the southeastern state of Chiapas and withdrew soldiers from the region. The leader of the Zapatista guerrillas, Subcomandante Marcos, agreed to restart peace talks on condition that the president order the evacuation of seven army bases, free all Zapatista prisoners held in federal jails since the 1994 uprising, and sign an Indian Bill of Rights to safeguard the area's marginalized Mayan tribes from exploitation.

In January 2001, the government closed four bases in the Chiapas region. In February, Marcos undertook a 15-day peaceful march across Mexico to Mexico City to raise support for the bill on Indian rights that President Fox had presented to Congress in December. The bill would give Indian communities a degree of autonomy to govern themselves by traditional customs and some control over the natural resources on their land. The rebels were cheered on their arrival in Mexico City, where they proposed to stay until the bill had been ratified. Fox welcomed the march, but was reminded by Marcos that peace could only be reached if the other Zapatista demands were met. Zapatista leaders addressed Mexico's Congress, but after ten days in the capital with no progress, the rebels retreated to the jungle. Congress approved the bill, which granted autonomy to 10 million Indians, in May. However, the Zapatistas pledged to continue their rebellion.

In May 2001, Fox proposed raising US$14 billion in new revenues, while cutting the top rate of corporate and personal tax from 40% to 32%. In the same month, Fox's ruling PAN won an election in the former PRI stronghold of Yucatán. In August, the PRI won a state election, Tabasco state, for the first time in two years. In December, Congress approved tax rises worth about 1.2% of GDP, but rejected long-standing proposals from President Fox to levy value-added tax (VAT) on food and medicine.

opposition leader elected In March 2002, Roberto Madrazo, a former state governor, won the election for the presidency of the PRI. However, the election was marked by claims of fraud, including alleged ballot-rigging.

In the same month, army special forces arrested Benjamin Arellano Félix, the head of the Tijuana cocaine cartel. The most powerful drug gang in Mexico, it accounted for an estimated 40% of all cocaine shipments to the USA.

Michael (1921–) King of Romania 1927–30 and 1940–47. The son of Carol II, he succeeded his grandfather as king in 1927 but was displaced when his father returned from exile in 1930. In 1940 he was proclaimed king again on his father's abdication, overthrew in 1944 the fascist dictatorship of Ion Antonescu (1882–1946), and enabled Romania to share in the victory of the Allies at the end of World War II. He abdicated and left Romania in 1947.

Micronesia, Federated States of country in the west Pacific Ocean, forming part of the archipelago of the Caroline Islands, 800 km/497 mi east of the Philippines.

Midway, Battle of in World War II, decisive US naval victory over Japan in June 1942 off Midway Island, northwest of Hawaii. The Midway victory was one of the most important battles of the Pacific war – Japanese naval air superiority was destroyed in one day, putting an end to Japanese expansion and placing them on the defensive thereafter.

Mihailovic, Draza (Dragoljub) (1893–1946) Yugoslav soldier, leader of the guerrilla Chetniks of World War II, a nationalist resistance movement against the German occupation. His feud with Tito's communists led to the withdrawal of Allied support and that of his own exiled government from 1943. He turned for help to the Italians and Germans, and was eventually shot for treason.

Mikoyan, Anastas Ivanovich (1895–1978) Armenian communist politician. He was Soviet minister of trade under Stalin and one of only nine members of the State Defence Committee during World War II (the country's supreme body at that time). He supported Khrushchev after Stalin's death and was a first deputy prime minister of the USSR 1955–64 and chairman of the Presidium of the Supreme Soviet (president of the USSR) 1964–65.

Milk, Harvey (1930–1978) US public official. As an experienced financial analyst, he was elected to San Francisco's Board of Supervisors in 1977. Instrumental in passing the city's gay rights ordinance, he was the first acknowledged homosexual official in the city. He was shot to death by a former city supervisor, who also killed Mayor George Moscone. When their assassin was given a light sentence, San Francisco's homosexual community rioted. Milk was born in New York City. He moved to San Francisco, California, in 1969 and at first operated a camera store.

Millerand, Alexandre (1859–1943) French prime minister in 1920 and president 1920–24. He formed a coalition government, the Bloc National, and supported Poland against the Russian invasion in 1920. He faced opposition from the Radical socialist majority, which, under Edouard Herriot, triumphed in the 1924 elections, and shortly afterwards was forced to resign.

Milner, Alfred, 1st Viscount Milner (1854–1925) British colonial administrator. As governor of Cape

Colony 1897–1901, he negotiated with Kruger but did little to prevent the second South African War (Boer War); as governor of the Transvaal and Orange River colonies 1902–05 after their annexation, he reorganized their administration. In 1916 he became a member of Lloyd George's war cabinet. KCB 1895, Baron 1901, Viscount 1902.

Milošević, Slobodan (1941–) Serbian communist politician; president of Serbia 1986–97, and president of the Federal Republic of Yugoslavia 1997–2000. Leader of the Socialisticka Partija Srbije (SPS; Socialist Party of Serbia) from 1986, he was widely believed to be the instigator of the conflict in *Bosnia-Herzegovina 1992–94. He adopted the public persona of peacemaker in 1994, putting pressure on his allies, the Bosnian Serbs, to accept negotiated peace terms; this contributed to the Dayton peace accord for Bosnia-Herzegovina in November 1995. As president of the Federal Republic of Yugoslavia, Milošević faced international condemnation for the brutal treatment of ethnic Albanians by Serbian forces in Kosovo. In March 1999, NATO aircraft began a bombing campaign in an attempt to force the Yugoslav government to end the persecution.

In June 1999, Milošević accepted NATO's peace agreement. He was replaced by Vojislav Koštunica in October 2000, and arrested in April 2001 and charged with abuse of power, corruption, and fraud. In June he was extradited to the United Nations (UN) War Crimes Tribunal in the Hague, the Netherlands, to face charges of crimes against humanity.

miners' strike British strike against pit closures that lasted almost a year from April 1984. The prime minister Margaret Thatcher was determined to make a stand against the miners and in April 1985 members of the National Union of Miners (NUM) returned to work.

The NUM, led by its Marxist president, Arthur *Scargill called the strike in April 1994 without a ballot, in protest against pit closures and as part of a campaign for a better basic wage. Support was strong in south Wales, Scotland, Yorkshire, and Kent but pits in Nottinghamshire and Leicestershire continued to operate. Some NUM members left the union and founded the Union of Democratic Mineworkers.

Mintoff, Dom(inic) (1916–) Maltese Labour politician; prime minister of Malta 1955–58 and 1971–84. He negotiated the removal of British and other foreign military bases 1971–79 and made treaties with Libya.

mir (Russian **'peace'** or **'world'**) in Russia before the 1917 Revolution, a self-governing village community in which the peasants distributed land and collected taxes.

Mitchell, (Sonny) James (FitzAllen) (1931–) St Vincent and the Grenadines centrist politician, prime minister 1972–74 and from 1984. Initially a St Vincent Labour Party (SVLP) representative, he became premier as an independent in 1972. He founded the centrist New Democratic Party (NDP) in 1975, and led it to power in 1984. As prime minister, he supported moves to integrate with Dominica, Grenada, and St Lucia into a Windward Islands Federation, encouraged agricultural diversification away from banana production, and promoted tourism and the 'offshore banking' sector, but was criticized for his failure to deal with money laundering and drug trafficking.

Mitsotakis, Constantine (1918–) Greek politician, leader of the conservative New Democracy Party (ND) 1984–93, prime minister 1990–93. Minister for economic coordination in 1965 (a post he held again 1978–80), he was arrested by the military junta in 1967, but escaped from house arrest and lived in exile until 1974. In 1980–81 he was foreign minister. He resigned the leadership of the ND after its 1993 election defeat; in January 1996 proposed corruption charges against him were dropped.

Mitterrand, François (1916–1996) French socialist politician. After a successful ministerial career under the Fourth Republic, holding posts in 11 governments 1947–58, Mitterrand joined the new Parti Socialiste (PS; Socialist Party) in 1971, establishing it as the most popular party in France before winning two successive terms as president, 1981–88 and 1988–95. From 1982 his administrations reverted from redistributive and reflationary policies to economic orthodoxy and maintenance of the 'strong franc' (linked to the Deutschmark), despite the high levels of unemployment this entailed, and vigorously pursued further European integration.

Mitterrand studied law and politics in Paris. During World War II he came to prominence in the resistance after initially working in Marshal *Pétain's Vichy adminstration. In 1945 he was elected as deputy for Nièvre, as the member of a small centre-left Resistance-based party. Opposed to General Charles *de Gaulle's creation of the Fifth Republic in 1958, he formed a Federation of the Left and as its candidate challenged de Gaulle unsuccessfully for the presidency in 1965. In 1971, as leader of the PS, he negotiated an electoral pact and Common Programme of Government with the Communist Party, 1972–77, but again failed to win the presidency in 1974, this time against Valéry *Giscard d'Estaing. He was finally elected president in 1981.

His ambitious programme of social, economic, and institutional reforms was hampered by deteriorating economic conditions after 1983. When the socialists lost their majority in March 1986, he was compelled to work with the Gaullist Jacques *Chirac as prime minister, and grew in popularity, defeating Chirac's bid for the presidency in May 1988. In 1993 he entered a second term of 'cohabitation' with the conservative prime minister Edouard Balladur. Towards the end of his presidency his failing health weakened his hold on power. Whereas he was able to enhance his reputation when 'cohabiting' with Chirac, the successful elements of Balladur's premiership contrasted with Mitterrand's waning popularity and weakened influence.

Mladic, Ratko (1943–) Bosnian Serb general, leader of the Bosnian Serb army 1992–96. His ruthless conduct in the civil war in Bosnia, including the widespread maltreatment of prisoners and the disappearance of many more, led to his being indicted for war crimes by the United Nations War Crimes Commission in 1995.

Mobutu, Sese Seko Kuku Ngbeandu Wa Za Banga (1930–1997) adopted name of **Joseph Desire Mobutu**, President of Zaire (now the Democratic Republic of Congo) 1965–97. The harshness of some of his policies and charges of corruption attracted widespread international criticism.

Model, Walter (1891–1945) German field marshal in World War II. He commanded Panzer units in France and on the Eastern Front before moving to the West to shore up the German defences following the Allied invasion of Europe.

Moi, Daniel arap (1924–) Kenyan politician, president 1978–2002. Leader of the Kenya African National Union (KANU), he became minister of home affairs in 1964, vice-president in 1967, and succeeded Jomo Kenyatta as president. He enjoyed the support of Western governments but was widely criticized for Kenya's poor human-rights record. His administration, first challenged by a coup attempt in 1982, became increasingly authoritarian. In 1991, in the face of widespread criticism, he promised the eventual introduction of multiparty politics. In 1992 he was elected president in the first free elections amid widespread accusations of vote rigging.

Moi was first nominated to the legislative council in 1955. In 1960 he became chair of the Kenya Africa Democratic Union (KADU) and opposition leader after independence in 1963. KADU merged with the ruling KANU party in 1964, and he was appointed vice-president of the party in 1966. He became president of the country following Kenyatta's death in 1978.

Moldova or **Moldavia**, country in east-central Europe, bounded north, south, and east by Ukraine, and west by Romania.

Mollet, Guy Alcide (1905–1975) French socialist politician, post-war leader of the Section Française de l'Internationale Ouvrière (SFIO) 1946–69, and prime minister 1956–57. He launched the Anglo-French Suez expedition with British prime minister Anthony *Eden, and in Algeria succumbed to settler pressures to remove the liberal governor general Georges Catroux.

Molotov, Vyacheslav Mikhailovich (1890–1986) adopted name of **Vyacheslav Mikhailovich Skriabin**, Soviet communist politician. He was chair of the Council of People's Commissars (prime minister) 1930–41 and foreign minister 1939–49 and 1953–56. He negotiated the 1939 non-aggression treaty with Germany (the Ribbentrop–Molotov pact), and, after the German invasion in 1941, the Soviet partnership with the Allies. His post-war stance prolonged the Cold War and in 1957 he was expelled from the government for Stalinist activities.

Molyneaux, Jim (1920–) Baron Molyneaux of Killead; born James Henry Molyneaux, Northern Ireland Unionist politician, leader of the Official Ulster Unionist Party (the largest Northern Ireland party)

1979–95. A member of the House of Commons from 1970, he temporarily relinquished his seat 1983–85 in protest at the *Anglo-Irish Agreement. He resigned as party leader in 1995 and retired from Parliament in 1997. Although a fervent supporter of the union between Britain and Northern Ireland, he was regarded as one of the more moderate Loyalists. He was knighted in 1996, and given a life peerage in 1997.

Momoh, Joseph Saidu (1937–2003) Sierra Leone soldier and politician, president 1985–92. An army officer who became commander in 1983 with the rank of major general. He succeeded Siaka Stevens as president when Stevens retired; Momoh was endorsed by Sierra Leone's one political party, the All-People's Congress. He dissociated himself from the policies of his predecessor, pledging to fight corruption and improve the economy. In April 1992 he fled to neighbouring Guinea after a military takeover.

Monaco small sovereign state forming an enclave in southern France, with the Mediterranean Sea to the south.

Monash, John (1865–1931) Australian civil engineer, army officer, and administrator. He was a colonel at the outbreak of World War I and commanded the 4th Infantry Brigade through the Gallipoli campaign. He then established a reputation as a commander in France 1916 and in 1918 succeeded William Birdwood (1865–1951) in command of the Australian Corps, becoming recognized as one of the most capable of the British corps commanders in battles such as Amiens, Mont St Quentin, and the breaking of the Hindenburg Line. KCB 1918.

Mondale, Walter Frederick (1928–) US Democrat politician, unsuccessful presidential candidate in 1984. He was a senator 1965–77 for his home state of Minnesota, and vice-president to

Jimmy Carter 1977–81. After losing the 1984 presidential election to Ronald Reagan, Mondale retired from national politics to resume his law practice.

Mondlane, Eduardo (1920–1969)
Mozambican nationalist, first president of *Frelimo 1962–69, the group aiming to achieve independence for Mozambique from the Portuguese. He was assassinated by unknown assailants.

Mongolia country in east-Central Asia, bounded north by Russia and south by China.

Mons, Battle of in World War I, German victory over the *British Expeditionary Force in August 1914. A planned attack on the German armies invading Belgium fell apart when French troops did not arrive, leaving the British to extricate themselves as best they could.

Montagu-Chelmsford reforms changes to the constitution of India in 1919, whereby Indians obtained greater control in local and some provincial matters such as health, education, and agriculture, while British administrators still controlled finance and law and order. Arguing that the reforms did not go far enough, Indian nationalists organized a concerted *noncooperation campaign 1920–22 in protest.

Montgomery, Bernard Law (1887–1976) 1st Viscount Montgomery of Alamein; called 'Monty', English field marshal. In World War II he commanded the 8th Army in North Africa in the Second Battle of El *Alamein in 1942. As commander of British troops in northern Europe from 1944, he received the German surrender in 1945.

At the start of World War II Montgomery commanded part of the British Expeditionary Force in France 1939–40 and took part in the evacuation from Dunkirk. In August 1942 he took command of the 8th Army, then barring the German

advance on Cairo. The victory of El *Alamein in October turned the tide in North Africa; it was followed by the expulsion of Field Marshal Rommel from Egypt and rapid Allied advance into Tunisia. In February 1943 Montgomery's forces came under US general Eisenhower's command, and they took part in the conquest of Tunisia and Sicily and the invasion of Italy. Montgomery was promoted to field marshal in 1944. In 1948 he became permanent military chair of the Commanders-in-Chief Committee for Western European defence, and 1951–58 was deputy Supreme Commander Europe. He was created 1st Viscount Montgomery of Alamein in 1946.

Montreux, Convention of international agreement of 1936 allowing Turkey to remilitarize the Dardenelles.

Morant, Harry Harbord (1865–1902) English-born Australian soldier and balladist, known as 'Breaker' Morant from the pen-name he used while writing verse for the *Bulletin* in the 1890s. During the Boer War he was court-martialled and shot by the British military authorities for the murder of a Boer prisoner. The strength of Australian protest ensured that in subsequent wars Australians were exempt from being sentenced to death by British military jurisdiction.

Morgan, John Pierpont, Jr (1867–1943) US banker and philanthropist. He became the head of the Morgan banking house after the death of his father, John Pierpont Morgan, in 1913. In World War I he organized a New York bankers' syndicate to underwrite a massive loan to the Allies. He acted for the British and French governments as agent for the purchase of supplies in the USA, and also for the US government when it entered the war in 1917. In his lifetime he gave $36 million to charitable and public institutions, including $9 million to the Metropolitan Museum of Art, New York City.

Morley-Minto reforms measures announced in 1909 to increase the participation of Indians in their country's government. Introduced by John Morley (1838–1923), secretary of state for India, and Lord Minto (1845–1914), viceroy of India, they did not affect the responsibility of government, which remained in British hands, but did give Indians wider opportunities to be heard.

Moro, Aldo (1916–1978) Italian Christian Democrat politician. Prime minister 1963–68 and 1974–76, he was expected to become Italy's president, but he was kidnapped and shot by Red Brigade urban guerrillas.

Moroccan Crises two periods of international tension in 1905 and 1911 following German objections to French expansion in Morocco. Their wider purpose was to break up the Anglo-French entente of 1904, but both crises served to reinforce the entente and isolate Germany. The first was resolved at the *Algeciras Conference. The second brought Europe to the brink of war and is known as the *Agadir Incident.

Morocco country in northwest Africa, bounded to the north and northwest by the Mediterranean Sea, to the east and southeast by Algeria, and to the south by Western Sahara.

Morrison, Herbert Stanley (1888–1965) Baron Morrison of Lambeth, British Labour politician. He was a founder member and later secretary of the London Labour Party 1915–45, and a member of the London County Council 1922–45. He entered Parliament in 1923, representing South Hackney in 1923, 1929–31, and 1935–45, and East Lewisham 1945–59. He organized the Labour Party's general election victory in 1945. He was twice defeated in the contest for leadership of the party, once by Clement Attlee in 1932, and then by Hugh Gaitskell in 1955. A skilful

organizer, he lacked the ability to unite the party. He was created baron in 1959.

Mosaddeq, Muhammad (1880–1967) Iranian prime minister 1951–53. A dispute arose with the Anglo-Iranian Oil Company when he called for the nationalization of Iran's oil production, and when he failed in his attempt to overthrow the shah, he was arrested by loyalist forces with support from the USA. From 1956 he was under house arrest.

Mosca, Gaetano (1858–1941) Italian jurist, politician, and political scientist. His best-known work *Elementi di scienza politica* (1896) (translated as *The Ruling Class* in 1939) set out his theory of the political elite. In all societies, the majority is ruled by a minority in the upper stratum of society and, in the endless struggle for power, the membership of the elite political class is determined by natural selection. Although his theory of the elite appears to justify fascism, Mosca spurned both Mussolini and Hitler.

Moscow, Battle for in World War II, a failed German attack on Moscow, October 1941–January 1942. The Soviet capital was a prime objective of the German invasion plan, Operation *Barbarossa, and the failure to capture the city was a severe setback for the German strategy.

Mosley, Oswald (Ernald) (1896–1980) British politician, founder of the British Union of Fascists (BUF) in 1932. He was a member of Parliament 1918–31. A Conservative MP for Harrow 1918–22, he joined the Labour party in 1924 and represented Shetwick 1926–31. He resigned in 1931 and founded the New Party. He then led the BUF until his internment 1940–43 during World War II. In 1946 Mosley was denounced when it became known that Italy had funded his prewar efforts to establish *fascism in the UK, but in 1948 he resumed fascist propaganda with his Union Movement, the revived BUF.

Mossad in full **Hamossad Lemodi'in Vetafkidim Meyuhadim**, in Israel, the organization responsible for secret national activities outside the borders of the state. Mossad's main spheres of responsibility are information collection on political, military, and security issues, research, and special operations, including intelligence warfare. Founded in 1951, Mossad assumed the tasks of the Political Department of the Ministry for Foreign Affairs. The chief of Mossad is directly subject to the prime minister.

Moulin, Jean (1899–1943) French Resistance leader. A government prefect at the outbreak of World War II, he joined General *de Gaulle in London in September 1941. He returned to France and, under his code-name Max, played a crucial role in securing the French internal resistance's loyalty to de Gaulle's leadership and unifying it under the National Committee of the Resistance in 1943. Captured in June 1943, and interrogated by the Gestapo officer Klaus *Barbie at his Lyon headquarters, Moulin died under torture. His body was reinterred in the Panthéon in 1964.

Mountbatten, Louis Francis Albert Victor Nicholas (1900–1979) 1st Earl Mountbatten of Burma, English admiral and administrator, a great-grandson of Queen Victoria. In World War II he became chief of combined operations in 1942 and commander-in-chief in southeast Asia in 1943. As last viceroy and governor general of India 1947–48, he oversaw that country's transition to independence. He was killed by an Irish Republican Army (IRA) bomb aboard his yacht at Mullaghmore, County Sligo, in the Republic of Ireland. He was knighted in 1922, became a viscount in 1945, and an earl in 1947.

Moynihan, Daniel Patrick (1927–2003) US Democrat politician and diplomat. A senator for New York from 1977, he became chair of the Senate Finance Committee in January 1993. In 1995 he led the opposition to Republican attempts to cut back on welfare spending. He concerned himself with the problem of poverty among urban black families, and was one of the authors of *The Negro Family: A Case for National Action* (1965), which came to be known as the Moynihan Report.

Mozambique country in southeast Africa, bounded north by Zambia, Malawi, and Tanzania; east and south by the Indian Ocean; southwest by South Africa and Swaziland; and west by Zimbabwe.

MPLA abbreviation for *Movimento Popular de Libertaçaõ de Angola*, 'Popular Movement for the Liberation of Angola', socialist organization founded in the early 1950s that sought to free Angola from Portuguese rule 1961–75 before being involved in the civil war against its former allies *UNITA and FNLA 1975–76. The MPLA gained control of the country in 1976 and in 1977 renamed itself the People's Movement for the Liberation of Angola-Workers' Party (**MPLA-PT**). It won the first multiparty elections in 1992, but UNITA disputed the result and guerrilla activity continued, escalating into full-scale civil war in 1993. A peace agreement was signed with UNITA in 1994.

Mubarak, Hosni (1928–) Egyptian politician, president from 1981. Vice-president to Anwar Sadat from 1975, Mubarak succeeded him on his assassination. He continued to pursue Sadat's moderate policies, and significantly increased the freedom of the press and of political association, while trying to repress the growing Islamic fundamentalist movement. He was re-elected (uncontested) in 1987 and 1993. He survived an assassination attempt in 1995. Mubarak, was re-elected in September 1999 to a fourth six-year term after taking nearly 94% of the vote in a poll whose result was never in doubt. Mubarak faced no challenger in the referendum.

He began his term by replacing his prime minister, Kamal Ganzouri, with an economist, Atef Obeid, who headed Egypt's privatization programme.

Mubarak commanded the air force 1972–75 and was responsible for the initial victories in the Egyptian campaign of 1973 against Israel. He led Egypt's opposition to Iraq's invasion of Kuwait in 1990 and played an instrumental role in arranging the Middle East peace conference in November 1991.

Mugabe, Robert (Gabriel) (1925–) Zimbabwean politician, prime minister from 1980 and president from 1987. He was in detention in Rhodesia for nationalist activities 1964–74, then carried on guerrilla warfare from Mozambique as leader of *ZANU (Zimbabwe African National Union; ZANU-PF (-Patriotic Front) after 1980). He became the first prime minister of an independent Zimbabwe. He was in an uneasy alliance with Joshua *Nkomo of ZAPU (Zimbabwe African People's Union) from 1976 until 1987, when the two parties merged under Mugabe's leadership. Mugabe came under increasing criticism in the 1990s and in 2000 as Zimbabwe suffered economic decline and growing political violence.

The merger of ZANU-PF and ZAPU in 1987 effectively established a one-party state, but Mugabe's proposals to establish this constitutionally were rejected in 1990. His failure to anticipate and respond to the 1991–92 drought in southern Africa adversely affected his popularity, but he was re-elected, unchallenged, in February 1996.

In May 1998, he faced student demonstrations against alleged government corruption and in November there were violent protests in Harare at the rise in fuel prices and the country's involvement in the

Congo war. Further protests followed in February 1999 and October 2000.

In 2000 Mugabe supported the invasion of white farms by veterans of the struggle for independence, and invoked special presidential powers in order to seize land without compensation. The policy was condemned as unconstitutional by the Supreme Court and further contributed to Zimbabwe's economic problems. In June the human rights group African Rights produced a scathing report on his government, accusing it of corruption, human rights abuse, and lack of respect for the rule of law.

In 2002 Mugabe was re-elected as president in controversial elections marred by corruption and violence.

Muhammad, Murtala Ramat (1938–1976) Nigerian army officer and politician. He succeeded Gen Yakubu Gowon as head of state in July 1975, but was assassinated in February 1976 in an abortive and irrational coup led by Lt-Col Dimka.

Muir, John Ramsay Brice (1872–1941) British historian and politician. He was a Liberal member of Parliament for Rochdale 1923–24, and chair 1931–33, then president 1933–36, of the National Liberal Federation. His chief historical work was *Short History of the British Commonwealth* (two volumes 1920–22).

Mukden incident a surprise attack on 18 September 1931 by the Japanese on the Chinese garrison of Mukden (now called Shenyang), capital city of Manchuria, that marked the beginning of their invasion of China.

Muldoon, Robert David (1921–1992) New Zealand National Party right-of-centre politician, prime minister 1975–84. He pursued austere economic policies such as a wage-and-price policy to control inflation, sought to introduce curbs on trade unions, was a vigorous supporter of the Western alliance, and was a proponent of reform of the international monetary system. A traditionalist and somewhat authoritarian conservative, Muldoon sought to maintain close links with the UK and the USA, gave state assistance to farmers and industrialists, and promoted traditional social values. He came into conflict with feminists, Maori rights campaigners, and anti-nuclear campaigners, who sought to prevent US nuclear-powered and nuclear-armed ships visiting New Zealand harbours. With the economy deteriorating, he was defeated in the general election of 1984 by the Labour Party, led by David *Lange. He stood down as National Party leader in 1984 and was knighted, but was to remain shadow foreign affairs spokesperson.

Born in Auckland, he fought in World War II as an infantry soldier in the Pacific and Italy, and worked after the war as a cost accountant. He joined the conservative National Party in 1947 and was first elected to the house of representatives in 1960, for Tamaki district. He served as finance minister in the National Party government of Keith *Holyoake 1967–72. In 1974 he became leader of the National Party, replacing John Marshall, who had been criticized for being insufficiently aggressive in opposition. Muldoon led the party to a decisive electoral victory in 1975 and was re-elected, with smaller majorities, in 1978 and 1981.

Mulroney, Brian (1939–) Canadian politician, Progressive Conservative Party leader 1983–93, prime minister 1984–93. He achieved a landslide victory in the 1984 election, and won the 1988 election on a platform of free trade with the USA, but with a reduced majority. Opposition within Canada to the 1987 Meech Lake agreement, a prerequisite to signing the 1982 Constitution, continued to plague Mulroney in his second term. A revised reform package in October 1992 failed to gain voters' approval, and in February 1993 he was forced to resign the leadership of the Conservative Party, though he remained prime minister until Kim Campbell was appointed his successor in June.

Munich Agreement pact signed on 29 September 1938 by the leaders of the UK (Neville *Chamberlain), France (Edouard *Daladier), Germany (Adolf *Hitler), and Italy (Benito *Mussolini), under which Czechoslovakia was compelled to surrender its Sudeten-German districts (the **Sudeten**) to Germany. Chamberlain claimed it would guarantee 'peace in our time', but it did not prevent Hitler from seizing the rest of Czechoslovakia in March 1939.

Muscovy Company company founded 1555 to foster trade with Russia via the Arctic seas, after attempts to find a northerly route to China in 1553 opened the way for trade with Russia. Furs, timber, and naval supplies were traded for cloth and weapons. The first voyage after Queen Mary granted a charter was financed by the sale of 250 shares at £25 each. The Company lost its monopoly 1698, but extended its trade overland through Muscovy to Persia. It survived until the Russian Revolution 1917.

Museveni, Yoweri Kaguta (1945–) Ugandan general and politician, president from 1986. He led the opposition to Idi *Amin's regime 1971–79, and became minister of defence 1979–80. Unhappy with Milton *Obote's autocratic leadership, he formed the National Resistance Army (NRA). When Obote was ousted in a coup in 1985, Museveni entered into a brief power-sharing agreement with his successor, Tito Okello, before taking over as president. Museveni led a broad-based coalition government.

Musharraf, Pervez (1943–) Pakistani general and military ruler, head of the army from 1998, emergency ruler from 1999, and president from 2001. He seized power from Prime Minister Nawaz Sharif in a bloodless coup in 1999 and suspended the national assembly. He pledged to turn around the near-bankrupt economy before allowing a return to democratic rule. From September 2001 he provided backing to the US-led military campaign against Afghanistan's Taliban regime.

Muskie, Edmund S(ixtus) (1914–1996) US Democrat politician. A moderate by ideology and nature, he was a senator from Maine 1959–81 and secretary of state 1980–81. As a senator he concentrated on the environment, specializing in legislation on clean air and water. In the 1968 presidential election he was Hubert Humphrey's vice-presidential candidate. In 1972 he failed in his bid to win the Democratic nomination for president. He became a member of the US Supreme Court 1981.

Muslim League Indian political organization. The All India Muslim League was founded in 1906 under the leadership of the Aga Khan. In 1940 the league, led by Muhammad Ali *Jinnah, demanded an independent Muslim state. The *Congress Party and the Muslim League won most seats in the 1945 elections for an Indian central legislative assembly. In 1946 the Indian constituent assembly was boycotted by the Muslim League. It was partly the activities of the League that led to the establishment of Pakistan.

Mussolini, Benito Amilcare Andrea (1883–1945) Italian dictator 1925–43. As founder of the Fascist Movement (see *fascism) in 1919 and prime minister from 1922, he became known as *Il Duce* ('the leader'). He invaded Ethiopia 1935–36, intervened in the Spanish Civil War 1936–39 in support of Franco, and conquered Albania in 1939. In June 1940 Italy entered World War II supporting Hitler. Forced by military and domestic setbacks to resign in 1943, Mussolini established a breakaway government in northern Italy 1944–45, but was killed trying to flee the country.

Mussolini was born in the Romagna, the son of a blacksmith, and worked in early life as a teacher and journalist. He became active in the socialist movement, notably as editor of the party newspaper *Avanti* 1912–14. He was expelled in 1914 for advocating Italian intervention in World War I. He served in the army 1915–17, and in 1919 founded the Fascist Movement, whose programme combined violent nationalism with demagogic republican and anti-capitalist slogans, and launched a campaign of terrorism against the socialists. Though anti-capitalist in origin, the movement was backed by agrarian and industrial elites in the context of post-war popular unrest. In October 1922 Mussolini came to power by semi-constitutional means as prime minister at the head of a coalition government. In 1925 he assumed dictatorial powers, and in 1926 all opposition parties were banned. During the years that followed, the political, legal, and education systems were remodelled on fascist lines. Fascism prefigured other 'totalitarian' regimes, in that it aspired to be an all-embracing ideology, but Mussolini faced constraints on his power – from monarch, church, and industrial elites – which had no real parallel in Hitler's Germany.

Mussolini's Blackshirt followers were the forerunners of Hitler's Brownshirts, and his career of conquest drew him into close cooperation with Nazi Germany. Italy and Germany formed the *Axis alliance in 1936. During World War II Italian defeats in North Africa and Greece, the Allied invasion of Sicily, and discontent at home destroyed Mussolini's prestige, and in July 1943 he was compelled to resign by his own Fascist Grand Council. He was released from prison by German parachutists in September 1943 and set up a 'Republican Fascist' government in northern Italy. In April 1945 he and his mistress, Clara Petacci, were captured by partisans at Lake Como while heading for the Swiss border, and shot. Their bodies were taken to Milan and hung upside down in a public square.

Mutesa II, Edward Frederick William Wulugembe Mutebi (1924–1969) Ugandan ruler, president 1963–66. He became *kabaka* (king) of Buganda in 1939 and was crowned in 1942. In a dispute with the British government he was deposed in 1953, but reinstated two years later. In 1963 he became commander-in-chief and president of Uganda when the country became a republic. He was forcibly replaced by Milton Obote in February 1966 and escaped to exile in England.

Muzorewa, Abel (Tendekayi) (1925–) Zimbabwean politician and Methodist bishop. He was president of the African National Council 1971–85 and prime minister of Rhodesia/Zimbabwe 1979–80. He was detained for a year in 1983–84. Muzorewa was leader of the minority United Africa National Council, which merged with the Zimbabwe Unity Movement (ZUM) in 1994. He pulled out of the 1996 presidential election contest at the last minute, claiming the electoral process was unfairly tilted in President Mugabe's favour.

Mwinyi, Ali Hassan (1925–) Tanzanian socialist politician, succeeding Julius Nyerere as president 1985–95. He began a revival of private enterprise and control of state involvement and spending, and also instituted a multiparty political system in 1995. However in October he lost the first free presidential elections, and was succeeded by Benjamin Mkapa.

Myanmar formerly **Burma (until 1989)**, country in Southeast Asia, bounded northwest by India and Bangladesh, northeast by China, southeast by Laos and Thailand, and southwest by the Bay of Bengal.

My Lai massacre killing of 109 civilians in My Lai, a village in South Vietnam, by US troops in March 1968. An investigation in 1969 produced enough evidence to charge 30 soldiers with war crimes, but the only soldier convicted was Lt William Calley, commander of the platoon.

Nadir Shah, (Khan) Muhammad (c. 1880–1933) King of Afghanistan from 1929. Nadir played a key role in the 1919 Afghan War, but was subsequently forced into exile in France. He returned to Kabul in 1929 to seize the throne and embarked on an ambitious modernization programme. This alienated the Muslim clergy and in 1933 he was assassinated by fundamentalists. His successor as king was his son *Zahir Shah.

Nagorno-Karabakh (Russian 'mountainous Qarabagh') autonomous region of *Azerbaijan; area 4,400 sq km/1,700 sq mi; population (1997 est) 204,800 (77% Armenian, 23% Azeri), the Christian Armenians forming an enclave within the predominantly Shiite Muslim Azerbaijan. The capital is Xankändi. The region lies on the eastern slopes of the Lesser Caucasus Mountains, partly covered with oak and beech forests. Main agricultural products include cotton, grapes, wheat, silk, and livestock (sheep, cattle, pigs, and horses). Since 1989 the region has experienced conflict between local Armenian troops and Azeri forces. By 1998, Nagorno-Karabakh was effectively an independent state.

Nagy, Imre (1895–1958) Hungarian politician, prime minister 1953–55 and 1956. He led the Hungarian revolt against Soviet domination in 1956, for which he was executed.

Nahas, Mustafa al- (1897–1965) Egyptian nationalist and politician, leader of the Wafd party. He was instrumental in the process leading to the establishment of the Arab League, one of his major achievements. The military failure in 1948 and the subsequent burning of Cairo in 1952 brought discredit to the whole political establishment, including the Wafd leaders. The 1952 military coup ended his political career.

Najibullah, Ahmadzai (1947–1996) Afghan communist politician, leader of the People's Democratic Party of Afghanistan (PDPA) from 1986, and state president 1986–92. Although his government initially survived the withdrawal of Soviet troops in February 1989, continuing pressure from the Mujahedin forces resulted in his eventual overthrow. He was executed in September 1996 by the Taliban (Islamic student army), who had seized control of most of Afghanistan.

Nakasone, Yasuhiro (1917–) Japanese conservative politician, leader of the Liberal Democratic Party (LDP) and prime minister 1982–87. He increased military spending and Japanese participation in international affairs, with closer ties to the USA. He was forced to resign his party post in May 1989 as a result of having profited from insider trading in the Recruit scandal. After serving a two-year period of atonement, he rejoined the LDP in April 1991.

Namboodiripad, Elamkulam Manakkal Sankaran (EMS) (1909–1998) Indian politician; leader of the Communist Party of India-Marxist (CPM) 1978–92. In 1934 he helped found the Congress Socialist Party (CSP). When it became the Communist Party of India in 1940 he remained a member of its politburo until it split in 1964. Namboodiripad headed the first Communist government ever elected in Asia when he was elected chief minister of Kerala in 1957. He became chief minister a second time in

1967–69, leading a seven-party coalition headed by the CPM. In his later years he was a columnist for the Communist Party of India-Marxist weekly *Deshabhimani*.

Namibia formerly **South West Africa (to 1968)**, country in southwest Africa, bounded north by Angola and Zambia, east by Botswana and South Africa, and west by the Atlantic Ocean.

Narayan, Jaya Prakash (1902–1979) Indian politician. A veteran socialist, he was an associate of Vinobha Bham in the Bhoodan movement for rural reforms that took place during the last years of British rule. He was prominent in the protest movement against Indira Gandhi's emergency regime 1975–77, and acted as umpire in the Janata party leadership contest that followed Indira Gandhi's defeat in 1977.

Nash, Walter (1882–1968) New Zealand Labour centre-left politician, prime minister 1957–60. He became Labour Party leader in 1950, succeeding Peter *Fraser, when the party was in opposition. He led Labour to a narrow victory, by one seat, in the 1957 general election to become prime minister. A moderate Christian Socialist, his premiership marked a period of consolidation rather than innovation. Although Labour was defeated in the 1960 general election, Nash remained the party's leader until 1963. GCMG 1965.

Nassau agreement treaty signed on 18 December 1962 whereby the USA provided Britain with Polaris missiles, marking a strengthening in Anglo-American relations.

Nasser, Gamal Abdel (1918–1970) Egyptian politician, prime minister 1954–56 and from 1956 president of Egypt (the United Arab Republic 1958–71). In 1952 he was the driving power behind the Neguib coup, which ended the monarchy. His nationalization of the Suez Canal in 1956 led to an Anglo-French invasion and the *Suez Crisis, and his ambitions for an Egyptian-led union of Arab states led to disquiet in the Middle East (and in the West). Nasser was also an early and influential leader of the non-aligned movement.

Nasser entered the army from Cairo Military Academy, and was wounded in the Palestine War of 1948–49. Initially unpopular after the 1952 coup, he took advantage of demands for change by initiating land reform and depoliticizing the army. His position was secured by an unsuccessful assassination attempt in 1954 and his handling of the Suez Crisis in 1956.

National Assembly for Wales devolved parliamentary body for Wales, comprising 60 members and based in Cardiff. The Assembly was created by the July 1998 Government of Wales Act, which was passed following the Welsh electorate's narrow approval of government proposals in an 18 September 1997 referendum on devolution. Its temporary base is the Cardiff University Council Chamber and Crickhowell House on Cardiff Bay. A new building, designed by the architect Richard Rogers, is to be built at Cardiff Bay to house the assembly from 2001.

National Association for the Advancement of Colored People **NAACP**, US civil-rights organization dedicated to ending inequality and segregation for blacks through nonviolent protest. Founded in 1909, its first aim was to eradicate lynching. Since then the NAACP has campaigned to end segregation and discrimination in education, public accommodations, voting, and employment, and to protect the constitutional rights of blacks. It has made the most significant gains for civil rights through groundbreaking judicial cases. NAACP lawyers led by Thurgood *Marshall were instrumental in the 1954 * *Brown* v. *Board of Education* decision, which officially ended segregation in public schools.

Desegregation was only fully achieved through the *civil-rights movement of the 1960s.

The NAACP was founded by a group of white liberals, including labour reformer William Walling, newspaper editor Oswald Villard, social worker Jane *Addams, philosopher John Dewey, and novelist William Dean Howells. Most of the officials were white, but most of the members were drawn from the ranks of the black middle class. In 1909 it merged with the Niagara Movement founded in 1905 by W E B *Du Bois, who went on to edit the NAACP journal *The Crisis* 1910–34. The NAACP Legal Defense and Education Fund was founded in 1939 to act as the legal arm of the civil-rights movement.

National Front in the UK, extreme-right wing political party founded in 1967. In 1991 the party claimed 3,000 members. Some of its members had links with the National Socialist Movement of the 1960s (see *Nazism). It attracted attention during the 1970s through the violence associated with its demonstrations in areas with large black and Asian populations and, in response, the left-wing Anti Nazi League was formed to mount counter protests.

National Guard militia force recruited by each state of the USA. The volunteer National Guard units are under federal orders in emergencies, and under the control of the governor in peacetime, and are now an integral part of the US Army. The National Guard has been used against demonstrators; in May 1970 at Kent State University, Ohio, they killed four students who were protesting against the bombing of Cambodia by the USA.

National Insurance Act UK act of Parliament of 1911, introduced by the Liberal chancellor Lloyd George, which first provided insurance for workers against ill health and unemployment.

nationalism in politics, a movement that consciously aims to unify a nation, create a state, or free it from foreign or imperialistic rule. Nationalist movements became an important factor in European politics during the 19th century; since 1900 nationalism has become a strong force in Asia and Africa and in the late 1980s revived strongly in Eastern Europe.

National Party of Australia Australian political party, favouring free enterprise and seeking to promote the interests of people outside the major metropolitan areas. It holds the balance of power between Liberals and Labor. It was formed in 1916 as the **Country Party of Australia** and adopted its present name in 1982. It gained strength following the introduction of proportional representation in 1918 and was in coalition with the Liberals 1949–83. Its leader from 1990 is Tim Fischer and its federal president John Paterson. In 1996 it entered into a coalition with the Liberal Party led by Prime Minister John Howard.

National Security Council US federal executive council that was established under the National Security Act of 1947. The statutory membership includes the president, vice-president, and secretaries of state and defence. Other officials, such as the directors of foreign operations administration and emergency planning, may attend by invitation of the president. Their special advisers include the head of the joint chiefs of staff and the director of the *Central Intelligence Agency. The operations coordinating board also reports to the council. The special assistant to the president for national security affairs is the chief staff officer, and the national security adviser heads the council's staff.

National Trust British trust founded in 1895 for the preservation of land and buildings of historic interest or beauty, incorporated by an act of Parliament in 1907. It is the largest private landowner in Britain. The National Trust for Scotland was established in 1931.

National Urban League US service organization established in 1911 to fight against racial discrimination and to increase the political and economic power of blacks and other minority groups. Its national headquarters is in New York, with around 115 local chapters throughout the USA.

Nation of Islam original name of the group popularly known as the *Black Muslims, now the title of a 100,000-member splinter group faithful to the Black Muslims' original principles led by Louis *Farrakhan. Members strive to improve their social and religious position in society, and the group has won praise for its work in deprived areas, although its reputation has been tarnished by Farrakhan's anti-Semitic and anti-white beliefs. In October 1995 the group demonstrated its political strength by organizing the 'Million Man March' – a march of around 400,000 black men in Washington.

Nauru island country in Polynesia, southwest Pacific, west of Kiribati.

Naxalite member of an Indian extremist communist movement named after the town of Naxalbari, western Bengal, where a peasant uprising was suppressed 1967. The movement was founded by Charu Mazumdar (1915–1972).

Nazarbayev, Nursultan (1940–) Kazakh politician, president of Kazakhstan from 1990. In the Soviet period he was prime minister of the republic 1984–89 and leader of the Kazakh Communist Party 1989–91, which established itself as the independent Socialist Party of Kazakhstan in September 1991. He was an advocate of free-market policies, and yet also enjoyed the support of the environmentalist lobby.

Nazism ideology based on racism, nationalism, and the supremacy of the state over the individual. The German Nazi party, the *Nationalsozialistische Deutsche Arbeiterpartei* (National Socialist German Workers' Party), was formed from the German Workers'

Party (founded in 1919) and led by Adolf *Hitler from 1921 to 1945.

During the 1930s many similar parties were created throughout Europe and the USA, such as the British Union of Fascists (BUF) founded in the UK in 1932 by Oswald *Mosley. However, only those of Austria, Hungary, and Sudeten were of major importance. These parties collaborated with the German occupation of Europe from 1939 to 1945. After the Nazi atrocities of World War II (see *SS, *concentration camp, *Holocaust), the party was banned in Germany, but today parties with Nazi or neo-Nazi ideologies exist in many countries.

Nazi state dictatorial government established in Germany by the National Socialist German Workers' Party (NSDAP), or Nazis, under Adolf *Hitler from 1933 onwards. The Nazi state was characterized by the concentration of absolute power in the hands of an individual (the *Führer*, or 'leader') and the violent suppression of all dissent. National socialist Germany is also known as the *Third Reich.

Once the Nazis became the largest party in the German parliament (though with no overall majority), and Hitler was named chancellor on 30 January 1933, the machinery of constitutional government and multiparty democracy that had operated in the *Weimar Republic was swiftly dismantled. In February the parliament building was burned down – an attack blamed on communists, but widely thought to have been staged by the Nazis – and the Enabling Act was passed, which gave the Nazi government sweeping powers to bypass parliament in drafting laws and conducting foreign affairs. Over the next year, regional assemblies were forced to adopt the same party make-up as the national parliament, so ensuring Nazi dominance, and finally all other political organizations were outlawed. A vast network of secret police (* *Gestapo*), aided by informers, enforced the new laws; political opponents were murdered or imprisoned in *concentration camps. The final phase in establishing a dictatorship came on June 1934, the *Night of the Long Knives, with an internal purge of the Nazi Party. To reassure the big-business interests that had funded his rise, Hitler ordered the murder of the leadership of the SA (*Sturmabteilung , or 'stormtroops') – the radical, populist wing of the party. The swift annihilation of any perceived opposition, a tactic known as *Blitzkrieg, confirmed Hitler's total hold over Germany. Power was now consolidated in the elite group around Hitler known as the *SS.

Neave, Airey Middleton Sheffield (1916–1979) British intelligence officer and Conservative member of Parliament 1953–79. He was a close adviser to Conservative Party leader (later prime minister) Margaret Thatcher. During World War II he escaped from Colditz, a German high-security prison camp. As shadow undersecretary of state for Northern Ireland from 1975, he became a target for extremist groups and was assassinated by an Irish terrorist bomb.

Neguib, Muhammad (1901–1984) Egyptian army general and politician; prime minister from 1952 and president 1953–54. After a distinguished military career, he led the coup of the Free Officers that ended King Farouk's reign in 1952 and abolished the monarchical system in 1953. Prime minister and then president of the newly emerged republic, he was deposed and succeeded by Gamal Abdel *Nasser and retired to Cairo.

Nehru, Jawaharlal (1889–1964) Indian nationalist politician, prime minister from 1947 until his death. Before the partition (the division of British India into India and Pakistan), he led the socialist wing of the nationalist *Congress Party, and was second in influence only to Mahatma Gandhi.

He was imprisoned nine times by the British 1921–45 for political activities. As prime minister from the creation of the dominion (later republic) of India in August 1947, he originated the idea of non-alignment (neutrality towards major powers). His daughter was Prime Minister Indira Gandhi. His sister, Vijaya Lakshmi *Pandit was the UN General Assembly's first female president 1953–54.

Nenni, Pietro (1891–1980) Italian Socialist politician. He was secretary general of the Italian Socialist party 1944–63 and in 1947 became leader of the main body of the party which refused to participate in the Christian Democrat prime minister Alcide De Gasperi's government. After the Soviet invasion of Hungary in 1956, Nenni broke with the Italian Communists and in 1964 supported the government formed by Aldo Moro. This led to a further split within the party, and in the elections of 1968 Nenni's faction lost votes heavily.

neo-Nazism the upsurge in racial and political intolerance in Eastern and Western Europe of the early 1990s. In Austria, Belgium, France, Germany, Russia, and Italy, the growth of extreme right-wing political groupings, coupled with racial violence, particularly in Germany, has revived memories of the Nazi period in Hitler's Germany. Ironically, the liberalization of politics in the post-Cold War world has unleashed anti-liberal forces hitherto checked by authoritarian regimes. The most significant parties in Western Europe described by the media as 'neo-nazi' were the National Front in France, led by Jean-Marie *Le Pen, and the National Alliance in Italy (although, by 1998, the National Alliance claimed to be a mainstream conservative party).

Nepal landlocked country in the Himalayan mountain range in Central Asia, bounded north by Tibet (an autonomous region of China), east, south, and west by India.

Netanyahu, Binyamin (1949–)
called **'Bibi'**, Israeli right-wing
politician and diplomat, leader of the
*Likud (Consolidation) party 1993–99
and prime minister 1996–99. A hardline politician, he succeeded Yitzhak
*Shamir to the Likud leadership in
March 1993, following the party's 1992
electoral defeat. Israel's first directly
elected prime minister, he persistently
frustrated progress in the
*Israel–Palestine peace process.

Netherlands, The   country in Western
Europe on the North Sea, bounded east
by Germany and south by Belgium.

government The Netherlands is
a hereditary monarchy. Its 1983
constitution, based on that of 1814,
provides for a two-chamber legislature
called the States-General, consisting
of a First Chamber of 75 and a Second
Chamber of 150. Members of the
First Chamber are indirectly elected
by representatives of 12 provincial
councils for a six-year term, half
retiring every three years. Members
of the Second Chamber are elected by
universal adult suffrage, through a
system of proportional representation,
also for a four-year term. Legislation
is introduced and bills amended in the
Second Chamber, while the First has
the right to approve or reject.

The monarch appoints a prime
minister as head of government, and
the prime minister chooses the cabinet.
Cabinet members are not permitted to
be members of the legislature, but they
may attend its meetings and take part
in debates, and they are collectively
responsible to it. There is also a council
of state, the government's oldest
advisory body, whose members are
intended to represent a broad cross-
section of the country's life, and
include former politicians, scholars,
judges, and business people, all
appointed for life. The sovereign is its
formal president but appoints a vice-
president to chair it.

Although not a federal state, the
Netherlands gives considerable
autonomy to its 11 provinces, each of
which has an appointed governor and
an elected council.

history The inhabitants of the
Netherlands are descendants of a
Germanic people called by the Romans
the Batavi, who lived on an island
between the two branches of the
River Rhine, and the Frisians who dwelt
further north. The land south of the
Rhine, occupied by Celtic peoples, was
brought under Roman rule by Julius
Caesar as governor of Gaul in 51 BC.

the Middle Ages Roman rule lasted
until the 4th century AD, when the
Franks overran the south. The Frankish
kings subdued the Frisians and Saxons
north of the Rhine in the 7th–8th
centuries and imposed Christianity on
them. Charlemagne's dominion in the
late 8th century extended to the
Netherlands, and he built a palace at
Nijmegen on the River Waal.

After the empire of Charlemagne
broke up, and with the establishment
of feudalism, the country was divided
into small sovereignties. In 922 Dirk
became count of Holland, and the
other Netherland provinces (such
as Namur, Hainaut, Limburg, and
Zutphen) were divided among various
barons and counts, autocratic rulers
who owed allegiance to the dukes
or earls of Lorraine, Brabant, and
Flanders. Holland, Zeeland, Utrecht,
Overijssel, Groningen, Drenthe, and
Friesland, which were afterwards to
form the United Provinces of the
Netherlands, were chiefly under the
rule of the counts of Holland and the
Bishop of Utrecht, who in turn owed
nominal allegiance to the German or
Holy Roman Empire.

Between the 11th and 15th centuries,
the cities of the Netherlands – notably
Bruges, Ghent, and Antwerp – became
important as commercial centres,
usually ruled by small groups of
merchants. Through the 15th century
all of the Low Countries (the modern-
day Netherlands, Belgium, and
Luxembourg, then collectively known

as the Netherlands) were brought under the rule of the dukes of Burgundy, by purchase, inheritance, and conquest.

Habsburg rule In 1477 Mary – following the death in battle of her father Charles the Bold, Duke of Burgundy – married Maximilian, the archduke of Austria, who later became Holy Roman emperor as Maximilian I. Through this, the Low Countries came into the possession of the Habsburgs. The Low Countries were passed on by Mary of Burgundy to her son, Philip, who married the daughter of Ferdinand and Isabella of Spain. Dying before his father, in 1506 Philip left the Low Countries to his son, Charles, who became king of Spain in 1516 and Holy Roman emperor in 1519 as Charles V. The Low Countries thus became the Spanish Netherlands.

the Dutch Revolt The struggle for freedom and for civic and religious independence came to a head in the reign of Philip II of Spain in the middle of the 16th century. The revolt was partly due to religious reasons: some of the people of the Low Countries were Protestant or Calvinist, and objected to the ardently Catholic policies of Philip II, including the imposition of the Inquisition. More important, there were also strong objections to the increasing centralization of government, the economic demands of the Spanish crown, and the maintenance of a standing army.

After an outbreak of image-breaking in churches by Dutch Calvinists in 1567, Philip dispatched a Spanish army under the Duke of Alba to restore order. Alba's brutally repressive actions sparked off a revolt. In 1573 William the Silent, prince of Orange – who was Philip's lieutenant in Holland, Zeeland, and Utrecht – became leader of the revolt against Spanish rule. William, although ambivalent towards religious disputes, came to rely upon the Dutch Calvinists for his chief support. William was one of the earliest champions of the principle of toleration, but the revolt against Spain became identified, especially by foreigners, with the cause of Protestantism, and William was regarded as a Protestant hero. The foundation of an independent Dutch state owes more to him than to any other individual.

By the capture of Brielle in 1572 Spain received its first serious reverse. In 1579 the Union of Utrecht was formed, by which the seven northern provinces banded together as the United Provinces to resist Spain, and in 1581 they declared their freedom. However, the south (now Belgium and Luxembourg) was reconquered by Spain.

After William's assassination by a Spanish agent in 1584 the Dutch continued fighting, receiving military aid from England. This in turn provoked the Spanish to send the Armada against England in 1588. William's sons, Maurice (1567–1625) and Frederick Henry (1584–1647), took prominent parts in the war against Spain, both succeeding in their turn to their father's offices. Maurice (Count Maurice of Nassau), in a series of brilliant campaigns, drove the Spanish from the northern Netherlands. The Dutch also won many sea battles against the Spanish, and in 1609 Philip III of Spain agreed to a twelve years' truce. The war, renewed in 1621 as part of the wider European conflict of the Thirty Years' War, was continued until 1648, when, by the peace of Westphalia, Spain recognized the independence of the United Provinces (also known as the Dutch Republic).

economic prosperity and trade rivalry The Dutch economy thrived in the 1590s; a prosperity based on the Baltic trade and herring fishery. Amsterdam expanded enormously, and science and the arts flourished. In 1602 the Dutch East India Company was formed, and a truce with Spain 1609–21 enabled the Dutch government to consolidate its gains. Having broken the Portuguese monopoly over the spice trade in the East Indies (modern Indonesia), they also took over many of Portugal's possessions in the East Indies and Africa. The Dutch also looked to the Americas, gaining control of Brazil 1630–45 and establishing a trading centre on Curaçao in the Caribbean. Fortunes were made from the slave trade.

By the middle of the 17th century, Dutch trading success prompted England to pass a series of Navigation Acts to protect English trade. These measures prevented freedom of Dutch trade with England and its colonies, and led to the Anglo-Dutch wars of 1652–54, 1665–67, and 1672–74. The wars were fought mostly at sea, although Admiral de Ruyter sailed up the Medway and the Thames to destroy English ships in 1667. The Dutch Republic was ultimately excluded from North America and West Africa, and Britain took over most of its overseas trade.

internal conflicts in the 17th century Success against Spain was followed by a struggle for power within the Dutch Republic, between the house of Orange-Nassau and the towns, in which Prince Maurice triumphed. Following the peace of Westphalia (1648) a struggle followed between the Orangist party, which favoured centralization under the Prince of Orange as chief magistrate (or stadholder), and the republican, oligarchical or states' rights party, headed by Johann de Witt.

The premature death of the stadholder William II of Orange, who died before the birth of his son, William III of Orange, allowed the republican party to seize control in 1650. De Witt became virtual prime minister, and soon found himself embroiled in the Anglo-Dutch Wars. De Witt was murdered in 1672 and William III of Orange recovered the office of stadholder. He secured British friendship by his marriage with his cousin, the future Mary II of England. This contributed to his subsequent elevation to the throne of England as King William III, when he was invited by Parliament to invade in 1688.

wars with Louis XIV The expansionist ambitions of the French king, Louis XIV, led to a series of wars with France. Louis attempted to annex the Spanish Netherlands (modern Belgium and Luxembourg) in 1667, alarming England and the Dutch Republic into an alliance with Sweden against France. Louis withdrew in 1668, but attacked the Dutch Republic in 1672, bringing it close to collapse. In the Peace of Nijmegen (1678), Louis made great gains in the north.

The Dutch allied with the British against Louis in the War of the League of Augsburg (1688–97). By the Treaty of Ryswick (1697) Louis gave up all conquests, with few exceptions, gained since 1678. In the War of the Spanish Succession (1701–14), the Dutch and British were once more allied against France. By the Treaty of Utrecht (1713) the Dutch were allowed to keep some of their barrier fortresses in the Spanish Netherlands, which were transferred to Austria.

decline in the 18th century The Treaty of Utrecht marked the end of the Dutch Republic as a major world power. The wars with France had proved expensive, and the French and British now dominated the trans-Atlantic trade, as well as encroaching on Dutch trade in the Baltic. Only the East Indies route continued to prosper.

The Dutch were also faced by domestic problems, including a declining population and erosion of the dykes that kept the sea from flooding large areas of land. In 1731 they gave way, causing widespread damage and incurring costly repair. William III's death in 1702, without an heir, brought about political unrest until, in 1747, a French invasion scare during the War of the Austrian Succession enabled the princes of Orange to reassert their authority and make their position hereditary. Attempts at constitutional reform in the 1780s were discouraged when the king of Prussia, the brother-in-law of William V of Orange, sent troops to invade the country.

the Revolutionary and Napoleonic period Many Dutch, who were anxious for reform, welcomed the arrival of French revolutionary forces in 1794–95. The United Provinces collapsed and were replaced by a French-sponsored 'sister republic', the Batavian Republic. Louis Bonaparte was made king of Holland in 1806, but abdicated when the country was attached to the French Empire (1810–13).

The Orange family had taken refuge in England when the French invaded the Netherlands, but on the fall of Napoleon they returned. By the Congress of Vienna the northern and southern provinces were formed into the kingdom of the Netherlands under King William I (son of Prince William V of Orange).

the 19th and early 20th centuries In 1830 the southern provinces seceded and *Belgium was formed into a separate kingdom. In 1840 William I abdicated in favour of his son William II (ruled 1840–49), who in 1848 granted a new and more liberal constitution to the people. During the reign of William III (1849–90) the question of Luxembourg was settled: since 1815 the king of the Netherlands had also been grand duke of Luxembourg, but in 1867 the grand duchy was established as an independent state.

From the middle of the 19th century, religious issues dominated Dutch domestic politics for many years, and several of the modern Dutch political parties have their basis in historical religious divisions. A beginning was made in the field of social legislation, which was considerably expanded in the 20th century. In 1890 Queen Wilhelmina, then still a child, came to the throne. The Palace of Peace, to which many nations contributed, was opened in The Hague in 1913, as the premises of the Permanent Court of Arbitration (now the UN International Court of Justice). From 1815 to 1939 the Netherlands played little part in European history, and maintained a policy of strict neutrality.

From the mid-19th century onwards there was great industrial and agricultural expansion in the Netherlands. The coalfields of south Limburg, which owed their later development to the fact that during World War I the supply of German coal became restricted, were exploited with considerable success; while the great scheme for the reclamation of the Zuider Zee (in order to add a new province to the country) was launched in 1923.

During World War I the Netherlands remained neutral, and on his abdication in November 1918, Kaiser William II of Germany went into exile there. After World War I, universal suffrage and proportional representation were introduced. At the same time the principle of equal public spending on secular and denominational schools was incorporated into the constitution.

occupation during World War II The Germans invaded the Netherlands on 10 May 1940. The following day, a German armoured column entered Brabant and fighting took place in The Hague. Queen Wilhelmina left on a British destroyer for England, and was followed by the Dutch cabinet. The Germans destroyed the centre of Rotterdam in an air bombardment in order to force the Dutch to surrender; within four hours 25,000 buildings were destroyed. The Dutch had little choice but to surrender.

Hitler appointed Arthur Seyss-Inquart, an Austrian Nazi, as commissioner for the occupied Netherlands. The country was soon crushed under the financial burdens imposed by the Germans and the standard of living rapidly declined. Produce was removed to Germany, and Dutch industry was geared to German war needs. Seyss-Inquart attempted to impose Nazi 'Nordic culture' on Dutch institutions. The fact that the Dutch proved to be immune to this cultural infiltration was partly due to the churches, which developed into strongholds of patriotism. There was active resistance too, and many Dutch people were executed for their activities against the Germans; others fled to Britain to continue the struggle from there.

the Allied liberation of the Netherlands In 1944 the Anglo-American chiefs of staff decided to use the newly constituted British and American Airborne Divisions to assist in seizing the Rhine crossings at Nijmegen and Arnhem, after the rapid advance by the land armies following the Normandy landings in June. The first landings of airborne troops were made on 17 September and reinforcements followed on successive days. There was heavy fighting in the area between Nijmegen and Arnhem during the ensuing days, and the position of the First Airborne Division became so precarious that on 25 September orders were given for the withdrawal of all forces across the Lower Rhine (see *Arnhem, Battle of).

After this the Allies turned their attention to opening up Antwerp. By 30 September 1944 the whole of South Beveland had been cleared by British and Canadian forces. By 9 November the stiff resistance had ceased and some 10,000 troops had been captured. Resistance in north Holland collapsed in the first week of April 1945 and the sea was reached on 15 April. By 21 April the whole area, apart from a small tip in the northeast, was cleared as far as Harderwijk and the eastern shore of the IJsselmeer. To the west the IJssel River line was stubbornly

defended at Deventer and Zutphen, but the former town fell on 10 April. In the southern part, the Canadian First Corps attacked from Nijmegen, and Arnhem was taken on 15 April. The Germans now withdrew into 'Fortress Holland' behind the Grebbe and New Water lines, protected by floods, beyond which no further Allied advance was made in this sector. The complete liberation of the country soon followed on the final collapse of all German resistance in Europe, though during the last weeks of the German occupation the Dutch suffered heavily from shortages of food and other commodities.

post-war reconstruction The enormous task of reconstruction was begun immediately after liberation. Further Dutch industrial expansion was greatly aided by the discovery of large quantities of gas under the North Sea off the Dutch coast. Side by side with material reconstruction the post-war governments pursued a full programme of social improvements. Those who had collaborated with the Germans were put on trial. In December 1945 the leader of the Dutch Nazis, Anton Mussert, was sentenced to death by a special court at The Hague. In April 1949 minor frontier modifications in the Netherlands' favour were made on the Dutch–German frontier.

Queens Wilhelmina, Juliana, and Beatrix On the national celebrations in honour of the fiftieth year of her reign and of her sixty-eighth birthday, Queen Wilhelmina in August 1948 resumed for a period of one week the royal authority that she had relinquished the previous May in favour of her daughter, Princess Juliana, who had since then acted as Princess Regent. In September Queen Wilhelmina formally signed an Act of Abdication.

Queen Juliana, the fifth monarch of the Netherlands and of the royal house of Orange-Nassau, was formally inaugurated in September in the Nieuwe Kerk in Amsterdam. Queen Wilhelmina after abdication took the title of princess of the Netherlands, living in retirement until her death in 1962.

Controversy arose in 1964 when Juliana's second daughter, Irene (1939–), became a Roman Catholic and married the Carlist claimant to the Spanish throne. She later renounced her succession right to the Dutch throne. In 1965 controversy revived when the heir to the throne, *Beatrix, became engaged to a West German diplomat. Many former resistance fighters strongly protested; but the Dutch parliament eventually approved the proposed marriage, which took place in 1966. Following the birth of three sons to Beatrix, the first male heirs to the House of Orange for a hundred years, the marriage won popular favour, and Beatrix became queen in 1980 on her mother's abdication.

decolonization The dominant issue in Dutch politics in the immediate post-war years was that of the Dutch East Indies, which had been occupied by the Japanese during World War II and was demanding independence as *Indonesia. After several years of abortive negotiation and intermittent fighting, the independence of Indonesia was finally established in 1949. The fighting stopped, and the transfer of sovereignty to the new state was approved by the Dutch and Indonesian parliaments. The question of Netherlands New Guinea remained unsettled, however, until 1963, when it was ceded to Indonesia.

Among the Netherlands' other colonies, Suriname became independent in 1975, while the Netherlands Antilles have full internal autonomy. The Netherlands absorbed large numbers of people from its former colonies.

regional cooperation and prosperity Dutch neutrality ended in 1940, and from 1945 the Netherlands became fully committed to the Western alliance. It became a member of the Western European Union, the North Atlantic Treaty Organization, the Benelux customs union, the European Coal and Steel Community, the European Atomic Energy Community (Euratom), and the European Economic Community.

The Netherlands prospered economically in the post-war years. Its currency, the guilder, became one of the most buoyant in the economy of Western Europe. The development, outside Rotterdam, of the Europoort, one of the greatest oil-refining centres in the world, contributed greatly to this prosperity. This concentration upon oil made the Europoort especially vulnerable in the aftermath of the 1973 Arab–Israeli War. The support of the Dutch government for Israel aroused considerable hostility from the Arabs and the trade in oil to the Netherlands was temporarily boycotted by Arab countries. The Dutch government introduced a variety of emergency measures to conserve energy, which were later adopted elsewhere.

politics and government Politically, the development of the Netherlands has been calm. All governments since 1945 have been coalitions, with the parties differing mainly over economic policies. In the 1970s the political balance shifted towards the left.

In the September 1989 elections, fought largely on environmental issues, Ruud Lubbers's Christen-Democratisch Appèl (CDA; Christian Democratic Appeal) won the most parliamentary seats. Lubbers formed a coalition government with the Partij van de Arbeid (PvdA; Labour Party). Both parties lost support in the May 1994 elections and eventually the PvdA leader, Wim Kok, formed a three-party coalition with the People's Party for Freedom and Democracy and the Democrats 66, both centrist in orientation.

In the May 1998 general election the PvdA made strong gains.

The Dutch government resigned in May 1999 after the smallest party, Democrats 66, withdrew. A row about giving citizens the right to vote in referendums had split the ruling coalition and led to the entire cabinet tendering its resignation. However, the government retracted its resignation a month later after mediation by Queen Beatrix.

euthanasia On 28 November 2000, the Netherlands parliament passed a bill legalizing euthanasia, which was ratified by the senate on 10 April 2001. The Netherlands is the first country to legalize euthanasia. Approximately 2,700 patients formally request euthanasia each year. Prior to legalization, doctors were not prosecuted, provided guidelines issued by the Royal Dutch Medical Association were followed.

homosexual marriage The Netherlands was the first country to legalize marriages between two people of the same sex. A bill passed in January 2001 came into effect on 1 April 2001.

In August 2001, Prime Minister Wim Kok announced that he would stand down as leader of the PvdA after elections in May 2002, and named parliamentary floor leader Ad Melkert as his chosen successor. On 1 January 2002, euro notes and coins were introduced as the national currency.

political assassination Pim Fortuyn, a far-right populist politician, was assassinated in the town of Hilversum, seemingly by animal rights activist Volkert van der Graaf. Fortuyn's anti-immigration and anti-Muslim stance brought his followers success in local elections in Rotterdam in March 2002 and his recently-formed Pim Fortuyn List party was expected to do well in the mid-May national elections.

general elections 2002 In the elections in May, the PvdA and its centre-left allies lost power. The centre-right CDA won 43 of the 150 parliamentary seats to become the largest party. The far-right Pim Fortuyn List came second with 26 seats.

Neto, (Antonio) Agostinho (1922–1979) Angolan nationalist and politician, president 1974–79. A member of the Popular Movement for the Liberation of Angola (*MPLA), he was imprisoned several times between 1952 and 1962, but escaped to the Congo where he became president and leader of the MPLA in the guerrilla war against Portuguese colonialism. His close ties with Fidel Castro gave him Cuban and Soviet backing, and enabled him to prevail in the civil war following the Portuguese withdrawal. In 1974 he became the first president of Angola, holding the post until his death.

Neurath, Baron Konstantin von (1873–1956) German politician and diplomat. In 1939 he became Reichsprotektor (governor) of Bohemia and Moravia, and set up an administration similar to that in Germany, but he was considered too lenient by Hitler and was recalled in 1941. He was tried at Nuremberg as a war criminal in 1946 and sentenced to 15 years' imprisonment, but died before his release.

Neves, Tancredo de Almeida (1910–1985) Brazilian politician. He was elected Brazil's first civilian president in 21 years in 1985 but died before his inauguration.

New Deal in US history, the programme introduced by President Franklin D Roosevelt in 1933 to tackle the *Great Depression, including employment on public works, farm loans at low rates, and social reforms such as old-age and unemployment insurance, prevention of child labour, protection of employees against unfair practices by employers, and loans to local authorities for slum clearance.

The centrepiece of the New Deal was the Social Security Act of 1935, which introduced a comprehensive federal system of insurance for the elderly and unemployed. The **Public Works Administration** was given $3.3 billion to spend on roads, public buildings, and similar developments (the *Tennessee Valley Authority was a separate project). The **Agricultural Adjustment Administration** raised agricultural prices by restriction of output. In 1935 Harry L *Hopkins was put in charge of a new agency, the **Works Progress Administration** (WPA), which in addition to taking over the public works created something of a cultural revolution with its federal theatre, writers', and arts projects. When the WPA was disbanded in 1943 it had found employment for 8.5 million people.

Some of the provisions of the New Deal were declared unconstitutional by the Supreme Court (1935–36). The New Deal encouraged the growth of trade-union membership, brought previously unregulated areas of the US economy under federal control, and revitalized cultural life and community spirit. Although full employment did not come until the military-industrial needs of World War II, the New Deal did bring political stability to the industrial-capitalist system. It also transformed the political landscape, making the Democratic Party the natural majority party and breaking Republican dominance since 1806.

New Democratic Party NDP, Canadian political party, moderately socialist, formed in 1961 by a merger of the Labour Congress and the Cooperative Commonwealth Federation. Its leader is Alexa McDonough.

New Frontier in US history, the social reform programme proposed by John F *Kennedy 1961–63. The phrase was coined in Kennedy's speech accepting the Democratic party's nomination 1960.

Newgate prison in London, which stood on the site of the Old Bailey central criminal court. Originally a

gatehouse (hence the name), it was established in the 12th century, rebuilt after the Great Fire of 1666, and again in 1780. Public executions were held outside it 1783–1868. It was demolished in 1903.

New Guard Australian right-wing paramilitary organization formed in Sydney 1931 with the philosophy of loyalty to the monarchy and the British Empire and the suppression of 'disloyal' elements, particularly communists. Its clearest purpose was the overthrow of New South Wales Labor premier Jack Lang, its most famous protest being the disruption of the premier's opening of the Sydney Harbour Bridge in 1932 by Francis De Groot (1888–1969). After Lang's dismissal, the New Guard's membership declined and it ceased to exist in 1935.

Ne Win (1911–2002) adopted name of **Maung Shu Maung, ('Brilliant Sun')** Myanmar (Burmese) politician, prime minister 1958–60, ruler from 1962 to 1974, president 1974–81, and chair until 1988 of the ruling Burma Socialist Programme Party (BSPP). His domestic 'Burmese Way to Socialism' policy programme brought the economy into serious decline.

New Right resurgence of conservative and anti-socialist thought in the UK, the USA, and other advanced industrial democracies that began in the mid-1970s. The term refers to a range of conservative and liberal ideas including principally a commitment to individualism and the primacy of capitalism and the free market in preference to state policies. Advocates of New Right theories were active in the UK and the USA since the early 1960s, but it was only after the economic crisis of 1973–74 and the electoral success of Margaret *Thatcher in 1979 and Ronald *Reagan in 1980 that the expression became common.

Newton, Huey P (1942–1989) US civil-rights activist who co-founded the Black Panther Party. In 1967, Newton was accused of killing an Oakland police officer. His trial attracted crowds of demonstrators chanting Panther slogans and demanding his release. Newton was convicted of voluntary manslaughter and sent to the California Men's Colony, but his conviction was later overturned by the California court of appeals. By the 1970s, the Black Panther Party had become a potent political force in California, but Newton was once again in serious trouble. He was charged with shooting a prostitute, after which the charges were dropped. He was retried and convicted for the 1969 death of the police officer. The conviction was later reversed.

new town in the UK, centrally planned urban area. New towns such as Milton Keynes and Stevenage were built after World War II to accommodate the overspill from cities and large towns, notably London, at a time when the population was rapidly expanding and inner-city centres had either decayed or been destroyed. In 1976 the policy, which had been criticized for disrupting family groupings and local communities, destroying small shops and specialist industries, and furthering the decay of city centres, was abandoned.

New Zealand or **Aotearoa, (Maori 'long daylight')** country in the southwest Pacific Ocean, southeast of Australia, comprising two main islands, North Island and South Island, and other small islands.

Nez Percé or **Sahaptini** or **Nimipu,** (French **'pierced nose'**) member of an American Indian people who inhabited the plateau between the Rocky Mountain and Coastal ranges (Idaho, Washington, and Oregon) until the mid-19th century. Their language belongs to the Penutian family. They were mistakenly named for another people, as nose-piercing was never a custom among them. Formerly sedentary and dependant on salmon-fishing, they adopted the nomadic buffalo-hunting lifestyle of the Plains Indians after acquiring horses in the 1730s. They were unique in selectively breeding horses, developing the Appaloosa into one of the largest herds in North America. The Nez Percé now live in Idaho and Washington and number about 1,500 (1990). Business concerns include logging, fishing, and commerce.

Ngo Dinh Diem (1901–1963) Vietnamese politician, president of South Vietnam 1955–63. He depended largely on US aid, but was able to suppress internal opposition until 1960–61, when the Communist-led National Liberation Front (Vietcong) began a guerrilla campaign against his government; this forced him to call for increased US support and led directly to the *Vietnam War. After causing unrest by embarking on a campaign against militant Buddhists, he was murdered by dissident army officers.

Nguyen Van Thieu (1923–2001) Vietnamese soldier and political leader. In 1963, as chief of staff of the armed forces of the Republic of Vietnam (South Vietnam), he was a leader in the coup against *Ngo Dinh Diem. He became deputy premier and minister of defence in 1964, and head of state in 1965. In 1967, as the war against the Vietcong escalated, he became president of the Republic of Vietnam, and in early 1973 was a signatory to the peace treaty that formally ended hostilities. Fighting between North and South continued until the communist victory in 1975 with the fall of Saigon (now Ho Chi Minh City), when Thieu took refuge first in Taiwan, then the UK, finally settling in the USA.

Nicaragua country in Central America, between the Pacific Ocean and the Caribbean Sea, bounded north by Honduras and south by Costa Rica.

government The constitution dates from 1987. The 92-member National Constituent Assembly is elected by universal suffrage through a system of proportional representation for a six-year term, and a president, similarly elected, serves a non-renewable five-year term, with the assistance of a vice-president and an appointed cabinet.

history The first European to reach Nicaragua was Gil González de Avila in 1522, who brought it under Spanish rule. It remained Spanish until 1821 and was then briefly united with Mexico. Nicaragua achieved full independence in 1838.

foreign investment After two decades of turmoil and invasions from other Central American states, Nicaragua experienced 30 years of relative tranquillity 1863–93 under Conservative rule. This long period of peace led to increasing foreign investment, especially in coffee plantations and railway construction. The Liberal dictator Santos Zelaya, in power 1893–1909, promoted state education, the separation of church and state, and civil marriage and divorce. He also led the movement for a brief union 1896–98 with El Salvador and Honduras.

US military presence In 1912, at the Nicaraguan government's request, the USA established military bases in the country. Their presence was opposed by a guerrilla group led by Augusto César Sandino. The USA withdrew its forces in 1933, but not before it had set up and trained a national guard, commanded by a trusted nominee, Gen Anastasio Somoza. Sandino was assassinated in 1934, but some of his followers continued their guerrilla activity.

Somoza rule The Somoza family began a near-dictatorial rule that was to last for over 40 years. During this time they amassed a huge personal fortune. Gen Anastasio Somoza was elected president in 1936 and stayed in office until his assassination in 1956, when he was succeeded by his son Luis. The left-wing Sandinista National Liberation Front (FSLN), named after the former guerrilla leader, was formed in 1962 with the object of overthrowing

the Somozas by revolution. Luis Somoza was followed by his brother Anastasio, who headed an even more notorious regime. In 1979, after considerable violence and loss of life, Somoza was ousted; see *Nicaraguan Revolution.

Sandinista reconstruction The FSLN established a provisional junta of national reconstruction led by Daniel Ortega Saavedra, published a guarantee of civil rights, and appointed a council of state, prior to an elected national assembly and a new constitution; assembly elections held in 1984 endorsed the FSLN.

relations with USA Nicaragua's relations with the USA deteriorated rapidly with the election of President Reagan. He froze the package of economic assistance arranged by his predecessor, Jimmy Carter, alleging that the Sandinista government was supporting attempts to overthrow the administration in El Salvador. In March 1982 the Nicaraguan government declared a state of emergency in the wake of attacks on bridges and petroleum installations. The Reagan administration embarked on a policy of destabilizing Nicaragua's government and economy by actively supporting the counter-revolutionary forces (the Contras) – known to have executed prisoners, killed civilians, and engaged in forced conscription – and by covert *Central Intelligence Agency operations, including the mining of Nicaraguan harbours in 1984. In February 1985 Reagan denounced Ortega's regime, saying that his objective was to 'remove it in the sense of its present structure'. The World Court ruled in 1986 that the USA was in breach of international law and ordered it to pay $17 billion in reparations. In June 1986 the US Congress approved $100 million in overt military aid to the Contras; total US aid to the Contras was $300 million. In 1988 a hurricane left 18,000 homeless.

Sandinista government defeated

Political parties were ostensibly legalized under the terms of a regional peace plan signed by the presidents of El Salvador, Guatemala, Costa Rica, Honduras, and Nicaragua in 1987, but the fighting continued. President Ortega entered into talks with the rebels in January 1988 and the US Congress rejected a request for additional military aid for the Contras. In October 1988 President Reagan announced that he would no longer seek military aid for the Contras. In February 1989 the presidents of Guatemala, El Salvador, and Honduras agreed to disarm the Contras, and in March 1989 1,900 members of the former National Guard of Anastasia Somoza were released. Elections held in February 1990 were won by Violeta Barrios de Chamorro of the US-backed National Opposition Union (UNO). The Bush administration spent $9 million on her election campaign. The USA lifted its economic embargo in March. By the end of June 1990 the Contra rebel army had been disbanded and the government had committed itself to reducing armed forces by 50%. In July violent riots occurred as people protested about land rights, inflation, and unemployment.

US pressure maintained

Chamorro's state visit to the USA in April 1991 was the first by a Nicaraguan president for over 50 years. In exchange for Nicaragua dropping its claim to the damages of $17 billion awarded it by the World Court against the USA, President Bush pledged economic support for Nicaragua, whose total international debt was almost $10 billion. The cost to Nicaragua of the US economic and Contra warfare was estimated at $15 billion, with 30,000 people killed. US aid was suspended in June 1992 because of concern about the extent of Sandinista's influence in Chamorro's government. In an effort to end the suspension, Chamorro dismissed

12 high-level police officers linked with Sandinista. An earthquake in September 1992 claimed 116 victims, with more than 150 people declared missing and over 16,000 made homeless.

In 1993 a state of emergency was declared in northern Nicaragua after renewed skirmishes between Contra and Sandinista rebel groups.

A peace accord was finally reached with the remaining Contra rebels, known as Recontras, early in 1994. Constitutional reforms, approved in November 1994, reduced the presidential term, ruled out re-election, and barred relatives of serving presidents from standing for the presidency.

In the October 1996 presidential elections Ortega was defeated, and the right-wing candidate Arnoldo Alemán Lacayo became president in 1997. In May 1998 and again in January 2001, Ortega was re-elected the Sandinista leader, but Enrique Bolaños, a 73-year-old entrepreneur and candidate of the ruling Liberal party, easily defeated Ortega in presidential elections in November 2001. The election was marked by a high turnout and none of the expected irregularities. Sandinista supporters blamed their Ortega's defeat partly on comments by US officials linking Ortega with terrorism. Bolaños suffered a setback in February 2002 when Lacayo was elected president of the National Assembly. In the same month the USA resumed military aid to Nicaragua for the first time since 1979.

Nicaraguan Revolution   the revolt 1978–79 in Nicaragua, led by the socialist **Sandinistas** against the US-supported right-wing dictatorship established by Anastasio *Somoza. His son, President Anastasio (Debayle) Somoza (1925–1980), was forced into exile in 1979 and assassinated in Paraguay. The Sandinista National Liberation Front (FSLN) was named after Augusto César Sandino, a guerrilla leader killed by the US-trained National Guard in 1934.

Nicholas II (1868–1918) tsar of Russia 1894–1917. He was dominated by his wife, Tsarina *Alexandra, who was under the influence of the religious charlatan *Rasputin. His mismanagement of the Russo-Japanese War and of internal affairs led to the revolution of 1905, which he suppressed, although he was forced to grant limited constitutional reforms. He took Russia into World War I in 1914, was forced to abdicate in 1917 after the *Russian Revolution, and was executed with his family.

Niger landlocked country in northwest Africa, bounded north by Algeria and Libya, east by Chad, south by Nigeria and Benin, and west by Burkina Faso and Mali.

Nigeria country in west Africa on the Gulf of Guinea, bounded north by Niger, east by Chad and Cameroon, and west by Benin.

  government The constitution was promulgated in 1989 to take effect in 1993. It provides for an elected executive president and a popularly elected two-chamber assembly, consisting of a 91-member Senate and a 593-member House of Representatives, each serving a four-year term. In 1993 the constitution was partly suspended and military rule imposed.

  Nigeria is a federal republic of 30 states, each with its own governor. There is also a coordinating federal body called the National Council of States, which includes the president and all the state governors.

  history Nigeria is named after the River Niger, its chief physical feature; the word means 'great river'. Nigeria has been inhabited since at least 700 BC. Many of the early inhabitants migrated across the Sahara Desert, since the delta barring the entrance to the Niger and the mangrove swamps and coastal forest belt made penetration from the sea difficult.

  early African states Trade, culture, and the Muslim religion also found their way over the caravan routes from Egypt and the Arab countries into northern Nigeria, especially around Bornu. The Hausa people in the northwest adopted Islam in the 13th century, and formed a number of city states at around the same time. In the 15th century the Yoruba people of the southwest established powerful city states. The Hausa and Yoruba states possessed complex administrative structures, headed by kings regarded as divine, superimposed on small agricultural communities. The influence of Islam helped preserve this hierarchical structure.

  The remarkable medieval kingdom of Benin (covering an area of southwest Nigeria) was an offshoot of the Yoruba states. It was visited by the Portuguese in 1486 and by the English in 1553, who found there a prosperous, well-organized society with well-developed art and culture.

  European contact Portuguese and British slave traders started to raid the coastal regions of Nigeria in the 15th and 16th centuries. The 17th and 18th centuries were a period of decline brought about by wars, political dissensions, famines, and the slave trade.

  British interest in the area increased in the later 18th century, and exploration began as a preliminary to the development of commerce. Mungo Park reached the Niger in 1796, Hugh Clapperton penetrated to Sokoto in 1823, and Richard and John Lander traced the course of the Niger in 1830. The British abolition of slavery in 1807 was a stimulus to legitimate trade and also to the missionaries who followed the explorers, and by the middle of the century they had reached Abeokuta, Ibadan, and Calabar.

  From the late 18th century the Hausa states suffered an invasion by the Fulani, an Islamic people originating from the upper Nile valley, who overran more than 259,000 sq km/10,000 sq mi of territory and further weakened the country.

the establishment of British rule
Infiltration by the British also began with the purchase by British traders of Lagos in 1861 from a native chief. In 1866 Lagos was placed under the government of Sierra Leone and later administered as part of the Gold Coast (modern Ghana) until 1886, when a separate colony and protectorate of Lagos was founded.

In 1885 a British claim to a protectorate over Nigeria was recognized by the Berlin Conference, and the southern part of the country, apart from the Lagos territories, was named the Oil Rivers Protectorate, later renamed the Niger Coast Protectorate. The northern part of the country, formerly chartered to the United African Company, was brought under government control in 1900, the northern part of its territories becoming the Northern Nigeria Protectorate and the southern part, together with the Niger Coast Protectorate, becoming the Southern Nigeria Protectorate, to which Lagos was added in 1906. In 1914 the north and south were united to form the Colony and Protectorate of Nigeria.

towards independence After World War II pressure for independence increased. Between 1946 and 1951 different constitutions were introduced, which gave Nigeria first representative government and then responsible government. The federal structure was first introduced in 1946, when the northern, eastern, and western regions were established.

The northern part of the former trusteeship territory of the Cameroons was administered by the northern region until 1961, when by a referendum it opted to become a part of the Region itself, while in the same referendum the southern part of the Cameroons territory, which had hitherto functioned as a Region of the federation, now elected to join the Cameroon Republic. The present midwestern region split off from western region after a referendum in 1963.

Regional self-government was achieved by the eastern and western regions in 1957 and by the northern region in 1959. In 1960 full independence was granted to the federation, which became a member of the Commonwealth. In 1963 Nigeria became a republic, retaining its federal structure so as to accommodate the many different ethnic groups, which include the Ibo, the Yoruba, the Aro, the Angas, and the Hausa.

democracy overthrown Nigeria's first president was Dr Nnami Azikiwe, an Ibo; he was a banker and proprietor of a newspaper group, and had played a leading part in the movement for independence. His chief rival was Abubakar *Tafawa Balewa, who was prime minister from 1957.

In January 1966, Nigeria, which was generally considered to be the most politically stable of the new African nations, suffered a military coup by young army officers, mainly Ibos from the eastern region, which had become richer after the discovery of oil there 1958. In the course of the coup the prime minister, the premier of the north region, and several other political leaders and army officers were assassinated. A military government was set up, led by Maj Gen Johnson Aguiyi-Ironsi. The revolt was sparked off by widespread suspicion that the recent general elections had been rigged, and by revelations of political corruption. A military government was set up comprising a Supreme Military Council and a Federal Executive Council.

Gowon seizes power In July 1966 there was a another military coup by a mostly Christian group from the north; several units of the army mutinied and a new head of the military government was installed. The Ironsi regime had been dominated by Ibo civil servants, and there had been a great deal of anxiety especially about where power lay. After the coup the new head of government was the army chief of staff, Lieut Col (later Gen) Yakubu *Gowon. The military government released a number of political prisoners, including chiefs Enaharo and Awolowo. The leaders of the coup stressed that the military government was an interim measure to be followed by free elections.

Biafra secedes While discussions on a future federal government structure were taking place in Lagos, open fighting and rioting broke out in northern Nigeria, the principal victims of murder and looting being Ibo civilians. The military governor of the eastern region, Lt Col Chukwuemeka Odumegwu Ojukwu, recalled all the Ibo people to their homeland, and the Ibos decided to secede from Nigeria and establish the independent state of Biafra (1967). At the last moment Gowon had announced a new federal structure for Nigeria, one composed of 12 states (each with a military governor), in an attempt to break the solidarity of the Ibo movement by quelling fears about a large and potentially aggressive northern region.

But Gowon's efforts failed to find a last-minute compromise; it has been suggested that there were also positive reasons for the Ibo secession – the potential oil revenues that were stronger incentives to break from the federal structure than simply fear of the north. In these terms, Gowon's appeasement had no hope of success; and in any case, Ibos could point to evidence of northern brutality as the best possible reason for rejecting the new federal compromise – by this time tens of thousands of Ibos in the north had been killed.

the Biafran War Gowon's federal government at first treated the Biafran secession as a matter for the civil police, but the seriousness of the situation became apparent to Gowon's government when the Ibo secessionists collaborated with Ibo officers in the Nigerian army and invaded the midwest region. The Nigerian army was placed immediately on a war footing, but could not prevent the Biafran advance into the midwest. A full scale civil war was now in progress, and the ability of the federal troops to recapture the midwest was checked temporarily when the Biafrans destroyed the main access point, the bridge at Onitsha.

The numerical and technical superiority of the federal forces eventually began to tell, especially after the opening up of new fronts in Bonny and Calabar. The federal troops were able to make territorial gains in fringe areas of Biafra that were less densely Ibo, but only gradually did the advance succeed, until resistance was concentrated in the core of Iboland. Yet the war could not be pushed easily to a conclusion, a state of affairs that owed much to the stubborness of Ibo resistance, but which intensified the sufferings of the people of Biafra. The war was concluded finally in January 1970, with the Biafran surrender after Ojukwu had fled to the Côte d'Ivoire.

The war left the economy gravely weakened, and warfare and famine had cost an estimated 1 million lives.

oil revenue and development The federal military government was anxious that there should be no recriminations after the civil war, and also that Nigeria should emerge as a stronger, united nation. Gowon was in the forefront of these initiatives, but ethnic loyalties have commanded people's first loyalties, and inhibited consistently the efforts made since 1960 to implement national development plans.

The finance for these development plans has been made available from the oil revenues, and the Nigerian government has increasingly claimed a larger stake in the oil industry, largely through the Nigerian National Oil Corporation (NNOC); Nigeria also became a member of the Arab-dominated Organization of Petroleum

Exporting Countries (OPEC). Oil revenue, channelled through the federal government to the regional governments, has given the central government increased power and influence, although the regions have behaved selfishly and competitively in the way they have devised and implemented development, welfare, and educational projects.

the overthrow of Gowon In 1972 Gen Gowon declared that the army would relinquish power, and the country return to civilian rule by 1976; but when he made the 14th independence anniversary speech on 1 October 1974, this deadline had been postponed, and Gowon announced that the army would continue to govern indefinitely, although it was stressed that the policy of a return to civilian rule had not been abandoned. The military government was able to justify such a declaration largely on the grounds that a national consensus did not exist on the subject of an appropriate civilian government system for Nigeria.

In fact, Gowon had contributed himself to an even more confused political and ethnic situation in Nigeria by stating consistently his commitment to the creation of more states, to supplement the 12 that had existed since 1968. On 29 July 1975 Gowon was overthrown while he was attending the Organization of African Unity (OAU; later African Union) Conference in Uganda.

military rule under Muhammad and Obasanjo, 1975–79 Nigeria's new head of state and commander-in-chief of the armed forces was Brig Murtala Ramat Muhammad, who announced immediate changes in the military leadership, and 'retired' all former members of the government, state governors, civilian federal commissioners, and all administrators of East Central State. New military governors were appointed for Nigeria's 12 states. Whereas

Gen Gowon's watchword had been 'Peace before Politics', Muhammad asserted that his predecessor had headed a regime that survived on 'nepotism, favouritism, and corruption'.

Muhammad established the Federal Council of States, which was given the brief of examining the suitability of Lagos as the federal capital, as well as assessing the possibilities for creating more states. In this latter respect Muhammad followed Gowon's policy in one direction, and 7 new states were created giving a total of 19.

Muhammad was not in power sufficiently long for his regime to make any fundamental changes or monumental mistakes, and the attempted coup that resulted in Gen Muhammad's death in February 1976 was probably an attempt by a group of officers to gain control within the Supreme Military Council, rather than an effort to reorientate Nigerian politics. The insurgence proved to be confined to a group of Lagos-based officers, led by Lieut Col Dimka, who were quickly arrested and later executed. Nigeria remained under the control of the Supreme Military Council, and the new head of state was Lt Gen Olusegun Obasanjo.

civilian rule overthrown Obasanjo announced a gradual return to civilian rule, and in 1979 the leader of the National Party of Nigeria, Shehu Shagari, became president. In December 1983, with the economy suffering from falling oil prices, Shagari's civilian government was deposed in another bloodless coup, led by Maj Gen Muhammadu Buhari. In 1985 another peaceful coup replaced Buhari with a new military government, led by Maj Gen Ibrahim Babangida, the army chief of staff. At the end of the year an attempted coup by rival officers was thwarted.

Babangida's reforms In an effort to end political corruption, President Babangida banned former and existing government officials from any future civilian administration.

A ban on political activity was lifted in May 1989, but the government rejected the applications of former political associations for recognition as political parties, instead creating two official parties, one to the left and one to the right of the political spectrum. In August 1991, 9 new states were created, bringing the total to 30. In the same month, the total of local government councils increased to 500 with the addition of 47 new ones. The changes were seen as moves towards the decentralization of power.

In December 1991 the ban prohibiting existing government officials running for office in a new government was lifted, and the federal government was moved from Lagos to Abuja, the new federal capital. The introduction of a system of primary elections, on the US model, was announced in 1992, and a delay in the return to civilian rule was expected.

first free presidential election declared void Babangida's Social Democratic Party (SDP) won the majority of seats when assembly elections were held in July 1992, but it was later announced that the assembly would not be opened until after presidential elections had taken place. The first free presidential election in June 1993 was won by the SDP candidate, Moshood Abiola (1938–98), but the results were suspended. Babangida promised fresh elections but later persuaded the SDP and the main opposition party, the National Republican Convention, to agree to talks aimed at establishing an interim government, excluding Abiola. In August Babangida postponed the talks and stepped down, nominating Ernest Shonekan, a civilian, as his successor.

military rule restored Shonekan headed an interim administration until November 1993, when he was replaced by the defence minister, Gen Sani Abacha (1943–98). Later that month all

political parties were banned. Abiola was arrested and charged with treason in June 1994, triggering an escalation of protests by the pro-democracy movement. In October 1994 the High Court ruled that Abiola's detention was illegal and in December 1994 a national constitutional conference recommended the continuation of military rule until 1996. During 1995 there was mounting international concern over human-rights abuses by the military regime. Some 100 human-rights activists were arrested, and in November 1995 Ken *Saro-Wiwa, an environmentalist and leading spokesperson for the Ogoni people, was executed along with eight of his colleagues. World leaders' pleas for clemency went unheeded, and following the executions, Nigeria was suspended from the Commonwealth.

social conditions An official population policy encouraging mothers to have no more than four children was ratified 1988, half the population being under 15.

political changes General Sani Abacha in mid-November 1997 dissolved his cabinet and said that he was granting an amnesty for some political prisoners. Abacha, whose government had been accused of holding hundreds of political prisoners, did not specify which detainees, or how many, would be freed. He promised to hold elections in 1998, handing power to a civilian government by 1 October. In April 1998 Sabacha won a crucial vote allowing him to stand unopposed in 'democratic' presidential elections planned for August. Nigeria's main opposition group, the United Action for Democracy, asked Nigerians to boycott the elections. Polling stations were closed late April 1998 after a very low turnout in Nigerian assembly elections. The vote had been boycotted by the opposition to protest against Abacha. Abacha died suddenly 8 June 1998, leaving no obvious successor.

General Abdulsalam Abubakar, the compromise choice of Nigeria's military government, was named the new head of state. Abubakar, former chief of defence staff, committed himself to General Abacha's programme to restore civilian government, but did not say whether this would happen by 1 October, as planned. In July Moshood Abiola died, reportedly of a heart attack, whilst still under house arrest. In August 1998 three new parties were formed: the People's Democratic Party (PDP), the People's Democratic Congress, and the Liberal Democratic Party. In September 1998, a Nigerian court freed 20 Ogoni activists imprisoned in 1994 (together with the writer Ken Saro-Wiwa who was later executed) on charges of murdering four pro-government chiefs.

Underlining the new political liberalization, in October 1998 Wole Soyinka, a leading dissident and Nobel prize-winning author, returned home, after four years of self-imposed exile.

The PDP was elected in mid-December 1998 to control most local councils. It was the first in a series of polls that would culminate in a presidential election in February 1999. The PDP also took a lead in elections for state governors and assemblies in January 1999, but the right-of-centre All Peoples Party (APP) took six key marginal states and the left-leaning Alliance for Democracy swept all six states in its southwestern stronghold.

In February 1999 the People's Democratic Party won 55 of the 109 Senate seats. In March 1999 Olusegun Obasanjo was elected president, ending 15 years of military rule, amid claims of fraud.

Nearly 16 years of military rule ended in Nigeria in May 1999 when Gen Abubakar handed over to Olusegun Obasanjo, and Nigeria rejoined the Commonwealth from which it was banned in 1995. Obasanjo attacked his military predecessors for corruption and put all government contracts made since January under review. Nigeria's new civilian president in June began a purge of the army. Obasanjo purged 29 senior officers from the military and seized hundreds of millions of dollars of stolen wealth from the allies of the late dictator Sani Abacha.

Fighting between Nigeria's two largest ethnic groups, Hausas and Yorubas, in the southwest of the country broke out in July 1999, resulting in many deaths. As fears spread of wider unrest, the president continued to purge some of the old guard, having nearly 200 new staff officers appointed. More ethnic fighting broke out in August in Ondo state in southwestern Nigeria.

The new civilian government in Nigeria began cracking down in October 1999 on multinational oil companies based in the Niger Delta, giving them six weeks to produce a firm environmental clean-up plan. The region accounted for 95% of the country's daily crude oil production. The six major multinational oil companies operating in Nigeria were Royal Dutch/Shell, Mobil, Chevron, Elf, Agip, and Texaco. The government of President Obasanjo blamed the multinational companies for the continuing unrest in the Niger Delta region, which had resulted in scores of deaths. After riots in both the Niger Delta (between the army and civilians) and in the capital, Lagos (between Nigeria's two biggest ethnic groups), throughout November and December 1999, President Obasanjo ordered that ethnic minority militants be shot on sight. Critics claimed that this heralded a return to a culture of human rights abuse and a reinstatement of military rule within Nigeria.

introduction of Islamic law
Zamfara, a state in northern Nigeria, formally adopted strict Islamic sharia law in January 2000, the third state to do so. President Obasanjo, a born-again Christian, refused to attend the

ceremony at which the law was proclaimed, declaring it unconstitutional. Ethnic and religious violence following the introduction of sharia law led to the deaths of over 1,000 people. In May a curfew was imposed upon the northern city of Kaduna after at least 200 people were killed in clashes between Muslims and Christians. In June similar violence broke out in the south of the country after the body of a murdered Christian was found in the region. Later in June, the governor of Kano, the largest city in north Nigeria, announced that sharia law would come into effect there in December, at the beginning of Ramadan, the ninth month of the Muslim calendar. Sharia law also came into effect in October in Yobe and (in a modified form) in Kaduna.

The same month, violence between the two largest ethnic groups, the militant Yoruba separatists' group Odua People's Congress (OPC), and the Hausas erupted again in Lagos. Over 100 people were killed. The OPC was outlawed and the security forces given the mandate to arrest anyone found to be backing the OPC or a tribal militia group. Over 200 people, including the leader of the OPC, Frederick Fashuen, were arrested.

In April 2001, the heads of Nigeria's army, navy, and air force all retired amid speculation that President Obasanjo might be trying to rid the armed forces of men loyal to the previous regime.

ethnic violence The killing of a traditional ruler of the Azara people of central Nigeria in June 2001 sparked off fighting between them and the neighbouring Tivs. Hundreds of people were reported dead, and some 70,000 people, mainly Tivs, were forced to leave their homes. The country was also shaken in early July by ethnic and religious fighting in both Nassarawa state in the centre of the country, and the northern Bauchi state. Hundreds of people were reported killed after

Christians rebelled against an attempt to impose Islamic law in the town of Tafawa-Balewa. Further clashes broke out between Christians and Muslims in the city of Jos in central Nigeria in September. Around 500 people were killed in a week-long bout of violence, and tens of thousands of people fled the fighting. Tensions had risen between the indigenous residents, who were mainly Christian or Animist, and the wealthier Hausa-Fulani Muslims.

After militants in central Nigeria killed 19 soldiers in October 2001, armed men in civilian clothing responded by attacking four villages, killing some 200 people. Nigerian soldiers were accused of carrying out the massacres. Tens of thousands of ethnic Tiv villagers began fleeing to escape the ensuing army crackdown. President Obasanjo had previously ordered the army to halt all military activity in the area, but his army chief said that the crackdown would continue until the Tiv militias blamed for killing the 19 soldiers were caught.

protests over petrol prices In January 2002, a general strike froze Nigerian cities, as unions protested against an 18% rise in the heavily subsidized price of petrol. The government declared the strike illegal and arrested several labour leaders after the protest paralysed the port city of Lagos, and disrupted commerce in several others, including Abuja, Ibadan, Kano, Kaduna, Makurdi, and the oil industry centre of Port Harcourt.

Night of the Long Knives purge of the German Nazi party to root out possible opposition to Adolf Hitler. On the night of 29–30 June 1934 (and the following two days) the SS units under Heinrich *Himmler were used by Hitler to exterminate the Nazi private army Sturmabteilung (SA or the Brownshirts) under Captain Ernst Röhm. Others were also executed for alleged conspiracy against Hitler (including Kurt von Schleicher). The Nazi purge enabled Hitler to gain the acceptance of the German officer corps and, when President Hindenburg died five weeks later, to become head of state.

Nimitz, Chester William (1885–1966) US admiral. In World War II he was commander-in-chief of the US Pacific fleet. He reconquered the Solomon Islands 1942–43, Gilbert Islands 1943, the Mariana Islands and the Marshall Islands 1944, and signed the Japanese surrender 1945 as the US representative.

Nitti, Francesco Saverio (1868–1953) Italian politician and economist. He was prime minister and minister of the interior 1919–20, during a time of economic and political crisis following World War I. He introduced proportional representation but failed to create a stable coalition government.

Nivelle, Robert Georges (1856–1924) French general. In World War I, he planned a massive offensive in the Craonne-Reims area for April 1917, but his public boasting forewarned the Germans and the offensive was a disaster, with enormous French casualties which precipitated the mutinies in the French army later that year. Nivelle was removed, replaced by General Pétain, and sent back to command the troops in North Africa.

Nixon, Richard M(ilhous) (1913–1994) 37th president of the USA 1969–74, a Republican. He attracted attention as a member of the *House Un-American Activities Committee in 1948, and was vice-president to Eisenhower 1953–61. As president he was responsible for US withdrawal from Vietnam, and the normalization of relations with communist China, but at home his culpability in the cover-up of the *Watergate scandal and the existence of a 'slush fund' for political machinations during his re-election campaign of 1972 led him to resign in 1974 when threatened with impeachment.

political career Nixon, a Californian, entered Congress in 1947, and rose to prominence during the McCarthyite era of the 1950s. As a member of the Un-American Activities Committee, he pressed for the investigation of Alger *Hiss, accused of being a spy. Nixon was senator for California from 1951 until elected vice-president. He played a more extensive role in government than previous vice-presidents, in part because of the poor health of President Dwight D Eisenhower. He narrowly lost the 1960 presidential election to J F Kennedy, partly because televised electoral debates put him at a disadvantage.

presidency He did not seek presidential nomination in 1964, but in a 'law and order' campaign defeated vice-president Hubert Humphrey in 1968. Facing a Democratic Congress, Nixon sought to extricate the USA from the war in Vietnam. He formulated the Nixon Doctrine in 1969, abandoning close involvement with Asian countries, but escalated the war in Cambodia by massive bombing, although the USA was not officially at war with neutral Cambodia.

resignation Nixon was re-elected in 1972 in a landslide victory over George McGovern, and immediately faced allegations of irregularities and illegalities conducted on his behalf in his re-election campaign and within the White House. Despite his success in extricating the USA from Vietnam, congressional and judicial investigations, along with press exposures of the Watergate affair, undermined public support. He resigned in 1974, the first and only US president to do so, under threat of impeachment on three counts: obstruction of the administration of justice in the investigation of Watergate; violation of constitutional rights of citizens – for example, attempting to use the Internal Revenue Service, Federal Bureau of Investigation, and Central Intelligence Agency as weapons against political opponents; and failure to produce 'papers and things' as ordered by the Judiciary Committee.

He was granted a pardon in 1974 by President Ford and turned to lecturing and writing.

Nkomati Accord nonaggression treaty between South Africa and Mozambique concluded in 1984, under which they agreed not to give material aid to opposition movements in each other's countries, which in effect meant that South Africa pledged itself not to support the Mozambique National Resistance (Renamo), while Mozambique was committed not to help the then outlawed African National Congress (ANC).

Nkomo, Joshua (1917–1999) Zimbabwean trade unionist and politician, vice-president 1990–99. As president of ZAPU (Zimbabwe African People's Union) from 1961, he was a leader of the black nationalist movement against the white Rhodesian regime. He was a member of Robert *Mugabe's cabinet 1980–82 and from 1987.

After completing his education in South Africa, Joshua Nkomo became a welfare officer on Rhodesian Railways and later organizing secretary of the Rhodesian African Railway Workers' Union. He entered politics in 1950, and was president of the African National Congress (ANC) in southern Rhodesia 1957–59. In 1961 he created ZAPU, of which he was president.

Arrested along with other black African politicians, he was kept in detention 1963–74. After his release he joined forces with Robert Mugabe as a joint leader of the Patriotic Front in 1976, opposing the white-dominated regime of Ian Smith. Nkomo took part in the Lancaster House Conference, which led to Rhodesia's independence as the new state of Zimbabwe, and became a cabinet minister and vice-president.

Nkrumah, Kwame (1909–1972) Ghanaian nationalist politician, prime minister of the Gold Coast (Ghana's former name) 1952–57 and of newly independent Ghana 1957–60. He became Ghana's first president in 1960 but was overthrown in a coup in 1966. His policy of 'African socialism' led to links with the communist bloc.

Originally a teacher, he studied later in both the UK and the USA, and on returning to Africa formed the Convention People's Party (CPP) in 1949 with the aim of immediate self-government. He was imprisoned in 1950 for inciting illegal strikes, but was released the same year. As president he established an authoritarian regime and made Ghana a one-party (CPP) state in 1964. He then dropped his stance of non-alignment and drew closer to the USSR and other communist countries. Deposed from the presidency while on a visit to Beijing (Peking) in 1966, he remained in exile in Guinea, where he was made a co-head of state until his death, but was posthumously 'rehabilitated' in 1973.

non-aligned movement countries with a strategic and political position of neutrality ('non-alignment') towards major powers, specifically the USA and former USSR. The movement emerged in the 1960s during the *Cold War between East and West 1949–89. Although originally used by poorer states, the non-aligned position was later adopted by oil-producing nations. Its 113 members hold more than half the world's population and 85% of oil resources, but only 7% of global GDP (1995).

noncooperation movement or **satyagraha**, in India, a large-scale civil disobedience campaign orchestrated by Mahatma *Gandhi in 1920 following the *Amritsar Massacre in April 1919. Based on a policy of peaceful non-cooperation, the strategy was to bring the British administrative machine to a halt by the total withdrawal of Indian support. British-made goods were boycotted, as were schools, courts of law, and elective offices. The campaign made little impression on the British government, since they could ignore it when it was peaceful; when it became violent, Gandhi felt obliged to call off further demonstrations. Its most successful aspect was that it increased political awareness among the Indian people.

nonviolence principle or practice of abstaining from the use of violence. The Indian nationalist leader Mahatma Gandhi adopted a campaign of passive resistance 1907–14 in response to the attempts by the Transvaal government to discriminate against Indians in South Africa. Later, in India, Gandhi again employed nonviolent methods, including the boycotting of British goods and hunger strikes (see *noncooperation movement). More recently, non-violent pro-democracy movement was led in the Philippines in 1986 by Corazon *Aquino, in Myanmar by Aung San *Suu Kyi, and in Indonesia in 1998 by Amien Rais.

Noriega Morena, Manuel (Antonio) (1940–) Panamanian soldier and politician, effective ruler of Panama from 1983, as head of the National Guard, until deposed by the USA in 1989. An informer for the US Central Intelligence Agency (CIA) from the late 1960s, he was known to be involved in drug trafficking as early as 1972.

He enjoyed US support until 1987. In the December 1989 US invasion of Panama, he was forcibly taken to the USA. He was tried and convicted of cocaine trafficking and money laundering in 1992.

Normandy French **Normandie**, former duchy of northwest France now divided into two regions: Haute-Normandie and Basse-Normandie; area 29,900 sq km/11,544 sq mi; population (both parts, 1999 est) 3,202,400. Normandy was named after the Viking Norsemen (Normans) who conquered and settled in the area in the 9th century. As a French duchy it reached its peak under William the

Conqueror and was renowned for its centres of learning established by Lanfranc and St Anselm. Normandy was united with England from 1100 to 1135. England and France fought over it during the Hundred Years' War, England finally losing it in 1449 to Charles VII. In World War II the Normandy beaches were the site of the Allied invasion on D-day, 6 June 1944.

North, Oliver (1943–) US Marine lieutenant colonel. In 1981 he joined the staff of the National Security Council (NSC), where he supervised the mining of Nicaraguan harbours in 1983, an air force bombing raid on Libya in 1986, and an arms-for-hostages deal with Iran in 1985, which, when uncovered in 1986 (*Irangate), forced his dismissal and trial.

North Africa Campaign Allied military campaign 1940–42 during World War II. Shortly after Italy declared war on France and Britain in June 1940, an Italian offensive was launched from Libya towards Egypt and the Suez Canal. In December 1940 Britain launched a successful counter-offensive and captured Cyrenaica. Following agreement between Mussolini and Hitler, the German Afrika Korps was established under General Rommel. During 1941 and early 1942 the Axis powers advanced, recaptured Tobruk, and crossed the Egyptian border before halting at El Alamein. The British 8th Army under General Montgomery won a decisive Allied victory against Rommel's forces at El Alamein on 4 November 1942, followed by advances across Libya towards Tunisia. British and US troops advanced from French northwestern Africa and the Allied armies in North Africa converged on Tunis. After a last-ditch defence, the Axis forces surrendered in May 1943.

North American Free Trade Agreement NAFTA, trade agreement between the USA, Canada, and Mexico, intended to promote trade and investment between the signatories, agreed in August 1992, and effective from January 1994. The first trade pact of its kind to link two highly-industrialized countries to a developing one, it created a free market of 375 million people, with a total GDP of $6.8 trillion (equivalent to 30% of the world's GDP). Tariffs were to be progressively eliminated over a 10–15 year period (tariffs on trade in originating goods from Mexico and Canada are to be eliminated by 2008) and investment into low-wage Mexico by Canada and the USA progressively increased. Another aim of the agreement was to make provisions on transacting business in the free trade area. The NAFTA Centre is located in Dallas, Texas.

North Atlantic Treaty Organization

NATO, military association of major Western European and North American states set up under the North Atlantic Treaty of 4 April 1949. The original signatories were Belgium, Canada, Denmark, France, Iceland, Italy, Luxembourg, Netherlands, Norway, Portugal, the UK, and the USA. Greece and Turkey were admitted to NATO in 1952, West Germany in 1955, Spain in 1982, and Poland, Hungary, and the Czech Republic in 1999. NATO has been the basis of the defence of the Western world since 1949. During the *Cold War (1945–89), NATO stood in opposition to the perceived threat of communist Eastern Europe, led by the USSR and later allied under the military *Warsaw Pact (1955–91). Having outlasted the Warsaw Pact, NATO has increasingly redefined itself as an agent of international peace-keeping and enforcement.

institutional structure NATO's chief body is the Council of Foreign Ministers (who have representatives in permanent session). There is an international secretariat in Brussels, Belgium, and also a Military Committee consisting of the Chiefs of Staff. The military headquarters SHAPE (Supreme Headquarters Allied Powers, Europe) is in Chièvres, near Mons, Belgium. In August 1999, George Robertson, then the UK defence secretary, was elected secretary general of NATO, replacing Javier Solana.

Both the Supreme Allied Commanders (Europe and Atlantic) are from the USA, but there is also an Allied Commander, Channel (a British admiral). In 1960 a permanent multinational **Allied Mobile Force** (AMF) was established with headquarters in Heidelberg, Germany, to move immediately to any NATO country under threat of attack. In May 1991, a meeting of NATO defence ministers endorsed the creation of a UK-commanded, 100,000-strong 'rapid-reaction corps' as the core of a new, streamlined military structure, based on mobile, multinational units adaptable to post-Cold War contingencies. The new force was to be used solely inside NATO territory, unless otherwise agreed by all members of the alliance. In 1992 it was agreed that the Organization for Security and Cooperation in Europe (OSCE) would in future authorize all NATO's military responses within Europe.

the Cold War NATO was formed at the start of the Cold War, at a time when the capitalist nations of the West were fearful of the potential for a communist Soviet invasion of Western Europe following the *Berlin blockade (1948–49) by Soviet forces. The Soviet leader Joseph *Stalin appeared to harbour expansionist ambitions and to be intent on forcing his rule on to the whole of Europe, not just the eastern portion that the Soviets had conquered in World War II. In response to the establishment of NATO, Stalin set up the Warsaw Pact in 1955 as the defensive alliance of the communist Eastern bloc nations.

Throughout the Cold War, NATO had at its disposal the combined military force of all its members, including the nuclear weapons of the USA, the UK, and France. But throughout this time, not a shot was fired in war. This fact is viewed as a great success by NATO's supporters, as it indicates that NATO acted as a strong deterrent to the perceived ambitions of the USSR in Europe.

NATO has encountered numerous problems since its inception over such issues as the dominant position of the USA, the presence in Europe of US nuclear weapons, burden sharing, and standardization of weapons.

after the Cold War The collapse of communism in eastern Europe from 1989 prompted the most radical review of NATO's policy and defence strategy since its inception in 1949. After the Warsaw Pact was disbanded in 1991, an adjunct to NATO, the **North Atlantic Cooperation Council** (NACC), was established. This included all the former Soviet republics, with the aim of building greater security in Europe.

At the 1994 Brussels summit a 'partnership for peace' (PFP) programme was formally launched, inviting former members of the Warsaw Pact and ex-Soviet republics to take part in a wide range of military cooperation arrangements, including training alongside NATO members and opening up defence plans. Romania was the first to join, followed by Estonia, Lithuania, Poland, and Russia the following year. By 1996 the partnership included 27 countries, comprising the 15 former Soviet republics, Austria, Hungary, the Slovak Republic, Bulgaria, Malta, Albania, the Czech Republic, Macedonia, Finland, and Sweden.

In May 1997, a NATO–Russia security pact, called the Founding Act on Mutual Relations, Cooperation and Security, was signed in Paris by all 16 NATO heads of government and Russian president Yeltsin. The charter gave Russia an assurance that NATO had no intention of siting nuclear weapons or allowing major troop deployments on the territories of new Eastern European member states. It also created a Russian–NATO advisory council, which, however, would have no veto over NATO actions.

In July 1997, Poland, Hungary, and the Czech Republic, who were former members of the Warsaw Pact, were invited to join the alliance, which they did at the Madrid summit in March 1999. The decision meant NATO's territory expanded by 14%.

the Balkans NATO engaged in its first major combat action August–September 1995 in Bosnia-Herzegovina. In December, a 60,000-strong, NATO-led 'International Implementation Force' was sent to police the Dayton peace settlement. The USA supplied one-third of the troops for the mission, termed 'Joint Endeavour'. In June 1999, NATO mounted the biggest military operation in Europe since World War II, when its forces took over the Serbian province of Kosovo to keep the peace in the region.

North Atlantic Treaty Organization, post-Cold War NATO, the collapse of communism in eastern Europe from 1989 prompted the most radical review of NATO's policy and defence strategy since its inception in 1949 during the *Cold War. After the Eastern European *Warsaw Pact was disbanded in 1991, an adjunct to NATO, the **North Atlantic Cooperation Council** (NACC), was established. This included all the former Soviet republics, with the aim of building greater security in Europe. In 1992 it was agreed that the Organization for Security and Cooperation in Europe (OSCE) would in future authorize all NATO's military responses within Europe.

At the 1994 Brussels summit a 'partnership for peace' (PFP) programme was formally launched, inviting former members of the Warsaw Pact and ex-Soviet republics to take part in a wide range of military cooperation arrangements, including training alongside NATO members and opening up defence plans. Romania was the first to join, followed by Estonia, Lithuania, and Poland; Russia agreed to participate in 1995. By 1996 the partnership included 27 countries, comprising the 15 former Soviet republics, Austria, Hungary, the Slovak Republic, Bulgaria, Malta, Albania, the Czech Republic, the Former Yugoslav Republic of Macedonia, Finland, and Sweden.

In May 1997, a NATO–Russia security pact, called the Founding Act on Mutual Relations, Cooperation and Security, was signed in Paris by all 16 NATO heads of government and Russian president Yeltsin. The charter gave Russia an assurance that NATO had no intention of siting nuclear weapons or allowing major troop deployments on the territories of new Eastern European member-states. It also created a Russian–NATO advisory council, which, however, would have no veto over NATO actions.

NATO's secretary general, Javier Solana, announced in July 1997 the historic decision to invite Poland, Hungary, and the Czech Republic to join the alliance, signalling the biggest single expansion in NATO's history. In December 1997 the 1949 Washington Treaty was amended to allow these countries to join NATO. The three states were invited during the Madrid summit to join NATO in 1999. The Madrid summit decision meant that countries with a population totalling 60 million, and armed forces of 382,000, would join NATO in 1999, increasing the military alliance's territory by 14%. The three countries officially became members of NATO in March 1999.

The US Senate voted in early May 1998 by a large majority to approve the inclusion of the Czech Republic, Hungary, and Poland in NATO. The vote was a foreign policy victory for President Clinton who had carefully steered the policy of NATO expansion through an initially sceptical political establishment. The vote made the USA the fifth country to ratify NATO expansion.

In June 1999 NATO mounted the biggest military operation in Europe after World War II, when its forces took over the Serbian province of Kosovo to keep the peace in the region. However, until its involvement in 1999 with the Kosovan crisis, the civil war between ethnic Albanians and Kosovan Serbs, NATO had never fired a shot in war.

In August 1999 George Robertson, then the UK defence secretary, was elected secretary general of NATO, replacing Javier Solana.

Northern Ireland Assembly power-sharing assembly based in Belfast, Northern Ireland. The Assembly came into being as a result of the 10 April 1998 Good Friday peace agreement between the contending Unionist and Irish Nationalist communities in Northern Ireland. The agreement negotiated the devolution (handing over) of a range of executive (administrative) and legislative (law-making) powers – in areas including agriculture, economic development, education, the environment, finance, health, and social security – from the secretary of state for Northern Ireland to an elected assembly. Elections were first held on 25 June 1998. The Assembly met for the first time on 1 July 1998, but following disagreements over the creation of a power-sharing executive, did not become fully operational until December 1999.

Northern Ireland Office NIO, UK government department established in 1972 to take responsibility for the direct government of Northern Ireland, including administration of security; law and order; and economic, industrial, and social policies.

The terms of the 1998 *Good Friday agreement established power-sharing with an executive drawn from an elected Northern Ireland Assembly. Following devolution on 2 December 1999, the secretary of state for Northern Ireland retained direct responsibility for political and constitutional matters, law and order, security, and electoral matters. The NIO has three executive agencies. Paul Murphy was appointed Northern Ireland secretary in 2002.

Northern Ireland peace process process leading to peace, the establishment of the *Northern Ireland Assembly, and the decommissioning of paramilitary arms in Northern Ireland, generally considered as beginning in 1993 when London and Dublin issued the *Downing Street Declaration. Ceasefire declarations by the *Provisional IRA followed in August 1994 and again in May 1997. Multiparty talks began in January 1998 culminating in the 'Good Friday agreement' on 10th April.

In November 1999, agreement was reached on the power-sharing executive of the Northern Ireland Assembly, and it met for the first time on 2 December 1999 as powers were devolved to the Assembly by the British government.

North Korea country in East Asia, bounded northeast by Russia, north and northwest by China, east by the Sea of Japan, south by South Korea, and west by the Yellow Sea.

Norway country in northwest Europe, on the Scandinavian peninsula, bounded east by Sweden, northeast by Finland and Russia, south by the North Sea, west by the Atlantic Ocean, and north by the Arctic Ocean.

Novotný, Antonín (1904–1975) Czech president 1957–68. He was a founder member of the Czech Communist Party in 1921 and worked in the underground movement during the German occupation of Czechoslovakia, imprisoned in concentration camps 1941–45. His resistance to reform caused his resignation from the presidency in 1968.

Nu, U (Thakin) (1907–1995) Myanmar politician, prime minister of Burma (now Myanmar) for most of the period from 1947 to the military coup of 1962. He was the country's first democratically elected prime minister. Exiled from 1966, U Nu returned to the country in 1980 and, in 1988, helped found the National League for Democracy opposition movement.

Nuclear Non-Proliferation Treaty treaty signed 1968 to limit the spread of nuclear weapons. Under the terms of the treaty, those signatories declared to be nuclear powers (China, France, Russia, the UK, and the USA) pledged to work towards nuclear disarmament and not to supply military nuclear technology to non-nuclear countries, while other signatories pledged not to develop or acquire their own nuclear weapons. The treaty was renewed and extended indefinitely May 1995.

nuclear warfare war involving the use of nuclear weapons. Nuclear-weapons research began in Britain in 1940, but was transferred to the USA after it entered World War II. The research programme, known as the Manhattan Project, was directed by J Robert Oppenheimer. The development of technology that could destroy the Earth by the two major superpowers, the USA and USSR, as well as by Britain, France, and China, has since become a source of contention and heated debate. The worldwide total of nuclear weapons in 1990 was estimated to be about 50,000, and the number of countries possessing nuclear weapons stood officially at five – USA, USSR, UK, France, and China; South Africa developed nuclear weapons in the 1980s but gave them up voluntarily in 1991. India and Pakistan exploded nuclear devices in 1998. Countries suspected of possessing or developing nuclear capability in the 1990s include Israel, North Korea, Iraq, and Iran.

Nujoma, Sam (1929–) Namibian left-wing politician, founder and leader of *SWAPO (the South West Africa People's Organization) from 1959, president from 1990. He was exiled in 1960, and controlled SWAPO's armed struggle against South Africa from Angolan bases in 1966. When the first free elections were held in 1989 under the United Nations peace plan, he returned to lead his party to victory, taking office in March 1990.

Nuremberg trials after World War II, the trials of the 24 chief Nazi war criminals November 1945–October 1946 by an international military tribunal consisting of four judges and four prosecutors: one of each from the USA, UK, USSR, and France. An appendix accused the German cabinet, general staff, high command, Nazi leadership corps, *SS, *Sturmabteilung, and *Gestapo of criminal behaviour.

Nye, Gerald P(rentice) (1892–1971) US senator. Originally appointed and then elected to the US Senate (as a progressive Republican from North Dakota 1925–45), he chaired a special committee 1934–37 investigating arms sales in World War I. The findings reinforced the US belief that the USA should remain neutral in World War II.

Nyerere, Julius Kambarage (1922–1999) Tanzanian socialist politician, president 1964–85.

He devoted himself from 1954 to the formation of the Tanganyika African National Union and subsequent campaigning for independence.

He became chief minister in 1960, was prime minister of Tanganyika 1961–62, president of the newly formed Tanganyika Republic 1962–64, and first president of Tanzania 1964–85.

Oakley, Annie (1860–1926) born
Phoebe Anne Oakley Moses, US
sharpshooter, member of Buffalo Bill's
Wild West Show. Even though she was
partially paralysed in a train crash
1901, she continued to astound
audiences with her ability virtually
until her death. Kaiser William of
Germany had such faith in her talent
that he allowed her to shoot a cigarette
from his mouth.

Obasanjo, Olusegun (1937–)
Nigerian politician and soldier; head of
state 1976–79 and president from 1999.
When Murtala Muhammad's brief
military rule of 1975–76 ended in his
death during a coup, Obasanjo
succeeded as head of state, and
oversaw the transfer of control back
to civilian rule. After that, he played
an important role internationally,
especially within the Commonwealth
and as founder and leader of the
African Leadership Forum. In 1998 he
announced that he would be a
candidate in the Nigerian presidential
elections, and in March 1999 Obasanjo
was elected president, ending 15 years
of military rule. In April, the Court of
Appeal ruled that the February 1999
presidential elections had been unfair,
but the result stood. He started his
term in May, pledging to put an end
to corruption and atrocities.

Obote, (Apollo) Milton (1924–)
Ugandan politician, prime minister
1962–66, and president 1966–71 and
1980–85. After forming the Uganda
People's Congress (UPC) in 1959, he
led the independence movement from
1961. As prime minister, his rule
became increasingly authoritarian, and
in 1966 he suspended the constitution
and declared himself president.
He was ousted by Idi *Amin in 1971,

fleeing to exile in Tanzania. Returning
in 1979 after the collapse of the Amin
regime, he was re-elected president in
1980 but failed to restore order and
was deposed by Lieutenant General
Tito Okello in 1985.

Obregón, Álvaro (1880–1928)
Mexican soldier and Constitutionalist
politician, president 1920–24. His
anticlerical measures prompted church
opposition and in 1923–24 Victoriano
*Huerta led a revolt against him.
This was crushed, and Plutarco Elías
Calles, Obregón's chosen candidate,
became president in 1924. Obregón
was chosen president again in 1928,
but was assassinated by a Roman
Catholic fanatic 16 days after the
election, before taking up office.

O'Brien, William (1852–1928) Irish
journalist and nationalist, born in
Mallow, County Cork. In 1880 O'Brien
established the journal *United Ireland* to
popularize the aims of Charles Stewart
Parnell and the Land League. He was
a leader of the Plan of Campaign
(1886–91), a nationalist proposal to
address tenant eviction and distress,
and in 1898 he founded the United
Irish League. O'Brien took the anti-
Parnellite side in the split in the Irish
Parliamentary Party, following Parnell's
citation in the O'Shea divorce case. A
leader of the tenant side in the Dunraven
Land Conference (1902–03), he directed
his influence towards the conciliation
policy which looked for the union of
Irishmen of all creeds and classes.

October Revolution second stage
of the *Russian Revolution 1917,
when, on the night of 24 October
(6 November in the Western calendar),
the Bolshevik forces under Trotsky,
and on orders from Lenin, seized the
Winter Palace and arrested members

of the Provisional Government. The following day the Second All-Russian Congress of Soviets handed over power to the Bolsheviks.

October War surprise attack on Israel October 1973 by Egypt and Syria; see *Arab-Israeli Wars.

Octobrists group of Russian liberal constitutional politicians who accepted the reforming October Manifesto instituted by Tsar Nicholas II after the 1905 revolution and rejected more radical reforms.

Oder–Neisse Line border between Poland and East Germany agreed at the Potsdam Conference in 1945 at the end of World War II, and named after the two rivers that formed the frontier.

Odinga, (Ajuma) Oginga (1912–1994) Kenyan politician. He promoted Kenyan independence and Jomo Kenyatta as the nationalist leader. In 1960 he became vice-president of the Kenya African National Union (KANU) and was involved in drafting the constitution for this new party. He was minister for home affairs, vice-president, and minister without portfolio in the government of the independent Kenya after 1964.

O'Duffy, Eoin (1892–1944) Irish politician and soldier. Born in County Monaghan, he joined the Irish Volunteers in 1917, and took a leading part in the *Sinn Fein movement and the *Irish Republican Army. He supported the Anglo-Irish Treaty (1921) and was appointed the first commissioner of the Garda Síochána (civic guard), established to police the Irish Free State in 1922. Following his dismissal by the president of the executive council (prime minister) Éamon de Valera in 1933, he joined the opposition, and became director general of the semi-fascist National Guard (formerly the Blueshirts).

Official Secrets Act UK act of Parliament 1989, prohibiting the disclosure of confidential material from government sources by employees; it remains an absolute offence for a member or former member of the security and intelligence services (or those working closely with them) to disclose information about their work. There is no public-interest defence, and disclosure of information already in the public domain is still a crime. Journalists who repeat disclosures may also be prosecuted.

Ojukwu, (Chukwuemeka) Odumegwu (1933–) Nigerian politician and soldier. Appointed military governor of the mainly Ibo-speaking Eastern Region of Nigeria following the 1966 coup, he proclaimed the Eastern Region the independent Republic of Biafra in May 1967, precipitating the Biafran civil war. After acting as head of government and supreme commander for three years, his forces were finally defeated in 1970, and he fled to Côte d'Ivoire. He returned to Nigeria in 1982, but an attempt to return to politics led to two years' imprisonment, and he was banned from standing for president in the 1993 elections.

Olaf V (1903–1991) King of Norway from 1957, when he succeeded his father, Haakon VII.

'Old Contemptibles' name adopted by British soldiers who survived the retreat from Mons in 1914 and other early battles of World War I.

Oman country at the southeastern end of the Arabian peninsula, bounded west by the United Arab Emirates, Saudi Arabia, and Yemen, southeast by the Arabian Sea, and northeast by the Gulf of Oman.

ombudsman (Swedish **'commissioner'**) official who acts on behalf of the private citizen in investigating complaints against the government. The post is of Scandinavian origin; it was introduced in Sweden in 1809, Denmark in 1954, and Norway in 1962, and spread to other countries from the 1960s.

O'Neill, Terence (1914–1990) Baron **O'Neill of the Maine**, Northern Irish Unionist politician. He was minister of finance 1956–63, then prime minister of Northern Ireland 1963–69. He expounded liberal policies and in 1965 exchanged visits with the Republic of Ireland's Taoiseach (prime minister) Seán Lemass to improve cross-border relations, but his government achieved little substantial reform. He resigned when opposed by his party on measures to extend rights to Roman Catholics, including a universal franchise in local elections.

O'Neill was born in London into a wealthy Anglo-Irish family. He was sent to Eton public school, then entered the Irish Guards, serving as a captain in World War II. He was a Unionist member of parliament at Stormont (the Northern Ireland parliament) from 1946–70 and was made a life peer in 1970.

O'Neill, Tip (1912–1994) born **Thomas Phillip O'Neill, Jr**, US Democratic politician, speaker of the House of Representatives 1977–86. An Irish-American 'New Deal' liberal, he was the last Democratic leader from the old school of machine politics. An insurance man when elected to the Massachusetts state legislature in 1936, he became its youngest Speaker in 1947 before going to the US House of Representatives in 1952.

O'Neill pushed liberal legislation while protecting his working-class constituents from budget cuts. In 1968 he supported Eugene McCarthy's antiwar candidacy and as majority leader in 1973 he voted to cut off funding of the air war in Vietnam. Elected Speaker (1977–87), he failed to muster an uneasy Democratic alliance of ageing Southern committee chairmen and impatient young liberals to resist President Reagan's conservative agenda.

Ordzhonikidze, Grigori Konstantinovich (1886–1937) Georgian communist. He became chair of the Central Control Commission of the Communist Party of the Soviet Union and deputy head of the government in 1926, chair of the

Supreme Council of National Economy and a Politburo member in 1930, and commissar for heavy industry in 1932. He was one of Stalin's chief lieutenants, but died in mysterious circumstances during the Great Purge of 1936–38.

Organization de l'Armée Secrète OAS, guerrilla organization formed in 1961 by French settlers devoted to perpetuating their own rule in Algeria (Algérie Française). It collapsed on the imprisonment 1962–68 of its leader, General Raoul Salan.

Organization for Economic Cooperation and Development OECD, international organization of 29 industrialized countries that provides a forum for discussion and coordination of member states' economic and social policies. Founded in 1961, with its headquarters in Paris, the OECD replaced the Organization for European Economic Cooperation (OEEC), which had been established in 1948 to implement the *Marshall Plan. The Commission of the European Union also takes part in the OECD's work.

Organization of American States OAS, association founded in 1948 at Bogotá, Colombia by a charter signed by representatives of North, Central, and South American states. It aims to maintain peace and solidarity within the hemisphere, and is also concerned with the social and economic development of Latin America.

Organization of Petroleum-Exporting Countries OPEC, body established in 1960 to coordinate price and supply policies of oil-producing states, protecting its members' interests by manipulating oil production and the price of crude oil. Its concerted action in raising prices in the 1970s triggered worldwide recession but also lessened demand so that its influence was reduced by the mid-1980s. However, continued reliance on oil re-strengthened its influence in the late 1990s. OPEC members are: Algeria, Gabon, Indonesia, Iran, Iraq, Kuwait,

Libya, Nigeria, Qatar, Saudi Arabia, the United Arab Emirates, and Venezuela. Ecuador, formerly a member, withdrew in 1993. OPEC's secretary general is Rilwanu Lukman of Nigeria.

Orlando, Vittorio Emanuele (1860–1952) Italian politician, prime minister 1917–19. He attended the Paris peace conference after World War I, but dissatisfaction with his handling of the Adriatic settlement led to his resignation.

Ortega Saavedra, Daniel (1945–) Nicaraguan socialist politician, head of state 1979–90. He was a member of the Marxist Sandinista Liberation Front (FSLN), which overthrew the regime of Anastasio *Somoza Debayle in 1979, later becoming its secretary general. US-sponsored *Contra guerrillas opposed his government from 1982.

Osborne Judgement UK legal ruling of 1909 that prevented trade unions from using membership subscriptions to finance the Labour Party. In 1913 the judgement was negated by the Trade Union Act, which permitted them to raise political levies and provide financial support to the Labour Party. Individual trade unionists could 'contract out' of the political levy by signing a form saying they did not wish to pay.

Ostpolitik (German 'eastern policy') German foreign policy introduced by Willy *Brandt in 1971, which sought reconciliation with Eastern Europe as a means of improving contacts between East and West Germany.

Ottawa Conferences two Imperial Conferences held in Ottawa, Canada, 1894 and 1932. The earlier meeting of leaders from the British Empire discussed improved communications between the dominions and Britain. The later meeting took place during the Depression, but instead of an empire-wide trading agreement, Imperial preference was negotiated through 12 separate agreements, ending any hopes of a self-sufficient Commonwealth.

Ottoman Empire Muslim empire of the Turks from 1300 to 1920, the successor of the *Seljuk Empire. It was founded by Osman I and reached its height with Suleiman in the 16th century. From 1453 its capital city was Istamboul (Istanbul; formerly Constantinople).

At its greatest extent the Ottoman Empire's boundaries were: in Europe as far north as Hungary and part of southern Russia; Iran; the Palestinian coastline; Egypt; and North Africa. From the 1600s the empire was in decline. There was an attempted revival and reform under the Young Turk party in 1908, but the regime crumbled when Turkey sided with Germany in World War I. The sultanate was abolished by Kemal Atatürk in 1922; the last sultan was Muhammad VI.

Overlord, Operation Allied invasion of Normandy 6 June 1944 (*D-day), during World War II.

Owen, David Anthony Llewellyn (1938–) British politician, Labour foreign secretary 1977–79. In 1981 he was one of the founders of the *Social Democratic Party (SDP), and became its leader in 1983. Opposed to the decision of the majority of the party to merge with the Liberals in 1987, Owen stood down but emerged in 1988 as leader of a rump SDP, which was eventually disbanded in 1990.

Oxfam acronym for **OX**ford **Committee for FAMine Relief**, charity working to relieve poverty and famine worldwide. It was established in the UK in 1942 by Canon Theodore Richard Milford (1896–1987), initially to assist the starving people of Greece. Its director since 1992 has been David Bryer.

Özal, Turgut (1927–1993) Turkish Islamic right-wing politician, prime minister 1983–89, and president 1989–93. He was responsible for improving his country's relations with Greece, but his prime objective was to strengthen Turkey's alliance with the USA.

P

Paardeburg, Battle of during the South African War, Boer defeat by the British in February 1900, at Paardeburg Hill, on the Modder River about 95 km/60 mi west of Bloemfontein.

Page, Earle Christmas Grafton (1880–1961) Australian politician, co-founder and leader of the Country Party 1920–39 and briefly prime minister in April 1939. He represented Australia in the British war cabinet 1941–42 and was minister of health 1949–55. GCMG 1938.

Pahlavi, Muhammad Reza (1919–1980) Shah of Iran 1941–79. He succeeded on the abdication of his father, Shah Reza Pahlavi, and soon embarked on a major programme of social reform. He invested lavishly in the armed forces and ruled in an authoritarian manner, greatly aided by security services.

Paisley, Ian (Richard Kyle) (1926–) Northern Ireland politician, cleric, and leader of the Democratic Unionist Party (DUP) from 1971. An imposing and deeply influential member of the Protestant community, he remains staunchly committed to the union with Britain. His political career was one of high drama, marked by protests, resignations, fierce oratory, and a pugnacious and forthright manner.

Pakistan country in southern Asia, stretching from the Himalayas to the Arabian Sea, bounded to the west by Iran, northwest by Afghanistan, and northeast and east by India.

government The 1973 constitution, suspended in 1977, was restored in part and amended in 1985 to make the president the dominant political figure. Primary power resides with the central government, headed by an executive president who is elected for five-year terms by a joint sitting of the federal legislature. The president must be a Muslim. Day-to-day administration is performed by a prime minister (drawn from the national assembly) and cabinet appointed by the president. From 1988, power shifted from the president to the prime minister in what became a dual administration. A military coup in 1999 dissolved the national assembly and the senate and gave the president complete authority.

Pakistan is a federal republic comprising four provinces: Sind, Punjab, North-West Frontier Province, and Baluchistan, administered by appointed governors and local governments drawn from elected provincial assemblies; Tribal Areas, which are administered by the central government; and the Federal Capital Territory of Islamabad. The federal legislature, the Majlis i-Shura, comprises two chambers: a lower house (national assembly) composed of 207 members directly elected for five-year terms by universal suffrage, with 10 further seats being reserved for minorities; and an upper house (senate) composed of 87 members elected, a third at a time, for six-year terms by provincial assemblies and Tribal Areas following a quota system. The national assembly has sole jurisdiction over financial affairs.

history The name 'Pakistan' for a Muslim division of British India was put forward in 1930 by Choudhary Rahmat Ali (1897–1951) from names of the Muslim parts of the subcontinent: *P*unjab, the *A*fghan Northwest Frontier, *K*ashmir, S*i*nd, and Baluchi*stan*. *Pak* means 'pure' in Urdu, and *stan* means 'land'.

Fear of domination by the Hindu majority in India led in 1940 to a serious demand by Muhammad Ali *Jinnah, the leader of the Muslim League, for a separate Muslim state. This contributed to the delay in Britain granting independence for some years, but in 1947 British India was divided into two dominions, India and Pakistan.

the formation of Pakistan The Islamic state of Pakistan was created, on Indian independence in 1947, out of the Northwest Frontier Region, the northwestern region of Punjab, Baluchistan, and Sind (making up West Pakistan), and the eastern region of East Bengal (making up East Pakistan). Jinnah became the first governor general and Liaquat Ali Khan, deputy leader of the Muslim League (1940–47), became the first prime minister.

Sectarian violence had been simmering for years, and at partition hundreds of thousands of Muslims and Hindus were massacred as they fled to the appropriate states. Punjab was the scene of the most violent fighting since there a third community, the Sikhs, was in the majority.

early conflicts with India Although Mahatma *Gandhi, the hero of Indian independence, forced the Indian National Congress (see *Congress Party) to divide the assets of the former government of India, there was no confidence between the two countries.

In the Muslim-majority state of Kashmir the Hindu maharaja opted to join India at partition, and called for Indian intervention when Muslims marched from the north on Srinagar. Fighting between Indian and Pakistani troops was brought to an end by a UN ceasefire on 30 October 1948, but Kashmir continued to be a source of tension and conflict between India and Pakistan.

Another source of tension between the two countries was the question of the use of the rivers of the Punjab. Problems also arose from the fact that the new frontiers divided the cotton and jute mills of Indian Bengal from their sources of supply in East Bengal (East Pakistan), and the consumers of Pakistan from the factories of India.

political developments to 1958 When Jinnah died in September 1948 the new leaders, mostly lawyers, were not always dedicated to Islam, and others wanted a theocratic state. The prime minister Liaquat Ali Khan laid emphasis on the Islamic nature of the state in order to gain popularity, provoking protest from the Hindus in the national assembly. However, he pursued a policy of making peace with India, and was assassinated in 1951 by objectors to this policy. The period was one of political intrigue and incessant polemic over the Islamic, or even theocratic, nature of Pakistan.

In 1954, in East Bengal, a United Front party led by H S Suhrawardy, leader of the Awami League, massively defeated the Muslim League, and in 1956 President Iskander Mirza was forced to accept Suhrawardy as prime minister, and the East Pakistan legislature voted for total autonomy, except in foreign affairs.

The new constitution introduced in 1956 declared Pakistan an Islamic republic (previously the British monarch had been head of state). The national parliament was to contain 300 members equally represented on both sides, and the prime minister and the cabinet were to govern according to the will of parliament.

Ayub Khan in power In 1958 Gen Muhammad *Ayub Khan led a military coup, suspended the constitution and all political parties, and declared martial law, with himself as the martial-law administrator. Ayub then assumed the presidency, and martial law lasted 44 months. To further his aim of 'blending democracy with discipline' he devised the system of 'basic democracies', elected by the people, as the local units of development. In the 1960 election the basic democrats gave him a massive mandate, although he received little support from the middle classes.

In 1962 a new constitution was introduced, which vested executive authority with the president, and the title of prime minister was abolished. The national assembly was divided into two provincial assemblies chosen by the basic democrats. Faced with orthodox Muslim opposition, Ayub retreated from early attempts at reform, such as the introduction of laws to restrict polygamy.

Although the economy grew rapidly – 6% per year between 1960 and 1965 – the imbalance between East and West Pakistan increased. The East contributed jute and tea, but most foreign aid, such as the Indus Basin scheme for hydroelectric development sponsored by the International Bank for Reconstruction and Development, went to the West. Pakistan received US military aid, which was used in 1965 in the war with India over Kashmir (see *India). Pakistan was also supported by China, whose own border disputes with India had led to war, and Pakistan has continued to have close relations with China.

Ayub's popularity waned. In 1968 his autocracy was challenged and there was an attempt on his life. The following year, after his attempts at conciliation had failed and under pressure from serious strikes and riots, he resigned and gave way to the army commander in chief Gen Agha Muhammad *Yahya Khan, who became president.

the creation of Bangladesh Regional tension had been mounting throughout the 1960s between demographically dominant East Pakistan and West Pakistan, where political and military power was concentrated. In the 1970 general election the separatist Awami League, led by Sheikh Mujibur *Rahman (Sheikh Mujib), won the majority of the East Pakistan seats in the national assembly, while Zulfikar Ali *Bhutto's

Pakistan People's Party (PPP) won a clear majority in the West.

Sheikh Mujib's demand for total autonomy for the East, and not merely in the field of foreign affairs, led Yahya to suspend the constitution in 1971. Mujib's call for a boycott of West Pakistan and a general strike received total support in the East. When the negotiations failed West Pakistan forces invaded the East, brutally suppressed the separatist movement, and arrested Mujib. Million of refugees fled to India from the fighting, and India decided to intervene militarily. The subsequent defeat of Pakistan by Indian forces led in the following year to East Pakistan becoming the independent state of *Bangladesh (1972). Despite being cut off from the jute and tea of the East, the Pakistan economy survived the loss.

When Bangladesh was accepted into the Commonwealth in 1972, Pakistan left, but rejoined in 1989.

the premiership of Zulfikar Ali Bhutto Yahya Khan resigned in 1971, passing power in West Pakistan to the People's Party leader Zulfikar Ali Bhutto, who became prime minister, with Chaudhri Fazal Elahi as president. Bhutto introduced a new federal parliamentary constitution in 1973 and a socialist economic programme of land reform and nationalization. The new constitution of 1973 formulated a federation with autonomous units, and a Council of Islamic Ideology was set up in order to bring existing laws into conformity with Islam. Prisoners of war were repatriated, and Bangladesh waived its intention of trying Pakistani 'war criminals' in exchange for an agreement in 1974 on the Pakistan external debt.

separatist movements The precedent set by Bangladesh led to a new danger of breakaway movements from other states. In 1973 a guerrilla war began in Baluchistan, and the Baluchi governor resigned. In the

North-West Frontier Province (NWFP) there was also unrest, with the Pathans campaigning for an independent Pakhtoonistan. The Pakhtoonkhwa National Awami Party leader was assassinated, and there was an assassination attempt on the NWFP Awami Party leader, Abdul Wali Khan.

By 1975 guerrilla activities had spread to Sind and the Punjab, and relations with Afghanistan, whose new government laid claim to the NWFP and Baluchistan, became strained when Afghanistan was seen to be supporting the Pakhtoonistan Liberation Front. In February 1975 the home minister Sherpao was assassinated. The NWFP National Awami Party was banned and Wali Khan was arrested, as well as other leaders who were agitating for state autonomy.

Zia seizes power Despite deteriorating economic conditions, the general election of March 1977 resulted in overwhelming victory for Prime Minister Bhutto, but the opposition parties alleged widespread ballot rigging. Demonstrations and riots followed, leading to the imposition of martial law. Opposition leaders were arrested, and a general strike was called. Eventually the two sides met for talks and agreed to another general election.

However, in July 1977 the army seized power in a bloodless coup, with army chief of staff Gen *Zia ul-Haq in control. Martial law was again imposed and political and trade-union activity banned. Bhutto was imprisoned for alleged murder and hanged in 1979.

Islamization and opposition Gen Zia became president in 1978 and introduced a broad Islamization programme aimed at deepening his support base and appeasing Islamic fundamentalists. Following the Soviet invasion of Afghanistan in 1979, Pakistan became a base for US-backed Afghani Islamic Mujahedin fighting

Soviet forces, and Pakistan's support led to closer relations with the USA. Pakistan also joined the *non-aligned movement in 1979, and has drawn closer to the Islamic states of the Middle East and Africa.

Zia's Islamization programme was opposed by middle-class professionals and by the Shiite minority. In 1981, nine banned opposition parties, including the PPP, formed the Movement for the Restoration of Democracy alliance to campaign for a return to parliamentary government.

The military government responded by arresting several hundred opposition politicians. A renewed democracy campaign in 1983 resulted in considerable anti-government violence in Sind province. From 1982, however, Gen Zia slowly began enlarging the civilian element in his government and in 1984 he held a successful referendum on the Islamization process, which was taken to legitimize his continuing as president for a further five-year term.

civilian government In 1985 direct elections were held to the national and provincial assemblies, but on a nonparty basis. A new civilian cabinet was formed and an amended constitution adopted. Martial law and the ban on political parties were lifted, military courts were abolished, and military administrators stepped down in favour of civilians. A government was formed by the Pagaro faction of the Pakistan Muslim League (PML) led by Muhammad Khan Junejo, which was subservient to Gen Zia. Benazir *Bhutto, the daughter of Zulfikar Ali Bhutto and leader of the PPP, returned in 1986 from self-exile in London to launch a popular campaign for immediate open elections. Riots erupted in Lahore, Karachi, and rural Sind, where troops were sent in, and PPP leaders were arrested.

Islamic law introduced In 1988, concerned with the deteriorating state of the economy and anxious to accelerate the Islamization process, President Zia dismissed the Junejo government and dissolved the national assembly and provincial legislatures, promising fresh elections within 90 days. Ruling by ordinance, Zia decreed that the sharia, the Islamic legal code, would immediately become the country's supreme law. A month later he was killed, along with senior army officers, in a military air crash near Bahawalpur. Sabotage was suspected.

Ghulam Ishaq Khan, the Senate's elderly chair, succeeded as president. In subsequent multiparty elections the PPP, which had moved towards the centre in its policy stance, emerged as the largest single party.

Benazir Bhutto's first premiership After forging a coalition with the Mohajir National Movement (MQM), Benazir Bhutto was sworn in as prime minister in November 1988, and Ghulam Ishaq Khan was elected president. The new Bhutto administration pledged itself to a free-market economic programme, and to leave the military budget untouched. It also pledged its support of the Islamic Mujahedin fighting the Soviet occupation forces in Afghanistan. In October 1989 the MQM withdrew from the ruling coalition and allied itself with the opposition Islamic Democratic Alliance (IDA). The Bhutto government narrowly survived a vote of no confidence a month later.

Nawaz Sharif's first premiership Benazir Bhutto's government was dismissed from office by President Ghulam Ishaq Khan in August 1990 on accusations of incompetence, corruption, and abuse of power. In October 1990 the opposition swept to victory and Nawaz Sharif, Bhutto's former chief minister of Punjab province, became prime minister. Sharif had headed the IDA, which incorporated the PML (led by former premier Muhammad Khan Junejo). The IDA captured 105 of the 207

parliamentary seats contested to the 45 of Bhutto's PPP. It also secured control of three of the four provincial assemblies, Bhutto's Sind stronghold being the exception. Sharif promised to pursue a free-market economic programme and was supported by the military, state bureaucracy, and mullahs.

During the Gulf crisis and war against Iraq of 1990–91, Pakistan sent 11,000 troops to Saudi Arabia to guard Islamic shrines, but there was considerable anti-Americanism within the country and popular support for the Iraqi leader Saddam Hussein.

Islamic law enforced In May 1991 a sharia bill enforcing Islamic law and designed to create an 'Islamic welfare state' was enacted. The opposition PPP, though welcoming parts of the social-reform programme, unsuccessfully voted against the bill. Nawaz Sharif also launched a privatization and deregulation programme, but these reforms were soon upset by labour unrest and terrorist incidents, and by the uncovering of a financial scandal involving Nawaz Sharif's family and members of the government.

In September 1992 floods devastated the northern region of Jammu and Kashmir, resulting in 2,000 deaths and the destruction of a fifth of the area's cotton crop. The Pakistani government came under attack for its handling of the disaster, which also caused 500 deaths in northern India.

political stalemate From early 1993 President Khan and Prime Minister Sharif were locked in a power struggle, contesting each other's authority at every level. Five months of political stalemate ended in July 1993 when the national assembly was dissolved and both Khan and Sharif resigned.

Benazir Bhutto's second premiership In the October 1993 general election Benazir Bhutto was sworn in as prime minister for a second time after the PPP and its allies secured a narrow victory over the PML, led by Sharif. The PPP was also able to form governments in Bhutto's home province of Sind and, in coalition, in the crucial state of Punjab. In November 1993 Farooq Leghari, drawn from Bhutto's PPP, was indirectly elected state president, promising to reduce the powers of the presidency and strengthen the prime-ministerial system.

From 1992 regional factional violence increased. In March 1995 two US diplomats were killed in an ambush in Karachi, an area that had seen escalating conflict between militant political, ethnic, and religious groups since 1994. There was also civil strife in North-West Frontier Province, where Islamic fundamentalism was on the increase.

In April 1996 the former Pakistan cricket captain Imran Khan formed the new Movement for Justice (Tehreek-e-Insaaf) to fight against corruption and injustice. Violent demonstrations, headed by fundamentalist Islamic parties, resulted when new tax increases, amounting to $1.2 billion, penalized poor people while the landed elite remained largely untaxed.

Benazir Bhutto dismissed again Amid allegations of corruption and mismanagement against Benazir Bhutto and her government, President Leghari tried to persuade her to resign. She denied the charges against her, refused to resign, and was dismissed in November 1996. The president also dissolved the national and provincial assemblies.

In January 1997, the Supreme Court upheld the constitutionality of President Leghari's dismissal of the Bhutto government, accepting the president's case that it had been characterized by nepotism, corruption, and misrule, and had been responsible for hundreds of extra-judicial killings in Karachi. In the same month Bhutto's father-in-law Hakim Ali Zardari was arrested on charges of fraud and tax evasion.

In January 1997 the interim government of Malik Meraj Khalid established a Council for Defence and National Security (CDNS) to advise the government on a range of security issues. By including chiefs of staff of the army, navy, and air force, along with the president, prime minister, and defence, interior, and foreign ministers, it gave the military a formal role in the political power structure for the first time since the death of Gen Zia ul-Haq in 1988.

the 1997 elections Nawaz Sharif, prime minister 1990–93 and leader of the right-of-centre Pakistan Muslim League–Nawaz (PML–N), secured a landslide victory in the February 1997 general election, winning 134 of the lower house's 204 directly elected seats: a further 13 seats were reserved for women and minorities. (Sharif enjoyed the support of 181 deputies in total). The centrist Pakistan People's Party (PPP) won only 18 seats – down from 86 at the previous election. The Movement for Justice (Tehreek-e-Insaaf) party, led by Imran Khan, won little support and no seats; however, the Mohajir Qaumi Movement, a Sind-based ethnic-rights party, polled strongly, winning 12 seats. Turnout slumped to 25%, reflecting disenchantment with the political process. Provincial elections were held simultaneously. Asif Zardari, the husband of Benazir Bhutto, was elected to the senate despite being still in detention in jail.

Nawaz Sharif's second premiership The new Prime Minister Nawaz Sharif pledged not to seek to 'victimize' his defeated opponents and promised market-centred economic reforms and improved relations with India. However, his room for manoeuvre was constrained by financial restrictions imposed by the International Monetary Fund, as the country was heavily in debt.

In April 1997 legislation was passed by parliament that curbed the power of the president – granted during an earlier period of military rule – to dismiss a government summarily and appoint provincial governors and top military officers. Tax rates and tariffs were also reduced; 13 state-owned companies were earmarked for privatization; and, as part of an 'accountability' drive against corruption, in April 1997 the head of the navy was dismissed and a number of bureaucrats suspended.

In 1998 Benazir Bhutto, at the time in self-imposed exile, was charged with corruption, which marked the beginning of lengthy judicial proceedings against her and her husband. In April 1999, she and her husband were found guilty of corruption and given five-year prison sentences. In November 1999 she was named as corrupt by the military government in Pakistan, as it fulfilled its threat to crack down on corruption among politicians and businesses.

nuclear capability The USA suspended military aid in 1990 after learning that Pakistan was seeking to develop nuclear weapons. Prime Minister Benazir Bhutto admitted in 1991 that Pakistan had the facilities for rapid construction of a nuclear weapon, and in 1994 Nawaz Sharif declared that the country had a nuclear bomb. In May 1998, in response to nuclear tests in India, Pakistan conducted five nuclear explosions on its territory. This further fuelled the tension between the two countries and angered public opinion worldwide.

In August 1998, two months after nuclear tests in Baluchistan, the government faced street protests against the growing economic crisis. This was brought about largely by the suspension of Western economic aid, credits from the IMF and investment, as a result of the tests. The value of the Pakistani rupee plunged and there was a sharp rise in the inflation rate and in government debt. In November 1998 US economic sanctions, which had

been imposed as punishment for Pakistan's May 1997 nuclear tests, were partially lifted. This was a reward for Pakistan's announcement of a voluntary moratorium on further tests, a commitment to adhere to the Comprehensive Test Ban Treaty, and the resumption of dialogue with India over disputed Kashmir. It paved the way for the government, on 25 November 1998, to agree a US$5.5 billion economic bailout package with the IMF and World Bank.

Throughout 1998 the increasing public disillusionment with the political class helped to strengthen the position of Islamic fundamentalists who, although still a clear minority, had growing influence, following the 1980s Islamization reforms, within the army and bureaucracy. In response, Prime Minister Sharif proposed, in September 1998, revising the constitution to introduce full Islamic law, but faced strong opposition within parliament. In October 1998 federal rule was imposed on Sind and the provincial government was dismissed, as a result of escalating violence, with around 800 people having been killed in Karachi during 1998. The deaths were the result of violent clashes between rival factions of the Muttahida Qaumi Movement (MQM), a party orientated towards Urdu-speaking Muslims who had migrated from India on partition in 1947. The MQM had ended its national and provincial level coalition with the ruling Pakistan Muslim League (PML) in October 1998. In June 1999 India agreed to enter peace talks on Kashmir.

Religious conflict and social unrest continued in Pakistan into 1999. Many people feared an upsurge in the wave of sectarian killings that had claimed more than 3,500 lives since the early 1990s. Thousands of opposition supporters held demonstrations in September 1999, calling on Prime Minister Sharif to step down. It was one of the biggest protests since he had been re-elected in 1997. Traders were also protesting against a new tax, which formed part of an agreement with the IMF.

takeover by Musharraf Pakistan's army in October 1999 overthrew Pakistan's government after Nawaz Sharif tried to sack General Pervez Musharraf from the top military job. Troops seized Sharif, government buildings in Islamabad, airports, and a TV studio as the general promised to maintain stability. Governments all over the world condemned the coup, while Pakistan's opposition leaders welcomed it. Gen Musharraf, who also appointed himself the country's chief executive, declared a state of emergency. The army general also dissolved Pakistan's legislature and suspended the constitution.

The Commonwealth said in October 1999 it would suspend Pakistan after the military coup led by Gen Musharraf. The success of his bloodless takeover was due largely to the fact that the army was solidly behind him. Furthermore, Musharraf demonstrated that despite the ousted prime minister Sharif sweeping back to power 32 months earlier with a big mandate, he had become so unpopular that the army could take over without soliciting any serious protest. He said the new regime would be largely civilian in character, but declared a state of emergency, suspended the country's constitution, and was holding Sharif, as well as an unknown number of ministers and other politicians, under house arrest.

Five days after taking power, General Musharraf announced a seven-point programme, which included reviving the economy and restoring the confidence of investors, insuring law and order, and 'rebuilding national confidence and morale'. A team from the Commonwealth visited Pakistan to ask when it would return to civilian and democratic rule. According to reports, Musharraf expected no change for a year.

In October Musharraf unveiled a 10-member civilian cabinet. The cabinet, to be known as the National Security Council, included Shaukat Aziz, a senior executive with Citibank in New York, as his finance minister, and the central bank governor, Mohammed Yaqub, who had worked at the IMF for 20 years. Although Musharraf, who had declared himself Pakistan's new Chief Executive, selected non-political figures to man the council, many had traditionally maintained close links with the army. He allowed President Rafiq Tarar to remain in post and did not restrict press freedom or impose military courts, although he did insist that civilian judges take an oath of allegiance to the military government (some refused to do so). The coup, which marked the first time in history that a military regime had taken over a nuclear power, was broadly supported within Pakistan. This was largely due to the unpopularity of Sharif's government, which was tainted by corruption and economic mismanagement.

Pakistan's junta in November laid treason charges against the deposed prime minister. Nawaz Sharif and seven others were accused of treason and kidnapping, which carried the death penalty. News of the charges came as diplomats attending the biennial Commonwealth Heads of State meeting in Durban, South Africa, were debating the fate of Pakistan, which had been suspended and faced further sanctions. The Pakistani military authorities had refused to give in to Commonwealth demands that they give a timetable for the restoration of democracy, and Pakistan was effectively suspended from the Commonwealth.

A month after the takeover, the military had been reassured only by what it had heard from US and IMF officials. In November 1999, Nawaz Sharif made a formal appearance in a court in Karachi. Although he denied the charges against him, the military government indicated in early December 1999 that he continued to face the charges. In January 2000 a Pakistani judge refused to let his trial proceed on the grounds that a fair trial would be impossible in the presence of the intelligence officials. Despite this and the refusal of six Supreme Court judges in Pakistan to swear an oath of allegiance to the new military government, the trial finally began in January 2000. The crisis for the country as a whole was marked by the simultaneous explosion of two bombs in Karachi, where the trial was taking place. One of the bombs was in the compound of the city court. During the trial, Sharif said that General Musharraf plotted his overthrow after they clashed over Pakistani policy in 1999 with regard to the dispute in Kashmir. Days before the closing arguments in the trial, one of Sharif's lawyers was shot dead by masked gunmen and the others demanded a safer venue. The government banned outdoor gatherings. Meanwhile, a police investigation was launched into the life of of Kulsoom Sharif, the wife of the deposed prime minister. She was accused of treason after criticizing the military government. Sharif was found guilty of terrorism and hijacking an aircraft, but acquitted of charges of conspiracy to murder and kidnapping. He was given two life sentences to run concurrently. He was later also sentenced on charges of corruption to 14 years' imprisonment, fined 20 million rupees/US$35,400, and banned from holding political office. In December 2000, he went into exile in Saudi Arabia, having his jail sentence pardoned by President Musharraf after appealing for permission to go abroad for medical help.

renewed Indian–Pakistani conflict
India continued to attack Pakistan-sponsored infiltrators with air strikes in Kashmir in June 1999, claiming it was winning the war which had began

in May. The warlike conflict between Pakistan and India appeared to have been averted in July 1999. However, in January 2000 relations with India worsened when India accused Pakistan of involvement in a week-long hijacking of an Indian airliner by Kashmiri militants who demanded the release of terrorists imprisoned by India. Pakistan denied any involvement. The Indian government agreed to release three prisoners, including the Islamic religious leader Maulana Masood Azhar, who subsequently appeared in public on Pakistani soil. Shelling and clashes in Kashmir heightened tension between India and Pakistan just before the scheduled visit to the area of US president Clinton. Both sides denied responsibility for attacks.

The possibility of a ceasefire and peace talks over Kashmir were denied when India refused any involvement from Pakistan in negotiations in August 2000, and hostile relations between India and Pakistan continued.

a return to democracy? In August, Musharraf announced non-party elections would be held between December 2000 and August 2001 to local councils which would in turn elect district councils. He reduced the voting age from 21 to 18 and reserved a third of the seats for women. He also decreed that those convicted of criminal offences or moral corruption would be disqualified from holding office. This banned over 100 political leaders, including ex-premiers Benazir Bhutto and Nawaz Sharif. In November, supporters of Bhutto and Sharif, formerly opponents, joined with 15 smaller parties to form the Alliance for the Restoration of Democracy, designed to achieve an early end to military rule.

In January 2001, the government announced that, from July, all bank transactions must be in strict accordance with sharia (Islamic law), which forbids the charging of interest.

In March the government arrested several opposition leaders who were members of the alliance, which had been planning a rally in April. The rally did not go ahead, and more than 1,600 activists were arrested the week it was planned to take place.

In April, the Supreme Court set aside the 1999 corruption conviction of the exiled former prime minister Benazir Bhutto, and ordered her retrial.

offer of talks with India accepted
India unexpectedly ended its six-month-old ceasefire in Kashmir on 24 May 2001, and invited Musharraf, to Delhi, India, to discuss the future of the disputed territory. The offer of talks was seen as a major diplomatic initiative, and the invitation by Indian prime minister Vajpayee was formally accepted.

Musharraf becomes president
Gen Musharraf had himself sworn in as president on 20 June 2001. Earlier, the general had dissolved the already suspended National Assembly and Senate, and dismissed President Rafiq Tarar, a primarily ceremonial figure who had little say in the running of the country. It was widely assumed that Musharraf wished to consolidate his authority ahead of his meeting with the Indian prime minister on 14 July. In August, Musharraf promised to hold provincial and federal elections in early October 2002, but gave no indication of intending to give up his position as leader. He was expected to introduce changes to the constitution to strengthen the position of president, and create a new political system – run by civilians but supervised by the army.

support for anti-terrorist coalition
In the wake of the terrorist attacks on the USA on 11 September, President Musharraf said he would support US military action against Afghanistan. However he faced widespread opposition on the streets, as anti-US riots took place across the country during the first week of US and UK military strikes 7–14 October, resulting in the death of four protestors in the Punjab town of Dera Ghazi Khan. Pakistan also faced a humanitarian crisis as hundreds of thousands of refugees fled Afghan cities and head for the Pakistani border. To forestall a general strike, called to protest against the US bombing of Afghanistan, the government ordered the Islamic leader Qazi Hussain Ahmed to be detained in a government rest house for a month. However, the strike went ahead on 9 November, with extremist religious parties trying to consolidate opposition to President Musharraf's pro-Western policies.

increased tension with India After five armed assailants broke into India's parliament building in December 2001, resulting in 14 deaths, India demanded that Pakistan take action against Lashkar-e-Taiba, the Pakistani-based Islamic militant group accused of carrying out the attack. India also accused Pakistan's intelligence services of actively supporting the attack. As political tension escalated, the two countries mounted large-scale military build-ups on their borders.

US reporter kidnapped and murdered Police searching for Daniel Pearl, a US reporter kidnapped in Pakistan in late January 2002, raided houses in Karachi, where he had been last seen. Six suspects were detained. Ahmed Omar Saeed Sheikh, a British-born extremist who became a kidnapping specialist for the militant group Islamic Jihad, was arrested on 12 February as chief suspect in Pearl's kidnapping. At first, Sheikh raised hopes that Pearl was still alive, but then told a court in Karachi on 14 February that he had kidnapped the US journalist and that he was dead. This was confirmed on 21 February when a videotape showing Pearl's murder was delivered to US officials in Karachi.

In March 2002, five people, including the wife and daughter of a US diplomat, were killed in a terrorist attack on a church in Islamabad. The attack on the church in the heart of the diplomatic enclave injured 45 people. It was the second attack on Christians in Pakistan since the US-led War on Terrorism began; in October 2001 armed assailants had killed 15 Christians and a Muslim in an attack on a church in the city of Bahawalpur.

In April, Musharraf won 98% backing in a referendum proposing the extension of his rule for five years.

threat of war In May 2002, Musharraf was accused by India of backing Islamic militant incursions into Indian-administered Kashmir. Musharraf denied the claims, and the countries came closer to war. Pakistan's test-firing of missiles capable of carrying nuclear warheads was seen as deliberately antagonistic by India, and troop build-ups on the Kashmir line of control continued. In June under diplomatic pressure from the USA, India announced a series of measures to reduce tension with Pakistan, including withdrawing its navy from waters near Pakistan and ending a ban on Pakistani civil aircraft entering its airspace.

In the same month a suicide bomber drove a van loaded with explosives into the US consulate in Karachi, killing 11 people and injuring at least 45 more. Islamic militants opposed to both the US military intervention in Afghanistan and the government's attempts to stop militant infiltration into Indian-controlled Kashmir were thought to be responsible.

Pal, Bipin Chandra (1858–1932) Indian nationalist and freedom fighter. He entered politics in 1877 and his association with the great reformist Brahma Samâj leader, Keshub Chunder Sen (1838–84), drew him into this movement in 1880. He was also greatly influenced by Bal Gangadhar Tilak (1856–1920), Lala *Lajpat Rai (with whom he formed the famous Congress trio 'Lal, Pal, and Bal'), and the religious writer and leader Aurobindo Ghose. In 1902 he launched a weekly journal, *Young India*, through which he championed the cause of Indian freedom.

Palau or **Belau**, country comprising more than 350 islands and atolls (mostly uninhabited) in the west Pacific Ocean.

Palestine Liberation Organization PLO, Arab organization founded in 1964 to bring about an independent state in Palestine. It consists of several distinct groupings, the chief of which is al-*Fatah, led by Yassir *Arafat, the president of the PLO from 1969. Another major faction is the Popular Front for the Liberation of Palestine, a Marxist party formed in 1967, which is more hard line, opposing negotiations with Israel and the 1993 peace accord. Recognized in 1973 by Arab nations as the 'sole representative of the Palestinian people', and given observer status by the United Nations in 1974, the PLO has played a central role in the *Israel–Palestine peace process.

Palme, (Sven) Olof Joachim (1927–1986) Swedish social-democratic politician, prime minister 1969–76 and 1982–86. As prime minister he carried out constitutional reforms, turning the Riksdag into a single-chamber parliament and stripping the monarch of power, and was widely respected for his support of developing countries. He was assassinated in February 1986.

Palmer, A(lexander) Mitchell (1872–1936) US public official. He held office in the US House of Representatives 1909–15. A Quaker, he declined an appointment as secretary of war under President Wilson, and served instead as custodian of alien property during World War I. As US attorney general 1919–21, he led the controversial 'Palmer raids' against alleged political radicals during the Red Scare.

pan-Africanism anticolonial movement that believed in the innate unity of all black Africans and their descendants overseas, and advocated a united Africa (see *African nationalism). It was founded in 1900 at the first pan-African Conference in London. Since 1958 pan-Africanism has become partially absorbed into wider movements of the developing world.

pan-Africanist Congress PAC, South African political party, formed as a militant black nationalist group in 1959, when it broke away from the African National Congress (ANC), promoting a black-only policy for Africa. PAC was outlawed 1960–90; its military wing was called Poqo ('we alone'). It suspended its armed struggle in 1994, and transformed itself into a political party to contest the first multiracial elections. It is more radical than the ANC, advocating a radical redistribution of land and a state-run economy.

Panama country in Central America, on a narrow isthmus between the Caribbean and the Pacific Ocean, bounded west by Costa Rica and east by Colombia.

government The constitution was revised in 1983, when a new, single-chamber legislative assembly of 72 members, elected by universal suffrage for a five-year term, was created. The president, similarly elected for a five-year term, is assisted by two elected vice-presidents and an appointed cabinet. The country is divided into nine provinces, each with its own governor, appointed by the president. There are also three Indian reservations, which enjoy a high degree of self-government.

history Panama was visited by Christopher Columbus in 1502. Vasco Núñez de Balboa found the Pacific from the Darien isthmus in 1513. Spanish settlements were sacked by Francis Drake 1572–95 and Henry Morgan 1668–71; Morgan destroyed the old city of Panama, which dated from 1519. Remains of Fort St Andrews, built by Scottish settlers 1698–1701, were discovered in 1976. Panama remained part of the viceroyalties of Peru and New Granada until 1821, when it gained independence from Spain; it joined Gran Colombia in 1822.

independence Panama achieved full independence in 1903 with US support. At the same time the USA bought the rights to build the Panama Canal (opened in 1914) and was given control of a strip of territory 16 km/10 mi wide, known as the Canal Zone, in perpetuity. Panama was guaranteed US protection and an annuity. In 1939 Panama's protectorate status was ended by mutual agreement, and in 1974 the two countries agreed to negotiate an eventual transfer of the canal to Panama. In 1977 two treaties were signed by Panama's president (1968–78), Gen Omar Torrijos Herrera, and US president Carter. One transferred ownership of the canal to Panama (effective from 1990) and the other guaranteed its subsequent neutrality, with the conditions that only Panamanian forces would be stationed in the zone, and that the USA would have the right to use force to keep the canal open if it became obstructed.

deterioration of economy
The 1980s saw a deterioration in the state of Panama's economy, with opposition to the austerity measures that the government introduced to try to halt the decline. In the 1984 general election, after a close result, Dr Nicolás Ardito Barletta, the Democratic Revolutionary Party (PRD) candidate, was declared president, but in 1985 he resigned amid speculation that he had been forced to do so by the commander of the National Guard. Relations between Panama and the USA deteriorated with the departure of President Barletta, and the Reagan administration cut and later suspended its financial aid.

Barletta was succeeded by Eric Arturo del Valle, but the country was, from 1983, effectively ruled by the army commander-in-chief, Gen Manuel Noriega. Although the 1977 Torrijos–Carter Canal Treaties specified that US forces in Panama were present purely to defend the canal, Noriega cooperated in allowing the USA to use Panama as an intelligence, training, resupply, and weapons base for the Reagan administration's campaigns in Nicaragua and El Salvador.

accusations against Noriega In 1987 Noriega was accused of corruption, election rigging, involvement in the cocaine trade, and the murder of a political opponent. Noriega's forces were allegedly responsible for up to a dozen political killings between 1983 and 1989. Political parties, labour and student unions, and business groups united as the National Civic Crusade to campaign for his removal; demonstrations were suppressed by riot police. In July 1987 Noriega successfully resisted calls for his removal, despite the suspension of US military and economic aid. He declared the May 1989 assembly elections invalid and in September Francisco Rodríguez, with army backing, was made president. In the following month an attempted coup against Noriega was put down.

US invasion In December 1989, US President Bush ordered an invasion of the country with the intention of arresting Noriega. Several hundred people were killed during the operation. Noriega sought refuge in the Vatican embassy but eventually surrendered and was taken to the USA, where he was convicted in 1992 of charges relating to drug trafficking. Guillermo Endara became president and worked to balance Panama's aims against pressures from the USA, its most important partner, in such areas as banking. In October 1991 an attempted antigovernment coup by former officers loyal to Noriega was

thwarted. Constitutional amendments approved by the assembly in 1991 included abolition of the army and, although this was rejected in a referendum in 1992, in 1994 the army was formally banned as a constitutional entity. A withdrawal date of 1999 was set for US troops stationed in Panama since the 1989 invasion.

In May 1994 Ernesto Pérez Balladares of the centre-left Democratic Revolutionary Party (PRD) was elected president.

In an August 1998 referendum, voters rejected a proposed change to the constitution that would have allowed President Balladares to run for a second term. In May 1999, Mireya Moscoso, widow of former president Arnulfo Arias, defeated Martín Torrijos, son of a former dictator, to become Panama's first female president, and was inaugurated in September. A populist, she pledged to tackle poverty, halt privatization, and raise tariffs to protect farmers. She inherited an economy in recession.

In December 1999, the USA closed its last military bases on the Panama Canal, in accordance with the 1977 agreement, and left the zone at the end of the month, enabling Panama to take control of the canal formally.

In December 2000, President Moscoso announced formation of a Truth Commission to determine the fate of 150 people who disappeared between 1968 and 1989 under military regimes.

Pandit, Vijaya Lakshmi (1900–1990) Indian politician, member of parliament 1964–68. She was involved, with her brother Jawaharlal *Nehru, in the struggle for India's independence and was imprisoned three times by the British. She was the first woman to serve as president of the United Nations General Assembly, 1953–54, and held a number of political and diplomatic posts until her retirement 1968.

pan-Germanism movement that developed during the 19th century to encourage unity between German- and Dutch-speaking peoples in Austria, the Netherlands, Flanders, Luxembourg, and Switzerland. Encouraged by the unification of Germany after 1871, the movement had an increasingly high profile in the period up to 1914.

Pankhurst, Christabel (1880–1958) English campaigner for women's suffrage. She was the daughter of the English suffragette Emmeline Pankhurst. After 1918 she devoted herself to a religious movement.

Pankhurst, Emmeline (1858–1928) born **Emmeline Goulden**, English *suffragette. Founder of the Women's Social and Political Union (WSPU) in 1903, she launched the militant suffragette campaign in 1905. In 1926 she joined the Conservative Party and was a prospective Parliamentary candidate for Whitechapel.

Pankhurst, Sylvia Estelle (1882–1960) English campaigner for women's suffrage. She was the daughter of the English suffragette Emmeline Pankhurst. She became a pacifist in 1914 and in 1921 was imprisoned for six months for seditious publications. After the Italian invasion of Ethiopia in 1935, she devoted her life to that country's independence, settling there permanently in 1956. Her works include *The Suffrage Movement* (1931) and a biography of her mother, published in 1935.

Papagos, Alexander (1883–1955) Greek soldier and politician. He served in the Balkan Wars, World War I, and the Graeco-Turkish War. From 1936–40 he was chief of the army general staff. He conducted Greek military operations from 1940–41. From 1943–45 he was a prisoner in Germany. In 1949 he was recalled from retirement to crush the communist rebellion, and, on his success, was promoted to field marshal. In 1951 Papagos entered Greek politics as leader of a new Greek Rally party. He appealed to all loyal Greeks, regardless of party, to support him in his efforts 'to save the country';

his party was returned as the most powerful single party in November 1951 and in November 1952 gained a sweeping majority. His administration was authoritarian, though resting on undoubted popular support, and succeeded in restoring a considerable measure of economic stability to Greece. Papagos was born in Athens, Greece.

Papandreou, Andreas (1919–1996) Greek socialist politician, founder of the pan-Hellenic Socialist Movement (PASOK); prime minister 1981–89, and again 1993–96. He lost the 1989 election after being implicated in an alleged embezzlement scandal, involving the diversion of funds to the Greek government from the Bank of Crete, headed by George Koskotas. In January 1992 a trial cleared Papandreou of all corruption charges.

Papandreou, George (1888–1968) Greek politician, prime minister 1944 and 1963–65. After escaping from Greece in 1942 during the German occupation, he returned in 1944 to head a coalition government. However, his socialist credentials were suspected by the army, and he held office for only a few weeks. In 1961 he founded the Centre Union Party, and returned as prime minister in 1963 and 1964. A disagreement with King Constantine II in 1965 led to his resignation, and in 1967, when a coup established a military regime, he was placed under house arrest. His son Andreas *Papandreou carried forward his political beliefs.

Papen, Franz von (1879–1969) German right-wing politician. As chancellor in 1932, he negotiated the Nazi–Conservative alliance that made Hitler chancellor in 1933. He was envoy to Austria 1934–38 and ambassador to Turkey 1939–44. Although acquitted at the *Nuremberg trials, he was imprisoned by a German denazification court for three years.

Papua New Guinea country in the southwest Pacific, comprising the eastern part of the island of New Guinea, the Bismarck Archipelago, and part of the Solomon Islands.

Paraguay landlocked country in South America, bounded northeast by Brazil, south by Argentina, and northwest by Bolivia.

Paris, Treaty of any of various peace treaties signed in Paris, including: **1763** ending the Seven Years' War; **1783** (also known as the Peace of Versailles) recognizing American independence; **1814** and **1815** following the abdication and final defeat of Napoleon I; **1856** ending the Crimean War; **1898** ending the Spanish-American War; **1919–20** the conference preparing the Treaty of *Versailles at the end of World War I was held in Paris; **1947** after World War II, the peace treaties between the *Allies and Italy, Romania, Hungary, Bulgaria, and Finland; **1951** treaty signed by France, West Germany, Italy, Belgium, Netherlands, and Luxembourg, embodying the Schuman Plan to set up a single coal and steel authority; **1973** ending US participation in the *Vietnam War.

Park Chung Hee (1917–1979) South Korean politician, president 1963–79. Under his rule South Korea had one of the world's fastest-growing economies, but recession and his increasing authoritarianism led to his assassination in 1979.

Parks, Rosa (Louise McCauley) (1913–) US civil-rights activist. Her refusal to surrender her seat on a bus to a white passenger and her subsequent arrest and imprisonment spurred the Montgomery bus boycott in 1955, which ignited the *civil-rights movement in the USA.

parliamentary reform in Britain, the aftermath of the Revolutionary Wars saw a period of political agitation for parliamentary reform that was met by government repression. However, there was a gradual reform of the clearly corrupt and archaic voting system in the 19th century, with Reform Acts in 1832, 1867, and 1884.

The Industrial Revolution empowered the middle classes, who demanded and received a say in government, and by the end of the 19th century the franchise had been extended to male agricultural labourers (full male franchise came in 1918). The women's movement won its battle for the full right to vote in 1928 (women were granted limited franchise in 1918).

parliamentary reform acts UK acts of Parliament 1918, 1928, and 1971. The 19th century witnessed the gradual reform of the voting system in Britain and suffrage was extended in the 20th century. In 1918 the Representation of the People Act gave the vote in the UK to men over 21 years and to women over 30. In 1928 a further act gave women the vote from the age of 21. In 1971 the voting age for men and women was lowered to the age of 18.

partition division of a country into two or more nations. Ireland was divided into Northern Ireland and the Irish Republic under the Government of Ireland Act 1920. The division of the Indian subcontinent into India and Pakistan took place in 1947. Other examples of partition include Korea 1953 and Vietnam 1954.

partition separation of Ireland into the *Irish Free State and Northern Ireland under the Government of Ireland Act (1920). This was recognized by the *Anglo-Irish Treaty (1921) following the *Anglo-Irish War (1919–21). In the south, the nationalists were given independence from Britain within the British Commonwealth, with the setting up of the mainly Roman Catholic Irish Free State. In the north the unionists gained control over six of the nine counties of Ulster, those with a Protestant majority, and remained part of the UK as Northern Ireland.

Passchendaele, Battle of in World War I, successful but costly British operation to capture the Passchendaele ridge in western Flanders, part of the third Battle of *Ypres October–November 1917; British casualties numbered nearly 310,000. The name is often erroneously applied to the whole of the battle of Ypres, but Passchendaele was in fact just part of that battle.

pass laws South African laws that required the black population to carry passbooks (identity documents) at all times and severely restricted freedom of movement. The laws, a major cause of discontent, formed a central part of the policies of *apartheid. They were repealed in 1986.

Patel, (Sardar) V(allabhbhai) J(averabhai) (1875–1950) Indian political leader. A fervent follower of Mahatma *Gandhi and a leader of the Indian National Congress, he was deputy prime minister 1947–50, after independence.

Patten, Chris(topher Francis) (1944–) British Conservative politician, governor of Hong Kong 1992–97. He was MP for Bath 1979–1992 and Conservative Party chair 1990–92, orchestrating the party's campaign for the 1992 general election, in which he lost his parliamentary seat. He accepted the governorship of Hong Kong for the crucial five years prior to its transfer to China in 1997. He went on to take part in the reform of the Royal Ulster Constabulary.

Patton, George Smith (1885–1945) US general in World War II, known as 'Old Blood and Guts'. During World War I, he formed the first US tank force and led it in action in 1918. He was appointed to command the 2nd Armored Division in 1940 and became commanding general of the 1st Armored Corps in 1941. In 1942 he led the Western Task Force that landed at Casablanca, Morocco. After commanding the 7th Army in the invasion of Sicily, he led the 3rd Army across France and into Germany, reaching the Czech frontier.

Paul (1901–1964) King of the Hellenes (Greece) from 1947, when he succeeded his brother George II. He was the son of Constantine I. In 1938

he married Princess Frederika (1917–), daughter of the Duke of Brunswick.

Paul, Alice (1885–1977) US women's suffrage leader, social reformer, and lawyer. She was the author of the first Equal Rights Amendment to the US Constitution (1923).

Paulus, Friedrich von (1890–1957) German field marshal in World War II, responsible for much of the detailed planning of Operation *Barbarossa, the German invasion of the Soviet Union 1941, and commander of the forces that besieged Stalingrad (now Volgograd) 1942–43. He was captured and gave evidence for the prosecution at the Nuremberg trials before settling in East Germany.

Pawnee (Caddoan *pariki* **'horn')** member of an American Indian people who inhabited the lower Mississippi River Valley until the 17th–18th centuries when they moved to Nebraska on the Platte River after acquiring horses. Their language belongs to the Caddoan family. They adopted the buffalo-hunting lifestyle of the Plains Indian for part of the year, but maintained their traditional agricultural settlements. Their society was hierarchical, and astronomical observations dictated practical events. They fought the Dakota *Sioux and worked as scouts for European settlers. The Pawnee now live on a reservation in Oklahoma and number about 2,000 (1990). Many are cattle farmers and most are Christian.

Paz, (Estenssoro) Victor (1907–2001) Bolivian president 1952–56, 1960–64, and 1985–89. He founded and led the Movimiento Nacionalista Revolucionario (MNR), which seized power in 1952. His regime extended the vote to Indians, nationalized the country's largest tin mines, embarked on a programme of agrarian reform, and brought inflation under control.

Peace Corps US organization of trained men and women, established by President Kennedy in 1961. The Peace Corps provides skilled volunteer workers for developing countries, especially in the fields of teaching, agriculture, and health, for a period of two years.

Pearl Harbor US Pacific naval base on Oahu island, Hawaii, USA, the scene of a Japanese aerial attack on 7 December 1941, which brought the USA into World War II. The attack took place while Japanese envoys were holding so-called peace talks in Washington. More than 2,000 members of the US armed forces were killed, and a large part of the US Pacific fleet was destroyed or damaged.

The local commanders Admiral Kimmel and Lt-Gen Short were relieved of their posts and held responsible for the fact that the base was totally unprepared at the time of the attack, but recent information indicates that warnings of the attack given to the USA (by British intelligence and others) were withheld from Kimmel and Short by President Franklin D Roosevelt. US public opinion was very much against entering the war, and Roosevelt wanted an excuse to change popular sentiments and take the USA into the war. The Japanese, angered by US embargoes of oil and other war material and convinced that US entry into the war was inevitable, had hoped to force US concessions. Instead, the attack galvanized public opinion and raised anti-Japanese sentiment to fever pitch; war was declared shortly thereafter.

Pearse, Patrick Henry (1879–1916) Irish writer, educationalist, and revolutionary. He was prominent in the Gaelic revival, and a leader of the *Easter Rising in 1916. Proclaimed president of the provisional government, he was court-martialled and shot after its suppression. Pearse was a founding member of the Irish Volunteers, and was inducted into the Irish Republican Brotherhood (the Irish wing of the Fenian movement) in 1913. He came to believe that a 'blood sacrifice' was needed to awaken the slumbering Irish nation. In a famous graveside oration in 1915, he declared that 'Ireland unfree shall never be at peace'.

He was commander-in-chief of the Volunteers during the Easter Rising in 1916, and read the declaration of the Irish Republic. The rebellion that he led emerged in short order as a defining moment in modern Irish history, its authors as founding martyrs of modern Ireland, and the words of the declaration as the sacred text of modern Irish republicanism.

Pearson, Lester Bowles (1897–1972) Canadian politician, leader of the Liberal Party from 1958, prime minister 1963–68. He was awarded the Nobel Prize for Peace in 1957 for playing a key role in settling the *Suez Crisis of 1956 when as foreign minister 1948–57, he represented Canada at the United Nations (UN).

Pelikan, Jaroslav (Jan, Jr) (1923–) US historian of religion. He wrote 22 books, including the monumental 5-volume *Christian Tradition* (1971, 1974, 1978, 1984, 1989). His *Riddle of Roman Catholicism* (1959) sold many copies during the presidential campaign of John Kennedy in 1960. He called for dialogue between Christianity and Judaism.

Peng Dehuai (or **Peng Teh-huai) (1898–1974)** Chinese communist military leader and politician. As deputy commander in Zhu De's 8th Route Army, he played a leading role in the liberation war against Japan 1937–45, successfully using guerrilla tactics. He was made defence minister in 1954, but clashed with party leader Mao Zedong in August 1959 over economic policy and military modernization and was replaced by Lin Biao. Peng was later formally purged in December 1966, during the 'Cultural Revolution', and was to spend the remainder of his life in prison.

Peng Pai (or **P'eng P'ai) (1896–1929)** Chinese rural revolutionary. In 1924 at the *Guomindang (nationalist party) base at Guangzhou (Canton), he became secretary of the Peasants' Bureau and director of the Peasant Movement Training Institute. In 1925 he had helped form the Guangdong Provincial Peasant Association, which claimed 200,000 members. During the Northern Expedition of 1926–28 Peng organized China's first rural soviet. In the wake of Chiang Kai-shek's counter-revolution against the communists, however, Peng's soviet was crushed in 1928. He was captured and executed by the Guomindang.

Peng Zhen (1902–1997) Chinese communist politician, mayor of Beijing 1951–66, who was purged at the start of the Cultural Revolution (1966–69). As mayor of the capital, Beijing, from 1951, Peng became an influential figure in the new People's Republic and, during the early 1960s, was singled out as one of Mao's 'close comrades-in-arms'. However, the two fell out at the beginning of the Cultural Revolution and by mid-1966, following criticisms of his 'rightist' leanings by the ultra-leftist Red Guards (he was accused by *Mao Zedong of protecting party intellectuals who had been critical of the policies of his Great Leap Forward), Peng became the first Politburo member to be purged.

Pentagon the headquarters of the US Department of Defense, Arlington, Virginia from 1947, situated on the Potomac River opposite Washington, DC. One of the world's largest office buildings (five storeys high and five-sided, with a pentagonal central court), it houses the administrative and command headquarters for the US armed forces and has become synonymous with the military establishment bureaucracy.

In September 2001, as part of a coordinated terrorist attack on the USA, the Pentagon was severely damaged when a hijacked aircraft was crashed into its northwest wall, bringing part of the structure down and killing 126 people.

Pentagon Papers top-secret US Defense Department report on the history of US involvement in the Vietnam War that was leaked to the *New York Times* by Defense Department employee Daniel Ellsberg in June 1971, fuelling the antiwar movement. President Richard Nixon tried to stop publication, but the Supreme Court ruled in favour of the press.

People's Budget in UK history, the Liberal government's budget of 1909 to finance social reforms and naval rearmament. The chancellor of the Exchequer David Lloyd George proposed graded and increased income tax and a 'supertax' on high incomes. The budget aroused great debate and precipitated a constitutional crisis.

Percival, Arthur (1887–1966) British general. He took command of British forces in Malaya June 1941 and barely had time to consolidate his position before the Japanese invaded December 1941. He was keenly aware of the deficiencies in his defences but could extract no further support from Britain and was forced to surrender 15 February 1942. He was imprisoned in Manchuria but was present aboard the USS *Missouri* to see the Japanese formally surrender 2 September 1945.

Peres, Shimon (1923–) Israeli Labour politician, prime minister 1984–86 and 1995–96. He was prime minister, then foreign minister, under a power-sharing agreement with the leader of the Likud Party, Yitzhak *Shamir. From 1989 to 1990 he was finance minister in a Labour–Likud coalition. As foreign minister in Yitzhak Rabin's Labour government from 1992, he negotiated the 1993 peace agreement with the *Palestine Liberation Organization (PLO). He shared the Nobel Prize for Peace in 1994 with Yitzhak *Rabin and PLO leader Yassir *Arafat for their agreement of an accord on Palestinian self-rule.

Following the assassination of Rabin in November 1995, Peres succeeded him as prime minister, and pledged to continue the peace process in which they had both been so closely involved, but in May 1996 he was defeated in Israel's first direct elections for prime minister.

perestroika (Russian 'restructuring') in Soviet politics, the wide-ranging economic and political reforms initiated from 1985 by Mikhail Gorbachev, finally leading to the demise of the Soviet Union. Originally, in the economic sphere, *perestroika* was conceived as involving 'intensive development' concentrating on automation and improved labour efficiency. It evolved to attend increasingly to market indicators and incentives ('market socialism') and the gradual dismantling of the Stalinist central-planning system, with decision-taking being devolved to self-financing enterprises.

Pérez de Cuéllar, Javier (1920–) Peruvian politician and diplomat, fifth secretary general of the United Nations 1982–91, prime minister of Peru from 2000. He raised the standing of the UN by his successful diplomatic efforts to end the Iran–Iraq War in 1988 and secure the independence of Namibia in 1989. He was a candidate in the Peruvian presidential elections of 1995, but was defeated by his opponent Alberto Fujimori. After Fujimori's resignation in 2000, Pérez de Cuéllar was appointed prime minister by President Valentín Paniagua.

Pérez Jiménez, Marcos (1914–2001) Venezuelan president 1952–58. He led the military junta that overthrew the Acción Democrática government of Rómulo Gallegos in 1948 and was made provisional president in 1952. In 1953 he was approved as constitutional president by congress. His regime had a reputation as the most repressive in Venezuelan history. It also encouraged European immigration and undertook massive public works in the capital, Caracas.

Perkins, Frances (1882–1965) US public official. She became the first female cabinet officer when she served as secretary of labour under F D Roosevelt 1933–45. Under Harry Truman she was a member of the federal civil service commission 1946–53.

Perón, (María Estela) Isabel (1931–) born **María Estela Isabel Martínez**, Argentine president 1974–76, and third wife of Juan Perón. She succeeded him after he died in office in 1974 (she had been elected vice-president in 1973), but labour unrest, inflation, and political violence pushed the country to the brink of chaos. Accused of corruption in 1976, she was held under house arrest for five years. She went into exile in Spain in 1981.

Perón, Eva ('Evita') Duarte de (1919–1952) born **María Eva Duarte**, Argentine populist leader. A successful radio actor, she became the second wife of Juan *Perón in 1945. When he became president the following year, she became his chief adviser and virtually ran the health and labour ministries, devoting herself to helping the poor, improving education, and achieving women's suffrage. She founded a social welfare organization called the Eva Perón Foundation. She was politically astute and sought the vice-presidency in 1951, but was opposed by the army and withdrew. After her death from cancer in 1952, Juan Perón's political strength began to decline.

Perón, Juan Domingo (1895–1974) Argentine politician, dictator 1946–55 and from 1973 until his death. His populist appeal to the poor was enhanced by the charisma and political work of his second wife Eva ('Evita') Perón. After her death in 1952 his popularity waned and, with increasing economic difficulties and labour unrest, he was deposed in a military coup in 1955. He fled to Paraguay and, in 1960, to Spain. He returned from exile to the presidency in 1973, but died in office in 1974, and was succeeded by his third wife, Isabel Perón.

Pershing, John Joseph (1860–1948)
US general. He served in the Spanish-American War in 1898, the Philippines 1899–1903, and Mexico 1916–17. In World War I, he stuck to the principle of using US forces as a coherent formation, and refused to attach regiments or brigades to British or French divisions. He commanded the American Expeditionary Force sent to France 1917–18.

Peru country in South America, on the Pacific, bounded north by Ecuador and Colombia, east by Brazil and Bolivia, and south by Chile.

government The 1993 constitution provides for a president, as head of state, elected by universal suffrage for a five-year term, renewable only once, and a single-chamber, 120-member national congress, similarly elected by proportional representation from a single national list of candidates for the same length of term. The president appoints a prime minister, as head of government, and a council of ministers.

history The Chimu culture flourished from about 1200 and was gradually superseded by the Inca empire, building on 800 years of Andean civilization and covering a large part of South America. Civil war had weakened the Incas when the conquistador Pizarro arrived from Spain 1531 and began raiding, looting, and enslaving the people. He executed the last of the Inca emperors, Atahualpa, 1533. Before Pizarro's assassination 1541, Spanish rule was firmly established.

independence A native revolt by Túpac Amarú 1780 failed, and during the successful rebellions by the European settlers in other Spanish possessions in South America 1810–22, Peru remained the Spanish government's headquarters; it was the last to achieve independence 1824. It attempted union with Bolivia 1836–39. It fought a naval war against Spain 1864–66, and in the Pacific War against Chile 1879–83 over the nitrate fields of

the Atacama Desert, Peru was defeated and lost three provinces (one, Tacna, was returned 1929). Other boundary disputes were settled by arbitration 1902 with Bolivia, 1927 with Colombia, and 1942 with Ecuador. Peru declared war on Germany and Japan February 1945.

dictatorships Peru was ruled by right-wing dictatorships from the mid-1920s until 1945, when free elections returned. Although Peru's oldest political organization, (the American Popular Revolutionary Alliance (APRA)), was the largest party in Congress, it was constantly thwarted by smaller conservative groups, anxious to protect their business interests. APRA was founded in the 1920s to fight imperialism throughout South America, but Peru was the only country where it became established.

military rule In 1948 a group of army officers led by General Manuel Odría ousted the elected government, temporarily banned APRA, and installed a military junta. Odría became president 1950 and remained in power until 1956. In 1963 military rule ended, and Fernando Belaúnde Terry, the joint candidate of the Popular Action (AP) and Christian Democrats (PDC) parties, won the presidency, while APRA took the largest share of the chamber of deputies seats.

After economic problems and industrial unrest, Belaúnde was deposed in a bloodless coup 1968, and the army returned to power led by General Velasco Alvarado. Velasco introduced land reform, with private estates being turned into cooperative farms, but he failed to return any land to Indian peasant communities, and the Maoist guerrillas of Sendero Luminoso ('Shining Path') became increasingly active in the Indian region of southern Peru.

economic and social crisis Another bloodless coup, 1975, brought in General Morales Bermúdez. A new constitution was adopted 1979. Elections were held for the presidency and both chambers of Congress 1980 and Belaúnde was re-elected. Belaúnde embarked on a programme of agrarian and industrial reform, but at the end of his presidency, in 1985, the country was again in a state of economic and social crisis. His constitutionally elected successor was the young Social Democrat, Alan García Pérez, who embarked on a programme to cleanse the army and police of the old guard. By 1986 about 1,400 had elected to retire. After trying to expand the economy with price and exchange controls, in 1987 he announced his intention to nationalize the banks and insurance companies but delayed the move, after a vigorous campaign against the proposal.

In 1989 the International Development Bank suspended credit to Peru because it was six months behind in debt payments. The annual inflation rate to April was 4,329%. García Pérez declared his support for the Sandinista government in Nicaragua and criticized US policy throughout Latin America. The party of Pérez, constitutionally barred from seeking re-election, saw its popularity slip in the November 1989 municipal elections. Novelist Mario Vargas Llosa, the presidential candidate of the centre-right Democratic Front coalition, was long considered the favourite to succeed García Pérez. However, Alberto Fujimori, the son of Japanese immigrants and leader of a new party, Change 90, forced a run-off in April 1990 elections. In June, Fujimori, a political novice, won a substantial victory. Soon after taking office he instituted a drastic economic adjustment programme in an attempt to halt Peru's inflation and to pay foreign debt. In August 1990 an attempt to assassinate him failed.

opposition to Fujimori In April 1992, faced with mounting opposition to the government and fears of a military coup, Fujimori allied himself with the army, suspended the constitution, and sacked half of the country's top judges, declaring them to be corrupt. The move, which he announced as a crackdown on rebel leaders and drug traffickers, brought international criticism (including a suspension of US humanitarian aid) and a challenge from his deputy, Máximo San Roman, who branded him a dictator. Fujimori said he would return to democratic rule within a year.

rebel leader arrested Sendero Luminoso guerrillas stepped up their campaign of terror July 1992 in response to a government crackdown. Their leader, Abimael Guzmán Reynoso, was arrested in September, along with several other high-ranking members of the group. All received life sentences in October, and terrorist attacks intensified in response. In July 1994 Fujimori issued an ultimatum to the guerrillas to surrender within four months under a so-called 'repentance law'.

constitutional reform The governing coalition won most seats in elections to a new unicameral congress November 1992, and in January 1993 the constitution was restored. A new constitution, allowing President Fujimori to seek re-election, was approved by referendum and adopted December 1993. In 1994 Fujimori dismissed his wife, Susana Higuchi, as first lady on the grounds of disloyalty. Higuchi later failed in her attempts to register a new political party as a vehicle for launching a presidential bid.

In February 1995 a long-standing border dispute with Ecuador, which had earlier erupted into armed military clashes, was resolved when the two countries signed a truce. With the economy improving, Fujimori was re-elected April 1995, easily defeating his main challenger, former United Nations secretary general Javier Pérez de Cuéllar. The controversial granting of an amnesty to those previously convicted of human rights abuses,

June 1995, was seen by some as an attempt by the president to win favour with the military. In March 1996 Dante Cordova resigned as prime minister in opposition to the rapid pace of free-market reforms being introduced by President Fujimori.

hostage crisis Marxist Tupac Amaru Revolutionary Movement (MRTA) guerrillas besieged the Japanese embassy in Lima December 1996, taking hostage around 500 diplomats, politicians, and business leaders. The rebels' demands were for up to 500 prisoners to be freed from prison, including their leader Victor Polay, and for President Fujimori to reverse his free-market economic policies. Over the ensuing weeks, several groups of hostages were released, leaving 74 still captive by January 1997. Education minister Domingo Palermo acted as Peru's official negotiator. Discussions between President Fujimori and the Japanese Prime Minister Ryutaro Hashimoto in February signalled some progress in that the Peruvian government agreed that rebel leader Nestor Cerpa could take part in negotiations. However, Fujimori's refusal to bow to the rebels' demand for the release of imprisoned comrades remained a stumbling block. In April 1997 the siege was dramatically ended and all the guerrillas killed by specially trained government forces, enhancing Fujimori's reputation.

In June 1998, Javier Valle Riestra, despite being a strong critic of the president, was appointed prime minister but in August he resigned and was replaced by Alberto Pandolfi, who had held the post before June. Also in August, President Alberto Fujimori sacked his armed forces chief, General Nicolás Hermoza. Amidst internal confusion, in October 1998 Peru signed a deal with Ecuador to end a 157-year long frontier dispute. In early January 1999 Fujimori appointed a new prime minister, Victor Joy Way, who also received the economics portfolio.

He was replaced, in October 1999, with Alberto Bustamante.

presidential elections 2000 In early 2000, President Fujimori sought an unprecedented and constitutionally unsound third term in office, and in May, was re-elected for a third term amid claims from the opposition candidate, his supporters, and from election monitors from the Organization of American States (OAS), that the counting system had been fraudulent. The US State Department branded the victory invalid, saying democracy was under serious threat. Fujimori pledged democratic and economic reforms and appointed an opposition leader, Federico Salas, as his new prime minister. He also appointed Carlos Bolona, a prominent free-marketeer, in an effort to calm foreign investors. In response to repeated protests, in September, he pledged to call new presidential elections in April 2001, in which he would not stand. Fujimori's vice-president, however, resigned in October after government plans to tie the promised elections to an amnesty for human rights abuses.

the Montesinos affair and Fujimori's resignation In September 2000, the opposition called for the arrest of Vladimiro Montesinos, head of the national intelligence service, who had been proved to have bribed a member of congress. He fled to Panama, which refused to accept him, and he returned to Peru as a fugitive in October. Fujimori ordered a manhunt for Montesinos, but continued to reject calls to resign. In order to prevent a coup, he fired his armed forces chief and three top generals. In November, a judge charged the still elusive Montesinos with corruption and abusing human rights (investigations in December revealed he was also involved in drug-trafficking and the arms trade), while Congress proposed to oust Fujimori on grounds on 'moral incapacity'. A new opposition president of Congress, Valentín Paniagua, was elected, and Fujimori, after fleeing to Japan, finally resigned. Paniagua was elected interim president on 22 November, appointed former United Nations secretary general Javier *Pérez de Cuéllar as prime minister, swore in a new cabinet, and purged the military of generals with close links to Montesinos. In January 2001, Paniagua established a Truth Council to investigate the disappearance of 4,000 people during the 1980s and 1990s 'dirty war' between security forces and leftist guerrillas.

It emerged that Fujimori had Japanese as well as Peruvian citizenship, making it unlikely he would be extradited. However, it emerged in March 2001 that, in addition to charges of dereliction of duty, Fujimori could face murder charges regarding the alleged execution of some of the rebels who were involved in the hostage siege at the Japanese embassy in Lima in 1997. The charges, if pressed, would increase pressure on Japan for Fujimori's extradition.

elections in 2001 Alejandro Toledo, an economist of Andean-Indian descent, was elected president of Peru in June 2001, narrowly defeating Alan García, a populist former president. Roberto Dañino became prime minister. International observers said the election was Peru's fairest in years and an important step on the road to democracy.

earthquake An earthquake measuring 7.9 on the Richter scale hit the cities of Arequipa and Moquegua in southern Peru, in June 2001. It killed more than 100 people, and left over 46,000 homeless.

Montesinos captured Vladimiro Montesinos was flown home on 25 June 2001 to face trial on charges of arms- and drug-dealing, embezzlement, directing death squads, and money-laundering. Montesinos had been arrested in Venezuela two days earlier and extradited to Lima.

car bomb in capital In March 2002 a powerful car bomb exploded near the US embassy in Lima, killing 9 people and injuring up to 40. The blast occurred three days before US president George W Bush was due to visit Lima as part of a Latin American tour. However, Bush said he would not be deterred by acts of terrorism and continued with his visit. The bomb was believed to be the work of the Sendero Luminoso.

Pétain, (Henri) Philippe Benoni Omer Joseph (1856–1951) French general and head of state. Voted in as prime minister in June 1940, Pétain signed an armistice with Germany on 22 June before assuming full powers on 16 July. His authoritarian regime, established at Vichy, collaborated with the Germans and proposed a reactionary 'National Revolution' for France under the slogan 'Work, Family, Fatherland'. Convinced in 1940 of Britain's imminent defeat, Pétain accepted Germany's terms for peace, including the occupation of northern France. In December 1940 he dismissed his deputy Pierre *Laval, who wanted to side with the Axis powers, but bowed to German pressures to reinstate him in April 1942. With Germany occupying the whole of France from that November, Pétain found himself head, in name only, of a puppet state. Removed from France by the German army in 1944, he returned voluntarily and was tried and condemned to death for treason in August 1945. He died in prison on the Ile d'Yeu, his sentence having been commuted to life imprisonment.

Peter II (1923–1970) King of Yugoslavia 1934–45. He succeeded his father, Alexander I, and assumed the royal power after the overthrow of the regency in 1941. He escaped to the UK after the German invasion, and married Princess Alexandra of Greece 1944. He was dethroned in 1945 when Marshal Tito came to power and the Soviet-backed federal republic was formed.

Petkov, Nicolai (1889–1947) Bulgarian politician. He was one of the founders of the Fatherland Front, signing the Moscow armistice which brought Bulgaria into the World War II on the side of the Allies in September 1944. When the Fatherland Front was formed, Petkov became deputy premier, but resigned in August 1945 and went into opposition, thus incurring the enmity of the communists, who had previously been his colleagues. He was arrested in June 1947 and charged with complicity in a military conspiracy, which he strenuously denied. The trial led to protests by Britain and the USA, but Petkov was sentenced to death and executed. He was born near Sofia, Bulgaria.

Petrie, (William Matthew) Flinders (1853–1942) English archaeologist who excavated sites in Egypt (the pyramids at El Gîza, the temple at Tanis, the Greek city of Naucratis in the Nile delta, Tell el Amarna, Naqada, Abydos, and Memphis) and Palestine from 1880. He was knighted in 1923.

Petrov case controversy in Australia resulting from the defection of two Soviet embassy officials, Vladimir and Evdokia Petrov, in 1954. Petrov claimed to have been a Russian spy and prime minster *Menzies set up a royal commission into Soviet espionage in Australia on the eve of a federal election. Full diplomatic relations between Australia and the Soviet Union were suspended until 1959 but the major repercussions were on the domestic political scene. Labor leader Herbert Evatt (1894–1965) and his staff were linked with communism and in 1955 the right wing of the Australian Labor Party split away to form the Democratic Labor Party. Subsequent evidence has suggested that Menzies manipulated the judges at the commission and has borne out Evatt's claim that the Menzies government orchestrated the whole affair for electoral advantage.

Phalangist member of a Lebanese military organization (**Phalanges Libanaises**), since 1958 the political and military force of the Maronite Church in Lebanon. The Phalangists' unbending right-wing policies and resistance to the introduction of democratic institutions were among the contributing factors to the civil war in Lebanon.

Phan Boi Chau (1867–1940) Vietnamese nationalist. Together with *Phan Chau Trinh, he dominated the anti-colonial movement in Vietnam in the early 20th century. In 1912, in China, he was involved in the establishment of the Revival Society (Quang Phuc Hoi), which sought to bring about a democratic republic in Vietnam. Following his arrest in 1925, he was sentenced to life imprisonment. The ensuing public outcry led to his release and he spent the rest of his life in gently guarded retirement at Hué.

Phan Chau Trinh (1872–1926) Vietnamese nationalist. Along with *Phan Boi Chau, he was a leading figure in the anti-colonial movement in Vietnam in the early 20th century. In contrast to Phan Boi Chau's commitment to a revolutionary monarchism, Phan Chau Trinh advocated Western-style republicanism. His funeral in 1926 was held in Saigon, provoking unprecedented mass demonstrations and student strikes. This heralded a new phase in the anti-colonial struggle in Vietnam, one that would involve greater popular participation.

Phibunsongkhram, Luang (1898–1964) Prime minister of Thailand (1938–44 and 1948–57). He became minister of defence (1934–38), and finally emerged as prime minister in 1938. He was pro-Japanese, and promoted a nationalistic policy which ended in his welcoming the Japanese armies that conquered South-East Asia in 1941–42. In 1944, faced with the prospect of Japanese decline, he was deposed by his rival Pridi Phanomyong. However, the difficulties of the country under Pridi's rule gave Phibun the opportunity to return to power. Pridi was overthrown in 1947 and a year later Phibun was again prime minister. He now pursued a policy of alliance with the United States, and became strongly anticommunist and anti-Chinese. Under his leadership, Thailand entered the American fold and became a leading member of SEATO (South-East Asia Treaty Organization) in 1954. In 1957 he was again deposed, this time after a corrupt election, and died in exile in Japan.

Philby, Kim (Harold Adrian Russell) (1912–1988) British intelligence officer from 1940 and Soviet agent from 1933. He was liaison officer in Washington 1949–51, when he was confirmed to be a double agent and asked to resign. Named in 1963 as having warned Guy Burgess and Donald Maclean (also double agents) that their activities were known, he fled to the USSR and became a Soviet citizen and a general in the KGB. A fourth member of the ring was Anthony Blunt.

Philip, Duke of Edinburgh (1921–) Prince of the UK, husband of Elizabeth II, a grandson of George I of Greece and a great-great-grandson of Queen Victoria. He was born in Corfu, Greece, but brought up in England.

Philippines country in southeast Asia, on an archipelago of more than 7,000 islands west of the Pacific Ocean and south of the Southeast Asian mainland.

Philippine Sea, Battle of in World War II, decisive US naval victory June 1944 in the Philippine Sea, east of the islands; the last of the great carrier battles, it broke the back of the Japanese navy.

phoney war the period in World War II between September 1939, when the Germans had occupied Poland, and April 1940, when the invasions of Denmark and Norway took place. During this time there were few signs of hostilities in Western Europe;

indeed, Hitler made some attempts to arrange a peace settlement with Britain and France.

Pieck, Wilhelm (1876–1960) German communist politician. He was a leader of the 1919 *Spartacist revolt and a founder of the Socialist Unity Party in 1946. He opposed both the Weimar Republic and Nazism. From 1949 he was president of East Germany; the office was abolished on his death.

Pierlot, Hubert (1883–1963) Belgian politician. A member of the Social Christian party, he was prime minister from 1939. After the capitulation of King Leopold in 1940, Pierlot became head of the Belgian government in exile in London, England. After Belgium was liberated, Pierlot headed a government from September 1944–February 1945. He was minister of state until 1954. Pierlot was born in Cugnon, Belgium, and educated at Louvain University.

Pigs, Bay of inlet on the south coast of Cuba about 145 km/90 mi southwest of Havana. It was the site of an unsuccessful invasion attempt to overthrow the government of Fidel *Castro by some 1,500 US-sponsored Cuban exiles 17–20 April 1961; 1,173 were taken prisoner. The failure of the invasion strengthened Castro's power in Cuba and his links to the USSR. It also sparked the *Cuban missile crisis of 1962.

The creation of this antirevolutionary force by the Central Intelligence Agency (CIA) had been authorized by the Eisenhower administration, and the project was executed under that of J F Kennedy. In 1962 most of the Cuban prisoners were ransomed for US$53 million in food and medicine. The CIA internal investigation report in the 1960s into the Bay of Pigs disaster was released for the first time after 36 years in February 1998. It blamed the agency for the failure, contending that Kennedy had been misinformed and poorly advised.

Piłsudski, Józef (Klemens) (1867–1935)
Polish nationalist politician, dictator
from 1926. Born in Russian Poland, he
founded the Polish Socialist Party in
1892 and was twice imprisoned for
anti-Russian activities. During World
War I he commanded a Polish force to
fight for Germany and evicted the
Russians from eastern Poland but fell
under suspicion of intriguing with the
Allies and was imprisoned by the
Germans in 1917–18. When Poland
became independent in 1919, he was
elected chief of state, and led a Polish
attack on invading Soviet forces in
1920, driving the Soviets out of Poland.
He retired in 1923, but in 1926 led
a military coup that established his
dictatorship until his death.

Pindling, Lynden (Oscar) (1930–2000)
Bahamian politician, prime minister
1967–92. In the 1960s he became leader
of the centrist Progressive Liberal Party
(PLP), formed in 1953. Attracting
support from the islands'
demographically dominant black
community, the PLP won the 1967
House of Assembly elections, the first
to be held on a full adult voting
register, and Pindling became the
Bahamas' first black prime minister.
He led the country to independence,
within the British Commonwealth,
in 1973 and successfully expanded the
tourist industry, but accusations of
government corruption grew in the
1980s and the PLP lost power in 1992.
After further electoral defeat in 1997,
Pindling retired as PLP leader.

Pinochet (Ugarte), Augusto (1915–)
Chilean military dictator 1973–89.
He came to power when a coup
backed by the US Central Intelligence
Agency (CIA) ousted and killed
President Salvador Allende. He
governed ruthlessly, crushing all
political opposition (including more
than 3,000 people who 'vanished' or
were killed), but also presiding over
the country's economic expansion in
the 1980s, stimulated further by free-
market reforms. He was voted out of
power when general elections were
held in December 1989, but remained
head of the armed forces until March
1998 when he became senator-for-life.
In January 2001, he was arrested on the
charge of organizing the killings of
77 left-wing activists and union
leaders. However, in July 2001,
Chile's appeal court ruled that he was
mentally unfit to stand trial, ending
lengthy efforts to prosecute him for
human rights abuses.

**Plaatje, Sol(omon) T(shekisho)
(1876–1932)** South African novelist,
journalist, and political campaigner.
Plaatje is best known for *Mhudi:
An Epic of South African Native Life
a Hundred Years Ago* (1930; written
c. 1920–21), the first novel in English
by a black South African. In 1912 he
was a founding member of the South
African Native National Congress
(SANNC; later the *African National
Congress (ANC)). He also produced
works on the Setswana language,
including a Setswana–English
dictionary, and translations of
Shakespeare into Setswana.

Plaid Cymru (Welsh **'Party of Wales'**)
Welsh nationalist political party
established in 1925. Its aim is
separation from and independence
of the UK, in order to safeguard the
culture, language, and economic life
of Wales. In 2001 it had about 15,000
members. In 1966 the first Plaid Cymru
member of Parliament was elected.
Four Plaid Cymru MPs were returned
in both the 1997 and 2001 general
elections. At Westminster, the Plaid
Cymru MPs form a single
parliamentary grouping with the
Scottish National Party, following a
formal pact signed in 1986. The party
has 17 seats in the Welsh Assembly,
and two members in the European
Parliament (2001).

**Plekhanov, Georgi Valentinovich
(1857–1918)** Russian Marxist
revolutionary and theorist, founder
of the *Menshevik party. He led the

first populist demonstration in St Petersburg, became a Marxist and, with Lenin, edited the newspaper *Iskra* ('Spark'). In 1903 his opposition to Lenin led to the Bolshevik–Menshevik split.

Plessy v. Ferguson US Supreme Court decision of 1896 that upheld the legality of racial segregation with the doctrine of 'separate but equal' public facilities. This standard for segregation legitimized the widespread *Jim Crow laws in the South and remained in force until 1954, when it was finally overturned by the * *Brown* v. *Board of Education* case.

Pleven, René (1901–1989) French centrist politician; prime minister 1950–51 and 1951–52, and holding ministerial office for much of the Fourth Republic. In October 1950 he put forward a plan for a European Defence Community (EDC) prepared by Jean Monnet. The proposal caused bitter rifts in France's parties and finally foundered when, under Pierre *Mendès-France's premiership, the National Assembly failed to ratify the EDC Treaty in August 1954. After a decade out of government, he served as justice minister under President Georges *Pompidou 1969–73.

PLO abbreviation for *Palestine Liberation Organization, founded in 1964 to bring about an independent state of Palestine.

pogrom (Russian **'destruction'**) unprovoked violent attack on an ethnic group, particularly Jews, carried out with official sanction. The Russian pogroms against Jews began in 1881, after the assassination of Tsar Alexander II, and again in 1903–06; persecution of the Jews remained constant until the Russian Revolution. Later there were pogroms in Eastern Europe, especially in Poland after 1918, and in Germany under Hitler (see *Holocaust).

Poincaré, Raymond Nicolas Landry (1860–1934) French moderate republican politician and president 1913–20. He served as prime minister

and foreign minister 1912–13, 1922–24 (when he ordered the occupation of the German Ruhr in lieu of reparations for war damage), and 1926–29 (when he successfully stabilized the franc).

Poindexter, John Marlane (1936–) US rear admiral and Republican government official. In 1981 he joined the Reagan administration's National Security Council (NSC) and became national security adviser in 1985. As a result of the *Irangate scandal, Poindexter was forced to resign in 1986, along with his assistant, Oliver North.

Poindexter, Miles (1868–1946) US representative and senator. Although he began as a Progressive, he opposed President Woodrow Wilson's international policies and became leader of the anticommunist 'Red Scare' of 1919. He was US ambassador to Peru (1923–28).

Poland country in eastern Europe, bounded north by the Baltic Sea, northeast by Lithuania, east by Belarus and Ukraine, south by the Czech Republic and the Slovak Republic, and west by Germany.

 government Under the revised constitution adopted 1990–91, Poland has a limited presidential political system. The executive president, directly elected for a maximum of two consecutive five-year terms in a two-round majority contest, has responsibility for military and foreign affairs and has the authority to appoint the prime minister, dissolve parliament, call referenda, veto bills, and impose martial law. There is a two-chamber legislature, comprising a 460-member lower assembly, the Sejm (parliament), and a 100-member upper chamber, the Senat (senate). Deputies are elected to the Sejm for four-year terms by means of proportional representation in free, multiparty contests. The Sejm passes bills, adopts the state budget and economic plan, and appoints a 24-member executive council of ministers, headed by a chair, or prime minister. The Senat is elected on a provincial basis, each province returning two senators, except Warsaw and Katowice, which elect three. The Senat has the power of veto in specified areas, which can be overridden by a two-thirds Sejm vote. There are 49 provinces under appointed governors and 2,348 elected local councils.

history Poland had been occupied by German forces during *World War II, and had been liberated by Soviet forces by March 1945. During the war some 6 million Polish citizens (including some 3 million Jews, and one third of the educated elite) had perished, and the country's economy and social structure had been shattered.

As the Soviet army had moved into central Poland in mid-1944, the USSR formed a Committee of National Liberation in Lublin. The Lublin administration started a programme of radical land reform, and in April 1945 a 20-year treaty of 'friendship, mutual assistance, and post-war cooperation' was signed between Poland and the USSR.

adjustments to Poland's borders As a result of the Tehran, Yalta, and Potsdam conferences (in November 1943, February 1945, and July–August 1945 respectively) the USA, the USSR, and Britain decided that the USSR would receive the eastern provinces of prewar Poland (including Wilno (Vilnius) and Lviv), and that Poland would acquire corresponding German territory in the west. A treaty between Poland and the USSR in August 1945 (ratified in 1946) established Poland's eastern frontier at the Curzon Line. Poland lost 181,350 sq km/70,000 sq mi in the east to the USSR, but gained 101,000 sq km/39,000 sq mi in the west from Germany.

In April 1945 the Oder and the Western Neisse rivers became the new western border, leaving nearly all Silesia and Pomerania and half of East Prussia in Poland. The German population of these provinces had fled

or was expelled, being replaced by Poles moved from the former eastern provinces. The new western border was recognized by the Soviet bloc, including East Germany (1951), and was later recognized as the de facto frontier by West Germany (1970).

the communists come to power Poland emerged from the war with few national minorities: the Jews had been almost totally exterminated, the Ukrainians and Belorussians absorbed into the USSR, and the Germans expelled. A Provisional Government of National Unity was formed as a short-lived compromise in June 1945 between the communist Lublin Committee, and the Polish Peasant Party of Stanislaw Mikołajczyk, who had been premier of the government-in-exile in London during 1943–44, after Gen *Sikorski's death in 1943. The Western powers recognized the new government in Warsaw.

The premier of the new government was the left-wing socialist Edward Osóbka-Morawski, with the communist Władysław *Gomułka and Mikołajczyk as deputy premiers. Mikołajczyk had the goodwill of many elements who adopted a negative attitude to the regime. His position was difficult, as he was the leader of the opposition, who had joined the government for a common purpose pending the promised general election. The key positions in the administration and economic affairs belonged to the communist Polish Workers' Party, which could rely, if necessary, on the support of Soviet troops. Manipulation and intimidation ensured that the communist-controlled 'Democratic Bloc' won the elections, held eventually in January 1947. Mikołajczyk fled the country.

Stalinist rule The Polish government of 1947 was not democratic in the Western sense. Reconstruction of the shattered country, especially its ruined cities, became a major task, and was helped by the industrial facilities acquired from Germany. The United Nations also provided aid. In December 1948 the few remaining socialists merged with the communists to form the Polish United Workers' Party (PUWP), which continued to rule Poland up to 1989. The two peasant parties merged into the United Peasant Party, and all political parties belonged to the communist-controlled National Unity Front.

The collectivization of farming, condemnation of Tito's Yugoslavia, and an extensive party purge that removed the moderate Gomulka from office (1948–49) indicated growing Stalinist tendencies and the dependence of the Polish government (headed by Bolesław Bierut) on the USSR. The new constitution of 1952 followed the Soviet model, only government-sponsored candidates standing at elections. Poland joined *Comecon in 1949 and the *Warsaw Pact in 1955.

Increasing friction between the government and the Catholic Church, the one powerful force still resisting Soviet penetration, led to the imprisonment of the primate, Cardinal Stefan Wyszynski, in October 1953. Although Poland increased its heavy industrial output, agriculture was undermined by collectivization. Discontent grew, owing to the scarcity of basic consumer goods, the harsh labour conditions, and the oppressive administration.

Poland under Gomułka After Khrushchev's denunciation of Stalin in the USSR serious rioting, leading to 53 deaths, broke out in the Polish city of Poznan in opposition to Soviet 'exploitation' and food shortages (June 1956). Control of the PUWP went in October 1956 to anti-Stalinist elements under the pragmatic Gomułka, who had previously been imprisoned. Soviet personnel were expelled, including the minister of defence, Marshal Rokossovsky, and some liberalizing reforms initiated. Most collective farms were dissolved, and relations with the church improved.

The initial liberal impetus of the Gomułka regime slackened as time went by, while Poland continued to industrialize. Church–state relations became uneasy, especially in 1966 over the Polish bishops' 'reconciliation gesture' to the German episcopate, a gesture that the Polish government interpreted as unpatriotic. Student riots in March 1968 and a power struggle within the party led to 'anti-Zionist' purges in the party, armed forces, and among intellectuals. Meanwhile economic performance worsened and disenchantment with Gomułka grew. An unexpected increase in food prices in December 1970 precipitated strikes, riots, and savage government reprisals in the Baltic ports of Gdansk, Gdynia, and Szczecin. Compelled to resign, Gomułka was replaced as PUWP leader by the Silesia party boss Edward *Gierek.

Gierek takes over Gierek calmed the deteriorating situation with price freezes, which were renewed in 1972. Gierek aimed at raising living standards, and increased technological imports from the West, although this added to the country's mounting foreign debt. The process by which Poland had been transformed from being a principally agricultural country in 1939 to a highly industrialized nation continued. Although remaining firmly allied to the Soviet Union, Gierek's regime was relatively tolerant and progressive by Eastern Bloc standards.

In the summer of 1976 proposals were made to increase the price of basic foodstuffs, but these were withdrawn in the face of widespread strikes and demonstrations. Opposition to the Gierek regime, which was accused of corruption, mounted in 1979 after a visit to his homeland by the recently elected Pope John Paul II.

the rise of Solidarity Strikes in Warsaw in 1980, following a poor harvest and meat-price increases, rapidly spread across the country. The government attempted to appease workers by entering into pay negotiations with unofficial strike committees, but at the Gdansk shipyards demands emerged for permission to form free, independent trade unions.

The government conceded the right to strike, and in Gdansk 1980 the *Solidarity (Solidarnosc) union was formed under the leadership of Lech *Wałęsa. In 1980 the ailing Gierek was replaced as PUWP leader by Stanisła Kania, but unrest continued as the 10-million-member Solidarity campaigned for a five-day working week and established a rural section.

martial law With food shortages mounting and PUWP control slipping, Kania was replaced as PUWP leader in 1981 by the prime minister, Gen Wojciech *Jaruzelski; the Soviet army was active on Poland's borders; and martial law was imposed in December 1981. Trade-union activity was banned, the leaders of Solidarity arrested, a night curfew imposed, and a Military Council of National Salvation established, headed by Jaruzelski. Five months of severe repression ensued, resulting in 15 deaths and 10,000 arrests. The USA imposed economic sanctions.

In June 1982, curfew restrictions were eased, prompting further serious rioting in August. In November Wałęsa was released, and in December 1982 martial law was suspended (lifted in 1983). The pope visited Poland in 1983 and called for conciliation. The authorities responded by dissolving the Military Council and granting an amnesty to political prisoners and activists. In 1984, 35,000 prisoners and detainees were released on the 40th anniversary of the People's Republic, and the USA relaxed its economic sanctions.

slow improvements The Jaruzelski administration pursued pragmatic reform, including liberalization of the electoral system. Conditions remained tense, however, strained by the continued ban on Solidarity and by a threat (withdrawn in 1986) to try Wałęsa for slandering state electoral officials. Economic conditions and farm output slowly improved, but Poland's foreign debt remained huge. During 1988 the nation's shipyards, coalmines, ports, and steelworks were paralyzed by a wave of Solidarity-led strikes for higher wages to offset the effect of recent price rises. With its economic strategy in tatters, the government of prime minister Zbigniew Messner resigned, being replaced in December 1988 by a new administration headed by the reformist communist Mieczysław F Rakowski, and the PUWP's politburo was infused with a new clutch of technocrats.

socialist pluralism After six weeks of PUWP–Solidarity–church negotiations, a historic accord was reached in April 1989 under which Solidarity was re-legalized, the formation of opposition political associations tolerated, legal rights conferred on the Catholic Church, the state's media monopoly lifted, and a new 'socialist pluralist' constitution drafted.

In the subsequent national assembly elections, held in June 1989, Solidarity captured all but one of the Sejm and Senate seats, for which they were entitled to contest (most seats were reserved for PUWP-backed candidates). Jaruzelski was elected president by parliament in July 1989.

conversion to a market economy In September 1989 a 'grand coalition' was formed with Tadeusz Mazowiecki, editor of Solidarity's newspaper, as prime minister. Jaruzelski continued as president, and was re-elected in July. The new government, which attracted generous financial aid from Western powers, proceeded to dismantle the command economy and encourage the private sector. A tough austerity programme approved by the International Monetary Fund (IMF) was also instituted to solve the problem of hyperinflation, which ran at 550% in 1989.

In January 1990 the PUWP voted to disband and re-formed as the Social Democracy Party. Censorship was abolished in April. During 1990 living standards in Poland fell by 40% and the number of unemployed rose to over 1 million. In July 1990, 40 members of the 259-strong Solidarity caucus, under the leadership of Zbigniew Bujak and Władysław Frasyniuk, established the Citizens' Movement–Democratic Action Party (ROAD) to provide a credible alternative to the Władysław-oriented Solidarity Centre Citizens' Alliance (SCA) established in May.

split in Solidarity Wałęsa accused the government of delaying political and economic reform and forcing workers to bear the brunt of the austerity programme. In July 100 SCA deputies and senators petitioned Jaruzelski to stand down to make way for Wałęsa. In September the Sejm passed a bill establishing a presidential term of five years. In the first round of presidential elections, held in November 1990, the rupture within Solidarity was exposed by both Prime Minister Mazowiecki and Lech Wałęsa contesting for the position. Having run a populist campaign, Wałęsa topped the poll with a 40% vote share, and Mazowiecki, defending an unpopular government, finished in third position, with 18% of the vote, behind Stanislaw Tyminski – a previously obscure, right-wing entrepreneur, who had returned to Poland from Canada – who captured 23% of the vote. In the second round, held in December, Wałęsa defeated Tyminski.

Wałęsa becomes president In December 1990 the defeated

Mazowiecki resigned as prime minister. Wałęsa resigned the Solidarity chair and was sworn in as president. He chose for prime minister an economist and former Solidarity activist, Jan Krzysztof Bielecki (1951–), and the new government included the IMF-backed finance minister Leszek Balcerowicz and other ministers from the outgoing administration. They pledged to consolidate the free market they had introduced, and the first privatization share sales were held in January 1991, with mixed success.

relations with the USSR and Germany Poland's relations with the USSR deteriorated in early 1991 over the issue of Soviet troop withdrawals: there were some 50,000 stationed on Polish territory, and the Poles wanted them to leave by the end of the year, coinciding with withdrawals from Hungary and Czechoslovakia. Told that it would take three years, Wałęsa refused to allow Soviet troops to pass through Poland on their way back to the USSR from other countries. In October 1991 a treaty was signed providing for the withdrawal of all Soviet combat troops by 15 November 1992 and the remainder by the end of 1993.

In June 1991 a treaty of good-neighbourliness and friendly cooperation was signed with Germany, confirming the Oder–Neisse border and recognizing the rights of the 500,000-strong German minority in Poland to their own culture, language, and religion.

public discontent The IMF approved further major loans in April 1991 in support of the Polish government's economic-reform programme. There was growing public discontent at the decline in living standards brought about by currency reform and the deepening recession. This led to industrial unrest as unemployment reached 1.5 million (8.4% of the working population) by June 1991.

political deadlock Bielecki offered his resignation at the end of August 1991, complaining that he no longer enjoyed the support of a Sejm that still contained many communists. Parliament refused to accept either the resignation or the government's crucial proposed budget cuts. President Wałęsa urged it to confer emergency powers to enable the government to rule by decree until the general election. This plea was rejected, creating an impasse, although Bielecki agreed to stay as prime minister until the elections.

first multiparty election The October 1991 general election was Poland's first post-communist, fully free, multiparty contest. No dominant party emerged from the voting, and Wałęsa proposed that he should combine the positions of president and prime minister for two years, heading a 'national unity' grand coalition government. However, this failed to gain broad support. An attempt was then made to construct a left-of-centre coalition led by Bronisław Geremek.

coalition governments This foundered, and in December 1991 Wałęsa reluctantly allowed Jan Olszewski, a former Solidarity defence lawyer and a representative of the SCA, to form a five-party, centre-right coalition government. This government pledged to pursue a more gradual approach to market-oriented reform and, in particular, to slow down the privatization programme by concentrating instead on helping ailing state industries. At the close of 1991 Poland's foreign debt stood at US$42 billion. GNP fell during 1990 and 1991 by 12% and 17% respectively and unemployment rose to more than 11%, with more than 2 million out of work. However, the annual rate of inflation fell from 684% in early 1990 to 60% at the end of 1991.

In June 1992 Olszewski was ousted on a vote of no confidence; Waldemar Pawlak succeeded him but failed to

hold together a workable coalition. In July Wałęsa nominated Hanna Suchocka at the head of a centre-right coalition as Pawlak's successor and Poland's first woman premier. Faced with public-sector unrest, Suchocka resigned in May 1993, after narrowly losing a vote of confidence. In June 1993 Wałęsa formed the Nonparty Bloc to Support Reform as a successor to the SCA. Poland was formally invited to apply for European Community (now European Union) membership in 1993, and in 1994 joined the North Atlantic Treaty Organization's 'partnership for peace' programme.

ex-communists return to power In October 1993, after an inconclusive general election, in which the ex-communist Democratic Left Alliance (SLD) and Polish Peasant Party (PSL) polled strongly, Pawlak was again appointed prime minister. Wałęsa sought to defend the post-communist market and social reforms in the face of the left-of-centre SLD–PSL administration, but was increasingly criticized for his autocratic style of leadership. In February 1995, claiming to be dissatisfied with the slow pace of economic reforms, he nominated Józef Oleksy to succeed Pawlak, who later resigned after losing a vote of no confidence. The ex-communist SLD leader, Aleksander Kwasniewski, narrowly defeated Wałęsa in the second round of the November 1995 presidential elections. In January 1996 Prime Minister Oleksy resigned, dogged by charges that he had been an informer to the Soviet and then the Russian secret service in 1982–95. Włodzimierz Cimoszewicz became premier in February 1996. Oleksy was subsequently appointed leader of the former communist Democratic Left Alliance. In April Lech Wałęsa, who had temporarily returned to his old job as an electrician at Gdansk shipyard, was granted a state pension in recognition for his services as president of Poland.

In February 1997, Marek Bełka, an independent economist, was appointed finance minister, with a brief to speed up the process of structural reform and privatization.

the 1997 constitution In March 1997 parliament passed a new constitution guaranteeing free education (to the age of 18) and basic health care, and committing Poland to a social market economy, respecting free enterprise and private ownership. The constitution was adopted, eight years after the fall of the Iron Curtain, in a referendum in May 1997. The constitution wiped out the last remnants of communism and sought to foster Poland's desire for integration into Europe. The new charter committed Poland to a market economy and private ownership, guaranteed personal freedoms necessary for entrance into the European Union (EU), and ensured civilian control of the military required for Poland's goal of NATO membership.

the 1997 general election In September 1997 the general election was won by Solidarity Electoral Action (AWS), a largely right-wing and Christian grouping of 36 parties based on the anti-communist Solidarity trade union and led by Marian Krzaklewski. It campaigned for faster privatization, decentralization, reform of pensions, and membership of the EU, and attracted 34% of the national vote. A coalition government with the centrist, pro-business Freedom Union (UW), which was led by Leszek Balcerowicz and won 13% of the vote, was formed in November, ending four years of rule by the Sojusz Lewicy Demokratycznej (SLD; Democratic Left Alliance), which won 27% of the vote, and the Peasants' Party, two parties with communist roots. The new prime minister was 58-year-old Jerzy Buzek, a Protestant chemical-engineering professor and Solidarity organizer in the 1980s, from the AWS. The Freedom Union's leader, Balcerowicz, resumed his position as

finance minister, which he held when he instituted 'shock therapy' liberalizing reforms in 1990, and also became a deputy prime minister. In October 1997 the former president and Solidarity leader, Lech Wałęsa, formed a new political party, Christian Democracy of Poland.

In February 1998, the new government put forward radical plans to decentralize government and created two tiers of elected government, overseeing half of the country's tax revenues. In July 1998 a reduction in the number of provinces from 49 to 16 was agreed by President Kwasniewski. By the autumn of 1998 the parliamentary majority of the new centre-right AWS–UW coalition government had been reduced to 17 seats. This followed defections by populists, nationalists and hard-line Roman Catholics from AWS, with some joining the Patriotic Movement for the Fatherland, an embryonic right-wing party formed by the former prime minister, Jan Olszewski.

European Union negotiations In December 1997 the EU decided to open membership talks with Poland. Poland commenced full EU membership negotiations in 1998, and in March 1999 Poland officially became a full member of NATO, along with the Czech Republic and Hungary.

the 1997 floods Severe flooding hit Poland in July 1997, causing an estimated 10 billion marks/£3.3 billions of damage. The River Oder (Odra) overflowed its banks, causing the evacuation of 140,000 people in Poland. About 62,000 people were made homeless. The floods also affected the Czech Republic and Germany.

opposition to prime minister In September 1999, 35,000 farmers and miners protested in Warsaw against the government's badly implemented reform of the health, education, and pensions systems, demanding the resignation of Prime Minister Jerzy

Buzek. In May 2000, Poland's centre-right coalition government broke down after its junior component, the Freedom Union, withdrew all five of its ministers. The party said it would not rejoin the government until Prime Minister Buzek was replaced. The Freedom Union formally withdrew from government in June 2000, leaving the Solidarity group, the coalition's main component, to form a minority government.

Having been cleared of charges of spying for the communist-era secret police, Poland's president, Alexander Kwasniewski was re-elected in October 2000 to another five years in office. The outcome was seen as a vote for continuity and reform at a time when Poland's economy was progressing well.

In January 2001, a new liberal-conservative party, known as the Citizens' Platform, was formed, seeking to offer an alternative to the ruling Solidarity group and the opposition Freedom Union. It quickly attracted considerable public support.

In May, a new right-wing coalition was formed from the three parties of the AWS ruling coalition and the Ruch Odbudowy Polski (ROP; Movement for the Reconstruction of Poland).

In May 2001, former president Gen Wojciech Jaruzelski, Poland's last communist leader, went on trial accused of ordering soldiers to fire on shipyard workers in 1970, killing 44, when he was defence minister. The trial was seen as an important symbol in Poland's attempts to reach closure with its communist past.

2001 elections Solidarity lost power in the general election held on 23 September 2001. The centre-right government, based on the Solidarity trade-union movement, took only 6% of the vote and no seats in parliament at all. The SLD won the election easily with 41% of the vote. Leszek Miller became prime minister.

EU membership Poland became a member of the EU on 1 May 2004, with a 2003 referendum finding 77% of the population to be in favour of accession.

Polish Corridor strip of land designated under the Treaty of *Versailles in 1919 to give Poland access to the Baltic. It cut off East Prussia from the rest of Germany. Germany resented this partition and one of the primary causes of tension with Poland in the build-up to World War II was the German demand to be permitted to build a road and rail connection across the Corridor, in a zone to be granted extra-territorial rights, a demand which the Poles implacably refused. When Poland took over the southern part of East Prussia in 1945, it was absorbed.

Pol Pot (c. 1925–1998) also known as **Saloth Sar, Tol Saut,** or **Pol Porth**, Cambodian politician and leader of the Khmer Rouge communist movement that overthrew the government in 1975. After widespread atrocities against the civilian population, his regime was deposed by a Vietnamese invasion in 1979. Pol Pot continued to help lead the Khmer Rouge despite officially resigning from all positions in 1989. He was captured in 1997 but escaped from Cambodia, reportedly to Thailand, in January 1998 to avoid facing an international court for his crimes against humanity. The Cambodian government announced mid-April 1998 that he had been captured inside Thailand. However, a few days later reports of Pol Pot's death were confirmed. He died following a heart attack, in a Cambodian village two miles from the Thai border.

Pompidou, Georges Jean Raymond (1911–1974) French Gaullist politician and head of state, President *de Gaulle's second prime minister 1962–68 and his successor as president 1969–74. As prime minister he played a key role in managing the Gaullist party but his moderate and pragmatic conservatism brought a rift with de Gaulle in May–June 1968, when he negotiated the Grenelle Agreement with employers and unions to end the strike movement. Their political divergences were confirmed when, during his own presidency, he authorized a devaluation of the franc (which de Gaulle had vetoed in 1968), agreed to British entry into the European Community (which de Gaulle had twice vetoed in the 1960s), and approved initial steps towards a European Monetary System. Pompidou died in office before completing his full seven-year presidential term.

poor law   English system for relief for the poor, established by the Poor Relief Act of 1601. Each parish was responsible for its own poor, paid for by a parish tax. The care of the poor was transferred to the Ministry of Health in 1919, but the poor law remained in force until 1929.

popular front   political alliance of liberals, socialists, communists, and other centre and left-wing parties. This policy was propounded by the Communist International in 1935 against fascism and was adopted in France and Spain, where popular-front governments were elected in 1936; that in France was overthrown in 1938 and the one in Spain fell with the defeat of the Republic in the Spanish Civil War in 1939.

Portal, Charles Frederick Algernon, 1st Viscount Portal of Hungerford (1893–1971)   British air chief marshal in World War II. Chief of the Air Staff 1940–45, he was an advocate of strategic bombing and at the Casablanca Conference January 1943 reached agreement with the US on a Combined Bomber Offensive to destroy German military industrial capability. Portal was unable to control *Harris, commanding RAF Bomber Command, who considered such a

policy a 'panacea' and instead preferred simple area bombing. KCB 1940, Baron 1945, Viscount 1946.

Port Arthur, Battle of   during the Russo-Japanese War, Japanese victory over the Russians after besieging the city of Port Arthur in Manchuria (now Lüshun, China) May 1904–January 1905. The Russian occupation of Port Arthur in 1897, later formalized as a lease in 1898, had been one of the main points of contention, and its loss was a significant blow to Russian morale.

Portugal   country in southwestern Europe, on the Atlantic Ocean, bounded north and east by Spain.

government The 1976 constitution, revised in 1982, provides for a president, elected by universal suffrage for a five-year term, renewable only once in succession, and a single-chamber 230-member assembly, elected through a party list system of proportional representation and serving a four-year term. The president, an active politician rather than a figurehead, appoints a prime minister who chooses a council of ministers. The prime minister and council of ministers are responsible to the assembly. A council of state, chaired by the president, acts as a supreme national advisory body. The relationship between president and prime minister is similar to the 'dual executive' in France.

history Portugal shares much of its early history with that of the whole Iberian peninsula. The dominance of Carthage in the south in the 3rd century BC gave place to that of Rome in the following century. Lusitania, comprising that part of Portugal south of the River Tagus, was formed into a Roman province during the reign of the Emperor Augustus (31 BC–AD 14), and the country prospered under Roman rule.

In the 5th century AD the area of what was to become Portugal was overrun by two Germanic tribes in succession, the Suebi (Suevi) and the

Visigoths, and then in the 8th century by the Muslim Moors from North Africa. By the 11th century the north of the country was subject to León, while the south was still ruled by the Moors.

the creation of Portugal Ferdinand (I) the Great, king of Castile, began the reconquest of the northwest of the Iberian peninsula from the Moors in the mid-11th century, a process continued by his son Alfonso VI of Castile-León. Alfonso VI arranged for the marriage of his illegitimate daughter to the brother of the duke of Burgundy, and their son, Afonso I, had by 1140 established Portugal as his kingdom on a basis of de facto independence, and established the Burgundian line. In 1179 Pope Alexander III acknowledged Afonso as king in return for an annual tribute. However, it was not until the late 13th century that the kingdom of Portugal was acknowledged by the kings of Castile-León. In 1147 Afonso captured Santarém from the Moors, and, with the assistance of English and German crusaders bound for the Holy Land, he also captured Lisbon.

the early kings Afonso I was succeeded by Sancho I (ruled 1185–1211), who was engaged during the earlier part of his reign in war with the Moors and with Alfonso IX of León, and later, by his encouragement of local self-government, won for himself the title of *O Povoador* (founder of cities). He opposed the claims of Pope Innocent III, but in 1210 submitted to papal authority.

Afonso II, the Fat (ruled 1211–23), is notable as the first king to summon the Portuguese Cortes (parliament). The Cortes, an assembly representing nobles, clergy, and cities, went on to secure control of taxation. Sancho II (ruled 1223–48) drove the Moors from Alentejo, and won many successes in the Algarve. He was forced to abdicate in favour of his brother, Afonso III (ruled 1248–79), who proclaimed himself king. Afonso III expelled the

Moors from the Algarve, united it with his other territories in 1253, and strengthened his kingdom by his marriage to the daughter of Alfonso X of Castile. Thus the kingdom of Portugal reached its present European boundaries.

the later Middle Ages Afonso III's son Diniz (ruled 1279–1325) devoted himself to the constitutional and social reconstruction of the kingdom. He encouraged agriculture, shipbuilding, and commerce, and was a patron of learning, founding the University of Coimbra (initially in Lisbon) in 1290. He negotiated a commercial treaty with England in 1294 and founded a Portuguese navy.

Afonso IV (ruled 1325–57) was chiefly occupied in wars with the Castilians and Moors, while his successor Pedro I, the Justicer (ruled 1357–67), endeavoured to lessen the power of the nobility and clergy. The claim of Ferdinand (1367–83) to the throne of Castile was contested by Henry of Trastamara. Ferdinand allied himself with the Aragonese and Moors and with England (the alliance with England dating from 1373).

On Ferdinand's death the Burgundian line established by Afonso I in the 12th century came to an end. In order to preserve Portugal's independence of Castile, the Cortes asserted its right to elect the new king, choosing John I (ruled 1385–1433), an illegitimate brother of Ferdinand and the first king of the house of Aviz. In 1385 the united Portuguese and English forces defeated the Castilians at Aljubarrota, securing Portugal's independence. The Anglo-Portuguese alliance was confirmed by the Treaty of Windsor in 1386, and John cemented the friendship between the two countries in 1387 by marrying Philippa, daughter of John of Gaunt (son of Edward III of England).

the era of exploration and expansion It was during the reign of John I that the great period of

Portuguese exploration and overseas expansion began, during which Portugal became for a while the greatest maritime country in the world.

This period began with the capture of Ceuta on the northwest coast of Africa in 1415 by John's fourth son Prince Henry the Navigator (1394–1460). Henry established a school for navigators in 1419, and under his patronage Portuguese sailors sailed around Cape Bojador (or Boujdour, in what is now the Western Sahara) in 1434, and discovered Madeira and the Azores in 1442, Senegal in 1445, and the Cape Verde Islands in 1446. The first consignment of African slaves was brought to Lisbon in 1434.

Exploration continued down the African coast in search of a route to India; in 1486 Bartolomeu Diaz sailed round the Cape of Good Hope, and in 1497 Vasco da Gama reached India. In 1494, by the Treaty of Tordesillas, Spain and Portugal agreed on the division between them of the uncharted world.

In 1500 King Manuel I (ruled 1495–1521) assumed the title of 'Lord of the conquest, navigation, and commerce of India, Ethiopia, Arabia and Persia'; in the same year Pedro Cabral claimed Brazil for Portugal, and Portuguese settlements were made on the west coast of India. Gaspar and Miguel Côrte-Real reached Greenland in 1500–01, and new colonies were established in east and north Africa. Afonso de Albuquerque conquered Goa (1510) in India and Malacca (now Melaka) in the Malay Peninsula (1511). Portuguese domination of the East Indies (modern Indonesia) was established in 1512–14, and commercial exchange began with China in 1517 and Japan in 1542. Portugal's commercial enterprise knew no limits, and Lisbon was recognized as the centre of European trade with southern and eastern Asia.

Spanish domination and rule

Portugal's pre-eminent position was not maintained. Alternative routes were opened up to the east by Portugal's rivals, while Portugal remained relatively weak and vulnerable. In addition, the commercial classes in Portugal were weak by comparison with the feudal nobility and the church.

Portugal's subsequent decline was at least partially due to its adoption of a fanatically orthodox Roman Catholicism, largely under the influence of Spain. This resulted in the persecution and, from 1497, the expulsion of the Jews, largely at the behest of Spain, which had expelled its own Jews in 1492. The Jews had contributed greatly to the wealth of the country, and many settled in the Netherlands, where their experience of the Portuguese trade was to prove invaluable.

During the reign of John III (ruled 1521–57) Catholic orthodoxy was rigorously imposed on the country, largely at the instigation of John's wife Catherine, the sister of the ardently Catholic Charles V, king of Spain and Holy Roman emperor. In 1536 the Inquisition was introduced, and from 1540 all education was in the hands of the Jesuits.

In 1578 the Portuguese army suffered a disastrous defeat at the Battle of Alcazarquivir, during an ill-advised crusade against the Moors of Morocco. The zealously religious King Sebastian, the young grandson of John III, died in the battle. Sebastian was succeeded by his uncle, the senile Cardinal Henry, last of the Aviz dynasty, who died in 1580.

Among the many claimants to the crown was Philip II of Spain, who marched into the country and had himself crowned king. From 1580 to 1640 Portugal remained under Spanish suzerainty, thus becoming involved in the Dutch Revolt in the Spanish Netherlands and the Thirty Years' War in Germany. England and the Netherlands seized the Portuguese possessions in South America and the

East Indies, although the Dutch seizure of Brazil was only temporary.

independence regained After several insurrections, Portugal regained its independence, and John, Duke of Braganza, a descendant of Manuel I, was crowned John IV in 1640. England recognized the Braganza dynasty in 1662 when Charles II of England married Catherine of Braganza, who brought in her dowry Bombay and Tangier. This confirmed the friendly relations between the two countries, which already dated back 500 years.

Portugal became involved in colonial wars with the Netherlands in Brazil and Angola, and a more serious conflict with Spain, which did not recognize Portugal's independence. In the reign of Afonso VI (1656–83), son of John IV, the Spanish were defeated at Elvas in 1659, Ameixial in 1663, Ciudad Rodrigo in 1664, and Montes Claros in 1665. The war concluded with the Treaty of Lisbon in 1668, by which Spain finally recognized Portugal's independence.

the reforms of Pombal The Anglo-Portuguese alliance was renewed by the Methuen Treaty (1703), and Portugal became involved in the War of the Spanish Succession as Britain's ally. However, Portugal had lost many of its colonies (a notable exception being Brazil, where gold and diamonds were discovered in the last decade of the 17th century), and was no longer one of the chief powers in Europe.

The Marquês de Pombal (1699–1782), chief minister throughout the reign of Joseph I (1750–77), tried to restore the kingdom to its former position by strengthening the monarchy and encouraging colonial development. His name is associated particularly with the rebuilding of the city of Lisbon, destroyed by the great earthquake of 1755. Pombal, an advocate of enlightened despotism, expelled the Jesuits in 1759, organized

education, encouraged industry and commerce, and reformed the army. However, his autocratic methods alienated many, and on the accession of the mad Queen Maria I, Pombal was deprived of office in 1777. In 1799, Maria's son, John, was appointed regent.

the Napoleonic period Following the French Revolution and outbreak of the Revolutionary Wars, in 1793 Portugal allied itself with Britain and Spain against France. In 1807 Napoleon sent a French army to invade Portugal and the royal family left the country for Brazil. Portugal then became a battleground in the struggle between the French and the British during the Peninsular War, until the French were finally ousted from Portugal in 1811.

Portugal in the 19th century In 1816, on the death of Maria I, John VI succeeded to the throne, but remained in Brazil, appointing the British army officer Marshal Beresford as his viceroy. The discontent that this caused among his subjects resulted in a revolution in 1820 and the establishment of a more democratic form of government. John hurried back to Lisbon, and promised to obey the 'constitution of 1822'. Meanwhile Brazil had obtained complete independence in 1822, with John's son having declared himself constitutional emperor as Pedro I of Brazil.

On the death of John VI in 1826, Pedro, who was now Pedro IV of Portugal, established the basis of the constitution that remained in force until 1910, and then, returning to Brazil, abdicated in favour of his seven-year-old daughter, Maria da Gloria, who ruled with her uncle Miguel as regent. The latter headed a reactionary movement, and with the aid of the nobility, military, and clergy proclaimed himself king in 1828.

A period of civil war followed, between the supporters of the autocratic Miguel and those of the more democratically and constitutionally minded Pedro. With the help of British troops, the constitutional party emerged victorious in 1834, and Pedro reinstated his daughter. However, political instability continued for much of the following two decades.

Maria's son, Pedro V (ruled 1853–61), was succeeded by his brother Luiz I (ruled 1861–89). He in turn was succeeded by Carlos I.

Towards the end of the 19th century Portugal was obliged to cede some of its territory in east and west Africa, giving up its claim to Nyasaland (modern Malawi) after a British ultimatum in 1890.

the foundation of the republic
Carlos I and the crown prince were assassinated in 1908. His second son, Manuel II, was dethroned in a revolution in October 1910, and a republic was proclaimed on 5 October.

The provisional government was under the presidency of Teófilo Braga, who was succeeded in 1911 by Manuel de Arriaga, the first president of the constitutional republic. A royalist counter-revolution under Paiva Couceiro in 1911 was suppressed, as was a leftist revolution in 1912. After three ineffective coalition cabinets, Afonso Costa, head of the majority democratic party, became prime minister. He ruled as a veiled dictator, although he respected parliamentary forms of government to some degree, effectively ruling by patronage.

Portugal in World War I In 1914 Costa was succeeded by the more moderate Bernardino Machado. When World War I broke out, Machado, who favoured the Allies, was succeeded by Azevedo Coutinho. The non-interventionist president, Arriaga, allowed the Germans to engineer a neutralist coup in 1915, which made Gen Pimenta de Castro a dictator, but he was quickly overthrown.

Costa returned to power, and, because he allowed the Allies the benefit of interned shipping, Germany

declared war on Portugal on 9 March 1916. Portugal's chief theatre of war was in Africa (where its colony of Mozambique bordered German East Africa), while Gen Tamagnini commanded the Portuguese Expeditionary Force (numbering 40,000 men) in France. In 1917 Costa was ousted by a coup led by the pro-German Sidónio Pais, who was assassinated in 1918.

Salazar's dictatorship Domestically, Portugal remained unstable after World War I; its economic situation was chronically bad, and corruption was rife. Government followed government until a military coup in 1926, and in 1928 Gen Carmona became president. Carmona appointed as his finance minister Dr António de Oliveira *Salazar, who stabilized the economy. President Carmona continued his dictatorship despite protests against it, leading to revolt and revolution in Madeira and the Azores. In 1932 Salazar became prime minister, with dictatorial powers, while Carmona remained as president until his death in 1951.

During World War II Portugal remained neutral, but in 1943, under the treaty of 1373, it granted Britain facilities to set up air and naval bases in the Azores. Britain returned these bases in 1946. Portugal became a founder-member of NATO in 1949.

The assembly set up under the constitution of 1933 provided a form of safety valve, but with the excesses of the later monarchy and of the republic still in his mind, Salazar was not prepared to entrust any substantial measure of power to an elected body, and that of the assembly was very limited. The constitution established Portugal as a corporative state, somewhat along the lines of Fascist Italy, and although social conditions were improved, this was at the cost of personal liberties.

colonial wars The constitution of 1933 adhered steadfastly to the idea that Portugal's overseas empire was an integral part of the nation. However, its remaining possession in India, Goa, was annexed by India in 1961, and during the 1960s, while Britain and France granted independence to their African colonies, Portugal refused to consider such a move. This resulted in the formation of armed liberation movements in Angola, Mozambique, and Portuguese Guinea (Guinea-Bissau), and Portugal became involved in long and costly colonial wars. The increasingly heavy demands made on the national budget by these wars limited the supply of capital for investment at home. In Africa itself Portugal's only friends were white-ruled South Africa, and, after the unilateral declaration of independence there in 1965, Rhodesia (Zimbabwe).

the 1974 revolution Salazar's successor as premier in 1968, Marcelo *Caetano, did not depart much from Salazar's policies. Domestic repression of workers' unions and of all criticism of the regime was exercised by the much-feared security police (PIDE).

On 25 April 1974 the Caetano regime was overthrown in a coup by the Armed Forces Movement (MFA) under the leadership of Gen António Ribeiro de Spínola, a critic of the regime's African policies. The MFA's stated aim was to 'save the nation from government'. One month later Spinola became president of the Junta of National Salvation, with a military colleague replacing the civilian prime minister.

Events moved rapidly in the first few months of the revolution. The African colonies were granted their independence; the following year Portugal also withdrew from East Timor (which was annexed by Indonesia in 1976). Political parties burgeoned, with the socialists and communists proving to be the best organized. Ministers of the former regime were purged, the PIDE dismantled, and business concerns nationalized.

After disagreements within the junta, Spínola resigned in September 1974 and fled the country. He was replaced by Gen Francisco da Costa Gomes. The leaders of the Armed Forces Movement drew ever closer politically to the Communist Party led by Alvaro Cunhal, and President Gomes narrowly avoided a communist coup by collaborating with the leader of the moderate Socialist Party (PS), Mario *Soares.

democracy restored National elections for the constituent assembly held in April 1975 (after the Armed Forces Movement had announced in advance their intention to retain control, whatever the outcome) gave the Socialist Party 38% of the vote and the Popular Democratic Party of Francisco Sá Caneiro 25% – a clear victory for more moderate policies. The military government's exclusion of the leaders of these parties from power exacerbated political tensions as Portugal entered its second year of post-Salazar rule.

In April 1976 further elections were held. The PS won 36% of the vote, and Soares formed a minority government. The fact that law-and-order policies appealed to the majority of Portuguese was confirmed in the summer of 1976 by the election of the army chief, Gen António Ramalho Eanes, to the presidency, with the support of centre and left-of-centre parties. The government headed by Soares faced a critical economic and political situation, and in December 1977 it was defeated in the assembly. The government survived precariously until Soares resigned in 1978. A period of political instability followed, with five prime ministers in two and a half years, until in December 1980 President Eanes invited Francisco Balsemão, a cofounder of the Social Democratic Party (PSD), to form a centre-party coalition.

the 1982 constitution Balsemão survived many challenges to his leadership, and in 1982 the assembly approved his new constitution, which reduced the powers of the president and moved the country towards a fully civilian government.

The PS won the largest number of seats in the 1983 elections and Soares formed a coalition with the PSD, led by former finance minister Aníbal Cavaco Silva. The coalition collapsed in 1985, and after an inconclusive election Cavaco Silva formed a minority PSD government. He increased economic growth and raised living standards, and favoured a free market and privatization.

In the 1986 presidential election Mario Soares became Portugal's first civilian president for 60 years. In the same year Portugal entered the European Community.

socialism abandoned In July 1987 the PSD won an absolute majority in parliament, with the left-of-centre Democratic Renewal Party and the communists both losing seats. In June 1989 parliament approved a series of measures that denationalized major industries and renounced the socialist economy. In January 1991 Soares was re-elected to a five-year term, and in October the PSD won the general election with a slightly reduced majority.

socialists returned to power Cavaco Silva stepped down as PSD leader prior to the October 1995 general election and was succeeded by former defence minister Fernando Nogueira. The elections were won by the PS, which had adopted a centre-left stance. Its leader Antonio Guterres formed a new minority PS administration, which pledged itself to continue the drive for closer European integration. In January 1996, PS candidate Jorge Sampaio won the presidential election. The PS Party easily won a second consecutive term at general elections in October 1999,

and Sampaio was re-elected in January 2001, although only 50% of eligible voters turned out. In July 2000, the parliament voted to decriminalize the possession and use of drugs such as heroin and cannabis, treating drug use as an illness instead.

In January 2001, a cattle slaughter programme was instituted in response to the growing problem of bovine spongiform encephalopathy (BSE), with 500 cases having been reported since 1998.

In March 2001, a bridge over the River Douro collapsed, killing around 70 bus and car passengers. The minister for public works, Jorge Coelho, who was warned the bridge was in a defective state the preceding year, resigned.

On 1 January 2002, euro notes and coins were introduced as the national currency.

Eduardo Ferro Rodrigues became leader of PS in January 2002, two months before a scheduled general election. Guterres announced he would stay on as caretaker prime minister until then. The PSD (Social Democratic Party) won the elections in March with a margin of just over 2% of the vote, but no overall majority of seats in parliament. The slim majority threw into doubt the ability of newly-elected prime minister José Manuel Durão Barroso to form a stable government on his own, and there was immediate speculation that he might seek an alliance with the right-wing PP. When Barroso named his ministers in early April, three were from the PP including its leader, Paulo Portas, as defence minister.

Potsdam Conference conference held in Potsdam, Germany, 17 July–2 August 1945, between representatives of the USA, the UK, and the USSR. They established the political and economic principles governing the treatment of Germany in the initial period of Allied control at the end of World War II, and sent an ultimatum to Japan demanding unconditional surrender on pain of utter destruction.

Poujade, Pierre-Marie (1920–) French entrepreneur and rightwing politician. His 'Poujadist' movement made a dramatic entry into French politics in the 1956 parliamentary elections (when the youngest deputy elected on Poujade's ticket was Jean-Marie *Le Pen) before fading in 1958. A salesman-turned-wholesaler in the rural department of Lot, Poujade came from a monarchist and anti-republican family. Beginning in 1953 with direct action against tax inspections and organized from 1954 as the Union for the Defence of Tradesmen and Artisans (UDCA), Poujadism came to denote a militant and nationalist protest against France's modernizing state, spreading out from its anti-taxation core to embrace the cause of a French Algeria. He published his political credo in *J'ai choisi le combat* (1956).

Poujadist member of an extreme right-wing political movement led by Pierre Poujade (1920–), which was prominent in French politics 1954–58. Known in France as the Union de Défense des Commerçants et Artisans, it won 52 seats in the national election of 1956. Its voting strength came mainly from the lower-middle-class, or petit-bourgeois, section of society. The return of Charles *de Gaulle to power in 1958, and the foundation of the Fifth Republic, led to a rapid decline in the movement's fortunes.

POUM acronym for *Partido Obrero de Unificación Marxista*, 'Workers' Marxist Union Party', a small Spanish anti-Stalinist communist party led by Andrés Nin and Joaquín Maurín, prominent during the Spanish Civil War. Since Republican Spain received most of its external help from the USSR, the Spanish communist party used this to force the suppression of POUM in 1937. POUM supporters included the English writer George

Orwell, who chronicled events in his book *Homage to Catalonia*.

Powell, Adam Clayton, Jr (1908–1972) US Democratic politician. A leader of New York's black community, he was elected to the city council in 1941. He was appointed to Congress in 1944, and later became chair of the House Education and Labor Committee. Following charges of corruption, he was denied his seat in Congress in 1967. Re-elected in 1968, he won back his seniority after a decision of the US Supreme Court in 1969.

Powell, Colin Luther (1937–) US general, chair of the Joint Chiefs of Staff 1989–93, and US secretary of state from 2001. A Vietnam War veteran, he first worked in government in 1972 and was national security adviser 1987–89. As chair of the Joint Chiefs of Staff, he was responsible for the overall administration of the Allied forces in Saudi Arabia during the *Gulf War of 1991. In December 2000 he was appointed the first black secretary of state by president-elect George W *Bush. He has generally been seen as a moderating influence on the hawkish elements of the administration, led by Defense Secretary Donald Rumsfeld, and favours working with international partners rather than unilaterally.

Powell, (John) Enoch (1912–1998) British Conservative politician. He was minister of health (1960–63), and contested the party leadership in 1965. In 1968 he made a speech against immigration that led to his dismissal from the shadow cabinet. He resigned from the party in 1974, and was Official Unionist Party member for South Down, Northern Ireland (1974–87).

Prague Spring the 1968 programme of liberalization, begun under a new Communist Party leader in Czechoslovakia. In August 1968 Soviet tanks invaded Czechoslovakia and entered the capital Prague to put down the liberalization movement initiated by the prime minister Alexander Dubcek, who had earlier sought to assure the Soviets that his planned reforms would not threaten socialism. Dubcek was arrested but released soon afterwards. Most of the Prague Spring reforms were reversed.

Prasad, Rajendra (1884–1963) Indian politician. He was president of the Indian National Congress several times between 1934 and 1948 and India's first president after independence 1950–62.

Premadasa, Ranasinghe (1924–1993) Sri Lankan right-wing politician, prime minister 1978–88, president from 1988, having gained popularity through overseeing a major house-building and poverty-alleviation programme. He sought peace talks with the Tamil Tiger guerrillas. He was assassinated in office by a suicide bomber in the centre of Colombo; the Tamil Tigers denied responsibility.

Prem Tinsulanonda (1920–) Thai general and politician, prime minister 1980–88. During the military administration of General Kriangsak Chomanam 1977–80, he served as deputy minister of the interior and, from 1979, as defence minister, before being appointed prime minister in March 1980. Prem formally relinquished his army office and established a series of civilian coalition governments. He withstood coup attempts in 1981 and 1985 and ruled in a cautious, apolitical manner, retaining the confidence of key business and military leaders.

Price, George Cadle (1919–) Belizean politician, prime minister 1954–84 and 1989–93. In 1950 he founded the country's first political party, the People's United Party (PUP), a left-of-centre grouping that grew out of a smaller group, the People's Committee, and called for the independence of Belize. Partial self-government was achieved in 1954 and Price became prime minister, continuing to lead his country until it

achieved full independence in 1981. A charismatic but ascetic politician, he became known as the 'father of the nation'. He unexpectedly returned to power in 1989 and remained there until 1993.

Primo de Rivera, Miguel, Marqués de Estella (1870–1930) Spanish soldier and politician, dictator from 1923 as well as premier from 1925. He was captain general of Cataluña when he led a coup against the ineffective monarchy and became virtual dictator of Spain with the support of Alfonso XIII. He resigned in 1930.

Primo de Rivera y Saenz de Heredia, José Antonio (1903–1936) Spanish fascist. He was the founder and leader of the *Falange party in 1933. A distinctive blend of poetry and thuggery characterized his speeches, with the latter quality more in evidence amongst his followers on the streets. No slavish follower of German or Italian nationalist models, he sought Spanish solutions for the problems facing Spain during the Second Republic. José Antonio (as he was universally known) was shot at Alicante in November 1936, having been found guilty of complicity in the rising against the Republic five months earlier.

Primrose League in the UK, quasi-masonic society founded in 1883 to promote the Tory democracy of the Fourth Party among working-class voters. It particularly opposed home rule for Ireland, and promoted the values of church, hierarchy, and empire. By 1910 it had attracted some 2 million members. It was supposedly named after Disraeli's favourite flower.

prisoner of conscience PoC, anyone confined for their opinions alone, usually a political dissenter or conscientious objector. In 1992, there were 4,500 PoCs in 62 countries according to the human rights organization *Amnesty International, which campaigns for their release.

Privy Council council composed originally of the chief royal officials of the Norman kings in Britain; under the Tudors and early Stuarts it became the chief governing body. It was replaced from 1688 by the cabinet, originally a committee of the council, and the council itself now retains only formal powers in issuing royal proclamations and orders in council. In 2003 there were over 500 privy counsellors. Cabinet ministers are automatically members, and it is presided over by the lord president of the council (Baroness Amos from 2003).

Prodi, Romano (1939–) Italian centre-left politician and Italian prime minister 1996–98. Prodi became president of the *European Union (EU) Commission following the resignation of Jacques *Santer in March 1999. A former academic and Christian Democrat, he was a founding member of the Partito Democratico di Sinistra (PDS; in English the Democratic Party of the Left) and 'Olive Tree' alliance in 1995. Prodi headed Italy's first left-of-centre government since the fall of *fascism in 1943. As Commission president, he oversaw reform of its bureaucracy and he sought to rebuild faith in EU institutions.

Profumo, John Dennis (1915–) British Conservative politician, secretary of state for war from 1960 to June 1963. He resigned following the disclosure of his involvement with Christine Keeler, mistress also of a Soviet naval attaché, and admitted he had deceived the House of Commons about the affair. The scandal caused great damage to the Macmillan government, contributing to its downfall. In 1982 Profumo became administrator of the social and educational settlement Toynbee Hall in London.

propaganda, Nazi in Germany between the 1920s and 1940s, the Nazi party pursued a systematic programme of propaganda, distorting facts and spreading lies to encourage particular attitudes. From 1933 the Ministry of Propaganda, under the direction of Joseph *Goebbels, took the use of propaganda as a means of mass communication to new heights, and propaganda became the science of moulding opinion rather than a medium for reliable information. Goebbels was able to manipulate every issue to fit with the ideology of *Nazism. Radio, newspapers, books, and even school lessons were moulded to spread Nazi messages of the racial superiority of German Aryans, and condemn the Jews as the scapegoats of Germany's problems.

propaganda, World War I the promotion of biased or misleading information was used on all sides in World War I to encourage recruitment and uphold morale among the civilian and military population. Information coming from the front had to be censored, and a constant flow of good news kept up through the newspapers and cinema. In the UK the *Defence of the Realm Act (DORA) of August 1914 ensured government control over information, the penalty for spreading uncensored information being imprisonment. The War Office Press Bureau was established in 1914 to control news about the war, along with the War Propaganda Bureau to produce positive posters and pamphlets. Letters home were heavily censored; eventually soldiers were provided with pre-printed postcards containing positive statements to tick and sign, allowing no indication of the terrible casualties and conditions on the Western Front.

Protocols of the Elders of Zion, the forged document containing supposed plans for Jewish world conquest, alleged to have been submitted by Theodor *Herzl to the first Zionist Congress at Basel in 1897, and published in Russia in 1905. Although proved to be a forgery in 1921, the document was used by Hitler in his anti-Semitic campaign 1933–45.

Provisional IRA radical faction of the *Irish Republican Army (IRA), now the main republican terrorist faction. In 1969, against a background of mounting violence in Northern Ireland, the IRA split between its left-wing (the Official IRA) and militarists (the Provisional IRA). In the violent 1970s the latter became the dominant force within Irish republicanism. In the 1980s the Provisional IRA adopted the strategy known as 'the armalite and the ballot box', which combined militarism with political activism. Use of the term Provisonal IRA has become synonymous with the IRA.

Prussia northern German state 1618–1945 on the Baltic coast. It was an independent kingdom until 1867, when it became, under Otto von Bismarck, the military power of the North German Confederation and part of the German Empire in 1871 under the Prussian king Wilhelm I. West Prussia became part of Poland under the Treaty of *Versailles, and East Prussia was largely incorporated into the USSR after 1945.

Pueblo US intelligence vessel captured by the North Koreans in January 1968, allegedly within their territorial waters. The crew, but not the ship, were released in December 1968. A naval court recommended no disciplinary action.

P'u-i (or Pu-Yi), Henry (1906–1967) Last Manchu Qing emperor of China (as Hsuan Tung) from 1908 until he was deposed in the republican revolution of 1912; he was restored for a week in 1917. After his deposition he chose to be called Henry. He was president 1932–34 and emperor 1934–45 of the Japanese puppet state of Manchukuo (see *Manchuria).

Punjab massacres in the violence occurring after the partition of India in 1947, more than a million people died while relocating in the Punjab. The eastern section became an Indian state, while the western area, dominated by the Muslims, went to Pakistan. Violence occurred as Muslims fled from eastern Punjab, and Hindus and Sikhs moved from Pakistan to India.

purge removal (for example, from a political party) of suspected opponents or persons regarded as undesirable (often by violent means). During the 1930s purges were conducted in the USSR under Joseph *Stalin, carried out by the secret police against political opponents, Communist Party members, minorities, civil servants, and large sections of the armed forces' officer corps. Some 10 million people were executed or deported to labour camps from 1934 to 1938.

Putin, Vladimir Vladimirovich (1952–) Russian politician, president 2000– , appointed prime minister in August 1999 and chosen by President Boris *Yeltsin as his preferred successor, Putin, a former KGB (Russian secret police) spy, was not a well-known figure either in Russia or abroad. A powerful and loyal ally of President Yeltsin, Putin became acting president following Yeltsin's resignation at the end of 1999, and was elected president in March 2000. Often described as a colourless bureaucrat and a poor public speaker, he seldom made television appearances, he was principally known for his loyalty and efficiency. The international community condemned his campaign of assaults against Chechnya.

putsch a violent seizure of political power, such as Adolf Hitler and Erich von Ludendorff's abortive Munich beer-hall putsch in November 1923, which attempted to overthrow the Bavarian government. The term is of Swiss-German origin.

Qaboos bin Said (1940–) Sultan of Oman, the 14th descendant of the Albusaid family. Opposed to the conservative views of his father, he overthrew him in 1970 in a bloodless coup and assumed the sultanship. Since then he has followed more liberal and expansionist policies, while maintaining his country's position of international non-alignment.

Qassem (or Qasim), Brigadier Abdul Karim al- (1914–1963) Iraqi soldier and politician, ruler 1958–63. In July 1958 Qassem led a successful coup and proceeded to establish himself as a dictator, appointing himself commander-in-chief, prime minister, and defence minister. In February 1963 he was overthrown by a combination of nationalist anti-communist military officers and civilian Ba'ath activists. This coup, which resulted in the death of Qassem and close associates, brought to power Abdul Salam Arif.

Qatar country in the Middle East, occupying Qatar peninsula in the Gulf, bounded southwest by Saudi Arabia and south by United Arab Emirates.

Qiu Jin (or Ch'iu Chin) (1875–1907) Chinese feminist and revolutionary. She left her family to study in Japan in 1904, where she became actively involved in radical Chinese student associations calling for the overthrow of the Manchu Qing (Ch'ing) dynasty. Returning to China in 1906, she founded a women's journal in which she argued that the liberation of women was an essential prerequisite for a strong China. In 1907 she was implicated in an abortive anti-Manchu uprising and was executed by the Qing authorities.

Quadros, Jânio da Silva (1917–1992) Brazilian politician and president 1961. He was a political independent who gained a huge majority in the 1960 presidential elections. His implementation of economic reforms on taking office encountered unprecedented opposition in congress with the result that he only served a seven-month term as president before resigning and seeking exile. His resignation caused national chaos; he was succeeded by his equally controversial vice-president João Goulart.

Quayle, (James) Dan(forth) (1947–) US Republican politician, vice-president 1989–93. A congressman for Indiana 1977–81, he became a senator in 1981.

Quezon (or Quezon y Molina), Manuel Luis (1878–1944) Filipino nationalist politician, president 1935–44. Quezon was elected the first president of the Philippine Commonwealth. He established a highly centralized government, verging on one-man rule, but displayed great courage during the Japanese onslaught on General Douglas *MacArthur's defences in 1941, refusing to evacuate to the USA until appealed to by President Franklin *Roosevelt. From 1942 he led a government in exile, until his death at Saranac Lake, New York, USA.

Quisling, Vidkun Abraham Lauritz Jonsson (1887–1945) Norwegian politician. Leader from 1933 of the Norwegian Fascist Party, he aided the Nazi invasion of Norway in 1940 by delaying mobilization and urging nonresistance. He was made premier by Hitler in 1942, and was arrested and shot as a traitor by the Norwegians in 1945. His name became a generic term for a traitor who aids an occupying force.

Quit India Movement campaign against British rule in India, begun in August 1942 under the leadership of Mahatma *Gandhi. In March 1942 Sir Stafford *Cripps had tried unsuccessfully to persuade the Congress Party of the need for it to participate in the war effort against Japan. Instead, Gandhi called on the British to leave India and let Indians deal with the Japanese by non-violent means. Calls to 'Quit India' were met with the arrest of Gandhi and other Congress leaders, which led to bloodshed, violence, and suppression.

R

Rabin, Yitzhak (1922–1995) Israeli Labour politician, prime minister 1974–77 and 1992–95. As a former soldier, he was a national hero in the Arab-Israeli Wars. His policy of favouring Palestinian self-government in the occupied territories contributed to the success of the centre-left party in the 1992 elections. In September 1993 he signed a historic peace agreement with the Palestinian Liberation Organization (PLO), providing for a phased withdrawal of Israeli forces. He shared the Nobel Prize for Peace in 1994 with Israeli foreign minister Shimon *Peres and PLO leader Yassir *Arafat for their agreement of an accord on Palestinian self-rule. He was shot and killed by a young Israeli extremist while attending a peace rally in Tel Aviv in November 1995.

Rabuka, Sitiveni (1948–) Fijian soldier and politician, prime minister 1992–99. When the April 1987 elections produced a new left-of-centre government, headed by Timoci Bavadra, which was determined to end discrimination against the country's ethnic Indian community, Rabuka staged two successive coups, in May and September 1987. Within months of the second coup, he stepped down, allowing a civilian government headed by Kamisese Mara, to take over. In 1992 Rabuka was nominated as the new Fijian premier. He was re-elected to the post in 1994 and, after revising the constitution so as not to discriminate against the ethnic Indian community, secured Fiji's re-admission to the Commonwealth in October 1997.

race-relations acts UK acts of Parliament of 1965, 1968, and 1976 to combat discrimination. The Race Relations Act of 1976 prohibits discrimination on the grounds of colour, race, nationality, or ethnic origin. Indirect as well as direct discrimination is prohibited in the provision of goods, services, facilities, employment, accommodation, and advertisements. The Commission for Racial Equality was set up under the act to investigate complaints of discrimination.

Radhakrishnan, Sarvepalli (1888–1975) Indian philosopher and politician. In 1946 he was chief Indian delegate to UNESCO, becoming its chairman in 1949. A member of the Indian assembly in 1947, he was appointed vice-president 1952–62 and president 1962–67.

Radic, Stjepan (1871–1928) Yugoslav nationalist politician, founder of the Croatian Peasant Party in 1904. He led the Croat national movement within the Austro-Hungarian Empire and advocated a federal state with Croatian autonomy. His opposition to Serbian supremacy within Yugoslavia led to his assassination in parliament.

Raeder, Erich (1876–1960) German admiral. Chief of Staff in World War I, he became head of the navy 1928, but was punished by Adolf Hitler 1943 because of his failure to prevent Allied Arctic convoys from reaching the USSR and resigned. Sentenced to life imprisonment at the Nuremberg trials of war criminals, he was released 1955 on grounds of ill health.

Rafsanjani, Hojatoleslam Ali Akbar Hashemi (1934–) Iranian politician and cleric, president 1989–97. When his former teacher Ayatollah *Khomeini returned after the revolution of 1979–80, Rafsanjani became the speaker of the Iranian parliament and, after Khomeini's death, state president and effective political leader. He was succeeded in 1997 by Seyyed Muhammad Khatami. In parliamentary elections in late February 2000 Rafsanjani failed to win a seat, while supporters of President Khatami and their reformist allies won a convincing majority. Following the pro-reformist election, it was disclosed that Rafsanjani was allegedly linked to government officials who had committed human rights abuses and executions of dissidents, intellectuals, and criminals during his presidency.

Rahman, Sheikh Mujibur (1920–1975) Bangladeshi nationalist politician, president in 1975. He was arrested several times for campaigning for the autonomy of East Pakistan. He won the elections in 1970 as leader of the Awami League but was again arrested when negotiations with the Pakistan government broke down. After the civil war in 1971, he became prime minister of the newly independent Bangladesh. He was presidential dictator January 1975 until August of that year, when he was assassinated.

Rahman, Tunku (Prince) Abdul (1903–1990) Malaysian politician, first prime minister of independent Malaya 1957–63 and of Malaysia 1963–70.

Rainier III (1923–) Prince of Monaco from 1949. He married the late US film actor Grace Kelly 1956.

Raj, the the period of British rule in India before independence in 1947.

Rajput or **Thakur**, member of a Hindu people, predominantly soldiers and landowners, widespread over northern India. The Rajput states of northwestern India are now merged in Rajasthan. The Rana family (ruling aristocracy of Nepal until 1951) was also Rajput. Rajastani languages belong to the Indo-Iranian branch of the Indo-European family.

Rakosi, Matyas (1892–1971) Hungarian communist. He joined the communists in 1918, was tried and imprisoned in 1925 and was extradited to the Soviet Union in 1940. He returned to Hungary in January 1945 as general-secretary of the Communist Party and after accumulating personal power he became a ruthless dictator in 1949, as 'Stalin's best Hungarian disciple'. He was forced to share power with Imre *Nagy for a period following Stalin's death in 1953, but regained sole control in March 1955 only to lose all his positions in June 1956. He retired to the Soviet Union where he died.

Ramaphosa, Cyril (1954–) South African politician, secretary general of the *African National Congress from 1991. He was a chief negotiator in the constitutional talks with the South African government that led to the first universal suffrage elections in May 1994, and was subsequently elected by parliament to chair the assembly that would write the country's new permanent constitution. He is seen by some as Mandela's natural successor. In July 1996 he announced his resignation from active politics to concentrate on a business career.

Ramgoolam, Navin Chandra (1947–) Mauritian politician, prime minister 1995–2000. He became leader of the centrist, Hindu-oriented Mauritius Labour Party (MLP) in 1991, becoming its president soon afterwards. Entering an electoral agreement with the Mauritian Militant Movement (MMM), the MLP and MMM secured a landslide victory and Ramgoolam was appointed prime minister.

Ramphal, Shridath Surendranath ('Sonny') (1928–) Guyanese politician. He was minister of foreign affairs and justice 1972–75 and secretary general of the Commonwealth 1975–90.

Randolph, Asa Philip (1889–1979) US labour and civil-rights leader. Devoting himself to the cause of unionization, especially among African-Americans, he was named a vice-president of the American Federation of Labor and Congress of Industrial Organizations

(AFL-CIO) 1957. He was one of the organizers of the 1963 civil-rights march on Washington.

Rankin, Jeannette (1880–1973) born **Jeannette Pickering,** US representative. She was the first woman elected to the US House of Representatives (Republican, Montana) in 1917 and became one of only 57 members to vote against US entry into World War I. Serving again in the House 1941–43, she was the only member of Congress to vote against US entry into World War II. She continued to lobby for peace in later years, particularly during the Korean and Vietnam wars.

Rapacki Plan proposal put to the United Nations 2 October 1957 by Polish foreign minister Adam Rapacki, for a zone closed to the manufacture or deployment of nuclear weapons in Poland, Czechoslovakia, East and West Germany. The ban was to be enforced by NATO and Warsaw Pact observers. The USA and Britain rejected the plan because it gave the USSR advantages owing to its superiority in conventional forces.

rapprochement improvement of relations between two formerly antagonistic states, such as the agreement between Britain and France in 1904 which ended decades of colonial rivalry.

Rasputin (1871–1916) born **Grigory Efimovich Novykh,** (Russian 'dissolute') Siberian Eastern Orthodox mystic. He acquired influence over the Tsarina *Alexandra, wife of *Nicholas II, and was able to make political and ecclesiastical appointments. His abuse of power and notorious debauchery (reputedly including the tsarina) led to his murder by a group of nobles.

Rathenau, Walther (1867–1922) German politician. He was a leading industrialist and was appointed economic director during World War I, developing a system of economic planning in combination with capitalism. After the war he founded the Democratic Party, and became foreign minister in 1922. The same year he signed the Rapallo Treaty of Friendship with the USSR, cancelling German and Soviet counterclaims for indemnities for World War I, and soon after was assassinated by right-wing fanatics.

rationing restricted allowance of provisions or other supplies in time of war or shortage. Food rationing was introduced in Germany and Britain during World War I. During World War II food rationing, organized by the government, began in Britain in 1940. Each person was issued with a ration book of coupons. Bacon, butter, and sugar were restricted, followed by other goods, including sweets, petrol, clothing, soap, and furniture. Many similar items were rationed in the USA, including sugar in both wars. The War Ration Book issued to Americans during World War II included meat, alcohol, and petrol. Some people in both countries tried to buy extra on the black market. In 1946, the world wheat shortage led to bread rationing. All food rationing finally ended in Britain in 1954. During the Suez Crisis of 1956, petrol rationing was reintroduced in Britain.

Rau, Johannes (1931–) German socialist politician, president from 1999. The son of a Protestant pastor, he was state premier of North Rhine-Westphalia (1978–98). In January 1987 he stood for chancellor of West Germany but was defeated by the incumbent conservative coalition. In March 1998 he announced his retirement from the premiership of North Rhine-Westphalia to be nominated, in November, as the party's candidate for the German presidency in the May 1999 election, which he won.

Ravensbruck German *concentration camp for female prisoners in Mecklenburg, northwest of Berlin, established in 1936. Medical experiments were carried out on Polish women at the camp and it was also the place of execution for Allied female agents.

Rawlings, Jerry (John) (1947–   ) Ghanaian politician, president 1981–2001. He first took power in a bloodless coup in 1979, and, having returned power to a civilian government, staged another coup in 1981. He then remained in power until 1992, when he was elected president under the new multiparty constitution. He was re-elected for a second term in December 1996.

Rayburn, Samuel Taliaferro (1882–1961) US Democratic politican. Elected to Congress in 1912, he supported President Roosevelt's New Deal programme of 1933, and was elected majority leader in 1937 and Speaker of the House in 1940. With the exception of two terms, he served as Speaker until his death.

Reagan, Ronald (Wilson) (1911–2004) 40th president of the USA 1981–89, a Republican. He was governor of California 1966–74, and a former Hollywood actor. Reagan was a hawkish and popular president. He adopted an aggressive foreign policy in Central America, attempting to overthrow the government of Nicaragua, and invading Grenada in 1983. In 1987, *Irangate was investigated by the Tower Commission; Reagan admitted that USA–Iran negotiations had become an 'arms for hostages deal', but denied knowledge of resultant funds being illegally sent to the *Contra guerrillas in Nicaragua. He increased military spending (sending the national budget deficit to record levels), cut social programmes, introduced the deregulation of domestic markets, and cut taxes. His *Strategic Defense Initiative (SDI), announced in 1983, proved controversial owing to the cost, unfeasibility, and opposition from the USSR. He was succeeded by Vice-President George *Bush.

Reagan became a Hollywood actor in 1937 and appeared in 50 films,

including *Knute Rockne, All American* (1940), *Kings Row* (1942), *Bedtime for Bonzo* (1951), and *The Killers* (1964).

He joined the Republican Party in 1962, and his term as governor of California was marked by battles against student protesters. Having lost the Republican presidential nomination in 1968 and 1976 to Richard Nixon and Gerald Ford respectively, Reagan won it in 1980 and defeated President Jimmy Carter. He was wounded in an assassination attempt in 1981. The invasion of Grenada, following a coup there, generated a revival of national patriotism, and this, along with his record of tax cutting, was one of the various causes of his landslide re-election in 1984. His last years in office were dominated by friction with the USSR over the SDI, popularly called Star Wars because incoming missiles would be intercepted in space.

rearmament re-equipping a country with new weapons and other military hardware. The Nazi dictator Adolf Hitler concentrated on rearmament in Germany after he achieved power in 1934.

Red Army the army of the USSR until 1946; it later became known as the Soviet Army. Founded by the revolutionary Leon *Trotsky, it developed from the Red Guards, volunteers who were in the vanguard of the Bolshevik revolution. The force took its name from its rallying banner, the red flag. At its peak, during World War II, it reached a strength of around 12 million men and women. The revolutionary army that helped the communists under *Mao Zedong win power in China in 1949 was also popularly known as the Red Army.

The early campaigns of the Red Army were marked by incompetence, and it suffered a number of humiliating defeats, notably in the Soviet–Polish war of 1920. Discipline, equipment, and general efficiency improved in the later 1920s and 1930s, though the army's leadership was seriously weakened by the Stalinist political purges of 1937 and 1938. The deficiencies of the Red Army were shown up in the Finnish 'Winter War' of 1939 to 1940, when the small, tenacious, and mobile Finnish Army inflicted early defeats on the invading force. Similarly, the first phases of the Nazi invasion of Russia in 1941 – beginning what is known there as the 'Great Patriotic War' – saw the Red Army driven back, incurring immense losses in soldiers and material. But the large human reserves at its disposal and increased output of tanks and guns enabled it to contain the Nazi forces, notably at the sieges of *Stalingrad and *Leningrad, and then drive them back across eastern Europe.

Red Brigades Italian **Brigate rosse**, extreme left-wing guerrilla groups active in Italy during the 1970s and early 1980s. They were implicated in many kidnappings and killings, some later attributed to right-wing *agents provocateurs*, including that of Christian Democrat leader Aldo Moro in 1978.

Red Cross or **International Federation of the Red Cross**, international relief agency founded by the Geneva Convention in 1863, having been proposed by the Swiss doctor Henri Dunant, to assist the wounded and prisoners in war. Its symbol is a symmetrical red cross on a white ground. In addition to dealing with associated problems of war, such as refugees and the care of disabled people, the Red Cross is concerned with victims of natural disasters – floods, earthquakes, epidemics, and accidents. It was awarded the Nobel Prize for Peace in 1917, 1944, and 1963.

Prompted by war horrors described by Dunant, the Geneva Convention laid down principles to ensure the safety of ambulances, hospitals, stores, and personnel distinguished by the Red Cross emblem. (The Muslim equivalent is the **Red Crescent**.) The organization consists of an International Committee (ICRC),

an Executive Board, and a General Assembly and Executive Council. The secretary general is Didier Cherpitel, appointed in 2001.

Red Guard one of the militant school and college students, wearing red armbands, who were the shock-troops of the *Cultural Revolution in China from 1966 to 1969. After killing many party officials and plunging the country into chaos, the Red Guards were outlawed and suppressed by the Chinese leader *Mao Zedong.

Redmond, John Edward (1856–1918) Irish nationalist politician, leader of the Irish Parliamentary Party (IPP) 1900–18. He rallied his party after Charles Stewart Parnell's imprisonment in 1881, and came close to achieving home rule for all Ireland in 1914. However, the pressure of World War I, Unionist intransigence, and the fallout of the 1916 *Easter Rising destroyed both his career and his party.

Rees-Mogg, Lord William (1928–) British journalist, editor of *The Times* 1967–81, chair of the Arts Council 1982–89, and from 1988 chair of the Broadcasting Standards Council. In 1993 he challenged the government over its ratification of the *Maastricht Treaty, notably the government's right to transfer foreign policy decisions to European Community (now European Union) institutions. His challenge was rejected by the High Court.

Rehnquist, William (1924–) US Supreme Court associate justice 1972–86, and chief justice from 1986. Under his leadership the court established a reputation for conservative rulings on such issues as abortion and capital punishment. This has been possible because a majority of its members have been nominated by Republican presidents; Rehnquist was nominated associate justice in 1972 by President Richard *Nixon and chief justice in 1986 by President Ronald *Reagan.

Reichstag German parliament building and lower legislative house during the German Empire 1871–1918 and Weimar Republic 1919–33. It was burned down in February 1933. Following the MPs' decision after reunification in 1991, German parliament was brought back to Berlin, and the Reichstag officially reopened in April 1999.

Reichstag Fire burning of the German parliament building in Berlin 27 February 1933, less than a month after the Nazi leader Hitler became chancellor. The fire was used as a justification for the suspension of many constitutional guarantees and also as an excuse to attack the communists. There is still debate over whether the Nazis were involved in this crime, of which they were the main beneficiaries.

Reid, James (Jimmy) (1932–) Scottish communist trade-union activist. In 1971, when the four shipyards of the publicly owned Upper Clyde Shipbuilders (UCS) consortium were threatened with closure, he led a 'work-in' that ultimately forced the Conservative government of Ted Heath to find a package to keep the yards open.

Reith, John Charles Walsham, 1st Baron (1889–1971) Scottish broadcasting pioneer, the first general manager 1922–27 and director general 1927–38 of the British Broadcasting Corporation (BBC). He was enormously influential in the early development of the BBC and established its high-minded principles of public-service broadcasting. He held several ministerial posts in government during World War II, including minister of information in 1940, transport in 1940, and minister of works 1940–42.

René, France-Albert (1935–) Seychelles left-wing politician. He became the country's first prime minister after independence, and president from 1977 after a coup.

He followed a nonnuclear policy of non-alignment. In 1993 René and his party, the People's Progressive Front, won the country's first free elections in 16 years. He was re-elected in 2001.

Rennenkampf, Paul Karlovich (1854–1918) Russian general. He served in China and the Russo-Japanese war before taking charge of the invasion of eastern Prussia in World War I.

Renner, Karl (1870–1950) Czech-born Austrian lawyer, Socialist, and statesman. He entered the Austrian parliament in 1907 and became leader of the Social Democrats. On the dissolution of the Empire he led the Austrian delegation to St Germain-en-Laye in 1919, where the frontiers of the Austrian Republic were settled. From 1919–20 he was chancellor. After World War II he headed the provisional government set up by the Allies, and at the end of 1945 he was elected president of the Austrian Republic. Renner's example of combined idealism and conciliation undoubtedly played a large part in the creation of a post-1945 Austrian republic on western European lines.

Reno, Janet (1939–) US lawyer, attorney general 1993–2001. Having been appointed to the post in 1993, she took full responsibility in the same year for the attack by the Federal Bureau of Investigation on the compound of the Branch Davidian cult at Waco, Texas, in which 86 died.

reparation compensation paid by countries that start wars in which they are defeated, as by Germany in both world wars. Iraq is required to pay reparations, under the terms of a United Nations resolution, after its defeat in the 1991 Gulf War.

Republican Party younger of the two main political parties of the USA, formed in 1854. It is more right-wing than the Democratic Party, favouring capital and big business, and opposing state financial assistance and federal controls. In the late 20th century most presidents have come from the Republican Party, but in Congress Republicans have generally been outnumbered. In 1992 Republican George Bush lost the presidency to Democrat Bill Clinton, who in 1996 was re-elected for a second term, although the Republicans retained control of Congress and had governors in 32 of the country's 50 states. The Republicans took the presidency in 2000, with George W *Bush slimly beating the Democrat Al Gore in a conflict-ridden election.

The party was founded by a coalition of slavery opponents, who elected their first president, Abraham Lincoln in 1860. The early Republican Party supported protective tariffs and homestead legislation for Western settlers, as well as abolitionism. Towards the end of the 19th century the Republican Party was identified with US imperialism and industrial expansion. With few intermissions, the Republican Party controlled Congress from the 1860s until defeated by the New Deal Democrats in 1932.

Conservative tendencies and an antagonism of the legislature to the executive came to the fore after Lincoln's assassination, when Andrew Johnson, his Democratic and Southern successor, was impeached (although not convicted), and General Ulysses S Grant was elected to the presidency 1868 and 1872. In the bitter period following the Civil War, the party was divided into those who considered the South a beaten nation and those who wished to reintegrate the South into the country as a whole, but Grant carried through a liberal Reconstruction policy in the South.

The party became divided during Theodore *Roosevelt's attempts at regulation and control of big business, and in forming the short-lived Progressive Party 1912, Roosevelt effectively removed the liberal influence from the Republican Party.

The Republican Party remained in eclipse until the election of Dwight D *Eisenhower 1952, more his personal triumph than that of the party, whose control of Congress was soon lost and not regained by the next Republican president, Richard *Nixon, 1968. Both Nixon and his successor, Gerald *Ford, pursued active foreign policies; the latter was defeated by Jimmy Carter in the presidential election of 1976.

The party, attracting increasing support from the Christian right and in the formerly Democrat-dominated southern states, enjoyed landslide presidential victories for Ronald *Reagan and also carried the Senate 1980–86. George *Bush won the 1988 presidential election but faced a Democratic Senate and House of Representatives, and in 1992 lost the presidency to the Democrat Bill Clinton. In the 1994 midterm elections Republicans regained control of both the Senate and the House of Representatives, but showed stresses between the more moderate wing and the rising far-right wing of the party, which, led by Newt Gingrich, relied increasingly on support from fundamentalist Christians, the Christian Coalition, and the pro-gun and anti-abortion lobbies. They retained control of Congress in the November 1996 election, and had governors in 32 of the country's 50 states, but their candidate Bob *Dole failed to win the presidency.

Republican George W Bush Jr, son of former president George Bush, won the presidency in 2000, in one of the most controversial elections in US history. The election was submerged in debate because Al Gore won the majority of popular votes, but fell three short of the 270 electoral votes necessary to win. Claims that media reports interfered with the electoral process and controversial ballots in the state of Florida resulted in a recount for Florida and a Supreme Court hearing.

reservation area of land allocated to American Indians by the US government from the 1860s. Apart from freeing the Plains Indians' lands for settlement by homesteaders, the reservation system had the advantage of confining its inhabitants to small, easily controlled areas of worthless land. Here their traditional way of life would be unsustainable and they would no longer be a threat to the settlers. The defeated image of the Plains Indian on a reservation is one of the most enduring in the history of the American West. The culture and community of whole groups came close to being destroyed by 1900. In recent decades, however, there has been a major revival in the rights and position of the American Indians in the USA.

Reuther, Walter Philip (1907–1970) US trade-union leader. He was vice-chair of the Union of United Automobile, Aircraft and Agricultural Implement Workers of America 1942–46 and its president from 1946. He was president of the Congress of Industrial Organizations 1952–56 and vice-president of the combined American Federation of Labor and Congress of Industrial Organizations 1955–70.

revolutions of 1989 popular uprisings in many countries of Eastern Europe against communist rule, prompted by internal reforms in the USSR that permitted dissent within its sphere of influence. By 1990 nearly all the Warsaw Pact countries had moved from one-party to pluralist political systems, in most cases peacefully but with growing hostility between various nationalist and ethnic groups.

Reynaud, Paul (1878–1966) French prime minister in World War II, who succeeded Edouard Daladier in March 1940 but resigned in June after the German breakthrough. He was imprisoned by the Germans until 1945, and again held government offices after the war.

Reynolds, Albert (1932–) Irish Fianna Fáil politician, Taoiseach (prime minister) 1992–94. He was minister for industry and commerce 1987–88 and minister of finance 1988–92. In December 1993 Reynolds and UK prime minister John Major issued a joint peace initiative for Northern Ireland, the Downing Street Declaration, which led to a ceasefire by both the Irish Republican Army (IRA) and the loyalist paramilitaries the following year.

Rhee, Syngman (1875–1965) Korean right-wing politician. A rebel under Chinese and Japanese rule, he became president of South Korea from 1948 until riots forced him to resign and leave the country in 1960. He established a repressive dictatorship and was an embarrassing ally for the USA.

Rhineland province of Prussia from 1815. Its unchallenged annexation by Nazi Germany in 1936 was a harbinger of World War II.

Rhodes, Cecil John (1853–1902) South African politician, born in the UK, prime minister of Cape Colony 1890–96. Aiming at the formation of a South African federation and the creation of a block of British territory from the Cape to Cairo, he was responsible for the annexation of Bechuanaland (now Botswana) in 1885. He formed the British South Africa Company in 1889, which occupied Mashonaland and Matabeleland, thus forming **Rhodesia** (now Zambia and Zimbabwe).

Ribbentrop, Joachim von (1893–1946) German Nazi politician and diplomat. As foreign minister 1938–45, he negotiated the nonaggression pact between Germany and the USSR (the Ribbentrop–Molotov pact of 1939). He was tried at Nuremberg as a war criminal in 1946 and hanged.

Rice-Davies, Mandy (Marilyn) (1944–) English model. She achieved notoriety in 1963 following the revelations of the affair between her friend

Christine Keeler and war minister John *Profumo, and his subsequent resignation.

Richthofen, Manfred, Freiherr von (1892–1918) called 'the Red Baron', German aviator. In World War I he commanded the 11th Chasing Squadron, known as **Richthofen's Flying Circus**, and shot down 80 aircraft before being killed in action.

Rimington, Stella (1935–) British public servant and director general of the counter-intelligence security service (MI5) 1992–96. She was the first head of MI5 to be named publicly, and in July 1993 published a booklet containing hitherto undisclosed details on the service, including its history, organization, and constitutional role.

Ríos Montt, Efraín (1927–) Guatemalan soldier and right-wing politician, president 1982–83. He launched a crackdown against corruption and guerrilla and left-wing activity, with thousands of native Indians being killed by the armed forces. Unpopular because of this repression and his Protestant fundamentalist beliefs, in what is a predominantly Catholic country, Ríos Montt was overthrown and forced into exile by an August 1983 coup led by General Oscar Humberto Mejía Victores.

River Plate, Battle of the in World War II, naval battle in the South Atlantic between a British cruiser squadron of three ships and the German 'pocket battleship' *Admiral *Graf Spee* December 1939. The British damaged the *Graf Spee* and pursued it as it sought refuge in Montevideo, Uruguay. The ship's captain was ordered to scuttle his vessel rather than risk it falling to the British.

Robertson, William Robert (1860–1933) British general in World War I, the only man ever to rise from private to field marshal in the British army.

Robinson, Mary (1944–) Irish Labour politician, president 1990–97. She

became a professor of law at the age of 25. A strong supporter of women's rights, she campaigned for the liberalization of Ireland's laws prohibiting divorce and abortion. In 1997 she became the United Nations (UN) high commissioner for human rights.

Robinson, Ray (Arthur Napoleon Raymond) (1915–) Trinidad and Tobago centre-left politician, prime minister 1986–92 and president 1997–2003. Leader of the National Alliance for Reconstruction (NAR), he won a landslide victory in 1986, becoming prime minister with portfolios for the economy and Tobago. However, economic recession caused political instability and in 1990 an attempted coup by Islamic fundamentalists ended in a six-day siege. Defeated in 1991 by the People's National Movement (PNM), led by Patrick Manning, Robinson returned to centre stage in 1995, as adviser to the coalition government of Basdeo Panday. In 1997 he was elected to the largely titular position of president.

Rocard, Michel (1930–) French socialist politician, prime minister 1988–91. Widely popular as the exponent of a moderate and modernizing social democracy, he was leader of the Parti Socialiste (PS; Socialist Party) 1993–94.

Rockefeller, Nelson (Aldrich) (1908–1979) US Republican politician, vice-president 1974–77. He was an official in the administrations of Roosevelt, Truman, and Eisenhower, and governor of New York 1958–73. He gained a reputation as a progressive and activist administrator.

Röhm, Ernst (1887–1934) German leader of the Nazi Brownshirts, the SA (*Sturmabteilung). On the pretext of an intended SA putsch (uprising) by the Brownshirts, the Nazis had some hundred of them, including Röhm, killed 29–30 June 1934. The event is known as the *Night of the Long Knives.

Roh Tae-woo (1932–) South Korean right-wing politician and general, president 1988–93. He held ministerial office from 1981 under President Chun, and became chair of the ruling Democratic Justice Party in 1985. He was elected president in 1988 amid allegations of fraud and despite being connected with the massacre of about 2,000 anti-government demonstrators in 1980. In October 1995 Roh admitted publicly to having secretly amassed £400 million during his term in office, of which he retained £140 million for personal use. He was arrested in November on corruption charges, along with former president Chun, and placed on trial in 1996, on charges of sedition and military rebellion in 1980. He was found guilty in August 1996, heavily fined, and sentenced to 22 years' imprisonment. In December 1996 an appeal court reduced his prison sentence to 17 years.

Rokossovski, Konstantin Konstantinovich (1896–1968) Polish-born Marshal of the Soviet Union. He came to prominence during World War II as commander of the 16th Army defending Moscow in 1941, and played an important role in pushing the Germans back from Soviet territory. He was Polish defence minister and commander-in-chief of the Polish armed forces (1949–56) and deputy prime minister of Poland (1952–56). In 1956 the new Władysław Gomułka regime dismissed him in response to widespread popular anti-Russian feeling, and he returned to the USSR. From 1961 he was a candidate member of the Central Committee of the Communist Party.

Roman Catholicism (Greek *katholikos* **'universal')** one of the main divisions of the Christian religion, separate from the Eastern Orthodox Church from 1054. It is headed by the pope, who traces his authority back through St Peter (the first bishop of Rome) to Jesus, through apostolic succession. Its headquarters

are in the *Vatican City State, in Rome. Membership is concentrated in southern Europe, Latin America, and the Philippines. In February 2000 Rome reported the number of baptized Roman Catholics to be 1.045 billion, an increase of 40 million since 1998, and more than half the Christians in the world.

Reformation and Counter-Reformation The Protestant churches separated from the Catholic church with the Reformation in the 16th century. In Germany, Switzerland, and other European countries, this came about as a result of fundamental divisions on matters of church doctrine and practice. However, in England, the Reformation was sparked primarily by disagreement over questions of royal marriage and succession. The Tudor monarch Henry VIII – once a staunch 'defender of the faith', who had written a pamphlet attacking the German Protestant reformer Martin Luther – established a separate Anglican Church with its own doctrine and liturgy after the pope had refused to sanction his divorce of Catherine of Aragon in order to marry Anne Boleyn.

In response to the Reformation, in the 16th and 17th centuries, the Catholic Church undertook the campaign of education and coercion known as the Counter-Reformation. An attempt to update Catholic doctrines was condemned by Pope Pius X in 1907, and more recent moves towards reform have been rejected by Pope John Paul II.

doctrine and worship The focus of liturgical life is the Mass, or Eucharist, and attendance is obligatory on Sundays and Feasts of Obligation such as Christmas and Easter. Inside the church is a formal setting, with the high altar (a table representing that of the Last Supper) as the focal point. Since the Second Vatican Council (1962–66), called by Pope John XXIII, the liturgy has been conducted in the vernacular or everyday language instead of Latin.

The Roman Catholic Church differs from the other Christian churches in that it acknowledges the supreme jurisdiction of the pope, and papal infallibility when he speaks *ex cathedra* ('from the throne'). The pope usually speaks in the name of the church on questions of faith and morals, and his declarations are infallible (without error). In 1854 the Immaculate Conception of the Virgin Mary, the mother of Jesus, was declared official doctrine; this states that she was conceived without the original sin with which all other human beings are born. The Virgin Mary is accorded a special place in the Roman Catholic Church. Declarations on moral issues include condemnation of artificial forms of contraception and abortion. Roman Catholics hold that the authority of the church has safeguarded God's teachings.

organization The Second Vatican Council was called by Pope John XXIII to bring the church up to date and make it more aware of 20th-century issues. Roman Catholic clerics attended from all over the world. Since the meeting of the Council, major changes have taken place, resulting in increased freedom among the religious and lay orders. The pope has an episcopal synod of 200 bishops elected by local hierarchies to collaborate in the government of the church. The priesthood is celibate and there is a strong emphasis on the monastic orders. Great importance is also attached to the mission of spreading the faith. Under John Paul II from 1978, power has been more centralized, and bishops and cardinals have been chosen from the more traditionally-minded clerics and from the developing world.

attitude to other religions The Second Vatican Council marked a more tolerant attitude to other world religions. Changes included the condemnation of religious persecutions. Pope John XXIII set up a committee to look at the relationship between the Roman Catholic and other Christian churches, and his work in the ecumenical movement continued after his death. Representatives have also attended meetings of the World Council of Churches as observers.

Romania country in southeast Europe, bounded north and east by Ukraine, east by Moldova, southeast by the Black Sea, south by Bulgaria, southwest by Serbia and Montenegro, and northwest by Hungary.

government Under the 1991 constitution, Romania has a limited presidential political system. There is a two-chamber legislature, comprising a 341-member chamber of deputies (lower chamber), in which additional seats are set aside for minorities, and a 143-member senate (upper chamber). Both are elected for four-year terms by means of proportional representation in multiparty contests. An executive president is directly elected for a four-year term in a two-round majority contest. The president appoints the prime minister, who in turn appoints a cabinet, or council of ministers.

history The earliest known inhabitants merged with invaders from Thrace. Ancient Rome made it the province of Dacia; the poet Ovid was one of the settlers, and the people and language were Romanized. After the withdrawal of the Romans in AD 275, Romania was occupied by Goths, and during the 6th–12th centuries was overrun by Huns, Bulgars, Slavs, and other invaders.

The principalities of Wallachia in the south, and Moldavia in the east, dating from the 14th century, fell to the *Ottoman Empire in the 15th and 16th centuries.

Turkish rule was exchanged for Russian protection 1829–56. In 1859 Moldavia and Wallachia elected Prince Alexander Cuza, under whom they were united as Romania from 1861.

He was deposed in 1866 and Prince Charles of Hohenzollern-Sigmaringen elected. After the Russo-Turkish war 1877–78, in which Romania sided with Russia, the great powers recognized Romania's independence, and in 1881 Prince Charles became King Carol I.

after independence Romania fought against Bulgaria in the Second *Balkan War in 1913 and annexed southern Dobruja. It entered World War I on the Allied side in 1916, was occupied by the Germans 1917–18, but received Bessarabia from Russia and Bukovina and Transylvania from the dismembered Habsburg empire under the 1918 peace settlement, thus emerging as the largest state in the Balkans. During the late 1930s, to counter the growing popularity of the fascist *Iron Guard movement, *Carol II abolished the democratic constitution of 1923 and established his own dictatorship.

World War II In 1940 he was forced to surrender Bessarabia and northern Bukovina to the USSR, northern Transylvania to Hungary, and southern Dobruja to Bulgaria, and abdicated when Romania was occupied by Germany in August. Power was assumed by Ion Antonescu (1882–1946, ruling in the name of Carol's son King *Michael), who signed the *Axis Pact in November 1940 and declared war on the USSR in June 1941. In August 1944, with the Red Army on Romania's borders, King Michael supported the ousting of the Antonescu government by a coalition of left and centre parties, including the Communists. Romania subsequently joined the war against Germany and in the Paris peace treaties in 1947 recovered Transylvania but lost Bessarabia and northern Bukovina to the USSR (they were included in Moldavia and the Ukraine) and southern Dobruja to Bulgaria.

republic In the elections 1946 a Communist-led coalition achieved a majority and proceeded to force King Michael to abdicate. The new Romanian People's Republic was proclaimed in December 1947 and dominated by the Romanian Communist Party, then termed the Romanian Workers' Party (RWP). Soviet-style constitutions were adopted in 1948 and 1952; Romania joined *Comecon in 1949 and co-signed the *Warsaw Pact in 1955; and a programme of nationalization and agricultural collectivization was launched. After a rapid purge of opposition leaders, the RWP became firmly established in power, enabling Soviet occupation forces to leave the country in 1958.

Ceausescu era The dominant political personality 1945–65 was RWP leader and state president Gheorghe *Gheorgiu-Dej. He was succeeded by Nicolae *Ceausescu, who placed greater emphasis on national autonomy and proclaimed Romania a socialist republic. Under Ceausescu, Romania adopted a foreign-policy line independent of the USSR, condemned the 1968 invasion of Czechoslovakia, and refused to participate directly in Warsaw Pact manoeuvres or allow Russian troops to enter the country. Ceausescu called for multilateral nuclear disarmament and the creation of a Balkan nuclear-weapons-free zone, and maintained warm relations with China. He was created president in 1974.

austerity programme At home, the secret police (Securitate) maintained a tight Stalinist rein on dissident activities, while a Ceausescu personality cult was propagated, with almost 40 members of the president's extended family, including his wife Elena and son Nicu, occupying senior party and state positions. Economic difficulties mounted as Ceausescu, pledging himself to repay the country's accumulated foreign debt (achieved in 1989), embarked on an austerity programme. This led to food shortages and widespread power cuts in the winters from 1985 onwards;

the army occupied power plants and brutally crushed workers' demonstrations in Brasov in 1987.

relations with neighbours From 1985 Ceausescu refused to follow the path of political and economic reform laid by Soviet leader Mikhail Gorbachev, even calling in the spring of 1989 for Warsaw Pact nations to intervene to prevent the opposition Solidarity movement from assuming power in Poland. Romania's relations with Hungary also reached crisis point 1988–89 as a result of a Ceausescu 'systematization plan' to demolish 7,000 villages and replace them with 500 agro-industrial complexes, in the process forcibly resettling and assimilating Transylvania-based ethnic Hungarians.

overthrow of Ceausescu The unexpected overthrow of the Ceausescu regime began in December 1989. It was sparked off by the government's plans to exile a dissident Protestant pastor, László Tökes (1952–), to a remote village. Ethnic Hungarians and Romanians joined forces in the city of Timisoara to form an anti-Ceausescu protest movement. Hundreds of demonstrators were killed in the state's subsequent crackdown on 17 December. Four days later, an officially sponsored rally in Bucharest backfired when the crowd chanted anti-Ceausescu slogans. Divisions between the military and Securitate rapidly emerged and on 22 December the army Chief of Staff, Gen Stefan Gusa, turned against the president and called on his soldiers to 'defend the uprising'. Ceausescu attempted to flee, but was caught and he and his wife were summarily tried and executed on Christmas Day.

National Salvation Front Battles between Ceausescu-loyal Securitate members and the army ensued in Bucharest, with several thousand being killed, but the army seizing the upper hand. A National Salvation Front was established, embracing former dissident intellectuals, reform communists, and military leaders. At its head was Ion Iliescu (1930–), a Moscow-trained communist; Petre Roman (1947–), an engineer without political experience, was appointed prime minister. The Front's council proceeded to re-legalize the formation of alternative political parties and draft a new constitution. Faced with grave economic problems, it initiated a ban on the export of foodstuffs, the abandonment of the 'systematization programme', the dissolution of the Securitate (a new intelligence service, accountable to parliament, was set up in its place), the abolition of the RCP's leading role, and the re-legalization of small-plot farming and abortion (all contraception had been banned by Ceausescu). It legalized the Orthodox Church, and the Vatican re-established diplomatic relations.

market economy In May 1990 Ion Iliescu won the country's first free elections since World War II. Moving towards a legal market economy, the government cut subsidies, the leu was devalued, and prices were allowed to float. Industrial exports slumped and strikes and protests increased until the government agreed to postpone its price-liberalization programme. Refugees continued to leave the country and there were demonstrations against the government during December 1990 and January 1991, especially in Timisoara and Bucharest.

The second stage of price liberalization commenced in April 1991, despite trade-union protests against the sharply rising cost of living and level of unemployment (over 1 million). At the same time the leu was devalued by 72% to meet the loan conditions set by the International Monetary Fund. President Iliescu signed a law in August to allow for the privatization of all state enterprises except utilities. In November 1991 the leu was made internally convertible. Prices rose 400% during 1991 and hundreds of thousands were on short-time work. GNP fell during 1991 to 12%. However, the annual inflation rate, which stood at 300% in 1993, was reduced to 28% by 1996 when the growth of the economy was reported to be 7% per annum.

In late September 1991 prime minister Petre Roman resigned after three days of riots in Bucharest by thousands of striking miners, protesting against soaring prices and a fall in living standards. Theodor Stolojan, the finance minister and a proponent of accelerated price liberalization, was appointed prime minister. He formed a new, cross-party coalition government in October 1991.

new constitution A national referendum in December 1991 overwhelmingly endorsed a new constitution which guaranteed pluralism, human rights, and a free market. Ethnic Hungarians, however, opposed the new constitution on the grounds that it failed to grant minority or language rights. Iliescu was re-elected in the September–October 1992 presidential election on a second ballot, promising more gradual market reforms; concurrent legislative elections resulted in a no majority parliament. A minority administration, formed under Nicolai Vacaroiu, only narrowly survived a series of no-confidence motions by the more reformist-minded opposition, and in March 1994 two far-right nationalist parties, Romania Mare and the Romanian National Unity Party, were brought into the coalition in an attempt to strengthen its position. In January 1995 a governing pact was signed with the anti-Semitic Romania Mare and the ex-communist Socialist Labour Party. These moves increased concern among ethnic Hungarians and raised doubts in the West over the future development of democracy in Romania.

Romania was formally invited to apply for European Community (now European Union) membership in 1993.

In 1994 a pact was signed with Bulgaria agreeing to joint military activities.

In local elections held in June 1996 support for Vacaroiu's government slumped with former communists making advances. Former tennis star Ile Nastase failed in his bid to be elected as PSD mayor of Bucharest.

new regime The former communists who had held power since the overthrow of Ceausescu in 1989 were defeated in the November 1996 elections. Emil Constantinescu, leader of the centre-right Democratic Convention (CDR) won the presidential election against Iliescu, heralding the advent of a new era of genuine democracy. The CDR also won parliamentary elections held in the same month. Former trade unionist Victor Ciorbea was appointed prime minister.

economic reform The new government was dominated by the CDR but also included representatives from the Social Democratic Union and the Hungarian Democratic Union of Romania. In February 1997 the government announced a radical 'economic shock therapy' reform programme, which included accelerated privatization and spending cuts, which would reduce average incomes in the short term, and reiterated the country's aim to enter NATO and the European Union. As part of the economic reform programme, the currency was freed and price controls ended, leading to a sharp increase in the inflation rate to an annualized 700%. In addition, a drive against official corruption was launched, with a quarter of county police chiefs being sacked and investigations launched into public–private mafias.

In February 1997 the former king, Michael, aged 75, returned to the country from exile in Switzerland, 50 years after having been forced to abdicate by the Communists. He promised to abide by the 1991 republican constitution and set about lobbying for the country's entry into NATO.

In October 1997 the government announced that the files of the Securitate, the former secret police who had been much feared during the communist era, would be opened. In November the Romanian Workers' Party (RMR) was renamed the Romanian Communist Party (RCR). In December the finance minister was dismissed by the reforming right-wing prime minister, Victor Ciorbea, leader of the Christian Democrat National Peasants Party (CDNPP), as part of a broader shake-up of the economic ministries.

Ciorbea loses backing of coalition
In February 1998, the Social Democratic Union (USD), the second-largest group in the ruling coalition, and which includes the Democratic Party, led by former premier Petre Roman, and many former communist bureaucrats-turned-entrepreneurs, criticized the government's slow pace of economic reform and withdrew its support. This forced Prime Minister Ciorbea to form a new coalition, which included the three member parties of the centre-right Democratic Convention of Romania (DCR) and members of the Hungarian Democratic Union of Romania (HDUR). The economy was experiencing difficulties, with the currency falling in value and inflation soaring. However, a privatization law was passed in February 1998.

Ciorbea resigned in March 1998 after the Social Democrats blocked his budget. He was replaced in April by Radu Vasile of the CDNPP, and the Social Democrats resumed their support of the coalition, which pledged faster economic reform. Romania commenced full EU membership negotiations in 1998.

civil unrest In January 1999 the government imposed roadblocks north of Bucharest to prevent 10,000 miners,

who were striking for a 35% pay increase, entering the capital.

The miners' leader, Miron Cozma, was an ally of Vadim Tudor, the populist leader of the xenophobic and protectionist Greater Romania Party, which called for a general strike and overthrow of the increasingly unpopular government of Prime Minister Radu Vasile.

In December 1999, Vasile was forced to resign, and was replaced by Mugur Isarescu, the head of Romania's central bank, and member of the Partidul National Liberal (PNL, National Liberal Party). The new government had the task of accelerating privatization (around 80% of the economy was still state-run), and of tackling corruption and the black market. This was a first step in preparing the country for entrance into the EU, having been invited to commence negotiations in February 2000.

presidential elections In August 2000, Isarescu announced he would contest the forthcoming presidential elections in November against the leader of his own party, the PNL, Theodor Stolojan. Isarescu's candidacy was supported by eight senior members of the party who broke away to form the 'true' National Liberal Party. In the event, the elections went to a second-round contest between former communist president Ion Iliescu and extreme nationalist candidate Corneliu Vadim Tudor, which Iliescu won in December. Parliamentary elections in November saw a decline for the PNL, with Iliescu's Social Democrats winning the largest share of the vote. The new government expressed an interest in joining the European Union.

In February 2001, the government announced plans to privatize 63 large state-owned enterprises. Since 1996 the previous government had privatized 4,000 small and medium-sized enterprises, so that the private sector accounted for 60% of GDP. However, GDP and average living standards had fallen by a fifth since 1996.

Rome, Treaties of   two international agreements signed 25 March 1957 by Belgium, France, West Germany, Italy, Luxembourg, and the Netherlands, which established the European Economic Community and the European Atomic Energy Commission (Euratom).

Rommel, Erwin Johannes Eugen (1891–1944)   German field marshal. He served in World War I, and in World War II he played an important part in the invasions of central Europe and France. He was commander of the North African offensive from 1941 (when he was nicknamed 'Desert Fox') until defeated in the Battles of El *Alamein and he was expelled from Africa in March 1943.

Roosevelt, (Anna) Eleanor (1884–1962)   US social worker, lecturer, and first lady. Her newspaper column 'My Day', started in 1935, was widely syndicated. She influenced *New Deal policies, especially those supporting desegregation. She was a delegate to the United Nations general assembly and chair of the UN commission on human rights 1946–51, and helped to draw up the Declaration of Human Rights at the UN in 1945. She was married to her cousin President Franklin D Roosevelt, and was the niece of Theodore *Roosevelt.

Roosevelt, Franklin D(elano) (1882–1945)   32nd president of the USA 1933–45, a Democrat. He served as governor of New York 1928–33. Becoming president during the *Great Depression, he launched the *New Deal economic and social reform programme, which made him popular with the people. After the outbreak of World War II he introduced *lend-lease for the supply of war materials and services to the Allies and drew up the *Atlantic Charter of solidarity.

Born in Hyde Park, New York, of a wealthy family, Roosevelt was educated in Europe and at Harvard and Columbia universities, and became a lawyer. In 1910 he was elected to the New York state senate. He held the assistant secretaryship of the navy in Wilson's administrations 1913–21, and did much to increase the efficiency of the navy during World War I. He suffered from polio from 1921 onwards but returned to politics, winning the governorship of New York State in 1928. When he became president in 1933, Roosevelt aroused a new spirit of hope with his skilful 'fireside chats' on the radio and his inaugural-address statement: 'The only thing we have to fear is fear itself.' Surrounding himself by a 'Brain Trust' of experts, he immediately launched his reform programme. Banks were reopened, federal credit was restored, the gold standard was abandoned, and the dollar devalued. During the first 100 days of his administration, major legislation to facilitate industrial and agricultural recovery was enacted. In 1935 he introduced the Utilities Act, directed against abuses in the large holding companies, and the *Social Security Act, providing for disability and retirement insurance. The presidential election of 1936 was won entirely on the record of the New Deal. During 1935–36 Roosevelt was involved in a conflict over the composition of the Supreme Court, following its nullification of major New Deal measures as unconstitutional. In 1938 he introduced measures for farm relief and the improvement of working conditions.

In his foreign policy, Roosevelt endeavoured to use his influence to restrain Axis aggression, and to establish 'good neighbour' relations with other countries in the Americas. Soon after the outbreak of war, he launched a vast rearmament programme, introduced conscription, and provided for the supply of armaments to the Allies on a 'cash-and-carry' basis. In spite of strong isolationist opposition, he broke a long-standing precedent in running for a third term; he was re-elected in 1940. He announced that the USA would become the 'arsenal of democracy'. Roosevelt was eager for US entry into the war on behalf of the Allies. In addition to his revulsion for Hitler, he wanted to establish the USA as a world power, filling the vacuum he expected to be left by the break-up of the British Empire. He was restrained by isolationist forces in Congress.

Roosevelt, Theodore (1858–1919)
26th president of the USA 1901–09, a Republican. After serving as governor of New York 1898–1901 he became vice-president to McKinley, whom he succeeded as president on McKinley's assassination in 1901. He campaigned against the great trusts (associations of enterprises that reduce competition), while carrying on a jingoist foreign policy designed to enforce US supremacy over Latin America. He was awarded the Nobel Prize for Peace in 1906 for his mediation at the end of the Russo-Japanese War in 1904.

As president, Roosevelt became more liberal. He tackled business monopolies, initiated measures for the conservation of national resources, setting aside 190 million acres for national forests, coal and water reserves, and wildlife refuges. Other highlights of his domestic policy were the passage of the Pure Food and Drug Act of 1906, which established the Food and Drug Administration, and the Hepburn Act of 1906, which enhanced the powers of the Interstate Commerce Commission. In 1904, he announced the Roosevelt Corollary to the Monroe Doctrine, to the effect that the USA assumed responsibility for intervening in Latin America when countries displayed 'chronic wrongdoing or impotence' (the Monroe Doctrine declared that European intervention in Latin America would be regarded as a threat to the USA).

Alienated after his retirement by the conservatism of his successor W H Taft, Roosevelt formed the Progressive or 'Bull Moose' Party. He unsuccessfully ran for the presidency in 1912. During World War I he strongly advocated US intervention.

Rosenberg, Alfred (1893–1946)
German politician, born in Tallinn, Estonia. He became the chief Nazi ideologist and was minister for eastern occupied territories 1941–44. He was tried at *Nuremberg in 1946 as a war criminal and hanged.

Rostov, Battle of in World War II, German defeat November 1941 by Soviet forces in fighting for Rostov, a city on the River Don in the southern USSR close to the Sea of Azov; the first military setback in the German invasion of the Soviet Union. The battle resulted in the resignation of Field Marshal Gerd von Rundstedt after a dispute with Hitler, a serious blow to the German Army.

Round Table conferences discussions on the future of India held in London 1930–32 between representatives of British India, the Princely States, and the British government. The Indian princes agreed to join a united India (including Pakistan) at the first conference 1930–31, but there was little progress in the second conference 1931 as Mahatma Gandhi demanded a wider franchise. After the third conference 1932, the British passed the Government of India Act 1935. See *India, *India Acts, **independence and partition**.

Rowlatt Bills in India 1919, peacetime extensions of restrictions introduced during World War I to counter the perceived threat of revolution. The planned legislation would inhibit individual rights and allow the Indian administration to arrest and detain people without a warrant. The bills were vigorously opposed by Indian nationalists, and the young Congress Party leader Mahatma *Gandhi called for a nationwide campaign for their repeal. Only one of the two bills was enacted, but it was never used and was later repealed.

Rowntree, B(enjamin) Seebohm (1871–1954) English entrepreneur and philanthropist. He used much of the money he acquired as chair (1925–41) of the family firm of confectioners, H I Rowntree, to fund investigations into social conditions. His writings include *Poverty, A Study of Town Life* (1901), a landmark in empirical sociology (study supported by observed evidence). The three **Rowntree Trusts**, which were founded by his father **Joseph Rowntree** (1836–1925) in 1904, fund research into housing, social care, and social policy, support projects relating to social justice, and give grants to pressure groups working in these areas.

Roy, Manabendra Nath (1887–1954) adopted name of **Narendranath Bhattacharya**, Indian politician, founder of the Indian Communist Party. He was exiled to Tashkent in 1920. Expelled from the Comintern in 1929, he returned to India and was imprisoned for five years. A steadfast communist, he finally became disillusioned after World War II and developed his ideas on practical humanism.

Royal Air Force RAF, the air force of Britain. The RAF was formed 1918 by the merger of the Royal Naval Air Service and the Royal Flying Corps.

Royal Armoured Corps RAC, British regiment formed 1939, when it consisted of 18 cavalry regiments and all the units of the Royal Tank Corps (later renamed the Royal Tank Regiment). Most of these cavalry regiments had already been mechanized, and their incorporation in the RAC confirmed the permanent substitution of the internal-combustion engine for the horse.

Royal Canadian Mounted Police RCMP; called **'Mounties'**, Canadian national police force, known for their uniform of red jacket and broad-brimmed hat. Founded as the North West Mounted Police in 1873, it was renamed in 1920 with the extension of its territory. It is the sole police force operating in the Northwest and Yukon territories. It is administered by the solicitor general of Canada, and its headquarters are in Ottawa, Ontario. The Mounties' Security Service, established in 1950, was disbanded in 1981 and replaced by the independent Canadian Security Intelligence Service.

Royal Flying Corps RFC, forerunner of the *Royal Air Force, created in 1912 from the Air Battalion, Royal Engineers, as the air arm of the British army.

Royal Naval Air Service RNAS, air arm of the British Royal Navy during World War I, formed in July 1914 from naval officers and elements of the *Royal Flying Corps.

Royal Navy the navy of Britain. Alfred the Great established a navy in the 9th century, and by the 13th century there was already an official styled 'keeper of the king's ships'. This office grew to become the Navy Board 1546, the body responsible for administering the fleet of Henry VIII, some 80 ships, with the *Great Harry* as his flagship. The Navy Board administered the navy until 1832, when the Board of Admiralty was instituted. The government head of the Admiralty was the First Lord of the Admiralty, while the senior serving officer in command of the navy was the First Sea Lord (now known as Chief of Naval Staff and First Sea Lord). The Admiralty was abolished 1964 and replaced by the naval department of the Ministry of Defence.

Royal Ulster Constabulary RUC, until 2001 the police force of Northern Ireland, established in 1922 following the *partition of Ireland. Its duties included those of a normal police force as well as protection against terrorist activity. Until 1969 it included an armed section known as the B-Specials. The RUC was 90% Protestant, and was often accused by Irish nationalists and republicans of bias against Roman

Catholics. In 2001, as part of reforms under the *Good Friday Agreement, a policy of 50–50 Protestant and Catholic recruitment was introduced, and the force changed its name to the Police Service of Northern Ireland (PSNI).

Ruby, Jack L (1911–1967) born Jacob Rubenstein, US assassin. After a life of petty crime, Ruby shot and killed Lee Harvey Oswald, the alleged assassin of President John F Kennedy. Ruby was sentenced to death in 1964 but died while awaiting a second trial.

Rundstedt, (Karl Rudolf) Gerd von (1875–1953) German field marshal in World War II. Largely responsible for the German breakthrough in France in 1940, he was defeated on the Ukrainian front in 1941.

As commander-in-chief in France from 1942, he resisted the Allied invasion in 1944 and in December launched the temporarily successful Ardennes offensive.

Rusk, (David) Dean (1909–1994) US Democrat politician. He was secretary of state to presidents J F Kennedy and L B Johnson 1961–69, and became unpopular through his involvement with the *Vietnam War.

Russian civil war bitter conflict in Russia (1918–21), which followed Russian setbacks in World War I and the upheavals of the 1917 *Russian Revolution. In December 1917 counter-revolutionary armies, the Whites, began to organize resistance to the October Revolution of 1917. The *Red Army (Bolsheviks), improvised by Leon *Trotsky, opposed them, resulting in civil war. The Bolsheviks eventually emerged victorious.

Russian Federation or **Russia**, country in northern Asia and eastern Europe, bounded north by the Arctic Ocean; east by the Bering Sea and the Sea of Okhotsk; west by Norway, Finland, the Baltic States, Belarus, and Ukraine; and south by China, Mongolia, Georgia, Azerbaijan, and Kazakhstan.

government The 1993 constitution is modelled on that of France, increasing presidential authority at the expense of the legislature and enhancing the centre's authority over Russia's 21 republics and 68 regions. The president, who is directly elected for a maximum of two five-year terms, serves as head of state and the armed forces and nominates the prime minister and council of ministers (cabinet). There is a two-tier legislature, the Federal Assembly, comprising the Council of the Federation (upper house), with 178 members (two from each of the regions and republics), and the State Duma (lower house), with 225 seats elected by proportional representation (parties must receive at least 5% of the total votes cast to secure any representation) and 225 seats elected by simple-majority voting in single-member constituencies. The president has the authority to dismiss the prime minister and may issue decrees and veto laws, although the veto may be overturned by two-thirds majorities in both houses. The president also appoints and heads a Security Council and proposes the chair of the Central Bank, the Prosecutor General, and key members of the judiciary. Since 1994 the interior, defence, and foreign affairs ministries have been directly subordinate to the president.

The powers of the Federal Assembly are relatively weak compared to those of the president. It may not consider presidential decrees and while it may oust a government through a vote of confidence, it must do so twice within three months before the president is forced to take action. The president may then either form a new government or dissolve the Assembly and call fresh elections. The Federal Assembly may, however, impeach the president if both chambers vote in favour and there is agreement from both the Supreme Court and the Constitutional Court. The State Duma has the right to reject two presidential nominees for the post of prime minister (it can be dissolved by the president if it rejects a third).

history For pre-1990 history see *Union of Soviet Socialist Republics. The Russian Federation declared its economic and political sovereignty in June 1990 and began to challenge Soviet authority. It held back revenue, embarked on a strategy of market reform, and established its own independent security and communications structures.

Commonwealth of Independent States formed In August 1991, communist hardliners attempted, but failed, to overthrow Soviet president Mikhail Gorbachev. After this, the Russian Federation, led by Boris Yeltsin, Russia's first-ever popularly elected leader, moved swiftly to break the political-institutional structures that had held together the USSR, in particular the Communist Party of the Soviet Union (CPSU). Russia sought to maintain some sort of confederal structure in order that economic ties might continue and territorial disputes be avoided, but was wary of Gorbachev's plan for a reorganized federation. Instead, after Ukraine's independence referendum on 1 December 1991, Russia proposed the *Commonwealth of Independent States (CIS). The USA officially acknowledged Russia's independence in the same month and accorded it diplomatic recognition, as did the European Community, and admission to the United Nations was granted. Gorbachev resigned on 25 December, effectively yielding power to Yeltsin.

the newly independent republic The Russian Federation contains almost half the population of the former USSR and around 70% of its agricultural and industrial output.

It is a vast federation, spanning 11 time zones, stretching 3,000 km/2,000 mi from the Arctic Ocean to China, and containing 21 'autonomous republics', five 'autonomous regions', and ten 'autonomous districts', each catering for a distinct non-Russian ethnic group, including Tatars, Chechens, Chuvash, Dagestanis, Buryats, Yakuts, Kalmyks, and Chuchi, and each with its own parliament and laws. After 1990 many of these made sovereignty or independence declarations, most conspicuously the oil-rich and predominantly Muslim Tataria (Tatarstan), where Russia's largest ethnic minority resides, gas-rich Bashkir, Siberian Yakutia, and Checheno-Ingush in the southwest, which made integration into the new federation difficult despite Russia's pledge to concede considerable autonomy. The Russian Federation also faced the threat of territorial claims and border conflicts with neighbouring republics.

The new Russian Federation, despite the weakness of its economy, remained a 'great power'. It inherited much of the former USSR's strategic and diplomatic assets, including a permanent seat on the United Nations Security Council (taken up in 1992), embassies overseas, and a considerable conventional and nuclear military arsenal.

Despite growing internal frictions, a federal treaty between Yeltsin and the leaders of 18 of Russia's 20 main political subdivisions was signed in March 1992 giving regional governments broad autonomy within a loose Russian Federation. Checheno-Ingush and Tatarstan refused to sign.

economic problems Russia's immediate concern was the rapid deterioration in living standards and shortages of food and consumer goods as a result of loosening price restraints and the restructuring of commerce, the military sector, and industry. In January 1992 nearly a dozen cities were rocked by rioting consumers protesting over the lifting of price controls. International efforts to stabilize the economy included a $2.5 billion loan from the International Monetary Fund (IMF) in August and the offer in September 1992 of more than $1 billion in food aid from the USA. During 1992, 46,815 small firms, mostly shops, were privatized. The country remained bedevilled by hyper-inflation (prices rising by 2000% during 1992) and declining output. A new IMF loan of $13 billion was negotiated in April 1993, dependent on the implementation of market reforms. The number of unemployed rose from none in 1985 to 1.7 million in 1995; the number of registered crimes doubled during the same period to 2.8 million.

arms control In the first official Russian-US summit in June 1992, Yeltsin and Bush agreed on a major reduction in strategic nuclear weapons. The pact would leave the two powers with less than one-half of the warheads they would have retained under the 1991 START agreement. In August 1992 an agreement was reached for joint control of the disputed Black Sea fleet by Russia and the Ukraine until 1995, after which time it would be divided between the two countries. The pact effectively removed the fleet from the command of the CIS. In December 1992, Yeltsin and Bush signed the START II arms-reduction treaty.

Congress of People's Deputies–Yeltsin power struggle In December 1992 the seventh session of the Congress of People's Deputies elected the conservative, former industrial manager, Viktor Chernomyrdin, to replace the young market reformer, Yegor Gaidar, as prime minister. The Congress met for its eighth session in March 1993 and attempted to limit President Yeltsin's powers to rule by decree and to cancel a constitutional referendum due to be held in April. President Yeltsin struck back by declaring temporary presidential 'special rule' and the referendum was held as planned. The results showed that, by a small majority, the Russian people supported President Yeltsin and approved the continuation of his

economic reforms and the proposed new constitution.

anti-Yeltsin coup thwarted In October 1993 an insurrection against President Yeltsin led by Alexander Rutskoi, the 'pretender president', and Ruslan Khasbulatov, the chairman of the former Russian parliament, was crushed by the Russian army, claiming at least 118 lives. The crisis started in September when, faced with continuing opposition to his reforms within the conservative-dominated Congress, Yeltsin dissolved parliament and announced that he would rule by decree until fresh assembly elections in December. Congress responded by voting to impeach him and electing Vice-president Rutskoi in his place. (Rutskoi had earlier been dismissed by Yeltsin but parliament had voted against the dismissal.) A siege of the parliament building ensued and on 4 October troops loyal to Yeltsin stormed the building. Rutskoi and Khasbulatov were imprisoned.

far-right gains In December 1993 elections to a new bicameral state legislature, the Federal Assembly, produced an inconclusive result, but the extremist Liberal Democratic Party (LDP), which was reported to have widespread backing among the military, captured the largest single share of the vote (23%). A new constitution, increasing the powers of the president and strengthening central government authority, was narrowly approved in a referendum later in the month. Following the far-right electoral gains, Yeltsin was obliged to compromise on the pace of his reforms and several prominent reformers quit the cabinet during early 1994, including former premier Yegor Gaidar. In February 1994, despite opposition from the president, an amnesty was granted to the leaders of both the 1991 and 1993 abortive coups. In the same month, an autonomy agreement was reached with Tatarstan. During 1994 Russia reached an economic accord with the European Union (formerly the European Community) and signed a 'partnership for peace' agreement with the North Atlantic Treaty Organization (NATO), which resulted in it participating in NATO exercises. The last Russian troops were withdrawn from eastern Germany and the Baltic states in August 1994, but peacekeeping forces were stationed in the Caucasus region and Tajikistan. The economy had contracted further during 1993, inflation remained high, and organized crime was on the increase. However, by 1994, 30% of state-owned enterprises had been privatized and 62% of GDP was produced by the private sector. Positive growth in GDP was at last registered in 1995.

civil war in Chechnya Russia's invasion of the breakaway republic of Chechnya (until June 1992 part of Checheno-Ingush) in December 1994 threatened to create another 'Afghanistan situation'. Indiscriminate bombing of the republic's capital, Grozny, in the face of fierce Chechen resistance resulted in high numbers of casualties, many of them civilian. As reports of low troop morale and lack of a unified command filtered back from the front, criticism of Russia's conduct of the war, estimated to have cost around £660 million a week, mounted both at home and abroad. On 30 July 1995 a peace deal, brokered by Prime Minister Chernomyrdin, was signed. It followed a hostage crisis in the southern Russian town of Budennovsk, in which 140 people had been killed, and the passing of a no-confidence motion by the State Duma (lower house) over the government's handling of the incident. Chernomyrdin agreed to enter into negotiations with the Chechen guerrillas in exchange for the release of the remaining hostages and the resultant deal provided for an immediate ceasefire, demilitarization of the republic, enhanced autonomy, and the holding of fresh elections in

December 1995. Fighting continued, however, in mountainous southern Chechnya prior to and during the elections and in January 1996 international outrage followed the Russian army's bombardment of a village on the Chechen border where 100 were being held hostage by 250 Chechen separatists. At least 150 Chechen lives were lost in the assault.

President Yeltsin's health had deteriorated noticeably during 1995, his public appearances became infrequent, and he appeared increasingly to be subject to the overall command of a conservative military-nationalist grouping (as had Gorbachev 1990–91). Voter disillusionment was reflected in the results of parliamentary elections in December 1995, in which the Communist Party attracted the largest share of the vote, 21%.

Vladimir Kadannikov replaced Anatoly Chubais as first deputy prime minister in January 1996. In February 1996, despite widespread concern over the Russian military's human-rights record in the Chechen conflict, Russia was admitted to the Council of Europe and in the same month the IMF agreed a three-year loan of $10 billion. The communist-dominated Russian parliament passed a resolution in March which denounced the December 1991 Belovezhsk Agreement which had broken up the Soviet Union. In April an agreement on economic union was signed with Belarus and closer ties were also established with Kazakhstan and Kyrgyzstan. The civil war in Chechnya continued and the rebel leader Jokar Dudaev was killed during a rocket attack in April. In May his successor Zelimkhan Yandarbiev agreed a peace deal with Yeltsin providing for a ceasefire to commence 1 June, followed by the withdrawal of Russian troops in August, the mutual release of detainees, and Chechen sovereignty within the Russian state. Also in May Yeltsin issued a proposal to phase out conscription to the Russian army by the year 2000.

Yeltsin re-elected Boosted by the Chechnya peace deal, Yeltsin won the first round of the presidential election in June 1996, defeating his main rival, Gennady Zyuganov, leader of the Russian Communist Party, with 35% of the vote compared to Zyuganov's 32%. Alexander Lebed, a former middle-ranking officer of Russian troops in Afghanistan, running on an anti-crime and anti-corruption platform, gained 15% of the vote. Quickly appointing Alexander Lebed as national security officer, Yeltsin went on to secure his re-election in the run-off race against Zyuganov in July.

Lebed negotiated a ceasefire and peace plan for Chechnya in August 1996, providing for the withdrawal of Russian troops, the formation of a transitional government, and the granting of 'special status' to Chechnya within the Russian Federation. Also in August a new 'super party', the Patriotic Popular Union of Russia (PPUR) was formed by the Russian Communist Party and the Agrarian Party. Leading figures in the new party included Rutskoi and former soviet prime minister Nikolai Ryzhkov.

In October 1996, less than four months after his appointment as national security adviser, Lebed was sacked by Yeltsin after he publicly feuded with interior minister Anatoly Kulikov, who had accused Lebed of planning a 'creeping coup'. Lebed was replaced by Ivan Rybkin. In the same month, Rutskoi was elected governor of Kursk in southwest Russia.

Yeltsin underwent heart bypass surgery in November 1996, and concern over his health continued after he returned to work a month later; he returned to hospital in January 1997, suffering from pneumonia.

Direct elections, held mid-1996–early 1997, brought to power a number of independents and communists; this weakened presidential control over the upper house of parliament, the Council of the Federation, whose representatives comprised the heads of the local legislature and executive.

In January 1997, all remaining Russian combat troops were withdrawn from Chechnya and Aslan Maskhadov, the comparatively moderate former chief-of-staff of the Chechen army and prime minister in the interim government, who had negotiated the August 1996 peace deal, was elected president of the separatist republic.

Critical of the ineffectiveness of his government, in March 1997 President Yeltsin promoted his reformist chief-of-staff, Anatoly Chubais, to the positions of first deputy prime minister and finance minister, and brought in Boris Nemtsov, the reforming governor of Nizhniy Novgorod province, as the other first deputy prime minister. In effect, they would take over control of the economy from prime minister Chernomyrdin in what was Russia's most reform-minded government for several years. The reduction of household subsidies and pensions reform were key priorities of the new government. Valentin Yumashev, a journalist, became the president's new chief-of-staff. Vladimir Potanin, who had been appointed first deputy prime minister in charge of the economy in August 1996, was sacked.

In March 1997, at a summit meeting in Helsinki with US President Clinton, President Yeltsin reluctantly accepted that NATO would expand to take in Central European members and agreed to push ahead with further cuts in nuclear, chemical, and conventional weapons. However, the START II treaty remained unratified by the Russian parliament.

In September 1997, President Yeltsin signed a controversial bill that endangered religious freedoms regained only since the collapse of the USSR. The new law meant that the churches needed documentary proof from the authorities that they had a legal entity in the USSR 15 years earlier, under Brezhnev's regime. The law caused an international outcry, particularly from minority religions in Russia, human-rights groups, the Vatican, and the USA. The new law was put into practice in October when the police stormed a Ukrainian Orthodox church near Moscow and arrested the church's archbishop. The Ukrainian Orthodox Church had broken away from the Russian Orthodox Church after the end of the USSR.

In October 1997, Russia's lower house of parliament voted to ratify the 1993 Chemical Weapons Convention, banning the development, production, and use of chemical weapons, an accord backed by over 160 countries. Russia is the largest possessor of such weapons, with stocks of over 40,000 tonnes. Also in October the opposition withdrew the threat of a vote of no confidence against the government of Prime Minister Chernomyrdin after President Yeltsin proposed round-table negotiations (involving nine members from the Federation Council, eight from the State Duma, and three each from the government and the presidency) on controversial policies, including household subsidies and land ownership.

corruption and instability
In November Boris Berezovsky, one of Russia's richest men, who had been condemned as the unacceptable face of new Russian 'crony capitalism', was sacked from his post as adviser to the president for allegedly seeking to further his own business interests.

In November the leading reformist politician, Anatoly Chubais, resigned as finance minister after it was revealed that he had accepted an advance of $90,000 for a planned book on privatization. The money came from a publishing house linked to a bank that had done well out of privatizations which Chubais had overseen in his ministerial capacity. Mikhail Zadornov, formerly head of

the budget committee of the Duma, and a member of the Yabloko liberal opposition party, became the new finance minister and Prime Minister Chernomyrdin regained more influence over economic policy. However, Chubais was persuaded by President Yeltsin to remain as a first-deputy prime minister since the country faced a difficult winter, with austerity continuing and economic growth only just starting.

relations with China President Yeltsin and the Chinese head of state, Jiang Zemin, in mid-November 1997 ended a long-running border dispute that had exploded into armed clashes during the 1960s. The agreement to implement a 1991 accord that mapped out the entire 4,480-km/2,800-mi frontier was reached during the fifth Sino-Russian summit in Moscow. Implementation of the border accord was delayed because of disagreements amongst experts as to where to place markers on the eastern frontier stretching in an arc from Mongolia to the Sea of Japan.

government sacked by Yeltsin
President Yeltsin surprised Moscow and the West in March 1998 by sacking his entire government, including two of its pivotal figures – Viktor Chernomyrdin, the prime minister, and his most aggressive free-marketeer, Anatoly Chubais, the first deputy prime minister. Yeltsin was quick to issue a reassurance that Russia would press ahead with its programme of economic reforms, which were widely blamed by the country's people for causing years of economic misery. The West was reassured by Yeltsin's appointment as acting prime minister of Sergei Kiriyenko, the Fuel and Energy Minister, who had a reputation as a committed reformist. Kiriyenko, a former banker and oil refinery manager, was finally accepted by the Duma in the third round of voting in late April. He formed a young cabinet by Russian standards – the three most

senior members of the cabinet – after the President himself – were no more than 40 years old. The reformist Boris Nemtsov, a close ally of the new prime minister, remained as deputy prime minister.

Overall, during the first half of 1998, the Russian government faced a mounting financial crisis caused by an inability to collect tax revenues, industrial unrest, and plummeting oil revenues; the stock market fell by more than 50% and the currency came under pressure from international speculators, forcing a hike in interest rates to 150%. Kiriyenko brought the reformist Boris Fedorov and Anatoly Chubais into his government team and in July 1998 Russia received the first half of an £11 billion IMF rescue package, with economic reform conditions attached. However, the government, faced by an obstructive legislature, made limited progress in achieving spending cuts and in August 1998, the rouble was devalued by 20% and a short-term moratorium placed on foreign debt repayments. In late August, President Yeltsin, on his return from holiday, unexpectedly sacked Kiriyenko and the entire government, and sought to restore to office his trusted ally, Viktor Chernomyrdin.

The communist-dominated Duma twice refused to ratify Chernomyrdin's appointment, leaving the country without a government. This forced Yeltsin to nominate as prime minister Yevgeny Primakov, his acting foreign minister and a cautious former spymaster who had served every Soviet and Russian leader since Khrushchev. The Duma endorsed his nomination in September 1998 and a new government was formed. It was notable for the lack of economic reformers in key positions and its inclusion, in charge of the economy, of Yuri Maslyukov, who had been the last head of the Gosplan state planning agency in the USSR.

In early November 1998 the government introduced a cautious economic restructuring programme, which was approved by the Communist-dominated Duma. With food stocks low, the USA promised aid of over 3 million tonnes of grain and meat, while Japan promised an $800 million aid package. GDP was expected to decline by 5% in 1998.

Also in November 1998 Galina Starovoitova, a prominent liberal Russian politician, human rights activist, and opponent of corruption, was shot dead in St Petersburg; and Yuri Luzhkov, the popular mayor of Moscow, formed a new centrist movement, Otechestvo (Fatherland).

Yeltsin threw Russian politics into turmoil in May 1999 by sacking the prime minister, Yevgeny Primakov, and the cabinet, as the country's lower house, the Duma, launched into a debate on whether to begin impeachment proceedings against the president. Sergei Stepashin, the interior minister, was named acting prime minister by Yeltsin. Later that month, the Duma confirmed Stepashin as prime minister and cancelled impeachment proceedings against the ailing president.

In June 1999, the Duma passed bills to reform banking and taxation, as demanded by the International Monetary Fund (IMF). This was followed by a summit between Russia and Group of Seven (G7) leaders in Cologne, Germany, later in June, who agreed to discuss rescheduling Russia's debt.

Prime Minister Stepashin visited Washington in July 1999 in an attempt to improve his country's relations with the USA. The IMF agreed to lend Russia $4.5 billion.

Boris Yeltsin in August 1999 sacked his fourth government in 18 months, discarding Sergei Stepashin, who had been in office just 82 days. He astonished the world by naming the head of Russia's federal security service, Vladimir Putin, as the next prime minister and his preferred successor. Also in August, Putin was confirmed as the country's new prime minister by the Duma.

Second Chechen War In August 1999, in Dagestan, a republic in the country's south, Islamic paramilitaries declared independence in an attempt to create a fundamentalist state, prompting a crackdown by the Russian army and a fierce battle for the region's mountain villages, forming the beginning of Russia's second war against Chechnya. In September 1999 an Islamic terrorist bombing campaign claimed around 350 lives, including 118 in an explosion in Moscow, and an explosion in Dagestan. Russia bombed alleged terrorist targets in Chechnya as a prelude to invasion by 30,000 troops. The military campaign was strongly supported by the Russian public. By November 1999 the Russian government claimed that it was close to taking the capital, Grozny. Yeltsin refused to act on Western criticism of his war with Chechnya which was directed at him when he attended a summit for the Organization for Security and Cooperation in Europe (OSCE) in Istanbul in November. Despite claims by Chechen guerrillas that they had made some advances in December 1999, Russian forces claimed to have surrounded the capital, Grozny, and issued an ultimatum to civilians that they must leave or die. After Western protests, and in a bid to deflate international pressure on Moscow, the Russian ultimatum was deferred by a week and it was claimed that the Russian military had arranged two safe corridors and a daytime ceasefire to enable civilians to flee without danger. By the end of January 2000, despite stiff resistance and heavy losses, Russian forces were reported to have taken control of the centre Grozny, and about 40% of the town.

Responding to increasing international criticism of mass arrests, torture, and killing by the Russian army fighting in Chechnya, at the end of February 2000, Moscow ordered an official investigation into possible war crimes. Permission was given for the Council of Europe's human rights commissioner to go to the region and investigate the allegations for herself. Meanwhile, Russian forces claimed that they had cornered Chechen rebels and killed hundreds, and at the same time reported some of the heaviest losses they had sustained during the five-month conflict.

Yeltsin resigns Boris Yeltsin resigned as president of the Russian Federation on 31 December 1999. Announcing that he was bowing out to give a younger generation a chance, he apologized to his country for failing to fulfil their hopes. The prime minister and acting president, Vladimir Putin, confirmed that the presidential poll would take place in March 2000. Putin looked like a strong candidate for president, as the party he endorsed, the Unity Party, became the second largest in the Duma in the December general election. Putin made his mark of departure from Yeltsin's rule by sacking some of the ex-president's leading ministers and officials, including Yeltsin's daughter, which suggests that he wanted to cut ties quickly with those holders of Kremlin posts who were tainted with corruption. He promoted a reformer, Mikhail Kasyanov, to first deputy prime minister, and in early January 2000 signed a decree radically changing the national security strategy to focus more upon fighting terrorism and organized crime. It also published a nuclear weapons strategy which was more suspicious of Western powers than the previous strategy. In February 2000 in the new Duma, the Communists and Unity Party, the party closest to the Kremlin, agreed to share most committees between them.

Putin as president In general elections in March 2000 Vladimir Putin, the acting president, was elected as president of the Russian Federation, and inaugurated in early May. Meanwhile, members of the Council of Europe condemned his campaign against Chechnya, and in April 2000 the Council of Europe's parliamentary assembly lifted Russia's voting rights and proposed suspending Russia from the Council. Russia vowed to continue the campaign; however President Putin, in a conciliatory gesture, told the EU that he would present a plan to settle the situation. At his inauguration in May 2000, Putin asked for approval of his choice of prime minister, Mikhail Kasyanov. Approval was given in May 2000, and Kasyanov was appointed to head a new government made up of several reformers, as well as some ministers who were close to Yeltsin.

Putin made his first official trip to the West since his election when he visited London, England, in April 2000. A few days earlier, Russia's Duma had ratified START II, the arms-control treaty which had been ratified by the USA in 1996, with the aim of reducing both countries' nuclear arsenals. Meanwhile, Putin rejected a plan from the Chechen president, Aslan Maskhadov, and the battle in Chechnya continued. By mid-May, 2,233 Russian soldiers had been killed and 6,575 wounded in the fighting since August 1999. The UN Human Rights Commission criticized Russia for using disproportionate force and for attacking civilians during the war, and requested that UN investigators be permitted to investigate the area.

control of the regions Despite continuing claims that Russia was in complete control of Chechnya, there was continuing violence in the region. Casualties included the deputy to Moscow's civilian administration in Grozny, Sergei Zverev, and the mayor of Grozny, Supyan Makhchayev, both of whom were the targets of attacks made by rebels. In spite of local resistance, President Putin imposed direct presidential rule on Chechnya

in June 2000, unveiling his plans to rebuild the country's shattered economy. Retaliation ensued, however, in the form of five suicide bomber attacks on Russian-controlled towns in Chechnya on 3 July 2000. The attacks resulted in 42 Russian soldiers and 11 civilians being killed. A month later, a bomb exploded in the centre of Moscow, killing seven people and injuring around 100. Although the Chechen president, Aslan Maskhadov, denied that his guerrillas were responsible, popular Russian opinion blamed Chechen rebels. President Putin tried to prevent anti-Chechen hysteria by vowing to see through the military campaign in Chechnya. The leader of the Chechen defence of Grozny until February, Lechi Islamov, was captured by Russian forces in August.

Putin's plan to create tighter control over Russia's regions was ratified in July 2000 as bills were passed to replace the regional governors with appointed legislators, and to strip the governors of their immunity from prosecution. The governors, who made up parliament's upper chamber, reluctantly voted in favour of this motion, as their opposition was likely to be vetoed by the lower chamber (the Duma), and by voting in favour, a confrontation with Putin was avoided. The reforms were intended to make the governors work more effectively, as well as affording moer power to Moscow, and, because they also included a new tax-reform package, they were intended to attract foreign investment.

disaster in 2000 Russian president Vladimir Putin faced criticism from his own country after he failed to return from his holiday when 118 men died on board a Russian nuclear-powered submarine, the *Kursk*, after it plunged to the bottom of the Barents Sea on 13 August 2000 during a naval exercise. Russia claimed that the accident was the result of a collision with a foreign submarine, and after several failed rescue attempts, accepted offers of foreign help, although too late to save the men on board. When foreign rescue divers finally reached the craft, they reported that it appeared that all crew members had died almost at once. The Russian government announced a policy of reducing forces by a third and of increasing pay for soldiers in an attempt to boost the Russian military. Only a week later, the Ostankino television tower in Moscow, one of the symbols of the capital, suffered a fire which gutted the interior of the tower, the world's second tallest free-standing structure. Three people were killed and programmes to viewers in the capital were halted for several days.

summit meetings In July 2000, the presidents of Russia, China, Kazakhstan, Kyrgyzstan, and Tajikistan met in Dushanbe, Tajikistan, and pledged cooperation in fighting terrorism, religious extremism, and drug trafficking. The following October, Russia agreed with Armenia, Belarus, Kazakhstan, Kyrgyzstan, and Tajikistan to form a 'Eurasian Economic Union'.

In November 2000, Russia's security council agreed to reduce its armed forces by 20% – 600,000 people – by 2005.

nationalist symbols In December 2000, the Duma voted to restore the old Soviet national anthem, though with different words, and re-instate the tsarist flag and double-eagle crest as national emblems.

Chechnya In January 2001, Putin announced plans to withdraw 80,000 troops from Chechnya, cutting Russian forces there by 75%. Overall control of the war in Chechnya would be transferred to the secret police. 3,500 troops left Chechnya in March. The same month, three bombs blamed on Chechen rebels killed 24 people and injured over 140 in southern Russia. In response, Putin replaced his defence and interior ministers with personal allies.

mounting tensions with the USA Differences between Russia and the USA had mounted during 2000 as President Putin had tried to rebuild Russian state power. He had visited former Soviet allies from Vietnam to Cuba, cultivated European leaders, and sought to re-energize the Russian armed forces. In February 2001, a US FBI agent was arrested for spying for Russia, and in March the USA expelled 6 Russian diplomats, giving a further 51 notice to leave. Russia retaliated by expelling 4 US diplomats, and giving another 46 notice to leave. Earlier in March, Russia had confirmed it would resume conventional arms sales to Iran, and also help it to complete a nuclear-power plant. The USA called on Russia not to supply Iran with advanced weapons.

media empire dismantled In April 2001, Gazprom, Russia's largest company and the world's biggest supplier of natural gas, took over NTV, the last national independent television channel, firing the director and top managers. About 400 journalists went on strike, and barred the doors of the television studios, claiming Gazprom's close connection to the Kremlin was a threat to free reporting. Public demonstrations occurred in Moscow and St Petersburg. Security forces secured the premises for the new management, and 40 journalists resigned and set up a new channel.

NTV was part of the Media-Most group, owned by Vladimir Gusinsky. Two of the group's leading publications were also shut down in April. Gusinsky, who was accused of fraud and money-laundering, was in exile in Spain, where a Spanish court refused to extradite him.

new party formed Liberal right-wing reformers, led by former deputy prime minister Boris Nemtsov, consolidated themselves in the Union of Right Forces (SPS), in May.

government extends influence over big business In May 2001, the Kremlin tightened its control over Gazprom by orchestrating the dismissal of its long-time chief executive. He was replaced by a senior government official associated with President Putin.

US missile tests denounced Russia denounced a missile test carried out by the USA on 15 July 2001, and accused it of threatening to undermine international efforts opposed to a new arms race. The test, 232 km/144 mi above the Pacific Ocean, appeared to be paving the way for further testing of the controversial US National Missile Defense (NMD) system. President Putin reiterated his concern that the NMD would breach the 1972 Anti-Ballistic Missile (ABM) treaty, considered one of the pillars of post-war arms control.

summit with North Korea President Putin met North Korean leader Kim Jong Il in the Kremlin on 4 August 2001. Putin pledged economic assistance to help modernize the North Korean economy, and Kim Jong Il promised no new missile tests until at least 2003.

The USA increased pressure on Russia in August 2001 by issuing what amounted to a November deadline for Moscow to agree to US President George W Bush's plan for a missile defence shield. As work was due to commence in late August to clear the ground for an eventual missile-defence testing site in Alaska, the USA insisted it would withdraw from the 1972 Anti-Ballistic Missile treaty unilaterally if necessary. Russia announced it was willing to make certain amendments to the treaty.

anti-terrorism coalition In the wake of the 11 September terrorist attacks on the USA, President Putin pledged support for US military action in Afghanistan. He said he would support the forces of Afghanistan's Northern Alliance in their fight against the Taliban.

further challenge to press freedom Russia's last independent television channel with a national reach, TV-6,

was shut down on 11 January 2002 in a surprise court decision by judges in Moscow. The court ordered TV-6 to be closed on grounds of bankruptcy, despite the station's claims that it was profitable. Bailiffs closed the network on 21 January, and handed its place on the airwaves to a sports channel. TV-6's coverage of the war in Chechnya and official corruption had angered the government, and it was suspected that the closure had been authorized by the Kremlin.

In May, President Putin signed a star signed a strategic arms-control agreement with George W Bush pledging to reduce long-range nuclear warheads by two-thirds over ten years. He also oversaw Russian commitment to a joint council with NATO to cooperate on terrorism and international crisis management.

In the same month, 34 people, including 12 children, were killed in a bomb explosion during a parade in Kaspiisk in the southern Russian republic of Dagestan, near the border with the neighbouring republic of Chechnya. Putin blamed Chechen separatists for the attack.

Russian Revolution two revolutions of February and October 1917 (Julian *calendar) that began with the overthrow of the Romanov dynasty and ended with the establishment of a communist soviet (council) state, the Union of Soviet Socialist Republics (USSR). In October Bolshevik workers and sailors, led by Vladimir Ilyich *Lenin, seized government buildings and took over power.

The **February Revolution** (March by the Western calendar) arose because of food and fuel shortages, continuing repression by the tsarist government, and military incompetence in World War I. Riots broke out in Petrograd (as St Petersburg was known 1914–24), which led to the abdication of Tsar Nicholas II and the formation of a provisional government, made up of liberals and a few social democrats, under Prince Gyorgy Yevgenevich Lvov (1861–1925). Lvov was then replaced as head of government by Alexander Kerensky, a respected orator who was concerned to stabilize the revolution. The government had little support, however, as troops, communications, and transport were controlled by the Petrograd Soviet of Workers, Peasants, and Soldiers, which was originally formed during the failed revolution of 1905. In April Lenin returned to Russia (after having been exiled since 1905) as head of the Bolsheviks, and under his command the Bolsheviks gained control of the soviets; advocated land reform (under the slogan 'All power to the Soviets'); and appealed for an end to Russian involvement in World War I, which Lenin characterized as an 'Imperialist' war.

The **October Revolution** was a coup on the night of 25–26 October (6–7 November by the Western calendar). Bolshevik workers and sailors seized the government buildings and the Winter Palace, Petrograd, where they arrested the ministers of the provisional government in the name of the people. The second All-Russian Congress of Soviets, which met the following day, proclaimed itself the new government of Russia, and Lenin became leader. In his speech to the Congress he announced an immediate end to Russian involvement in the war and advocated the return of the land to the peasants. The Bolsheviks soon took control of the cities, established worker control in factories, and nationalized the banks. They also set up the *Cheka (secret police) to silence the opposition, and, in 1918, concluded peace with Germany through the Treaty of *Brest-Litovsk. The Western Allies, with the exception of some leftists, were alarmed by the Russian Revolution from the beginning, seeing the threat of Russia's departure from the war. The treaty with Germany realized the Allies' fears. Germany achieved great

economic gains by acquiring large amounts of Russian land and resources. Furthermore, it was also now able divert troops from Russia to the Western front, where Allied armies in France were facing exhaustion (see *World War I).

In the same year the *Russian civil war broke out, when anti-Bolshevik elements within the army attempted to seize power. The war lasted until 1922, when the Red Army, organized by Leon *Trotsky, finally overcame White (tsarist) opposition, but with huge losses, after which communist control was complete. Some 2 million refugees fled from Russia during these years.

Russian revolution, 1905 political upheaval centred in and around St Petersburg, Russia (1905–06), leading up to the February and October revolutions of 1917. On 22 January 1905 thousands of striking unarmed workers marched to Tsar Nicholas II's Winter Palace in St Petersburg to ask for reforms. Government troops fired on the crowd, killing many people. After this 'Bloody Sunday' slaughter the revolution gained strength, culminating in a general strike which paralysed the whole country in October 1905. Revolutionaries in St Petersburg formed a 'soviet' (council) called the Soviet of Workers' Deputies. Nicholas II then granted the Duma (parliament) the power to pass or reject proposed laws. Although these measures satisfied the liberal element, the revolution continued to gain ground and came to a head when the army crushed a serious uprising in December 1905.

Russo-Japanese War war between Russia and Japan 1904–05, which arose from conflicting ambitions in Korea and *Manchuria, specifically, the Russian occupation of Port Arthur (modern Lüshun) in 1897 and of the Amur province in 1900. Japan successfully besieged Port Arthur May 1904–January 1905, took Mukden (modern Shenyang) on 29 February–

10 March, and on 27 May defeated the Russian Baltic fleet, which had sailed halfway around the world to Tsushima Strait. A peace treaty was signed on 23 August 1905. Russia surrendered its lease on Port Arthur, ceded southern Sakhalin to Japan, evacuated Manchuria, and recognized Japan's interests in Korea.

Rwanda landlocked country in central Africa, bounded north by Uganda, east by Tanzania, south by Burundi, and west by the Democratic Republic of Congo (formerly Zaire).

Rykov, Aleksei Ivanovich (1881–1938) Soviet communist. He was chairman of the Supreme Council of National Economy (1918–20 and 1923–24), deputy chairman of the Council of People's Commissars (1921 24), and succeeded Lenin as chairman (1924–30). He was also a member of the Communist Party's Politburo.

Ryzhkov, Nikolai Ivanovich (1929–) Russian politician. He held governmental and party posts from 1975 before being brought into the Politburo and serving as prime minister 1985–90 under Gorbachev. A low-profile technocrat, Ryzhkov was the author of unpopular economic reforms. In August 1996 he became a leading member of the communist-led Patriotic Popular Union of Russia, one of the main left-wing factions in Russia's Duma.

S

Sabah, Sheikh Jabir al-Ahmad al-Jabir al- (1928–) Emir of Kuwait from 1977. He suspended the national assembly in 1986, after mounting parliamentary criticism, ruling in a feudal, paternalistic manner. On the invasion of Kuwait by Iraq in 1990 he fled to Saudi Arabia, returning to Kuwait in March 1991. In 1992 a reconstituted national assembly was elected.

Sabah, Sheikh Saad al-Abdullah al-Salim al- (1930–) Kuwaiti Crown Prince and politician, prime minister 1978– . Sheikh Saad, eldest son of the former emir of Kuwait, Sheikh Abdullah al-Salim al-Sabah was named Kuwait's crown prince and prime minister at the beginning of 1978, after Sheikh Jabir al-*Sabah, the cousin of Sheikh Saad, became emir, thus assuring that the emirship would pass once again to the Salim side of the family. More gregarious and less austere than his cousin, Sheikh Saad's personality made him popular in some quarters, although his background in police and security matters, and his reported suspicion of parliament, led him to be disliked by others.

Sacco, (Ferdinando) Nicola (1891–1927) Italian anarchist. Sacco emigrated to the USA in 1908. In 1920 he was accused, with Bartolomeo *Vanzetti, of murdering two men while robbing a shoe factory in Massachusetts. Although the evidence was largely circumstantial, the two men were tried in 1921 and sentenced to death. They were executed in 1927 after a controversial and lengthy appeal. It has been claimed that they were punished for their political sympathies, but experts now believe that Sacco was guilty, and Vanzetti innocent.

Sacco–Vanzetti case murder trial in Massachusetts, USA, 1920–21. Italian immigrants Nicola Sacco (1891–1927) and Bartolomeo Vanzetti (1888–1927) were convicted of murder during an alleged robbery. The conviction was upheld on appeal, with application for retrial denied. Prolonged controversy delayed execution until 1927. In 1977 the verdict was declared unjust because of the judge's prejudice against the accuseds' anarchist views.

Sadat, (Muhammad) Anwar (1918–1981) Egyptian politician, president 1970–81. Succeeding *Nasser as president in 1970, he restored morale by his handling of the Egyptian campaign in the 1973 war against Israel. In 1974 his plan for economic, social, and political reform to transform Egypt was unanimously adopted in a referendum. In 1977 he visited Israel to reconcile the two countries, and he shared the Nobel Prize for Peace in 1978 with Israeli prime minister Menachem *Begin for their efforts towards the Israel-Egypt peace treaty of 1979. Although feted by the West for pursuing peace with Israel, Sadat was denounced by the Arab world. He was assassinated by Islamic fundamentalists and succeeded by Hosni Mubarak.

Saigon, Battle of during the Vietnam War, battle 29 January–23 February 1968, when 5,000 Vietcong were expelled by South Vietnamese and US forces. The city was finally taken by North Vietnamese forces 30 April 1975, after South Vietnamese withdrawal from the central highlands.

St Kitts and Nevis country in the West Indies, in the eastern Caribbean Sea, part of the Leeward Islands.

St Lucia country in the West Indies, in the eastern Caribbean Sea, one of the Windward Islands.

St Quentin, Battle of in World War I, alternative name for the Battle of Guise 29–30 August 1914.

St Valentine's Day Massacre the murder in Chicago, USA, of seven unarmed members of the 'Bugs' Moran gang on 14 February 1929 by members of Al Capone's gang disguised as police. The killings testified to the intensity of gangland warfare for the control of the trade in illicit liquor during Prohibition.

St Vincent and the Grenadines country in the West Indies, in the eastern Caribbean Sea, part of the Windward Islands.

Saipan island of the Marianas group about 1,900 km/1,200 mi north of New Guinea. It was occupied by the Japanese in World War II and when US troops recaptured it June 1944, several hundred Japanese civilians committed mass suicide rather than be captured.

Sakharov, Andrei Dmitrievich (1921–1989) Soviet physicist. He was an outspoken human-rights campaigner, who with Igor Tamm developed the hydrogen bomb. He later protested against Soviet nuclear tests and was a founder of the Soviet Human Rights Committee in 1970. In 1975 he was awarded the Nobel Prize for Peace for his advocacy of human rights and disarmament. For criticizing Soviet action in Afghanistan, he was sent into internal exile 1980–86.

Salan, Raoul Albi Louis (1899–1984) French general. As commander-in-chief of France's forces in Algeria 1956–58 he was instrumental in securing Charles *de Gaulle's return to government in the crisis of 1958. However, after the failure of his Algiers putsch with General Challe in April 1961, Salan founded the terrorist Organization de l'Armée Secrète (OAS) from his base in Spain, plotting de Gaulle's assassination. Arrested, tried and sentenced to life imprisonment in 1962, he was amnestied by President de Gaulle in 1968.

Salandra, Antonio (1853–1931) Italian politician and prime minister, March 1914– June 1916. After Giovanni Giolitti's resignation in March 1914, he became prime minister; rejecting the former's policy of neutrality, he began working for Italy's intervention in World War I. The intractable problem of the Italian irredenta led Salandra to desert the Central Powers. By the secret Treaty of London (April 1915) Italy was committed to join the Allies and in return was promised territorial compensation in Trentino, Trieste, and Dalmatia. Parliamentary opposition to the war led to Salandra's resignation in May 1915 in order to avoid an open debate, but the pressure of pro-intervention demonstrations in the country led to his reinstatement by the king. In this way the parliamentary majority was over-ridden and war was declared on Austria on 23 May. In the same year Salandra justified Italy's rupture with the Triple Alliance on the grounds of *sacro egoismo*. Criticism of the management of the war led to Salandra's resignation in June 1916.

Salazar, António de Oliveira (1889–1970) Portuguese prime minister 1932–68 who exercised a virtual dictatorship. During World War II he maintained Portuguese neutrality but fought long colonial wars in Africa (Angola and Mozambique) that impeded his country's economic development as well as that of the colonies.

Saleh, Ali Abdullah (1942–) Yemeni politician and soldier, president from 1990. He became president of North Yemen on the assassination of its president (allegedly by South Yemen extremists) in 1978, and was re-elected to the post in 1983 and 1988. In 1990 he was elected president of a reunified Yemen, but within three years differences between north and south had resurfaced and civil war re-erupted in 1994. Saleh's army inflicted a crushing defeat on the southern forces of Vice-President al-Baidh, who fled into exile, and a new ruling coalition was formed. He was re-elected in 1999.

Salote Tupou III, Mafili'o Pilolevu (1900–1965) Queen of Tonga 1918–65. Her prosperous reign saw the reunion, for which she was mainly responsible, of the Tongan Free Church majority with the Wesleyan Church in 1924. There were also significant improvements in education, health, and agriculture. Education was made mandatory from 1929, a central medical school was established in 1929, and the economy was diversified to lessen dependence on the production of copra.

Salt March demonstration 11 March–4 May 1930 during the period of Indian nationalist agitation against British rule, forming part of Mahatma Gandhi's campaign of civil disobedience.

Samoa country in the southwest Pacific Ocean, in Polynesia, northeast of Fiji Islands.

Samsonov, Aleksandr Vassilievich (1859–1914) Russian general. He joined the cavalry 1875, served in the Russo-Turkish war, became a general 1902 and commanded a Siberian Cossack brigade in the Russo-Japanese war 1905. In 1914 he was given command of the Army of the Narev and invaded eastern Prussia. After some initial victories, advancing as far as Allenstein (now Olzstyn, Poland), he was completely defeated at Tannenberg and committed suicide 31 August 1914.

Samuel, Herbert Louis (1870–1963) 1st Viscount Samuel of Mount Carmel and Toxteth, British Liberal politician and administrator. He was leader of the Liberal Party 1931–35, held several ministerial offices, and served as high commissioner of Palestine 1920–25.

Sandinista member of a Nicaraguan left-wing organization (Sandinist National Liberation Front, FSLN) named after Augusto César Sandino, a guerrilla leader killed in 1934. It was formed in 1962 and obtained widespread support from the trade unions, the church, and the middle classes, which enabled it to overthrow the regime of General Anastasio Somoza in July 1979.

The FSLN dominated the Nicaraguan government and fought a civil war against US-backed Contra guerrillas until 1988. The FSLN was defeated in elections of 1990 by a US-backed coalition, but remained the party with the largest number of seats.

Sandino, Augusto César (1895–1934) Nicaraguan revolutionary and guerrilla leader. He made the mountains of northern Nicaragua his stronghold and led guerrilla resistance to the US forces occupying the country from 1912. His success in evading them and the Nicaraguan National Guard generated sympathy for his cause, and a great deal of anti-US feeling. After the withdrawal of US marines in 1933, the National Guard leader, Anastasio Somoza, arranged a meeting with him, apparently to discuss peace. This, however, was a ruse, and Sandino was murdered on Somoza's orders near Managua.

Sands, Bobby (1954–1981) born **Robert Sands**, Irish republican. Born in Belfast, Northern Ireland, Sands came of age at the height of 'the Troubles' in the early 1970s. Intimidation by loyalists and the introduction of internment in 1971 radicalized his politics and by 1972 he was an active service member of the *Provisional IRA. Imprisoned in the H Blocks of Long Kesh for arms offences in 1976, Sands became the leader of a prisoner's protest demanding the restoration of 'political status'. In 1981 he joined a hunger strike and subsequently was elected to the UK Parliament. He died 66 days after first refusing food.

Sandys, (Edwin) Duncan, Baron Duncan-Sandys (1908–1987) British Conservative politician. As minister for Commonwealth relations 1960–64, he negotiated the independence of Malaysia in 1963. Baron 1974.

San Francisco conference conference attended by representatives from 50 nations who had declared war on Germany before March 1945; held in San Francisco, California, USA. The conference drew up the United Nations Charter, which was signed 26 June 1945.

Sanger, Margaret Louise (1883–1966) born **Margaret Higgins**, US health reformer and crusader for birth control. In 1914 she founded the National Birth Control League. She founded and presided over the American Birth Control League 1921–28, the organization that later became the Planned Parenthood Federation of America, and the International Planned Parenthood Federation in 1952.

Sanguinetti, Julio María (1936–) Uruguayan politician and president 1985–90 and from 1994. His liberal and progressive government was characterized by the consolidation of democracy, human rights and economic restructuring, particularly in relation to Latin American integration.

San Marino small landlocked country within northeast Italy.

Santer, Jacques (1937–) Luxembourg politician, prime minister 1984–94, and president of the European Commission 1995–99. He resigned his EC presidency along with the rest of the Commission, following a scandal over fraud and mismanagement.

São Tomé and Príncipe country in the Gulf of Guinea, off the coast of West Africa.

Saro-Wiwa, Ken (1931–1995) Nigerian writer, environmentalist, and political leader of the Ogoni, an ethnic minority occupying Nigeria's oil-rich delta region. In 1991 he founded the Movement for the Survival of the Ogoni People (MOSOP) and began a vigorous international campaign against the environmental damage caused by oil exploitation. Arrested for the murder of four prominent Ogoni activists in May 1994, Saro Wiwa and eight others were executed by the military leadership in November 1995. Nigeria was suspended from the Commonwealth and condemned by the United Nations in a General Assembly vote as a result of the executions.

Sarrail, Maurice Paul Emmanuel (1856–1929) French general. He was appointed commander of the Army of the Orient, the French element in the Salonika expedition, August 1915 and became commander-in-chief of the Allied forces in Salonika January 1916. He made little impression in this role and was replaced 1917, then placed on the reserve early 1918.

Sassau-Nguesso, Denis (1943–) Congolese socialist politician, president 1979–92 and from 1997. He progressively consolidated his position within the ruling left-wing Congolese Labour Party (PCT), at the same time as improving relations with France and the USA. In 1990, in response to public pressure, he agreed that the PCT should abandon Marxism-Leninism and that a multiparty system should be introduced. He returned to power in November 1997.

Sastri, V(alangunian) S(ankarana-Rayana) Srinvasa (1869–1946) Indian politician. He was secretary of the Madras session of Congress in 1908 and took an active part in drawing up the Lucknow pact between the Congress and Muslim League, which demanded 'responsive government' for India, and was opposed to Mahatma Gandhi's policy of non-violence and noncooperation. Elected to the Madras Council in 1913, he became a member of the Imperial Legislative Council in 1915 and the Council of State in 1921.

Sato, Eisaku (1901–1975) Japanese conservative politician, prime minister 1964–72. He ran against Hayato Ikeda (1899–1965) for the Liberal Democratic Party leadership and succeeded him as prime minister, pledged to a more independent foreign policy. He shared the Nobel Prize for Peace in 1974 (with Seán *MacBride) for his rejection of nuclear weapons. His brother **Nobusuke Kishi** (1896–1987) was prime minister of Japan 1957–60.

satyagraha (Sanskrit 'insistence on truth') nonviolent resistance to British rule in India, as employed by Mahatma *Gandhi from 1918 to press for political reform; the idea owes much to the Russian writer Leo Tolstoy.

Saud (1902–1969) in full **Saud ibn Abdul Aziz al-Saud**, King of Saudi Arabia 1953–64. He initially maintained warm relations with Egypt's new ruler Gamal Abdel *Nasser, but became concerned at Nasser's growing power in the region from 1956, and thus developed close ties with the UK and the USA, which he visited in March 1957. His younger half-brother, *Faisal, was Crown Prince from 1953 and, after Saud's extravagant spending had produced a financial crisis, was made prime minister in 1958. Saud, as an Arab traditionalist, was uneasy with Faisal's advocacy of gradual Westernization, including the education of women. This led to conflicts and Faisal's resignation in 1960. However, he returned as prime minister in November 1962, after Saud fell ill. Faisal immediately published a ten-point reform and development programme that was designed to take the country into the modern age, through using the country's increasing oil wealth to provide social welfare benefits to Saudi citizens. In early 1964 Faisal became regent and in November 1964, after a meeting of a council of the senior members of the al-Saud family, Saud was persuaded to abdicate. Faisal became king and Saud lived the remainder of his life in exile.

Saudi Arabia country on the Arabian peninsula, stretching from the Red Sea in the west to the Gulf in the east, bounded north by Jordan, Iraq, and Kuwait; east by Qatar and United Arab Emirates; southeast by Oman; and south by Yemen.

government Saudi Arabia is an absolute monarchy with no written constitution, no legislature, and no political parties. The king rules, in accordance with Islamic law, by decree. He appoints and heads a council of ministers, whose decisions are the result of a majority vote but always subject to the ultimate sanction of the king. In 1992 the formation of a 60-member consultative council, the Majlis al-Shura, to be appointed every four years, suggested moves towards a more democratic form of government.

history The sultanate of Nejd in the interior came under Ottoman rule in the 18th century. Present-day Saudi Arabia is almost entirely the creation of King *Ibn Saud who, after the dissolution of the *Ottoman Empire in 1918, fought rival Arab rulers until, in 1926, he had established himself as the undisputed king of the Hejaz and sultan of Nejd. In each of these provinces he appointed one of his sons as viceroy, though Asir had a separate administration. There were three ministers, for foreign affairs, defence, and finance. In Riyadh and Mecca and in other places there were councils of notables. In 1932 Nejd and Hejaz became the United Kingdom of Saudi Arabia. Asir was incorporated in 1934.

Despite the fact that the majority of the population are Sunni Muslims (with a Shiite minority), the country since unification has been dominated by the puritanical Muslim Wahabi sect. Under the leadership of successive kings, the Wahabis keep the holy places and control the pilgrimage to Mecca, and are responsible for the country's very strict legal and social codes.

oil wealth Soon after the integration of Saudi Arabia oil was discovered, and Ibn Saud granted exploration and drilling rights to various US oil companies. Oil was first produced in commercial quantities in 1938, realizing large sums in royalties and added greatly to the kingdom's revenue, although in 1952 the Saudi Arabia Monetary Agency, a modified form of state bank, was set up in an attempt to keep the country solvent, because the extravagant demands of members of the royal family outstripped the revenue. Oil has continued to be the basis of the country's great prosperity.

foreign relations up to the 1960s
In 1936 Ibn Saud formed alliances with Iraq and Egypt. In World War II Saudi Arabia remained nominally neutral until March 1945 when it came in on the side of the Allies. In the same year the *Arab League (League of Arab States) was formed, with Saudi Arabia as a leading member.

Thereafter relations with the West deteriorated for a period, although traditionally relations with the West, especially Britain and the USA, have been among the best of any Arab country. Saudi Arabia was involved in a quarrel with Britain over the boundary of Muscat and Oman that led to fighting in the disputed Buraimi Oasis area. The country also rejected US military aid, and aligned its defence policy with Egypt, which it supported in the *Suez Crisis in 1956. Relations with the West were further strained when Saudi Arabia made use of the income from US oil concessions to sponsor international anti-Western propaganda.

the reign of King Faisal Ibn Saud died in November 1953 and was succeeded by the crown prince, Saud (1902–69). Some modernizing of the government was initiated but the king was grossly corrupt, and in 1958 Saud's brother Faisal became the effective leader of the country. Tensions developed with Egypt. Saud was deposed in favour of Faisal in

November 1964, and he took refuge for a time in Egypt, with which Saudi Arabia was by this time in direct conflict through the civil war in Yemen.

After the 1967 Arab–Israeli War Saudi Arabia gave aid to Egypt and Jordan. An abortive coup was foiled in 1969, and in the east relations were developed with Iran to establish stability in the Gulf after the British withdrawal from the area in 1971. While the country was kept tightly within traditional strictness, its global standing increased through the presence of the Islamic holy cities of Mecca and Medina, the enormous growth in earnings from oil, the close alliance with Egypt, and respect for King Faisal. Relations with the West deteriorated again during the 1973 Arab–Israeli War, and Saudi Arabia, by now the leading Arab oil producer, led in the use of oil as a crucial political weapon.

In March 1975 Faisal was assassinated by a nephew, and his half-brother, Khalid, succeeded him. Khalid was in failing health and increasingly relied on his brother Fahd to perform the duties of government. Khalid died in 1982 and was succeeded by Fahd.

Middle East affairs Saudi Arabia gave financial support to Iraq in its war with Iran. The *Iran–Iraq War (1980–88) also prompted Saudi Arabia to buy advanced missiles from the USA. Islamic fundamentalists staged demonstrations in Mecca in 1979 and 1987, leading to violence and worsening relations with Iran. In 1989 Saudi Arabia assumed a leading role in the search for a settlement of the Lebanese civil war, hosting a constitutional convention of Lebanese legislators in Taif.

participation in the Gulf War
In August 1990 the security of Saudi Arabia was threatened when Iraq invaded and occupied neighbouring Kuwait. King Fahd turned to the USA and UK for assistance and a massive build-up of ground and air strength

began, alongside Saudi Arabia's own forces, culminating in the *Gulf War of 1991 and Iraq's forced withdrawal from Kuwait. In return, King Fahd agreed to increase his oil output to offset the loss of Kuwaiti and Iraqi production, and to pay a substantial part of the cost of maintaining US and British forces. During the Gulf War, Saudi Arabia served as the staging ground for the air and ground assaults on Iraqi forces. The country was hit by Iraqi missile strikes but suffered no serious damage. However, the war is estimated to have cost Saudi Arabia $60,000 million.

limited democracy In May 1991 religious leaders demanded the creation of a consultative council to assist in the government of the kingdom, as proposed by King Fahd a month earlier. In November 1991, Saudi Arabia was one of the main participants in the historic Middle East peace conference in Spain. The eventual formation of a consultative council, Majlis al-Shura, in March 1992 did little to aid democracy, and in 1993 the introduction of regional advisory assemblies was countered by the disbanding of a committee for the protection of human rights. In October 1994 the government announced a crackdown on Islamic militants, appointing a Higher Council for Islamic Affairs as an 'ombudsman of Islamic activity in education, economic, and foreign policy'. Following a stroke in December 1995, King Fahd transferred control to Crown Prince Abdullah, a traditionalist, but in February 1996 King Fahd returned to power.

In September 2001, Saudi Arabia severed diplomatic relations with the Taliban regime in Afghanistan, in response to the 11 September terrorist attacks on the USA, believed to have been orchestrated by the Afghanistan-based terrorist leader Osama bin Laden.

In December the interior minister announced that identity cards,

carrying pictures of their unveiled faces, would be issued to Saudi women for the first time – previously a woman had been named only as a dependent on the card of her father or husband.

Savage, Michael Joseph (1872–1940) New Zealand Labour left-of-centre politician, prime minister 1935–40. He introduced much social security legislation and a popular marketing act, which helped Labour secure re-election in October 1938. He was also concurrently minister in charge of broadcasting and relations with the Maori peoples and, as foreign minister, pledged support to the UK during World War II. He died in office and was succeeded as prime minister by Peter *Fraser.

Savimbi, Jonas Malheiro (1934–2002) Angolan soldier and right-wing revolutionary, founder and leader of the National Union for the Total Independence of Angola (UNITA). From 1975 UNITA, under Savimbi's leadership, tried to overthrow the government. A peace agreement was signed in 1994. Savimbi rejected the offer of vice-presidency in a coalition government in 1996; however, in 1998, UNITA was demilitarized and accepted as a national political party.

Saxony German **Sachsen**, administrative region (German *Land*) in eastern Germany; area 18,412 sq km/ 7,109 sq mi; population (1999 est) 4,459,700. The capital is Dresden, and other major towns include Leipzig, Chemnitz, and Zwickau. The region is on the plain of the River Elbe north of the Erzgebirge mountain range. Industries include electronics, textiles, vehicles, machinery, chemicals, and coal.

Scargill, Arthur (1938–) British trade-union leader. Elected president of the National Union of Miners (NUM) in 1981, he embarked on a collision course with the Conservative government of Margaret Thatcher. The damaging strike of 1984–85 split the miners' movement. In 1995, criticizing what he saw as the Labour Party's lurch to the right, he announced that he would establish a rival party, the independent Socialist Labour Party. This proved to be largely ineffectual, and made little impact in consequent elections. By 1997 membership of the NUM had fallen to 10,000.

Schacht, Hjalmar Horace Greely (1877–1970) German financier. As president of the Reichsbank from 1923–29, he founded a new currency that ended the inflation of the Deutschmark. In 1933 he was recalled to the Reichsbank by the Nazis and, as minister of economics, restored Germany's trade balance. Dismissed from the Reichsbank after a dispute with Hitler over expenditure on rearmament, he was charged with high treason and interned; he was later acquitted of crimes against humanity at Nuremberg in 1945 and cleared by the German de-Nazification courts in 1948.

Scharnhorst German battle cruiser in World War II. Launched 1936, it took part in the Norway campaign 1940, and cruised the North Atlantic sinking 22 merchant ships. It was based at Brest in France until February 1942 when it broke out in the Channel Dash and returned to Germany. It was finally sunk in the Battle of the North Cape December 1943.

Scheer, Reinhard (1863–1928) German admiral in World War I, commander of the High Sea Fleet from 1915 and commander of the German forces at the Battle of *Jutland.

Scheidemann, Philipp (1865–1939) German politician and journalist. In 1903 he was elected to the Reichstag, and in 1911 joined the executive committee of the Social Democratic party. During World War I he was, with Friedrich Ebert, leader of the Majority Social Democrats, who voted for the government's war credits, but nevertheless worked for a peace of reconciliation. When, in 1918, Ebert became chancellor, Scheidemann, on his own initiative, proclaimed Germany a republic. In February 1919 Scheidemann was elected prime minister by the National Assembly at Weimar. A few months later he resigned, following his failure to obtain amendments of the Allies' peace conditions, and his refusal to sign the Treaty of Versailles. When Hitler came to power he left the country, and died in Denmark. Scheidemann was born in Kassel, Germany.

Schindler, Oskar (1908–1974) Czechoslovak industrialist and Jewish benefactor. A flamboyantly successful businessman, he set up a factory in Kraków, Poland, soon after the German invasion of 1939. He established good relations with the occupying forces and, through gifts and lavish entertainment, persuaded them to let him employ Jewish workers. He saved many hundreds of Jews from death in concentration camps by bribing the Nazis to release them into his 'custody'.

Schleicher, Kurt von (1882–1934) German soldier and chancellor. A member of the Prussian nobility, he held staff posts throughout World War I, afterwards joining the Reichswehr ministry, where he became the link between the army and politicians. Schleicher engineered the elimination of the Socialists from government in 1930, then played a major role in Heinrich Brüning's fall two years later. He was minister of defence in 1932, and in December of the same year he became chancellor of Germany in succession to Franz von Papen. His government lasted only until 28 January 1933, as a result of the hostility fomented by Adolf Hitler and the Nazis. President Hindenburg refused to authorize him to dissolve the Reichstag and appointed Hitler as chancellor, and Schleicher then retired into private life. Together with his wife he was murdered during the Nazi purge of 30 June 1934.

Schlieffen Plan military plan finalized in December 1905 by the German chief of general staff, General Count Alfred von Schlieffen, that formed the basis of German military planning before World War I, and inspired Hitler's plans for the conquest of Europe in World War II. It involved a simultaneous attack on Russia and France, the object being to defeat France quickly and then deploy all available resources against the Russians.

Schlüter, Poul Holmskov (1929–) Danish right-wing politician, leader of the Conservative People's Party (KF) from 1974 and prime minister 1982–93. His centre-right coalition survived the 1990 election and was reconstituted, with Liberal support. In January 1993 Schlüter resigned, accused of dishonesty over his role in an incident involving Tamil refugees. He was succeeded by Poul Nyrup Rasmussen.

Schmidt, Helmut Heinrich Waldemar (1918–) German socialist politician, member of the Social Democratic Party (SPD), chancellor of West Germany 1974–83. As chancellor, Schmidt introduced social reforms and continued Brandt's policy of *Ostpolitik. With the French president Giscard d'Estaing, he instigated annual world and European economic summits. He was a firm supporter of NATO and of the deployment of US nuclear missiles in West Germany during the early 1980s.

Schmidt was elected to the Bundestag (federal parliament) in 1953. He was interior minister for Hamburg 1961–65, defence minister 1969–72, and finance minister 1972–74. He became federal chancellor (prime minister) on Willy *Brandt's resignation in 1974. Re-elected in 1980, he was defeated in the Bundestag in 1982 following the switch of allegiance by the SPD's coalition allies, the Free Democratic Party. Schmidt retired from federal politics at the general election of 1983, having encountered growing opposition from the SPD's left wing, who opposed his stance on military and economic issues.

Schumacher, Kurt (1895–1952) German socialist politician. He was arrested in 1933, and spent 11 years in concentration camps. In 1945 he reorganized the German Social Democratic Party (SPD), and in 1949 became leader of the opposition in the West German parliament.

Schuman, Robert Jean-Baptiste Nicolas (1886–1963) French Christian-Democrat politician, prime minister 1947–48 and foreign minister 1948–55. He was a member of the post-war Mouvement Républicain Populaire (MRP). His Schuman Declaration of May 1950, drafted by Jean Monnet, outlines a scheme for pooling coal and iron ore resources. The resultant European Coal and Steel Community, established by France, Belgium, Germany, the Netherlands, Italy and Luxembourg under the 1951 Paris Treaty, was the forerunner of the European Community (now the European Union).

Schuschnigg, Kurt von (1897–1977) Austrian chancellor 1934–38, in succession to Engelbert *Dollfuss. He tried in vain to prevent Nazi annexation (*Anschluss*) but in February 1938 he was forced to accept a Nazi minister of the interior, and a month later Austria was occupied and annexed by Germany. He was imprisoned in Germany until 1945, when he went to the USA; he returned to Austria in 1967.

Schwarzkopf, Norman (1934–) called 'Stormin' Norman', US general. He was supreme commander of the Allied forces in the *Gulf War 1991. He planned and executed a blitzkrieg campaign, 'Desert Storm', sustaining remarkably few Allied casualties in the liberation of Kuwait. He was a battalion commander in the Vietnam War and deputy commander of the US invasion of Grenada in 1983.

Scopes monkey trial trial held in Dayton, Tennessee, USA, 1925. John T Scopes, a science teacher at the high school, was accused of teaching, contrary to a law of the state, Charles Darwin's theory of evolution. He was fined $100, but this was waived on a technical point. The defence counsel was Clarence Darrow and the prosecutor William Jennings *Bryan.

scorched earth in warfare, the policy of burning and destroying everything that might be of use to an invading army, especially the crops in the fields. It was used to great effect in Russia in 1812 against the invasion of the French emperor Napoleon and again during World War II to hinder the advance of German forces in 1941.

Scotland Office formerly **Scottish Office (1885–1999)**, UK government department, charged with ensuring that Scottish interests are represented within the UK government. It has been part of the Department for Constitutional Affairs since June 2003. Established in 1707 in England and in 1938 in Scotland, it is based at Dover House, in London. The elected *Scottish Parliament and Scottish Executive, comprising ministers drawn from and accountable to the Parliament, took over its role from 1 July 1999 in the case of devolved matters. The secretary of state for Scotland (from 2003) is Alistair Darling.

Scottish National Party SNP, nationalist party that supports the separation of Scotland from the UK as an independent state within the European Union. It was formed by the combining of several early nationalist parties in 1934 and at first advocated only autonomy (self-government) within the UK. It gained its first parliamentary victory in 1945 but did not make serious headway in Parliament until the 1970s when it became an influential bloc at Westminster, and its support was crucial to James Callaghan's Labour government. The SNP won 6 of Scotland's 72 seats and over one-fifth of the Scottish vote in the 1997 general election, and 35 of 129 seats in the 1999 election to the new Scottish Parliament, in which it forms the main opposition. It is now second only to the Labour Party in Scotland. Its share of the vote fell only slightly in the 2001 general election, when it won five seats.

Scottish Parliament devolved legislative (law-making) body of Scotland. It comprises 129 members and was created by the November 1998 Scotland Act, which was passed following the Scottish electorate's overwhelming approval of government proposals in a referendum on devolution held on 11 September 1997. The first elections to the Parliament were held on 6 May 1999 and the Parliament opened on 1 July 1999.

Scud Soviet-produced surface-to-surface missile that can be armed with a nuclear, chemical, or conventional warhead. The **Scud-B**, deployed on a mobile launcher, was the version most commonly used by the Iraqi army in the Gulf War 1991. It is a relatively inaccurate weapon.

Scullin, James Henry (1876–1953) Australian Labor politician, prime minister 1929–32. Scullin entered the House of Representatives in 1910. He lost his seat in 1913 and was re-elected in 1922, becoming Labor leader in 1928. With the electoral victory over the *Bruce government in 1929 he became prime minister. His period in power was dominated by the economic depression and his government was rendered virtually powerless by a hostile Senate, uncooperative state premiers, and internal divisions. Numerous defections forced him to an election in 1932, at which Labor was defeated by the newly formed United Australia Party under *Lyons. He stepped down as Labor leader in 1925 and retired from parliament in 1949.

Seaga, Edward Philip George (1930–)
US-born Jamaican centre-right politician, prime minister 1980–89. Leader of the Jamaican Labour Party (JLP) and the opposition from 1974, he defeated Michael Manley's People's National Party (PNP) in 1980. Abandoning his predecessors' socialist and non-aligned stance, he promoted free enterprise, severed diplomatic ties with communist Cuba in 1981, and developed close US links. In 1983 Seaga's JLP won all 60 seats in the House of Representatives, but lost power to the PNP, led by a more moderate Manley, in 1989; the JLP was defeated again in 1993 and 1997.

secession Latin secessio, in politics, the withdrawal from a federation of states by one or more of its members, as in the secession of the Confederate states from the Union in the USA 1860, Singapore from the Federation of Malaysia 1965, and Croatia and Slovenia from the Yugoslav Federation 1991.

Second Front in World War II, battle line opened against Germany on 6 June 1944 by the Allies (Britain and the USA). See *D-day. Following Germany's invasion of the USSR June 1941 (the 'first front'), Soviet leader Josef Stalin constantly pressured Britain to invade the European mainland, to relieve pressure on Soviet forces.

Seeckt, Hans von (1866–1936)
German general. In World War I, he planned the German offensive against Soissons, the Austro-German campaign in Galicia, and the conquest of Serbia 1915. Following the war, he became commander-in-chief of the new German Army 1921 and throughout the 1920s concentrated upon building up the 100,000 strong army into a highly-trained cadre which, from 1933 onward, was able to expand into the Reichswehr.

Seipel, Ignaz (1876–1932) Austrian statesman. A Catholic priest and professor of theology, he became minister of welfare in the last Cabinet before the collapse of old Austria in October 1918. From 1921 he led the Christian Socialists, the largest party in the new Austrian parliament, becoming chancellor the following year, and helping the republic to a period of reasonable stability. Surviving an assassination attempt in 1924, he resumed the premiership in 1926 and held it until 1929. Austria's strong man in the 1920s, Seipel nevertheless failed to consolidate its political institutions. He so mistrusted the Social Democrats that he encouraged the paramilitary forces of the Right, especially the Heimwehr, and toyed with the idea of an *Anschluss with Germany. Seipel was born in Vienna, Austria.

Seljuk Empire empire of the Turkish people (converted to Islam during the 7th century) under the leadership of the invading Tatars or Seljuk Turks. The Seljuk Empire (1055–1243) included Iran, Iraq, and most of Anatolia and Syria. It was a loose confederation whose centre was in Iran, jointly ruled by members of the family and led by a great sultan exercising varying degrees of effective power. It was succeeded by the *Ottoman Empire.

Senanayake, Don Stephen (1884–1952)
Sri Lankan politician; first prime minister of independent Sri Lanka (formerly Ceylon) 1948–52. Active in politics from 1915, he became leader of the United National Party and negotiated independence from the UK in 1947. A devout Buddhist, he promoted Sinhalese–Tamil racial harmony and rural development.

Senanayake, Dudley Shelton (1911–1973) Sri Lankan politician; prime minister 1952–53, 1960, and 1965–70. The son of Don Senanayake, he sought to continue his father's policy of communal reconciliation.

Sendero Luminoso or Shining Path, Maoist guerrilla group active in Peru, formed 1980 to overthrow the government; until 1988 its activity was confined to rural areas. From 1992 its attacks intensified in response to a government crackdown. By 1997 the 17-year war had caused 30,000 deaths. In 1999 the movement was believed to have fewer than 1,000 fighters.

Senegal country in West Africa, on the Atlantic Ocean, bounded north by Mauritania, east by Mali, south by Guinea and Guinea-Bissau, and enclosing the Gambia on three sides.

Senghor, Léopold Sédar (1906–2001) Senegalese politician and writer, the first president of independent Senegal 1960–80. Previously he was Senegalese deputy to the French national assembly 1946–58, and founder of the Senegalese Progressive Union. He was also a well-known poet and a founder of *négritude*, a black literary and philosophical movement.

Septennial Act act 1716 extending the term of a parliament from three to seven years. It was designed to bolster the Whig government, by postponing the election due 1718 to 1722, but in the long term it led to greater stability but also increased the opportunities for corruption. The Parliament Act 1911 reduced the life of a parliament to five years.

Serbia and Montenegro country in southeast Europe, with a southwest coastline on the Adriatic Sea, bounded west by Bosnia-Herzegovina, northwest by Croatia, north by Hungary, east by Romania and Bulgaria, and south by the Former Yugoslav Republic of Macedonia and Albania.

government The present constitution was adopted in 1992 for the 'rump federation' of the republics of Serbia and Montenegro. There is a two-chamber federal assembly, the Savezna Skupstina, consisting of a 138-member Chamber of Citizens – 108 of whose members are directly elected from Serbia and the rest from Montenegro – and a 40-member Chamber of the Republics, with 20 members selected by each republic

to reflect party strengths. The combined assemblies elect a federal president, who chooses a prime minister to head a cabinet of some 15 members. The constitution provides for the president and prime minister to be drawn from different republics.

The two constituent republics, Serbia and Montenegro, have their own presidents and assemblies. The federal assembly is supreme in defence matters and can declare a state of emergency in a constituent republic. However, in practice, the authority of the individual republics, which function as virtually independent states, is greater than that of the federal government.

history Until 1992 Serbia and Montenegro – along with Bosnia-Herzegovina, Croatia, Slovenia, and Macedonia – were constituent republics of Yugoslavia. When Bosnia-Herzegovina, Croatia, Slovenia, and Macedonia declared independence and seceded from the federation in the period 1991–92 Serbia and Montenegro declared the Federal Republic of Yugoslavia.

Servan-Schreiber, Jean Jacques (1924–) French publisher and radical politician, founder in 1953 of the magazine *L'Express*, which supported and popularized Pierre *Mendès-France's modernizing republicanism in the mid-1950s. He was the author of the widely influential polemic, *Le Défi Américain* (1967).

Sèvres, Treaty of the last of the treaties that ended World War I. Negotiated between the Allied powers and the Ottoman Empire, it was finalized August 1920 but never ratified by the Turkish government.

Seychelles country in the Indian Ocean, off east Africa, north of Madagascar.

Seyss-Inquart, Arthur (1892–1946) Austrian lawyer and politician. He joined the Nazi party in 1928. He was minister of the interior and security in the Schuschnigg Cabinet from

February to March 1938. Seyss-Inquart became governor of Austria in 1938 and deputy-governor general of Poland in 1939. As Reich commissioner for the Netherlands he became notorious for his cruelty, and after the war was executed as a war criminal. Seyss-Inquart was born in Moravia.

Sforza, Carlo (1873–1952) Italian diplomat and statesman. In 1919 he became under-secretary of state, and in 1920 foreign minister under Giovanni Giolitti. He was ambassador to France in 1922. After Mussolini's March on Rome, he resigned and returned to Italy, where he was an active opponent of fascism. By 1928 he was forced into exile, first in Belgium, and later in the USA. He returned to Italy in 1943, and made a dramatic re-entry into European diplomacy at the Paris Conference of 1947, once more becoming Italy's foreign minister. His efforts to restore Italian influence in world politics and to bring Italy into the Western alliance occupied the last years of his life. By the time he resigned, owing to ill-health, in 1951, he had seen his policies brought to a successful fruition.

SHAEF abbreviation for **Supreme Headquarters Allied Expeditionary Force**, World War II military centre established 15 February 1944 in London, where final plans were made for the Allied invasion of Europe (under US general Eisenhower).

Shagari, (Alhaji) Shehu (Usman Aliyu) (1925–) Nigerian politician, president 1979–83. An experienced minister prior to the 1966 coup, he became both state commissioner for education in Sokoto province and federal commissioner for economic development and reconstruction 1968–70, and then commissioner for finance 1971–75. He was a member of the constituent assembly that drew up the constitution for the Second Republic, and in 1979 was the successful presidential candidate for the National Party of Nigeria. He was overthrown in a military coup in 1983.

Shamir, Yitzhak Yernitsky (1915–) Polish-born Israeli right-wing politician; prime minister 1983–84 and 1986–92; leader of the Likud (Consolidation Party) until 1993. He was foreign minister under Menachem Begin 1980–83, and again foreign minister in Shimon *Peres's unity government 1984–86.

Sharett, Moshe (1894–1965) Israeli Labour politician, prime minister 1954–55. He was responsible for the volunteering of Palestinian Jews into the British army during World War II, and following the establishment of the state of Israel in 1948, Sharett became foreign minister and a Knesset (parliament) deputy, gaining a reputation as a moderate. In January 1954 he replaced Ben-Gurion as prime minister, and remained foreign minister. He was replaced as prime minister in November 1955, when, following parliamentary elections, Ben-Gurion was returned to power.

Sharon, Ariel (1928–) Israeli right-wing Likud politician, prime minister from 2001. Initially a soldier, he left the army in 1973 to help found the Likud party with Menachem *Begin. He was elected to the Knesset (Israeli parliament) in 1977, and held a succession of influential posts. A leading member of the staunchly nationalist new right, he took over Likud's leadership from Binyamin *Netanyahu after the party's defeat in the 1999 general election. His electoral victory over Labour's Ehud *Barak in February 2001 endangered the *Israel–Palestine peace process, as it was his controversial visit to Jerusalem's Haram al-Sharif (Temple Mount) in September 2000 that precipitated a second Palestinian intifada (uprising) against Israeli forces that claimed hundreds of lives.

Sharpeville black township in South Africa, 65 km/40 mi south of Johannesburg and north of

Vereeniging; 69 people were killed here when police fired on a crowd of anti-apartheid demonstrators 21 March 1960.

Shastri, Lal Bahadur (1904–1966) Indian politician, prime minister 1964–66. He campaigned for national integration, and secured a declaration of peace with Pakistan at the Tashkent peace conference in 1966.

Sheehy-Skeffington, Hannah (1877–1946) born **Hannah Sheehy**, Irish patriot and feminist. One of the first women in Ireland to study at, and teach in, a university, she was a founder member of the Irish Women Graduates' Association (1901) and campaigned ardently for votes for women. Her husband, the pacifist Francis Sheehy-Skeffington, was murdered by troops during the 1916 Easter Rising.

Shevardnadze, Edvard Amvrosievich (1928–) Georgian politician, president 1992–2003. He was Soviet foreign minister 1985–91. A supporter of Mikhail *Gorbachev, he was first secretary of the Georgian Communist Party from 1972 and an advocate of economic reform. In 1985 he became a member of the Politburo, working for détente and disarmament. In July 1991 he resigned from the Soviet Communist Party (CPSU) and, along with other reformers and leading democrats, established the Democratic Reform Movement. In March 1992 he was chosen as chair of Georgia's ruling military council, and in October was elected speaker of parliament (equivalent to president). He survived assassination attempts in 1995 and 1998.

Shidehara, Kijuro (1872–1951) Japanese politician and diplomat, prime minister 1945–46. As foreign minister 1924–27 and 1929–31, he promoted conciliation with China, and economic rather than military expansion. After a brief period as prime minister 1945–46, he became speaker of the Japanese Diet (parliament) 1949–51.

Shinwell, Emmanuel (1884–1986) **Baron Shinwell;** called '**Manny'**, British Labour politician. In 1935 he defeated Ramsay MacDonald at Seaham Harbour, Durham, in one of the most bitterly contested British election battles of modern times. From 1942 he was chair of the Labour Party committee which drafted the manifesto 'Let us face the future', on which Labour won the 1945 election. As minister of fuel and power (1945–47) he nationalized the coal mines in 1946.

Shore, Peter David (1924–2001) **Baron Shore of Stepney**, British Labour politician. Member of Parliament for Stepney 1964–97, he was parliamentary private secretary to Harold Wilson, and held several government posts, including secretary of state for economic affairs 1967–69, for trade 1974–76, and for the environment 1976–79. After holding various opposition posts, he became shadow leader of the Commons 1984–87. A persistent critic of European economic union, he launched a 'No to Maastricht' campaign in 1992.

Siad Barre, Mohamed (1921–1995) Somalian soldier and politician, president of Somalia 1969–91. Seizing power in a bloodless coup, with promises to solve clan rivalries and regenerate his country through a policy of 'scientific socialism', he exploited those rivalries to promote his own regime and presided over a socialist government that degenerated into an autocracy based on a ruthless personality cult.

Siam former name (until 1939 and again 1945–49) of *Thailand.

Siegfried Line in World War I, a defensive line established in 1917 by the Germans in France, really a subdivision of the main *Hindenburg Line; in World War II, the Allies' name for the West Wall, a German defensive line established along its western frontier, from the Netherlands to Switzerland.

Sierra Leone   country in West Africa, on the Atlantic Ocean, bounded north and east by Guinea and southeast by Liberia.

Sihanouk, Norodom (1922–) Cambodian politician, king 1941–55 and from 1993. He was prime minister 1955–70, when his government was overthrown in a military coup led by Lon Nol. With *Pol Pot's resistance front, he overthrew Lon Nol in 1975 and again became prime minister 1975–76, when he was forced to resign by the *Khmer Rouge. He returned from exile in November 1991 under the auspices of a United Nations-brokered peace settlement to head a coalition intended to comprise all Cambodia's warring factions (the Khmer Rouge, however, continued fighting). He was re-elected king after the 1993 elections, in which the royalist party won a majority; in 1996, however, it was announced that he was suffering from a brain tumour and might abdicate. In October 1997, three months after a successful coup by communists, he left for China and his return was uncertain. In March 1998 he pardoned his son, prince Norodom Ranariddh, who had been sentenced to 30 years' imprisonment for smuggling arms and colluding with the Khmer Rouge.

Sikandar Hayat Khan (1892–1942) Indian politician. He was elected to the Punjab legislative council in 1921, and was appointed chair of the Punjab Reforms Committee to work with the Somon Commission. Elected chief minister of the Punjab at the start of World War II, he launched rural reconstruction programmes, extended irrigation facilities, laid new roads, and established and strengthened the roles of panchayats (local councils). After his death the Punjab was plunged into political turmoil.

Sikorski, Władysław Eugeniusz (1881–1943)   Polish general and politician; prime minister 1922–23, and 1939–43 in the Polish government in exile in London during World War II.

He was killed in an aeroplane crash near Gibraltar in controversial circumstances.

Silesia   region of Europe that has long been disputed because of its geographical position, mineral resources, and industrial potential; now in Poland and the Czech Republic with metallurgical industries and a coalfield in Polish Silesia. Dispute began in the 17th century with claims on the area by both Austria and Prussia. It was seized by Prussia's Frederick the Great, which started the War of the Austrian Succession; this was finally recognized by Austria in 1763, after the Seven Years' War. After World War I, it was divided in 1919 among newly formed Czechoslovakia, revived Poland, and Germany, which retained the largest part. In 1945, after World War II, all German Silesia east of the Oder-Neisse line was transferred to Polish administration; about 10 million inhabitants of German origin, both there and in Czechoslovak Silesia, were expelled.

Simeon II (1937–)   born **Simeon Borisov Saxe-Coburg-Gotha;** also known as **Simeon Koburgotski**, prime minister and former king of Bulgaria, whose political party won the country's 2001 general election. Simeon succeeded to the throne at the aged of six in 1943, after his father *Boris III's death. Simeon was a puppet king, under first German and then, from 1944, Russian occupation. In 1946 Simeon fled to Egypt after the communists rigged a referendum and declared a republic. He subsequently lived in exile in Spain. Simeon returned permanently to Bulgaria in 2001, after the Constitutional Court ruled that his family properties should be returned but that he could not stand for president. In April 2001 he formed the National Movement (NM), a populist political party. The NM won half the parliament's seats in 2001, and although he was not originally a candidate, Simeon accepted a nomination in July 2001 to become prime minister, taking the family name Simeon Koburgotski.

Simmonds, Kennedy Alphonse (1936–) St Kitts' centre-right politician, prime minister 1980–95. He helped form the centre-right People's Action Movement (PAM) in 1965 and became its leader in 1976, challenging the dominant St Kitts Labour Party (SKLP). In 1980 he became prime minister over a PAM-led coalition with the Nevis Reformation Party (NRP). After defusing secessionist demands on Nevis Island by establishing a federation in 1982, he led the country through independence in 1983, and sought to promote tourism and diversification of agriculture. In 1995 he lost power to the SKLP, led by Denzil Douglas.

Simon, John Allsebrook, 1st Viscount Simon (1873–1954) British Liberal politician. He was home secretary 1915–16, but resigned over the issue of conscription. He was foreign secretary 1931–35, home secretary again 1935–37, chancellor of the Exchequer 1937–40, and lord chancellor 1940–45. Knighted 1910, Viscount 1940.

Simpson, Wallis Warfield, Duchess of Windsor (1896–1986) US socialite, twice divorced. She married *Edward VIII 1937, who abdicated in order to marry her. He was given the title Duke of Windsor by his brother, George VI, who succeeded him.

Sinai, Battle of battle 6–24 October 1973 during the Yom Kippur War between Israel and Egypt. It was one of the longest tank battles in history. Israeli troops crossed the Suez Canal 16 October, cutting off the Egyptian 3rd Army.

Singapore (Sanskrit *Singa pura* 'city of the lion') country in southeast Asia, off the tip of the Malay Peninsula.

Singh, V(ishwanath) P(ratap) (1931–) Indian politician, prime minister 1989–90. As a member of the Congress (I) Party, he held ministerial posts under Indira Gandhi and Rajiv Gandhi, and from 1984 led an anti-corruption drive. When he unearthed an arms sales scandal in 1988, he was ousted from the government and party and formed a broad-based opposition alliance, the *Janata Dal, which won the November 1989 election. Mounting caste and communal conflict split the Janata Dal and forced him out of office in November 1990.

Sing Sing name until 1901 of the village of **Ossining**, New York, USA, with a state prison of that name 1825–1969, when it was renamed the Ossining State Correctional Facility.

Sinn Fein (Irish 'we ourselves') Irish political party founded in 1905, whose aim is the creation of a united republican Ireland. The driving political force behind Irish nationalism between 1916 and 1921, Sinn Fein returned to prominence with the outbreak of violence ('the Troubles') in Northern Ireland in the late 1960s, when it split into 'Provisional' and 'Official' wings at the same time as the *Irish Republican Army (IRA), with which it is closely associated. From the late 1970s 'Provisional' Sinn Fein took on a more active political role, putting up candidates to stand in local and national elections. Sinn Fein won two seats in the 1997 UK general election and one seat in the 1997 Irish general election. In the 2001 UK general election, it increased its number of seats to four. Gerry *Adams became party president in 1978. Sinn Fein took part in the multiparty negotiations (known as the Stormont Talks) and became a signatory of the agreement reached on Good Friday, 10 April 1998. The party gained 17.6% of votes in the June 1998 elections to the 108-seat Belfast assembly. In September a historic meeting between Gerry Adams and the Ulster Unionist leader, David Trimble, took place at Stormont; Sinn Fein also agreed to appoint a contact with the international body overseeing the decommissioning of arms – the party's chief negotiator, Martin McGuinness.

In October 2001 Gerry Adams made an unprecedented plea to the IRA to proceed with decommissioning in order to save the peace process and the devolved power-sharing administration of Northern Ireland from collapse; on 22 October it was verified that the IRA had put some arms beyond use.

Sino-Soviet split period of strained relations between the two major communist powers, China and the USSR, during the early 1960s, thus dividing the communist world. The tension was based partly on differences in ideology but also involved rivalry for leadership and old territorial border claims. The Chinese communists also criticized the USSR for supplying aircraft to India and for withdrawing technical and military aid to China in 1960. The USSR supported India in its border warfare with China between 1961 and 1962.

Sioux or **Lakota, Dakota,** or **Nakota,** (Chippewa *nadowessioux* 'snake' or 'enemy') member of an American Indian people who inhabit the Great Plains region; the largest group of Plains Indians. Their language belongs to the Siouan family, and they are divided into three groups: Dakota, Nakota, and Lakota. Originally hunter-gatherers living around Lake Superior, Michigan, they were forced into North and South Dakota by the Cree and Chippewa around 1650, and took up a nomadic, buffalo-hunting lifestyle. They developed a warrior culture in which status was achieved by bravery in warfare. With reservations in the Dakotas, and other parts of the USA and Canada, they now number about 108,200 (2000) in the USA and 60,000 in Canada (1991).

Sirhan, Sirhan (c. 1943–) Palestinian assassin. He came with his family to California in 1956. He was enraged by Senator Robert Kennedy's pro-Israeli stance. He shot and killed Kennedy in 1968 and was found guilty of premeditated murder. His death sentence was commuted to life imprisonment due to a plea for leniency by Senator Edward Kennedy.

Sisulu, Walter Max Ulyate (1912–2003) South African civil-rights activist, deputy president of the African National Congress (ANC). In 1964 he became, with Nelson Mandela, one of the first full-time secretaries general of the ANC. He was imprisoned following the 1964 Rivonia Trial for opposition to the apartheid system and released in 1989, at the age of 77, as a gesture of reform by President F W *de Klerk. In 1991, when Mandela became ANC president, Sisulu became his deputy.

Sithole, Ndabaningi (1920–2000) Zimbabwean politician. With Robert *Mugabe he founded the Zimbabwe African National Union (ZANU) in 1963, the members of which originally formed the core of the Rhodesian guerrilla movement. In 1964 he was arrested for alleged incitement to violence and was later accused of plotting political assassinations. In 1974 he was conditionally released in order to participate in talks about Rhodesia's (modern-day Zimbabwe) future. In 1975 he sought refuge abroad, returning in July 1977 to help bring about a Rhodesian settlement. Following independence he became leader of the Ndonga faction of ZANU. In 1998 he was sentenced to two years' imprisonment for his involvement in an assassination attempt on Mugabe in August 1995; while appealing the sentence he was suspended from Parliament.

Slapton Sands beach in Devon, England, where during World War II, on the night of 27–28 April 1944 a convoy of landing craft carrying US troops on a pre-D-day exercise was by chance attacked by German E-boats (fast, armed boats). There were nearly 1,000 casualties, but the incident was not made public in case the Germans realized that Normandy was the intended Allied landing place, rather than the Pas-de-Calais.

Slim, William Joseph, 1st Viscount Slim (1891–1970) British field marshal in World War II. He served in the North Africa campaign 1941 then commanded the 1st Burma Corps 1942–45, stemming the Japanese invasion of India, and then forcing them out of Burma (now Myanmar) in 1945. He was governor general of Australia 1953–60. He was created a KCB in 1944 and a Viscount in 1960.

Slovakia one of the two republics that formed the Federative Republic of Czechoslovakia. Settled in the 5th–6th centuries by Slavs; it was occupied by the Magyars in the 10th century, and was part of the kingdom of Hungary until 1918, when it became a province of Czechoslovakia. Slovakia was a puppet state under German domination 1939–45, and was abolished as an administrative division in 1949. Its capital and chief town was Bratislava. It was re-established as a sovereign state, the *Slovak Republic, after the break-up of Czechoslovakia in 1993.

Slovak Republic or **Slovakia**, landlocked country in central Europe, bounded north by Poland, east by the Ukraine, south by Hungary, west by Austria, and northwest by the Czech Republic.

Slovenia or **Slovenija**, country in south-central Europe, bounded north by Austria, east by Hungary, west by Italy, and south by Croatia.

Slovo, Joe (1926–1995) South African lawyer and politician, general secretary of the South African Communist Party 1987–91; chief of staff of Umkhonto we Sizwe (Spear of the Nation), the armed wing of the African National Congress (ANC) 1985–87; and minister of housing in President Mandela's government 1994–95. He was one of the most influential figures in the ANC, and spent 27 years in exile.

Smersh the main administration of counterintelligence in the USSR, established 1942; a subsection of the *KGB.

Smith, Al(fred Emanuel) (1873–1944) US political leader who served four terms as governor of New York. The first Roman Catholic to receive a presidential nomination, he unsuccessfully fought for the 1924 presidency as a Democrat, on a platform of liberalizing Prohibition. In his lively, yet unsuccessful, campaign against Herbert Hoover he was called the 'Happy Warrior'. His defeat nonetheless forged a breakthrough for the Democrats, re-establishing support in the larger cities and attracting support from the farm states of the West.

Smith, Ian (Douglas) (1919–) Rhodesian politician. He was a founder of the Rhodesian Front in 1962 and prime minister 1964–79. In 1965 he made a unilateral declaration of Rhodesia's independence and, despite UN sanctions, maintained his regime with tenacity.

In 1979 he was succeeded as prime minister by Bishop Abel Muzorewa, when the country was renamed Zimbabwe. He was suspended from the Zimbabwe parliament in April 1987 and resigned in May as head of the white opposition party. In 1992 he helped found a new opposition party, the United Front.

Smith, John (1938–1994) British Labour politician, party leader 1992–94, born on the Scottish island of Islay. He was trade and industry secretary 1978–79 and from 1979 held various shadow cabinet posts, culminating in that of shadow chancellor 1987–92. When Neil Kinnock resigned the leadership after losing the 1992 general election, Smith was readily elected as his successor. During his two years as leader, building on Kinnock's efforts, he drew together the two wings of the Labour Party to make it a highly electable proposition. He won the trust and support of colleagues of all shades of opinion, and built a formidable front-bench team. His sudden death from a heart attack shocked British politicians of all parties.

Smith, Walter Bedell (1895–1961)
US soldier and diplomat. From 1942 to 1945 he was Eisenhower's chief of staff, in which position he helped plan and carry out the invasions of North Africa, Sicily, and Normandy. President Truman appointed him ambassador to the Soviet Union 1946–49 and then director of the Central Intelligence Agency 1950–53. Under President Eisenhower he served as under secretary of state 1953–54.

smoking   inhalation (breathing in) of the fumes from burning substances, generally tobacco in the form of cigarettes. The practice is habit-forming and dangerous to health, since carbon monoxide and other toxic materials result from the combustion process. Smoking is addictive because of the presence of the drug nicotine in the smoke. A direct link between lung cancer and tobacco smoking was established in 1950; the habit is also linked to respiratory and coronary heart diseases. In the West, smoking is now forbidden in many public places because even **passive smoking** – breathing in fumes from other people's cigarettes – can be harmful. Some illegal drugs, such as crack and opium, are also smoked. In 2001, it was estimated that there were 1.1 billion smokers worldwide.

Smuts, Jan Christian (1870–1950)
South African politician and soldier; prime minister 1919–24 and 1939–48. He supported the Allies in both world wars and was a member of the British imperial war cabinet 1917–18.

Snowden, Philip (1864–1937)   1st Viscount Snowden, British right-wing Labour politician, chancellor of the Exchequer in 1924 and 1929–31. He was MP for Blackburn 1906–31 and entered the coalition National Government in 1931 as Lord Privy Seal, but resigned in 1932. Viscount 1931.

Soares, Mario Alberto Nobre Lopes (1924–)   Portuguese socialist politician, president 1986–96. Exiled in 1970, he returned to Portugal in 1974, and, as leader of the Portuguese Socialist Party, was prime minister 1976–78. He resigned as party leader in 1980, but in 1986 he was elected Portugal's first socialist president.

Sobchak, Anatoly (1937–2000)
Russian centrist politician, mayor of St Petersburg 1990–96, cofounder of the Democratic Reform Movement (with former foreign minister *Shevardnadze), and member of the Soviet parliament 1989–91. He prominently resisted the abortive anti-Gorbachev coup of August 1991.

Sobibor   German extermination camp northwest of Lublin, established March 1942. An estimated 250,000 Jews were sent there and murdered before the camp was closed 1943. Its closure was unique since it was forced by a rebellion of prisoners led by a Soviet prisoner-of-war.

Sobukwe, Robert (1924–1977)   South African nationalist leader. Originally a member of the African National Congress (ANC) Youth League, he was dismissed from his teaching post in 1952 because of his participation in the defiance campaign, and in 1959 helped found the *pan-Africanist Congress (PAC), being elected its president. PAC was banned in 1960 and he was imprisoned until 1969.

Social and Liberal Democrats   SLD, original name for the British political party formed in 1988 from the former Liberal Party and most of the Social Democratic Party. Since 1989 the party has been called the *Liberal Democrats.

Social Democratic and Labour Party   SDLP, Northern Ireland left-of-centre political party, formed in 1970. It aims ultimately at Irish unification, but has distanced itself from violent tactics, adopting a constitutional, conciliatory role. Its leader, John Hume, played a key role in the negotiations which ended in the 1998 Good Friday Agreement on power-sharing. It secured 24 of the 108 seats in the new Northern Ireland

Assembly, elected in June 1998; the party's deputy leader, Seamus Mallon, was voted deputy first minister (to Ulster Unionist David Trimble) by the first meeting of the Assembly. Mallon resigned with Trimble in July 2001, following the failure of the IRA to proceed with decommissioning. In October 2001, after it was confirmed that the IRA had put some arms beyond use, the SDLP nominated its leader elect, Mark Durkan, to the post of deputy first minister.

Social Democratic Party SDP, British centrist political party 1981–90, formed by members of Parliament who resigned from the Labour Party. The 1983 and 1987 general elections were fought in alliance with the Liberal Party as the Liberal/SDP Alliance. A merger of the two parties was voted for by the SDP in 1987, and the new party became the Social and Liberal Democrats, which became the *Liberal Democrats, leaving a rump SDP that folded in 1990.

social exclusion the emergence in modern Western societies of the increasing group, or underclass, who do not have the means, material and otherwise, to participate in social, economic, political, and cultural life. The term was invented in France and applied to people who fell through the social security net. More recently, it has been used by the UK Labour government, which, in December 1997, set up a special Social Exclusion Unit, based at 10 Downing Street, to deal with the problem.

'socialism in one country' concept proposed by the Soviet dictator Stalin in 1924. In contrast to Leon Trotsky's theory of permanent revolution, Stalin suggested that the emphasis be changed away from promoting revolutions abroad to the idea of building socialism, economically and politically, in the USSR without help from other countries.

social security state provision of financial aid to reduce poverty.

The term 'social security' was first applied officially in the USA, in the Social Security Act of 1935. In Britain it was first used officially in 1944, and following the *Beveridge Report of 1942 a series of acts was passed from 1945 to widen the scope of social security. Basic entitlements of those paying National Insurance contributions in Britain include an old-age pension, unemployment benefit (known as jobseeker's allowance from October 1996), widow's pension, incapacity benefit, and payment during a period of sickness in one's working life (Statutory Sick Pay). Other benefits, which are non-contributory, include family credit, income support, child benefit, and attendance allowance for those looking after sick or disabled people. It was announced in the March 1998 budget that family credit and the disabled working allowance would be replaced from October 1999 by a working families tax credit and disabled persons tax credit, to be administered by the Inland Revenue.

Sokolovsky, Vasily (1897–1968) Soviet general in World War II. Chief of staff to the West Front Army from 1941, he took command of it 1943, led it in the counteroffensive after the Battle of Kursk, and liberated Smolensk. His progress then slowed and he was removed from command and became chief of staff to the 1st Ukrainian Front. In 1945 he became deputy commander of 1st Belorussian Front for the attack on Berlin, captured the *Führerbunker*, and verified Hitler's corpse from dental records. After the war he became commander-in-chief of Soviet Forces in Germany.

Solidarity Polish **Solidarnosc**, national confederation of independent trade unions in Poland, formed under the leadership of Lech *Wałęsa September 1980. An illegal organization from 1981 to 1989, it was then elected to head the Polish government. Divisions soon emerged in the leadership and in 1990 its political wing began to fragment (Wałęsa resigned as chairman in December of that year). In the September 1993 elections Solidarity gained less than 5% of the popular vote but, in September 1997, under the leadership of Marian Krzaklewski, Solidarity Electoral Action (AWS) won 34% of the vote and led the subsequent coalition government with Jerzy Buzek as prime minister.

Solomon Islands country in the southwest Pacific Ocean, east of New Guinea, comprising many hundreds of islands, the largest of which is Guadalcanal.

Somalia country in northeast Africa (the Horn of Africa), on the Indian Ocean, bounded northwest by Djibouti, west by Ethiopia, and southwest by Kenya.

Somme, Battle of the Allied offensive in World War I July–November 1916 on the River Somme in northern France, during which severe losses were suffered by both sides. It was planned by the Marshal of France, Joseph Joffre, and UK commander-in-chief Douglas Haig; the Allies lost over 600,000 soldiers and advanced approximately 8 km / 5 mi (13 km/8 mi at its furthest point). It was the first battle in which tanks were used. The German offensive around St Quentin March–April 1918 is sometimes called the Second Battle of the Somme.

Somoza Debayle, Anastasio (1925–1980) Nicaraguan soldier and politician, president 1967–72 and 1974–79. The second son of Anastasio *Somoza García, he succeeded his brother Luis *Somoza Debayle as president of Nicaragua in 1967, to head an even more oppressive and corrupt regime, characterized by tightened press censorship and rising popular discontent as the economic situation deteriorated. He was removed by Sandinista guerrillas in 1979 and assassinated in Paraguay in 1980.

Somoza Debayle, Luis (1923–1967) Nicaraguan nationalist liberal politician, president 1956–63. He took over the presidency on the assassination of his father, Anastasio *Somoza García. He introduced a number of social reforms, including low-cost housing and land reform, and reduced the level of political repression, but remained a staunch anti-Communist, supporting the USA in its 1961 Bay of Pigs invasion of Cuba.

Somoza (García), Anastasio (1896–1956) Nicaraguan soldier and politician, president 1937–47 and 1950–56. As head of the Nicaraguan army, he deposed President Juan Bautista Sacasa, his uncle, in 1936 and assumed the presidency the following year, ruling as a virtual dictator from 1937 until his assassination in 1956. He exiled most of his political opponents and amassed a considerable fortune in land and businesses. Members of his family retained control of the country until 1979, when they were overthrown by popular forces.

Song Jiaoren (or Sung Chiao-jen) (1882–1913) Chinese revolutionary and champion of parliamentary government. Song was the principal spokesperson of the *Guomindang (nationalist party) in the elections of 1912, carrying out a vigorous western-style electioneering campaign which called for a figurehead presidency, a responsible cabinet system, and local autonomy. The Guomindang won the elections and Song was widely tipped to become prime minister. His programme, however, was a direct challenge to the hegemonic ambitions of the president, *Yüan Shikai, and he was assassinated at Shanghai railway station by Yüan's henchmen.

Soong, T V (or Tse-Ven) (1894–1971) also known as **Tzu-Wen Sung** or **Ziwen Song,** Chinese nationalist financier and politician. He was finance minister of the nationalist government at Guangzhou (Canton) 1925–27 and at Nanjing 1928 to 1933.

He westernized Chinese finances, standardized the Chinese currency, and founded the Bank of China in 1936. Soong was foreign minister from 1942–45. In 1949, following the Communist revolution, he went to the USA.

Soong Ching-ling (or **Sung Qingling) (1890–1981)** Chinese politician, wife of the Kuomintang (*Guomindang) nationalist leader *Sun Zhong Shan (Sun Yat-sen); she remained a prominent figure in Chinese politics after his death, being appointed one of the three non-communist vice-chairs of the People's Republic of China in 1950, and serving as acting head of state of communist China 1976–78.

Souphanouvong, Prince (1902–1995) Laotian politician, president 1975–86. After an abortive revolt against French rule in 1945, he led the guerrilla organization Pathet Lao (Land of the Lao), and in 1975 became the first president of the Republic of Laos.

South Africa country on the southern tip of Africa, bounded north by Namibia, Botswana, and Zimbabwe and northeast by Mozambique and Swaziland.

government In November 1993 the South African government and the *African National Congress (ANC) agreed on an interim constitution, which was adopted by the Transitional Executive Council in December 1993 and took effect after the first multiracial elections in April 1994. It provides for a National Assembly of 400 members, elected by a system of proportional representation through national and regional party lists, and a 90-member Senate, consisting of 10 members from each regional assembly. Elections are by universal adult suffrage. The president, who is head of state and government, is elected by the National Assembly and appoints a first deputy president, to act as premier, from the majority party within the Assembly, and a second deputy president from the second-largest party. Any party with 20% of

the national vote is entitled to nominate a deputy president, to be appointed by the president. The appointments are subject to confirmation by the National Assembly.

The earlier 1984 constitution was based on racial discrimination in the context of *apartheid, with black Africans completely unrepresented at national level.

towards the Union of South Africa The Second South African, or Boer, War 1899–1902 was ended by the Peace of Vereeniging of 1902. The defeat of the Boers (now known as Afrikaners) was to lead to the creation of the Union of South Africa, but it also stimulated Afrikaner nationalism. Britain annexed the South African Republic (the Transvaal) and the Orange Free State, but both were given responsible government in 1906 and 1907. Their constitutions did not mention a non-racial qualified franchise, which, though weakly implemented in practice, had been a feature of the earlier constitutions of the Cape and Natal.

The National Convention of 1908–10 was dominated by the British colonial administrator Lord Alfred *Milner, and the former Boer commanders Jan *Smuts and Louis *Botha. The Convention, which was composed of white representatives of the four colonies, drafted a constitution for the Union of South Africa, and the draft constitution deliberately deferred the question of the non-racial franchise, except for the Cape, which was allowed to retain its existing constitution in this respect.

The British parliament endorsed the proposals of the National Convention, embodied in the South Africa Act 1909, and on 31 May 1910 the Union of South Africa achieved independence within the British Empire under the premiership of Louis Botha.

the continuance of Afrikaner nationalism Smuts and Botha believed that the healing of the breach between Afrikaner and Briton was essential to South Africa's future, and did not favour Afrikaner nationalism. However, there were many who did. In a famous speech at De Wildt, near Pretoria, in 1912 the former Boer general James *Hertzog announced that in a conflict of interests between Britain and South Africa he would place the interests of South Africa first.

The apparent anti-British tone of the speech caused Botha to resign and reform his government without Hertzog, who in 1914 founded the National Party in opposition to the governing South African Party (SAP). Also in opposition were the South African Labour Party (founded in 1910 by Col F.H.P. Cresswell) and the British-oriented Unionist Party.

The outbreak of World War I in 1914 sparked a small-scale Boer rebellion, which was speedily crushed by Smuts. South African forces occupied German South West Africa (now Namibia), and also served elsewhere with the Allies. Some 6,700 South Africans died in the war.

industrial unrest From 1913 to 1922 there were several major strikes in the South African gold and coal mines – in the earlier period mainly to gain recognition of white trade unions from the mine owners. In 1922, however, the white miners struck over the use of blacks in jobs previously done by whites. For a brief period a revolutionary council controlled the Rand, until Smuts brought in troops to quell it. Three ringleaders were hanged and others temporarily imprisoned or deported.

As a consequence in the 1924 election Smuts's SAP was defeated by a Nationalist–Labour Pact government and Hertzog became prime minister – a position he was to hold until 1939.

Hertzog's first government Hertzog's first government introduced a number of measures aimed at preserving white dominance, and others that sought to reconcile Anglo-Boer antagonisms.

The Industrial Conciliation Act 1924 and the Wages Act 1925 were both aimed at protecting the white unions and workers from black encroachment, and the government also tried to introduce measures to remove black Africans from the Cape electoral roll. The English and Afrikaans languages were given equal status in education and government, and a compromise solution was found to the 'flag issue', whereby the orange, white, and blue of the 17th-century Dutch Republic had a centrepiece of the Union Jack and the flags of the former Boer republics. In the economic sphere, state capital was injected into industry, and semi-public industrial bodies such as the Iron and Steel Industrial Corporation (ISCOR) were formed.

Hertzog continues in power At the 1929 general election, though the Labour Party was split, the Pact held. Hertzog's National Party, however, won enough seats to form a government on its own, but in refusing, in the midst of world recession, to go off the gold standard, Hertzog nearly brought the country to economic ruin. Pressurized by the veteran politician Tielman Roos, who emerged from retirement to demand abandonment of the gold standard and the formation of a national government, Hertzog's government conceded, and there was an almost immediate improvement in the country's economic position.

In 1933 Hertzog's National Party and Smuts's SAP fused, eventually to form the United South African National Party (United Party). Dr D F *Malan of the Cape National Party broke away in 1934 but reunited with Hertzog and some of his followers in 1939 to form the Reunited National Party (Herenigde Nasionale Party), the forerunner of the later National Party in South Africa.

In 1934 the House of Assembly passed two bills that confirmed the understanding under the 1931 *Statute of Westminster that South Africa was independent of legislative control by the British Parliament, and that the British crown acted solely on the advice of South African ministers in matters concerning South Africa.

In 1936 by 169 votes to 11 the South African parliament adopted the Bantu Representation Act, removing black Africans in Cape Province from the voters' roll. It also passed the Native Land and Trust Act 1936, allocating less than 14% of South Africa's land as black African 'reserves'.

the beginnings of black nationalism The *African National Congress (ANC) had been formed in 1912 by Dr Pixley Seme and the Rev John Dube as a multiracial nationalist organization. Its aims were to extend voting rights to the entire population, and to end racial discrimination. In the 1920s Clement Kadalie's Industrial and Commercial Union (ICU) – with a peak membership of 100,000 – temporarily superseded the ANC, but it collapsed in 1929 partly through internal feuding but also through government intervention. In the 1930s an All African Convention campaigned without success against the Hertzog Bill to deprive Cape Africans of the franchise. In the 1940s the Congress Youth League sought to influence the ANC towards more 'Africanist' policies.

South Africa divided in World War II At the outset of World War II Hertzog declared that South Africa would remain neutral. He was challenged by Smuts and on 4 September 1939 was defeated in parliament by 80 votes to 67. Hertzog resigned and Smuts became premier. The South African army fought alongside the British, and played an important part in the Ethiopian and North African campaigns. Many fell prisoner at Tobruk, but South African armoured units participated in the British Eighth Army advance under Gen Alexander.

At home Afrikaners were deeply divided, and by 1941 it was clear that a majority of Afrikaners were against the war effort and in favour of a republic. Hertzog retired from politics in 1940 and a few of his supporters under Havenga, disillusioned with the Reunited National Party, formed the Afrikaner Party. The Ossewa-Brandwag ('Sentinels of the Ox Wagon'), which had been formed as a cultural organization following the Voortrekker centenary celebration of Dingaan's defeat at Blood River in 1838, developed into a strongly pro-Nazi political force, and many Afrikaners were interned.

At the general election of 1943, however, Smuts won an overwhelming victory with 105 seats to the 43 gained by Malan's National Party.

South Africa had benefited economically during the war years, but between 1945 and 1948 the Smuts government was condemned at the United Nations for South Africa's racial policies (particularly towards its Indian population). It was also attacked at home for appearing, under the liberal guidance of Jan H Hofmeyr, to seek to blur racial divisions between black and white.

In 1947 Malan and Havenga entered into an electoral pact. At the general election of 1948 the National and Afrikaner parties gained 79 seats and Smuts' United Party 74. To many Afrikaners the Nationalist victory atoned for a 'century of wrong'.

the introduction of apartheid Up to 1948 the predominant racial struggle in South Africa had been between the English speakers and the Afrikaners. Since Union in 1910 legislation under successive governments had increasingly restricted the civil rights and movement of Indians and blacks, but it was the Malan government that developed an all-encompassing theory of *apartheid ('apartness') or 'separate development'. The latter term was later replaced by 'multinational development', but the basic policy remained.

In the early post-war period ANC leaders – encouraged by UN anti-racial policies and the gaining of independence by former British and other colonies – combined with the coloureds (people of mixed-race origin) and Indians to demonstrate peacefully against such apartheid measures as the Pass Laws and the Group Areas Act of 1949, which gave legal status to traditional residential segregation. In 1952 the Defiance Campaign, a non-violent mass movement aimed by blacks at drawing attention to the worst of their grievances, collapsed in a few months, and its leaders, including the Zulu chief Albert *Luthuli, were banned or imprisoned and new legislation introduced to make it almost impossible for such a demonstration to occur again. However, the campaign had brought into the open South Africa's key racial issues.

The government's decision to abolish the political rights of the Cape coloureds was hotly contested by the Torch Commando, initially led by ex-servicemen's organizations, but in 1953 the Nationalist Party was returned with an enhanced majority despite an electoral pact between the United and Labour parties, a pact that had operated at general elections since 1943.

In 1954 J G Strijdom succeeded Malan as prime minister, and Dr Hendrik *Verwoerd succeeded Strijdom in 1958. The Nationalist government pressed ahead with further apartheid legislation, including the Separate Representation of Voters Act 1956, which removed coloureds from the electoral roll. Following the Tomlinson Commission Report of 1955, legislation was introduced to implement the 'homeland' (or Bantustan) policy, by which certain – mostly arid – areas were set aside for development towards self-government by particular ethnic black groups. Additional legislation banned mixed marriages, limited the number of Africans allowed in urban areas, and denied

Africans the right to strike. The effect was to make anything other than official contact between black and white in South Africa almost impossible.

parliamentary opposition In 1958 the Labour Party lost all parliamentary representation and ceased to exist. Another opposition party had emerged in 1953, when a small group broke with the United Party to form the Liberal Party. It was multiracial and eventually included unqualified universal suffrage among its aims. It never won a parliamentary seat and eventually disbanded in 1968 when the government brought in legislation forbidding mixed political organizations. The only other multiracial political party in South Africa, the Communist Party, was disbanded under the Suppression of Communism Act 1950.

In 1959 another group broke with the United Party to form the Progressive Party. Although for many years Helen *Suzman was its only MP, in 1974 seven members were returned to parliament. In 1975 the Progressive Party joined with another splinter group from the United Party to form the South African Progressive Reform Party, with Colin Eglin as leader. The new party had 12 seats in parliament in 1977 (out of a total of 171) and aimed to replace the United Party as the official opposition. The basic policy of the party was power-sharing between black and white.

the beginnings of radical black opposition In the mid-1950s the Congress Alliance, a body representative of all races, including whites, had sought to reorganize the resistance movement, and in 1955 a Freedom Charter was adopted at Kliptown. Later, differences led to a breakaway movement, the pan-Africanist Congress (PAC), being formed in 1959 with Robert Sobukwe as president.

The PAC launched a peaceful demonstration against the Pass Laws (restricting the movements of nonwhites within the country) at *Sharpeville and Lange on 21 March 1960. White police, panicking, fired on the unarmed crowds and killed 69 people. The repercussions were worldwide, and the flight of capital and withdrawal of investment temporarily rocked the South African economy. The government introduced stronger measures to deal with opponents, including the banning of the ANC and the PAC.

Many black leaders went into exile, and many of their followers joined guerrilla forces outside South Africa believing that armed struggle was the only way to achieve black-majority rule in South Africa. In 1964 the ANC leader Nelson *Mandela was sentenced to life imprisonment for alleged sabotage. He became a central symbol of black opposition to the apartheid regime, remaining in prison until 1990.

South Africa becomes a republic
A referendum on 5 October 1960 showed 52% of eligible voters in favour of a republic and 48% against – a numerical majority of 74,580 out of a total vote of 1,626,336. In 1961 Verwoerd attended the Commonwealth Conference to put South Africa's case for remaining a member of the Commonwealth as a republic. The attack on its racial policies made him withdraw his application. The attack was particularly severe because of African unrest, the massacres at Sharpeville and Lange, and the subsequent repressive legislation. On 31 May 1961 South Africa became a republic outside the Commonwealth.

Vorster's premiership At every election the Nationalists maintained their majority. In 1966 Verwoerd was assassinated by a parliamentary messenger and John *Vorster became prime minister. While maintaining the apartheid policies of his predecessors he deliberately sought to improve the Republic's relations with black Africa and, under strict control, to promote the homelands. Partly due to the buoyant economy in the 1970s, a shortage of white industrial workers forced change in relations with black workers, particularly in their efforts to form trade unions. The Durban strikes by African workers in 1972–73 in particular resulted in limited amended legislation in favour of black workers. In 1975, in cooperation with President Kaunda of Zambia, Vorster sought to find a peaceful solution to achieving black-majority rule in Rhodesia (now *Zimbabwe), but these talks broke down and guerrilla war continued.

At the United Nations South Africa's racial policies continued to be condemned, as was its refusal to relinquish control of South West Africa (Namibia), which it had originally administered as a mandate from the League of Nations after taking it from Germany in World War I. Black African states particularly resented South Africa's military intervention from 1975 in Angola in support of UNITA in its civil war with the Soviet- and Cuban-backed MPLA. South African raids were also made to attack bases in southern Angola of SWAPO, the Namibian liberation movement. South African military interventions in Angola continued through much of the 1980s.

Internally, the government introduced new security laws to give it powers to ban any individual or organization that 'endangers the security of the state'. In addition, early in 1976, the government introduced legislation empowering South African armed forces to cross the country's borders to counteract any threat to security south of the Equator.

renewed opposition to the regime In the 1970s several homeland leaders such as Chief *Buthelezi of KwaZulu and Chief Phatudi of Lebowa emerged as national African leaders urging a common programme of reform. Nominal independence was achieved by a number of the black homelands, or bantustans, starting with Transkei in 1976. However, these Black National States were not recognized internationally, and were regarded as puppet regimes by more militant black nationalists.

New African-orientated organizations such as the South African Students' Organization (SASO) and the Black Peoples' Convention (BPC) had sprung up, backed by Black Community Programmes, an offshoot of the Christian Institute of Southern Africa. All had their activities circumscribed by the banning of able leaders or limitation of funds.

Militant opposition to the regime erupted in June 1976 with rioting in Soweto township near Johannesburg, which led to the deaths of 176 people, a number of whom were students demonstrating against the compulsory use of the Afrikaans language as the medium of instruction. Further unrest continued periodically in Soweto and other townships. In 1977 international condemnation of police brutality followed the death in detention of the black community leader Steve *Biko, who had founded SASO in 1968.

By the 1980s thousands of the apartheid regime's opponents had been imprisoned without trial and more than 3 million people had been forcibly resettled in black townships.

In the arena of parliamentary politics, efforts were made late in 1976 and early in 1977 to achieve unity amongst the white opposition parties, and in March 1977 Sir De Villiers Graaff, the UP leader, and Theo Gerdener, the leader of the Democratic Party, expressed their agreement to form a new party called the New Republic Party. Earlier in the year, six members on the right wing of the UP had formed the new South Africa Party. However, in a general election in November 1977 the National Party (NP) won a landslide victory.

constitutional reform In 1978 Vorster resigned and was succeeded as prime minister by his NP colleague P W *Botha. Botha embarked on constitutional reform to involve coloureds and Asians, but not blacks, in the governmental process. This led to a clash within the NP, and in March 1982 Dr Adries Treurnicht, leader of the hardline (*verkrampte*) wing, and 15 other extremists were expelled. They later formed a new party, the Conservative Party of South Africa (CPSA). Although there were considerable doubts about Botha's proposals in the coloured and Indian communities as well as among the whites, they were approved by 66% of the voters in an all-white referendum and came into effect in September 1984.

In 1986 a number of apartheid laws were amended or repealed, including the ban on sexual relations or marriage between people of different races and the ban on mixed racial membership of political parties, but the underlying inequalities in the system remained and the dissatisfaction of the black community grew. In the 1986 cabinet of 21, including Botha, there were 19 whites, 1 coloured, and 1 Indian. The NP continued to increase its majority at each election, with the white opposition parties failing to unseat it.

state of emergency In May 1986 South Africa attacked what it claimed to be guerrilla strongholds in Botswana, Zambia, and Zimbabwe. The exiled ANC leader Oliver *Tambo was receiving increasing moral support in meetings with politicians throughout the world, and Winnie *Mandela, during her husband's continuing imprisonment, was 'banned' repeatedly for condemning the system publicly. Nonviolent resistance was advocated by Bishop *Tutu, the *Inkatha movement, and others.

A state of emergency was declared in June 1986, a few days before the tenth anniversary of the first Soweto uprising, marked by a strike in which millions of blacks participated. Serious rioting broke out in the townships and was met with police violence, causing hundreds of deaths. Between 1980 and 1990 some 1,070 people were judicially executed.

sanctions imposed Abroad, calls for the economic and cultural boycott of South Africa, in particular economic sanctions against South Africa, grew during 1985 and 1986. At the Heads of Commonwealth conference in 1985 the Eminent Persons' Group (EPG) of Commonwealth politicians was conceived to investigate the likelihood of change in South Africa without sanctions. In July 1986 the EPG reported that there were no signs of genuine liberalization. Reluctantly, Britain's prime minister, Margaret Thatcher, agreed to limited measures. Some Commonwealth countries, notably Australia and Canada, took additional independent action. The US Congress eventually forced President Reagan to move in the same direction. Between 1988 and 1990 economic sanctions cost the South African treasury more than $4 billion in lost revenue. The decisions by individual multinational companies to close down their South African operations may, in the long term, have had the greatest effect.

promise of reform At the end of 1988 South Africa signed a peace agreement with Angola and Cuba, which included the acceptance of Namibia's independence, and in 1989, under United Nations supervision, free elections took place there. In February 1989 state president Botha suffered a stroke that forced him to give up the NP leadership and later the presidency. He was succeeded in both roles by F W de Klerk, who promised major constitutional reforms. Meanwhile the nonracist Democratic Party (DP) was launched, advocating universal adult suffrage, and, together with the

Conservative Party, made significant gains in the September 1989 whites-only assembly elections. The ruling NP lost one-quarter of its seats. Its new total was only nine seats more than was required for a majority, its worst electoral showing since coming to power in 1948.

Despite de Klerk's release of the veteran ANC activist, Walter Sisulu, and some of his colleagues in October 1989, the new president's promises of political reform were treated with scepticism by the opposition until he announced the lifting of the ban on the ANC, followed by the release of Nelson Mandela on 11 February 1990. In September President de Klerk declared membership of the NP open to all races. In December ANC president Oliver Tambo returned triumphantly and in January 1991 Nelson Mandela and Zulu leader Chief Buthelezi both urged their followers to end attacks on one another, but revelations of government financial support and police funding for Inkatha political activities, for example to counter the ANC and foment division among blacks, threatened ANC cooperation.

Mandela was subsequently elected ANC president.

abandonment of apartheid announced In February 1991 President de Klerk announced the intended repeal of all remaining apartheid laws. In March he announced legislation to abolish all racial controls on land ownership, enabling all South Africans to purchase land anywhere. In June 1991 all the remaining racially discriminating laws were repealed. As a result the USA lifted its trade and investment sanctions against South Africa in July and the country was readmitted into international sport by the International Olympic Committee. In September President de Klerk announced a draft constitution, giving black people the franchise but providing strong safeguards for the white minority. It was immediately criticized by the ANC because it served to perpetuate the white hegemony. However, the ANC agreed to negotiate and it joined with the pan-Africanist Congress (PAC) to form a united front against the government. In December, however, the PAC withdrew, claiming that the planning of the negotiations was undemocratic. A whites-only referendum held in March 1992 gave de Klerk a clear mandate to proceed with plans for the new constitution, which would end white-minority rule.

An obstacle to constitutional reform occurred when in June 1992 more than 40 people were killed in the black township of Boipatong by Inkatha, aided and abetted by police. The ANC called a halt to the constitutional talks until the government took steps to curb township violence.

proposed government of national unity In February 1993 de Klerk and Mandela agreed to the formation of a government of national unity after free nonracial elections in 1994. Inkatha leader Chief Buthelezi complained of not having been consulted and warned that he would oppose such an arrangement.

Radical ANC leader Chris Hani was assassinated by a white extremist in April 1993. In the same month President de Klerk apologized for apartheid for the first time in public and announced April 1994 as the date for the first nonracial elections. An escalation in township violence followed, initiated by groups opposed to the proposed constitutional changes and to the ANC's dominant role in negotiating them. In September 1993 it was agreed that a multiracial Transitional Executive Council would be established (to comprise one member from each of South Africa's political parties) in the run-up to the elections. In October 1993 a new Freedom Alliance was formed by Inkatha leader Chief Buthelezi, white

right-wing groups, and the leaders of the black homelands of Ciskei and Bophuthatswana, all opposed to the creation of a single democratic state and seeking greater autonomy for their respective areas. In the same month, Mandela and de Klerk were jointly awarded the Nobel Prize for Peace.

interim nonracial constitution In November 1993 the government and the ANC agreed on an interim constitution, providing for multiracial elections to a 400-member National Assembly in April 1994 and incorporating a fundamental bill of rights. Under the new constitution, South Africa would be divided into nine provinces (the existing homelands were to be dissolved and progressively integrated), and, in addition to English and Afrikaans, Xhosa and eight other languages would be made official. The constitution was approved by South Africa's Transitional Executive Council in December 1993, but the vote was boycotted by the right-wing Freedom Alliance.

pre-election violence South Africa was invited to rejoin the Commonwealth in January 1994. Chief Buthelezi continued his campaign to derail the democratization process, calling on Inkatha supporters to boycott the forthcoming elections. In March Bophuthatswana was annexed following a popular uprising against its leader, Lucas Mangope, and an attempted takeover of the capital, Mmbatho, by white right-wing extremists. The Freedom Alliance rapidly disintegrated. First Ciskei registered, then the leader of the far-right Volksfront, General Constand Viljoen, left his party to form and register a new right-wing Freedom Front.

Buthelezi remained intransigent, and politicially motivated killings increased. A temporary state of emergency was imposed in KwaZulu/Natal, where violence had escalated following the shooting of

Inkatha demonstrators in Johannesburg. Within days of the start of the elections, Buthelezi agreed to call a halt to Inkatha's campaign of violence in return for the status of the Zulu king being enshrined in the new constitution. The violence abated to some extent, but the ultra-right (the only group still refusing to participate) carried out pre-election bombings in Johannesburg and Pretoria.

first multiracial elections In the first nonracial elections in April 1994, the ANC captured 62% of the popular vote and won seven out of South Africa's nine new provinces.

The NP came second with 20% (winning Western Cape), and Inkatha (IFP) third with 10%. Despite reports of ballot-rigging in KwaZulu/Natal (where the IFP received most support), the Independent Electoral Commission declared the elections free of fraud. The following month Nelson Mandela was inaugurated as president of South Africa, with his ANC colleague Thabo Mbeki as first deputy president (premier), and the former president and NP leader F W de Klerk as second deputy president. The post of home affairs minister went to Zulu leader Chief Buthelezi.

South Africa under Mandela In June 1994 South Africa rejoined the Commonwealth, and in August it was announced that a 40-member select committee would be set up to oversee the drafting of a new, permanent constitution. A bill was passed restoring land to dispossessed blacks in November 1994.

Crime and violence escalated during 1995, particularly in KwaZulu/Natal province, and although the ANC won local elections in November, turnout was at barely 30%. A Truth and Reconciliation Commission was appointed, also in November, to investigate abuses of human rights in the apartheid era.

In March 1996 the divorce of Nelson and Winnie Mandela was formally completed. In the same month, ANC's Trevor Manuel replaced Chris Liebenberg as the country's first non-white finance minister. De Klerk withdrew the NP from the government of national unity in May 1996 after the adoption of a new constitution, which made no provision for power-sharing after 1999. The NP went into opposition.

In August 1996, unrest concerning the rise in crime in South Africa came to a head when members of a Muslim community group beat, shot, doused in petrol, and set ablaze a repeated arms and drugs offender. Threat of further vigilante action prompted President Mandela to increase the security forces' presence in the region. In September 1996 the Constitutional Court rejected the new draft constitution on the grounds that it lacked sufficient safeguards to protect regional and union interests. An amended version was submitted to the court a month later and Mandela formally signed the new constitution in December 1996.

In August 1997, de Klerk resigned as leader of the NP. He claimed that his retirement was intended to rectify the 'unjustified perception' that the party was still linked to the past, which had been obstructing political realignment in the country. In September Marthinus van Schalkwyk, a white Afrikaner, succeeded de Klerk as leader of a divided and weakened National Party.

President Mandela handed over the leadership of the ANC to his deputy Thabo Mbeki at the party's national conference in December 1997. In late April 1998 Mandela named a former anti-apartheid guerrilla leader to South Africa's top military post, making him the first black ever to lead the armed forces. Lieutenant General Siphiwe Nyanda, who once led ANC fighters, would succeed General Georg Meiring as head of the South African National Defence Force.

In September 1998, in its first military intervention since the end of apartheid, South African troops were sent troops into Lesotho in support of the government, beleaguered by an army mutiny. In January 1999, the assassination of Sifiso Nkabinde, leader of the opposition United Democratic Movement, and revenge attacks on ANC members that followed, increased concern over the country's stability in preparation for general elections planned for June.

The ANC won 66% of the vote in the country's second nonracial election in June 1999. The election marked the end of the Mandela era, in which the accent was on racial reconciliation. He was succeeded on 16 June by the ANC president, Thabo Mbeki. Mbeki pledged his government to end poverty and to fight against racism, corruption, and crime. Jacob Zuma was appointed deputy president after Buthelezi declined the post.

AIDS crisis The 13th international AIDS conference opened on 9 July 2000, in Durban, South Africa, one of the countries most affected by the disease. The United Nations estimated that 20% of South Africans are HIV positive. The unorthodox stance on AIDS in South Africa was called into question, as President Mbeki did not alter his stance that immune deficiency is caused by poverty and not by the HIV virus, nor did he alter his refusal to allow treatment with AZT, an immune boosting drug. The conference reported that more than 34 million people in the world are HIV positive, 70% of whom were in Africa. In October, the South African government launched a new campaign to inform the public about AIDS. In April, a group of 39 pharmaceutical companies dropped their court case against the South African government over the provision of cheaper generic drugs for AIDS. A report by South Africa's Medical Research Council in October 2001 revealed that AIDS had become the single biggest killer in the country, with 25% of all deaths in 2000, and 40%

of all adult deaths, being AIDS-related. The report predicted that, without effective treatment, up to 7 million people would die of the disease by 2010, halting population growth.

housing crisis A political stunt organized on 4 July 2001 by the pan-African Congress (PAC) to highlight South Africa's housing crisis got out of hand when tens of thousands of homeless people flocked to a piece of wasteland east of Johannesburg and demanded to buy a plot each for the equivalent of £2.50. The protest was staged on land near Johannesburg airport that belonged to the provincial government. However, a court ordered the squatters to leave and the South African government sent police to evict them.

racism conference A week-long United Nations conference on racism that opened on 31 August 2001 in Durban, South Africa, descended into chaos and recrimination. Rows over the Middle East, anti-Israeli language, and reparations for slavery threatened to ruin the conference. The USA and Israel walked out on 3 September, demanding that language branding Israel as a racist and apartheid state be removed from documents. After an extra day of diplomatic wrangling, the conference adopted a final declaration on 8 September that ignored the Israel-Palestine tensions. Britain and the other former colonial powers also escaped any commitment to pay reparations for slavery. At the insistence of Western countries, there was no explicit apology for the slave trade, but only acknowledgment and regret.

The ANC party suffered a blow in October 2001 when Tony Yengeni, the party's chief whip, was arrested, charged with corruption and perjury, and forced to resign. He had been investigated over a US$6 billion arms deal, and was accused of lying over his acceptance of a luxury car from the European Aeronautical Defence Space Company (EADS), an arms manufacturer.

South Africa's opposition alliance finally collapsed in October 2001 after weeks of infighting. The New National Party (NNP), which had split from the Democratic Alliance led by the Democratic Party (DP), began discussions with the ANC about joint rule in the Western Cape province and a possible role in central government. In November, the ANC agreed to joint rule despite widespread reservations from members of both parties.

In January 2002, the government promised to set up a commission of inquiry into the collapse of the rand. The currency lost 37% of its value in 2001.

Southern African Development Community SADC, organization of countries in the region working together initially to reduce their economic dependence on South Africa and harmonize their economic policies, but from 1995 to promote the creation of a free-trade zone by 2000. It was established in 1980 as the **Southern African Development Coordination Conference (SADCC)**, adopting its present name in 1992, and focuses on transport and communications, energy, mining, and industrial production. The member states are Angola, Botswana, Lesotho, Malawi, Mauritius, Mozambique, Namibia, South Africa, Swaziland, Tanzania, Zambia, and Zimbabwe; headquarters in Gaborone, Botswana.

South Korea country in East Asia, bounded north by North Korea, east by the Sea of Japan, south by the Korea Strait, and west by the Yellow Sea.

government Under the 1988 constitution, executive power is held by the president, who is directly elected by popular vote. The president is restricted to one five-year term of office and governs with a cabinet (state council) headed by a prime minister. Legislative authority resides in the single-chamber, 299-deputy national assembly, the Kuk Hoe, 237 of whose members are directly elected for four-

year terms by universal suffrage in single-member constituencies, and the remainder of whom are appointed in accordance with a formula designed to reward the largest single assembly party. The assembly has the authority to impeach the president and to override presidential vetoes. There is also a nine-member constitutional court, and guarantees of freedom of speech, press, assembly, and association are written into the constitution.

history The Republic of Korea was formed out of the zone south of the 38th parallel of latitude, the area occupied by US troops after Japan's surrender in 1945. The US military government controlled the country until, following national elections, an independent republic was declared on 15 August 1948.

Dr Syngman *Rhee, leader of the right-wing Liberal Party, was the nation's first president in a constitution based on the US model. To begin with, the republic had to cope with a massive influx of refugees fleeing the communist regime in North Korea, in addition to problems concerning the repatriation of over a million forced workers who had been sent to Japan during World War II.

the Korean War In June 1950 the North launched a massive invasion of South Korea, with the aim of reunifying the country. This began the three-year *Korean War, which, after intervention by US-led United Nations forces (on the side of the South) and by China (on the side of the North), ended in stalemate. The 38th parallel was re-established as the border between North and South by the armistice agreement of July 1953, and a UN-patrolled demilitarized buffer zone was created. South Korea was devastated by the war, and lost 226,000 troops.

Park Chung Hee in power, 1961–79 South Korea's economic recovery was hindered under Syngman Rhee by poor planning and inefficient execution, involving widespread corruption. Syngman Rhee's government was overthrown by popular demonstrations in April 1960, and a Democratic Party prime minister, Chang Myon, came to power. A new parliamentary-style constitution gave greater power to the legislature, and the ensuing political instability precipitated a military coup led by Gen *Park Chung Hee in May 1961.

A presidential system of government was re-established, with Park, who had meanwhile retired from the army, elected president in October 1963. Although in theory civilian government had been restored, South Korea remained a very closely controlled one-party state. Park was re-elected in May 1967, and, after amendment of the constitution, again in April 1971.

Opposition to the repressive Park regime mounted during the 1970s. In response, martial law was imposed. In October 1972 Park suspended the South Korean constitution and in November a national referendum approved what was called the Yushin, or 'Revitalisation', constitution, which strengthened the president's powers. A clampdown on political dissent, launched in 1975, was partially relaxed for the 1978 elections, but brought protests in 1979 as economic conditions briefly deteriorated. President Park was assassinated later that year, and martial law was reimposed.

economic development in the 1960s and 1970s From the beginning of Park's rule in 1961 successive economic plans were more capably worked out than in the 1950s, and implemented with increasing confidence. Capital was provided almost entirely by foreign loans, mainly from the USA and Japan. The resumption of diplomatic relations with Japan in 1964 was a major factor in this recovery.

From 1971 South Korea's industrial growth was one of the fastest in the world, particularly in international trade, with the country becoming a major exporter of light and heavy industrial goods. The Saemaul, or 'New Communities' campaign, inaugurated in the spring of 1971, spread the benefits of increasing prosperity into the rural areas.

continuing tensions with the North In August 1971 North Korea proposed political discussions with the South, and the Red Cross Societies of the two halves of the country began talks on humanitarian problems arising from the division of Korea. Despite the establishment in 1972 of a North–South coordinating committee to promote peaceful unification, relations with the South remained tense and hostile. Border incidents were frequent, and in October 1983 four South Korean cabinet ministers were assassinated in Rangoon, Burma (now Myanmar), in a bombing incident organized by two North Korean army officers.

The perceived threat of invasion from the North continued to be a key factor in South Korean politics, helping to justify stern rule. The country devoted large resources to modernizing its armed forces, which were supported by more than 35,000 US troops, assuring US intervention in the event of an invasion. Political and economic relations with the USA have remained close – the USA currently provides a market for 40% of South Korea's exports – but anti-US sentiment has always been strong among opposition groups.

developments after Park's death Following President Park's assassination in 1979 an interim government, led by former prime minister Choi Kyu-Hah, introduced liberalizing reforms, releasing opposition leader Kim Dae Jung in 1980. However, as antigovernment demonstrations developed, a new dissident clampdown began, involving the arrest of 30 political leaders, including Kim Dae Jung. After a severely suppressed insurrection in Kim's home city of Kwangju, President Choi resigned in 1980 and was replaced by the leader of the army, Gen Chun Doo Hwan. A new constitution was adopted, and, after Chun Doo Hwan was re-elected president in 1981, the new Fifth Republic was proclaimed.

cautious liberalization in the 1980s
Under President Chun economic growth resumed, but internal and external criticism of the suppression of civil liberties continued. Cautious liberalization was seen prior to the 1985 assembly elections, with the release of many political prisoners and the return from exile of Kim Dae Jung. After the 1985 election the opposition parties launched a campaign for genuine democratization, forcing the Chun regime to frame a new, more liberal constitution, which was adopted after a referendum in October 1987.

The ensuing presidential election was won by the ruling party's candidate, Roh Tae Woo, amid opposition charges of fraud. He took over in February 1988, but in the national assembly elections in April 1988 the ruling Democratic Justice Party (DJP) fell well short of an overall majority. Only in February 1990, when the DJP merged with two minor opposition parties to form the Democratic Liberal Party (DLP), was a stable governing majority secured.

continuing unrest In December 1990 the government launched a 'purification' campaign designed to improve public morals and reduce materialism. In May 1991 at least 250,000 people demonstrated and six attempted suicide in protests triggered by the beating to death of a student by police. Protests continued, and the police and security services were given emergency powers to deal with student-led unrest.

The country's two-party structure was restored in September 1991 when the opposition New Democratic Party, led by Kim Dae Jung, and the small Democratic Party, led by Lee Ki Taek, merged to form the Democratic Party, headed jointly by the two leaders. The ruling DLP lost its majority, and Roh resigned as leader.

civilian government restored
In December 1992 Kim Young Sam, candidate of the ruling DLP, won the presidential election, becoming the first president without a military background to be elected since 1960. The new civilian government pursued a strategy of gradual deregulation of South Korea's bureaucratic economy, including some privatizations, and pushed through reforms aimed at curbing political corruption. Despite a temporary slowdown in GDP growth in 1992–93, President Kim remained popular and the number of student protests diminished significantly.

From 1994 the government encouraged greater competition, privatization, and deregulation within the still booming economy, as part of a *segyehwa* ('globalization') initiative. However, in June 1995 the ruling DLP, which had been weakened by a split in its ranks March 1995, polled poorly in the country's first-ever local elections, with the opposition DP performing strongly.

In September 1995 a new centre-left opposition party, the National Congress for New Politics (NCNP), was formed by veteran politician Kim Dae Jung. It immediately attracted more than 50 defectors from the DP, making it the largest opposition party in the national assembly. In December 1995 the ruling DLP had renamed itself the New Korea Party (NKP) with Lee Soo Sung as prime minister. The party lost its majority in elections to the national assembly in April 1996.

corruption and treason charges
In October 1995 former president Roh Tae Woo was charged with corruption, after having publicly admitted to having amassed 500 billion won (£400

million) in a party slush fund during his term in office and to having retained 170 billion won for personal use. He was arrested, along with former president Chun Doo Hwan, in November 1995, and in January 1996 both men were charged with treason for their alleged role in the massacre of more than 200 antigovernment demonstrators in the military rebellion that brought Chun to power in 1980.

Chun Doo Hwan and Roh Tae Woo were respectively sentenced to death and 23 years' imprisonment in August 1996. They were also fined, between them, more than $610 million for receiving bribes from industry while in office. Chun and Roh immediately appealed against the convictions, and in December Chun's sentence was commuted to life imprisonment and Roh's to 17 years' imprisonment.

economic crisis In December 1996 and January 1997 there was large-scale industrial unrest across the country, especially in the car- and ship-building industries, and street protests over a new labour law that would end job security guarantees, making it easier for companies to dismiss workers, and empower businesses to alter workers' hours and employ temporary staff. Fears of a major economic crisis were confirmed in January with the collapse of Hanbo, the country's second-largest *chaebol* ('conglomerate') based on steel-making, with debts of $6 million. In late January 1997 President Kim Young Sam, whose popularity rating had fallen to 18%, met opposition leaders and agreed to revise the law. A revised bill was passed in March 1997. Hanbo's collapse, however, revealed widespread corruption which led, within a year, to the imprisonment of the son of President Kim Young San on charges of accepting bribes and tax evasion and to a jail sentence for the former president of the Bank of Seoul.

In February 1997 Kim Woo Suk resigned from the cabinet and, along with two other close political allies of

President Kim Young Sam, was arrested after claims that he took bribes to secure loans for Hanbo. President Kim made a televised public apology for the affair and, in March 1997, appointed Koh Kun, a career technocrat with a reputation for high integrity, as the country's sixth prime minister since 1993. However, the scandal, connected with a son of President Kim, severely tarnished the President's reputation and weakened his authority during his last year in power. In March 1997 Lee Hoi Chang, a former prime minister who had been sacked in 1994, was appointed chairman of the ruling New Korea Party. The same month witnessed the collapse of Sammi steel corporation, another of the top thirty *chaebol*.

Economic crisis continued through 1997. In July, Kia, the country's third biggest car maker and eighth biggest *chaebol* was reported to be in difficulties. A cabinet reshuffle in August did not change the overall situation. In November the country faced a major currency crisis and submitted an application to the International Monetary Fund (IMF) for an emergency loan package of $60 billion (£38 billion). In December veteran opposition leader Kim Dae Jung was elected president at his fourth attempt. One of his first acts was to confirm the release from prison of ex-presidents Chun Doo Whan and Roh Tae Woo ordered by outgoing president Kim Young Sam. Meanwhile patriotic Koreans responded to an official appeal by donating gold to be turned into hard currency to support the country's ailing financial structure. By April 1998 the won, which had stood at about 900 to the US$ in April 1997, appeared to be stabilizing at around the 1,400 level.

Although South Korea's economic difficulties occurred in the context of major crises afflicting Thailand, Malaysia, and Indonesia, its standing as the 11th greatest economy in the world meant that any major Korean collapse posed a greater threat to the stability in the South East Asian region. These political and economic developments were being played out against the background of mounting tensions with North Korea, arising out of the catastrophic famine gripping that country.

relations with the North South Korea was admitted to the United Nations along with North Korea in September 1991. Despite concerns over North Korea's nuclear aspirations, the prime ministers of the two Koreas met in Seoul in December 1991 and signed a non-aggression and confidence-building pact, which provided for the restoration of cross-border communications, the reunion of divided families, and the free movement of people, commerce, and ideas. On 31 December 1991 a further pact was signed in Panmunjom in which both states agreed to ban the testing, manufacture, deployment, or possession of nuclear weapons. In response, the USA agreed to withdraw its nuclear weapons from South Korea and to reduce its troop strength, although in 1994, in response to a perceived threat from North Korea, it again stepped up its military presence.

In 1995 South Korea donated two 'safe' nuclear reactors to North Korea, in an attempt to persuade the latter to abandon its suspected atomic-weapons programme, and also supplied the North with emergency shipments of rice. In April 1996 a joint US–South Korean proposal was announced for peace talks involving the two Koreas together with the USA and China in an attempt to bring a *rapprochement* to the peninsula. In August 1996 more than 5,000 students were arrested following their demands for unification with North Korea and the withdrawal of US troops.

US and North and South Korean officials began talks in March 1997 that mediators hoped would lead to peace

on the peninsula. Delegations gathered in New York for a briefing by the USA and South Korea on proposals for talks aimed at formally ending the Korean War. It was the first time since 1972 that North and South Koreans had met for peace talks. Talks between North and South continued in Beijing, China, but collapsed in April 1998 over Seoul's insistence that aid for the famine-stricken North be linked to the reuniting of families divided since the 1950–53 Korean war.

South Korea said in June 1999 that it was 'gravely concerned' that North Korea had sent its warships into southern territorial waters, allegedly to protect fishing fleet. A tense stand-off in the Yellow Sea exploded later in June when the South Korean navy sank a North Korean torpedo boat and damaged several other vessels. North Korea's accused the South of provoking the incident. In the same month, talks between the North and South Korean governments about the possible reunification of families separated by the 54-year-old split were suspended.

foreign affairs Other notable developments in foreign affairs during the 1990s include the establishment of full diplomatic relations with the USSR in 1990, the beginning of diplomatic links with communist China in 1992, and the development of closer political and economic links with Japan. In January 1997 South Korea joined the Organization for Economic Cooperation and Development (OECD).

start of Kim Dae Jung's presidency In February 1998 Kim Dae Jung was sworn in as president. He pledged his administration's goals as revitalizing the troubled economy, political and economic reform, and reconciliation with the North, starting with an exchange of envoys and a summit meeting. Kim Jong Pil was appointed prime minister; the leader of the conservative United Liberal Democrats (ULD) and a former premier 1971–75, he had agreed in November 1997 not to stand for the presidency in return for this position. However, the Grand National Party (GNP), formed in November 1997 through the merger of the Democratic Party and the New Korea Party, which held 162 of the national assembly's 299 seats, opposed Kim Jong Pil's appointment.

In February 1998 new labour laws were introduced, ending the Korean tradition of lifetime employment by allowing companies to introduce redundancies, which had previously been prohibited. However, 6 trillion won ($4.3 billion) was to be spent on welfare provision and retraining for the unemployed, since unemployment was expected to rise during the coming year as a result of the economic crisis in Southeast Asia. In addition, there were reforms to open South Korea's financial markets to foreigners. In May there were large-scale strikes as workers demanded an easing of the austerity reforms agreed with the IMF and more generous benefits for the unemployed.

In March 1998 President Kim Dae Jung freed 2,304 prisoners, as part of a broader amnesty. This figure included 74 political prisoners, but international human-rights organizations claimed that around 400 'prisoners of conscience' remained in jail.

In August 1998 there was serious labour unrest and violence continued at Hyundai, the country's largest car maker, which was seeking to lay off workers in the face of slumping sales and financial losses. GDP was set to contract by at least 5% in 1998, as a result of austerity measures.

Kim Jong Pil's appointment as prime minister was finally ratified by the legislature in August 1998, after sufficient deputies had switched sides to President Kim Dae Jung's ruling coalition a national assembly majority.

renewed North-South talks

In October 1998 representatives of North and South Korea, the USA, and China met in Geneva in a renewed effort to bring permanent peace to the peninsula. However, it was not until April 2000 that both North and South Korea simultaneously announced the arrangement of the first summit meeting between the divided countries. Kim Dae Jung and the hereditary leader of North Korea, Kim Jong Il, planned to meet in June 2000 in Pyongyang, the capital of North Korea. Just days after the announcement, South Korea's ruling party failed to secure a majority in parliamentary elections. When Kim Dae Jung was welcomed by Kim Jong Il, leader of North Korea, in Pyongyang, capital of North Korea, the two leaders came to some agreement, including a plan for South Korea to speed up economic investment in North Korea, and a plan to open rail links between the two countries. Following the agreement that links between the two countries would be forged, in August 2000, 100 elderly people from either side of the border were reunited with their families from whom they had been separated for 50 years. In September 2000, the defence ministers of North and South Korea met for the first time in more than 50 years. Kim Dae Jung was awarded the Nobel Peace Prize on 13 October 2000 for his work in bringing about reconciliation with the communist government of North Korea.

In September 2001, South Korea's parliament passed a vote of no confidence in Lim Ding Won, the minister in charge of negotiations with North Korea, triggering the resignation of the entire cabinet. A government spokesman said that the policy of reconciliation with the North would still continue.

In June 2002, in the worst clash between North and South Korea in three years, naval vessels fired on each other in disputed coastal waters in the Yellow Sea. Four South Korean sailors were killed and 19 injured, while around 30 North Korean casualties were reported. The incident threatened to derail Kim Dae Jung's policy of engagement with the North.

soviet (Russian **'council'**) originally a strike committee elected by Russian workers in the 1905 revolution; in 1917 these were set up by peasants, soldiers, and factory workers. The soviets sent delegates to the All-Russian Congress of Soviets to represent their opinions to a future government. They were later taken over by the *Bolsheviks.

Spaak, Paul-Henri (1899–1972) Belgian socialist politician. From 1936 to 1966 he held office almost continuously as foreign minister or prime minister. He was an ardent advocate of international peace.

Spain country in southwestern Europe, on the Iberian Peninsula between the Atlantic Ocean and the Mediterranean Sea, bounded north by France and west by Portugal.

government The 1978 constitution provides for a hereditary monarch as formal head of state. The monarch appoints a prime minister, called president of government, and a council of ministers, all responsible to the national assembly, Las Cortes Generales. The Cortes consists of two chambers, the chamber of deputies, with 350 members, and the senate, with 257. Deputies are elected by universal suffrage through a system of proportional representation; 208 of the senators are directly elected to represent the whole country and 49 to represent the regions. All serve a four-year term.

Spain has developed a form of regional self-government whereby each of the 50 provinces has its own council (Diputación Provincial) and civil governor. The devolution process was extended in 1979 when 17 autonomous communities were approved, each with a parliament elected for a four-year term.

history For the history of Spain before 1945, see *Spain: history 1492–1936.

Following his victory in the *Spanish Civil War (1936–39) Gen Francisco *Franco had become leader of a right-wing military dictatorship in Spain. Immediately after World War II the fascist *Falange (the only legal party), the army, the Roman Catholic Church, and the upper classes were united in their support of Franco, because they were haunted by the spectre of left-wing revolution.

Spain was economically still very weak, as World War II had inhibited its own reconstruction programme in the wake of the Civil War. In addition, for some years after 1945, Spain suffered political isolation. It was not a member of the United Nations, and in December 1946 the UN recommended the withdrawal of all embassies from Spain, a decision complied with by most nations.

the plan to restore the monarchy Anxious to consolidate his internal position, Franco adopted a conciliatory attitude towards some of his former opponents. In 1947 he announced that Spain would become a monarchy, with a regency council and himself as head of state. If the head of state died the regency council should propose a successor, a king or regent, to be approved by a two-thirds majority of the Cortes (parliament). A referendum later that year approved this decision. Prince *Juan Carlos, the son of Don Juan (the latter named by ex-King *Alfonso XIII as his successor) lived most of his early life in Spain, close to Franco.

This implication of an eventual restoration of the Bourbon monarchy probably consolidated Franco's regime in the country as a whole, but caused considerable misgivings among a section of the Falange. In July 1957 the Spanish parliament was officially informed that the monarchy would be restored in Spain on the death or withdrawal from power of Franco.

the ending of isolation By 1948 the Western powers were re-examining their attitude towards Spain; in the light of the Cold War, Soviet communism was perceived as a far greater threat than Franco's Spain.

The UN removed the ambassadorial ban on Spain, and in 1952 Spain joined UNESCO. In 1951 it received a loan from the US Export-Import Bank, and in 1953, under a ten-year defence agreement signed with the USA, Spain was to receive arms and economic aid and to allow the USA the use of naval and air bases in its territory. This agreement was periodically renewed, with the Spanish government driving a harder bargain on each occasion.

Until the end of the 1960s it appeared that Spain stood a good chance of reintegrating itself within the community of Western European countries and of achieving a smooth political succession. But both possibilities depended largely on Franco's willingness and ability to relinquish office and power, and this failed to happen, except during a few weeks in the summer of 1974 when ill health obliged him to transfer his functions as chief of state to Prince Juan Carlos.

Franco's hold weakens The regime faced numerous problems. The worldwide economic recession of the mid-1970s exposed the weaknesses of the Spanish economy, which was also hit when Britain, Spain's major trading partner, joined the European Community in 1973. Tourism, which had developed in the 1960s, also saw a decline. The government's emphasis on its historic links with the Arab nations (dating from the period of Muslim rule in Spain in the Middle Ages) and with its former colonies in South America (which it had lost in the early 19th century) brought few benefits other than cultural ones. At the same time, soaring domestic inflation politicized large sections of the hitherto complacent middle class.

The militant *Basque separatist movement, ETA (*Euskadi ta Askatasuna, 'Basque Homeland and

Liberty') began to wage guerrilla warfare in the north in the late 1960s, and Catalan nationalism, though less active, was no less well established. Thus the two economically most advanced areas of Spain presented the most critical political problems for Madrid.

Unrest in the universities and among the industrial workers became endemic from the late 1960s. The number of industrial workers had grown with the large-scale movement away from the land, and these workers made numerous attempts to establish authentic trade unions in opposition to the state-controlled syndicates. Both students and workers received aid from increasing numbers of priests, whose actions reflected the dissatisfaction of the new generation of Spanish clergy with the Roman Catholic Church's traditionally acquiescent role in Spain; the clergy was also acting in response to the social teachings of Pope John XXIII and to its fears for the future after Franco's death.

The assassination, allegedly by members of ETA, of Franco's vice-president, Carrero Blanco, in 1973, and the overthrow of the friendly regime in Portugal in 1974 presented the government with new problems. Franco's age and ill health exacerbated the struggle for power between the anti-monarchical and anti-liberal old-style Falangists, the more outward-looking members of the right-wing Roman Catholic organization Opus Dei, and the cautiously pragmatic politicians represented by the prime minister, Carlos Arias Navarro.

the return to democracy In 1975 the death of Gen Franco brought a restoration of the monarchy (in the person of King Juan Carlos), and the renewal of open political debate and party activity for the first time since the 1930s. There followed a slow but steady progress to democratic government.

A more liberal cabinet was formed, but left-wing discontent continued when the expected amnesty for political prisoners was not granted. Early in 1976 mass rallies were held, and communist- and socialist-led groups united in the Democratic Formation. Later, the Cortes approved bills lifting restrictions on political meetings, a revised amendment to the Penal Code was passed, and Adolfo *Suárez replaced Navarro as prime minister. A partial amnesty was granted, and the proposal for an elected two-chamber parliament was approved by a popular referendum in December 1976.

In February 1977 legislation was enacted legalizing most political parties, the Communist Party being legalized in April. The National Movement – Spain's state political party under Franco – was abolished in April.

In June 1977 the first general elections since 1936 were held. Pre-election tension had run high in the Basque provinces, with several people losing their lives in demonstrations and kidnappings. The centre-left coalition Union of the Democratic Centre (UCD), headed by Suárez, won 165 of the 350 seats in the Congress of Deputies, and 105 of the 207 elected seats in the Senate. King Juan Carlos subsequently nominated a further 41 senators. The inaugural session of the Cortes was opened by the king in July. A new constitution was endorsed by referendum in 1978.

regional demands and the right-wing threat Spain faced two main internal problems: the demands for independence by regional extremists and the possibility of a right-wing military coup. Suárez suddenly resigned in 1981 and was succeeded by his deputy, Leopoldo Calvo Sotelo. He was immediately confronted with an attempted army coup in Madrid, while at the same time the military commander of Valencia declared a state of emergency there and sent tanks out on the streets. Both uprisings failed, and the two leaders were tried and imprisoned.

Calvo Sotelo's decision to take Spain into the North Atlantic Treaty Organization (NATO) in 1982 was widely criticized, and he was forced to call a general election in October 1982. The result was a sweeping victory for the Partido Socialista Obrero Español (PSOE; Spanish Socialist Workers' Party), led by Felipe González. At the same time ETA had stepped up its campaign for independence with widespread terrorist activity, spreading in 1985 to the Mediterranean holiday resorts and threatening Spain's lucrative tourist industry.

the González administration
The PSOE had fought the 1982 election on a policy of taking Spain out of NATO and carrying out extensive nationalization. Once in office, however, González showed himself to be a pragmatist. His nationalization programme was highly selective, and he left the decision on NATO to a referendum.

In January 1986 Spain became a full member of the European Community, and in March the referendum showed popular support for remaining in NATO despite the special conditions attached to its membership. These included a bilateral treaty with the USA for the presence of its troops in Spain and for the limited use of Spanish troops away from Spanish soil.

In the 1986 election González returned for another term as prime minister. In 1988 Spain, with Portugal, became a member of the Western European Union. In the 1989 general election the PSOE won only 175 seats in the 350-member national assembly but retained power under González, who formed a 'tactical alliance' with the Basque and Catalan parties. Major tax reforms were passed in 1991 in an effort to help the nation's struggling economy.

After an unofficial truce, ETA's armed struggle resumed in August 1992. González announced in October 1992 that he would seek a fourth term of office and contest the next elections. During 1993 the PSOE was plagued by a series of corruption scandals prompting González to call an early general election in June. The PSOE narrowly won, with 38.8% of the vote to the opposition Popular Party's (PP) 34.8%, but lost its parliamentary majority. In August, on the king's request, González formed a new minority government.

Further revelations of corruption during 1994 increased pressure on González to reform his government or step down, and in 1995 the party came under attack for its alleged involvement in a 'dirty war' against ETA activists in the 1980s. Local elections in May 1995 were won by the conservatives and in September the Catalan nationalist party withdrew its support from the governing coalition, following allegations that González had himself been involved in the setting up of an anti-ETA hit squad in the 1980s.

the end of the González era
Although a probe into the role González and other members of parliament had played was subsequently abandoned, the loss of Catalan support forced him to call an early election in March 1996, in which the conservative PP triumphed, ending 13 years of Socialist government. However, the margin was narrower than expected, and 20 seats short of a majority, forcing the party's leader, José María Aznar, to begin talks with moderate Catalan nationalists to form a coalition government. Aznar formed a minority PP government in May.

In December 1995 the Spanish foreign minister, Javier Solana Madariaga, became NATO secretary general, and in November 1996 parliament agreed to Spain's full integration within NATO, limiting the 1982 limitations to membership.

ETA continued its separatist fight, and in July 1997 Spain was swept by an unprecedented mass mobilization against the organization's terrorist activities. The government called for the isolation of the pro-ETA Herri Batasuna (HB) Party, which generally wins up to 15% of the Basque vote.

In December 1997 Spain's Supreme Court jailed 23 HB leaders. It was the first time in HB's legal existence that a legal judgement recognized a link between the army and armed Basque separatists. Spain's Supreme Court in July 1998 sentenced a former Socialist interior minister, his deputy, and a former civil governor to 10 years each in jail for their involvement in a 'dirty war' against the Basque guerrilla group ETA in the 1980s.

In September 1998 ETA called a 'total and indefinite' ceasefire. The government eventually responded by announcing, in November, that it would begin peace talks with ETA. Spain's constitutional court in July 1999 freed the leaders of HB, jailed in 1997. It was hoped that the move would help to consolidate the Basque peace process. After a 14-month suspension of violence, in November 1999 the group announced that it would resume actions against the government. Two factors appeared to be behind the decision: the arrest of an ETA negotiator, Belén Gonzalez, the previous month, and the failure of the moderate Basque parties to work with ETA in pressing for an independent Basque state by political means. The announcement frustrated hopes for a gradual peace in the Basque Country and prompted protests from Spaniards fearing a return to violence. In late January 2000, the ceasefire was brought to an end when two car bombs exploded in the Spanish capital, Madrid, killing an army officer and damaging vehicles and buildings. Two days after the blast, more than one million people demonstrated against

Basque separatist violence on the streets of Madrid.

2000 election Two political parties, the Socialists and the Communist-led United Left agreed in February 2000 to form their first alliance since the 1936 civil war, in order to fight the ruling conservative People's party in the March general election. They agreed to form a coalition government if they won. However, the elections recorded a decisive victory for the centre-right People's Party, led by Prime Minister José María Aznar, which was also the biggest conservative victory in Spain's 25-year-old democracy.

ETA violence continues ETA's violence continued into 2000; bombings and assassinations marked ETA's most violent wave of terror for a decade, and brought the total number of deaths to 800 since 1968 in the campaign for Basque independence. In September, 37 suspected ETA terrorists, including its military commander Ignacio Gracia Arregui, were arrested by Spanish and French police in a concerted cross-border initiative. The violence continued, however, and a Supreme Court judge and his two bodyguards were killed in late October. The following month, Ernest Lluch, a former socialist minister, was shot dead. Nationwide protests against terrorism followed the next day. On 12 December, Spain's two biggest political parties, the ruling People's Party and the opposition Socialists, agreed to cooperate against ETA.

In March 2001, the socialist deputy mayor of Lasarte, in the Basque region, was killed by ETA, a week after they set off two car bombs in Mediterranean resorts. In May the Basque Nationalist Party celebrated their best election victory in Basque elections for 20 years. However, the pro-ETA party suffered its worst defeat. A Spanish general and 15 other people were injured when a bomb exploded in central Madrid, Spain, on 28 June in an apparent assassination attempt blamed on ETA. ETA was also blamed for two car bomb explosions, one in Madrid on 10 July that killed a policeman and injured 13 others, the other in a small village near Pamplona, northern Spain, on 14 July that killed a local councillor. It was the 10th killing in 2001 and the 33rd to be attributed to ETA since the terrorist group ended its ceasefire. Public demonstrations against the killings were held on 15 July in cities and towns throughout Spain and in parts of the Basque Country.

tentative talks Prime Minister Aznar met Basque president Juan José Ibarretxe in July 2001, to discuss the future of the Basque region and the continuing ETA violence. No agreements were reached, but the meeting was widely viewed as a step forward. However, a massive car bomb planted by ETA prompted the evacuation of hundreds of holidaymakers from a busy hotel in the Spanish resort of Salou on the Costa Brava in August. ETA had warned months earlier it would target tourist spots to damage Spain's leading economic sector and make an international impact. In towns nearby, police later seized weapons, 160 kg/350 lb of explosives and a car-bomb ready for use. Police later struck a blow against ETA, arresting six members of a commando unit in and around Barcelona. ETA hit back with a bomb in the car park of Madrid airport; it caused extensive damage but no injuries.

A car bomb in a busy residential part of Madrid on 6 November 2001 wounded 90 people. The attack, blamed on ETA, was apparently aimed at Juan Junquera, a senior government scientist and former defence official, who was passing in his car when the device was detonated.

On 1 January 2002, euro notes and coins were introduced as the national currency. In February 2002, the Spanish government and the opposition PSOE agreed to ban political parties with links to violent groups. The decision initially affected only the Basque separatist party Euskal Herritarrok (EH), which has links with ETA.

Following an occupation by Moroccan soldiers of the uninhabited rocky outcrop of Perejil in the Strait of Gibraltar in July and the subsequent recapture of the islet by Spanish forces, the Spanish and Moroccan governments declared a truce in their ownership dispute under an accord brokered by the USA. However, Morocco continued to claim a number of other Spanish-held territories, including the north African city enclaves of Ceuta and Melilla.

Spain: history 1492–1936 In 1936, Spain was heading towards civil war. For Spanish history since 1945 see *Spain.

By the 13th century the smaller Christian kingdoms of Spain had all been absorbed by the two dominant kingdoms, Castile and Aragón. The marriage of Ferdinand of Aragón to Isabella of Castile in 1469 led to the unification of Spain, which was completed when Granada, the last Moorish stronghold in Spain, was conquered in 1492.

the achievements of Ferdinand and Isabella The reign of Ferdinand and Isabella marks the beginning of Spain's emergence as one of the great powers of Europe, and, indeed, the world. Spain reached its greatest power under their successors Charles I (the Holy Roman Emperor Charles V), and Philip II.

Under Ferdinand and Isabella the various kingdoms and provinces of Spain were united under one central authority, and gradually the independent cortes (parliaments) of the various provinces, although nominally still holding power, became subservient to that authority. In 1504 the Spanish crown acquired Naples and Sicily, which had earlier belonged to the house of Aragón.

In 1492 Ferdinand and Isabella sponsored the voyage of Christopher Columbus, whose early exploration of the Americas opened up potentially vast overseas dominions for Spain. The Portuguese were also active in the exploration of the New World, and by the Treaty of Tordesillas in 1494 Spain and Portugal agreed to divide the uncharted world between them. Spanish *conquistadores* went on to conquer Mexico in 1519–21 (Hernán Cortés), Peru in 1531 (Francisco Pizarro), and most of the rest of Central and South America, bringing large amounts of gold and silver back across the Atlantic to enrich the Spanish exchequer and stimulate the Spanish economy. This in turn contributed to the Europe-wide inflation of the 16th century.

the enforcement of Catholic orthodoxy A marked feature of the Spanish monarchy was its ardent Catholicism. The consequence of this was not only to weaken Spain economically, but to stifle the intellectual and cultural life of the country.

In 1478 Ferdinand and Isabella secured the pope's permission to establish an Inquisition (there had been one in Aragón but not in Castile) to suppress heresy in Spain, and especially the Jews. Isabella's confessor, the monk Tomás de Torquemada , became Inquisitor-General throughout Spain in 1483. Any divergence from strict orthodoxy was brutally repressed, and in the first decade some 2,000 'heretics' were burned. In 1492, the year of the conquest of Granada, the Jews were expelled from Spain, which thereby lost some of its most commercially active citizens. In its possessions in the New World, the Spanish embarked on a process of mass conversions, often imposed forcibly.

The Spanish monarchs, emerging from centuries of war against the Muslims, regarded themselves as the Catholic sovereigns of Europe, and when Protestantism became widespread in Europe, Spain took a leading role in the Counter-Reformation. The remaining Spanish Muslims – known as Moriscos – were expelled in 1609.

Charles V and the extension of Spanish power On the death of Isabella in 1504, the crown of Castile passed to her daughter Joanna the Mad, who had married Philip of Burgundy, the son of the Habsburg Holy Roman Emperor, Maximilian I. For a time Castile and Aragón were ruled separately, but on the death of Philip, Ferdinand again administered Spain and finally, on his death, left the whole of his kingdom to his daughter and to her son Charles as regent.

Charles had already received the Netherlands from his father in 1506. On Ferdinand's death in 1516 he succeeded to all the possessions of the Spanish crown, not only in Spain, but also in Italy and the Americas. On Maximilian's death in 1519, Charles inherited the Habsburg family lands in Austria and was elected Holy Roman Emperor as Charles V. The duchy of Milan in Italy was also acquired by the Spanish crown in 1535.

During Charles's reign the history of Spain, or at least of the Spanish king, is the history of Europe. (For further information see, for example, articles dealing with the histories of the Netherlands, Belgium, Luxembourg, France, Germany, Austria, and Italy.) The importance of this reign to Spain itself, however, lies in the fact that during it the royal power was definitely established. Charles continued, however, to respect the rights of his various Spanish realms.

the reign of Philip II Worn out by the internal troubles of the empire, in 1555 Charles abdicated the Netherlands, and in 1556 Spain, to his son Philip. The position of Holy Roman Emperor passed to Charles's brother Ferdinand I, who also retained the Austrian Habsburg lands, but the rest of Charles's hereditary possessions were passed to his son, who reigned as Philip II of Spain.

Philip (ruled 1556–98) was a man of tenacious purpose, but lacked political flair and imagination. He regarded himself as, above all else, the Catholic champion of Europe. This position was the keystone of his life's work, and he died still pursuing this policy and having ruined Spain in its pursuit. He ruled over the empire of Spain at its greatest. His power extended over Spain, the Spanish Netherlands (the present-day Netherlands, Belgium, and Luxembourg), the greater part of Italy, Portugal (annexed in 1580), the whole of South America, a large part of North America, and possessions in the East Indies and in Africa. As the (largely absent) husband of Mary I of England, he also influenced her anti-Protestant policies. He possessed the finest fighting machine in Europe, both military and naval, and his great victory over the Turks at Lepanto helped contain the westward expansion of the Ottoman Empire.

Philip's position in Europe as the greatest monarch was unquestioned, partly because France was divided by the Wars of Religion (1562–89). However, since Spanish territory encircled France, Philip faced the continued hostility of France. In addition, the cruelties of the Duke of Alva in repressing the Calvinists, and Philip's authoritarian policies, led to the outbreak of the Dutch Revolt in 1568 (see the *Netherlands). The English sent military aid to their fellow Protestants in the Netherlands, and this provoked Philip to send the Spanish Armada against England (1588), which ended in the destruction of the Spanish fleet. The greatest days of Spain passed with Philip's death in 1598.

the beginnings of Spanish decline The century that followed Philip's death was a time of decline. Plague, population decrease, economic recession, and constant wars (and the means used to finance them, which caused serious inflation) all greatly reduced Spain's wealth and power. In the reign of Philip III (1598–1621), the remaining Moors (the Moriscos) were expelled from Spain (1609). Spain's efforts to prevent other countries trading with its American dominions were increasingly ineffective.

The Dutch Revolt was temporarily interrupted by the Twelve Years' Truce (1609–21), but continued during the reign of Philip IV (1621–65) as part of the wider European conflict of the Thirty Years' War (1618–48). Spain took an active role in this war, in which it had become embroiled for religious and strategic reasons but from which it gained little. Its soldiers, however, were still the finest in Europe. The military history of the closing stages of the war in the Netherlands suggests that Spain finally was defeated through lack of resources and not because of military deficiency; almost at the end of the struggle it could still win ephemeral military triumphs, as in the recapture of Breda in 1625.

European wars and the expense of maintaining empire placed an increasing burden on Spain, and in 1640 both Portugal and Catalonia revolted against the financial demands of the Spanish crown. Spanish rule was restored in Catalonia (1652), but by the Peace of Westphalia (1648) Spain was obliged to recognize the independence of both Portugal and the United Provinces (the northern provinces of the Spanish Netherlands, which had first declared their freedom in 1581).

The power of France had been steadily increasing during the whole of this period, and the entry of France into the Thirty Years' War in 1635 had been for entirely political, rather than religious, reasons. By the end of the 17th century France, under Louis XIV, had become the dominant power in Europe. Spain became involved in most of the wars during the reign of

Louis XIV, but it generally lost ground with each war, although in 1697 Louis XIV returned Luxembourg.

the War of the Spanish Succession
During the whole of the reign of Charles II of Spain (1665–1700) Europe waited for the division of the spoils at his death. It was known that Charles II would die childless, and France, the Austrian Habsburgs, and Bavaria had claims to the Spanish throne.

Two partition treaties were arranged. The first provided for the accession of the young son of the Elector of Bavaria to the Spanish throne, and the two other powers were to be compensated by acquiring shares of the still large extraterritorial possessions of Spain. The second treaty, following the death of the Bavarian prince, gave the throne to Austria, and again compensated France from the residue of the Spanish Empire.

The Spanish king and people, however, repudiated both treaties, and by the will of Charles II the whole of the Spanish dominions were left to Philip of Anjou, grandson of Louis XIV, and the founder of the Bourbon dynasty in Spain. Philip was proclaimed king of Spain in November 1700 as Philip V (ruled 1700–46). This led to the War of the Spanish Succession (1701–14). By the Treaty of Utrecht (1713) all Spain's Italian possessions, the remaining Spanish Netherlands (present-day Belgium and Luxembourg), Minorca, and Gibraltar were taken from it, dismantling its empire in Europe. But Spain's extensive oversease empire remained intact. In the course of the war, Philip V had suppressed the independence of Catalonia, recreating an absolute monarchy.

Spain in the 18th century Spain's relations with Britain continued to be bad, and again culminated in war in 1739. This was the War of Jenkins' Ear, which merged into the War of the Austrian Succession (1740–48), in which Prussia, France, and Spain were allied against Austria, Britain, and the Netherlands.

The 18th century was a period of great change for Spain. Ferdinand VI (ruled 1746–59) and Charles III (ruled 1759–88) initiated wide reforms, reformed the revenues, and placed Spain again upon a satisfactory financial basis. Roads were improved, commerce encouraged, banks firmly established, and the revenues from the colonies carefully and wisely supervised.

During the Seven Years' War (1759–63) Spain was again allied with France against Britain, and in 1763 lost Florida to Britain, regaining it in 1783 at the end of the American Revolution, in which France and Spain helped the colonists against Britain.

In 1788 Charles IV became king, and Spain quickly reverted to a state of affairs similar to that which had existed in the reign of Charles II. The ministers of Charles III were replaced by the royal favourite Manuel de Godoy, who was corrupt and unpopular.

the Revolutionary and Napoleonic Wars Following the outbreak of the French Revolution (1789) and the execution of the French king (1793), Spain declared war on France. However, in 1796 it was forced to sign a treaty with France by which it promised aid to the French. The result was that its fleet was defeated by the British off Cape St Vincent and its trade practically annihilated. Another French and Spanish fleet was defeated by the British at the Battle of Trafalgar in 1805.

In 1807 a quarrel between Charles IV and his son Ferdinand culminated in an appeal to Napoleon. Charles and Ferdinand were both summoned to Bayonne, where the crown of Spain was ceded to Napoleon. Napoleon made his brother, Joseph Bonaparte, king of Spain in 1808, and French armies occupied Spain. But the Spanish people recognized only their own chosen king, Ferdinand VII, and

the War of Liberation began. The British, allied with Spanish resistance, finally drove out the French in 1814. A constitution for Spain was drawn up in 1812 in Cádiz, and Ferdinand promised to be faithful to it. In 1814, however, when he returned to Spain he restored the old Spanish absolute monarchy.

the turbulent 19th century Throughout the 19th century conflict raged between monarchists and liberals; revolutions and civil wars took place in 1820–23, 1833–39, 1868, and 1872–76, besides many minor revolts. The century was also marked by the loss of Spain's American colonies, all of which fought for, and achieved, independence in the period 1810–30.

In 1833 Ferdinand VII's daughter Isabella II succeeded him, and in 1843 signed the constitution of 1836, which had been modelled on that of Cádiz (1812). Isabella's reign was chaotic, her ministers were weak, and she was not able to keep the country in order. From 1833 to 1839 the country was in a state of civil war (the First *Carlist War), when supporters of Don Carlos (1788–1855), Isabella's uncle, sought unsuccessfully to establish their leader's claim to the throne. The administration became increasingly corrupt, and finally in 1868 there was a revolution and Isabella was obliged to abdicate.

From 1868 to 1870 a provisional government was set up, and many experiments were tried in order to bring peace to the country. Various candidates were put forward for the Spanish throne. These included the Hohenzollern Prince Leopold (a member of the Prussian royal house), whose candidature provoked France. This resulted in the Franco-Prussian War of 1870, which, as the Prussian chancellor Bismarck had calculated, persuaded the remaining German states to join the Prussian-led German Empire. The Prussian candidate was withdrawn, and Amadeus I of Savoy was finally elected. Amadeus remained in Spain for three years, then abdicated and left the country. For a year (1873–74) Spain became a republic, and in 1875 Isabella's son Alfonso became king as Alfonso XII (ruled 1875–85).

In 1872 the Second Carlist War had broken out, and in 1876 it ended with the withdrawal of Don Carlos (grandson of the first Carlist claimant) to France. In 1885 Alfonso XII died, and in the following May his son, *Alfonso XIII, was born and was recognized as king). His mother, Queen Maria Christina, acted as regent.

After the Spanish-American War in 1898 Spain ceded Cuba, Puerto Rico, Guam, and the Philippines to the USA. Spain's navy was destroyed, and the huge cost of the war was a very heavy burden on an impoverished country.

the 20th century The early 20th century saw a growth of republicanism, socialism, anarchism, and regional separatism. On 17 May 1902 Alfonso XIII was crowned. A host of troubles called for a stable government. The Moroccan question, however, was patched up by a Franco-Spanish treaty (1904), recognizing Spanish rights there. In Catalonia hatred was developing between the Catalan nationalists and the radical centralists. During the 1905 elections antagonism to the military in Catalonia resulted in the Law of Jurisdictions, allowing military tribunals to try offences against military institutions. The power of the military in Spanish politics, in which the king concurred, was thus increased. The Catalan movement also intensified.

From 1905 to 1907 the Liberals held office. By 1910 José Canalejas had come to the front as the Liberal leader. Although a Catholic, he curbed the power of the church in Spain, and in Morocco he successfully countered a French military bid for supremacy, against which the Germans also sent the cruiser *Panther* to Agadir (see

*Agadir Incident). His work towards a settlement of the Catalan question was ended by his assassination in Madrid by an anarchist on 12 November 1912. During World War I Spain was neutral, being divided between the pro-Allies liberal anticlerical left and the pro-German reactionary clerical right.

A military bid for power was brewing, pressure being put upon the government by the secret military committees of defence, organized by army officers. On 10 August 1917 a general strike, aiming at the creation of a socialist democratic republic, spread across the whole country. In suppressing it, the army became the strongest force in the state. Juan la Cierva (who, as the then minister of the interior, was responsible for the execution of Francisco Ferrer, the extremist anticlerical and socialist, in 1909), became war minister and practical dictator of a new cabinet, with García Prieto as premier. La Cierva's conflict with Spanish *syndicalism brought about his downfall. On 3 December 1918 the liberal Conde de Romanones returned to power, and secured the entry of Spain to the Council of the League of Nations.

the dictatorship of Primo de Rivera Political chaos followed, and government succeeded government. A military revolt broke out on 13 September 1923, under Miguel *Primo de Rivera. The government resigned, and the king was forced by the army to recognize a military directorate, with Primo de Rivera as president.

The functions of the Cortes (parliament) were suspended and the control of departments was left to undersecretaries, who were later (1925) raised to the status of ministers. Industry and agriculture prospered under the dictatorship, but culture did not. The Spanish joined the French in suppressing a revolt in Morocco. In Spain the dictatorship depended on censorship, and from 1926 to 1927 on martial law. Eventually, the dictatorship brought the throne into such disrepute that the king dismissed Primo de Rivera in 1930.

the Second Republic When municipal elections in April 1931 resulted in a sweeping Republican victory, the king left the country without, however, renouncing any of his rights. A provisional Republican government was set up under Niceto Alcalá Zamora, head of a conservative group within the Republican Party. On 14 April a Catalan Republic was proclaimed, with Francesc Macià as president.

The provisional Republican government was confirmed by the general elections held on 28 June 1931. On 14 July the Cortes began the task of drawing up the constitution, which was completed by December. In the five years between the overthrow of the monarchy and the Civil War, democracy under the Second Republic was very fragile, attacked by both right (monarchist) and left (communist and anarchist) extremists.

There were many strikes and communist riots, and in October 1931 the government was split on the issue of the separation of the church and the state, which the Cortes voted in favour of. Alcalá Zamora resigned, and a new cabinet was formed by Manuel Azaña. In November ex-King Alfonso was formally outlawed, and in December Alcalá Zamora was elected president of the Republic.

A month after the proclamation of the Republic a mob set fire first to the Jesuit church in the centre of Madrid, then to other churches and convents in the city and suburbs. The government took no effective action, being content to attach the blame not to the mob but to the monarchists. This incited further violence, and soon churches and convents in most of the large cities of Spain were set on fire. By a decree in January 1932 the Society of Jesus (the Jesuits) was dissolved on Spanish territory, and its property taken by the state.

Between the general election of November 1933 and 1936 Spain was under a centre-right government. In early 1934 the government overcame a general strike and uprisings in Asturias and Catalonia. In the general elections of February 1936 the newly formed Popular Front, a centre-left alliance, was swept into power. Out of 470 seats they held 260 (166 more than after the 1933 elections), while the right and centre had 214. The new cabinet, under Manuel Azaña, consisted of republican left and republican union ministers, and some socialists, syndicalists, anarchists, Marxists, and communists.

Under the Popular Front government another outburst against the church took place. Spain was moving towards complete chaos. In the streets, left-wing extremists fought those on the right, mostly members of the fascist *Falange. Paramilitary formations were being trained by both extremes: the Falangist groups operated clandestinely, while the socialists, communists, and others were organizing openly.

Spandau suburb of Berlin, Germany. It was the site of Germany's principal arsenal in World War I; 'Spandau' machine guns (actually German-made Maxims) were named after it. The chief war criminals condemned at the Nuremberg Trials 1946 were imprisoned in the fortress here. The last of them was the Nazi leader Rudolf Hess, and the prison was demolished after his death 1987.

Spartacist member of a group of left-wing radicals in Germany at the end of World War I, founders of the **Spartacus League**, which became the German Communist Party in 1919. The league participated in the Berlin workers' revolt of January 1919, which was suppressed by the Freikorps on the orders of the socialist government. The agitation ended with the murder of Spartacist leaders Karl *Liebknecht and Rosa *Luxemburg.

Special Air Service SAS, specialist British regiment recruited from regiments throughout the army. It has served in Malaysia, Oman, Yemen, the Falklands, Northern Ireland, and during the 1991 Gulf War, as well as against international urban guerrillas, as in the siege of the Iranian embassy in London in 1980.

Special Operations Executive SOE, British intelligence organization established in June 1940 to gather intelligence and carry out sabotage missions inside German-occupied Europe during World War II.

Spee, Maximilian Johannes Maria Hubert (1861–1914) Count von Spee, German admiral, born in Copenhagen. He defeated a British squadron in a naval battle at Coronel in November 1914 but went down with his flagship in the 1914 battle of the Falkland Islands. The *Graf Spee* battleship was named after him.

Speer, Albert (1905–1981) German architect and minister in the Nazi government during World War II. He was appointed Hitler's architect and, like his counterparts in Fascist Italy, chose an overblown classicism to glorify the state, for example, his plan for the Berlin and Nuremberg Party Congress Grounds in 1934. He built the New Reich Chancellery, Berlin, 1938–39 (now demolished), but his designs for an increasingly megalomaniac series of buildings in a stark classical style were never realized.

Spengler, Oswald (1880–1936) German philosopher whose *Decline of the West* (1918) argued that civilizations go through natural cycles of growth and decay.

He was admired by the Nazis.

Spion Kop, Battle of during the South African War, Boer victory over the British 24 January 1900 at Spion Kop, a small hill a few miles southwest of Ladysmith, Natal. British troops attempting to relieve Ladysmith under

General Sir Redvers Buller were repulsed by a smaller Boer force.

Springfield rifle US Army service rifle, adopted in 1903 and retained in service until the 1940s.

Sri Lanka island in the Indian Ocean, off the southeast coast of India.

SS (German *Schutz-Staffel*, 'protective squadron') Nazi elite corps established 1925. Under *Himmler its 500,000 membership included the full-time **Waffen-SS** (armed SS), which fought in World War II, and spare-time members. The SS performed state police duties and was brutal in its treatment of the Jews and others in the concentration camps and occupied territories. It was condemned as an illegal organization at the Nuremberg Trials of war criminals.

Stakhanov, Aleksei Grigorievich (1906–1977) Soviet miner who exceeded production norms; he gave his name to the **Stakhanovite** movement of the 1930s, when workers were offered incentives to simplify and reorganize work processes in order to increase production.

Stalin, Joseph (1879–1953) adopted name of **Joseph Vissarionovich Djugashvili,** (Russian **'steel'**) Soviet politician. A member of the October Revolution committee of 1917, Stalin became general secretary of the Communist Party in 1922. After *Lenin's death in 1924, Stalin sought to create 'socialism in one country' and clashed with *Trotsky, who denied the possibility of socialism inside Russia until revolution had occurred in Western Europe. Stalin won this ideological struggle by 1927, and a series of five-year plans was launched to collectivize industry and agriculture from 1928. All opposition was eliminated in the Great *Purge 1936–38. During World War II, Stalin intervened in the military direction of the campaigns against Nazi Germany. He managed not only to bring the USSR through the war but to help it emerge as a superpower, although only at an immense cost in human suffering to his own people. After the war, Stalin quickly turned Eastern Europe into a series of Soviet satellites and maintained an autocratic rule domestically. His role was denounced after his death by Khrushchev and other members of the Soviet regime.

Stalin was born in Georgia, the son of a shoemaker. Educated for the priesthood, he was expelled from his seminary for Marxist propaganda. He became a member of the Social Democratic Party in 1898, and joined Lenin and the Bolsheviks in 1903. He was repeatedly exiled to Siberia 1903–13. He then became a member of the Communist Party's Politburo, and sat on the October Revolution committee. Stalin rapidly consolidated a powerful following (including Molotov); in 1921 he became commissar for nationalities in the Soviet government, responsible for the decree granting equal rights to all peoples of the Russian Empire, and was appointed general secretary of the Communist Party in 1922. As dictator in the 1930s, he disposed of all real and imagined enemies. His anti-Semitism caused, for example, the execution of 19 Jewish activists in 1952 for a 'Zionist conspiracy'.

Stalingrad, Siege of in World War II, German siege of Soviet city of Stalingrad (now Volgograd) August 1942–January 1943. The siege of Stalingrad was a horrific campaign, with both sides sustaining heavy casualties – the Germans lost some 400,000 troops while there were over 750,000 Soviet military casualties and an unknown number of civilian deaths. The Germans were finally driven out by a massive Soviet counterattack launched in November 1942.

Star Wars popular term for the *Strategic Defense Initiative announced by US president Reagan in 1983.

Statute of Westminster in the history of the British Empire, legislation enacted in 1931 which gave the dominions of the British Empire complete autonomy in their conduct of external affairs. It made them self-governing states whose only allegiance was to the British crown.

Stauffenberg, Claus von (1907–1944) German colonel in World War II who, in a conspiracy to assassinate Hitler (the *July Plot), planted a bomb in the dictator's headquarters conference room in the Wolf's Lair at Rastenburg, East Prussia, on 20 July 1944. Hitler was merely injured, and Stauffenberg and 200 others were later executed by the Nazi regime.

Stavisky, Alexandre (1886–1934) Russian-born Frenchman responsible for a financial scandal in France in 1934. He floated a very large sum in bogus bonds, in the name of the municipal credit establishment of Bayonne, France. Stavisky committed suicide after a warrant for his arrest had been issued. The scandal caused the fall of two governments, a general strike, and riots in the French capital, Paris.

Steel, David Martin Scott (1938–) British politician, leader of the Liberal Party 1976–88 and presiding officer (speaker) of the Scottish Parliament from 1999, born in Kirkcaldy, Fife, Scotland. He entered into a compact with the Labour government 1977–78, and into an alliance with the Social Democratic Party (SDP) in 1983. Having supported the Liberal–SDP merger (forming the Social and Liberal Democrats, which later became the Liberal Democrats), he resigned the leadership in 1988, becoming the party's foreign affairs spokesperson. At the 1994 party conference, he announced that he would not seek re-election to the next parliament. He is the president of Liberal International. He entered the House of Lords in 1997 as Lord Steel of Aikwood. He was knighted in 1990.

Stefanik, Milan Ratislav (1884–1919) Slovakian general. He joined the French army as a private soldier in

1914 and rapidly rose to the rank of general. He went to the Italian front in 1916 and flew several missions to drop propaganda pamphlets on Czech troops in the Austro-Hungarian army. Active in rallying Czech and Slovak troops from all areas, he worked with the Czech legion in Siberia in 1918 and, on the formation of the Czechoslovakian republic in 1918, he became commander-in-chief and war minister. He was killed in a flying accident while on his way to Prague.

Stern Gang or **Fighters for the Freedom of Israel**, Zionist guerrilla group founded 1940 by Abraham Stern (1907–1942). The group carried out anti-British attacks during the UK mandate rule in Palestine, both on individuals and on strategic targets. Stern was killed by British forces in 1942, but the group survived until 1948, when it was outlawed with the creation of the independent state of Israel.

Stevens, Siaka Probin (1905–1988) Sierra Leone politician, president 1971–85. He was the leader of the moderate left-wing All People's Congress (APC), from 1978 the country's only legal political party.

Stevenson, Adlai Ewing (1900–1965) US Democratic politician. As governor of Illinois 1949–53 he campaigned vigorously against corruption in public life, and as Democratic candidate for the presidency in 1952 and 1956 was twice defeated by Dwight D Eisenhower. In 1945 he was chief US delegate at the founding conference of the United Nations (UN) and in 1961 he was ambassador to the UN.

Steyn, Marthinus Theunis (1857–1916) South African statesman. He was a lawyer and a judge in Free State, and became state president in 1896. He led guerrilla forces in the South African War, but later supported the British government. Steyn was born in Free State, South Africa. He was educated in Holland and England, and was called to the Bar at the Inner Temple in London, England, in 1882.

Stilwell, Joseph Warren (1883–1946) called '**Vinegar Joe**', US general in World War II. In 1942 he became US military representative in China, when he commanded the Chinese forces cooperating with the British (with whom he quarrelled) in Burma (now Myanmar). He later commanded all US forces in China, Burma, and India until recalled to the USA in 1944 after differences over nationalist policy with the *Guomindang (nationalist) leader Chiang Kai-shek. Subsequently he commanded the US 10th Army on the Japanese island of Okinawa.

Stimson, Henry Lewis (1867–1950) US politician. He was war secretary in President Taft's cabinet 1911–13, Hoover's secretary of state 1929–33, and war secretary 1940–45.

Stock Market Crash panic selling on the New York Stock Exchange in October 1929; see *Wall Street Crash, 1929.

Stonehouse, John Thomson (1925–1988) British Labour Party politician. An active member of the Cooperative Movement, he entered Parliament in 1957 and held junior posts under Harold Wilson before joining his cabinet in 1967. In 1974 he disappeared in Florida in mysterious circumstances, surfacing in Australia amid suspicions of fraudulent dealings. Extradited to Britain, he was tried and imprisoned for embezzlement. He was released in 1979, but was unable to resume a political career.

Stormont suburb 8 km/5 mi east of Belfast, Northern Ireland. It is the site of the new Northern Ireland Assembly, elected as a result of the Good Friday agreement in 1998 and functioning from 1999 when some powers were transferred back to Northern Ireland from Westminster. It was previously the seat of the government of Northern Ireland 1921–72.

Strategic Arms Reduction Talks START, phase in peace discussions dealing with *disarmament, initially involving the USA and the Soviet Union, from 1992 the USA and Russia, and from 1993 Belarus and the Ukraine.

It began with talks in Geneva, Switzerland, in 1983, leading to the signing of the Intermediate Nuclear Forces Treaty in 1987. In 1989 proposals for reductions in conventional weapons were added to the agenda. As the Cold War drew to a close from 1989, negotiations moved rapidly. Reductions of about 30% in strategic nuclear weapons systems were agreed in Moscow in July 1991 (START) and more significant cuts were agreed in January 1993 (START II); the latter treaty was ratified by the US Senate in January 1996. Russia's Duma ratified START II in April 2000. just following the inauguration of Russian President Vladimir Putin. Under the treaty, which applies to inter-continental rockets, the USA and Russia will both halve their stocks of atomic warheads to between 3,000 and 3,500 each by 2007. A START III treaty, currently being negotiated, would increase arms reduction even further.

Strategic Defense Initiative SDI or **Star Wars**, US programme (1983–93) to explore the technical feasibility of developing a comprehensive defence system against incoming nuclear missiles, based in part outside the Earth's atmosphere. The programme was started by President Ronald Reagan in March 1983, and was overseen by the Strategic Defense Initiative Organization (SDIO). In May 1993, the SDIO changed its name to the Ballistic Missile Defense Organization (BMDO), to reflect its focus on defence against short-range rather than long-range missiles. SDI lives on today in the less ambitious National Missile Defense (NMD) programme.

Strauss, Franz Josef (1915–1988) German conservative politician, leader of the West German Bavarian Christian Social Union (CSU) party 1961–88, premier of Bavaria 1978–88.

Straw, Jack (1946–) British Labour lawyer and politician, foreign secretary from 2001. Situated on the right wing of the Labour party, Straw was home secretary during the Labour government's first term 1997–2001 and introduced crime reduction programmes, while also facing a rising level of political asylum applications. As foreign secretary, he backed Prime Minister Tony *Blair during the US-led Iraq War in 2003, although he had reservations about proceeding without broader United Nations support.

Streicher, Julius (1895–1946) German politician. After World War I, he began a violent anti-Semitic and nationalistic movement at Nuremberg, Germany. He founded a special weekly paper for 'the struggle for the truth against traitors' entitled *Der Sturmer*, which specialized in Jew-baiting. After Hitler's triumph in 1933 the views of *Der Sturmer* soon prevailed throughout Germany, and when Hitler decided on boycotting Jewish shops, Streicher was made Aktionsführer (riot leader). Later he became governor of Franconia. Streicher was born in Fleinhausen near Augsburg, Germany. He was sentenced to death at the Nuremberg trial in 1946 and executed.

Stresemann, Gustav (1878–1929) German politician; chancellor in 1923 and foreign minister 1923–29 of the Weimar Republic. During World War I he was a strong nationalist but his views became more moderate under the Weimar Republic. His achievements included reducing the amount of war reparations paid by Germany after the Treaty of Versailles of 1919, negotiating the Locarno Treaties of 1925, and negotiating Germany's admission to the League of Nations. He shared the Nobel Prize for Peace in 1926 with Aristide *Briand for their work for European reconciliation.

Strijdom, Johannes Gerhardus (1893–1958) South African politician. He was prime minister of the Union of South Africa and leader

in chief of the National party
(1954–58). Strijdom was member of
Parliament for Waterberge (1929–58).
He was born in Willowmore, Cape
Province, South Africa.

Stroessner, Alfredo (1912–)
Paraguayan military dictator and
president 1954–89. As head of the
armed forces from 1951, he seized
power from President Federico Chávez
in a coup in 1954, sponsored by the
right-wing ruling Colorado Party.
Accused by his opponents of harsh
repression, his regime spent heavily on
the military to preserve his authority.
Despite criticisms of his government's
civil-rights record, he was re-elected
seven times and remained in office
until ousted in an army-led coup in
1989, after which he gained asylum
in Brazil.

**Struve, Petr Berngardovich
(1870–1944)** Soviet economist,
sociologist, and politician of German
descent. In the 1890s he was the
leading Marxist theorist in Russia,
and in 1898 drafted the manifesto
of the Russian Social Democratic
Workers' party.

Sturmabteilung SA, (German 'storm
section') German militia, also known
as **Brownshirts**, of the *Nazi Party,
established in 1921 under the leadership
of Ernst *Röhm, in charge of physical
training and political indoctrination.

Suárez González, Adolfo (1932–)
Spanish politician, prime minister
1976–81. A friend of King Juan Carlos,
he was appointed by the king to guide
Spain into democracy after the death
of the fascist dictator Franco.

Sudan country in northeast Africa,
bounded north by Egypt, northeast
by the Red Sea, east by Ethiopia and
Eritrea, south by Kenya, Uganda, and
the Democratic Republic of Congo
(formerly Zaire), west by the Central
African Republic and Chad, and
northwest by Libya. It is the largest
country in Africa.

Sudeten mountainous region in
northeast Bohemia, Czech Republic,
extending eastwards along the border
with Poland. Sudeten was annexed by
Germany under the *Munich
Agreement 1938; it was returned to
Czechoslovakia in 1945.

Germany and the Czech Republic
sought to bury decades of mutual
antagonism in January 1997 by signing
a joint declaration aimed at drawing
a line under the vexed issue of the
Sudetenland. Germany apologized
for the suffering caused during the
Nazi occupation. For their part, the
Czechs expressed regret over the
'injustices' that took place during
the expulsion of more than 2.5 million
Sudetenland Germans after World
War II. It took over two years to reach
agreement.

Suez Canal artificial waterway from
Port Said to Suez, linking the
Mediterranean and Red Seas;
160 km/100 mi long and with a
minimum width of 60 m/197 ft.
The canal was built at sea level, with
no locks, and can accommodate vessels
of up to 150,000 tons. It separates
Africa from Asia and provides the
shortest eastward sea route from
Europe. It was opened in 1869,
nationalized in 1956, blocked by Egypt
during the Arab-Israeli War in 1967,
and not reopened until 1975.

The French Suez Canal Company
was formed in 1858 to execute the
scheme of Ferdinand de Lesseps.
The canal was opened in 1869, and
in 1875 British prime minister Disraeli
acquired a major shareholding for
Britain from the khedive of Egypt.
The 1888 Convention of Constantinople
opened it to all nations. The Suez
Canal was administered by a company
with offices in Paris controlled by a
council of 33 (10 of them British) until
1956 when it was forcibly nationalized
by President *Nasser of Egypt.
The Damietta port complex on the
Mediterranean at the mouth of the
canal was inaugurated in 1986.
The port is designed to handle
16 million tonnes of cargo.

Suez Crisis military confrontation from October to December 1956 following the nationalization of the Suez Canal by President Nasser of Egypt. In an attempt to reassert international control of the canal, Israel launched an attack, after which British and French troops landed. Widespread international censure forced the withdrawal of the British and French. The crisis resulted in the resignation of British prime minister Anthony *Eden.

At a London conference of maritime powers the Australian prime minister Robert Menzies was appointed to negotiate a settlement in Cairo. His mission was unsuccessful. The military intervention met Soviet protest and considerable domestic opposition, and the USA did not support it. *Cold War politics came into play during the Suez Crisis, and the UK and France found themselves unable to act independently of the USA in a way that they could have done before World War II. British, French, and Australian relations with the USA were greatly strained during this period. The USSR was seeking to extend its influence in Africa at the time and saw Egypt as a key country with which it could establish friendly relations. The support given to Egypt by the Soviets during the Suez Crisis increased their influence in the region, and this was sealed during the 1960s when the USSR provided much of the funding for the Aswan High Dam project in Egypt. The Suez Crisis, therefore, had a significant role in the Cold War as well as in the conflict between Egypt and the former colonial powers of Britain and France.

See also *United Kingdom, **the Suez Crisis**; *Egypt, **towards the Suez Crisis** and **Suez and the Second Arab–Israeli War**; and *Israel, **the Suez Crisis and the Second Arab–Israeli War**.

suffragette woman fighting for the right to vote. In the UK, the repeated defeat in Parliament of *women's suffrage bills, introduced by supporters of the women's movement between 1886 and 1911, led to the launch of a militant campaign in 1906 by Emmeline *Pankhurst and her daughters, founders of the Women's Social and Political Union (WSPU). In 1918 women were granted limited franchise; in 1928 it was extended to all women over 21.

Suffragettes (the term was coined by a *Daily Mail* reporter) chained themselves to railings, heckled political meetings, refused to pay taxes, and in 1913 bombed the home of Lloyd George, then chancellor of the Exchequer. One woman, Emily Davison, threw herself under the king's horse at the Derby horse race in 1913 and was killed. Many suffragettes were imprisoned and were force-fed when they went on hunger strike; under the notorious 'Cat and Mouse Act' of 1913 they could be repeatedly released to regain their health and then rearrested. The struggle was called off on the outbreak of World War I.

Suharto, Thojib I (1921–) Indonesian politician and general, president 1967–98. His authoritarian rule met with domestic opposition from the left, but the Indonesian economy enjoyed significant growth until 1997. He was re-elected in 1973, 1978, 1983, 1988, 1993, and, unopposed, in March 1998. This was despite his deteriorating health and the country's economy being weakened by a sharp decline in value of the Indonesian currency (the rupiah), which had provoked student unrest and food riots. After mounting civil unrest reached a critical point, on 21 May 1998 he handed over the presidency to the vice-president, Bacharuddin Jusuf Habibie.

Suhrawardy, Hussein Shaheed (1893–1963) Indian and Pakistani politician, prime minister of Pakistan 1956–57. In 1945 Suhrawardy became chief minister of the Muslim League, which argued for the partition of India after the British left. In 1946 he was elected chief minister of Bengal in a landslide victory and was in large part responsible for the deaths in August 1946 of hundreds of Hindu workers by middle-class Muslims in what is known as 'The Great Calcutta Killing'.

Sukarno, Achmed (1901–1970) Indonesian nationalist, president 1945–67. During World War II he cooperated in the local administration set up by the Japanese, replacing Dutch rule. After the war he became the first president of the new Indonesian republic, becoming president-for-life in 1966; he was ousted by *Suharto.

summit or **summit conference**, in international diplomacy, a personal meeting between heads of state to settle international crises and other matters of general concern. 'Summit' was first used in this sense by Winston Churchill in 1950, although it could be applied to the meetings between himself, Roosevelt, and Stalin at Tehran and Yalta during World War II. During the *Cold War, the term 'superpower summit' was applied to meetings between the Soviet Union's Communist Party leader and the US president.

Sunningdale Agreement pact of December 1973 between the UK and Irish governments, together with the Northern Ireland executive, drawn up in Sunningdale, England. The agreement included provisions for a power-sharing executive in Northern Ireland. However, the executive lasted only five weeks before the UK government was defeated in a general election, and a general strike in May 1974 brought down the Northern Ireland government.

Sun Zhong Shan (or **Sun Yat-sen**) **(1867–1925)** Chinese revolutionary leader. He founded the *Hsin Chung Hui* ('New China Party') in 1894, one of the political groups that merged to form the Kuomintang (*Guomindang, nationalist party) in 1912 after the overthrow of the Manchu Empire.

He was elected provisional president of the Republic of China in December 1911 and played a vital part in deposing the emperor, who abdicated in February 1912. He was president of a breakaway government from 1921.

superpower state that through disproportionate military or economic strength can dominate smaller nations. The term was used to describe the USA and the USSR from the end of World War II, when they emerged as significantly stronger than all other countries. With the collapse of the Soviet Union in 1991, the USA is, arguably, now the world's sole superpower.

Suriname or **Surinam**, country on the north coast of South America, bounded west by French Guiana, south by Brazil, east by Guyana, and north by the Atlantic Ocean.

Sutton Hoo archaeological site in Suffolk, England, where in 1939 a Saxon ship burial was excavated. It may be the funeral monument of Raedwald, King of the East Angles, who died about 624 or 625. The jewellery, armour, and weapons discovered were placed in the British Museum, London.

Suu Kyi, Aung San (1945–) Myanmar (Burmese) politician and human-rights campaigner, leader of the National League for Democracy (NLD), the main opposition to the military junta. She is the daughter of former Burmese premier *Aung San, who fought for the country's independence. Despite Suu Kyi being placed under house arrest in 1989, the NLD won the 1990 elections, although the junta refused to surrender power. She was awarded the Nobel Prize for Peace in 1991 in recognition of her 'nonviolent struggle for democracy and human rights' in Myanmar. Although officially released from house arrest in 1995, she was banned from resuming any leadership post within the NLD by the junta.

Her liberties continued to be restricted by the Myanmar government, which refused visas to enable her family to visit her, while Suu Kyi believed that she would be refused re-entry to her country if she was to leave. Her situation grabbed international attention in 1998, when it was announced that her husband, Oxford academic Michael Aris, whom she met when she too was at Oxford University, England, was dying of cancer. He was refused a visa and died in March 1999, having not seen his wife for two years.

In August 2000, Suu Kyi was prevented from leaving the capital, Yangon (Rangoon), to go a nearby town to meet members of her League. She was involved in a nine-day roadside protest after which she was put under house arrest for two weeks, as she had been held from 1989 to 1995. This latest restriction on Suu Kyi, who has not been allowed to move freely since 1989, prompted renewed international condemnation of the military government, who also searched the offices of her party, and failed to enter into dialogue with Suu Kyi, or to take any other steps towards reform. She was released from a further 20 months of house arrest in June 2002.

Suzman, Helen Gavronsky (1917–) South African politician and human-rights activist. A university lecturer concerned about the inhumanity of the *apartheid system, she joined the white opposition to the ruling National Party and became a strong advocate of racial equality, respected by black communities inside and outside South Africa. In 1978 she received the United Nations Human Rights Award. She retired from active politics in 1989.

Suzuki, Zenko (1911–) Japanese politician. Originally a socialist member of the Diet in 1947, he became a conservative (Liberal Democrat) in 1949, and was prime minister 1980–82.

Sverdlov, Yakov Mikhailovich (1885–1919) Russian politician. He joined the Russian Social Democratic Workers' party in 1901, and worked from 1902–17, as a professional revolutionary in the Bolshevik organizations, always strictly following Lenin's policy. In 1913 he was co-opted onto the Bolshevik Central Committee. After the February Revolution of 1917, Sverdlov became the party's main organizer. Soon after the seizure of power by the Bolsheviks, he succeeded Lev Kamenev as chairman of the All-Russian Central Executive Committee of the Soviets, and was thus titular head of the state. For a time, in 1918–19, Sverdlov, together with Stalin, was Lenin's closest collaborator.

Swadeshi movement (Bengali 'from one's own country') in India, a boycott of foreign-made goods orchestrated by Indian nationalists in response to the partition of Bengal 1905. Huge bonfires of imported cloth, especially Lancashire cotton, were lit throughout Bengal. Protesters vowed to use only domestic (Swadeshi) cottons and other goods manufactured in India. The boycott spread throughout the subcontinent, providing a stimulus to indigenous Indian industry and nationalist protest.

SWAPO acronym for **South West Africa People's Organization**, organization formed 1959 in South West Africa (now *Namibia) to oppose South African rule. SWAPO guerrillas, led by Sam Nujoma, began attacking with support from Angola. In 1966 SWAPO was recognized by the United Nations as the legitimate government of Namibia, and won the first independent election in 1989.

Swarajiya or **Self-Government Party**, political party established in India in 1922 as an attempt to reinforce the position of the Congress Party in the Indian legislature. In 1923, it became the largest party in the central assembly and also in some provincial assemblies, but its tactics of obstruction against British colonial rule were only partially successful. Recognized by the Congress Party in 1924, Swarajiya continued until 1929 and was revived to help the Congress Party to contest the 1934 elections.

Swaziland country in southeast Africa, bounded east by Mozambique and southeast, south, west, and north by South Africa.

Sweden country in northern Europe, bounded west by Norway, northeast by Finland and the Gulf of Bothnia, southeast by the Baltic Sea, and southwest by the Kattegat strait.

government Sweden has a hereditary monarch as formal head of state, and a popularly elected government. The constitution is based on four fundamental laws: the Instrument of Government Act 1809, the Act of Succession 1810, the Freedom of the Press Act 1949, and the Riksdag Act 1974. The constitution provides for a single-chamber parliament, the Riksdag, comprising 349 members, elected by universal suffrage, through a system of proportional representation, for a three-year term.

The prime minister is nominated by the speaker of the Riksdag and confirmed by a vote of the whole house. The prime minister chooses a cabinet, and all are then responsible to the Riksdag. The monarch now has a purely formal role; the normal duties of a constitutional monarch, such as dissolving parliament and deciding who should be asked to form an administration, are undertaken by the speaker.

history The earliest traces of human presence, dating from around 10,000 BC, have been found at Segebro near Malmö, and a small population of hunters probably inhabited the southern part of Sweden at this time. During the Mesolithic period, the Maglemosian culture (around 6000 BC) found all over Scandinavia is represented at sites such as Lilla Loshult Mosse and round Ringsjö. Pottery appears first on sites of the Ertebolle culture (around 4000 BC). Evidence of Neolithic agriculture

has been found in settlements in Skåne, Blekinge, and elsewhere. Remains of the Via culture, in the form of houses as well as pottery and stone tools, have been found at Östia Viå and Mogetorp in Sodermanland. In the later Neolithic period a megalithic culture emerged.

the Bronze and Iron Ages In the middle of the 2nd millennium bronze weapons and tools were imported and also made locally in the Lake Mälaren area. Burial mounds and cairns of the Bronze Age are common in southern Sweden. Few remains have been found from the period of transition from the Bronze Age to the Iron Age (600–400 BC), and it is possible that the harsher climate at this time caused widespread emigration.

In the Middle or Roman Iron Age the return of a better climate brought about an expansion of culture, and the many Roman imports suggest a higher standard of living. The Migration period (around AD 400–550) shows a marked increase in prosperity and is one of the great periods of Swedish art. Important gold hoards have been found at Timboholm and near Tureholm. The goldsmiths' work is of fine quality, as can be seen in the collars from Ålleberg and Möne.

the Middle Ages The early history of Sweden is contained in legend and saga. The country appears to have been inhabited by two separate but closely related peoples, the Swedes in the north and the Goths in the south. In the Viking era, the Swedish Vikings penetrated many parts of the Baltic, and sailed down the great rivers of Russia. In Russia they founded the principality of Novgorod and traded as far south as the Black Sea.

Although Christianity was first introduced at a much earlier period, it was not until the mid-12th century that the Swedes were united with the Goths and accepted Christianity. A series of crusades from the 12th to the 14th centuries brought Finland under Swedish rule. The later Middle

Ages in Sweden are marked by a centralization of power in the country, but also by clashes between rival claimants to the throne and between the king and the nobility.

the union with Denmark By the Union of Kalmar in 1397 the kingdoms of Denmark, Norway, and Sweden came under the common regency of Margaret of Denmark. Margaret's successors were not, however, always able to assert their authority in Sweden. There was a popular revolt in 1434 led by Engelbrekt Engelbrektsson, and during several periods Swedish noblemen were in effective control of Sweden, even taking the title of king.

The union finally came to an end in the reign of Christian II, after his massacre of the leaders of a Swedish rebellion (the Stockholm Bloodbath, 1520). Gustavus Vasa, a Swedish noble, started a revolt in Dalarna in 1521 and, with help from Lübeck (one of the most powerful cities of the Hanseatic League), made Sweden independent of Denmark–Norway. He was elected king as Gustavus I by the Riksdag (parliament) in 1523 and survived a series of revolts to leave Sweden a financially and politically stable country on his death in 1560. He exploited the arrival of Lutheranism in Sweden to destroy the power of the Roman Catholic Church and to appropriate its possessions in 1527, but Lutheran services only gradually replaced Catholic ceremonies in Sweden. The Vasa dynasty continued to rule Sweden until 1818.

towards Baltic domination Gustavus's son Eric XIV (ruled 1560–68) embarked on a campaign of expansion in the southern Baltic and took Estonia under Swedish protection in 1561, but otherwise had little success in a debilitating seven-years war with Denmark. His half-brother, John III (ruled 1568–92), continued the Baltic campaign. Married to a Polish princess, he brought up his son Sigismund as a Roman Catholic and

had him elected king of Poland in 1587. Sigismund's religion, however, proved a serious handicap on his accession to the Swedish throne in 1592, and he was opposed by his ruthless and ambitious uncle Charles, who finally had Sigismund deposed and himself hailed as king by the Riksdag in 1600. As Charles IX he too fought in the Baltic states with little success, and on his death in 1611 he left to his 16-year-old son, Gustavus II (Gustavus Adolphus), a country that was at war with Denmark, Poland, and Russia.

Gustavus Adolphus Sweden in 1611 was lacking in population, internal communications, and material resources, and its geographical position was unfavourable for the expansion of its trade, since its way to the North Sea and the Atlantic was controlled by Denmark. Gustavus Adolphus, 'the Lion of the North', continued the policy of turning the Baltic into a 'Swedish lake'. He ended the war with Denmark, recovering territory lost by his father. War with Russia gave Sweden control of what is now the Baltic coast of Russia, while war with Poland ended in a truce in 1629, which confirmed Sweden in possession of Livonia (most of present-day Latvia and Estonia) and gave it a grip on the mainland of Germany.

In 1630 Gustavus Adolphus intervened in the Thirty Years' War to champion the Protestant cause in Europe. Following his landing in Germany, he won a series of spectacular triumphs in 1631 and 1632: the Catholic League was defeated; the Catholic general, Tilly, was out-manoeuvred and finally killed; and Gustavus Adolphus was able to penetrate to the south. He was obliged to turn north again by the attacks of the Habsburg general Wallenstein in Saxony, and defeated Wallenstein at Lützen, although he himself was killed in the battle.

Gustavus Adolphus was the real founder of the greatness of Sweden.

He strengthened the country internally by his domestic and financial reforms; the government was centralized and strong; the army was reformed; and Sweden for the next century was one of the great powers in Europe. In fact its resources were always strained to the utmost to maintain this position, and its Baltic possessions were to embroil it in a series of wars that it could not afford – but without which it could not hope to keep them.

the later 17th century Gustavus Adolphus was succeeded by his daughter, six-year-old Christina. Christina's minority was made famous by the achievements of the regent and chancellor, Axel Oxenstjerna, who pursued her father's foreign policy and maintained Swedish interests during and after the Thirty Years' War. The success of Sweden was seen in the Treaty of Westphalia (1648) that ended the war and marked the zenith of Swedish power. Sweden became an important power in Germany, and was recognized as the leader of Protestant Europe, and the greatest power of the north. In 1645 Denmark was forced to give up its right to tolls in the Sound, and ceded Gotland, Jämtland, Härjedalen, and, temporarily, Halland to Sweden.

In 1654 Christina became a Catholic and abdicated in favour of her cousin, Charles X. He continued the work of Gustavus Adolphus. He attacked Denmark and incorporated the provinces of Skåne, Blekinge, Halland, and Bohuslän into Sweden, thus establishing Sweden's natural frontiers along the western and southern coasts. Charles X died in 1660 and was succeeded by his son, Charles XI, who was only four years old.

Charles XI proved to have inherited the military genius of the Vasas. When he assumed the crown in 1672 he fought a series of wars by which he was able to preserve intact the territories of Sweden, and then turned his attention to domestic reform. He curbed the power of the nobility, and left Sweden reformed and restored at his death in 1697.

Charles XII and the end of the Swedish empire Charles XI was succeeded by his son, Charles XII, 'the wonder of Europe'. He spent the 20 years of his reign in almost constant warfare, and it was at this stage that the strain of maintaining a scattered empire, harassed by ambitious states with large populations and resources, began to tell on a country that had only a small population.

Charles astonished Europe with his boldness and enterprise, and won many brilliant victories, penetrating, on one occasion, deep into Russia. But ranged against him was a formidable coalition of powers, and his schemes were too grandiose to be fulfilled, even by a military genius of his calibre. In the end he was clearly defeated, and probably only his death in 1718 saved Sweden from utter disaster. The Swedish empire was dismembered in a series of treaties, 1719–21. Most of the German provinces were ceded to Britain, Hanover, and Prussia, while Russia was confirmed in its possession of Livonia, Estonia, and Ingermanland (or Ingria, an area around the head of the Gulf of Finland, northeast of Estonia).

On Charles XII's death the Swedish monarchy lost its absolute power, and under Frederick I (king 1720–51) and Adolphus Frederick (king 1751–71) a form of parliamentary government prevailed. This system, with its bitter party quarrels between the factions known as the 'Hats' and the 'Caps', was brought to an end after a coup d'état by the young Gustavus III in 1772, under whom science and culture flourished. However, Gustavus proved less successful in his political ventures, and he was assassinated at a masked ball in 1792.

the Napoleonic era and the advent of the Bernadottes Gustavus III was succeeded by his son, Gustavus IV, an implacable opponent of Napoleon. After entering into alliance with France, Russia invaded and occupied Finland, and in 1809 this part of the Swedish kingdom had to be ceded to the tsar. Shortly before this Gustavus IV was deposed.

Gustavus's uncle, who succeeded as Charles XIII in 1809, was infirm, and to secure the goodwill of Napoleon the Riksdag accepted Napoleon's marshal, Bernadotte, as Crown Prince Charles John in 1810. He took over the government, but did not further Napoleon's ambitions against Britain and Russia. He became a truly national Swedish leader, and brought Sweden into the alliance against Napoleon in 1813. He made war on Denmark to secure Norway as recompense for the loss of Finland, and then later invaded Norway, whose union with Sweden was confirmed by the great powers in 1814.

In 1818 Charles XIII died and Bernadotte succeeded as Charles XIV, initiating the dynasty that still reigns in Sweden. His son, Oscar I, who reigned from 1844 to 1859, introduced many democratic reforms. In the reign of Oscar II (1872–1907) Norway seceded from Sweden in 1905, a peaceful settlement being made at Karlstad.

Sweden enters the 20th century During the 20th century Sweden maintained its long tradition of neutrality and political stability, and introduced a highly developed system of social welfare. The office of ombudsman is a Swedish invention, and Sweden was one of the first countries to adopt a system of open government.

Oscar II was succeeded by his son Gustavus V (1907–50), during whose reign democracy was further extended, social services introduced or expanded, and a universal franchise introduced. The acknowledgement of the growth of party politics dates from the dissolution of the union with Norway. Industrialization had encouraged the

growth of socialism, which, in its Swedish manifestation, took on a moderate, social democratic bent.

During World War I Sweden was neutral, and in 1920 it entered the League of Nations. In the 1920s party politics were irritated by the prohibition question, which completely split the Liberals and caused divisions on the left. There was a series of different governments. The problem of unemployment helped to increase the prestige of the Social Democrats. Total prohibition was rejected in 1922, but a liquor-control system was enforced, which had some success in the rural districts, but was finally abolished in 1955.

Sweden in World War II Sweden was neutral during World War II, although, when the USSR invaded Finland, Sweden showed its sympathy by opening its frontiers to Finnish refugees and enrolling volunteers to fight for the Finns. When the Germans made a demand in 1940 for transit facilities for troops and supplies through Sweden to Norway (which the Germans had recently occupied), the Riksdag complied, but Sweden really had no choice in the matter. The Swedish prime minister, however, rejected Germany's invitation to Sweden to join its 'New Order'.

Throughout 1943 Sweden continued to remain on friendly terms with all the belligerents, though public opinion had been largely pro-British since the occupation of Norway and Denmark by Germany in 1940. In 1943 the government obtained Germany's consent to the cancellation of the transit agreement, and transport of German material and military personnel through Sweden ceased.

In September 1944 the Swedish government announced that all Swedish Baltic ports and waters would be closed to foreign shipping, owing to the new situation in the Baltic brought about by the Soviet–Finnish armistice of that year. This resulted in the virtual stoppage of Swedish–German trade for the duration of the war.

Sweden's international role After World War II Sweden took part in the relief work and reconstruction of the war-ravaged countries. It joined the United Nations in 1946 and has played an important part in the work of the organization. The Swedish diplomat Dag Hammarskjöld was secretary general of the UN 1953–61, and Sweden regularly contributed troops to UN peace-keeping forces in areas such as the Middle East, the Congo, and Cyprus. Sweden promoted the UN conference on environmental protection in Stockholm in 1972.

Sweden maintained its neutrality throughout the Cold War, refusing to follow Norway and Denmark in joining the North Atlantic Treaty Organization (NATO). In 1952 it became a founder member of the Nordic Council, an organization established to further the mutual interests of the Scandinavian countries. It also became a founder member of the European Free Trade Association (EFTA) in 1959, but because of its neutrality it did not seek membership of the European Economic Community (EEC) – although eventually joined the European Union (EU) in 1995, following the end of the Cold War.

the Social Democrats and the welfare state At home the Social Democrats (the Social Democratic Labour Party, or SAP) remained in power after the war continuously until 1976, under prime ministers Tage Erlander (PM 1946–69) and Olof *Palme (PM 1969–76, and again in 1982–86). However, as a minority party for most of this period, they either were in coalition with, or relied on, the support of other parties. A national health service was introduced in 1955 and a generous state pension scheme in 1959. Overall, Sweden developed one of the world's most comprehensive welfare systems, and achieved oneof the highest standards of living in Europe.

During Palme's first premiership there were two major reforms of the constitution. In 1971 the chambers in parliament were reduced from two to one, and in 1975, following the death of Gustavus VI (ruled 1950–73), the last of the monarch's constitutional powers were removed. Gustavus was succeeded by his grandson Carl XVI Gustaf, who only has a symbolic function. In the general election of 1976 Palme was defeated over the issue of the level of taxation needed to fund the welfare system.

the end of Social Democratic hegemony A coalition of the Centre (C), Conservative, and Liberal (Fp) parties, with Thorbjörn Fälldin, the leader of the Centre Party, as prime minister, took office in 1976, ending 44 years of Social Democratic rule. The government operated a mixed economy in close cooperation with private industry, and central wage negotiations between employers and trade unions produced almost unbroken industrial peace.

The Fälldin administration fell in 1978 over its wish to follow a non-nuclear energy policy, and was replaced by a minority Liberal Party government. Fälldin returned in 1979, heading another coalition, and in a referendum the following year there was a narrow majority in favour of continuing with a limited nuclear-energy programme.

Palme's second premiership Fälldin remained in power until 1982, when the Social Democrats (SAP) under Olof Palme returned as a minority government. Palme was soon faced with deteriorating relations with the USSR, arising from suspected violations of Swedish territorial waters by Soviet submarines. However, the situation had improved substantially by 1985. In February 1986 Palme was murdered by an unknown assailant. His deputy, Ingvar Carlsson, took over as prime minister and leader of the SAP.

economic problems In the September 1988 general election Carlsson and the SAP were re-elected with a reduced majority. In February 1990, with mounting opposition to its economic policies, the government resigned, leaving Carlsson as caretaker prime minister. In December 1990 the Riksdag supported the government's decision to apply for European Community (EC) membership, but in the September 1991 elections Carlsson's government was defeated.

He was succeeded as prime minister by Carl Bildt who led a minority coalition government, comprising the Moderate Party, the Fp, the C, and the Christian Democratic Community Party (KdS). In September 1992 an unprecedented agreement between Bildt's coalition and the right-wing populist party, New Democracy, pledged cooperation in solving the country's economic problems. In the September 1994 general election the SAP won most seats, although not an overall majority, and Ingvar Carlsson returned to power at the head of a minority government. In August 1995 it was announced that Carlsson would step down as prime minister in March 1996, once his party had chosen a replacement. In December 1995 Göran Persson, the finance minister, was chosen to succeed him.

A national referendum in November 1994 narrowly supported the country's application for European Union (EU) membership, and in January 1995 Sweden became a full EU member.

In March 1996 Persson replaced Carlsson as planned. Persson, acknowledging that Sweden faced several more years of austerity and welfare cutbacks, appointed Erik Asbrink as finance minister. He also pledged to close nuclear power plants within two years.

The ruling Social Democrats, led by Persson, won the September 1998 general election, but with their lowest share of votes, at 37% (down 8%), for 40 years. The ex-communist Left Party, which doubled its vote to 12%, agreed to support the government in return for more spending on welfare and a referendum on joining Europe's single currency. In September 1999, Carl Bildt, the former representative to Bosnia, stepped down as leader of the opposition Moderate Party and was replaced by Bo Lundgren.

In January 2002, Prime Minister Persson said that Sweden might hold a referendum on the euro in 2003, after polls suggested that Swedish public opinion had recently swung in favour of joining the single currency.

Switzerland landlocked country in Western Europe, bounded north by Germany, east by Austria and Liechtenstein, south by Italy, and west by France.

government Switzerland is a federation of 20 cantons and six half-cantons (canton is the name for a political division, derived from Old French). The constitution dates from 1874 and provides for a two-chamber federal assembly, consisting of the National Council and the Council of States. The National Council has 200 members, elected by universal suffrage, through a system of proportional representation, for a four-year term. The Council of States has 46 members, each canton electing two representatives and each half-canton one. Members of the Council of States are elected for three or four years, depending on the constitutions of the individual cantons.

Federal government lies with the Federal Council, consisting of seven members elected for a four-year term by the assembly, each heading a specific federal department. The federal assembly also appoints one member to act as federal head of state and head of government for a year, the term of office beginning on 1 January. The federal government is allocated specific powers by the constitution with the remaining powers left with the cantons, each having its own constitution, assembly, and government. At a level below the cantons are more than 3,000 communes. Direct democracy is encouraged through communal assemblies and referenda.

history In the 1st millennium BC Switzerland was inhabited by Celts. From the 5th century BC the country, especially the south, became a centre of the Celtic La Tène culture of the Early Iron Age. The La Tène culture continued to the Roman conquest, at which time there were two main Celtic tribes, the Helvetii (or Transalpine Gauls) in the northwest, and the Rhaetians in the southeast. The Roman conquest of these tribes began as early as 107 BC, when they were defeated in southern Gaul (modern France), and was completed by Julius Caesar in 58 BC at the Col d'Armecy.

the early Middle Ages The ancestors of many of the modern Swiss are the Germanic tribes who overran this part of the Roman Empire in the 5th century AD: the Alemanni east of the River Aar about AD 406, and the Burgundians in the southwest in 443. They became Christian about 600–650, but the Helvetii were not converted until later.

Charlemagne, king of the Franks from 768 and crowned emperor by the pope in 800, incorporated Switzerland into his domains. At his death the region fell into confusion, and in the subsequent partition of his lands half of modern Switzerland was allotted to the Eastern Frankish kingdom and half to Lotharingia (Lorraine).

In 888 Rudolf of the Guelphic family founded the kingdom of Burgundy, of which west Switzerland formed a part, while the German regions fell to the duchy of Swabia in 917. In the 11th century Switzerland was united under the German (Holy Roman) Empire, but in the 12th century many autonomous feudal holdings developed as the power of the Empire declined. Several

local dynasties rose to power, such as the houses of Zähringen (1097–1218), Lenzburg, Kyburg, Savoy, and Habsburg. The cities of Fribourg (1178) and Bern (1191) were founded by the Zähringens to secure their supremacy against the attacks of the rural nobility.

the formation of the Swiss Confederation A period of chaos ensued, until in 1273 Rudolf I of Habsburg became Holy Roman emperor, with control of what is now German Switzerland, and subsequently extended Habsburg rule over Austria.

The extension of Habsburg power in Switzerland caused alarm and resistance in the regions round the Lake of Lucerne, and a few days after Rudolf's death in 1291 the first Perpetual (or Everlasting) League of the three 'forest cantons' (Uri, Schwyz, and Unterwalden) was formed, which, in 1315, defeated the Austrian Habsburg forces at the Battle of Morgarten.

War with the Austrian Habsburgs continued off and on, and Austria was defeated again at Sempach and Nafels. Other cantons joined the League: Lucerne in 1332, Zürich in 1351, Zug and Glarus in 1352, and Bern in 1353. As a result, the League extended its influence and lands, and from this time is usually referred to as the Swiss Confederation. Switzerland began to prosper, and education, art, and industry all began to develop during this period.

From 1474 to 1477 the Confederation was at war with Charles the Bold of Burgundy, defeating him at Grandson and Morat in 1476. In 1481 Fribourg and Solothurn came into the confederation. In 1499 the Austrian Habsburg emperor, Maximilian I, attempted to reassert his rule over the eastern region of Rhaetia – which as the Grey League (Grisons or Graubünden) had asserted its independence – but he was defeated at Calven.

Later, during the Reformation, Austria was more successful, but the Grey Leaguers retained their independence until they at last joined the Swiss Confederation in 1803. Switzerland's de facto independence dates from the Swiss victory over the Empire at Dornach in 1499, after which the Confederation was released from its obligation to pay the imperial tax.

the Reformation in Switzerland The Reformation led to internal dissension in Switzerland. During the period 1523–29 the northern cantons of Zürich, Berne, and Basel accepted the reformist teachings of Ulrich Zwingli, while the forest cantons remained Roman Catholic. In the hostilities that resulted the Catholic troops were victorious, Zwingli was killed in 1531, and a truce was arranged, whereby each canton was left free to determine its own religion.

In 1536 Bern took the Vaud from the dukes of Savoy, and in the same year a French theologian, John Calvin, arrived in Geneva and established a college of pastors there. After a long battle with some of the leading citizens, Calvin eventually turned the city into a theocratic republic, which had such influence that it became known as the 'Protestant Rome'. The city was visited by John Knox and other Scottish and English theologians. Calvin was succeeded by Théodore Beza.

Calvin's doctrines were far stricter than Zwingli's, and the Calvinists tolerated no opposition, either from Catholics or from dissident Protestants within their territory. So while Zwingli introduced Protestantism into the country and by his struggle and death ensured its survival, Calvin's doctrines reaped much of the benefit of his efforts.

complete independence From the early 16th century Swiss mercenaries were widely employed in Europe, and fighting for foreign kings became a flourishing trade. The Swiss themselves became involved in the Italian wars, and were defeated by the French at Marignano in 1515. After this, good relations were established with France, and the Swiss saw that to keep their linguistically and religiously fragmented Confederation together they needed to adopt a policy of neutrality in European wars. Switzerland managed to maintain its neutrality in the Thirty Years' War (1618–48), and at the end of the war the Treaty of Westphalia (1648) recognized the final separation of Switzerland from the Habsburg Empire.

Through the 17th and 18th centuries, continued peace helped the growth of industry and general prosperity, although during this period the peasantry were much oppressed, and their attempt in 1653 to secure better conditions was crushed. This confirmed the hold on power in the various cantons of the patrician oligarchies.

the Helvetic Republic For 150 years after 1648, the Swiss were able to maintain their neutrality in Europe's many wars. Following the French Revolution the French invaded Switzerland in 1798, and established the Helvetic Republic, a 'sister republic' with a centralized government, under French control. This centralization did not conform to the Swiss tradition of local self-government; nevertheless it created for the first time a national unity, though imposed from outside. The Helvetic Republic introduced a uniform Swiss monetary system, using Latin inscriptions, so as not to conflict with any of the various language groups – a device still in use today.

In the Act of Mediation (1802–03), Napoleon recognized the sovereignty of the cantons, making Switzerland a democratic federation. But only in 1815 was Switzerland's independence fully restored, and its permanent neutrality guaranteed, at the Congress of Vienna. Switzerland also received Geneva and other territories, increasing the number of cantons to 22.

religious conflict and constitutional reform During the 19th century religious differences led to bitter controversy and conflict. In 1847 war broke out between Liberal Protestants and the seven Roman Catholic cantons, the latter having formed a separatist league or Sonderbund (1845), as a result of the suppression of various monasteries by the Liberals in the canton of Aargau. After a short campaign, Gen G H Dufour, at the head of the federal army, defeated the Catholics.

In 1848 a new federal constitution was adopted, and peace signed, giving the Protestants nearly all they had fought for. Switzerland was transformed from a confederation of independent states into one federal state, with the central government possessing wide powers. Bern was chosen as the capital. In 1874 a revision of the federal constitution was introduced, giving wider powers to the state, especially in military matters, but also introducing the principle of the referendum.

Manufacturing industry continued to develop in the 19th century, which also witnessed the introduction of the railways, and tourism began to emerge as an important industry; these factors led to growing prosperity.

the early 20th century Surrounded by belligerent countries during World War I, Switzerland nevertheless retained its neutrality, though the French-speaking and German-speaking populations naturally differed in their sympathies. Switzerland participated in a non-military capacity by organizing Red Cross units, tracing the missing, and permitting incapacitated prisoners of war to be interned within its frontiers.

In 1920 Switzerland joined the League of Nations, which made its permanent headquarters in Geneva. For the next 19 years Switzerland was therefore at the centre of international politics. In 1923 Switzerland formed a customs union with Liechtenstein.

Switzerland in World War II
In World War II the conquest of France by Germany in 1940 made Switzerland economically dependent upon the latter, and in August 1940 a new trade agreement between the two countries was signed. In the same year the Federal Council dissolved the Swiss Nationalist Movement, a totalitarian organization connected with the Nazis, and soon afterwards the Communist Party was also dissolved. When the war spread to the USSR and the Balkans the trade agreement Switzerland had made with the USSR earlier in 1941 became worthless.

Germany then brought pressure on Switzerland to enter into the closest possible economic association, and, as a reprisal against this second agreement, Great Britain intensified its blockade against Switzerland. The country's position was made more difficult by attempts to subvert it from within by the highly organized German Nazi Party in Switzerland itself. After the German invasion of the USSR, Germany demanded that Switzerland participate in the 'fight for Europe' and adhere to the 'New Order'. Only very few Swiss fought in the German army, however, and these were condemned by Swiss military courts for serving with a foreign power.

Switzerland's international role
Switzerland did not become a member of the United Nations (UN) after World War II, but joined UNESCO and other international organizations, and took part in the *Marshall Plan, the programme of US economic aid to post-war Europe. Switzerland joined the European Free Trade Association (EFTA) in 1960, but has not sought membership of the European Union (EU).

A referendum in 1986 rejected the advice of the government and came out overwhelmingly against membership of the UN, and in 1992 another referendum rejected closer ties with the European Community. A further referendum in June 1994 rejected a proposal for Switzerland to participate in UN peacekeeping operations. Nevertheless, the headquarters of many UN and other international bodies (such as the World Health Organization and the International Red Cross) are based in Switzerland, which has also been the site of many peace conferences.

social and economic affairs Switzerland's economic development has been peaceful and prosperous, and political stability has helped it to become, per person, one of the world's richest countries. Switzerland absorbed large numbers of migrant workers, who account for about one-sixth of the country's labour force. In a referendum held in 1975 the Swiss electorate, following the advice of the federal government, rejected the idea of repatriation of migrant workers.

Tourism has continued to be a growth industry in Switzerland, bringing in large amounts of foreign currency.

The formation of a new canton, Jura, along the Franco-German linguistic frontier caused some friction, and even violence, between the two communities. The French-speaking Catholic inhabitants of the area had pressed for separation from the predominantly German-speaking Protestant canton of Bern, and in 1979 Jura officially became the 23rd canton.

political stability The country's domestic politics have been characterized by coalition governments and stability. In 1971 women gained the right to vote in federal elections, and, in 1991, 18-year-olds were allowed to vote for the first time.

The October 1987 election returned a four-party coalition to power, although there was a significant increase in the number of seats held by the Green Party. Flavio Cotti was selected president of the Confederation for the year 1991 by the United Federal Assembly, in December 1990. The

October 1991 election saw little change in the resulting seat distribution, with the four-party coalition again retaining control. Kaspar Villiger was president in 1995. Jean-Paul Delamuraz (1936–98) succeeded Villiger as head of state in January 1996. In late 1996 Arnold Koller was elected president, and began his term in 1997. Flavio Cotti was elected president, for a second term in his political career, in December 1997 and took office in January 1998. On 8 December 1997, the Federal Assembly elected Ruth Dreifuss, head of the Federal Department of Home Affairs since 1993, to the vice-presidency of the Federal Council for 1998.

On 9 December 1998 she was elected to the Presidency of the Swiss Confederation for 1999, the first woman to hold this office.

Swiss banks and wartime gold In 1997 Switzerland came under international pressure over allegations that its banks were holding deposits worth billions of pounds made by Jewish families during World War II. The three banks principally implicated, Crédit Suisse, the Union Bank of Switzerland, and Swiss Bank Corp, agreed in February 1997 to set up a $70 million/£43 million compensation fund for heirs of the Holocaust victims.

In March 1997 the government announced plans to endow a £3 billion foundation for victims of Nazi genocide. With threats that Swiss businesses would be boycotted unless the question of 'lost' Jewish bank accounts and wartime gold dealing was addressed, politicians and diplomats were forced to meet the growing crisis with concrete action.

elections Switzerland's far-right People's Party, which was hostile to immigration and against joining the EU, made spectacular electoral gains in parliamentary elections held in October 1999, emerging as the second strongest force in parliament. The party, which drew its strongest support in predominantly German-speaking cantons, jumped from fourth to second place with 23% of the vote, winning 45 seats in the 200-member lower house. A further tightening up of the laws on immigration looked likely, and the People's Party was certain to see the vote as an endorsement of the anti-foreigner sentiments it expressed during the election campaign. Despite these gains by the People's Party, the four-party ruling coalition remained in office. It is made up of the Social Democratic Party, the Radical Democratic Party, the People's Party, and the centre-right Christian Democratic People's Party.

On 1 January 2001, Moritz Leuenberger was inaugurated as president. In March 2001, in the third referendum on the issue since 1992, voters overwhelmingly rejected a proposal to open European Union membership negotiations.

In September, the upper house of parliament voted to join the United Nations (UN). However, even those in favour stated that the country would not forgo its neutrality in world affairs. However, in a referendum held in March 2002, Switzerland voted to join the UN – membership was supported by 54.6% of the popular vote and 12 of the 23 cantons.

In December 2001, Swiss voters rejected a referendum proposal to disband their armed forces. Campaigners estimated that the neutral country spends 9 billion Swiss francs/£3.9 billion a year (almost a fifth of the national budget) on its army.

In January 2002, Kasper Villiger became president for a second time.

syndicalism (French *syndicat* **'trade union'**) political movement in 19th-century Europe that rejected parliamentary activity in favour of direct action, culminating in a revolutionary general strike to secure worker ownership and control of industry. After 1918 syndicalism was absorbed in communism, although it continued to have an independent existence in Spain until the late 1930s.

Syria country in western Asia, on the Mediterranean Sea, bounded to the north by Turkey, east by Iraq, south by Jordan, and southwest by Israel and Lebanon.

government The 1973 constitution provides for a president, elected by universal adult suffrage for a seven-year term, who appoints and governs with the help of a prime minister and a council of ministers. There is a single-chamber, 250-member legislature, the Majlis al-Sha'ab, also elected by universal adult suffrage. It serves a four-year term.

history Since the earliest times Syria's strategic geographical position – controlling the trade routes from the Mediterranean to the interior – has made it the gathering point for successive waves of immigrants. Prosperous city states emerged in the 3rd millennium BC, especially on the coast. Damascus claims to be the world's oldest continuously inhabited city (over 4,000 years) and Aleppo claims to be even older. It was in Syria that some of the earliest forms of writing evolved. Ugaritic, one of the earliest known alphabets, dating from the 2nd millennium BC, was discovered at Ugarit near the port of Latakia. Around 2000 BC the nomadic Amorites from the Syrian desert swept west, establishing several kingdoms. The Amorites were followed by the Hurrians from the northeast, who established the extensive kingdom of Mitanni, itself defeated by the Hittites in around 1350 BC and incorporated into their empire.

From around the middle of the 2nd millennium BC the Egyptians attempted to control the area, coming into conflict with both Mitanni and the Hittites. Major disruptions occurred around 1200 BC with the invasions of the mysterious Sea Peoples, who appear to have brought about the sudden demise of the Hittite Empire. Subsequently the Arameans, another nomadic people, established kingdoms in the area, while several 'Neo-Hittite' states survived in the north.

a succession of empires Both the Aramean and Neo-Hittite states were conquered by the Assyrians in the 9th and 8th centuries BC. The Assyrian Empire was itself defeated by the Babylonians towards the end of the 7th century BC, who in turn fell to the Persians in the late 6th century BC. The Macedonian Greeks under Alexander the Great had subdued the Persian Empire by the time of Alexander's death in 323 BC, when his conquests were divided among his generals. Syria became part of the Seleucid Empire founded by Seleucus I, Nicator, and came to prominence under Antiochus the Great. During the reign of the last Seleucid king, Antiochus XIII (69–65 BC), Syria became a Roman province (64 BC), and subsequently part of the Byzantine Empire.

Syria fell in AD 636 to the Muslim Arabs as they expanded out of Arabia. The Umayyad dynasty ruled its vast empire between 661 and 750 from Damascus, and thereafter local and externally supported dynasties disputed control. In the 11th to 13th centuries Syria was the scene of many battles between Muslims and European Crusaders. With the fall of Acre in 1291 the last Crusader foothold was removed by the Mamelukes, who ruled until defeated by the Ottoman Turks in 1517. The period spent within the Ottoman Empire (1517–1918) was one of slow decay. Egypt (at this time only notionally part of the Ottoman Empire) conquered Syria between 1831 and 1840. Nevertheless Syria became a centre for the revival of Arab culture and of the drive for Arab self-determination.

the French mandate Arab nationalists were disappointed following the defeat of the Ottoman Empire (Turkey) at the end of World War I. Instead of obtaining independence, they were used as pawns of Allied diplomatic bargaining. Under the terms of the Sykes–Picot Agreement of 1916 – by which the Allies secretly decided on how to partition the Ottoman Empire – Syria and Lebanon were assigned to the French area of influence, and at the San Remo Conference of April 1920 France was granted a League of Nations mandate to govern these two territories.

The French carried out considerable modernization in the main population centres, but nationalist-inspired uprisings made clear the Syrians' feeling of betrayal. Some progress was made towards self-government, but attempts by France to reorganize Syria politically by according special administrative status to the various sections of the population met with hostility, and there was a major national rising against French rule in 1925–27.

towards independence In September 1936 the principle of Syrian independence was acknowledged in a treaty that was never ratified, and real moves towards independence were disrupted by World War II. French and British troops invaded Syria in order to drive out a commander loyal to the pro-German Vichy government. Independence was granted in theory in September 1941, but it was not until elections had been held in August 1943 (as a result of which Shukri Kuwatli became president) that it arrived in fact in April 1946.

Syria since independence The first two decades following independence were marked by political instability, and frequent interventions by the military. This instability ended with the coming to power of Lt-Gen *Assad in 1970, since when the country's internal divisions along tribal, ethnic, and religious lines have largely been suppressed. In foreign affairs Syria took a militant attitude towards the Arab–Israeli conflict (see *Arab–Israeli Wars), although this has gradually moderated. Syria has also varied in its attitude towards pan-Arabism, with periods of stressful relations with its Arab neighbours alternating with attempts at union with them.

the decades of upheaval, 1946–70 Syrian forces took part in the 1948–49 war with Israel, and the country shared the sense of Arab disillusionment at the outcome. Col Husni Zaim seized power briefly in March 1949, but internal and external pressure led to his overthrow and Col Adib Shishakli took over in December and remained until 1954. Several economic projects were initiated in the comparative political tranquillity. Kuwatli was returned after an army insurrection, and the Soviet Union increased its influence.

At the same time there was growing pressure for union with Egypt, many Syrians being inspired by the militant Arab nationalism of its president Gamal Abdel *Nasser – especially following his stand in the *Suez Crisis of 1956. The union came into being under the name of the United Arab Republic in February 1958, but growing discontent with Egyptian domination led to a military coup in September 1961, followed by the break-up of the union and the formation of the independent Syrian Arab Republic.

The secessionists were in turn ousted in March 1963 by officers belonging to the *Ba'ath Party, led by Gen Amin Hafez, who became president. The new regime instituted socialist policies such as nationalization, and adopted a foreign policy orientated towards

the communist countries. But the Ba'athists themselves were divided and the sequence of coup and counter-coup continued, with the radical wing staging a military coup in February 1966.

This new government survived a disastrous involvement in the 1967 war with Israel. The war followed a long history of border incidents and resulted in the loss of territory on the Golan Heights, the strategically important plateau overlooking northern Israel. After the war Syria remained among the militants in the Arab world, refusing negotiations, and backing the claims of the Palestinians.

Assad comes to power Involvement in the 1970 war in Jordan exacerbated divisions in the Ba'ath party, and the moderate wing, led by Lt-Gen Hafez al *Assad, secured power in a bloodless coup in November 1970. In the following year Assad was elected president, and introduced the longest period of stable government in Syria since independence, although marred by his suppression of an Islamic extremist uprising in Hama in 1982 with the loss of 5,000–10,000 lives. He also became head of government, secretary general of the Ba'ath Arab Socialist Party, and president of the National Progressive Front, an umbrella organization for the five main socialist parties. Syria is therefore in reality, if not in a strictly legal sense, a one-party state, underpinned by the military.

Middle East affairs, 1970–80 In September 1971 an agreement was signed to form, with Egypt and Libya, a 'Confederation of Arab Republics', but this broke up in 1979.

Syria's military performance was improved in the 1973 war with Israel, even though more land was lost. Syria did not abandon its hard line on the Palestinians' claims and on a total Israeli withdrawal. Relations between Syria and Egypt cooled after President

Sadat's Israel peace initiative in 1977 and the subsequent *Camp David Agreements (1978 and 1979). Distinct strains also emerged in Syria's relations with Iraq because of a dispute over the headwaters of the River Euphrates. In 1981 Israel formally annexed the Golan Heights.

involvement in Lebanon Syria became deeply involved in 1975–76 in Lebanon's civil war, at first as a mediating influence and then on the side of the right-wing Christians against the Muslims and Palestinians. Syria eventually committed 50,000 troops to the operations. Its aim was to create an area of influence consisting of Lebanon, Syria, and Jordan (with which close relations were established) approximating to the idea of a 'Greater Syria'. Assad opposed US-sponsored peace moves in Lebanon, arguing that they infringed upon Lebanese sovereignty. He also questioned Yassir Arafat's leadership of the Palestine Liberation Organization and supported opposition to him.

In 1984 President Assad and the Lebanese president Amin Gemayel approved plans for a government of national unity in Lebanon, which would give equal representation to Muslims and Christians, and secured the reluctant agreement of Nabih Berri of the Shiite Amal Militia and Walid Jumblatt, leader of the Druze. Fighting still continued, and Assad's credibility suffered, but in 1985 his authority proved sufficient to secure the release of 39 US hostages from an aircraft hijacked by the extremist Shiite group Hezbollah.

In November 1986 Britain broke off diplomatic relations after claiming to have proof of Syrian involvement in international terrorism, when a Syrian citizen attempted to blow up an Israeli plane at Heathrow airport, London. In July 1987 Syria instigated a crackdown on the pro-Iranian Hezbollah party.

leaning towards the West Syria leant increasingly towards the West, its policies in Lebanon in direct conflict with Iran's dream of an Islamic republic, and its crumbling economy was promised Arab aid if Damascus switched allegiance. In June 1987, following a private visit by the former US president Jimmy *Carter, Syria's relations with the USA began to improve, and efforts were made to arrange the release of Western hostages in Lebanon, a process that continued through 1991. In 1990 Syrian troops defeated the forces of the Maronite Christian leader Michel Aoun, helping to bring to an end the civil war in Lebanon. After Iraq's invasion of Kuwait in August 1990, Syria sided with other Arab states and the United Nations (UN) coalition against Iraq, contributing troops for the *Gulf War. In November 1990 full diplomatic relations with Britain were resumed, and in 1991 President Assad agreed to a US Middle East peace plan.

In December 1991, Assad was re-elected, unopposed, for a fourth term. In the August 1994 assembly elections the Ba'ath Party was returned to its dominant position.

In 1993 Syria joined other Arab countries, including Iraq, in boycotting a UN treaty banning production and use of chemical weapons. In 1997, three border points with Iraq, closed since 1980, were re-opened.

discussions with Israel 1994–2000 In 1994 Israel offered partial withdrawal from the Golan Heights area, as part of a wider-ranging peace treaty between the two countries, and in 1995 a security framework agreement was reached. However, peace talks did not progress further. One issue of contention was the war between Israel and Hezbollah guerrillas in southern Lebanon in 1996. Together with the USA, Syria tried to agree a ceasefire between Israel and Lebanon, but violence continued.

In January 1998, relations with Israel deteriorated after Israeli forces in the Golan Heights seized land cultivated by Arab farmers, which led to violence. In November, the Syrian-backed Islamic Jihad movement claimed responsibility for a bomb attack in Jerusalem.

In 1999 peace talks between Israel and Syria were resumed after a break of more than three years. Issues of the Golan Heights, as well as of Syria's role in Lebanon, where it still had 30,000 troops, and the Middle East, were discussed, and a date for more peace talks set for early 2000. Israeli Prime Minister Ehud *Barak and Syrian Foreign Minister Farouk Sharaa returned to the USA, but concluded their talks with only the outline of an agreement. While in talks, Syria accused Israel of a lack of good faith after Israel negotiated for the disarmament of Hezbollah, the Islamic militia in Lebanon, and Syria distanced itself from Iran, to form part of the security arrangements. When Barak arrived back in Israel, he was met with strong opposition to a withdrawal from the Golan Heights from Israeli politicians and civilians.

Peace talks over the Golan Heights were postponed indefinitely by Israel in January 2000. No reason was given, although Israel rejected a demand from Syria to commit to a full Israeli withdrawal from the Golan Heights, saying that negotiations would not be resumed until Syria was seen to control Hezbollah guerrillas operating in southern Lebanon. This preceded renewed fighting between Israel and Lebanon after Israel withdrew from the 1996 ceasefire agreement, bombing three power transformers providing power to Lebanese cities in retaliation for the recent killings of six Israeli soldiers in Lebanon. Following the fighting, Israeli prime minister Ehud Barak defeated a motion of no confidence and insisted that, before Israel pulled out from Lebanon, he

would exhaust all chances of a deal with Syria and Lebanon.

After Arab-Israeli peace talks were reopened in March 2000, Israel's cabinet confirmed Prime Minister Barak's commitment to withdraw Israeli troops from south Lebanon by July 2000. However, the bombing campaign which had gained strength since Israel bombed three Lebanese power stations in February continued despite, and perhaps as a result of, unanimous condemnation of Israel's actions at a recent meeting of the 22-nation Arab League. In an attempt to prevent Israel's withdrawal from the Golan Heights being under fire, US president Clinton and Syrian president Assad attempted to frame a deal which would lead to a peaceful withdrawal, and would include the UN Security Council. However, Israel remained determined to withdraw, despite Syrian warnings that a unilateral move could provoke an escalation of violence in the region.

political prisoners In November 1995, 1,200 political prisoners, including members of the banned Muslim Brotherhood, were released as part of an amnesty to commemorate President Assad's seizure of power 25 years previously. In January 1999, Amnesty International called for the further release of 300 political prisoners, condemning Syria's human-rights record. In July 2000, there were further releases, coinciding with Bashar al Assad becoming president.

changes in government Having been re-elected in 1999, in March 2000, President Assad carried out his first major cabinet shuffle since 1992, appointing Muhammad Mustafa Miro to the position of prime minister.

President Assad died in June 2000. His son Bashar was named commander-in-chief of the army and was nominated to succeed as president. His presidency was confirmed in a referendum held on 10 July 2000 which afforded him 97% of the popular vote.

economic changes In November the Iraq–Syria border was re-opened and Iraq began pumping oil to Syria through a pipeline that had been closed for a decade. In early December, President Bashar Assad approved the establishment of private banks and took preliminary measures to establish a stock market and float the Syrian pound. The measures reversed the nationalization of banks that had occurred in the early 1960s. In January 2001, Syria signed a free-trade accord with Iraq.

In March 2001, Assad renewed relations with the *Palestine Liberation Organization, after ten years.

A vote by the UN General Assembly in October 2001 gave Syria a two-year seat on the Security Council. Despite appeals from the US Congress – Syria was on the US State Department terror list for funding militant Islamic groups – the Bush administration did not publicly oppose the result, because as one of ten non-permanent members, Syria would not hold any veto power in the council.

**Tafawa Balewa, Alhaji Abubakar
(1912–1966)** Nigerian politician,
prime minister 1957–66. In September
1957 he was appointed prime minister,
a post he retained at Nigerian
independence three years later.
He was knighted in 1960. In 1962 he
declared a state of emergency in
response to a political crisis in the
Western Region. He was assassinated
four years later in a coup.

Taff Vale case decision in 1901 by the
British Law lords that trade unions
were liable for their members' actions,
and could hence be sued for damages
in the event of a strike, picketing, or
boycotting an employer. It followed
a strike by union members for higher
wages and union recognition against
the Taff Vale Railway Company.
The judgement resulted in a rapid
growth of union membership, and
was replaced by the Trade Disputes
Act 1906.

Taft, Robert Alphonso (1889–1953)
US right-wing Republican senator
from 1939, and a candidate for the
presidential nomination 1940, 1944,
1948, and 1952. He sponsored the
Taft–Hartley Labor Act of 1947,
restricting union power. He was the
son of President William Taft.

Taft, William Howard (1857–1930)
27th president of the USA 1909–13,
a Republican. He was secretary of war
1904–08 in Theodore Roosevelt's
administration, but as president his
conservatism provoked Roosevelt to
stand against him in the 1912 election.
Taft served as chief justice of the
Supreme Court 1921–30.

Taiwan country in east Asia, officially
the Republic of China, occupying the
island of Taiwan between the East
China Sea and the South China Sea,
separated from the coast of China by
the Taiwan Strait.

government The 325-member
National Assembly, the Kuo-Min
Ta-Hui, has the power to amend the
constitution of 1947. Until the 1991
elections, its membership was
dominated by veterans who, originally
elected from mainland China in 1947,
were allowed to retain their seats as
'life members' after their constituencies
fell under communist Chinese control
in 1949.

Taiwan's president, directly elected
for a four-year term, is head of state
and commander-in-chief of the armed
forces, and promulgates laws. (Until
1996 the president was elected by the
national assembly for a six-year term.)
The president works with a cabinet,
the Executive Yuan, headed by a prime
minister, responsible to a single-
chamber legislature, the Legislative
Yuan. The Legislative Yuan comprises
164 members, directly elected for a
three-year term on the basis of
proportional representation. Before
1972, it was dominated by mainlander
'life members'. Now, however, all its
deputies have been elected in Taiwan.
The Legislative Yuan has the power to
hear administrative reports presented
by the Executive Yuan and can amend
government policy. Three Control,
Judicial, and Examination Yuans also
exist, with the tasks of investigating
the work of the executive, interpreting
the constitution, and overseeing
entrance examinations for public offices.

history Taiwan, then known as
Formosa ('the beautiful'), was settled
by China from the 15th century, briefly
occupied by the Dutch during the mid-
17th century, and annexed by the
Chinese Manchu dynasty in 1683.

It was ceded to Japan under the terms of the Treaty of Shimonoseki after the 1895 Sino Japanese war and not regained by China until the Japanese surrender in August 1945.

Chinese nationalist government In December 1949 Taiwan became the refuge for the Chinese nationalist government forces of *Chiang Kai-shek who were compelled to evacuate the mainland after their defeat by the communist troops of Mao Zedong. Chiang and his nationalist followers dominated the island and maintained an army of 600,000 in the hope of reconquering the mainland, over which they still claimed sovereignty. They continued to be recognized by the USA as the legitimate government of China, and occupied China's United Nations and Security Council seats until October 1971, when they were expelled and replaced by the People's Republic.

economic growth Taiwan was protected by US naval forces during the Korean War 1950–53 and signed a mutual defence treaty with the USA in 1954. Benefiting from such security, the country enjoyed a period of rapid economic growth during the 1950s and 1960s, emerging as an export-oriented, newly industrialized country. Political power during these years was concentrated in the hands of the Kuomintang or KMT (*Guomindang) and the armed forces led by President Chiang Kai-shek, with martial law imposed and opposition activity outlawed.

external changes During the 1970s the Taiwanese government was forced to adjust to rapid external changes as the USA adopted a new policy of détente towards Communist China. In January 1979 this culminated in the full normalization of Sino-US relations, the severing of Taiwanese-US diplomatic contacts, and the annulment of the USA's 1954 security pact. Other Western nations followed suit in ending diplomatic relations with Taiwan during the 1970s and early 1980s.

democratization and 'Taiwanization' These developments, coupled with generational change within the KMT, prompted a slow review of Taiwanese policies, both domestic and external. Chiang Kai-shek died in April 1975 and his son Chiang Ching-kuo (1910–1988) became party chair and, from 1978, state president. Under his stewardship, a programme of gradual democratization and 'Taiwanization' was adopted, with elections being held for 'vacated seats' within the national assembly and Legislative Yuan and with native Taiwanese being more rapidly inducted into the KMT. In the December 1986 elections a formal opposition party, the Democratic Progressive Party (DPP), led by Chiang Peng-chien, was tolerated and captured 22% of the vote to the KMT's 69%. In July 1987 martial law was lifted and replaced with a national security law under which demonstrations and the formation of opposition parties were legalized, provided they forswore communism, and press restrictions were lifted.

accelerating reform President Chiang was succeeded on his death by *Lee Teng-hui, the Taiwanese-born vice-president from 1984. The new president accelerated the pace of reform. Many 'old guard' figures were retired 1988–89 and a plan for phasing out by 1992, through voluntary retirement, up to 200 mainland constituencies and replacing them with Taiwanese deputies was approved.

In the December 1989 Legislative Yuan elections the KMT's vote share fell to 59% and from September 1990 the 'ancient guard' Chinese-born KMT members became a minority within Taiwan's parliament.

relations with China normalized In May 1991 President Lee Teng-hui officially declared an end to the 42 years of 'civil war' ('Period of

Communist Rebellion') between the KMT government of the Republic of China (Taiwan) and the People's Republic of China. For the first time, the existence of a Communist Party-led government in Beijing was formally recognized and in April 1991 the first official Taiwanese delegation visited Beijing.

calls for independence rejected
In October 1991 the opposition party, the DPP, introduced a new clause into its charter advocating Taiwanese independence and calling for a plebiscite on the issue, despite the fact that calling for independence remained a seditious offence.

At the end of 1991 the 566 last remaining 'life members' formally resigned from their legislative posts.

In December 1991 a new national assembly was elected and became the first to be controlled by Taiwan-elected members. The KMT won a landslide victory, capturing 71% of the vote and securing the required majority to push through fundamental reform of the constitution. The DPP was damaged by its technically illegal pro-independence stance; the Taiwanese remained concerned that a declaration of independence might prompt invasion by mainland China or an uprising by internal factional divisions.

first democratic election
In December 1992, in the country's first fully democratic elections, the ruling KMT lost considerable support to the DPP but still, with a 53% vote share, secured a clear majority of seats in the Legislative Yuan. In February 1993 the island-born Lien Chan was appointed prime minister following the resignation of Hau Pei-tsun, who led a conservative 'mainlander' faction within the KMT.

In 1993, Taiwan applied to become a member of the United Nations (UN), but the application was blocked by China. Taiwan renewed its application each year, but still had not achieved

membership by 2001, as China blocked the request every time.

In the December 1995 elections, the ruling KMT retained its majority in the Legislative Yuan by a slim margin, with the DPP winning 33% of the vote and the New Party, a breakaway faction of the KMT led by diehard Chinese mainlanders, 13%.

In March 1996 the incumbent Lee Teng-hui was directly elected president in Taiwan's first-ever democratic election, attracting 54% of the vote in spite of nearby large-scale military exercises by China intended to intimidate Taiwan's voters. Peng Ming-min, leader of the pro-independence DPP, finished second with 21% of the vote. In 1997 he appointed Vincent Siew as his prime minister.

In August 1998 Lin Yi-shiung became the new chairman of the opposition, the pro-independence DPP.

foreign relations Following a diplomatic pact between China and South Korea in 1992, Taiwan severed relations with the latter. South Africa was left as the only major country with full diplomatic links with Taiwan. However, in 1993, a cooperation pact was signed with China.

In December 1998 President Lee Teng-hui snubbed China's call for early talks by announcing that reunion with the mainland was impossible until Beijing adopted democracy. Lee's ruling KMT, which had begun to champion a distinct Taiwanese identity separate from mainland China, increased its majority in parliamentary and local elections, and won the mayorship of Taipei. With voter turnout at 68%, the KMT secured 46% of the vote and won 123 of the 225 seats in the newly-expanded Legislative Yuan. The main opposition party, the DPP, with 30% of the vote, won 70 seats, while the pro-unification New Party, with 7% of the vote, won 11 seats. 168 of the 225 seats were directly elected from multi-member constituencies, 41 were elected by proportional representation, 8 were elected from aboriginal constituencies and 8 were elected by party appointment from overseas Chinese communities. DPP general-secretary Chiou I-jen resigned after the election and was replaced by You His-kun.

In July 1999 Taiwan was recognized by the government of Papua New Guinea. The recognition was, however, retracted later that month.

question of independence in 2000 China threatened Taiwan with invasion in February 2000 if it continued to put off discussions about reunification, in a move which seemed to be pre-empting pro-independence sentiment in Taiwan's presidential elections scheduled for 18 March. However, China denied that it was threatening Taiwan, saying that it had long been attempting to move Taiwan to negotiate its future. As presidential candidate Chen Shui-bian and his Min-chu Chin-pu Tang (MCT; Democratic Progressive Party) emerged as possible victors in March, China renewed threats that it would take Taiwan by force if moves were made towards official independence.

In general elections in March 2000, Taiwan elected Chen Shui-bian as its next president. A member of the Democratic Progressive Party, which has favoured a formal declaration of independence from China, Chen's election posed a threat to relations between Taiwan and the Chinese government. His election ended 55 years of nationalist rule by the KMT, and in a gesture of conciliation both to the KMT and to China, Chen chose as his prime minister the current KMT defence minister, Tang Fei, and pushed through legislation voting to lift a 50-year ban on direct trade, investment, and postal links with China. In his inaugural address in May 2000, President Chen Shui-bian sought to reassure China in saying that he would not issue a formal declaration of

independence for the island. However, the resignation on 3 October 2000 of Taiwan's prime minister, Tang Fei, after only four and a half months in office, shook Taiwan's government. His sudden resignation, officially attributed to poor health, sparked a political storm and raised questions over the stability of the government. Chang Chun-Hsiung, a veteran of the MCT, was named premier the following day. The following month, President Chen Shui-bian faced mounting criticism from the KMT for his handling of the economy and relations with China, and was threatened with impeachment.

ban lifted As of 1 January 2001, Taiwan lifted its 52-year ban on direct trade and communications with China, but only for business between the mainland's Fujian province and the Taiwanese islands of Kinmen and Matsu.

In March 2001, the traditionalist Lien Chan, who supported reunification with China, was elected chairman of the Kuomintang party, replacing Lee Teng-hui.

2001 elections Taiwan's pro-independence MCT achieved victory in the general elections on 2 December 2001, winning 87 of the 225 seats. The KMT suffered a landslide defeat, taking 68 seats, down from 114. In January 2002, Yu Shyi-kun was appointed prime minister. In the same month Taiwan became a member of the World Trade Organization (WTO).

Tajikistan formerly **Tadzhikistan (to 1991)**, country in central Asia, bounded north by Kyrgyzstan and Uzbekistan, east by China, and south by Afghanistan and Pakistan.

Takeshita, Noboru (1924–2000) Japanese conservative politician. Elected to parliament as a Liberal Democratic Party (LDP) deputy in 1958, he became president of the LDP and prime minister in 1987. He and members of his administration were shown in the Recruit scandal to have been involved in insider trading and he resigned in 1989.

Taliban or **Talibaan, ('the Seekers')** Afghan political and religious military force that seized control of southern and central Afghanistan, including the country's capital, Kabul, in September 1996. An Islamic regime was imposed, and by the end of 1996 the Taliban controlled two-thirds of the country. In 1997, the Taliban changed the country's official name to the Islamic Emirate of Afghanistan. The Taliban receives financial support from Saudi Arabia, but the regime was, as of mid-1998, recognized by only three states: Saudi Arabia, the United Arab Emirates, and Pakistan. In September 2000, the Taliban claimed to control 95% of Afghanistan and declared that it deserved international recognition as the country's government. In October 2001, US-led forces launched military strikes on Afghanistan in an attempt to force the Taliban to give up Osama bin Laden, the terrorist leader named as the prime suspect in the 11 September terrorist attacks on the USA.

Talmadge, Eugene (1884–1946) US Democrat governor (1933–37, 1941–43, 1946). A states rights governor (1933–37), he attacked individuals and agencies opposed to him, and, with Huey *Long, he led Southern opposition to President Franklin Roosevelt, even mounting an abortive campaign to replace Roosevelt in 1936. Governor again (1941–43), he lost favour after demanding that the University of Georgia regents fire a pro-integration dean. He was re-elected governor in 1946 but died before assuming office.

Tambo, Oliver (1917–1993) South African nationalist politician, in exile 1960–90, president of the *African National Congress (ANC) 1977–91. Because of poor health, he was given the honorary post of national chair in July 1991, and Nelson *Mandela resumed the ANC presidency.

Tamil Tigers or **Liberation Tigers of Tamil Eelam (LTTE),** Tamil separatist guerrilla movement based in northen *Sri Lanka with a stronghold in the Jaffna peninsula. It was formed by Velupillai Prabhakaran in 1975. The movement's civil war against the country's Sinhalese majority community and governments began in the late 1970s with demands for an autonomous Tamil state in northern and eastern Sri Lanka, known as Eelam (the Tamil name for the island that used to be called Ceylon).

Tanaka, Kakuei (1918–1993) Japanese conservative politician, leader of the dominant Liberal Democratic Party (LDP) and prime minister 1972–74. In 1976 he was charged with corruption and resigned from the LDP but remained a powerful faction leader.

Tanganyika African National Union TANU, moderate socialist national party organized by Tanzanian politician Julius *Nyerere in the 1950s. TANU won electoral successes 1958 and 1960, ensuring that Nyerere was recognized as prime minister on 1 May 1961, when Tanganyika prepared for independence from Britain.

tank armoured fighting vehicle that runs on tracks and is fitted with weapons systems capable of defeating other tanks and destroying life and property. The term was originally a code name for the first effective tracked and armoured fighting vehicle, invented by the British soldier and scholar Ernest Swinton, and first used in the Battle of the Somme in 1916.

A tank consists of a body or hull of thick steel, on which are mounted machine guns and a larger gun. The hull contains the crew (usually consisting of a commander, driver, and one or two soldiers), engine, radio, fuel tanks, and ammunition. The tank travels on caterpillar tracks that enable it to cross rough ground and debris. It is known today as an MBT (main battle tank).

Tannenberg, Battle of in World War I, victory of German forces led by field marshal Paul von Hindenburg over Russian forces under General Aleksander Samsonov in August 1914 at a village in East Prussia (now Grunwald, Poland) 145 km/90 mi northeast of Warsaw.

Tanzania country in east Africa, bounded to the north by Uganda and Kenya; south by Mozambique, Malawi, and Zambia; west by the Democratic Republic of Congo (formerly Zaire), Burundi, and Rwanda; and east by the Indian Ocean.

Tardieu, Andre Pierre Gabriel Amedee (1876–1945) French premier and journalist.

Tarnopol, Battle of in World War I, Austro–German victory over the Russians July 1917 at a town in Polish Galicia (now Ternopol, Ukraine) about 110 km/70 mi southeast of Lemberg (Lviv, Ukraine); one of the first instances of the more general collapse of the Russian armies following the Russian Revolution 1917.

Taylor, A(lan) J(ohn) P(ercivale) (1906–1990) English historian and television lecturer. His books include *The Struggle for Mastery in Europe 1848–1918* (1954), *The Origins of the Second World War* (1961), and *English History 1914–1945* (1965).

Taylor, Albert Davis (1883–1951) US landscape architect. Trained by Warren Manning, he opened a firm in Cleveland, Ohio (1916–51), drafting plans that combined naturalistic parks with formal gardens near buildings for clients like the Pentagon and Forest Hill Park in Cleveland. Taylor was born in Carlisle, Massachusetts.

Tchelitchew, Pavel (1898–1957) Russian-born painter. He is noted for his intricate surrealistic work, as in *Hide and Seek* (1940–42). Tchelitchew was born in the district of Kaluga, Russia. After study in Russia, he worked in Berlin (1921–23), moved to Paris (1923–c. 1934), where he was a scenic designer for ballets, and then to New York City in 1934, before finally settling in Italy in 1950.

Teapot Dome Scandal US political scandal that revealed the corruption of President *Harding's administration. It centred on the leasing of naval oil reserves in 1921 at Teapot Dome, Wyoming, without competitive bidding, as a result of bribing the secretary of the interior, Albert B Fall. Fall was tried and imprisoned in 1929.

Tedder, Arthur William (1890–1967) 1st Baron Tedder, UK marshal of the Royal Air Force in World War II. As deputy supreme commander under US general Eisenhower 1943–45, he was largely responsible for the initial success of the 1944 Normandy landings. He was made a KCB in 1942, and became a baron in 1946.

Tehran Conference conference held in 1943 in Tehran, Iran, the first meeting of World War II Allied leaders Churchill, Roosevelt, and Stalin. The chief subject discussed was coordination of Allied strategy in Western and Eastern Europe.

Templer, Gerald Walter Robert (1898–1979) British field marshal. He served in both world wars, but is especially remembered for his work as high commissioner in Malaysia 1952–54, during the period of fighting against communist insurgents. KBE 1949.

Tennessee Valley Authority TVA, US government corporation founded in 1933 to develop the **Tennessee River basin** (an area of some 104,000 sq km/40,000 sq mi) by building hydroelectric power stations, producing and distributing fertilizers, and similar activities. The TVA was associated with President F D Roosevelt's *New Deal, promoting economic growth by government investment.

Te Puea, Herangi (1883–1952) Princess, New Zealand Maori nationalist leader. Born in Waikato, on North Island, into a chiefly family, she became a leading figure, from 1911, within the Maori nationalist movement, the Kingitanga. During the inter-war period, the Kingitanga became an important instrument for the settlement of Maori grievances against colonial rule and for social and cultural advance.

Territorial Army British force of volunteer soldiers, created from volunteer regiments (incorporated in 1872) as the **Territorial Force** in 1908. It was raised and administered by county associations, and intended primarily for home defence. It was renamed the Territorial Army in 1922. Merged with the Regular Army in World War II, it was revived in 1947, and replaced by a smaller, more highly trained Territorial and Army Volunteer Reserve, again renamed the Territorial Army in 1979.

Test Ban Treaty agreement signed by the USA, the USSR, and the UK on 5 August 1963 contracting to test nuclear weapons only underground. All nuclear weapons testing in the atmosphere, in outer space, and under water was banned. In the following two years 90 other nations signed the treaty, the only major nonsignatories being France and China, which continued underwater and ground-level tests. In January 1996 France announced the ending of its test programme, and supported the implementation of a universal test ban. The treaty did not restrict or regulate underground testing, or the possession or use of nuclear weapons during wartime.

Tet Offensive in the Vietnam War, a prolonged attack mounted by the *Vietcong against Saigon (now Ho Chi Minh City) and other South Vietnamese cities and hamlets (including the US Marine base at Khe Sanh), which began on 30 January 1968. Although the Vietcong were finally forced to withdraw, the Tet Offensive brought into question the ability of the South Vietnamese army and their US allies to win the war and

added fuel to the antiwar movement in both the USA and Australia. From this political perspective, the Tet Offensive might be considered the watershed of the Vietnam War.

Of 84,000 communist Vietcong who took part in the offensive, 32,000 were killed by mid-February. The fighting in Saigon was especially fierce, and in Hué, which the Vietcong controlled for almost a month, 3,000 civilians were executed. The US Marine base at Khe Sanh was besieged for almost three months, and although the Vietcong were finally repulsed with heavy losses, the USA later abandoned the base.

Thailand formerly **Siam (to 1939 and 1945–49)**, country in southeast Asia on the Gulf of Siam, bounded east by Laos and Cambodia, south by Malaysia, and west by Myanmar (Burma).

government A hereditary monarch is head of state. A number of constitutional changes were implemented through the 1990s. There is a two-chamber national assembly, comprising a 500-member house of representatives, the Saphaphutan, elected by universal suffrage for a four-year term, and a 200-member senate, the Wuthisapha. The senate used to be appointed by the monarch (and traditionally drawn from the armed forces and police), but is known also democratically elected for a four-year term.

The monarch retains significant political power, having the authority to dissolve the national assembly and to veto bills, with a two-thirds assembly majority being required for a royal veto to be overturned. On the advice of the national assembly, the monarch appoints a prime minister, and cabinet ministers. Since 1992, the prime minister and ministers may not be simultaneously members of the national assembly.

The military's influence is now much reduced. The 1997 constitution sets out a wide range of political, religious, and social rights.

history Archaeological evidence suggests that the area of modern Thailand was the centre of a significant Neolithic culture as early as 3500 BC, and of iron-working as early as 2000 BC.

early empires The Thai peoples were relatively late arrivals in the area. The earliest historical evidence suggests that the area was mostly under the control of the Funan Empire, centred on Cambodia, in the 5th century AD, although by the 7th century various kingdoms of Mon peoples had been established in the Chao Phraya valley. The northeast region on the other hand remained in the hands of the Khmer empires that followed Funan, notably that of Angkor after the 8th century.

the first Thai kingdoms The Thais themselves began to move into their present territory in the 8th and 9th centuries from the kingdom of Nan Chao in the Yunnan area of southwest China. Small states were established in the 11th century, and in 1238 the first major kingdom was founded at Sukhothai in north-central Thailand. Mongol invasions of Nan Chao forced greater migrations, and, under King Rama Khamheng, Sukhothai expanded to overcome the Mon kingdoms of the lower Chao Phraya valley and extend its rule down the southern peninsula.

The Sukhothai kingdom was, however, short-lived, and by 1350 power had passed to the south where another prince, Ramatipadi, founded Ayuthya. From this capital much of Thailand became united, and the country was involved in a protracted power struggle with first Cambodia and then Burma (Myanmar). The contest with Burma was particularly long, and after successes on both sides it led in 1767 to the destruction of Ayuthya. Order in Thailand was subsequently restored, and in 1782 the present Chakri dynasty came to power in the new capital of Bangkok.

European contacts Siam (as the country was known until 1939, and again in 1945–49) was reached by Portuguese traders in 1511. The 17th century witnessed the arrival of the British East India Company, the Dutch, and the French, and trading rivalries between the three countries developed rapidly. France was particularly active and sought domination in Siam, which brought a wary Siamese reaction.

This circumspection continued into the 19th century. Although a treaty of friendship and trade was signed with Britain in 1826, it was only with the accession of King Mongkut (Rama IV) in 1851 that Siamese attitudes changed. In 1855 another treaty was signed with Britain, establishing Britain as the paramount power in the region and opening Siam to foreign commerce. Similar arrangements with other powers followed.

independence maintained King Mongkut and his successor, King Chulalongkura (Rama V; reigned 1868–1910), employed Western advisers to assist in the modernization of the country's administration and commerce, and managed to maintain Siam's independence by playing off the British interests to the west and south against those of the French to the east. Anglo-French diplomatic agreements of 1896 and 1904 established Siam as a neutral buffer kingdom between the British territories of Burma and Malaya and French Indochina. Some territorial concessions were made by Siam in order to maintain its independence: the Laotian territories east of the River Mekong went to France along with the Cambodian provinces of Battambang and Siem Reap, while in 1909 rights to four Malay states of southern Siam were transferred to British Malaya.

Siam in the early 20th century Siam remained a British sphere of influence in the early 20th century, becoming Britain's ally in World War I in 1917. After World War I a movement for national renaissance developed, and this, combined with the worldwide depression of the 1930s, precipitated a political coup against the absolute monarch King Prajadhipok in 1932. The coup created a constitutional monarchy and parliamentary government, and the name of Muang Thai ('land of the free') was adopted for the country in 1939.

Throughout the 1930s politics were marked by considerable unrest and by increasing nationalism. In 1938 the pro-Japanese military leader Phibun Songkhram seized power. In 1940, taking advantage of the defeat of France and encouraged by Japan, Phibun annexed the Indochinese territories lost in 1893 and 1907. In December 1941 Japanese forces entered Thailand, requesting the right to advance through the country preparatory to their attack on British Malaya and Singapore. This was refused, but after a brief struggle Phibun signed a treaty with the Japanese, and by 1942 Thailand had declared war on the Allies. However, there was an anti-Japanese guerrilla movement, the Free Thai, which succeeded in forcing the resignation of Phibun in 1944.

military control After World War II Thailand restored the French territories and signed treaties with its former enemies, but another period of unstable government followed, particularly as a result of the assassination of King Ananda Mahidol (Rama VIII) in 1946. The year 1947 saw a military coup by the wartime leader Phibun Songkhram, and the army retained control during the next two decades, with the leader of the military junta periodically changed by a series of bloodless coups: Field Marshal Phibun Songkhram 1947–57, Field Marshal Sarit Thanarat 1957–63, and Gen Thanom Kittikachorn 1963–73. The monarch, King *Bhumibol Adulyadej, was only a figurehead.

Thailand followed a steady anti-communist line under the influence of its alliance with the USA, and was a founder member of the Southeast Asia Treaty Organization (SEATO). It encountered serious communist guerrilla insurgency along its borders with Laos, Cambodia, and Malaysia.

From time to time experiments at liberalization were made, with elected assemblies in 1957–58 and 1968–71. The results were fractious and further military coups resulted. Thanom ruled through a National Executive Council until 1973, when growing unrest over foreign policy and the lack of basic freedoms led to student riots in Bangkok, culminating in the fall of the government in October. Free elections were held in 1975 and 1976. A series of coalition governments lacked stability, and in 1976 the armed forces, led by Admiral Chaloryoo, took over, with Thanin Kraivichien becoming prime minister.

The government succeeded in reorienting the country's foreign policy in the aftermath of the Vietnam War. The USA withdrew all its substantial military presence in Thailand, and diplomatic relations were established with the communist regimes in China, North Korea, and Cambodia. Disputes with communist Laos and Vietnam continued, and Thailand remained firmly within the non-communist *Association of South East Asian Nations (ASEAN).

towards civilian government
The army supreme commander, Gen Kriangsak Chomanan, held power 1977–80 and established a mixed civilian and military form of government under the monarch's direction. Having deposed Kriangsak in October 1980, Gen Prem Tinsulanonda (1920–) formally relinquished his army office and headed an elected civilian coalition government from 1983.

Attempted coups in April 1983 and September 1985 were easily crushed by Prime Minister Prem, who ruled in a cautious apolitical manner. With an economic growth averaging 9%–10% a year, Thailand emerged as an export-oriented, newly industrializing country. Chatichai Choonhavan, leader of the Thai Nation Party, was elected prime minister in 1988.

foreign affairs The civil war in Cambodia and Laos, which resulted in the flight of more than 500,000 refugees to Thailand 1975–90, provided justification for continued quasi-military rule and the maintenance of martial law. Thailand drew closer to its allies in the Association of South East Asian Nations, who jointly supported the Cambodian guerrilla resistance to the Vietnamese-imposed government. The country was drawn more deeply into the Cambodian civil war with the shelling July 1989 of a refugee camp in Thailand, but tensions eased after the Cambodian peace agreement of 1991.

the 1991 military coup In February 1991 Prime Minister Chatichai Choonhavan was overthrown in a bloodless coup led by Gen Sunthorn Kongsompong, the supreme military commander, and army chief Gen Suchinda Kraprayoon. It was the country's 17th coup or attempted putsch since the abolition of the absolute monarchy in 1932. A civilian, Anand Panyarachun, was appointed interim prime minister, subject to the ultimate control of the military junta, but after new elections in March 1992 he was replaced by Gen Suchinda. The latter's appointment sparked the largest street demonstrations for two decades, forcing him to resign.

constitutional reforms and the return of democracy In May 1992 the ruling coalition agreed to a package of constitutional reforms, including the proviso that the prime minister should not come from the ranks of the military. Anand was again made interim prime minister in June, but after the September 1992 general election gave a Democrat coalition

185 seats in the 360-member parliament, Chuan Leekpai became prime minister.

In January 1995 further constitutional amendments were approved, lowering the voting age to 18, reducing the size of the senate, and giving women equal rights in law to men. The ruling coalition collapsed in May 1995 as a result of a land-reform scandal, and a general election was called for July.

coalition governments, 1995–97 The July 1995 election was narrowly won by the opposition Thai Nation Party, amid allegations of vote-buying in rural areas. Its leader Banharn Silpa-archa formed a new seven-party coalition. In March 1996 Banharn Silpa-archa appointed a new 260-member senate – the first to be appointed by a democratically elected prime minister. Only 39 of its members were active military officers compared with 139 in the outgoing senate.

In August 1996 Banharn was left with a narrow majority after Palang Dharma, the third-largest party in the seven-party coalition, withdrew from the government. Banharn resigned in September after losing the support of the other six parties.

In November 1996, a general election – the fourth in four years – brought to power a new, reshuffled six-party coalition led by Gen Chavalit Yongchaiyudh of the New Aspiration Party (NAP). The new coalition comprised the NAP, Chart Patthana, the Social Action Party (SAP), Prachakorn Thai, Muan Chon, and Seritham. In November 1997, Chuan Leekpai was again elected prime minister as well as minister of defence. His Democratic Party hastily cobbled together a coalition, and began to implement economic reforms.

economic reform In February 1998, Prime Minister Chuan Leekpai warned that the economy was expected to contract by 3.5% in 1998, as a result of the austerity measures instituted since the devaluation of the baht (Thai currency) in July 1997. Plans were also announced for the repatriation of 500,000 foreign workers (drawn chiefly from neighbouring Myanmar) each year for the next three years; by April 1998, 100,000 had already been sent back. Plans to restructure the country's stricken financial institutions were unveiled in August 1998, and in September, the IMF approved an aid package of US$135 million. In October the opposition Chart Patthana party was brought into the coalition government, with the aim of increasing its majority to help push through reforms. The reforms achieved some success in the following years.

elections in 2001 Thai Rak Thai (TRT; Thais Love Thais), the party of Thaksin Shinawatra, a telecommunications tycoon, initially won over half the seats in the 500-seat lower house of Thailand's parliament in a general election held on 6 January 2001. The elections were marred by vote-buying and other irregularities, and a rerun of disputed seats deprived the party of its overall majority. It formed a coalition government with two other parties. TRT had run a populist campaign, promising a grant of 1 million baht for each of Thailand's 70,000 villages and a generous health insurance plan. In March, a bomb destroyed an aircraft at Bangkok airport minutes before Shinawatra was due on board. In early April, secessionist Muslims in southern Thailand were blamed for bomb attacks in two cities that killed one and injured 40.

The National Counter-Corruption Commission opened its case in the Constitutional Court against Prime Minister Thaksin Shinawatra in April. Shinawatra, who was accused of concealing the full extent of his wealth when earlier in government, appeared before the court in June, but was acquitted in August.

Thalmann, Ernst (1886–1944) German Communist politician and associate of Stalin.

Thani, Sheikh Khalifa bin Hamad al- (1932–) Qatar political leader, emir (ruler) 1972–95. He utilized the small state's burgeoning oil revenues to modernize the bureaucratic structure, diversify the economy, and develop education and the social services. He also sought to curb the extravagances of the royal family and pursued a pro-Western foreign policy, joining the UN-coalition forces in the 1990–91 Gulf War against Iraq. However, although he appointed an advisory council, he continued to rule in an authoritarian manner. In June 1995 he was deposed as emir by his son, Sheikh **Hamad bin Khalifa al-Thani** (1950–), who had been crown prince and defence minister since 1977.

Thant, U (1909–1974) Burmese diplomat, secretary general of the United Nations 1962–71. He helped to resolve the US–Soviet crisis over the Soviet installation of missiles in Cuba, and he made the controversial decision to withdraw the UN peacekeeping force from the Egypt–Israel border in 1967 (see *Arab-Israeli Wars).

Thatcher, Margaret Hilda (1925–) Baroness Thatcher; born **Margaret Hilda Roberts,** British Conservative politician, prime minister 1979–90. She was education minister 1970–74 and Conservative Party leader 1975–90. In 1982 she sent British troops to recapture the Falkland Islands from Argentina. She confronted trade-union power during the miners' strike 1984–85, sold off majority stakes in many public utilities to the private sector, and reduced the influence of local government through such measures as the abolition of metropolitan councils, the control of expenditure through 'rate-capping', and the introduction of the community charge, or poll tax, in 1989. In 1990, splits in the cabinet over the issues of

Europe and consensus government forced her resignation. An astute parliamentary tactician, she tolerated little disagreement, either from the opposition or from within her own party.

theocracy political system run by priests, as was once found in Tibet. In practical terms it means a system where religious values determine political decisions. The closest modern examples have been Iran during the period when Ayatollah Khomeini was its religious leader, 1979–89, and Afghanistan under the Islamic fundamentalist Taliban regime, 1996–2001. The term was coined by the historian Josephus in the 1st century AD.

Third Reich or **Third Empire**, Germany during the years of Adolf *Hitler's dictatorship after 1933. Hitler and the Nazis wanted to place their government into the history of Germany for both historical precedent and legitimacy. The idea of the Third Reich was based on the existence of two previous German empires: the medieval Holy Roman Empire, and the second empire of 1871 to 1918.

38th parallel demarcation line between North (People's Democratic Republic of) and South (Republic of) Korea, agreed at the Yalta Conference in 1945 and largely unaltered by the Korean War 1950–53.

Thompson, 'Big Bill' (1869–1944) born **William Hale Thompson**, US mayor. He was elected mayor for two terms 1916–24; he then dropped out of politics because his financial backer was indicted for fraud and race riots marred his term. He managed to get himself re-elected for another term (1928–32), this time backed by Al *Capone. Thompson's campaign to purge the school board and school libraries of all 'pro-British' elements resulted in his being derided throughout America. His political career faded out and he was the target of a number of suits charging corruption.

Thorez, Maurice (1900–1964) French communist politician. As leader of the French Communist Party (PCF) 1930–64, Thorez took it into the Popular Front alliance in the 1930s and was one of France's first three communists ministers when he joined General *de Gaulle's Provisional Government in November 1945.

Thorpe, (John) Jeremy (1929–) British Liberal politician, leader of the Liberal Party 1967–76.

thousand-bomber raid in World War II, massive air raid on the German city of Cologne, 31 May 1942. Some 898 RAF bombers actually arrived over Cologne and dropped 1,455 tons of bombs, starting 1200 fires; 18,440 buildings were destroyed and over 56,000 people made homeless.

three-day week in the UK, the policy adopted by Prime Minister Edward *Heath in January 1974 to combat an economic crisis and coal miners' strike.

A shortage of electrical power led to the allocation of energy to industry for only three days each week. A general election was called in February 1974, which the government lost.

Thurmond, J(ames) Strom (1902–2003) US governor and senator, a Democrat. He served as governor of South Carolina 1947–51. Although relatively progressive, especially in matters of education, he was staunchly opposed to the Democrats' civil-rights programme in 1948; at that year's convention he led the walkout of the Southern Democrats and ran as the presidential candidate of the State's Rights Democratic Party or 'Dixiecrats'. The split in the Democratic Party and disruption of the concept of the 'solid South' ultimately benefitted Truman, who went on to win an unexpected victory.

Tiananmen Square (Chinese 'Square of Heavenly Peace') paved open space in central Beijing, China, the largest public square in the world (area 0.4 sq km/0.14 sq mi). On 3–4 June 1989 more than 1,000 unarmed protesters were killed by government troops in a massacre that crushed China's emerging pro-democracy movement.

Tibet Chinese **Xizang**, autonomous region of southwestern China; area 1,221,600 sq km/471,700 sq mi; population (2000 est) 2,620,000 (many Chinese have settled in Tibet; 2 million Tibetans live in China outside Tibet). The capital is Lhasa. Although Tibet has its own People's Government and People's Congress, Tibetan nationalists regard the province as being under colonial rule. The controlling force in Tibet is the Communist Party of China, since China's occupation of Tibet in 1950. There is a government-in-exile in Dharmsala, Himachal Pradesh, India, where the Dalai Lama lives. The religion in the region is traditionally Lamaism (a form of Mahyna Buddhism).

Tikhonov, Nikolai Aleksandrovich (1905–1997) Soviet politician. He was a close associate of President Brezhnev, joining the Politburo 1979, and was prime minister (chair of the Council of Ministers) 1980–85. In April 1989 he was removed from the Central Committee.

Tilak, Bal Gangadhar (1856–1920) Indian nationalist politician and philosopher who was the leading campaigner for full independence before *Gandhi. Tilak gathered popular support by linking political action with an appeal to Hindu religious and cultural identity. He was twice imprisoned for anti-British activities, and founded the Home Rule League in 1914. In 1916, he signed the Lucknow Pact with the Muslim leader Muhammad Ali Jinnah, which united the Hindu and Muslim communities in the independence struggle.

Tilghman, William (Matthew) (1854–1924) US lawyer. An outstanding lawman in Kansas and Oklahoma (1877–1914), he also supervised the production of a motion picture, *The Passing of the Oklahoma*

Outlaws. He came out of retirement during the Prohibition period and was killed in Cromwell, Oklahoma. Tilghman was born in Fort Dodge, Iowa.

Tillett, Ben(jamin) (1860–1943) English trade union leader and politician. He became general secretary of the powerful Dockers' Union, and was a principal organizer of national strikes that hit Britain's docks in 1889 and 1911. He sat as Labour MP for North Salford, Lancashire, 1917–24 and 1929–31.

Tilsit, Treaty of peace treaty between Russia and France (under Napoleon I) 7 July 1807; also a treaty between Prussia and France 9 July 1807. The treaties were signed in the eastern Prussian town of Tilsit, which passed to Russia 1945 and was renamed Sovetsk.

Timoshenko, Semyon Konstantinovich (1895–1970) Soviet general in World War II; he was an old companion of Stalin and one of the few people he was prepared to trust.

Tindemans, Leo (1922–) Belgian politician. A regular holder of cabinet posts from 1968, he led the government from 1974 to 1978, and was appointed chair of the Christian People's Party (CVP) in 1979. A prominent role-player in the European Community, he was president of the Group of the European People's Party from 1992, and in 1993 was the first holder of the Jacques Delors chair in Maastricht.

Tinian, Battle of in World War II, successful US Marines operation in July 1944 to capture a Japanese-held island in the Marianas group.

Tirpitz German battleship in World War II, launched 1939 as a sister ship to the *Bismarck*. It sailed to Norway January 1942 and remained there, a permanent threat to Allied convoys bound for the USSR until it was sunk by the RAF November 1944.

Titanic British passenger liner, supposedly unsinkable, that struck an iceberg and sank off the Grand Banks of Newfoundland on its first voyage on 14–15 April 1912; estimates of the number of lives lost, largely due to inadequate provision of lifeboats, vary between 1,503 and 1,517. In 1985 it was located by robot submarine 4 km/2.5 mi down in an ocean canyon, preserved by the cold environment, and in 1987 salvage operations began.

Tito (1892–1980) adopted name of **Josip Broz**, Yugoslav communist politician, in effective control of Yugoslavia from 1943. In World War II he organized the National Liberation Army to carry on guerrilla warfare against the German invasion in 1941, and was created marshal in 1943. As prime minister 1945–53 and president from 1953, he followed a foreign policy of 'positive neutralism'.

Born in Croatia, Tito served in the Austrian army during World War I, was captured by the Russians, and fought in the Red Army during the civil wars. Returning to Yugoslavia in 1923, he became prominent as a communist and during World War II as partisan leader against the Nazis. In 1943 he established a provisional government and gained Allied recognition (previously given to the Chetniks) in 1944, and with Soviet help proclaimed the federal republic in 1945. As prime minister, he settled the Yugoslav minorities question on a federal basis, and in 1953 took the newly created post of president (for life from 1974). In 1948 he was criticized by the USSR and other communist countries for his successful system of decentralized profit-sharing workers' councils, and became a leader of the *non-aligned movement.

Tlatelolco, Treaty of international agreement signed in 1967 in Tlatelolco, Mexico, prohibiting nuclear weapons in Latin America.

Tobruk (or Tubruq) port, and only natural harbour, in Libya, 96 km/60 mi west of Bardia; population (1995 est) 127,000. The town has an oil refinery linked by a 560 km/348 mi pipeline to the Spirit oilfield. Another local industry is ship repair. Occupied by Italy in 1911, it was taken by Britain in 1941 during World War II, and unsuccessfully besieged by Axis forces April–December 1941. It was captured by Germany in June 1942 after the retreat of the main British force to Egypt. It was finally recaptured by the British in November 1942.

Todd, (Reginald Stephen) Garfield (1908–1992) New Zealand-born Rhodesian politician, prime minister of Southern Rhodesia (now Zimbabwe) 1953–58. He founded and led the United Rhodesia Party, but was removed as its leader by opponents of his liberal policies, which were also rejected by an increasingly right-wing White electorate. He was placed under restriction by the Rhodesian Front regime of Ian Smith 1965–76.

Togliatti, Palmiro (1893–1964) Italian politician who was a founding member of the Italian Communist Party in 1921 and effectively its leader for almost 40 years from 1926 until his death. In exile 1926–44, he returned after the fall of the Fascist dictator Mussolini to become a member of Badoglio's government and held office until 1946.

Togo country in West Africa, on the Atlantic Ocean, bounded north by Burkina Faso, east by Benin, and west by Ghana.

Tojo, Hideki (1884–1948) Japanese general and premier 1941–44 during World War II. Promoted to chief of staff of Japan's Guangdong army in Manchuria in 1937, he served as minister for war 1940–41 where he was responsible for negotiating the tripartite Axis alliance with Germany and Italy in 1940. He was held responsible for defeats in the Pacific in 1944 and forced to resign. After Japan's defeat, he was hanged as a war criminal.

Tolbert, William Richard (1913–1980) Liberian politician and 19th president of Liberia, 1971–80. He succeeded the long-standing president William V S Tubman, and was the last president to come from the American-African elite that had ruled Liberia for 160 years since its foundation. Tolbert was executed in a coup by African Liberians under Master Sergeant Samuel Doe in 1980.

Tonga country in the southwest Pacific Ocean, in Polynesia.

Tonkin Gulf Incident clash that triggered US entry into the Vietnam War in August 1964. Two US destroyers (USS *C Turner Joy* and USS *Maddox*) reported that they were fired on by North Vietnamese torpedo boats. It is unclear whether hostile shots were actually fired, but the reported attack was taken as a pretext for making air raids against North Vietnam.

On 7 August the US Congress passed the **Tonkin Gulf Resolution**, which formed the basis for the considerable increase in US military involvement in the Vietnam War.

totalitarianism government control of all activities within a country, openly political or otherwise, as in fascist or communist dictatorships. Examples of totalitarian regimes are Italy under Benito *Mussolini 1922–45; Germany under Adolf *Hitler 1933–45; the USSR under Joseph *Stalin from the 1930s until his death in 1953; and more recently Romania under Nicolae *Ceausescu 1974–89.

Touré, (Ahmed) Sékou (1922–1984) Guinean trade-union leader and politician, long-serving first president of the Republic of Guinea 1961–84. In 1958, de Gaulle wished France to retain its west African colonies as self-governing units within a French Community, but Touré successfully organized an overwhelming rejection of this in favour of full independence.

Townsend, Francis E(verett) (1867–1960) US physician and social reformer. Almost destitute as a result of ill health, he conceived of his old-age revolving pension plan for the elderly; its essential feature was that every American over 60 would be given a pension to be financed by a national sales tax. Within two years the so-called Townsend plan spawned a social movement with 2.25 million members throughout the USA and its own newspaper (1935). Several bills incorporating the Townsend plan were introduced in Congress in 1935–36, but his plans were later discredited by financial scandals.

Toynbee, Arnold Joseph (1889–1975) English historian whose *A Study of History* 1934–61 was an attempt to discover the laws governing the rise and fall of civilizations.

Trades Union Congress TUC, voluntary organization of trade unions, founded in the UK in 1868, in which delegates of affiliated unions meet annually to consider matters affecting their members. In 1997 there were 67 affiliated unions, with an aggregate membership of 6 million.

trade unionism, international worldwide cooperation between unions. In 1973 a European Trade Union Confederation was established, with a membership of 29 million, and there is an International Labour Organization, established in 1919 and affiliated to the United Nations from 1945, which formulates standards for labour and social conditions. Other organizations are the International Confederation of Free Trade Unions (1949) – which includes the American Federation of Labor and Congress of Industrial Organizations and the UK Trades Union Congress – and the World Federation of Trade Unions (1945).

Trail of Tears route traversed by 16,000 Cherokee in 1838 from their ancestral lands in North Carolina, Georgia, Tennessee, and Alabama to Indian Territory under the Indian Removal Act of 1830. Held initially in stockades by the US army, they were forced to march under military escort nearly 1,600 km / 1,000 mi in winter with little food; over 4,000 died from disease, hunger, and exposure. The Trail of Tears became a national monument in 1987.

Transport and General Workers' Union TGWU, UK trade union founded in 1921 by the amalgamation of a number of dockers' and road-transport workers' unions, previously associated in the Transport Workers' Federation. With more than 900,000 members, it ranks behind the public employees' union, UNISON, as the second-largest trade union in Britain.

transportation punishment of sending convicted persons to overseas territories to serve their sentences. It was introduced in England towards the end of the 17th century and although it was abolished in 1857 after many thousands had been transported, mostly to Australia, sentences of penal servitude continued to be partly carried out in Western Australia up until 1867. Transportation was used for punishment of criminals by France until 1938.

Traore, Moussa (1936–) Malian army officer and politician who seized power to become president of Mali in 1968 (and prime minister from 1969). He restored civilian government by 1979 and remained as president, but internal unrest continued and he was himself overthrown by the military in 1991. He was sentenced to death in 1993 for human rights abuses, but the sentence was reduced to life imprisonment. In 1999 he was sentenced to death for embezzlement, but the sentence was again commuted to life imprisonment by President Konare.

Treblinka German extermination camp 80 km/50 mi northwest of Warsaw. About 800,000 prisoners were killed here before a mass escape took place April 1943 in which many of the SS guards were killed by the inmates. After severe reprisals the camp was closed down and dismantled in November 1943.

Trenchard, Hugh Montague (1873–1956) 1st Viscount Trenchard, British aviator and police commissioner. He commanded the Royal Flying Corps in World War I 1915–17, and 1918–29 organized the Royal Air Force, becoming its first marshal 1927. As commissioner of the Metropolitan Police 1931–35, he established the Police College at Hendon and carried out the Trenchard Reforms, which introduced more scientific methods of detection. KCB 1918, baronet 1919, Baron 1930, Viscount 1936.

Treurnicht, Andries Petrus (1921–1993) South African Conservative Party politician. A former minister of the Dutch Reformed Church, he was elected to the South African parliament as a National Party member in 1971 but left it in 1982 to form a new right-wing Conservative Party, opposed to any dilution of the *apartheid system.

Trevelyan, George Macaulay (1876–1962) British historian. Regius professor of history at Cambridge 1927–40, he pioneered the study of social history, as in his *English Social History* 1942.

Trinidad and Tobago country in the West Indies, off the coast of Venezuela.

Triple Alliance pact from 1882 between Germany, Austria-Hungary, and Italy to offset the power of Russia and France. It was last renewed in 1912, but during World War I Italy's initial neutrality gradually changed and it denounced the alliance in 1915. The term also refers to other alliances: in 1668 – England, Holland, and Sweden; in 1717 – Britain, Holland, and France (joined in 1718 by Austria); in 1788 – Britain, Prussia, and Holland; in 1805 – Britain, Russia, and Austria (also known as the Third Coalition).

Triple Entente alliance of Britain, France, and Russia 1907–17. In 1911 this became a military alliance and formed the basis of the Allied powers in World War I against the Central Powers, Germany and Austria-Hungary.

Tripolitania   former province of *Libya, stretching from Cyrenaica in the east to Tunisia in the west, and from the Mediterranean some 1,300 km/809 mi into the Sahara Desert. It came under Turkish rule in the 16th century; Italy captured it from Turkey in 1912, and the British captured it from Italy in 1942 and controlled it until it was incorporated into the newly independent United Kingdom of Libya, established in 1951. In 1963 Tripolitania was subdivided into administrative divisions.

Trotsky, Leon (1879–1940)   adopted name of **Lev Davidovitch Bronstein**, Russian revolutionary. He joined the Bolshevik party and took a leading part in the seizure of power in 1917 and in raising the Red Army that fought the Civil War 1918–20. In the struggle for power that followed *Lenin's death in 1924, *Stalin defeated Trotsky, and this and other differences with the Communist Party led to his exile in 1929. He settled in Mexico, where he was assassinated at Stalin's instigation. Trotsky believed in world revolution and in permanent revolution, and was an uncompromising, if liberal, idealist.

Trotsky was isolated by Stalin, who used the opposition to Trotsky's belief that socialist revolution had to be exported by the USSR to the rest of the world, as well as the personal feud between Trotsky and Grigory *Zinovyev, head of the communist *International, to oust him. Trotsky was left without support and lost his power in the party. Trotsky had been described as capable but arrogant by Lenin, and it was this perceived arrogance and intellectual capacity that made him unpopular with many of the other Bolshevik leaders after Lenin's death in 1924. Stalin was then able to use Trotsky's ideas for the rapid industrialization of the Soviet Union through five-year plans, despite attacking the idea when Trotsky promoted it before his exile from Russia.

Truck Acts   UK acts of Parliament introduced 1831, 1887, 1896, and 1940 to prevent employers misusing wage-payment systems to the detriment of their workers. The legislation made it illegal to pay wages with goods in kind or with tokens for use in shops owned by the employers.

Trudeau, Pierre Elliott (1919–2000) Canadian Liberal politician. He was prime minister 1968–79 and 1980–84. In 1980, he was re-elected by a landslide on a platform opposing Québec separatism, and the Québec independence movement was later defeated in a referendum. He repatriated the constitution from the UK in 1982, but by 1984 had so lost support that he resigned.

Trujillo Molina, Rafael Leonidas (1891–1961)   Dominican Republic right-wing politician, dictator 1930–61, and president 1930–38 and 1942–52. As commander of the Dominican Guard, he seized power from President Horacio Vásquez and was elected president unopposed. He established a ruthless autocracy, aided by a powerful terroristic police force and murder squads, his personal control over much the economy, and his manipulation of 'puppet presidents'. There was economic progress and impressive public works projects, but at the cost of political repression and strained relations with neighbouring states, where he tried to foment right-wing revolutions. He was assassinated by military leaders in May 1961.

Truman Doctrine   US president Harry *Truman's 1947 dictum that the USA would 'support free peoples who are resisting attempted subjugation by armed minorities or by outside pressures'. It was used to justify sending a counter-insurgency military mission to Greece after World War II, and evolved into the policy of *containment of Soviet expansion. See also *United States of America, **the Truman Doctrine**.

Truman, Harry S (1884–1972)
33rd president of the USA 1945–53,
a Democrat. In January 1945 he became
vice-president to Franklin D Roosevelt,
and president when Roosevelt died in
April that year. He used the atomic
bomb against Japan to end World War
II, launched the *Marshall Plan to
restore Western Europe's post-war
economy, and nurtured the European
Community (now the European
Union) and NATO (including the
rearmament of West Germany).

Truth and Reconciliation Commission
South African government commission
established in August 1994 to
investigate state-sanctioned murders
and other human rights abuses under
the former apartheid regime. Its
chairman, since 1995, has been former
Archbishop Desmond *Tutu. The aims
of the Commission, as its title suggests,
are to discover the truth about what
happened in the era of apartheid and,
in so doing, to bring about a
reconciliation between both sides of
the divide.

Tsushima, Battle of during the
Russo–Japanese War, Japanese naval
victory over the Russians 27–28 May
1905, in the Strait of Tsushima between
Japan and Korea. This battle, the only
engagement between Dreadnought-
type battleships, was arguably one of
the greatest naval battles ever fought.

**Tubman, William Vacanarat Shadrach
(1895–1971)** Liberian politician.
The descendant of US slaves, he was a
lawyer in the USA. After his election to
the presidency of Liberia in 1944 he
concentrated on uniting the various
ethnic groups. Re-elected several times,
he died in office of natural causes,
despite frequent assassination attempts.

Tuchman, Barbara (1912–1989) US
historian. Her career as a nonacademic,
best-selling historian began in earnest
with her fourth book, the Pulitzer
prize-winning *The Guns of August*
(1962). *Stillwell and the American
Experience in China, 1911–45* (1971) won
a second Pulitzer. Her six best-sellers

sold many millions of copies. Tuchman
was born in New York City. After
graduating from Radcliffe College
(1933) and reporting on the Spanish
Civil War for the *Nation* (1937–38),
she turned to the study of history.

Tudjman, Franjo (1922–1999)
Croatian nationalist leader and
historian, president from 1990.
As leader of the centre-right Croatian
Democratic Union (CDU), he led the
fight for Croatian independence.
During the 1991–92 civil war, his
troops were hampered by lack of arms
and the military superiority of the
Serb-dominated federal army, but
Croatia's independence was recognized
following a successful United Nations-
negotiated ceasefire in January 1992.
Tudjman was re-elected in August 1992
and again in October 1995. Despite
suffering from stomach cancer, he was
re-elected president in June 1997. He died
in December 1999 while still president.

Tunisia country in North Africa, on the
Mediterranean Sea, bounded southeast
by Libya and west by Algeria.

government The 1959 constitution,
amended in 1988, provides for a
president, who is both head of state
and government, elected by universal
suffrage for a five-year term. The
president cannot serve more than three
terms. There is a single-chamber,
163-member national assembly, also
directly elected for a five-year term
(144 by simple majority voting and,
from 1993, 19 reserved for parties
failing to win a majority in each of the
country's 25 constituencies, so as to
ensure the presence of an opposition
in the national assembly).

The president appoints a prime
minister and a council of ministers.

history Founded as Carthage by the
Phoenicians in the 8th century BC,
Tunisia was under Arab rule from the
7th century AD until it became part
of the *Ottoman Empire in 1574.
It harboured the Barbary Coast pirates
until the 19th century. It became a
French protectorate in 1883.

The Destour Socialist Party (PSD), founded in 1934 by Habib Bourguiba, led Tunisia's campaign for independence from France. The country achieved internal self-government in 1955 and full independence in 1956, with Bourguiba as prime minister. A year later the monarchy was abolished, and Tunisia became a republic, with Bourguiba as president. A new constitution was adopted in 1959, and the first national assembly elected. Bourguiba was made president for life in 1975. Between 1963 and 1981 the PSD was the only legally recognized party, but others were subsequently formed. In November 1986 the PSD won all the assembly seats, while other parties boycotted the elections.

foreign affairs President Bourguiba followed a distinctive foreign policy, establishing links with the Western powers, including the USA, but joining other Arab states in condemning the US-inspired Egypt–Israel treaty. He allowed the Palestine Liberation Organization to use Tunis as its headquarters, provoking an Israeli attack in 1985 and straining relations with the USA. Diplomatic links with Libya were severed in 1985, and not restored until 1988.

Bourguiba's firm and paternalistic rule, and his long period in Tunisian politics, made him a national legend. However, in November 1987 he was deposed and replaced by Zine el-Abidine Ben Ali. In July 1988, a number of significant constitutional changes were announced, presaging a move to more pluralist politics, but in the April 1989 elections the renamed PSD, now the Constitutional Democratic Rally (RCD), won all 141 assembly seats. During the Gulf War January-February 1991 which followed Iraq's invasion of Kuwait, there were anti-US protests in Tunisia.

crackdown on Islamic militants Ben Ali's active repression and alleged torture of Islamic fundamentalists provoked criticism from Western nations in January 1992. The West saw the government crackdown as a major setback in Tunisia's progress towards democracy.

Changes to the electoral system were approved in 1993, introducing proportional representation for 19 of the 144 seats in the national assembly. In the March 1994 presidential election Ben Ali, as the only candidate, won 99% of the vote. The RCD won more than 90% of the vote in the concurrent assembly elections.

In March 1996, the leader the Movement of Social Democrats (MDS), the main opposition party, was jailed for his secret contacts with Libyan agents.

The government of Tunisia in November 1999 released several hundred political prisoners. It was the largest release since the crackdown on Islamist activists and sympathizers in the early 1990s.

In December 1999 Ben Ali, the re-elected president, named the head of his new government to be Mohamed Ghannouchi, an economist, and the interior minister to be Abdallah Kallel, who had taken a hard line against Islamists in the early 1990s. In December 2000, a leading human-rights activist, Moncef Marzouki, was imprisoned for one year.

In April 2002 the international islamic terrorist group al-Qaeda claimed responsibility for an explosion at a synagogue on the island of Djerba that killed 16 people, 10 of them German tourists.

Tupamaros urban guerrilla movement operating in Uruguay, aimed at creating a Marxist revolution, largely active in the 1960s and 1970s, named after 18th-century revolutionary Túpac Amaru. It was founded by Raúl Sendic (died 1989); he served more than 13 years in prison.

Turkey country between the Black Sea to the north and the Mediterranean Sea to the south, bounded to the east by

Armenia, Georgia, and Iran, to the southeast by Iraq and Syria, to the west by Greece and the Aegean Sea, and to the northwest by Bulgaria.

government The constitution of 1982 provides for a single-chamber, 550-member national assembly, elected by a system of proportional representation for a five-year term, and an executive president, elected by the assembly for a seven-year term. The president appoints a prime minister who works with the president in a somewhat diluted version of the French 'dual executive'. The president is obliged to work in conjunction with the prime minister.

the establishment of the republic In July 1922 Rauf Bey, who with Kemal Atatürk had been mainly instrumental in launching the Nationalist revolution, became prime minister. On 1 November 1922 the sultanate was abolished. The National Assembly then elected the cousin of the deposed sultan, Abdul Mejid Effendi, to be caliph, the 'Commander of the Faithful', but with no secular powers. This 'spiritual' caliphate was finally abolished in 1924, and the Muslim religion was disestablished in 1928. Meanwhile, on 2 October 1923, the foreign occupation of Constantinople (now Istanbul) terminated, and on 29 October Turkey was declared a republic with Atatürk as president.

The republic took the form of a powerful oligarchy led by a dictator and depending on press censorship. The westernization of Turkey was forcibly and rigorously carried through, and a new legal code introduced. Once the work of westernizing Turkey was more or less completed, Atatürk, now known as the 'Ghazi' (conqueror), relaxed his methods of dictatorial reform, although his position always remained unassailable. In the new economic system the state reserved the right to plan the general economic course and,

while allowing private enterprise, owned the leading industries and supervised and coordinated the activities of private concerns.

Atatürk's foreign relations Atatürk largely restricted the new Turkish state to the area actually inhabited by Turks, although it also included some of the Kurdish lands in the east. The Kurdish rebellion in 1925 aggravated the question of the Turkish–Iraqi boundary in the area of Mosul. Eventually, on 6 June 1926, almost the whole area was given by treaty to Iraq. Relations with Iran were also stabilized.

In 1934 Turkey joined in a regional pact with Greece, Yugoslavia, and Romania, each country guaranteeing each other's frontiers, and in the same year, by the Pact of Saadabad, Turkey strengthened its political cooperation with Iraq, Iran, and Afghanistan. Following the restoration of Turkish sovereignty over the Dardanelles in 1936 and the cession of Alexandretta (now Iskenderun) by Syria to Turkey in 1939, Turkish relations with the Western democracies became closer. An Anglo-French guarantee against aggression was given to Turkey in May 1939, and this was followed on 19 October by an Anglo-French–Turkish pact of assistance, effective for 15 years.

Turkey in World War II Atatürk's death in 1938 was a major shock to the republic. But the regime of his Republican People's Party, now under President Ismet *Inönü, was sufficiently sturdy to survive.

In World War II Turkey's position became difficult following the German successes in the Balkans in 1941, and Turkey found a semicircle of Axis forces round its western borders. Turkey came under great pressure from Germany, and in June 1941 the Turkish government had little option but to sign a 'Treaty of Friendship' with Germany. However, the situation changed with the victories won by the

Allies in 1942–43 at El Alamein and Stalingrad, and eventually, in February 1945, the Turkish parliament decided to declare war on Germany and Japan.

Turkey joins the Western alliance
In 1945 the USSR denounced the treaty of friendship that it had made with Turkey in 1925, and in the following year made a demand for a revision of the 1936 Montreux convention by which Turkey had gained the right to remilitarize the Straits between the Black Sea and the Mediterranean. This marked the end of a distinct phase in Turkish–Soviet relations: following the revolutions in both countries friendly relations had been established in the 1920s, accompanied by economic cooperation, but after World War II this gave way once more to the traditional grouping of Turkey in the Western European sphere of influence.

The USA recognized the important position that Turkey held as a barrier against the spread of communism into the Middle East and Asia, and made substantial loans in order that Turkey could utilize to the full its economic resources and strengthen its defences. In 1950 Turkey dispatched troops to form part of the US-led UN forces in the Korean War, and in 1952 it became a member of NATO.

In 1953 Turkey signed a treaty of friendship with Greece and Yugoslavia (the latter having split from the Soviet bloc). Turkey's treaty in 1954 with Pakistan was the foundation stone of the subsequent *Baghdad Pact (1955), which later became the *Central Treaty Organization (CENTO). During the *Suez Crisis of 1957 Turkey remained on good terms with both Britain and France.

the Menderes era, 1950–60 Until 1945 the Republican People's Party tolerated virtually no opposition parties; but after that date genuine opposition parties were allowed to be formed and greater democratic liberties permitted. In Turkey's first free elections in 1950 the leading opposition party, the Democratic Party, gained power under Celal Bayar and Adnan Menderes. Bayar became president, and Menderes prime minister. In the elections of 1954 the Democratic Party virtually obliterated all the other opposition parties. Turkey's foreign policy, based on cooperation with Western Europe, remained unchanged, but as time passed the Menderes regime appeared increasingly reactionary and intolerant in home affairs, particularly towards other parties.

From 1953 onwards Greek–Turkish relations suffered a steady deterioration, owing to their very different approaches to the *Cyprus question. Relations reached a low point in 1955, when serious anti-Greek rioting broke out in Turkey, causing substantial damage and loss of life. The 1959 London and Zürich agreements between Greece, Turkey, and Britain, which set up an independent Cyprus with guarantees for the Turkish minority there, led to a marked improvement in Greek–Turkish relations for a time.

In 1957 the Democratic Party was again returned to power, but with a reduced majority. Discontent was, however, growing among the army and the intellectuals, who saw Atatürk's Turkey threatened by Menderes's economic incompetence, corruption, authoritarianism, and increasing partiality to Islam. In May 1960 the Menderes regime was overthrown in an army coup led by Gen Cemal Gürsel. Menderes, President Bayar, and others were tried for treason; Menderes was executed, but Bayar's sentence was commuted to imprisonment.

Inönü returns to power, 1961–65
Parliamentary government was reestablished during 1961, and elections were held in October. Gürsel became president, and former

president Ismet Inönü, of Atatürk's Republican People's Party, became premier. The main opposition group, the Justice Party, adopted many of the policies formerly held by the proscribed Democratic Party.

Inönü's government worked for friendlier relations with the USSR, while retaining Turkey's Western alliances. This policy was partially influenced by Turkish suspicions that Britain and the USA were pro-Greek in their attitude to the Cyprus question, which flared up again in December 1963, when Archbishop Makarios, the Cypriot president, declared Cyprus's intention of repealing the London and Zürich agreements unilaterally. For a time the whole NATO structure in the Mediterranean was threatened by Greek–Turkish hostility, and Turkish aircraft raided Cyprus in a defensive action to protect the Turkish Cypriots there. With the acceptance by Turkey and Greece of United Nations intervention and mediation in Cyprus, an uneasy lull followed.

Many Turks considered that their government had been too compliant over Cyprus, and this increased the difficulties of Inönü's coalition government. Between 1961 and 1965, through successive coalitions, Inönü had just succeeded in keeping the political system in being, staving off two coup attempts in 1962 and 1963, but in 1965 Inönü resigned.

Demirel and the return of military rule, 1965–73 Elections were held in October 1965, and the right-wing Justice Party won an absolute majority over all other parties. Its leader, Süleyman *Demirel, became premier.

In March 1966 Gen Sunay was elected president in succession to Gursel, who had become incurably ill. The Justice Party experienced increasing difficulties with its allies at home in parliament and, in the case of the USA, abroad. A further crisis in 1967–68 over Cyprus almost led to war with Greece.

From 1968 clashes between political extremists and with the army became more violent. In 1969 the Justice Party was returned in the election, but, because the party split, it had a reduced majority. Prompted by strikes and student unrest, the army forced Demirel to resign in March 1971, and for the next two years the country was under military rule again. During this period Turkey's reputation suffered because of the curtailment of civil liberties, and a war was fought against urban guerrillas.

the invasion of Cyprus and its aftermath, 1974–76 After the lifting of martial law, elections were permitted in October 1973, and the Republican People's Party (RPP) under Bulent *Ecevit, who had opposed military domination, won a slim, but not overall, majority. He succeeded in forming a coalition, which lasted between January and September 1974.

Ecevit's reputation was greatly enhanced at home as a result of the invasion and occupation of northern Cyprus in July 1974 to protect the Turkish-Cypriot community, following the coup against Makarios by Greek Cypriots in favour of union with Greece. The Turkish invasion resulted in the effective partition of the island.

Ecevit resigned because of difficulties in his coalition in September 1974, largely due to his refusal to annex northern Cyprus. Only in March 1975 did Demirel succeed in forming another coalition government. This polarization in politics resulted in a new growth of disorders beween left- and right-wing forces on the university campuses, and an inability of the government to cope with Turkey's economic problems.

Relations were inevitably strained with Greece, over the sovereignty of the Aegean islands as well as over Cyprus, and inertia over the search for a solution in Cyprus led to a crisis with the USA. An embargo was imposed on arms supplies for a time, and Turkey retaliated with closer control over US bases. The Soviet prime minister paid a successful visit in December 1975. However, with instability and political deadlock dominating the domestic front, the renewed intervention of the armed forces seemed a possibility. Following an embargo on arms by the USA and the closure of the US defence installations in 1975, a new defence agreement was signed in March 1976. In July and August of that year military confrontation arose between Greece and Turkey as a result of Turkish explorations for oil in areas of the Aegean Sea to which Greece laid claim. With rejection by the International Court of Justice of Greece's request for an injunction on further Turkish prospecting the crisis passed.

political instability and military rule, 1977–83 At elections held in June 1977, the RPP won 221 seats in the national assembly, but Ecevit was unable to form a government, and in July Demirel became prime minister. His government was a coalition of his Justice Party, the National Salvation Party, and the Nationalist Action Party. Demirel precariously held on to power until 1978, when Ecevit returned, leading another coalition. He was faced with a deteriorating economy and outbreaks of sectional violence, and by 1979 had lost his working majority and resigned.

Demirel returned in November, but the violence continued, and in September 1980 the army stepped in and set up a national security council, with Bulent Ulusu as prime minister. Martial law was imposed, political activity suspended, and a harsh regime established.

democracy restored, 1983–91 Strong international pressure was put on Turkey to return to a more democratic system of government, and in May 1983 political parties were allowed to operate again. The old parties reformed under new names and in November three of them contested the Assembly elections: the conservative Motherland Party (ANAP), the Nationalist Democracy Party (MDP), and the Populist Party (SDPP). The ANAP won a large majority and its leader, Turgut Özal, became prime minister. Özal and the ANAP retained their majority in the 1987 election. In 1989 Özal was elected president, with Yildirim Akbulut as prime minister. In 1991 Mesut Yilmaz replaced Akbulut as head of the ANAP and became prime minister.

By 1987 Turkey was making overtures to join the European Community (EC; the predecessor of the European Union or EU). Long criticized for its violations of human rights, at the end of 1989 Turkey learned that its application for membership of the EC had been refused and would not be considered again until at least the mid-1990s. During the 1990–91 Gulf War, Turkey supported the US-led forces, allowing use of vital bases in the country.

the Kurdish conflict Ethnic Kurds had long suffered discrimination in Turkey, and from 1984 there had been guerrilla fighting in Kurdistan, and a separatist *Workers' Party of Kurdistan (PKK) was active.

During the early 1990s Kurdish separatist activity escalated both within Turkey and in Europe, where Turkish businesses were targeted in several leading cities. In March 1995 the government launched a full-scale offensive into northern Iraq in an attempt to eliminate PKK bases there. This, along with a second action in July 1995, was widely condemned by the international community.

By the end of 1995 it was estimated that a total of 19,000 people had been killed since the hostilities began in 1984. A government crackdown was announced, but in April 1996 some of the bloodiest fighting of the separatist campaign took place, with a new Turkish offensive that claimed the lives of over 130 combatants – the Turkish government having ignored the rebel leader's unilateral ceasefire declaration in December 1995.

Support for the PKK appeared to be decreasing inside Turkey; a Kurdish nationalist party endorsed by pro-PKK media won only 4% of the vote in the December 1995 elections. The PKK, however, has an effective financial base among the half-million-strong Kurdish diaspora in Europe, and is aided by covert support from Syria and other rivals of Turkey.

In late 1998 Abdullah Ocalan, the leader of the PKK, who had been under house arrest in Italy for a month, was freed. In a ruling that looked likely to worsen the diplomatic crisis between Italy and Turkey, an appeals court in Rome ruled that restrictions on Ocalan's movements were no longer justified. Ocalan, whom Turkey wanted extradited from Italy as a terrorist, had requested political asylum, provoking a Turkish embargo on imports from Italy.

Turkish politics in the 1990s
Following an inconclusive general election in October 1991, Demirel formed a coalition government with the support of the Social Democratic Populist Party, becoming premier for the seventh time.

President Turgut Özal died suddenly of a heart attack in April 1993. Demirel was elected president in May, and Tansu Ciller of the True Path Party (DYP) became Turkey's first female prime minister. In the 1994 assembly elections, the Islamicist Welfare Party made substantial gains.

In an attempt to boost the economy, the lira was devalued in January 1994. Following a rise in annual inflation to more than 70%, the government announced measures designed to stabilize the nation's economy, but by the end of 1994 the annual inflation rate had risen to 149%. During 1994, Turkey borrowed $742 million from the International Monetary Fund.

In September 1995, the governing coalition collapsed. A customs deal was agreed with the EU (formerly EC) in December. The December elections proved inconclusive, with the Islamicist Welfare Party winning the largest numbers of seats. After weeks of negotiation, Ciller and ANAP leader Mesut Yilmaz agreed in February 1996 on a rotating five-year ANAP–DYP coalition, with Yilmaz as premier. In May 1996 the DYP withdrew from the coalition.

In March 1997 Prime Minister Erbaken bowed to public pressure for measures to stamp out Muslim fundamentalism and in the following month concluded a 18-point agreement with senior military officers that would further curb the growth of the Islamic movement at the expense of the secular state.

The broad-based coalition government of Mesut Yilmaz won a vote of confidence in July 1997, proclaiming a government of national unity and promising to reduce the influence of Islamists. After 11 months of Islamist-led government, the new government showed an understanding of secularism which appeared to be in line with that prevalent in Western Europe. The government, however, collapsed in November 1998 when Mesut Yilmaz this time lost a vote of confidence. After Yalim Erez, an independent politician, failed in early January 1999 to form a government, he was replaced as prime minister by Bulent Ecevit. Ecevit's centre-left party won most seats in a general election in April 1999. The far-right nationalist National Action Party came second and an Islamist party third. Ecevit's coalition government, which included the National Action Party, won a vote of confidence in June.

The trial of Abdullah Ocalan, the leader of the PKK, who had been arrested in Europe, began in May 1999. He was charged with treason and attempting to divide the state by force, and sentenced to death in June. Across Europe, Kurds protested and governments condemned the verdict.

In November 1999 the death sentence was upheld by a Turkish appeal court, leading Ocalan to appeal to the European Court of Human Rights.

Ocalan told his fighters in August 1999 to withdraw from the country's southeast and ordered them to halt all attacks. The PKK announced that it would lay down its arms and end 15 years of violence. The USA then told Ankara that, with the PKK all but defeated, it must recognize the rights of Turkey's Kurdish minority. At the same time, the US administration called on the PKK to end the violence. Ocalan appealed to the Turkish government to begin a dialogue with the PKK, saying his guerrillas were prepared to hand over their arms in exchange for Kurdish rights. The PKK turned itself into a legitimate political organization in February 2000, announcing that it renounced the armed struggle it had waged against the Turkish government for the past 15 years.

In December 1999, Turkey was at last declared a candidate for entry to the EU, but in order to become a full member it would need to meet EU criteria on human rights and settle its territorial dispute with Greece. Hopes for joining the EU were jeopardized, and domestic peace troubled in February 2000, when the leader of the only legally recognized Kurdish party, the People's Democracy Party (Hadep), and the mayors of three cities in Turkey's Kurdish southeastern region (also members of Hadep), were charged with helping the outlawed PKK. Turan Demir, head of Hadep,

was sentenced to three years and nine months' imprisonment. The president of the European parliament urged Turkey to free the mayors, and although her request was initially rejected, the mayors were set free at the end of February, pending the outcome of their trial.

The Turkish parliament voted in April 2000 to prevent a change to the constitution that would have allowed the president, Suleyman Demirel, run for a second term. Officially the position of the Turkish president is largely ceremonial, but Demirel's predecessor, Turgut Ozal, made the role more influential. In May 2000 Judge Ahmet Necdet Sezer was sworn in as the new president. He pledged reform to push the country towards EU acceptance, which would involve sweeping legal reform in order to implement European standards on Turkish law. In August, he overruled a decree that had allowed the government to dismiss bureaucrats deemed too pro-Kurdish or insufficiently secular.

amnesty Nearly 20,000 prisoners were freed in late December 2000 under an amnesty law designed to reduce crowding in prisons. The amnesty was criticized because it did not apply to Turkey's many political prisoners.

financial crisis During November 2000, Turkey fell into a financial and banking crisis, triggered by an investigation into corruption among bankers. After two and a half weeks, the International Monetary Fund (IMF) stepped in with a US$10 billion aid package, which reversed the stock market fall. However, in February 2001, criticisms of Prime Minister Bulent Ecevit by President Ahmed Necdet Sezera over a corruption investigation led to another stock market crash, thousands of job losses, and the decision to float the lira, the value of which then plummeted. The collapse of Turkey's exchange-rate policy forced the government to abandon the IMF programme and announce new reforms, including the sale of debt-ridden state companies. More than 50,000 people stormed barriers and tried to march on Turkey's parliament in Ankara in April when Ecevit refused to step down.

Also in March, the government unveiled planned changes to the justice system to meet European Union conditions for membership. In April the human rights group Amnesty International urged Turkish authorities to end the abuse of prisoners. Many inmates, 17 of whom had died, were on hunger-strike in protest of their conditions. Others were on hunger-strike to highlight their transfer to isolation. In May the European Court of Human Rights ruled that Turks had violated almost every article of the European Human Rights Convention after their invasion of Cyprus in 1974. In June, European MPs again urged Turkey to conform to human rights laws on prisons, after 23 inmates died in hunger strikes protesting at the smaller cells they said subjected them to isolation and mistreatment.

political party banned In June 2001, Turkey's Constitutional Court banned the pro-Islamic opposition party, Fazilet Partisi (FP; Virtue Party), on the grounds that it had flouted the country's strictly secular political system. In August, the popular politician Tayyib Erdogan, a former mayor of Istanbul, set up a new Islamic party, the Justice and Development Party (AK), from the moderate faction of the FP.

In October, Turkey's parliament approved a package of 34 amendments to the constitution to help pave the way for membership of the EU. Among other reforms, restrictions against the use of the Kurdish language were to be relaxed. But the package fell short of EU hopes as the

death penalty was retained, although its use was restricted to cases of terrorism, and under threat or in times of war. Further reforms were enacted the following month, with women being formally recognized in law. In early December, Turkey lifted its objections to the formation of a 60,000-strong EU rapid-reaction force. Turkey, a member of NATO, had wanted to deny the EU access to the alliance's assets unless it was given a veto over their use.

In July 2002 parliament voted to hold elections in November, 18 months early, despite the objections of Prime Minister Ecevit who headed a disintegrating coalition government of his own Democratic Party, the right-wing Nationalist Movement Party, and the Motherland Party. The political turmoil followed the resignation from the Democratic Party of foreign minister Ismail Cem and other senior party figures earlier in the month.

Turkmenistan country in central Asia, bounded north by Kazakhstan and Uzbekistan, west by the Caspian Sea, and south by Iran and Afghanistan.

Tutu, Desmond Mpilo (1931–) South African priest, Anglican archbishop of Cape Town 1986–96 and secretary general of the South African Council of Churches 1979–84. One of the leading figures in the struggle against *apartheid in the Republic of South Africa, he was awarded the Nobel Prize for Peace in 1984 for encouraging peaceful reconciliation between the black and white communities.

In November 1995 Tutu was named as the head of the *Truth and Reconciliation Commission, a commission set up in June 1995 by Nelson Mandela to investigate abuses by both government and opposition groups during the apartheid era.

Tuvalu country in the southwest Pacific Ocean; formerly (until 1978) the Ellice Islands; part of Polynesia.

Twenty-one demands Japanese attempt 18 January 1915 to make China a virtual protectorate if 21 'outstanding questions' were not resolved. China's president *Yüan Shikai submitted to the extension of Japanese power in Manchuria, Shandong, the Chang Jiang valley, and the southeast, but refused to appoint Japanese political and financial advisers to his government.

Typhoid Mary (c. 1870–1938) born **Mary Mallon**, US typhoid carrier.

Working as a private cook while carrying the bacteria that cause typhoid fever, she infected wealthy New York families with the disease (1904–07). Never ill herself, she was finally tracked down and hospitalized in New York City (1907–10) to protect others. Discovered cooking again for a New Jersey sanatorium in 1914, she was hospitalized for life. It is estimated that Mallon passed the disease on to at least 50 people, three of whom died.

U

U-2 US military reconnaissance aeroplane, used in secret flights over the USSR from 1956 to photograph military installations. In 1960 a U-2 was shot down over the USSR and the pilot, Gary Powers, was captured and imprisoned. He was exchanged for a US-held Soviet agent two years later.

Uganda landlocked country in East Africa, bounded north by Sudan, east by Kenya, south by Tanzania and Rwanda, and west by the Democratic Republic of Congo (formerly Zaire).

government The 1969 constitution was suspended following a military coup in 1985 and a National Resistance Council (NRC) set up, consisting of 210 elected and 68 presidentially appointed members. In 1994 a constituent assembly, comprising 214 elected and 74 nominated members, was formed to review a proposed new multiparty constitution. The president governs in collaboration with the NRC, through a cabinet whom he appoints.

history Uganda was a British protectorate 1894–1962. It became an independent member of the *Commonwealth in 1962, with Dr Milton Obote, leader of the Uganda People's Congress (UPC), as prime minister. In 1963 it was proclaimed a federal republic; King Mutesa II became president, ruling through a cabinet. King Mutesa was deposed in a coup in 1966, and Obote became executive president. One of his first acts was to end the federal status. After an attempt to assassinate him in 1969, Obote banned all opposition and established what was effectively a one-party state.

Idi Amin's regime In 1971 Obote was overthrown in an army coup led by Maj-Gen Idi *Amin Dada, who suspended the constitution and all political activity and took legislative and executive powers into his own hands. Obote fled to Tanzania. Amin proceeded to wage what he called an 'economic war' against foreign domination, resulting in the mass expulsion of people of Asian ancestry, many of whom settled in Britain. In 1976 Amin claimed that large tracts of Kenya historically belonged to Uganda and accused Kenya of cooperating with the Israeli government in a raid on Entebbe airport to free hostages held in a hijacked aircraft. Relations with Kenya became strained, and diplomatic links with Britain were severed. During the next two years the Amin regime carried out a widespread campaign against any likely opposition, resulting in thousands of deaths and imprisonments. The East African Community consisting of Tanzania, Kenya, and Uganda, formed in 1967, collapsed in 1977.

military coups In 1978, when Amin annexed the Kagera area of Tanzania, near the Ugandan border, the Tanzanian president, Julius Nyerere, sent troops to support the Uganda National Liberation Army (UNLA), which had been formed to fight Amin. Within five months Tanzanian troops had entered the Uganda capital, Kampala, forcing Amin to flee, first to Libya and then to Saudi Arabia. A provisional government, drawn from a cross-section of exiled groups, was set up, with Dr Yusuf Lule as president. Two months later Lule was replaced by Godfrey Binaisa who, in turn, was overthrown by the army. A military commission made arrangements for national elections, which were won by the UPC, and Milton Obote came back to power.

Obote's government was soon under pressure from a range of exiled groups operating outside the country and guerrilla forces inside, and he was only kept in office by the presence of Tanzanian troops. When they were withdrawn in June 1982 a major offensive was launched against the Obote government by the National Resistance Movement (NRM) and the National Resistance Army (NRA), led by Dr Lule and Yoweri Museveni. By 1985 Obote was unable to control the army, which had been involved in indiscriminate killings, and he was ousted in July in a coup led by Gen Tito Okello. Obote fled to Kenya and then Zambia, where he was given political asylum.

national reconciliation Okello had little more success in controlling the army and, after a brief period of power-sharing with the NRA, fled to Sudan in January 1986. Museveni was sworn in as president and announced a policy of national reconciliation, promising a return to normal parliamentary government within three to five years. He formed a cabinet in which most of Uganda's political parties were represented and worked at consolidating his hold domestically, reviving the economy, and improving African relations, as in the nonaggression treaty signed with Sudan in 1990. Ugandan Asians were encouraged to return and reclaim their businesses, and in 1993 the Baganda monarchy was reinstated, in the person of Ronald Muwenda Mutebi II. A draft multiparty constitution was published in March 1993 and twelve months later Museveni's supporters won the majority of seats in elections to a constituent assembly, which was to review the proposed new constitution.

In May 1996 Yoweri Museveni had a landslide victory in the country's first direct presidential elections.

In October 1997 rebel forces, led by the Allied Democratic Forces (ADF), threatened the country's stability.

The end of 1999 saw a rise in diplomatic successes for the country, when in November Musevini signed an agreement with the leaders of Tanzania and Kenya to establish the East African Community, which was intended to create a common market and political federation similar to that of the European Union. In December 1999, Musevini signed a treaty with Sudanese president Omar al-Bashir, promising to halt support to rebel groups in each other's countries, attempting to bring an end to five years of rebel wars across their mutual border, and to restore diplomatic ties between Sudan and Uganda. However, despite the peace deal between Sudan and Uganda, rebels in Sudan attacked towns in northern Uganda, and battles continued along the Congo–Uganda border between rebels and the Ugandan army. The new wave of violence forced the United Nations (UN) to halt deliveries of food to 100,000 displaced people. Violence in the Democratic Republic of Congo continued as troops from Uganda and Rwanda, supporting different factions of the Congolese rebels, ignored an agreement to an internationally supervised withdrawal from the rebel-held city of Kisangani, and continued to fight. UN secretary general Kofi Annan urged the UN to impose sanctions on Uganda and Rwanda, to force them out of Congo.

Voters, in a referendum in June 2000, chose to remain with President Musevini's 'no party' system, in which parties are allowed to exist, but are unable to support candidates in elections.

Domesday cult killings 2000
After a fire at the headquarters of the Restoration of the Ten Commandments of God cult in western Uganda killed up to 500 people in March 2000, it was

revealed that the cult may also have been responsible for the kidnapping and murder of children, and for more than 400 bodies which have been exhumed from mass burial sites. The Ugandan government, which had at first considered the March incident to be mass suicide, issued the cult leaders' arrest warrants for mass murder. The government and the police force faced mounting pressure to explain how the activities of the cult could have gone unchecked.

ebola outbreak In Uganda's first recorded outbreak of the ebola virus, over 160 people were known to have died from the deadly and highly contagious virus between September and December 2000, with a further 405 confirmed cases of the disease.

presidential elections President Museveni of Uganda was re-elected with 69% of the vote in presidential elections held in March 2001. Observers estimated that up to 15% of the vote had been affected by serious irregularities, but that the result did reflect the voters' wishes. The main challenger to Museveni, Kizza Besigye, did not accept the result and petitioned the Supreme Court to annul the poll. The poll was seen as a democratic litmus test for Museveni.

Fighting in the Congo lessened as the first armed UN troops arrived in late March 2001. 2,500 UN troops in all were deployed. Uganda withdrew some of its troops from the east of the country, and Ugandan-backed rebels in the north ended their violence.

In November, a peace agreement was signed with Rwanda following talks in London, England. It aimed to prevent further hostilities by cracking down on cross-border support for dissidents.

Ukraine country in eastern central Europe, bounded to the east by Russia, north by Belarus, south by Moldova, Romania, and the Black Sea, and west by Poland, the Slovak Republic, and Hungary.

Ulbricht, Walter (1893–1973) East German communist politician, in power 1960–71. He lived in exile in the USSR during Hitler's rule 1933–45. A Stalinist, he became first secretary of the Socialist Unity Party in East Germany in 1950 and (as chair of the Council of State from 1960) was instrumental in the building of the Berlin Wall in 1961. He established East Germany's economy and recognition outside the Eastern European bloc.

Ulster Defence Association UDA, Northern Ireland Protestant paramilitary organization responsible for a number of sectarian killings. Fanatically loyalist, it established a paramilitary wing (the Ulster Freedom Fighters) to combat the *Irish Republican Army (IRA) on its own terms and by its own methods. No political party has acknowledged any links with the UDA. In 1994, following a cessation of military activities by the IRA, the UDA, along with other Protestant paramilitary organizations, declared a ceasefire.

Ulster Unionist Party or **Official Unionist Party (OUP)**, the largest political party in Northern Ireland. Right-of-centre in orientation, its aim is equality for Northern Ireland within the UK, and it opposes union with the Republic of Ireland. The party has the broadest support of any Northern Irish party, and has consistently won a large proportion of parliamentary and local seats. Its central organization, dating from 1905, is formally called the Ulster Unionist Council. Its leader from 1995 is David Trimble. It secured 28 of the 108 seats in the new Northern Ireland Assembly, elected in June 1998, and Trimble was elected Northern Ireland's first minister at the Assembly's first meeting on 1 July (he resigned in June 2001, but agreed to stand for re-election in October 2001).

Ulster Volunteer Force UVF, in Northern Ireland, most recently a loyalist (pro-Union) paramilitary group, especially active in the 1970s, 1980s, and early 1990s. Originally a paramilitary wing of the Ulster Unionists, the first UVF was formed in 1912 to coordinate ad hoc paramilitary activity. A second UVF, active in the Anglo-Irish War, became part of the Ulster Special Constabulary. The name was revived in 1966 for a Belfast-based group, which was legalized in 1974 but banned the following year. In 1994 the UVF was one of the signatories to a loyalist ceasefire.

Ulundi   joint capital of KwaZulu-Natal Province in the Republic of South Africa; population (1991 est) 11,100. It was the capital of the Zulu kingdom and site of the battle that ended the Anglo-Zulu War in July 1879. The defeated Zulu king, Cetewayo, was captured and banished to Cape Town. Ulundi was razed to the ground and Zululand annexed by the British. It was rebuilt in the 1970s as capital of the former independent homeland of KwaZulu, and became joint capital of KwaZulu-Natal with Pietermaritzburg after South Africa's first multiracial elections in 1994.

Umberto II (1904–1983)   King of Italy May–June 1946. When his father *Victor Emmanuel III abdicated in May 1946, he was proclaimed king, and ruled 9 May–13 June 1946. He was forced to abdicate as the monarchy's collusion in the rise of fascism made him highly unpopular, and a referendum decided in favour of a republic. He retired to Portugal, where he died.

unequal treaties   series of agreements drawn up 1842–58 through which Western powers won diplomatic privileges and territorial concessions in China and Japan. Under the threat of coercion, the enfeebled Chinese Qing dynasty was forced to sign the agreements, which established the treaty ports. Nationalist resentment at this fuelled the *Boxer movement 1900.

UNESCO   acronym for **United Nations Educational, Scientific, and Cultural Organization**, specialized agency of the United Nations, established in 1946, to promote international cooperation in education, science, and culture, with its headquarters in Paris.

Unilateral Declaration of Independence   UDI, unnegotiated severing of relations with a colonial power; especially, the declaration made by Ian Smith's Rhodesian Front government 11 November 1965, announcing the independence of Rhodesia (now Zimbabwe) from Britain.

Unionist Party   grouping established in the Cape Colony 1908 from elements of Dr Leander Starr Jameson's Progressive Party. Upon the unification of South Africa 1910, it transformed itself into a national party representing the English-speaking community in South Africa, and hence its large mining and business interests. Regarded by the National Party as the mouthpiece of British imperial interests, the Unionist Party merged with Smuts's moderate and predominantly Afrikaner South Africa Party 1920 to help stave off J B M Hertzog's nationalist challenge.

Union Movement   British political group. Founded as the **New Party** by Oswald *Mosley and a number of Labour members of Parliament in 1931, it developed into the **British Union of Fascists** in 1932. In 1940 the organization was declared illegal and its leaders interned, but it was revived as the Union Movement in 1948, characterized by racist doctrines including anti-Semitism.

Union of Soviet Socialist Republics   USSR, former country in northern Asia and Eastern Europe that reverted to independent states in 1991; see *Armenia, *Azerbaijan, *Belarus, *Estonia, *Georgia, *Kazakhstan, *Kyrgyzstan, *Latvia, *Lithuania,

*Moldova, *Russian Federation, *Tajikistan, *Turkmenistan, *Ukraine, and *Uzbekistan.

UNITA acronym for **União Nacional para a Independência Total de Angola** (National Union for the Total Independence of Angola), Angolan nationalist movement founded by Jonas *Savimbi in 1966. Backed by South Africa, UNITA continued to wage guerrilla warfare against the ruling People's Movement for the Liberation of Angola (MPLA) after the latter gained control of the country in 1976. A peace agreement was signed in May 1991, but fighting recommenced in September 1992, after Savimbi disputed an election victory for the ruling party, and escalated into a bloody civil war in 1993. A peace agreement was signed in 1994. Savimbi later turned down the vice-presidency in a coalition government. In 1998 UNITA was demilitarized and formally legalized. In February 2002, the Angolan army killed Savimbi, and two months later the government and UNITA signed a ceasefire. Savimbi was succeeded as leader by Paulo Lukamba.

United Arab Emirates federation in southwest Asia, on the Gulf, bounded northwest by Qatar, southwest by Saudi Arabia, and southeast by Oman.

government A provisional constitution has been in effect since December 1971. The drawing-up of a permanent constitution has been deferred four times, the last occasion being in 1991. The provisional constitution provides a federal structure for a union of seven sheikdoms. The highest authority is the Supreme Council of Rulers, which includes all seven sheiks. Each is a hereditary emir and an absolute monarch in his own country.

The council elects two of its members to be president and vice-president of the federal state for a five-year term. The president then appoints a prime minister and council of ministers.

There is a federal national council of 40 members appointed by the emirates for a two year term, and this operates as a consultative assembly. There are no political parties.

history In 1952 the seven sheikdoms of Abu Dhabi, Ajman, Dubai, Fujairah, Ras al Khaimah, Sharjah, and Umm al Qaiwain set up, on British advice, the Trucial Council, consisting of all seven rulers, with a view to eventually establishing a federation. In the 1960s the Trucial States, as they were known, became extremely wealthy through the exploitation of oil deposits.

The whole area was under British protection, but in 1968 the British government announced that it was withdrawing its forces within three years. The seven Trucial States, with Bahrain and Qatar, formed the Federation of Arab Emirates, which was intended to become a federal state, but in 1971 Bahrain and Qatar seceded to become independent nations. Six of the Trucial States then combined to form the United Arab Emirates (UAE). Sheikh Zayed bin Sultan al-Nahayan, the ruler of Abu Dhabi, became the first president. The remaining sheikdom, Ras al Khaimah, joined the UAE in February 1972.

In 1976 Sheikh Zayed, disappointed with the slow progress towards centralization, was persuaded to accept another term as president only with assurances that the federal government would be given more control over such activities as defence and internal security. In recent years the UAE has played an increasingly prominent role in Middle East affairs, and in 1985 it established diplomatic and economic links with the USSR and China. Diplomatic relations were restored with Egypt in 1987.

In 1990–91, the UAE opposed Iraq's invasion of Kuwait and contributed troops and economic support to the UN coalition that defeated Iraq in the *Gulf War. The international financial scandal surrounding the 1991 collapse of the Bank of Commerce and Credit International (BCCI) had serious implications for the UAE because Abu Dhabi's ruler held a controlling interest in the bank. In 1994 the Abu Dhabi government agreed to pay a sum amounting to $1.8 billion to creditors and depositors of the former BCCI.

During 1992 the UAE became embroiled in a border dispute with Iran.

United Arab Republic union formed in 1958, broken in 1961, between *Egypt and *Syria. Egypt continued to use the name after the break-up until 1971.

United Australia Party Australian political party formed by Joseph *Lyons 1931 from the right-wing Nationalist Party. It was led by Robert Menzies after the death of Lyons. Considered to have become too dominated by financial interests, it lost heavily to the Labor Party 1943, and was reorganized as the *Liberal Party 1944.

United Democratic Front moderate multiracial political organization in South Africa, founded 1983. It was an important focus of anti-apartheid action in South Africa until 1989, when the African National Congress and pan-Africanist Congress were legalized.

United Kingdom UK, country in northwest Europe off the coast of France, consisting of England, Scotland, Wales, and Northern Ireland.

government The UK is a constitutional monarchy with a parliamentary system of government. There is no written constitution. Cabinet government, which is at the heart of the system, is founded on rigid convention, and the relationship between the monarch as head of state and the prime minister as head of government is similarly based. Parliament is sovereign, in that it is free to make and unmake any laws that it chooses, and the government is subject to the laws that Parliament makes, as interpreted by the courts. Since the UK joined the European Union (EU), the supremacy of Parliament has been challenged and it has become clear that domestic legislation can in certain circumstances be overridden by that of the EU as a whole.

Parliament has two legislative and debating chambers, the House of Lords and the House of Commons. The House of Lords has three main kinds of members: those who are there by accident of birth, the hereditary peers; those who are there because of some office they hold; and those who are appointed to serve for life, the life peers. In 1999 the House of Lords Act restricted the membership of hereditary peers from some 800 to 92. Among those sitting by virtue of their position are the spiritual peers (2 archbishops and 24 bishops of the Church of England) and 9 senior judges, known as the law lords. The majority of members are life peers. Membership of the House of Lords changes more frequently than the Commons; in May 2001 it stood at 675. The House of Commons has 651 members, elected by universal adult suffrage from single-member geographical constituencies, each constituency containing, on average, about 65,000 electors.

Although the House of Lords is termed the upper house, its powers, in relation to those of the Commons, have been steadily reduced so that now it has no control over financial legislation and merely a delaying power, of a year, over other bills. Before an act of Parliament becomes law it must pass through a five-stage process in each chamber – first reading, second reading, committee stage, report stage, and third reading – and then receive the formal royal assent. Bills, other than financial ones, can be introduced in either house, but most begin in the Commons.

The monarch appoints as prime minister the leader of the party with most support in the House of Commons, and he or she, in turn, chooses and presides over a cabinet. The voting system, which does not include any form of proportional representation, favours two-party politics, and both chambers of Parliament are physically designed to accommodate two parties, the ruling party sitting on one side of the presiding Speaker and the opposition on the other. The party with the second-largest number of seats in the Commons is recognized as the official opposition, and its leader is paid a salary out of public funds and provided with an office within the Palace of Westminster, as the Houses of Parliament are called.

history For earlier periods of the history of the British Isles see *United Kingdom: history 1815–1914 and *United Kingdom: history 1914–45.

In 1945 the UK was still nominally at the head of an empire that covered a quarter of the world's surface and included a quarter of its population, and, although two world wars had gravely weakened it, many of its citizens and some of its politicians still saw it as a world power. The reality of its position soon became apparent when the newly elected Labour government confronted the problems of rebuilding the war-damaged economy. This renewal was greatly helped, as in other Western European countries, by support from the USA through the *Marshall Plan.

the 1945 election The ending of *World War II in Europe in May 1945 was quickly followed by the dissolution of Winston *Churchill's coalition government. The general election in July resulted in the return of a Labour government with a large absolute majority, and Clement *Attlee became prime minister. This was the third Labour government in Britain's history, but the first that held both office and effective power.

The Labour Party put forward an industrial programme for the nationalization of the coal, gas, and electricity industries, of inland transport services, and of the iron and steel industries. They also advocated public ownership of the Bank of England and the creation of a National Investment Board. The Conservatives, under the leadership of wartime prime minister Winston Churchill, opposed this domestic policy, and the electoral battle was fought mainly on the issue of nationalization. The Conservatives suffered one of the severest defeats in their whole history; for in a House of Commons of 640 members the Labour Party won 393 seats as against 166 in the previous Parliament; the Conservatives dropped from 358 to only 213 seats; while the Liberal Party, who had put forward 307 candidates, had only 12 elected.

post-war austerity The keynote of life in Britain in the years following the end of the war was austerity. The sudden end of the war with Japan (September 1945) hastened the rate of demobilization, and by 30 November over 955,000 men and 147,000 women had been discharged from the armed forces, freeing them to take part in Britain's export drive to earn US dollars. Financial stringency had become doubly necessary in Britain following the cessation on 2 September of the US *lend-lease programme. Because Britain had sold off its foreign investments to finance the war effort, and had converted a great proportion of its industry to munitions and other war supplies, the country had relied on lend-lease to feed its people.

Until Britain could restore its export trade, it needed to secure a large credit in US dollars to survive the period of reconstruction, and after many weeks of negotiation in Washington a loan of £1,100 million was arranged, but with certain stringent conditions attached.

Increased production both for domestic needs and export was

essential. However, when by 1947 production had still not come up to requirements, there was an economic and financial crisis, since the large US loan was rapidly being exhausted. In the effort to restore the balance of trade, austerity measures were increased and the resultant hardships resulted in a fall in the government's popularity.

In the course of 1948 there was a rapid increase in production, coupled with a slowing down of inflation and an improvement in the balance of payments. The economic situation was also improved by the start of US aid under the Marshall Plan. Taxation remained high in 1949 and was even increased in several directions, the chancellor of the Exchequer, Stafford *Cripps admitting that it was impossible to reduce it so long as defence commitments and the social services continued on the existing scale. By 1951 rationing of various staple foods still existed in Britain, although not in most other West European countries, and this, coupled with the continuous housing shortage, caused increasing irritation in the country at large.

nationalization and the welfare state Despite the great difficulties of the economic situation, the Labour government pressed ahead with a radical restructuring of British society. In the first session of the new Parliament alone, no fewer than 84 acts were passed. The system of national insurance was extended by the National Insurance Act, which also provided for the making of payments towards the cost of a national health service. Complementary to this the National Health Service Act established a free national health service (NHS) for England and Wales. The National Insurance (Industrial Injuries) Act made new provision for compensation for industrial casualties.

The government proceeded with its programme of nationalization, completing legislation to bring the coal mines, all inland transport, and the electricity and gas industries under state control. The government deferred their intention to extend nationalization to the iron and steel industry, and instead declared preventive war on the House of Lords in the shape of a bill to amend the Parliament Act 1911. It was proposed to reduce from two years to 12 months the period during which the House of Lords might delay the enactment of a bill that it refuses to pass. The Parliament Bill came up for second reading in the House of Lords (27 January 1949). It was defeated there, and the government then decided to resort to the procedure of the Parliament Act 1911 to carry their new bill into law. The bill was passed by the Commons in September 1949.

An Iron and Steel Bill introduced in the 1948–49 session of Parliament proposed to nationalize the principal firms engaged in the basic processes of the iron and steel industry. This bill was particularly strongly opposed by the Conservatives, but eventually became law. The Conservatives, however, undertook to denationalize the iron and steel industry as soon as they returned to power. Altered circumstances induced the government to increase from 12 to 18 months the period of compulsory full-time military service.

In 1950 the general election saw a bitter struggle between the two main parties, Labour and Conservative, and a further decline in the number of Liberals returned. The Labour Party fought the election on the legislative record of the preceding five years, promising, in addition, a future programme involving more nationalization. The Conservatives alleged that the government had seriously increased Britain's economic difficulties. In the election Labour retained power, with a greatly reduced majority (of 8, as against 186 in 1945).

For the next 18 months the party battle in the House of Commons was continuous and bitter. There were also splits within the Labour government, and in April 1951 Aneurin (Nye) *Bevan and Harold *Wilson left the government over the introduction of prescription charges in the NHS.

post-war foreign and imperial policy Ernest *Bevin, the Labour foreign secretary, for the most part continued Churchill's foreign policy, in particular sharing Churchill's distrust of the USSR. Although Britain, the USA, France, and the USSR had divided the defeated Germany into four occupation zones, and agreed on the post-war treatment of Germany at the *Potsdam Conference (July–August 1945), the wartime alliance did not long survive the end of hostilities. As the Cold War intensified, Britain's close relationship with the USA continued. Britain played an important role in the formation of the post-war Western alliance, and became a founder-member of the *North Atlantic Treaty Organization (NATO) in 1949. Britain also began to develop its own nuclear deterrent, leading to the test explosion of its first atomic bomb in 1952.

In June 1950 the Cold War heated up with the outbreak of the *Korean War. In Britain the Conservative opposition supported Attlee in his policy of full cooperation with the USA and the United Nations on this issue. Before the end of the year British troops were serving in Korea, and they played an important part in holding the Chinese offensive of April 1951. Chinese intervention in Korea raised the problem of Communist China's status in the world, and at the UN Britain had already recognized the Beijing government as the de facto government of China; but the USA had not done so. In many quarters in Britain and Western Europe US policy in east Asia was occasionally viewed with misgiving, as being too ready to be interventionist. Truce talks began in

Korea in 1951, although an armistice was not concluded until two years later.

Finally, it was the post-war Labour government that saw through the granting of independence to India, Pakistan, Ceylon (Sri Lanka), and Burma (Myanmar), and the restyling of the British Empire as the British *Commonwealth. Although this was the fruition of long-term imperial policies, Britain's greatly weakened economic power meant that the shedding of its empire had become as necessary as it was politically desirable.

the Conservatives return to power In the autumn of 1951 there was another general election. The result was a Conservative victory, with a majority of 16, and Winston Churchill became the new prime minister. Early in 1952 George VI died suddenly and was succeeded by his elder daughter as Queen *Elizabeth II, who was crowned on 2 June 1953.

The Conservative government concentrated on the economic plight of the country. They had accepted the bulk of the nationalization carried out by their predecessors, but they did repeal the acts that had nationalized iron and steel and road transport. The internal economic situation showed steady improvement: full employment was maintained, and many controls were abolished.

The international situation appeared to have eased since the death of the Soviet leader Stalin (1953). In 1954 the foreign secretaries of the major powers (including Communist China) met at Geneva and agreed a settlement that concluded the Indochina War. In the same year the French Assembly, fearing the re-creation of a German army, finally rejected the proposed European Defence Community, but subsequently the agreements signed in London (1954) solved the problems of West European defence and led to the creation of the Western European Union.

Though there were serious internal troubles in two British colonies, *Kenya and *Cyprus, settlements of two other outstanding problems were reached in 1954. In July Britain and Egypt signed an agreement by which British troops were to leave the Suez Canal zone within 20 months, while in August the dispute with Iran over the latter's nationalization of British oil interests (dating from 1951) was settled, compensation being paid to Britain.

Eden takes over from Churchill
On 5 April 1955 Churchill resigned from the premiership and was succeeded by Anthony *Eden. At the general election in May 1955 Eden's government was returned with an increased majority. In December Attlee resigned from leadership of the parliamentary Labour Party and was granted an earldom. The new Labour leader was Hugh *Gaitskell, elected in preference to Herbert *Morrison and Nye Bevan.

By 1956 the economic situation in Britain was uncertain. Anti-inflationary measures produced a temporary rise in unemployment, and in September the TUC rejected wage restraint. In foreign affairs, relations with the USSR appeared to be easing. In July 1955 a meeting of the heads of government of Britain, France, the USSR, and the USA took place at Geneva, the first meeting of this kind since the Potsdam Conference ten years earlier, while in April 1956 the Soviet leaders Bulganin and Khrushchev visited Britain. However, later in the year the unrest in Poland and the Hungarian uprising cast a cloud over East–West relations.

the Suez Crisis In Britain the European news was soon overshadowed by the growing crisis in the Middle East, following the announcement on 26 July 1956 by President Nasser that Egypt was nationalizing the Suez Canal. The seizure of the canal was regarded as illegal in Western Europe and the USA,

but only in Britain and France was there any serious demand for stern action against Egypt.

Israel reached a secret understanding with Britain and France, and invaded Egypt on 29 October 1956, advancing into Sinai. France and Britain called on both belligerents to cease fighting, and when this did not occur Anglo-French forces began to bomb Egyptian military targets (31 October) and launched an airborne invasion (5 November). The British and French governments claimed their main objective was the protection of the Suez Canal, and the maintenance of free navigation, which they said was threatened by the invading Israeli forces. Egypt responded to these attacks by blocking the Suez Canal and making it impassable, the very thing that Britain and France had tried to avoid. World opinion, including the USA and USSR, condemned the Anglo-French action. The Arab states united in their support of Egypt, which emerged as the leader of Arab nationalism, and thereafter turned increasingly to the USSR for support, putting paid to Western influence in the Middle East for several years. Britain, France, and Israel were branded as aggressors at the UN and called upon to cease their military activities. A ceasefire was declared from midnight on 6 November, and US pressure brought about a gradual withdrawal of Anglo-French forces, which were replaced by a special UN force.

Britain's action in Egypt aroused the most bitter controversy in the country and was condemned by the Labour Party. The government justified their action on the grounds that it had prevented a war in the Middle East and ensured active UN intervention. There was no doubt, however – whatever the merits of the case – that Britain's prestige had suffered severely, and the blocking of the canal and the consequent disruption of oil supplies increased Britain's economic difficulties. In January 1957 Eden announced his resignation from the premiership and retirement from political life on account of ill-health.

Macmillan succeeds Eden Eden was succeeded as premier and leader of the Conservative Party by Harold *Macmillan. After the shambles of Suez, Britain's steady withdrawal from empire continued in a more measured way. Sudan had become independent at the beginning of 1956, and in 1957 both Ghana (March) and Malaya (August) became dominions within the Commonwealth. There was a conference of Commonwealth prime ministers in London in June 1957; and in January 1958 Macmillan made history by embarking on a highly successful Commonwealth tour – the first such tour undertaken by a British premier in office.

In December 1957 Macmillan attended the NATO heads of government conference in Paris. Here agreement was reached in principle on the US offer to supply European members with nuclear weapons; this agreement was much criticized by the Labour Party in Parliament.

At home the government's unpopularity showed no apparent improvement. Inflationary pressure continued, and by autumn there were rumours of an impending devaluation of the pound. On 19 September 1957 the bank rate was raised from 5 to 7% (the highest rate since 1920). Subsequently Britain's international currency position improved. A major (and very controversial) piece of legislation enacted in 1957 was the Rent Act, which freed a large number of privately owned properties from rent control altogether and made rent increases possible in many others.

Macmillan's second administration By 1959 a marked improvement in Britain's economic situation helped to return the Conservatives to power once again at the general election in October, with a larger majority than before.

More and more of Britain's colonies became independent: Cyprus (1959), Nigeria (1960), Jamaica, Trinidad and Tobago, and Uganda (all in 1962), and several more followed within the next two years. Macmillan had made clear his commitment to decolonization and his opposition to apartheid in his 1960 'wind of change' speech to the South African parliament, and in 1961 South Africa, refusing to compromise on its policy of apartheid, left the Commonwealth and became an independent republic outside it.

Beyond the Commonwealth, Macmillan established working relationships with the US presidents Eisenhower and Kennedy, but was sufficiently realistic to see that the UK's long-term economic and political future lay in Europe. The framework for the European Economic Community (EEC) had been created by the mid-1950s, with the UK an onlooker rather than a participant.

In November 1959 the agreement under which *European Free Trade Association (EFTA) was set up (of which Britain was a leading member) was initialled in Stockholm. The government's opening of negotiations to join the EEC (August 1961) caused controversy within its own ranks, and also within the Labour Party and among Commonwealth members. Distrusting Britain's closeness to the USA – particularly after the 1962 agreement by which the USA would supply the UK with Polaris nuclear missiles – the French president, Charles de Gaulle, blocked the British application (1963). The period of high East–West tension came to an end with the diffusion of the Cuban missile crisis (November 1962), and a new era of 'peaceful coexistence' was marked by the signing of the Nuclear Test-Ban Treaty (August 1963) At home, Macmillan showed his commitment to 'one-nation' Conservatism by the establishment in 1961 of the National Economic Development Council, which involved government, management, and trade unions in joint consultations over economic issues. In 1960 the economic situation had again begun to cause concern. A wages pause began in July 1961, and there were tax increases in an effort to curb home demand and avert inflation. The government's popularity declined as a result. There were also balance-of-payments problems. The winter of 1962–63 was the worst in Britain since 1947, and unemployment rose sharply, though temporarily.

Despite rising living standards, the UK's economic performance was not as successful as that of many of its competitors, such as West Germany and Japan. There was a growing awareness that there was insufficient investment in industry, that young talent was going into the professions or financial institutions rather than manufacturing, and that training was poorly planned and inadequately funded.

the defeat of the Conservatives In June 1963 the government barely survived the scandal that centred on the minister of war, John *Profumo (who resigned on 7 June), and which led to a judicial enquiry by Lord Denning into the security aspects of the affairs. In October Macmillan suddenly resigned on the grounds of ill health. The Conservatives then chose as their new leader, and prime minister, Lord Home, who then disclaimed his peerage to become Sir Alec Douglas-Home.

The internal controversy caused by Douglas-Home's succession further weakened the Conservative Party, which had now held office for 12 years. Though Douglas-Home continued his predecessor's progressive Commonwealth policy, and carried through domestic reforms such as the bill abolishing resale price maintenance (1964), a significant

proportion of voters turned to the Liberals and to the Labour Party, which now presented a much more dynamic image under Harold *Wilson, its leader since Gaitskell's death early in 1963. As a result, Labour won the general election in October 1964, though only by a majority of four, subsequently reduced to three. Wilson became prime minister, and early in 1965 Edward *Heath replaced Douglas-Home as Conservative leader, under a new system of selection by election.

Wilson's Labour government, 1964–66 The election had been fought on the issue of the economy. Wilson created the Department of Economic Affairs (DEA) to challenge the short-term conservatism of the Treasury (although the DEA was disbanded in 1969), and brought in a leading trade unionist to head a new Department of Technology. The new government inherited from its predecessor a serious balance of payments crisis, and its own initial pronouncements and actions exacerbated this by creating a crisis of confidence in sterling abroad. Devaluation was only narrowly avoided, and huge international loans were obtained and import surcharges levied.

By the autumn of 1965 Britain's balance of payments position appeared healthier than for some years past. This position had been reached, however, by imposing measures such as credit restrictions, which hampered Labour's development plans and alienated some of its supporters. Despite government efforts to establish an effective prices and incomes policy, and the National Plan for future economic development, announced by secretary of economic affairs George Brown in September 1965, the basic British post-war problem of combining domestic expansion with international solvency, and of maintaining full employment without creating persistent inflation, remained. Other separate issues, such as the housing shortage, and the immigration issue, were still pressing in 1966, while overseas the Vietnam War and Rhodesia's unilateral declaration of independence in November 1965 (see *Zimbabwe) all affected Britain directly or indirectly.

Labour continues in power, 1966–70 In March 1966 the Labour Party won the general election with a greatly increased majority. A subsequent budget included the novel proposal of a Selective Employment Tax and a promise that Britain would change to decimal coinage in 1971. Two issues dominated foreign and Commonwealth affairs: the question of whether Rhodesian sovereignty could be handed over to a white minority, and Britain's renewed application to join the EEC. By 1969 the rupture with Rhodesia was almost complete, but the resignation of President de Gaulle in France renewed hopes of Britain's eventual membership of the EEC.

But economic issues rather than foreign affairs dominated political life. Between 1958 and 1965 Britain's gross national product had increased by only a third, while that of the EEC had gone up by more than a half. To improve the economy the government sought to impose a pay freeze, later changed to a pay pause, to increase exports and reduce imports, to modernize technology, and to increase production. Its measures proved insufficient to maintain the pound at 2.8 to the dollar and in November 1967 the pound was devalued to 2.4 to the dollar. Public spending was cut, particularly on defence. This virtually committed Britain to abandoning its military presence east of Suez by 1971.

A monetary squeeze, applied with varying severity by all British governments during the 1960s, became steadily more severe. The bank rate rose again to 7% in 1966, but was cut to 6% in 1967, avoiding a sterling crisis. These monetary policies made it increasingly difficult for industry to raise new capital. It became more difficult to reconcile plans for economic expansion with the policy of seeking a permanent solution to Britain's balance of payments problem. The second consideration was given priority and by 1969 the banks were virtually forbidden to make loans outside terms imposed by the Bank of England. More and more, Britain's economic policy had to be brought into line with international trends. With this aim in mind the government attempted to introduce an ambitious plan for the reform of industrial relations, but this was dropped in the face of trade-union opposition.

The economic situation improved in 1969 and a surplus in the balance of payments was achieved for the first time in years. This surplus was maintained in 1970 and a general election called, in which the franchise was extended to people aged 18–21. However, Wilson's promises of fundamental changes in economic planning, industrial investment, and improved work practices had not been fulfilled, and the Labour Party was defeated. In June 1970 a Conservative government was formed under Edward Heath, with an overall majority of 30.

social developments in the 1960s A number of liberalizing reforms had been introduced in the 1960s. Both abortion and homosexuality became legalized in 1967, with certain qualifications. Capital punishment was abolished in 1965; there was a simplification of the divorce laws; majority juries were introduced; and road-safety legislation enacted that resulted in a decrease in accidents.

In 1968 race relations became strained as a result of agitation by Enoch *Powell, who came to the fore as a critic of immigration policy, even after a Commonwealth Immigrants Act imposed severe restrictions on entry to Britain. The Race Relations Act introduced legal penalties for manifestations of race prejudice, and was possibly successful in subsequently improving race relations.

Catholic grievances in Northern Ireland over inadequate civil liberties and economic deprivation became so serious that British troops were sent there in 1969 to restore and maintain order. The situation in Northern Ireland was soon to deteriorate into serious intercommunal violence, and was to prove an intractable problem for successive British governments.

Heath's Conservative government, 1970–74 Like Harold Wilson, the new Conservative prime minister Edward Heath saw institutional change as one way of achieving industrial reform and created two new central departments (Trade and Industry, Environment) and a think tank to advise the government on long-term strategy, the Central Policy Review Staff. He also attempted to change the climate of industrial relations through a long and complicated Industrial Relations Bill. He saw entry into the European Community (EC, as the EEC had now become) as the 'cold shower of competition' that industry needed, and membership was negotiated in 1972.

In the early 1970s British politics were dominated, as before, by serious inflation, now accompanied by rising unemployment (which reached the million mark in 1972), industrial unrest, and a series of commodity crises, notably in oil. The situation in Northern Ireland deteriorated steadily, and violence spread to the UK and the Republic of Ireland. The Rhodesian problem remained insoluble, despite various efforts to reach a settlement and the testing of Rhodesian opinion by the Pearce Commission. The promise of the government to sell arms to South Africa in defiance of a UN resolution threatened the unity of the Commonwealth.

In 1972 Conservative policies produced strikes in the mining industry and by railway workers,

the beginning of a dispute about fishing limits, the 'cod war', with Iceland (which was concluded in Iceland's favour in 1976), and constant confrontations between workers and the National Industrial Relations Court. The year 1973 began auspiciously with the entry of Britain into the European Community, which was generally acclaimed as a triumph for Edward Heath. Reactions to this event were varied, but in a referendum held in 1974 by the newly elected Labour government Britain voted to stay in the Community.

Heath's 'counter-revolution', as he saw it, was frustrated by the trade unions, and the sharp rise in oil prices following the 1973 Arab–Israeli War forced a U-turn in economic policy. Instead of abandoning 'lame ducks' to their fate, he found it necessary to take ailing industrial companies, such as Rolls-Royce, into public ownership. The situation was exacerbated by both miners' and railway workers' strikes, precipitated by the introduction of a statutory incomes policy. A state of emergency was proclaimed in November 1973 with restrictions on the use of power and blackouts throughout the country. A huge trade deficit was announced and at the beginning of 1974 the country was working a three-day week. In February 1974 the Heath government fell at a general election at which the major issue was, inevitably, the confrontation with the trade unions and, after a brief period during which Heath tried to form a coalition with the Liberal Party (Labour did not have an overall majority), Wilson returned to power.

Wilson's second premiership, 1974–76 The minority Labour government relied heavily on the Liberals and on the Scottish and Welsh Nationalists, all of whom had greatly increased their vote in the election. However, a second general election in November 1974 gave Labour an overall, if small, majority.

Wilson had taken over a damaged economy and a nation puzzled and divided by the events of the previous years. He turned to Labour's natural ally and founder, the trade-union movement, for support and jointly they agreed on a 'social contract': the government pledged itself to redress the imbalance between management and unions created by the Heath industrial-relations legislation, and the unions promised to cooperate in a voluntary industrial and incomes policy. The fight against inflation continued, through voluntary wage restrictions and, in 1975, wage restraint, which limited increases to £6 per week for everyone. The economic situation began to look slightly brighter when the first of the North Sea oil came into production and some check was given to rising prices.

In Northern Ireland the political solution worked out at Sunningdale in 1973 produced the new Ulster Executive in January 1974, but this fell within the year as a result of a massive Protestant workers' strike against it. Irish politics continued to have their effect in Britain with sporadic bombings and shootings.

On a more positive note Labour legislation included the Equal Pay and Sex Discrimination Acts (both major achievements for the women's movement), the reorganization of local government outside Greater London, and the reorganization of the National Health Service. The programme of changing over to a system of comprehensive schools was advanced.

Wilson met criticism from a growing left-wing movement within his own party, impatient for radical change, and in March 1976, apparently tired and disillusioned, he took the nation by surprise by retiring in midterm.

Callaghan's Labour government, 1976–79 Wilson was succeeded by the political veteran James *Callaghan. In the other two parties, Heath had unexpectedly been ousted in 1975 by

Margaret *Thatcher, and the Liberal Party leader, Jeremy *Thorpe, had resigned after a personal scandal and been succeeded by the young Scottish MP David *Steel.

Callaghan was now leading a divided party and a government with a dwindling parliamentary majority. Later in 1976 an unexpected financial crisis arose from a drop in confidence in the overseas exchange markets, a rapidly falling pound, and a drain on the country's foreign reserves. After considerable debate within the cabinet, both before and afterwards, it was decided to seek help from the International Monetary Fund and submit to its stringent economic policies. Within weeks the crisis was over and within months the economy was showing clear signs of improvement.

In 1977, to shore up his slender parliamentary majority, Callaghan entered into an agreement with the new leader of the Liberal Party, David Steel. Under the 'Lib–Lab Pact' Labour pursued moderate, nonconfrontational policies in consultation with the Liberals, who, in turn, voted with the government, and the economy improved dramatically. The Lib–Lab Pact had effectively finished by the autumn of 1978, and soon the social contract with the unions began to disintegrate. Widespread and damaging strikes in the public sector badly affected essential services during what became known as the 'winter of discontent'.

At the end of March 1979, following the rejection of devolution proposals by referendums in Scotland and Wales, Callaghan lost a vote of confidence in the House of Commons and was forced into a general election.

Conservatives come to power under Thatcher The Conservatives returned to power under the UK's first woman prime minister, Margaret Thatcher. Thatcher rejected the 'concensus politics' that had dominated Britain since 1945, and introduced her own more right-wing ideology ('Thatcherism'), combining belief in market forces, monetarism, anti-collectivism, strong government, and nationalism.

Thatcher inherited a number of inflationary public-sector pay awards that, together with a budget that doubled the rate of value-added tax (VAT), resulted in a sharp rise in prices and interest rates. The Conservatives were pledged to reduce inflation and did so by mainly monetarist policies, which caused the number of unemployed to rise from 1.3 million to 2 million in the first year. Thatcher had experience in only one government department, and it was nearly two years before she made any major changes to the cabinet she inherited from Heath. In foreign affairs Zimbabwe became independent 1980 after many years, and without the bloodshed many had feared.

the creation of the SDP
Meanwhile, changes were taking place in the other parties. Callaghan resigned the leadership of the Labour Party in 1980 and was replaced by the left-winger Michael *Foot, and early in 1981 three Labour shadow cabinet members, David *Owen, Shirley *Williams, and William Rodgers, with the former deputy leader Roy *Jenkins (collectively dubbed the 'Gang of Four'), broke away to form a new centrist group, the *Social Democratic Party (SDP).

The new party made an early impression, winning a series of by-elections within months of its creation. From 1983 to 1988 the Liberals and the SDP were linked in an electoral pact, the Alliance. They advocated the introduction of a system of proportional representation, which would ensure a fairer parity between votes gained and seats won.

the Falklands factor
Unemployment continued to rise, passing the 3 million mark in January 1982, and the Conservatives and their leader received low ratings in the public-opinion polls.

An unforeseen event rescued them: the invasion of the Falkland Islands by Argentina in April 1982. Thatcher's decision to send a task force to recover the islands paid off (see *Falklands War). The general election in 1983 was fought with the euphoria of the Falklands victory still in the air, and the Labour Party, under its new leader, divided and unconvincing. The Conservatives won a landslide victory, winning more Commons seats than any party since 1945, although with less than half the popular vote. Thatcher was able to establish her position firmly, replacing most of her original cabinet, among whom had been many 'one-nation' Conservatives.

domestic problems The next three years were marked by rising unemployment and growing dissent: a dispute at the government's main intelligence-gathering station, GCHQ; a bitter and protracted miners' strike; increasing violence in Northern Ireland; an attempted assassination of leading members of the Conservative Party during their annual conference; and riots in inner-city areas of London, Bristol, and Liverpool. The government was further embarrassed by its own prosecutions under the Official Secrets Act and the resignations of two prominent cabinet ministers. With the short-term profits from North Sea oil and an ambitious privatization programme, the inflation rate continued to fall and by the winter of 1986–87 the economy was buoyant enough to allow the chancellor of the Exchequer to arrange a pre-election spending and credit boom.

party leadership changes
Leadership changes took place by 1987 in two of the other parties. Michael Foot was replaced by his Welsh protégé Neil *Kinnock; Roy Jenkins was replaced by David Owen as SDP leader, to be succeeded in turn by

Robert MacLennan in September 1987, when the SDP and Liberal parties voted to initiate talks towards a merger.

The merger of the Liberal and Social Democratic parties was an acrimonious affair, with the SDP, led by David Owen, refusing to join the merged party and operating as a rival group. Paddy *Ashdown emerged as the leader of the new party.

Thatcher's last years Despite high unemployment and Thatcher's increasingly authoritarian style of government, the Conservatives were re-elected comfortably in June 1987, with a slightly reduced majority.

In a cabinet reshuffle in July 1989, Geoffrey *Howe was replaced as foreign secretary by John *Major. In October 1989 the chancellor of the Exchequer, Nigel Lawson, resigned because of disagreements with the prime minister, and Major replaced him. Douglas *Hurd took over the foreign office.

The government was widely criticized for its decisions forcibly to repatriate Vietnamese 'boat people' and to give right of abode in the UK to the families of 50,000 'key' Hong Kong citizens after the transfer of the colony to China in 1997. David Owen announced that the SDP would no longer be able to fight in all national constituencies and would only operate as a 'guerrilla force'. The Green Party polled 2 million votes in the European elections.

Thatcher challenged In September 1990 the House of Commons was recalled for an emergency debate that endorsed the government's military activities in the Gulf, and UK forces played an important role in the *Gulf War launched the following January. In October 1990 the government announced that it was joining the European Exchange Rate Mechanism (ERM). In November the deputy prime minister, Geoffrey Howe, gave a dramatic resignation speech, strongly

critical of Thatcher. Michael *Heseltine then announced his candidacy for the leadership of the Conservative Party. Having failed to gain a clear victory in the first ballot of the leadership election, Thatcher was persuaded by her colleagues to withdraw from the contest. In the subsequent second ballot Michael Heseltine (131 votes) and Douglas Hurd (56) conceded that John Major (185) had won. He consequently became party leader and prime minister.

Major's leadership Major was initially popular for his consensual style of leadership, but dissatisfaction with the poll tax continued and was seen as the main cause of a 25% swing away from the Conservatives in a March 1991 by-election. A hastily constructed replacement of the poll tax did little to repair the damage done to the Conservative Party, which sustained heavy losses in the May 1991 local elections. The deterioration of the National Health Service was also an issue.

Despite the apparent waning popularity of the Conservative government and almost two years of economic recession, the party won its fourth consecutive victory in the April 1992 general election, with a reduced majority. Neil Kinnock announced his resignation as leader of the Labour Party and Roy Hattersley resigned as deputy. John *Smith was elected as the new Labour leader in July 1992.

the recession deepens With a deepening recession and international pressure on the pound, the government was forced to devalue in September 1992 and leave the ERM. Further criticism in October forced it to review its economic strategy and, in the same month, Trade and Industry Secretary Michael Heseltine announced a drastic pit-closure programme, involving the closure of 32 collieries and the loss of 30,000 miners' jobs. The announcement initially met with massive public opposition, but the closure programme eventually went ahead.

the Conservatives lose ground In November 1992, the government won a narrow majority (3) in a 'paving debate' on ratification of the *Maastricht Treaty on closer European economic and political union. The vote went in favour of the government motion because of the support of the Liberal Democrats. In May 1993 the Conservatives lost a key seat to the Liberal Democrats in a by-election. Norman Lamont, who was largely blamed for the 1992 ERM fiasco, was subsequently replaced as chancellor of the Exchequer by home secretary Kenneth *Clarke, but this failed to prevent a second Conservative by-election defeat in July. In the same month the Maastricht Treaty was finally ratified by parliament.

In December 1993 Prime Minister John Major and Irish premier Albert Reynolds issued a joint peace proposal on Northern Ireland, the *Downing Street Declaration, which offered all-party constitutional talks in return for a cessation of violence.

the sleaze factor During 1994 the Conservative Party was plagued by a series of personal scandals, further eroding public confidence and undermining the party's Back to Basics campaign for a return to traditional family values. Revelations of British arms sales to Iraq prior to the 1991 Gulf War and the alleged complicity of senior Conservative figures, including John Major, further embarrassed the government, as did reports that certain Conservative MPs, including junior ministers, had been paid by clients to ask helpful parliamentary questions. Responding to public concern, Major announced the setting up of a committee, under Lord Justice Nolan, 'to oversee standards in public life'.

the European dimension In March 1994 the government's failure to retain the full extent of the UK's blocking vote in negotiations held on wider European union enraged Conservative 'Euro-sceptics', leading to calls for Major to resign or call a general election.

new Labour leader The Liberal Democrats made substantial gains in the May 1994 local elections. In the same month Labour leader John Smith died suddenly. Tony *Blair, young and articulate, with a clear view of the direction he wished the party to follow, emerged as the new leader after the first fully democratic elections for the post in July. The impact of Blair's election was instantaneous, and his party's popularity rating immediately soared. Meanwhile, the Conservatives were recovering from further losses in the June European elections.

the Anglo-Irish peace process In August 1994 Major, in a dual initiative with Irish premier Albert Reynolds, secured a ceasefire by the Irish Republican Army (IRA) in Northern Ireland, as an initial step towards a negotiated peace process. Differences subsequently arose between the UK and Irish governments over the interpretation and implementation of a report on decommissioning of weapons in Northern Ireland, which was published in January 1996, and the peace process was disrupted when the IRA renewed its bombing campaign in London in February 1996. The Major government responded by sending more troops to Northern Ireland.

Major's re-election bid In Scottish local elections in April 1995 the Conservatives failed to win a single seat, and in June 1995, faced with a right-wing rebellion over his policies on Europe, Major dramatically resigned the Conservative Party leadership. He was re-elected the following month, his sole challenger, John Redwood, a prominent 'Euro-sceptic', having resigned as Welsh secretary in order to challenge him.

Major carried out an immediate

cabinet reshuffle and, in an unexpected move, promoted president of the Board of Trade Michael Heseltine to the post of deputy prime minister. Following publication of the Nolan Committee's initial report on standards in public life in November 1995, MPs voted to require members to declare all outside earnings resulting from their positions in parliament and to ban all paid lobbying.

the government's diminishing majority In March 1996 the government announced that Creutzfeld–Jakob disease in humans could be passed from BSE-infected beef to humans, precipitating a collapse in beef sales and a Europe-wide ban on the import of UK beef.

The Conservative Party had been losing seats at by-elections since 1993, and in February 1997 the Wirral South seat was won by Labour from the Conservatives in a by-election, driving the Conservatives again into a Commons minority and bolstering Labour's hopes of an outright majority in the general election in May.

At the elections for representation at the Northern Ireland all-party talks held in May 1996, the Official Ulster Unionist Party (OUP) won 30 seats, the Democratic Unionist Party (DUP) 24 seats, the Social Democratic Labour Party (SDLP) 21 seats, and Sinn Fein 17. In February 1997 there were reports of a rift between SLDP leader, John *Hume, and Sinn Fein leader, Gerry *Adams.

Labour's landslide victory After an unusually long election campaign, the country went to the polls on 1 May 1997. The opinion polls, which had predicted a clear win for Labour, proved to be accurate, and the election resulted in a landslide victory for Tony Blair and his party, with a House of Commons majority of 179. The Conservative Party had its lowest share of the vote since 1832 and the smallest number of seats since the 1906 general election. A number of cabinet

ministers lost their seats and Major immediately conceded and announced his resignation as Conservative Party leader. He was succeeded by William Hague, aged only 36.

The new government took office and immediately announced a number of policy initiatives, derived from its election manifesto, and a significant change in its attitude towards Europe. As expected, the key appointments were John Prescott as deputy prime minister, Gordon Brown as chancellor of the Exchequer, and Robin Cook as foreign secretary.

resignation and reshuffling In July 1998 Prime Minister Blair made a major reshuffle of his cabinet. In the following months, however, three senior cabinet members would resign their posts. In October the Secretary of State for Wales, Ron Davies, resigned from the cabinet following an incident in London. Alun Michael, who had previously been Minister of State at the Home Office, replaced him, but was resigned in February 2000 just before a vote of no confidence, and later stepped down as Labour leader in Wales. Davies also withdrew his candidacy for the post of First Minister in the Welsh assembly, which was due to be elected in May 1999. Prime Minister Blair was forced to endorse Rhodri Morgan as First Secretary of the Welsh Assembly in February 2000; Blair had previously blocked his appointment to this position in favour of Michael. In December 1998 the Secretary of State for Trade and Industry, Peter Mandelson, and the Paymaster General, Geoffrey Robinson, both resigned following revelations that Robinson, a millionaire, had in October 1996 made a loan to Mandelson of £373,000 to assist him in buying a house. Mandelson's post was filled by the Chief Secretary to the Treasury, Stephen Byers, who was succeeded by Alan Milburn, and Robinson's post was filled by Dawn Primarolo. In June 1999 former cabinet minister, Jonathan Aitken, was given an 18-month prison sentence for perjury.

devolution In September 1997 Scottish voters backed the idea of a Scottish Parliament by 75% of votes, and of its tax-varying powers by 63% (the total turnout was 61.4%). This marked the beginning of the way towards devolution. The results of a referendum held in Wales, also in September 1997, gave approval to devolution proposals by a much narrower vote (50.3%).

Elections for the new Scottish Parliament and Welsh Assembly were held in May 1999. The Scottish Parliament opened on 1 July. Labour was the largest party in both chambers but did not achieve an overall majority.

moves towards peace in Northern Ireland The UK and Ireland took the significant step in late August 1997 of signing an international agreement on arms decommissioning in preparation for Anglo-Irish political talks in September. The British government then confirmed that six weeks of IRA ceasefire had qualified Sinn Fein for a place at the talks table. The development was historic in that it represented the first time a British government had invited the republican movement to take part in round-table talks.

Northern Ireland multiparty talks (known as Stormont talks) resumed in January 1998. All parties involved – including Sinn Fein – agreed on a document jointly proposed by the British and Irish governments as a basis for negotiation. Despite political difficulties and incidents of violence, the negotiations continued, culminating in the release of the Northern Ireland Political Talks Document on 10 April. The 'Good Friday' agreement, heralded as a historic breakthrough, granted a range of executive and legislative powers to a Northern Ireland Assembly; proposed the establishment of a North–South Ministerial Council and a British-Irish Council; and was concerned with human rights, policing service, decommissioning of illegal weapons, and the release of political prisoners. Voters in Northern Ireland and the Republic of Ireland gave their overwhelming support to the agreement in a referendum held on 22 May.

In the June 1998 elections to the new Northern Ireland assembly the Ulster Unionists and the SDLP polled strongly and the UUP leader, David Trimble, became first minister.

In August 1998 a dissident IRA group, calling themselves the 'Real IRA', exploded a large bomb in the shopping centre of Omagh, Northern Ireland, killing 28 civilians. New security measures were passed by Parliament, which was specially recalled. However, the 'Real IRA' announced a permanent ceasefire in September 1998. In October 1998 David Trimble and the SDLP leader, John Hume, were jointly awarded the Nobel Prize for Peace.

In June 1999 Prime Minister Blair, in an effort to make progress in implementing the Good Friday Peace Agreement, publicly stated that he did not consider it necessary for the IRA to begin disarming before Sinn Fein could join the proposed Northern Ireland executive so long as the intention to do so was made clear. The same month Patrick Magee, who was given eight life sentences in 1986 for terrorist offences – including the planting of a bomb at the Grand Hotel, Brighton, during the Conservative Party conference in 1984 – was released from the Maze Prison in Northern Ireland under the terms of the Good Friday Agreement. His release angered Unionist politicians and threatened the peace process.

devolution of power in Northern Ireland The Northern Ireland peace negotiations resumed in July 1999. Although talks foundered on the issues of decommissioning of arms and prisoner release, the IRA agreed to begin decommissioning discussions, and consequently a coalition government was able to be established, and powers were devolved to the province by the British government in December. However, after a report on the decommissioning of paramilitary groups in Northern Ireland revealed that there had been no arms handover, the Secretary of State for Northern Ireland, Peter Mandelson, declared in February 2000 that he had begun the process of suspending the Northern Ireland Assembly. David Trimble, the Ulster Unionist leader and first minister of the Assembly, indicated that he was on the brink of resigning because of the failure to decommission. The IRA announced that it would not respond to such pressure, and on 11 February Mandelson began to enact legislation to reintroduce direct rule, but within hours of the suspension of the Assembly, the British government announced a new IRA initiative on arms decommissioning. This did not appear to have averted the crisis, as on 15 February the IRA pulled out of disarmament talks and withdrew all decommissioning propositions.

Following an IRA announcement that it would put its weapons out of use, members of the Ulster Unionist party agreed to return to work at the Northern Ireland assembly, and the power-sharing executive resumed operations at the end of May 2000. David Trimble persuaded his Ulster Unionist party to re-enter the coalition with Sinn Fein, saying that the IRA was expected to implement its promise of disarmament immediately. The IRA opened its arms dumps to independent inspection.

elections to the European Parliament Widespread voter apathy in the elections to the European Parliament in June 1999 resulted in the lowest ever turnout in any national poll in the UK – just 23% of the electorate in England and Wales voted.

The Conservatives made sweeping gains in the elections. The Tories won 36 seats in the European Parliament, Labour 29, the UK Independence Party 3, and the Scottish National Party, Plaid Cymru, and the Greens 2 each.

The UK restored full diplomatic relations with Libya, broken off after a British policewoman was shot outside the Libyan embassy in London in 1984. The move came after Libya accepted 'general responsibility' for the murder of Yvonne Fletcher and offered to pay compensation to her family.

beef crisis The three-year-old worldwide ban on the export of British beef was formally lifted in July 1999, allowing meat exporters to start the difficult task of rebuilding their foreign markets from 1 August.

The resumption of worldwide sales applied only to de-boned meat and meat products from animals born after 1 August 1996 – the date the ban on feeding meat and bonemeal to animals in the UK became fully effective. The crisis had cost British exporters more than £1 billion and taxpayers an estimated further £3 billion.

Relations between Britain and France soured in October 1999 as the French government refused to lift a ban on imports of British beef. British supermarkets responded with bans on French food after an EU report revealed that sewage had been used to make animal feed in France. However, Prime Minister Blair refused to ban French meat, saying scientific advice did not justify on health grounds. Angry French farmers responded to Britain's consumer boycotting by blockading the Channel Tunnel.

An EU panel of scientists decided that France had produced no new evidence to justify keeping its ban on imports of British beef. The ban stayed nonetheless. France's government said early November it would face legal action through the European Commission rather than lift its ban on imports of British beef. Britain offered a compromise, possibly involving more tests of its beef and a voluntary labelling scheme for British beef which could lead to France lifting its ban and allay consumer fears in Germany. Britain and France engaged in a last-ditch round of talks over beef mid-November, with the European Commission warning that legal action against Paris would start later in the month if the ban on UK exports remained in place.

Cabinet reshuffle In a wide-ranging Cabinet reshuffle in October 1999 Tony Blair appointed Peter Mandelson secretary of state for Northern Ireland. Mo Mowlam, who left the Northern Ireland Office, took over as minister for the cabinet office and chancellor of the Duchy of Lancaster. Alan Milburn moved up from the Treasury to the post of secretary of state for health, and Geoffrey Hoon was appointed secretary of state for Defence. The defence secretary, George Robertson, left the cabinet to become NATO secretary-general, and Frank Dobson resigned his post as health secretary to become the government's favoured candidate for the Labour Party nomination for the first elections for the post of mayor of London. This post was filled in 2000 by Ken *Livingstone, who stood as an independent candidate.

The hereditary peers who would retain their ancient rights to sit and vote in the House of Lords into the next millennium were announced in November 1999. In a historic ballot, 75 peers were elected by their fellow hereditaries under the so-called Weatherhill compromise that allowed them to stay until stage two of House of Lords reform. More than 600 other hereditaries lost their rights as members of the House of Lords when the House of Lords Bill became law in November.

Northern Irish prisoners In July 2000, a further 80 prisoners were released from Northern Ireland's Maze prison, taking the total number released to 420. Only 20 remain inside. After violence between the two loyalist paramilitary groups the Ulster Volunteer Force (UVF) and the Ulster Defence Association (UDA), Johnny Adair of the UDA was returned to prison for violating the terms of his early release. British troops also returned to the streets of Belfast after two years absence.

crises in Africa 2000 The biggest British task force since the Falklands War was dispatched to Sierra Leone to oversee the evacuation of foreigners from Freetown, as rebels moved towards the capital and a UN peacekeeping mission came under attack. The British government insisted that their troops would not become embroiled in the civil war, although it was expected that British troops would remain in the region until the UN could assemble a bigger task force. In Zimbabwe, Britain was criticized by South African political leaders including those of South Africa, Mozambique, and Namibia, who claimed that Britain and other Western countries had sparked the crisis over land which was leading to widespread and government-backed violence, by failing to honour promises made in 1998 to fund a land redistribution programme. When Zimbabwean ministers arrived in London in April, Britain offered to fund land reform over the next two years, under the proviso that the money go to the poorest sector of society and not personal allies of government ministers, and that fair law be reinstated in the country; the Zimbabwean ministers refused to agree to the conditions, saying that they went back on the 1998 agreement and that they represented British colonialism.

petrol crisis 2000 A wave of disruptive protests over fuel prices supplemented by high taxes upon petrol and other oil products hit

Europe in August and September 2000. Popular protests began in France at the end of August and then spread to Germany, Spain, the UK, Ireland, and Belgium. In France, protests by lorry drivers, farmers, ambulance workers, and taxi drivers were successful as the government made tax concessions on fuel. The actions of the French government inspired similar protests across much of Europe, but in the UK protesters were unsuccessful as Tony Blair ruled out immediate concessions to the protesters despite their blockading of refineries which prevented fuel deliveries to petrol stations throughout the UK. After the protest began to affect employment and the economy, the protesters started to lift their blockades, but threatened to resume their tactics if no tax concessions were made within 60 days. In November, the chancellor of the Exchequer, Gordon Brown, announced some concessions on fuel duties.

rail accident An accident at Hatfield, Hertfordshire, in October 2000 caused by an old and faulty rail killed four people. It led to the massive disruption on the railways for several months as Railtrack imposed speed limits wherever track needed repair.

asylum Home Office figures released in January 2001 show that applications for political asylum in the UK rose in 2000 to a record 76,040, representing a quarter of all applications made in the EU. The backlog of outstanding applications had fallen to 66,195, which was 35% less than at the end of 1999.

legislation Legislation in the last months of 2000 included the planned privatization of 51% of the air traffic control service, the reduction of the homosexual age of consent from 18 to 16, a freedom of information act establishing a public right of access to certain government documents, and changes in election funding.

foot-and-mouth crisis Foot-and-mouth disease, a highly infectious virus that affects pigs, cows, sheep, and other cloven-hoofed animals, spread rapidly across the UK from late February 2001. Livestock, meat, and dairy exports were banned, much of the countryside was virtually shut down, seriously affecting the tourist industry as well as farming, and many sports fixtures were cancelled. In mid-March, the British government began a mass cull of healthy animals in affected areas in an attempt to contain the spread of the disease. The existing vaccine for the disease left vaccinated animals as carriers that could infect those animals that remained unvaccinated, although a more effective vaccine was under development in the USA. Severe curbs on the movement of livestock in Europe were announced, as some cases were discovered in France, and Canada and the USA banned all meat imports from Europe. By the end of April, over 2 million animals had been slaughtered, and new outbreaks of the disease had significantly reduced.

The first day with no new cases reported since the outbreak came in mid-May. By the end of May, 3 million animals had been slaughtered, and movement restrictions remained across the country.

2001 general elections On 7 June 2001, Blair gained a second general election victory, with Labour maintaining a considerable majority over the Conservatives. The Conservative Party embarked on a leadership battle after the immediate resignation of its leader, William Hague. Blair reshuffled his cabinet: Robin Cook was demoted from the Foreign Office and replaced by Jack Straw, while David Blunkett was promoted to Home Secretary. Women held 7 out of 23 cabinet seats. Iain Duncan Smith, a right-wing Eurosceptic, won a decisive victory over the former chancellor of the Exchequer Kenneth Clarke in the Tory leadership election in September, winning 61% of the vote.

asylum seeker policy condemned
In August 2001, the UN condemned the UK's policy of jailing asylum seekers while they waited to have their cases heard. Responding to revelations that more than 1,000 refugees were detained in prison alongside convicts, the UN High Commissioner for Refugees, Ruud Lubbers, demanded an immediate end to the policy. Britain was the only country in Europe to put innocent asylum seekers in jail.

anti-terrorist coalition In the wake of the 11 September terrorist attacks on the USA, Tony Blair pledged military and diplomatic support for US President George W Bush, and actively sought support for an international coalition against terrorism. British fighter planes and special forces were deployed for strikes against Afghanistan and its Taliban regime that commenced on 7 October.

In April 2002, facing criticism over the deterioration of public services, the government introduced a tax-raising budget to finance improvements to the NHS. This was followed by a £61 billion boost for UK public spending to 2005–06 in a review in July. Education was the main beneficiary, and there were also substantial rises in funding for transport, policing, housing, defence, and overseas aid.

transport crisis A series of departmental communications errors, continuing inefficiencies in the national transport system, and alleged untruthfulness in public statements forced the transport secretary Stephen Byers to resign from his cabinet post in May 2002. The public transport crisis was further compounded by a high-speed train derailment at Potters Bar railway station in Hertfordshire that killed seven people. Byers's resignation led to a reshuffle that resulted in a cabinet post for Paul Boateng, who as chief secretary to the Treasury became Britain's first black cabinet minister.

United Kingdom history 1815–1914
The period that followed the Napoleonic Wars was one of great internal stress in Britain. The new machinery of the Industrial Revolution was attacked by those made unemployed by its introduction, and the large numbers of soldiers returning from the war made the unemployment situation worse. Demand for parliamentary reform from the increasingly radical middle classes emerged again, but those in power had, since the French Revolution, adopted a reactionary stance, fearing any concession to the would-be reformers would bring about full-blooded revolution.

King George III had been permanently insane from 1811, and his son, the future George IV, had taken over as Prince Regent. The death of George III in 1820 was in itself unimportant, but it marked the end of an era. The rate of technological progress that followed in the 19th and early 20th centuries was remarkable. Constitutional and social changes were equally sweeping; within 110 years of George III's death Britain became a democracy in a sense fuller than the most extreme reformers of his age could have believed either possible or desirable.

the epoch of reaction The Tory Lord Liverpool, who had become prime minister in 1812, continued in office until 1827. His government's repression of freedom of speech and of the press aroused such opposition that during 1815–20 revolution did indeed seem imminent. Public hostility was directed in particular at Liverpool's foreign secretary, Lord Castlereagh, one of the architects of post-Napoleonic reaction across Europe. Castlereagh was blamed for the Peterloo massacre of 1819, in which soldiers broke up a meeting in Manchester in support of parliamentary reform, leaving 11 people dead and 500 wounded. In the wake of this event, the home secretary, Henry Addington, introduced the notorious Six Acts, which further curtailed civil liberties.

After 1820, however, the aura of reaction began to lift somewhat. Following his suicide in 1822, Castlereagh was succeeded as foreign secretary by his arch-rival George Canning, who showed some sympathy towards nationalist and liberal aspirations abroad by lending significant support to the independence struggles in Greece and South America. At home, in 1824 the radical Francis Place secured the repeal of the Combination Acts that had banned trade unions, although strikes still remained illegal. Canning briefly succeeded Liverpool as prime minister, in coalition with the Whigs, but died in office (1827). He in turn was briefly succeeded in 1827–28 by a liberal Tory, Viscount Goderich (later created Earl of Ripon).

In 1828 another Tory, the Duke of Wellington, became prime minister. Although generally reactionary in attitude, under pressure Wellington carried through some notable reforms, including the achievement of Catholic Emancipation and the repeal of the Test Act and the Corporation Act, both of which had excluded any but members of the established Church of England from holding public office. His government, which lasted until 1830, also modified the Corn Laws, whose effect of driving up food prices had made them extremely unpopular with the growing urban population. However, agitation for the complete repeal of the Corn Laws was to continue, and Wellington's resistance to parliamentary reform, and his lack of opposition to Catholic Emancipation, made him unpopular.

the great Reform Act of 1832

In 1830 George IV died and was succeeded by his brother, William IV. In the same year a reforming Whig government was formed by Charles Grey. The agitation for a parliamentary Reform Bill at last resulted in the passing of the great Reform Act of 1832 – to the aristocracy of the time the beginning of the end of all things.

Hitherto, the franchise had been limited to certain classes of property owner. Moreover, the distribution of parliamentary constituencies had remained unchanged for generations, and had failed to take account of the great demographic shifts that had been taking place over the previous century. This resulted in many 'rotten boroughs' with insignificant numbers of voters returning members to parliament, while some of the newly grown industrial cities, such as Birmingham and Manchester, had little or no parliamentary representation. There were also many 'pocket boroughs', so-called because they were 'in the pocket' of patrons, who by bribery or influence could ensure the election of their favoured candidates. In addition, the absence of a secret ballot meant that electors were open to pressure by others to vote for a particular candidate.

The existing electoral system was thus largely geared to the interests of the mostly aristocratic landed classes, who viewed any attempt to change the system as an attack on their property rights. By this stage the Whigs had lost the support of many aristocrats, but found new support among progressive industrialists, the followers of the utilitarian reformer Jeremy Bentham, Nonconformists, and the middle classes. These groups were referred to collectively as the 'Liberals', although the Whig Party was not officially known as the Liberal Party until after 1840. The Liberals had developed a new ideology of free trade and a policy of nonintervention (laissez-faire) in economic affairs – and parliamentary reform. Parliamentary reform was also campaigned for by the radical leader of the working-class movement, William Cobbett.

The Reform Act of 1832 did not actually go as far as many reformers would have liked. However, rotten and pocket boroughs were abolished, and parliamentary seats redistributed to reflect new demographic realities. The Act extended the (male) franchise on the basis of certain property-related qualifications, but fell far short of granting universal male suffrage, and Parliament continued to be dominated by the landed classes. Nevertheless, the principle that Parliament could be reformed had been established.

further reforms under Grey and Melbourne Grey's government also introduced a number of humanitarian measures, including the abolition of slavery throughout the British Empire (1833), and the introduction of factory inspectors (also 1833) to regulate working conditions. The *poor law of 1834, however, was a harsh manifestation of laissez-faire ideology, and extended the use of *workhouses.

In 1834 Grey was briefly succeeded as prime minister by Lord Melbourne, who again became prime minister of a Whig government in 1835–41. During the period of his premiership the young Queen Victoria came to the throne (1837) in succession to her uncle William IV. Victoria much admired Melbourne, and regarded him a her political mentor. But apart from addressing the abuses of local government in the Municipal Corporations Act (1835), the introduction of the penny postage (1840), and the ending of the employment of children as chimney sweeps (the Climbing Boys Act, 1840) his government did not achieve that much, and the zeal for further reform seemed to have left the Whig Party.

Britain in the early Victorian era Commercially Britain continued to prosper, and great technological progress was being made. Britain from the mid-18th century had been the first country to embark upon the Industrial Revolution, and continued to benefit from this head start. By the middle of the 19th century Britain had become the first country in which the urban population outnumbered the rural population. The Napoleonic Wars had left it the 'workshop of the world', and for a time it had no competitors of any importance – it was not until the last quarter of the century that Britain's industrial power began to be surpassed by that of Germany and the USA. Transport was revolutionized by the introduction of the steamship and the railways, and heavy engineering began to emerge as one of Britain's most important industries. The first public railway in Britain was opened in 1825, and others soon followed. The rapid proliferation of the railways not only assisted in the spread of industrialization, but also had social and cultural impacts, increasing the mobility of labour and opening up new horizons for many people.

For the mass of the population, however, industrialization had resulted in few benefits. Living conditions in the new cities were crowded and unhealthy, and working conditions in the mines and factories were often appalling, with men, women, and children working extremely long hours in often dangerous environments. Wages were low, and trade union activity still circumscribed by law. The efforts of a few idealistic industrialists such as Robert Owen to improve the lot of their workers had little wider impact, although Owen's efforts did give rise to the cooperative movement.

Politically the two great parties still remained fairly true to the old ideas; nevertheless the *Liberal Party, evolving from the Whigs, and the *Conservative Party, evolving from the Tories, were both being permeated by more democratic attitudes. The people were at last being recognized as a real factor in political existence, though the majority of the adult male population still had no parliamentary vote after 1832, and the power of the crown and of the landed proprietors was still very great.

Radical agitation for wider parliamentary reform in the later 1830s and 1840s manifested itself in the mainly working-class Chartist movement, which included among its aims the achievement of universal adult male suffrage. However, Chartism had lost its momentum by 1850, and the progress towards full democracy was slow: universal male adult suffrage was not to be achieved until 1918, and that for women not until a decade later. Nevertheless, gradually from this period the power and prestige of the House of Commons increased, and its representative character was broadened, until it became the greatest power in the legislature.

Peel and the Corn Laws In 1841 Robert Peel became prime minister. As home secretary in the 1820s he had founded the modern police force and reformed the prisons and the criminal law, and he had briefly been prime minister in 1834–35. Peel realized that his party needed to attract votes from the ever-growing middle classes, and his Tamworth Manifesto of 1834 had marked the beginnings of the transformation of the Tories into the Conservative Party.

Peel's second premiership saw the reintroduction of income tax (1842), which had first been introduced as a temporary measure during the Revolutionary and Napoleonic Wars, and the Coal Mines Act (1842), which forbade the employment of women and children underground. However, his premiership is most notable for the repeal of the Corn Laws (1846). Although his government was protectionist in principle, the Irish potato famine forced Peel's hand, and he was obliged to introduce the greatest free-trade measure hitherto achieved in Britain. The repeal of the Corn Laws had been pressed for by the Anti-Corn Law League, led by the laissez-faire Liberals, John Bright and

Richard Cobden. The government was nevertheless slow in providing famine relief in Ireland, and this contributed further to Irish hostility towards British rule. In addition, the removal of protection for Irish wheat-growers led to the eviction of many smallholders by the impoverished landowners, adding to the distressed state of Ireland.

The Tories were split by the repeal of the Corn Laws, and Peel resigned (1846), never to hold office again. The Peelites, chief among whom were William Ewart Gladstone and Lord Aberdeen, ultimately joined forces with the Whigs to form the Liberals, while the protectionists, under George Bentinck and Benjamin Disraeli, ultimately formed the modern Conservative Party.

the beginning of the Palmerston era Peel was succeeded by the Whig Lord John Russell. His premiership (1846–52) was marked by the suppression of Chartist riots, and the Ten Hours Act of 1847, which introduced the ten-hour working day for women and young people in certain industries (1847). This last measure, as with the earlier Coal Mines and Climbing Boys acts, owed much to the efforts of the reforming Tory Lord Shaftesbury.

Russell's foreign secretary was Lord Palmerston, a former Tory who had served in the same capacity in two previous Whig cabinets. Palmerston's populist nationalism and his championing of liberal and national causes in Europe (for example, supporting the independence of Belgium from France) made him liked by the public, but his high-handed methods alienated other ministers and Queen Victoria. He resigned from Russell's government in 1851, and brought it down by defeating the Militia Bill in 1852. Russell was briefly succeeded by the Conservative, Lord Derby.

Derby's ministry lasted only 10 months, after which time there was a Peelite–Liberal coalition under the leadership of Lord Aberdeen, whose chief ministers included Russell, Palmerston (as home secretary), and Gladstone, the last of whom abolished all remaining protectionist duties, making Britain a completely free-trade country.

Palmerston had in particular distrusted the ambitions of Russia, which appeared to be intent on filling the vacuum as the Turkish Ottoman Empire declined, and whose advance into Central Asia seemed to threaten British India. Russia's invasion of the Turkish Balkans in 1853 led to the outbreak of the Crimean War, but Aberdeen's government handled the war so badly that it was forced to resign in 1855.

Palmerston as prime minister Palmerston took over as prime minister, and saw the war to a more or less successful conclusion (1856). Over the following decade Palmerston dominated British politics. After two years he was defeated, but appealed to the country and was returned by a large majority. Later, in 1858, his Conspiracy to Murder Bill was thrown out, and Lord Derby formed his second administration, which lasted for only 15 months, after which Palmerston again came into power, remaining as prime minister until his death in 1865.

Foreign and imperial affairs continued to occupy Palmerston to the end of his life. In 1856–60 the Second Opium War was launched against China to protect British commercial interests, while his suppression of the Indian Mutiny in 1858 was followed by the government of India being transferred from the East India Company to the British crown (this last measure being carried through by Derby's government). During the American Civil War (1861–65), despite official British neutrality, Palmerston favoured the South, and incidents such

as the Trent Affair – in which a Union warship seized two Confederate commissioners from a British ship – and the furore over the British-built Confederate warship the *Alabama* almost involved Britain in the war on the side of the Confederacy. In contrast, many textile workers in Lancashire boycotted slave-grown cotton from the South, at the risk of their own livelihoods.

Disraeli and the second Reform Act Palmerston was succeeded by Lord John Russell, who attempted to pass a further parliamentary Reform Bill (a measure Palmerston had refused to countenance during his lifetime), but was so bitterly attacked by many members of his own party that he resigned and was succeeded by Lord Derby (1866).

In Derby's government Disraeli was chancellor of the Exchequer and leader of the Commons, and in this capacity in 1867 he introduced a Reform Bill, and, 'educating his own party' up to it, passed it. It was described by Lord Derby as 'a leap in the dark', and contained many amendments proposed by Gladstone. The second Reform Act made a further redistribution of parliamentary seats, and extended the franchise to all male heads of households in towns and cities, but effectively continued to exclude agricultural labourers. The fact that it was a Conservative government that introduced the successful Reform Bill allowed them to take the credit for it, but it was also a landmark in Disraeli's development of 'one-nation' Conservatism.

For the next decade and a half the field of politics was dominated by the duel between Gladstone and Disraeli. In 1868 Disraeli became prime minister following the retirement of Lord Derby, but a few months later was defeated in the general election.

Gladstone's first government, 1868–74 Disraeli was succeeded by Gladstone, whose policies embodied

19th-century Liberal ideology: free trade, reduction in government intervention in the free market, and social reform. As chancellor of the Exchequer in two earlier governments (1852–55 and 1859–66) he had reduced government expenditure and cut tariffs. During his first period as prime minister (1868–74) his government passed more reforming measures than almost any previous one. Elementary (primary) education was made universally available in 1870 (although it did not become compulsory until 1880, and not free until 1891). The secret ballot in general elections was introduced (the ballot act 1872), and trade unions were more fully legalized (1871), following the formation of the Trades Union Congress (TUC) in 1868. The minister for war, Edward Cardwell began to modernize the organization of the army.

However, Ireland continued to be an intractable problem for British governments. Following the potato famine of 1845–48 Irish resentment at what was seen as the callousness of the Anglo-Irish land-owning classes and the indifference of the British government had led to a renewal of nationalist unrest, including an unsuccessful uprising in 1867 by the Fenian movement. In 1870 the Irish Home Rule Association was formed (see *home rule, Irish), and the question of Irish home rule was to dog Gladstone to the end of his political career. In his first government Gladstone was opposed to any such move, but attempted to address Irish nationalist and economic grievances by the Irish Church Act of 1869 (which ended the position of the Anglican Church of Ireland as the established church there) and the first of the Irish Land Acts. However, growing agitation on the land question in Ireland at that time led to the introduction of repressive Coercion Acts, and from this time Irish nationalist MPs in the House of

Commons began a campaign of deliberate obstruction as a tactic for achieving home rule.

The foreign policy of Gladstone's government was unpopular; Britain's attitude towards Prussia during the Franco-Prussian War and towards the USA's claims for compensation relating to the *Alabama* affair were thought to be decidedly weak. Also unpopular were Gladstone's Licensing Acts, putting restrictions on the sale of liquor. In 1874 the Liberal government was defeated in the election, 'borne down in a torrent of gin and beer', as Gladstone put it. The Conservatives were returned to power, having for the first time since 1841 a real majority in the House of Commons.

Disraeli's second government, 1874–80 Disraeli demonstrated the 'one-nation' nature of the his brand of Conservatism by introducing such social-reform measures as the Artisans' Dwelling Act, which encouraged slum clearance, and the Public Health Act (1875), which strengthened earlier legislation. A further Trade Union Act of 1875 legalized peaceful picketing, and the 56-hour working week was introduced in 1878. Above all, however, his government is remembered for its commitment to British imperialism. From around this time Britain's industrial monopoly was being challenged by Germany and the USA, and to seek new markets and sources of raw materials the Conservatives under Disraeli launched the UK on a career of imperialist expansion.

A great upholder and flatterer of the monarchy, Disraeli conferred on Queen Victoria the title of empress of India, and personally secured for Britain the majority of shares in the Suez Canal – thus securing a crucial connection to British India, and paving the way for British control in Egypt.

Fear of Russian expansionism continued to dominate British policy in the Balkans, and overrode humanitarian considerations. Thus Gladstone fiercely attacked Disraeli in 1875 when the latter appeared indifferent to the atrocities committed by Turkish troops in Bulgaria. The atrocities led to the intervention of Russia in support of its fellow Slavs in Bulgaria, and Turkey was defeated in a short war (1877–78). Russia obliged Turkey to agree to a humiliating peace at San Stefano (March 1878), by which Turkey recognized the independence of some of its Balkan possessions, including an enlarged Russian-dominated Bulgaria, and ceded a large area in the Caucasus region to Russia.

The other European powers, including Britain, put pressure on Russia to revise this settlement, and at the Congress of Berlin (June–July 1878), although the independence of Serbia, Romania, and Montenegro was recognized, the enlarged Bulgaria was reduced, Bosnia–Herzegovina was handed to Austria-Hungary, and Russia was forced to return a portion of the Caucasus territory.

Disraeli returned from the Congress claiming he had achieved 'peace with honour'. He had in addition achieved the transfer of Cyprus from Turkish to British rule, thus further increasing the British presence in the eastern Mediterranean region. In 1880, however, Disraeli was badly defeated at the election, and resigned.

Gladstone's second and third governments, 1880–86 Gladstone now formed his second administration, and again remained in power for about five years. Britain continued to extend its imperial ambitions, although in South Africa Britain's attempt to annex the Boer republic of the Transvaal from 1877 ended with the British defeat at Majuba Hill in 1881. In 1882 a nationalist uprising in Egypt was suppressed by British troops, and British control was more thoroughly imposed, although the khedive of Egypt still ruled under the nominal suzerainty of the Turkish Ottoman

Empire. In Sudan, which was ruled by Egypt, and in which Britain therefore had an interest, the revolt by the Mahdi led to the death of Gen Gordon at Khartoum (1885). Meanwhile, British representatives met in Berlin with representatives from Germany, France, Portugal, and Belgium in 1884–85 to decide on the partition of Africa, and also agreed to abolish slavery on the continent.

At home, the second Irish Land Act was introduced in 1881, and an act of 1882 empowered local authorities to provide proper services for sewage, water supply, and street lighting. A further parliamentary Reform Act, which extended the franchise to male agricultural workers, became law in 1884, increasing the franchise to about 5 million voters. In 1885 Gladstone resigned following criticism of his government's failure to relieve Gordon at Khartoum. He was succeeded by Lord Salisbury, but his Conservative government was only in office for a short time.

In 1886 at the general election the Liberals were again returned to power. Gladstone formed his third ministry, but his majority was dependent on the Irish nationalist MPs, under the leadership of Charles Stewart Parnell. Gladstone determined to introduce a Home Rule Bill for Ireland, which led to a split in his own party. The dissidents, such as Spencer Hartington, Joseph Chamberlain, and the veteran John Bright, became known as the Liberal Unionists, and the bill was defeated by a majority of 30. Gladstone appealed again to the country, but was defeated in the election.

the Conservative era, 1886–1906 Lord Salisbury now formed his second administration. Generally acting as foreign secretary as well as prime minister during his premierships, Salisbury espoused a policy of 'splendid isolation' for Britain, while other European powers involved themselves in complex alliances and counter-alliances.

From 1886 to 1906, broken only by a short Liberal administration, the Conservatives were constantly in power. The introduction of the Home Rule Bill had seriously split the Liberal Party, and later, on the retirement of Gladstone, differences became still more marked – although the dissident Liberal Unionists at first refused to cooperate with the Conservatives.

This period, although dominated by the Conservatives in the House of Commons, also witnessed the politicization of the labour movement. Unskilled workers began to become unionized, a process encouraged by the success of the London dockers' strike of 1889. The first socialist MP, Keir *Hardie, was elected in 1892, and the following year Hardie founded the *Independent Labour Party (ILP). In 1900 the ILP combined with trade unionists and members of the *Fabian Society to form the Labour Representation Committee, the nucleus of the *Labour Party, which was formed in 1906.

In 1892 the Liberals succeeded to office. Gladstone introduced a second Home Rule Bill, which passed through the Commons, but was rejected by the House of Lords. After this defeat Gladstone finally retired and was succeeded as prime minister by Lord Rosebery.

In 1895 the Conservatives again came to power, and the Liberal Unionists formed a coalition with them, the Duke of Devonshire (Hartington), Lord Lansdowne, and Joseph Chamberlain accepting office. Chamberlain, an ardent imperialist, quickly made a name for himself as colonial secretary, and was responsible for relations with the Boer republics of South Africa. In 1899 the Boer War (the second of the South African Wars) broke out, and ended in 1902 with the annexation of the Boer republics by Britain. However, Britain subsequently

pursued a conciliatory policy towards the Boers (Afrikaners), leading to the Union of South Africa in 1910. Britain's other white-settled colonies had already become self-governing dominions: *Canada in 1867, *Australia in 1901, and *New Zealand in 1907.

On a wave of wartime patriotism, the Conservatives had again been returned to power at the 'khaki' election of 1900. In 1902 Lord Salisbury died and was succeeded by Arthur Balfour. Queen Victoria, who had celebrated her diamond jubilee in 1897, died in 1901 and was succeeded by her son, Edward VII.

During Balfour's administration the highly controversial Education Act was introduced, which replaced the school boards (which had been dominated by the Church of England) with local education authorities (LEAs). There was also a further Irish Land Act (the Wyndham Act, 1903). The foreign secretary, Lord Lansdowne, ended British isolationism by forming an alliance with Japan and the *Entente Cordiale with France. In 1903 Chamberlain put forward a tariff-reform scheme, which succeeded in dividing the Conservative Party, and Chamberlain resigned to campaign for imperial preference.

Asquith's Liberal government The Conservative split contributed to the overwhelming Liberal victory of 1906. Sir Henry Campbell-Bannerman formed the new administration, which rapidly introduced the Trades Disputes Act (1906). This replaced the judgement reached by the House of Lords in the *Taff Vale case (1901) that trade unions could be made financially liable by their members' actions. Campbell-Bannerman was succeeded shortly before his death by Herbert *Asquith (1908). Edward VII died on 6 May 1910 and was succeeded by his eldest surviving son, *George V.

Asquith's chancellor of the Exchequer, David *Lloyd George, introduced a number of radical measures that marked the beginnings of the welfare state in Britain. Old-age pensions were introduced in 1908, and health and unemployment insurance in 1911. The rejection by the House of Lords of Lloyd George's 1909 budget – which included proposals for graduated income tax and the taxation of land values – led to a constitutional crisis. Asquith retaliated by introducing the Parliament Act 1911, which severely curtailed the power of the Lords. The Act only came into being after Asquith had obtained from the king a reluctant promise to create enough peers to swamp the Conservative majority in the House of Lords if it were rejected.

In 1912 Asquith introduced a third Irish *Home Rule Bill. This was vehemently opposed by the Protestants in the north of Ireland, who feared domination by the Catholic south. The Ulster Unionists under Edward *Carson threatened to resort to armed struggle if necessary, which in turn led to the *Curragh 'Mutiny' of March 1914. However, the crisis was put on hold by the outbreak of World War I in August 1914.

One other major domestic issue dominated the prewar years in Britain: that of votes for women. This was pressed for by the radical *suffragettes, whose treatment at the hands of the authorities, together with the government's refusal to consider extending the franchise to women, showed the illiberal side of an otherwise fairly enlightened administration. The campaign of the suffragettes was called off with the outbreak of war in 1914.

the road to war The causes of World War I are complex. For Britain, Germany was an imperial and commercial rival, and the decision by the Germans to build up their navy to protect their colonial and trading interests was regarded as a direct threat by Britain, and a naval arms race ensued. The precipitating event was the assassination of the Austrian Archduke Francis Ferdinand by a Serbian nationalist in Sarajevo. Following this event, the elaborate sequence of alliances in Europe led to a domino effect, as country after country was drawn into the conflict. When Austria-Hungary went to war with Serbia, Russia became involved on behalf of its fellow Slavs in the Balkans, then Germany in support of Austria-Hungary, then France in support of Russia. As part of their strategy against France, German forces invaded Belgium. As a guarantor of Belgian neutrality since 1839 Britain demanded that the Germans withdraw. When no response to this request was received, Britain declared war on Germany (4 August 1914).

Asquith was to continue until 1915 as prime minister of a Liberal government, and then as head of a coalition until 1916.

For the later history of Britain see *United Kingdom: history 1914–45. For British history since 1945 see *United Kingdom.

United Kingdom history 1914–45 for earlier periods of the history of the British Isles see *United Kingdom: history 1815–1914.

Britain in World War I In 1914, for the first time for a century, Britain became involved in a European war.

In the political field, Herbert *Asquith, prime minister since 1908, was to continue until 1915 as head of a Liberal government, and then as leader of a coalition until 1916. With the outbreak of war divisive issues such as Irish *home rule and women's suffrage (see *suffragettes) were put aside, and the wave of industrial strikes that had marked the immediate prewar years came to a halt, as the nation united in patriotic fervour for what everybody believed would be a short war.

The new war minister, Gen Horatio Kitchener – one of the few who were expecting an extended war – immediately set about forming a volunteer army, which by the end of 1915 had recruited some 2.6 million men. However, the skilled industrial workforce became dangerously diluted, and this, together with the failure of the government to implement central planning to put the economy on a war footing, led to shortages of such vital supplies as shells.

The resultant political scandal forced Asquith to form a coalition government in May 1915, in which eight Conservatives and one Labour minister joined the cabinet. Control of munitions production was taken away from Kitchener and placed in the hands of a new munitions ministry under David *Lloyd George. From this point the government began to impose tighter controls on industry, the workforce, and society in general, and in January 1916 compulsory military conscription was introduced.

As 1916 progressed public optimism decreased. The failure of such major offensives as that at *Gallipoli and on the Somme (see *Somme, Battle of the), together with food shortages caused by the success of German submarines, all contributed to dissatisfaction with the government, and in December Asquith's coalition collapsed. It was replaced by a new coalition under the premiership of Lloyd George (who had been war minister since the death of Kitchener in June), with the close support of the Conservative Bonar *Law.

Lloyd George pursued the war with aggressive energy. Government control of the economy and society became more all-embracing, and so-called 'war socialism' was introduced, although in reality this was principally a close alliance between government and private industry, which did well under the arrangement. Shortages in the workforce continued to be a problem, especially after the upper age for conscription was raised to 50 in May 1918 in response to the German Spring

Offensive. However, women had been increasingly encouraged to join the workforce – a significant social innovation – and were rewarded with the promise of the vote once the war was over.

The war eventually came to an end in November 1918 with the collapse of the Central Powers. The Allied victory probably had more to do with the success of the British naval blockade on Germany, starving it of resources, than with the military conduct of the war. In the end it was a war of attrition, in which the side whose resources (both material and manpower) lasted out emerged victorious. British losses were lower than those of the other major combatants, but nevertheless amounted to some three-quarters of a million deaths.

the struggle for Irish independence
With the prospect of home rule shelved for the duration of the war, many Irish nationalists rallied around the radical *Sinn Fein movement. In April 1916 Sinn Fein launched the armed Easter Rising in Dublin against British rule. The rising was suppressed and the leaders executed, but hostilities resumed in 1918. Guerrilla attacks on the British army, especially by members of the Irish Republican Army (IRA), continued until 1921. A truce was declared in 1921, and following the Anglo-Irish Treaty of 6 December the southern counties of Ireland achieved self-governing dominion status as the Irish Free State, while Northern Ireland remained a part of the United Kingdom, but with its own parliament. For more details of these and subsequent events in Ireland, see *Ireland, Republic of.

Lloyd George's post-war government The war had transformed British society, and had in particular given many women a new degree of social and economic freedom. The beginnings of political freedom came with the 1918 Representation of the People Act, which gave the vote to all women over 30 with residential or business qualifications, as well as all men over 21.

In the December general election Lloyd George's coalition was returned with a massive majority, amid popular clamour for revenge against Germany. The Liberal Party had been split since 1916 between the followers of Lloyd George and the followers of Asquith, and at the election the success of the Labour Party put it in a position to challenge the Liberal Party as the official opposition. Irish nationalists practically disappeared, while the 73 Sinn Feiners refused to take their seats, among them being Countess Markievicz, the first woman MP.

Foreign affairs were largely taken up with the Paris Peace Conference, and the peace treaty with Germany was signed on 28 June 1919 (see *Versailles, Treaty of). The harsh terms of the treaty were forced through by the French, against more pragmatic arguments for moderation by the British representatives. The treaty aroused long-lasting resentment in Germany, and was to contribute to the later rise of national socialism. Dealing with the repercussions of the treaty was to occupy successive British governments right up to World War II.

One more positive result of the treaty was the creation of the *League of Nations, of which Britain became a founder member. The League awarded to Britain various former German colonies – Tanganyika and parts of Togo and Cameroon – to administer under mandate, as well as parts of the dismantled Turkish Empire, namely Palestine and Transjordan.

At home, the end of the war was followed by a short-lived economic boom, followed by economic decline as wartime demand for industrial supply evaporated. This was accompanied by high unemployment and the resumption of industrial unrest. The Miners' Federation called for nationalization of mines and

formed, with railway and transport workers, the Triple Alliance. The miners' strike of 1921 was settled by the Sankey coal commission, which recommended nationalization, though its recommendation was not to be adopted for another quarter of a century. An industrial court, composed of employees and employers, was established to settle industrial disputes.

the rise of the Labour Party
In 1922 confidence in the Lloyd George's coalition government diminished, a general election took place, and a Conservative ministry under Bonar Law was returned. Labour became the second-largest party in the House of Commons, and from this point was to replace the Liberal Party as the official opposition. The Conservatives, however, had no clear majority. Law resigned owing to ill health in May, and was succeeded as prime minister by Stanley *Baldwin. Baldwin proposed to abandon free trade and restore import duties as a response to the economic slump, and on this issue another general election was held in December.

Again no one party had an overall majority, but in January 1924 the Labour Party assumed office under Ramsay *MacDonald, but the new government was dependent on the support of the Liberals. In its short period in office the first Labour administration managed to achieve little. In February the government formally recognized the USSR – Britain had earlier backed the anti-communist White forces in the Russian Civil War – and MacDonald was continually attacked for his supposed soft attitude towards communism abroad and at home. Over this issue the Liberals withdrew their support from the government in October 1924. Labour's defeat in the subsequent election was partly due to the forged *Zinovyev letter, which appeared to be an appeal by Soviet communists to their British counterparts to launch an uprising.

The Conservatives, under Baldwin, were returned to power with a large majority.

the period of the general strike
In industry class feeling had become bitter, and unemployment gave rise to increasing alarm. In the coal industry many mines were closed and many areas were reduced to destitution, especially in south Wales and in the north of England.

By 1926 the mine-owners were demanding that the miners accept lower wages and longer hours. The miners went on strike in early May, and the miners asked the Trades Union Congress (TUC) to call a *general strike. More than 2 million workers in transport, newspapers, and the iron and steel industries came out in sympathy, and the government responded by invoking the Emergency Powers Act of 1920, and used troops to control essential supplies. The TUC called off the general strike after nine days, although the miners did not return to work until November.

The following year the government introduced the Trades Disputes Act, which made general strikes illegal. Baldwin's chancellor of the Exchequer, Winston *Churchill – who had played a prominent part in the defeat of the general strike – included in his 1928 budget a policy of granting rating (local taxation) relief to depressed industries. However, the government refused requests for aid from the agricultural sector, which was also in a depressed state.

Britain in the depression
The general election of May 1929 was the first in which all women over 21 were entitled to vote, this right having been granted by the 1928 Franchise Act. The election resulted in Labour returning to power under MacDonald, although without a working majority. Unemployment, already serious, became considerably worse following the Wall Street crash in October 1929,

which was followed by a worldwide depression.

Unemployment figures reached over 2.8 million in 1931, while a budget deficit of £40 million was shown to be imminent. The government could only obtain foreign loans if it cut its spending, and the Labour cabinet resigned when it was proposed to cut unemployment payments. MacDonald remained in office and formed a coalition 'National Government' with the Liberals and Conservatives. One of the first acts of the new government was the abandonment of the gold standard in order to avert the collapse of the pound. After the National Government had been returned a second time and by a great majority, Neville *Chamberlain, the Conservative chancellor of the Exchequer, reversed the country's traditional free-trade policy by introducing the Import Duties Bill 1932, under which Britain's fiscal policy became definitely protectionist.

By now the country's financial outlook had improved, but no appreciable decline in unemployment came until 1934. In 1935 MacDonald was succeeded as prime minister by the Conservative Stanley Baldwin, and by 1936 unemployment showed a further decline. This was partly attributable to the improvement in the iron and steel industry, which was helped by the government's plans for rearmament in response to developments in Nazi Germany.

the abdication crisis King *George V died on 30 January 1936 and was succeeded by Edward, Prince of Wales, as *Edward VIII. The new king reigned for less than a year, abdicating on 10 December 1936, uncrowned, in consequence of his proposed marriage to Mrs Wallis Simpson, an American citizen whose two previous marriages had ended in divorce. Such a marriage was felt by many to be unsuitable for the head of the Church of England, and Edward left Britain immediately afterwards and married Mrs Simpson in France the following year. He was created Duke of Windsor after his abdication. His brother succeeded to the crown as *George VI.

British foreign policy to 1935 Much of British foreign policy in the period up to 1935 was aimed at ameliorating the consequences of the Treaty of Versailles, and rehabilitating Germany into the community of nations. This policy was often conducted in the face of French resistance. The Dawes Plan of 1924 and the Young Plan of 1929 were attempts to lessen Germany's crippling burden of reparation payments, and the Locarno Pact of 1925 contributed to European security and allowed Germany to enter the League of Nations (see *Locarno, Pact of). Following the introduction of the Young Plan the Allies agreed to end their occupation of the German Rhineland.

In the wake of World War I, there was much discussion concerning disarmament. International agreement on limitations to naval power was reached at the Washington Conference of 1921, and an Anglo-American naval treaty was signed in 1930. The World Disarmament Conference in Geneva began to meet in 1932, headed by Arthur Henderson, who had been foreign secretary in Ramsay MacDonald's second Labour government.

In imperial affairs, the Statute of Westminster of 1931 granted to the self-governing dominions (Canada, Australia, New Zealand, and South Africa) complete autonomy in external as well as internal affairs, in effect making those countries completely independent of Britain. In India nationalist pressure brought about slow constitutional progress, and from 1937 nationalist politicians began to participate in provincial government.

the Abyssinian crisis From 1935 domestic politics in Britain were overshadowed by growing threats to world peace. Japanese aggression in China led Britain to reassess its naval policy, while the invasion of Abyssinia (Ethiopia) by the Italian fascist dictator Mussolini appeared to pose an implicit threat to British interests in the Near East. Although the League of Nations imposed sanctions against Italy, they had little effect, partly owing to the backward state of British rearmament.

At this juncture Sir Samuel Hoare, the British foreign secretary, and Pierre Laval, the French premier, concluded the *Hoare–Laval Pact, by which Italy was to receive substantial concessions at the expense of Abyssinia. There was a public outcry against these proposals, however, and Hoare was replaced by Anthony *Eden. Eden was himself to leave the government early in 1938 following a disagreement with his colleagues over Anglo-Italian relations.

the policy of appeasement Early in 1936 the international situation underwent further deterioration following Germany's denunciation of the Locarno Pact. Italy had by now completed the conquest of Abyssinia. Britain began to carry out rearmament on a larger scale, but the pace remained slow, and popular feeling – as a result of what many now regarded as the senseless slaughter of World War I – was strongly pacifist. Germany, having already embarked on a massive rearmament programme, seized its chance to occupy the Rhineland, which had been declared a demilitarized zone.

During 1937 the international situation grew worse. Two wars were in progress: the Sino-Japanese War and the Spanish Civil War. Japan and Germany both left the League of Nations before the year ended. Regarding the civil war in Spain, the British government, like the French, pursued a policy of 'nonintervention', and at the same time strove unsuccessfully to bring about the withdrawal from Spain of Italian, German, and Soviet 'volunteers' representing the rival ideologies of fascism and communism.

The policy of appeasement towards aggressor nations was continued by Neville Chamberlain, who succeed Baldwin as prime minister in 1937. Easy enough to criticize as weak and naïve in retrospect, appeasement at the time had few critics in Britain, a notable exception being Winston Churchill, who had been excluded from government since 1929. Initially few people believed Hitler's expansionist threats were anything but bluster, and Hitler himself had many admirers in the British establishment. By the end of 1937, however, Britain was more united on the main issue of rearmament, and to raise the money for this the rate of income tax was increased. But the German pace of rearmament continued to draw further ahead of the British effort.

the Munich Agreement The threats to peace grew more specific in 1938, and the year was marked by successive crises. Hitler assumed command of all the armed forces of the German Reich, thus proclaiming the restoration of Germany to its full military strength and its reliance upon that strength in seeking a remedy for its grievances.

Events were by now moving too swiftly for conciliatory action, and, by the beginning of September the countries of Europe were ranging themselves for conflict. Hitler's demands that Czechoslovakia cede the *Sudeten to Germany seemed to make war inevitable and, as France had guaranteed the integrity of Czechoslovakia, and Britain was committed to uphold the security of France, Britain was immediately involved.

In September Chamberlain resolved to make a personal effort to avert the catastrophe. Travelling for the first

time by aeroplane, he sought a direct interview with Hitler at his home at Berchtesgaden, and followed this journey by two other flights to Germany in order to secure the acceptance of a plan agreed upon with France, which, in effect, called upon Czechoslovakia to make heavy sacrifices in the cause of peace. In the same month the Munich Conference was held, at which Chamberlain signed (29 September) with Hitler a declaration pledging their two countries to seek peaceful means of settling any future differences arising between them. Chamberlain sincerely believed that he had, in his own words, 'brought back peace in our time'. But most neutral opinion justifiably regarded the declaration on Hitler's part as worthless and hypocritical and the whole transaction as a betrayal of Czechoslovakia.

preparations for war In 1939 foreign policy still dominated all other political issues in Britain, and nominally the government was still wedded to appeasement. The first sign of any change in the government's policy was the opening of consultations with the USSR on the possibility of German aggression in southeastern Europe, but the discussion had no concrete result.

On 31 March, when the air was full of rumours of German designs on Poland, Chamberlain announced that Britain would lend its support to Poland if that country were attacked. Again, when Italy overran Albania, the prime minister announced that, in the event of any action that threatened Greece or Romania, Britain would lend those countries all the support in its power.

These pledges marked the end of the much-criticized appeasement policy, and the government now introduced a limited measure of conscription and by doubling the strength of the Territorial Army. Having given guarantees to Greece and Romania, the government realized the importance of securing the assistance of Turkey, and negotiations with that country were successful. Chamberlain was in fact making every effort to build up a 'peace front', but his hopes of getting the support of the USSR were disappointed.

With the German threat to Danzig (Gdansk) in July and flagrant violations of Polish rights there, the approach of war was now obvious. The British people had by now become inured to the prospect of war, and on all sides it was recognized that Nazi methods were incompatible with any settled order in Europe. On 24 August Lord *Halifax (the foreign secretary) reiterated Britain's resolve to stand by Poland. However, Hitler ignored this, and German armies invaded Poland on 1 September. On 3 September Britain declared war.

the phoney war On the outbreak of war the government immediately introduced a number of measures. Under the National Service Bill nearly all men from the age of 18 to 41 became liable to be called up for military service. An Emergency Powers Act was passed at the same time, which empowered the government to do almost anything to secure public safety, maintain order, and prosecute the war. Large-scale evacuation of women and children was carried out from London and other big cities, leading to serious educational and social problems.

Owing, however, to the fact that there were no air raids in the early months of the war many of these returned to their former homes. For many months – during the so-called phoney war, when there was no fighting in Western Europe – the people of Britain largely followed their normal peacetime way of life, a state of things that was destined to be rudely interrupted by Hitler's offensives in Western Europe, starting with the attack on Norway in April 1940, and ending with the defeat of France in June.

It was increasingly felt during the first nine months, while Chamberlain was prime minister, that the war was not being prosecuted with the efficiency or vigour necessary to ensure even the possibility of ultimate victory. Matters came to a head with the utter failure of the Norwegian expedition, and the various elements of discontent boiled up in a debate in the House of Commons in which Leo Amery summed up the feeling of the effective majority when he addressed to the prime minister the words of Oliver Cromwell to the Long Parliament, ending in the cry 'In God's name go!'.

retreat from Dunkirk Within a few hours of this speech a new coalition administration had been formed, and Winston Churchill – who had joined the government on the outbreak of war as first lord of the admiralty – became prime minister. Clement *Attlee, the leader of the Labour Party, became deputy prime minister, and other senior Labour figures entered the government as members of the war cabinet, and to head up the crucial ministries of labour and supply. Churchill's leadership was to make an immense contribution to the successful conduct of the war, and, through his speeches to the country, broadcast on the radio, he also played a vital role in maintaining the morale of the British people.

On 22 May Parliament passed the Emergency Powers (Defence) Act, which gave the government complete power of control over persons and property for the prosecution of the war. Thus full mobilization of the country's resources was begun much more promptly and more efficiently than it had been in World War I.

Following the sweep of the German armies across France, the British Expeditionary Force began to be evacuated at Dunkirk from 26 May, being forced to leave behind virtually all of its equipment. France surrendered shortly afterwards, and

Britain appeared to be faced with imminent invasion, as the Germans massed their armies in and about the Channel ports and assembled a large fleet of transports and barges. A *Home Guard of part-time soldiers was hastily enrolled in Britain to assist in the defence of their factories and homes.

the Battle of Britain and the Blitz But it was evident that as the Germans did not command the sea, they could not hope to land an invading army with any chance of success unless they first secured supremacy in the air over the Channel and the British Isles. In the middle of August they began daylight air operations on a large scale with the aim of destroying British airfields, and air battles between large forces occurred almost daily for over a month (see *Britain, Battle of).

By the middle of September it was clear that the Germans were suffering ruinous loss and were no nearer to their objective. They then abandoned the massed assaults by daylight and adopted the policy of night raiding, in which they avoided heavy casualties at the cost of giving up their hope of destroying the defending air force and also at the sacrifice of anything like accuracy of aim. Their attacks fell principally on the major cities, especially London. The main ports were also heavily attacked, a great deal of damage being done. The *Blitz in its most intense phase lasted till the end of spring 1941, and accounted for some 40,000 civilian deaths.

the widening of the anti-Axis alliance By this stage Britain was the only country left in Europe still resisting Hitler, although the self-governing dominions and the rest of the British Empire had all also declared war on Germany. Throughout 1941 Churchill made strenuous efforts to broaden Britain's support. The increasing scale of US aid for Britain before the USA formally declared war on the Axis, and the growth of

collaboration in every sphere between the two countries, owed much to Churchill's handling of Anglo-American relations. His meeting with President Roosevelt of the USA at sea in August led to the *Atlantic Charter, a statement of joint aims, and following the German invasion of the USSR in June Churchill had set aside all ideological differences to declare Britain's full support for the Soviet Union – although for geographical reasons this was largely restricted to the supply of arms and munitions via the Arctic convoys.

Over the broad field of strategy throughout 1941 the ultimately dominant factor was British sea power. The problem for Germany was how to consolidate its conquests in Western Europe while under the constant pressure of the British naval blockade. If the blockade could be maintained it was evident that the Germans during the year must attempt to break out of the encirclement, whether by invasion of Britain, by a thrust towards the Mediterranean at either end, or by pushing further east than Poland. In the event, the Germans chose the eastern and southern options. The weakest link in the British chain of encirclement was the Mediterranean, and the contest for its control was to be long drawn out and fluctuating.

At the same time the attempt to set up a German counter-blockade continued throughout 1941 in the Atlantic, where the Germans hoped, by means of unrestricted submarine warfare based on the French ports, to cut off Britain from US food supplies and munitions. By this time the USA had become convinced that its own national future depended upon sustaining Britain's resistance to aggression, and embarked upon the *lend-lease programme, by which Britain and the USSR received vast amounts of material aid.

In December 1941 Japan launched its attacks on US and British bases in the

Pacific and Southeast Asia, bring the USA into the war alongside Britain, but its initial territorial and military losses in the Asia–Pacific theatre were as disastrous as Britain's. It was to be some time before British and US naval power could rally and restore the balance.

At home, the National Service Act passed at the end of 1941 conscripted for military or other vital war purposes all men between 18 and 50, and all unmarried women between 20 and 30 (later extended to 50).

the tide begins to turn During the first six months of 1942 Parliament reflected the uneasiness of the nation at a disheartening series of military reverses and disasters. The British Eighth Army was driven out of Libya, and with the Germans threatening Egypt Parliament was anxious and critical. Churchill, for the first time, had to meet the challenge of a motion of no confidence in the 'central direction of the war' in the House of Commons, but the vote of censure motion was defeated by 476 to 25 votes.

Although German air activity over Britain had declined greatly from the weight of the 1940 raids, the Germans, during April–May, carried out a number of heavy raids on the cathedral cities of Exeter, Bath, Norwich, and York (Canterbury was attacked in October), doing considerable damage to life and property (see *Baedeker raids).

However, by the time a new session of Parliament opened in November, the Germans were in full retreat from Egypt (see *Alamein, El, Battles of), a large Anglo-American expeditionary force had successfully landed in French North Africa, and the whole outlook in the Mediterranean had changed. In addition, Britain was now waging more effective war against the German submarines, and British bombers began massed attacks on German factories and cities. In 1943 Anglo-American forces invaded Italy, and Churchill, with the foreign secretary,

Eden, took part in a series of international conferences at which t he Allied war plans were coordinated and provision was made for continued collaboration after the war – a collaboration that, in the result, was to be far from whole-hearted.

reshaping society The needs of total war mobilization had a great levelling effect on society in Britain. Free medical care was more widely available, and food rationing actually resulted in the poorer sectors of society being much better fed than before the war.

With the war progressing favourably, Parliament turned its attention increasingly to post-war policies, particularly in physical and social reconstruction. In February 1943 the government accepted in principle the plan for social security expounded in the *Beveridge Report, and in a broadcast to the nation on 21 March Churchill outlined a four-year plan of post-war social policy to be carried out by a national government, representing all parties. Late in December R A *Butler, then minister of education, introduced his new Education Bill, which completely recast the national system of education, introducing compulsory, free education to the age of 16, and reorganizing secondary schools into grammar schools, secondary modern schools, and technical schools. There were also considerable reforms in the field of social security, which laid the foundations of the post-war welfare state.

The housing problem, however, was to prove intractable, both as to immediate needs and regarding long-term programmes. The bombardment by German flying bombs and V2 rockets from 1943 prevented an early resumption of building. The Town and Country Planning Act, giving local authorities wider power to purchase compulsorily land required for the reconstruction of blitzed and blighted areas, became law after an acrimonious passage through Parliament.

the cost of the war The great industrial effort behind the armed forces assured the success of the invasion of Normandy on D-Day, 6 June 1944 – and ultimately the success of the Allies in Europe, culminating in the German surrender in May 1945. Although the maximum mobilization of the population had been reached in 1943, the accumulation of armed strength in men and munitions continued. On D-Day there were 4.5 million men in the British armed forces and 500,000 women in the auxiliary forces.

Up to this date war production had been more than twice that achieved in World War I. Britain itself had produced 70% of the munitions supplied to the British Empire, other Empire countries had produced another 10%, while the balance came from the USA. From the beginning of the war to the end of 1943 Britain built 6,858,313 tonnes/tons of new merchant shipping and, in agriculture, the ploughing up of 28,000 sq km/ 11,000 sq mi of grassland had resulted in halving food imports.

By the end of the war 202,000 houses in Britain were totally destroyed, and another 255,000 rendered uninhabitable. At sea nearly 3,000 British ships had been sunk. Exports had been reduced to less than a third of the 1938 figure. Direct taxation had increased from £494 million in 1938 to £1,781 million in 1943, and indirect from £582 million to £1,249 million. Total war expenditure had now reached the great sum of £25,000 million. To pay for imports of war materials the government had to sell overseas assets worth £1,065 million, while incurring fresh overseas debts totalling £2,300 million.

Nearly a quarter of a million members of the British armed forces and over 58,000 civilians lost their lives during the war.

Although the war in the Asia–Pacific theatre was to continue until August 1945, victory in Europe was followed by a general election, in which the Labour Party won a landslide victory.

For British history from 1945 see *United Kingdom.

United Nations UN, association of states for international peace, security, and cooperation, with its headquarters in New York City. The UN was established on 24 October 1945 by 51 states as a successor to the *League of Nations. Its Charter, whose obligations member states agree to accept, sets out four purposes for the UN: to maintain international peace and security; to develop friendly relations among nations; to cooperate in solving international problems and in promoting respect for human rights; and to be a centre for the harmonizing the actions of nations. The UN has played a role in development assistance, disaster relief, cultural cooperation, aiding refugees, and peacekeeping. Its membership in 2001 stood at 189 states, and the total proposed budget for 2000–01 (raised by the member states) was US$2.5 billion, supporting more than 50,000 staff.

The UN has six principal institutions. Five are based in New York: the General Assembly, the Security Council, the Economic and Social Council, the Trusteeship Council, and the Secretariat. The sixth, the International Court of Justice, is located at the Peace Palace in the Hague, Netherlands. Kofi Annan, from Ghana, became secretary general in 1997, and was re-elected for a second term in 2001. In January 1998, Louise Fréchette, a Canadian, was elected its first deputy secretary general. In October 2001, Annan and the UN itself were awarded the 2001 Nobel Prize for Peace. There are six official working languages: English, French, Russian, Spanish, Chinese, and Arabic. The name 'United Nations' was coined by US president Franklin D Roosevelt.

United States: history 1861–77 for
events after 1945 see *United States of
America.

the outbreak of the Civil War
As state after state in the South
seceded to form the Confederacy, their
senators and congressmen withdrew
from Congress. In many of the
Southern states, forts, arsenals, and
munition supplies belonging to the
national government were taken over
by the Southerners. Before President
James Buchanan left office this was the
case everywhere with a few striking
exceptions, the chief of which were
the forts guarding the harbour of
Charleston, South Carolina, where
secession began. Here Maj Robert
Anderson left Fort Moultrie and took
its guns to the stronger Fort Sumter,
where he prepared to hold out with
the regular (Union or Federal) soldiers.

In March 1861 the Republican
Abraham Lincoln was inaugurated as
president. In his speech he affirmed
that he did not propose to interfere
with slavery where it already existed.
But he also asserted that no state could
withdraw from the Union, and that it
would be his duty to preserve, protect,
and defend the Union. A little more
than a month later, Lincoln, against the
advice of a majority of his cabinet,
decided that Fort Sumter must be
relieved, and in accordance with a
promise made to the governor of South
Carolina, notified him, on 8 April 1861,
of this intention.

The Confederate cabinet was also
divided, but militant counsels finally
prevailed, and Gen Pierre Beauregard,
who was now in charge of the
Charleston forces, was ordered to take
the fort. The bombardment began on
12 April, and 34 hours later the fort
was surrendered. Two days later
Lincoln issued a call for 75,000 troops.
Northern Democratic leaders rallied
to the cause.

In the South, Virginia, which had
at first been against secession, now
joined the Confederacy together with

Arkansas, Tennessee, and North
Carolina, and soon all the 11 Southern
states were united. The states of the
Confederacy were North Carolina,
South Carolina, Georgia, Florida,
Alabama, Louisiana, Mississippi,
Texas, Virginia, Tennessee, and
Arkansas. There were four border
states that were also slave states:
Delaware, Maryland, Kentucky, and
Missouri. Special efforts were made
by the South to win Missouri and
Kentucky. The governors of these
states favoured secession, but their
legislatures defeated them.

**the North's advantages over the
South** In the conflict that was now
beginning the North had certain
advantages that were ultimately
to weigh decisively in the balance.
Its population were more educated,
and it had greater wealth. It was
immeasurably more advanced
industrially, the South being mainly
agricultural and dependent for most
other things on purchases from the
North and from Europe. The North
also had better railways. It was
completely self-contained, and could
meet all its own needs and those of
its armies. If there was to be a lengthy
war, the Northern numbers would tell.
The North, too, had the stronger
navy and soon had command of the
sea, enabling the Union government
to blockade the ports of the South.
As Lincoln called for 75,000 troops,
Jefferson Davis, president of the
Confederacy, asked for 100,000, and at
the same time moved the capital of the
Confederacy from Montgomery, Alabama,
to Richmond, Virginia, in July 1861.

international reactions The first
real clash of arms came on 21 July 1861
between the Northern army under
Irvin McDowell and the Southerners
under Beauregard and Albert Johnston,
at the First Battle of Bull Run. The
Union forces were routed, retreating
as far as Washington, DC.

While the fighting was going on in
Virginia and Missouri, relations with

Britain assumed great importance. There was dismay in the North when on 13 May 1861 a proclamation of neutrality was issued by Britain that accorded to the Confederacy belligerent rights such as are granted to a sovereign nation. Most of the European nations soon followed. Nor was the situation improved when the so-called 'Trent Affair' occurred, in which a Union warship seized two Confederate commissioners from a neutral British ship.

the war in 1862: Fort Donelson to Fair Oaks The North was beginning to gather strength. Nearly half a million men had come to the colours, when only about half that number had responded so far in the South. In 1862 Federal strength first began to show. In the West Ulysses S Grant captured Fort Donelson on the Cumberland River; the Confederate Simon Bolivar Buckner was forced to accept Grant's stipulation of unconditional surrender, and gave up an army of 15,000 men.

The opposing forces next met in the Battle of Shiloh on 6–7 April 1862. The first day's fighting favoured the Confederates, but Albert S Johnston, one of the best of the Confederate commanders, was killed. In the second day's fighting the Union forces won and the Confederates retreated to Corinth. Another blow was struck at the Confederates when a fleet under David G Farragut ran past the forts protecting New Orleans and captured it.

In March 1862 George McClellan and the Army of the Potomac began the principal Federal advance against Richmond up the Virginia Peninsula, first coming upon the Confederates at Yorktown. His army had been weakened by the sudden withdrawal of 25,000 men to defend Washington, DC, and he settled down for a siege, only to find that the enemy had retreated. He met them in battle at Williamsburg, where once more the enemy retreated towards Richmond.

McClellan was again ready to move, when the officials at Washington conceived the idea of crushing 'Stonewall' Jackson, who was in the Shenandoah Valley. Jefferson Davis, the Confederate president, sent reinforcements to Jackson, who defeated Gen Nathaniel P Banks at Winchester, evaded the other two Union armies that were seeking him, and triumphantly led his men back to join the forces in line near Richmond.

In the meantime, on 31 May and 1 June, McClellan's army fought a great battle at Fair Oaks. At first it seemed as if the Union force had lost the day but the timely arrival of a new corps resulted in the Confederates being put to flight.

the war in 1862: the Seven Days' Battle to Antietam McClellan was now only 10 km/6 mi from Richmond, but Davis now appointed Robert E Lee as commander-in-chief of the Southern armies. Lee was quick to take advantage of the pause in McClellan's movement. He rushed up reinforcements from all over the South until he had an effective fighting force of 90,000 men against his enemy's 100,000.

Then ensued the Seven Days' Battle. Two severe engagements were fought in the last days of June at Mechanicsville and Gaines Mill, and on 1 July was fought the Battle of Malvern Hill. The Union forces settled down at last on the bank of the James River, while Lee withdrew to the defences of Richmond. Once more McClellan was ready to attempt the capture of Richmond. But all his plans came to nothing, because the government ordered him to return with his army to defend Washington. The administration made Henry Halleck commander-in-chief and gave Gen John Pope the best part of McClellan's army.

The Second Battle of Bull Run was fought on 29 August 1862, and the Union armies were beaten. Another defeat at Chantilly completely destroyed Pope's reputation as a general. Lincoln called on McClellan to resume command of the Army of the Potomac once more.

Lee had moved into Maryland, thinking to win that state to the Confederacy, to capture Baltimore, and then advance into Pennsylvania, thus carrying the war into Union territory. The stage was now set for the bloody struggle at Antietam (17 September 1862). The battle was a stalemate, 23,000 dead being left on the field. Lee retreated across the Potomac and McClellan delayed in following his enemy. He was now relieved of his command for good.

the Emancipation Proclamation and the last battles of 1862 Lincoln then took one of his most important steps. Hitherto he had merely struggled to preserve the Union intact. The slavery question had been held in abeyance for fear of alienating the Democrats in the North and the people in the border states. But now, on 22 September 1862, he issued his famous Emancipation Proclamation, declaring that the slaves in all states in rebellion against the government should be free on and after 1 January 1863.

The reaction in Europe was immediate, most nations being in sympathy with the abolition of slavery. But there was a reaction in the North itself. The Democrats made big gains in the November elections, and it was only New England and the border states that kept the House of Representatives Republican.

In the autumn of 1862 the Union general William Rosecrans won victories at Corinth and Murfreesboro, and most of Tennessee was in his possession. In the East, on 13 December 1862, Lee severely defeated Ambrose Burnside in the Battle of Fredericksburg.

the war in 1863: Chancellorsville to Chattanooga In the first days of May 1863 the Confederates won a great battle at Chancellorsville, but it cost them the life of 'Stonewall' Jackson. In the West Grant besieged Vicksburg with his army and a fleet of ironclads. The siege lasted six weeks and on 4 July 1863 the town was surrendered.

While the siege was still in progress the greatest battle of the war was fought at Gettysburg, Pennsylvania (1–3 July), after which Lee retreated to Virginia. This ended Lee's invasion of the North, and was the turning point of the war. In September 1863 Braxton Bragg beat the Union forces under Rosecrans at Chickamauga in Tennessee, but the Confederates suffered heavily at Chattanooga in November, forcing them to retreat into Georgia. This was one of the most important actions in the war, ensuring ultimate Federal success in the West.

the war in 1864: the Wilderness to Nashville These last battles had been fought with Grant as commander-in-chief. In February 1864 Lincoln made him lieutenant general in charge of all the armies. Grant now planned to end the war. He himself would face Lee in Virginia, seek to destroy his army, and take Richmond. At the same time he would send William Sherman to face Gen J E Johnston in Georgia.

In May 1864 began the two indecisive battles of the Wilderness in Virginia, and of Spotsylvania. On 3 June 1864 the enemies met at Cold Harbor, and here in less than an hour over 12,000 Union soldiers were killed or wounded. Grant had lost 60,000 men in his campaign; and the Confederates 40,000; but he knew that the South could not replace its losses in manpower, whereas the North could.

In the early autumn months Philip Sheridan won victories over the Confederates at Winchester and Cedar Creek and then laid waste the entire Shenandoah Valley. While Grant was fighting in the Wilderness Sherman began his march from Chattanooga. On 2 September 1864 he entered Atlanta. In the meantime, in August,

Admiral Farragut had won his famous victory of Mobile Bay, which had been the harbour for the Confederate blockade runners, a victory that destroyed the Confederate fleet.

In November, after strong opposition in his own party, Lincoln was renominated for president by the Republicans, and Andrew Johnson, a war Democrat from Tennessee, was nominated for vice-president. Gen McClellan was nominated by the Democrats. Lincoln was easily re-elected.

Less than two weeks after the election Sherman set out on his famous march to the sea from Atlanta. The army of 62,000 men accomplished the 480-km/300-mi journey, leaving destruction in its wake, and on 21 December Sherman entered Savannah unopposed. George H Thomas won the Battle of Nashville in December 1864 and thus drove the last of the Confederates out of Tennessee.

1865: the conclusion of the war
In January 1865 Wilmington, North Carolina, was taken by joint naval and military action, and the last remaining port of the Confederacy was closed. Sherman began his march back from the sea. Columbia was burned down, and Charleston was deserted by the Confederates. On 2 April the Union forces attacked Petersburg and captured it. At length, on 3 April 1865, the Union armies entered Richmond.

Lee was completely surrounded. At Appomattox Court House on 9 April he surrendered. Johnston surrendered his army to Sherman on 26 April, and by the end of May all the rest of the organized forces in the far South had also laid down their arms.

the aftermath of war In this costly civil war over 620,000 lives had been lost, while tens of thousands of soldiers returned with health permanently impaired. The public debt of the Union had risen to nearly $3,000 million. What it cost the Confederacy has never been definitely estimated.

Despite all this, the North was stronger than ever; but the South was ruined.

The victory of the Union did not bring real reconciliation between the sections. Reconstruction was only finally achieved at tremendous social and political cost, and many of the problems, especially racial, that plagued 20th-century America stemmed from the post-Civil War period.

On 14 April 1865 Lincoln was assassinated. He had been ready to accord the rebel states generous treatment; but his views did not meet with the approval of the Radical Republicans in Congress. Lincoln had been succeeded by his vice-president, Andrew Johnson, who maintained Lincoln's attitude towards the South. On 29 May 1865 he issued a pardon proclamation to the entire South. Under him, too, the Thirteenth Amendment to the Constitution, forbidding slavery in the USA, was adopted.

the Reconstruction period
But Johnson had not reckoned with Congress, which met on 4 December 1865 and at once passed a bill for the appointment of a committee whose function was to inquire into the question of the Southern states. In March they passed, over Johnson's veto, a bill giving blacks full rights as citizens, and this was afterwards embodied in the Fourteenth Amendment to the Constitution. Johnson's failure to work with moderate Republicans in guaranteeing basic rights and protection for the freed slave caused a Radical Republican triumph in the elections of 1866, and opened the way for the military enforcement of Reconstruction.

The Southern states, except Tennessee, were divided into five military districts. Civilian rule and full state rights were to be restored after the creation of constitutions based upon universal male suffrage and after ratification of the Fourteenth

Amendment. By 1868 all but three states were readmitted under these conditions, and Mississippi, Texas, and Virginia finally re-entered in 1870. The Fifteenth Amendment, ratified in March 1870, aimed to guarantee black male suffrage in the South.

Radical Reconstruction, however, was short-lived. One by one the Southern states were 'redeemed' by conservative political groups, and the Republican Party ceased to exist as a viable entity in the South. Corruption and incompetence had certainly been a part of Radical Reconstruction, but its defeat marked the end of attempts to elevate the freed slaves. Southern whites moved swiftly to disenfranchise freed slaves, who were increasingly subjected to violence by such organizations as the Ku Klux Klan. The lack of an independent economic base, moreover, meant that blacks would not advance significantly in the decades after the war. In 1877 the last of the Federal troops were removed from the South, ending the era of Reconstruction.

For black American history see *civil-rights movement.

United States of America   USA, country in North America, extending from the Atlantic Ocean in the east to the Pacific Ocean in the west, bounded north by Canada and south by Mexico, and including the outlying states of Alaska and Hawaii.

  government The USA is a federal republic comprising 50 states and the District of Columbia. Under the 1787 constitution, which took effect 1789 and has had 27 amendments, the constituent states are reserved considerable powers of self-government. The federal government concentrated originally on military and foreign affairs and the coordination of interstate concerns, leaving legislation in other spheres to the states, each with its own constitution, elected legislature, governor, supreme court, and local taxation powers. Since the

1930s, however, the federal government has become increasingly active and has therefore impinged upon what were previously state affairs. It has become the principal revenue-raising and spending agency. This activism was criticized during the 1980s, and Republican administrations professed a desire to reverse the process.

  The executive, legislative, and judicial branches of the federal government are deliberately separate from each other, working in a system of checks and balances. At the head of the executive branch is a president elected every four years in a national contest by universal adult suffrage, but votes are counted at the state level on a winner-takes-all basis, with each state (and the District of Columbia) being assigned seats (equivalent to the number of its congressional representatives) in a national electoral college that formally elects the president. The president serves as head of state, of the armed forces, and of the federal civil service. He or she is restricted to a maximum of two terms and, once elected, cannot be removed except through impeachment and subsequent conviction by Congress. The president works with a personally selected (appointed) cabinet team, subject to the Senate's approval, whose members are prohibited from serving in the legislature.

  The second branch of government, Congress, the federal legislature, comprises two houses, the 100-member Senate and the 435-member House of Representatives. Senators serve six-year terms, and there are two from each state regardless of its size and population. Every two years a third of the seats come up for election. Representatives are elected from state congressional districts of roughly equal demographic sizes and serve two-year terms.

  Congress has sole powers of legislation and operates through a system of specialized standing, select, and investigative committees, which are composed of members drawn from parties in accordance with their relative strength in each chamber. The Senate is the more powerful chamber of Congress, since its approval is required for key federal appointments and for the ratification of foreign treaties. The president's policy programme needs the approval of Congress, and the president addresses Congress in January for an annual 'State of the Union' speech and sends periodic 'messages' and 'recommendations'. The success of a president to carry out his or her platform depends on voting support in Congress, bargaining skills, and public support. Proposed legislation, to become law (an Act of Congress), requires the approval of both houses of Congress as well as the signature of the president. If differences arise, 'joint congressional committees' are convened to effect compromise agreements. The president can impose a veto, which can be overridden only by two-thirds majorities in both houses. Constitutional amendments require two-thirds majorities from both houses and the support of three-quarters of the nation's 50 state legislatures.

The third branch of government, the judiciary, headed by the Supreme Court, interprets the written US constitution; its function is to ensure that a correct balance is maintained between federal and state institutions and the executive and legislature and to uphold the constitution, especially the civil rights described in the first ten (the Bill of Rights) and later amendments. The Supreme Court comprises nine judges appointed by the president with the Senate's approval, who serve life terms and can only be removed by impeachment, trial, and conviction by Congress.

The USA administers a number of territories, including American Samoa and the US Virgin Islands, which have local legislatures and a governor.

These territories, as well as the 'self-governing territories' of Puerto Rico and Guam, each send a non-voting delegate to the US House of Representatives.

The District of Columbia, centred around the city of Washington DC, is the site of the federal legislature, judiciary, and executive. Since 1971 it has sent one non-voting delegate to the House and since 1961 its citizens have been able to vote in presidential elections (the District having three votes in the national electoral college).

history For the Civil War, and the period of Reconstruction, see *United States: history 1861–77.

the USA after World War II
The USA under the Democratic Party President Harry S *Truman emerged from World War II as a superpower, and maintained its internationalist stance during the prosperity of the post-war era. However, adjusting to peace was not without its domestic problems.

With the end of hostilities, in US industry the struggle between management and labour was renewed. Trade-union membership had increased during the war, and attempts to reduce wartime wages or at least to resist any increase – although prices remained high – were met by a series of strikes during 1945 and 1946 in the coal, automobile, steel, and electrical industries. Wages were bound up with prices, and the country was divided on the question of price control. The Price Control Act lapsed in June 1946, and by the end of the year President Truman had reluctantly to give way to the public agitation for the removal of controls. All controls were swept away except for those on rent, rice, and sugar.

attitudes towards the USSR
Against this domestic background of labour disputes, rapid demobilization, and sometimes violent readjustment to peacetime conditions, US foreign policy was conducted with the support

of Republicans and Democrats alike. The secretary of state, James F Byrnes, represented the USA at a series of international conferences beginning with the General Assembly of the United Nations in January 1946, and ending with the Peace Conference in Paris from July to October.

US foreign policy was largely united by suspicion of the USSR's intentions. Reacting from the unfavourable reception given by the USSR to his plans for four-power control of Germany for 25 years, Byrnes in a speech at Stuttgart in September 1946 spoke in terms of German unity and cooperation with the West. Henry *Wallace resigned as secretary of commerce, denouncing Byrnes's policy of resistance to the USSR, a policy that Wallace believed was merely in the interests of British imperialism. This controversy aggravated the difficulties that the Democratic Party had to face in the Congressional elections in November. The Republicans gained a majority in both the House of Representatives and the Senate, the first Republican majority in Congress since 1930.

the Truman Doctrine and Marshall Aid In foreign affairs relations with the USSR continued to occupy the State Department. Early in 1947 Byrnes was succeeded as secretary of state by Gen George C *Marshall. Events in Greece (where there was a civil war between communists and royalists) provided the occasion for an important speech by President Truman in March 1946, calling for US aid to Greece and Turkey (where the USA also feared Soviet interference), and laying down the policy, later known as the *Truman Doctrine, of helping any country in danger of coming under communist rule.

In May $350 million authorized for relief work through the United Nations Relief and Rehabilitation Association was taken over to be administered

direct by the US government itself in Europe and China. The way was thus prepared for the most significant event of the year, the speech by Gen Marshall at Harvard University in June 1947 advocating US aid to enable Europe to recover its normal economy. The speech was recognized as an invitation to the countries of Europe to examine their needs and to jointly form a plan of development that US aid would make possible.

The foreign ministers of the UK, France, and the USSR met in Paris in June 1947 to discuss Marshall's offer. Soviet participation was later withdrawn. In spite of this a conference on European economic cooperation opened in Paris, and as a result of its recommendations the Economic Cooperation Bill was passed by Congress in April the following year. The *Marshall Plan, which thus came into effect in 1947, was designed to strengthen the capitalist economies of the USA's allies, enabling them to resist any similar ideologically related aid offers from the USSR, which already dominated the countries of Eastern Europe that it had liberated at the end of World War II. The *Cold War was under way.

Events in Europe, particularly the communist coup d'état in Czechoslovakia in February 1948, gave considerable impetus to the project for aid to Europe. In June the Senate adopted a resolution proposed by Arthur *Vandenberg, chair of the Senate Foreign Relations Committee, with the intention of giving aid to Europe in defence as well as in economic affairs, and thus admitting the possibility of regional defence pacts within the framework of the UN Charter. In the same year the USA helped to create the *Organization of American States (OAS).

domestic politics in the later 1940s At home, the administration had been at odds with Congress over its budget proposals in 1947. Congress proposed a greater measure of tax reduction than President Truman considered safe in view of the possibility of inflation, but the congressional proposals were successfully vetoed. The president's veto was, however, unable to prevent the anti-labour legislation contained in the Taft-Hartley Labor Act of June 1947.

Both the Republican and Democratic parties supported Truman's foreign policy, which was not an issue in the presidential election due to take place in 1948. At the Democratic convention in July Truman was nominated, but with no general conviction of success on the part of his supporters. T E *Dewey was nominated as Republican candidate (as he had been in 1944).

Truman, himself confident, confounded the prophets by polling 24,105,812 votes in the popular ballot, against 21,970,005 for Dewey. The party position in both houses of Congress was reversed, the Democrats gaining a majority. The results put Truman in a position to launch his 'Fair Deal' programme, which included the repeal of the Taft-Hartley Act (pressed for by organized labour, which had given strenuous political support to the Democrats), and the introduction of civil-rights legislation. He was, however, disappointed by the unwillingness of Congress to embark on either of these measures during 1949.

The economic situation was depressed in 1948–49, but improved after October 1949, and at the turn of the year there was a marked if short-lived boom, unemployment being appreciably reduced.

the formation of the Western alliance In foreign affairs, the *Vandenberg Resolution of June 1948 had provided the initiative for consultations between the USA and the Five Powers (the UK, France, the Netherlands, Belgium, and Luxembourg), which in March 1948 had signed a treaty of mutual assistance (see *Brussels, Treaty of).

Other countries (Italy, Portugal, Denmark, Norway, and Iceland) were invited to participate, and these ten countries with the USA and Canada concluded the North Atlantic Treaty, which was signed in Washington in April 1949, thus creating NATO as a Western military alliance against the perceived Soviet threat.

The passage of the second year's appropriations for the Marshall Plan, acceptance of the North Atlantic Treaty and the Mutual Assistance Act for European defence, and the renewal of the Reciprocal Trade Agreements Act were features of a constructive foreign policy that afforded significant evidence of continued appreciation by both political parties of the new position of the USA in world affairs.

Then came the Korean crisis, and in July 1949 Truman, in his message to Congress, asked for $10,000 million for the US armed forces and said he would request further sums for military aid to the NATO powers and other nations vital to US security. He also reported to Congress that he had authorized the secretary of defence to call up as many men as might be needed, and he asked for the statutory limits of the strength of the armed forces to be removed.

the Korean War In June 1949 the forces of communist North Korea crossed the 38th parallel and launched an attack against the republic of South Korea (*Korean War). Truman announced that US forces would intervene, and immediately afterwards the Security Council of the UN decided to invoke military sanctions against the aggressors. British and Australian naval and air forces were placed at the disposal of the US commander, Gen Douglas *MacArthur, who assumed command of all UN forces. At the same time the Seventh US Fleet was placed between Taiwan (which was in the hands of the Chinese Nationalists) and mainland (communist) China to prevent further acts of aggression against that island by organized communist troops.

During June–July 1950 the UN troops in Korea were driven farther south, eventually centring their defence on Taegu, in positions extending over a perimeter of 200 km/ 125 mi from Pohang to Pusan. In September, US troops were landed behind the communist lines at Inchon, in a major UN counteroffensive. Landings were made at several other points on the occupied coast, and other troops advanced north from the Pusan perimeter. Troops in the north had captured Seoul by the end of September, and the UN forces were on the Yalu River on the border of China by November, having crossed the 38th parallel a month before.

In January 1951, after repeated warnings to the UN forces to withdraw, the Chinese communists intervened and launched a large-scale offensive, sweeping deep into South Korea. But by April the UN forces had checked the advance and pushed the communists back beyond the 38th parallel again. In April 1951 MacArthur was replaced by Gen Ridgway, who in turn was replaced, in 1952, by Gen Mark *Clark. Bitter fighting continued, while truce negotiations, begun in July 1951, took their slow course. An armistice was eventually signed in July 1953.

Truman's second term The Korean War contributed to the wave of anti-communist hysteria that swept the USA from 1950, spearheaded by Senator Joe *McCarthy. Truman and his secretary of state Dean *Acheson (who had succeeded Marshall in 1949) were accused of being 'soft on communism', and Truman's second term as president ended somewhat stormily. In November 1950 an unsuccessful attempt on his life had been made by Puerto Rican nationalists. Through 1951 and 1952 inflationary pressures upset the domestic life of the nation, and there were several major strikes.

There were also disturbing cases of criminal corruption on a large scale. The growing fear of communist infiltration into the USA showed itself in retrograde and restrictive legislation such as the McCarran–Walter Immigration Act, which was enacted despite Truman's veto.

Eisenhower comes to power For the 1952 presidential election the Republicans chose Gen Dwight D *Eisenhower as their candidate, with Richard *Nixon as vice-presidential candidate. Eisenhower's nomination was the subject of bitter controversy within the Republican Party itself, the influential right wing preferring Robert *Taft. Once nominated, however, Eisenhower swept into office on a wave of popularity, easily defeating his Democratic rival, Adlai *Stevenson. The rightward shift in US public opinion, together with Eisenhower's image as the hero of World War II, contributed to his becoming the first Republican president since Hoover. The Republicans also gained control of Congress by a very narrow margin.

Eisenhower adhered to the Truman–Acheson doctrine of 'containment of communism', while at home he pursued a policy of 'progressive conservatism' designed to encourage business enterprise. The Eisenhower era was one of economic growth, involving the migration of southern blacks to the northern industrial cities, and rapid expansion in the educational sector.

Eisenhower's first term Eisenhower's first term proved generally successful at home. The administration weathered a threatened economic recession in 1953–54, and a Korean ceasefire was signed in July 1953 (Eisenhower had visited Korea in December 1952 in fulfilment of his election promises). To the black population the decision of the Supreme Court in May 1954 that racial segregation in schools was unconstitutional was very naturally associated with the prevailing Republican administration.

In 1954 the Democrats regained control of Congress, and after this date the influence of Senator Joe McCarthy declined rapidly, and his anti-communist witch hunt came to an end. Democratic critics of Eisenhower have suggested, with some justification, that the president found it easier to work with a Democratic Congress than with one controlled by his own party. By the end of the Eisenhower's first term the administration's most obvious domestic problem was the relatively weak position of the farming community in an otherwise flourishing economy.

In foreign affairs tension in eastern Asia eased after the Geneva Conference of 1954 had ended the Indochina War, even though the USA continued to refuse recognition to the communist government in Beijing. In European matters, the death of Stalin was interpreted as the beginning of an easing of the Cold War, an idea strengthened in the popular mind by the meeting of heads of government (including Eisenhower and Soviet premier Nikolai Bulganin) in Geneva in 1955.

Eisenhower's second term In 1956, in spite of recent serious illness, Eisenhower ran for the presidency again, once more with Nixon as vice-presidential candidate, and with Stevenson again his Democratic opponent. The last days of the election campaign were overshadowed by the anti-communist rising in Hungary, and by the *Suez Crisis (which Eisenhower did much to defuse). The ominous foreign news possibly made many Americans cling more than ever to a president who seemed to have transcended party ties and to have become a national idol. Eisenhower was elected by a landslide vote, but it was essentially a personal victory, and the Republicans failed to gain control of Congress.

In the southern states, where racial segregation and discrimination were openly practised, a new civil-rights movement developed under the leadership of Dr Martin Luther *King, Jr. Further steps towards civil rights were made by the 1957 Civil Rights Act, which set up a Civil Rights Commission. In the same year Eisenhower sent federal troops to Little Rock, Arkansas, to enforce racial desegregation in schools.

During 1957–58 the Anglo-American alliance, which had been jeopardized by the Suez crisis, was largely rebuilt, and the USA showed increasing willingness to take the initiative in Middle East affairs, intervening militarily when stability in the Lebanon seemed threatened, July–October 1958. But to most Americans 1958–59 was dominated by the severe business recession, which caused a steep rise in unemployment. It further affected the Republicans' already declining popularity. In addition, Americans felt increasing insecurity from the Soviets' lead in the space race (they had launched the first artificial satellite into space in 1957), though a US 4-tonne missile was fired into orbit in December 1958.

In April 1959 John Foster *Dulles resigned as secretary of state, and died a month later. Eisenhower had allowed him considerable scope in foreign affairs, and US foreign policy had been strongly tinged by his rigidly anti-communist views, which had led to the creation of two anti-communist military alliances: the *Central Treaty Organization in the Middle East, and the Southeast Asia Treaty Organization. A future improvement in US–Soviet relations seemed possible early in 1960, but was nullified in May, when Eisenhower was faced, at the Summit Conference in Paris, with a demand from Soviet leader Nikita Khrushchev for a US apology for the *U-2 incident some days earlier, when a US reconnaissance plane was shot

down over the USSR. The break-up of
the conference inevitably followed.

Kennedy comes to power Richard
Nixon, the vice-president, was chosen
as Republican candidate for the 1960
presidential elections. The Democrats
nominated John F *Kennedy, with
Lyndon B *Johnson, Kennedy's bitter
rival for the presidential nomination,
as vice-presidential candidate. Popular
reaction after eight years of Republican
administration swung the polls in
Kennedy's favour, though in the event
he won the presidency only by a very
narrow margin. He was the USA's first
Roman Catholic president.

At his inauguration Kennedy
referred to a 'new frontier' challenging
the American nation, and he initiated
a vigorous programme of social
reform, which included proposals for
some state-aided medical care, and the
establishment of full civil rights for all
US citizens, regardless of religion or
race. The end of the recession and a
new period of economic boom gave
impetus to Kennedy's programme; but
opposition to his reforms was
prolonged and powerful, and the
actual enactment of his major domestic
measures was not to be achieved by
Kennedy, but by his successor.

Kennedy, the Cold War, and Cuba
Foreign affairs dominated Kennedy's
presidency. The US space programme
began to catch up with that of the
USSR: the first American was rocketed
into space in May 1961, and in
February 1962 John *Glenn became
the first American to orbit the Earth.
In 1961 Kennedy made a triumphal
progress of Western Europe, and met
Khrushchev in Vienna; in September
1961 the USA and Russia agreed on
the principles for disarmament
negotiations.

In April 1961 there was an
unsuccessful anti-Castro invasion of
Cuba by Cuban exiles based in Florida
(see *Bay of Pigs); this, a commitment
that Kennedy had largely inherited
from the previous administration, and

whose ignominious failure showed up
the weaknesses of American
intelligence, had the effect of driving
Cuba further to the left and into a
closer relationship with the USSR.

Throughout 1962 there was a Soviet
arms build-up in Cuba. In October
Kennedy alleged that Soviet offensive
missile sites were being erected in
Cuba, and announced that a US naval
blockade of the island would be
maintained until the bases were
dismantled. His firmness paid off.
Khrushchev announced that the USSR
would dismantle the rocket bases in
Cuba and return them to the USSR (see
*Cuban missile crisis). The president's
handling of this explosive situation
brought him widespread acclaim, even
though the confrontation had brought
the two countries close to nuclear war,
and extreme Republicans continued to
press for even stronger action on Cuba.

In 1963 Kennedy was able to
announce major tax reductions, and
in August the USA signed the Nuclear
Test-Ban Treaty in Moscow, ushering
in a new era of 'peaceful coexistence'.
However, Kennedy also increased the
US military commitment to Vietnam
(see below). Then, in November,
Kennedy was assassinated in Dallas,
Texas. His loss was mourned
throughout the world.

**Johnson succeeds to the
presidency** Kennedy was
automatically succeeded as president
by the vice-president, Lyndon B
Johnson, who, in 1964, was elected
president in his own right. Johnson
gained an overwhelming victory over
the right-wing Republican, Barry
*Goldwater, whose nomination had
caused many traditional Republicans
to vote Democrat. The Republican
Party had, in fact, reached a low ebb,
and was threatening to become
the preserve of the states' rights
supporters, and, by implication,
of the segregationists. Subsequently,
however, the rise to power of men like
John Lindsay, elected Republican

mayor of New York in 1965, indicated that a revival of liberal Republicanism might be imminent (although Lindsay himself subsequently became a Democrat).

Johnson and the 'Great Society' Following Kennedy's death it was left to Johnson to oversee the passage of additional liberal reforms, called the 'Great Society' by Johnson. During 1965 Johnson managed to carry through Congress three liberalizing acts that owed their inspiration to Kennedy: the *Medicare Act, the Immigration Act, and the Voting Rights Act. His success in handling the legislature was to make him one of the most effective of modern US presidents in domestic affairs. Other pieces of liberal legislation included the Equal Opportunities Act and the Housing Act. All these measures combined to guarantee black Americans their civil rights and extended the reach and responsibilities of the federal government.

Increasing concern for the political status of black people was shown by some impressive civil-rights demonstrations in many US cities. The 1955 bus boycott in Montgomery, Alabama, organized by Martin Luther King, had marked the beginning of a new dynamic phase in the fight against Southern segregation, involving greater use of direct-action tactics, including the 'sit-in' after 1960. The complexity of the racial problem in the USA was highlighted also by sporadic but serious racial riots – for example, in Rochester, New York State, in the summer of 1964, and in Los Angeles in 1965 and 1966. However, the black migration to the northern cities was to go into reverse from 1970, stimulated by new economic opportunities in US Sunbelt states, new black political influence, and a feeling of returning to earlier roots.

escalation in Vietnam By mid-1965 the civil-rights issue was being overshadowed by the *Vietnam War. The USA had first sent military

'advisers' to South Vietnam in 1956, when Eisenhower was president. In 1960 Kennedy had increased the number of these advisers. By 1965 the communist threat to South Vietnam was regarded as so serious, and the South so clearly incapable of meeting it alone, that Johnson in May committed US troops to the Asian mainland in strength. By March 1966 nearly 250,000 Americans were fighting in Vietnam.

The US policy was queried by a number of its traditional allies, notably France, but was supported by Harold Wilson, the British premier, and by Australia, New Zealand, and South Korea, the three last-named of whom all sent token contingents to South Vietnam. The US policy was based on the American desire to 'contain' communism, and stemmed from memories of other areas in the world, such as Cuba, where US action had been too little and had come too late to prevent a communist takeover. (The controversial US military intervention in the Dominican Republic in 1965 was also influenced by these factors.) Nevertheless, as time passed, liberal elements in the USA itself challenged the government's policy on Vietnam, fortified by the recognition that the war was not being won. The war polarized public opinion and deeply divided the Democratic Party into 'hawks' and 'doves'. The communist *Tet offensive of February 1968 caused great alarm in government circles, and in March, as domestic opposition to the war intensified, Johnson simultaneously announced a new peace initiative and his decision not to stand for re-election in the autumn.

the 1968 presidential election The 1968 election was fought on the issues of inflation and law and order, as well as the war in Vietnam. The violence that accompanied the Democratic convention in Chicago, when antiwar demonstrators clashed with police and troops, was a timely reminder of the relationship between America's foreign and domestic tensions.

The previous four years, moreover, had witnessed a progression of violent race riots in northern and western cities, the most serious being in Watts (Los Angeles) in 1965, and in Newark and Detroit in 1967. The summer of 1968 brought the assassination of two leading figures, the black civil-rights leader Martin Luther King in April, and in June Senator Robert *Kennedy, a brother of the former president and a leading contender for the Democratic nomination.

In the event, the election proved very close, with the former Republican vice-president, Richard Nixon, narrowly triumphing over the Democrat Hubert Humphrey, who had been Johnson's vice-president.

disengagement and détente
Foreign affairs and the continuing war in Vietnam dominated Nixon's first term. Working closely with his national security adviser, Henry *Kissinger, the president pledged continued commitment to the USA's allies, but made it clear that US troops would no longer be readily available.

Nixon escalated the Vietnam conflict by invading neighbouring Cambodia – giving rise to increased antiwar demonstrations at home, some of which were dealt with violently – before he began a gradual disengagement. In Vietnam itself the US military presence was to be phased out, and Vietnamese nationals were to take over the American role. 'Vietnamization', as the new policy was called, was to prove a failure, however, and Nixon's search for a satisfactory peace formula in Southeast Asia was yielding few results. In the spring of 1972, after a new communist offensive, the president announced resumed intensive bombing of the North and the mining of North Vietnamese harbours.

At the same time, Nixon was reversing the USA's traditional hostility towards China and the Soviet Union.

In February 1972 he undertook a massively publicized trip to Beijing, and quickly followed this with a visit to Moscow. Despite the continuing failure to find a peace settlement in Vietnam, therefore, the apparent dramatic thawing in the Cold War as indicated by the new détente with China and the Soviet Union made Nixon extremely popular. The Strategic Arms Limitation Talks resulted in the SALT I accord in 1972.

Nixon's domestic policies Although an economic conservative, Nixon accepted both budget deficits and economic controls when faced with the twin problems of unemployment and inflation. In August 1972 the president announced a 90-day freeze on prices, wages, and rents. Nixon later rejected mandatory controls in favour of a voluntary policy. In other areas of domestic affairs he was less successful. In 1969, for example, he proposed a Family Assistance Plan to replace the existing welfare system, but it failed to pass Congress. He suffered a further political setback when the Senate rejected two of his nominations for the Supreme Court.

the 1972 presidential election
During the summer of 1972 Nixon's popularity steadily increased. His opponent in the autumn election was Senator George *McGovern of South Dakota, an antiwar liberal, whom the Republicans succeeded in labelling a 'radical'. Through a combination of ill-fortune and ineptitude, McGovern never managed to establish his credibility with the American public. Moreover, his major weapon – the continuing war in Vietnam – was taken from him when a week before the election Henry Kissinger announced, prematurely as it turned out, an imminent ceasefire agreement with the North Vietnamese. Nixon won a shattering victory, gaining 61.3% of the vote and winning every state except Massachusetts and the District of Columbia.

the Watergate scandal The period from 1972 to 1974 was dominated by the series of political scandals collectively known as the *Watergate affair. Throughout the summer of 1973 Americans watched as a Senate committee conducted dramatic and revealing hearings into illegal government activities during and after the 1972 elections – in particular the break-in by some of Nixon's staff at the Democratic Party's headquarters at the Watergate Hotel. In October 1973, moreover, Vice-president Spiro Agnew was forced to resign after conviction on a tax-evasion charge and on the presentation of other evidence relating to political corruption.

Nixon's own position became increasingly precarious. As evidence accumulated that men close to the president had actively engaged in criminal concealment of evidence relating to the Watergate burglary, the House of Representatives initiated impeachment investigations. The focus of interest quickly became tape recordings that Nixon had made of his private conversations in the White House. In July 1974 the Supreme Court unanimously decreed that the remaining tapes must be surrendered, denying the president's claim of executive privilege. Finally, in August, when it became apparent that Nixon had lied in previous statements, the president resigned his office and was succeeded by Vice-president Gerald *Ford.

Ford's presidency With the last US forces having been withdrawn from Southeast Asia in 1973, and the end of the Watergate affair (the USA's most serious political crisis of the century), there began a period of relative calm in the United States. Ford pardoned Nixon, and kept the services of Kissinger and the policy of détente when he became president. Watergate had shaken the US public's confidence in the Washington establishment, and Ford faced a hostile, Democrat-dominated Congress that introduced legislation curbing the unauthorized power of the presidency, attempting to mend fences both at home and abroad. Ford also had to deal with the economic recession and increased OPEC oil prices that began under Nixon following the 1973 Arab–Israeli War, which Kissinger had played an important role in ending. Generally speaking, however, Ford's term of office proved uneventful.

the Carter presidency Ford ran in the presidential election of November 1976, but was defeated by Washington outsider and Democrat Jimmy *Carter, who promised open and honest government. Carter was a fiscal conservative but a social liberal, who sought to extend welfare provision through greater administrative efficiency. He substantially ended the fuel crisis through enforced conservation in the energy bills of 1978 and 1980.

In foreign relations President Carter emphasized human rights. In the Middle East, he moved close to a peace settlement in 1978–79 (the *Camp David Agreements) and in January 1979 the USA's diplomatic relations with communist China were fully normalized.

The Carter presidency was, however, brought down by two foreign-policy crises in 1979–80: the fall of the shah of Iran and the Soviet invasion of Afghanistan. The president's leadership style, military economies, and moralistic foreign policy were blamed by the press for weakening US influence abroad. There was a swell of anticommunist feeling and mounting support for a new policy of rearmament and selective interventionism.

President Carter responded to this new mood by enunciating the hawkish *Carter Doctrine in 1980 and supporting a new arms-development programme, but his popularity plunged during 1980 as economic recession gripped the country and US embassy staff were held hostage by Shiite Muslim fundamentalists in Tehran.

the Reagan administration The Republican Ronald *Reagan benefited from Carter's difficulties and was elected to the presidency in November 1980, when the Democrats also lost control of the Senate. The new president had risen to prominence as an effective, television-skilled campaigner. He purported to believe in a return to traditional Christian and family values and promoted a domestic policy of supply-side economics, decentralization, and deregulation.

The early years of the Reagan presidency witnessed substantial reductions in taxation, with cutbacks in federal welfare programmes that created serious hardships in many sectors as economic recession gripped the nation. Reagan rejected détente and spoke of the USSR as an 'evil empire' that needed to be checked by a military build-up and a readiness to employ force. This led to a sharp deterioration in Soviet–US relations, ushering in a new cold war during the Polish crisis of 1981. In 1983 US forces invaded the Caribbean island of *Grenada to oust the left-wing regime that had seized power.

Reagan was re-elected on a wave of optimistic patriotism in November 1984, defeating the Democrat ticket of Walter *Mondale and Geraldine *Ferraro by a record margin.

A radical tax-cutting bill was passed in Congress, and in 1986 a large budget and trade deficit developed (as a spending economy was developed to control Congress). At home and overseas the president faced mounting public opposition to his interventions in Central America. The new Soviet leader Mikhail Gorbachev pressed unsuccessfully for arms reduction during superpower summits in Geneva (November 1985) and

Reykjavik (October 1986), but a further summit in December 1987, with an agreement to scrap intermediate-range nuclear missiles, appeared to promise a new détente.

the Irangate scandal In November 1986 the Republican Party lost control of the Senate in the midterm elections, just before the disclosure of a scandal concerning US arms sales to Iran in return for hostages held in Beirut, with the profits illegally diverted to help the Nicaraguan 'Contra' (anticommunist) guerrillas. The *Irangate scandal briefly dented public confidence in the administration and forced the dismissal and resignation of key cabinet members.

During the last two years of his presidency, a more consensual Reagan was on view and, helped by his December 1987 arms-reduction deal, he left office with much of his popular affection restored.

Bush comes to power Reagan's popularity transferred itself to Vice-president George Bush who, despite selecting the inexperienced Dan Quayle as his running-mate and despite opposition charges that he had been indirectly involved in the Irangate proceedings, defeated the Democrats' candidate Michael Dukakis in the presidential election of November 1988.

Bush came to power, after six years of economic growth, at a time of uncertainty. Reagan's tax-cutting policy had led to mounting federal trade and budget deficits, which had served to turn the USA into a debtor nation for the first time in its history and had precipitated a stock-market crash in October 1987. Retrenchment was concentrated during 1989–90 in the military sphere, helped by continuing Soviet moves towards reductions in both conventional and nuclear forces. Domestically, Bush spoke of the need to create a 'kinder, gentler nation', and unveiled minor initiatives in the areas of education, drug control, and the environment, where problems had surfaced during the Reagan years. (In 1990, almost 500,000 children were suffering from malnutrition and at least 100,000 people were homeless.) The start of his presidency was marred by the Senate's rejection of his nomination for Defense Secretary, John Tower, following criticisms of Tower's lifestyle and his links to military contractors. With his overthrowing of the corrupt Panamanian leader, Gen Manuel Noriega, in December 1989, Bush began to establish his presidency.

the Gulf War The USA responded to Iraq's invasion and annexation of Kuwait in August 1990 by coordinating, in the UN, the passage of a series of resolutions demanding Iraq's unconditional withdrawal and imposing comprehensive economic sanctions. By late November the USA had sent more than 230,000 troops and support personnel to Saudi Arabia to form the core of a 400,000-strong Western and Arab 'desert shield' with the object of defending the Saudi frontier and, if necessary, dislodging Iraq from Kuwait. A further 150,000 US troops were sent in early December and the *Gulf War was fought in January–February 1991.

US reaction to the demise of the USSR In July 1991 Bush and Gorbachev held the first superpower summit since the end of the Cold War and signed the long-awaited START treaty (see *Strategic Arms Reduction Talks). The USA condemned the attempted Moscow coup in August 1991 which briefly removed Gorbachev, and backed Boris *Yeltsin's efforts to restore the Soviet president. Bush's reaction to later developments – the resignation of Gorbachev, the demise of the USSR, and the creation of the Commonwealth of Independent States – was initially cautious. Having granted recognition to the independence of the Baltic States in September 1991, Bush announced that

although he would acknowledge the independence of all remaining 12 republics, he would establish formal international relations with only six – the Russian Federation, Ukraine, Kazakhstan, Belarus, Armenia, and Kyrgyzstan. However, by January 1992 all the former Soviet republics had been granted admission to the Conference on Security and Cooperation in Europe (CSCE, from 1994 the Organization for Security and Cooperation in Europe, OSCE).

Bush followed US success in the Gulf War by convening a Middle East peace conference in Spain in November 1991. Domestically, the economic recession continued. Bush's approval rating slumped and he faced increased public criticism. In another foreign-policy move, in December 1992, he sent US Marines to intervene in Somalia, a country weakened by civil war and famine.

Clinton assumes the presidency Bill *Clinton won the November 1992 presidential election for the Democrats, having campaigned on a platform of improved health-care provision, cautious state intervention to boost the economy, increased protection for the environment, and defence of minority rights. Although he had only a 5% lead over Bush in the popular vote, he won 33 states, plus the District of Columbia, to Bush's 17 states, and 370 electoral-college votes to Bush's 168. The independent candidate, Ross Perot, won nearly 20% of the vote but no electoral-college votes.

domestic reforms Despite initial criticism of his uncertain style of leadership and apparent lack of principles, President Clinton's record of success in Congress during 1993, in terms of votes won, was the best of any president since 1953. His medium-term budget was passed in August, introducing spending cuts and tax increases intended to reduce the federal budget deficit by $496,000

million over a five-year period.
The *North American Free Trade
Agreement, which had encountered
fierce opposition from protectionist
forces within the Democratic Party
and labour movement, was ratified
in November, and wide-ranging anti-
crime measures passed. Plans for a
radical reform of the health-care
system, guaranteeing coverage for all
US citizens and legal aliens under a
'managed competition system', were
unveiled in September 1993.

foreign policy shifts Initial
assertiveness in foreign policy in the
form of a US-led offensive against
forces of the Somali warlord Gen Aidid
(June 1993) gave way to a period of
uncertainty and introspection
following international criticism of the
Somali operation, which had resulted
in mounting casualties. The majority of
US troops had been withdrawn from
Somalia by March 1994.

midterm election losses At the start
of 1994, with an improving economy,
President Clinton's popularity improved
dramatically. However, a downward
slide began when allegations of the
Clintons' involvement in irregular
financial dealings in the 1980s (the
'Whitewater' affair) led to a special
inquiry being launched. As the year
progressed, the Clinton team
experienced mounting opposition to
their health-care reform plan, which
was eventually blocked by Congress.
Tensions were high in the run-up to
the November 1994 midterm elections,
which in the event left both chambers
of Congress in the hands of the
Republicans, as well as 30 of the
country's 50 governorships. Newt
Gingrich, a radical-right Reaganite
who had spearheaded the Republican
campaign, became House Speaker and
effective leader of the opposition.

**Clinton versus the Republican
Congress** From January 1995 the
Republicans, led by Gingrich, fought
to secure passage of their ten-point

populist electoral manifesto, 'Contract
with America', which recommended
radical measures for reducing federal
powers, cutting the budget deficit, and
reducing crime. By mid-April, all but
one of the ten points had cleared the
lower chamber, although the Senate,
led by Republican majority leader
Bob *Dole, had passed only two.
Clinton exercised the first veto of his
presidency, and in December 1995
presented his own proposals for
balancing the budget by 2002.
A compromise health-care reform
package cleared Congress the same
month, but was opposed by Clinton,
who vowed again to use his veto.

In foreign policy, the Clinton
administration achieved two
considerable diplomatic successes in
the autumn of 1995, overseeing the
signing of the second phase of the
agreement on Palestinian self-rule and
brokering the Dayton peace agreement
for Bosnia–Herzegovina in September–
December 1995.

By the end of 1995, Clinton appeared
well placed to challenge Republican
frontrunner, Bob Dole, in the
forthcoming presidential elections.
However, in January 1996, allegations
of financial and sexual impropriety
resurfaced to plague the president.
The first lady, Hillary Clinton, was
subpoenaed to appear before a grand
jury investigating the Whitewater
affair, and a federal appeals court ruled
that a sexual-harassment case against
President Clinton, filed by Paula Jones,
a former state employee in Arkansas,
could proceed to trial. In March Bob
Dole officially clinched the Republican
Party nomination to run for the
presidency; Clinton secured the
Democrat nomination unopposed.
In April Clinton signed into law an act
giving future presidents a veto over
individual spending items within bills,
which looked likely to shift the balance
of power in Washington. The 'line-
item' veto was likely to face a Supreme

Court challenge. Also in April commerce secretary Ron Brown, a close aide of Clinton's, was killed in an aircrash over Croatia.

A $160-billion budget deal for 1996 was agreed by the White House and Congressional Republicans in May, involving an overall $20-billion cut in money terms, but providing an extra $5 billion, shifted from other programmes, to fund increases in the areas of education, police, job training, and environment.

In May 1996 Bob Dole announced his resignation from the Senate in order to concentrate on the presidential campaign. At the end of the same month, the jury in Little Rock, Arkansas, returned verdicts of guilty of conspiracy and fraud against two defendants connected with the Whitewater affair, in spite of the president's testimony for the defence. The final report of the Senate Whitewater committee concluded that Hillary Clinton had probably played a role in limiting the investigation into the suicide of Vince Foster, a White House aide, at the beginning of the affair, and that Bill Clinton, when governor of Arkansas, had given 'inappropriate assistance' to an Arkansas bond dealer.

In June 1996, in an effort to win back control of Congress in the November 1996 elections, the Democrats published a moderate policy programme entitled 'Families First'. In August 1996 Clinton signed into law a Republican bill that abolished automatic federal welfare entitlements to poor families. The bill devolved the job of designing welfare programmes to the individual states, who were instructed to limit welfare payments to a duration of two years and for a maximum of five years during the course of a person's lifetime. Clinton also introduced a new minimum wage of $4.75 per hour, and a small extension of health insurance coverage.

In September 1996 the USA launched a cruise missile attack on military targets in southern Iraq in retaliation for Saddam Hussein's earlier attacks on Kurdish safe havens within Iraq.

Clinton re-elected In November 1996 Clinton emerged victorious in the presidential elections, taking a place in history as one of only 13 presidents to win two straight terms. In December 1996 the final composition of the House of Representatives, after the November elections, was confirmed as 227 Republicans, 207 Democrats, and one independent.

From December 1996 wide publicity was given to a scandal concerning the funding of the Democratic Party's election campaign and President Clinton's legal defence fund by Asian nationals, and possibly the Chinese government, which led to an FBI inquiry and ongoing congressional investigations. Clinton responded by announcing tougher regulations on the sources of Democratic Party funding, including a ban on accepting donations from foreign citizens.

Clinton's inauguration address in January 1997 was centrist in tone, emphasizing the limitations of presidential power and the need for a 'new kind of government' that works through empowerment rather than through bureaucracy and 'lives within its means and does more with less'. In his State of the Union address a month later, he announced that higher educational standards would be the top priority of his second term.

Madeleine *Albright, the former US representative at the UN, became the country's first female secretary of state, replacing Warren Christopher, while former Republican senator William Cohen became secretary of defence. The former national security adviser, Anthony Lake, was initially nominated as director of the CIA, but withdrew after facing 'nasty and brutish' confirmation hearings before the Senate. The CIA's acting director,

George Tenet, was nominated instead. Janet Reno and Robert Rubin were retained as attorney general and treasury secretary respectively.

The congressional leaders were, in the Senate, the Republican Trent Lott (majority leader), and in the House of Representatives, the Republican Newt Gingrich (speaker).

Gingrich was narrowly re-elected as speaker after admitting that he had improperly used tax-exempt charitable donations to fund a politically partisan college course. He was reprimanded and fined $300,000 dollars by the House's ethics committee. Bob Dole, the Republicans' unsuccessful presidential challenger in 1996, provided Gingrich with the $300,000 to pay off the fine in the form of an eight-year interest-bearing loan. In April 1997 James McDougal, a former business partner of President Clinton, was sentenced to three years' imprisonment for fraud and conspiracy in the 'Whitewater' affair.

In October 1997 President Clinton made the first concerted use of his new line-item veto powers to delete 38 projects worth $287 million from a military construction bill. In the same month the attorney-general, Janet Reno, ordered an expanded investigation into President Clinton's and Vice-president Gore's fund-raising for the 1996 election campaign, concentrating on the issue of telephone calls from the White House. However, in December 1997 Reno announced, to Republican outrage, that she had decided not to appoint an independent counsel to investigate the alleged campaign finance abuses by Clinton and his vice-president.

Republican re-elected mayor of New York In 'off-year' state governorship elections held in November 1997 in Virginia and New Jersey, the Republicans scored victories. Meanwhile, in New York, the Republican mayor, Rudolph Giuliani, fighting on a record of sharply reduced crime, was comfortably re-elected, the first Republican to do so since Florio La Guardia in 1937.

Clinton accused of sexual impropriety President Clinton faced damaging accusations, in January 1998, that he had had a sexual relationship with Monica Lewinsky, a White House intern, had lied under oath by denying the affair, and had encouraged Miss Lewinsky to perjure herself. The president firmly denied the allegations and, receiving strong support from the first lady, retained high public-approval ratings (around 60%).

In February, Kenneth Starr, the Whitewater affair special prosecutor, subpoenaed witnesses (including White house aides) to appear before a Washington grand jury. In January, Clinton became the first serving president to be interrogated as a defendant in a court case, when he testified in his lawyer's office in his defence against allegations of sexual harassment made by Paula Jones, a former Arkansas state employee. However, in April 1998 this case was brought to an end when a district judge dismissed the case as, it was ruled, Miss Jones suffered nothing worthy of redress. This ruling did not affect the continuing investigations by Starr. In August 1998 President Clinton testified under oath for four hours to a grand jury, and later admitted in a television broadcast that his relationship with Monica Lewinsky, who had testified in July, had not been 'appropriate' and that he had 'misled people' about it publicly for seven months. Nevertheless, Clinton's job approval ratings remained above 60%.

In September 1998 Kenneth Starr delivered to Congress his report on the 'Whitewater' and 'Monicagate' scandals, stating that it contained 'substantial and credible information' that might support impeachment. Two dozen of the country's newspapers called for Clinton's resignation. However, a *New York Times*/CBS poll showed that 62% of the public still approved of his work as president and believed that, for the sake of the country, he should remain in office. A videotape of the President's private testimony to the grand jury about Monica Lewinsky was controversially shown on national television. In October 1998 the House of Representatives voted to proceed with an impeachment inquiry against President Clinton. In November 1998 the House Judiciary Committee heard testimony from special prosecutor Kenneth Starr, who conceded that he had found no significant evidence against Clinton in the original focus of his investigation, the Whitewater affair. However, in the Lewinsky case, Starr stated that the President had been guilty of obstruction of justice and perjury and had 'repeatedly used the machinery of government and the powers of his office to conceal his relationship with Monica Lewinsky from the American people ... and from the grand jury.' On 13 November 1998, Paula Jones agreed to drop her long-running sexual harassment suit against President Clinton in return for $850,000, but no apology or admission from the President that her allegations were well founded.

Clinton's impeachment trial
On 19 December 1998 the US Congress voted to impeach President Bill Clinton on two charges – of perjury and obstruction of justice – over his relationship with Monica Lewinsky. The impeachment trial, the first since that of Andrew Johnson in 1868, opened in the Senate on 7 January 1999. Chief Justice William Rehnquist was sworn in to preside amid much confusion. The impeachment trial proceedings in the Senate began on 14 January. In the meantime, two separate opinion polls showed that Clinton's job-approval rating was at a record 73%, and the President announced a projected 1999 federal

budget surplus of $76 billion – $22 billion more than estimated earlier. On 12 February 1999 Clinton was acquitted of impeachment charges, with a 55–45 vote against the conviction on the charges of perjury and a 50–50 vote on the obstruction of justice charge. In October 1999 Kenneth Starr resigned as independent counsel and was replaced by Robert Ray, and although President Clinton had been acquitted over the Lewinsky affair, the Whitewater affair remained to be completed by the presentation of a formal report into the matter. The statute which established independent counsels expired in June 1999, but already authorised investigations such as Whitewater were required to run their course.

first balanced budget since 1969
In his January 1998 annual State of the Union address, President Clinton proposed that future projected federal budget surpluses – commencing with a $39 billion surplus for fiscal 1998, the first surplus since 1969 – should be used to strengthen the social security (state pensions) system rather than to reduce taxes, as the Republican opposition proposed. In February the president presented to Congress a proposed budget which, with lower spending on defence and transport and increases for childcare, reduced class sizes, and the Medicare health programme, would establish a balanced budget for 1999. This was three years ahead of the 2002 target date set in August 1997 bipartisan budget agreement, and was the first balanced budget plan in the USA for nearly 30 years. There were three chief reasons for the improved state of the federal finances: reduced defence spending with the end of the Cold War (16% of federal spending went on defence in 1998 compared with 27% in 1989); rising tax receipts from continuing economic growth; and a slowing in health-care costs.

In February 1998 a federal judge ruled that the line-item veto powers extended to the president in 1996 were unconstitutional since they excessively delegated part of Congress's legislative role to the executive. In July of the same year, the Supreme Court ruled that the line-item veto, which had enabled the president to strike out particular tax and spending items within legislation, was unconstitutional since it violated the constitutional principle of the separation of executive and presidential powers. President Clinton had used the line-item veto 82 times since August 1997 to veto $355 million in public spending.

In May 1998, the Senate restored food stamps to a quarter of a million legal immigrants and refugees; they had been withdrawn in 1996 as part of welfare reform.

In August 1998, the House of Representatives voted to outlaw unregulated 'soft money' donations to political parties during election campaigns.

In October 1998 Congress agreed a budget for fiscal 1999, which included of tax cuts of $80 billion and $18 billion in new funding for the IMF.

Two bombs exploded at the US embassies in Dar es Salaam, Tanzania and Nairobi, Kenya on 7 August 1998. Six people were killed in the Tanzania explosion, none of them Americans, and 60 injured. In Kenya the death toll was expected to exceed 230, including 12 US nationals, and 5,000 people were injured. In both cases, the massive explosions were caused by car bombs. The USA retaliated, bombing alleged terrorist sites in Sudan and Afghanistan.

Midterm Congressional elections
The Republican Party's attempts to profit from the Lewinsky scandal, including a $10 million advertising blitz, backfired in the Congressional elections of November 1998. With President Clinton's public approval rating remaining high, and with turnout among blacks and Latinos unusually high, the Democrats reduced the Republicans' majority in the House of Representatives by five seats: the final outcome was Republicans 223 seats, Democrats 211, and independent, one seat. The Democrats' performance in the House mid-term elections was the strongest of any party of a sitting president since 1934. There was no net change in the Senate where, with 34 seats being contested, the Republicans finished with 55 seats to the Democrats' 45. This left the Republicans 12 votes short of the 67 needed to secure impeachment in the upper chamber. Overall, turnout, at 36%, was at its lowest level since 1942, and there was evidence of a reaction against Republicans who had sought to exploit the Lewinsky issue. The outcome was seen as a triumph for Vice-president Al Gore and First Lady Hillary Clinton, who both campaigned vigorously on the President's behalf. It was also interpreted as an indication that voters, content with Clinton's handling of the still booming economy, did not wish to see the President impeached. Accepting responsibility for his party's poor performance, the Republicans' partisan House Speaker, Newt Gingrich, resigned on 6 November 1998 and announced he would leave politics. The speaker-elect also withdrew after admitting to a series of adulterous affairs.

renewed attacks on Iraq
In December 1998 the USA and the UK launched an artillery attack on Iraq, named Operation Desert Fox, which lasted four days and ended with President Clinton's and UK prime minister Tony Blair's declaration of policy of confinement in relation to Saddam Hussein. Following further escalation of tensions in the region (mostly over the no-fly zone over northern and southern Iraq), US forces renewed their attacks in January 1999. Also in January, President Clinton announced an overall $110 billion

increase in defence budget by 2005, including the biggest rise in military pay since 1984.

In February 1999, President Clinton's proposed budget for 2000 predicted a surplus of $117 billion, much of it to be reserved for the Social Security (pensions) system.

natural disasters As Hurricane Floyd hit the east coast of America in September 1999, some three million people fled inland. It was the largest evacuation in US history. President Clinton pre-emptively declared the states of Florida and Georgia disaster areas. States of emergency were also declared in the Carolinas, Virginia, Maryland and Delaware. During August 2000, the wildfires, the worst in 30 years, struck the west of the USA, and consumed 4.4 million acres/ 6,875 sq mi of land.

foreign trade relations In July 2000, a trade agreement between the USA and Vietnam was signed, clearing the way for normal relations for the first time since the Vietnam War. The agreement would reduce tariffs on goods and services, protect intellectual property, and improve investment relations. Sanctions on exporting food and medicine to Cuba were lifted, although they remained in place on other goods.

record trade deficit The US trade deficit hit a record US$34.26 billion in October 2000. The increase of 15% over the previous month was partly due to the US economy being stronger than those of its trading partners.

2000 presidential elections By March 2000, the two remaining candidates in the presidential race were George W Bush, son of former President George Bush, for the Republicans, and for the Democrats, the current vice-president, Al Gore. Both gained their parties' nominations in March after winning primary elections in six southern states. In July, the two candidates' vice-presidential running-mates were announced.

George W Bush chose Dick Cheney, a former chief of staff to President Gerald Ford, and secretary of defence for Bush's father during the Gulf War. Al Gore chose Joseph Lieberman, a senator and outspoken critic of Bill Clinton. Lieberman, a political moderate, became the first Jew in US history to compete for the vice-presidency.

The presidential elections were the closest ever, Gore winning 49% of the vote to Bush's 48.7%, but losing on the electoral college system. The result hung on the outcome in Florida. The vote there separated Bush and Gore by only a few hundred votes and a recount was ordered. In the elections for Congress, the Republicans retained a majority in the House of Representatives, but lost it in the Senate, where both Republicans and Democrats won 50 seats. Democrat Hillary Clinton, wife of outgoing President Clinton, won a Senate seat for New York.

After disputes of hand recounting, Florida's Supreme Court ruled that hand recounts should continue in three heavily Democratic counties, but imposed a deadline. One county stopped the recount when officials realized they could not count all the votes by the deadline. On 26 November, Florida's secretary of state certified that Bush had won, but Gore appealed against the result, and the court extended the deadline.

The debate continued in the US Supreme Court, which declared, on 12 December, that there could be no further recounts in Florida. The following day Gore conceded defeat, putting Bush in the White House and ending the most bitterly disputed election for more than a century. In April 2001, a study revealed that Bush would in fact have won by a greater majority if the hand count had been completed.

a new government Bush announced his cabinet appointments over

December 2000–January 2001. All but one of the posts was given to a Republican, despite Bush's post-election pledge of bipartisanship, and a high proportion to people from ethnic minorities. Colin Powell became the first African American to be appointed secretary of state and Condoleezza Rice the first woman and first African American to become national security adviser. The staunchly Christian conservative senator John Ashcroft was controversially appointed attorney general. After being sworn in as the USA's 43rd president in late January 2001, Bush proposed sweeping changes to US schools, ended federal aid to international agencies that performed or advocated abortion, and unveiled the core project of his 'compassionate conservatism', the creation of a White House Office for Faith-Based Action that would distribute billions of dollars over ten years to religious groups for charitable and social work.

the Fed takes emergency action
The US Federal Reserve Board (the Fed) made a surprise cut in interest rates in January 2001. The cut amounted to emergency action by the Fed to avert an excessive slowdown after markets fell sharply in December 2000 and consumer confidence reached a two-year low. The Fed said it would cut rates again if that were necessary to ward off recession.

California blacks out US federal and state officials met with representatives of the power industry in Washington, DC, as California's electricity crisis deepened in January 2001. Two of the largest power utility companies in California were on the brink of bankruptcy due to the 10-fold increase over the last year in the price electricity distributors pay generators, a cost the law forbids the companies to pass on to customers. Electricity was deregulated in California in 1996, and the federal government expressed concern that the crisis could derail

plans for deregulation in other states. Inability of companies to meet demand and difficulties in finding supplies outside the state led to the first mandatory blackouts on 18 January. Further electricity blackouts were imposed in mid-March, as demand exceeded supply. In response, regulators raised the upper limit on the retail price of electricity to help the struggling power companies. Demand was expected to increase as summer approached and air-conditioners started to be turned on.

diplomatic expulsions Following the arrest in February 2001 of a US FBI agent for spying for Russia, 6 Russian diplomats were expelled in March, and another 51 given notice to leave. Russia responded by expelling 4 diplomats and giving another 46 notice to leave. Differences between the two countries had mounted over the preceding year as Russian President Vladimir Putin had tried to rebuild Russian state power.

Bush's early policies In February, Bush presented his budget plan to Congress. It included US$1.6 billion tax cuts over ten years (approved by the Senate in May), and increased spending on defence and education. In mid-March, President Bush abandoned a campaign promise to regulate American power plants' carbon-dioxide emissions, saying he wanted to increase domestic energy production. In May he unveiled a national energy strategy that called for more coal mines, oil refineries, and nuclear reactors. Carbon dioxide is implicated in global warming, and the decision was criticized by environmentalists across the world, who accused Bush of selling out to the energy industry. The policy was in contradiction of the 1997 *Kyoto Protocol.

Bush also expressed support for the early deployment of the National Missile Defense (NMD) system, wanting to develop the project with new technologies. He revealed plans for the system in May, while also promising to cut the USA's nuclear arsenal

2000 census The census for 2000 showed that, since 1990, the Latino population of the USA had increased by 60% to 12% of the total population. Blacks also made up 12% of the population, while Asians increased by 50% to 3.7%. Whites made up 69%, down from 74% in 1990.

crisis in China A US spy plane and a Chinese fighter jet collided in mid-air on 1 April 2001. The fighter crashed and the pilot was killed, while the US EP-3 surveillance plane was forced to make an emergency landing on China's Hainan Island. Who was at fault was not resolved, and the Chinese demanded an apology and an explanation, while the USA demanded the return of the plane and its 24 crew members. The apology and release of the crew occurred on 11 April, but China did not return the plane. The crisis was resolved on 24 May, when China accepted US proposals to dismantle the plane and fly it out of the country in crates. China had insisted that allowing the plane to be flown out of the country would be regarded as a national humiliation.

President Bush strained relations with China further by selling Taiwan military equipment and stating that the USA had an obligation to help Taiwan defend itself against Chinese attack. Visits by the Dalai Lama and Chen Shui-bian, the president of Taiwan, to the White House in late May 2001 prompted China to protest that the USA was interfering in its domestic affairs.

Republicans lose control of the Senate In May 2001, Senator James Jeffords of Vermont announced that he was leaving the Republican Party to serve as an Independent. His departure overturned Republican control of the Senate, and Democrats took control for the first time in six years. The move threatened to jeopardize President Bush's

conservative political programme, but the Democrat leader, Tom Daschle, promised to adopt a cooperative approach towards the Republican agenda.

Bush in Europe In June 2001, on his first official visit to Europe, President Bush faced diplomatic criticism and public demonstrations over his rejection of the Kyoto Protocol on climate change, and his plans for the US missile shield. Meeting with the European Union (EU) and NATO, he portrayed himself as an ally and friend, but stood firm on the controversial issues, winning implicit support for NMD from Britain, Spain, and Italy. His first meeting with Russian president Vladimir Putin was unexpectedly amicable. Bush spoke of Russia as an ally, and insisted it had nothing to fear from the future expansion of NATO. At a summit in Göteborg, Sweden, the EU attempted to persuade the USA to accept the Kyoto Protocol on climate change. However, five hours of talks between Bush and EU leaders yielded no movement from the USA, and the EU member states declared that they would ratify the protocol without US involvement.

diplomatic tensions with Japan Relations between the USA and Japan were strained in July 2001 by a delay in handing over to the Japanese authorities a US pilot suspected of raping a Japanese woman in Chatan, Okinawa. The attack had threatened to overshadow a meeting at Camp David, Maryland, between President Bush and the Japanese prime minister, Junichiro Koizumi, and prompted renewed calls for a reduction in the numbers of US troops on the island of Okinawa.

political party finance restrictions On 25 June 2001, the Supreme Court ruled that the US government could restrict the amount of money that political parties spend in coordination with individual congressional candidates. In a 5–4 split decision, the court emphasized that large contributions of money tend to corrupt. Contributors will be allowed to give up to US$20,000 annually to a political party, but only US$2,000 to a candidate for a primary or general election. The court's ruling therefore prevents up to US$22,000 going to a single candidate.

illegal immigrant concessions A committee led by Secretary of State Colin Powell and Attorney General John Ashcroft recommended in July that some of the 3 million Mexicans living illegally in the USA should be allowed to gain permanent residence through a guest-worker programme.

ban on human cloning In July, the US House of Representatives approved a comprehensive ban on human cloning, even for scientific research, and promised severe penalties for those caught flouting it. Although President Bush announced in August that he would allow federal funds to be used for research on existing lines of embryonic stem cells, he said he would not allow any cloning to create new embryos.

military base closures proposed In August, the Pentagon asked Congress to approve an independent commission that would close and consolidate military bases in the USA. It said that the military had 20–25% more base capacity than was needed, and that the closures would eventually save around US$3.5 billion.

controversial energy plan approved The House of Representatives approved President Bush's energy plan in August, including controversial proposals to allow oil drilling in the Arctic National Wildlife Refuge, Alaska. The plan, passed by only 17 votes, was seen as a devastating blow to the environmental movement.

Bush accepts electoral reform proposals President Bush broadly accepted recommendations for electoral reform put forward in August by former US presidents Jimmy Carter and Gerald Ford. The proposals were designed to avoid a repeat of the confusion in the 2000 presidential election over the Florida ballot count.

terrorist attacks The USA suffered the worst terrorist attack ever on 11 September 2001. Suicide hijackers crashed two fuel-laden passenger jets into the twin towers of the World Trade Center in New York City, both of which caught fire and collapsed, killing office workers and rescue workers alike. The entire southern end of Manhattan was evacuated. Another hijacked aircraft was flown into the Pentagon in Washington, DC, and a fourth plane crashed near Pittsburgh, Pennsylvania. The total death toll was estimated to be around 3,000. Airports, borders, and stock markets in the USA were closed, and flights to, from, and within the USA were grounded. On 13 September Congress and President Bush agreed on an initial emergency spending package of US$20 billion to help reconstruct New York and strengthen security. Politicians around the world had immediately condemned the attacks and promised help in finding the terrorists. President Bush promised to hunt down the perpetrators of what he called 'an act of war' and put US armed forces on high alert. No terrorist group claimed responsibility for the attacks but Western intelligence agencies blamed Saudi-born dissident Osama bin Laden, based in Afghanistan. The Bush administration set out to build an international coalition of forces against bin Laden and his terrorist network, the al-Qaeda organization. Bush declared a War on Terrorism on 16 September against both al-Qaeda and any state that sponsored or harboured terrorists. After Afghanistan's ruling Taliban regime refused to hand over bin Laden, US and British forces launched military strikes on the country on 7 October.

As the USA's exchanges stayed closed in the wake of the terrorist action, financial markets across the world slumped as the fear of a deep recession grew. The New York Stock Exchange reopened on 17 September, after its longest shutdown since World War I. The US Federal Reserve injected US$38.25 billion of cash into the banking system, about ten times the daily average and, on 17 September, announced a half-point cut in the base interest rate.

On 26 September, the International Monetary Fund (IMF) said a recession in the USA was a foregone conclusion since the terrorist attacks. US airlines resumed business, but cut some 20% of flights anticipating a severe drop in business, and announced thousands of job losses. The federal government agreed an aid package of grants and loans totalling US$15 billion for US airlines. President Bush also unveiled plans for greater safety in the air, including armed marshals on planes and increased airport security, to increase public confidence in air travel.

Meanwhile, fear of biological attack increased in the USA as eight anthrax cases were confirmed in Florida on 14 October, resulting in the death of one man. There were also anthrax cases in New York and Nevada, with powder containing manufactured anthrax spores sent in letters to media organizations. However, there was no specific evidence linking the cases to either bin Laden or the al-Qaeda network by the end of October. Following the death of an elderly woman in Connecticut in late November from the inhalation form of anthrax, suspicions deepened that the source of the anthrax threat was US-based, rather than the work of foreign terrorists. In the same month a letter to Senator Patrick Leahy of Vermont tested positive for the disease, as did the offices of two other senators.

Despite objections voiced by civil libertarians, President Bush signed a military order in November allowing non-US citizens suspected of terrorism to be tried before a military commission instead of in civilian courts. The Justice Department also requested police across the USA to question 5,000 men, mostly from the Middle East, who had entered the country legally in the past two years. Bush submitted a US$2.13 trillion budget to Congress in February 2002. It included a 12% increase in military spending (the biggest rise in military spending since 1982), and allocated US$11 billion dollars to protect the USA from biological terrorism. However, there was widespread criticism that the government would post deficits of US$106 billion in 2002, US$80 billion in 2003, and US$14 billion in 2004.

In March 2002, the USA imposed tariffs of up to 30% for three years on most steel imports from many of the world's biggest producers, who greeted the move with outrage. In its bid to revive its ailing steel industry, the USA was accused of setting back the cause of free trade. The EU responded by promising an immediate complaint to the WTO and imposing tariffs of its own of up to 26% on some steel products. It also drew up a list of US goods on which it would impose sanctions worth US$2 billion if the USA refused to provide compensation. The government reacted by threatening action through the WTO.

In May, during a European tour taking in Germany, Russia, France, and Italy, President Bush visited Moscow, Russia, and signed a strategic arms-control agreement with Russian president Vladimir Putin pledging to reduce long-range nuclear warheads by two-thirds over ten years.

Unrepresented Nations' and Peoples' Organization UNPO, international association founded in 1991 to represent ethnic and minority groups unrecognized by the United Nations and to defend the right to self-determination of oppressed peoples around the world. The founding charter was signed by representatives of Tibet, the Kurds, Turkestan, Armenia, Estonia, Georgia, the Volga region, the Crimea, the Greek minority in Albania, North American Indians, Australian Aborigines, West Irians, West Papuans, the minorities of the Cordillera in the Philippines, and the non-Chinese in Taiwan. UNPO is based in the Netherlands and its general secretary is Michael Van Walt van Praag.

urbanization process by which the proportion of a population living in or around towns and cities increases through migration and natural increase. The growth of urban concentrations in the USA and Europe is a relatively recent phenomenon, dating back only about 150 years to the beginning of the Industrial Revolution (although the world's first cities were built more than 5,000 years ago). The UN Population Fund reported in 1996 that within ten years the majority of the world's population would be living in urban conglomerations. Almost all urban growth will occur in the developing world, creating ten large cities a year.

Uruguay country in South America, on the Atlantic coast, bounded north by Brazil and west by Argentina.

US Constitution the framework of US federal government, drafted at the Constitutional Convention in Philadelphia in 1787, and ratified in 1788 to take effect from 1789. It replaced the Articles of Confederation (1781). Although the framers of the Constitution sought to increase the power of central (federal) government, they included safeguards against possible tyranny, and the states retain considerable powers of self-government. Certain powers are reserved to the states or forbidden to central government, and the legislative, executive, and judicial branches are separate and hold powers to check and balance each other. Since 1788, the Constitution has had 27 amendments, including the Thirteenth Amendment (1865) abolishing slavery and the Nineteenth Amendment (1920) giving women the vote. Article VI establishes the Constitution as the 'supreme law of the land'.

Ustaše Croatian nationalist terrorist organization founded 1929 and led by Ante Pavelic against the Yugoslav state. During World War II, it collaborated with the Nazis and killed thousands of Serbs, Romanies, and Jews. It also carried out deportations and forced conversions to Roman Catholicism in its attempt to create a 'unified' Croatian state.

Uzbekistan country in central Asia, bounded north by Kazakhstan and the Aral Sea, east by Kyrgyzstan and Tajikistan, south by Afghanistan, and west by Turkmenistan.

V

V1, V2 (German *Vergeltungswaffe* 'revenge weapons') German flying bombs of World War II, launched against Britain in 1944 and 1945. The V1, also called the **doodlebug** and **buzz bomb**, was an uncrewed monoplane carrying a bomb, powered by a simple kind of jet engine called a pulse jet. The V2, a rocket bomb with a preset guidance system, was the first long-range ballistic missile. It was 14 m/47 ft long, carried a 1-tonne warhead, and hit its target at a speed of 5,000 kph/3,000 mph.

The V2 was developed by the rocket engineer Wernher von Braun (1912–1977). After the war captured V2 material became the basis of the space race in both the USSR and the USA.

Vance, Cyrus Roberts (1917–2002) US Democratic politician, secretary of state 1977–80. He was United Nations negotiator in the peace talks on *Bosnia-Herzegovina 1992–93, resigning from the post due to ill health. Together with European Community negotiator David Owen, he devised the Vance–Owen peace plan for dividing the republic into ten semi-autonomous provinces. The plan was rejected by the Bosnian Serbs.

Vandenberg, Arthur Hendrick (1884–1951) US politician. A Republican, he was elected to the US Senate in 1928 and remained there for the next 23 years. Although initially an isolationist, he supported F D Roosevelt's war policies and was a supporter of the United Nations in 1945. He became the Republican party's chief spokesperson on foreign affairs, and was chair of the Senate Foreign Relations Committee 1946–48.

Vanderbilt, Harold Stirling (1884–1970) US bridge innovator. He helped contract bridge spread from 1926 to 1929 by espousing the game, and modernized it with bidding and scoring changes. He presented the Vanderbilt Cup team trophy in 1928 and twice won it. Vanderbilt was born in Oakdale, New York; he was also Harvard Law School graduate and railroad magnate.

Van Dyke, Willard Ames (1906–1986) US film-maker and photographer. Trained by Edward Weston, he moved on to work in film in 1939, producing, directing, and photographing social documentary films with American Documentary Film (1940–68). Van Dyke was born in Denver, Colorado.

Vansittart, Robert Gilbert (1881–1957) 1st Baron Vansittart, British diplomat, noted for his anti-German polemic. He was permanent undersecretary of state for foreign affairs 1930–38 and chief diplomatic adviser to the foreign secretary 1938–41. KCB 1929, Baron 1941.

Vanuatu group of islands in the southwest Pacific Ocean, part of Melanesia.

Vanzetti, Bartolomeo (1888–1927) Italian anarchist. Vanzetti emigrated to the USA in 1908, finding work as a fish pedlar. In 1920 he was accused, with Nicola *Sacco, of murdering two men while robbing a shoe factory in Massachusetts. Although the evidence was largely circumstantial, the two men were tried in 1921 and sentenced to death. They were executed in 1927 after a controversial and lengthy appeal. It has been claimed that they were punished for their political sympathies, but experts now believe that Sacco was guilty, and Vanzetti innocent.

Vargas, Getúlio Dornelles (1883–1954) Brazilian president 1930–45 and 1951–54. Following his presidential election failure in 1930, he overthrew the republic and in 1937 set up a totalitarian, profascist state known as the Estado Novo. Ousted by a military coup in 1945, he returned as president in 1951 with the support of the labour movement but, amid mounting opposition and political scandal, committed suicide in 1954.

Vasilevsky, Alexandr M (1895–1977) Soviet general, Marshal of the Soviet Union. Appointed Chief of Staff 1942 he was responsible for planning most major Soviet operations of World War II, including the Stalingrad counteroffensive and the defence of the Kursk salient. In March 1945 he took command of the 3rd Belorussian Front when its commander was killed and completed the conquest of eastern Prussia and the Baltic states. He was appointed commander-in-chief Far East May 1945, and planned and executed the invasion of Manchuria, Korea, and the Kurile and Sakhalin islands of Japan.

Vatican City State sovereign area within the city of Rome, Italy.

government The pope, elected for life by the Sacred College of Cardinals, is absolute head of state. He appoints a pontifical commission to administer the state's affairs on his behalf and under his direction.

history The pope has traditionally been based in Rome, where the Vatican has been a papal residence since 1377; the Vatican Palace is one of the largest in the world and contains a valuable collection of works of art.

The Vatican City State came into being through the Lateran Treaty of 1929, under which Italy recognized the sovereignty of the pope over the city of the Vatican. The 1947 Italian constitution reaffirmed the Lateran Treaty, and under its terms, Roman Catholicism became the state religion

in Italy, enjoying special privileges. This remained so until, under a new 1984 Concordat (ratified in 1985), Catholicism ceased to be the state religion. Karol Wojtyla, formerly archbishop of Kraków in Poland, has been pope since 1978 under the title of John Paul II.

Since his accession John Paul II has travelled widely and done much to restore relations with former Soviet bloc countries. His moral and social views, however, have been deeply conservative, particularly on issues such as contraception and abortion.

Veil, Simone (1927–) French centrist politician, the first woman to hold a full cabinet post under the Fifth Republic, as Valéry *Giscard d'Estaing's minister for health 1974–79. A survivor of Hitler's concentration camps (where she lost both her parents and her brother), she trained for the judiciary and worked in the justice ministry prior to her appointment as a full cabinet minister. She was widely respected and popular as a politician despite the French right's hostility to her legalization of abortion in 1975. Veil chose then to develop her political career at the European level. Elected to the European Parliament (EP) 1979–93, and its first president 1979–82, she presided over the EP liberal-democratic group 1982–93 before returning as French minister for health, urban, and social affairs under Edouard Balladur 1993–95. She was appointed to the Constitutional Council in February 1998.

Venezia Giulia e Zara former region of northeast Italy which comprised the provinces of Carnaro, Gorizia, Istria, and Zara; area 8,950 sq km / 3,456 sq mi. At the end of World War II, by the peace treaty signed in Paris on 10 February 1947, the greater part of the region was ceded to Yugoslavia; Italy retained 466 sq m / 180 sq mi, now incorporated into Friuli-Venezia Giulia.

Venezuela country in northern South America, on the Caribbean Sea, bounded east by Guyana, south by Brazil, and west by Colombia.

Venizelos, Eleuthérios Kyriakos (1864–1936) Greek politician born in Crete, leader of the Cretan movement against Turkish rule until the union of the island with Greece in 1905. He later became prime minister of the Greek state on five occasions, 1910–15, 1917–20, 1924, 1928–32, and 1933, before being exiled to France in 1935.

Ventris, Michael George Francis (1922–1956) English architect. Deciphering Minoan Linear B, the language of the tablets found at Knossos and Pylos, he showed that it was a very early form of Greek, thus revising existing views on early Greek history.

Verdun fortress town in northeast France in the *département* of the Meuse, 280 km/174 mi east of Paris. During World War I it became a symbol of French resistance and was the centre of a series of bitterly fought actions between French and German forces, finally being recaptured September 1918.

Versailles, Treaty of peace treaty after World War I between the Allies (except the USA and China) and Germany, signed on 28 June 1919. It established the *League of Nations, an international organization intended to solve disputes by arbitration. Germany surrendered Alsace-Lorraine to France, and large areas in the east to Poland, and made smaller cessions to Czechoslovakia, Lithuania, Belgium, and Denmark. The Rhineland was demilitarized, German rearmament was restricted, and Germany agreed to pay reparations for war damage. The treaty was never ratified by the USA, which signed separate treaties with Germany and Austria in 1921. The terms of Versailles and its reshaping of Europe contributed to the outbreak of *World War II.

Verwoerd, Hendrik (Frensch) (1901–1966) South African right-wing Nationalist Party politician, prime minister 1958–66. As minister of native affairs 1950–58, he was the chief promoter of apartheid legislation (segregation by race). He banned the *African National Congress (ANC) in 1960 and withdrew South Africa from the Commonwealth in 1961, making the country a republic. He was assassinated in 1966.

Vichy health resort and spa town in Allier *département*, central France, situated on the River Allier 320 km/200 mi southeast of Paris; population (1990) 60,000. From 1940 to 1944, during World War II, it was the seat of the French general *Pétain's government (also known as the *Vichy government), which collaborated with the Nazis.

Vichy government in World War II, the right-wing government of unoccupied France after the country's defeat by the Germans in June 1940, named after the spa town of Vichy, France, where the national assembly was based under Prime Minister Pétain until the liberation in 1944.

Vichy France was that part of France not occupied by German troops until November 1942. Authoritarian and collaborationist, the Vichy regime cooperated with the Germans even after they had moved to the unoccupied zone in November 1942. It imprisoned some 135,000 people, interned another 70,000, deported some 76,000 Jews, and sent 650,000 French workers to Germany.

Victor Emmanuel III (1869–1947) King of Italy from the assassination of his father, Umberto I, in 1900. He acquiesced in the Fascist regime of Mussolini from 1922 and, after the dictator's fall in 1943, relinquished power to his son Umberto II, who cooperated with the Allies. Victor Emmanuel formally abdicated in 1946.

Vietcong (Vietnamese 'Vietnamese communists') in the Vietnam War

(1954–75), the members of the communist National Front for the Liberation of South Vietnam, founded in 1960, who conducted a guerrilla campaign against South Vietnamese and US forces. Their name was coined by the South Vietnamese government to distinguish them from the *Vietminh, who had liberated North Vietnam from Japanese occupation and then French colonial rule in 1941 and 1954. Supplied and reinforced by the North along the 'Ho Chi Minh Trail', the insurgents ultimately forced the withdrawal of US troops and reunified Vietnam by 1975.

Vietminh   the Vietnam Independence League, founded 1941 to oppose the Japanese occupation of Indochina and later directed against the French colonial power. The Vietminh were instrumental in achieving Vietnamese independence through military victory at Dien Bien Phu 1954.

Vietnam   country in Southeast Asia, on the South China Sea, bounded north by China and west by Cambodia and Laos.

    government Under the 1992 constitution, the supremacy of the Communist Party is declared and the highest state authority and sole legislative chamber is the National Assembly, the Quoc Hoi, composed of a maximum of 400 members directly elected every five years by universal suffrage. The assembly elects from its ranks a permanent, 15-member council of state, whose chair acts as state president, to function in its absence. The executive government is the council of ministers, headed by the prime minister, which is elected by and responsible to the National Assembly.

    The dominating force in Vietnam is the Communist Party. It is controlled by a politburo, and is prescribed a 'leading role' by the constitution.

    history Originally settled by Southeast Asian hunters and agriculturalists, Vietnam was founded in 208 BC in the Red River delta in the north, under Chinese overlordship. Under direct Chinese rule 111 BC–AD 939, it was thereafter at times nominally subject to China.

It annexed land to the south and defeated the forces of Mongol emperor Kublai Khan in 1288. European traders arrived in the 16th century.

The country was united under one dynasty in 1802.

    Vietnam was conquered by France between 1858–84, and it joined Cambodia, Laos, and Annam as the French colonial possessions of Indochina. French Indochina was occupied by Japan 1940–45.

north/south division *Ho Chi Minh, who had built up the Vietminh (Independence) League, overthrew the Japanese-supported regime of Bao Dai (1913–1997), the former emperor of Annam, in September 1945. French attempts to regain control and restore Bao Dai led to bitter fighting 1946–54, and final defeat of the French at Dien Bien Phu. At the 1954 Geneva Conference the country was divided along the 17th parallel of latitude into communist North Vietnam, led by Ho Chi Minh, with its capital at Hanoi, and pro-Western South Vietnam, led by Ngo Dinh Diem, with its capital at Saigon.

    Vietnam War Within South Vietnam, the communist guerrilla National Liberation Front, or Vietcong, gained strength, being supplied with military aid by North Vietnam and China. The USA gave strong backing to the incumbent government in South Vietnam and became, following the August 1964 *Tonkin Gulf Incident, actively embroiled in the *Vietnam War. The years 1964–68 witnessed an escalation in US military involvement to 500,000 troops. From 1969, however, as a result of mounting casualties and domestic opposition, the USA gradually began to withdraw its forces and sue for peace. A ceasefire agreement was negotiated in January 1973 but was breached by the North

Vietnamese, who moved south, surrounding and capturing Saigon (renamed Ho Chi Minh City) in April 1975.

socialist republic The Socialist Republic of Vietnam was proclaimed in July 1976, and a programme to integrate the south was launched. The new republic encountered considerable problems. The economy was in ruins, the two decades of civil war having claimed the lives of more than 2 million; it had maimed 4 million, left more than half the population homeless, and resulted in the destruction of 70% of the country's industrial capacity.

foreign relations In December 1978 Vietnam was at war again, toppling the pro-Chinese Khmer Rouge government in Kampuchea (now Cambodia) led by *Pol Pot and installing a puppet administration led by Heng Samrin. A year later, in response to accusations of maltreatment of ethnic Chinese living in Vietnam, China mounted a brief, largely unsuccessful, punitive invasion of North Vietnam in February–March 1979. These actions, coupled with campaigns against private businesses in the south, induced the flight of about 700,000 Chinese and middle-class Vietnamese from the country 1978–79, often by sea (the 'boat people'). Economic and diplomatic relations with China were severed as Vietnam became closer to the USSR, being admitted into the Eastern-bloc economic organization Comecon in June 1978.

economic reform Despite considerable economic aid from the Eastern bloc, Vietnam did not reach its planned growth targets 1976–85. This forced policy adjustments in 1979 and 1985. Further economic liberalization followed the death of Le Duan (1907–1986), effective leader since 1969, and the retirement of other prominent 'old guard' leaders in 1986. Under the pragmatic lead of Nguyen Van Linh, a *doi moi* ('renovation') programme was

launched. The private marketing of agricultural produce and formation of private businesses were now permitted, agricultural cooperatives were partially dismantled, foreign 'joint venture' inward investment was encouraged, and more than 10,000 political prisoners were released. Economic reform was most successful in the south. In general, however, the country faced a severe economic crisis from 1988, with inflation, famine conditions in rural areas, and rising urban unemployment inducing a further flight of 'boat people' 1989–90, predominantly to Hong Kong; some of these were forcibly repatriated from December 1989.

Nguyen Van Linh resigned his leadership of the Communist Party at the congress held in June 1991 and Do Muoi, a supporter of Linh's policies, was elected the party's new general secretary. Vo Van Kiet, a leading advocate of capitalist-style reform, replaced him as prime minister in August 1991. In April 1992 a new constitution was adopted, which guaranteed economic freedoms and citizens' right to own property, while emphasizing the Communist Party's dominant role. Le Duc Anh became president in September 1992. An announcement in March 1996 stated that GDP had expanded by 9.5%. In June–July the Communist Party revamped its leadership at its eighth congress but Do Muoi was re-elected general secretary, with Le Duc Anh and Vo Van Kiet remaining in the Politburo at the hub of the country's leadership triumvirate.

improved foreign relations In 1989 Vietnam withdrew the last of its troops from Cambodia and the peace agreement in October 1991 helped improve Vietnam's external image. Relations with China were normalized, after a 12-year breach, in November 1991, when Do Muoi and Vo Van Kiet paid a state visit to Beijing and signed a series of commercial and diplomatic agreements. Commercial links were also established with members of the Association of South East Asian Nations (ASEAN). In 1992 relations were normalized with anticommunist South Korea. The USA formally lifted its 30-year-old trade embargo in 1994, and re-established full diplomatic relations in 1995. Vietnam became a full member of ASEAN in July 1995.

Vietnam affected by economic crisis In September 1997 President Le Duc Anh and Prime Minister Vo Van Kiet, both in their seventies, were replaced by the younger Tran Duc Luong (aged 60) and Phan Van Khai (aged 63), at a time when the *doi moi* economic reform programme was running into difficulties. Losses by state firms were draining the budget, foreign investment was 20% down on 1996, and the economic growth rate had slumped amid problems of corruption and bureaucratic red tape. The new prime minister pledged to cut state subsidies. However, in October the dong (Vietnamese currency) had to be effectively devalued as Vietnam was affected by the financial crisis that was sweeping Southeast Asia.

Do Muoi retires In October 1997 it was reported that, since military withdrawal from Cambodia in 1989, Vietnam's standing army had been reduced by two-thirds to around 500,000. In December the 80-year-old Do Muoi, the communist party's general secretary and controlling power in Vietnam, announced his retirement. He was replaced by 66-year-old Gen Le Kha Phieu, who was viewed as more ideologically hardline and conservative than the pragmatic Muoi.

In August 1998 Pham The Duyet, one of the five most senior members of the ruling Communist Party of Vietnam (CPV), faced allegations of corruption. Meawnhile, the country's currency was devalued by a further 7% in the same month.

In November 1998 the government placed new emphasis on agricultural development, after export growth had slumped to 3% (against 24% in 1997), as a result of the Asian economic crisis. Inflation had increased to around 10% and the World Bank predicted that GDP growth would be only 3% in 1998. In December 2000, a UN report revealed that more than 2.6 million Vietnamese children under five were malnourished.

improved relations with the USA In July 1999, the USA and Vietnam approved a trade agreement, marking the first major economic cooperation between the two countries since the end of the war. It came into effect in July 2000, The USA had lifted its trade embargo on Vietnam in 1994. The new agreement, which lowers export duties, encourages US companies to invest in Vietnam and opens up the USA, the world's largest market, to Vietnamese products. In August 1999 the USA opened a consulate in Ho Chi Minh City, 24 years after the forced US flight from the city. The following year, in November, US president Clinton visited Vietnam, becoming the first serving US president to do so since Nixon in 1969, and gave a live television broadcast on capitalism and democracy.

In April 2001, Nong Duc Manh became the new secretary general of the ruling Communist party. A modernizing reformist, he proposed to tackle bureacracy, corruption, and wastefulness. As a Tay, he was the first member of a Vietnamese ethnic minority to hold a senior party post.

Vietnam War 1954–75 war from 1954–1975 between communist North Vietnam and US-backed South Vietnam, in which North Vietnam aimed to conquer South Vietnam and unite the country as a communist state. North Vietnam was supported by communist rebels from South Vietnam, the *Vietcong. The USA, in supporting the South against the North, aimed to prevent the spread of communism in Southeast Asia, but at the end of the war North and South Vietnam were reunited as a socialist republic.

Vietnam War protests
demonstrations, marches, and acts of civil disobedience in protest to US involvement in the *Vietnam War (1954–75), beginning around 1965. Anti-war sentiment arose from the question of the morality of participation in what many regarded as a civil war; the growing human and environmental costs; and doubts that the US war effort would succeed.

Vigdís Finnbogadóttir (1930–)
President of Iceland 1980–96. She was first elected president in 1980, the first woman ever to be democratically elected president of a republic, and was re-elected in 1984 and 1988. In 1996 she stepped down and was replaced by Ólafur Ragnar Grímsson.

Villa, Pancho (Francisco) (1877–1923)
born **Doroteo Arango**, Mexican revolutionary. The Mexican Revolution of 1911 made him famous as a military commander. In a fierce struggle for control of the revolution, he and Emiliano *Zapata were defeated in 1915 by Álvaro *Obregón and Venustiano *Carranza, with whom Villa had earlier allied himself against the dictatorship of General Victoriano *Huerta. Both Villa and Zapata withdrew to mountain strongholds in north and central Mexico and continued to carry on guerrilla warfare. In 1916 Villa was responsible for the shooting of a number of US citizens in the town of Santa Isabel, Chihuahua, as well as an attack on the city of Columbus, New Mexico, USA, which precipitated the sending of a US punitive force by President Woodrow *Wilson. He eventually made peace with the government in 1920, being pardoned in return for agreeing to retire from politics, but was murdered in Parral.

Vimy Ridge hill in northern France, taken in World War I by Canadian troops during the battle of Arras, April 1917, at the cost of 11,285 lives. It is a spur of the ridge of Notre Dame de Lorette, 8 km/5 mi northeast of Arras.

Vittorio Veneto, Battle of official Italian name for the third battle of the Piave, the Italian victory over Austrian October–November 1918 which heralded Austria's final defeat.

Vlasov, Andrey Andreyevich (1900–1946) Soviet general in World War II. He was captured by the Germans May 1942 and, feeling he had been badly treated by Stalin, began making anti-Soviet broadcasts for the Germans. In November 1944 he began forming a 'Russian Liberation Army' from disaffected prisoners-of-war. He was captured by the Soviets May 1945 and executed for treason.

Vogel, Hans-Jochen (1926–) German socialist politician, chair of the Social Democratic Party (SPD) 1987–91. A former leader of the SPD in Bavaria and mayor of Munich, he served in the Brandt and Schmidt West German governments in the 1970s as housing and then justice minister and then, briefly, as mayor of West Berlin.

Volstead Act US legislation passed in 1919 designed to enforce Prohibition under the Eighteenth Amendment to the US Constitution. Officially the National Prohibition Act, it was popularly named after its proponent, Minnesota congressman Andrew Volstead.

Voroshilov, Klement Efremovich (1881–1969) Marshal of the USSR. He joined the Bolsheviks in 1903 and was arrested many times and exiled, but escaped. He became a Red Army commander in the civil war 1918–20, a member of the central committee in 1921, commissar for war in 1925, member of the Politburo in 1926, and marshal in 1935. He was removed as war commissar in 1940 after defeats on the Finland front and failing to raise the German siege of Leningrad.

He was a member of the committee for defence 1941–44 and president of the Presidium of the USSR 1953–60.

Vorster, John (1915–1983) born **Balthazar Johannes Vorster**, South African National Party politician, prime minister 1966–78, and president 1978–79. During his term as prime minister some elements of apartheid were allowed to lapse, and attempts were made to improve relations with the outside world. He resigned the presidency because of a financial scandal.

Vranitzky, Franz (1937–) Austrian socialist politician, federal chancellor 1986–97. A banker, he entered the political arena through the moderate, left-of-centre Socialist Party of Austria (SPÖ), and became minister of finance in 1984. He succeeded Fred Sinowatz as federal chancellor in 1986, heading an SPÖ-ÖVP (Austrian People's Party) coalition, which was returned in the October 1994 and December 1995 general elections. He resigned in January 1997.

Vyshinsky, Andrei Yanuaryevich (1883–1954) Soviet politician. As commissar for justice, he acted as prosecutor at Stalin's treason trials 1936–38. He was foreign minister 1949–53 and often represented the USSR at the United Nations.

Wafd (Arabic 'deputation') the main Egyptian nationalist party between World Wars I and II. Under Nahas Pasha it formed a number of governments in the 1920s and 1930s. Dismissed by King Farouk in 1938, it was reinstated by the British in 1941. The party's pro-British stance weakened its claim to lead the nationalist movement, and the party was again dismissed by Farouk in 1952, shortly before his own deposition. Wafd was banned in January 1953.

Waffen SS military arm of the *SS, by the end of 1944 the Waffen SS numbered 600,000 men in 34 divisions. In general the Waffen SS fought as motorized infantry, but by the end of 1944 the 6th Panzer Army was a Waffen SS formation.

Wagner, Robert F(erdinand) (1877–1953) US Democratic senator 1927–49, a leading figure in the development of welfare provision in the USA, especially in the *New Deal era. He helped draft much new legislation, including the National Industrial Recovery Act 1933, the Social Security Act 1936, and the National Labor Relations Act 1935, known as the Wagner Act.

Waldheim, Kurt (1918–) Austrian politician and diplomat, president 1986–92. He was secretary general of the United Nations 1972–81, having been Austria's representative there 1964–68 and 1970–71.

He was elected president in spite of revelations that during World War II he had been an intelligence officer in an army unit responsible for transporting Jews to death camps. His election therefore led to some diplomatic isolation of Austria, and in 1991 he announced that he would not run for re-election.

Wałęsa, Lech (1943–) Polish trade union leader, president of Poland 1990–95. One of the founding members of the *Solidarity free-trade-union movement, which emerged to challenge the communist government during strikes in the Gdansk shipyards in August 1980. Wałęsa led the movement to become a national force. He was awarded the Nobel Prize for Peace in 1983 for his work with the Solidarity movement. After his election as president, he gradually became estranged from Solidarity. In 1997 he formed a Christian Democratic party, which was, however, unlikely to make a significant impact on Polish political life.

A brilliant orator and negotiator, as an electrician at the Lenin Shipyard in Gdansk, Wałęsa became a trade-union organizer and led a series of strikes in 1970 and 1976. In August 1980 he successfully challenged the government to improve working conditions and grant political concessions. After the imposition of martial law in December 1981 he was interned. A devout Catholic, he obtained the support of the Church hierarchy in his negotiations with the authorities.

In 1990 he became president but lost his power base due to his apparent inability to work with the freely elected parliament and conflicts with previous allies and advisers, most notably Tadeusz Mazowiecki. In 1995 he was defeated in the presidential elections by the Social Democrat Aleksander Kwasniewski. Although he continues to take an active part in Poland's political life, his influence is not significant. The leader of the

Solidarity trade union, Marian Krzaklewski, effectively blocked all Wałęsa's efforts to use it as a springboard for further involvement in the country's politics.

Wales Office or **Office of the Secretary of State for Wales**, UK government department, established as the Welsh Office in 1965, which was responsible until 1999 for administration in Wales of policies on agriculture, education, health and social services, local government, planning, sport, and tourism. In July 1999 most of its powers passed to the *National Assembly for Wales. Based in Whitehall, and part of the Department for Constitutional Affairs since June 2003, the secretary of state for Wales (Peter Hain from 2002) is the main government figure liaising with the devolved administration and represents Wales's interests in the government and in Parliament.

Wallace, George Corley (1919–1998) US politician; governor of Alabama 1963–67, 1971–79, and 1983–87. Wallace opposed the integration of black and white students in the 1960s.
He contested the presidency in 1968 as an independent (the American Independent Party) and in 1972 campaigned for the Democratic nomination but was shot at a rally and became partly paralysed.

Wallace, Henry Agard (1888–1965) US politician and journalist. Appointed secretary to the Treasury by Franklin Roosevelt in 1933, he served as vice-president during Roosevelt's third term 1941–45. He later broke with Truman and, after serving as editor of the *New Republic* 1946–47, was the unsuccessful Progressive Party candidate for president in 1948.

Wallenberg, Raoul (1912–c. 1947) Swedish business executive who attempted to rescue several thousand Jews from German-occupied Budapest in 1944, during World War II. He was taken prisoner by the Soviet army in 1945 and was never heard from again.

Wall Street Crash, 1929 panic selling on the New York Stock Exchange following an artificial boom from 1927 to 1929 fed by speculation.
On 24 October 1929, 13 million shares changed hands, with further heavy selling on 28 October and the disposal of 16 million shares on 29 October. Many shareholders were ruined, banks and businesses failed, and in the depression that followed, unemployment rose to approximately 17 million.

The repercussions of the Wall Street Crash, experienced throughout the USA, were also felt in Europe, worsened by the reduction of US loans. A world economic crisis followed the crash, bringing an era of depression and unemployment.

Wang Jingwei (or Wang Ching-wei) (1883–1944) Chinese politician. In 1927, after the death of *Sun Zhong Shan (Sun Yat-sen), he was appointed head of the new *Guomindang (nationalist party) government at Wuhan, and between May and December 1931 led an alternative Guomindang government based in Guangzhou. In 1932 became the party's president, with his main rival for control of the Guomindang, *Jiang Jie Shi (Chiang Kai-shek), in charge of the military. A rapprochement with Jiang ended after Wang was seriously injured in an assassination attempt in November 1935. In 1938, after the outbreak of war with Japan, Wang offered to cooperate with the Japanese, and in 1940 he became head of a puppet regime ruling the occupied areas, centred on Nanjing.

war crime offence (such as murder of a civilian or a prisoner of war) that contravenes the internationally accepted laws governing the conduct of wars, particularly the Hague Convention of 1907 and the Geneva Convention of 1949. A key principle of the law relating to such crimes is that obedience to the orders of a superior is no defence. In practice, prosecutions are generally brought by the victorious side.

Ward, Joseph George (1856–1930) Australian-born New Zealand Liberal politician, prime minister of New Zealand 1906–12 and 1928–30. In his various posts, he was noted for introducing welfare reforms, for example the provision of pensions for widows and the formation of the world's first ministry of public health.

warlord in China, any of the provincial leaders who took advantage of central government weakness, after the death of the first president of republican China in 1912, to organize their own private armies and fiefdoms.

They engaged in civil wars until the nationalist leader Jiang Jie Shi's (Chiang Kai-shek's) Northern Expedition against them in 1926, and they exerted power until the communists seized control under Mao Zedong in 1949.

War Office former British government department controlling military affairs. The Board of Ordnance, which existed in the 14th century, was absorbed into the War Department after the Crimean War and the whole named the War Office. In 1964 its core became a subordinate branch of the newly established Ministry of Defence.

War Powers Act legislation passed in 1973 restricting the US president's powers to deploy US forces abroad for combat without prior Congressional approval. The president is required to report to both Houses of Congress within 48 hours of having taken such action. Congress may then restrict the continuation of troop deployment despite any presidential veto.

Warsaw ghetto area in the centre of Warsaw established by the Nazis in 1940 into which some 433,000 Jews were crowded.

Warsaw Pact or **Eastern European Mutual Assistance Pact**, military defensive alliance 1955–91 between the USSR and East European communist states, originally established as a response to the admission of West Germany into NATO. Its military structures and agreements were dismantled early in 1991; a political organization remained until the alliance was officially dissolved in July 1991.

The Warsaw Pact was signed on 1 May 1955 in Warsaw, the capital of Poland. The date was significant as 1 May is May Day, the traditional festival day of the socialist calendar. Warsaw was chosen as the site for signing the Warsaw Pact as this allowed the USSR to present itself as merely one of a group of equally concerned nations, rather than the single dominant power. The member countries were the USSR, Poland, Czechoslovakia, Hungary, Romania, Bulgaria, Albania, and East Germany.

Warsaw rising in World War II, uprising against German occupation of Warsaw August–October 1944 organized by the Polish Home Army. The rebellion was brutally quashed when anticipated Soviet help for the rebels did not arrive.

The German army had begun withdrawing from Warsaw in anticipation of the arrival of the Soviets when the Home Army rose to keep the German troops occupied and so make it easier for the Soviets to enter the city. Street fighting began 1 August, but on the following day the Soviet attack was halted and the Germans were free to turn their full power against the rebellion.

In spite of appeals for help the Soviets made no move to assist the Poles and would not permit Allied aircraft flying in arms and supplies to the Poles to land in Soviet territory.

Home Army detachments from outside Warsaw which attempted to go to the city's aid were surrounded and disarmed by the Soviets. Eventually the Poles realized the Soviets were waiting for the Poles and Germans to wear each other out so they could impose their own regime with no resistance and they surrendered 2 October 1944.

Washington, Booker T(aliaferro) (1856–1915) US educationist, pioneer in higher education for black people in the South. He was the founder and first principal of Tuskegee Institute, Alabama, in 1881, originally a training college for blacks, and now an academic institution. He maintained that economic independence was the way to achieve social equality.

Washington argued that blacks should abandon their struggle for immediate civil rights and instead concentrate on acquiring wealth, culture, and education, and that these in turn would bring respect, acceptance, and eventual equality for blacks. This stance caused him to be shunned by many black intellectuals and civil-rights leaders such as W E B *du Bois.

Washington Conference international diplomatic meeting 1921 to avert a naval arms race between the principal maritime powers – Britain, the USA, Japan, France, and Italy. China, the Netherlands, Portugal, and Belgium were also represented. The resultant treaty 1922 put a stop to naval competition by limiting the battleship strength of the five powers.

Washington, Treaties of any of four international agreements.
(1) Between the USA and Britain 1846, by which the boundary west of the Rocky Mountains was established.
(2) Between the USA and Britain 1854 concerning fisheries, duties, and navigation in British North America; often called the Reciprocity Treaty.
(3) Between the USA and Britain 1871 for the settlement of all causes of difference.
(4) The *Washington Conference agreement 1922, limiting international naval competition.

Watergate US political scandal, named after the building in Washington, DC, which housed the headquarters of the Democratic National Committee in the 1972 presidential election. Five men, hired by the Republican Committee for the Re-election of the President (popularly known as CREEP), were caught after breaking into the Watergate with complex electronic surveillance equipment. Investigations revealed that the White House was implicated in the break-in, and that there was a 'slush fund' used to finance unethical activities, including using the CIA and the Internal Revenue Service (IRS) for political ends, setting up paramilitary operations against opponents, altering and destroying evidence, and bribing defendants to lie or remain silent. In August 1974, President *Nixon was forced by the Supreme Court to surrender to Congress tape recordings of conversations he had held with administration officials, which indicated his complicity in a cover-up. Nixon resigned rather than face impeachment for obstruction of justice and other crimes. See also *United States of America, **the Watergate scandal**.

Wavell, Archibald Percival, 1st Earl Wavell (1883–1950) British field marshal in World War II. As commander-in-chief in the Middle East, he successfully defended Egypt against Italy in July 1939 and successfully conducted the North African war against Italy 1940–41. He was transferred as commander-in-chief in India in July 1941, and became Allied Supreme Commander after Japan entered the war. He was unable to prevent Japanese advances in Malaya and Burma (now Myanmar), and Churchill became disillusioned with him. He was made viceroy of India 1943–47. He was honoured as a KCB in 1939, created Viscount in 1943, and Earl in 1947.

Waverley, John Anderson, 1st Viscount Waverley (1882–1958) British administrator, born in Scotland. He organized civil defence for World War II, becoming home secretary and minister for home security in 1939. Anderson shelters, home outdoor air-raid shelters, were named after him. He was chancellor of the Exchequer 1943–45. He was made a KCB in 1919, and Viscount in 1952.

Wei, Jingsheng (1951–) Chinese pro-democracy activist and essayist, imprisoned 1979–97 for attacking the Chinese communist system. He is regarded as one of China's most important political dissidents.

Weil, Simone (1909–1943) French writer who became a practising Catholic after a mystical experience in 1938. Apart from essays, her works (advocating political passivity) were posthumously published, including *Waiting for God* (1951), *The Need for Roots* (1952), and *Notebooks* (1956).

Weimar Republic constitutional republic in Germany from 1919 to 1933, which was crippled by the election of antidemocratic parties to the *Reichstag (parliament), and then subverted by the Nazi leader Hitler after his appointment as chancellor in 1933. It took its name from the city where in February 1919 a constituent assembly met to draw up a democratic constitution.

Weinberger, Caspar Willard (1917–) US Republican politician. He served under presidents Nixon and Ford, and was Reagan's defence secretary 1981–87.

Weizmann, Chaim Azriel (1874–1952) Zionist leader, the first president of Israel 1948–52. He conducted the negotiations leading up to the Balfour Declaration, by which the UK declared its support for an independent Jewish state.

Weizsäcker, Richard, Baron von (1920–) German Christian Democrat politician, president 1984–94. He began his career as a lawyer and was also active in the German Protestant church and in Christian Democratic Union party politics. He was elected to the West German Bundestag (parliament) in

1969 and served as mayor of West Berlin from 1981, before being elected federal president in 1984.

Welensky, Roy (1907–1991) born Roland Welensky, Rhodesian politician. He was instrumental in the creation in 1953 of the Central African Federation, comprising Northern Rhodesia (now Zambia), Southern Rhodesia (now Zimbabwe), and Nyasaland (now Malawi), and was prime minister 1956–63, when the federation was disbanded. His Southern Rhodesian Federal Party was defeated by Ian Smith's Rhodesian Front in 1964. In 1965, following Smith's unilateral declaration of Southern Rhodesian independence from Britain, Welensky left politics. He was knighted in 1953.

West Bank area (5,879 sq km / 2,270 sq mi) on the west bank of the River Jordan; population (1997 est) 1,873,500. Its main cities are Jenin, Tulkarm, and Nablus in the north; Jerusalem, Jericho, and Ramallah in the centre; and Bethlehem and Hebron in the south. The area was captured by Israel from Jordan in 1967; Jordan finally renounced any claim to it in 1988. Israel refers to the area as Judaea and Samaria, and in 2001 75% of the area of the West Bank remained under Israeli military control, protecting the 180,000 Israeli settlers.

The West Bank was held by the Jordanian army in 1948 at the end of the First *Arab-Israeli War following the creation of the state of Israel, and formally annexed in 1950. The area was integrated into the kingdom of Jordan, with Palestinians there being given Jordanian passports and citizenship. The West Bank was captured by Israel during the Six-Day War (5–10 June 1967) and placed under military government. There was initially little resistance from the resident Arab Palestinian population, in part due to Israeli improvements in the standard of living, and in part lack of affinity with Jordanians in Jordan's

East Bank. However, Israeli settlement of the area picked up pace in the 1980s, creating tensions, and after 1987 as the *Intifada (uprising) gained strength in the occupied territories, Israeli military presence increased significantly. In July 1988 Jordan renounced responsibility for the West Bank, having previously recognized the main representative of Palestinians to be the *Palestine Liberation Organization (PLO).

In 1993 Israel and the PLO began negotiations in the *Israel–Palestine peace process. They agreed to a phased withdrawal of Israeli troops from the *Gaza Strip and Arab towns and villages in the West Bank and to limited self-rule for Palestinians. The West Bank was divided into three zones: A, where PLO devolved authority was greatest; B, where the Palestine National Authority (PNA) had some limited authority but Israel maintained a security presence and 'overriding security responsibility'; and C, under military occupation.

In May 1994 the PLO assumed control over the Jericho area of the West Bank; in September 1995 Israeli armed forces withdrew from Nablus, Ramallah, Jenin, Tulkarm, Qalqilya, and Bethlehem; and in December 1995 the PLO took over civil administration in Hebron. However, numerous Jewish settlements remained in place in the West Bank under Israeli military protection. The October 1998 Wye Memorandum envisaged, after full implementation, that 17% of the West Bank would fall into Zone A, 24% into Zone B, and 59% into Zone C. The final status of the West Bank has yet to be resolved, with the issue of Jerusalem, claimed as a national capital by both peoples, remaining particularly contentious. There are around 170,000 armed Israeli settlers in the West Bank

During the second Intifada, in 2000–01, Israeli troops temporarily sealed off several West Bank towns, in retaliation for Palestinian bomb explosions in Israel, and there was fierce fighting in Nablus and Ramallah, involving Israeli tanks and helicopter gunships.

In August 2001 Israeli troops entered Jenin in the far north, marking the first incursion into a city under full Palestinian control since the 1994 transfer of control.

Westmoreland, William Childs (1914–) US general who served as commander of US forces in Vietnam 1964–68. He was an aggressive advocate of expanded US military involvement there.

Westphalia independent medieval duchy, incorporated in Prussia by the Congress of Vienna in 1815, and made a province in 1816 with Münster as its capital. Since 1946 it has been part of the German *Land* (region) of North Rhine-Westphalia.

West Point former fort in New York State, on the Hudson River, 80 km / 50 mi north of New York City, site of the US Military Academy (commonly referred to as West Point), established 1802. Women were admitted in 1976. West Point has been a military post since 1778.

Weygand, Maxime (1867–1965) French general. In World War I he was chief of staff to Marshal Foch and chief of the Allied general staff in 1918. In 1940, as French commander-in-chief, he advised surrender to Germany, and was subsequently high commissioner of North Africa 1940–41. He was a prisoner in Germany 1942–45, and was arrested after his return to France; he was released in 1946, and in 1949 the sentence of national infamy was quashed.

Wheatley, John (1869–1930) British Labour politician, born in County Waterford, Ireland. He grew up in the former county of Lanarkshire, Scotland, became a Lanarkshire councillor, and was elected member of Parliament for Glasgow Shettleston in 1922, holding the seat until his death. In the 1924 Labour government,

Wheatley served as housing minister, introducing an act designed to enable local authorities to build large stocks of council houses at affordable rents.

Wheeler, (Robert Eric) Mortimer (1890–1976) English archaeologist. After a number of distinguished excavations in Britain, he was director general of archaeology in India 1944–48, and later adviser to the government of Pakistan. He excavated sites of the forgotten Indus Valley civilization, which flourished in the later 3rd millennium, and helped to popularize archaeology by appearances on television, even on entertainment programmes such as *Animal, Vegetable or Mineral.*

White Australia Policy Australian government policy of immigration restriction, mainly aimed at non-Europeans, which began in the 1850s in an attempt to limit the number of Chinese entering the Australian goldfields and was official until 1945.

Whitehead, Edgar (Cuthbert Fremantle) (1905–1971) Rhodesian politician, leader of the United Rhodesia Party and prime minister of Southern Rhodesia (now Zimbabwe) 1958–62. He gained the premiership when his predecessor Garfield *Todd was dropped by his party for his liberal views. However, even Whitehead's more conservative programme was rejected in 1962 by the White electorate in favour of the racist Rhodesian Front.

Whitlam, (Edward) Gough (1916–) Australian politician, leader of the Labor Party 1967–78 and prime minister 1972–75. He ended conscription and Australia's military commitment in Vietnam, introduced the Medibank national health service, abolished university fees, expanded Aboriginal rights, attempted redistribution of wealth, raised loans to increase national ownership of industry and resources, and recognized mainland China.

When the opposition blocked finance bills in the Senate, following a crisis of confidence, Whitlam refused to call a general election and was dismissed by the governor general, John *Kerr. He was defeated in the subsequent general election by Malcolm *Fraser. He served as ambassador to UNESCO 1982–86.

Wilhelmina (Helena Paulina Maria) (1880–1962) Queen of the Netherlands, 1898–1948. Following the Nazi invasion of Holland in May 1940, she and her government went into exile in London for five years. Her daughter *Juliana (b.1909) succeeded her when she abdicated for reasons of ill-health in 1948.

William II (1859–1941) German Wilhelm II, Emperor of Germany from 1888, the son of Frederick III and Victoria, daughter of Queen Victoria of Britain. In 1890 he forced Chancellor Bismarck to resign in an attempt to assert his own political authority. The result was an exacerbation of domestic and international political instability, although his personal influence declined in the 1900s. He was an enthusiastic supporter of Admiral Tirpitz's plans for naval expansion. In 1914 he first approved Austria's ultimatum to Serbia and then, when he realized war was inevitable, tried in vain to prevent it. In 1918 he fled to Doorn in the Netherlands after Germany's defeat and his abdication.

Williams, Eric (1911–1981) Trinidad and Tobago centre-left politician and historian, prime minister 1956–81. After a career as a university lecturer and professor in the USA he founded the People's National Movement (PNM) in 1956. As chief minister, he took Trinidad and Tobago into the Federation of the West Indies in 1958, but seceded in 1961, and achieved full independence within the British Commonwealth in 1962. Economic downturn and increasing authoritarianism led to Black Power riots in 1970, but during the 1970s rising oil prices provided the basis for large-scale industrialization and nationalization by his government. In 1976 Williams oversaw Trinidad and Tobago's shift to republican status.

Williams of Crosby, Shirley Vivien Teresa Brittain (1930–) Baroness, British Liberal Democrat politician, leader of the party in the House of Lords from 2001. She was Labour minister for prices and consumer protection 1974–76, and education and science 1976–79. She was a founder member of the *Social Democratic Party (SDP) in 1981 and served as its president 1982–88. In 1988 she joined the newly merged Social and Liberal Democrats, which became the *Liberal Democrats in 1989.

Wilson, (James) Harold (1916–1995) Baron Wilson of Rievaulx, British Labour politician, party leader from 1963, prime minister 1964–70 and 1974–76. His premiership was dominated by the issue of UK admission to membership of the European Community (now the European Union), the social contract (unofficial agreement with the trade unions), and economic difficulties.

Wilson, born in Huddersfield, West Yorkshire, studied at Jesus College, Oxford, where he gained a first-class degree in philosophy, politics, and economics. During World War II he worked as a civil servant, and in 1945 stood for Parliament and won the marginal seat of Ormskirk. Assigned by Prime Minister Clement Attlee to a junior post in the ministry of works, he progressed to become president of the Board of Trade 1947–51 (when he resigned because of social-service cuts). In 1963 he succeeded Hugh Gaitskell as Labour leader and became prime minister the following year, increasing his majority in 1966. He formed a minority government in February 1974 and achieved a majority of three in October 1974. He resigned in 1976 and was succeeded by James Callaghan. He was knighted in 1976 and made a peer in 1983.

Wilson, (Thomas) Woodrow (1856–1924) 28th president of the USA 1913–21, a Democrat. One of the USA's most successful presidents and world's most respected statesmen, he was known for his humanity, honesty, and integrity. He kept the USA out of *World War I until 1917, and in January 1918 issued his *Fourteen Points as a basis for a just peace settlement, which included the formation of a *League of Nations. He was awarded the Nobel Peace Prize in 1919. Congress later refused to commit the USA to the League.

Wilson was born in Staunton, Virginia, and educated at Princeton University, of which he became president 1902–10. In 1910 he became governor of New Jersey. Elected US president in 1912 against Theodore Roosevelt and William Taft, he initiated antitrust legislation and secured valuable social reforms in his progressive 'New Freedom' programme, and was re-elected in 1916. He also instituted a federal income tax, the first since the Civil War. A champion of peace and neutrality, he strove to keep the USA out of World War I, a policy popular with most Americans. However the German U-boat campaign, sensationalized by the sinking of the British liner *Lusitania* (with 128 Americans lost), forced him to declare war in 1917. At the peace conference in Paris he secured the inclusion of the League of Nations in individual peace treaties, but his refusal to compromise on its text contributed to its defeat in Congress. In 1919 Wilson suffered a stroke during a nationwide campaign to gain support for the League and retired from public life.

Windsor, House of official name of the British royal family since 1917, adopted in place of Saxe-Coburg-Gotha. Since 1960 those descendants of Elizabeth II not entitled to the prefix HRH (His/Her Royal Highness) have borne the surname Mountbatten-Windsor.

Wingate, Orde Charles (1903–1944)
British soldier. In 1936 he established
a reputation for unorthodox tactics in
Palestine. In World War II he served
in the Middle East and organized
guerrilla forces in Ethiopia, and later
led the Chindits, the Third Indian
Division, in guerrilla operations
against the Japanese army in Burma
(now Myanmar).

winter of discontent the winter of
1978–79 in Britain, marked by a series
of strikes that contributed to the defeat
of the Labour government in the
general election of spring 1979.
The phrase is from Shakespeare's
Richard III: 'Now is the winter of our
discontent / Made glorious summer
by this sun of York.'

Winter War the USSR's invasion of
Finland 30 November 1939–12 March
1940, also called the Russo-Finnish War.

women's suffrage women's right to
vote in elections. After a prolonged
struggle women were finally given the
right to vote on equal terms with men
in 1920 in the USA and in 1928 in
Britain. Women's suffrage was granted
at different times in different countries;
for example Norway granted women
the vote in 1913; Belgium in 1948.
Swiss women won the right to vote
only in 1971.

Workers' Party of Kurdistan PKK,
Kurdish guerrilla organization, active
in Turkey from 1974. Initially it aimed
to secure an independent Kurdish
state, Kurdistan, but has since
modified its demands, indicating
a preparedness to accept autonomy
within a federal system. Responsible
for many civilian deaths and bombings
of private as well as government
buildings, the PKK has been the
subject of a prolonged and unrelenting
campaign of suppression by the
Turkish authorities (more than
11,000 people died in fighting between
government and PKK forces 1978–94).
The PKK was banned in Germany and
France in 1993 after attacks on Turkish
premises in those countries. The PKK

turned itself into a legitimate political
organization in February 2000,
announcing that it renounced the
armed struggle it had waged against
the Turkish government for the past
15 years.

workhouse in the UK, a former
institution to house and maintain
people unable to earn their own living,
established under the *poor law.
Groups of parishes in England
combined to build workhouses for
the poor, the aged, the disabled, and
orphaned children from about 1815
until about 1930.

Works Progress Administration
WPA, in US history, a government
initiative to reduce unemployment
during the Depression (11 million in
1934). Formed 1935, it provided useful
work for 8.5 million people during
its eight-year existence, mainly in
construction projects, at a total cost of
$11 billion, and was discontinued only
in 1943 when the change to a war
economy eliminated unemployment.
The WPA was renamed the Works
Projects Administration in 1939.
The WPA was an integral part of
President Roosevelt's *New Deal.

World Health Organization WHO,
specialized agency of the United
Nations established in 1946 to prevent
the spread of diseases and to eradicate
them. From 1996 to 1997 it had a budget
of US$842.654 million. Its headquarters
are in Geneva, Switzerland. The
WHO's greatest achievement to date
has been the eradication of smallpox.

World Trade Organization WTO,
specialized, rules-based, member-
driven agency of the United Nations,
world trade monitoring body
established in January 1995, on
approval of the Final Act of the
Uruguay round of the *General
Agreement on Tariffs and Trade
(GATT). Under the Final Act, the WTO,
a permanent trading body with a
status comparable with that of the
International Monetary Fund or the

World Bank, effectively replaced GATT. The WTO oversees and administers agreements to reduce barriers to trade, such as tariffs, subsidies, quotas, and regulations which discriminate against imported products. Other functions of the WTO include: handling trade disputes, offering a forum for trade negotiations, technical assistance and training for developing countries, and monitoring national trade policies.

World War I 1914–18, war between the Central European Powers (Germany, Austria-Hungary, and allies) on one side and the *Triple Entente (Britain and the British Empire, France, and Russia) and their allies, including the USA (which entered in 1917), on the other side. An estimated 10 million lives were lost and twice that number were wounded. It was fought on the eastern and western fronts, in the Middle East, in Africa, and at sea.

World War II 1939–45, war between Germany, Italy, and Japan (the *Axis powers) on one side, and Britain, the Commonwealth, France, the USA, the USSR, and China (the *Allies) on the other. An estimated 55 million lives were lost (20 million of them citizens of the USSR), and 60 million people in Europe were displaced because of bombing raids. The war was fought in the Atlantic theatre (Europe, North Africa, and the Atlantic Ocean) and the Pacific theatre (Far East and the Pacific).

It is estimated that, during the course of the war, for every tonne of bombs dropped on the UK, 315 tonnes fell on Germany.

In 1945 Germany surrendered (May), but Japan fought on until the USA dropped atomic bombs on Hiroshima and Nagasaki (August).

World War II, Atlantic theatre 1939–45, following *Hitler's invasion of Poland on 1 September 1939, Britain, the Commonwealth, and France declared war on Germany. In June 1940 Germany's *Axis ally Italy entered the conflict, and in June 1941 Hitler broke its non-aggression pact with the USSR to invade Soviet territory, bringing the USSR onto the side of the Allies. The USA declared war on the Axis powers in December 1941 after the Japanese attack on Pearl Harbor. By the end of 1941, war was being fought in the Atlantic, North Africa, and on all fronts in Europe, either through open warfare or, in defeated countries such as Norway, Poland, and France, through their resistance movements. The battlefront had also extended to the Pacific theatre.

World War II, Pacific theatre 1941–45, in late 1941 Germany's *Axis ally Japan attacked the US Pacific naval base at *Pearl Harbor bringing the USA into the war, and turning what had been largely a European war into a global conflict. China, which had been waging the Sino–Japanese War since 1931, also joined the Allied effort. Japan pushed rapidly forward, reaching the eastern frontier of India and the island gateway to Australia by spring 1942, before its expansionist aims were thwarted. Japanese surrender was finally forced by the dropping of atomic bombs on *Hiroshima and Nagasaki in August 1945.

Worner, Manfred (1934–1994) German politician, NATO secretary general 1988–94. He was elected for the centre-right Christian Democratic Union (CDU) to the West German Bundestag (parliament) in 1965 and, as a specialist in strategic affairs, served as defence minister 1982–88. He was a proponent of closer European military collaboration.

Wrangel, Peter Nicolaievich, Baron von (1878–1928) Russian general, born in St Petersburg. He commanded a division of Cossacks in World War I, and in 1920, after succeeding Anton Denikin as commander-in-chief of the White Army, was defeated by the Bolsheviks in the Crimea.

Wyszynski, Stepan (1901–1981)
Polish Roman Catholic churchman, archbishop of Gniezno and Warsaw and Primate of Poland from 1948 until his death. He was appointed a cardinal in 1952, but before he could take up his office, he was imprisoned for criticizing the Polish communist government and detained for three years. He finally became a cardinal in 1957, and concluded an uneasy truce between the Church and the administration of Władysław Gomułka.

Xi'an Incident   kidnapping of the Chinese generalissimo and politician *Jiang Jie Shi (Chiang Kai-shek) in Xi'an on 12 December 1936, by one of his own generals, to force his cooperation with the communists against the Japanese invaders.

Yahya Khan, Agha Muhammad (1917–1980) Pakistani president 1969–71. His mishandling of the Bangladesh separatist issue led to civil war and he was forced to resign.

yakuza (Japanese 'good for nothing') Japanese gangster. Organized crime in Japan is highly structured, and the various syndicates between them employed some 110,000 people in 1989, with a turnover of an estimated 1.5 trillion yen. The *yakuza* have been unofficially tolerated and are very powerful.

Yalta Conference strategic conference held 4–11 February 1945 in Yalta (a Soviet holiday resort in the Crimea) by the main Allied leaders in World War II. At this, the second of three key meetings between the 'Big Three' – Winston Churchill (UK), Franklin D Roosevelt (USA), and Joseph Stalin (USSR) – plans were drawn up for the final defeat and disarmament of Nazi Germany, the post-war partition of Europe (see *Cold War), and the foundation of the *United Nations.

Yalu River, Battle of during the Russo–Japanese War, Russian defeat by the Japanese 1 May 1904 in the vicinity of Antung (now Dandong), Manchuria.

Yamamoto, Isoroku (1884–1943) Japanese admiral in World War II. Long convinced that Japan would eventually fight the USA he began planning the attack on *Pearl Harbor early 1940. After the raid he was quick to appreciate the significance of the US carrier force escaping the damage, and prepared plans to entrap and destroy them, but this backfired and instead he lost most of his own carriers in the Battle of Midway.

Yamani, Ahmad Zaki al- (1930–) Saudi Arabian politician, oil minister

1962–86. An exemplar of a new generation of young, Western-trained technocrats who came to serve the ruling al-Saud family, al-Yamani rose to prominence as the government's legal adviser from 1958, and in 1962 became minister of oil and natural resources. He remained in this post until October 1986 and during these years was the most influential figure within the Organization of Petroleum-Exporting Countries (OPEC), the cartel of oil-producing states formed in 1960. He played a key role in orchestrating, through restrictions on output, the surge in world oil prices during the 1970s, which saw Saudi annual oil revenues rise from $2.7 billion in 1972 to $102 billion in 1981. During the early 1980s al-Yamani changed strategy and advocated increased Saudi, and OPEC, oil production, in an effort to maintain the cartel's share of world output. The consequence was a fall in world oil prices, which raised al-Yamani's popularity in the West, but led to his dismissal in 1986.

Yamashita, Tomoyuki (1885–1946) Japanese general in World War II. He commanded the 25th Army in the invasion of Malaya and *Singapore 1941, conducting a quick and effective campaign which earned him the title 'Tiger of Malaya' in Japan. He was arrested for war crimes and executed 1946.

Yanayev, Gennady (1937–) Soviet communist politician, vice-president of the USSR 1990–91. He led the August 1991 anti-Gorbachev attempted coup, after which he was arrested and charged with treason. He was released in 1994 under an amnesty.

Yang Shangkun (1907–1998) Chinese communist politician. He held a senior position in the Central Committee of the Communist Party of China (CCP) 1956–66 but was demoted during the *Cultural Revolution. He was rehabilitated in 1978, elected to the Politburo in 1982, and served as state president 1988–93.

Yeltsin, Boris Nikolayevich (1931–) Russian politician, president of the Russian Soviet Federative Socialist Republic (RSFSR) 1990–91, and president of the newly independent Russian Federation 1991–99.

He directed the Federation's secession from the USSR and the formation of a new, decentralized confederation, the *Commonwealth of Independent States (CIS), with himself as the most powerful leader. A referendum in 1993 supported his policies of price deregulation and accelerated privatization, despite severe economic problems and civil unrest. He survived a coup attempt later the same year, but was subsequently forced to compromise on the pace of his reforms after far-right electoral gains, and lost considerable public support.

He suffered two heart attacks in October and November 1995, yet still contested the June 1996 presidential elections, in which he secured re-election by defeating Communist Party leader Gennady Zyuganov in the second round run-off. Yeltsin resigned as president on 31 December 1999. Announcing that he was bowing out to give a younger generation a chance, he apologized to his country for failing to fulfil their hopes. He relinquished his power six months early to his chosen successor, Vladimir Putin, in return for receiving guarantees of immunity from any future prosecution for any of his actions in the Kremlin.

Yemen country in southwest Asia, bounded north by Saudi Arabia, east by Oman, south by the Gulf of Aden, and west by the Red Sea.

Yezhov, Nikolai Ivanovich (1895–1939) Soviet politician and party functionary.

As head of the NKVD (the Soviet secret police) 1936–38, he was a major figure in Stalin's ruthless *purges of the Communist Party. The bloody suppression of all dissent in this period came to be known after him, as the 'Yezhovshchina', but he himself was arrested in 1938–39 and never seen again.

Yom Kippur War the surprise attack on Israel in October 1973 by Egypt and Syria; see *Arab–Israeli Wars; *Israel, the Fourth Arab–Israeli War; and *Egypt, the Fourth Arab–Israeli War. It is named after the Jewish national holiday on which it began, the holiest day of the Jewish year.

York, Alvin Cullum 'Sergeant' (1887–1964) US war hero. Although a conscientious objector, York was drafted as a private in the 82nd Infantry Division in World War I and promoted to the rank of sergeant. At the Battle of the Argonne Forest 8 October 1918, York led a charge against a German position in which he and his comrades captured 132 prisoners and 35 machine guns. He was awarded the Congressional Medal of Honour and the French *Croix de Guerre*. A film biography, *Sergeant York*, appeared 1940.

Yoshida, Shigeru (1878–1967) Japanese diplomat and conservative Liberal politician who served as prime minister for most of the period 1946–54, including much of the US occupation 1945–52. Under Yoshida, Japan signed the San Francisco Peace Treaty with the USA and its allies in 1951.

Young Plan scheme devised by US entrepreneur Owen D Young to reschedule German payments of war reparations 1929.

Young Turk member of a reformist movement of young army officers in the Ottoman Empire founded 1889. The movement was instrumental in the constitutional changes of 1908 and the abdication of Sultan Abd al-Hamid II 1909. It gained prestige during the

Balkan Wars 1912–13 and encouraged Turkish links with the German empire. Its influence diminished after 1918. The term is now used for a member of any radical or rebellious faction within a party or organization.

Ypres, Battles of Flemish **Ieper**, in World War I, three major battles 1914–17 between German and Allied forces near Ypres, a Belgian town in western Flanders, 40 km/25 mi south of Ostend. Neither side made much progress in any of the battles, despite heavy casualties, but the third battle in particular (also known as Passchendaele) July–November 1917 stands out as an enormous waste of life for little return. The Menin Gate (1927) is a memorial to British soldiers lost in these battles.

Yüan Shikai (1859–1916) Chinese soldier and politician, leader of Republican China 1911–16. He assumed dictatorial powers in 1912, dissolving parliament and suppressing Sun Zhong Shan's (Sun Yat-sen's) Kuomintang (*Guomindang). He died soon after proclaiming himself emperor.

Z

Zaghlul, Saad (1857–1927) Egyptian nationalist and politician, prime minister in 1924. Leader of the Wafd party, he came to be regarded as the 'father' of an independent Egyptian nation-state. His intransigent, uncompromising attitude to, and open criticism of, the negotiations with the British, costing him deportation to Malta in 1919 and Seychelles in 1921, made him the symbol and hero of the Egyptian nationalist cause to end the protectorate. He became prime minister of the first elected government in January 1924 and resigned 11 months later in protest against the British ultimatum to his government.

Zahir Shah, Muhammad (1914–) King of Afghanistan 1933–73. Zahir, educated in Kabul and Paris, served in the government 1932–33 before being crowned king. He was overthrown in 1973 by a republican coup and went into exile. He became a symbol of national unity for the Mujahedin Islamic fundamentalist resistance groups.

Zambia landlocked country in southern central Africa, bounded north by the Democratic Republic of Congo (formerly Zaire) and Tanzania, east by Malawi, south by Mozambique, Zimbabwe, Botswana, and Namibia, and west by Angola.

government Zambia is an independent republic within the *Commonwealth. The 1991 multiparty constitution provides for a president as head of state and government and a single-chamber, 150-member national assembly. Both are elected by universal suffrage for a five-year term, renewable only once. The president governs with an appointed cabinet and is advised by a 27-member House of Chiefs, consisting of four chiefs from each of the country's nine provinces.

history The country was visited by the Portuguese in the late 18th century and by Scottish explorer David Livingstone in 1851. As Northern Rhodesia it became a British protectorate in 1924, together with the former kingdom of Barotseland (now Western Province), taken under British protection at the request of its ruler in 1890.

independent republic From 1953 the country, with Southern Rhodesia (now Zimbabwe) and Nyasaland (now Malawi), was part of the Federation of Rhodesia and Nyasaland, dissolved in 1963. Northern Rhodesia became the independent Republic of Zambia in 1964, within the Commonwealth, with Dr Kenneth *Kaunda, leader of the United National Independence Party (UNIP), as its first president. Between 1964 and 1972, when it was declared a one-party state, Zambia was troubled with frequent outbreaks of violence because of disputes within the governing party and conflicts among the country's more than 70 tribes.

relations with Rhodesia Zambia was economically dependent on neighbouring white-ruled Rhodesia but tolerated liberation groups operating on the border, and relations between the two countries deteriorated. The border was closed in 1973, and in 1976 Kaunda declared his support for the Patriotic Front, led by Robert Mugabe and Joshua Nkomo, which was fighting the white regime in Rhodesia. Despite his imposition of strict economic policies, Kaunda was re-elected in 1983 and again in 1988, unopposed, for a sixth consecutive term.

end of Kaunda presidency In 1990, in response to the growing strength of the opposition Movement for Multiparty Democracy (MMD), President Kaunda announced the introduction of a multiparty system for in October 1991. The MMD applied for formal registration as a political party and the formation of a National Democratic Alliance (NADA) was announced. Elections took place, on schedule, and the MMD won an overwhelming victory. Frederick Chiluba was sworn in as Zambia's new president in November 1991, bringing to an end the 27-year leadership of Kaunda.

drought During 1991–92 southern Africa experienced its worst drought of the 20th century and as a result Zambia suffered dire food and water shortages (1992–93). In 1993 a state of emergency was declared in response to reports of a planned anti-government coup.

further developments In May 1996, the constitution was controversially amended to require future presidential candidates to be second-generation Zambians. The amendment barred the nomination of Kenneth Kaunda. Kaunda himself was jailed in late December 1997 in the capital, Lusaka, five days after he returned to his country for the first time since an attempted coup. South African President Mandela joined Britain and the USA in criticizing Zambian President Chiluba for having detained his political rival.

On 31 December Kaunda was released from prison and immediately put under house arrest. In June 1998 charges against him were dropped and he was released.

In April 2001, Zambia's ruling party was divided over President Chiluba's attempts to change its constitution so as to run for a third term in office. In defiance of a court order, the vice-president and eight ministers who opposed the change were expelled

from the party. Having secured the constitutional change, Chiluba then announced he would not stand as a candidate in the presidential elections. However, Chiluba lost one of his closest allies in September when Michael Sata left the government and his job as national secretary of the MMD claiming that Chiluba's choice of candidate for the election was illegal, as it violated the party's constitution.

Levy Mwanawasa, Chiluba's chosen successor, was sworn in as president on 2 January 2002, after a high court rejected an opposition appeal to delay the inaugural ceremony until allegations of electoral fraud were investigated. Opposition parties said they would continue to challenge the results, which foreign observers agreed were flawed.

ZANU acronym for **Zimbabwe African National Union**, political organization founded in 1963 by the Reverend Ndabaningi Sithole and later led by Robert Mugabe. It was banned in 1964 by Ian Smith's Rhodesian Front government, against which it conducted a guerrilla war from Zambia until the free elections of 1980, when the ZANU Patriotic Front (ZANU-PF) party, led by Mugabe, won 63% of the vote. In 1987 it merged with *ZAPU in preparation for making Zimbabwe a one-party state.

Zapata, Emiliano (1879–1919) Mexican Indian revolutionary leader. He led a revolt against dictator Porfirio Díaz from 1910 under the slogan 'Land and Liberty', to repossess for the indigenous Mexicans the land taken by the Spanish. By 1915 he was driven into retreat, and was assassinated in his stronghold, Morelos, by an agent of Venustiano *Carranza.

Zapatista National Liberation Army Spanish **Ejército Zapatista de Liberación Nacional (EZLN)**, guerrilla movement in Mexico, led by the mysterious masked figure of Subcomandante Marcos. It has campaigned especially for the rights of indigenous Maya people in the southeast province of Chiapas since January 1994.

ZAPU acronym for **Zimbabwe African People's Union**, political organization founded by Joshua *Nkomo in 1961 and banned in 1962 by the Rhodesian government. It engaged in a guerrilla war in alliance with *ZANU against the Rhodesian regime until late 1979. In the 1980 elections ZAPU was defeated and was then persecuted by the ruling ZANU Patriotic Front party. In 1987 the two parties merged.

Zeebrugge raid in World War I, daring British attack on German naval base on the coast of Belgium April 1918.

zemstvo Russian provincial or district council established by Tsar Alexander II 1864. These councils were responsible for local administration until the revolution of 1917.

Zhao Ziyang (1919–) Chinese politician, prime minister 1980–87 and leader of the Chinese Communist Party 1987–89. His reforms included self-management and incentives for workers and factories. He lost his secretaryship and other posts after the Tiananmen Square massacre in Beijing in June 1989.

Zhdanov, Andrei Aleksandrovich (1896–1948) Soviet politician. As Secretary of the Central Committee of the Communist Party from 1934 onwards, he was largely responsible for formulating the ideology of Stalinism. During World War II, he played a leading role in the defence of the besieged city of Leningrad (now St Petersburg), 1941–44.

Zhivkov, Todor Hristo (1911–1998) Bulgarian Communist Party (BCP) leader 1954–89, prime minister 1962–71, and president 1971–89. His period in office was one of caution and conservatism. In 1990 he was charged with embezzlement during his time in office and in 1992 sentenced to seven years under house arrest. He was released in January 1997.

Zhou Enlai (or Chou En-lai) (1898–1976) Chinese communist politician. Zhou, a member of the Chinese Communist Party (CCP) from the 1920s, was prime minister 1949–76 and foreign minister 1949–58. He was a moderate Maoist and weathered the *Cultural Revolution. He played a key role in foreign affairs.

Zhu De (or Chu The) (1886–1976) Chinese communist military leader, 'father' and commander of the Chinese Red Army 1931–54. He devised the tactic of mobile guerrilla warfare and organized the *Long March to Shaanxi 1934–36. He was made a marshal in 1955.

Zhukov, Georgi Konstantinovich (1896–1974) Marshal of the USSR in World War II and minister of defence 1955–57. As chief of staff from 1941, he defended Moscow in 1941, counterattacked at Stalingrad (now Volgograd) in 1942, organized the relief of Leningrad (now St Petersburg) in 1943, and led the offensive from the Ukraine March in 1944 which ended in the fall of Berlin.

Zia, Begum Khaleda (1945–) Bangladeshi conservative politician, prime minister 1991–96. As leader of the Bangladesh Nationalist Party (BNP) from 1984, she successfully oversaw the transition from presidential to democratic parliamentary government, but faced mounting opposition from 1994.

Zia ul-Haq, Muhammad (1924–1988) Pakistani general, in power from 1977 until his death, probably an assassination, in an aircraft explosion. He became army chief of staff in 1976, led the military coup against Zulfikar Ali *Bhutto in 1977, and became president in 1978. Zia introduced a fundamentalist Islamic regime and restricted political activity.

Zimbabwe landlocked country in south central Africa, bounded north by Zambia, east by Mozambique, south by South Africa, and west by Botswana.

   government Zimbabwe is an independent republic within the

*Commonwealth. The 1980 constitution, revised 1990, provides for an executive president, who is head of state and government, and a single-chamber House of Assembly. Under the revised constitution, the president, formerly elected by parliament, is directly elected for a six-year term and appoints a vice-president and cabinet. The House of Assembly has 150 members – 120 directly elected, 12 nominated by the president, plus ten traditional chiefs and eight provincial governors. It serves a six-year term and is subject to dissolution within that period.

history There was a Bantu-speaking civilization in the area that is now Zimbabwe before AD 300. By 1200 Mashonaland (now in eastern Zimbabwe) was a major settlement of the Shona (or Mashona) people, who had moved in from the north. The Shona derived their wealth from mining and trading minerals. They built in stone, and the most famous remains of their civilization are at Great Zimbabwe (the name Zimbabwe means 'stone house' in Bantu). In the 15th century the Shona empire, under Mutota, expanded across Zimbabwe before it fell to the Rozwi, who ruled until the 19th century. Portuguese explorers reached the area in the early 16th century.

In 1837 the pastoral Shona were conquered by the disciplined armies of another Bantu people, the Matabele (or Ndebele), a branch of the Zulu. The Matabele were in retreat after unsuccessful battles with the Boers (Afrikaners) in South Africa, and settled in western Zimbabwe (Matabeleland), where they established a military despotism.

the establishment of British rule Mashonaland and Matabeleland, together with what is now Zambia, were granted to the British South Africa Company in 1889, largely owing to the efforts of Cecil *Rhodes. The whole region was named Rhodesia in 1895 in honour of Rhodes. King Lobengula of Matabeleland accepted British protection in 1888 but rebelled in 1893; he was defeated, but in 1896 after the *Jameson Raid the Matabele once more unsuccessfully tried to regain their independence.

In 1911 the territory under the British South Africa Company's administration was divided into Northern Rhodesia (now Zambia) and Southern Rhodesia (now Zimbabwe). In 1922 Southern Rhodesia voted for responsible government, and also rejected a proposal for a merger with South Africa. A government was established under a governor with an executive council and legislative assembly in October 1923. Although technically a colony, Southern Rhodesia was, from the outset, regarded in practice as a quasi-dominion, enjoying virtual self-government by its white minority.

Southern Rhodesia after World War II The country's prosperity, founded on the tobacco crop, grew rapidly; many Africans from what are now Zambia and Malawi flocked there to work, attracted by the higher wages and living standards. There was steady immigration to Southern Rhodesia from both South Africa and Britain, particularly after World War II.

Pressures for full dominion status increased from 1945 onwards, the situation now being complicated by the rise of an African nationalist movement in Southern Rhodesia.

The South-African based African National Congress had been present since 1934, and there was growing dissatisfaction among urbanized black Africans with their lack of political status. The attitude of the average white Rhodesian to the black Africans was paternal. It failed to gauge the rapid change that the African attitude to white domination in Africa was undergoing, while, at the same time, few white Rhodesians were in favour of implementing *apartheid measures as fully as in South Africa.

the Federation of Rhodesia and Nyasaland The idea of federating Southern Rhodesia and the neighbouring territories of Northern Rhodesia and Nyasaland (now Malawi) had first been examined by a royal commission in 1938. As a consequence, the Central African Council was created in 1945. There was strong support for federation in ruling circles in Southern Rhodesia, for economic links with Nyasaland and Northern Rhodesia were close, and the Southern Rhodesian cities of Salisbury (Harare) and Bulawayo were the principal business centres for all three territories.

The Federation of Rhodesia and Nyasaland, which was established in 1953, lasted for ten years. In 1958 the progressive premier of Southern Rhodesia, Garfield Todd, was swept from power by the more conservative United Federalists under Sir Edgar Whitehead.

In 1963 the Federation was dissolved, though economic bonds between its three former components remained close. Nyasaland and Northern Rhodesia became independent African states, as Malawi and Zambia respectively. Southern Rhodesia, with its relatively large and long-established white ruling minority (although still outnumbered 23:1 by black Africans), remained theoretically a British colony.

black African opposition From the outset, African leaders in all three territories had opposed the Federation, believing it implied perpetual domination by the white minority. Despite the federal government's efforts to dispel these fears by advocating 'partnership' between the races, this opposition remained implacable. The African leaders regarded the great economic benefits derived from federation as irrelevant compared with their continuing lack of political power.

The African National Congress had been reconvened in 1957 under the leadership of Joshua *Nkomo. It was banned in 1959, and Nkomo went into exile to become leader of the National Democratic Party (NDP), which had been formed by some ANC members. When the NDP was banned in 1961, Nkomo created the Zimbabwe African People's Union (ZAPU). In 1963 a splinter group developed from ZAPU, the Zimbabwe African National Union (ZANU), led by the Rev Ndabaningi Sithole, with Robert *Mugabe as its secretary general.

independence talks Demand by the white Rhodesians for immediate dominion status had become vociferous. After lengthy discussions with Britain, a new constitution had been introduced for Southern Rhodesia in December 1961. It allowed for minority African representation, but because of its limitations it was violently opposed by the black African political leaders in Southern Rhodesia. In September 1962 ZAPU, the principal African opposition party, was banned, and its leaders subsequently placed 'under restriction', after various acts of terrorism and intimidation had allegedly occurred.

The UN voted for the suspension of the Southern Rhodesian constitution, but Britain maintained, as it was to do subsequently on all occasions, that as a British colony, Southern Rhodesia was not within the UN's competence. In November 1962 the governing United Federal Party under Whitehead pledged an end to racism in Southern Rhodesia. This pledge probably helped to bring about the party's total defeat in the elections of December 1962, which were won by the right-wing Rhodesia Front, led by Winston Field, who became prime minister of Rhodesia (as Southern Rhodesia was now known).

Field visited London to press for immediate independence for Rhodesia. It had been assumed by both Britain and Rhodesia that the 1961 constitution was the prelude to Rhodesian independence, but whereas

Britain wished to write into it safeguards to ensure ultimate majority rule (in other words, rule by black Africans) within a specified period, the Rhodesian government was not prepared to do this, although it conceded the principle of ultimate majority rule at some unspecified time in the future.

UDI and the British reaction

In April 1964 Field, regarded by his party as too moderate, was replaced as premier by Ian *Smith, and in May Smith won overwhelming support at the elections, and all the opposition groups were decimated. Four months later ZANU was banned, and Nkomo and Mugabe were imprisoned. Following protracted and unsuccessful negotiations, on 11 November 1965 Smith issued his Unilateral Declaration of Independence (UDI), announcing that Rhodesia was now an independent dominion within the Commonwealth, and reiterated his country's loyalty to the British crown.

Britain at once declared the UDI and the Smith regime illegal, and the latter to be in a state of rebellion against the crown. The British Parliament passed the Southern Rhodesia Enabling Act on 16 November 1965, and introduced exchange-and-control restrictions against Rhodesia. In December Britain imposed a total embargo on trade with Rhodesia. To prevent Zambia suffering from the effects of the sanctions imposed on Rhodesia, Britain provided economic aid, and an airlift of oil. Britain hoped that the measures adopted would inflict sufficient hardship in Rhodesia to bring about 'a return to constitutional government' (in other words, the fall of the Smith regime).

Many African states felt that the measures did not go far enough, and that Britain should settle the matter by force. This the British prime minister, Harold Wilson, refused to contemplate. At the UN there was bitter Afro-Asian criticism of Britain, but no action was agreed upon. A Commonwealth prime ministers' conference at Lagos in 1966 discussed the Rhodesian question at length, and Wilson defended Britain's policies.

failed negotiations with Britain

In December 1966 Harold Wilson and Ian Smith met on HMS *Tiger* to discuss a settlement. This included six principles, the major one of which insisted on 'unimpeded progress to majority rule', but the proposals were unacceptable to the Rhodesian Front. The British government then sponsored a resolution in the UN Security Council calling for selective mandatory sanctions against specified Rhodesian exports. In May 1968 the Security Council went further and imposed, under Chapter VII of the UN Charter, comprehensive mandatory economic sanctions against Rhodesia and established a UN Sanctions Committee to supervise their effectiveness. These sanctions were in fact bypassed by many multinational companies.

In October 1968 Wilson and Smith met again on HMS *Fearless*, but the talks broke down. In 1969 Rhodesia declared itself a republic and adopted a new constitution, with white-majority representation in a two-chamber legislature.

In 1971 the new British Conservative government reopened negotiations and agreement was reached between Sir Alec Douglas-Home and Smith in November of that year. The settlement was based on the 1969 republican constitution with certain amendments to allow for the (remote) possibility of African representation increasing to parity and from there to majority rule through a combination of elected and chiefly representatives. A British stipulation of the agreement was that it must be seen to be 'acceptable to the people of Rhodesia as a whole'. A royal commission, under the chairmanship of Lord Pearce, was sent to Rhodesia to test opinion. Africans overwhelmingly rejected the proposals and this was confirmed in the Pearce commission's report (May 1972).

the failure of the proposed constitutional conference Following the withdrawal of Portugal from its African territories in 1974 and the growing, if still limited, success of guerrilla raids on Rhodesia's northern borders, the Rhodesian government, under pressure from Zambia and South Africa, in 1974–75 released Joshua Nkomo, leader of ZAPU, and the Rev Ndabaningi Sithole and Robert Mugabe of ZANU, from detention. This was followed by discussions with them and Bishop Abel *Muzorewa, president of the African National Council (the ANC, which had been formed in 1971 to oppose the earlier independence arrangements), with the aim of setting up a national conference to work out a new constitution.

Rifts soon developed, however, within the ANC, but under pressure from the leaders of Zambia, Tanzania, and Mozambique, in July 1975 Nkomo and Sithole agreed to cooperate under the leadership of Bishop Muzorewa, and the unity problem was apparently resolved. All agreed 'to intensify the liberation struggle' although it soon became clear that neither the ANC nor Smith had any enthusiasm for a constitutional conference.

the Victoria Falls conference Under joint pressure from John Vorster, prime minister of South Africa, and President Kenneth Kaunda of Zambia, representatives of the Smith government and of the ANC met on 25 August 1975 in a South African Railways passenger coach in the middle of Victoria Falls Bridge. Smith made it clear beforehand that he had no intention of handing over Rhodesia to black-majority rule, while the ANC insisted that the issue of majority rule was not negotiable and the alternative to an immediate handover of power was war. There were other problems,

but the unexpected presence of Kaunda and Vorster, who acted as joint chairs at the opening conference sessions, ensured that some attempt at discussion ensued. After two days, however, the talks collapsed, each side blaming the other for failure.

Nkomo's talks with Smith Following the Victoria Falls conference, the rift between ZANU and ZAPU supporters within the ANC intensified, the former under Sithole, supported by Muzorewa, insisting that military struggle was the only solution to majority African rule in Rhodesia, and ZAPU, under Nkomo, urging a continuation of the constitutional talks. Eventually Nkomo was excluded from the ANC Zimbabwe Liberation Council, based in Zambia; establishing himself in Salisbury (Harare), he became chairman of the inside-Rhodesia branch of the ANC, much to the anger of the other factions.

Nkomo began secret talks with Smith in October 1975, resulting in a first public session on 15 December. This ended with the announcement that special committees were to be set up to investigate aspects of the constitutional issue; but as the talks dragged on into March 1976, despite reports of the moderate proposals put forward by the Nkomo side, it became clear that the basic issue, early transfer of power to black-majority rule, would not be resolved. The talks finally broke down on 19 March 1976, despite British offers to mediate, provided that Smith was prepared to accept the principle of majority rule.

the escalation of the liberation war During the talks, the African presidents had tried to restrain guerrillas operating from their soil, but with the breakdown of the talks they threw their weight firmly behind the military struggle in Rhodesia. Following border clashes Samora Machel, president of Mozambique, closed the Rhodesia–Mozambique border at the beginning of March 1976, causing some dislocation to the Rhodesian economy by cutting off access to the ports of Beira and Maputo (formerly Lourenço Marques).

Estimates of the numbers of Zimbabwe guerrillas in training varied from 12,000 to 15,000. Those based in Mozambique were being trained by Chinese instructors, while others were reported to be abroad in the USSR, Algeria, and elsewhere. By mid-1976 clashes with the guerrillas were expected to develop into a bitter race war in Rhodesia, the political and military impact of which could not fail to affect South Africa as well. Thus the pressures for Smith to reach an accommodation with the moderate Nkomo wing of the ANC increased.

further international discussions At the end of April 1976, Henry Kissinger, US secretary of state, on a first visit to Africa, announced that, short of military aid, the USA was willing to help African countries bring about majority rule in Rhodesia. Pressure was also put on Botswana and South Africa to tighten the sanctions against Rhodesia. Coinciding with the Kissinger visit to black Africa, Smith announced that four tribal chiefs were to be created ministers in his government, but Nkomo made it plain that this stratagem was unacceptable as a substitute for majority rule. In September 1976, following discussions with Vorster and Kissinger, Smith announced that his government agreed to majority rule within two years and accepted proposals for government in the interim, subject to lifting of sanctions and cessation of guerrilla activities.

The announcement was welcomed by African leaders, but there were divergencies of opinion between them and Smith (and among themselves), and the armed struggle for the independence of Zimbabwe continued. Rhodesian troops made retaliatory assaults on guerrilla camps in Mozambique in October and November.

In October 1976 a conference was held in Geneva at which Britain, the Smith regime, and the three main nationalist parties were represented; but it broke down on several issues and was indefinitely adjourned on 11 January 1977. By this stage Nkomo and Mugabe had patched up their differences and jointly formed the Patriotic Front (PF). Subsequent proposals by Britain on interim government leading to majority rule were categorically rejected by Smith, and increased military expenditure and a wider call-up were announced by the Rhodesian government. An amendment to the Land Tenure Bill, giving all sections of the community the right to purchase land owned by whites, and gradual reduction of some racial-discrimination measures took effect in 1977.

Muzorewa becomes premier of Zimbabwe-Rhodesia In March 1978 the Smith government and some African nationalist leaders agreed to form an interim government, including black members, while working towards majority rule. At the beginning of 1979 Smith produced a new 'majority rule' constitution, which contained an inbuilt protection for the white minority but which he had managed to get Bishop Muzorewa to accept. In June 1979 Muzorewa was pronounced prime minister of what was to be called Zimbabwe-Rhodesia. The new constitution was denounced by Mugabe and Nkomo as another attempt by Smith to perpetuate white domination, and they continued to lead the Zimbabwe African National Liberation Army from bases in neighbouring Mozambique.

the Lancaster House Agreement In August 1979 the new British prime minister Margaret Thatcher, under the influence of her foreign secretary Lord Carrington and President Kaunda of

Zambia, agreed to the holding of a constitutional conference in London at which all shades of political opinion in Rhodesia would be represented. The conference, held in September 1979, resulted in what became known as the *Lancaster House Agreement and paved the way for full independence.

A member of the British cabinet, Lord Soames, was sent to Rhodesia as governor general to arrange a timetable for independence. Economic and trade sanctions were lifted. A small Commonwealth monitoring force supervised the disarming of the thousands of guerrilla fighters who brought their weapons and ammunition from all parts of the country.

independence achieved A new constitution was adopted and elections were held under independent supervision in February 1980. They resulted in a decisive win for Robert Mugabe's ZANU–PF party. The new state of Zimbabwe became fully independent in April 1980, with the Rev Canaan Banana as president and Robert Mugabe as prime minister.

During the next few years a rift developed between Mugabe and Nkomo and between ZANU–PF and ZAPU supporters. Nkomo was accused of trying to undermine Mugabe's administration and was dismissed from the cabinet. Fearing for his safety, he spent some months in the UK. ZAPU was opposed to the 1984 proposal by the ZANU–PF for the eventual creation of a one-party socialist state.

Zimbabwe under Mugabe
Mugabe's party increased its majority in the 1985 elections with 63 seats against 15, and early in 1986 he announced that the separate seats for the whites in the assembly would be abolished within a year. Relations between ZANU–PF and ZAPU and the two leaders eventually improved, and by 1986 discussions of a merger were under way. When President Banana retired in 1987 Mugabe combined the

posts of head of state and prime minister, and Nkomo returned to the cabinet as vice-president.

In December 1989 a draft constitution was drawn up that renounced Marxism–Leninism as the state ideology and created a one-party state, fusing the governing party and opposition groups; the ZANU–PF abandoned its Marxist ideology in 1991. A new opposition group headed by former Mugabe ally, Edgar Tekere, was launched in 1989, with the intention of challenging the ZANU–PF in the 1990 elections. Tekere announced that his Zimbabwe Unity Movement would advocate capitalism and multiparty democracy. However, the ZANU–PF won a comfortable victory in the elections of March 1990 and Mugabe was re-elected president. The state of emergency, in force since 1965, was ended in July 1990. Mugabe's proposals in August 1990 for a one-party state were strongly opposed.

During 1991–92 Zimbabwe was one of the countries hit by the worst drought of the century to plague southern Africa. In March 1992 Mugabe declared the drought a national disaster and appealed for foreign aid. The effects of the drought continued into 1993.

In July 1992 Rev Sithole and Ian Smith formed a United Front to oppose the ZANU–PF. In April 1993 the Forum Party, a moderate, centrist party composed largely of intellectuals and business people, was formed. ZANU–PF were re-elected in 1995, having won support in rural areas through its land redistribution scheme. In March 1996 Mugabe was re-elected president by default when the other candidates withdrew from the contest.

civil unrest President Mugabe late January 1998 called in the army as thousands looted and rioted in Harare, the capital, in the country's worst civil unrest since independence. The unrest started with one of the biggest labour strikes ever held in the country, called by the Zimbabwe Congress of Trade Unions to protest against tax increases. At an emergency cabinet meeting, Mugabe declared that price controls would be introduced. Important issues revolved round Mugabe's proposals to redistribute much land from white farmers to black farmers. In September 1998, after pressure from aid donors, the government announced that it would redistribute only 118, rather than the originally planned 1,470, large (and mainly white-owned) farms to landless farmers. In November 1998 there were violent protests in Harare against the rise in fuel prices and the country's involvement in the war in the Democratic Republic of Congo. In February 1999 there were more violent protests against President Mugabe. In June the human-rights group African Rights produced a scathing report on Mugabe's government, accusing it of corruption, human-rights abuse, and lack of respect for the rule of law.

In a surprise change the Zimbabwean President, Robert Mugabe, announced in October 1999 that the government was ready to compensate the families of an estimated 25,000 people killed in an opposition stronghold during the civil war in the early 1980s.

For 10 years President Mugabe had vowed to never apologize or compensate the victims of the feared North Korean-trained Five Brigade army unit, originally deployed in 1981 to track down armed bandits but which ended up killing thousands of civilians in Matabeleland, home to the country's second-largest Ndebele tribal group. Ndebeles constituted about 15% of Zimbabwe's population.

In 1999 Zimbabwe was in the throes of its worst economic crisis in two decades. The crisis was widely blamed on government mismanagement, and Mugabe was expected to face his strongest opposition yet at parliamentary elections scheduled for 2000. Opposition activists elected a trade union leader to lead their election campaign. The threat to President Mugabe's 20-year rule was worsened by Zimbabwe's worst economic crisis of his rule, including fuel shortages, power cuts, and 60% inflation, as well as involvement in the war in the Democratic Republic of Congo. His popularity was in decline; this was consolidated when a referendum showed that Zimbabwean voters had rejected a new constitution which was considered to reinforce his power.

farm invasions 2000 In early 2000 white-owned farms experienced a wave of invasions by veterans from the country's war of independence, who claimed that the land on which the farms stood was their own land by right. The farmers claimed that the action was orchestrated by the government in order to promote fear prior to the elections scheduled for April. However, a leader of a veterans' group maintained that his members were willing to go back to guerrilla warfare, and to overthrow President Mugabe, to defend their claims to the land. President Mugabe dissolved his parliament in mid-April 2000, giving no date for the delayed parliamentary elections, despite having previously said that elections would be held in May. Around 500 farms had been seized by war veterans paid by the government, and the country was embroiled in a deepening economic crisis, as well as rising violence.

Speaking on the 20th anniversary of Zimbabwe's independence, President Mugabe said that he was determined to resolve the question of land, and in doing so he declared that the white farmers were the enemies of Zimbabwe and that they were to blame for the recent farm invasions and rising violence. Meeting at a crisis summit at Victoria Falls, Zimbabwe, Mugabe and several South African political leaders including those of South Africa, Mozambique, and

Namibia, claimed that Britain and other Western countries had sparked the crisis by failing to honour promises made in 1998 to fund a land redistribution programme. When Zimbabwean ministers arrived in London, England, in April, Britain offered to fund land reform over the next two years, under the proviso that the money go to the poorest sector of society and not Mugabe's personal allies, and that fair law be reinstated in the country; the Zimbabwean ministers refused to agree to the conditions, saying that they went back on the 1998 agreement and that they represented British colonialism.

In May 2000, Mugabe denounced Britain and launched his ruling party's election manifesto, in which he reiterated his support for the seizure of land. Continuing violence from hit squads trained and funded by the government began to target school teachers who were accused of being supporters of the opposition, as well as intimidating any others suspected of opposing government policy. In the middle of May, it was announced that elections would take place the following month, although international concern was levelled at the effect of intimidation tactics on democracy. At the end of May 2000, Zimbabwe's President Mugabe fulfilled his threat to seize land without compensation to owners, despite proposals from South Africa's President Mbeki under which $14 million/£8.75 million was to be made available by donor countries to buy 118 of the 841 disputed farms in order to use them for land redistribution. The seizure of the farms without compensation meant that the farmers owed millions to the Zimbabwean banks, placing the country's financial sector in turmoil. This compounded economic difficulties from earlier in the month after the World Bank suspended any new loans to Zimbabwe following its failure to keep up with repayments

to existing debts. Furthermore, Mugabe announced his plan to seize the assets of foreign mining companies in his attempt to nationalize his country's economy.

Mugabe re-elected UN involvement in coordinating observers for the imminent parliamentary elections was withdrawn in June as Mugabe accused the UN of attempting to hijack the monitoring process. Terror and intimidation tactics which had been employed by government-controlled gangs in the previous three months of land invasions led human-rights organization Amnesty International to announce that free and fair elections were no longer possible in Zimbabwe's political climate. Mugabe's ruling ZANU–PF Party was elected to remain in parliament at the end of June 2000. Under the constitution, Mugabe had the right to appoint 30 MPs of his choice, but his party was elected with a majority of only five, not reaching the two-thirds majority needed for him to change the constitution. Mugabe's new cabinet, which had to be drawn solely from members of his own party, dropped many of his long-standing political allies and included economists and business leaders in an attempt to heal Zimbabwe's shattered economy. However, commuters in Harare rioted in early September in protest against the doubling of public transport fares, and the central bank again devalued the Zimbabwean dollar, by 3%. Further protests against the rising cost of living were planned by the main opposition party, and in October 2000, rioters blocked roadways near Harare, threw stones at police, and set fire to buses, in protest against soaring food prices. Bread and sugar prices rose by an average of 30% the previous week in the country.

In October, the opposition moved for Mugabe's impeachment, but the effort was fruitless as Mugabe's ZANU-PF held an absolute majority in parliament. Mugabe said he would put on trial for genocide those whites who were guilty of atrocities during Zimbabwe's liberation war in the 1970s. He had already expanded his land acquisition programme in August, which the supreme court later declared illegal. The government said it would defy the ruling, though in December Mugabe publicly signalled an end to the land invasions, and the government agreed to meet representatives of commercial farmers to discuss ending the crisis. However, in February 2001, Mugabe's party unanimously agreed to remove all white judges from Zimbabwe's judiciary and decided to replace the five members of the Supreme Court. The court was internationally thought of as the main barrier between Mugabe and the imposition of absolute tyranny.

In early March, Zimbabwe's chief justice, Anthony Gubbay, was driven to resign by threats, and replaced by President Mugabe's ally, Godfrey Chidyausiku. The move followed a further crackdown on Mugabe's critics, including the expulsion of 14 accredited foreign reporters and the charging of the main opposition leader, Morgan Tsvangirai, with inciting violence in a speech made five months previously. In May Tsvangirai succeeded in having his case referred to the Supreme Court, which cleared him in November.

In late April 2001, the so-called war veterans who had invaded white-owned farms in 2000 turned their attention to private businesses. They occupied premises and demanded compensation for workers who had been laid off over the last three years of recession. In a rare attempt to curb their activities, 26 war veterans were arrested in May and charged with trying to extort money from private businesses.

In June, Chenjerai Hunzvi, the leader of Zimbabwe's war veterans, died of malaria. Giving himself the nickname 'Hitler', Hunzvi had led violent attacks on Mugabe's opponents and encouraged the occupation of white-owned farms. He led attacks on commercial farmers, industries and factories, opposition parties, and aid agencies. In the process, he became one of Mugabe's most trusted lieutenants. He was buried at the national heroes shrine.

economic crisis worsens The danger of civil unrest increased on 13 June when the government raised the price of fuel by nearly 70%, the sharpest rise for 20 years. The country's main trade union said that over three-quarters of Zimbabweans already lived below the poverty line.

Mugabe reassesses land reform In June 2001, in an abrupt change of heart, President Mugabe declared himself willing to accept a visit by a group of Commonwealth ministers – including the British foreign minister, Jack Straw – in a bid to settle the explosive issue of land reform in his country. Although diplomats were encouraged by Mugabe's decision, many Zimbabweans feared that his hints that he wanted to end the country's land crisis were a ploy to regain credibility ahead of the presidential elections expected in 2002.

Mugabe extends institutional influence In July 2001, the Zimbabwean Justice Minister announced the appointment of three additional judges to the Supreme Court, the first time that the country had had more than five judges sitting. The move was seen as an attempt by President Mugabe to put compliant judges into a court that had often ruled against the government. Mugabe also appointed seven other judges, most with strong links to his ZANU-PF party, to the Zimbabwe High Court.

war veteran violence continues At least 10 whites were seriously injured when mobs of war veterans went on the rampage in Chinhoyi, an important tobacco-farming town northwest of Harare, in August 2001. 23 white farmers were charged with inciting violence. President Mugabe brushed off suggestions that he was forcing white farmers out of the country, despite the fact that around 300 farmers and their families had fled from about 100 raided farms in the Chinhoyi area in one week alone.

At Commonwealth talks in Nigeria in September 2001, Robert Mugabe's government agreed to carry out land reform fairly and legally in Zimbabwe in return for a pledge by Britain to provide £36 million to help finance the new programme. Although Mugabe endorsed the deal, he said it would need to pass through his ruling ZANU-PF party and cabinet. At a special southern African summit in Harare, governments of neighbouring countries extracted similar promises from Mugabe and blamed Zimbabwe for spreading economic and political disorder in the region. However, attacks on white-owned farms in Zimbabwe continued throughout September.

In September, Zimbabwe's central bank said the country's economy was in a downward spiral and would shrink by about 8% that year. At least 570 large-scale tobacco farms had already been forced to close. Meanwhile, in an interim ruling in October that reversed an earlier decision, Zimbabwe's expanded Supreme Court told the government that it could proceed with the seizure of white-owned farms and redistribution of the land. The ruling threatened to unravel the land reform deal brokered at the Commonwealth meeting in Nigeria. The risk of mass starvation in Zimbabwe increased as militant war veterans and government supporters invaded nine white-owned farms on 3–4 November. Aid agencies warned of starvation due to the declining crop output, and at least 3 million people out of a population of 12.6 million had registered for food aid with the government. A group of about 500 militants from ZANU-PF beat whites on the streets of Bulawayo on

16 November and firebombed the offices of the main opposition party, the Movement for Democratic Change (MDC). Arson attacks the following day escalated dangerously as police riot squads clashed with opposition supporters; by the third day, the riots had spread to other cities. The MDC's leader, Morgan Tsvangirai, was cleared of treason charges in late November, allowing him to run against President Mugabe in the March 2002 presidential election. In early December Mugabe, in the continuing campaign against white farmers, threatened to break up all farms larger than 2,000 ha/4,940 acres. He was supported by Zimbabwe's reconstituted Supreme Court, which, in a final ruling on 4 December, that the controversial land programme was legal.

Zimbabwe's parliament passed two laws – the Public Order and Security Bill and the General Laws Amendment Act – in January 2002 that curbed free speech and tightened restrictions on political opposition, thereby threatening the legitimacy of the presidential election due in March. The commander of the armed forces, Gen Vitalis Zinavashe, also said that the army would not recognize the result of the elections if Mugabe lost. In response, Britain's foreign secretary Jack Straw announced that the UK would press for Zimbabwe to be suspended from the Commonwealth. In February the row continued over the monitoring of the March elections. An advance party of 30 European Union observers, including the Swedish diplomat Pierre Schori, arrived in Harare, the capital, but the Zimbabwean government insisted that it would allow representatives of only nine specified European countries to monitor elections and that Sweden was not among them.

presidential elections 2002
Presidential elections in Zimbabwe in March 2002 were marred by violence, intimidation, and claims by hundreds

of thousands of opposition supporters that they had been obstructed from voting. The High Court halted the election after three days of chaotic voting, and police were forced to fire tear gas to disperse hundreds of disappointed voters. Mugabe was re-elected, but Morgan Tsvangirai vowed to challenge the defeat of the MDC. Mugabe's election to a further six-year term after a poll characterized by blatant irregularities was widely condemned by many Western countries, including the UK and the USA. Following Mugabe's re-election, Zimbabwe was suspended from the Commonwealth on 19 March 2002 for one year. Nigeria and South Africa both backed the decision, the first time the influential African states had condemned Mugabe unambiguously. However, a defiant Mugabe promised to carry on seizing white-owned farms regardless of the suspension, and charged Morgan Tsvangirai with treason the following day.

In June, the government ordered 2,900 white commercial farmers, whose farms had been targeted for seizure and redistribution to poor black workers, to stop work with immediate effect under threat of imprisonment. The farmers were given 45 days to vacate their homes. At the same time, Zimbabwe faced its worst food shortage in 60 years.

Zimmerman, Arthur (1864–1940) German politician. As foreign secretary, he sent the notorious Zimmermann Telegram to the German minister in Mexico in January 1917. It contained the terms of an alliance between Mexico and Germany, by which Mexico was to attack the USA with German and Japanese assistance in return for the 'lost' states of New Mexico, Texas, and Arizona. Publication of the message in March

1917 finally brought the hesitant USA into the war against Germany, and Zimmermann 'resigned' shortly afterwards.

Zinovyev (or Zinoviev), Grigory Yevseyevich (1883–1936) Russian communist politician whose name was attached to a forgery, the **Zinovyev letter**, inciting Britain's communists to rise, which helped to topple the Labour government in 1924.

Zionism national liberation movement advocating the re-establishment of a Jewish homeland (the *Eretz Israel*) in Palestine. Here, in the 'Promised Land' of the Bible, its adherents called for the Jewish people to be granted a sovereign state with its capital at Jerusalem, the 'city of Zion'. The movement was founded by the Hungarian writer Theodor *Herzl, who in 1897 convened the First Zionist Congress in the Swiss city of Basel. Zionism was the driving force behind the creation of the state of Israel in 1948.

In 1917, the Zionist leaders Chaim Weizmann and Nahum Sokolow gained from Great Britain (which controlled Palestine after the collapse of the Ottoman Empire in World War I) a promise of support for a Jewish homeland. This was enshrined in the *Balfour Declaration. Before and during World War II, escalating persecution in Europe led many Jews to embrace Zionism and emigrate. After the war, the United Nations sanctioned the establishment of a Jewish state alongside a homeland for the Arab Palestinian people.

Zog, Ahmed Bey Zogu (1895–1961) King of Albania 1928–39. He became prime minister of Albania in 1922, president of the republic in 1925, and proclaimed himself king in 1928. He was driven out by the Italians in 1939 and settled in the UK.

APPENDIX – Web Resources

American history of the 20th century from the Internet Public Library:
http://www.ipl.org/div/subject/browse/hum30.55.85.10/

Award-winning series with archive footage gathered from 31 countries, a comprehensive online site on the Cold War:
http://www.cnn.com/SPECIALS/cold.war/guides/about.series/

People's Century 1900 – 1999, based on the television series with special content for students:
http://www.pbs.org/wgbh/peoplescentury/

World War I – an international archive of documents concerning the Great War:
http://www.lib.byu.edu/~rdh/wwi/

World War I – consists of events surrounding the First World War:
http://www.worldwar1.com/tgws/tgws2.htm

Exhibition from the US National Archives on all aspects of the First World War:
http://www.learningcurve.gov.uk/greatwar/default.htm

The Russian-Japanese War Research Society:
http://www.russojapanesewar.com/

Written by a teacher for the Schools History Project GCSE:
http://www.historygcse.org/

History, as witnessed by those who lived it:
http://www.eyewitnesstohistory.com/20frm.htm

Comprehensive website with informative articles, timelines, famous people, wars etc:
http://www.worldhistory.com

A collection of the most famous broadcasts and recordings of the 20th Century including Martin Luther King's "I have a dream…" to Oppenheimer's views on government secrecy:
http://www.historychannel.com/speeches/archive/speech_214.html

Includes the discovery of nuclear fission, hydrogen bomb development, the
Manhattan Project and the ensuing Cold War:

http://www.atomicarchive.com/historymenu.shtml

Science and achievement in the early half of the 20th century from Marconi's
early transmission of radio waves to Alexander Fleming's discovery of penicillin:

http://www.bbc.co.uk/history/timelines/britain/cen_science.shtml

Comprehensive website on all aspects of the Holocaust of World War II:

http://www.ushmm.org/wlc/en/

The Nuremburg War Crimes Trial, documents held at Yale Law School:

http://www.yale.edu/lawweb/avalon/imt/imt.htm

Documents of World War I:

http://www.mtholyoke.edu/acad/intrel/ww2.htm

The official archives of the US government:

http://www.archives.gov/welcome/index.html

Library and Museum for President John F Kennedy and the times in which
he lived:

http://www.cs.umb.edu/jfklibrary/index.htm

Stalinism: Its Origins & Future:

http://home.mira.net/~andy/bs/index.htm

Websites on Hiroshima:

http://www.dannen.com/hiroshima_links.html

Website containing information on the Vietnam War, ethnic groups of Vietnam
and current events including travel tips:

http://www.vwam.com/

An overview of the Vietnam War and relevant documents:

http://vietnam.vassar.edu/

This site contains declassified Soviet documents from 1917 to 1991:

http://www.ibiblio.org/expo/soviet.exhibit/soviet.archive.html

An informative site on the Russian people including a timeline, glossary, further links and a chat forum:

http://www.pbs.org/wcta/faceofrussia/series-index.html

Multilingual European Museums website containing information on the First World War, the Spanish Civil War and the Second World War:

http://www.lescheminsdelamemoire.net/lcdlm.asp

With more than 400 histories on this website, you can search on a particular time period and theme

http://www.historyworld.net/wrldhis/wrldhis_results.asp?HWtype=HISTORY

British History Online can be browsed by subject, period, place and people:

http://www.british-history.ac.uk/period.asp

Institute for Historical Research, part of the University of London:

http://www.history.ac.uk/welcome.html

Website for the Royal Historical Society

http://www.rhs.ac.uk/welcome.html

Website for the American Historical Association:

http://www.historians.org/

Based at the Women's Library, London, the GENESIS project is organising access to women's history collections in the British Isles:

http://www.genesis.ac.uk/index.html

Australian Historic Records register is a database concerning Australian life from the early years of European settlement until 1988:

http://www.nla.gov.au/ahrr/

Biographies of people who have helped shape all aspects of the modern world:

http://www.bbc.co.uk/history/historic_figures/

Quizzes, games and articles all on history:

http://www.bbc.co.uk/history/lj/

Historical documents held in the National Archives of the United Kingdom:
http://www.nationalarchives.gov.uk/about/

National Archives of Ireland:
http://www.nationalarchives.ie/

National Archives of Scotland:
http://www.nas.gov.uk/

Review of part of the 20th century in Africa:
http://www.channelafrica.org/english/2000/1945_1959.html

Africa in the 20th century:
http://husky1.stmarys.ca/~wmills/course317/his317.html

Chronology of American History:
http://www.digitalhistory.uh.edu/historyonline/chron20.cfm

African American History including migration and Black Culture in the early 20th century:
http://encarta.msn.com/encyclopedia_761595158_4/African_American_History.html

Genocide in the 20th century:
http://www.historyplace.com/worldhistory/genocide/
http://www.scaruffi.com/politics/dictat.html
http://www.globalwebpost.com/genocide1971/

Top 10 Infectious diseases of the 20th century:
http://hopkins-id.edu/idfun/topten/events.html

Wellcome Library's History of medicine internet gateway:
http://medhist.ac.uk/browse/mesh/C0012652L0012652.html

In-depth specials from CNN on the 20th century:
http://www.cnn.com/SPECIALS/1999/century/

Source list and detailed death tolls for the 20th century hemoclysm:
http://users.erols.com/mwhite28/warstat1.htm

Website devoted to the impact of disease-carrying bugs on world history:
http://scarab.msu.montana.edu/historybug/